FOR REFERENCE

NOT TO BE TAKEN FROM THE ROOM

Twentieth-Century Literary Criticism

Guide to Gale Literary Criticism Series

For criticism on	Consult these Gale series
Authors now living or who died after December 31, 1999	**CONTEMPORARY LITERARY CRITICISM (CLC)**
Authors who died between 1900 and 1999	**TWENTIETH-CENTURY LITERARY CRITICISM (TCLC)**
Authors who died between 1800 and 1899	**NINETEENTH-CENTURY LITERATURE CRITICISM (NCLC)**
Authors who died between 1400 and 1799	**LITERATURE CRITICISM FROM 1400 TO 1800 (LC)** **SHAKESPEAREAN CRITICISM (SC)**
Authors who died before 1400	**CLASSICAL AND MEDIEVAL LITERATURE CRITICISM (CMLC)**
Authors of books for children and young adults	**CHILDREN'S LITERATURE REVIEW (CLR)**
Dramatists	**DRAMA CRITICISM (DC)**
Poets	**POETRY CRITICISM (PC)**
Short story writers	**SHORT STORY CRITICISM (SSC)**
Literary topics and movements	**HARLEM RENAISSANCE: A GALE CRITICAL COMPANION (HR)** **THE BEAT GENERATION: A GALE CRITICAL COMPANION (BG)**
Asian American writers of the last two hundred years	**ASIAN AMERICAN LITERATURE (AAL)**
Black writers of the past two hundred years	**BLACK LITERATURE CRITICISM (BLC)** **BLACK LITERATURE CRITICISM SUPPLEMENT (BLCS)**
Hispanic writers of the late nineteenth and twentieth centuries	**HISPANIC LITERATURE CRITICISM (HLC)** **HISPANIC LITERATURE CRITICISM SUPPLEMENT (HLCS)**
Native North American writers and orators of the eighteenth, nineteenth, and twentieth centuries	**NATIVE NORTH AMERICAN LITERATURE (NNAL)**
Major authors from the Renaissance to the present	**WORLD LITERATURE CRITICISM, 1500 TO THE PRESENT (WLC)** **WORLD LITERATURE CRITICISM SUPPLEMENT (WLCS)**

ISSN 0276-8178

Volume 151

Twentieth-Century Literary Criticism

Criticism of the
Works of Novelists, Poets, Playwrights,
Short Story Writers, and Other Creative Writers
Who Lived between 1900 and 1999,
from the First Published Critical
Appraisals to Current Evaluations

Linda Pavlovski
Project Editor

Detroit • New York • San Francisco • San Diego • New Haven, Conn. • Waterville, Maine • London • Munich

Twentieth-Century Literary Criticism, Vol. 151

Project Editor
Linda Pavlovski

Editorial
Jessica Bomarito, Tom Burns, Kathy D. Darrow, Jeffrey W. Hunter, Jelena O. Krstović, Michelle Lee, Ellen McGeagh, Joseph Palmisano, Thomas J. Schoenberg, Lawrence J. Trudeau, Russel Whitaker

Data Capture
Francis Monroe, Gwen Tucker

Indexing Services
Laurie Andriot

Rights and Acquisitions
Margaret Abendroth, Margaret Chamberlain, Lori Hines

Imaging and Multimedia
Mary Grimes, Lezlie Light, Mike Logusz, Denay Wilding

Composition and Electronic Capture
Kathy Sauer

Manufacturing
Rhonda Williams

© 2004 Thomson Gale, a part of The Thomson Corporation. Thomson and Star Logo are trademarks and Gale is a registered trademark used herein under license.

For more information, contact
Thomson Gale
27500 Drake Rd.
Farmington Hills, MI 48331-3535
Or you can visit our internet site at
http://www.gale.com

ALL RIGHTS RESERVED
No part of this work covered by the copyright herein may be reproduced or used in any form or by any means—graphic, electronic, or mechanical, including photocopying, recording, taping, Web distribution, or information storage retrieval systems—without the written permission of the publisher.

This publication is a creative work fully protected by all applicable copyright laws, as well as by misappropriation, trade secret, unfair competition, and other applicable laws. The authors and editors of this work have added value to the underlying factual material herein through one or more of the following: unique and original selection, coordination, expression, arrangement, and classification of the information.

For permission to use material from the product, submit your request via the Web at http://www.gale-edit.com/permissions, or you may download our Permissions Request form and submit your request by fax or mail to:

Permisssions Department
Thomson Gale
27500 Drake Rd.
Farmington Hills, MI 48331-3535
Permissions Hotline:
248-699-8006 or 800-877-4253, ext. 8006
Fax 248-699-8074 or 800-762-4058

Since this page cannot legibly accommodate all copyright notices, the acknowledgments constitute an extension of the copyright notice.

While every effort has been made to secure permission to reprint material and to ensure the reliability of the information presented in this publication, Thomson Gale neither guarantees the accuracy of the data contained herein nor assumes any responsibility for errors, omissions or discrepancies. Thomson Gale accepts no payment for listing; and inclusion in the publication of any organization, agency, institution, publication, service, or individual does not imply endorsement of the editors or publisher. Errors brought to the attention of the publisher and verified to the satisfaction of the publisher will be corrected in future editions.

LIBRARY OF CONGRESS CATALOG CARD NUMBER 76-46132

ISBN 0-7876-7050-2
ISSN 0276-8178

Printed in the United States of America
10 9 8 7 6 5 4 3 2 1

Contents

Preface vii

Acknowledgments xi

Literary Criticism Series Advisory Board xv

S. Y. Agnon 1888-1970 1
Austro-Hungarian-Israeli novelist, short story writer, and poet

James Dickey 1923-1997 87
American poet, novelist, critic, essayist, scriptwriter, and author of children's books

Knut Hamsun 1859-1952 228
Norwegian novelist, playwright, and short story writer
Entry devoted to Hunger (1890)

Joseph Heller 1923-1999 292
American novelist, playwright, and autobiographer

Literary Criticism Series Cumulative Author Index 345

Literary Criticism Series Cumulative Topic Index 443

TCLC Cumulative Nationality Index 455

TCLC-151 Title Index 461

Preface

Since its inception more than fifteen years ago, *Twentieth-Century Literary Criticism* (*TCLC*) has been purchased and used by nearly 10,000 school, public, and college or university libraries. *TCLC* has covered more than 500 authors, representing 58 nationalities and over 25,000 titles. No other reference source has surveyed the critical response to twentieth-century authors and literature as thoroughly as *TCLC*. In the words of one reviewer, "there is nothing comparable available." *TCLC* "is a gold mine of information—dates, pseudonyms, biographical information, and criticism from books and periodicals—which many librarians would have difficulty assembling on their own."

Scope of the Series

TCLC is designed to serve as an introduction to authors who died between 1900 and 1999 and to the most significant interpretations of these author's works. Volumes published from 1978 through 1999 included authors who died between 1900 and 1960. The great poets, novelists, short story writers, playwrights, and philosophers of the period are frequently studied in high school and college literature courses. In organizing and reprinting the vast amount of critical material written on these authors, *TCLC* helps students develop valuable insight into literary history, promotes a better understanding of the texts, and sparks ideas for papers and assignments. Each entry in *TCLC* presents a comprehensive survey on an author's career or an individual work of literature and provides the user with a multiplicity of interpretations and assessments. Such variety allows students to pursue their own interests; furthermore, it fosters an awareness that literature is dynamic and responsive to many different opinions.

Every fourth volume of *TCLC* is devoted to literary topics. These topics widen the focus of the series from the individual authors to such broader subjects as literary movements, prominent themes in twentieth-century literature, literary reaction to political and historical events, significant eras in literary history, prominent literary anniversaries, and the literatures of cultures that are often overlooked by English-speaking readers.

TCLC is designed as a companion series to Thomson Gale's *Contemporary Literary Criticism,* (*CLC*) which reprints commentary on authors who died after 1999. Because of the different time periods under consideration, there is no duplication of material between *CLC* and *TCLC*.

Organization of the Book

A *TCLC* entry consists of the following elements:

- The **Author Heading** cites the name under which the author most commonly wrote, followed by birth and death dates. Also located here are any name variations under which an author wrote, including transliterated forms for authors whose native languages use nonroman alphabets. If the author wrote consistently under a pseudonym, the pseudonym will be listed in the author heading and the author's actual name given in parenthesis on the first line of the biographical and critical information. Uncertain birth or death dates are indicated by question marks. Single-work entries are preceded by a heading that consists of the most common form of the title in English translation (if applicable) and the original date of composition.

- A **Portrait of the Author** is included when available.

- The **Introduction** contains background information that introduces the reader to the author, work, or topic that is the subject of the entry.

- The list of **Principal Works** is ordered chronologically by date of first publication and lists the most important works by the author. The genre and publication date of each work is given. In the case of foreign authors whose works have been translated into English, the English-language version of the title follows in brackets. Unless otherwise indicated, dramas are dated by first performance, not first publication.

- Reprinted **Criticism** is arranged chronologically in each entry to provide a useful perspective on changes in critical evaluation over time. The critic's name and the date of composition or publication of the critical work are given at the beginning of each piece of criticism. Unsigned criticism is preceded by the title of the source in which it appeared. All titles by the author featured in the text are printed in boldface type. Footnotes are reprinted at the end of each essay or excerpt. In the case of excerpted criticism, only those footnotes that pertain to the excerpted texts are included.

- A complete **Bibliographical Citation** of the original essay or book precedes each piece of criticism. Source citations in the Literary Criticism Series follow University of Chicago Press style, as outlined in *The Chicago Manual of Style,* 14th ed. (Chicago: The University of Chicago Press, 1993).

- Critical essays are prefaced by brief **Annotations** explicating each piece.

- An annotated bibliography of **Further Reading** appears at the end of each entry and suggests resources for additional study. In some cases, significant essays for which the editors could not obtain reprint rights are included here. Boxed material following the further reading list provides references to other biographical and critical sources on the author in series published by Thomson Gale.

Indexes

A **Cumulative Author Index** lists all of the authors that appear in a wide variety of reference sources published by Thomson Gale, including *TCLC*. A complete list of these sources is found facing the first page of the Author Index. The index also includes birth and death dates and cross references between pseudonyms and actual names.

A **Cumulative Nationality Index** lists all authors featured in *TCLC* by nationality, followed by the number of the *TCLC* volume in which their entry appears.

A **Cumulative Topic Index** lists the literary themes and topics treated in the series as well as in *Classical and Medieval Literature Criticism, Literature Criticism from 1400 to 1800, Nineteenth-Century Literature Criticism,* and the *Contemporary Literary Criticism* Yearbook, which was discontinued in 1998.

An alphabetical **Title Index** accompanies each volume of *TCLC*. Listings of titles by authors covered in the given volume are followed by the author's name and the corresponding page numbers where the titles are discussed. English translations of foreign titles and variations of titles are cross-referenced to the title under which a work was originally published. Titles of novels, dramas, nonfiction books, and poetry, short story, or essay collections are printed in italics, while individual poems, short stories, and essays are printed in roman type within quotation marks.

In response to numerous suggestions from librarians, Thomson Gale also produces a paperbound edition of the *TCLC* cumulative title index. This annual cumulation, which alphabetically lists all titles reviewed in the series, is available to all customers. Additional copies of this index are available upon request. Librarians and patrons will welcome this separate index; it saves shelf space, is easy to use, and is recyclable upon receipt of the next edition.

Citing *Twentieth-Century Literary Criticism*

When citing criticism reprinted in the Literary Criticism Series, students should provide complete bibliographic information so that the cited essay can be located in the original print or electronic source. Students who quote directly from reprinted criticism may use any accepted bibliographic format, such as University of Chicago Press style or Modern Language Association (MLA) style. Both the MLA and the University of Chicago formats are acceptable and recognized as being the current standards for citations. It is important, however, to choose one format for all citations; do not mix the two formats within a list of citations.

The examples below follow recommendations for preparing a bibliography set forth in *The Chicago Manual of Style,* 14th ed. (Chicago: The University of Chicago Press, (1993); the first example pertains to material drawn from periodicals, the second to material reprinted from books:

Morrison, Jago. "Narration and Unease in Ian McEwan's Later Fiction." *Critique* 42, no. 3 (spring 2001): 253-68. Reprinted in *Twentieth-Century Literary Criticism.* Vol. 127, edited by Janet Witalec, 212-20. Detroit: Gale, 2003.

Brossard, Nicole. "Poetic Politics." In *The Politics of Poetic Form: Poetry and Public Policy,* edited by Charles Bernstein, 73-82. New York: Roof Books, 1990. Reprinted in *Twentieth-Century Literary Criticism.* Vol. 127, edited by Janet Witalec, 3-8. Detroit: Gale, 2003.

The examples below follow recommendations for preparing a works cited list set forth in the *MLA Handbook for Writers of Research Papers,* 5th ed. (New York: The Modern Language Association of America, 1999); the first example pertains to material drawn from periodicals, the second to material reprinted from books:

Morrison, Jago. "Narration and Unease in Ian McEwan's Later Fiction." *Critique* 42.3 (spring 2001): 253-68. Reprinted in *Twentieth-Century Literary Criticism.* Ed. Janet Witalec. Vol. 127. Detroit: Gale, 2003. 212-20.

Brossard, Nicole. "Poetic Politics." *The Politics of Poetic Form: Poetry and Public Policy.* Ed. Charles Bernstein. New York: Roof Books, 1990. 73-82. Reprinted in *Twentieth-Century Literary Criticism.* Ed. Janet Witalec. Vol. 127. Detroit: Gale, 2003. 3-8.

Suggestions are Welcome

Readers who wish to suggest new features, topics, or authors to appear in future volumes, or who have other suggestions or comments are cordially invited to call, write, or fax the Project Editor:

Project Editor, Literary Criticism Series
Thomson Gale
27500 Drake Road
Farmington Hills, MI 48331-3535
1-800-347-4253 (GALE)
Fax: 248-699-8054

Acknowledgments

The editors wish to thank the copyright holders of the criticism included in this volume and the permissions managers of many book and magazine publishing companies for assisting us in securing reproduction rights. We are also grateful to the staffs of the Detroit Public Library, the Library of Congress, the University of Detroit Mercy Library, Wayne State University Purdy/Kresge Library Complex, and the University of Michigan Libraries for making their resources available to us. Following is a list of the copyright holders who have granted us permission to reproduce material in this volume of *TCLC*. Every effort has been made to trace copyright, but if omissions have been made, please let us know.

COPYRIGHTED MATERIAL IN *TCLC*, VOLUME 151, WAS REPRODUCED FROM THE FOLLOWING PERIODICALS:

American Poetry Review, v. 6, July, 1977 for "Review of *The Zodiac*" by Stanley Plumly. Copyright © 1977 by American Poetry. Reproduced by permission of the author.—*Carolina Quarterly,* v. 22, spring, 1970. Copyright © 1970 by The University of North Carolina Press. Reproduced by permission.—*Chicago Review,* v. 20, November, 1968. Copyright © 1968 by *Chicago Review*. Reproduced by permission.—*Commentary,* v. 89, February, 1990 for "Agnon without End" by Alan L. Mintz. Copyright © 1990 by the American Jewish Committee. All rights reserved. Reproduced by permission of the publisher and the author.—*Commonweal,* v.122, February 24, 1995. Copyright © 1995 Commonweal Publishing Co., Inc. Reproduced by permission of Commonweal Foundation.—*Contemporary Literature,* v. 39, winter, 1998. Copyright © 1998 The Board of Regents of the University of Wisconsin System. All rights reserved. Reproduced by permission.—*English Language Notes,* v. 26, December, 1998. Copyright © 1998 by Regents of the University of Colorado. Reproduced by permission.—*Georgia Review,* v. 32, summer, 1978. Copyright © 1978 by the University of Georgia. Reproduced by permission.—*Hebrew Annual Review,* v. 10, 1986 for "S. Y. Agnon's Art of Composition: The Befuddling Turn of the Compositional Screw" by Yair Mazor. Copyright © 1986 by the Division of Hebrew Language and Literature, Ohio State University. All rights reserved. Reproduced by permission of the author.—*Hudson Review,* v. 52, summer, 1999. Copyright © 1999 by The Hudson Review, Inc. Reproduced by permission.—*Interdisciplinary Literary Studies,* v. 1, fall, 1999 for "Literature, Politics, and the Law: On Blacksmiths, Tailors, and the Demolition of Houses" by Shulamit Almog. Copyright © 1999 by Interdisciplinary Studies. All rights reserved. Reproduced by permission of the author.—*Intertexts,* v. 7, spring, 2003. Copyright © 2003 by Texas Tech University Press. Reproduced by permission.—*James Dickey Newsletter,* v. 7, fall, 1990 for "To Rise Above Time: The Mythic Hero in Dickey's *Deliverance* and *Alnilam*" by Angelin Brewer. Copyright © 1990 by Angelin Brewer. Reproduced by permission of the author./v. 8, fall, 1991. Copyright © 1991 by James Dickey Newsletter. Reproduced by permission of the publisher.—*Modern Hebrew Literature,* v. 9, spring-summer, 1984; v. 11, spring-summer, 1986; v. 14, spring-summer, 1995. Copyright © 1984, 1986, 1995 by the Institute for the Translation of Hebrew Literature (Tel Aviv). All rights reserved. Reproduced by permission.—*Modern Language Studies,* v. 13, winter, 1983, for "Biblical Substructures in the Tragic Form: Hardy, *The Mayor of Casterbridge*; Agnon, *And the Crooked Shall Be Made Straight*" by Nehama Aschkenasy, v. 15, fall, 1985 for "Wherefrom Did Gediton Enter Gumlidata?: Realism and Comic Subversiveness in 'Forevermore,'" by Esther Fuchs. Copyright © 1983, 1985 by the Northeast Modern Language Association, all rights reserved. Both reproduced by permission of the publisher and the respective authors.—*Modern Poetry Studies,* v. 5, autumn, 1974. Copyright © 1974 by Jerome Mazzaro. Reproduced by permission.—*New Criterion,* v. 18, May, 2000 for "Review of Crux: The Letters of James Dickey" by Jeffrey Meyers. Copyright © 2000 by The Foundation for Cultural Review. Reproduced by permission of the author.—*New Republic,* v. 157, September 23, 1967. Copyright © 1967 by *New Republic*. Reproduced by permission.—*New Statesman,* March 20, 1998. Copyright © 1998 Statesman & Nation Publishing Company Limited. Reproduced by permission.—*New York Review,* v. 46, November 18, 1999. Copyright © 1999 by *New York Review*. Reproduced with permission from The New York Review of Books.—*Northwest Review,* v. 7, fall-winter, 1965-66. Copyright © 1965-66 by Northwest Review. Reproduced by permission.—*Papers on Language and Literature,* v. 31, fall, 1995. Copyright © 1995 by The Board of Trustees, Southern Illinois University at Edwardsville. Reproduced by permission.—*Parnassus,* v. 8, 1980 for "Double Dutch" by Turner Cassity; v. 13, spring-summer, 1986 for "Toward the Abyss: James Dickey at Middle Age" by Paul Christensen. Copyright © 1980, 1986 by Poetry in Review Foundation, NY. Both reproduced by permission of the publisher and the respective authors.—*Poetry,* v. 105, November, 1964 for "James Dickey's New Book" by Wendell Berry. Copyright © 1964 by *Poetry*. Reproduced by permission of the editor of POETRY and the author.—*Prairie Schooner,* v. 52, spring, 1978. Copyright © 1978 by University of Nebraska Press. Reproduced from *Prairie Schooner* by permission of the University of Nebraska Press.—*Prooftexts,* v. 9, September, 1989. Copyright 1989 by Johns Hopkins University. All rights reserved. Reproduced by permission.—*Publishers Weekly,* v. 247, May 29, 2000. Copyright © 2000 by Reed Publishing USA. Reproduced from *Publishers Weekly,* published by the

Bowker Magazine Group of Cahners Publishing Co., a division of Reed Publishing USA., by permission.—*Review of Contemporary Fiction,* v. 20, fall, 2000. Reproduced by permission.—*Scandinavian Studies,* v. 71, fall, 1999 for "Writing on the Wall: The Language of Advertising in Knut Hamsun's *Sult*" by Mark Sandberg. Copyright © 1999, by *Scandinavian Studies.* Reproduced by permission of the publisher and the author.—*Scandinavica: An International Journal of Scandinavian Studies,* v. 14, November 2, 1975. Copyright © 1975, 1989, by the editors of *Scandinavica.* Both reproduced by permission.—*Sewanee Review,* v. 77, April, 1969. Copyright © 1969 by The University of the South. Reproduced with permission of the editor./v. 108, winter, 2000. Copyright © 2000 by Harry Hart. Reproduced with permission of the editor and the author.—*South Carolina Review,* v. 3, June, 1971; v. 26, spring, 1994. Copyright © 1971, 1994 by Clemson University. All reproduced by permission.—*Southern Literary Journal,* v. 28, spring, 1996. Copyright © 1996 by the University of North Carolina Press. Reproduced by permission.—*Southern Quarterly,* v. 33, winter-summer, 1994-1995. Copyright © 1994-1995 by the University of Southern Mississippi. Reproduced by permission.—*Southern Review,* v. 36, spring, 2000 for "James Dickey: Journal to War" by Henry Hart. Copyright © 2000 by *Southern Review.* Reproduced by permission of the author.—*Studies in Contemporary Satire,* v. 17, 1990. Reproduced by permission.—*Studies in Short Fiction,* v. 12, 1975; v. 34, summer, 1997. Copyright © 1975, 1997 by Newberry College (South Carolina). All rights reserved. Reproduced by permission.—*Virginia Quarterly Review,* v. 63, winter, 1987. Copyright © 1987 by the *Virginia Quarterly Review,* The University of Virginia. Reproduced by permission of the publisher.—*War, Literature, and the Arts,* v. 6, fall-winter, 1994. Reproduced by permission./v. 14, 2002 for "Cathcart and the Magazine" by W. Brett Wiley. Reproduced by permission of the author.—*World Literature Today,* v. 72, 1998. Copyright © 1998 by the University of Oklahoma Press. Reproduced by permission of the publisher.

COPYRIGHTED MATERIAL IN *TCLC*, VOLUME 151, WAS REPRODUCED FROM THE FOLLOWING BOOKS:

Auster, Paul. From ***The Art of Hunger: Essays, Prefaces, Interviews and The Red Notebook.*** Sun & Moon Press, 1992. Copyright © 1991, by Paul Auster. All rights reserved. Reproduced by permission of Green Integer Books, Los Angeles.—Axelrod, Mark. From ***The Poetics of Novels: Fiction and Its Execution.*** St. Martin's Press, Inc., 1999. Copyright © 1999, by Mark Axelrod. All rights reserved. Reprinted by permission of St. Martin's Press, LLC.—Band, Arnold. From "The Kafka-Agnon Polarities," in ***The Dove and the Mole: Kafka's Journey into Darkness and Creativity.*** Edited by Moshe Lazar and Ronald Gottesman. Undena, 1987. Copyright © 1987 by Undena Publishing. All rights reserved. Reproduced by permission of the publisher and the author.—Baughman, Ronald. "*Deliverance*," in ***Understanding James Dickey.*** University of South Carolina Press, 1985. Copyright © 1985 by University of South Carolina Press. Reproduced by permission.—Calhoun, Richard J. and Robert W. Hill. From "The Literary Criticism, Lately Neglected," in ***James Dickey.*** Twayne Publishers, 1983. Copyright © 1983 by Twayne Publishers. Reproduced by permission of the Gale Group.—Ferguson, Robert. From "1888-1890: The Breakthrough: *Hunger*," in ***Enigma: The Life of Knut Hamsun.*** Hutchinson, 1987. Copyright © 1987, by Robert Ferguson. All rights reserved. Reproduced by permission of the author.—Gershon, Shaked. From "Midrash and Narrative: Agnon's 'Agunot'," in ***Midrash and Literature.*** Edited by Geoffrey H. Hartman and Sanford Budick. Chapter translated by Lois Bar-Yaacov. Yale University Press, 1986. Copyright © 1986 by Yale University Press. All rights reserved. Reproduced by permission.—Hassan, Ihab. From "The Spirit of Quest in Contemporary American Letters," in ***Rumors of Change: Essays of Five Decades.*** University of Alabama Press, 1995. Copyright © 1995 by University of Alabama Press. All rights reserved. Reproduced by permission.—Hoffman, Anne Golomb. From "Introduction: 'Like a Man Who Is Exiled from the Palace of His Father'," in ***Between Exile and Return: S. Y. Agnon and the Drama of Writing.*** State University of New York Press, 1991. Copyright © 1991 by the State University of New York Press. All rights reserved. Reproduced by permission of the State University of New York Press.—Nagel, James. From ***Biographies of Books: The Compositional Histories of Notable American Writings.*** Edited by James Barbour and Tom Quirk. University of Missouri Press, 1996. Copyright © 1996 by the Curators of the University of Missouri. All rights reserved. Reproduced by permission.—Ozick, Cynthia. From ***Metaphor and Memory.*** Vintage, 1991. Copyright © 1989 by Cynthia Ozick. All rights reserved. Reproduced by permission of Alfred A. Knopf, a division of Random House, Inc. In the UK by permission of the author.—Pratt, John Clark. From ***Fourteen Landing Zones: Approaches to Vietnam War Literature.*** Edited by Phillip K. Jason. University of Iowa Press, 1991. Copyright © 1991 by the University of Iowa. All rights reserved. Reproduced by permission.—Roskies, David. From "Essay on 'The Sense of Smell'," in ***Reading Hebrew Literature.*** Edited by Alan Mintz. Brandeis University Press, University Press of New England, 2003. Copyright © 2003 by Brandeis University Press. All rights reserved. Reproduced by permission.—Sokoloff, Naomi B. From "Expressing and Repressing the Female Voice in S. Y. Agnon's *In the Prime of Her Life*" in ***Women of the World: Jewish Women and Jewish Writing.*** Edited by Judith R. Baskin. Wayne State University Press, 1994. Copyright © 1994 by Wayne State University Press. Reproduced with permission of the Wayne State University Press.—Starr, William W. "*Alnilam*: James Dickey's Novel Explores Father and Son Relationships," in ***The Voiced Connections of James Dickey: Interviews and Conversations.*** Edited by Ronald Baughman. University of South Carolina Press, 1987. Copyright © 1987 University of South Carolina Press. Reproduced by permission.—Van Ness, Gordon. From "Other Prose: *Jericho, God's Images, Wayfarer,* and *Southern Light*," in ***Outbelieving Existence: The Measure Motion of James Dickey.*** Camden House, 1992. Copyright © Camden House. Reproduced by permission.

PHOTOGRAPHS AND ILLUSTRATIONS APPEARING IN *TCLC,* VOLUME 151, WERE RECEIVED FROM THE FOLLOWING SOURCES:

Agnon, S. Y., photograph. Copyright © David Rubinger/Corbis. Reproduced by permission.—Dickey, James, photograph taken in 1990. AP/Wide World Photos. Reproduced by permission.—Hamsun, Knut, photograph. The Library of Congress.— Heller, Joseph, photograph. AP/Wide World Photos. Reproduced by permission.

PHOTOGRAPHS AND ILLUSTRATIONS APPEARING IN *TCLC*, VOLUME 151, WERE RECEIVED FROM THE FOLLOWING SOURCES:

Agnon, S. Y., photograph. Copyright © David Rubinger/Corbis. Reproduced by permission.—Dickey, James, photograph taken in 1990. AP/Wide World Photos. Reproduced by permission.—Hamsun, Knut, photograph. The Library of Congress.— Heller, Joseph, photograph. AP/Wide World Photos. Reproduced by permission.

Thomson Gale Literature Product Advisory Board

The members of the Thomson Gale Literature Product Advisory Board—reference librarians from public and academic library systems—represent a cross-section of our customer base and offer a variety of informed perspectives on both the presentation and content of our literature products. Advisory board members assess and define such quality issues as the relevance, currency, and usefulness of the author coverage, critical content, and literary topics included in our series; evaluate the layout, presentation, and general quality of our printed volumes; provide feedback on the criteria used for selecting authors and topics covered in our series; provide suggestions for potential enhancements to our series; identify any gaps in our coverage of authors or literary topics, recommending authors or topics for inclusion; analyze the appropriateness of our content and presentation for various user audiences, such as high school students, undergraduates, graduate students, librarians, and educators; and offer feedback on any proposed changes/enhancements to our series. We wish to thank the following advisors for their advice throughout the year.

Barbara M. Bibel
Librarian
Oakland Public Library
Oakland, California

Dr. Toby Burrows
Principal Librarian
The Scholars' Centre
University of Western Australia Library
Nedlands, Western Australia

Celia C. Daniel
Associate Librarian, Reference
Howard University
Washington, D.C.

David M. Durant
Reference Librarian
Joyner Library
East Carolina University
Greenville, North Carolina

Nancy Guidry
Librarian
Bakersfield Community College
Bakersfield, California

Steven R. Harris
English Literature Librarian
University of Tennessee
Knoxville, Tennessee

Mary Jane Marden
Collection Development Librarian
St. Petersburg College
Pinellas Park, Florida

Heather Martin
Arts & Humanities Librarian
University of Alabama at Birmingham, Sterne Library
Birmingham, Alabama

Susan Mikula
Director
Indiana Free Library
Indiana, Pennsylvania

Thomas Nixon
Humanities Reference Librarian
University of North Carolina, Davis Library
Chapel Hill, North Carolina

Mark Schumacher
Jackson Library
University of North Carolina
Greensboro, North Carolina

Gwen Scott-Miller
Assistant Director
Sno-Isle Regional Library System
Marysville, Washington

Donald Welsh
Head, Reference Services
College of William and Mary, Swem Library
Williamsburg, Virginia

S. Y. Agnon
1888-1970

(Born Shmuel Yosef Czaczkes) Austro-Hungarian-Israeli novelist, short story writer, and poet.

The following entry provides criticism on Agnon's works from 1975 through 2003.

INTRODUCTION

Agnon was known for his ironic and lyrical fiction, based largely on Hebrew folklore and tradition.

BIOGRAPHICAL INFORMATION

Agnon was born Shmuel Yosef Czaczkes in Buczacz, Galicia (then Austria-Hungary, now Poland) 17 July, 1888. His father, a rabbi, taught him the Talmud and Hasidic literature, along with secular Hebrew and Yiddish writings, while his mother recited German stories. His love for literature led him to publish stories in Hebrew and Yiddish while still a teenager. In 1908 he settled in Palestine, but was rejected both by the Russian-Jewish population and the new settlers who prized manual labor above intellectual rigor. Agnon took his pen name, which later became his legal name, from the title of his first published story, "Agunot," which was published in Jaffa, Israel, in 1909. "Agnon" is based on a Hebrew word meaning abandoned or forsaken. In 1912 he settled in Germany, finding a more comfortable life there for around twelve years and forming friendships with well-known Zionists. In 1919 he married Esther Marx, with whom he had two children. Agnon became well known among German Jews and achieved literary success when his Hebrew works were translated into German. He also built a notable collection of ancient Hebrew manuscripts and was devastated in 1924 when a fire in his home destroyed them, along with his personal manuscripts. Agnon then returned to Palestine, settling in Jerusalem. In 1929 his personal library was again destroyed by fire when Arabs rioted in the city. Agnon won the Israel Prize in 1954 and the Nobel Prize in 1966. He died in 1970.

MAJOR WORKS

Agnon was virtually unknown to Western readers until his works began to be translated from Hebrew into English after he won the Nobel Prize in 1966. Unlike

many other modernist Jewish writers of his era, he emphasized original folk sources and dwelled on the lessons of the Torah. His earlier short stories and novellas concerned Jewish life in Eastern Europe, but after his immigration in 1924 until his death, he wrote almost exclusively about life in Palestine. Agnon's work has been compared to that of Cervantes and Kafka in its air of mystery and its imaginative power. His short stories are remarkably diverse, some magical fables, some accounts of modern-day alienation and exile. Others attempt to deal with the ways Judaism has survived throughout history in periods of political turmoil. His first successful work was a novella, *Ve-Hayah he-'Akov le-Mishor* (1912; *And the Crooked Shall Be Made Straight*). After the manuscript for his first novel was destroyed in a fire, he produced *Hakhnasath Kallah* (1931; *The Bridal Canopy*), a novel set in the eighteenth century about a Jewish man who travels about seeking dowries for his daughters. While continuing to write short fiction, he published the novel *Sipur Pashut* (1935; *A Simple Story*), an account of the development of a psychosis and its ultimate cure. *Ore'ah Nata Lalun* (*A Guest for the Night*) appeared in 1937 and in 1945, *Tmol Shilshom* (*Only Yesterday*). The former novel, a comment on the waning spirit of European Judaism, was written just before World War II; the latter is a picaresque and imaginative story set in Jerusalem, told from the point of view of a dog whose astute social and political commentary exceeds that of most his human counterparts. *Bi-levav Yamim* (1948; *In the Heart of the Seas: A Story of a Journey to the Land of Israel*), which follows a group of Jews in their journey from Galicia to Palestine, was followed by *Edo ve-Enam* (1950; *Edo and Enam*), a tale of the supernatural. *Shirah* (*Shira*), posthumously published in 1971, is a story of a bourgeois German exile in 1930's Palestine who seeks an escape from the conformity of his life. Several editions of Agnon's short stories and a collection of his poetry also were published after his death.

CRITICAL RECEPTION

Critical discussion of Agnon's work has truly been what one commentator called an "industry." Agnon's multifaceted writings, concurrent with the growth of Hebrew as an accepted language in American and British universities, have also substantially increased interest in literature in modern Hebrew. The wealth of Hebrew and German criticism during Agnon's earlier career presaged a still-growing American and British critical following, encouraged by scholarly journals such as the *Hebrew Annual Review, Judaism,* and *Prooftexts.* Early English-language Agnon critics, such as Arnold Band, used New Critical and comparative literature approaches or discussed the dilemmas of relating modern Jewish culture to the past. From the late 1970s through the early 2000s, critical approaches to Agnon came in what eminent Agnon scholar Alan Mintz called "a polyphony of voices," following the general trends of scholarly inquiry. Gershon Shaked and other critics emphasized the rich intertextuality of Agnon's fiction, which has provided a rich vein for further critical analysis. A variety of approaches to Agnon's work, including poststructuralism, psychoanalysis, deconstruction, postcolonialist theory, reader-response criticism, and feminist criticism, have developed among Agnon scholars. The close text-centeredness most Agnon critics embrace, Mintz says, suggests "the hovering spirit of classical Jewish learning."

PRINCIPAL WORKS

Ve-Hayah he-'Akov le-Mishor (novella) 1911-12
Das Buch von den Polnischen Juden [editor, with Ahron Eliasberg] (folk tales) 1916
Giv 'at ha-Hol (short stories) 1920
Be-Sod Yesharim (short stories) 1921
"Me-Hamat ha-Metsik" (short story) 1921
'Al Kapot ha-Man'ul (short stories) 1922
Bidmi yameha [*In the Prime of Her Life*] (novella) 1923
Ma'aseh he-meshulah meerets ha-Kedosha (short stories) 1924-25
Polin: Sipure agadot (short stories) 1924-25
"Ma'aseh rabi Gadiel ha-Tinok" (short story) 1925
Al Olam [*Forever More*] (novel) 1926
"Ha-Nidah" (short story) 1926
Sipur ha-Shanim ha-Tovot [*Ma'aseh ha'Rav Veha-Orah*] (short stories) 1927
Agadat hasofer (short stories) 1929
Laylot (short stories) 1930-31
Hakhnasath Kallah [*The Bridal Canopy*] (novel) 1931
Me-Az ume-Ata (short stories) 1931
Sippurei Ahayim (novel) 1931
Sefer HaMa'asim [*The Book of Deeds*] (short stories) 1932
Be-Shuva u-ve-Natat (short stories) 1935
Sipur Pashut [*A Simple Story*] (novel) 1935
Kovets Sipurim (short stories) 1937
Ore'ah Nata Lalun [*A Guest for the Night*] (novel) 1937
Yamim Nora'im [*Days of Awe: Being a Treasury of Traditions, Legends and Learned Commentaries Concerning Rosh ha-Shanah, Yom Kippur and the Days Between. Culled from Three Hundred Volumes, Ancient and New*] [*A Treasury of Jewish Wisdom for Reflection, Repentance, and Renewal on the High Holy Days*] (nonfiction) 1938
"Pi Shenaim: O me-Husar Yom" (short story) 1939
Elu va-Elu [*A Dwelling Place of My People: Sixteen Stories of the Chassidim*] (short stories) 1941
Shevu'ath Emunim [*The Betrothed*] (novella) 1943
"'Al Berl Kaznelson" (character sketch) 1944
Sipurum ve-Agadot (short stories) 1944
Sipurim (short stories) 1945
Tmol Shilshom [*Only Yesterday*] [*Just Yesterday*] (novel) 1945
Bi-levav Yamim [*In the Heart of the Seas: A Story of a Journey to the Land of Israel*] (novel) 1948
Edo ve-Enam (novel) 1950
Samukh ve-Nireh (short stories) 1950
Ad Heinah (short stories) 1953
"Sifrehem shel Anshe Butshatsh" (article) 1956
Tihella, and Other Israeli Tales [with others] (short stories) 1956
Atem re'item [editor] (collection of rabbinic sources) 1959
Kelev Hutsot (excerpts from *Temol shilshom*) 1960
Sihfrehem shel Tsadikim [compiler] (articles) 1961
Ha-Esh ve-Ha'etsim (short stories) 1962
Sipurum (short stories) 1966
Two Tales: "Betrothed" and "Edo and Enam" (novellas) 1966
Sipure Yom-ha-Kipurim (short stories) 1967
Selected Stories of S. Y. Agnon (short stories) 1970
Shirah [*Shira*] (novel) 1971

Twenty-One Stories (short stories) 1971

Ir u-Melo'ah [*A City and Its Fullness*] (short stories) 1973

Mr. Lublin's Shop (novel) 1975

A Book That Was Lost and Other Stories (short stories) 1995

Present at Sinai: The Giving of the Law (non-fiction) 1996

Agnon's Aleph Bet: Poems (poetry) 1998

*These works published in the collected works, *Kol Sipurav Shel Agnon* (Jerusalem, Tel Aviv), 1947-1957; standard edition, edited by Agnon (Schocken Books) 1953-1962; [*Kol sipurav shel Sh. Y. 'Agnon*] 8 vols., 1968.

CRITICISM

Bernard Knieger (review date 1975)

SOURCE: Knieger, Bernard. "Shmuel Yosef Agnon's 'The Face and the Image'." *Studies in Short Fiction* 12, no. 2 (1975): 184-85.

[*In the following review of an Agnon short story, Knieger calls attention to the Hebrew meaning of the phrase "face-to-face," concluding that the narrator is facing his own isolation from traditional faith.*]

One of the Agnon stories in *Twenty-One Stories* (New York: Schocken, 1970) is **"The Face and the Image."** But this title is a metaphorical translation of the Hebrew **Ha-panim la-panim,** which literally translates into "The Face to the Face." The editor Nahum N. Glatzer in his "Editorial Postscript" writes (on page 283) that the "Hebrew title of the story is taken from Proverbs 27:19, which the standard translations render as, 'As in the water face answereth to face, so the heart of man to man.'" But what is the relevance of this proverb to the story? Presumably the reference exists to establish an ironic contrast: the proverb asserts that man comforts man, but the narrator of the Agnon story is an isolated individual.

As is characteristic of many titles, the title **Ha-panim la-panim** provides crucial guidance to the central meaning of the story. But we do not realize the full nature of this guidance unless we recognize that this phrase not only appears in Proverbs; more crucially, it appears in a variant form—*panim el panim,* "face to face"—in Genesis and in Exodus. In Genesis 32:30, after his famous wrestling match where he has been renamed Israel, Jacob says, "I have seen God face to face, and my life is preserved." And in Exodus 33:11 it is written, "And Jehovah spoke unto Moses face to face, as a man speaketh unto his friend." These are well-known passages: *panim el panim* is as famous a phrase to a Hebrew speaker with a minimum knowledge of Jewish culture as, say, "Home of the Brave" would be to the average American. Therefore, part of the content of the Agnon title is in its echo of *panim el-panim*: that is, in the contrast between the face confronted by its mirror-image and with "God."

The central plot situation in the story is the narrator's failure to be able to visit his ill—dying or perhaps already dead—mother as a result of a series of awkward mishaps set up by the narrator himself. **"The Face and the Image"** is from the collection *The Book of Deeds,* and the characteristic story there is non-realistic, as the English reader can judge for himself, for Glatzer has included nine other stories from this source in the *Twenty-One Stories*. In any event, the mixture of realism and surrealism in **"The Face and the Image"** encourages a symbolic interpretation of this story in which the mother emerges as, say, the "old faith," certainly as its representative. As Glatzer writes in a general comment on *The Book of Deeds*: "Deep faith is a matter of the past . . ." (pp. 277-278). Thus the narrator at the end of the story is not sitting face to face with his mother, the representative of the old faith, but rather in strange surroundings. He is surprised by a mirror-image of himself "reflecting back every movement of the hand and quiver of the lips, like all polished mirrors, which show you whatever you show them, without partiality or deceit." Significantly, the "image rose" when he is trying to avoid recognizing the consequences of his not being by his mother's side. In the final line of the story, the "I" says that "it, namely, the revelation of the thing, surprised me more than the thing itself, perhaps more than it had surprised me in my childhood, perhaps more than it had ever surprised me before." Presumably what is revealed to him is his isolation, his folly, his impotence.

Instead of wrestling with God or speaking to Him face to face, the narrator at the end is speaking with himself and wrestling with his own self-image: man in his folly, his self confusion and isolation, in his impotence, and perhaps in his vanity as well, cannot return to the old faith—some such statement emerges as the central theme of this story, a meaning that is anticipated by the title **Ha-panim la-panim,** and by its echo of the more famous *panim el panim*.

Nehama Aschkenasy (essay date winter 1983)

SOURCE: Aschkenasy, Nehama. "Biblical Substructures in the Tragic Form: Hardy, *The Mayor of Casterbridge*; Agnon, *And the Crooked Shall Be Made Straight*." *Modern Language Studies* 13, no. 1 (winter 1983): 101-10.

[*In the following essay, Aschkenasy compares biblical references in* The Mayor of Casterbridge *and* And the

Crooked Shall Be Made Straight, *concluding that Agnon's use of the biblical dimension is more subtle than Hardy's.*]

Bringing together Hardy's *The Mayor of Casterbridge* (1886)[1] and Agnon's **And the Crooked Shall Be Made Straight** (1912),[2] a novella not yet translated into English, may seem an arbitrary yoking of different social milieus, cultural frames of reference, and verbal associations. But the apparent gap between Hardy and Agnon, and especially between these two particular works, is reduced considerably once we become aware of striking similarities in a number of artistic motifs and dramatic coincidences, as well as in the central tragic vision. Though both stories first appeared in serialized forms, they manifest an unmistakably Aristotelian "unity of action" in their unremitting focus on the decline and fall of their respective protagonists. In both stories, an initial act of "shame and horror," to use Dorothea Krook's tragic formula,[3] triggers a series of dramatic coincidences that, abetted by forces of fate and chance that seem to have been let loose, contribute to the inevitable tragic catastrophe.

While it is impossible to establish a direct influence, the glaring affinities between the two works call our attention to the sometimes mysterious ways in which folk motifs and literary patterns travel across countries and cultures and find themselves in different settings.[4] The fair as a grotesque reflection of moral and social chaos, and as the actual and symbolic backdrop for the protagonist's intoxicated surrender to temptation, is a powerful vision in both stories. A wrongful, immoral "business transaction" is at the heart of the tragic entanglement in both. In Hardy's story, the selling of the wife in a moment of drunken rashness, with which the novel starts, sets off a series of coincidences beyond the protagonist's control. In Agnon's tale, the "act of shame and horror" is not one single episode but rather a protracted state; it starts with the protagonist's ill-advised departure from his hometown and wife for the purpose of collecting alms, and culminates in his selling the letter of recommendation given to him by his rabbi. In both stories, the protagonists' final failures are tied to the obscure vicissitudes of the business world as well as to the uncertainty of harvest. The reappearance of a person thought lost and dead, the mishandling of letters, the motif of the "double," and the case of the wife who is married to a second "husband" while her lawful first husband is alive are elements of fateful significance in both stories.

But it is not only in the plot that the similarities between the two stories are so provoking. In fact, in terms of plot line alone, Agnon's tale seems to be a prose version of Tennyson's poem "Enoch Arden" (1864).[5] Like Enoch Arden, Menashe-Hayim, Agnon's protagonist, comes home to find his wife nursing a child by a second husband whom she married when the first husband was declared dead. Like Enoch Arden, Menashe-Hayim chooses to spend the rest of his life in self imposed exile and complete anonymity, away from human community, rather than ruin the happiness and reputation of his wife, who is unaware of the sinfulness of her second marriage. But while Tennyson's hero does not offer any philosophical observations regarding his personal experience, both Henchard, the deposed mayor of Casterbridge, and Menashe-Hayim, Agnon's hapless protagonist, comment on the moral and theological implications of their tragic predicament. The central situation is similar: in both cases: the first marital union, sanctified by God and community, was fruitless. Henchard's child died in infancy, and Menashe-Hayim's marriage never produced an offspring. However, the wife's second marriage, though impure and unlawful, seems to have been blessed by nature; the wives of both protagonists bear children to their second "husband." In both works, the bewildered protagonists question the moral order of the universe in words which reverberate with Jobian echoes. Hardy says of his protagonist: "Part of his wish to wash his hands of life arose from his perception of its contrarious inconsistencies—of Nature's jaunty readiness to support unorthodox social principles."[6] Agnon's protagonist expresses a similar sentiment while at the same time accepting God's verdict.[7] In fact, the Jobian stature of both protagonists, while not fully developed in either story, is quite apparent; Hardy's Henchard "cursed himself like a less scrupulous Job,"[8] while Agnon's hero is described in words taken from The Book of Job (14:1): "Man that is born of a woman is of few days, and full of trouble."[9] Moreover, both Henchard and Menashe-Hayim find solace in The Book of Psalms, and see in it a reflection of their own predicaments.

Both stories are saturated with Scriptural citations and references that are not just isolated allusions that illuminate individual episodes. In both, a specific Biblical pattern provides the structural meaning of the total work, and serves as a scaffold that supports the entire narrative. The main dramatic situation in Hardy's novel, the conflict between Henchard, the old mayor of Casterbridge, and Farfrae, his successor, is described as analogous to the Saul-David conflict in 1 Samuel. In Agnon's story, the protagonist who leaves his home and wanders among strangers is seen as reenacting his nation's destiny of dispossession and exile, a major Biblical theme. But the differences between Hardy's and Agnon's treatment of the Biblical structures are of great significance. Let us first see how the Biblical materials are evoked in these two stories and incorporated into the narrative.

On several occasions in *The Mayor of Casterbridge* Hardy likens his protagonist to specific Biblical characters. At times, it is only the writer who is aware of the analogy, while his protagonist remains oblivious to the

Biblical dimension of his own predicament. In addition to the reference to Job, Hardy also tells us that Henchard felt "like Saul at his reception by Samuel,"[10] and at another point he depicts him as "Samson shorn."[11] On other occasions, it is Henchard who suggests the similarity between himself and a Biblical character: "I—Cain—go alone as I deserve—an outcast and a vagabond";[12] and, "I felt quite ill . . . and, like Job, I could curse the day that gave me birth."[13]

But the only parallelism that extends to the entire plot and is sustained throughout the story is undoubtedly that between Henchard and Saul.[14] To delineate briefly the major features of this analogy: Henchard is a Saul-like figure in his potential of greatness as well as in his lapses into rages and depressions. Gloomy and lonely, he is drawn to the younger man, Farfrae, who, like his Biblical counterpart David, possesses musical skills. But the loving relationship between the two men deteriorates into suspicion and animosity when their fortunes change. Henchard loses his business, his social position, and even his daughter; while Farfrae gains the admiration of the townspeople, prospers financially, and marries first Henchard's fiancee and then his beloved stepdaughter. Eventually, the younger man will inherit the older man's position as the mayor of Casterbridge. The Biblical parallels are obvious. Saul, too, felt betrayed by people whose loyalty he demanded on the basis of their natural ties to him: his son Jonathan and his daughter Michal. The loving friendship between the two Biblical characters also sours when the older man is threatened by the younger man and sees in him the potential usurper of his title and power. Henchard's secret visit to the weather caster parallels Saul's nocturnal trip to the witch who raises the prophet Samuel from the dead. It is in this scene that Hardy himself draws the readers' attention to the parallelism between Henchard and Saul. In the modern story, as well as in its ancient counterpart, the encounter with the prophet bodes ill for the seeker of the future and marks his final doom.

Since Hardy's focal point is Henchard and not Farfrae, the correspondence between Henchard and Saul is much closer than that between Farfrae and David. While Farfrae possesses David's good looks, fine voice and social charm, he ultimately emerges as lackluster, a pale reflection of his glamorous counterpart in the Bible. Furthermore, while in the central conflict Henchard's role parallels that of Saul, Hardy attributes to Henchard some of the qualities of David. In one instance, Henchard fights with Farfrae, yet at the last moment he refrains from destroying him; this is reminiscent of two Biblical incidents in which David has a chance to kill Saul, yet he decides to spare the king's life. In another scene, Henchard identifies with the "Servant David" and asks the church choir to recite Psalm 109 to him.[15]

Henchard, then, incorporates in his character a variety of Biblical figures: the ill-fated Saul, the strong Samson rendered powerless, the puzzled sufferer Job, and the prototypical sinner, Cain. While each Biblical figure illuminates one aspect of Henchard's personality, the most dominant is that of king Saul.

At the same time, a different frame of reference that becomes apparent in the novel links the mayor of Casterbridge to another ancient king, Oedipus of Thebes. While the Biblical parallelism is established by the actual naming of Biblical figures, the analogy between Henchard and Oedipus is done mainly through a series of incidents as well as imagery. One of the first scenes in the novel portrays the arrogant mayor confronting the embittered townspeople who complain about the damaged wheat that the mayor had sold to the bakers and that produced debased bread. The theme of pollution and the protagonist as responsible for it suggests an analogy with the first scene in *Oedipus Rex,* in which the people of Thebes complain about the plague to Oedipus, who turns out to be the source of it. Hardy, then, draws the image of the diseased monarch from both Hebraic and Hellenic sources.[16] The analogy with Oedipus reinforces the tragic framework of the novel and suggests the existence of malevolent forces in the universe. Henchard's one act of violence has unleased those irrational forces and, no matter how much he tries to make amends for his initial act of "shame and horror," those forces, in the form of chance coincidences, fatal reappearance of people, and the vicissitudes of nature, will finally defeat and destroy him. "Tragedies end badly," says George Steiner, the tragic personage "is broken by forces which can neither be fully understood nor overcome by rational prudence."[17]

On the other hand, the introduction of the Biblical pattern takes the novel away from the exclusively tragic domain and anchors Henchard's predicament in a sphere that emphasizes human responsibility and free will, and calls for a just punishment for man's sin. If the analogy with Oedipus implies that Henchard's universe is a vicious circle in which he is trapped regardless of what he will do, the Biblical dimension offers another vision that sees human life in terms of progress and change and views time as a healing mechanism.

The Greek conception of time recognizes no historical development says Tom Driver, "and the changes come about not through the guilt of man but through the will of the gods."[18] The Judeo-Christian consciousness of time, on the other hand, emphasizes "the significance of action taken in the historical present."[19] The Hellenic element in Hardy's novel would suggest that Henchard's tragedy lies in his imperfect human nature, in his inability, as man, to alter or control the powers around him. And the novel offers many instances of Henchard's sense of entrapment. The Hebraic presence, on the other hand, sees Henchard's predicament in the context of a dynamic moral frame in which human suffering is a consequence of the wrong human action. Henchard accepts his role as sinner and understands the nature of his punishment in Biblical terms when he likens himself to Cain and adds: ". . . But my punishment is not greater than I can bear."[20] The Hebraic conception of human life as determined by human action is certainly present in the story. Hardy, who read Matthew Arnold,[21] was undoubtedly acquainted with the chapter "Hebraism and Hellenism" in *Culture and Anarchy* (1869) in which Arnold sees the polarity between Hellenism and Hebraism as that between pursuing knowledge ("right thinking," in his words) and choosing moral action ("right acting").[22]

It is hard to say which vision ultimately wins in *The Mayor*. Both the Hellenic and the Hebraic are present as optional conceptions of man and his place in the universe; one is stark and uncompromising, the other demanding but reconciliatory. It is not surprising that there is no critical consensus as to whether Hardy's novel achieves full tragic proportions.[23] The Biblical figures who function as the archaic prototypes of Henchard are remote from the tragic sphere.[24] However, one may wonder why Hardy chose Saul as the main counterpart of his protagonist. While the Biblical vision as a whole is non-tragic, as Steiner explains, it is undeniable that there are tragic moments in the Bible. Moreover, of all Biblical characters, it seems that Saul comes closest to the tragic.[25] In fact, the tragic potential of the Saul story has been fully utilized by the Hebrew poet Tchernichovsky in two ballads which emphasize the heroic stature of Saul, the starkness of his fate, and the sense of doom that accompanies him. In one ballad ("Shaul B'Ein Dor"), Tchernichovsky recreates the scene of Saul's painful confrontation with the ghost of Samuel the prophet. The king emerges as an appealing figure, attempting to understand his fate, trying to impose order over chaos. The prophet speaks in the name of an irrational, obscure power, the laws of which are arbitrary and inscrutable. This episode is reminiscent of the Oedipus-Tiresias bitter exchange in *Oedipus Rex*. Interestingly Hardy has also anchored the analogy between Henchard and Saul in the protagonist's attempt to gain knowledge with the aid of a soothsayer.

It seems that while Hardy used the Biblical prototypes for the non-tragic dimension that they would introduce in the novel, he singled out the character of Saul as Henchard's ancient counterpart because of an intuitive perception of the tragic potential of this particular Biblical figure.

The protagonist that Agnon has chosen to carry the weight of the tragic predicament is different from Hardy's hero. Henchard's personal traits immediately suggest that he is likely to come under the tragic pall: he exhibits a capacity for great rages as well as a hubristic defiance of the laws of nature and man; yet he is not evil. Agnon's protagonist, Menashe-Hayim, is colorless by comparison. While Agnon couches his story in an archaic idiom and sets it in an old-fashioned, dying folk culture, he seems to offer the modern idea that even the "little" man, the man of no special "character," is capable of the tragic experience. Indeed, Menashe-Hayim's act of defiant impiety, the selling of the letter of recommendation, is not less outrageous than Henchard's selling of his wife, especially in the light of the dramatic events that it triggers: Menashe-Hayim will lose his wife, who will unwittingly enter a marriage that is sinful and defiled in the eyes of Jewish law.

Unlike Hardy, Agnon does not name any Biblical figure as the ancient prototype of his protagonist; nor does he recreate a particular Biblical episode of dramatic potential in his story. Instead, the Biblical language of exile and redemption that suffuses the narrative, and that is implied in the title itself, suggests that Menashe-Hayim reenacts his nation's entire historical destiny of punishment and restoration. Menashe-Hayim thus relives not an isolated Biblical episode, but the main drama that underlies the total Old Testament vision. The title, which is an exact quotation of Isaiah 40:4 (. . . and the crooked shall be made straight, and the rough places plain"), sets the tone; it offers an eschatological vision of national redemption, and establishes the Biblical terms of the story.

However, the Biblical structure is only one of several layers of verbal and cultural associations that exist in the story. In fact, the nineteenth century protagonist and his milieu serve as the middle point of a number of concentric circles of ideas and concepts. The other prominent layers are: the Talmudic, marked by the use of Aramaic as well as of legal-halachic terms such as "deserted wife" ("Agunah"), "halachic problem" ("sugiah"), "borrower" ("shoel"), "legal evidence" ("siman"), "testimony" ("eduth"), "transgression" ("averah"), "adultery" ("Issur Arayoth"); the Literature of Ethics, identifiable by wise sayings and ethical aphorisms which are either quoted from actual Rabbinic texts, or imitate their style; the Hassidic-mystical, made up of tales of miraculous, last minute rescues, in which words such as "faith," "salvation," "miracle," and "fate" are predominant; and the popular layer, which represents the ambiance of the contemporary folk culture and is marked by the language of superstition ("the devil," "shed mi'shahat"), premonitions (the protagonist kissing the empty mesusah space, the ballads sung in the fair), and the callous, mocking voice of the community that sometimes intrudes into the tale.[26]

The Biblical layer of the story cannot be read in isolation; it is inextricably tied to the other circles of associations which, together, exhibit the mutation, transformation, and even corruption of specific Biblical concepts. For example: the most predominant concepts within the Biblical orbit are those of redemption and exile. Indeed, the root g'l, to redeem, is the most frequently used in the story; the root glh, to go on exile, also appears quite often. The husband's departure from his home and wife is described as going on exile, and his return is viewed as the redemption of both himself and his wife ("ki yavo v'yigaaal," he will return and redeem).[27] The concept of redemption in this context echoes the prophetic language, hence Menashe-Hayim is reenacting his national destiny. But the word "redeemer" is later used in the narrow legal meaning in which it appears in the Bible (i.e. the kin who redeems the blood, or the property, or the wife, of another family member). Ironically, it is not the lawful husband who will be the redeemer of his wife, but the second husband ("nimtsa la goel," a redeemer was found for her).[28] Furthermore, the verb "to redeem" is used within the Talmudic-halachic context, too, when the rabbis try to "redeem," or free, the wife from the limbo status of "agunah" ("l'gaolah mi'kavlei ha'aigun," to free her from the bonds of "iggun").[29] Again the irony is apparent: the rabbis think that they redeemed the woman, while actually they have enabled her to commit adultery. As the story moves towards its resolution, words deriving from the root g'l, to redeem, appear in greater frequency. At this point, Menashe-Hayim wishes for the redemption of his soul in mystical terms;[30] yet the word redemption is now stripped of all its associations and narrows down to one meaning only—death.[31]

A similar mutation occurs in the root glh, to go on exile. Initially, Menashe-Hayim's wife prepares for him "the gear for exile," a phrase repeatedly used in the Book of Ezekiel chapter 12. This prophetic phrase creates the grand setting for the protagonist's departure from home, and anchors his private experiences in the collective, national destiny. Together with the title of the story, that describes the return of the exiles, the Biblical echoes suggest the Hebraic quality of historical remembrance of past events, and the conception of the future as open and redeemable, that Tom Driver sees as the main traits of the Judaic consciousness of time.[32] As the story progresses, however, the relationship between the wandering of the exiled nation and the begging from door to door of our protagonist becomes merely satirical. Menashe-Hayim deteriorates into a greedy, gluttonous vagabond, and Agnon marks this change in his protagonist by adding the Biblical phrase that describes Cain's wanderings: "a fugitive and a vagabond," ("na vanad").[33] At this point, the wandering of the protagonist no longer parallels that of his nation's, since it does not mean an expiation of sin but, rather, sinking more and more into sin. Furthermore, to justify his failure to return home, Menashe-Hayim uses the excuse that he deliberately "exiles himself" ("oseh golah"). He is thus distorting the concept of "exile" as used in the Literature of Ethics and in Hassidic sources. In the former, it is suggested that an individual should temporarily leave his family and wander among strangers in order to perfect his soul. In Hasidic tradition, the Zaddik, spiritual leader, goes on exile as a way of preparing himself for his leadership role. Menashe-Hayim, however, corrupts the Biblical, Rabbinic, and Hasidic meanings of the concept of exile, thus revealing both his depravity and comic pretentiousness.

Towards the end of the story, Agnon abandons altogether the verbs that derive from the root glh, go on exile, and uses repeatedly the verb "wander," ("na vanad") associated with Cain. This time, it is the protagonist, in a moment of illumination, who views himself not in terms of the individual who fulfills his nation's destiny, but as the sinner Cain. He asserts that, just as he has been wandering in this world, so his soul will continue its restless wandering in the other world.[34] Thus the theme of the return of the exiles, described in the title of the story, comes full circle in an ironic reversal of its Biblical meaning; instead of restoration into harmony, we have the vision of Menashe-Hayim's tormented soul, forever in exile, eternally wandering.

Agnon's story abounds with many other Biblical allusions that introduce motifs from Genesis, Lamentations, The Psalms, Job, and The Book of Esther. Generally, the biblical language creates a comic discrepancy between the sublime and the mundane, as when the grotesque musicians in the fair are described in the language with which the psalmist envisions the return of the exiles.[35] In other instances, a Biblical verse is quoted word by word, or slightly paraphrased, and incorporated into the language of the narrative only to reinforce the protagonist's estrangement from the Biblical world, and to foretell disaster. For example: Menashe-Hayim expresses his wish to visit the fair with the phrase used by Moses when he begs God to see the promised land: ". . . let me go over and see" (Deuteronomy, 3:25). Besides the inherent irony, these words suggest Menashe-Hayim's eventual failure to enter his own promised land, i.e., his home.

The reversal of the Biblical context is a satirical device; the Biblical idiom dwarfs the protagonist and exposes his faults and pretensions. At the same time, the Biblical dimension reveals the tragic loneliness of modern man, cut off from the ancient source of meaning and comfort.[36] While the Biblical language in the story creates a world filled with the promise of redemption, the actual plot, especially the ending in which the protagonist acts against Biblical law and dies a sinner, reveals a world empty of the main Biblical premises.

On the other hand, Agnon's story does not commit itself totally to the tragic vision. While the tragic structure of the plot is undeniable, Agnon rejects the Hellenic conception of man as a plaything at the hands of the gods. The first chapter of the story uses repeatedly various words that signify "fate" (such as "mazal"—fate, "gzeira"—predestination, "galgal"—the wheel of fortune), and creates the impression that the protagonist is exposed to the capriciousness and irrationality of a malevolent force that governs human life. Yet it soon becomes clear that the term "fate" is used as an excuse by a protagonist who is unable to face up to his own inadequacies. Furthermore, the Hasidic stories inserted early into the narrative prove that it is man's own inner resources that determine the happy outcome of events, not outside forces. Therefore, Menashe-Hayim's predicament cannot be fully defined in tragic terms since he is not controlled by hidden, evil forces; nor is he seen as gaining dignity and nobility by spitefully challenging the injustice of these forces. Thus, at the end of the story, Agnon's protagonist is not only denied redemption in Biblical terms, but is also deprived of the grandeur of the tragic hero.

And yet, Menashe-Hayim does ultimately achieve a measure of redemption, though it takes place outside both the Hebraic and the Hellenic orbits. A "dissociation of sensibility" occurs at the end of the story that allows us to separate the concept of "sin" as a Biblical-legal term, from the idea of "guilt" as a psychological state. In the Biblical sphere, within which Menashe-Hayim still moves, he continues to be a sinner; yet he rids himself of his guilt feelings and experiences an emotional tranquility at the end of the story. His redemption is defined in psychological terms as that of a man who has made the courageous decision to sacrifice his own life for the happiness of another human being. His reward is also emotional. He dies convinced of his wife's love and assured of being buried in the grave, and under the tombstone, designated for him.[37] If the crooked is being made straight at the end, it is not in Biblical terms, but in modern, secular, psychological terms. Redemption is located in the subjective consciousness of the individual who has finally made peace with himself, but it is not bound up with his fulfilling the divine destiny of his community.

It is quite apparent that while the Biblical presence functions as a supportive substructure in both works, the two writers differ in their use of the Biblical material. For Hardy, the Scriptures serve as a large storehouse of archaic legends that contain prototypical characters and situations. The relationship between the Biblical universe and the Wessex environment is, therefore, metaphorical: Henchard felt *like* Job, acted *like* Saul, etc. Furthermore, for Hardy the architect the Biblical plot offered a structure that could be used as a direct parallel of the modern plot-line. The symmetrical neatness and the almost geometric precision of the analogy are essential to the narrative form of Hardy's novel. There is no structural tension, no paradoxical or satirical relationship between the Biblical story and its nineteenth century counterpart. True, the Saul-David precedence expands the insular, regional story both spatially and chronologically; thus the Henchard-Farfrae conflict is the Biblical tale writ small. But the architectural support that the Biblical frame offers Hardy is mechanical, imposed by a skilled artisan to perfect his fictional creation.

In Agnon's story, the Biblical element is embedded in the language itself and is thus inseparable from the very fabric of the narrative. While Hardy's plot is independent of the Biblical structure, Agnon's tale has no life of its own but that which is inextricably tied to the Biblical dimension. The language of exile and redemption places the individual story in a larger framework of universal significance where the personal and the historic meet, and creates expectations that are eventually defeated. The crux of the narrative is the constant tension between the Biblical frame and the modern plot. Thus the language of absolute justice and eschatological promise constantly challenges the temporal, relative, and enclosed reality of the protagonist and is, in turn, challenged by it. Both the Biblical and the modern are tested against each other; the correlation between them is simultaneously direct and reverse, genuine and ironic. Agnon does not need the adjective "like" because the Biblical presence asserts itself as an organic part of the verbal life of the tale, rather than as a structure extraneous to the actual dramatic web. For Agnon, the Bible exists not as an archaic layer that the artist can draw on to reinforce his narrative, but as a ubiquitous presence, constantly claiming attention and provoking the imagination.

Notes

1. Hereafter, *The Mayor*. All page references will be made to the Harper edition (1950).

2. Hereafter, *The Crooked*. All page references will be made to Schoken's 1971 edition, volume "Elu V'Elu."

3. *Elements of Tragedy* (New Haven: Yale University Press), p. 8.

4. Agnon was an avid reader of German letters (See: S. Y. Agnon, *M'Atsmi El Atsmi,* Schoken, 1976, pp. 113, 115, et passim). It is possible that he became aware of the works of Hardy through critical reviews that appeared in Germany before he left for Israel (in 1907). It seems that Hardy was popular in Germany even before the turn of the century. Carl. J. Weber, in *The First Hundred Years of Thomas Hardy 1840-1940* (New York: Russel and Russel, 1965), lists works on Hardy that appeared in Germany as early as 1889, 1894, 1901, 1902, and 1903. An indirect source through which Agnon could have heard of Hardy's works

was the Hebrew writer Y. H. Brenner. Brenner spent some time in England and, as Agnon himself testifies (*M'ATsmi El Stsmi*, p. 121), was a voracious reader. Brenner read also English and used to have long talks with Agnon on world literature.

5. "Enoch Arden" was translated into German by Carl Hessel in 1874(?) (Leipzig: P. Reclam jun). Another translation, in an illustrated edition, appeared in Berlin in 1883, published by G. Grote.

6. *The Mayor*, p. 368.

7. *The Crooked*, p. 122.

8. *The Mayor*, p. 330.

9. *The Crooked*, p. 123.

10. *The Mayor*, p. 214.

11. *The Mayor*, p. 373.

12. *The Mayor*, p. 361.

13. *The Mayor*, p. 90.

14. The close parallelism between the Henchard-Farfrae drama and the Biblical story has been closely studied by Julian Moynahan in "*The Mayor of Casterbridge* and 1 Samuel," *PMLA*, 71 (1956), 118-30.

15. *The Mayor*, p. 269.

16. See D. A. Dike, "A Modern Oedipus: *The Mayor of Casterbridge*," *Essays in Criticism*, 2 (1952), 169-79.

17. *The Death of Tragedy*, (London: Faber, 1961), p. 8.

18. *The Sense of History in Greek and Shakespearean Drama* (New York: Columbia University Press, 1967), p. 27.

19. Driver, p. 39.

20. *The Mayor*, p. 361.

21. See Carl J. Weber, *Hardy of Wessex* (New York: Columbia University Press, 1965), p. 42.

22. Matthew Arnold, *Culture and Anarchy* (New York: Bobbs-Merrill, 1971), p. 109.

23. See John Paterson, "*The Mayor of Casterbridge* as Tragedy," in A. J. Guerard (ed.), *Hardy: A Collection of Critical Essays* (Englewood Cliffs: Prentice-Hall, 1963), p. 95.

24. Milton, of course, treated Samson as a tragic character in "Samson Agonistes." The Book of Job was also "rewritten" as tragedy.

25. On the tragic dimension of Saul's figure and career see: Hillel Barzel, "Moses: Tragedy and Sublimity," in R. R. Gros Louis (ed.), *Literary Interpretations of Biblical Narratives* (New York: Abingdon, 1974), pp. 125-6.

26. This is not an attempt to differentiate between the historical layers of the Hebrew language used by Agnon, but rather, between the areas of cultural connotations and symbols present in this story.

27. *The Crooked*, p. 112.

28. *The Crooked*, p. 116.

29. *The Crooked*, p. 113.

30. Gershom G. Scholem shows how the concepts of exile and deliverance have been converted in Kabbalah, and later in Hasidic thought, into terms denoting personal-psychological processes or mystical-cosmic ideas. See *Major Trends in Jewish Mysticism* (New York: Schoken, 1974), pp. 286, 305, 341 et passim.

31. *The Crooked*, p. 123.

32. *The Sense of History*, p. 39-66.

33. *The Crooked*, p. 88.

34. *The Crooked*, p. 127.

35. *The Crooked*, p. 99 offers a comic paraphrase of Psalm 126:6 "He that goeth forth and weepeth, bearing precious seeds, shall doubtless come again with rejoicing, bringing his sheaves with him."

36. The idea that Agnon's troubled protagonists represent modern man's tragic predicament and sense of estrangement is one of the main premises that runs through Baruch Kursweill's works on Agnon. See *Massot Al Sipurei Agnon* (Tel Aviv: Schoken, 1963).

37. Arnold Band argues that the ending of the story takes it away from the tragic sphere. See *Nostalgia and Nightmare* (Berkeley: University of California Press, 1968), p. 87.

Jeffrey M. Green (review date spring-summer 1984)

SOURCE: Green, Jeffrey M. "Inside Agnon." *Modern Hebrew Literature* 9, no. 3-4 (spring-summer, 1984): 80-4.

[*In the following review of* Estherlein, *a compilation of Agnon's letters to his wife from 1924-1931, Green states that Agnon reveals few literary secrets but offers insights into his thinking about other matters.*]

For those of us whom he captivates, Agnon is incomparable. While they might seem to be limited to a narrow realm of experience and interests, his writings have an emotional range extending from the depths of tragedy to the most caustic of wit. His works include Hassidic legends, astonishing surrealistic dreams, allegory-like fantasies as well as realism, and they always remain enigmatic. A basic reason for this is that Agnon's narrators, whether omniscient or personalized, tend to be unreliable. They do not tell all they know, nor do they have a well-defined opinion about what they are telling. For that reason it is difficult to say just where the Apparent Author stands. Those features of Agnon's works are what give them such a modern cast, even though he often deals with pre-modern life.

The unreliability of Agnon's narrators is apparently connected to a feature of his public personality in life. A major problem for any writer is what to do with his real self, how to use it without compromising it, how to put it into his works without depleting it, and how to protect it from the curious world. That problem is mirrored in the somewhat naive approach of many readers, who take fiction for confession and imagination for gossip. Yet even the least naive of us develop a certain curiosity about the people who wrote the books that most engross us.

For Agnon the problem of both revealing and concealing himself from his audience was compounded by the nature of that audience. A great many of his readers knew him personally, at least slightly, Jerusalem and the Yishuv being such small communities at that time. Apparently Agnon put up a deceptive public front in order to preserve his creative privacy. At least that is the way the late Gershom Scholem interpreted his friend's behavior in his 1981 interview with Dan Miron (published in translation in *Ariel,* No. 52).

Agnon gives away his own game at the end of one of his first letters from Jerusalem, dated November 12, 1924:

> Since I have an empty page, I will write you an amusing little story.
>
> On the ship I saw a man sitting with a young woman, and they were both talking Hebrew. The man was dressed like a gentleman, and the maid was also dressed well. I introduced myself to them, saying my name was Czaczkes, and as for them . . . he is an American citizen, and she is from Warsaw. After that introduction both of them together informed me that in Vienna they had heard that Agnon was also travelling on the ship, and as hard as they tried, they had not found him. They had sought and inquired after him both in the first and the second classes, and also in the third and in the fourth, and they had not found him. I turned the conversation to another topic. On the second day the young man (not really so young) was in a rush, and when I addressed him he answered me as if under duress: he was hurrying because he had been told that Agnon was strolling here! I saw that he had no time for a simple person like myself and let him go. But after a few minutes he returned, deeply upset, because he had not found Agnon, and he expressed his sorrow to another gentleman, an English Jew, not an important personage, but very smart, and he told our man, "But Mr. Agnon is sitting right here." I too was startled, and I asked the Englishman how he knew I was Agnon, and he said that first of all he could tell by my face that I was a poet, and secondly he had seen that many Hebrews were rushing about seeking Agnon, and you, that is, I, were not looking for him, etc.
>
> (p. 29).

Now that he is no longer living, of course, Agnon has no need to protect his creative privacy, and our own curiosity about the man who wrote his books can become disinterested, transcending gossip and becoming an inquiry into the nature of a supremely creative individual personality. These letters offer us insight into that personality.

From a literary point of view, Agnon is still a dynamic presence in the life of Israeli letters, not only because of the great works published during his lifetime, but also because of the large body of writings that have been published posthumously. Since his death in 1970, Agnon's daughter, Emuna Yaron, has been editing his literary estate, and this collection of letters to his wife, also including several letters from his wife to him, is the ninth volume in that enterprise. Her introduction and notes are indispensable for the understanding of the letters, placing them in the context of events to which they do not refer.

When reading personal correspondence not intended for oneself, one's interest is quite different from that of the original correspondents. What Agnon had to tell his wife about the quality of the food served in a vegetarian restaurant in Leipzig is of little immediate interest to us. While some writers, such as Flaubert, used their correspondence to explore the nature of literature in general and their own literary efforts in particular, Agnon has very little to say about his art in these letters, except about the physical circumstances in which he worked, how hot and noisy or pleasant and comfortable his room was, how the Tel Aviv sun dried the ink in his fountain pen, how he dropped and broke it, and whether or not he was working hard. He occasionally tells Esther that a story came out quite nicely, and he mentions the need to keep writing while the writing was good and exploit moments when stories flowed from his pen, but he never discusses a story in detail or explains what he was trying to do in it or why. The names of many writers crop up in these letters: Hebrew writers whom he frequented (although he preferred the company of rabbis and young *halutzim*), Traven, whose book, *Das Totenschiff,* he read and recommended to his wife, and Balzac (he asks Esther to send him a German translation of *Le Cousin Pons*). Yet not once does he give his critical opinion of these writers or their works at any length. Esther, his first reader, the one who typed his manuscripts and helped him prepare them for publication, was apparently not, at least not in his letters, a literary confidante. At best the letters tell us a great deal about the life surrounding his work, but about the essence of that work, that is, the reason why we are interested in Samuel Josef Czaczkes today, nothing is directly revealed.

Indirectly one can learn a great deal. No reader of Agnon could fail to be curious about his real attitudes towards religion, and on that topic these letters are enlightening, although the basic question remains unresolved. We hear of his going to synagogue, and of his strong sense of the holiness of Jerusalem, as well as of the standards of dress and behavior he demanded of himself out of respect for that city. He frequently visited the graves of famous rabbis in the Land of Israel and abroad. But in the very sentence in which he tells how, in Leipzig, he visited the graves of both Rabbi Jacob Emden and Rabbi Jonathan Eybeschuetz, a famous pair of antagonists (the former suspected the latter of Sabbateanism), he mentions that he also visited the tomb of Friedrich Gottlieb Klopstock, not a renowned *Tsadik,* in fact not even a Jew.

We get further insight into the sincerity of his religious attitudes from the instructions he gives Esther about the children's religious education, making sure they recite the *Shema* before they go to sleep. On the other hand, Esther herself was not orthodox. She did not pretend to be, nor, apparently, did her husband expect her to be. In one letter Agnon tells her to be prepared to observe the Sabbath strictly so as not to offend potential landlords in Jerusalem. But in an earlier one he tells her that he is more comfortable being an *"Epikoros"* (heretic) among the religious than a *"Tsadik"* in the eyes of the *"Epikorsim"*. He enjoyed being accepted by the Hassidim, attending their celebrations and conversing with their sages, and he marvels at being honored by them even though he was clean shaven and without *pe'ot*. In life, as in his writing, he seems to have been above all a man of many reservations, deeply committed, but in his own way, to his work, to the Land of Israel and Jerusalem, to the Hebrew language, and to his immediate family.

At the time these letters were written, Agnon was already a prominent Hebrew writer. It is interesting to see his ambivalence about fame. In several of the letters he boasts that he is being paid five times what other writers were receiving for their stories. In other letters he marvels that he is read by the orthodox, including several extremely religious rabbis. He loves to be with the young pioneers and values their appreciation of his writing. He tells about being asked to read to groups and accepting or refusing, and once, about starting and being unable to continue. He also tells about the more official and ceremonial side of being a Hebrew author, and for that he had very little patience.

In the summer of 1930, after overseeing the printing of his collected works in Leipzig,—a project underwritten by Salman Schocken—Agnon travelled to his native Galicia, where he received a hero's welcome. To describe his emotions he resorts to Yiddish: *"hob zikh gerissen dos beser funm punim far busho"* (I could have torn the flesh off my face for shame). He does not explain.

One major virtue of these letters is that the narrator is a reliable one. We know who is talking and what his intentions are. That helps us anchor ourselves in reading Agnon's fiction. It is amusing to think of him, apparently so unworldly in his fictional disguise, attending plays in Germany, wishing he could bring Esther to Vienna and show her the sights, and rushing off to visit the pyramids on his way to Palestine. Agnon, so Jewish, did not wall himself up among his fellow Jews. He enjoyed meeting gentiles and mentions befriending a good number of them, including sailors on the ship he took from Alexandria to Genoa. In short, these letters flesh out the somewhat disembodied personality one glimpses through Agnon's fiction. Another one of their major virtues is the Hebrew itself, Agnon's style in life, unpremeditated, unrevised, and flowing naturally. Finally, they are full of news and information. As in his stories, Agnon frequently tells more in a single sentence than other writers tell in a whole page.

Esther Fuchs (essay date fall 1985)

SOURCE: Fuchs, Esther. "Wherefrom Did Gediton Enter Gumlidata? Realism and Comic Subversiveness in 'Forevermore'." *Modern Language Studies* 15, no. 4 (fall 1985): 64-79.

[*In the following essay, Fuchs deconstructs an Agnon story emphasizing the central irony, which she claims other critics have neglected.*]

1. INTRODUCTION

S. Y. Agnon's story **"Ad Olam"** "Forevermore" has stirred much critical controversy over its ideological meaning. Meshulam Tochner sees the story as a polemic against modern Biblical criticism and modern Hebrew literature.[1] Eddy Zemach claims that the story argues against secular Judaism.[2] Hillel Barzel maintains that the story demonstrates the transience of secular political statehood by displaying the way in which "one secular civilization is destroyed by another."[3] Despite the considerable differences between these interpretations they all agree that the story is a vehicle for an ideological message, and that the "overt text" is of secondary importance. The allegorical method of interpretation underlying these analyses focuses on the intention of the author and the meaning of the story but ignores the *form* of the story, e.g., the way in which the hero is characterized and the structure of the plot.

Since in narrative fiction, or for that matter, in any work of art form and content are inseparable, the ideological-allegorical approach misses not only the aesthetic impact of the form, but the meaning generated by it. The critic who concentrates on the ideological implications of the story to the exclusion of its other elements runs the risk of imposing his own preconceived ideas on the work. Criticizing Tochner's approach to Agnon, Dan Miron gives expression to this problem by asking, "Did the research precede the conclusion, or was it the conclusion which determined the research?"[4] In the case of ironic works, such as **"Ad Olam,"** neglect of the formal aspect incurs far-reaching repercussions because it prevents the critic from noticing the incongruity between, for example, the point of view of the protagonist and that of the implied author. Most of the interpretations mentioned above indeed identify these distinct points of view; hence the interpretations ascribing to Agnon anti-Zionist or anti-secular conceptions. Furthermore, because of the obsessive concern with ideology, the ironic treatment of the protagonist and his field of research—the central metonymy of the story—was all but missed. It is ironic indeed that a story dedicated to questioning meaning and undermining the validity of academic research and logic in general should be presented as a rational-ideological allegory. By focusing on the two largely neglected aspects of characterization and the structure of the central metonymy, the present analysis will demonstrate the underlying irony of the story, which is its most salient feature.

2. THE CHARACTERIZATION OF THE PROTAGONIST

Adiel Amzeh, the protagonist of the story, enjoys a considerable popularity among critics. He is presented as a tragic hero who reaches the highest human destination: liberation from material constraints and a true dedication to the spiritual and moral goals of life.[5] The mythical stature of the hero endows the story with high points not found in Agnon's other stories, which fail to offer an equal "epic, mythic and archaic development" of their heroes.[6] Adiel Amzeh is praised not only for his moral stature but for his scholarly achievements as well, in stark contrast to Agnon's other scholars and scientists.[7] Furthermore, Amzeh is presented both as the author's alter ego—his direct mouthpiece—and as the symbolic embodiment of the Jewish people.[8]

The enthusiastic reception of Adiel Amzeh considers his actions *in vacuo*. It disregards the context and motivations of his praiseworthy behavior. A man who joins a leprosarium elicits immediate admiration because one supposes that only a humane motivation can inspire him to do so. But this is not Amzeh's reason for joining the suffering lepers. The unanimous critical applause also ignores the *manner* in which Amzeh performs his supposedly humane actions, as well as the way in which the author characterizes him.

Despite his central role in the story, Amzeh is characterized as a type rather than a full-fledged character. The expositional material gives little information about his past or about any activities that are not directly related to his research. Amzeh exemplifies the type of the monomaniac, obsessed by his work and completely controlled by it:

> The years during which he worked on his research made him a slave to his work, controlling him from the early hours of the day till bedtime. Everyday, immediately on waking up, his legs dragged him to his desk, and pen and papers, and his eyes, if not absorbed in mental pictures and visions would fix themselves in the books or photographs or maps of Gumlidata or in the maps of the battles which destroyed Gumlidata.[9]

The syntactic structure of this excerpt emphasizes the idea that Amzeh is a slave to his work by presenting him as a direct object in both complex sentences (made him, controlled him, dragged him). His actions are described synecdochically: his legs, his eyes act for him. The synecdochic description emphasizes the physical, rather than volitional aspect of his actions, so much so that the protagonist seems more like a mechanical automaton than a human being. The mechanization of the human produces a comic effect, as explained by Bergson:

> The attitudes, gestures and movements of the human body are risible to the extent that this body makes us think of a simple mechanism . . . We laugh whenever a person gives us the impression that he is a thing . . . we laugh at any arrangement of acts and events which gives us . . . the illusion of life and the clear sensation of a mechanical agency.[10]

Although Amzeh deals with an activity that requires intellectual concentration and emotional involvement he is presented as a mechanical object activated by the very thing he is expected to control—his work. The author could have created empathy for the protagonist had he explained Amzeh's attachment to the history of Gumlidata, psychologically and/or intellectually. But he does not do so. Amzeh's obsession with Gumlidata continues to be just that: an arbitrary involvement with an outlandish topic. The description of Amzeh's writing and erasing, adding and subtracting adds to this impression of arbitrariness:

> At times he would add to *what he wrote* on the previous day, and *at times* he erased in one day *what he wrote* in many days. Similarly at night, often after going to bed, he would get up and return to the desk and check what he wrote, *sometimes with* a nod and *sometimes with* satisfaction and *sometimes* laughing at himself and his mistakes which caused him to investigate further and re-examine and correct.[11]

The repetitions in this excerpt reinforce the repetitive actions of writing and erasing, rewriting and rechecking. This presents Amzeh's actions as circular and reversible, just like his going to bed and getting up. By omitting specific references to what is written and erased the author succeeds in presenting Amzeh's actions as vacuous motions, nothing more than insipid and mechanical gestures. Repetitiveness, reversibility, and circularity are rudimentary ingredients in all comic actions.

The compulsive behavior of the protagonist could have turned him into a tragic hero had he been aware of his absurd situation. Amzeh is capable of laughing at his silly mistakes, but he is incapable of perceiving the overall inanity of his life. The causal link between action and consciousness can turn a clown into a victim, as Unamuno says.[12] Amzeh remains a clown because he is unconscious of his ridiculous conduct. In one of the climactic points of the plot, when Amzeh finds out that the wealthy Gerhard Goldenthal is interested in publishing his book on Gumlidata, the protagonist's conduct changes abruptly: "Suddenly he changed entirely and became like those famous scholars, who neglect their research work for the sake of the honor that people who do not deal with research give them."[13] The radical change in Amzeh's attitude is comic because it is abrupt and arbitrary; it signifies the opposite of all the values associated with him previously. The sudden reversal contributes to the characterization of Amzeh as an automaton. The mechanical and obsessive manner in which he previously worked now typifies his anxious anticipation of his visit with Mr. Goldenthal: "And so he sat and glanced at his book and looked at the mirror, and glanced at the watch and checked his clothes and examined his movements, for he who seeks the presence of a rich man must take pains to look graceful in his clothes, and graceful in his face and graceful with his movements."[14] Amzeh's new obsession with his appearance highlights the arbitrary quality of his previous obsession with his work. The series of synonymous verbs—look, glance, check, examine—intimates that Amzeh's activities are inherently static and bring about little progress. Despite the new direction of his obsession, the manner in which he acts does not change. It remains compulsive, mechanical, unconscious. This reversal foreshadows the arrival of Ada Eden, the old nurse from the leprosarium. When the nurse first appears, inconveniently right before the scheduled appointment with Mr. Goldenthal, Amzeh apologizes for not being able to pay attention to her. But when he hears of the book "which has become rotten with age and tears"[15] he changes his mind. He offers her a seat and implores her to continue talking about the extraordinary book at the leprosarium, and when it finally becomes clear that the ancient book is indeed related to Gumlidata, he decides to join the nurse on her way back to the leprosarium. *It is clear that Amzeh acts out of academic curiosity, not out of altruistic compassion for the poor, segregated, and ailing people.* We are confronted with an insatiable desire to accumulate information, which is vastly different from a Kierkegaardian leap into transcendence, as some critics believe it to be. Amzeh's questions revolve around the book, not the lepers: "What did you hear of that manuscript? How did it end up with you? You made me curious, madame, curious hungry for knowledge, practically like a psychoanalyst."[16]

Amzeh's attitude does not change even after his arrival at the leprosarium. His interaction with the lepers is not motivated by his will to alleviate their suffering but by his excitement over the things he finds in the book. The book is the aim, the lepers function at best as an audience with whom to share his discoveries: "And when he discovered something appropriate for everybody he entered the hall and gathered its residents and said to them brothers and friends sit down and I shall read for you."[17]

The only time Amzeh cries is not at all related to the anguish of the lepers, but to the heroic act of the city scribe who, despite the danger to his life, continued to write the history of Gumlidata even during the final attack on the city.[18] The protagonist joins the leprosarium for purely egotistical reasons; he does it in order to find out more information about Gumlidata, the ancient city he has been investigating for twenty years.

Still, the author could have diminished the ironic distance between Amzeh and the reader by describing the subjective perspective of the protagonist. Even the most irrational actions can be justified if their cause is understandable. It is evident, however, that the author does not wish to justify his monomaniac protagonist. The descriptions of Amzeh's excitement over the ancient manuscript focus on his facial features, not on his feelings. This is his reaction to Ada Eden's news: "Suddenly his face changed and his voice changed and his mouth became distorted and he burst into a stuttering laughter."[19] When he sees the ancient book in the leprosarium: "He stared at it till his eyes grew as big as half of his face and he did not stop staring at it till he jumped to open it."[20] When the lepers warn him not to touch the book with his bare hands and tell him about the dangers of contagion, the author adds sardonically; "I do not know whether he heard or did not hear. I know this: that his eyes grew till they stretched over his face and a part around his face."[21] The description of Amzeh's physiognomical expressions deploys the technique of caricature which exaggerates a certain facial feature beyond recognition and distorts normal proportion. Amzeh's exaggerated response to the book contrasts with his indifference to the lepers, whose sufferings ought to have elicited at least some reaction in the visitor. The caricatural description reflects the preposterous incongruity between reality and Amzeh's reaction.

The parody of Amzeh's speech increases further the ironic distance between him and the reader. Through repetition, digression, and cumbersome syntax the author manages to undercut Amzeh's run-on speech:

> I will tell you approximately about the matter; for twenty years I have dealt with the research of the history of that city; there is no piece of paper which mentions the city's name which I have not read, *if* I were a king I could reconstruct the city and rebuild it just as it was before its destruction, *and if* you want I will tell you about all the trips I take through it—I walk *in its* markets *and its* busy alleys, *and its* streets *and its* roads *and its* palaces *and its* temples. Oh, my good nurse the headache—from the trips I take there, and *I also know the order of its destruction, and I know how they destroyed it, and also* the name of every troop which worked on its destruction, *and how* many were killed by sword *and how many* died of hunger *and* thirst, *and how many* perished in the plague which followed the war, except for one thing that I do not know, from which *side* entered the troops of Gediton the hero, *whether from* the *side* of the great bridge which used to be called the Bridge of Courage or *whether* they came indirectly from the *side* of the valley of Aphardat, the Valley of the Cranes—the plural of crane is Aphardat in the language of Gumlidata, and not ravens *or* chestnuts *or* galoshes as linguists, such as Mr. X and Mr. True Advisor, Professor Y *and* all the other professors, whose pictures you saw in the illustrated newspapers when they received medals and honorable titles from the royal court.²²

This enormous period, which includes numerous inadequately punctuated complex and combined sentences, reflects the confused and desultory thought processes of the scholar. From the topic of his research, he goes on to describe the thoroughness of his research, mentions in passing the headaches caused by his imaginary trips in Gumlidata, elaborates on the trips he takes, returns to the things he knows concerning the controversial grammatical form of a certain word in the language of Gumlidata, while throwing in a disparaging comment about his colleagues. The incompatibility of these issues emphasizes the absurdity of lumping all of them into one prolonged period. The incongruity between the tragic destruction of the city, which seems to be the most troublesome issue in the period, and the academic problem that haunts the scholar (from which side did the enemy enter) reflects the skewed academic perspective that gives priority to knowledge over human suffering. Gumlidata's destruction is one of the many things Amzeh *knows* about the city and so it becomes peripheral, conceding the central place to Amzeh's eruditions ("there is not a piece of paper . . . I have not read . . . if I were a king I could reconstruct the city . . . and I know the order . . . and also the name . . . and how many were killed . . ."). For the running theme in this run-on period is what Amzeh knows and does not know about the city of Gumlidata. The subject is Amzeh, not Gumlidata. But the scholar's attempt to prove his superior knowledge by tediously enumerating the city's sites ("its markets, its busy alleys, and its streets and its roads . . .") and the macabre listing of the forms of destruction and death ("and I know how they destroyed it . . . and how many were killed . . . and how many died . . . and how many perished") undercuts the thrust of his speech because it reduces Amzeh's erudition to an insipid series of petty details. The reduction reaches the point of absurdity when it lists the plural forms of the word "crane," which Amzeh affirms to be "Aphardat," not "ravens," "chestnuts," or "galoshes." Not only is this linguistic discussion completely irrelevant to the main subject, but the incongruity among the terms as well as the phonetic incompatibility of the singular and plural formations overreaches all the other inanities in the speech. The repetition of conjunctions (if, and, whether, or), nouns (trip, side, destruction), and pleonastic constructions ("I also know the order of its destruction, and I know how they destroyed it") underlines the extraneous and trivial quality of Amzeh's knowledge. Above all, the numerous digressions in the jumbled speech point up the illogical nature of the professor's thought processes, presenting him as a buffoon rather than a serious scholar.²³

Amzeh's monologue alludes to the only causal link between the character and his academic curiosity. This curiosity remains an enigma because the emotional or psychological motives for it are still unclear. Amzeh's insatiable thirst for additional information on Gumlidata is his exclusive motivation throughout the story. As a monomaniac, Amzeh exemplifies what is, according to Auden, the quintessential comic character: "The comic butt of satire is a person who, though in possession of moral faculties, transgresses the moral law beyond the moral call of temptation, . . . The commonest object of satire is a monomaniac."²⁴ The author satirizes Amzeh by creating a grotesque incongruity between the context of his life and his perception; there is no correlation between the suffering of the lepers and Amzeh's unabated passion for Gumlidata. He further distorts the relationship between reality and the hero's perception by exaggerating Amzeh's interest in Gumlidata while trivializing his objects of interest. When Amzeh takes his imaginary trips in the city he "talks with the dogs of its temples about their prices."²⁵ Had Amzeh held his imaginary discussions with Gumlidata's ministers about the city's political predicament, had he argued with its philosophers about Gumlidata's religion, the reader might have forgiven and perhaps even admired the scholar's exclusive obsession with his city. The ironic effect is produced by the incongruity between Amzeh's seriousness and the identity of his imaginary interlocutors—dogs.

Amzeh does not change in the course of the story. His obsession with Gumlidata continues unabated after his arrival at the leprosarium. Not even the sight of the most wretched of human sufferers brings about a change in his limited perception of the world. Amzeh remains a monomaniac throughout the story, a flat and static type.

grotesque in **"Ad Olam"** dramatizes for readers the precariousness of their own position as readers of a fictional tale, mediated by an arbitrary language.[52] Readers soon realize that the troublesome 'a and g recur not only in the names of Gumlidata's heroes but also in the names of "their" story. In essence, 'Adiel 'Amzeh, 'Ada 'Eden, and Gebhard Goldenthal are not different from 'Eldag, the hero Gediton, and the king Gifyon Golaskinon.

The limited irony directed at scholarly pretentiousness, the "science" of history, and the monomaniac obsession with one's work expands in **"Ad Olam"** to encompass the precariousness of fictional writing, of art, and of language. If we construe **"Ad Olam"** as an ideological "historiosophical" allegory about Judaism and Zionism, then most of the disquieting elements in the story will naturally be considered as superfluous and oppressive "riddles serving a private myth."[53] If, on the other hand, we approach **"Ad Olam"** as a work of art, these riddles become essential, for they make the reader aware of the tensions between fiction and fact, word and meaning, perception and reality. The riddles of **"Ad Olam"** may be frustrating to those who search for ideological reassurances; they are indispensable to readers who prefer far-reaching questions to restrictive answers.

Notes

1. Meshulam Tochner, *Pesher agnon,* (The Meaning of Agnon), (Ramat Gan, 1968, pp. 130-132.

2. Eddy Zemach, "Hatefisa hahistoriosofit bishnayim misipuravhame ha meuharim shel Agnon" (The Historiosophic Outlook in Two of Agnon's Later Stories), *Hasifrut,* Vol. 1, no. 2 (April-May, 1968), p. 418.

3. Hillel Barzel, *Sipurei ahavah shel shai agnon,* (Ramat Gan, 1975), p. 160.

4. Dan Miron, "Tsiyun derekh vetamrur azhara bevikoret agnon" (A Signpost and a Warning Signal in the Criticism of Agnon), *Moznayim,* Vol. 27, no. 5-6, (April-May, 1968), p. 352.

5. Gavriel Moked, *Shivhei adiel amzeh* (The Praises of Adiel Amzeh), (Tel Aviv, 1957).

6. *Shivhei adiel amzeh,* p. 88.

7. *Sipurei ahavah,* p. 163.

8. "Adiel Amzeh is, then, at the same time the scholar of the overt text of the story, and the creator-author's biographical personality in the covert test," *Pesher Agnon,* p. 128. For the allegorical interpretation of Amzeh as the Jewish people see Hillel Barzel, *Sipurei ahava,* p. 127.

9. S. Y. Agnon, "Ad Olam" (Forevermore) in *Ha'esh ve'haetsim* (The Fire and the Wood) (Tel Aviv and Jerusalem: Schocken, 1962); "Forevermore," tr. Joel Blocker in *Israeli stories* ed. Joel Blocker (New York: Schocken, 1965). The following references to the work are based on my own translation. E. F.

10. Henri Bergson, "Le Rire," *Oeuvres,* (Paris, 1959), pp. 401, 414, 419; My translaton—E. F.

11. "Ad olam," pp. 315-316. The italics are mine—E. F.

12. Miguel de Unamuno, *The Tragic Sense of Life,* tr. J. F. Crawford, (New York, 1954), p. 323.

13. "Ad olam," p. 318.

14. "Ad olam," p. 318.

15. "Ad olam," p. 320.

16. "Ad olam," p. 325.

17. "Ad olam," p. 333.

18. "Ad olam," p. 333.

19. "Ad olam," p. 324.

20. "Ad olam," p. 329.

21. "Ad olam," p. 329.

22. "Ad olam," pp. 323-324. The italics are mine—E. F.

23. Koestler explains the comic effect of the digression as follows:

    "The abrupt transfer of a train of thought from one operative field to another leads to its separation from its original emotional charge . . . This sudden dissociation of intellectual and emotional state, the rupture between knowing and feeling is a fundamental characteristic of the comic,"

24. W. H. Auden, "Notes on the Comic," *The Dyer's Hand and Other Essays,* (New York, 1962), pp. 371-385.

25. "Ad olam," p. 319.

26. "The comic element is the incorrigible element in every human being; the capacity to learn from experience or instruction is forbidden to all comic creations and to what is comic in you and me." Mary MacCarthy, "Characters in Fiction," *On the Contrary,* (New York, 1951), p. 289.

27. "Ad olam," p. 334.

28. *Pesher agnon,* p. 134.

29. *Pesher agnon,* p. 136.

30. *Pesher agnon,* pp. 136, 148; My translation—E. F.

31. Eddy Zemach, "Hatefisa," pp. 381-385.

32. Shlomo Zucker, "Be'ayathap ha-perush shel 'edo ve'enam' ve'ad olam' le-shai agon," (On the Problem of Interpreting S. Y. Agnon's 'Edo and Enam' and 'Forevermore," *Hasifrut,* Vol. 2, no. 2, (January, 1970), pp. 415-417.

33. On the metaphorical and metonymic functions of objects in narrative, see W. J. Harvey, *Character and the Novel,* (Ithaca, New York, 1965), p. 35.

34. Matthew Hodgart, "Origins and Principles," *Satire,* (Toronto and New York, 1969), pp. 12-32. Concerning the function of animals in satire, Hodgart says:

> "The animal world is continually drawn on by the satirist; he reminds us that homo sapiens despite his vast spiritual aspirations is only a mammal that feeds, defecates, menstruates, ruts, gives birth and catches unpleasant diseases,"

35. "Ad olam," p. 331.

36. "Ad olam," p. 330.

37. "Ad olam," p. 315.

38. Baruch Kurzweil believes that the alliterative game is unproductive and amounts to "riddles serving a private myth." *Masot al sipurei shay agnon,* [Essays on the stories of S. Y. Agnon], (Jerusalem and Tel Aviv, 1975), p. 325. Gavriel Moked's interpretation of the alliterative 'a and g is offered in "Bein 'Edo ve-enam le 'Ad Olam," [Between 'Edo and Enam and Forevermore], *Akhshav,* Vol. 25-28, (Spring, 1973), pp. 77-93.

39. Heinrich Schneegans, *Geschichte der grotesken Satire,* (Strussburg, 1894), p. 40.

40. *Pesher agnon,* p. 134.

41. "Ad olam," p. 324.

42. "To be comic, the two things they, [the words], they denote must either be so incongruous with each other that one cannot imagine a real situation in which a speaker would need to bring them together, or so irrelevant to each other, that they could only become associated by pure chance." *The Dyer's Hand,* p. 380.

43. Meshulam Tochner interprets both the neologisms and the names of Gumlidata's gods by drawing on Hebrew homonyms, *Pesher Agnon,* p. 134.

44. In reference to the verbal grotesque in the work of Rabelais, Spitzer calls attention to the critics' oversights in this regard: "But by explaining every coinage separately, by dissolving the forest into trees, the commentators lose sight of the whole phenomenon; they no longer see the forest—or rather jungle that Rabelais must have had before his eyes . . . He [Rabelais], creates word families, representative of gruesome fantasy-beings, which have reality only in language, which are established in an intermediate world between reality and irreality, between the nowhere that frightens and the 'here' that 'reassures.'" *Linguistics and Literary History—Essays in Stylistics,* (New York, 1962), pp. 16-17.

45. "Ad olam," pp. 328-329.

46. "Ad olam," p. 326.

47. "Ad olam," p. 332.

48. "Ad olam," p. 332.

49. "Ad olam," pp. 316-317

50. "Ad olam," p. 328.

51. "Ad olam," p. 318.

52. Leo Spitzer describes the effect of verbal grotesque as

> ". . . a moment of shock followed by a feeling of reassurance; to be swept towards the unknown frightens, but realization of the benignly fanciful results gives relief; laughter, our physiological reaction on such occasions, arises precisely out of a feeling of relief following upon a temporary breakdown of our assurance,"

53. *Masot,* p. 325.

Yair Mazor (essay date 1986)

SOURCE: Mazor, Yair. "S. Y. Agnon's Art of Composition: The Befuddling Turn of the Compositional Screw." *Hebrew Annual Review* 10 (1986): 197-208.

[*In the following essay, Mazor examines the paradoxical nature of the composition of two Agnon stories.*]

> "Do forgive me. Perhaps I cast a shade upon Agnon . . . but I came here to speak about agony and about love and about pain in Agnon that Qohelet who put on various appealing disguises. And because of loving him so dearly, I spoke about him this way and not another."
>
> (Amos Oz, *Under This Blazing Sun*)[1]

1. Preamble

A remarkably intriguing aspect in S. Y. Agnon's art of composition[2] is that in a considerable number of his works, the reader is confronted by a strikingly confusing organization. As the story's plot seems to reach its climax and move toward its denouement, and all the conflicts of the fictional world face resolution, an unexpected, intrusive plot development is presented, which disrupts the natural concluding momentum of the piece and forces seemingly arbitrary continuation. The confused reader is forced to surmise that the writer (or implied author, following Booth, 1961) has clumsily violated his own aesthetics by inserting unrelated material into his story and consequently upset the story's composition, undermined its integrity, and subverted its coherence. Furthermore, the flimsy nature of the casual sequence is not exposed in the overture of the piece itself. Many of Agnon's stories deliberately lead the reader astray. Significant portions of the piece's expositional sequence goad the reader to assume a traditional plot causality. Only in a relatively late stage of the text continuum does the reader realize that he has been misled; the commencing causal order is found to be only a thin veneer that conceals a "deep structure" which deviates from the surface causality, forming a disengaged sequence. But once the reader becomes thoroughly familiar with the nature of Agnon's structure, ideology and aesthetic rationale, however, he realizes that his *prima vista* was, in fact, erroneous; it was just a conscious authorial ploy perpetrated by Agnon. An examination of the composition in the piece and its literary motivation sheds new light upon the alleged compositional fallacy, which is an adroitly performed device that generates sophistication for the piece.

It is the aim of this paper to examine this attractive aspect of Agnon's compositional *ars poetica* through a close reading of two of his stories, **"Bên šetê 'arîm"** ("Between Two Cities") and **"Šnê talmîdê ḥăkāmîm šehāyû be 'îrênû"** ("Two Scholars Who Lived in Our Town").[3]

2. "BETWEEN TWO CITIES"—A TALE OF TWO COMPOSITIONAL SYSTEMS

In examining this story's composition, the apparent looseness of which is caused by the disruptive intrusion of an unexpected turn of plot, it is essential to summarize the fictional features of the two allegedly conflicting parts of the story. The story opens with a tale of two small towns located in a region in Bavaria. Both of the towns have the same name, Katsenau. One of them is rather grey and oppressed, a working-class town of little splendor. Among its population is a small Jewish congregation, consisting of shopkeepers. The other town is much more appealing, being a resort town famous for medical baths and springs that attract many people, especially in the summer. The distance between the two towns is not great, and many Jewish people from the less-attractive Katsenau indulge themselves on Sabbath by walking to the more attractive twin town. Here they escape their labors for a short while and enjoy the refreshing air and the animated beauty of the woods.

One day, during World War I, Isidor Shaltheiz, a Jewish teacher from Frankfurt, arrives in the resort of Katsenau for a vacation. He soon becomes idle and restless. He begins spending his hours walking, and one day he arrives at the neighboring, poorer Katsenau. This Katsenau is not as alluring as the resort-Katsenau, but its faded features are compensated for by the kindness of its Jewish congregation. When these generous people find out that the recuperating teacher has a family in the big city that is deprived of the good food they can easily provide, they give him parcels stuffed with delicious food to send to his family. (The fact that the recuperating teacher is pampering himself with dainties and idleness while his family lives in destitution is later poignantly juxtaposed.) One day, during his journeying between the two cities, the bored teacher begins to count his footsteps, trying to pass the time between meals. While counting his footsteps, the teacher realizes that the distance between the two cities exceeds the bounds of the Sabbath limit (in Hebrew: *Těḥûm Šabbāt*)—the prescribed distance Jewish people may not exceed on the Sabbath without violating the sacred laws of the Sabbath. The teacher feels that it is his duty to notify the Jewish congregation in Katsenau that their refreshing weekly walks to the baths of Katsenau should be strictly prohibited since they constitute a severe religious transgression. Subsequently, the Sabbath walks cease and the few enjoyable hours the hardworking Jewish people have are taken away. The teacher continues to relish the luxury of his daily walks and to accept food from the Jewish people, while they have lost their one pleasure in life. At this point, the story's woeful conclusion seems to be reached. The plot's climax, which is a typical anti-climax of the teacher's recompensive discovery, passes; the peripety has been committed and the plot moves toward its turning point. Still, an unexpected surprise awaits the reader.

The story does not end. Instead, it develops a continuation with a new channel. This unanticipated development becomes even more surprising as the reader learns that the new episode does not proceed from the previous events. On the contrary, its content seems to have no connection to the story's previous fictional trends. Thus, the impression of a loose composition seems a judicious criticism.

The unexpected addition deviates from the story's plot by concentrating on the grief-filled misfortunes that the war caused the people of the two cities. The vicissitudes of war, mentioned only obliquely in the story's first part, become prominent in the second. Thus, the excessive addition is, in fact, a major thematic element of the story's second part which has been anticipated in the first portion of the story. Hence, it may be considered a foreshadowing integrative element which knots the two detached story parts.

In the second part of the story, the reader becomes acquainted with the aggravating distress of the baker's family. The family's only son has volunteered for the war, despite his physical limitations; he was severely injured and lost both legs. From this point in the story, the blemished leg, or the *Oedi-pus* (in Greek, swell-foot), acts as a leading element in the story. The sister of the baker's wife lived in resort-Katsenau, but because of the amassed daily troubles, the two sisters are deprived of getting together. Here one encounters another integrative element that glues the story's parts together. In both the story parts, the short distance between the two cities is important and seems longer, because of the disturbing occurrences associated with the distance. Thus, the short distance between the two cities is extended far beyond its geographical measure. The two sisters decide to meet in the forest midway between the two cities. Once the reader is acquainted with the symbolic meaning of the forest in Agnon's works (for instance, Hershel, the chastised lover in **"Simple Story"** [*"Sippûr pāšût"* in Hebrew] goes insane in the forest), he is aware that the forest usually symbolizes a place of impending danger or a pessimistic outcome. The fact that a dog's bark is echoing in the entangled thicket as the meeting is about to take place reinforces the premonition of doom; in Agnon's writings, evil is associated with the figure of the dog (note, for instance, the prominent role of the mad dog in *Těmôl šilšôm* [*Yesterday Heretofore*]).[4] When the baker's wife reaches the meeting place in the forest, she is disappointed because her sister has not yet appeared. Although her sister does arrive at the end, her anxiety is indeed well-founded.

Suspense in Agnon's *ars poetica* is manifested by the flood of late buses, postponed trains and tardy streetcars demonstrated in **"The Doctor and His Divorced Wife,"** *Šîrāh,* **"The Last Bus"** and many other works. These suspenseful incidents are always associated with neglected opportunities, agonizing misadventures, crumbling relationships or other misfortunes.

It has been noted that references to the deficient leg are central to the story's second part. The leg motif extends to the sisters as well. The sister who is waiting in the forest runs impatiently to and fro or stands as if her legs are chained to the ground. It appears that almost all the legs' potential functions are enumerated in Agnon's description of her: "She was *stepping* to and fro, *returning* and *standing,* as if her *legs were bound* to the ground, and she didn't know why she was *standing* there and not *running* toward her sister as her heart was *running* and pining toward her."

Similar descriptions, saturated with references to legs, are repeated as the two sisters meet: "Were those her *legs* that were *running*? It was her heart that was *running* and her *legs* followed it." There are even more references to legs in the short, added chapter, but the most significant is the one that closes the story: "The day was fading . . . the two sisters were standing in mute silence. At last one turned in her place and the other turned in her place and between them the forest's trees blackened until the stars came out and lit the way for the two sisters . . . who just parted from each other for many days . . . as one walks to one side and the other walks to the other side."

The gloomy atmosphere that permeates the scene is excessively oppressive and not likely to be overlooked by the reader. Consequently, the leg references mentioned in this closing paragraph of the story are evidently "oedipal". Once the reader couples the leg references portraying the sisters' grim fortune with the opening reference to the soldier's felled legs, he is in a better position to diagnose the meaning of the disfigured leg metonym in the story's addition; it is a symbol of the character's woeful distress.

In contrast with many of Agnon's other stories in which the leg metonym functions as a symbol of an erotic deterioration (see Yael's limping leg in **"The Hill of Sand"** [*"Gib'at haḥôl"*]; the lame woman in Hartman's dream in **"Different Faces"** [*"Pānîm aḥērôt"*]; Manfred's torn and ripped shoes in *Šîrāh*; the wooden leg of Mintshey, the rejected lover in **"Simple Story"** [*"Sippûr pāšût"*] and more), Agnon deletes the sexual connotations of the legs metonym in **"Between Two Cities"** limiting its reference to human misfortune. Thus, Agnon's literary fabric is not arbitrary. He attentively selects and, in this case, remolds his symbols to adjust to the alternating literary needs.

However, the metonym of the leg, inserted in a context of distress, acts as a benchmark of the story's seemingly clumsy addition. Yet, Agnon's capacity to remold a common symbol with a new meaning in order to harmonize with new subject matter does not initially seem to account for the disrupted composition of the story or the disturbing gulf between its parts. But the fact is that it does, indeed.

The leg metonym has already been alluded to as the integrative element which binds the two story parts. The major source of the Jewish congregation's distress is caused by the sudden divulgence that the resort-Katsenau is beyond the Sabbath limit, and consequently the enjoyable walks to it on the Sabbath are forbidden. The unexpected prohibition of these walks means the town's people are deprived of even the humblest chance for pleasure in their hard lives. The act of walking is an obvious reference—though indirect—to the leg metonym. Thus, the misfortune of the Jewish community in the story's first part is conspicuously attached to the metonym of the marred leg. Furthermore, the story's second part is sprinkled with references to the marred-leg metonym (the amputated legs of the soldier, the two sisters' restlessly running legs, their feeling that their legs are confined to the ground, their sombre walking in two different directions) and the major thematic trends also relate the the marred-leg metonym (the agony of the baker's wife because of her only son's felled legs, and the deficiency of the two sisters' capacity to meet with each other despite the short distance between their two cities). All these factors make the analogous strands between the two parts of the story very tight.

In both parts of the story, the metonym of the marred leg permeates the heart of the characters' agony. The characters are deprived of their only feeble chance to gain life's joy: the prohibited Sabbath walking between the two cities conspicuously foreshadows the sisters' inability to walk between the two cities. Hence, the absence of a causal connection between the two parts of the story is fully compensated for by a cogent, analogous connection: the dominant thematic trend of each part is metaphorically reflected by that of the other. The integrity of the complete story is deftly maintained. Beyond the seemingly clumsy surface of loose organization, a sound inner unity is very much *in esse*.

The analogous metaphorical relationship between the two parts of the story is not limited to its composition; it is also harnessed to the major ideological goal of the story, which is the perpetual anguish that clings to human disunion. The two components of the analogous equation, the Jews' prohibited walk between the two cities in the first part and the sisters' avoided walk between the cities in the second, are both reflections of anguish caused by human disharmony.

The second part of the story, then, does not deviate from the trend of the first. On the contrary, it acts as a mirror that radiates and enriches the first part with another angle of presentation. The two parts of the story are actually identical sides of the same thematic coin, two literary standpoints for the same idea. The authorial ploy has been pulled off; the first impression of a disrupted composition is replaced with a dexterously spun organization. Thus, the tale of the two cities is a tale of two systems—one is anchored in the story's compositional structure and evokes a delusional impression of loose organization, while the other system is concealed in the story's foundation and solidifies both parts through a well-intertwined analogy. The story benefits from a sense of controlled harmony which helps its artistic integrity.

The conflicting trends of the two compositional systems prevent an undesirably rigid and mechanical relationship between the story's two parts. The deviation from a strict analogy, on the other hand, made possible by the seemingly loose compositional system, supplies the story with a rhetorical flexibility by bridling its tightness and inhibiting artificial impact. Consequently, a well-measured authenticity prevails in the story.

3. "Two Scholars Who Have Lived in Our Town": One Plus One Make One

Like **"Between Two Cities," "Two Scholars Who Have Lived in Our Town"** is founded upon two parts which seem at odds with each other—the second part deviating from the first in terms of plot and focus. As in the previous case, the writer adds a second part which seems to display poor craftsmanship. This second part seems to disrupt the first part and, consequently, violate its coherence and subvert its integrity. But a close reading of the thematic trends within the story's two parts shows that the first impression of an unorganized piece is incorrect. The initial perception of a redundant and shaky composition, caused by a superfluous patch, gives way to a well-constructed composition.

The first part of the story is devoted to the tense conflict between two celebrated scholars, Rabbi Moshe-Pinchas and Rabbi Shlomo, in a small Jewish congregation. The differences between these two scholars is apparent in every facet of their beings. Rabbi Moshe-Pinchas is unattractive and has a coarse physique; he is moreover exceedingly meticulous, sullen, irascible and demonstrably unsocial. Rabbi Shlomo appears as the alter ego of Rabbi Moshe-Pinchas. Rabbi Shlomo is attractive, tolerant, highly social, tender and affable, and he possesses amicable manners. The unbridgeable gulf between them is reminiscent of the differences between Shammai and Hillel.[5] Yet, despite their differences, a solid friendship thrives between them. Moshe-Pinchas' personal barrier prohibits others from getting close to him, but it seems to fade around Shlomo. Perhaps their differences yield attraction; perhaps their reciprocal scholarly excellence is the basis of their friendship. For whatever reason, the friendship between Moshe-Pinchas and Shlomo is evident.

However, friendship requires a delicate balance, and the relationship between Moshe-Pinchas and Shlomo deteriorates drastically. The cause of this decline seems fairly trivial, but it is sufficient to destroy their friendship forever. Oddly enough, the amicable Rabbi Shlomo seems to cause the clash. At the peak of a Talmudic debate, Moshe-Pinchas intones his arguments in a tempestuous manner, raising his voice and waving his arms furiously; this casts him in a rather ridiculous light. Attempting to pacify and calm him down the agitated Moshe-Pinchas, Shlomo used an idiomatic expression which might be considered teasing. It is obvious that Shlomo has not intended to insult Moshe-Pinchas. On the contrary, he probably thought that a touch of humor would be a delicate way of sparing Moshe-Pinchas any embarrassment. But Moshe-Pinchas is profoundly hurt and perplexed; he blushes, holds his words, and returns dejectedly to his seat. After that moment, he refuses to speak to Shlomo. Despite the divine commandment, Moshe-Pinchas bears a grudge and seeks to take vengeance.

Countless attempts by Shlomo to gain Moshe-Pinchas' forgiveness are rejected; his constant appeal falls on deaf ears. The rift between the two prominent scholars, which occurs early in the plot, casts a shadow upon the subsequent events of the story's first part. Moreover, the unresolved split not only leaves its grim mark on the rest of the occurrences in the story's first part, it seems to mold the characters in this grief-ridden state.

For instance, when Shlomo is elected to serve as the chief rabbi of a neighboring Jewish congregation, Moshe-Pinchas disrupts Shlomo's scholarly acceptance speech with insults, attempting to contradict Shlomo's arguments and to shame him. But Shlomo does not take vengeance. On the contrary, he continues to laud Moshe-Pinchas' scholarly virtues in an effort to win his forgiveness. Still, his mulish adversary denies and rejects him.

The feud between the town's two venerable spiritual leaders inspires all the events in the plot of the story's first part. Thus, Moshe-Pinchas turns down an appealing offer to serve as a chief rabbi in a neighboring Jewish congregation when he learns that Shlomo has recommended him. Also, Shlomo is invited to serve as a chief rabbi in his hometown, but he turns down the tempting offer since Moshe-Pinchas' signature can't be obtained for the commission.

Moshe-Pinchas' animosity toward Shlomo also produces a well-designed thematic composition. Occurrences involving Moshe-Pinchas and Shlomo are intermittently mentioned, always calling attention to their unmended quarrel. For each event that happens to Shlomo which is caused by his bitter antagonist, there is a counter-occurrence that happens to Moshe-Pinchas which is effected by his grudge against Shlomo.

This well-coordinated equation of theme and composition is underscored by another equation in the story's first part, the inverted character pattern—a pattern founded upon a chiasmic motion. Shlomo's success is balanced inversely by Moshe-Pinchas' deterioration. As Shlomo ascends, becomes more esteemed, respected and famous, Moshe-Pinchas descends, declines and ultimately is excommunicated. The conflict between the two equations of the story's first part—a well-coordinated balance versus a chiasmic-reverse balance—defines an important thematic-ideological function as it evokes a sense of a split that reflects the split between the distinguished scholars, a split which injects a biting gloom in both their lives, drains their spiritual potency, and consequently deprives their congregations of full inspiration. Thus, the split between the two equations radiates the essence of the story's prevailing idea—the devastating power of a senseless feud and the powerful role of irrationality in human life.

The conflicting nature of the two equations is of rhetorical merit also, as it evokes a sense of authentic flexibility and prevents an undesirably rigid and mechanical effect. Thus, an effective dialectical pattern is obtained. On one hand, the two equations reinforce the composition of the story's first part as they yield compositional firmness. On the other hand, the conflicting trends of these two equations block a rigid stiffness by deviating from the tight compositional firmness.

The withdrawal of Moshe-Pinchas from the story's arena seems to violate the composition of the story and dismiss the story's major conflict—its dramatic essence. Moshe-Pinchas' death should move the story toward its conclusion. The nature of the split between the two scholars produces a paratactic sequence. From a theoretical standpoint, Moshe-Pinchas' enduring hostility toward Shlomo could produce an endless, horizontal sequence that lacks an ascending principle capable of extricating the plot from the sequential momentum and channelling it toward a climax. Theoretically, more and more fictional components (occurrences between Moshe-Pinchas and Shlomo) could join this horizontal continuum without drawing it closer to a climactic resolution. In this vein, Moshe-Pinchas' death plays the role of *deus ex machina*, or redeeming element which relieves the plot of its enduring momentum, disrupts the paratactical continuum and propels the plot toward its conclusion. The lack of a natural, inner extricating mechanism to deliver the culminating point of the fictional sequence is fully compensated for by the invasion of this external component, forcing a finale upon the plot by disregarding its most fundamental trend.[6]

In spite of this, the story does not climax with Moshe-Pinchas' death, but evolves into an extended continuation. Furthermore, this unexpected continuation seems to abuse a leading thematic track in the story's first part. Shlomo's undeniably firm authority in the story's first part is severely shaken in the second. Though he is far from being completely powerless, he is certainly enfeebled. Thus, continuing the story after it seemed to reach its ultimate conclusion, and by patching a second part which violates a major thematic trend in the first part, appears questionable and upsetting. However, as with the story previously discussed, this impression of a poor composition is unjust: the seemingly botched composition is prudently motivated by sense, idea and well-wrought aesthetics.

The demise of Shlomo's authority seems to be an outgrowth of his reluctance to abandon justice for the sake of the brazen demands of the congregational members who wish to dominate and exploit weaker members. More than once, Shlomo is exposed to the impudence of the sanctimonious disputants, who openly display their disfavor and seek to subvert his position by insolent brawls. Yet Shlomo refuses to compromise his moral values.

Oddly enough, this grave situation comes into existence after Shlomo's arch rival, Moshe-Pinchas, has passed away. One would expect that Shlomo's foes would fade since his mighty adversary is no longer there to support their impertinence. Still, they are most insolent. Their denigration is no more than a delusion which will be fully deciphered in light of the comprehensive interpretation of the story, as the underlying knot between its two conflicting parts is untied.

The relative demise of Shlomo's authority seems to be translated into compositional concepts. As already mentioned, the story's first part exhibits a compact, solid composition.

In the second part of the story, the undermining of Shlomo's authority is expressed by the crumbling of the composition. Attempts by the powerful, dissatisfied rivals to demolish Shlomo's authority, moving demonstrations of Shlomo's gracious attitude toward the late Moshe-Pinchas' family, the decline of Shlomo's health and his refusal to act as a chief rabbi in his old hometown are all plot fragments that bespeak a shattered, fragmentary composition.

Thus, the deterioration of Shlomo's authority is piously mirrored in the compositional layer, which widens the seemingly unbridged gulf between the story's two halves. Another difficulty is that as long as Moshe-Pinchas lived, Shlomo's other adversaries didn't dare threaten him. A strong support for Shlomo could easily have been raised. But once this support, Moshe-Pinchas, was no longer available, the opponents of Shlomo mysteriously began to offend and insult him.

The nature of this enigmatic paradox challenges the reader to decode its concealed rationale. Accordingly, this paradox is the clue to solving the riddle of the perplexing relationships between the story's parts. The reciprocity evoked by two adversary forces engaged in a perpetual conflict produces a balanced parallelogram of forces, which is related in both thematic and compositional strategies of the story's first part. But when Moshe-Pinchas passed away, the tightly balanced parallelogram of forces is nullified. This parallelogram's nullification earns a literary reflection in the story's second part: the well-coordinated theme and composition that characterize the story's first part are countered by a fragmentary theme and composition in the story's second part. The splintered theme and composition of the story's second part flows from the ending of the story's first part—Moshe-Pinchas' death, which upsets the parallelogram of forces. Hence, the story's unity is dexterously maintained by a causal mending of its two parts. The story's seemingly disparate parts generate a solid integrity: one plus one makes one. The aesthetic features of a literary work of art may inform its ideological message. The bisected portrait of the story presents two polar positions in an ageless conflict that everlastingly haunts human life. The conflict may manifest itself as embittered, mordant, caustic, and yet somehow impressively august, like the conflict between Shlomo and Moshe-Pinchas in the story's first part. On the other hand, the conflict may manifest itself as mean-spirited, loathsome and ignominious, like the conflict inflamed by Shlomo's impertinent rivals in the story's second part. The pattern of everlasting human conflict is the constant; the variable is the specific human expression of those engaged in the conflict.

In this vein, the halved portrait of the story aims to portray the essence of *la condition humaine*; it draws together the potential, different poles of the eternal human conflict—the lofty and the base. As in the previously examined story, the first impression of a remissly patched composition does not lead one astray in vain: it draws the reader's attention to the aesthetic and ideological undercurrents of the piece. Agnon's befuddling turn of the compositional screw is highly shrewd indeed.

Notes

1. All translations from Hebrew are by the writer of this paper.

2. Agnon's compositional craft has been discussed by many critics, especially Arnold Band, Hillel Barzel, Baruch Kurtzveil, Gabriel Moked, Dov Sadan, Gershon Shaked. Others, too, have an attentive interest in Agnon's art of composition and have produced many stimulating observations which shed a valuable light upon this challenging aspect of Agnon's writing. For a detailed bibliography of works by the critics mentioned above, see Mazor (1979, pp. 122-126).

3. These stories may be found in Agnon (1971, pp. 5-53, 78-91).

4. Both the mad dog and the forest motifs have been previously probed by many of Agnon's critics (cf. David, 1972, p. 22) A recent consideration of these motifs is included in Fleck (1983) and Wineman (1983).

5. Shammai and Hillel were two leading scholars who conducted the Sanhedrin, an assembly of 71 ordained scholars, which was the supreme court and legislature during the Roman regime period in Israel during the last years of King Herod's reign and after his death (4 B.C.). Shammai gained his fame for being extremely severe in judgment, while Hillel gained his fame for his tolerant consideration.

6. The aesthetic-rhetorical features of the paratactical literary sequence and the function of the foreign extricating element have been thorughly discussed in Herenstein-Smith (1968).

Bibliography

'Agnôn, Š. Y. 1971. *Sāmû' wenir'eh*. Jerusalem & Tel-Aviv.

Band, A. J. 1968. *Nostalgia and Nightmare*. Los Angeles.

Barzel, H. 1973. *Sippûrê 'aha̱bāh šel Š. Y. 'Agnôn*. Ramat-Gan.

Barzel, H., ed. 1982. *Š. Y. 'Agnon: Mibḥar ma'ămārîm 'āl yeṣîrātô*. Tel-Aviv.

Booth, W.C. 1961. *The Rhetoric of Fiction*. Chicago.

David, J. 1972. *Sepārîm wum'ămārîm 'āl S. Y. 'Agnôn wîṣîrôtāw*. Jerusalem.

Fleck, J. 1983. "Fiction, Fable and the Face of a Generation: S. Y. Agnon's *Only Yesterday*." *Hebrew Annual Review* 7: 69-88.

Herenstein-Smith, Barbara. 1968. *Poetic Closure*. Chicago.

Kurtzweil, B. 1975. *Massôt 'āl sippûrê Š. Y. 'Agnôn*. Tel-Aviv.

Mazor, Y. 1979. *Haddînāmîqā šel môṭibîm bîṣîrôt Š. Y. 'Agnôn*. Tel-Aviv.

———. 1985. "A. Strindberg and S. Y. Agnon: Scandinvnian Cantons in the Regions of Hebrew Literature". *Scandinavica* 24/1: 35-55.

———. 1986. "Between Hebrew and Scandinavian Literature: Where Oscillating Structures Become Osculation Points". *Modern Judaism* 6/1: 51-77.

Moked, G. 1957. *Šibḥê 'ădi 'ēl 'amzāh*. Tel-Aviv.

Sadan, D. 1963. *'Āl Š. Y. 'Agnôn*. Tel-Aviv.

Shaked, G. 1973. *'Omānût hassippûr šel Š. Y. 'Agnôn*. Tel Aviv.

Wineman, A. 1983. "Agnon's Forest: The Case of '*Ôrē'aḥ ñaṭā lālûn*. *Hebrew Annual Review* 7: 251-257.

Gershon Shaked (essay date 1986)

SOURCE: Shaked, Gershon. "Midrash and Narrative: Agnon's 'Agunot." In *Midrash and Literature,* edited by Geoffrey H. Hartman and Sanford Budick; chapter translated by Lois Bar-Yaacov, pp. 285-303. New Haven, Conn.: Yale University Press, 1986.

[*In the following chapter from a collection of essays discussing literary manifestations of Midrash, an ancient biblical form of exegesis, Shaked demonstrates how Agnon's early story "Agunot" uses forms of intertextuality borrowed from old Hebrew traditions.*]

I

From love of our language and adoration of holiness I abase myself before the words of the Torah, and starve myself by abstaining from the words of the Sages, keeping these words within me so that they may be fitted altogether upon my lips. If the Temple still stood, I should take my place on the dais with my fellow poets and daily repeat the song which the Levites used to chant in the Holy Temple. Now, when the Temple is still in ruins, and we have neither priests at their holy work nor Levites chanting and singing, I occupy myself with the Torah, the Prophets, and the Writings, the Mishnah, the Halakhah and the Haggadot, Toseftot, Dikdukei Torah, and Dikdukei Soferim. When I look into their words and see that from all our goodly treasures which we had in ancient days nothing is left us but a scanty record, I am filled with sorrow, and this same sorrow causes my heart to tremble. Out of this same trembling I write my fables, like a man who has been exiled from his father's palace, who makes himself a little booth and sits there telling of the glory of his forefather's house.

("The Secret of Writing Fables. The Sense of Smell")

This is a poetic expression of Shmuel Yosef Agnon's fundamental attitude towards the relationship between modern literature and ancient texts.[1] For Agnon, intertextuality is neither a mere literary device nor an unconscious phenomenon. Rather it is the very source of his creativity, perhaps even its main subject. Modern Hebrew literature, according to Agnon, is nothing less than a substitute for the sacred texts; the absence of sacred literature is the source of his inspiration. Moreover, the author sees himself as the heir of the holy scribes whose works were only a communal creation, and whose anonymity, which foregrounded the texts and hid the identity of the individual authors, was an integral part of their work.

As a modern author, therefore, Agnon continues the ancient tradition in his work because it has become part of his cultural heritage. But as a modern author, who can only imitate the language of the canon and cannot enact its content as part of a living ritual, he cannot be the true bearer of that canon. Therefore, Agnon does not see himself as a transmitter of a great cultural lineage, built layer upon layer, beginning with the Bible and continuing through the Mishnah, the Talmud, and all the works which stem from them. Instead he views himself as belonging to a different culture altogether, one which inherits a multi-textual tradition it can no longer carry on. This culture relates to these earlier texts, but, because of the new social context, these texts can be made real only by means of invented fables—fables, in other words, which are not the sacred fables that the righteous of each generation were accustomed to tell, but which are, rather, secular chambers, in which only the echoes of the canon are heard. Hence the work of the modern writer, claims Agnon, serves as a secular substitute (a "booth") for sacred tradition (the "palace"). In order to understand Agnon's works in general, and the story with which I shall be concerned in particular, this connection between holy origins and secular expression must be kept in mind.

II

To a greater degree than that of any other writer in modern Hebrew literature, Agnon's work is based upon intertextual connections.² Indeed, Agnon conceives of an ideal addressee for whom the traditions of sacred literature are totally native, one who can discern the relationship between the fable and the holy canon. Agnon's implied addressee, however, is not simply the reader who is close to those traditions and is able to recognize them. He is one who is able, like the author himself, to distinguish among them and even to create oppositions between them.³ In order to understand Agnon's work, one must read his text not only as a link in the chain of sacred tradition, but also as an anti-text to this traditional literature.

Agnon's text will be misunderstood, therefore, not only by the addressee who is completely unfamiliar with the textual tradition to which the author is referring, but also by the addressee who credulously reads the text as a link in a chain of sacred texts. The author writes a great many stories which *appear* to be sacred texts or "quasi-sanctified" texts (or even a kind of Apocrypha), stories in which the author, by various devices, hints that his text is indeed a link in the chain of sacred texts. **"Agunot" ["Deserted Wives"]** (1908), and ***Ve-Haya he-Akov le-Mishor*** [***And the Crooked Shall Be Made Straight***] (1912) are two such works. The first is prefaced by a kind of pseudo-midrash, while in the second Agnon opens each chapter with quotations from the traditional literature, the narrative as a whole (through the use of the introduction, the style, and the inserted tales) being structured on the frame of "tales of believers" (the name given to traditional religious and moral stories dealing with awe of heavenly power and deep religious faith). The same literary approach can be found in many later stories as well. But whether, in fact, Agnon's works only contain hints pointing towards sacred texts or are actually written "as if" they themselves are quasi-sanctified, it is clear that the tales' creative power arises from the constant tension between the text itself and the sanctified or semi-sanctified literary tradition (if we take into account the later literature of the religious community) which it invokes. To examine this tension in Agnon's work, let us turn to his first story, **"Agunot,"** which in many ways determined Agnon's subsequent literary development, thematically, structurally, and stylistically.⁴

III

"Agunot," by Shmuel Yosef Czazkes, was the first story published by the young author in Palestine, where he had immigrated in 1908. It appeared in one of the first periodicals of the Second Aliyah, *Ha-Omer,* vol. II, no. 1, 1908. It is significant that the author used part of the title of this story for his nom de plume and his surname. This is a symbolic act which, to my knowledge, is without parallel in Hebrew literature. Indeed, Agnon so identified himself with the name of his story that what we have here is an extension of the fictional into the real, the fictional narrative becoming a kind of *perush* (interpretation) on the existential and poetic experience of the author, an interpretation which has forced him to displace the chief element in his identifying sign. The story, then, might be thought of as a form of midrash on the new name of the author.

Taking the name from the deed or the deed from the name is, of course, a well-known technique in Jewish literature: "And Joseph called the name of the firstborn Menasheh; For God, said he, hath made me forget all my toil, and all my father's house. And the name of the second called he Ephraim; For God hath caused me to be fruitful in the land of my afflictions" (Gen. 41:51-52). (The play here is upon *Menasheh* and *nashani*—"made me forget," and *Ephraim* and *hifrani*—"caused me to be fruitful.") The two names are used to summarize two events which happened to the father of the family. The name is a sign of the deed. When, therefore, Agnon relates the title of his story to himself, he continues this tradition of the ancient literature, implicitly declaring that his life is a commentary on the story, just as the story is a commentary on his life. By affiliating what seems to be a legendary or fictional experience with the actual identity of a person who is within and without the fiction at one and the same time, the author, especially through his signature, identifies the text as something which belongs to him, and to no one else.

IV

This phenomenon of the text as commentary, mediating between fact and fiction, is replicated in a number of ways in **"Agunot."** The most important of these for our purposes is the relationship that is established between the opening or introduction to the story and what the "author" (as he refers to himself) calls "the fable," "a great tale and terrible, from the Holy Land." The opening section is built along the same lines as many Ḥasidic tales, which open with "a quotation from the writings," pointing, generally, towards the works of the holy Ari, Rabbi Isaac son of Solomon Luria (1534-72), the head of the kabbalistic community in Safad.⁵ The Ari's works were left unpublished. But the "quotations" from the Ḥasidic books which were attributed to him were cited with a show of great authority, even though it was widely acknowledged that their authenticity was quite often doubtful. Agnon revives this form of the "quotation from the writings," what I would call the pseudo-quotation, supporting his fable with words which seem to have a sanctified status, almost an ordination. Furthermore, the sacred authority of these citations extends itself into the fable, the fable becoming a kind of exemplum of the imaginary quotation. The quotation, however, is not reducible to the purely imaginary. Imaginary *in fact,* and yet constructed of similarly "authentic" passages of sacred literature (which are themselves of dubious authority), it is, we may say, a genuine pseudo-quotation because the well-informed reader can grasp not only the authenticity of the unfolding of its elements, but also the spirit in which it is invoked. It is a text derived from sacred texts, which has many of the characteristics of those texts, but which is itself outside the sacred context.

The opening of **"Agunot,"** therefore, continues the midrashic form of writing signalized by Agnon's choices of name and title. The addressee, as he reads, is half-willing to suspend his disbelief and imagine that this is not a secular work by a secular author, but a religious work in which the implied author carries on the midrashic activity of former generations. The pseudo-sacred opening imitates a tradition in which, the relationship between a secular story and the sacred canon having been revealed, the story itself takes on a species of sacred and sanctified significance. The fictionality is self-fulfilling: secular and sacred are interwoven, and we do not know if the sacred sanctifies the secular, or the secular sanctifies the sacred. Indeed, the relationship between secular and sacred, and the fictive or real status of each, are perhaps the central themes of the tale.

Specifically, the opening follows in a tradition of midrashic writing which depended upon the Song of Songs and the midrash on the Song of Songs. It renews the general motif of the relationship between a metaphorical (or symbolic) character who represents the Jewish people and an anthropomorphic image of God, while it recapitulates a particular stage in the midrashic exegesis of that text where, in Song of Songs Rabbah, this connection is made suggestively to express the intimate and even reciprocal relationship between the people and their God. This relationship is made explicit later in the exegetical tradition, as, for example, in the Lurianic Kabbalah where we find a detailed reciprocity between the deeds of the people and the deeds of God.

Now, the midrash that Agnon writes is simultaneously an interpretation of the Song of Songs and of the midrash on the Song of Songs. In the opening of Agnon's midrash the following phrases from the Song of Songs appear: "Behold, thou art fair, my love, behold, thou art fair" (4:1); "they smote me, they wounded me, they took away my veil" (5:7); "my beloved withdrew and was gone" (5:6); "I am lovesick" (5:8). Citations from the Song of Songs, furthermore, appear not only in the opening but also in the body of the story where they take on increasingly complex significance. On the one hand, their application, like the fable as a whole, moves from the abstract or conceptual level of interpretation to a more literal or reified one. On the other hand, they draw into the body of the story the conceptual significance they had possessed in the opening. (I am referring to such verses as "My beloved descended into the garden," as implied in **"Agunot,"** p. 31, "the time of the singing of birds is come," p. 31, "I sleep but my heart waketh," p. 35).[6]

These verses, and phrases close to them, are the central elements of the intertextual connection. By appearing first in the opening and then returning in the body of the tale they suggest that the story as a whole looks in two directions. On the one hand, it refers to the nearer context of its own secular or fictional elements. And, on the other hand, it points toward the more remote context of its pseudo-sacred opening.[7] The more remote context establishes the relationship between the events of the near context and the traditional literature of past generations. It accumulates the interpretative meanings of the generations and causes them to issue in new events and new interpretations.

The introduction, of course, does not remain on the literal level of the love story told in Song of Songs. It quickly proceeds to evoke the midrash of the Song of Songs, which compares the people of Israel to the "fair one," God to the "beloved," and which interprets other elements of the love story in the light of this comparison. In this way, for example, "Behold, thou art fair, my love, behold thou art fair," elicits the following midrash: "Behold, thou art fair with precepts, behold thou art fair with deeds of kindness, behold thou art fair in positive precepts, behold thou art fair in negative precepts; behold thou art fair in the religious duties of the house, with the *ḥallah,* terumah, and tithes, behold thou art fair in religious duties of the field, with the gleanings, the forgotten sheaf, the corner, etc." (Midrash Song of Songs 4:1). Or another example: "I adjure you, O daughters of Jerusalem . . . what will ye tell him? That I am love-sick. As a sick person yearns for healing, so the generation in Egypt yearned for deliverance" (5:8).

These midrashim do not appeal in their original form in Agnon's text. They are, however, painstakingly implied in a discourse of authorial asides which compounds new expressions out of the interpretative echoes of many different sacred texts. This process begins in the opening of the story, where, for example, the pseudo-midrash being created substitutes the expression "a thread of grace" (which, so far as I have been able to determine, is not found in the traditional texts) for the phrase "a thread of mercy," which is indeed repeated in various well-known midrashic contexts, as, for example, in Ḥagigah 12b:

> *Look down from heaven, and see, even from Thy holy and glorious habitation.* Ma'on *is that in which there are companies of Ministering Angels, who utter (divine) song by night, and are silent by day for the sake of Israel's glory, for it is said: By day the Lord doth command His lovingkindness, and in the night his song is with me.*
>
> Resh Lakish said: Whoever occupies himself with (the study of) the Torah by night, the Holy One, blessed be He, draws over him a chord of lovingkindness ["a thread of mercy"] by day, for it is said: *"By day the Lord doth command His lovingkindness"*? Because *"by*

night His song is with me." And there are some who say: Resh Lakish said: Whoever occupies himself with the study of the Torah in this world, which is like the night, the Holy One, blessed be He, draws over him a chord of lovingkindness in the world to come, which is like the day, for it is said: *"By day the Lord doth command His lovingkindness, for by night His song is with me."*

(Compare also B. Megillah 13a and B. Tamid 29a.)

The motifs of the "prayer shawl, the hangings, and the weaving," which appear in the concrete image of *the prayer shawl* which is woven from the good deeds of the people of Israel by God Himself for *the Congregation of the people of Israel,* are similarly found in various forms in different midrashic sources. For example, the motif of "the apparel of the Shekhinah" appears in the Zohar III, Shelach Lecha 163b: "When the Shekhinah is in the pale blue she prepares for herself an outer covering of the same pale blue which was found in the Sanctuary, etc." And it appears in earlier and later versions, for example in *The Book of Comfort* by the tenth-century writer R. Nissim of Kairouan, or in the kabbalistic book of morals, *Shevet Musar,* by R. Elijah, son of Solomon Ha-Kohen from Izmir, where good deeds are compared to a garment which the naked soul is awarded as a consequence of its fulfillment of the commandments and for other praiseworthy deeds:

> Precious is the light and the upper (heavenly) garment created by the light of the Torah and the performance of its commandments, for through the commandments a precious, spiritual garment is woven, lighting the body of heaven in its clearness; the soul, leaving this world naked of bodily cover, hovering, ashamed, seeing itself naked, immediately puts on this clear, light-giving garment, a garment it had made for itself in the world of flesh through Torah and the commandments, and is overjoyed, seeing itself in the garment of Kingdom.

(*Shevet Musar* 35, 274-75.)

One could present a long list of sources which would show clearly that Agnon's pseudo-midrash is assembled from authentic materials which themselves provide varying contexts and interpretations. Concepts such as "grace and mercy," "the Congregation of Israel," "in her youth in her Father's house," "the Temple of her Sovereign and the city of sovereignty," "neither been sullied nor stained," "the power and the glory and the exultation," "the prayer shawl is damaged," "evil winds [spirits] blow," "and they know they are naked," "wandering and howling," "groans and cries," "darkest melancholy-Mercy shield us!"—all these and more acquired different meanings at different moments in sacred literature, from the midrash through to the late mystic literature (of the Ḥasidim). There is no need to go over each concept, nor to make a detailed analysis of the compounding of several concepts into units. But as these multiple perspectives come together in Agnon's text—indeed, as they exist separately within different midrashim—they hint at a relationship of reciprocity between the heavenly and the secular, between the Congregation of Israel or the Shekhinah (or the heavenly Spheres) and the Holy-One-Blessed-Be-He (or other Spheres in the scheme of Spheres) as He manifests Himself in affairs of this world. As long as the stream flows from below (the stream of commandments and good deeds), the stream from above continues to flow (the testing of immanence) and harmony exists, a harmony which the Congregation as a whole, and every individual in it, feels. When this stream is impeded, generally because of an event in the lower world of flesh, an interruption of the flow occurs. Harmony, which is simultaneously erotic and cosmic, is disrupted, and there is a kind of fall in the lower world, which will not be corrected until, miraculously, the harmony is restored. This disharmony has multiple manifestations: in the area of personal relations (where pairing becomes separation); in the area of the Spheres (where the masculine Spheres are alienated from the Sphere of Kingdom, which is the Shekhinah, while Judgments and the strength of the devil's camp increase); and in the area of the relations between the people and its God (where Exile overcomes Redemption).

Some of these patterns stand out in the quotations cited above (good deeds lead to unification of Creation, to the satisfaction of the Creator, and to the weaving of the garment which clothes the soul in good deeds), while others are to be found in the general store of meanings known to every "ideal" addressee, one who is intimate with this literature. Agnon's pseudo-midrashic opening, therefore, is both a precis of a sacred text and a narrative of a cosmic story. It suggests that a state of harmony, which originates in the reciprocal relations between the two heroes of the drama (God and the Congregation of Israel, or the Sphere of Glory and Majesty and the Sphere of Kingdom), gives way to the destruction of this harmonic state because of some negative, human factor and to a condition of longing for restoration of the original state (very much as in Romantic longings for lost perfection). Agnon accepts the premise that in sacred literature we find the permanent and known laws of the cosmic drama. These laws govern, as well, the strange game played between the midrashic assumption that "all is foreordained" and "we are free to choose." The cosmic process is realized in human action, just as every human action is an expression of the cosmic process. Reciprocal relations between these two processes are themselves expressed in the relationship between the opening and the tale.

V

As I have begun to show, semantic elements which link **"Agunot"** with sacred literature are found not only in the opening but throughout the story. Some of these are developed into motifs. Others stand on their own and, by virtue of the opening, are rendered open to conceptual glossing, based on the significance of their appearance in combination in the sources. Since the alternatives for explicating them cannot be limited with any certainty, the text's meaning remains unfixed within a field of intelligible significance.[8] The polysemousness of the textual units leads one back to a multitude of integral cultural contexts (such as the Bible, midrash, Talmud, Zohar, kabbalah more generally, the Ari, the Moral Books, Ḥasidic writings). The choice of one specific implied text as the base line of explication (a choice often reflecting the limitations of the addressee) leads to one kind of interpretation, but it does not necessarily eliminate others suggested by other implied texts. Examples of such exegetical quantities are: "ante-room and mansion of glory" (31), "the harp of David" (31), "but all this pride was inwards" (31), "the garden" (31), "the evil one intervened" (32), "a great mansion" (32), "a hall for prayer" (32), "no part of him was free of it" (34), "an empty vessel" (34), "on her couch in the night" (35), "the taper" (35), "like a lyre whose strings are rent" (36), "the Guardian of Night" (36), and many others. Each phrase has a rich and differentiated semantic history in Jewish culture and religion. The intervention of the devil in Job is not the same as the intervention of the devil in the kabbalistic literature and later Ḥasidic works, and so on. In **"Agunot"** this lattice of cited and pseudo-cited phrases creates an intertextual network, drawing after it entire systems of connotations and values. The opening implies that the tale reflects back on a paradigmatic situation and leads forward to a paradigmatic meaning (not fully specified or fulfilled) which replicates the evolution of meanings in the intertextual field. The story, therefore, is not only the tale of Ben Uri, Dinah, Ezekiel, and Freidele. These characters express as well a sacred drama of harmony and disharmony, redemption and exile, unity and disintegration, innocence and the fall, all of which unfolds in the ongoing history of Jewish literary forms, where sacred becomes continuous with secular, divine reality with fictional representation. The continuum grows on and on but the principle of its growth—as perhaps of midrash as a whole—is a denial or blockage of fulfillment, what Agnon conceptualized as *aginut*.

VI

To explain this as clearly as possible I turn now to the mysterious concretization of the title, **"Agunot,"** in the tale itself. On the face of it the title may be regarded as a misnomer. *Agunah* is defined in the halakhah as a married woman separated from her husband who may not divorce him because it is not known whether he is dead or alive. Agnon does not apply this halakhic meaning in his story. The four possible couples in the story either do not marry or marry and divorce in accordance with halakhah. Ben Uri does not marry Dinah; Ezekiel does not marry Freidele; Freidele marries a man in the distant diaspora; Ezekiel and Dinah marry and divorce.

In other words, there are no clear cases of *aginut* in this story. And yet a condition of disharmony such as might be thought to be created by aginut does exist; and, as is appropriate to the concept of aginut, it seems to be related to the improper pairing of couples. Thus, according to the story, it is not the law which determines proper pairing—and its consequences. Rather it is the emotional relationship of the individuals to these pairings. Had each of the participants found his or her true partner, harmony might have been established. Had Dinah married Ben Uri and Freidele married Ezekiel, all would have been well. The disharmony of the state of aginut, therefore, must be said to be here actually created, and not, as one might expect, palliated, by law and custom, and the major antinomy emphasized by the structure of the tale is thus the conflict between true marriage and marriage arranged by society. It is for this reason that the rabbi, who has been an agent of these disharmonious couplings, must be exiled.

If we return from the tale itself to the opening, it becomes apparent that cosmic order has been deranged because of a disturbance in the emotional order which is itself a faithful account of an order of cosmic coupling. The customs and norms generally accepted in the congregation bring about a tragic shift in the cosmic order, which is also the order of redemption. According to Agnon, the inherent conflict is between the Jewish tradition in its social form and a system of saving values embedded deep within this same tradition.

The tale itself evokes three additional conflicts which might also be likened to the state of aginut: that between Diaspora and the Land of Israel, between Exile and Redemption, and between Life and Art. These conflicts are connected, first and foremost, to the ghostly insubstantiality of the characters' representational value. Each of them beckons onward to a wider circle of meanings. But much as the title of the story, from which the ghostlike author derives his family name,[9] remains without a definite referent in the events of the story, so the ever-widening circles of reference frequently invert or subvert their previously suggested meanings. Clearly, for example, there is a relationship between Ben Uri and the biblical Bezalel Ben Uri, the builder of the Ark, who is a kind of archetypal craftsman in Israel, a craftsman who built for all time—or did he? Ezekiel's name is connected to the Prophet of God's word—and to the doom of Exile. ("But Rabbi Ezekiel? His feet are planted in the gates of Jerusalem and stand on her soil, but his eyes and his heart are pledged to houses of study and worship abroad, and even now, as he walks in the hills of Jerusalem, he fancies himself among the scholars of his own town, strolling in the fields to take the evening air": p. 41.) Dinah's name is related to frivolous behavior between man and woman, as in the story of Dinah and Shechem the son of Hamor, and as in the midrashic commentary on that story: "And Dinah went forth, the daughter of Leah, of whom it is written, 'The king's daughter is all glorious within'" [Ps. 45]—"And Dinah, the daughter of Leah went forth; she was not the daughter of Jacob. The daughter of Leah: as it is written about her mother that she is a gadabout so she, too, is a gadabout, etc." (Midrash Tanḥuma, Vayishlakh, 5-7). Freidele's name, while unrelated to any specific textual antecedent, is significant for its Yiddish form. The Yiddish diminutive unquestionably locates her among the Dispersed.

In similar ways the attraction between Ben Uri and Dinah holds out the promise of building the sanctuary and the Ark in the Land of Israel. Ben Uri is a native of the Land. His Ark may bring about the establishment of Sire Ahiezer in the Land, Sire Ahiezer who went up from the Diaspora in order to become established in the Land of Israel and to strengthen both learning and holy work there. But all these hopes are cut off totally. The failure, in fact, of the pairing of Dinah and Ezekiel, whom Sire Ahiezer chooses as her groom, is also the failure of his "redemption." Further, the failure of this pairing also becomes the failure of the return to Zion, just as Ezekiel's return to the land of Israel is the failure of his "pairing" and his failure as a scholar. Students will no longer come to him. The Ark, which is a sort of metamorphosis of the female figure (according to Midrash Song of Songs 4:4, and also 12: "And through whom did he give the Torah, through his two breasts—these are Moses and Aaron"—and later on, they are "the two Tables of the Covenant"), becomes an inverted metaphor. Instead of the woman being compared to the Ark of the Law, the Ark is compared to a woman ("To what might the Ark have been compared at that moment? To a woman who extends her palms in prayer, while her breasts—the Tables of the Covenant—are lifted with her heart, beseeching her Father in Heaven": p. 36).

The pattern of inversion continues. Analogies between Dinah and the Ark appear throughout the story. Thus, it is said of Dinah: "the doves fluttered about her in the twilight, murmuring their fondness in her ears and shielding her with their wings, like the golden cherubs on the Ark of the sanctuary" (pp. 31-32); and of the Ark: "On the hangings that draped the doors of the Ark, eagles poised above, their wings spread, to leap toward the sacred beasts above" (p. 34). The two exist side by side, and Ben Uri imbues the Ark with spirit, until Dinah (after the Ark has been overturned) causes it to lie like "a body without a soul," and she herself becomes "an unspotted soul gone forth naked into exile" (p. 36).

A tragic exchange occurs here: Ben Uri is matched with the Ark in place of the woman who it would seem is intended for him; Dinah harms the Ark as if it were a woman, her rival. The same exchange has other consequences. The sanctuary is not built properly; the grandee from the Diaspora does not establish himself in the Land of Israel; Redemption recedes further into the distance.

In the tale itself we find a concatenation of unfulfilled matches, characters who do not establish themselves in the Land of Israel, Redemption which has been postponed, and the failure to grasp a chance of human fulfillment. The artist, who because of his work does not devote himself to the human connection which might have brought harmony into the world, epitomizes all these. The breakdown of possible harmonious relationships, which does not permit the community to fulfill its social and national objectives, is figured in the reciprocal relationship between the tale itself and intertextual elements that appear in the tale, which, in turn, returns us to the meaning of the opening. The obstruction represented in the paradigm of the fall, which causes cosmic or metaphysical disharmony, also causes social disharmony and the delay of national redemption.

VII

Underlying both opening narrative and the tale there is a text which, even as it does not appear explicitly, is implied both in the opening and the tale. Finally, this text is also rendered implicit in the epilogue, which once again introduces what we might call a superreal component into the story and, in fact, creates the deepest connection between the different elements of the text. In various midrashic commentaries we find a motif of the perfect pairing similar to that which we find in Plato's *Symposium*. Thus, for instance, the development of the well-known parable in Genesis Rabbah 8: "Rabbi Jeremiah, son of Eleazar, said: 'At the hour that the Holy-One-Blessed-Be-He created the first man, he created him as an androgyne, as it is written "male and female created He them."'" Rabbi Samuel, son of Naḥman, said: 'At the hour that the Holy-One-Blessed-Be-He created the first man, He created him with two faces, and sawed him through, and made him double-backed, one facing this direction and one in the other.'" And in the continuation of the same chapter: "He said, 'in the past Adam (man) was created from earth and Eve created from Adam (man).' From here onwards it is said: 'in our image and after our likeness.' There is no man without a woman; there is no woman without a man. And both of them do not exist without the Shekhinah." And in chapter 68: "A matron asked R. Jacob son of Halafta: 'In how many days did the Holy-One-Blessed-Be-He create the world?' He said unto her: 'In six days, as it is written (Exodus 31) "For in six days the Lord made heaven and earth."'" She said unto him, 'What has he been doing from that hour to this day?' He said unto her: 'The Holy-One-Blessed-Be-He sits and makes matches, this man's daughter with that man. That man's wife with this man, etc.'"

These early sayings are elaborated in mystical ways in later midrash, frequently endowing the relations between man and woman with cosmic meaning. The following well known example of such elaboration is from the Zohar I 5b:

> Another explanation refers "His fruit was sweet to my taste" (Song of Songs 2:3)—to the souls of the righteous who are the fruit of the handiwork of the Almighty and abide with him above. Listen to this: All the souls in the world, which are the fruit of the handiwork of the Almighty, are all mystically one, but when they descend to this world they are separated into male and female, though these are still conjoined. And look at this: the desire of the female for the male creates a soul, and the desire of the male for the female, and his clinging to her, bring(s) forth a soul; and he incorporates the desire of the female and takes it in; and the lower desire is taken up into the higher desire and becomes one thing, without separation. And then the female takes in all and is impregnated by the male; their two desires are conjoined. And because of this all is mixed together, this in that.
>
> When the souls issue forth, they issue forth as male and female together. Subsequently, when they descend (to this world) they separate, one to one side and the other to the other, and the Holy-One-Blessed-Be-He mates them—He and no other, He alone knowing the mate proper to each. Happy is the man who is upright in his works and walks in the way of truth, so that his soul may find its original mate, for then he becomes indeed perfect, and through his perfection the whole world is blessed.
>
> And for this reason it is written: "His fruit is sweet to my taste" because He blesses through making whole, and "that the whole world will be blessed through him," because everything depends upon the actions of the human being, if he is righteous or not righteous.[10]

Even without a detailed explication of this passage it is clear that its meaning is based squarely on a quotation from the Song of Songs, and on several of the chapters of midrash which we quoted above. The topics have been transposed from a conceptual exegesis, backwards one might say, to a level of understanding that is concerned with the movements of the Heavenly Spheres. Here abstractive commentary has been recycled into the processions of phenomenal-noumenal being. Thus, for instance, Tishby explains the first portion: "Souls are created in the coupling of the Holy-One-Blessed-Be-He—Glory—with the Shekhinah. And of the overabundance given to the Shekhinah by the Holy-One-Blessed-Be-He for the creation of souls, she says: 'And his fruit was sweet to my taste.'" In the next section the chapter describes what happens, what results, in the world of human souls as a consequence of the events in the heavenly Spheres. The coupling of the Holy-One-Blessed-Be-He, says Tishbi, brings about the coming-together of the souls which were united above in the world of spirits, but those who are not deserving may lose their rightful partner, the one created with them in the holy coupling. A whole man is one who returns to his former paired-unity. (See above "he becomes indeed perfect.") And the perfect couple brings blessing to the Shekhinah and draws from her blessing to the world in their coupling. Of them the Shekhinah says: "And his fruit was sweet to my taste," which means, the coupling of the souls which are the fruit of the Holy-One-Blessed-Be-He gives me pleasure.[11]

This is a harmonious and phenomenological understanding of the erotic ideal which connects perfection created in the heavenly Spheres with perfection in relations between men and women. In a correctly ordered world, all species should have existed in permanent pairs, but Adam and Eve's sin caused a breakdown of this harmonic order. The coming-together of split souls in this world is fraught with manifold difficulties. Only he whose acts are desirable can be blessed in coming-together with his ancient partner without hardships, with the help of the Holy-One-Blessed-Be-He.[12]

This myth is at the foundation of our story and is perhaps more important than all the other implied texts, both in the opening and in the tale itself. It determines that the ideal coupling is the desired state, while the imperfect coupling is the state of the world. The tale itself does not tell an unusual story; it reflects a given, everyday situation. The need to correct this situation creates the eternal longing for harmony which characterizes all "deserted" souls (agunot). Ben Uri's music, a social order which creates improper matches, the conflict between art and reality—all of these are necessary obstacles through which the myth is concretized, the myth which hints at a desired harmony but points to the reality of disharmony. In Agnon's hands this myth expresses romantic agony and romantic irony: the suffering of deserted souls, those who cannot find their partners, and the irony created by the gap between longings and the frustration of longings. It recreates the internal connection between the opening narrative and "the tale itself," between the paradigm and the concretization of the paradigm, which in itself incorporates the mythic foundation of that same paradigm.

VIII

The unraveling of the tale is important insofar as it establishes the connection between the tale and everything which emerges from the implied paradigm of the opening, which is based upon the kabbalistic coupling myth. The unraveling of the tale begins with the marriage of Ezekiel and Dinah. The saying of the Sages, "When a person takes a wife to himself, all his sins fall away," through which the rabbi absolves Dinah after her confession, is not fulfilled in her own life. The coupling does not take place ("And neither drew near to the other all that night"); the marriage is not consummated because the two souls are not meant for one another. Each was meant for another. The divorce contract presented by the rabbi is nothing more than an halakhic expression of what actually exists in the domestic life of the couple. The match of the two souls fails. It throws up a barrier which causes the community (through the rabbi) to accept responsibility for the breakdown.

The opening narrative and its mythic foundation forge a connection between the tale and the life of the community. Erotic disharmony is a disharmony between parts of the community (the Land of Israel and the Diaspora) which brings about a breakdown in the process of communal redemption. ("It was not long that Sire Ahiezer left Jerusalem with his daughter. He had failed in his settlement there; his wishes had not prospered": p. 42.)[13]

The rabbi who, it would seem, is responsible for the breakdown in the marital order accepts responsibility for the fact that the community, through enforcing its norms (i.e., marrying a rich man's daughter to a scholar), caused a breakdown in the coupling of souls (the erotic attraction of the woman toward the creative figure). Ben Uri, logically then, is exiled to a foreign place because he too has participated in the breakdown of the coupling of souls in his preference for a woman-substitute (the replacement of the soul by the work of art) to the real woman. And so all of the characters in Agnon's story become agunot, lose their rightful partners and places. The rabbi himself becomes a lost soul, searching for that which will restore to the world what has been lost because of him (or because of the community). All of the stories of the rabbi in the epilogue—searching for a young painter (the reincarnation of Ben Uri), wandering across the sea on a red kerchief with an infant child in his arms, or staring into the eyes of little children in the houses of study—all these are stories with a strange messianic character. Whoever imposes upon himself "the obligation of exile" is looking for a way to emerge from the state of exile, inasmuch as he lifts up his eyes to a messianic solution which will bring redemption to the whole world. "Do not touch my messiahs. These are the babes of the house of study" (B. Shabbat 119b). It is possible to understand the search for the lost child as the rabbi's attempt to atone for the sin of placing an obstacle before true coupling, thereby preventing a child from coming into the world (who might have been the messiah). On the cosmic level the obstacle in the path of the coupling creates the universal disharmony which delays the Redemption and increases the burden of the Diaspora in the life of the nation.

IX

There are no direct parallels between the paradigm of the opening or the mythic paradigm which functions as the foundation of the whole story and "the tale itself." The tale of the pairings which failed (as a consequence of the norms of society and its failure to absorb the creativity of the artist into a pattern of human creativity) stands on its own and is a story of "the deserted souls" who have not found their proper partners and place. The story as a whole is also a concretization of the experience of the author who associates himself with the essence of the tale. By identifying himself as a romantic figure, cast about from Exile to Redemption, and from the Land of Israel to the Diaspora, the author repeatedly hints that he too is engaged in an eternal erotic quest which will never find satisfaction.

On the other hand, the opening and the myth of a mystic coupling that is left unconsummated, as well as the intratextual relationship that is transformed into an endlessly intertextual one, emphasize that the tale is a concretization of a tragic paradigm. This is the paradigm of the text, or of the pseudo-sacred text, which connects the actions of the people of Israel with the Lord of Creation, or connects the coupling in this world with the ongoing coupling in the Spheres. This relationship secures the connection between the concepts of "love," "art," "exile," "redemption," "diaspora," and "the Land of Israel," on the one hand, and such concepts as "the exile of the Shekhinah," "days of Messiah," "the Shekhinah," and "the Holy-One-Blessed-Be-He," on the other.

The extraordinarily complex intertextuality of this story makes it susceptible to a form of criticism which Hebrew literature, with its tradition of midrash upon midrash, invites in a particularly urgent way. In this work, and in other works of Agnon, intertextuality of a special kind is patently the condition and the theme of its literary being. Only an author who declares that he is a kind of heir to the "poets of the Temple," and who "occupies himself with the Torah, the Prophets, the Writings, the Mishnah, the Halakhah and the Haggadot" can write works which extend the continuum of sacred literature, even while those newly composed works stand in direct contradiction to it. Agnon's is the intertextuality of aginut. By actualizing "the holy paradigm" in the tale, he creates a story of frustrated love which profanes the sacred and sanctifies the profane.

Notes

1. On the general question of Agnon's poetics see G. Shaked, *Agnon's Narrative Art* (Hebrew) (Tel Aviv: Sifri'at Po'alim, 1973), pp. 13-29.

2. Many fine scholars have taken up the question of intertextuality in Agnon's writing, whether they give it this name or some other. On intertextuality in "Agunot" see H. Weiss, *Between Open and Hidden Levels of Meaning in Hebrew Short Stories* (Hebrew) (Tel Aviv: Open University, 1979).

3. I clarified this concept in my book, cited above, pp. 89-132.

4. See the important interpretation of Arnold Band, *Nostalgia and Nightmare* (Berkeley: University of California Press, 1968), pp. 57-63.

5. I would like to thank Yehuda Leibes, who kindly assisted me in the identification of these texts and in defining some of their functions.

6. All the quotations in the Hebrew text are from "Agunot," *Elu Ve-Elu* (Jerusalem and Tel Aviv: Schocken, 1953), pp. 406-16. All quotations in the English are from "Agunot," trans. Baruch Hochman, *Twenty-One Stories,* ed. Nahum Glatzer (London: Victor Gollancz, 1970), pp. 30-44.

7. I am using the term intertextuality here according to the propositions described by Jonathan Culler in the work of Lourent Jenny: "he proposes to distinguish intertextuality proper from 'simple allusions or reminiscence': in the latter case a text repeats an element from a prior text without using its meaning; in the former it alludes to or redeploys an entire structure, a pattern of form and meaning from a prior text": *The Pursuit of Signs* (Ithaca: Cornell University Press, 1981), p. 104.

8. We can thus harmonize two different interpretations such as those presented by Isaac Bacon and Orna Golan. Bacon understands the story in terms of the problems of the artist and bases his argument mainly on the connection between "grace and mercy," art and love, using midrashim which support this interpretation. Golan interprets the story as the failure of the Second Aliyah (Ben Uri!) which built the sanctuary (the place) before the Ark (Jewish values). She cites various midrashim on the "Ark of the Covenant," and on the characters of Dinah (as the daughter of the tribe of Dan) and Ben Uri (the tribe of Judah), who could have been the parents of the Messiah. See O. Golan, "'Agunot' and the Second Aliyah" (Hebrew), *Mozna'im* 32 (1971): 215-23; and I. Bacon, "On Shai Agnon's 'Agunot'" (Hebrew), *Mozna'im* 46 (1978): 167-79.

9. This is a technique which reaches its peak in the stories "Edo and Enam" and "Ad Olam" ("For evermore"), in which Agnon uses the first letters of his name, *ayin* and *gimmel,* to indicate that the characters in the story are part of his personality. In *And the Crooked Shall Be Made Straight* (1912) he also uses this technique in the character of Menashe (Mashkiaḥ) Chaim (the "Forgetter of Life"), and Kreindel Charny ("Atarah Sheḥorah" = Black Crown).

10. *Mishnat ha-Zohar,* ed. I. Tishbi (Jerusalem, 1961), pp. 627-28.

11. Ibid.

12. Ibid.

13. Another myth, that of H. N. Bialik in *Scroll of Fire,* also creates a connection between the erotic separation of men and women and Exile.

Arnold Band (essay date 1987)

SOURCE: Band, Arnold. "The Kafka-Agnon Polarities." In *The Dove and the Mole: Kafka's Journey into Darkness and Creativity,* edited by Moshe Lazar and Ronald Gottesman, pp. 151-60. Malibu, Calif.: Undena, 1987.

[*In the following chapter from a book of essays on Franz Kafka, Band reviews previous criticism comparing Kafka's and Agnon's writings, arguing that many of the alleged similarities in the works of the two writers have been overemphasized.*]

The comparison of Kafka with other writers of the modern period has become such a beaten path in Kafkakunde that one often shudders upon encountering another "Kafka and . . ." study. Despite this academic ennui, we should, nevertheless, discriminate between comparisons that are gratuitous and those that are grounded and illuminating. In referring to the Kafka-Agnon polarities, I am attempting to avoid the tedious "Kafka and . . ." formula while calling attention to an area of research virtually unknown in Kafkaist circles since it is mainly written in Hebrew, but is, nevertheless, potentially rewarding.

The attribution of a certain strain in Agnon's writing to the influence of Franz Kafka first appeared in the early 1930's. In 1932, Agnon, who had recently solidified his reputation as a modern version of the traditional Jewish teller of pious tales in a four-volume Berlin edition of his collected works, published a startling new cluster of five stories, titled enigmatically **Sefer HaMa'asim (The Book of Tales)** which dismayed and confused his readers. They found them impenetrable since they suspended the realistic canons of time, space, and causality in ways which even his most fantastic quasi-Hasidic tales did not do. Several critics who knew both German literature well and the extent of Agnon's library smiled and declared: "He's been reading Kafka," and their articles referred to influences rather than comparisons or contrasts.

Though Kafka was by no means a well-known writer in the early 1930's, certainly not one of the unavoidable prooftexts he is today, the attribution was logical—given the literary situation in Jerusalem and Tel Aviv. By the late twenties and early thirties, there had formed in those two cities a veritable colony of sophisticated German-reading émigrés, many from Berlin and Prague, some of them Kafka's close associates. Hugo Bergmann, for instance, came in 1920; Leo Hermann, the editor of *Selbstwehr,* in 1926; Max Brod and the two Weltsches arrived in 1939 and 1940. Together with such luminaries as Gershom Scholem who came in 1923 and Martin Buber, who came in 1933, they formed one of the first centers of Kafka enthusiasts. Their personal libraries and those of hundreds of other intellectuals, all refugees from German-speaking centers, contained at least the three novels, published in the late twenties, some of the short stories, and, if they left after the Anschluss or Kristallnacht, the first edition of *Gesammelte Werke,* 1936-37.

Agnon, though an Ost-Jude, was part of this circle since he had spent 11 years (1913-24) in Germany, was an Austrian citizen (since he came from Galicia), and shrewdly capitalized on the romanticization of the Ost-Jude which begins to surface in Germany in the first decade of the century and is manifest in such periodicals as *Der Jude* (edited by Martin Buber from 1917-1929) and several popular anthologies of the period where Agnon had published translations of his early Hebrew scripts. While Agnon protested that he had never read Kafka except for *Der Verwandlung,* he probably did. It is also probable that Kafka, at least in his later years, read some of Agnon's tales of Eastern European Jewry since he became deeply interested in that world, particularly in Bratslav Tales which, interestingly enough, Agnon admitted were one of the formative influences in his writing career. I cite these biographical facts—as I will cite others—not to prove influence, but rather to establish common contacts, partial "grounds for comparison."

Once coined, the Agnon-Kafka nexus became common currency in Hebrew literary criticism and circulated unexamined and unspecified. It was reaffirmed forcefully by the prestigious critic, Baruch Kurzweil (also a Prague Jew), in the 1950's and 1960's; Kurzweil wrote extensively on Agnon and, in arguing that religious doubt lurks under the deceptively pious surface of Agnon's prose, compared him repeatedly to other modern writers such as Kafka, Musil, and Joyce. Kurzweil correctly noted the obvious fact that while Kafka was only marginal to the Jewish tradition, Agnon was fully in the tradition (despite all his doubts), and herein lay the difference. While placing the two writers in the same modernist tradition, Kurzweil essentially constricted and subverted the grounds for comparison.

Kurzweil's criticism, in general, was theologically oriented and deliberately avoided literary history. In my own work on Agnon, which, for the first time, set Agnon in his historical milieu, I demonstrated, for instance, that Agnon had in fact written a story in Yiddish in 1907 with the intriguing name **"Totem-tants,"** which manifested many of the calculated indeterminacies of Kafka's mature style, and that Agnon had read widely in neo-Romantic German and Scandinavian authors during his adolescence in Galicia.[1] When one observes both writers from the perspective of general literary history, the comparison is far from gratuitous: both were born in the 1880's (Kafka 1883, Agnon 1888) and reared in the homes of relatively successful businessmen (both in marketing) in the last decades of the Hapsburg Empire. While Kafka's Prague was far more westernized than Agnon's Buczacz, connections of the latter with Lemberg and Vienna were well established; the latest newspapers and books were available and political life was intense. If one were to compare the news of the Jewish world published in *Selbstwehr,* the Zionist weekly whose centrality in Kafka's life has been well established by Hartmut Binder, with the Hebrew and Yiddish newspapers which Agnon was reading (and in which he published) one finds a remarkable commonalty of content and concern: reports of Zionist activities, the settlement of Palestine, antisemitism as in reports of pogroms in Russia, blood libels throughout all of eastern Europe, and, between 1911-13, the Beiliss Trial which reopened the wounds of the Dreyfus Affair which had hardly healed. The availability of relatively inexpensive newsprint and improved communication are technological advances which contributed mightily to the formation of an international sense of Jewish solidarity: the death of Herzl or the Kishinev pogrom were widely covered and the news was immediately available in Jewish homes everywhere. Kafka's diaries, Evelyn Beck's study of his interest in the Yiddish theatre,[2] my own research into the impact of the Beiliss Trial[3] and, more recently, the perceptive psychoanalytic of study Marthe Robert,[4] or Ronald Hayman's biography on Kafka's obsession with trials and judgments, are adequate proof of his deep interest, even obsession with Jewish affairs.[5] Kafka often talked of settling in Palestine, but was characteristically incapable of making such a radical move. Agnon, on the other hand, did make a move and resided in Jaffa and Jerusalem between 1908 and 1913.

During Agnon's stay in Germany between 1913 and 1924, mostly in Berlin, but also in Leipzig, Frankfurt and Bad-Homburg, the intellectual circles of our two writers actually intersected in some places. Agnon probably read *Der Verwandlung* during this period and it is inconceivable that Kafka did not come across the name of Agnon since the latter was very popular in the circle of German Jews who were Zionists and disposed to harbor a strange nostalgia for anything that smacked of Ostjudentum, as manifested in Buber's *Der Jude* which certainly reached Kafka who published "Ein Bericht für eine Akademie" in it in 1917. Agnon published six stories between 1917-24, several translated from the Hebrew manuscript by Gershom Scholem (no less!) and one, **"Agadat HaSofer"** ("Die Erzählung vom Toraschreiber") appeared in the same volume, though not in the same issue, as "Ein Bericht. . . ." Agnon also published stories in three anthologies which were very popular in the same circles: 1. ***Chad Gadja: Das Pesachbuch,*** ed. Hugo Hermann. Berlin, 1914. 2. ***Treue: Ein Jüdisches Sammelsschrift,*** ed. Loe Hermann. Berlin, 1915. 3. ***Das Buch von den Polnischen Juden,*** ed. S. J. Agnon and A. Eliasberg. Sensitized to the ethos of what—perhaps in polite language—was being called "Polish Jewry" by his encounters with Izak Loewy and his Yiddish troupe, or Mordecai Georg Langer, Kafka would have seen in Agnon the modern incarnation of the classical Hasidic storyteller. Kafka might also have read Agnon's novella ***Vehaya He'akov Lemishor*** (***Und das Krumme wird gerade***) published first in 1918, but twice republished after Kafka's death. This was one of the most popular books in those German-Jewish circles which Kafka frequented. Ironically, Agnon, the leading Hebrew prose writer of the twentieth century, was first more appreciated in German translation than in the Hebrew originals.

With the historical grounds for comparison firmly established, we can define the areas worthy of comparison and subject them to critical scrutiny. Before doing so, we should refer to the Hebrew study by Hillel Barzel (1972) which is totally dedicated to a comparative study of Agnon and Kafka (actually the name of the book)[6] and more or less represents the state of the field. Other Hebrew critics, such as G. Shaked of the Hebrew University have recently offered seminar courses on this topic, but since they have not yet published anything on this matter, we cannot address ourselves to them.

Barzel unfortunately follows his predecessor in the chair at Bar-Ilan University, Baruch Kurzweil, and persists in emphasizing the theological/metaphysical motif as the main message of both writers, a position which few would subscribe to today. All aspects of these writers are then assayed with this touchstone. Barzel thus finds Agnon more religious, open to possibilities of redemption, and clearly rooted in the Jewish tradition. Kafka is therefore metaphysical but secular, monothematic, closed to all possibility of redemption, particularly since he can find no refuge in home or family, usually areas of security—or at least, struggle—in Agnon's fiction. While Barzel finds both writers masters of allegory and symbol (not fully explained), or of a subtle mixture of the comic and the tragic, Agnon always seems to possess the wider range. After over 100 pages of equally vacuous comparisons, Barzel spends some 200 pages (eight chapters) comparing works, or parts of them under a variety of rubrics: similar similes, the use of archetypes, authorial presence, the wandering Jew, the concept of the artist, etc. Here, it must be said, that Barzel is saved by the presence of the texts and that his insights, though limited by his initial concept, are at times interesting. It is, for instance, illuminating, to compare **"Agadat HaSofer"** with "Ein Hungerkünstler"

under the rubric "the concept of art," but this assumes that this is the only interpretation of the two stories or that they are comparable to begin with—a contention which is never established. I cite Barzel's difficulty as emblematic of the problems of such a comparative study: the enormity of the subject, the narrow, inflexible method, and the apologetic desire to demonstrate that Agnon is in the same league with Kafka combined to subvert Barzel's study. What I hope to do in the remainder of this paper is more modest: I would like to establish some guidelines for research in this area by defining what is possible and productive.

What, we should ask, are the perimeters of our investigation? Do we compare—or contrast—all of Agnon with all of Kafka? Obviously this is impossible, not only because of the limitations of time and interest, but because much of Agnon bears no resemblance whatsoever to Kafka's normative mode of expression—assuming we can agree upon such a stylistic phenomenon. Even if we were to go beyond the twenty-odd stories of **"Sefer HaMa'asim"** (ordinarily recognized as "Kafkaesque") to include such formidable pieces as **"Shevu'at Emunim," "Ido ve'Enam," "Ad Olam," "Hadom ve'Khiseh,"** and the **"Kelev Meshuga"** (**"Mad Dog"**) portions of the novel ***Temol Shilshom,*** altogether some 600 pages of dense fiction, we would still be left with several thousands pages of stories, novels, quasi-historical compilations of tales, collections of rewritten customs interlarded with anecdotes, eulogies, commemorative pieces, etc., etc. Not only Agnon lived twice as long as Kafka, but he happened to spend most of his adult life in Jerusalem, a city with specific implications for a Hebrew writer, not only in its historical resonances, but in that it was the vital center of the Jewish world in one of the most dynamic periods in Jewish history. One simply could not escape into one's burrow—however one may want to interpret that metonym. This does not mean that Agnon was a better or a worse writer, but rather one who was more vulnerable to the pressures of overwhelming historical forces. When we speak of Agnon's resemblance to Kafka, we are actually referring to about ten per cent of the former's work. Once the perimeters have been established, we should turn to the all important questions of language and thematics which are often intertwined. To focus on these problems, we turn to two stories, one by each writer, both written in 1912—not that these stories have much in common, but that each, in its own way, was crucial in the artistic development of the author: Kafka's *Das Urteil* and Agnon's ***Vehaya He'akov Lemishor,*** (***And the Crooked Shall Become Straight***), the same story which was so popular in its German translation of 1918, ***Und das Krumme wird gerade.*** In each case, the story represents an artistic "breakthrough"—to use Politzer's term, a breakthrough from fragments and experimentation to a sudden mastery involving decisions regarding stylistic and thematic features which subsequently mark the author's work for the rest of his career.

In that *Das Urteil* is well known to Kafkaists, I can be brief. It was, according to Kafka's testimony, written in the night of September 22-3, 1912, and deals with the clash between a son, Georg Bendemann, and his seemingly ailing, aged father, who, by the end of the story, condemns his son to death by drowning. Bound by this injunction ("Urteil"), Georg jumps off the bridge near their apartment. In this story we already find the seemingly lucid sentence which, upon examination, is often indeterminate, the obsession with guilt and trials, the subject-object inversion, the varied and often contrary identifications, and the unique fusion of disparate experiences which are characteristic features of Kafka's art.

Politzer has attributed the force of the breakthrough to Kafka's meeting with Felice Bauer. Finding this attribution inadequate, I have suggested elsewhere that many of the specifics of the story become more integrated when we understand that Kafka organized his story around a nuclear concept which could hold together disparate, centrifugal elements. Here as in some Kafka's other well integrated stories, a central, generalized concept is presented as the title and the narrative is a taut examination of the term, situation by situation. The term may have several mutually contradictory meanings and the story is then a narrative concretization of the frustrating yet exhilarating complexities of language. I have traced the term *Urteil* to both the Beiliss Trial (1911-1913) and the Jewish High Holiday Prayer Book.[7] Echoes of Rosh HaShanah or Yom Kippur service illuminate the process of judgment, the figure of the father or of all systems of authority which, by their very nature, must fail, despite their oppressiveness. In the service, as exemplified in the "Unetaneh Tokef" prayer where the term "Urteil" is in a dramatic, key position, the divinity addressed has the personality traits of Georg Bendemann's father (or Hermann Kafka as portrayed in the famous "Brief an der Vater"): the domineering king and judge of the world—yet addressed by "Du," the source of all authority and thus of guilt, the all-seeing eye form which we can never hide, the unquestioned power which controls man's destiny. Echoes of the Beiliss enrich the figure of the friend in Russia, the lonely failure pitied by Georg yet to whom he feels accountable, the exiled person with whom the father has an enigmatic relationship and whose fall seems to threaten the newly won security of Georg both in business and in love. Given Kafka's family background and his recently rekindled Jewish consciousness (as demonstrated by Evelyn Beck) an event so central to the consciousness of Prague Jewry could not have left him unaffected. Identification with Mendel Beiliss, or even a remote though prolonged observation of his plight, could have provided Kafka with the necessary validation of his own feelings of insecurity and loneliness, an expansion and objectification of his Oedipal torment, corroboration of his doubts about the validity and viability of language, and a moral justification for the bewildering dialectic between self-corrosive guilt and subtle imposture which marks so many of his protagonists. *Der Verwandlung,* a further development of these themes, we should recall, was written several weeks later, in November, 1912.

All the features mentioned above are the product of deliberate artistic choices: the tight, Flaubertian style which leaves nothing to chance; the plot strategies which take the reader from an apparently orderly bourgeois setting into the abyss which lurks beneath it; in all, a departure from the limitations of realistic prose writing. Agnon, at the same time, made several decisions concerning his craft—which he cultivated with the same intensity as Kafka—that took him in a somewhat different direction. Though six years younger than Kafka, Agnon published about 70 pieces in Yiddish and Hebrew, both in Buczacz and Jaffa, before writing **Vehaya He'Akov Lemishor.** Most of these were, to be sure, embarrassingly clumsy and were published only because the editor of a provincial newspaper often has to fill space. Those published in Jaffa attest to experiments in more serious writing, usually macabre neoromantic tales of frustrated love, bizarre deaths, strange women—all conveyed in an agitated, often lush Hebrew prose style. Agnon, himself, obviously realized that this was not the medium he was seeking since, after the success of **Vehaya He'Akov Lemishor**—written, according to his testimony in only four days, though it covers some 80 pages—he scrapped most of what he had written previously and either rewrote or totally discarded every line he had previously published. Few of these 70 items were ever published in the many collections of his works.

Instead of paring down contemporary prose style to the threshold of meaning, Agnon adopted the late rabbinic style his great grandfather might have used, but kept it under a scrupulously tight control. The lexical, morphological, and phrasing features are clearly late rabbinic; the sentence, however, is carefully measured and modern in its stratagems. Agnon could thus generate the tension he sought between historical linguistic resonance (so important in an ancient, text-oriented culture), and a controlled reticence which often conceals more than it tells. The sensitive reader is thus forced to share the implied author's ambivalence about the world he has chosen to describe.

The technique worked wonders in **Vehaya He'Akov Lemishor,** a tale set in mid-nineteenth century Galicia where the norms of traditional piety and the bourgeois ethos are subtly at odds. The hero, Menashe Hayyim, a pious shopkeeper of some means, is forced into bankruptcy by a new competitor. To recoup his capital, he reluctantly takes to the road as an itinerant beggar armed with a letter of recommendation certifying his identity, his former position in society, and his rectitude. This seemingly bizarre technique for recovering lost capital was both common in earlier centuries, but had become the butt of satire by the nineteenth century. By using this ambiguous style, Agnon does not allow the reader to know what the author thinks about it since he wants to defuse this social issue. Menashe Hayyim's humiliating enterprise achieves its goal—at first: he does recoup enough capital to return home and reopen a business. Unfortunately, once he thinks his fate has turned, he succumbs to temptation by selling his letter to another beggar. As one might anticipate, he then loses his money and all his possessions at an inn during a country fair with its grotesque side-shows and gluttony and must return to the road to beg, sans letter of recommendation. The beggar who bought the letter naturally dies and is buried as Menashe Hayyim; the latter's wife, now a widow, remarries and bears children. When Menashe Hayyim finally does return home, he discovers his wife married and a mother. Herein lies the moral problem of the Novella: according to Jewish law, he should reveal that he is alive, thus embarrassing his wife and condemning her child to bastardy; but since he loves his wife, a bourgeois-romantic sentiment, he leaves town beset by the guilt of his concealment. To prevent disclosure, he often hides in forests and becomes a denizen of cemeteries. One day he noticed the cemetery guard engraving a handsome tombstone with the name "Menashe Hayyim" on it. The guard told him it was ordered by a lady for the grave of a certain beggar, her husband. Realizing that it was his wife, Krendel Tcharni, who had ordered the stone for him since she thought him dead, Menashe Hayyim finally confessed the story of his life to the guard. Several days later, happy in thought that his wife still loved him and that he had resisted to reveal the truth, thereby ruining her life, Menashe Hayyim dies and the guard places over his grave the stone ordered by his wife for the other grave which she thought was his. Though childless, his name was not forgotten because his wife would come to weep over his grave.

Even in bad plot-outline, this Novella does not sound like the pious tale it was taken to be by most critics for over 30 years: the quasirabbinic style, the pious milieu, succeeded in deflecting the reader from such obvious points as the loss of identity and the descent into hell, let alone the ambiguous ending in the graveyard. Kurzweil noticed in the late 1950's that there are, indeed, many discordant elements in the story, but following his theological bias, reads this story and much of modern Hebrew literature as a literary manifestation of secularism. The story, for him, implies an accusation against the cruelty of God who lets Menashe Hayyim descend into a world chaos for no glaring sin, if any at all. The hero is forced to leave his home and wife, to depart on a journey from which there is no return, since his return can be effected only by a miracle. But there are no miracles today. Some fifteen years later I argued that Kurzweil, as usual, never addressed himself to the totality of the study, to the title which (taken from Isaiah, 40) implies that "crooked is made straight" and to the ending, which definitely vindicates the hero and restores the reader's confidence in the possibility of justice in this world. Menashe Hayyim does die happy in the knowledge that he has withstood temptation (to reveal his true identity: that he was still alive) and has been rewarded with the two gifts most important to him, after he had despaired of ever recouping his fortune and his status, i.e., assurance of his wife's continuing love for him, and confidence that he would have his posterity even if it were merely his name on a tombstone.

Today I would extend my argument further. While it is undeniable that Agnon was interested in a popular tale which he probably had read or heard, and delighted in entertaining his audience with what seemed to be a pious tale, he made several deliberate decisions which imply a conscious sense of direction and lead us to certain conclusions concerning his attitude towards his craft.

1. After four years of experimentation in a neo-romantic style with themes taken from the world of Jaffa where he lived, he abandoned both his stylistic and thematic course. He obviously realized that this direction did not afford him the opportunities to exploit his prodigious knowledge of Hebrew or confront the cultural problems which obsessed him. Ultimately, these Jaffa stories were frivolous, and remained so until recast in his new style. (Many, as said, were never recast, but merely discarded.)

2. He chose both a theme and style which were patently not the norm of fiction then being written in Hebrew.

3. He mixed features of the pious tale with points familiar to the German Romantic tradition and the bourgeois novel.

4. He adopted a manneristic, late-rabbinic style for a Novella which has many passages of bourgeois and psychological realism.

Here the contrast with Kafka is instructive. Kafka selected situations which were, to him, either intolerable, or absurd, or comically grotesque, and struggled to fashion an unmediated linguistic medium which, while contemporary, teetered on the threshold of human consciousness. Agnon's style beginning with *Vehaya*

He'Akov Lemishor immediately directs the reader to a world of texts and textuality, a specific textuality at that, one that embodies in all its features a traditional, recognizable milieu. Briefly, no competent reader of Hebrew could conceivably miss the multifarious implications of this style. Realizing that he could not fashion a neutral text, "free" of referentiality to previous texts—for such is the nature of the Hebrew language in the beginning of the century and, to a lesser degree, even today—Agnon fashioned an artful pastiche of an older style so convincing that it took most readers some thirty years to realize that under the pious text of the Novella lay a sub-text which qualified, ironized, or even subverted the text. Though criticized by such formidable figures as Berdiczewski and S. Tsemah, Agnon succeeded admirably in creating a voice which allows for a wide range of authorial attitudes towards the text and the situations created, a subtle modulation between authorial and narrative voice, hence the possibility of a variety of unreliable narrators. Applied to those stories which most closely resemble those of Kafka, the manneristic style adds another level of indeterminacy. If one, furthermore, were to speak of Kafka and Agnon in terms of self-referentiality, one could say that Kafka creates the space for "play" by precluding clear signification of the represented world, while Agnon creates space for "play" by precluding clear signification of the textual world. While, on the surface, the texture—particularly in translation—may seem to be the same, it is totally different.

In sum, while the worlds of Kafka and Agnon overlap in fiction as they did in actual life, extreme caution must be exercised in making comparisons. The question hinges not upon whether Agnon read *Der Verwandlung* or both read Nahman of Bratslav, but rather upon the specific nature of the texts they produced. For a quick proof of my argument, I suggest a simple test: read the modern Hebrew translation of a Kafka passage and you get a Hebrew approximation of Kafka, similar to the English approximations of Kafka you get in the English translation. Read, however, a translation of the same passage into Agnon's manneristic, late-rabbinic Hebrew, and you produce an entirely different reader's response. It is no longer an approximation of Kafka, but distinctively an Agnonic text.

Notes

1. A. J. Band, *Nostalgia and Nightmare: A Study in the fiction of S. J. Agnon* (Berkeley and Los Angeles: University of California Press, 1968).

2. Evelyn T. Beck, *Kafka and the Yiddish Theatre* (Wisconsin: University of Wisconsin Press, 1971).

3. A. J. Band, "Kafka and the Beiliss Affair," *Comparative Literature,* 32/2 (Spring, 1980), pp.168-183.

4. Marthe Robert, *Seul, comme Franz Kafka* (Paris: Calmann-Lévy, 1979).

5. Ronald Hayman, *K: A Biography of Franz Kafka* (London: Weidenfeld and Nicholson, 1981).

6. Hillel Barzel, *Agnon ve-Kafka* (Tel Aviv, 1972).

7. See note 3.

Cynthia Ozick (essay date December 1988)

SOURCE: Ozick, Cynthia. "Agnon's Antagonisms." *Commentary* 86 (December 1988): 43-8.

[*In the following essay, Ozick uses Agnon's novella* Edo and Enam *to reflect on the ambiguities of translation and on the oppositions between ideas of safety and destruction, redemption and illusion, and exile and return.*]

Shmuel Yosef Agnon, the 1966 Nobel winner for literature, was born one hundred years ago, in Galicia, Poland, and died in Jerusalem in 1970. Not long after his death, I wrote a story about Agnon, a kind of parable that meant to toy with the overweening scramble of writers for reputation and the halo of renown. It was called "Usurpation" and never mentioned Agnon by name. Instead, I pretended he was still alive, not yet a laureate: "It happens that there lives in Jerusalem a writer who one day will win the most immense literary prize on the planet." I referred to this writer as "the old man," or else as "the old writer of Jerusalem"—but all the while it was Agnon I not-so-secretly had in mind; and I even included in my story, as a solid and unmistakable clue, one of his shorter fables: about why the messiah tarries.

To tell the truth, this midrashic brevity (God knows where I came upon it) was the only work of Agnon's I had ever read. Nothing could have tempted me to look more extensively into Agnon, not even the invention of a story about him: though I was enchanted by the dazzlements his great name gave off, my story was nevertheless substantially blind to the illuminations of his pen.

I could hardly blame myself for this. For decades, Agnon scholars (and Agnon is a literary industry) have insisted that it is no use trying to get at Agnon in any language other than the original. The idea of Agnon in translation has been repeatedly disparaged; he has been declared inaccessible to the uninitiated even beyond the usual truisms concerning the practical difficulties of translation. His scriptural and talmudic resonances and nuances, his historical and textual layers, his allusive and elusive echoings and patternings, are so marvelously multiform, dense, and imbricated that he is daunting even to the most sophisticated Hebrew readers.

What, then, can a poor non-Hebraist possibly make of an Agnonic masterwork when, willy-nilly, it is stripped of a quarter or a half of its texture and its substance, when the brilliant leaves are shaken off the spare, bare, naked-toed trunk? A writer in monolingual America, confined to writing and reading wholly in English, will clearly have no Agnon other than the Agnon who has been Englished. If the prodigal Agnon can be present only in Hebrew, to read him in any other tongue is to be condemned to paucity. The Hebrew prince is an English-language pauper.

So, drawn almost exclusively to the lustiness of literary blue blood, unwilling to see it ransacked and pauperized, I have kept my distance from the translated Agnon.

But Agnon himself has a different idea of translation and its possibilities. The anecdote that illustrates Agnon's position is consummately sly—a sort of play, or paradigm, or Oscar Wildean joke. Saul Bellow tells the joke on himself in his introduction to *Great Jewish Short Stories,* a popular paperback anthology he edited in 1963, some years before either writer had captured the Nobel Prize.

> In Jerusalem several years ago [Bellow recounts], I had an amusing and enlightening conversation with the dean of Hebrew writers, S.Y. Agnon. This spare old man, whose face has a remarkably youthful color, received me in his house, not far from the barbed-wire entanglements that divide the city, and while we were drinking tea, he asked me if any of my books had been translated into Hebrew. If they had not been, I had better see to it immediately, because, he said, they would survive only in the Holy Tongue. His advice I assume was only half serious. This was his witty way of calling my attention to a curious situation. I cited Heinrich Heine as an example of a poet who had done rather well in German. "Ah," said Mr. Agnon, "We have him beautifully translated into Hebrew. He is safe."

Now the "curious situation" Bellow alludes to is the fact (as he comments a moment later) that "Jews have been writing in languages other than Hebrew for two thousand years." No one could have been more aware of this variety of language-experience than Agnon—which is why Bellow understood Agnon's remark to be "only half serious."

But there are two entirely serious elements to take note of in Agnon's response. The first is his apparent confidence in the power of "beautiful translation." A case can be made that Heine, too, with all *his* strata of sources, from medieval ballads to chivalric romances to French satire, will not readily yield to successful translation—perhaps even less so than Agnon, because a poet is always more resistant to translation than a writer of prose, however complex the prose. And yet Agnon does not doubt that "we have him," that Heine can be genuinely Heine even in a language as distant from German, and as alien to European literary styles, as Hebrew.

All the same, it is not the translator's skill, much as Agnon seems willing to trust in it, that preserves Heine for Agnon. It is Heine's "return," so to speak, as a Jewish poet, to the sacred precincts of the Land of Israel—his return via the Holy Tongue. For Agnon it may be that Heine in German is less fully Heine than he is in Hebrew: to be "safe" is to have entered into the influences of holiness; redemption is signified by the reversal of exile. Whatever happens outside the Land of Israel, whatever ensues in the other languages of the earth, is, to be sure, saturated in its own belongingness, and may indeed be alluring, and without question "counts" in the world of phenomena; but counts differently, because it is outside the historic circle of redemption that only the Land possesses. The world beyond the Land, however gratifying or seductive, is flavored with the flavor of exile.

At first glance Agnon's witticism, "he is safe," appears to be in praise of translation as a relatively easy triumph of possibility—but only, it seems, if the text in question is drawn from the tongues of exile into the redemptiveness of Hebrew. Presumably, translation *out* of Hebrew would be considered not so much a linguistic as a metaphysical lessening. Or else, since the original continues to stand, Agnon Englished would strike Agnon as irrelevant. The calculated remark, "he is safe," is a joke that recognizes, after all, the chanciness of translation, that in fact *not* all translation "saves"; and it is this contradiction that makes the joke, since the redemptiveness of translation can work in one direction only. A flawed rendering of Heine into Hebrew may nevertheless partake of redemption; a brilliant rendering of Agnon into English backslides into the perilous flavor of exile.

And that is the second serious point. When you reverse the direction—when translation becomes *yeridah* (descent from the heights of Jerusalem; desertion) rather than *aliyah* (ascent to the sublime; return)—the witticism collapses, a different tone takes hold, and a chink opens into dread, into the regions of the unsafe, of the irrational, into the dark places of alien myth, of luring mermaid and moon-dazed mountain nymph, of Pan and unbridled Eros. The Lorelei will chant her deadly strains out of the bosom of the Rhine, but never out of Lake Kinneret (the Hebrew name for the Sea of Galilee). And Saul Bellow's domesticated metaphysical anecdote—Agnon drinking tea and speculating about Heine's salvation—becomes a parable that, when set to run in reverse, can turn into a tale of baleful exilic potency.

Imagine, for instance, that it is not the Land of Israel that is the magnet, but all the lands beyond. Imagine that the longing of heroic temperaments is for exile rather than for redemption. Imagine everything seen upside down and inside out: a yearning for abroad instead of for Jerusalem; a pilgrimage in search of holy talismans that leads away from the Land toward half-pagan scenes. Imagine a sacred tongue that is not Hebrew. Imagine an Exodus undertaken for the sake of returning to the wilderness. Imagine trading the majestic hymns of Scripture for wild incantations and magical ululations. Imagine the Land of Israel as a site of drought and dearth and death and crumbling parapets and squatters and muteness, while faraway countries flow with rivers and songs and color and grace and beauty and joy.

All these ominous reversals of "he is safe," Agnon has made; he has made them in a work of fiction. If the Land of Israel assures immortality for Jewish poets, the corollary must be that exile can shore up only the short term, the brief lease, until the final slide into oblivion. But what of the opposite proposition? The proposition that the old, old myths, the legends that precede Sinai by a millennium and more, the fables that continue to girdle and enthrall the world, will outlive all? The proposition that compared to the loud song of the Lorelei, out of whose strong throat beat the hypnotic wing-whirrs of a hundred birds, the biblical Hannah's murmured prayer—unaesthetic, humble, almost not there—falls into insignificance?

Such a proposition may be an unlikely meditation for the pen of the "old writer of Jerusalem," "the dean of Hebrew writers," who in 1950, when he delivered up the tale called *Edo and Enam*,[1] had reached the lively age of sixty-two; sixteen years later we see him flying to Sweden, exultant in a *yarmulke*. Does the pious *yarmulke* contradict the tale? The tale may be said to hang on the case of the translation into Hebrew of a pair of newly-discovered ancient languages; and yet no redemption will come of it. Heine's *"Die Lorelei,"* a song about death through allurement, is transmuted into a Hebrew ballad, and is thereby deemed "safe." But the Enamite Hymns carry, and carry out, the real power of death by allurement: they are all peril. Transported to the Land of Israel they have the capacity to kill, though they too are "beautifully translated" into the Holy Tongue.

Their devoted translator in the story is Dr. Ginath, a scholar without a *yarmulke*, a wholly secularized scientific philologist and ethnographer, who will go to any length to get hold of lost languages: once, for example, he posed as a mystical holy man from Jerusalem, "Hacham Gideon," in order to pry out the secret tongue of the living vestige of the tribe of Gad. "These days," remarks the narrator of *Edo and Enam*, "it is as if the earth had opened up and brought forth all that the first ages of man stored away. Has not Ginath discovered things that were concealed for thousands of years, the Edo language and the Enamite Hymns?" Dr. Ginath is the author of "Ninety-nine Words of the Edo Language," and also of an Edo grammar, but

> the Enamite Hymns were more: they were not only a new-found link in a chain that bound the beginnings of recorded history to the ages before, but—in themselves—splendid and incisive poetry. Not for nothing, then, did the greatest scholars come to grips with them, and those who at first had doubted that they were authentic Enamite texts began to compose commentaries on them. One thing, however, surprised. . . . All these scholars affirmed that the gods of Enam and their priests were male; how was it that they did not catch in the hymns the cadence of a woman's song?

"I could hear," continues the narrator, "a kind of echo from my very depths . . . ; ever since the day I had first read the Enamite Hymns that echo had resounded. It was a reverberation of a primal song passed on from the first hour of history through endless generations."

That "cadence of a woman's song" belongs to the autochthonous enchantresses, among them the Lorelei; it is the voice of the intoxicated sibyls who speak for what we may call the First Religion, which is the poetry of Eros and nature, of dryad and nymph and oread, of the sacred maidens whose insubstantial temples are the sea, the rivers, the forests, the meadows, and the hills. In *Edo and Enam,* Agnon experiments with importing the hymns of this First Religion into the Land of Israel, into the marrow of Jerusalem itself, where such hymns cannot flourish, where they will grow lethal; and he also imports the singer of the hymns, the enchantress Gemulah, who, when she sang in her native realm, "stirred the heart like . . . the bird Grofith, whose song is sweeter than that of any creature on earth."

Gemulah is from a distant mountainous region, though her people originally lived among springs. According to their tradition, they derive from the tribe of Gad, which in the Bible once received a blessing of "enlargement." As warriors, they "advanced into the lands of the Gentiles, for they misconceived the text" of the blessing— "they did not know that the blessing refers only to the time when they lived in the Land of Israel, not to their exile in the lands of other peoples." But it is exile itself they have misconceived; they take it for eternity, and have succumbed to the First Religion.

While at least formally they maintain their ancestral hope for the return to Jerusalem, and while Gemulah's father, a learned elder of the tribe, is still able to read to the people from the Midrash and the Jerusalem Targum, "which they have in its complete text, and which he translated into their language," the Gadites are by now profoundly separated. Their speech is unlike any other. In fulfillment of their name, Gad, or Luck, they depend on the stars and deal in charms and talismans and magical texts. Though they continue to circumcise their sons, their alien funeral rites are observed "with songs and dances full of dread and wonder." Gemulah herself is "accomplished in all their songs, those that they had once sung . . . by the springs and also those of the mountains." Gemulah's father hands on to her a "secret knowledge laid up by his ancestors," as well as an arcane private language, an antic invention that separates the two of them even from Gad itself; they are a pair of oracles and sorcerers.

In order to "learn from the eagles how they renew their youth," Gemulah's father ascends into the mountains, where he is attacked and devoured by an eagle. Following a long mourning, Gemulah will be taken by her bridegroom to the Land of Israel, to the city of Jerusalem, where she will sicken and fall mute. The First Religion, woven out of filaments of purest nature poetry, is silenced in the domain of monotheism.

A dumbstruck Lorelei, a somnambulist who "walks wherever the moon leads her," like a mermaid drawn by the tides, Gemulah will at last become equal to the letters of her name when their positions are set free to recombine: a female golem. And indeed at the tale's opening we are privy to some banter about just such a creature—"Wasn't it you who said Dr. Ginath had created a girl for himself?"—and we hear the name of Solomon Ibn Gabirol invoked, the Hebrew poet of medieval Spain who is said to have carpentered a woman out of wood.

Gemulah's bridegroom is Gavriel Gamzu, a man in a *yarmulke,* a dealer in rare books and manuscripts. He began as an ordinary yeshiva student, but discovered himself in thrall to "intrinsic beauty," hence to poetry. In youth once, intending to purchase a copy of the *Shulkhan Arukh,* the major compendium of religious laws, he emptied his pockets instead for the sake of an exotic *divan* of pure verse. "Because he was so fastened to poetry, he came unfastened at the yeshiva," and was driven to wander the world in search of the ravishments of anonymous hymns. The lure of primeval song has brought him to Gemulah's country. A sandstorm in that region, however, leaves him blind in one eye, perhaps as a divine judgment for preferring intrinsic beauty to the discipline of the codes of conduct.

From now on Gamzu's vision is halved, strangely narrowed. Wearing his *yarmulke,* he lectures against "read[ing] the Law beyond the text," and keeps a stern eye out for "those Bible critics who turn the words of the living God upside down"; but the next instant this one and only eye abandons piety and fixes on the holiness of poets, whose "hallowed hands" have the power to save from the demons of hell. It appears that intrinsic beauty and the Law cannot rest together in peace within the range of a single eye, and may not wed and live together under a roof in Jerusalem. The bewitchment-seeking spirit of Gavriel Gamzu is for the moment more at home away from home, in the lands of exile. Only there do enchantments thrive unrestrained.

Consequently Gamzu's pursuit of rapture can be fulfilled only outside the Land of Israel, in separated communities compromised by long periods of exile. If the uncanniness of Gemulah's song electrifies him into seizing her as his bride, it is not Gadite poetry alone that stirs Gamzu. In his incessant travels he has happened on other deposits of wondrous lyricism—for instance, exilic Jews whose forefathers in the time of the First Temple were young men driven from Jerusalem by the Babylonian ruler Nebuchadnezzar. Riding on millstones, they were carried aloft to their rescue in the isolation of a mysterious new settlement, where "they saw maidens coming up from the sea," and married them; and not long afterward they "forgot Jerusalem." When the priestly scribe Ezra subsequently summoned them to be restored to the Land of Israel, they hung back. Like the Gadites, they mistook exile for permanence. This lost society, the children of mermaids, has developed rites and songs over the generations that deviate signally from the practices of Israel. The close presence of women in their synagogue and the singing of unfamiliar hymns of startling sweetness derive, no doubt, from the habits of their ancestresses the sea-maidens.

In delineating these legendary distant tribes sunk in attrition and dilution, can Agnon have had in mind the real precedent of the Jews of Elephantine? A community founded on an island in the Nile by Jewish mercenaries under Persian governance, even after Ezra's return to Jerusalem in the 5th century B.C.E., they defied the ban on multiple temples and insisted on erecting a separate and rival edifice. The Elephantine Papyri testify to the strong position of women among them: bridegrooms had to provide dowries, for example. But the statuary that crept into their temple architecture, and the customs that invaded their practice, including the outright worship of goddesses, severely divided the Elephantinians from the Jewish mainstream, and they disappeared into the belly of exile, leaving behind a mere archeological vapor. In **Edo and Enam,** Agnon condenses the vapor of wayward paganized Jews into the honeyed elixir of Gamzu's hymns—but when the hymns are introduced into the place where the Temple once stood, havoc rules, and Jerusalem begins to unbuild.

Consider the condition of Jerusalem when Gamzu brings into the city his wife Gemulah and her father's talismans—mystical leaves, at first sight colorful, then drained of color, on which certain charms are inscribed. These leaves, long buried in a jar in a cave beneath a mountain crag in Gemulah's country, were given to Gamzu by Gemulah's father; they have the power to retrieve her when she escapes to sleepwalk under a full moon, a malady that occurs chiefly when she is away from her native surroundings.

When the charms, in the company of the now ailing Gemulah, settle into Jerusalem, their influence sets off a rash of departures, a rush back down into exile, an explosion of *yeridah,* signifying a descent from lawful holiness. The narrator's wife and children have left Jerusalem for another town; we are not told why. Gerda and Gerhard Greifenbach, who rent part of their house to the scholarly Dr. Ginath, are yearning for foreign lands, and are about to go on a tour. They are described as "dark and distracted," restless and discontent; it is likely that they suffer from the exilic emanations of the two mystical leaves in their possession, gifts from the itinerant Dr. Ginath—perhaps he found them in a bundle of manuscripts purchased from Gamzu, or perhaps he obtained them in Gemulah's country while impersonating Gideon, the Jerusalem Hacham. The Greifenbachs' house is itself tainted by exilic flaws. It was once inhabited by a quarrelsome sectarian from Germany, who ended by abandoning Jerusalem; and again by a couple named Gnadenbrod: the wife refused to live in Jerusalem, and they reentered exile in Glasgow—immediately after which an earthquake undermined the house and permanently weakened the roof.

Gemulah's presence insinuates exile into the everyday life of Jerusalem, if exile is understood to mean deterioration, peril, and loss. The water supply dries up in tanks, pipes, and taps. Angry Arabs appear out of nowhere to stab young lovers. The city is overrun with housebreakers and squatters. In the general homelessness, newlyweds find it impossible to live together under one roof. All this happens when Gemulah is loosed from her sickbed into Jerusalem, somnambulant, released from muteness only to sing her magical song, *yiddal, yiddal, yiddal, yah, pah, mah.* The body of the city is there, but only as a shell: the spirit of peace is gone from it. Jerusalem itself becomes a kind of golem—which may account for the prevalence of the letter "g"—*gimel*—in all the names of the tale, Gemulah's among them, since *gimel* too is an anagram for golem.

In the last scenes we see Gamzu himself turned into a golem at the sound of Gemulah's private language, the language belonging only to herself and her sorcerer father. When Gamzu first heard Gemulah's voice, on a mountaintop in her own country, he was entranced: Gemulah stood before him as "one of the twelve constellations of the Zodiac, and none other than the constellation Virgo"—an oracle, one of the minor divinities of the First Religion, an enchantress, an alien nymph displaced. Now, in a manner reminiscent of the mystical leaves that initially showed brilliant colors and then grew brown as earth, "suddenly the colors began to change in Gamzu's face, until at last all color left it, and there remained only a pale cast that gradually darkened, leaving his features like formless clay."

It is displacement that governs the imaginings of **Edo and Enam.** Displacement—the grim principle of exile—is what distinguishes Agnon's fictive commentary on the First Religion from, say, the visionary work of the Sicilian Giuseppe di Lampedusa or the Swedish Pär Lagerkvist, each of whom has written a remarkable modernist novella on the subject of the primal enchantress—or, perhaps, on the theme of ecstatic beauty.

Lampedusa's enchantress in "The Professor and the Mermaid" is Lighea, "daughter of Calliope," a siren who appears to a student of ancient Greek and couples with him, hoping to lure him to oblivion. Like her mother the muse of poetry, in the name of rapture she urges the erasure of all distinctions: "ignorant of all culture, unaware of all wisdom, contemptuous of any moral inhibitions, she belonged, even so, to the fountainhead of all culture, of all wisdom, of all ethics, and could express this primigenial superiority of hers in terms of rugged beauty. 'I am everything [she chants] because I am simply the current of life, with its detail eliminated.'"

Lagerkvist's parable, "The Sibyl," has a Christian lining, and offers a darker view of the ecstatic: all the same, the oracle's power of annihilation (and self-annihilation) is unmistakable, and her utterances in the pit at the temple of Delphi are, like Gemulah's, in a recondite tongue never before heard by mortal ears:

> I began to hiss forth dreadful, anguished sounds, utterly strange to me, and my lips moved without my will; it was not I who was doing this. And I heard shrieks, loud shrieks; I didn't understand them, they were quite unintelligible, yet it was I who uttered them. They issued from my gaping mouth. . . . Not long afterward it happened that I was carried out of the oracle pit unconscious, violated by [the] god . . . my ecstasy, my frenzy, was measureless. . . . I smelled a sour stench of goat; and the god in the shape of the black goat, his sacred beast in the cave of the oracle, threw itself upon me and assuaged itself and me in a love act in which pain, evil, and voluptuousness were mingled.

The siren and the sibyl, potent representatives of the First Religion, swallow up all things—every achievement, every desire, every idea—into the poetry of ecstatic obliteration, Eros joined with degradation and death. Gemulah's bewitchment of Gamzu is no different, though Agnon's voice, like Gemulah's, is airier:

> Because songs are conjoined, they are linked up with one another, the songs of the springs with the songs of high mountains, and those of high mountains with the songs of the birds of the air. And among these birds there is one whose name is Grofith; when its hour comes to leave the world, it looks up to the clouds and raises its voice in song; and when its song is ended, it departs from the world. All these songs are linked to-

gether in the language of Gemulah. Had she uttered that song of Grofith, her soul would have departed from her, and she would have died.

Yet finally Gamzu opposes Gemulah's sorcery in a way imagination would never dream of opposing the siren's song or the oracle's cry. Who, in the gossamer realms of the First Religion, which knows nothing of exile, and where all the world is home to all divinities, would dare to stop the mouths of Delphic sibyls or glittering mermaids? But Gamzu puts his hand over Gemulah's mouth to save her from singing the notes of Grofith, the poetry of ecstatic frenzy, which can kill. It is the hand of anti-myth.

And still Gemulah dies. She dies for magic, for voluptuous longing, for ecstasy; she dies singing the song of the bird Grofith after all, bidden to do so by Dr. Ginath, whom she mistakes for the Jerusalem Hacham, the magus who once sojourned in her country. As an act of science, the philologist Ginath transcribes the strange syllables of her mysterious language; but Gemulah has no science; she is the antithesis of science. Spellbound under the moon, she walks on the roof of Ginath's part of the Greifenbachs' house—the very roof weakened long ago by an earthquake that came as a judgment upon those who abandon Jerusalem to run after exile. Ginath pursues her, and together they fall to their deaths.

Scanning the obituary notices in the newspaper, the narrator happens on a curious misprint: the announcement of the death of a Dr. Gilath. The letter "l" has been substituted for the letter "n." Agnon's Hebrew readers can readily guess the reason. "Ginath" (which means "garden") suggests the bower of esoteric knowledge, the fatal *pardes* ("paradise") into which, according to legend, four scholars, all prodigious and original, ventured; only one of them, Rabbi Akiva, came out alive—perhaps because he more than the others revered the Law. And "Gilath"? Omitting the vowels, the root-consonants spell out the letters of *galuth*: Hebrew for exile, displacement.

Gemulah is in exile from her country of charms and talismans and conjury and divination and necromantic hymn; Jerusalem, the city of the Law, is inimical to all of these. In her native land, Gemulah blooms unharnessed, under the mild rule of poetry and play and random rapture. But in Jerusalem wizards and their hymns weaken and perish; so Gemulah sickens, and takes to her bed spiritless and speechless; it is well-known that a golem lacks the capacity for speech. When the moon calls her, she rises up to meander through Jerusalem, infiltrating her omens and influences through the city, and then Jerusalem too sickens with the sickness of exilic ailments: dread and dryness and departure.

But as soon as Gemulah is destroyed, disordered and disconsolate Jerusalem comes to healthy life again: the water begins to flow freely in the pipes, the exiles stream home, *yeridah* gives way to *aliyah*—the narrator's family returns, the Greifenbachs hurry back from abroad, nothing more is heard of housebreakers, squatters, marauders, or separated couples. The First Religion is routed, and Jerusalem is restored.

How is it, though, that Gemulah's husband Gamzu escapes death? Like Ginath, who is punished for flying after the enticements of the languages of exile, Gamzu has been an enamored soul possessed by the music of the First Religion; and yet Gamzu lives. Like Akiva, he survives the penetration into *pardes*. Gamzu is safe—ultimately he can keep his eye, his only eye, on Jerusalem's principle of Law; he wears his *yarmulke,* and has the power to stop up Gemulah's mouth, so that (at least temporarily) she will not lose herself in the song of the deadly bird of beauty. Only in the regions beyond Jerusalem is he powerless before savage beauty.

The principle of Jerusalem versus the principle of exile; *aliyah* versus *yeridah*; redemption versus illusion; seeking to be "safe" versus finding oneself swallowed up by the forces of obliteration. A fugue of antagonisms. One cannot even be sure of Agnon's definitive passion, whether he leans finally to the side of lyrical sorcery or of Torah. Near the close of **Edo and Enam,** the narrator learns that Dr. Ginath has burned all his papers, among them the record of Gemulah's inchoate utterances. Jerusalem, it would seem, has won over the wilderness. But in the very last sentences of the tale, the Enamite Hymns are lauded for their "grace and beauty," and Dr. Ginath is celebrated for saving them for the world: is this jubilant praise rendered in the narrator's voice or in Agnon's own? And in the end how do we know whether Jerusalem itself is really safe, even after the destruction of the enchantress Gemulah? Heine's Lorelei, after all, now sings in the Holy Tongue, the better to sabotage the citizens of Jerusalem.

Note

1. "Edo and Enam," together with a second novella, "Betrothal," is available in English (*Two Tales*, translated by Walter Lever, Schocken Books).

Nitza Ben-Dov (essay date September 1989)

SOURCE: Ben-Dov, Nitza. "Discriminated Occasions and Discrete Conflicts in Agnon's *A Simple Story.*" *Prooftexts* 9, no. 3 (September 1989): 213-27.

[*In the following essay, Ben-Dov discusses the "assertive mother" theme in* A Simple Story *and describes Agnon's use of repetition or variation of motifs to highlight the rivalry between two women for one man's attention.*]

The powerful influence of Agnon's Jewish mothers on their sons has long been observed by his critics. Yet the psychology of the mother herself—her motives, thoughts, words, and actions—has not been explored. *A Simple Story,* the novel that is Agnon's masterpiece of psychological realism,[1] offers an excellent opportunity to delve into the mother's mind. Unlike Jacob Rechnitz's mother in **"Betrothed"** and Yitzhak Kumer's in *Just Yesterday,* Hirshl's mother belongs to the fictive present of the novel. Rechnitz and Kumer's mothers, though they doubtless have a pervasive and devastating influence on their sons' lives, especially upon their later relationships with women, belong only to the suggestive biographical background of the work. However, Hirshl's mother Tsirl is not only an authoritative figure who is responsible for her son's character and predicament—a recurrent theme in Agnon's works—but she has a psychological depth of her own.

Although the protracted conflict between an assertive mother and a submissive son is the core of the novel, in this study I will concentrate on a more discrete conflict, the one between Tsirl and Blume, his mother and the woman he desires. By focusing on this underlying drama, I will try to expose both the psychology of the mother and Agnon's subtle technique for revealing it. It is this technique which makes *A Simple Story,* with its unpretentious title, Agnon's most intricate work. The novel, which deals with the well-worn theme of a young man disappointed in love, emerges upon closer reading as a stunningly original piece of work.

A Simple Story relates the story of Hirshl Hurvitz's unrequited love for Blume Nacht, his orphaned second cousin on his father's side. Unrequited love, another prominent theme in Agnon's fiction, is inextricably linked to the theme of the mother-son relationship; possessive and forceful mothers tend to make weak and passive sons, unsuccessful in fulfilling their erotic desires. Blume, who is to become the object of Hirshl's desires, travels to Szybusz to join the prosperous Hurvitz family—Boruch Meir, his wife Tsirl, and their only son Hirshl—in accordance with her dying mother's suggestion: "When I die, go to our cousin Boruch Meir. I'm sure he'll have pity and take you in" (3). But, alas, during Blume's first evening in the Hurvitz household, Tsirl, Boruch Meir's wife, is resentful of the intrusion of the newcomer; and Boruch Meir himself does not appear until breakfast on the following morning to welcome his cousin. At the outset, then, the gap between the promise of the influential cousin and his delayed appearance in the text hints at Boruch Meir's secondary role in his own household. Indeed, Blume's abiding sense of alienation in her relatives' home is directly attributable to the combination of Boruch Meir's self-effacement and Tsirl's domineering presence.

Nevertheless, Blume's arrival comes at an opportune time for the Hurvitzes and for Tsirl in particular. The latter, busy with the family business inherited from her father, needs a reliable person to run her house; that is, she needs a new maid. Thus, in a less than charitable gesture this wealthy cousin takes in Blume as a servant, an unsalaried one at that, on the grounds that the girl is a relative and not some "hired hand." Although Tsirl seems to be satisfied with the services rendered, she finds herself faced with the irritating fact of her son's growing love for the poor relation. Seeking to stave off the ill effects of such a situation Tsirl decides to marry her son off to Mina Ziemlich, the daughter of nearby wealthy farmers with whom the Hurvitzes have business connections. Having acquiesced in the marriage, Hirshl goes mad and he is taken by his parents to the sanatorium of one Dr. Langsam in Lemberg (Lvov). True to his name, Langsam—"slowly" in German—step by step and with sensitivity guides Hirshl to recovery and back to the bosom of his family.

Now we may return to the meeting at the breakfast table around which the whole Hurvitz family gathers and encounters Blume for the first time—a scene treated at length and in minute detail. Through this "discriminated occasion"[2] I intend to illustrate how dramatized scenes in Agnon come to assume large dimensions on both a symbolic and an allusive scale, and how seemingly inconsequential episodes, the most routine events, continue to resonate throughout the text. This use of recurring elements, or motifs, is one of Agnon's strategies of indirection, which are, in turn, the essence of his art.[3]

On her first morning in the Hurvitz household Blume rises early. By the time the relatives are up and about breakfast is waiting for them. As a final touch, Blume has set out a tray of cakes she had brought with her from home after her mother's death. The Hurvitz family looks at the breakfast table in the scene that follows.

> Soon Boruch Meir appeared, rubbing his hands. He said good morning to Blume, lifted the tails of his jacket, and sat down at the table, where he poured himself some coffee and regarded his cousin and the cakes she had brought with approval. He was followed into the dining room by his son Hirshl, who declared:
>
> "Those cakes look awfully good!"
>
> He took one of them, ate it, and said, "These deserve a special blessing."
>
> "Who baked them?" asked Tsirl, breaking off a little piece and tasting it. "Did you?"
>
> "No," Blume said, looking at her. She too tasted a piece. "But I can bake just as good."
>
> "Thanks be to God," said Tsirl, her tone of voice changing, "that we aren't cake eaters and pastry nibblers here. Plain ordinary bread is good enough for us."
>
> Blume looked down at the table. The munching of cake did not stop.

> "Mama dear," said Hirshl, leaning toward his mother, "I have something to say to you."
>
> Tsirl looked at her son. "Then say it," she said.
>
> "It's a secret," said Hirshl with a smile.
>
> Tsirl bent an ear toward him.
>
> Hirshl put his mouth to it as though intending to whisper and said in a loud voice, "You must admit, Mother, that these cakes are delicious."
>
> Tsirl frowned. "All right," she said.
>
> (6)

The abundance of detail lavished on Blume's cakes elevates the conversation about them to something more than idle chitchat. Indeed, in the context of so mundane an episode this conversation functions as a portentous exchange in which are announced in embryonic form the interpersonal relationships that impel this novel: Tsirl's ambivalence toward Blume, the rivalry of these two women for Hirshl's affection, and the latent friction between Hirshl and his mother over Blume. The prepared and ready breakfast provides the unequivocal response to Tsirl's semi-hopeful, somewhat offensive remark to Blume the day before: "But I do hope that you were also taught a few things that a woman ought to know" (4)—Blume, that is, is to serve as a maid. Tsirl had been quick to drop the hint, and just as quickly Blume responded. As much as this tacit understanding, obviating the need for direct talk, may have pleased the lady of the house, she was greatly displeased by the relish with which her husband, and especially her son, greeted Blume's cakes. Sensing that Blume might rise above the humble station she has in mind for her—a mere maid—Tsirl voices misgivings about the girl's talents, culinary and otherwise: "Plain ordinary bread is good enough for us."

Henceforth, the breakfast episode recurs as a haunting refrain in the novel. The essence of the problematic relationships uniting and dividing the principal figures is captured immediately in their placement around the table. The cake episode will resurface allusively over and over, in telling acts and vignettes and in Hirshl's dreams. Cake (plus puddings, pancakes, and other confections) and servant girls placed in everyday scenes will function as metonymic representations of Blume. Such scenes, far from being innocuous, are supercharged with portent; the memory of Blume and her cakes will cast a long shadow on them all, for Blume is conspicuous even in her absence.

A symmetrical structure is evident in the breakfast scene, an early symptom of the conflicts entangling the characters. Tsirl cuts a piece of cake, tastes it, and then speaks, after which Blume does exactly the same—the deliberate slow-motion ritual of two rivals testing each other's mettle in the first stages of a duel. (Such symmetry will also mark the last days of Blume's stay in the Hurvitz home. Before deciding to find her son a wife, Tsirl notices that Hirshl is quietly but desperately pining for Blume: "Tsirl saw what she saw." And when Blume, aware that Hirshl is about to be married off by his mother, decides to look for work elsewhere, the narrator comments: "Blume saw what she saw" [35, 45].)

The early scene is already fraught with ironic comments on the relationship and rivalry between the two women. Even as Tsirl makes her tactless remark, "Thanks be to God we aren't cake eaters and pastry nibblers," everyone continues munching on the cake. (In fact, the Hebrew text states literally that as Blume lowers her eyes in embarrassment, the sound of uninterrupted "chomping" grows progressively louder, or "explosive.") And the rest of Tsirl's comment, that "plain ordinary bread is good enough for us," is mocked as well, but later in the novel. As the narrator mentions the visits of Gedalia Ziemlich, Hirshl's prospective father in-law, he elaborates: "At one time this had been accompanied by a slice of fried bread; since Blume's arrival, however, the coffee was drunk with a piece of such cake as she had learned to bake from her mother" (42). Lastly, Tsirl's declaration of restrained eating habits is set in glaring contrast to the facts, for "what Tsirl liked best was a proper meal: a good roast, stew, or cut of rare beef" (26). How ironic, then, that such disingenuous words of domestic frugality are directed against a poor girl who nursed a sick mother from an early age and never knew a pampered day in her life.

Blume eventually leaves her cousins' home. But the taste of her homemade cakes lingers long after she is gone. A hint about them is dropped, for example, at a festive dinner given by the Ziemlichs in honor of their future in-laws. As dinner is served, Tsirl and Hirshl, mother and son, indulge in private ruminations about Blume and the first encounter with her. Everyone but Hirshl attacks the sumptuous meal with gusto. All the while a serving girl comes and goes with platters of food, until at last she brings in the dessert.

> The serving girl reappeared with a large cornmeal pudding in the shape of a derby hat, stuffed with plums and walnuts and sprinkled with sugar coins. Though everyone except Hirshl was bursting at the seams, the aroma proved irresistible. Even Hirshl took a large slice and ate it with gusto.
>
> "You must admit, Hirshl," said Tsirl, flashing him a smile, "that this pudding is delicious." Hirshl blushed. After priding himself on his self-restraint, here he was being a pig like the rest of them. Nor was that the worst of it. The worst of it was that his mother's words were the same as those he had spoken to her on the day of Blume's arrival in their house, when she had brought with her the most delicious home-baked cakes.
>
> (81)

The picture of the serving girl with her pudding could not but conjure up instantaneously, for both Tsirl and

when his wife becomes pregnant and gives birth to a new daughter. In the hospital's maternity ward, Herbst meets a nurse named Shira and begins an affair with her on the very day of his wife's delivery. Although he sleeps with her only a few times and she herself disappears midway through the novel, Herbst becomes obsessed with Shira. His work grinds to a halt; his family life becomes intolerable to him; and his psyche is delivered over to grotesque sadomasochistic dreams.

The main body of the novel in its present state leaves Herbst sucked into the downward spiral of obsession. The unfinished portion was apparently intended to lead up to the fragmentary concluding chapter Agnon attached to the manuscript, in which Shira is discovered to have contracted leprosy and to be living in a leprosarium. Herbst joins her there; embracing and kissing her, he willingly becomes infected with her disease in order to be with her always.

Adultery has been a staple of the novel since *Madame Bovary* and *Anna Karenina*; for Agnon, it serves less as an erotic theme than as a device for portraying the breakdown of a world view: the liberal German Jewish culture embodied in Manfred Herbst. Jerusalem of the 1930's as it is depicted in **Shira** is awash in German Jews—scholars, physicians, daughters of good families—who have fled Nazism only to find themselves at loose ends in an unfamiliar Zion. Their displacement is emblematized by many rare volumes and first editions of German classics that have come into the hands of Jerusalem booksellers as the impoverished refugees sell off their libraries to keep body and soul together. Although Herbst himself came earlier, before the rise of Hitler, out of vaguely Zionist motives and on the strength of an offer of a post at the new Jerusalem university, and although he has learned Hebrew and feels at home in Palestine, he remains very much the creation of German Jewish culture.

This is nowhere more evident than in Herbst's commitment to the vocation of scientific humanism as expressed in his scholarship. His researches into early Byzantine Church history are impelled by the conviction that the path to truth lies through the careful and dispassionate investigation of past events, no matter how seemingly removed from the exigencies of the present. This pursuit is undertaken in the esteemed and cherished company not of persons but of books, which become eroticized objects. (The novel abounds in vignettes of bibliomania and bibliophilia.) Yet Herbst's soul has nothing of the arid pedantry of George Eliot's Casaubon in *Middlemarch.* His mind is steeped in German romantic poetry, and he makes notes toward the writing of a dramatic tragedy of his own. Politically, his liberalism extends to an identification with the Brith Shalom group, which in the Palestine of those days favored a binational accommodation with the Arabs. Even the family circle partakes of the German Jewish ethos: an intelligent and solicitous wife who insulates her scholar-husband from the nuisances of domestic life, and strong-willed daughters raised to be useful and independent.

For all its attractiveness, however, this blossoming of late bourgeois intellectual culture curiously displaced to Jerusalem is presented in the novel as being ripe for destruction. It is being obliterated at its source as the forces of nonrationality triumph in Germany. Herbst's wife Henrietta wanders among the offices of the British Mandatory bureaucracy in a vain search for immigration certificates for her relatives at home. The Arab attacks against Jews, which intensified in 1936, come uncomfortably close to the Herbsts' house in an Arab neighborhood of Jerusalem. Unbeknownst to Herbst, his daughter Tamara has become a member of an underground group set upon evicting the British by force. Even the world of the Hebrew University, with its largely German or German-trained professoriate, is less bent on the discovery of truth, however rarefied, than it is preoccupied with jealousies of rank and reputation. The utter secularity of Herbst's world, its radical and complacent alienation from the sources of Jewish faith, is underscored obliquely by the novel's intrusive narrator, who observes his subjects from a point of view much closer to the religious tradition.

The agent who precipitates the disintegration of this world view is unlikely indeed. The nurse Shira, the object of Herbst's obsession, is neither young nor conventionally appealing. What attracts Herbst about her seems to be the mannishness of her sexuality, its freedom and nihilism. She is disdainful of religion and ideology and finds her only fulfillment in caring for the sick and suffering. In contrast to Herbst's German civility, she, who comes from Eastern Europe, fascinates him with an account of her flight naked into the Polish snows in escape from her lover on their wedding night.

As a character, Shira is both overdetermined and underrealized. This touches directly on what makes **Shira** a problem novel, and on what makes the novel as a genre a problem for Agnon. We know little about the nurse. Herbst's contact with her is very limited, and midway through the novel, as I have mentioned, she disappears altogether. (The freckle-like protuberances on her skin, noticed in the first chapter, turn out to be the early signs of leprosy.) Yet the temptation to underestimate her role in the novel, to see her as, in essence, merely the exotic catalyst of Herbst's undoing, is contradicted by Agnon's naming the novel for her, by the narrator's insistence that his story is as much about her as about Herbst, and by the fragmentary conclusion in which the two are united in a leprosarium. Shira is clearly very important to what Agnon wants to do in the novel, but the nature of that importance is never entirely demonstrated.

Most critics have sought to resolve this dilemma by invoking allegory, as Robert Alter has done in his eloquently argued afterword to the new English translation. Thus Shira, whose name means "poetry" in Hebrew, is understood as a figure for the subversive modernist fusion of eros and art; what circulates in Herbst's mind, then, is not the 19th-century poetry of sentiment, but a Nietzschean melody fueled by the darker forces of life and death. It is exposure to this troubling power that pulls down the foundations of the world built by German Jewish culture.

Such a reading of Agnon's novel, as with most allegorical solutions to literary puzzles, produces in the uninitiated reader a momentary thrill of recognition as the pieces suddenly appear to come together in a profound, overarching scheme. But the *frisson* of comprehension soon dissipates when one attempts to analyze *how* the pieces fit together. Whatever the meaning of Shira's name, it is hard to see how so perverse and sketchily rendered a character can bear the weight of such large designs.

Still, in the end we cannot do without allegory of some kind. In ***Shira*** one senses that the inherent limitations of Herbst's world view are being exposed by Agnon not out of any pleasure in documenting its dissolution but out of a belief in the existence of some transcendent, alternative realm. The identity of that realm is never named, but its latent power is everywhere suggested. The transfiguring idea—call it what you may: art, eros, purity, spirituality—can simply not be accommodated by the this-worldly resources of the novel as a genre. For this reason I believe the novel could not be finished. Agnon's deathbed instruction to publish ***Shira*** in its incomplete state may thus have signaled his final acknowledgment and acceptance of that impasse.

We must be grateful, however, for his last-minute instruction, for there can be no other work of literature, however, fully realized, which presents the contradictions of the modern Jewish imagination as powerfully as this incomplete masterpiece.

Anne Golomb Hoffman (essay date 1991)

SOURCE: Hoffman, Anne Golomb. "Introduction to *Between Exile and Return: S. Y. Agnon and the Drama of Writing,* edited by Sarah Blacher Cohen, pp. 1-20. Albany: State University Press of New York, 1991.

[*In the following excerpt from the introduction to her full-length semiotic study of Agnon's writings, Hoffman reviews her complex textual approach, encompassing psychoanalysis, traditional Hebrew criticism, and poststructuralist literary theory. (Hoffman's book contains a complete bibliography of primary and secondary sources.)*]

S. Y. AGNON: MODERN JEWISH WRITER

Each of these terms—"modern," "Jewish," "writer"—provides structure to this inquiry. S. Y. Agnon, the subject of my study, ranks with the major modernists of this century, but differs from his European peers in his intense engagement in a universe of sacred language. The modernism of the early part of this century consisted of a revolt against inherited norms and conventions, along with a self-conscious search for new forms of expression. The literary experiments of Shmuel Yosef Agnon are the more striking within this context, insofar as they appropriate and transform elements of the ongoing religious and cultural traditions of Judaism.

Agnon's is a restless writing that resists easy classification. He has been read by some as a pious storyteller, by others as a modern ironist. He is both and more. Shifting between exile and return, Agnon's writing cannot simply be identified with the ideological enclosures of traditional world views; nor is it characterized by the complete absence of inherited structures. Because Agnon writes in Hebrew, the very language that he uses maintains a connection to the language of Scripture and commentary; that relationship is made inescapable by the many ways in which the writing uses Jewish themes and sources. Sharply modern disjunctions within self, social world and tradition are all the more startling for their interaction with a deeply rooted mystique of the wholeness inherent in sacred language.

Agnon explores structures that are not so much those of European history and society as they are those of traditional eastern European culture surrounding sacred Jewish texts, whose study and elaboration had been the binding force of the people in its dispersion. The modern Jewish imagination, with its collective memory of dispersion and the experience of return, carries the history of a people inscribed in its language. On the eve of the return to a physical homeland through the Zionist movement in which Agnon participated, we find the writer engaged in fictions that oscillate ambivalently between old world and new, filial rebellion and a return to the father (and the identity of the "father" is not constant), and between extreme positions in relation to the texts at the center of the community's identification of itself.

Images of books and writing express a central tension and offer a rich starting point for a study of Agnon's modernism. These images offer an emblem of the writing's link to a text-centered tradition; at the same time, they make visible the displacement of authority and the decentering of the text that is the writing's break with tradition.

My study approaches the fertile field of writing that is Agnon's art to examine questions of authority and voice, self and other, text and language. The deep allusiveness to Jewish sources in texts that call themselves into question prompts my inquiry into the nature of textuality and the place of the modern, secular text in a tradition of sacred writing. I use the term "textuality" to suggest that issues of boundary and transgression, exile, and return are acted out within the domain of the writing itself.

This is a study *of* writing *in* the writing of S. Y. Agnon. "Writing" here can be understood as a process of signification, or communication in language, a multi-leveled process with conscious and unconscious components to it. Agnon's writing brings into the foreground dimensions of the text that might otherwise go unnoticed by the reader, signaling a revision of relations among writing, text, language, and subject.

Language becomes the issue and writing the scene of the action in the dramas of signification that I propose to discuss. I am less interested in a representational approach that ignores or suppresses the writing in the interests of examining the purported external reality to which it refers. In making this claim, I do not mean to overlook the impact of political or historical factors on texts. I propose rather to examine historical and cultural trends and developments through their inscription in the text. They are part of the writing, not external to it.

Periods of cultural breakdown and renascence produce intensified self-consciousness in literary works, as if the processes involved in the production of the text and the relationship of the text to its historical-cultural context have come up for question and so make themselves more strongly felt in our reading. "Modernity . . . is about the loss of narrative," observes Alice Jardine [1985, 100]; modernist writers valorize the loss, making it the occasion for moves in new directions. The modernists of the first part of the twentieth century, among whom Agnon has a place, take on the project of renewing literature out of the disclosure of new territories in language. For some, this process involves exploration of territory that is as much psychological as topographical and in which the unconscious exerts a disruptive force. Joseph Conrad goes upriver into the heart of darkness to uncover a bestiality that is not only the horror of colonialism, but is also just as much the lawlessness buried in the depths of civilized men. Thomas Mann takes hyper-disciplined Gustave von Aschenbach on a southward journey that undoes repressive constraints, allowing for emergence of an Eros that destroys the careful structures of an Apollonian consciousness. Franz Kafka explores the penal colony, crumbling the distances between archaic and modern, primitive and civilized, that his European traveler relies upon.

In each of these modernist fictions, language discloses multiple referents for the journey that is occurring. Landscape and setting become charged with implication that cannot be located simply in the point of view of a particular character. As a result, the reader suffers a loss of privilege; no longer can the reader assert the vantage point of a superior knowledge or claim the text for the territory of a particular set of beliefs.[1]

One might compare S. Y. Agnon to James Joyce. If Joyce's project is the absorption and reformulation of the English language, his texts make us aware of the languages within language, the play of polysemy in any verbal utterance. The mythic and the mundane are made to interact through the medium of language. In a revolutionary transformation that is comparable in scope but different in substance, Agnon blurs the boundaries of sacred and secular, enlarging the domain of the literary, and implying a claim for writing that approaches the collective.

Agnon writes during the period of the renewal of Hebrew as a language of daily use. In the context of political and social upheavals that the nineteenth century brought to European and Russian Jewry, we find a coalescence of some currents of Jewish life into a nationalist movement in which the revival of Hebrew constituted a significant feature of national identity. The precipitous pace of events of the last century, including not only the rise of Jewish nationalism but also the Nazi effort at genocide, has made of modern Jewish identity less a stable set of concepts than an ongoing field of forces. Agnon's texts are inscribed within that cultural-political upheaval. Registering the impact of the competing tendencies of modern Jewish thought, including questions of language choice and use, nationalism, piety, and skepticism, the writing gives access to the main currents of this last century of Jewish modernization and modernism. At the same time, Agnon's writing sustains a detachment from the immediacy of solutions or the urgency of contemporary pressures, allowing itself an exploration of the ways in which cultural constructs and ideologies derive from deeper levels of subjectivity and collectivity.

The conflict between sacred and secular has proved in many ways to be an energizing source for the modern Hebrew writer. Agnon's writing responds to the question of secularization of a sacred tongue and can be studied in relation to other texts of the modern period for its treatment of issues surrounding that effort. Mendele Mokher Seforim prepared the way with novels and tales that put traditional sources to parodic use in biting social satires. Mendele's writing registers the impact on the eastern European Jewish community of Enlightenment expectations and their frustration, nationalist aspirations, and the rise of state anti-Semitism. In H. N. Bialik's essays, as well as his poetry, we find indications of profound cultural dislocation; the writer experiences language as a realm of promise as well as terror. (See, for example, Bialik's exploration of mundane and poetic language in "Revelation and Concealment in Language" and more recent discussions by Scholem, 1972; Hartman, 1985.) For Agnon, as for Bialik, language forms a charged field of operations.

While Agnon's strength as a writer was heralded early on by Y. H. Brenner, full acknowledgment of his importance to modern literature came in the 1930s with Dov Sadan's emergence as a critic; Sadan directed readers to the psychological dimensions of the writing and demonstrated the complexity of Agnon's relationship to the past. During the 1940s, Baruch Kurzweil explored many of the conflicts central to Agnon's fiction; following Sadan, Kurzweil (1970, 76) made a particular claim for the surrealistic *Sefer hama'asim* (*The Book of Deeds*) as the "psychological key" to Agnon. In 1968, Arnold Band provided an overview of the life and work that constituted an important initiative in the study of artistic development. Since the late 1970s, Gershon Shaked has led the way in examining theme, structure, and intertextuality through close reading of texts. The present study brings current literary theory to bear on a reading of Agnon in a comparative context. In doing so, it builds upon previous work, while drawing on more recent developments in post-structuralist thought.

To enter Agnon's fictive universe, one must acknowledge the very central place occupied by Torah as the fabric of the world that both contains Creation and binds God to Israel. At the mythic center of Agnon's fictive universe, Torah constitutes a text of presence where word and thing join. Within this emblematic geography, two sorts of movement can be discerned, movement away from or toward the source. More interesting than any simple linear movement of departure and return is the expression of both movements simultaneously in the text. "Like a man who is exiled from the palace of his father": the phrase, which forms the title of this introductory chapter (taken from a 1934 story called **"Ḥush hareaḥ"** or **"The Sense of Smell"**), signals the ambivalence that informs the relationship of text and writing to a rich linguistic patrimony.[2]

Mystical and rabbinic approaches to language and writing constitute an attractive source for Agnon, insofar as they retrieve a relationship to the letters of a holy alphabet out of which the world was formed. The Midrash tells us, for example, that "God consulted the Torah and created the world" [Genesis Rabbah I.1]. As the blueprint for Creation, Torah is understood to be literally the world-forming text, one indication of a "mystique of language" [Scholem 1972, 70] that pervades Judaism. A sense of the rich inherence of meaning in the text, as well as the infinite interpretability of that text, manifests itself in the talmudic conviction that all Torah was given to Moses at Sinai [Avot 1:1].

Through his own formative immersion in Jewish sources, Agnon gains access to this linguistic domain and uses it as a primary source for his art. There are moments in reading Agnon that suggest a restoration of presence in text and word. The text evokes the horizon of a golden age that it can only point to, so that the reader is made to feel loss, while glimpsing a wholeness that cannot be achieved. Like Kafka, Agnon writes for a restoration he knows to be unattainable in writing. His writing activates both a sense of the inherence of meaning in language and the testimony to loss of a prior plenitude. In a geography of language and text, his writing moves between exile and return.

This study of the tensions that inform Agnon's literary art begins by comparing Agnon to two other twentieth-century Jewish writers, in order to identify some central questions concerning inscription, utterance, and authority. The chapters that follow examine the production of an autobiographical myth in the writing, as well as stories of writing that play with the relationship of later texts to their predecessors; the book concludes with readings of several major novels that both raise and subvert some fundamental cultural assumptions. While not intended as a survey of Agnon's art, this study does demonstrate the diverse moves of texts in relation to inherited or traditional structures, as well as the range of the writing through the significant components of modern Jewish experience. The thematic continuity of my work is supplied by a focus on representations of writing and books, considered as components of an ongoing drama of textuality, and also by an approach to reading and writing as related processes in the production of meaning.

. . . . .

Language, Literature and Subjectivity

No longer the transparent medium in which story is given, language has become visible in the texts of our modernity. For writers and anatomists of various persuasions, from the linguist to the psychoanalyst, and the literary critic, language is the dense medium of cultural expression in which subjectivity takes shape. As a preface, I would like to suggest some theoretical coordinates for the questions that structure this study of textuality in Agnon. Realizing that this brief discussion risks offering too much to the novice and too little to the more experienced reader, I would also simply direct readers to the body of the book, where theoretical issues come out of the readings themselves.

Agnon's texts make manifest problems in communication that involve the transmission and decoding of messages. In order to enter the domain of signification in which signs are produced, I make use of a model of communication that situates the sender of the message in relation to the addressee and notes also the code in which the message is communicated. The notion of "message" is complicated, however, insofar as literary or poetic language defies our ability to detach any simple "message" from the text we read. The poetic aspects of language acquire communicative function of their own, directing our attention to the play of language. This self-referential quality constitutes the poetic function of language [Jakobson, 1960, 356].

Extending this notion of the reflexive nature of poetic language, I argue that the effect of self-reference is intensified in texts that contain within them representations of writing, books, and structures of communication. My starting point in reading Agnon is to look at representations of structures of communication in order to see what they have to tell us about the texts in which they are to be found, about ourselves as readers, and about the nature of the experiences we call "literary."

As readers and critics, we can draw upon linguistics and psychoanalysis to investigate the ways in which texts call into question concepts of identity, self, and ego as unitary fictions. This is particularly a feature of modernist texts such as Agnon's, where voice and utterance, the relationship of an "I" to a "you," become major sites of conflict and supply the dramatic material of plot. This study demonstrates the ways in which Agnon's writing posits varieties of wholeness, which it then calls into question. Agnon's writing calls our attention not only to narration as an ordering activity aimed at producing coherence, but also to self as a construction out of disparate impulses. By reminding us of the constructedness of story and character, the writing demonstrates the often tenuous nature of the coherence that such concepts allow.

We should note at the outset that use of the terms "subject" and "subjectivity" reflects the impact of linguistics and psychoanalysis on understanding the nature of the self. The concept of "self," as it is commonly used, suggests the undivided presence of consciousness to itself. This assumption of coherence can be maintained, however, only at the cost of overlooking or erasing difference [Derrida 1982, 16]. Rather than assume the self to be a coherent and integrated entity, we have come to understand that the knowledge of self supplied by consciousness is only part of the story. The term "subject" takes the place of unitary terms like "identity," "individuality," or "person," because it provides greater acknowledgement of the constructedness of the self, as well as of the role of cultural and unconscious factors in its construction of the world [Silverman 1983, 130].

The interaction of psychoanalysis and literature makes possible rich examinations of subjectivity in language. We can understand why this should be so, if we remind ourselves that it is through the acquisition of language that we gain the possibility of subjectivity. By assuming the personal pronoun "I" in relation to the "you" of another person, each of us enters the social realm of language [Benveniste 1971, 224, 227]. Discourse is the arena in which subjectivity takes shape. Nevertheless, no one of us can claim ownership of the pronoun "I." Those pronouns are "shifters": "I" and "you" change their reference with each user. The interpersonal realm of pronouns demonstrates the dependence of a sense of self on another person's corroborative participation in discourse.

Texts do not mirror the subjectivity either of author or of reader, but texts are produced and read out of processes and structures that are inherent to subjectivity. In Jacques Lacan's hypothesis of the mirror stage, for example, we find suggestive indications of "the *méconnaissances* that constitute the ego, the illusion of autonomy to which it entrusts itself" [1977, 6]. In that hypothetical moment, the infant gains a rudimentary sense of self by assuming an absolute identification with its mirror image, overlooking the mediating other in that transaction. Lacan uses the term "imaginary" for this illusory or specular identification of self with other. While the mirror stage constitutes a theoretical moment in development, it suggests also an emblematic account of the achievement of self at the very cost of alienation from self. Lacan's approach to Freud demonstrates the alienation of the subject in the very utterance that affirms his/her subjectivity.

Our experiences with language testify to the workings of the unconscious. In this respect, Lacan's attention to linguistic manifestations of unconscious processes has opened up new possibilities for our reading of texts. Using the Saussurean structure of the sign, J. Laplanche and J.-B. Pontalis [1973, 210] refer to a coalescence of signifier with signified in the imaginary. That illusory coalescence corresponds to the infant's experience of a one-to-one correspondence, or the illusion of perfect fit in the early mother-child dyad. That specular identification or mirroring is disrupted by the intrusion of a third term, the paternal, which brings about the advent to the symbolic order, a pre-existing cultural order or world of signs in which the relation of signifier to signified is arbitrary.[3]

Despite the inevitable move into the symbolic order, the residual effects of the "imaginary" inhabit our use of language and make themselves felt in forms of cultural expression. Myths of a primal language such as the Eden story posit the original unity of word and object, expressive of a magical relationship to environment [Cassirer 1944, 109-10]. These are fantasies of an original and originary presence, fictions of a lost wholeness. While we may be tempted, as readers, to identify this "recollection" of wholeness as Edenic, pre-Oedipal, prelinguistic or imaginary, we should keep in mind that these are verbal tags, retrospective efforts to retrieve in language that to which language attests our loss.[4]

The literary text may bring about experiences of language for the reader that reflect both the imaginary and the symbolic order. In particular, Agnon's writing may activate in the reader a nostalgia for the imaginary coalescence of signifier with signified, as well as a sense of their inevitable separation and dislocation in discourse. Thus, fictional texts provide a unique access to processes of subjectivity, not only in their representations of character, but in the reader's own engagement with the text. While the reader's distance from the text may supply the illusion of safety, we find on closer examination that these borderlines are indeterminate: any reading reflects both text and reader. The reader actualizes the text in a reading that is shaped by conscious and unconscious presuppositions and by cultural codes [Eco 1979].

The linguistic structures of the text betray traces of the cumulative impact of developmental struggles and long lost battles in the formation of subjectivity. These paradigmatic stages and ruptures shape our use of language, and we can try to assess their impact on our reading. Rather than view development as a smoothly continuous process, J. Laplanche and J.-B. Pontalis [1973, 427] regard the abundance of references to ruptures or "splittings" of one sort or another in psychological writings of the last century as indicative of a pervasive sense that human beings are inherently divided within themselves. Indeed, if we survey the territory that Freud and his French followers have disclosed to us, we may be struck by the succession of "splits" or decisive ruptures that begins with the trauma of birth, separation from the body of the mother, and the hypothesis of a primal repression through which the unconscious is formed.

Texts may recall stages in the formation of the subject, not sequentially, but cumulatively, so that we can try to read the register of the unconscious both in texts and in ourselves as readers. Julia Kristeva observes that theory enables us to "'situate' such processes and relations diachronically within the process of the constitution of the subject precisely because they function synchronically within the signifying process of the subject himself" [1986, 96]. These synchronic operations dominate the signifying process in texts, particularly those we call "literary." My reading attends to echoes in the writing of earlier stages in the formation of subjectivity that, contrary to popular belief and everyday functioning, have not been superseded.

The notion of "inscription," in particular, is crucial to my study, insofar as it resonates with the impact of early stages in the formation of subjectivity. "Inscription" denotes the action of writing upon something; more concretely, it indicates that which is inscribed or written into a surface. It carries the sense of a formative writing and has been used as a metaphor for the formation of the unconscious [Freud 1925; Derrida 1978].

"Inscription" suggests something of the incisive impact with which cultural processes shape and gender individuals. My study focuses on inscription in a textual field constituted by male Jewish writers, for whom it has a different significance than it would for a female reader, evoking as it does writing, incision, and a relation to the body. Turning to Agnon and Kafka, I argue that dramas of inscription in literary texts register the impact of difference in our knowledge of ourselves, disclosing as well the uncertainties of our positions in culture.

From the perspective of a female reader, I draw attention to issues in the writing that carry explicitly masculine labels. The order of culture is patriarchal; the terms we use and the positions we occupy are gendered. Nevertheless, "male" and "female" should be understood not as essences, but as mutually dependent terms in an opposition that is constitutive of culture. I would like to think that this study is sensitive to issues of gender in the domain of textuality; that territory, however, is neither exclusively masculine nor feminine, and, in some ways, challenges or resists those classifications.

In *Beyond the Pleasure Principle* [1920], Freud describes the child's game of *"Fort-da,"* that is born out of the experience of loss of the mother. (The child overcomes the impact of the mother's absence by constructing a game in which he repeatedly throws away a spool and retrieves it, uttering *"fort"* and *"da"* triumphantly.) The anecdote shows language to be a form of mastery that responds to loss and attests to the absence of the object, even as it asserts its presence in words [Silverman 1983, 169]. This play of absence and presence persists into later language games, including those we call literary. Thus, for example, representations of books and writing in Agnon give access to a drama of presence and absence, attachment and loss. Not at all secondary to the ideas it conveys, writing moves into the foreground as the scene of the action. This book is an effort to render a reading of the writing.

Jacques Derrida calls for a psychoanalysis of literature that would study the "becoming literary of the literal," an approach that would respect the "originality of the literary signifier," rather than privileging "nonliterary signified meanings." This approach undoes the assumption of a fixed distance between sign and referent and directs our attention back to the writing in order to work towards a "psychoanalytic graphology" which would study the relation between writing and repression [1978, 226, 229-30]. Drawing our attention to the ways in which texts subvert their own manifest statements, deconstruction demonstrates that the position of the observer is implicated in the structure it purports to survey. There is no privileged vantage point from which one can arrive at conclusive statements about a text. This loss of privilege opens up new possibilities of reading by directing us to a study of constructions of authority either in the text or in ourselves.

As object and as concept, "book" suggests an authoritative definition of a discursive field that is orderly and bounded. If we look at the development of western literature, we find the "book" as metaphor has a rich history. E. R. Curtius [1953] traces the history of the metaphor of the Book in European culture from its first flowering in Hellenistic Greece (with some earlier appearances), through Rome, attributing to Christianity "a religion of the Holy Book" [1953, 310] and noting a rich history of metaphors of writing and of the book.

We stand to amplify that history with a study of textuality in the history of Judaism. Susan Handelman [1982] offers an important initiative in this area by considering rabbinic methods of exegesis in light of postmodern theories of language and text. In Jewish traditions of interpretation, the sacred text is regarded as both definitive and inalterable and, at the same time, unbounded, in the sense that it already contains all later interpretations within it. Furthermore, rabbinic strategies of interpretation utilize the potential for polysemy in language. Here we see the grounds for the attraction of postmodern theorists to rabbinic exegesis: rabbinic approaches to Scripture appear to anticipate and confirm the postmodern reader's sense of polysemy and indeterminacy in the text. It must be noted that rabbinic exegesis takes the play of language as a manifestation of divine plenitude, while for the postmodernist, polysemy indicates the instability of the text that is the product of multiple discourses. Nevertheless, although a comparison of these two approaches to textuality may risk overlooking significant epistemological differences, it should also be evident that comparison can amplify our readings of both modern and ancient texts.

The Talmud tells us that after the destruction of the second Temple, God was left with the four cubits or ells of the law [Berakhot 8a], a suggestion that the activity of interpretation of the law supplies the architecture of the faith. Simon Rawidowicz, Gershom Scholem, and, most recently, Susan Handelman and José Faur delineate the drama inherent in interpretation and assert its importance to understanding the nature of the text in Jewish tradition. Rawidowicz refers to rabbinic interpretation as "the second house of the Jews," and describes the breaking up and building from within that the process of interpretation involves; he argues that the very structure of the "house" (subordination to the "four ells of the Law") provides the "limitation which leads to expansion" (1974, 50, 52, 100, 102].

Gershom Scholem asserts that "tradition" is itself a revisionary process in which claims of fidelity to prior texts are made for "interpretations" of great originality. He characterizes the biblical commentator in terms of both his awe of the sacred text and the boldness of his intrusion upon it; from the interpreter's stance, the text is not monolithic in its consistency, but shows itself to be "diversified, multifold, and full of contradictions" [1971, 285, 288-90]. Recuperating strategies of interpretation and a focus on the very letters of the sacred text, Scholem examines approaches that belong as much to rabbinic interpretation as to specifically mystical movements. Scholem's work constituted a response to the rationalist enterprise of nineteenth-century German *Wissenschaft des Judentums* (as David Biale, 1979, has shown), which may also help to explain its appeal to poststructuralist thinkers. Jacques Derrida, Harold Bloom and others have used the work of Scholem as access to rabbinic and mystical approaches to interpretation and writing. These theorists incorporate elements of a loosely defined Jewish textuality into the critical enterprise of demonstrating the fierce dramas that occur in and between texts.

Thus, Scholem's work on Jewish mysticism, with its consistent focus on writing, texts, and issues of interpretation, has served as an energizing source for current theorists. They find in his discussions of language and textuality the transitional space in which to consider rabbinic attitudes to textuality together with contemporary theory. This commingling of current literary theory, on the one hand, with, on the other, rabbinic exegesis and mystical approaches to language has proved controversial, to say the least. Nevertheless, the discussion of textuality is a valuable one that should be kept from territorializing attempts on the part of contemporary theorists or from isolationist defenses on the part of rabbinic scholars. Certainly, there is little point to ignoring historical and ideological differences in order to claim the identity of rabbinic and postmodern modes of interpretation. At the same time, however, as long as we remain alert to the dangers of collapsing significant differences, we stand to gain in understanding the linguistic universes we inhabit, by extending our knowledge of the interpretive modes and traditions that have contributed to them.

My study fits into this general area by considering some of the ways in which Agnon's modernist writing draws on a history of interpretive strategies. This approach to Agnon both acknowledges the participation of his writing in traditional structures, but understands that it can never be completely identified with them. I read Agnon with a sense of his participation in a drama of language use that is deeply rooted in Jewish learning, however marginalized and ambivalent his activities in that domain may be.

I have not made the author the focus of study, because it seems to me that is not the task of the literary critic, whose effort it is to understand what constitutes the "literary." While the author is technically the subject of the enunciation as producer of the text, he or she is lost to us as direct speaker; we encounter instead a voice or play of voices in the text. Language speaks through the text in ways the author may not have imagined.[5] I have, however, studied the production of a persona of the author, a "literary" Agnon, who is the production of bits of narrative found in a variety of texts—speeches, interviews, reminiscences, not to mention in the margins of the texts that are properly designated as literary themselves. That "Agnon" is literary insofar as it is a rich "text," constructed over time, open to different readings. It is a construction on the reader's part out of material that the writer has made available over time, material that accumulates to form the larger "text" that is the life of the writer in relation to the community in which he writes.

A last point of reference for this study concerns feminism's further revision of the relationship of the subject to language through recuperation of the lost and fragmented body of the woman, the subtext so long repressed in western culture. That subtext makes itself felt in Agnon in images of relationship to the body that may subvert the ostensible metaphysics of sacred writing. That writing has been, until very recently, a male province in a tradition that developed rules and practices to the specific exclusion of women. Without arguing that Agnon was a feminist, we can examine the ways in which his writing evokes a patriarchal writing, but does not rest within theologically defined structures. It subjects that patriarchal writing to the play that is literature, play that is at least disruptive, if not subversive. My readings are attentive to the Oedipal dramas that shape Agnon's literary art, but I am equally aware of issues surrounding fusion with an archaic maternal body that may disrupt that linguistic order. Those issues of relationship to the female body reflect a level of experience prior to the positioning of the subject in culture that occurs through the Oedipus complex.

Feminist theory argues for recontextualizing knowledge in personal relations and the body. While I agree with the attempt to contextualize knowledge in the personal, it seems to me that such an effort cannot simply discredit or replace the "objective" with a new way of knowing. Rather, it must modify the seemingly objective by incorporating an acknowledgment of the perspective of the observing "I." I have attempted to find a base for discussion in the texts of Agnon that acknowledges the role of the reader in selecting and designating as noteworthy particular elements of texts. Nevertheless, the text remains the primary, though ultimately indefinable, object of study for me. It takes its place in a continuum that runs from author to reader, in a series of interactions whose boundaries cannot be definitively determined.

Criticism must explore that interactive process, thereby modifying the old sense of the text as autonomous artifact and the reader as invisible interrogator. At the same time, critics who attempt to subvert academic discourse and shake its epistemology by writing in the personal, as opposed to the presumably "objective" mode of academic discourse, may forget that any discourse produces its subject, a subject that can never be identical with the subject of the enunciation. If current theorists attempt to move beyond what they criticize as an outmoded humanism, that effort strikes me as an alteration of the focus on the human subject, rather than a repudiation of it.

Ultimately it is reading that interests me. Part of the value of literary criticism is to give access to the workings of the process by which texts are received, assimilated, and reformulated in readers' statements about them. While we may want to ignore the process of reading in order to arrive at statements of meaning, reading is the interaction in which such statements take shape. Reading reflects indeterminacies that are inherent in any communicative process, however much we may need to assume a stable identification of sender, message, and addressee.

RABBI NAHMAN AND "THE MENORAH": TOWARD A MODEL OF READING

My introduction comes to an end with a brief reference to Rabbi Nahman of Bratslav, whose "Tale of the Menorah," can be read as a depiction of the reading process. Agnon and Kafka find a common source in Rabbi Nahman of Bratslav.[6] Indeed, Rabbi Nahman figures as both a model and a source for modern Jewish writing: he draws interest both for his enigmatic tales, with their parabolic qualities, and for the fiercely experienced contradictions within his personal life, a "highly complex inner dialectic," as Arthur Green [1981, 106] describes it, that gave rise to a new definition of the *zaddiq* or righteous man in terms of "conflict and controversy."

For our purposes, Rabbi Nahman's "Tale of the Menorah" [1981, 239-40; 1983, 231-32] can be read for the ways in which it conceptualizes the variable relationships between artist, created object, and viewer. This is the story of a young man who returns home to his father after a long absence and "prides himself on his mastery of the craft of making a hanging lamp or menorah." He has his father invite to their home all the "masters of this craft," so that he, the son, can demonstrate his mastery to them. But the craftsmen are not impressed with the son's skill. The father approaches each and each admits that he has found fault with the menorah. When the father tells his son that all have found the menorah to be flawed, the son turns to his father and says: "By this I have shown my greatness. For I have shown to all of them their defects. For in this menorah are to be found the defects of each and every one of the craftsmen who are here. [. . .] What one sees as ugly, the other sees as lovely. And vice versa.

And I made this menorah of mine from defects alone, in order to show to all of them that they lack perfection, and to each there is a defect: for what is lovely in the eyes of one is a flaw in the eyes of his friend. But in truth I can make a menorah properly."

The parabolic qualities of this short tale lead the reader or listener to play with applications beyond the story itself. For the contemporary reader, "The Tale of the Menorah" is particularly self-reflexive insofar as it offers a depiction and an enactment of the reading process. One could argue that the menorah, as a created work, is analogous to a text that a reader reads in its openness to the reader's construction of it. Considered as a text, the menorah is not fixed or invariable, but rather is shaped by the response of the viewer or reader. (This effect is intensified once we realize that we possess no stable text of the parable itself, which comes down to us through its transmission by the Bratslaver Hasidim.[7])

The flaw that each observer finds in the menorah mirrors the observer to himself, confusing subject and object, and suggesting an important dimension of the process of reading: the reader finds his/her reflection in the text, but with a difference that disrupts the comfort of an easy identification. The menorah or work of art disturbs the observer's comfortable self-assurance and initiates a process of self-criticism. In effect, if the reader were to follow through to complete the interactive process that the text initiates, he/she would be working towards an understanding of subjectivity on the model of self-reflection that the parable prompts. To begin the process of "restoration" is to participate in *tiqqun,* that is, to carry out human action, directed towards return, under the sign of the Father.

Two concepts of the text operate in this short tale. On the one hand, we find indications of radical indeterminacy: the menorah as text is what the viewer says it is. It reflects each viewer to himself. On the other hand, the craftsman's statements assume a notion of the text as invariable. He stands outside the reader-text interaction and comments on it from a privileged vantage point that suggests a higher perspective. His statements imply a judgment of those variable readings according to an unchanging standard that classifies them as flaws. In effect, the craftsman's words raise the ideal of a fully restored menorah (presumably a stable text) that would subsume all variant readings into it.

Whether the reader chooses to identify the craftsman as Creator, as Rabbi Nahman, or simply as the artist, the suggestion is that the role of this craftsman is to make the interaction between viewer and object possible. The menorah as text is stabilized, implicitly, through its participation in a divinely authorized structure. That theological structure nevertheless allows and even provides for individual experiences or readings. Within the larger structure of religious values, variables are termed "flaws" or "shortcomings," a designation which makes viewers or participants aware of a higher standard, while acknowledging the "difference" of each that is his or her humanness.

This is a tale that thematizes its own efforts and opens out towards the reader or listener. It works to engage the reader with the object of which the narrative speaks and to bring about an experience of the text for the reader similar to the viewer-menorah interactions that the story describes. Rabbi Nahman's narrative initiates an elaborate dance of textuality, whose participants define and illuminate each other in their interaction.[8]

While literary criticism involves the effort to articulate the interaction between reader and text, the focus remains on the text itself. Although the roots of any reading are always personal, reading sustains a vital connection with the text that we hold in common, however varied our responses to it may be. The challenge is to make public a reading, demonstrating its derivation from a configuration of texts and a particular angle of approach. I want to emphasize the non-exclusivity of the approach I take, while making a strong case for the importance of a study of writing and textuality to our understanding of Agnon.

We can only use our language, constructs that shape our thought and our relation to the world. No critic stands apart from culture. Nevertheless, while we cannot think outside of the signifying systems, conscious and unconscious, that have formed us, texts do offer a unique medium through which we can read ourselves in culture. Rather than hold up the goal or the promise of a "revolutionary" or revolutionized language, we may agree that our participation in culture is now accompanied by a degree of self-consciousness that enables us to assume the dual stance of participant-observers. The literary art of S. Y. Agnon offers to us complex dramas of textuality and consciousness, through which we may move to interrogate some of the constitutive assumptions in our knowledge of the world.

Notes

1. This is along the lines of the "deterritorialization" of which Gilles Deleuze and Felix Guattari [1986] speak: there is no firm ground for definitive interpretation of the text; the text resists the claim of any ideology.
2. "Ḥush hareaḥ," or "The Sense of Smell," is discussed in chapter 6. For a discussion of the pervasive influence of this image of the son's exile in the formation of the identities of Hebrew writers at the turn of this century, see Alan Mintz, 1989.
3. Jacques Lacan notes that "the paternal function concentrates in itself both imaginary and real relations, always more or less inadequate to the symbolic relationship that essentially constitutes it" [1977, 67].

4. "Not only does language provide the agency of self-loss, but cultural representations supply the standard by which that loss is perceived," observes Kaja Silverman [1983].

5. M. M. Bakhtin examines this quality of polyphony and values texts in which the play of voices is particularly rich and unconstrained. Julia Kristeva develops the concept of intertextuality out of this play of voices or fragments of utterances in any text.

6. Hillel Barzel describes Agnon's familiarity with tales of the Baal Shem Tov and the shared affinity of Kafka and Agnon to Rabbi Nahman of Bratslav [1972, 168-70, 177]. Arnold Band notes that Agnon read *Shivhe Haran,* tales of Rabbi Nahman, as an adolescent; he emphasizes the impact of Rabbi Nahman's style on Agnon. Y. H. Brenner was the first to notice the influence of Rabbi Nahman on Agnon's "'Agunot" [Band 1968, 9, 60, 92]. Franz Kafka knew Rabbi Nahman's tales through Martin Buber's work.

7. I compared Hebrew editions by Yisrael Har [1981] and Yehudit Kuk [1973] and translations by Martin Mantel [1977] and Howard Schwartz [1983]. "The Tale of the Menorah," also titled as "The Tale of the Menorah of Defects," is not among the original thirteen collected by Rabbi Nahman's disciple Rabbi Nathan. See editions prepared by S. A. Horodetzky [1922] and Band [1978].

8. One further note: In the tradition of the Bratslaver Hasidim, the prayer that is recited before one of R. Nahman's tales is told breaks down distinctions between teller, listener, and text [Schwartz, 223]. Through the telling of the tale, teller and listeners participate in and transmit traditional tales of the deeds of holy men. The act of telling brings the teller closer to those deeds, imparting to teller and audience a measure of the holiness of the deeds themselves. The teller participates actively in the realization of the tale and draws his audience into the narrative fabric that he weaves. The Bratslaver prayer is an invocation of the power of narrative to transform the experience of its participants.

Naomi B. Sokoloff (essay date 1994)

SOURCE: Sokoloff, Naomi B. "Expressing and Repressing the Female Voice in S. Y. Agnon's *In the Prime of Her Life.*" In *Women of the Word: Jewish Women and Jewish Writing,* edited by Judith R. Baskin, pp. 216-35. Detroit: Wayne State University Press, 1994.

[*In the following essay, Sokoloff applies a feminist critique to an Agnon novella, which she says associates the tradition and uncertain future of the Hebrew language with its repressed and unfulfilled female characters.*]

While the last fifteen years have witnessed an upsurge of interest in feminist critical thought and literary interpretation, few attempts have been made to explore the implications of gender as a thematic concern in modern Hebrew texts.[1] Yet Hebrew warrants special feminist examination because of its exceptional history as a holy tongue that for many centuries was studied almost exclusively by men. It was only the major cultural upheavals and transformations of the Jewish Enlightenment and Zionism—sources, as well, of the Hebrew linguistic and literary renaissance of the last two centuries—that led to significant changes in women's social and intellectual roles. The inevitable tensions between a male-dominated tradition and modern cultural change have left their mark on literary representations of women in Hebrew writing by men, even as they have fostered a singular set of obstacles and stimuli for the creation of a female literary tradition in modern Hebrew literature. In light of these considerations, ***In the Prime of Her Life*** (*Bidmi yameha,* 1923) invites a feminist rereading, since this novella by Shmuel Yosef Agnon, Nobel Prize winner and preeminent Hebrew novelist of the first half of the twentieth century, is centrally concerned with the sounding and silencing of female voice.

Much of the feminist critical agenda has aimed at documenting ways in which female figures have been represented by men, as well as ways in which women have spoken back, representing themselves through their own vocal self-assertion.[2] Agnon's novella, which features a female narrator, a young woman who marries her mother's former suitor and recounts her life story in the form of a written memoir, raises questions of interest for both modes of reading. Consequently, even as ***In the Prime of Her Life*** represents women through the filter of male perceptions, the text poses as a woman's account of her own experience and so calls attention directly to women's expression and language.

In this fiction such issues develop explicitly through insistent treatment of tensions between suppressed and emergent voices. Though critical appraisals have been curiously silent on this matter, Agnon in effect structures the entire novella around a series of verbal exchanges and keen thematic attention to talk. Virtually every paragraph centers on obtrusive reference to or citation of conversations, interior monologues, and varieties of written messages. In this way the text endorses the primacy of linguistic acts as plot actions that regulate matters of will, power, and social relations. It is noteworthy, too, that the representations of language, like the social conflicts they imply or convey, are marked by sexual difference. Just as men and women behave differently, so they express themselves differently, and their uses of words illuminate contrasting privileges and predicaments. The novella in this way highlights the protagonist's attempt to make herself heard by stating her convictions and expressing her own desires. This is not to say that the text necessarily applauds her efforts. At times it clearly decries them. Agnon himself was by no means a feminist nor an advocate of women's liberation, and he sometimes casts his character in a distinctly unflattering light. The narrative nevertheless maintains an intense scrutiny of women's voices, and for this reason feminist theory may provide a productive critical framework for examining *In the Prime of Her Life,* illuminating aspects of the text that have been overlooked, underestimated, or marginalized by critics.

From the start, *In the Prime of Her Life* concentrates on the silence of a female character, Tirza's ailing mother, Leah. In the process the text associates subdued voice with death and confinement. Describing the period of Leah's declining health, the opening paragraph relates: "Our house stood hushed [*dumam*] in its sorrow and its doors did not open to a stranger"(167).³ The next paragraph reiterates and augments this introductory announcement: "The winter my mother died our home fell silent [*damam*] seven times over." Both passages play on the Hebrew root *d-m-m,* recalling the sounds of the title and the first sentence of the novella: "In the prime of her life [*bidmi yameha*] my mother died." *Demi,* "silence," functions in this last phrase to signify "in the prime" of her days. Submerged within it, too, heightening its ironic nuances, is reference to blood (*dam*). These lines thereby connect silence with the snuffing out of vitality in a young woman who died too soon. Subsequently the narrative illustrates the cruelty of Leah's fate by relating another image of suppressed language: letters Mother received from her true love, Akaviah Mazal, have been kept under lock and key for years. She opens them, it is recounted, only to destroy them, burning them in a room whose windows are locked tight. In this stifling setting of enclosure and repression, smoke rises in an allusion to the sacrifice of Leah's true desires.

After her death, Father's arrangements for the inscription on Leah's tombstone reconfirm the entire pattern of her life as silenced and suppressed desire. To understand this episode we should remember the feminist claim that patriarchal culture has often defined woman according to its needs rather than hers; it has also frequently represented females as passive beings unable to produce their own meanings. In this way, as Susan Gubar argues, men have attempted to create woman through masculine discourse, and women, serving as secondary objects in someone else's scheme of things, have been perceived as blank pages on which to write and be written.⁴ In Agnon's story, these descriptions are apt; men have been writing the script for Leah all her life. Not allowed to sound her wishes, she has been denied intentionality. Most importantly, her father marries her to the wrong man, one who is better off financially and considered more socially desirable than the suitor she herself prefers. As a result she dies at an early age, her heart physically and metaphorically weakened because deprived of love. Through the incident of the tombstone Agnon creates a startling, culminating illustration of this phenomenon. The woman, her spirit extinguished, has been transformed into an object, her identity reduced to a name carved in stone. It is pointed out, moreover, that her husband thinks more about her epitaph than about her. Though he is genuinely and deeply aggrieved at the loss of his wife, in choosing the lettering for the grave he "all but forgot" (172) the woman. The writing, his defining of her, eases his pain. To Mintz's credit he does reject a highly formulaic epitaph, one which Mr. Gottlieb has prepared, in favor of one more meaningful. The first inscription is very clever; it is based on an acrostic of Leah's name that also incorporates the year of her death into every line of the poem, but there is nothing personal in it. Recognizing this shortcoming, the husband opts for something more authentic. He goes to Mazal, the former beau and author of those now burnt love letters, to commission a second inscription. Though it is finally too late, and though he acts only through an intermediary who is a man, Mintz makes at least some concession toward acknowledging his wife's suppressed desires and inner life: her ardent feelings for Mazal.⁵

Tirza, the daughter, who is at once the narrator and the primary focus of the narrative, establishes her own significance in opposition to these actions on the part of the men. Her initial introduction of herself, for example, in the first paragraphs of the story, serves as a celebration of her mother's voice: "Lying on her bed my mother's words were few. But when she spoke it was as though limpid wings spread forth and led me to the Hall of Blessing. How I loved her voice. Often I opened her door to have her ask, who is there?" (167). While the rest of the paragraph insists on suffocation and enclosure, rendering the mother's thoughts inaudible, Tirza here emphasizes aperture (the outspread wings and the open door) along with sound, self-assertion, listening, and response. These emphases evolve into question about Tirza's identity ("Who is there?") and so constitute an affirmation of her own presence.

Tensions between the suppression and emergence of female voice develop further as the plot unfolds into a story of the daughter's search for independence. Tirza sets her heart on marrying Akaviah Mazal, falls ill in a kind of duplication or reenactment of her mother's final illness, and, surviving this, convinces her father that she and Mazal should be wed. The assertion of her desires, as a recuperation of her mother's lost life, progresses through any number of verbal encounters that disclose identifiably distinctive masculine and feminine aspects. When, for example, Mrs. Gottlieb invites Tirza to spend the summer at her home, the narrator recounts: "My father readily agreed, saying 'Go now.' But I answered, 'How will I go alone?' and he said, 'I will come and visit.' Kaila stood dusting by the mirror and she winked at me as she overheard my father's words. I saw her move her lips and grimace in the mirror, and I laughed to myself. Noticing how my face lit up with cheer my father said, 'I knew you would heed my words,' and he left the room" (175).

This passage could be a textbook illustration of sociolinguistic observations on female verbal behavior. Women, because of the more vulnerable status they occupy in many societies, often tend to avoid language that threatens or endangers the stability of relationships. Consequently, they rely heavily on a range of politeness strategies meant to deflect attack and help maintain interpersonal equilibrium. These include attentiveness, approval, flattery or indirectness, the use of honorifics, appeals to a higher law, generalizations, and excuses of exigence.[6] In the passage cited, Tirza, too, is deferential because of her subordinate position. Accordingly, she restricts her comments to a question. Despite her unhappiness about the plans for the summer, she leaves the father's decision open and does not impose her own mind or views on him. The housekeeper likewise avoids straightforward declaratives. Trying to convince Tirza to agree with her father and respect his desires, Kaila expresses herself only by indirections and distortions. Tirza, aware of the preposterous incongruity of her servant's actions, laughs with amusement at the linguistic inequity prevailing in this exchange. Only fourteen, she does not yet take her own powerlessness quite seriously. She remarks innocently in the next paragraph: "Kaila, God be with you, speak up, don't remain silent, please stop torturing me with all your hints and riddles." For this she is reprimanded and reminded of the gravity of the situation: this trip is for the father's well-being, not hers, and would she but look at him closely she would realize that he is lonely and needs the opportunity to visit the Gottliebs in the country. In short, Kaila first acts on the conviction that she mustn't express herself directly, and then, when pressed, conveys this same message more overtly to Tirza. The girl's personal desires must remain unspoken. As a result of all the indirectness, Mintz for his part misreads Tirza entirely. "I knew you would heed my words (*lishmoa' bekoli*)," he says, thus reinscribing her back into his code of understanding. Using an expression typical of biblical discussions on obedience to God, he reinforces his patriarchal authority and reconfirms his failure to appreciate the inner thoughts of the women in his life.[7]

Other incidents as well contrast the discourse of men and women, demonstrating an imbalance of power between them. For instance, the matchmaker who comes to visit talks at great length, making tiresome chitchat and keeping Tirza a captive but courteous audience (193). Tirza's father, for his part, unselfconsciously exercises strategies to dominate conversations. Not only does he direct talk to his own preferred topics (generally, his personal misfortune due to Leah's death); he also extends his own words to encompass everyone: "We are the miserable widowers," he laments, and Tirza comments, "How strange were his words. It was as though all womankind had died and every man was a widower" (186).

In addition to these scenes in which Agnon neatly contrasts masculine communicative prerogatives with the women characters' cautions and insecurities about speaking, on other occasions male characters explicitly impute negative qualities to or give misogynistic interpretations of female speech. In an embedded tale recounting Mazal's past, Leah's father is quoted as chiding his wife for engaging in "woman's talk"—that is, talk he deems to be idle and impious (19). A comparably condemnatory comment surfaces when the doctor comes to visit the Mintz family after Mother's death. Remarking that the daughter has grown and that she has on a new dress, he asks if she knows how to sew. Tirza responds with a maxim, "Let another man praise thee, and not thine own mouth" (174). Restricting herself to a nonassertive stance, this character offers a formulaic reassurance of the male interlocutor's initiative in conversation. All the same he responds by saying, "A bold girl and looking for compliments." What the man takes as an act of boldness is more properly an evasion of confrontation and a highly reticent hint at a topic the daughter is actually eager for others to acknowledge: her budding sexuality, her own growing up which has been overlooked because everyone is preoccupied with mourning. This incident, like the scolding Leah's father gives his wife, underscores attention in the text to the characters' stereotypic notions of women's speech and to a conviction that female expression should remain sharply circumscribed.

In a pivotal scene concerned with these issues, Tirza at first submits to the discourse of men characters. Quelling her own impulses, she molds her expression to conform to their expectations. However, the episode quickly becomes a turning point, a moment of rupture in which she attempts to emancipate herself from male-dominated patterns of verbal interaction. This happens when Mintshi Gottleib, her hostess, discloses that Akaviah and Leah were once in love. Tirza, struck by melancholy and confusion, is then approached by Mintshi's husband, and the following exchange ensues: "'Look, our friend is boring a hole through the heavens,' Mr. Gottlieb said laughing as he saw me staring up at the sky. And I laughed along with him with a pained heart" (77). Afterwards, although she has humored him, Tirza remains deeply troubled by Mrs. Gottlieb's revelations about the past and she cannot let the matter rest: "Night after night I lay on my bed, asking myself, 'What would now be if my mother had married Mazal? And what would have become of me?' I knew such speculations to be fruitless, yet I did not abandon them. When the shudders which accompanied my musings finally ceased, I said: Mazal has been wronged. He seemed to me to be like a man bereft of his wife yet she is not his wife" (177). Shortly after that her ruminations resume:

> How I loathed myself. I burned with shame and did not know why. Now I pitied my father and now I secretly grew angry at him. And I turned my wrath upon Mazal also. . . . Sometimes I told myself: Why did Mintshi Gottlieb upset me by telling me of bygone memories? A father and mother, are they not man and woman and of one flesh? Why then should I brood over secrets which occurred before my time? Yet I thirsted to know more. I could not calm down, nor could I sit still for a moment's quiet. And so I told myself, if Mintshi knows what happened surely she will tell me the truth. How though will I open my mouth to ask? For if I but let the thoughts come to mind my face turns crimson let alone when I speak out my thoughts aloud. I then gave up all hope. More I could not know.
>
> (178)

Tirza's lengthy internal monologue offers an explicit meditation on her fears of speaking up. In its very length the passage itself is an act of verbal self-assertion—a muffled voicing of her anxieties, to be sure, but at least a way of formulating and sounding her preoccupations in her own mind. Here once more the character's remarks consist of questions rather than declaratives or imperatives, but, in contrast to her earlier silences and deferential reserve, these questions are angry and searching. Language, moreover, serves specifically as a way of constituting a self. Probing her origins, Tirza asks overtly, who am I? and ponders what she might have been had her mother married somebody else.

This character's progress toward self-expression is subsequently impeded but then also spurred on by her engagement, engineered by the matchmaker Gotteskind, with a young man in whom she takes no interest. Recoiling at the prospects of an arranged match, Tirza dreams that her father has married her off to an Indian chief and that her body is "impressed with tattoos of kissing lips" (193). If, as feminist criticism has argued, the female predicament entails the imposition of a male cultural script onto woman, a writing of her that determines her sexual life and social status, in this passage we find a graphic image of a woman whose destiny is being inscribed directly onto her body. The verbal and sexual power so prominently featured in ***In the Prime of Her Life*** as part of the male domain converge in this scene. They are presented through a single dramatic symbol of female disempowerment: the mouth, locus of both kisses and speech, appears here as tattoo, sealing the young woman's dreaded fate of being married off by force to someone entirely foreign and alien to her. This episode makes Tirza all the more determined to have Akaviah Mazal, whom she perceives as the true object of her desire.

As she pursues Akaviah and so expresses her own will, Tirza again resorts to speech characterized by indirection and generalization. She does so, though, with a new flare. According to accepted protocol, she cannot easily speak with her beloved. Mazal is not only older than she; he also becomes her teacher when, turning sixteen, Tirza begins attending a teachers seminary. With increasing daring she devises pretexts for making conversation with Akaviah. To reach him she pretends that a dog has bitten her hand, and so, under the guise of soliciting compassion and protective care, she dupes him into allowing her to reveal her erotic intent. (As many readers have noted, the dog in Agnon's texts is frequently an indicator of uncontrolled sexuality and also of madness, that is, of impulses threatening to the accepted limits of society.[8])

Tirza's most extreme declaration of desire occurs when societal constraints are further removed. During her illness, at the height of feverish delirium, she etches the name "Akaviah Mazal" many times into her mirror. She also writes Akaviah a letter, noting, "You shall dwell in my thoughts all day" (209). In both instances the young woman is trying to write him, to inscribe him, into her inner self or subsume his signature into the image of herself which she receives from the mirror. In this way Tirza attempts to reverse that early pattern, epitomized by the episode with the tombstone, in which the men inscribed Leah's name in their discourse. It is significant that she does this at a time when she is sick and suffering delusions. Literary equations of woman's rebellion with madness have been noted recurrently in feminist criticism. At times, too, feminist interpretations have considered this identification of aggression or self-assertion with insanity as an attempt to discredit female protest.[9] Tirza's temporary derangement conforms in part to such a pattern; her daring is a function of illness and irrationality. Agnon's text, however, is subtle in its judgment of her. The scene serves less as an attempt to trivialize Tirza's situation than as a sensitive acknowledgment of how profound are the disorders that plague the entire family and culminate in the events of the daughter's life. Yet, by contrast with those gravely disturbing matters, her efforts at self-expression do come to seem of diminished seriousness. What remains certain is that, opening a Pandora's box of emotional troubles, this character courts disaster. Something has gone fundamentally wrong in this home, and Tirza's sickness is highly overdetermined. Not only the occasion for speaking out, the fever is an expression of psychic dis-ease. Tirza invited a chill by wearing inappropriate attire (a summer dress in winter), and her illness then is instrumental in manipulating her father's (and perhaps Mazal's) sympathy. That this partially unwitting ploy is effective results from the susceptibility of the older generation to emotional blackmail as well as from their complicity, their willingness to arrange a new marriage to settle old scores. Each for his own reasons agrees to the match. Therefore, because of the complicated interpersonal context in which Tirza's development takes place, *In the Prime of Her Life* is only in part the story of a young woman's rebellion against social mores; beneath the surface there is another agenda, one in large measure pessimistic about the ability of a young woman to free herself of patriarchal imperatives.

Tirza's name has been understood as both "will" (*ratson*, from the Hebrew root *r-ts-h*) and "pretext" (*teruts*, from the root *t-r-ts*). A range of meanings delimited by these concepts underlies the events of her life and complicates the rather straightforward examples of incipient self-assertion brought forward in the first half of this essay. At issue, most crucially, is the protagonist's dangerous psychic involvement in the events of the past and in the unresolved tensions of her parents' youth. Her reliving of Mother's life turns out to be less a renewal than a repetition of mistakes, and in this light determination becomes a pretext for passivity and determinism. Agnon explores these matters by combining attention to mother/daughter relations—a central topic in current feminist criticism—with one of his own major thematic preoccupations: struggles between individual will and forces beyond the control of the individual, be those explained as destiny, divine intervention, or the workings of the unconscious.[10]

Many critics have claimed that Tirza's recreating of her mother's life enacts a variation on the familiar Agnon theme of the love triangle.[11] The young woman marries a father figure and continues to yearn for her father's company, even as Mazal marries the daughter instead of the mother he loved. Leah similarly married Mintz instead of her beloved, and Mintshi, enamored of Mazal, married Gottlieb and buried herself in ceaseless activity. Each case creates a three-some that interferes with the attainment of intimacy or displaces love from one object of passion to a dissatisfying substitute. What has not been sufficiently recognized and stated, though, is the degree to which Tirza's problems are those of an adolescent, specifically a female who must deal with the death of her mother, and the connection between these issues and that of emergent voice.

Adolescence is a time of gradually letting go, of loosening bonds with parents in preparation for making choices of all sorts, but most importantly erotic. As Katherine Dalsimer notes, this withdrawal from parents accounts for the unique place this stage of life occupies in psychoanalytic writing.[12] Deemed at once to be a time of possibility and aperture, it is also an age of pain. Because tensions present since earliest childhood are reactivated in adolescence, this is a moment of awakening that permits new resolution to old conflicts. At the same time, pulling away from parents is felt subjectively by youngsters as a profound loss or emptiness not unlike mourning. The actual death of a parent, occurring at this juncture, inevitably heightens that inner loss experienced in the normal course of growing up. It can also influence the reworking of psychic conflicts essential for the young person to attain new maturity. If all deaths are greeted by the living with some degree of denial, the impulse to disbelieve the finality of the loss proves that much more intractable for children or teenagers.[13] Unchallenged, unmodified by day-to-day experience, such wishful fantasy may prove even more difficult to abandon and may result in further magnified esteem for the lost figure.

Tirza's life is decisively affected by just such a turn of events. Matters are complicated further, because she is female. The field of psychoanalysis has increasingly recognized the enduring nature of a daughter's relation to her mother.[14] In adolescence there is heightened need for mother as the individual who provided crucial primary intimacy, and much as was true in the earliest days of childhood, the daughter often looks to her mother as a mirror through whose approval and disapproval she can recognize, define, validate, delimit, and forge herself. Tirza Mintz moves toward maturity with difficulty, for in her case the pull to identify with the mother is at once unhealthily strong and also exacerbated by Leah's death. Tirza's father, for his part, cannot compensate for the mother's absence. He is singularly unable to provide his daughter the mirroring she needs because he is deeply self-absorbed, preoccupied always with his mourning and his business dealings. Not only does he misread his daughter, as in the passage examined earlier; in addition he overlooks her awareness of her own emerging womanliness. When, for instance, concerned with her appearance, she puts on festive new clothes, his reaction of surprise leads her to feel deeply guilty; though the mourning period has passed, she comes to perceive her attentions to herself as a failure of devotion to Leah. As she moves one step toward embracing life, he encourages her to prolong mourning for her mother. Tirza notes explicitly: "In my grief I said, my father has forgotten me, he has forgotten my existence" (170). This passage alludes neatly to the two kinds of grief the reader can identify in Tirza's adolescent experience: she suffers a natural loss of intimacy, a withdrawal between parents and children, but this is a blow intensified many times over by the physical death of the mother. Both are made worse by the father's self-centered reactions.

It is in this context that Tirza tries to realize the fantasy of reenacting and revising her mother's life; she wishes to redress the (perceived) wrong done Mazal, even as she would like to reverse her mother's romantic disappointment, and so she tries to make the crooked straight (that is, *letaretz*—"to straighten"—a word that again recovers the sound of the protagonist's name). She attempts, too, to preserve a memory, to deny Leah's absence, and to find validation of herself as a woman. The implication raised by this set of circumstances is that, though Tirza believes she is pining away for love of Mazal, in effect and at a deeper level she attempts to hold onto childhood and maternal intimacy. That highly important psychic business of adolescence, the need to develop autonomy, is retarded and distorted by confusion of her own identity with that of her mother. The tragedy of this excessive attachment is then compounded by the incestuous quality inherent in the solution Tirza seeks out: her marriage to Mazal. Altogether, Tirza's adolescence, far from an emancipation, has become a subjugation to the parents' past and to her continuing need to imitate her mother. In a chilling scene Tirza, now pregnant, foresees for herself an early death parallel to Leah's. Part of this fantasy, moreover, is that she prays for a daughter—to take care of Mazal. This eventuality would result yet again in a displacement onto another of the maternal role; her wish hints that Tirza wants less to be a mother than to implore someone else to do some mothering.

The full extent of the protagonist's tragedy becomes apparent, like many other developments in the narrative, through the treatment of dialogue, talk, and matters of voice. For example, one of the first signs that Tirza has made a serious mistake in pursuing Mazal occurs early on in their courtship. She feels attracted to him precisely because she expects she can confide in him. Overcome with ennui at the seminary she notes, "I saw there wasn't a person to whom I could pour out my heart; and I then said, I will speak to Mazal." Her projected scenario does not materialize. Welcoming her into his house, Akaviah latches onto her as a listener and, telling her his life story, doesn't allow her to get a word in edgewise. Tirza, instead of speaking up, is drawn into his discourse. It is the long ago that remains dominant here, and not Tirza's newly emergent young life. It is significant that Mazal's monologue is presented as a long interpolated sequence in the novella; the very status of his speech as embedded narrative indicates that it is essentially extrinsic to Tirza's story, yet absorbs her attention and displaces the novella's focus from her present onto the past. Subsequently, in another scene that relies on pointed reference to voice, Tirza's description of her illness testifies to the increasing intensity of her problems. She has come more and more to resemble her mother. The text observes, "My heart beat feebly and my voice was like my mother's voice at the time of her illness" (211). A similar remark appears, too, when her marriage fails to bring her the happiness she had expected. Pregnancy precipitates a crisis of depression that confirms and clarifies the nature of Tirza's discontent. She has not progressed to a mature autonomy, and when her father brings presents for the new baby, the mother-to-be speaks as if she were herself the child: "'Thank you, grandfather,' I said in a child's piping voice."

This scene also makes strikingly clear that forces operating in Tirza's life invalidate, alter, or bring additional layers of meaning to her vocal self-assertions. Noting, "The child within me grows from day to day" (215), the text here recalls the first description of Tirza listening to her mother's voice, which stated "I was still a child." Though the young woman is not aware of it, the reference to the child within may include Tirza as much as her offspring. Here, as throughout the narrative, what is said aloud is quite different from what the characters mean. If at first woman's speech is indirect, a kind of deferential duplicity determined by relations of power and powerlessness, later on words also function in another way to both conceal and reveal. They contain hidden significations, and Tirza at times unknowingly discloses deep motivations she herself would not recognize.[15] For such reasons voice cannot in any simple sense be synonymous with will. While Tirza's early attempts to make herself heard were intended to help her wield some power, it becomes clear in the course of the text that her unconscious desires, deeply powerful ones, exceed and elude the goals she has defined and willed for herself.[16] Nor does the birth of her child signal joy; her final melancholy is one more manifestation of the crooked that cannot be made straight.

At the end of *In the Prime of Her Life* the question of voice reasserts itself, complicated by such matters. Tirza seeks out a new kind of expression by composing a memoir. This fact has several implications. On a simple dramatic level, the effort to chronicle is plausibly motivated by Tirza's adolescence. Given the enlarged self-preoccupations typical of teenagers, keeping a diary is a natural activity for this time of life.[17] In Tirza's case such writing is a more formal attempt at the task begun earlier in the story: to constitute a self through language, to puzzle over her life and ask, who am I? (For Tirza this self-definition is crucial if she is not to subsume her identity totally within that of someone else.) That she is a female brings additional meaning to this act. She is, after all, a figure who has sought and is still seeking to assert her own voice in a society which discourages out-spokenness by women. She turns, significantly, to the form of writing often favored by women: the diary or memoir not intended for publication but meant to provide an outlet for emotion and a forum for self-expression. Her purposes of self-definition and self-expression are stymied, though, because she finds herself unhappily trapped in a situation much larger than her own imagined script of events. Since other powerful forces are at play, and since even her public speaking up has led her to an all-encompassing, seemingly preordained pattern of relations, writing serves as a last resort, a way for her to seek solace and not as a way for her to arrive at an unambiguous enunciation of identity. As her persistent unhappiness and continuing restlessness lead her to one last act of speaking out, she brings the uncertainties of her stance to the fore in her closing comments: "Sometimes I would ask myself to what purpose have I written my memories, what new things have I seen and what do I wish to leave behind? Then I would say, it is to find rest in my writing, so did I write all that is written in this book" (216). Caught between the new and the old, she is left still searching for a context for her own voice, establishing it—only ambiguously—in a private realm of writing.

Yet Agnon's purposes extend beyond Tirza's private female predicaments to his concern with larger collective issues. Throughout the history of Hebrew writing, female figures have often served to symbolize an entire reality or the Jewish people as a whole—from the desolate widow of Lamentations, to the personification of Zion as beloved in medieval poetry, to A. B. Yehoshua's contemporary psychohistories of Zionism. While Agnon deals in depth with Tirza's personal tale specifically as a woman's experience, he also uses her to alert readers to a series of questions, both historical and linguistic, connected with national rebirth. Tirza lives in an East European shtetl at the turn of the century. From an enlightened family, she receives a Hebrew education that is unusual for a girl of this time. As Agnon, at various junctures in the novella, brings out the theme of Enlightenment and transformations of tradition, there emerges a parallel between his protagonist's individual efforts to revive the past and the communal effort to create a Jewish cultural renaissance and to forge a rebirth of the Hebrew language. Tirza's psychological dilemmas—especially her struggle for a context in which to make her own voice heard—parallel the struggle of the Hebrew language to achieve a new audience and new vitality. In addition, attention to Tirza's Hebrew schooling makes for a specific dramatic situation, in this sociohistorical milieu, that turns questions about women's social roles into an integral part of the collective issues treated here. It is a novelty for a woman to have the opportunities Tirza has—to study and to insist on her own wishes in rebellion against her father's plans for her marriage. Her audacity becomes possible in a climate that has begun to encourage human beings to shape their own future. Within that context, where the question of individual freedom looms so large, Agnon examines the possibility of freedom for a woman whose expected lot in life is very different from that of the men around her.[18]

Two major thematic concerns thus coincide and enrich one another in *In the Prime of Her Life*: the return of what has been repressed, and the repression of female voice. The past of the mother resurfaces even as the daughter's early inclinations reemerge in adolescence with destructive force. Agnon's use of a woman's struggle for emancipatory language, together with the portrayal of the female adolescent as partially emergent voice, effectively symbolizes and conveys the drives at once present and absent in these lives. Tirza takes remarkable initiatives, but they become enmeshed in cultural and historical circumstances that irrefutably oppose her willfulness.

In *In the Prime of Her Life* it is the past both personal and mythic that fatalistically overshadows the future, leaving Tirzah Mintz Mazal incapable of determining her own fate. Yet, while he does not champion her cause, Agnon does pay serious attention to female predicaments and grants them credence as a legitimate topic for literary art, bringing remarkable insight and what can only be described as a brilliant synthesis of themes, narrative strategies, and stylistic sensitivities to his representation of a woman's voice. While designed to serve his own artistic aims, the treatment of women's speech and silence in this narrative renders *In the Prime of Her Life* exceptionally responsive to feminist readings.

Notes

This essay is an abridged and somewhat altered version of my "Narrative Ventriloquism and Muted Feminine Voice: Agnon's *In the Prime of Her Life*," *Prooftexts* 9 (1989), 115-37. I am grateful to the Johns Hopkins University Press for permission to print this new version of the essay here. Research for this study was supported by a National Endowment for the Humanities Travel to Collections Grant and by the University of Washington Graduate School Fund for Overseas Travel. Thanks go also to Janet Hadda, Yael Feldman, Esther Fuchs, and Judith Baskin for their reactions to drafts of this paper.

1. Several books examining feminist perspectives have been published recently in English, including Nehama Aschkenasy, *Eve's Journey: Feminine Images in Hebraic Literary Tradition* (Philadelphia, 1986); Esther Fuchs, *Israeli Mythogynies: Women in Contemporary Hebrew Fiction* (New York, 1987); and *Gender and Text in Modern Hebrew and Yiddish Literature,* ed. Naomi B. Sokoloff, Anne Lapidus Lerner, and Anita Norich (New York, 1992). This last volume contains my annotated bibliography of feminist criticism and gender studies in the field of modern Hebrew literature.

2. Women's silences and the suppression of female voice, both as literary theme and as political dynamic in matters of canon formation, have been primary concerns of contemporary feminist theory. For an overview of such issues see, for example, Tillie Olsen, *Silences* (New York, 1978), Adrienne Rich, *On Lies, Secrets and Silence: Selected Prose 1966-1978* (New York, 1979), Elaine Showalter, "Toward a Feminist Poetics," and *idem,* "Feminist Criticism in the Wilderness," in *The New Feminist Criticism,* ed. Elaine Showalter (New York, 1985), 125-43 and 243-76.

3. Hebrew citations are drawn from *'Al kapot haman'ul* in *Kol sipurav shel Shmuel Yosef Agnon* (Jerusalem, 1975). Quotations in English come from the translation by Gabriel Levin in *Eight Great Hebrew Short Novels,* ed. Alan Lelchuk and Gershon Shaked (New York, 1983), 165-216.

4. Susan Gubar, "'The Blank Page' and the Issues of Female Creativity," in Showalter, *New Feminist Criticism,* 292-313.

5. Yizhak Akaviahu, "Craft of Engraving and the Craft of Creating" [Hebrew], *Yediot ahronot* (September 4, 1976), offers a problematic reading of Mintz's reaction to the tombstone as an illustration of the artistic personality while overlooking the specificity of this episode as a comment on relations between the sexes.

6. See, for example, Robin Lakoff, *Language and Woman's Place* (New York, 1975); Dale Spender, *Man Made Language* (London, 1980); and Sally McConnell-Ginet, Ruth Borker, and Nelly Furman, *Women and Language in Literature and Society* (New York, 1980).

7. Yosef Ewen, "The Dialogue in the Stories of S. Y. Agnon" [Hebrew], *Hasifrut* (1971), 281-94, discusses at length how dialogue throughout Agnon's work functions to indicate failed communication.

8. See especially Baruch Kurzweil, *Masot 'al sipurei agnon (Essays on Agnon's Stories)* (Jerusalem, 1975), 104-15, and, in response, Avraham Kariv, "And the Straight Shall Be Made Crooked" [Hebrew], *Moznayim* (January 1978): 83-95.

9. Sandra Gilbert and Susan Gubar, *The Madwoman in the Attic: The Woman Writer and the Nineteenth-Century Literary Imagination* (New Haven, Conn., 1979), offer lengthy exploration of connections between madness and rebellion in literary images of women. According to this account, the woman who refuses to be selfless, takes initiatives, or has a story to tell is perceived to be monstrous or insane.

10. On mother/daughter relations see *The Lost Tradition: Mothers and Daughters in Literature,* ed. Cathy N. Davidson and E. M. Broner (New York, 1980). On the role of individual will in Agnon's writing see Dan Miron, "Domesticating a Foreign Genre," *Prooftexts* 7 (1987), 1-28.

11. For discussion see Eli Shweid, "In Way of Return" [Hebrew], *Gazit* 3 (1960): 17-20; Yair Mazor, *Hadinamika shel motivim (The Dynamics of Motives in Some Works by S. Y. Agnon)* (Tel Aviv, 1970); and David Aberbach, *At the Handles of the Lock: Themes in the Fiction of S. Y. Agnon* (London, 1984).

12. Katherine Dalsimer, *Female Adolescence: Psychoanalytic Reflections on Literature* (New Haven, Conn., 1986).

13. Dalsimer, *Female Adolescence,* 124.

14. See Nancy Chodorow, *The Reproduction of Mothering: Psychoanalysis and the Sociology of Gender* (Berkeley, Calif., 1978), and Dorothy Dinnerstein, *The Mermaid and the Minotaur: Sexual Arrangements and Human Malaise* (New York, 1976).

15. On Tirza's confusion about her own motives and about those of Mintshi and Mintz, see Gideon Shunami, "Gap in Consciousness as a Key to the Story" [Hebrew], *'Al hamishmar* (September 22, 1972); and Arnold Band, "The Unreliable Narrator in *My Michael* and *In the Prime of Her Life*" [Hebrew], *Hasifrut* 3 (1971): 30-47.

16. For overviews of the feminist angle on these issues see, for instance, Toril Moi, *Sexual/Textual Politics* (London and New York, 1985); Alice Jardine, *Gynesis: Configurations of Woman and Modernity* (Ithaca, N.Y., and London, 1985); and Kaja Silverman, *The Subject of Semiotics* (New York and London, 1983).

17. Dalsimer, *Female Adolescence,* 20.

18. The extent to which the particularity of women's experience has been recognized as a valid literary topic is a central and knotty problem for much feminist criticism.

Aharon Appelfeld (essay date spring-summer 1995)

SOURCE: Appelfeld, Aharon. "Between Shelter and Home." *Modern Hebrew Literature* 14 (spring-summer 1995): 9-11.

[*In the following essay, Appelfeld disputes other critics who say that Agnon exemplifies the "sacred" in Judaism vs. the "profane" of secularism, asserting that Agnon had a more holistic approach which combined both tradition and change.*]

It has become commonplace to describe Agnon's writings as representing the tension between the sacred and the profane, or as the critics put it, between the traditional and the secular. In other words, between the polar opposites that were deeply rooted in the souls of the writer and his contemporaries. This interpretation of his work was first proposed more than half a century ago, and was spread enthusiastically by Baruch Kurzweil: Agnon of the traditional-patristic world, versus the secularized, sceptical Agnon, striving to bridge the unbridgeable.

This interpretation appeared to be grounded in Agnon's writings. It seemed especially evident in ***Only Yesterday***: Jerusalem versus Jaffa; Sonia, the queen of the sea and the workaday life, versus Shifra, whose life runs down in stifling rooms; the dark fanatical alleys of Jerusalem, as opposed to the open sea and the pioneers of Jaffa and the settlements—while the protagonist Yitzhak dreams and struggles to find himself in these two worlds. It seems to be a strong, almost symmetrical, opposition of the sacred and the profane.

But the symmetry itself is suspicious. True, it may be found in nature, but things are different where the soul is concerned. Let it be said at once: even in ***Only Yesterday***, where the sacred/profane model appears so vividly, it is an illusion. Jerusalem is a city of paupers, of fanatical traditionalists, and not at all a place of genuine faith. Yet in that fossilised city lives the painter Blaukopf, a Jew who does not observe the Law but is full of intense religiosity. Meanwhile, in Jaffa and the settlements, which purport to be building a new Jewish world, things are far from perfect. Wealthy pompous patrons on the one hand, humbug activists on the other, and some bubble-headed flirts in between. Yet the pious Hasid Malkhov also lives in Jaffa, an old-world Jew with something of the pioneers' innocence about him. In other words, things that appear to be either sacred or profane are not necessarily so.

As I see it, there is another way of juxtaposing Jerusalem and Jaffa. Jerusalem has its specious preachers and Jaffa its busybodies. In Jerusalem there is exterior piety, and in Jaffa hollow secularity. Nonetheless, there exist truly religious people in Jaffa as in Jerusalem. Indeed, Agnon did not divide people into religious and secular, but held that some Jews had a spiritual Jewish quality that others lacked.

Agnon was not an author of sharp contrasts, but of nuances. He did not set one thing against another. His characters are presented not by means of monologues and arguments, but through observation of their behaviour, with an occasional comment. In that, he differed from the writers of his generation. The critics have strained to make him fit in with his contemporaries and to point out their common qualities, but there is no avoiding it—Agnon stands apart. He did not swim with the current of his age, which arose in the Enlightenment and continued during the Revival, which stressed the contrast, the tension and hostility, between religion and life, Judaism and humanity. His contemporaries maintained, in loud or subdued voices, that old Judaism had reached a dead-end and was doomed to extinction. Berdyczewski and Brenner also felt affection for Judaism, but accepted the verdict. Agnon did not. He, who wrote ***A Guest for the Night***, which is a litany of doom, who had witnessed the protracted death throes of the Jewish townlet, could not accept the demise of Judaism. Throughout his life he felt a part of it, and strove to restore it to its birthplace, Jerusalem.

After the great destruction Agnon set out in search of lost Jewry. His writings are, in effect, a prolonged gathering of fragments. Curiously, it was *Eretz Israel,* the physical distance, which enabled him to see his native town not only affectionately, but in a new perspective. *Eretz Israel* of the early decades of the century represented a protest against everything that the diaspora stood for. And yet in this place, which in those days tried so hard to shed the burden of the past, he succeeded in giving voice to his forefathers better than any of his predecessors.

Agnon differed from his contemporaries in almost every aspect—his language, the Hebrew sources he drew on, the syntax, the tone. . . . His writing was not qualitatively but substantially different. This may be explained in a variety of ways, but I believe it will remain a mystery. His mental pattern created a different poetics. Perhaps we may still usefully apply Schiller's old distinction between the two types of writers, the sentimental and the naïve. The sentimental writer can never accept reality as he finds it, but strives for the perfect and the ideal. He is a rebel with an idea, in the light of which he views the flaws of the real world. Most of the Hebrew writers since the Enlightenment were sentimental, and saw Jewish reality as fundamentally flawed. The original idea, Enlightenment, was succeeded by the Bund and Communism, and later by Zionism. These represented resistance not only to the social conditions of the diaspora, but to Judaism itself, its moral and religious values.

The naïve writer (naïve not in the sense of unsophisticated, but of a certain integral innocence) accepts reality as he finds it, with all its charm and ugliness, past and present, the material and the spiritual. He never says: this society is hopeless and must be changed, root and branch. He will say: this society in which I live, which is so full of suffering and sorrow, deserves to be carefully observed, right back to its origins. Life, such as it is, is worthy of a little charity. The naïve writer does not place an idea before the face of reality. He is concerned with reality, with its ailments and deformities, and not because he dotes on misfortune. He knows that his society has not wilfully adopted these faults, but had them imposed upon it by reality. Agnon may be one of the few writers of his generation, if not the only one, to meet this definition of the naïve writer. The others were characterised by their conflict with the fathers, with Jewish history, and above all, with the Jewish religion. Though most Hebrew writers were not Zionists, their message amounted to a pragmatic Zionist one: we have to change.

Agnon had no use for this message. He had an unsentimental affection for the world of his fathers, its physical nature, the Jewish house and the synagogue, and Jewish creation through the ages. Whatever was created in the Jewish world was embedded in him and his writings. T. S. Eliot stated that the essence of a writer lies in his tribe's collective memory, which he stores and renews. In that sense, Agnon was unique among our writers. We have had thinkers and writers who were captivated by Judaism, people like Martin Buber and Gershom Scholem, but they did not accept it as a whole. They chose the aspects that appealed to them. Agnon, on the other hand, saw Judaism as an indivisible cultural entity. Any attempt at division jeopardised its integrity. His writings embraced everything: the Enlightenment and Hasidism, assimilationism and Zionism. He blended the modern and the Jewish experiences, which is why his world is not really divided into the sacred and profane, but into that of values and their absence, the genuine and the false. He is a post-assimilatory artist in search of himself, and he attempted to construct bridges across the gulf that opened up between the generations. Unlike his contemporaries, he felt no enmity for the tribal beliefs. He was one of the few who understood that the core of Jewish culture lies in its religion, which may take on different features, as indeed happened, but remains the infrastructure underlying the tribe's very existence.

In common with Rabbi Kook, Agnon viewed the emergent Jewish community in Israel not as a culmination, but as the beginning of a new Jewish life. He was quite free of modern orthodoxy, its self-confidence and pretensions. He had the inner freedom to observe himself and his fathers clearly, without rancour or pity. Of course, his world differed from theirs, but that did not mean it was superior. He wrote in a minor key, without outbursts of rage and jeremiads. The action is almost inward, but make no mistake—the quiet conservative tone was itself a major revolution. While his contemporaries went out to search for treasures, Agnon stayed home and communed with his fathers and their writings. It was this ability to remain true to himself, this loyalty, that made Agnon what he was.

He has been compared to Kafka, which is a great mistake. Kafka was concerned with the individual, his inner depths, his inconsolable despair. Agnon's protagonist, even in moments of bitter despair, is never alone. The tribe, or what is left of it, will take pity on him and gather him to its bosom in the darkest hour. That was what happened to Yitzhak Kummer and to the guest in ***A Guest for the Night.*** Even the individual who has strayed far from the tribe can seek the path and try to rejoin it. Zionism sought to provide a shelter and a foothold for the persecuted Jew, and Agnon sought to achieve the impossible—to gather up the fragments of the tribal soul and bring them back to their ancient source. It was an unattainable mission.

To return to the point of departure. The critics and scholars of Agnon's day, (with the exception of Dov Sadan), saw Agnon in their own image. Being uprooted, and preoccupied with their uprootedness, they saw in him and his protagonists reflections of their own personae, namely, people swaying between loyalty to their tradition and its utter rejection. Agnon had nothing to do with all that. He was years ahead of this conflict. He was at peace with his fathers, not because he was weak, needing shelter and oblivious of the gulf. The return to the fathers was a return to himself, and Jerusalem closed the cycle of wandering. After years on the roads, the wanderer returned home.

Mark Bernheim (review date summer 1997)

SOURCE: Bernheim, Mark. Review of *A Book That Was Lost and Other Stories,* by S. Y. Agnon. *Studies in Short Fiction* 34, no. 3 (summer 1997): 397-99.

[*In the following review, Bernheim offers a mostly positive assessment of a new edition of Agnon short stories.*]

In modern Jewish literature, S. Y. Agnon has long occupied a particular place. Undeniably the great Hebrew language craftsman of the century, this 1966 Nobel Laureate has been relatively inaccessible in the English-speaking world. Two other Nobel winners—I. B. Singer and Saul Bellow—are far more widely read and viewed as the voice of Yiddish literature on the one hand and explorer of besieged cultural values on the other. But Agnon, born Shmuel Yosef Czaczkes in 1888 in Galician Buczacz, then part of Austria-Hungary, and dead in 1970, may find his awaited audience in English more easily thanks to this handsome 1995 anthology bringing us twenty-five of his stories, many not previously translated, gathered from Agnon's long and varied lives in Poland, Palestine, Germany, and Israel.

Much credit should go to Professors Alan Mintz and Anne Golomb Hoffman; these Agnon scholars give us not an ordinary "Selected Stories of . . ." but rather an engrossing tool for gaining serious understanding of Agnon's scope and achievement. The book divides into seven principal parts, plus a thorough Glossary of Terms used from Hebrew, extensive notes when needed for each story, and an excellent "Bibliographic Note" on previous Agnon translations, critical studies having already appeared, and sources for the Hebrew originals.

The seven parts are coherently structured for the reader: the editors choose to follow Agnon's migrations and relate them to each story. Before actually beginning to chart the author from Galicia to Palestine to World War I Germany, back to Palestine and eventually to Israel through the stories selected, Mintz and Hoffman present the rightly-famous early "signature" sketch **"Agunot"** (1908) from which Agnon later invented his own pseudonym. The term is well known to represent in Orthodox Judaism an abandoned wife who has lost all rights and must remain undivorced by the husband who will not free her, as is traditionally required. For Agnon, forever the outsider positioned among east European Orthodoxy, early Zionism, German assimilationism, and eventual Israeli identity as the literary lion of Jerusalem and greatest Hebrew writer of his day, this **"Agunot"** fits perfectly into his multidimensional self.

But note: the long introduction by both editors is, I found, a bit disjointed. One senses the two scholars jockeying for position and credibility, as the introduction stops and starts several times annoyingly, beginning with an analogy to Joyce and Faulkner (at least we are spared the familiar comparisons with Borges and Kafka for the most part) that is dropped much too soon to be really stimulating later on when the reader comes to the stories themselves. They are on safer ground with a historical overview of Agnon's connections with Gershom Scholem and Salman Schocken, and their interesting comments on Agnon's reluctance to deal with the Holocaust significantly in his fiction. Choosing the life histories of his vanished Polish culture rather than the death agonies of its inhabitants, they suggest, was his only solution to affirm life.

The editors' divisions propel us seamlessly from Tales of Childhood, to the Artist in the Land of Israel, to the Ancestral World, to Buczacz: from The Epic Life of One Town, to Stories of Germany, to The Search for Meaning. Mintz and Hoffman have selected and combined convincingly, in each chapter justifying the inclusion of each story with a brief gloss on the position it holds in Agnon's universe. Brief parables stand alongside longer works that even stretch occasionally to novella length.

My favorite? In the "Buczacz" chapter of tales from Galicia (and surely the reader will sense the voice of I. B. Singer and his Krochmalna Street characters from the childhood stories) we find the previously untranslated gem simply called **"Pisces."** I wanted ten times its forty-five pages: poignant and haunting, comically sardonic at points, **"Pisces"** follows the bizarre intersecting fates of a huge fish about to be devoured by one gross Fishl Karp, the town glutton and usurer whose voraciousness for this prize catch he has bought ultimately leads them both to ruin. Serious biblical allusions and themes stand alongside visually memorable mythic scenes, archetypes, and folklore. The novella runs along superbly on these various legs; if one reads nothing else, heaven forbid, by Agnon, this tale would assure great appreciation.

As for the title story, **"A Book That Was Lost,"** the editors locate it roughly one-third of the way through the anthology, in the Palestine section. It too has tremendous resonance, telling of a precious rabbinical commentary that has been in transit—seemingly forever—from Galicia to the Holy Land. As Mintz and Hoffman relate,

> Not so much a story of the writer as a story of the writer's devotion to the town, **"A Book That Was Lost"** uses its narrative frame to construct a home for the lost book, the book that never makes it to the new national library of the Jewish people. . . . The story is as much a record of what has been destroyed or lost over the years as it is of Zionist achievement. . . . It becomes the mission of the writer to record loss . . . and thus to make a place for a traditional text in a new society, even if that "place" consists of the notation of its absence.

Agnon's stories in fact encapsulate the last two centuries' tumultuous Jewish history—traditional isolation giving way to "Aliyah," to assimilation and to final literary and personal redemption in an uncertain homeland. It is Mintz's and Hoffman's achievement as well to have found, like the giant fish in **"Pisces,"** a place in the net that captures both the freedom and the limited destiny of a people in transit. Cynthia Ozick has noted the "complexity hidden in seeming innocence" that links Agnon with Flaubert and other masters of ambiguities. *A Book That Was Lost and Other Stories* show this depth of surfaces and other paradoxes that make it an important addition to the modern fiction world.

William Riggan (essay date 1998)

SOURCE: Riggan, William. Introduction: "Hebrew Literature in the 1990s," *World Literature Today* 72, no. 3 (1998): 479-84.

[*In the following excerpt from an essay on contemporary Hebrew literature, Riggan calls Agnon the best of the "conservatives" who appreciated the nuances of the Hebrew language tradition.*]

To read the creative and critical texts gathered here in this special issue of *World Literature Today* commemorating the fiftieth anniversary of the founding of the State of Israel is to witness, by and large, precisely such a turn from the collective to the personal, from state-building to the construction and protection of one's own private, personal space, from questions writ large about the history and nature of Jewry to concern with one's individual love life or education or domestic dilemmas or damaged psyche and soul. . . .

The fundamental importance of Hebrew as a sociocultural medium is self-evident. First, it is the bond of the individual with Jewish history, cerebration, and values that cannot be duplicated by any other medium. Second, it is the bond uniting the potpourri of Israelis, regardless of religion, country of origin, political posture, educational level, et cetera. The vexing question, however, is the degree to which Hebrew can be altered, transformed, and inundated with foreignisms and yet retain its ability to bond a Hebrew-speaker or Hebrew-reader to a Jewish past, a Jewish present, and a Jewish future, however these be defined. And on the pragmatic level, the question is whether the present trend can be ameliorated and possibly even reversed. For Hebrew, like any other language, is not merely a means of communication; it is a virtual organ of perception, despite the necessity of distinguishing between the world and our means of symbolizing it. Hebrew is not a neutral mechanism through which our evolving culture transacts its affairs. It is, by its very form and content, a shaper of values, an advocate of ideologies, a stimulus of senses, and an instructor of the mind.

Today, as in the past, the single most positive architect of the Hebrew language is the serious writer of poetry and of prose. A host of erudite and creative authors have coined neologisms, revived long-dormant terms and phrases, adapted Hebrew to modern use, and re-created it as a language with a rich treasury and variety of expression. This endeavor has involved both linguistic conservatism and creativity. The most successful of the conservatives was Israel's Nobel laureate S. Y. Agnon (1888-1970), who, more than any other writer, utilized to good advantage the Hebrew language from its biblical origins, through its rabbinic continuation, onward through medieval diction, to its modern renaissance. His style is not simply eclectic. Rather, "It is an artistic blend of various strands of language at an unusual pitch of intensity. Any paragraph in any story or any novel of Agnon's teems with half-phrases and quarter-phrases from the Bible, the Talmud, the medieval tract, the hassidic tale, the philosophic homily. And these language pebbles form a mosaic of unusual splendor and unusual brilliance. How they do this is Agnon's secret. In an age which has enriched but also vulgarized the Hebrew language, Agnon stands out as the self-appointed guardian of its purity, its wealth and its Semitic character."[1] . . .

Note

1. See Eisig Silberschlag, *From Renaissance to Renaissance,* Vol. 2: *Hebrew Literature in the Land of Israel, 1870-1970* p. 185. If Agnon is not as widely read as his magnificent writing deserves, it is not solely because he is basically a *lauditor temporis acti,* but because his myriad allusions escape modern readers.

Shulamit Almog (essay date fall 1999)

SOURCE: Almog, Shulamit. "Literature, Politics, and the Law: On Blacksmiths, Tailors, and the Demolition of Houses." *Interdisciplinary Literary Studies* 1, no. 1 (fall 1999): 37-52.

[*In the following essay, Almog draws linguistic comparisons between a story by Agnon and the transcript of an actual legal case in modern-day Israel, concluding that the literary text reveals more of the true nature of human conflict.*]

I. INTRODUCTION

In 1962, Haim H. Cohn, at the time the Attorney General of the State of Israel, approached Shmuel Yosef Agnon and asked him to contribute to a collection of articles being prepared to commemorate the seventy-fifth birthday of Pinhas Rosen, then Minister of Justice. Agnon, who had not as yet been awarded the Nobel Prize but was nevertheless the most widely acclaimed living author in Israel, agreed, and the same year contributed a collation consisting of seventeen short stories, entitled *A Small Book of Tales.*[1] One of the stories in this collation is **"The Kilikov Trial or a Life for a Life,"** which is quoted here almost in full.[2]

> I have still not concluded all my praise for Kilikov, for not for its worldly qualities alone is Kilikov to be extolled, but it is to be praised for the judicial decisions of its judges. What are the decisions of its judges? It is told that once, during the Polish wars, a gentile killed his friend in Kilikov. Maliciously or accidentally? From the judgment it emerges that he was killed with malice. He was put in jail and convicted of killing, as a man is convicted when murdering another with malice.
>
> When the murderer was taken out to be hanged it was remembered that he was a blacksmith by profession and that in all Kilikov there was no other blacksmith. And indeed a city cannot cope without a blacksmith, who serves the needs of many.
>
> They investigated and found that in the city there were two tailors but that they could make do with one. The judges reconvened and said: instead of the blacksmith we shall hang one tailor and we shall let the blacksmith live, for the city cannot manage without a blacksmith but one tailor will suffice.
>
> They acquitted the blacksmith and brought him back from the hangman's house and in his stead they hanged one of the two tailors living in the city. Which of the two I do not know, but I do know a poem which the wise man Mordechai Ben David Starlisker, known as Marbad Set, composed about it, the conclusion of which hints at its beginning:
>
> Here there are two who are tailors
> One is put on trial and he will be punished severely
> Then shall the country see your wisdom and be fearful
> And thereafter no man shall willfully offend.

We shall let Kilikov be for the time being, and move to Jerusalem, where the Supreme Court was asked to deal with the issue of the demolition of a house belonging to a terrorist. In March 1997, Mussa Abed al-Kadr J'enimat left the village of Zurif in the Hebron District and blew himself up in a coffee house in Tel Aviv. Three women sitting in the coffee house were killed and several others were injured, many of them children and infants. As had occurred in many other cases in the past, the Military Commander of Judea and Samaria made use of the powers conferred upon him by Regulation 119 of the Defense (Emergency) Regulations 1945 (hereinafter, Regulation 119) and issued an order for the demolition of the house in the village of Zurif, where the terrorist, his wife, and four children lived.[3] The terrorist's family petitioned the High Court of Justice for an injunction to prevent the demolition. The petition was dismissed by a majority of two judges to one.[4] The short judgment was primarily comprised of the opinions of President Aharon Barak and Justice Mishael Cheshin. President Barak dismissed the petition. For him, the decisive factor was that the demolition of the houses of suicide-terrorists would be likely to deter other terrorists from committing terrorist acts in the future. Justice Goldberg agreed with President Barak.[5] Justice Cheshin, in the minority, upheld the petition. In his view, demolition of the house was contrary to the fundamental principle of law that the courts will only punish a person who has actually committed a crime.

Let us now return to the fictional Kilikov, where, following the committal of the murder, the judges held that it was necessary to take the life of the innocent tailor, whose connection to the murderer was completely coincidental: bad luck led him to live in the same city as the murderer. In Kilikov, too, so it appears from the story, the killing of the tailor had a deterrent effect: so that "thereafter no man [would] willfully offend."

There is, of course, a significant difference between the demolition of houses belonging to innocent persons and the taking of innocent lives. Indeed, the taking of life is infinitely worse than the confiscation of property or its destruction. However, it would seem that the special gravity associated with the taking of life does not negate the basic similarity between the issues emerging from the judgment and Agnon's story, respectively. In both cases society is required to cope with the need to harm innocent people in order to defend the peace and security of that society. The degree of harm caused to the innocent aggravates the dilemma, but does not change its essence. This conclusion also emerges from the stance taken by Justice Cheshin, whose judgment in the *J'enimat case* includes a number of references to the implied analogy between the demolition of the house of persons who have not committed any crime and the taking of lives of persons who are innocent.

The purpose of this article is to consider Agnon's short story alongside the opinions of two justices of the Supreme Court in the *J'enimat case*—those of President Barak and Justice Cheshin. The purpose of this combined investigation is not to engage in an analysis of the legal issues relating to the demolition of houses, a highly complex matter which lies at the center of the *J'enimat case* as well as in the center of a number of other decisions of the Supreme Court;[6] it is also not an attempt to find an answer to this question through any literary context. The combined discussion which follows aims to examine the manner in which artistic expression accentuates the central dilemma with which both the legal and the literary texts are concerned, as well as to discuss a number of points of similarity and dissimilarity in the effects and functions of legal versus literary texts.

II. THE DEMOLITION OF HOUSES IN JERUSALEM

We all tell stories in order to present our case, to persuade, to gain respect and confirmation. All of these stories "are based on selections, distortions, suppressions and emphases which are both deliberate and non-deliberate," which are jointly "means of emphasis and deletion."[7]

To the list of human stories, one can, of course, add the stories told by jurists, and among them the judgments, which are the legal stories emanating from the judges.[8] The judgments, like other stories, make continuous use of the same methods: selections, emphases, suppressions, and the like, whose purpose is to lead or direct to the objective which the author desires to attain. Naturally, the "means of emphasis and deletion" which every judge selects, whether knowingly or not, help blur one facet of the matter being considered by the judgment, emphasize another and draw the author closer to the objectives which he wishes to reach. This is also the situation in the *J'enimat case*. President Barak and Justice Cheshin start from the same premise—the need to decide the legality of the demolition of the terrorist's house—however, each one creates a text of an entirely different character by emphasizing certain factors, ignoring others, and choosing certain rhetorical tools. I shall illustrate this phenomenon by referring in detail to the respective opinions of the judges.

The judgment of President Barak is written in a dry, factual style. It is free of any personal or emotional overtones or display of feeling on the part of the writer concerning the horrifying terrorist act in consequence of which the court was required to sit in judgment, or in relation to the need to decide on the destruction of the home of a woman and her children. In contrast, these feelings are clearly reflected in the parallel choice of language of Justice Cheshin. Thus, in his judgment, President Barak calls J'enimat a "terrorist" (and not a "suicmurderer," as Justice Cheshin chooses to call him); the acts of the terrorist and their terrible consequences are described by President Barak in a purely factual manner (whereas Justice Cheshin describes them as "the murder of innocent souls"); President Barak chooses to define the demolition of the house as an outcome which is indeed "grave" for the family of the terrorist, but states that it is not a "punishment"; it is rather a "deterrent." He prefers not to refer to the issue of the innocence or guilt of the family members. Possibly, the reason for this choice of dry, unemotional language is the desire of the writer not to appear to have been spurred by emotion in his judgment, nor to be seen as one whose anger and feelings following the murder have led him to authorize the demolition. However, for the reader, the very brevity of the descriptions acts as a rhetorical tool which gives rise to an extremely powerful emotional reaction. It should be remembered that the words of President Barak are directed towards a particular community. Among this community of Israelis, who are well-aware of the circumstances in which the text is written and its background—repeated acts of terrorism, as a result of which hundreds of Israelis have lost their lives or have been injured—the dry descriptions of President Barak make a statement which tends to emphasize and accentuate the horror of terrorism, whereas it is likely that the use of extravagant descriptions would have tended to lessen the effect. Accordingly, the restrained descriptions actually help to create an emotional atmosphere or climate which makes it easier to accept the result reached by the judgment: the need to demolish the house because of the deterrent value of that act.

The sentences selected by President Barak in his judgment are short, sharp, and follow one after another in a concise and direct logical process—which does not permit delays or diversions—towards their goal. This linguistic structure is particularly prominent in the final paragraph of the judgment, which summarizes the rationale behind the general principle of law applied in Israel in relation to the demolition of houses:

> We are aware of the fact that the demolition of the structure damages the home of the first Petitioner and her children. That is not the purpose of the demolition order. It is not a punishment. Its purpose is deterrence. At the same time, its consequences are grave for the family members. The Respondent believes that this is vital in order to prevent further harm to the lives of innocent persons. He is of the view that pressure from the families is likely to deter the terrorists. There is no complete guarantee that this measure is efficacious. But within the framework of the few measures which are left to the State to defend itself against "living bombs," this measure too should not be scorned.

Barak's linguistic selections direct the readers to a single conclusion. When "grave consequences" are set opposite the possibility of "preventing further harm to the lives of innocent persons" a simple equation is established which has an inescapable result: the demolition of the house. President Barak introduces a statement which is in essence a narrative amounting to a clear, simple, and inevitable determination, both from a legal and moral point of view; it possesses a simple theoretical nature and at least the semblance of being devoid of emotional considerations. Helping to achieve this result is the stress which the judgment places on the foreign dimensions of the event. The village of Zurif, it would appear from the judgment, is part of an area in which the decisions are made by the "Military Commander" who has jurisdiction in that area only, and who derives his powers from old mandatory legislation which also is valid only in that area. In contrast, Justice Cheshin neutralizes the foreign elements of the situation by means of the nexus which he establishes between the incident, a Basic Law—which in fact comprises a chapter of the constitution of the State of Israel (Basic Law: Human Dignity and Liberty)—and local traditions (his citations from religious sources). The result of the "means of emphasis and deletion" adopted by President Barak and his choice of drafting and text is the blurring of the dilemma lying at the heart of the situation being adjudicated by him, or at least the transformation of a dilemma which in reality is extremely complex and difficult into one which is one-dimensional in nature.

As will be seen below, Justice Cheshin chooses to define the issues otherwise, and, making use of the same materials as are before President Barak, creates a completely different narrative. The two sides of the equation applied by President Barak (damaging the home of the terrorist's family compared to saving the lives of innocent people) are not mentioned by Justice Cheshin. In contrast, he introduces into the legal arena, with great stress, a component which in his view is central and which is completely absent from President Barak's judgment. Reference here is to the "fundamental principle of law," namely the principle that only a person who has committed a crime is to be punished. Justice Cheshin indeed points to the legal grounds leading him to uphold the petition,[9] but the legal argument is far from being at the center of his thinking. The judgment leads us down a surprisingly winding path towards a final result which is at polar extremes to that reached by President Barak. It commences with a paragraph a few sentences long—all of which reiterate the same concept: Regulation 119 of the Defense (Emergency) Regulations confers on the Military Commander power not only to order the demolition of one house in the village of Zurif, but also the destruction of all the houses in the village, or all the houses in the street in which the terrorist lived, or larger portions of the house in which the terrorist's dwelling was located. If this is the case, he states at the end of the passage, "*prima facie,* the Commander acted within the boundaries of his powers, and why, therefore, should the claim of the Petitioner be heard?" The irony in this statement is clear. On the face of it, it appears to support the position of the Military Commander and confirm that he acted within his powers; however, in fact, the deliberate reiteration of the significance of this power instills in the reader a harsh impression of the draconian nature of that power, which in practice enables the demolition of an entire village in response to the crimes of a single person. From here, it is a short way to the conclusion which Justice Cheshin wishes to reach: the introduction of grave reservations about the very use of powers under Regulation 119, even if used only with respect to the demolition of a single house. From this premise, Justice Cheshin leads us towards a selection of well-known quotations from ancient sources:

> This fundamental principle we have all known and repeated from the beginning of time: a man will bear his iniquities and for his own sins shall he be put to death. As the prophet said: "The soul that sinneth, it shall die. The son shall not bear the iniquity of the father, neither shall the father bear the iniquity of the son: the righteousness of the righteous shall be upon him, and the wickedness of the wicked shall be upon him" (Ezekiel 18:20). No one is punished unless he is given due warning and no one is sanctioned save the guilty party alone. This is the law of Moses and it is written in the book of the law of Moses: "The fathers shall not be put to death for the children, nor the children be put to death for the fathers; but every man shall be put to death for his own sins."
>
> (II Kings 14:6)
>
> These values lead us directly towards the early days of our people, and current times are like those days: it shall no longer be said that "the fathers have eaten sour grapes and the children's teeth are on edge."
>
> (Jeremiah 31:29)

This combination of sources, as set out by Justice Cheshin, give his words a powerful moral foundation. By means of this combination the author directs us towards a fundamental and profound level, possessing a mythical and axiomatic value which extends beyond Regulation 119, and which in the judge's view supersedes it. Justice Cheshin seems to point us towards treasuries of ancient wisdom in order to draw from them the truth which must be applied in the case at hand. From this level, located in the national-collective but at the same time universal dimension, Justice Cheshin returns surprisingly to the personal dimension, and with it he closes his judgment:

> I experienced great mental turmoil before I was able to say the things I am saying now. This is the law [*Torah*] I learned from my teachers and this is the law I know. I can do no other.

The contents of this paragraph reveal the feelings of the judge and the emotional and mental processes which he underwent prior to reaching his determination. This disclosure has the power to carry with it even those who hold a contrary view when starting to read the judgment; opponents to the judgment may find themselves swayed as awareness, understanding, and even support for the opposite view emerge from the judgment, feelings which may once have been the province of the writer until that "great turmoil" which swept through him caused him to make the decision which he eventually rendered. Justice Cheshin succeeds in creating a very personal narrative, and together with its primary purpose—formulating and rationalizing a judicial determination—it possesses appreciable aesthetic value and strength. However, the resulting effect is similar to the effect which is created by the judgment of President Barak: the obfuscation of the quandary lying at the heart of the situation being considered. The rhetoric of the judgment diverts the attention of the reader from the specific dilemma, namely, injury to the innocent versus protection of the public, towards the fascinating picture of a judge struggling with the dictates of his conscience, his fundamental legal and moral values and personal sense of justice, and the dictates of the hour, that "great turmoil," described by Justice Cheshin, which in essence is the heart of the judgment. It is fascinating, and beautiful and important, but it diverts us from the quintessence of the dilemma with which the judgment should deal.

III. "Literary Stories" versus Other Stories

I have considered the various choices made by President Barak and Justice Cheshin in their judgments. These are choices which certainly possess good and proper grounds from the subjective view points of the writers; however, it should be remembered that they include, as do all choices, an element of personal preference. Thus, in the same way as Justice Cheshin prefers to concentrate on the question of the supremacy of a fundamental principle of law and elaborate on his personal judicial difficulties, this time President Barak prefers not to give any hint of his doubts or personal feelings.[10]

One may ask whether—when considering the process of adjudication—there is room for this type of accentuated preference. Do not choices and preferences concerning the shaping of text, necessarily create a certain distortion of reality, whereas adjudication and the process leading towards it are actually supposed to reflect reality? Is not a judge required to describe things as they actually are, and refrain from any preconceptions or use of measures which may "falsify" his description of the true state of affairs? Is not the judge required to refrain from various selections and choices, which help him reach the results which suit him, but which at the same time do not permit a true and "pure" perception, in so far as possible, of the issue which he is judging? Is not the creation of a narrative of one type or another contrary to the very nature of the judge's function? This is not the place to expand on these complex issues, which apparently do not have an easy answer.[11] Similarly, it would seem that even if this is an undesirable phenomenon, judges are incapable of delivering judgments free from all of these personal choices and preferences.[12] In any event, the significant point is that there is no room for questions of this type when we are dealing with artistic texts (literary or otherwise), and only when we are dealing with such texts.

In this context, there is a distinction between "literary" stories and all other stories. When reference is to an artistic, literary text it is clear from the beginning that authors are not required to limit themselves in any way. They are not required to reflect any reality whatsoever and are entitled and permitted to "distort" reality as they wish. Their choices and preferences, their deletions and emphases, and their rhetorical tools are all fitting means which are subject to their free and full personal choice. This is the nature of literary writing. This, in the terminology of Jacques Derrida, is "the lawless law of fiction."[13]

In this context, Dan Miron writes:

> All these stories [the stories which are not literary] being based on selections, "distortions," repressions, and deliberate emphases, the artistic story contains great power in presenting the fundamental essence of the tale and the act of narrative, as all these means of emphases and deletion are part of its declared character, with a right to selection and "arbitrariness" which is embedded in its aesthetic substance.[14]

On this basis, I would like to examine the literary text in comparison with the legal text and consider whether the former is indeed more powerful in presenting the fundamental essence of the story.

IV. THE HANGING OF THE TAILOR IN KILIKOV

The tale of **"The Kilikov Trial"** is primarily constructed from a short and tight factual description of a number of incidents. It does not contain an express determination of the propriety of the result—the hanging of the tailor. In this way it is, of course, distinguishable from the judgment in the *J'enimat case,* which discloses, as is required of every judicial decision, the clear stance of every one of the judges in relation to the question of the demolition of the house. At the same time, this limited story itself emphasizes the essence of the problem with which the judgment is concerned, as well as the dialectic connected with it, in a sharp and powerful manner which is absent from the judgment. Accordingly, from certain points of view, it is more disturbing than the judgment.

Initially, I shall consider some of the linguistic and plot choices in the story. The story tells of an event which took place "once during the Polish wars," not in a Jewish area nor in a Jewish community, but in a Polish community. At the same time, the incident occurred in an area where there was a Jewish community. It is told that the event itself was known to the members of the Jewish community, and one of them, as is pointed out at the conclusion of the story, even composed a poem about it. By means of these choices, the story creates a complex synthesis between elements which are both local and foreign. The result is the positioning of the plot in a dimension which is at one and the same time both near and far. On one hand, it is characterized by a foreignness which enables us to examine the incident in an objective manner, free of inter-communal, religious, cultural, and other contexts; and on the other hand, it is positioned close enough to enable us to accept the story as something conceivable, which is likely to take place even in the community of the storyteller, as a matter which has local significance alongside its foreign significance.

This complexity is also presented in another way. I have mentioned Agnon's choice of a minimalist narrative structure. The story does not refer to the question of the innocence or contributory guilt of the non-Jew who is murdered. The circumstances of the murder are not mentioned. Nothing is said of the character or personality of the murderous blacksmith nor indeed of the tailor hanged in his stead. The story as a whole is free of any hint of emotional or psychological attributes. However, there is a good reason for all these choices: all these details are subordinate to the essence. They are not necessary to the question which arises. On the contrary, had they been mentioned, they would have tended to obscure that question. Similarly, the story does not contain any commentary on the facts being related. The hanging of the tailor is not defined as punishment, nor is it defined as an act which is not punishment. The story merely states that these are the facts. This is what happened in Kilikov. Every woman and man will decide their own position with regard to these facts.

What is left is only the refined narrative, at the center of which stands a man brought to his death by circumstances outside his control. This man is every woman and every man. The innocent tailor, the gentile Pole, could also be a Jewish tailor, or an Arab woman in the village of Zurif.

From one vantage point, the story may be considered part of the long literary tradition which contains satirical descriptions of legal systems, whose purpose is to emphasize the power of law to do wrong or distort, and through which is presented, in the words of Jean-Jacques Lecercle, "an *a contrario* defense of an ideal of judicial fairness and the correct administration of justice."[15]

The satire is directed, *inter alia,* towards ridiculing the mistakes and wrongdoing of society, in order to cause us to react with the appropriate disapproval towards various deviations from proper and desirable norms.[16] Indeed, it seems that in the light of the outrageous reversal of justice in Kilikov, the reader's conviction of the vital importance of the principle *nullum crimen nulla poena* is significantly strengthened. This principle, which means that only the performer of a certain act is subject to punishment, is a fundamental principle recognized in every system of law and in every cultured society (hereinafter, "the principle of personal responsibility"). Deviation from this principle, such as that described in the story, violates our sense of justice, and causes us moral outrage.

Agnon's short story awakens and strengthens the rationale underlying the principle of personal responsibility by the use of irony. The expression "praise for Kilikov" in the opening sentences of the story possesses, so it seems, a clear ironic significance, as does the poem concluding the story, and indeed as does the story as a whole. The irony is created by the incongruity between the act (the murder committed by the blacksmith) and the consequences of that act (the hanging of the tailor).[17] This incongruity cries out. To those exposed to it, it gives rise to the feeling that they are witnesses to a moral abomination. This is the "fundamental essence" of the story and the dilemma which lies at its center; the same dilemma which became blurred in the judicial decision in the *J'enimat case*. In this manner, Agnon managed to achieve the result which we often see in the legends and parables of Talmudic sages: the clear and sharp presentation of a complex situation, by means of a brief and sparing sketch.

I have noted that the story of **"The Kilikov Trial"** does not contain an express determination of the question of the propriety of the result reached by the judges—the hanging of the tailor. However, it still remains to be examined whether one may infer a certain stance from it. It seems that the hanging of the tailor is portrayed in the story as an act which is abhorrent from the moral point of view. Nevertheless, one cannot ignore a number of details which emerge from the story, which have the effect of emphasizing the dilemma bound up within the issue. In this brief text, Agnon twice asserts that the blacksmith is essential to the welfare of the community: "And indeed a city cannot cope without a blacksmith, who serves the needs of many" and "for the city cannot manage without a blacksmith." Similarly, the final line of the poem that concludes the story reveals that following the hanging of the tailor the "rule of law" strengthened and "thereafter no man shall willfully offend." Accordingly, one may ask the specific question whether ultimately the public good required the hanging of the tailor, as well as the more general question: should an innocent man be killed in order to prevent consequences more serious than his death?[18] That was, for example, the dilemma of Agamemnon: whether to sacrifice his daughter Iphigenia in order to save his ships or whether to refrain from doing so, even at the price of the lives of other people.

The story of **"The Kilikov Trial"** is rife with expressions which direct the reader towards Jewish *Halachic* sources: "A Life for a Life" (*nefesh tachat nefesh*), which is the subtitle of the story, "accident" (*shogeg*), and "malice" (*zadon*). These expressions refer to the same Jewish-cultural sources to which Justice Cheshin alludes in his judgment, the literature of the sages and Biblical sources. However, contrary to the implications emerging from Justice Cheshin's judgment, these sources also do not provide a definitive answer to the questions posed above nor does it resolve the question of the relationship between violations of the rights of an individual and the good of the public. On one hand, there are the Biblical sources which are quoted by Justice Cheshin in his judgment, which proclaim a complete commitment to the principle of personal responsibility—and one should also point out the *Halacha* from the era of the *Mishnah* forbidding the killing of even one Jewish soul to save the lives of many[19]—but alongside these are *Halachic* sources which justify certain deviations from both principles when it becomes necessary for the public good. Thus, the *Talmud* tells of a man who rode on a horse on Saturday in the days of the Greeks, and the court ordered that he be punished by stoning, even though according to the *Halacha* the court could not order a man to be stoned for such an offense. The grounds for the decision were the needs of the hour. The court wished, by means of this extraordinary punishment, to deter and prevent future offences.[20] The *Rambam* (Rabbi Moshe Ben Maimonides) held that on occasion it is permitted to violate the rights of an individual where this is necessary for the public good: "In the same way as a doctor amputates the arm or leg of a person in order that he should live, thus, the court may hold at a certain time that some commandments may be temporarily disobeyed."[21] These examples are indeed not identical to the facts of the story, but they point to a certain ambivalence on the part of Jewish law with regard to the need to injure an individual beyond the requirements of the law, where such an injury is vital to the public good.

Does the ironic dimension of **"The Kilikov Trial"** assist us to identify the definitive determination or position taken on the issue being considered by the story? In my view, the use of irony in **"The Kilikov Trial"** is primarily a way of perceiving the complexities of the situation. This perception includes a criticism concerning the morally problematic nature of the situation being described, but does not advocate a positive stance, such as a stance proclaiming that there is a duty to refrain from hanging the tailor. Thus, it is possible to imagine an ironic description of a situation, which even if perceived to be undesirable or morally outrageous, leaves one no choice but to resign oneself to it, perhaps in accordance with the position of the author who, for example, perceives the human condition as a whole as ironic. In other words, irony does not necessarily propose a definitive operative determination or course of action which conforms to the moral feelings which arise as a result of the ironic description. Indeed, it seems that the story leads to a certain mode of thinking which

nized in every system of law and in every cultured society (hereinafter, "the principle of personal responsibility"). Deviation from this principle, such as that described in the story, violates our sense of justice, and causes us moral outrage.

Agnon's short story awakens and strengthens the rationale underlying the principle of personal responsibility by the use of irony. The expression "praise for Kilikov" in the opening sentences of the story possesses, so it seems, a clear ironic significance, as does the poem concluding the story, and indeed as does the story as a whole. The irony is created by the incongruity between the act (the murder committed by the blacksmith) and the consequences of that act (the hanging of the tailor).[17] This incongruity cries out. To those exposed to it, it gives rise to the feeling that they are witnesses to a moral abomination. This is the "fundamental essence" of the story and the dilemma which lies at its center; the same dilemma which became blurred in the judicial decision in the *J'enimat case*. In this manner, Agnon managed to achieve the result which we often see in the legends and parables of Talmudic sages: the clear and sharp presentation of a complex situation, by means of a brief and sparing sketch.

I have noted that the story of **"The Kilikov Trial"** does not contain an express determination of the question of the propriety of the result reached by the judges—the hanging of the tailor. However, it still remains to be examined whether one may infer a certain stance from it. It seems that the hanging of the tailor is portrayed in the story as an act which is abhorrent from the moral point of view. Nevertheless, one cannot ignore a number of details which emerge from the story, which have the effect of emphasizing the dilemma bound up within the issue. In this brief text, Agnon twice asserts that the blacksmith is essential to the welfare of the community: "And indeed a city cannot cope without a blacksmith, who serves the needs of many" and "for the city cannot manage without a blacksmith." Similarly, the final line of the poem that concludes the story reveals that following the hanging of the tailor the "rule of law" strengthened and "thereafter no man shall willfully offend." Accordingly, one may ask the specific question whether ultimately the public good required the hanging of the tailor, as well as the more general question: should an innocent man be killed in order to prevent consequences more serious than his death?[18] That was, for example, the dilemma of Agamemnon: whether to sacrifice his daughter Iphigenia in order to save his ships or whether to refrain from doing so, even at the price of the lives of other people.

The story of **"The Kilikov Trial"** is rife with expressions which direct the reader towards Jewish *Halachic* sources: "A Life for a Life" (*nefesh tachat nefesh*), which is the subtitle of the story, "accident" (*shogeg*), and "malice" (*zadon*). These expressions refer to the same Jewish-cultural sources to which Justice Cheshin alludes in his judgment, the literature of the sages and Biblical sources. However, contrary to the implications emerging from Justice Cheshin's judgment, these sources also do not provide a definitive answer to the questions posed above nor does it resolve the question of the relationship between violations of the rights of an individual and the good of the public. On one hand, there are the Biblical sources which are quoted by Justice Cheshin in his judgment, which proclaim a complete commitment to the principle of personal responsibility—and one should also point out the *Halacha* from the era of the *Mishnah* forbidding the killing of even one Jewish soul to save the lives of many[19]—but alongside these are *Halachic* sources which justify certain deviations from both principles when it becomes necessary for the public good. Thus, the *Talmud* tells of a man who rode on a horse on Saturday in the days of the Greeks, and the court ordered that he be punished by stoning, even though according to the *Halacha* the court could not order a man to be stoned for such an offense. The grounds for the decision were the needs of the hour. The court wished, by means of this extraordinary punishment, to deter and prevent future offences."[20] The *Rambam* (Rabbi Moshe Ben Maimonides) held that on occasion it is permitted to violate the rights of an individual where this is necessary for the public good: "In the same way as a doctor amputates the arm or leg of a person in order that he should live, thus, the court may hold at a certain time that some commandments may be temporarily disobeyed."[21] These examples are indeed not identical to the facts of the story, but they point to a certain ambivalence on the part of Jewish law with regard to the need to injure an individual beyond the requirements of the law, where such an injury is vital to the public good.

Does the ironic dimension of **"The Kilikov Trial"** assist us to identify the definitive determination or position taken on the issue being considered by the story? In my view, the use of irony in **"The Kilikov Trial"** is primarily a way of perceiving the complexities of the situation. This perception includes a criticism concerning the morally problematic nature of the situation being described, but does not advocate a positive stance, such as a stance proclaiming that there is a duty to refrain from hanging the tailor. Thus, it is possible to imagine an ironic description of a situation, which even if perceived to be undesirable or morally outrageous, leaves one no choice but to resign oneself to it, perhaps in accordance with the position of the author who, for example, perceives the human condition as a whole as ironic. In other words, irony does not necessarily propose a definitive operative determination or course of action which conforms to the moral feelings which arise as a result of the ironic description. Indeed, it seems that the story leads to a certain mode of thinking which

In this context, there is a distinction between "literary" stories and all other stories. When reference is to an artistic, literary text it is clear from the beginning that authors are not required to limit themselves in any way. They are not required to reflect any reality whatsoever and are entitled and permitted to "distort" reality as they wish. Their choices and preferences, their deletions and emphases, and their rhetorical tools are all fitting means which are subject to their free and full personal choice. This is the nature of literary writing. This, in the terminology of Jacques Derrida, is "the lawless law of fiction."[13]

In this context, Dan Miron writes:

> All these stories [the stories which are not literary] being based on selections, "distortions," repressions, and deliberate emphases, the artistic story contains great power in presenting the fundamental essence of the tale and the act of narrative, as all these means of emphases and deletion are part of its declared character, with a right to selection and "arbitrariness" which is embedded in its aesthetic substance.[14]

On this basis, I would like to examine the literary text in comparison with the legal text and consider whether the former is indeed more powerful in presenting the fundamental essence of the story.

IV. THE HANGING OF THE TAILOR IN KILIKOV

The tale of **"The Kilikov Trial"** is primarily constructed from a short and tight factual description of a number of incidents. It does not contain an express determination of the propriety of the result—the hanging of the tailor. In this way it is, of course, distinguishable from the judgment in the *J'enimat case*, which discloses, as is required of every judicial decision, the clear stance of every one of the judges in relation to the question of the demolition of the house. At the same time, this limited story itself emphasizes the essence of the problem with which the judgment is concerned, as well as the dialectic connected with it, in a sharp and powerful manner which is absent from the judgment. Accordingly, from certain points of view, it is more disturbing than the judgment.

Initially, I shall consider some of the linguistic and plot choices in the story. The story tells of an event which took place "once during the Polish wars," not in a Jewish area nor in a Jewish community, but in a Polish community. At the same time, the incident occurred in an area where there was a Jewish community. It is told that the event itself was known to the members of the Jewish community, and one of them, as is pointed out at the conclusion of the story, even composed a poem about it. By means of these choices, the story creates a complex synthesis between elements which are both local and foreign. The result is the positioning of the plot in a dimension which is at one and the same time both near and far. On one hand, it is characterized by a foreignness which enables us to examine the incident in an objective manner, free of inter-communal, religious, cultural, and other contexts; and on the other hand, it is positioned close enough to enable us to accept the story as something conceivable, which is likely to take place even in the community of the storyteller, as a matter which has local significance alongside its foreign significance.

This complexity is also presented in another way. I have mentioned Agnon's choice of a minimalist narrative structure. The story does not refer to the question of the innocence or contributory guilt of the non-Jew who is murdered. The circumstances of the murder are not mentioned. Nothing is said of the character or personality of the murderous blacksmith nor indeed of the tailor hanged in his stead. The story as a whole is free of any hint of emotional or psychological attributes. However, there is a good reason for all these choices: all these details are subordinate to the essence. They are not necessary to the question which arises. On the contrary, had they been mentioned, they would have tended to obscure that question. Similarly, the story does not contain any commentary on the facts being related. The hanging of the tailor is not defined as punishment, nor is it defined as an act which is not punishment. The story merely states that these are the facts. This is what happened in Kilikov. Every woman and man will decide their own position with regard to these facts.

What is left is only the refined narrative, at the center of which stands a man brought to his death by circumstances outside his control. This man is every woman and every man. The innocent tailor, the gentile Pole, could also be a Jewish tailor, or an Arab woman in the village of Zurif.

From one vantage point, the story may be considered part of the long literary tradition which contains satirical descriptions of legal systems, whose purpose is to emphasize the power of law to do wrong or distort, and through which is presented, in the words of Jean-Jacques Lecercle, "an *a contrario* defense of an ideal of judicial fairness and the correct administration of justice."[15]

The satire is directed, *inter alia*, towards ridiculing the mistakes and wrongdoing of society, in order to cause us to react with the appropriate disapproval towards various deviations from proper and desirable norms.[16] Indeed, it seems that in the light of the outrageous reversal of justice in Kilikov, the reader's conviction of the vital importance of the principle *nullum crimen nulla poena* is significantly strengthened. This principle, which means that only the performer of a certain act is subject to punishment, is a fundamental principle recog-

cannot be ignored. Perhaps, looked at broadly and comprehensively, it was right to sacrifice the tailor on the altar of the general good? Can there be situations where it is proper to protect the public at any price, even where the price entails relinquishing moral logic? Agnon demonstrates how hopeless are such questions.[22]

This dialectic, which brings to the fore the problematic nature of the situation and simultaneously points to it as being incapable of being proper land definitively resolved, does not allow us the relative tranquillity achieved by virtue of a legal decision, whether it is a decision such as the one reached by President Barak or a decision such as that of Justice Cheshin. The Agnon story poses the question, with all its force, with all its moral unpleasantness, stripped of any pretense of being directed towards securing the interests of the whole. In the same way, Yoseph Dan comments: "Questions to which the answer is very easy when one talks of national interests, become insoluble when one talks of the fate of an individual."[23] Accordingly, this story—which comes to no conclusion and which from a certain point of view perhaps hints at an inability to reach an absolute, correct conclusion in this type of dilemma—is more disturbing than the judgment.

Paradoxically, the reason for this difference is the influence of the artistic design expressed by the literary text. It is actually this design, which is *prima facie* intended to distance the text from its realistic, down-to-earth dimensions, which transforms the dilemma lying at the heart of the story of **"The Kilikov Trial"** to one which is clear and powerful, and gives it depth and layers which are absent from other texts. It makes us focus on the individual, and it gives that individual's fate depth and meanings that are absent from other kinds of texts. While the legal text "translates" the conflict into several general "closed truths," almost every sentence in Agnon's story opens new directions of thought and considerations. It makes us look at the conflict as a part of a web, which cannot be fully conceived, a web which remains hidden in the judgment. These examples illustrate in a highly expressive and powerful manner the vital character and important function of the literary statement within the context of a legal determination.

V. Conclusion

The issue of the demolition of houses is, in actual fact, a political one. The political situation, which represents the current power relationship equations, makes the legal outcome possible. The judgment gives the issue a legal garment which hides those dimensions. But this pretext is upset by Agnon's short story, which demonstrates how a similar situation is resolved by means of exposed power. Thus, literature reveals the true nature of the conflict, which itself overpowers the ethical and humanistic questions that are inevitably a part of it.

Martha C. Nussbaum explains the manner in which good literature influences us:

> Good literature is disturbing in a way that history and social science writing frequently are not. Because it summons powerful emotions, it disconcerts and puzzles. It inspires distrust of conventional pieties and exacts frequently painful confrontation with one's own thoughts and intentions. One may be told many things about people in one's own society and yet keep that knowledge at a distance. Literary works that promote identification and emotional reaction cut through those self-protective stratagems, requiring us to see and to respond to many things that may be difficult to confront—and they make this process palatable by giving us pleasure in the very act of confrontation."[24]

Possibly, a person who, in certain circumstances, permits the violation of the rights of an individual innocent of any guilt, where he believes that this is required for the good of the whole, stands at the top of a slippery slope. Possibly, one who stands at the top of such a slope cannot help but slide to its depths. Agnon sketches for us the bottom of such a slope. He does not propose a definitive solution to the question of the inevitability of the slide, however; he forces us to look at the slope and consider the significance of the descent to its depths. This perception is the painful confrontation between goals which must be achieved and the moral feelings which stand as an obstacle to their achievement, the confrontation which is hinted at in the words of Nussbaum: the confrontation between the safety of the whole and the rights of an individual, which is left indistinct in the legal text, and exposed in all its sharpness in the artistic text. The internal result of such confrontations, as is demonstrated by the judgment in the *J'enimat case,* is always personal. There are those who will halt at the peak of the slope in the light of this internal confrontation. There are those who will say that there is no choice, and on occasion that we are obliged, even at the tremendous price which was accepted by the judges of Kilikov, to reach the bottom. And there are those who, luckily, will not be required to render a normative and binding judgment in this matter, but will wish to point out to us the sheerness of the slope.

Notes

*I would like to thank the former Deputy President of the Supreme Court of Israel, Haim H. Cohn, who introduced me to the story of "The Kilikov Trial" and was kind enough to share his insights with me during several conversations; thanks are also due to Zipora Kagan and Ariel Bendor for their useful comments on the draft of this article and to Rahel Rimon for translating the story of "The Kilikov Trial."

1. See *Commemorative Volume for Pinhas Rosen,* edited by Haim H. Cohn (13-23).
2. The story was republished in Shmuel Yosef Agnon's *Takhrikh shel sipurim* (196).

3. The Defense (Emergency) Regulations are mandatory legislation valid in the area of Judea and Samaria. What follows are relevant sections from Regulation 119(1): "A Military Commander may by order direct the forfeiture to the Government . . . of any house, structure or land situated in any area, town, village, quarter or street the inhabitants or some of the inhabitants of which he is satisfied have committed, or attempted to commit, or abetted the commission of, or been accessories after the fact to the commission of any offence against these Regulations. . . . And when any house, structure or land is forfeited as aforesaid, the Military Commander may destroy the house or the structure or anything in or on the house, the structure or the land."

4. H.C.J. (High Court of Justice) 2006/97 *Ganimat v. OC Central Command* (hereinafter, the *J'enimat case*). This document has not yet been published.

5. Justice Goldberg, in a judgment comprising only four lines, also refers to the consideration of deterrence, and holds that it is sufficient that it is believed that demolition has a certain deterrent effect in order to preclude interference with the discretion of the Military Commander regarding the necessity for the demolition.

6. Other judgments rendered by the Supreme Court of Israel on this issue include: H.C.J. 4772/91 *Hizran v. Military Commander of Judea and Samaria,* 46(2) P.D. 150; H.C.J. 2722/92 *Alamrin v. Military Commander of the Gaza Strip,* 46(3) P.D. 693; H.C.J. 6026/94 *Nazal v. Military Commander of Judea and Samaria,* 48(5) P.D. 338; and H.C.J. 1730/96 *Sabiah v. Military Commander of Judea and Samaria,* 50(1) P.D. 353.

7. See Dan Miron, *Histaklut be-ravnekher* (276).

8. The place of the narrative and its various functions in legal texts is a subject which in recent years has received considerable attention. See, for example, Richard Delgado's "Story-Telling for Oppositionists and Others: A Plea for Narrative" (*Michigan Law Review,* 1989); David Ray Papke's *Narrative and the Legal Discourse* (1991); Bernard S. Jackson's *Law, Fact, and Narrative Coherence* (1991); Robert Cover's *Narrative, Violence, and the Law* (1992); Gary Minda's *Postmodern Legal Movements* (1995); Robin West's *Narrative, Authority, and the Law* (1993); Ian Ward's *Law and Literature: Possibilities and Perspectives* (1996); Thomas Ross's *Just Stories* (1996); Linda H. LaRue's *Constitutional Law as Fiction: Narrative in the Rhetoric of Authority* (1995); Barry R. Schaller's *A Vision of American Law: Judging Literature and the Stories We Tell* (1997); Shulamit Almog's *Law and Literature, Halacha and Aggadah* (1997); *Law's Stories: Narrative and Rhetoric in the Law,* ed. Peter Brooks and Paul Gerwitz (1996); Bert van Roermund's *Law, Narrative, and Reality* (1997); and Michael Thompson's *Reproducing Narrative* (1998).

9. In his view, Regulation 119 of the Defense (Emergency) Regulations (1945) must be interpreted in accordance with the Basic Law: Human Dignity and Liberty and the values of the State of Israel as a Jewish, free, and democratic State. In the light of this doctrine, he held that the demolition order must be invalidated.

10. It is interesting to note that President Barak does not always refrain from referring to his personal feelings. Thus, for example, in a judgment dealing with the censorship of plays, President Barak includes a description of his difficult experiences as a Jewish child during the Holocaust, and of the impact of these experiences on the shaping of his beliefs with regard to the issues being adjudicated. See H.C.J. 14/86 *Laor v. The Council for the Censorship of Films and Plays,* 41(1) P.D. 421. From this one may conclude that President Barak does not refrain from exposing his feelings in his judgments as part of an overriding policy, but refrains from such exposure or chooses to make use of his feelings as may suit his particular needs in shaping the judgment at hand.

11. Those issues are elaborated in my article, "'The Appellant's Eyes Grew Dim': Between Narrative and Normative," which is forthcoming in *Bar-Ilan Law Studies*.

12. Indeed, there is a contention to the effect that we always reach judgments or decisions on the basis of our personal world-view or communal-cultural context and not only on the basis of the entire body of information which may be gathered in relation to a particular matter. See, for example, the writings of Jerome Frank, especially "The Judging Process and the Judge's Personality" (100-18), from *Law and the Modern Mind* (1930), as well as Frank's *Courts on Trial: Myth and Reality in American Justice* (1950).

13. See Jacques Derrida's "How to Avoid Speaking: Denials" (23).

14. See Miron (276).

15. See Jean-Jacques Lecercle's *Philosophy of Nonsense* (87). Examples of descriptions of this type may be found in Voltaire's *Candide,* Charles Dickens's *Bleak House,* and William Goodwin's *Caleb Williams.*

16. See J. A. Cuddon's *The Penguin Dictionary of Literary Terms and Literary Theory* (828).

17. For the definition of irony in this spirit, see Cuddon (460). This incongruity, which ensues from the reader's reasonable expectations being disturbed, also provides the story with its comic impact.

18. For a description of the philosophical debate in this connection, see Daniel Statman's *Moral Dilemmas* (28-31).

19. *Tosefet Terumah* (7, 23). This example is also cited by Statman, who adds that this rule of law has certain reservations (29).

20. See *Babylonian Talmud, Yebamoth* (2). See also *Yerushalmi, Hagiga* (Chapter 2, Rule 2).

21. *Mishne Torah, Mamrim* (B.D.).

22. Perhaps Agnon acts here as Richard Rorty's "liberal ironist," the person who knows that the question "Is it right to deliver *n* innocents over to be tortured to save the lives of *mXn* other innocents?" and other questions of this kind are unanswerable. See Rorty's *Contingency, Irony, and Solidarity* (xv).

23. See Yoseph Dan's *The Foreigner and the Mandarin* (171).

24. See Nussbaum's *Poetic Justice: The Literary Imagination and Public Life* (7-8).

Works Cited

Agnon, Shmuel Yosef. *Takhrikh shel sipurim.* Jerusalem: Schocken, 1984.

Cohn, Haim H., ed. *Commemorative Volume for Pinhas Rosen.* Jerusalem: Students Union of the Hebrew University Publishing House, 1962.

Cuddon, J. A. *The Penguin Dictionary of Literary Terms and Literary Theory.* 3rd ed. London: Penguin, 1992.

Dan, Yoseph. *The Foreigner and the Mandarin.* Masada: Ramat-Gan, 1975.

Derrida, Jacques. "How to Avoid Speaking: Denials." *Languages of the Unsayable: The Play of Negativity in Literature and Literary Theory.* Ed. Sanford Budick and Wolfgang Iser. New York: Columbia UP, 1989. 3-70.

Frank, Jerome. *Courts on Trial: Myth and Reality in American Justice.* 1950. New York: Atheneum, 1967.

———. *Law and the Modern Mind.* 1930. Garden City: Doubleday, 1963.

Lecercle, Jean-Jacques. *Philosophy of Nonsense: The Intuitions of Victorian Nonsense Literature.* London: Routledge, 1994.

Miron, Dan. *Histaklut be-ravnekher.* Tel Aviv: ha-Kibuts ha-me'uha, 1996.

Nussbaum, Martha C. *Poetic Justice: The Literary Imagination and Public Life.* Boston: Beacon, 1995.

Statman, Daniel. *Moral Dilemmas.* Atlanta: Rodopi, 1995.

David G. Roskies (essay date 2003)

SOURCE: Roskies, David G. "Essay on 'The Sense of Smell'." In *Reading Hebrew Literature,* edited by Alan Mintz, pp. 118-25. Hanover, N.H.: Brandeis University Press, 2003.

[*In the following essay from a collection which offers several commentaries about specific works of Hebrew literature, Roskies discusses the complexities of an Agnon short story, "The Sense of Smell."*]

Despite its brevity, Agnon's **"The Sense of Smell"** combines disparate elements that are not easily reconciled. The story's homiletic structure, storybook headings, archaic style, and anecdotal plot, and its coincidental encounters, dream sequence, and moment of mystical reverie bespeak a world of all-too-perfect harmony. Yet the narrative is riddled with riddles. Is the writer/protagonist a pious raconteur or a misanthrope? Does not the closed and self-referential world of Torah study, with its obsessive search for authority, clash with the solipsism of the artist, who lives in the subjective realm of the senses? The sukkah, furthermore, is both lowly and sublime; the "sense of smell" of the story's title implies a sensibility at once neotraditional and radically innovative. Having lavished so much attention upon the wording of a single phrase chosen, almost erased, and ultimately validated, what is Agnon trying to say about the relationship between writing as a craft and writing as a religious calling?

[1]

To begin with, the linguistic medium would seem to be the story's manifest message. Just as the homiletic style of chapters 1 through 3 avoids all signs of modernity, the message is resolutely antisecular. Hebrew cannot be confused with any other national language. It is *leshon hakodesh,* the language that predates Creation and that will usher in the messianic age. It is the vehicle of past, present, and future; of the Torah; the Holy One, blessed be He; the angels and seraphim; the people Israel; of Jacob, the exiles, the mourners of Zion, the Messiah. It is the language of prayer, the language that God most longs to hear; the language of Song of Songs, in which God sings the praises of His people, Israel; and the language of the Psalms, in which Jews seek solace through their long night of exile.

This is vintage Agnon, just the kind of densely allusive, sermonlike preamble that he made famous with **"Agunot,"** his signature story of 1908. For the narrator is convinced that we live in an age of stammerers and skeptics. His opening homily is a preemptive strike, a polemic against all those who deride the revival of Hebrew as a spoken language; who fail to master even the rudiments of the holy tongue; who revert to writing in the languages of exile; who "put worldly matters first and words of Torah second." "If [scholars] would make Torah their basis," the narrator proclaims, "the Torah would come to their aid." *She'ilu 'asu hatorah 'ikkar haytah hatorah mesay'atam.* Indeed, this extravagant credo is borne out by story's end: the Torah will literally come to the author's aid. But not before he pulls out all the stops. So holy is the holy tongue, he polemicizes at the end of chapter 2, that it overrides even the wickedness of the worst Gentile. To wit, Balaam, whose most extreme act of betrayal was forgiven on account of his immortal Hebrew words in praise of Israel, *ma tovu ohalekha Ya'akov.* For this one poem, he merited having a Torah portion named after him and having the morning prayers open with his words.

Never mind that the Balaam of folk memory flies in the face of this seemingly irrefutable proof; that, quite to the contrary, when you teach someone a lesson, *lernt men mit im Bolok,* you teach him "the Torah portion Balak". Never mind that the man who colluded in the downfall of 158,600 men of Israel should be forgiven and immortalized simply because he uttered his prophetic words in Hebrew. And never mind that, looking ahead to the Middle Ages, some of the great Jewish sages composed their works not in Hebrew but in Arabic. The narrator has this to say in rebuttal: These works (the *Kuzari*? the *Guide for the Perplexed*?) were but pabulum for babies! Besides, there is divine reason for the choice of Arabic. The Holy Land has been entrusted to Arab hands by God, until such time as God returns it to the Jewish exiles.

So what began as an exalted invocation of the cosmic merits of the holy tongue has ended with a rearguard, rednecked attack on:

1] Jewish scholars who refuse to master their ancient tongue;

2] the culture of the Gentiles;

3] the Golden Age of Spanish Jewry;

4] the attempt to liberate Palestine by political means; and

5] the whole secular enterprise.

Meanwhile, the lyrical tone of chapter 1, with its seductive and seamless rhetorical structure, has given way to the strident rhetoric of intellectual debate: *shema yomar . . . kol ha'omer ken . . . kol sheken . . . umipnei mah . . . mipnei she . . . teda'lekha sheken . . . shema tomar . . . lefikhakh . . . veshoneh . . . velamah.* The narrator signals a further shift in tone in chapter 3, as he turns his attention inward, to his own state of exile. *Me'ahavat leshonenu umihibbat hakodesh ani mashhir panai 'al divre torah umar'iv 'atsmi 'al divrei hakhamim umeshamram bevitni kdei sheyakhonu yahdav 'al sfatai.* Not a Levite is he, officiating at the Temple among his singing brothers, but a lone Nazirite, on a self-imposed diet of Torah and the words of our sages. He lives in spatial and spiritual exile. Anne Hoffman calls this section Agnon's "imaginative geography," reading "sukkah" of the author's parable not as "lowly hut," but as "sanctuary," the word that houses.[1] This may be true in retrospect; but at this point in our reading, what we hear is a litany of loss: the solitary study of Torah replaces the communal singing of psalms; the living word is replaced by *zikhron devarim*; the resplendent house of God is replaced by a makeshift hut; and the ultimate expression of loss is the writing of *sippurei ma'asiyot,* mere *mayselekh* that tell obsessively of a world that is no more.

Thus, the first three chapters form a kind of triptych: praise, polemic, and lament. Since the diction and cadence remain so firmly rooted in traditional discourse, the shift to the first-person singular in chapter 3 is almost imperceptible. The craft of writing is here depicted as a tragic surrogate for the exalted Levitical calling, yet so long as the storyteller can on occasion construct a lowly sukkah, fiction still partakes of the same universe of faith and meaning that was once the preserve of the Temple brotherhood. As a Nazir, furthermore, dedicated solely to the preservation of the holy tongue and feeding exclusively off words of Torah, the narrator must honor and preserve each and every word.

How brutal, then, the fall from even this demoted status, when the narrator is forced from his solitary ministrations by a public accusation on the part of an unnamed grammarian. To make matters worse, the narrator is described in the chapter heading as a mere *mehabber,* or "author," no better than his opponent, who challenges him on the most hallowed ground, the aforementioned sukkah. Can one speak of a sukkah "smelling"? Not much to hook a story on, much less, a quest narrative. But a quest it becomes, "mock heroic" perhaps, but a quest nonetheless. And here we see the narrator at his most misanthropic. He is radically mistrustful of *sifrei shimush,* the tools of modern scholarship, as he is of the scholars themselves, who "know everything except that particular thing you are looking for." And he finds no answer even among his fellow Jerusalemites, native speakers of Hebrew, because each is motivated solely by ego and personal whim. Just as he is about to erase the offending word, however, the sukkah itself miraculously intervenes, its aromatic smells validating the narrator's linguistic usage.

What this last episode means is never explained, and is anyway superseded by an even greater miracle, announced in the heading of chapter 5: "The Righteous from Paradise Come to the Author's Aid." What has the narrator done to warrant such a miracle? He has gone out of his way to honor a descendant of Rabbi Jacob of Lissa. He has also engaged a scholar in dialogue, in the course of which he has praised the Sage of Lissa for the exceptionally useful prayer book that he had compiled. The narrator then falls into a sweet slumber and is visited by the sage himself, who holds the aforementioned siddur in his hands. Dream merges with reality when the narrator awakens, consults his own copy of the prayer book, and rediscovers in its pages the very words he has been seeking. Searching through another sacred tome, he finds additional linguistic proof. He ends the chapter with sweet thoughts of revenge.

Properly, the quest is over. All told, the author has found textual validation in three separate sources, and his credo, "If scholars would make Torah their basis, the Torah would come to their aid" has been borne out in fact. What's more, the quest has taken him out of his glorious isolation and allowed for meaningful interactions on a social and trans-temporal plane. Hoffman calls the dream sequence "something of a family romance," in which the narrator discovers kinship not in life, but in texts, the dream suggesting a community "where, ultimately, it is language that joins together sages of the past and the figure of the writer" (119-20). Again, paraphrasing Hoffman, the sage instructs his progeny that true innovation through the Torah means discovering what is already there, already written, already read, already copied.

The author makes much of the fact that he was able to identify the face of the sage in his dream; this, despite the absence of any known pictures and despite the well-known rule that "the great among Israel just don't look like their relatives, because their Torah gives their faces a special glow." What was so special about the Sage of Lissa's Torah? "Our holy rabbis have left us lots of prayer books," the narrator had said earlier, "filled with directions and commentaries both hidden and revealed, with matters grammatical or sagacious, with permutations of letters, secrets, and allegories, all to arouse the hearts of worshipers as they enter the King's palace." Yet none could match the prayer book of the Sage of Lissa for usefulness. None but he had made himself a true servant of the Torah, or had written "in such an accessible way." Does this not suggest an elective affinity between him and the dweller in a mere sukkah, a match for any man in scholarship, who nonetheless stooped to conquer in order to produce accessible stories of supreme usefulness?

If the true sage and he are revealed to be *mishpokhe*, members of a select brotherhood who "darken their faces over study of Torah," then why the reverie at daybreak, the pious recitation of psalms, and the discovery of a fourth and final proof, in Rashi's commentary? The Torah has already come to his aid. The anal grammarian has already been vanquished. Why the repetition? Why isn't the Sage of Lissa a good enough *yikhes*? Because Rashi's intervention comes against the backdrop of something new, the intrusion of real smells and real sounds emanating from a particular natural landscape. Whatever happened before, when a sukkah came and its aroma rose before him until he really saw that it was smelling, what happens now is acutely sensory and sensual.

Yet this most personal, overtly autobiographical, moment in the story is also the most intertextual. In a scene reminiscent of Bialik's "Hamatmid," the scholar is seated indoors poring over a sacred tome while nature beckons outdoors. Recalling an episode in the *Tales of Nahman of Bratslav*, he hears birds singing exquisite melodies to one another. And in the language of the Song of Songs, the same passage, in fact, with which he began the story, the voice of the second bird "was just sweeter than the other bird's"; *vehayah kolah 'arev mikolah shel ḥavertah*, and together, the two birds "sang new songs, the likes of which no ear had ever heard." Pretending not to hear, the author sets their singing to the words of Psalm 45, the Psalm for the Chief Musician upon Lilies, and although he identified this psalm earlier as "a song of praise of the sages' disciples, those who are soft as lilies and pleasant as lilies," it is clear that he is reading the words as he has never read them before, nonmetaphorically, and in a way unsanctioned by tradition. That is when Rashi comes to the rescue, and glosses the words *kol bigdotekha* (45:9) in two different ways: contextually, as "all thy garments smell like fragrant spices," and midrashically, as "all your betrayals and foul deeds will be forgiven and will smell sweet before me." Whereupon the sukkah reappears in all its aromatic glory, and his mind is eased "like a person smelling flowers that smell."

On the manifest, homiletic, plane, one that is clearly privileged from beginning to end, the author is rescued by the Torah. On a psychological plane, he is rescued by his own sense of smell. Alongside the ideal portrait of the Torah scholar, modeled by Jacob of Lissa, who, for all his relative obscurity, had served his flock so much better than any other scholar, there is the real portrait of the contemporary Hebrew writer, living in a diminished world, at odds with his surroundings, reduced to writing *mayselekh* in an embattled language.

Why did Agnon write this story? Why did he write it in 1937? Why, sitting in Talpiot, Jerusalem, did he prefer the company of the sages long since dead? How credible is it that one sense of smell does not subvert, betray, the other?

[2]

Agnon is the master of what Bakhtin calls the "double-voiced utterance." Agnon appropriates the utterance of another as the utterance of another and uses it for his own purposes. His stylized tales are designed to be interpreted as the utterances of two speakers. The audience hears in a version of the original utterance the collective voice of the Jewish past and a second, contemporary, speaker's evaluation of that utterance. Left to their own devices, the two speakers would be in essential agreement, so that the success of the stylization would derive from the utterances of the second speaker corroborating the utterances of the first. The narrator functions here as a latter-day scribe, a *sofer stam*, as is the case in such late works as *'Ir umlo'ah*. Devoid of inner tension, these stories are eminently forgettable.

Not so **"The Sense of Smell."** Here, the first utterance, the collective voice of the past, is under attack. Its whole authority and semantic position are being questioned. This is why the writer must up the ante and pre-empt his attackers with a tour de force in praise of the holy tongue. Conscious throughout of an audience for whom Hebrew is neither holy nor viable, the speaker of the second utterance objectifies, personifies, hallows the first utterance in every way conceivable: through lyrical, polemical, tragic, and mock-heroic passages. The ultimate purpose of his discourse is not self-validation, not the quest, but the revival of the authority and vitality of the first utterance. If Rashi can speak to the present, then the present can speak through the past.

Hebrew, in Agnon's scheme, becomes the language of polyphony. The real enemy, therefore, is the grammarian, who insists upon using Hebrew monologically: one word, one meaning. God forbid that the revival of Hebrew as a living language be entrusted to people like him! If truth is dialogic, then Hebrew is the one true language. Note that Hebrew precedes Creation, precedes God, as it were, thus freeing the text of Torah for dialogue, commentary, agreement, and disagreement. Why, even the author, for all his erudition, doesn't understand everything he reads in Scripture! Agnon displays his genius by conjuring up a dialogue that works vertically instead of horizontally. On the horizontal plane of politics, society, and academic scholarship, language is debased and monologic. Only when one gives voice to the past, crediting each individual utterance and its author, recognizing that author's unique face, does Hebrew regain its openendedness, its unfinalizability, its cosmic potential. Each recaptured utterance, moreover, rests upon an ethical event, upon the author / hero owning, or signing an act: praying, studying, helping a stranger, talking words of Torah with another scholar. In this way, *leshon hakodesh* becomes both the vehicle and tenor of true dialogue.

How does individual creativity enter into the system of sanctioned dialogue? Creativity begins when one feels at home in the world of the past. Creativity is predicated upon mobilizing the whole personality. Creativity comes when the recitation of the received words is accompanied by something unexpected, a birdsong unlike any that was ever sung. Creativity begins when nature comes to the rescue of culture, when the utterance beyond space enters into dialogue with the utterance beyond time.

[3]

Agnon's best stories are not stylizations at all. They are a species of "creative betrayal." As such, they belong in the mainstream of Jewish literary history, midway between Der Nister and I. B. Singer.[2] Agnon shares Der Nister's sense of election. The artist is a Nazir, who dedicates his life to the service of his craft. The measure of his self-discipline is the distance between mundane, profane speech and the carefully wrought language of his literary art. The plot is always the tale of a symbolic quest, undertaken by a lone hero who meets with many obstacles. Both writers swore allegiance to Reb Nahman. Both came of age in the heady atmosphere of Weimar Germany.

Even if there were no genetic link between them, both Der Nister and Agnon arrived at the art of creative betrayal via the same three-act drama of rebellion, loss, and negotiated return. In Agnon's case, each act played itself out in and through a different setting.

Act 1, the rebellion, as a member of the Second Aliyah.

Act 2, when he experienced the profound loss of Buczacz and all that it stood for.

Act 3, the negotiated return to the severed past, during Agnon's sojourn in Weimar Germany.

Creative betrayal was the art of triage, the art of rescuing what little could still be saved in an age of skepticism, fragmentation, and gross materialism: archaic language, storytelling, the figure of the sage. Creative betrayal was an artistic bulwark against national despair. What else could a Hebrew writer hold out to his audience in 1937, at the height of the Arab revolt, and against the rising specter of Hitler and Stalin? A little sukkah, and nothing more.

But the strength of creative betrayal lay in the very combination of its disparate strands: rebellion and retrieval, nature and culture, the sensual present and the spiritual past. When the Agnon narrator says, "There is nothing especially wondrous or praiseworthy about this," you know that something extraordinary has just happened. His coy modesty at story's end just about gives the game away, "because the psalm played itself like an instrument of many strings. A Song of Love, next to which all other songs are as nothing." This is a song that can be heard only by someone who has returned to the study house of Buczacz via the cultural revolution of Tel Aviv/Jaffo. This is a song rooted as much in the senses of the beholder as in the language of psalms.

And lest there be any doubt about this, Rashi himself comes out of the Academy on High in the Garden of Eden and explicates the key passage: *bigdotekha* from the root *bgd* means "thy garments," but it can also mean "your betrayals," from the word *begidah*. Like the art of creative betrayal, derived from the Hebrew *begidah yotseret,* the art of creative recloaking is preceded by the act of betrayal. Agnon, perhaps the greatest of the born-again storytellers, has written a fantasy about a writer, all of whose betrayals and foul deeds were forgiven, and who, in the midst of his anger, isolation, and despair, was granted a miracle: the early morning breezes, the sweet fragrances, and the birdsong emanating from his own garden suddenly endowed the language of Creation with new meaning and gave new promise to the language of redemption.

Notes

1. Anne Golomb Hoffman, *Between Exile and Return: S. Y. Agnon and the Drama of Writing* (Albany: SUNY Press, 1991), 117.

2. See David G. Roskies, *A Bridge of Longing: The Lost Art of Yiddish Storytelling* (Cambridge, Mass.: Harvard University Press, 1995).

FURTHER READING

Biographies

Goldberg, Isaac. "Shmuel Yosef Agnon: Israel's Nobel Laureate." *AB Bookman's Weekly* 87 (April 1 1991): 1267.
    Brief overview of Agnon's life and work.

Lutske, Harvey. "S. Y. Agnon." In *History in Their Hands: A Book of Jewish Autographs,* pp. 173-74. Northvale, N.J.: Jason Aronson Inc., 1996.
    Brief sketch about Agnon.

Criticism

Aberbach, David. *At the Handles of the Lock: Themes in the Fiction of S. Y. Agnon.* New York: Oxford University Press, 1984, 221 p.
    A study of themes in Agnon's fiction, emphasizing the blurring of distinctions among author, narrator, and character.

Almog, Shulamit. "Literary Legal Utopias—Alexander's Visit to Kasiah and Law at the End of Days." *Utopian Studies* 12, no. 2 (2001): 164-173.
    Comparison between an ancient legend about Alexander the Great and a short story by Agnon, indicating that the idea of a utopia is not inherently lawless.

Alter, Robert. "On S. Y. Agnon." *Commentary* 56 (fall, 1989): 619-30.
    Discusses Agnon's unfinished novel, Shira, as a commentary on the role of art in relation to reality.

Bar-Adon, Aaron. "S. Y. Agnon and the Revival of Modern Hebrew." *Texas Studies in Literature and Language* 14 (1973): 147-75.
    A study of Agnon's importance to the renewed interest in modern Hebrew.

Baumgarten, Murray. "Mirror of Words: Language in Agnon and Borges." *Comparative Literature* 31, no. 4 (fall 1979): 351-66.
    Compares the works of Agnon and Jorge Luis Borges, with emphasis on each author's theories of and uses of language.

Ben-Dov, Nitza. *Agnon's Art of Indirection: Uncovering Latent Content in the Fiction of S. Y. Agnon.* Leiden, The Netherlands: E. J. Brill, 1993, 167 p.
    Study of hidden meanings in Agnon's fiction.

Bodoff, Lippman. "Kabbalistic Feminism in Agnon's *Betrothed.*" *Judaism* 42 (fall, 1993): 423-37.
    A look at the ways Agnon uses kabbalistic themes in his portrayal of Jewish women.

Fisch, Harold. "The Dreaming Narrator in S. Y. Agnon." *Novel: A Forum on Fiction* 4 (1970): 49-68.
    Lengthy article about the role of the narrator in Agnon's fiction.

Fleck, Jeffrey. "Fiction, Fable, and the Face of a Generation: S. Y. Agnon's *Only Yesterday.*" *Hebrew Annual Review* 7 (1983): 69-88.
    Discusses Only Yesterday and its portrayal of conflicts between tradition and modernity, as well as the dialectic between history and symbol, in postwar Palestine.

Green, Sharon. *Not a Simple Story: Love and Politics in a Modern Hebrew Novel.* Lanham, Maryland: Lexington Books, 2001, 167 p.
    Study of the manifestations and frustrations of love relationships in Agnon's fiction.

Greenstein, Michael. "Breaking the Mosaic Code: Jewish Literature vs. the Law." *Mosaic* 27 (September 1994): 87-106.

    A discussion of the ways several Jewish writers, such as Agnon, Sigmund Freud, Walter Benjamin, and Saul Bellow, both embrace and undermine Jewish law.

Hoffman, Anne Golomb. "Agnon for All Seasons: Recent Trends in Criticism." *Prooftexts* 11, no. 1 (January 1991): 80-94.

    Summarizes the wealth of Agnon criticism which appeared from the 1970s through the late 1980s.

———. "Topographies of Reading: Agnon through Benjamin." *Prooftexts* 21, no. 1 (winter 2001): 71-89.

    Reader-response criticism emphasizing the "topographies" each reader brings to the text, with emphasis on several Agnon novels.

Hoshen, Dalia. "Midrash and the Writing of Agnon." *Review of Rabbinic Judaism* 5, no. 3 (October 2002): 332-66.

    Detailed treatment of Judaism in the works of Agnon, the tension between skepticism and faith, the link with midrashic literature, and Agnon's style of writing.

Katsman, Roman. *The Time of Cruel Miracles: Mythopoesis in Dostoesvky and Agnon.* Frankfurt am Main, Germany: P. Lang, 2002, 236 p.

    Study of the use of myth in Dostoevsky and Agnon.

Katz, Stephen. *The Centrifugal Novel: S. Y. Agnon's Poetics of Composition.* Madison, N.J.: Fairleigh Dickinson University Press, 1999, 219 p.

    Study of the multi-level texts used in the composition of three Agnon works.

Mazor, Yair. *The Triple Cord, Agnon, Hamsun Strindberg: Where Scandinavian and Hebrew Literature Meet,* Tel Aviv, Israel: Papyrus, 1987, 250 p.

    Study of supposed Scandinavian influences on Agnon's writing.

Parfitt, Tudor. "Agnon and Germany." In *The Great Transition: The Recovery of the Lost Centers of Modern Hebrew Literature,* edited by Glenda Abramson and Parfitt, p. 176. Totowa, N.J.: Rowman, 1985.

    An examination of Agnon's relationship to German culture, with particular attention to his novel *Ad Heinah.*

Shaked, Gershon. *Shmuel Yosef Agnon: A Revolutionary Traditionalist,* translated by Jeffrey M. Green. New York: New York University Press, 1989, 293 p.

    Examines Agnon as a "modern" writer whose unique literary forms expressed the conflict between tradition and the anarchy created by contemporary life. Includes a bibliography of Hebrew works, translated works, and criticism in Hebrew, English, and German.

Weiss, Hillel. "Analytic Index for the Complete Works of Agnon: A Scholarly Tool in Preparation." *Literary and Linguistic Computing: Journal of the Association for Literary and Linguistic Computing* 4, no. 3 (1989): 169-173.

    Discussion of the application of the Poetic Linguistic and Analytic Index (PLAI) to the works of Agnon.

Weizman, Elda. "Building True Understanding via Apparent Miscommunication: A Case Study." *Journal of Pragmatics* 31, no. 6 (June 1999): 837-46.

    Study of the treatment of misunderstanding in *A Simple Story.*

Werses, Samuel. *Relations between Jews and Poles in S. Y. Agnon's Work.* Jerusalem, Israel: Magnes Press, Hebrew University, 1994, 128 p.

    Study of the ways Agnon treats Polish Jews in his fiction.

Additional information on Agnon's life and career is published in the following sources by the Gale Group: *Contemporary Authors,* **Vols. 17-18;** *Contemporary Authors New Revision Series,* **Vols. 60, 102;** *Contemporary Authors—Obituary,* **Vols. 25-28R;** *Contemporary Authors Permanent Series,* **Vol. 2;** *Contemporary Literary Criticism,* **Vols. 4, 8, 14;** *Encyclopedia of World Literature in the 20th Century,* **Ed. 3;** *Literature Resource Center;* *Major 20th-Century Writers,* **Eds. 1, 2;** *Reference Guide to Short Fiction,* **Ed. 2;** *Reference Guide to World Literature,* **Eds. 2, 3; and** *Short Story Criticism,* **Vol. 30.**

James Dickey
1923-1997

(Full name James Lafayette Dickey) American poet, novelist, critic, essayist, scriptwriter, and author of children's books.

INTRODUCTION

A prominent figure in contemporary American literature, Dickey is best known for his intense exploration of the primal, irrational, creative, and ordering forces in life. Often classified as a visionary Romantic in the tradition of Walt Whitman, Dylan Thomas, and Theodore Roethke, Dickey emphasized the primacy of imagination and examined the relationship between humanity and nature. He frequently described confrontations in war, sports, and nature as a means for probing violence, mortality, creativity, and social values. In his poetry, Dickey rejected formalism, artifice, and confession, favoring instead a narrative mode that features energetic rhythms and charged emotions.

BIOGRAPHICAL INFORMATION

Dickey was born February 2, 1923, in the Atlanta suburb of Buckhead. In 1942 he attended Clemson College, but left to enlist in the U.S. Army Air Corps. During World War II, he logged nearly 500 combat hours, serving in the South Pacific. After the war, Dickey attended Vanderbilt University, graduating with his B.A. in 1949, and earning his M.A. in 1950. In 1956 Dickey, then a successful advertising copywriter and executive, cultivated a friendship with Ezra Pound, whose essays on poetry were to have a considerable influence on Dickey's image-centered approach to poetry. During the 1960s, Dickey won wide acclaim and several major literary awards for his poetry. He also was appointed Consultant in Poetry to the Library of Congress. He continued to be active during the 1980s and 1990s, teaching until five days before his death January 19, 1997.

MAJOR WORKS

Dickey's poetry was often inspired by crucial events in his own life. His early poetry, for example, is infused with guilt over his role as a fighter pilot in World War II and the Korean War, ruminations on his older brother's death, and reflections upon his Southern heritage. In his first three volumes of verse—*Into the Stone and Other Poems* (1960), *Drowning with Others* (1962), and *Helmets* (1964)—Dickey explores such topics as war, family, love, death, spiritual rebirth, nature, and survival. These poems are generally arranged in traditional stanzaic units and are marked by an expansive tone. These volumes also contain several poems about the wilderness in which Dickey stresses the importance of maintaining the primal physical and imaginative powers that he believes are suppressed by civilization. *Buckdancer's Choice* (1965), which won a National Book Award, signaled a shift in Dickey's verse to freer, more complex forms. Employing internal monologues, varied spacing between words and phrases in place of punctuation, and subtler rhythms, *Buckdancer's Choice* investigates human suffering in its myriad forms.

Throughout his later poetry, Dickey laments the loss of youth, expresses a profound fear of mortality, and explores visionary qualities and creative energies. This verse evidences a more self-reflexive voice and an increasingly restrained, meditative style. He also began to employ what he termed "country surrealism," a technique by which he obscures distinctions between dreams and reality to accommodate the irrational. For example, "The Zodiac" is a long, self-referential poem about an intensely visionary alcoholic artist who has difficulty distinguishing between illusion and reality. The title poem of *The Strength of the Fields* (1979), which Dickey read at Jimmy Carter's presidential inauguration, affirms faith in humanity while addressing various human dilemmas.

In *Deliverance* (1970), which was adapted into an acclaimed film, Dickey reiterates several themes prevalent in his verse, primarily the rejuvenation of human life through interaction with nature. The novel describes four suburban men who seek diversion from their unfulfilling lives by canoeing down a remote and dangerous river. They encounter natural threats and human violence, forcing them to rely on primitive instincts in order to survive. Dickey's second novel, *Alnilam* (1987), is an ambitious, experimental work centering on a blind man's attempts to uncover the mysterious circumstances of his son's death. His last novel, *To the White Sea* (1993), is the story of a seemingly sociopathic soldier forced to parachute into Japan during World War II. In addition to his writing, Dickey also is an esteemed poetry critic. In such volumes of essays and journals as *Babel to Byzantium* (1968), *Self-Interviews* (1970), *Sorties* (1971), and *Crux* (1999), he offers subjective viewpoints of poetry and asserts his preference for artistic intensity and intuition.

CRITICAL RECEPTION

Dickey is considered one of the major figures in American literature during the latter half of the twentieth century. Lauded as a significant American poet, he might be the most frequently discussed poet of his generation. Much has been written about Dickey's controversial public persona and pursuit of celebrity, and the ways in which his legendary personality affected his work and literary reputation. The role of his Southern heritage is also a rich area of critical discussion, as several reviewers have explored Dickey's place within the pantheon of Southern poets. Another area of debate has been Dickey's interest in primitivism, the concept that civilized man should maintain contact with nature, sensations, and primal impulses often suppressed by modern society. This theme was viewed as a recurring one in Dickey's oeuvre and was embodied in the best-selling novel, *Deliverance*.

PRINCIPAL WORKS

Into the Stone, and Other Poems (poetry) 1960
Drowning with Others (poetry) 1962
Helmets (poetry) 1964
The Suspect in Poetry (criticism) 1964
Two Poems of the Air (poetry) 1964
Buckdancer's Choice (poetry) 1965
Babel to Byzantium: Poets and Poetry Now (criticism) 1968
Poems, 1957-1967 (poetry) 1968
Deliverance (novel) 1970
The Eye-Beaters, Blood, Victory, Madness, Buckhead, and Mercy (poetry) 1970
Self-Interviews (monologues) 1970
Sorties: Journals and New Essays (essays) 1971
Tucky the Hunter (children's poetry) 1978
The Strength of Fields (poetry) 1979
Scion (poetry) 1980
Falling, May Day Sermon, and Other Poems (poetry) 1981
Puella (poetry) 1982
The Central Motion (poetry) 1983
Night Hurdling: Poems, Essays, Conversations, Commencements, and Afterwords (poetry, essays, and interviews) 1983
Alnilam (novel) 1987
The Eagle's Mile (poetry) 1990
The Whole Motion: Collected Poems, 1945-1992 (poetry) 1992
To the White Sea (novel) 1993
Striking In: The Early Notebooks of James Dickey (notebooks) 1996
James Dickey: Selected Poems (poetry) 1998
Crux: The Letters of James Dickey (correspondence) 1999
The James Dickey Reader (poetry, essays, monologues, and criticism) 1999

CRITICISM

Wendell Berry (review date November 1964)

SOURCE: Berry, Wendell. "James Dickey's New Book." *Poetry* 105 (November 1964): 130-31.

[*In the following review, Berry describes some of the poems in* Helmets *as clumsy and mechanical.*]

Going into this book [*Helmets*] is like going into an experience in your own life that you know will change your mind. You either go in willing to let it happen, or you stay out. There are a lot of good poems here. **"The Dusk of Horses," "Fence Wire," "Cherrylog Road," "The Scarred Girl," "The Ice Skin, Drinking from a Helmet,"** and **"Bums, on Waking"** aren't the only poems I thought moving and good, but they are the ones I keep the firmest, clearest memory of.

Thinking just of the poems I've named, I realize to what an extent sympathy is the burden of this book, how much there is of seeing into the life of beings other than the poet. The reader is moved imaginatively and sympathetically into the minds of horses at nightfall, of farmer and animals divided and held together by fences, of a young girl scarred in a wreck, of bums waking up in places they never intended to come to.

"Drinking from a Helmet" represents not the fact of sympathy, but the making of it. The poet moves from his own isolated experience of war into an almost mystical realization (and assumption) of the life of the dead soldier from whose helmet he drinks. A tense balance is held between the felt bigness of the war and the experience of the one young man.

"Cherrylog Road" is a funny, poignant, garrulous poem about making love in a junk yard. It surely owes a great deal to the country art of storytelling. It's a poem you want to read out loud to somebody else, and it's best and most enjoyable when you do.

But I think that Mr. Dickey is also capable of much less than his best. There are poems that seem to have been produced by the over-straining of method, ground out in accordance with what the poet has come to expect he'll do in a given situation. **"Springer Mountain"** will illustrate what I mean. The poem tells about a hunter who, on impulse, pulls off his clothes and starts running after a deer. I can't help believing that the power of insight and feeling that is the *being* of a poem like **"The Dusk of Horses"** becomes *equipment* in **"Springer Mountain."** The poet seems to be using capabilities developed elsewhere, and to be using them deliberately and mechanically. The hunter's gesture, or transport or whatever it is, seems to have been *made* to happen, and isn't seen with enough humor to mitigate its inherent silliness and clumsiness. After a good many readings I don't yet feel I know how it is meant or what it means. And more than that, I have no faith in it, no belief that anybody ever did any such thing. It's like watching a magician's act that, in spite of a certain brilliance, remains flatly incredible.

Usually involved in the weakness of the weaker poems is a dependence on a galloping monotonous line-rhythm (nine syllables, three or four stressed, five or six unstressed, the last unstressed) that can be both dulling and aggravating. The point isn't that this happens, but that it happens often. And when it happens it acts as a kind of fence, on the opposite sides of which the poem and the reader either give each other up or, worse, go on out of duty.

But I want to end by turning back to the goodness of the book. There are poems here of such life that you don't believe they're possible until you read them the second time, and I've got no bone to pick with them.

William C. Strange (essay date fall-winter 1965-1966)

SOURCE: Strange, William C. "To Dream, To Remember: James Dickey's *Buckdancer's Choice*." *Northwest Review* 7, no. 2 (fall-winter 1965-1966): 33-42.

[*In the following essay, Strange identifies dream and memory as the main thematic concerns of the poems comprising* Buckdancer's Choice.]

Dream, memory, and poem are an ancient knot in a web of tempting correspondencies: image and event, possibility and necessity, wish and commandment, future and past. At one time or another and in various measure, all of these pairs have been used to explain that tense presence which is a poem, and they are still useful, permitting one to describe handily the tendency of modern poetry as a shift from memory and its coordinates to dream. Of course, there are exceptions. Old Ovid seems a poet of the dream while David Jones clearly writes for us out of a remarkable memory. Still, our time is distinguished by poet-theorists such as André Breton, who talks of "*l'homme, ce rêveur définitif*," and we support with our prizes the *Seventy-seven Dream Songs* of John Berryman. And when the drift of western poetry is seen in large perspective, as the pitch of its weight slips from heroic to lyric, then its direction is unmistakable. The Greeks called memory the mother of poetry; we moderns know a deep well of the unremembered where poetry and dreams are born.

James Dickey's most recent book, **Buckdancer's Choice,** stands out sharply in this context as a collection of modern poems in which one can feel both the lure of dream and the thrust of memory. In single poems and in the ordering of the whole, it displays a breadth of concern and a balance of energies that are notable in themselves and full of promise for the future.

Most simply, **Buckdancer's Choice** can be sorted into one set of recognizably modern poems that are dreams in fact or in technique and another set of poems that are "remembered" rather than dreamed. Indeed, this division is so much a part of this book that quite often a poem from one category will be paired off with a poem from the other. **"Fathers and Sons,"** for example, consists of two poems printed together: the first describes a boy asleep and dreaming while his father dies, and the second a father haunted by his memories of a dead son. Other poems may not be so explicitly joined, but they, too, will draw together to enforce a balance between timeless dream and time remembered. **"Pursuit from Under"** and **"Sled Burial, Dream Ceremony"** or **"Faces Seen Once"** and **"The Common Grave"** co-operate in this way. However, the most striking moments in the dialectic occur when these opposites meet within one large poem such as **"The Firebombing"** or within a short and remarkably compressed piece like **"The War Wound."** One comes to read *Buckdancer's Choice* for such compounding poems as these, but the collection is best met in its simples.

Of the two categories, Dickey's dream poems are by far the less impressive. Sometimes they are too dependent upon other poems, even upon poems from other collections. **"Sled Burial, Dream Ceremony"** is scarcely intelligible without **"Pursuit from Under,"** and **"Fox Blood"** drives us all the way back to **"Listening to Foxhounds"** and **"A Dog Sleeping on my Feet"** in Dickey's second book, *Drowning with Others.* More often, these poems fail to impress because we know their moves too well. Dreaming transformations of men into appropriate beasts is old hat though Dickey can vary his tired totems effectively, reporting the metamorphosis as fact when it suits him, as in **"Reincarnation,"** or using it boldly in **"Gamecock"** to stage a conceit. His style, too, is masterful, reaching with suitable ease to the brittle clarity of nightmare. And his bag of dream tricks contains all the turns of a neo-Freudian rhetoric: condensation, displacement, reversal, etc. Indeed, the more clinical these poems are, the more effective they seem to be. Witness the depth and power of Dickey's conception in **"Them, Crying"** where compulsion is his subject. In something less than eighty lines, he brings to life a truck-driver, "unmarried, unchildlike, / Half-bearded and foul-mouthed," who is drawn irresistibly to the children's ward of a large hospital by the sound of children crying *within him.* Or witness the perfectly realized counterpoint of hallucination and reality in Dickey's presentation of a voyeur in **"The Friend."**

> He has learned what a plant is like
> When it moves near a human habitation   moving
>   closer the
>   later it is
> Unfurling its leaves near bedrooms   still keeping
>   its wilderness life
> Twigs covering his body with only one way out   for
>   his
>   eyes into inner light
> Of a chosen window. . . .

The dreams of damaged minds seldom have been rendered better than this. But the real surprise is to find that Dickey can make of these clinical materials poems that are gracious and charming. Such qualities are not common in those whose work is the dream, be they poets or psychoanalysts, and they have been too rare in Dickey's earlier verse. But he broke through with **"Cherrylog Road"** in his last collection, *Helmets,* and he breaks through in this book with a poem such as **"The Celebration."**

This last is as clinical a dream poem as one could wish for. Surely, no tenets are more basic to the art of psychoanalysis than these: We all carry within us a record, written in scars, of the inevitable frustrations met by our growing appetites. Of necessity, these frustrations are usually sexual and often involve our parents. Adjustment, maturity, wisdom, or whatever you choose to call the achievement of a sound life, depends in part upon our becoming aware of past pain and its effects in the present; and this past is recovered most easily through the symbols that we dream. Now, Dickey could have tailored **"The Celebration"** to these propositions. In it, the poet describes himself moving through symbols to a quite literal anamnesis of his parents as lovers and then back from this vision of the primal scene to a new sense of himself and his responsibilities in the present. What the poet learns, he feels along the body more than knows—"[I] stepped upon sparking shocks / Of recognition when I saw my feet . . . knowing them given"—, but he does try to state what he has recognized as clearly and as directly as he can. He talks of learning to understand

> the whirling impulse
> From which I had been born,
> The great gift of shaken lights,
> The being wholly lifted with another,
> All this having all and nothing
> To do with me.

The final lines of the poem are even more explicit in pointing the moral of all this seeing: the poet sees and becomes as a consequence "a kind of loving, / A mortal, a dutiful son." It is hard to conceive of a poem more properly psychoanalytic in its recognitions and consequent moralizings.

The details which earn this recognition, making the "whirling impulse" known and truly told within the poem, also are heavy with the modern craft of dreams. In its first lines the poem looks like a phantasmagoria of lust:

> All wheels; a man breathed fire,
> Exhaling like a blowtorch down the road
> And burnt the stripper's gown
> Above her moving-barely feet.
> A condemned train climbed from the earth

> Up stilted nightlights zooming in a track.
> I ambled along in that crowd. . . .

Most of us have met such carnal nightmares before, in the *Commedia* or in *The Rape of the Lock,* but this one is distinctly modern. More savage than Pope's, more narrowly psychological than Dante's, this fantasy is twin to the cases reported in Freud's *The Interpretation of Dreams* or to George Grosz's drawings of Berlin. Reason can stumble through this queer pastiche but is sent spinning when we find that all this fantasy is simple fact. The blowtorch-man is a fire-eater in a side show, the stripper just that, the condemned train a roller-coaster, and the crowded scene, Lakewood Midway at carnival time. With some care Dickey has led us into his poem, forcing us to see both the literal and the figurative dimensions of its sense, refusing to let us simplify.

In the second stanza Dickey quickly re-asserts the figurativeness of the carnival setting. Just in case his realistic explanation of the hallucinatory first stanza may have been too surprising and too distracting, he makes another ride, the dodgem cars, explicitly figurative by using them as one term of a simile: "each in his vehicle half / In control, half-helplessly power-mad / As was in the traffic that brought him." After this reminder, the poem need not be so explicit with its images; Dickey has prepared us for the symbols that he must use. In the literal scene, the poet is walking quietly and alone in the carnival crowd when he sees with surprise that his mother and father are there, "he leaning / On a dog-chewed cane, she wrapped to the nose / In the fur of exhausted weasels." Age and sexuality are finely caught here as the phallic symbols of cane and wrap are modified by their worn, literal substance. More than anything else, it is precisely this shadow of sexual energy in his parents that surprises the poet. They are so old. What can they celebrate? "I believed them buried [that verb is no accident] miles back / In the country, in the faint sleep / Of the old, and had not thought to be / On this of all nights compelled / To follow where they led. . . ."

In the stanza which follows, similar details reinforce this effect of tired fact scarcely covering powerful fancy. His mother carries a teddy bear that is as insistently symbolic as weasel wrap and dog-chewed cane; she holds it as if it were a child, and it was won for her "on the waning whip" of his father's right arm. The "crippled Stetson" which his father wears may not be so suggestive, except in its bobbing movement, but even here one could cite a section of Freud's dream book headed simply "A Hat as a Symbol of a Man (or of Male Genitals)." The poem's central image, of the old couple riding on a ferris wheel, needs no such footnoting:

> They laughed;
> She clung to him; then suddenly
> The Wheel of wheels was turning
> The colored night around.
> They climbed aboard. My God, they rose
> Above me, stopped themselves, and swayed
> Fifty feet up; he pointed
> With his toothed cane, and took in
> The whole Midway till they dropped,
> Came down, went from me, came and went
> Faster and faster, going up backward,
> Cresting, out-topping, falling roundly.

"The Wheel of wheels" is a perfectly apt description of a ferris wheel, but here it is also an intensive and a symbol. The cane, too, has become ambiguous with a new-old strength, for "toothed" may still mean "dog-chewed" but it suggests "possessing teeth." And all of the verbs that move these lines carry into them a phallic significance that nearly obliterates their letter. The whole passage is rich with a sense that scarcely requires glossing, even though it is this large image that elicits from the poet those attempts at direct statement our analysis began with.

But working our way up to these statements as the poem meant us to, we find that the lesson read is something more than a moral tag at its close. Recognition sparks within and without this poem, for **"The Celebration"** is peculiarly reflexive. Its images know themselves as they would be known, and the "whirling impulse" this poet sees, he teaches us to see, with all the fervent pragmatism of a revivalist. "Believers, I have seen / The wheel in the middle of the air. . . ." Though such language is borrowed from an old faith and testament, with some wit it calls a new generation of dreamers back to the constant task of prophecy: in omens find a responsible joy, and let it find you.

> Believers, I have seen
> The wheel in the middle of the air
> Where old age rises and laughs,
> And on Lakewood Midway became
> In five strides a kind of loving,
> A mortal, a dutiful son.

With this poem and others like it, Dickey seems to be saying to his contemporaries, "Look, I can do it too," and also "Look, how narrow this thing that we have done." **"The Celebration"** is a first-rate product of our time's craft of dreams, but it is also ours in ways that are not so admirable: in the passivity and in the privacy of its vision. Dreams happen to a person, and if you live in and for them, you wait and are paid for your waiting in coin of no man's realm. Clearly, a balanced art demands visions that one chooses as well as those that one is chosen by, and visions *of more than one's self.* Poetry, at least, should be dreams that one can trade in. Concern with the trap of solipsism, that Wordsworth and Sartre both know so well, and concern for a poetry that is performance as well as visitation run throughout *Buckdancer's Choice.* One finds it in certain implications of **"The Celebration"**'s moral close: in seeing others oblivious of me, I see myself and my responsibilities, my "duty." One finds it in the way that this small book is crammed with the full reality of other persons: generations of family, friends, an old teacher with a bad heart, a truck driver drowning in tenderness, a voyeur, a slaveowner, enemies from an old war, and victims. One finds it in Dickey's appetite for

> those things that, once
> Established, cannot be changed by angels,
> Devils, lightning, ice, or indifference:
> Identities! Identities!

in a context where these "Identities" are both the mathematics that Mangham teaches and the man that he is as the poet's remembering "establishes" him. One finds it, conversely, in Dickey's reaction to "an angel's too-realized / Unbearable memoryless face." One finds it, particularly, in his sense of memory as counter-weight to dream, public and willed, and in such poems as **"Buckdancer's Choice."**

Intended or not, the use of this poem as title piece flaunts such a book as John Berryman's *Seventy-Seven Dream Songs,* for **"Buckdancer's Choice"** is a song, too, but not a dream song. It is an old song that minstrels once danced to, shuffling and flapping their arms like stunted wings, and the poem remembers it as it was performed. The poem begins by recalling the poet's mother, "dying of breathless angina" but finding breath and life of a sort in whistling to herself "the thousand variations" of this one song. It also remembers the poet as a boy who "crept close to the wall / Sock-footed, to hear the sounds alter, / Her tongue like a mockingbird's beak / Through stratum after stratum of a tone. . . ." Behind this spot of time lies another evoked by it: the house in which the boy listens is "barnlike, theatrelike," he is "sock-footed," and his mother's whistle calls up in him "a sight like a one-man band, / Freed black, with cymbals at heel, / An ex-slave who thrivingly danced / To the ring of his own clashing light. . . ." Together, these two moments of time past form a metaphor of sorts whose point is most immediately that time does pass. "For years, they have all been dying / Out, the classic buck-and-wing men / Of traveling minstrel shows; / With them also an old woman / Was dying of breathless angina. . . ."

But there are three faces to this metaphor—the minstrel's, the mother's, and the boy's—and only the first two are stained by death. The song speaks for each of them in different ways proclaiming

> what choices there are
> For the last dancers of their kind,
> For ill women and for all slaves

> Of death, and children enchanted at walls
> With a brass-beating glow underfoot,
> Not dancing but nearly risen
> Through barnlike, theatrelike houses
> On the wings of the buck and wing.

Choices and *risen* are the most difficult terms in this last and fullest statement of the metaphor. Clearly, they are meant to give the image its final shape by opposing the dying mother and the last dancer to the boy who does not die and, apparently, to the poet who remembers him with this poem. The alignment is clear, if not its sense. Why *choices*?

To choose is to be free, and the buckdancer is a freed slave who celebrates his freedom by dancing out "The thousand variations of one song," thriving all the while in the choices of his dance. His dying art remembered frees the woman who is slave to the nearness of her death, for his song is both a literal artifact making it possible for her to partake of a joy her dying body denies her and a kind of emblematic definition of its own use. Joy is the one song, but she cannot simply identify with it; rather, she must achieve her own identity as a kind of thousand-and-first variation of it. Art's long memory has saved for her the fact of joy, but she must join with it, finding herself in her own performance of this joy as a dancer finds identity in the strict measure of his dance or as variations find themselves in a sounding theme.

The boy and the poet who remembers him complete the literal scene by making something nearly heroic out of the invalid's ultimate lyricism. In listening to his mother "warbling all day to herself," the boy reverses the movement from minstrel show to muffled sickroom by transforming the house into a kind of theatre, while the poet remembering this three-personed song in his poem restores it entirely to the public domain so that we, too, may use it. Perhaps this is one justification for the poem's claim that the vanishing dancer and the dying woman are countered by a "risen" boy: the song she appropriates—and what could be more private than the "prone music" of an invalid's whistle—he takes back for himself and in time performs, that others may for the moment find themselves, and company, in **"Buckdancer's Choice."**

But "risen" makes figurative sense as well as literal, as it must when it involves even such mimic wings as the buckdancer's elbows suggest. At first glance, "risen" looks like more of that southern evangelical baroque that is such an engaging quality of Dickey's imagination, but here I think the religious implications are more precise and more serious. "Risen" is but the end of something that has been building from the first lines of the poem. For example, why should his mother's whistle have split the air into just "nine levels"? Is the number meant to remind us of the nine muses, or of the nine heavens through which Dante rose as the blessed were manifest to him under the conditions of space and time? When this same fracted air, in *terza senza rima,* is offered as proving "some gift of tongues of the whistler," the reference is more certainly religious and more illuminating.

Speaking in tongues is described several times in the *New Testament*. In *Acts* St. Peter defends the authenticity of the experience in terms which could suggest Dickey's poem: "your sons and daughters shall prophesy, / And your young men shall see visions, / And your old men shall dream dreams" (2:17). However, St. Paul's discussion of the gift of tongues seems more clearly relevant to a reading of Dickey's poem. In *I Corinthians 14,* he develops at some length the distinction between tongues and prophecy that St. Peter hints at with his young prophets and aged dreamers. According to St. Paul, the man with the gift of tongues speaks in mysteries to his God; his spirit prays, but his understanding is not fruitful unless his words are interpreted for him and for others. To the unbelievers, speaking in tongues will seem testimony only of madness in the speaker. (In this context, the address "Believers, I have seen . . ." at the close of **"The Celebration"** acquires further ironic bite.) Describing his mother's whistle as a gift of tongues, Dickey draws heavily upon St. Paul's conception and even language, for St. Paul calls this a "speaking into the air" and expands his claim with a series of musical metaphors. More important, Dickey's reference seems to involve St. Paul's valuation of the experience: speaking in tongues is a valid gift of the spirit, but the gift of prophecy is much greater. The prophet is a tuned pipe and harp, a certain trumpet; he speaks to all for the sake of all. He is a bearer of public visions. If the old woman has received the gift of tongues, her son hopes for the gift of tuned speech, for the gift of prophecy; and in time he receives it, as this poem testifies most powerfully.

No wonder, then, that Dickey chooses **"Buckdancer's Choice"** as the title piece for this collection: it is a perfect emblem of the art he would achieve. Modern poetry has been content too long with an invalid's private song. Dickey is reaching once more for the time that was and the time that is to be. He is reaching for prophecy.

Dickey's verbal skills were always considerable; they have grown more sure. In his earlier books the fluent movement of his verse was overwhelmed at times by a surge of anapests, and diction was marred by conventional insincerities. Those poems had a brother dying "ablaze with the meaning of typhoid" and fell too often into the cadence of "O grasses and fence wire of glory / That have been burned like a coral with depth. . . ." Now, such cadences are modulated by carefully indicated pauses within the line: "He has only to pass by a tree moodily walking head down . . ." and his familiar elegiac and meditative vocabulary includes new tones, like the impeccable gaucherie of "Homeowners unite. / All families lie together, though some are burned alive. / The other try to feel / For them. Some can, it is often said." Still, these are not the clearest measure of Dickey's growth or of his achievement in this new book. Poems of real substance may be recognized by what they do to our commonplaces about poetry, not cancelling them out but making them more true than they were before. We have known for a long time that the modern poet seeks in "la plénitude du grand songe" for "memorable speech." The virtue of **Buckdancer's Choice** is to insist that the deepest dreams belong to languages not to men and that the best poetry is speech remembering.

Paul Carroll (review date November 1968)

SOURCE: Carroll, Paul. "James Dickey as Critic." *Chicago Review* 20 (November 1968): 82-7.

[*In the following favorable review of* Babel to Byzantium, *Carroll examines the critical backlash against Dickey's work.*]

After I talk about this collection of book reviews and essays on modern poets—which seems to me the sanest, most invigorating and most fun to read since Randall Jarrell's *Poetry and the Age* (1953)—I want to try and put into perspective a nasty attempt at poetic fratricide in which James Dickey has been the target. Why I bother with such dirty literary linen is simple: I want everybody to read and enjoy Mr. Dickey without the distraction encouraged by the scuttlebutt resulting from the attempt at fratricide, which was manufactured, for the most part, by envy, it would seem. Not only has James Dickey shown the unmistakable "blue sign of his god on the forehead," as St.-John Perse describes the true poet, which holds the promise that we may have a major poet in our midst (indeed, why his collected **Poems: 1957-67** failed to win the 1968 Pulitzer Prize remains, to my mind, more baffling than the intricacies displayed in most of the theories regarding John F. Kennedy's assassination) but he also writes the kind of criticism I admire—namely, direct, personal talk about this poet or that poem in his or its own skin, as it were.

What commends the prose in **Babel to Byzantium** is similar to what makes the best of Mr. Dickey's poems memorable: the honesty and authority of the insight, unburdened by literary fashion or even by the critic's previous judgment; and the originality and power of the imagination at work on material that counts.

When I suggest that the insight is honest and has authority I mean that it is the last thing from that type of tidy, judicious opinion one reads (only during Lent, hopefully) in so many reviews and essays. One learns to trust Dickey to say only what he feels. What he feels can compel you, in turn, to reread a writer whom you may have dismissed as an adolescent infatuation or to open yourself to one whom you've never read. Of Kenneth Patchen for instance, Dickey says: "It is wrong of us to wish Patchen would 'pull himself together.' He has never been together. He cannot write poems, as this present book (*When We Were Here Together*) heartlessly demonstrates. But his authentic and terrible hallucinations infrequently come to great good among the words which they must use. We should leave it at that," he concludes, "and take what we can from him." Or of John Logan and the lack of wider recognition his work merits but hasn't received: "His strange kind of innocence, walking in and out of his ecclesiastical and literary knowledgeableness, is not an easy thing to talk about, though anyone who reads Mr. Logan cannot fail to be excited and uplifted by it." Then the insight blazes: "(Logan) is far beyond the Idols of the Marketplace and works where the work itself is done out of regard for the world he lives in and the people he lives among because he is helplessly and joyously what he is."

Fluctuating quotations on the literary stock market obviously do not interest Dickey. He refuses to take on faith alone, for example, the veneration afforded Charles Olson and his poetics of "composition by field" by some of the poets associated with the old Black Mountain College and by some of the Beat poets, as well as by some of the younger poets, longing, it would seem, for apostolic succession. Examining Olson's theory and its practice in *The Maximus Poems,* Dickey finds both second-hand and not too interesting news. But he is not out to hatchet another poet, granting that Olson's mind "seems to me quite a capable one, and at all points working hard to say what it has been given it. That is enough, because it has to be." On the other hand, J. V. Cunningham, John Frederick Nims, Elder Olson, and Reed Whittemore are treated as poets and not as "minor voices from the '40s." Nims, for one, is often dismissed by fellow poets and critics as a virtuoso. Not by Dickey: "Mr. Nims has worked hard for a good many years to achieve his style of unremitting brilliance, and it behooves us to look closely at what he is doing"—which he does, with care and energy.

And the originality and power of the imagination seem without equal, in my opinion, among practicing critics. "Opening a book by Robert Penn Warren is like putting out the light of the sun," Dickey observes, "or like plunging into the labyrinth and feeling the thread break after the first corner is passed." His is an imagination which leaps beyond mere critical insight: "One will never come out the same Self as that in which one entered. When he is good, and often when he is bad, you had as soon read Warren as live." Truths such as this, arrived at only through the imagination, occur again and again throughout this book.

In addition, Dickey almost always exhibits that rare gift: he is able to transcend a fundamental antipathy to some poet's work—which he describes, however, clearly and forcefully—and to discover what he feels is genuine in the poems. After arguing that Robert Duncan, for instance, is "certainly one of the most unpityingly pretentious poets I have ever come across," he also praises Duncan's "ingenuousness," the originality of his intellect, and several "marvelous" Duncan poems. Richard Wilbur, James Merrill, Allen Ginsberg, and Gene Derwood are other poets whom Dickey dislikes. In each, however, he finds nuggets of genuine poetry.

In brief, these book reviews of some 65 American and British poets are free of that myopia, parochialism and occasional smugness or patronizing tone found in much criticism. Instead, Dickey's reviews are clear-sighted, catholic in taste, and exuberantly respectful as only one poet can be towards the effort of one of his fellows. Best of all, Dickey ignores what he calls the critic's expected "System of Evaluation," which he is supposed to defend not only on its practical and local instances but in its broader theoretical and philosophical implications as well. On the contrary, Dickey explores only his immediate, existential experience of this poet or that poem. And he does so in clear, masculine prose. (His lack of a critical system is the only possible fault I can find in this book. As far as I'm concerned, however, such lack is a virtue.)

In addition to the book reviews, there are longer essays on Edward Arlington Robinson—a valuable discussion which I know will send me back to Robinson soon—and on Robert Frost—an analysis so accurate in defining both Frost's genius and his spiteful, egocentric personality that one feels like laughing and weeping at once. Then there are five good shorter essays on individual poems, ranging from Smart's "A Song of David" to Francis Thompson's "The Hound of Heaven" to Williams' "The Yachts." (An entire book on individual poems he loves would be a happy event, I think, from which everybody would benefit.)

Finally, three essays are grouped under the umbrella, "The Poet Turns on Himself." **"Barnstorming for Poetry"** delineates what it feels like for a middleaged man suddenly to find himself a literary lion overnight as he sings, staggers, and suffers from college to college during an exhausting, exhilarating reading tour. Every poet who has ever run such a curious gauntlet will read this piece with (what Melville called in a far different context, I'm afraid) "that shock of recognition." **"Notes on the Decline of Outrage"** should be read, and read carefully, by anyone who likes to think of James Dickey as a Georgia redneck. He isn't. What we come to know instead is a man, who was born white and raised in the Georgia of 40 years ago, trying to explore, as much in touch with his feelings as he can get, what it means *to him* to think about abandoning inherited, familial attitudes towards Negroes. What that man decides, as well as how he reaches the decision, will not satisfy those addicted to easy abstract slogans; but I suspect the essay will be admired by those who care more about individuals than abstractions or clichés or finding a mirror which will reflect their opinions and prejudices. I know I admire the essay almost as much as James Baldwin's masterpiece, "Down at the Cross: Letter from a Region in My Mind," and for the same reason: both offer one man, feeling and thinking with his own heart, memories, and brains.

Now, I'd like to turn to the attempt at poetic fratricide mentioned at the beginning of this review.

"The Hunting of the Dickey" has become a popular, if vulgar, sport among a growing number of poets and poetasters. A few weeks ago, for example, I heard one of the younger poets, who is bright and well-read, dimiss Dickey as being the David Ogilvy of American verse. When asked if he'd read such magnificent Dickey poems as **"The Sleep Child," "Slave Quarters"** or **"The Heaven of the Animals,"** he admitted, rather sheepishly, he had not; even more depressing, the poet confessd that, due to bad-mouthing against Dickey he'd heard along the literary grapevine, he'd decided not to bother with the criticism collected in **Babel to Byzantium.**

Exactly what *are* Dickey's crimes or sins? I thought, after this melancholy encounter. Most of the charges I've heard poets make against Dickey seem to have been brought into melodramatic focus by Robert Bly in his well-read essay, "The Collapse of James Dickey" (*The Sixties,* Spring, 1967). In that piece, Mr. (I almost said Captain) Bly tries to secure Dickey to the yardarm and flog him because some of the poems in **Buckdancer's Choice** (National Book Award, 1966) exhibit "a gloating about power over others." According to Bly, this gloating manifests itself most clearly in such poems as **"Slave Quarters"**—that almost classic work depicting the sensibility of a contemporary white Southerner enmeshed in the cunning bondage of memory and fantasy of what an antebellum plantation owner might have felt—and in **"Firebombing"**—a long, often tedious poem which, with considerable honesty and power, embodies an attempt by a middleaged suburbanite to relive in memory the excitement and youthful virility felt when he was a bomber pilot flying missions over Japan during World War II. Both are poems of "memory and desire": haunting, masculine, poignant. Clearly the first is not the apologia pro rednecks Mr. Bly discovers, nor is the latter a paean to "the American habit of firebombing Asians." But Bly shows little interest in reading them as poems: instead, he chooses to bully poems into being flagrantly "repulsive" examples of what he claims is their author's moral leprosy.

The Bly essay concludes, then, with a libel against Mr. Dickey. The poet is branded as "a sort of Georgia cracker Kipling," presumably because he earns an annual $25,000 from activities resulting from his being a poet, publishes some of his verse in *The New Yorker,* allegedly supports the Vietnam war, and reveals himself in general as "a toady to the government, supporting all movement toward Empire."

Frankly, the Bly essay appalled me. How could a critic with his sensibility and extremely wide reading, I wondered, allow his argument to be grounded on the silly assumption that since the Dickey poems espouse few of the virtues cherished by white Northern liberals, the poems were "repulsive" and their author an Establishment stooge and moral pariah? Mr. Bly's essay is so shrill and wrong-headed that it almost seems unnecessary to recall that Ezra Pound and T. S. Eliot despised equalitarian democracy and, by implication, most, if not all, liberal goals; or that Apollinaire adored the war on the Western Front; or that Dante firmly believed that unless one were a baptized believer in the One, Holy, Roman, Catholic, and Apostolic Church one was destined for eternal misery in either hell or limbo.

Here, then, are the crimes for which Mr. Dickey stands accused by Mr. Bly and other devotees of "The Hunting of the Dickey" clan. In his poems, he explores feelings and memories of one man existing in his own flesh and bone, instead of using poetry to elicit attention by mouthing this or that current liberal or Far Left attitude about the Negro revolution or the Vietnam conflict. In addition, he earns a decent living for his family by doing what he can do with consummate skill: write poetry, read it in public, and teach it in the classroom. In other words, his crimes or sins are the ancient ones: talent, independence of attitude, and recognition and reward. Worst of all, he is only 45. Ten years ago, he was unpublished and unknown. Today, he stands as the first of his generation to have published a collected poems and a volume of criticism on modern and contemporary poets. Success is, as Ambrose Bierce reminds us, "the one unpardonable sin against one's fellows."

(Regarding Mr. Dickey's views on Vietnam, I know only that when we talked about that wretched war one afternoon in September, 1967, the poet said that, after a lot of hard thought, he hadn't made up his mind as yet. In my opinion, our involvement in Vietnam is murder—barbarous, immoral, infectuous—and I told Dickey as much. But I also remembered that Camus refused to join the supporters of the Algerian rebels in 1957, stating that he hadn't made up his mind, thereby provoking vicious denunciations from intellectuals of the Left, including Sartre. Moreover, Dickey mentioned the possibility that he might become a speech writer for Senator Eugene McCarthy. What began as a casual acquaintanceship in 1966, when the poet assumed his responsibilities as poet to the Library of Congress, had matured into what Dickey implied was a closer relationship. At that time, he clearly was a McCarthy man; I don't know how he feels today, and it doesn't matter, of course, in so far as the irresponsible smear that he's a toady of the Pentagon and White House is concerned.)

I've spent time in describing this inept attempt at poetic fratricide by Mr. Bly—most of whose criticism and work as editor, translator and gadfly-at-large to the literary community, and whose exemplary public stands against the Vietnam war I admire without reservation—in order to say to him and to other members of "The Hunting of the Dickey" society, including that young poet: If you allow such popular but false images of James Dickey as "redneck" or "war-lover" or "careerist" to keep you from reading **Babel to Byzantium,** or from reading it with an unclouded eye, you'll be depriving yourself of criticism as it should be written. The man who wrote this book clearly loves and serves the god of poetry and the god's faithful disciples with (as the Baltimore Catechism prescribes with regard to another deity) his whole heart, and his whole soul, and whole mind, and whole strength.

Harry Morris (essay date April 1969)

SOURCE: Morris, Harry. "A Formal View of the Poetry of Dickey, Garrigue, and Simpson." *Sewanee Review* 77, no. 2 (April 1969): 318-22.

[*In the following excerpt, Morris provides a negative assessment of* Poems, 1957-1967, *calling the poems in the volume dull, awkward, and stylistically inferior.*]

James Dickey, Jean Garrigue, and Louis Simpson are ready apparently for an assessment of their work to date; for each poet, the current book is a selection from all his past work plus a final section containing new poems.

Traditionally we have expected poets to develop their powers of observation, to give form to their utterance; to be concise and precise, to seek a verbal music, and to enrich the texture of their verse with the devices of rhetoric. In Mr. Dickey's verse [in ***Poems, 1957-1967***] I find the observation myopic, sometimes filmed completely over; form is adhered to but so meaninglessly or inexactly as to suggest casual concern only or incredibly inept management. In addition to what seems a total inability to achieve conciseness within a single poem, Mr. Dickey appears unable also to conclude a poem in under thirty lines. Of the 108 pieces in this volume, only seven comprise fewer than thirty lines. The majority of the poems are close to fifty lines or over. Precision in diction is of so little concern to the poet that in many cases even prepositions are employed awkwardly or improperly. With the two foregoing misdeeds, music can be at best only a tiresome jangle, harsh and out of tune. Rhetoric in our fashionable age is out at heels and many will applaud Mr. Dickey's avoidance of all the old devices, but will they clap also for the resulting threadbare fabric of the verse?

Mr. Dickey is a poet of nature; he looks at a wide range of wildlife; shark, fox, wolverine, deer, cattle, big cat at the zoo, rabbit, sheep, dog, and mostly unidentified birds. But I wish to test Mr. Dickey's observation of snakes, reptiles being among the few creatures I know anything about.

"**Reincarnation (I)**" presents a former county judge reborn as a rattlesnake. Mr. Dickey does not know that the rattlesnake, like all pit vipers, is viviparous, not oviparous.

> . . . disappearing into the egg buried under the sand
> And wakened to the low world being born . . .

Mr. Dickey has heard that snakes employ their tongues in sensory perception, in some manner other than to taste. The scientists, much at odds about the matter, say that snakes smell through their tongues or feel through them or do indeed, like other creatures, taste through them. None that I have ever heard or read has suggested that snakes hear through their tongues:

> With his tongue he can hear them in their concerted
> effort. . . .

Mr. Dickey believes that snakes can pass through the grass without a telltale wavering of blades.

> he moves through, moving nothing,
> And the grass stands as never entered.

Such skill is rarely, if ever, true of the rattlesnake. Add to this recital his error in believing that rattlesnakes rattle as a warning and that they will attack a man unprovoked.

Perhaps more a failure in logic or in preciseness than in observation is the age of Mr. Dickey's snake. Observation would come into play, however, in a person's having noted that a new-born rattlesnake is rarely twelve inches long, whereas the snake in the poem would have to be several feet:

> Still, passed through the spokes of an old wheel, on
>   and

around
The hub's furry rust in the weeds and shadows of the riverbank.

Logic fails the writer when he presents us with a mature snake, one who has already "drawn from bird eggs and thunderstruck rodents", and yet tells us that the reincarnated judge is in the "new/Life of resurrection". Would not reincarnation be as a new-born creature rather than as something already existing, already full-grown?

I know very little about other animals of which Mr. Dickey writes, but when he makes six errors of considerable magnitude on a creature I know something about, I am reluctant to accept his teachings on others.

I have condemned the writer's casual nod to the conventions of form. In his earlier work, most of his pieces may be said to be stanzaic: pattern is observed in the number of lines to the stanza. Favored stanza lengths are five and six lines per unit, although couplets, tercets, quatrains, septenaries, and octets are frequently used. But why Mr. Dickey has observed such regularity in this one matter is beyond me. Since he employs no rhyme pattern, it is not rhyme that determines the length of a stanza. Since stanza units are not thought units, image units, or sound units, these factors do not dictate the length of a stanza. In fact, there is no justification for any of his groupings. Line length, at first glance, appears regular; but on scanning we find that Mr. Dickey ignores the number of feet in any given line whenever he pleases.

In his later work, Mr. Dickey is apparently experimenting with very long lines, broken on the printed page by extra spacing to indicate pauses or rhythm groupings. He is not attempting an alliterative revival as some reviewers have suggested, for no convention of Anglo-Saxon or Middle English verse with which we are familiar is observed. I suppose he is writing by phrases—wanting cadences that to him must be attractive—but to get cadences he employs a good many loose constructions, a weakness that leads to my next objection.

Mr. Dickey writes verse so loosely that he may do anything in it, commit any dispersal, admit any discourse, follow any digression. In **"The Escape",** the title of which refers to arranging burial in a plot other than the family mausoleum in Fairmount, Mr. Dickey employs twenty-one lines to describe some of the surroundings the corpse will "escape". Mr. Dickey or the "over-witty in other mens Writings" will justify these excursions as scenes of life and death not to be encountered in the county graveyard in Alabama to which the corpse escapes; even as such the tableaux are loosely written, with much unnecessary verbiage. But they do not belong in the poem at all; a finer poet would achieve a greater poignancy through symbolic correlatives, delivered in the focused materials themselves.

Illustrations of Mr. Dickey's lack of verbal precision may be taken from almost any poem (my italics):

Bleary with ointments

("**Sun**")

With a ring of *convulsive* rubber

("**Adultery**")

With dew our *porous* home
Is *dense,* wound up like a spring,

Which is solid as motherlode
At night.

("**Hedge Life**")

Especially are his pronouns difficult. As in the last quotation above, where the antecedent for the relative pronoun *which* is impossibly ambiguous, poem after poem employs all the different classes of pronouns—personal, possessive, demonstrative, and relative—in bewildering uncertainty; see for instance **"The Wedding"**. So often is dedicated search a necessary labor that a reader wearies and concludes the pains have outcost the truffles. Especially distasteful is the repeated use of *you* as an indefinite pronoun.

And, finally, Mr. Dickey's avoidance of all but a few of the devices of rhetoric, his eschewal of most of those things which would give density to his verse—and herein most especially symbolic action—leave his work so thin that a reader is left unsatisfied, and one who endures the full three hundred pages of ***Poems 1957-1967*** suffers a dulling tedium through which poetry should never put its faithful.

Unfortunately I find little or no growth in this collection of the work of ten years; the only change is in the direction of greater dispersal, to be found both in the author's self-permissiveness in greater rambling and in his adoption of the long line. And although no single poem satisfies altogether, here are the pieces that are least discomforting: **"The Performance"**, **"The Lifeguard"**, **"Chenille"**, **"Cherrylog Road"**, **"Pursuit from Under"**, **"Gamecock"**, **"Mangham"**, **"Angina"**, **"The Sheep Child",** and **"Bread"**.

George Lensing (review date spring 1970)

SOURCE: Lensing, George. A review of *The Eye-Beaters, Blood, Victory, Madness, Buckhead and Mercy,* by James Dickey. *Carolina Quarterly* 22, no. 2 (spring 1970): 90-1.

[*In the following essay, Lensing offers a negative review of* The Eye-Beaters, Blood, Victory, Madness, Buckhead, and Mercy.]

When James Dickey's ***Poems 1957-1967*** appeared three years ago, the poet found himself suddenly promoted to the front ranks of American versifiers: Louis Untermeyer described the volume as the "outstanding collection of one man's poems to appear in this decade," while Peter Davison suggested that Dickey might well nudge his way onto the niche of eminence with Robert Lowell as a "major" poet. Dickey's next volume, therefore, has been awaited with some anticipation, and ***The Eye-Beaters, Blood, Victory, Madness, Buckhead and Mercy***, it seems to me, does not forcibly advance his reputation.

Dickey's power as a poet has depended upon a fairly repetitive technique: a human psyche is situated in some natural setting and proceeds surrealistically toward a metaphorical merger with any of various forms of plant, animal or human life. The process is always accompanied by an accumulative verbal intensity and excitement. As Dickey himself has said of his own work, "I meant to try to get a fusion of inner and outer states, of dream, fantasy and illusion where everything partakes of the protagonist's mental processes and creates a single impression." Most of the poems in the new volume are projections of this technique.

I would suggest, however, two reasons why Dickey's newer poems do not reach the mark of some of his earlier work. The energizing power of Dickey's language has always depended upon the free flow of successive participial and gerund phrases, long, loose lines, frequently run-on: the effect must be accumulative. One poem in the new volume, **"In the Pocket,"** describes a game of football phatasmagorically reenacted. The poem's crescendo builds toward the conclusion:

> . . . throw it hit him in the middle
> Of his enemies   hit move scramble
> Before death and the ground
> Come up   LEAP STAND KILL DIE STRIKE
> Now.

The failure lies in the excessive dependence on uppercase letters, verbal arrangement on the page, and a weak anticlimactic redundancy with the terminal adverb. In short, verbal power has succumbed to artificial gimmickry.

Secondly, and perhaps more pervasive, the focus of a number of these poems is blurred by a tendency toward verbosity and overstatement. **"Turning Away"** and **"Pine"** are examples of poems too discursive to sustain interest. Part of this is the result of the almost total prose-like effect of many of these poems: Dickey has moved far away indeed from the anapestic cadences of his earlier poems. The poet himself seems to sense the nature of the problem by his insertion of a marginal gloss in **"The Eye-Beaters"** or a brief plot-summary epigraph in **"Madness."**

These weaknesses do not obscure Dickey's continuing power as a poet—though ***The Eye-Beaters***, etc. seems to me a falling off from the success of ***Buckdancer's Choice*** and the preceding volumes. One poem, **"The Eye-Beaters,"** reminiscent of the earlier **"The Owl King,"** describes blind children whose hands are tied to prevent their striking their eyes in angry frustration. Though flawed by discursiveness and a trite conclusion, the poem is a powerful statement. Finally, no one expects Dickey to be able to sustain through every poem the authentic lyric force of poems like **"The Lifeguard"** and **"Hunting Civil War Relics at Nimblewill Creek."** The nature of his poetry is such that it demands strong emotive risks, but it should be undertaken with acute consciousness of the dangers along the way.

Richard J. Calhoun (essay date June 1971)

SOURCE: Calhoun, Richard J. "'His Reason Argues with His Invention': James Dickey's *Self-Interviews* and *The Eye-Beaters*." *South Carolina Review* 3, no. 2 (June 1971): 9-16.

[*In the following essay, Calhoun surveys the weakness in Dickey's* Self-Interviews *and* The Eye-Beaters.]

James Dickey's first novel, ***Deliverance***, was such a phenomenal success that anything else he produced in 1970 must by comparison seem rather neglected. Early last year he published his sixth volume of poems, a slim paperback with one of the most ungainly titles in the history of American publishing—***The Eye-Beaters, Blood, Victory, Madness, Buckhead and Mercy***. Then just as the excitement over ***Deliverance*** was abating, a third 1970 volume, ***Self-Interviews***, appeared, simpler in its title but unique in its conception. It seems that Dickey had agreed to expound via the tape recorder on a series of topics outlined for him by two young teachers, Barbara and James Reiss, who feel that they have midwifed something "neither quite like a typical tape-recorded interview nor autobiography" but rather "a new genre, the tape recorded self-interview."

This new genre of the McLuhan era does have a much older literary antecedent which it may not quite equal for literary style or drama, the dialogue in which the writer creates two voices, one his, the other in opposition, in dialectical counterpoint. Dickey has used this form effectively in an essay on Randall Jarrell reprinted in ***Babel to Byzantium***. Perhaps this kind of essay reveals more of a duality in Dickey as poet-critic and virile sophisticate than ***Self-Interviews***, but with James Dickey as the protagonist the Reisses could hardly fail to produce a volume that is both entertaining and informative.

I would have to say, however, that, no matter how entertaining this spoken Dickeyese may be, the prose is not quite up to the standards of the essays in Dickey's volume of literary criticism, ***Babel to Byzantium,*** where Dickey's critical judgments are occasionally enlivened by a stylistic barb of true wit. Nothing comes across on the tape recorder to equal the preciseness of his epigram on the poetry of J. V. Cunningham.

> Cunningham is a good, deliberately small and authentic poet, a man with tight lips, a good education and his own agonies. His handsome little book should be read, and above all by future Traditionalists and confessors; he is their man.

The microphone is also not quite conducive to audacious but carefully worded opening paragraphs like that with which Dickey began his essay on William Carlos Williams.

> William Carlos Williams is now, dead, and that fact shakes one. Has any other poet in American history been so actually useful, usable, and influential? How many beginning writers took Williams as their model, were encouraged to write because . . . Well, if that is poetry, I believe I might be able to write it too!

The only comparable passage that filters through the tape recorder to the pages of ***Self-Interviews*** is Dickey's account of a poem written in an advertising office and typed by a new secretary.

> I wrote this poem **"The Heaven of Animals"** in an advertising office. I had a new secretary and I asked her to type it for me. She typed up the poem letter-perfect and brought it to me.
>
> Then she asked, "What is it? What company does it go to?"
>
> "This is a poem," I said.
>
> "It is?"
>
> "Yes, it is, I hope."
>
> "What are we going to sell with it?" she asked.
>
> "God," I said, "We're going to sell God."
>
> "Does this go to a religious magazine or something?"
>
> "No, I'm going to publish it in *The New Yorker,*" I told her.
>
> And, as it happened, that's where it came out.

If ***Self-Interviews*** seldom equals the wit of Dickey's best critical prose, it has the true sound of Dickey speaking, a marvel in itself as anyone who has heard him read will testify; and it is a handbook of information about Dickey and his poems, compiled not by some assistant professor at a midwestern university but by the poet himself. Part one, "The Poet at Mid-Career," provides details about Dickey's creative psyche from the first awakenings of his interests in poetry through the publication of ***Poems 1957-1967.*** Part two, "The Poem as Something That Matters," consists of five sections, one each on Dickey's first five volumes of poetry. Dickey's critical pretensions are very modest. He makes it clear that he is not trying "to impose an official interpretation on the poems or "to preclude anybody else's interpretation. . . . I have been asked on this occasion, though, what my poems are supposed to be about from my standpoint and what I have tried to do in them."

What *is* surprising is that Dickey's comments are not too surprising. Very little transpires which would show that his explicators have ever been dead wrong. Instead, in part one we have further evidence for what his critics have assumed all along. Dickey has "never been able to dissociate the poem from the poet." He doesn't "believe in Eliot's theory of autotelic art." He feels that the value of literature "must be maintained if we're going to have any humanity left at all." He regards a poem as "that kind of personal connection of very disparate elements under the fusing heat of the poem's necessity." He just doesn't "have beautiful Mozartian flights of the imagination." He is not surprisingly "much more interested in a man's relationship to the God-made world, or the universe-made world, than to the man-made world." He is drawn "to a philosopher like Heraclitus" and has as "personal heroes of the sensibility John Keats, James Agee, and Malcolm Lowry." The last two items may be news.

Part two is of greater use to students of Dickey's poems. It is informative and useful and often good reading, even if Dickey fails to evoke any sense of a critical recreation of the creative process as Stephen Spender did in "The Making of a Poem" and Allen Tate did in his essay on his own "Ode to the Confederate Dead."

Some reviewers have complained that Dickey reveals himself very cautiously, giving his reader "a routine milking of the glands" rather than the "total act of the body" that he feels meaningful communication should involve. I would not call ***Self-Interviews*** or anything that James Dickey's imagination produces routine, but the reader may well feel that the Dickey he encounters here is the public Dickey speaking on the level of good conversation and that the voice of the inner man is not heard.

The passage in ***Self-Interviews*** that best provides a lead for a description of ***The Eye-Beaters, Blood, Victory Madness, Buckhead and Mercy*** is Dickey's comment on his poem **"The Lifeguard"** from his early volume, ***Drowning With Others.***

> Allen Tate once said that he thought of his poems as commentaries on those human situations from which there was no escape. **"The Lifeguard"** is my idea of a poem about one of those human situations from which there is no escape.

There are seventeen poems in ***The Eye-Beaters.*** An even dozen are concerned with situations from which there is no escape—aging, illness, and death; and it is these poems which have attracted the attention of the reviewers. This part of Dickey's book seems to be his "no exit," that is, (if Dickey will pardon the trite phrase) his most existential volume.

Dickey has indicated in a recent interview that he is pleased with *The Eye-Beaters,* regarding it as perhaps his most successful single volume. His reviewers have not been exactly unanimous in their agreement with Dickey's judgment. Some have objected to it on thematic grounds, feeling that Dickey at his best is a poetic celebrant of the life force and that he cannot handle darker themes as successfully. Other critics have found a falling off in style. Dickey, the poet of "open forms," has not quite successfully mated the freedom of his split line with the discipline of more nearly regular stanzaic forms, *etc.* Critics always seem to voice a feeling of having been betrayed when poets change a successful style or theme.

There is some truth to these charges, however, and I must agree partially with the complaints about Dickey's style. Dickey is a bit too often both rhetorical and commonplace. I do not detect the note of hysteria that the ears of some critics have caught, but I was bothered by an overuse of rhetorical devices which tend to make Dickey sound somewhat melodramatic. Several of Dickey's poems in this volume bear a heavy freight of interjections ("Ah, it was then, Chris," *etc.*) and apostrophes ("O son," "O Chris," "O parents," "O justice scales") as well as rhetorical questions. Occasionally—and only occasionally—Dickey sounds like Randall Jarrell, who was a bit too fond of such devices.

In fact, it seems that stylistically Dickey is heading in two opposite directions in this volume. In a poem like **"The Eye-Beaters"** he seems to be moving impressively ahead, even beyond the "big forms" of his earlier poems, toward archetypal images; whereas in other poems he seems to revert to the direct statements of his early poems and to come up with something too commonplace.

> . . . Not bad! I always knew it would have to be
> somewhere around
> The house . . .
>
> **("Diabetes, I")**

> . . . I'm going in Tyree's toilet
> and pull down my pants and take a shit.
>
> **("Looking for the Buckhead Boys")**

When he touches on his illnesses, real and imaginary, his style suggests that of Robert Lowell in *Life Studies* rather than the expansive imagination of James Dickey evident in his previous volumes.

> My eyes are green as lettuce with my diet,
> My weight is down. . . .
>
> **("Under Buzzards")**

But in spite of such tatters in his poetic garments James Dickey is still a very fine poet, and his most recent volume of poetry does not represent as abrupt a change in his style or thematics as some of his reviewers have assumed or as my few examples might have suggested. A central concern of Dickey's poetry has always been contact with the Other, represented variously as animalistic natural forces, the dead, Being itself.

In his first volume, *Into the Stone,* death is regarded as a change of being, not a thing to be feared; and the dead are accessible through the imagination. An exchange of being with the dead is a part of Dickey's obsession to understand through an act of faith in his imagination events which reason alone cannot comprehend. In *Drowning with Others* this "way of exchange" is a chief preoccupation of Dickey's, but here he seems for the first time reluctant to commune with the dead, and the exchange is predominantly with vital animal forces. In his next volume, *Helmets,* even the communion with the Other has become suspect as something only temporary and even potentially dangerous, since the *persona* may lose power as well as gain it. In *Buckdancer's Choice* there are, for the first time, unsuccessful attempts at communion. In one of the finest poems in the volume, **"The Firebombing,"** Dickey tries to transpose himself from his airplane down to the destruction he is creating below. This time, however, his imagination is incapable of penetrating such barriers as the aesthetic distance created by the space barrier, the beauty of the flight, and peacetime, middle-class comfort.

In the "Falling" section of *Poems 1957-1967* there is a further stage in Dickey's movement away from a concern with vital forces to the threat of destructive forces. Here he becomes concerned with the problem of how to face death and other threats to vitality and with the resources and rituals the merely human being has to draw on in such encounters. In the title poem **"Falling,"** an airline hostess falling to her death realizes under the extreme pressures of her contracted life-span that the only possibility of transcendence lies in making her death a mystery for the farm boys below. Consequently, she affirms her life at the very moment of her death, stripping herself naked and preparing her body for the last fatal and sacrificial reunion with the fertile earth. She discovers within herself a resource which permits transcendence.

In another poem, **"Power and Light,"** there is a suggestion that the pole climber represents a new concept that Dickey has of the poet, in that he is able to find the sources of his power—his ability to make connections for "the ghostly mouths" carried over the lines—*underground,* in the silent dark of his basement. Dickey seems to suggest that the "secret" of existence that he has been pursuing comes from a confrontation not with the natural world but with the "dark" of one's own death. A key passage in the poem seems to look back toward his earliest personal poems and ahead to new directions.

> . . . Years in the family dark have made me good
> At this   nothing else is so good   pure fires of the Self
> Rise crooning in lively blackness. . . .

In *Self-Interviews* Dickey provides further evidence of continuity by confirming what his reviewers have always known, that there is a connection between the chronology of his poems and that of his life. In *The Eye-Beaters* the reader encounters a person who is aware that his own youth is gone, that his life-space, like that of the air hostess in **"Falling,"** has narrowed. **"Two Poems of Going Home"** invokes rather effectively the inmost secret fears of a middle-aged man who finds only memories left at the locale of his youth.

> . . . Why does the Keeper go blind
> With sunset? The mad, weeping Keeper who can't keep
> A God-damned thing   who knows he can't keep everything
> Or anything alive: none of his rooms, his people
>   His past, his youth, himself,
>   But cannot let them die? . . .
>
>   **("Living There")**

"The Cancer Match" uses that prerogative of the poet that Dickey describes in *Self-Interviews* of lying convincingly and projects a fatal illness.

>   I see now the delights
>   Of being let "come home"
> From the hospital.
>   Night!
>   I don't have all the time
>   In the world, but I have all night.
>   I have space for me and my house,
>   And I have cancer and whiskey
>   In a lovely relation.

In *Self-Interviews* Dickey describes his celebration of life forces in his earlier poems as the reaction of a survivor of two very destructive wars. Rather than hysteria, the emotions that make themselves known to the reader in the poems of *The Eye-Beaters* are gratitude at having survived so far the destructive forces of nature and praise of the courage to take risks as a means of coping with the fear of death.

In the poem **"The Eye-Beaters"** Dickey implies the new poetics of the present volume. The poet must describe encounters with the most basic life experiences, including destructive as well as life-giving forces. He must see the image of the blind children as archetypal and imagine the reason for the children beating their eyes.

>   Therapists, I admit it; it helps me to think
> That they can give themselves, like God from their scabby fists,
>   the original
> Images of mankind: . . .

In *The Eye-Beaters,* consequently, Dickey presents situations, real and imaginary, where his *persona* is faced with the fear of death. He must imagine ways to cope with this fear. One solution, already indicated, is to take risks. In **"Giving a Son to the Sea,"** the father urges his son to take to the sea to affirm life even though the sea may swallow him up. In **"Under Buzzards,"** the diabetic drinks the beer that could kill him.

At any rate, Dickey makes it clear that the reality of death must be confronted. In **"Looking Up the Buckhead Boys,"** the poet feels the compulsion to look into his school yearbook of more than thirty years before—"The Book of the Dead"—and to go out to face what has happened to the "Buckhead Boys." Like some of his reviewers, I regret the loss of those powerful notes of Dickey's celebration of life; every poet today must have his existential volume, and, for better or worse, this is Dickey's. Here he seems to be attempting to say that a confrontation with death and its associated destructive forces (aging, disease, violence, and madness) may lead to fear but it may also lead to a realization of and an appreciation of the value of life. It should be noted that the volume includes a unique and almost semi-official celebration of the courage to take risks. Dickey reprints opposite a black, blank page the two poems from *Life Magazine* in honor of the Apollo astronauts who first walked on the dead surfaces of the moon and, from that perspective, appreciated in the black sky of the universe the blue life-light of their own planet.

>   . . . To complete the curve   to come back
> Singing with procedure   back through the last dark
>   Of the moon, past the dim ritual
> Random stones of oblivion, and through the blinding edge
>   Of moonlight into the sun
>   And behold
>   The blue planet steeped in its dream
> Of reality, its calculated vision shaking with
>   The only love.

Joyce Carol Oates (essay date autumn 1974)

SOURCE: Oates, Joyce Carol. "Out of Stone into Flesh: The Imagination of James Dickey." *Modern Poetry Studies*, 5, no. 2 (autumn 1974): 97-144.

[*In the following excerpt from an essay, Oates traces Dickey's poetic development.*]

> Despair and exultation
> Lie down together and thrash
> In the hot grass, no blade moving . . .
>
> —Dickey, **"Turning Away"**

> A man cannot pay as much attention to himself as I do without living in Hell all the time.
>
> —Dickey, *Sorties*

The remarkable poetic achievement of James Dickey is characterized by a restless concern with the poet's "personality" in its relationships to the world of nature and of experience. His work is rarely confessional in the sense of the term as we have come to know it, yet it is always personal—at times contemplative, at times dramatic. Because Dickey has become so controversial in recent years his incredible lyric and dramatic talent has not been adequately recognized, and his ceaseless, often monomaniacal questioning of identity, of the self, of that mysterious and elusive concept we call the personality, has not been investigated.

Yet this is only natural: it is always the fate of individuals who give voice to an era's hidden, atavistic desires, its "taboos," to be controversial and therefore misunderstood. Dickey's poetry is important not only because it is so skillful, but because it expresses, at times unintentionally, a great deal about the American imagination in its response to an increasingly complex and "unnatural" phase of civilization. (To Dickey, mental processes have come to seem "unnatural," in contrast to physical acts: hence the "Hell" of the quote from his journal, *Sorties.*) He has said, quite seriously, that "the world, the human mind, is dying of subtlety. What it needs is force" (*Sorties*, p. 85). His imagination requires the heroic. But the world cannot and will not accommodate the Hero, no matter how passionately he believes he has identified himself with the fundamental, secret rhythms of nature itself. One comes to loathe the very self that voices its hopeless demands, the "I" that will not be satisfied, and will never be silent. *I myself am hell* (Milton's Lucifer, in Book IV of *Paradise Lost*) is a philosophical statement, though it is expressed in the poetic language of personal emotion.

The volumes of poetry Dickey has published so far—***Into the Stone*** (1960), ***Drowning With Others*** (1962), ***Helmets*** (1964), ***Buckdancer's Choice*** (1965), ***The Eye-Beaters, Blood, Victory, Madness, Buckhead and Mercy*** (1970)—present a number of hypothetical or experimental personae, each a kind of reincarnation of an earlier consciousness, through which the "self" of the poet endures. He moves, he grows, he suffers, he changes, yet he is still the same—the voice is a singular one, unmistakable. It asks why, knowing the soul heroic, the man himself is so trapped, so helpless? Dickey's central theme is the frustration that characterizes modern man, confronted with an increasingly depersonalized and intellectualized society—the frustration and its necessary corollary, murderous rage. Dickey is not popular with liberals. Yet one can learn from him, as from no other serious writer, what it is like to have been born into one world and to have survived into another. It might be argued that Dickey is our era's Walt Whitman, but a Whitman subdued, no longer innocent, baptized by American violence into the role of a "killer/victim" who cannot locate within his society any standards by which his actions may be judged. A personality eager to identify itself with the collective, whether nature or other men, can survive only when the exterior world supports that mystical union of subject and object. Dickey speaks from the inside of our fallen, contaminated, guilt-obsessed era, and he speaks its language.

This was not always so: his earliest poems are lyric and meditative. They present a near-anonymous sensitivity, one hypnotized by forms, by Being, in which dramatic and ostensibly intolerable truths are resolved by a formal, ritualistic—essentially magical—imagination, into coherent and well-defined unities; his later poems submit this sensitivity to a broken, over-heated, emotionally and intellectually turbulent world. The "stoneness" of the first volume undergoes an astonishing variety of metamorphoses until, in **"The Eye-Beaters"** and **"Turning Away: Variations on Estrangement,"** it emerges as stark, isolated, combative self-consciousness, in which "A deadly, dramatic compression / Is made of the normal brow." The poet begins as Prospero knowing all and forgiving all and, through a series of sharply-tested modes of perception, comes to seem like Hamlet of the great, tragic soliloquies.

Who can tell us more about ourselves?—about our "American," "masculine," most dangerous selves? Even more than Whitman, Dickey contains multitudes; he cannot be reproached for the fact that some of these aspects of a vast, complex self are at war with the others. He experiments with the art of poetry, and with the external world and the relationships it offers him (will he be lover?—murderer?—observer?), but what is most moving about his work is his relentless honesty in regard to his own evolving perception of himself, the mystery of his "personality." He refuses to remain in any explored or conquered territory, either in his art or in his personality. Obsessed with the need to seek and to define, he speaks for those who know that the universe is rich with meaning, but are not always able to relate the intellectual, conscious aspect of their natures to it. Thus, the need to reject the "conscious" mind and its public expression, civilization itself, which is so disturbing in Dickey. Indeed, *Sorties* (1971) is very nearly a confession of despair—the poet seems unable to integrate the various aspects of his nature, conceiving of the world of the intellect and art as "hell." "Believe me, it is better to be stupid and ordinary," Dickey tells us early in the book. What such a temperament requires, however, is not less intelligence, but more.

Dickey has not always expressed himself in such extreme terms, and he has been, all along, a careful craftsman, knowing that meaning in poetry must be expressed through language, through a system of mental constructs. In fact, it must be invented anew with each poem; it must be rigorously contracted, abbreviated, made less explosive and less primitive. In an excellent essay in *The Suspect in Poetry* (1964), he cautions young poets against abandoning themselves to their unconscious "song," which he defines as "only a kind of monstrousness that has to be understood and ordered according to some principle to be meaningful."[1] The unrestrained and un-imagined Self must be related syntactically to the external world in order to achieve meaning.

Yet the phenomenal world changes; language shifts, evolves, breaks free of its referents; and the human ego, mysteriously linked to both, is forced to undergo continuous alterations in order simply to survive. In the poem **"Snakebite"** (1967), the "stage of pine logs" and the "role / I have been cast in" give way suddenly and horribly to the dramatic transition from the pronoun "it" to the pronoun "me," as the poet realizes he is confined in his living, breathing, existential body: he is not playing a role, after all. If he wants to survive he will have to drain that poison out of his bloodstream. Therefore, one of the burdens of the poet's higher awareness is to discover if there is any metamorphosis, any possible reincarnation, that is ultimately more than a mode of perception, *a way of arranging words.* Otherwise we begin to imagine ourselves as totally "estranged." To deny that estrangement, we must deny our very framework of perception—language and sanity and logic—as if, by annihilating the mental construct of Incarnation, we might somehow experience it on a level far below consciousness. Certainly, Dickey has emphasized the poem as physical experience; he has set up opposing pseudo-categories of the poetry of "participation" and the poetry of "reflection" (*Sorties,* p. 59). Such an estrangement rests, however, upon the metaphysical assumption that man's intellect is an intruder in the universe, and that the language-systems he has devised are not utterly natural, natural to his species. Surely the human invention or creation of language is our species' highest achievement; some psycho-linguists speculate that human beings are born with a genetic endowment for recognizing and formulating language, that they "possess genes for all kinds of information, with strands of special, peculiarly human DNA for the discernment of meaning in syntax."[2] Failing to accept the intellect as triumphantly human, rather than somehow unnatural, the poet is doomed to endless struggles with the self. **"Variations on Estrangement"** at the end of *Eye-Beaters* deals with countless battles and meadows strewn "with inner lives," concluding with the hope that the poet's life may be seen "as a thing / That can be learned, / As those earnest young heroes learned theirs, / Later, much later on."

An objective assessment of one's situation must be experienced apart from life itself, then. And only "much later on." To use a critical term Dickey appropriated from William Wordsworth, he is a poet of the "Second Birth," not one who, like Arthur Rimbaud or Dylan Thomas, possesses a natural instrument for poetry, but one who eventually reduces the distinction between "born" and "made" poets only by hard work, by the "ultimate moral habit of trying each poem, each line, each word, against the shifting but finally constant standards of inner necessity" (*The Suspect in Poetry,* pp. 55-57). Contrary to his instinct for direct, undiluted self-expression, the poet has tried to define and develop his own personality as a "writing instrument"; he has pared back, reduced, restrained the chaotic "monstrousness" of raw emotion, in order to relate his unique experience to common experience. He contradicts T. S. Eliot's ideal of an impersonal poetry, yet paradoxically refuses to endorse what he would call the monstrousness of confessional verse: "The belief in the value of one's personality has all but disappeared."

But what is personality, that a belief in it might save us?

Not a multi-levelled phenomenon, Dickey's sense of "personality," but rather a series of imagined dramas, sometimes no more than flashes of rapport, kinships with beasts or ancient ancestors—as in the apocalyptic **"The Eye-Beaters,"** in which personality is gained only when "Reason" is rejected in favor of primitive action. The process of increasing self-consciousness, as image after image is explored, held up like a cask to the poet's face,[3] absorbed, and finally discarded, comes to seem a tragic movement, as every existential role in the universe must ultimately be abandoned.

"INTACT AND INCREDIBLE LOVE"

Dickey has said that the century's greatest phrase is Albert Schweitzer's "reverence for life." This conviction runs through his work, but is strongest in the earlier volumes. *Into the Stone* consists of contemplative, almost dream-like poems that investigate the poet's many forms of love: beginning with the mythical, incantatory dissolution of the individual personality into both "dark" and "light," and concluding with the book's title poem, which emphasizes the poet's confident "knowing" and his being "known," through his relationship with a woman.

"Sleeping Out at Easter" is terse, restrained, as the "Word rising out of darkness" seems to act without the deliberate involvement of the poet. As dawn arrives in the forest, the "Presences" of night turn into trees and "One eye opens slowly without me." Everything moves in its own placid, non-personalized pattern, out of darkness and into the sunlight, and the world is "made good" by the springing-together of wood and sun. The metamorphosis of Presences into daytime trees is one that could occur without the poet's song, yet the poet voices a total acceptance, as if he knew himself uniquely absorbed in the cycle of night/day, his "magical shepherd's cloak . . . not yet alive on [his] flesh." In other, similarly incantatory poems, the poet lies at the edge of a well, contemplating himself and his smile and the "grave face" of his dead brother, or lies "in ritual down" in a small unconsecrated grove of suburban pines—trying to get back, to get down, beneath both gods and animals, to "being part of the acclaimed rebirth" of spring (**"The Vegetable King"**). (Years later, when his poetry has undergone tremendous changes, Dickey will deal again with the transformation of a human being into a tree in **"The Field,"** one of his most eccentric poems.)

Into the Stone contains a number of war poems, but in spite of their subject they absorb the poet's personality much as the nature poems do, locating in confusion and panic certain centers of imagination, of decision, which the poet is able to recall years later when "at peace." **"The Enclosure"** is the first of Dickey's many poems which "enclose" and idealize women: a group of war-nurses on a Philippine island are protected by a compound with a wire fence, but the poet imagines them whispering to the soldiers outside "to deliver them out / Of the circle of impotence." In lines of curious, ceremonial calm, the poet declares how, after the war, this vision led him to "fall / On the enemy's women / With intact and incredible love." Of the war poems, the most vivid is **"The Performance,"** which celebrates the paradox of pain and triumph in the memory of David Armstrong, executed by the Japanese; Dickey remembers Armstrong doing a handstand against the sun, and his death by decapitation is seen as another kind of "performance." Even here there is a sense of acquiescence, finality, as if the cycle of nature could absorb this violent death as easily as it could absorb the shapes of trees back into primordial Presences.

The reverential awe of **"Trees and Cattle"** places the poet's consciousness in a "holy alliance" with trees, cattle, and sunlight, making his mind a "red beast"—his head gifted with ghostly bull's horns, by the same magic that allowed D. H. Lawrence to imagine his head "hard-balanced, antlered" in "A Doe at Evening"; the sun itself burns more deeply, because trees and cattle exist. A miracle of some kind has occurred, though it cannot be explained, and the poet half-believes he may be saved from death; as, in a later poem, **"Fog Envelopes the Animals,"** the poet-hunter is somehow transformed into the "long-sought invisibility" of pure things or events or processes: "Silence. Whiteness. Hunting." But *Into the Stone* is characterized by passivity and no hint of the guilty, pleasurable agitation of physical life, whether hunting or love; the title poem describes the poet "on the way to a woman," preoccupied with a mystical absorption into the "stone" of the moon. The woman is outside the concern of the poem, undefined, not even mythologized; the poet is not vividly portrayed, as in **"Cherrylog Road"**; he could be any man, any lover, believing that "The dead have their chance in my body." All is still, mysterious, calm. The poet "knows" his place and his love, quite unlike the moon-drawn men of a later poem, **"Apollo,"** who are seen as "floating on nothing / but procedure alone," and who symbolize "all humanity in the name / Of a new life." This later poem makes the "stone" of the moon into "stones," breaks up a seamless cosmology into a universe of "craters" and "mountains the animal / Eye has not seen since the earth split" (the earth-moon split an ancient and honored moon-theory, of obvious symbolic, if not scientific, value)—not the Platonic oneness of stone, but stones: "We stare into the moon / dust, the earth-blazing ground. We laugh, with the beautiful craze / Of static. We bend, we pick up stones" (**"Apollo"**).

A more dramatic sense of self is evident in Dickey's second book, *Drowning With Others*. Here, he imagines the torturous memories of a lifeguard who failed to save a drowning child, he imagines himself inside the hunting dream of a dog sleeping on his feet, he contemplates fish in **"The Movement of Fish"** with the alert, awed scrutiny of Lawrence himself, making a judgment, like Lawrence's, that arises from the distant otherness of the fish's world, where its sudden movement has the power to "convulse the whole ocean" and teach man the Kierkegaardian terror of the leap, the "fear and trembling" of great depths that are totally still, far beneath the superficial agitation that men see or float upon in their boats.

Yet the hunted/hunting animals of **"The Heaven of Animals"** are poetic constructions, Platonic essences of beasts wholly absorbed in a mythical cycle of life-death-rebirth: at the very center of nature these beasts "tremble," "fall," "are torn," "rise," and "walk again," like Ralph Waldo Emerson's red slayer and his perpetual victim. **"The Heaven of Animals"** is all but unique in Dickey's poetry because the poet himself has no clear position in it, as if its Unity of Being somehow excluded an active intellectual consciousness; if we look back at the poem from **"Fog Envelopes the Animals"** and other hunting poems, and from Dickey's statements in *Self-Interviews* about the mysterious "renewal" he experiences when hunting, we can assume that his deepest sympathies are with the predators, but this is not evident from the poem itself, which is one of his finest, most delicate achievements. The owl of **"The Owl King"** is another poetic (and not naturalistic) creature, a form of the poet himself who sits "in my shape / With my claws growing deep into wood / And my sight going slowly out, / Inch by inch." Superior forces belong to those who, like the owl, can see in the dark; or to those who, like Dickey himself, possess extraordinary powers of vision[4] that set him apart from other, average men. But the forces are benevolent, godly, and restrained—the Owl-King participates in a mysterious ceremony with the Blind Child, "as beasts at their own wedding, dance," and is not the symbol of cold, savage violence of the owl perched upon the tent in **Deliverance,** just as the poet-narrator of the volume **Drowning With Others** is not the helplessly eager murderer of **Deliverance.** Here, in the Owl-King's Roethkean kingdom, all nature is transformed by mind, its brutal contingencies and dramas suppressed, the possible "monstrousness" of its song made into a child-like lyric. Its final stanzas link it to earlier poems of Dickey's in which tension has been resolved by an act of impersonal, godly will:

> Far off, the owl king
> Sings like my father, growing
> In power. Father, I touch
> Your face. I have not seen
> My own, but it is yours.
> I come, I advance,
> I believe everything, I am here.

Through the child's (blind) acceptance, Dickey accepts the world; just as, in the anguished **"The Eye-Beaters"** (of 1970), he rejects the world of normal, rational vision, having been shaken by the experience of seeing blind children beat at their eyes in order to "see." In **"The Owl-King,"** the transcendent, paternal bird withdraws into the darkness of his own vision, while the lost child's father emerges "In love with the sound of my voice" to claim his child; both aspects of the poetic consciousness are required if the child is to be saved, cherished, and yet both are dependent upon the child's acquiescence. (Just as, for the hunter, the imagined "acquiescence" of the hunted)—the slain—is a ritualistic necessity; see Dickey's attempted justification of his love of hunting, in **Self-Interviews.**) This poem is a "song of innocence" whose unearthly simplicity—the child moves from tree to tree as if blessing them—will be transformed, years later, into the nightmarish "song of experience" of the crazed blind children in **"The Eye-Beaters."** Then, the objects of the poet's pity being, in themselves, hopeless, not even human children, beyond all love or language, the poet himself will narrowly escape madness. But this is years later, years deeper into flesh.

Entering History

In his third book, **Helmets,** Dickey begins to move out of the perfected world of Eternal Recurrence, no longer the awed, alert but essentially passive observer, now ready to experience history. It is clear that Dickey desires to take on "his" own personal history as an analogue to or a microcosmic exploration of twentieth-century American history, which is one of the reasons he is so important a poet. In his inspired, witty, and ingeniously-balanced essay on Randall Jarrell in **The Suspect in Poetry,** Dickey allows that he can discover in Jarrell's poetry very little excellence of technique, but he insists that Jarrell's contribution—"that of writing about real things, rather than playing games with words"—is a valuable one. Dickey indicates implicitly that *he* will take on both the challenge of being an artist and a historian of our era, which he has, applying a superior poetic talent to Jarrell's "realm . . . of pity and terror . . . a kind of non-understanding understanding, and above all of helplessness."[5]

Once he is released from the sacred but bloodless cycle of Nature, Dickey is concerned with giving life to this "non-understanding understanding" of creatures simpler than himself, or of an earlier form of himself, as in the beautiful, perfect poem **"Drinking from a Helmet."** In **"The Dusk of Horses,"** the emphasis has shifted from acceptance to a sharper awareness of distinctions between self and object, the need for the human participant in an action to judge it:

> No beast ever lived who understood
>
> What happened among the sun's fields,
> Or cared why the color of grass
> Fled over the hill while he stumbled,
>
> Led by the halter to sleep
> On his four taxed, worthy legs.
>
> ("The Dusk of Horses")

In this and similar poems in **Helmets,** the graceful fluidity of the lines is like the fluidity of the earlier poems: the god's-eye vision set to music. As the theme of "helplessness" grows, however, Dickey loses interest in well-made and sweetly-sounding poetry, and pours his remarkable energies into such extravaganzas of shouts and shrieks as **"The May-Day Sermon."** And, whereas death might once have been resolved by a mystical affirmation of unity, in the recent poem **"Diabetes"** it is resolved by a surreptitious drink of beer; in **"The Cancer Match,"** by whiskey.

Throughout **Helmets** there is an increasing growth, as if the subjects long loved by the poet are now shifting out of the hypnosis of love itself, beginning to elude his incantatory powers: coming alive and separate. In a poem reminiscent of Wallace Stevens' "Anecdote of the Jar," Dickey stands by a fence with his palm on the top wire, and experiences a vision or a nervous hallucination of the disorder that would result if the tension of the wire were broken:

> If the wire were cut anywhere
> All his blood would fall to the ground
> And leave him standing and staring
> With a face as white as a Hereford's.
>
> ("Fence Wire")

The "top tense wire" is like a guitar string "tuned to an E," whose humming sound arranges the acres of the farm and holds them "highstrung and enthralled." Suddenly, the poet in his human role must accept a position in nature which is superior to that of trees and cattle, an intellectual responsibility that will involve both exultation and the risk of despair. But because of Dickey's hand on this fence wire,

> The dead corn is more
> Balanced in death than it was,
> The animals more aware
>
> Within the huge human embrace
> Held up and borne out of sight
> Upon short, unbreakable poles
> Where through the ruled land intones
> Like a psalm . . .

Because of the sensational aspects of some of his later poems, Dickey is not usually known to have concerned himself so seriously, and so perceptively, with the metaphysics behind aesthetic action; it is characteristic of his energy and his pursuit of new challenges that a very few poems about "poetry" are enough for him. If read in its proper chronological place in Dickey's work, **"Fence Wire"** is a moving as well as a significant poem; it is the first clear statement of the poet's sense of himself as involved responsibly in history. In his most powerful poems the tension between that "top thread tuned to an E" and the abandonment to one's own possible, probable "monstrousness" provides a dramatic excitement generally lacking in these early, though entirely admirable poems, and, less content with lyric verse itself, Dickey will experiment with wildly imaginative monologues in which words float and leap all over the page.

. . . . .

Monsters

After *Helmets,* Dickey's poetry changes considerably. The colloquial tone and unserious rhythms of **"Cherrylog Road"** are used for deadly serious purposes, as Dickey explores hypothetical selves and the possibility of values outside the human sphere. Where in an early poem like **"The Performance,"** a mystical placidity rendered even a brutal execution into something observed, now most actions, most states of being, are examined bluntly, brutally, emotionally, as the poet subjects himself to raw life without the sustaining rituals of Being.

Dickey has many extraordinary poems, fusions of "genius" and "art," but the central poem of his work seems to be **"The Firebombing."** No reader, adjusted to the high, measured art of Dickey's first three volumes, can be ready for this particular poem; it is unforgettable, and seems to me an important achievement in our contemporary literature, a masterpiece that could only have been written by an American, and only by Dickey.

"The Firebombing" is an eight-page poem of irregular lines, abrupt transitions and leaps, stanzas of varying length, connected by suburban-surreal images, a terrifying visionary experience endured in a "well-stocked pantry." Its effort is to realize, to *feel,* what the poet did twenty years before as a participant in an "anti-morale raid" over Japan during the closing months of World War II. Its larger effort is to feel guilt and finally to feel anything. One of the epigraphs to the poem is from the *Book of Job*: "Or hast thou an arm like God?" This is Dickey's ironic self-directed question, for it is he, Dickey, the homeowner/killer, the Job/God, who has tried on the strength of vast powers and has not been able to survive them. Irony is something altogether new in Dickey:

> Homeowners unite.
>
> All families lie together, though some are burned alive.
> The others try to feel
> For them. Some can, it is often said.

The detachment is not godly, but despairing. Though he is now Job, he was at one time the "arm of God," and being both man and God is an impossibility. Dickey's earlier war poems always show him a survivor, grateful to survive, rather boyish and stunned by the mystery of a strange rightness beneath disorder; it seems to have taken him many years to get to this particular poem, though its meaning in his life must have been central. Now the survivor is also a killer. What of this, what of killing?—what is a release from the sin of killing? Confession, but most of all guilt; if the poet cannot make himself feel guilt even for the deaths of children, how will it be possible for him to feel anything human at all?—

> . . . some technical-minded stranger with my hands
> Is sitting in a glass treasure-hole of blue light,
> Having potential fire under the undeodorized arms
> Of his wings, on thin bomb-shackles,
> The "tear-drop-shaped" 300-gallon drop-tanks
> Filled with napalm and gasoline.

This stranger is, or was, Dickey himself, who made 100 combat missions through the South Pacific, the Philippines and Okinawa, and participated in B-29 raids over Japan; but he is only a memory now, an eerily aesthetic memory. He exists in the mind of a suburban husband and father, worrying about his weight and the half-paid-for pantry that is part of his homeowning and his present "treasure-hole":

> Where the lawn mower rests on its laurels
> Where the diet exists

> For my own good   where I try to drop
> Twenty years . . .

So many years after the event, what remains? He is now a civilian, a citizen, an American who understands himself in ironic, secret charge of all the necessary trivia of unaesthetic life—the purchasing of golf carts and tennis shoes, new automobiles, Christmas decorations—which he knows as the "glue inspired / By love of country," the means by which the possibly atomistic or death-bound ego is held fast in its identity. Though the wonder remains, he is far from the moon-hypnotized, somnambulistic rhythms of the past; **"The Firebombing"** is what Dickey would call an "open poem," one in which a certain compulsiveness in the presentation of the subject matter precludes or makes peripheral an aesthetic response,[6] and the poet's own recollection of his action is mocked, if it must be assessed in stylized terms:

> As I sail artistically over
> The resort town followed by farms,
> Singing and twisting
> All the handles in heaven   kicking
> The small cattle off their feet
> In a red costly blast
> Flinging jelly over the walls
> As in a chemical war-
> fare field demonstration.

Remembering this, he knows that "my hat should crawl on my head" and "the fat on my body should pale"—but one of the horrors of this bombing raid is that it has somehow destroyed a normal human response, as if the "arm of God" the pilot had assumed had also annihilated him. Having shown us so convincingly in his poetry how natural, how inevitable, is man's love for all things, Dickey now shows us what happens when man is forced to destroy, forced to step down into history and be an American ("and proud of it"). In so doing, he enters a tragic dimension in which few poets indeed have operated. Could, Walt Whitman's affirmation hold out, if he were forced to affirm not just the violence of others, but his own? If war is necessary, warriors are necessary; someone must sacrifice his cosmic love; and not only is the traditional life-praising song of the poet savagely mocked by his performance as a patriot in wartime, but the poet cannot even experience his own deeds, for he has acted as a machine inside a machine. In **"The Firebombing,"** everything must remain remote and abstract, not experienced in any vital way. The Machine Age splits man irreparably from his instinctive need to see, to feel, to *know* through the senses. The Whitmanesque affirmation of man is difficult to sustain if the poet can see the objects of his love only from a great height, through an intellectual telescope. When Whitman feels he is "on the verge of a usual mistake" ("Song of Myself," stanza 38), it is only an emotional mistake; he could never have considered the nihilism of a self without emotions, in which his inventiveness could really attach itself to nothing because it could experience nothing.

After this dream-like unleashing of "all American fire" the poet states flatly that *Death will not be what it should*—a counter-statement, perhaps, to Albert Schweitzer's *Reverence for life*. It is this poet's unique vision:

> Ah, under one's dark arms
> Something strange-scented falls—when those on earth
> Die, there is not even sound;
> One is cool and enthralled in the cockpit,
> Turned blue by the power of beauty,
> In a pale treasure-hole of soft light
> Deep in aesthetic contemplation
> Seeing the ponds catch fire
> And cast it through ring after ring
> Of land. . . .
> It is this detachment,
> The honored aesthetic evil,
> The greatest sense of power in one's life,
> That must be shed in bars, or by whatever
> Means, by starvation
> Visions in well-stocked pantries. . . .

These "visions" will inspire in the poet wilder and wilder imaginings in his own creative life, and an abandonment of the ego as "homeowner" in favor of the ego as "hunter" or "primitive." The mechanized State tempts one to an aesthetic evil, and so perhaps salvation may be found in a pre-aesthetic, pre-historical animality that will seize upon possible rites (the structural basis of **Deliverance**) in order to exorcise the despairing and suicidal violence of the animal self. Whether Dickey's themes are explorative rather than absolute, whether his work traces an autobiographical query or a record, the function of his poetry seems to be the demonstration of the failure of such a vision. And yet it is certainly tempting, to take on the viciousness—and the innocence—of the animal, to take for our totems owls, snakes, foxes, wolverines, and to reject forever the possibilities of detachment and evil that are inherent in civilization.

Like Dostoyevsky, Dickey considers the helplessness of the *killer*. But, unlike Dostoyevsky, he cannot imagine a transformation of the killer into a higher form of himself: the mysterious process by which Raskolnikov grows, and by which Smerdyakov can be seen as a rudimentary form of Father Zossima. But Dickey cannot operate through metaphor, as Dostoyevsky did, for he was the man, he did these things, *he* and no one else. Though his poetry charts a process of wonders, a changing of selves, finally he is only himself, a particular man, trapped in a finite and aging body with memories that belong to him and not to the rest of us, not to any liberalized concept of the guilt we all "share." (Like Herbert Marcuse, Dickey could probably feel no more than scorn for the "repressive tolerance" of some aspects of liberalism.) If made general and universal, in order to be shared, is guilt itself not made an aesthetic event?—a luxury?—a perversion?

But the narrator of the poem cannot concern himself with such abstractions:

> All this, and I am still hungry,
> Still twenty years overweight, still unable
> To get down there or see
> What really happened.
> . . . . .
> It is that I can imagine
> At the threshold nothing
> With its ears crackling off
> Like powdery leaves,
> Nothing with children of ashes, nothing not
> Amiable, gentle, well-meaning. . . .

A poetry of Being can move to perfect resolutions, but this poetry of anguished Becoming cannot. ("Some can, it is often said," Dickey has remarked, ironically and sadly.) The narrative and confessional elements of **"The Firebombing"** demand a totally different aesthetic: the aesthetic-denying open form. No reconciliation of opposites is possible here because the poet cannot reconcile himself to his earlier self. And so what of "Absolution? Sentence?" These do not matter, for "The thing itself is in that."

"The Firebombing" is central to an understanding of Dickey's work. It could not have been prophesied, on the basis of the earlier, Roethke-inspired poems; but once it appears, unsuppressed, it is so powerful an illumination that it helps to explain a great deal that might remain mysterious and puzzling. **Buckdancer's Choice, Falling,** and above all **Eye-Beaters** deal with mortality, decay, disease, perhaps attributable in part to the poet's actual aging, but only in part, for the descent into a physically combative and increasingly unaesthetic world is not the usual pattern our finest poets follow, as both Roethke and Yeats, and other poets of the "Second Birth," suggest. Yet the emphasis Dickey places upon mortality, his self-consciousness about it, is a motif that begins to appear even in his literary criticism. How is it possible that the man who believes in nature—in natural processes—should feel uneasy about the natural process of aging? It is a paradox in Ernest Hemingway also, but perhaps it is to be understood in Rainer Maria Rilke's terms: our fear is not of death, but life unlived. In an introduction to Paul Carroll's *The Young American Poets* (1968), Dickey makes a statement that totally contradicts the contemplative, balanced criticism of *The Suspect in Poetry,* of only four years previously:

> . . . the aging process almost always brings to the poet the secret conviction that he has settled for far too little. . . . The nearer he gets to his end the more he yearns for the cave: for a wild, shaggy, all-out, all-involving way of speaking where he (or, now, someone: some new poet) engage each other at primitive levels, on ground where the issues are not those of literary fashion but quite literally those of life and death. All his lifelong struggle with "craft" seems a tragic and ludicrous waste of time.

One would imagine, from such remarks, that the speaker is far older than forty-five; "the nearer he gets to his end" is a visionary statement that might be comprehensible in the Yeats of *Last Poems,* but astonishing in a poet who is the same age as the Yeats of *The Green Helmet.* But if a denial of "craft" (or civlization) is needed in order to release spontaneous energy, then one can see why, for Dickey, it must be done.

Entropy

Buckdancer's Choice received the National Book Award in 1965, and in 1967 Dickey put together his ***Poems, 1957-1967,*** for Wesleyan University Press. It does not observe strict chronological order, however, beginning with the demonic "May Day Sermon To The Women of Gilmer County, Georgia, By a Woman Preacher Leaving the Baptist Church," one of Dickey's most flamboyant poems. Clearly, Dickey does not want the reader to enter the world of **Into the Stone** with the innocence he himself had entered it; that celebration of forms is all but out-shouted by the eleven-page sermon, which is about violence done to and by a young girl in Georgia, and about her escape with her motorcycle-riding lover, "stoned out of their minds on the white / Lightning of fog"—

> singing   the saddlebags full of her clothes
> Flying   snagging   shoes hurling away   stocking grabbed-off
> Unwinding and furling on twigs: all we know   all we could follow
> Them by was her underwear was stocking after stocking where it tore
> Away, and a long slip stretched on a thorn all these few gave
> Out.   Children, you know it: that place was where they took
> Off into the air   died   disappeared   entered my mouth   your mind

It is an incredible achievement, with the intonations of a mad, inspired sermon, the flesh elevated beyond the spirit, but both elevated into myth. It is a myth that transforms everything into it: everything turns into everything else, through passion. The intellect exercises very little control in this "wild, shaggy, all-out, all-involving" work, and though Dickey has expressed doubt over the value of Allen Ginsberg's poetry,[7] one is forced to think of certain works of Ginsberg's and of how, under ether-sniffing or morphine injection, Ginsberg wrote all of *Ankor Wat* and that extravaganza, "Aether," in which a preaching voice proclaims certain truths to us: "we are the sweepings of the moon / we're what's *left over* from perfection"—"[my] Madness is intelligible reactions to / Unintelligible phenomena"—

And—
What can be possible
in a minor universe
in which you can see
God by sniffing the
gas in a cotton?

("Aether," in *Reality Sandwiches*)

Dickey is much more violent, more heartless, than Ginsberg, of course, since he is driven by energies more archaic than is Ginsberg, who is a philosopher with a respect for the syntax of the imagination if not of superficial grammar; the **"May Day Sermon"** is at once revenge for and repetition of the helplessness of the bomber pilot, a mythic annihilation of a punishing, near-invisible Father, and an escape off into space, the girl's clothing cast off behind her like the airline stewardess' clothing in **"Falling."** In all the exuberant spurts of language there is violence, but especially here:

> And she comes down   putting her back into
> The hatchet   often   often   he is brought down laid out
> Lashing   smoking   sucking wind: Children, each year at this time
> A girl will tend to take an ice pick in both hands   a lone pine
> Needle   will hover   hover: Children, each year at this time
> Things happen quickly   and it is easy for a needle to pass
> Through the eye of a man bound for Heaven she leaves it   naked goes
> Without further sin through the house

After countless readings, the **"May Day Sermon"** still has the power to shock: consider the "needle-eye-Heaven" joke. The maniacal repetitions make one wince ("get up up in your socks and rise"), and the Dylan Thomas-surreal touches sometimes seem forced ("Dancing with God in a mule's eye"), but the poem's shrieking transmutation of murder, nakedness, eroticism, fertility, and poetry into a single event has an irresistible strength: "everything is more *more* MORE." Nature itself becomes active in the process of transmutation, as even "peanuts and beans exchange / Shells in joy" and in a poetic sleight-of-hand reminiscent of Thomas' *Ballad of the Long-Legged Bait* at its apocalyptic conclusion, "the barn falls in / Like Jericho." The countryside itself is speaking through the woman preacher "as beasts speak to themselves / Of holiness learned in the barn." It is mysticism, but existential and ribald, noisy, filled with the humming of gnats and strange prophecies:

> Each May you will crouch like a sawhorse to make yourself
> More here   you will be cow chips   chickens croaking. . . .
>   . . . . .
>   and every last one of you will groan

> Like nails barely holding   and your hair be full of the gray
> Glints of stump chains.   Children, each year at this time you will have
> Back-pain, but also heaven.

In **"May Day Sermon"** Dickey creates a patchwork of images that go beyond the "not wholly sane" images of **"Chenille."**

However, ***Buckdancer's Choice*** contains several very personal and moving poems dealing with mortality, the title poem and **"Angina"** (which deal with Dickey's mother, an invalid "dying of breathless angina"), **"Them, Crying," "The Escape,"** and one which reasserts the mystical possibility of transcending death, its certainties expressed in a steady three-beat line:

> All ages of mankind unite
> Where it is dark enough.
>   . . . . .
> All creatures tumbled together
> Get back in their wildest arms
> No single thing but each other. . . .

(**"The Common Grave"**)

But the most passionate poems are counter-statements, concerned with developing images adequate to express horror; in **"Pursuit from Under,"** the poet summons up a terrifying image that does not have its place in his own experience, or even in his probable experience, but is a conscious re-creation of a memory. He is standing in a meadow, in August, and imagines he hears the "bark of seals" and feels "the cold of a personal ice age." Then he recalls having once read an account of Arctic explorers who died of starvation and whose journal contained a single entry of unforgettable horror:

> . . . under the ice,
> The killer whale darts and distorts,
> Cut down by the flawing glass
>
> To a weasel's shadow,
> And when, through his ceiling, he sees
> Anything darker than snow
> He falls away
> To gather more and more force
>   . . . . .
>   then charges
> Straight up, looms up at the ice and smashes
> Into it with his forehead. . . .

And so the killer whale pursues the poet, even in this familiar meadow in the South, and he thinks of "how the downed dead pursue us"—"not only in the snow / But in the family field." It is interesting to note that Norman Mailer's nihilistic and very deliberately "literary" novel, *Why Are We in Vietnam?*, also transports its protagonist/victim to the Arctic in order to allow him a vision of God-as-beast: this "vision" is then imposed upon all of American (universal?) experience, and can allow for no possibilities of transcendence. If God is a beast (as Dickey concludes in **"The Eye-Beaters"**), then the beast is God, and one must either acquiesce to him and experience the helplessness of terror in an ordinary southern meadow, or imitate him, taking on some of his powers. But, increasingly, the poet reaches out beyond his own geographical and historical territory to appropriate this vision. It demands a distortion or a rejection of naturalistic life; at times, as he admits, a kind of necessary theatricality, as he explains in *Self-Interviews* why hunting is so important to him: ". . . the main thing is to re-enter the cycle of the man who hunts for his food. Now this may be playacting at being a primitive man, but it's better than not having any rapport with the animal at all . . . I have a great sense of renewal when I am able to go into the woods and hunt with a bow and arrow, to enter into the animal's world in this way." And, in *Deliverance,* the experience of "renewal" or deliverance itself is stimulated by a hunt for other men; simple animals are no longer enough, and the whole of the novel is constructed around those several intensely dramatic moments in which the narrator sights his target—a human and usually forbidden target—and kills him with an arrow from his powerful bow: The arrow is at least real; the napalm and gasoline bomb is not, since it is dropped upon abstractions. And, too, the necessary intimacy of the besieged men in *Deliverance* approximates a primitive brotherliness, excluding the confusion that women bring to a world of simple, clear, direct actions. For women, while mysterious and unfathomable, are also "civilization."

But if women are objects, goddess-objects, they too can be assimilated into the mystique of primitive power-worship. One of the most striking poems in all of Dickey's work is **"The Fiend,"** which magically transforms a voyeur/lover into a tree, into an omnipotent observer, back into a voyeur again, while throughout he is the poet who loves and desires and despairs of truly knowing his subjects; the poem is a long, hushed, reverential overture to murder. Yet the equation of the voyeur with the poet is obvious, and the poem concludes ominously by remarking how "the light / Of a hundred favored windows" has "gone wrong somewhere in his glasses." Dickey is remarkably honest in acknowledging the value he puts upon his own fantasies, in contrast to the less interesting world of reality. What is important is *his* imaginative creation, *his* powers of seeing. In praise of what a Jungian would call the "Anima," Dickey has said in *Sorties* that "poor mortal perishable women are as dust before these powerful and sensual creatures of the depths of one's own being" (p. 4). A dangerous over-estimation of the individual's self-sufficiency, one might think, especially since there is always the possibility of that interior light going "wrong somewhere in his glasses."

In fact, in Dickey's later poems eyesight becomes crucial, aligned with the mysterious grace of masculinity itself. When one's vision begins to weaken, there is an immediate danger of loss of control; conversely, "sight" itself can be rejected, denied, as a prelude to glorious savagery. Or the denial of vision can facilitate a more formal, sinister betrayal, as Dickey imagines himself as, simultaneously, a slave-owner on a Southern plantation and the white father of an illegitimate black son and the father-who-denies-his-son, a Master driven to madness by his role as an Owner, in the poem **"Slave Quarters."** Dickey's question concerns itself with many forms of paternal betrayal, a betrayal of the eyes of others:

> What it is to look once a day
> Into an only
> Son's brown, waiting, wholly possessed
> Amazing eyes, and not
> Acknowledge, but own . . .

How take on the guilt . . . ? is the poem's central question.

In the section, "Falling," in ***Poems, 1957-1967,*** Dickey explores further extensions of life, beginning with **"Reincarnation (II),"** in which the poet has taken on the form of a bird. His first reincarnation was into a snake, which we leave waiting in an old wheel not for food, but for the first man to walk by—minute by minute the head of the snake becoming "more poisonous and poised." But as a bird the poet undergoes a long, eerie, metaphysical flight that takes him out of mortality altogether—

> to be dead
> In one life is to enter
> Another to break out to rise above the clouds

But **"Reincarnation (II)"** is extremely abstract and does not seem to have engaged the poet's imaginative energies as deeply as **"Reincarnation (I)"** of ***Buckdancer's Choice.*** It is balanced by the long **"Falling,"** an astonishing poetic feat that dramatizes the accidental fall of an airline stewardess from a plane, to her death in a cornfield. "The greatest thing that ever came to Kansas" undergoes a number of swift metamorphoses—owl, hawk, goddess—stripping herself naked as she falls. She imagines the possibility of falling into water, turning her fall into a dive so that she can "come out healthily dripping / And be handed a Coca-Cola" but ultimately she is helpless to save herself; she is a human being, not a bird like the spiritual power of **"Reincarnation (II)"** and she comes to know how "the body will assume without effort any position / Except the one that will sustain it enable it to rise live / Not die." She dies, "driven well into the image of her body," inexplicable and unquestionable, and her clothes begin to come down all over Kansas; a kind of mortal goddess, given

And green of insects   or the therapist suffering kindly   but
            a tribal light old
Enough to be seen without sight?

The vision he imagines for them is pre-historic; a caveman artist, "Bestial, working like God," is drawing beasts on a cave wall: deer, antelope, elk, ibex, quagga, rhinoceroses of wool-gathering smoke, cave bear, mammoth, "beings that appear / Only in the memory of caves." The niches of the children's middle brain, "where the race is young," are filled not with images of the Virgin, but with squat shapes of the Mother, or with the bloody handprint on the stone "where God gropes like a man" and where the artist "hunts and slashes" his wounded game. Then, the Visitor's rational, skeptical nature argues with him, addressing him as "Stranger"; perhaps the children want to smash their eyes in order to see nothing, and the Visitor's invention of the caveman artists is an expression of his own blindness, his hope for magic that might "re-invent the vision of the race." He admits his desire to believe that the world calls out for art, for the magical life-renewal of art, and not for the blankness of nothing save physical pain. Otherwise, it is possible that he will go mad. Otherwise, what can he value in his own poetry? The artist must be a therapist to the race, and not simply to himself; but Dickey concludes this complex poem by acquiescing to his own self-defined "fiction," a kind of lie that enables him to identify himself with the caveman artist, and to escape the deadening truths of his Reason by choosing "madness, / Perversity." He projects himself back into a dim racial memory, a hideous vision that puts history out and annihilates him as a man of the present. No salvation, except by way of a total surrender to the irrational and uninventive:

        Beast, get in
My way. Your body opens onto the plain. Deer, take
  me into your
            life-
lined form. I merge, I pass beyond in secret   in perversity and
            the sheer
Despair of invention   my double-clear bifocals
  off   my reason gone
Like eyes. Therapist, farewell at the living end. Give
  me my spear.

The prayer, addressed to a "Beast," necessarily involves the poet in a transformation downward, into a kind of human beast whose "despair of invention" forces him to inarticulate, violent action. It is possible that the conclusion is an ambiguous one—the artist denying his art through a self-conscious work of art—or, as Raymond Smith has seen it, in an essay called "The Poetic Faith of James Dickey,"[8] the poet rejecting any art-for-art's-sake aesthetic. However, the final words of the poem seem the expression of a suicidal loss of faith in anything but action, and that a primitive, bloody action.

Dickey has diagnosed this action as **"Perversity,"** and the poem has a passionate, religious feel about it, the testament of a loss of faith in one religion (Art) and the tentative commitment to another religion (that of the "Beast"). This is the mystical leap that Dickey's imagination has yearned for, the defiance of his higher, artistic, moral self, experienced in middle-age as a banality from which he must—somehow—be delivered.

The forms of Dickey's "heroism" are anachronistic, perhaps, but his despair may be prophetic.

In these later poems, the poems of "flesh," there is a dramatic ferocity that goes beyond even the shimmering walls of words he created for **"Falling"** and **"May-Day Sermon."** Dickey is there, inside the poem; reading it, we are inside his head. He is willing to tell everything, anything, he is willing to become transparent, in war now against his own exquisite sensibility. *Help help Madness help*: the book's shameless cry.

Society did not always shy away from the self-expression of its most sensitive and eccentric members. Much has been written about the relationship of so-called primitive people with their priests and shamans: these societies benefited from their leaders' ecstasies and bizarre revelations, and did not destroy them as heretics or castrate them by interpreting their visions as "only poetry." What value can the visionary give to his own experience if, returning to the world with it, he is at the very most congratulated for having invented some fascinating, original metaphors? Dickey, so disturbing to many of us, must be seen in a larger context, as a kind of "shaman," a man necessarily at war with his civilization because that civilization will not, cannot, understand what he is saying. Mircea Eliade defines the shaman as a "specialist in ecstasy": traditionally, he excites himself into a frenzy, enters a trancelike state, and receives the power of understanding and imitating the language of birds and animals. He is not a "normal" personality, at least at these times. He participates in what is believed to be divine.

If the shaman, or the man with similar magical powers, has no social structure in which to interpret himself, and if he is obviously not normal in the restrictive sense of that word, his instincts will lead him into a rebellion against that world; at his most serene, he can manage a cynical compromise with it. Irony can be a genteel form of savagery, no less savage than physical brutality. In some intellectuals, irony is the expression of disappointed hopes; in others, it is a substitute for violence. It *is* violent. If the release offered by words no longer satisfies the intense need of the sufferer, he will certainly fall into despair, estrangement. Hence a preoccupation, in Dickey, with physical risk, a courting of the primitive in art and in life (in carefully restricted areas, of course), and a frantic, even masochistic need continually to test and "prove" one's self.⁹ The ritual of hunting cannot ultimately work, because it is so obviously a "ritual"—a game—and bears no relationship at all to what hunting was, and is, to people who must hunt for their food. It is just another organized adventure, another "timid poem." Consciousness is split on a number of levels: the sensual keenness inspired by adultery and guilt, the excitement inspired by near-death, the mindless rage of the beast who fears extinction, the plight of the overweight suburban homeowner, the husband, the father, the poet . . . and yet the truest self seems somehow detached, uninvolved. **"Turning Away,"** the last poem in *Eye-Beaters,* deals with aspects of estrangement not simply in terms of marriage, but in terms of the self, which hopes to see "Later, much later on" how it may make sense—perhaps as a fictional creation, in a book.

If regression cannot be justified by calling it "ritual"—hunting, fighting, excessively brutal sports—it must be abandoned. If the poet can no longer evoke the "primitive," since his body cannot keep pace with the demands of his imagination, the primitive ideal must be abandoned. Physical prowess—extraordinary keenness of eyesight—can be undermined by that baffling human problem, mortality and disease. Death waits. Yet one is not always prepared for it. If it is seen as an embarrassment, another obscure defeat, it will never be accepted at all; better to pray for the Apocalypse, so that everyone can die at once, with no one left to think about it afterward. The stasis celebrated in much of contemporary literature, the erecting of gigantic paranoid-delusion systems that are self-enclosed and self-destructing, argues for a simple failure of reasoning: the human ego has too long imagined itself the supreme form of consciousness in the universe. When that delusion is taken from it, it suffers. Suffering, it projects its emotions outward onto everything, everyone, into the universe itself. Our imaginative literature has largely refused to integrate ever-increasing subtleties of intuitive experience with those of intellectual experience; it will not acknowledge the fact that the dynamism of our species has become largely a dynamism of the brain, not the body. Old loves die slowly. But they die.

The concluding poem in *Eye-Beaters* differs from the rest in many ways. It is a meditation, primarily. It is almost entirely speculative, an abstract seventeen-stanza work dealing with the mystery of the soul. The familiar theme of battle and certain specific images involved (helmets, meadows of "intensified grass") are used in a way new to Dickey; its tone of hard, impassive detachment contrasts with the despairing ferocity of **"Eye-Beaters"** and the poems of disease.

The immediate occasion for the poem is evidently dissatisfaction with an "old peaceful love." Another person, nearby, is "suddenly / Also free . . . weeping her body away." But the confessional quality of the poem is not very important; the poet's detachment approaches that of T. S. Eliot's in "Four Quartets." He could very well be writing about himself—his relationship with his "soul" (which is usually identified with the feminine, in mystical literature) though that interpretation is probably not necessary. The poet's problem is how, as a "normal" man, to relate his predicament with the human condition generally. As in **"Reincarnation (II),"** the poet discovers himself released from one life and into another, where he feels himself "Like a king starting out on a journey / Away from all things that he knows." Outside the "simple-minded window" is a world of ordinary sights, from which one may take his face; yet this world is one of danger and "iron-masked silence." In utter stillness, the poet stands with his palm on the windowsill (as he once stood with his palm on the fence wire) and feels the "secret passivity" and "unquestionable Silence" of existence: man wears the reason for his own existence as he stands and, in such a confrontation, the "tongue grows solid also."

Imagined then as a kind of Caesar (Dickey would like to "see with / the eyes of a very great general," here as elsewhere), he realizes he has nothing to do in his own life with his military yearnings and his hope for himself to be utterly free of any finite time or place, an omnipotent life-force released from identity to "breed / With the farthest women / And the farthest also in time: breed / Through bees, like flowers and bushes: / Breed Greeks, Egyptians and Romans hoplites / Peasants caged kings clairvoyant bastards." His desire is so vast as to exclude the personal entirely; he must turn away, at least in imagination, from the domesticity of his life, so that his soul can achieve the release it demands. It is nothing less than the wide universe that is the object of its desire; like the wolverine, the poet's soul hungers to "eat the world." This desire is in itself a kind of miracle or reincarnation:

> Turning away, seeing fearful
> Ordinary ground, boys' eyes manlike go,
>   The middle-aged man's like a desperate
>   Boy's, the old man's like a new angel's. . . .

Dreaming, the poet sees horses, a "cloud / That is their oversoul," and armed men who might spring from his teeth. He must speak of battles that do not stain the meadow with blood but release "inner lives"—as if through a pure concentration of will, of artistic creation, the poet realizes:

> So many things stand wide
>   Open!   Distance is helplessly deep
> On all sides   and you can enter, alone,
>   Anything   anything can go
> On wherever it wishes   anywhere in the world or in
> time
>   But here and now.

What must be resisted is the "alien sobbing" nearby; the poet's attachment to a finite self, a domestic existence, must be overcome, as if he were a guard on duty to prevent the desertion of the higher yearnings of his soul. The most abstract charge of all is his sense that he might be, even, a hero in a book—his life might be "a thing / That can be learned, / As those earnest young heroes learned theirs, / Later, much later on."

"**Turning Away**" is a tentative reply to the despairing vision of "**The Eye-Beaters**," and it concludes a collection of widely varying poems with a statement about the need to transcend the physical life by an identification with the timeless, "physical life" having been examined frankly and unsparingly and found to be generally diseased. The poem's immediate occasion is marital discord, but Dickey's imagery of battle is a very generalized one—"So many battles / Fought in cow pastures fought back / And forth over anybody's farm / With men or only / With wounded eyes—" Dickey's most inclusive metaphor for life is life-as-battle; for man, man-as-combatant.

The emphasis Dickey places in his later poems upon decay, disease, regression, and estrangement suggest that they may constitute a terminal group of poems: terminal in the sense that the poet may be about to take on newer challenges. Having developed from the mysticism of Stone into and through the mysticism of Flesh, having explored variations on unity and variations on dissolution, he seems suspended—between the formal abstractions of "**Turning Away**" and the jagged primitive-heroic music of "**The Eye-Beaters**," perhaps still seeking what Blake calls the "Image of wonder" that allows man to "meet the Lord in the air & . . . be happy."

In any case Dickey's work is significant in its expression of the savagery that always threatens to become an ideal, when faith in a human, specifically human ideal is difficult to come by—or when a culture cannot accommodate man's most basic instincts, forcing them backward, downward, away from the conscious imagination and back into the body as if into the body of an ancient ancestor: into the past, that is, forbidding intelligent entry into the future.

Notes

1. *The Suspect in Poetry* (Madison, Minnesota: The Sixties Press, 1964), p. 47.
2. Lewis Thomas, M.D., "Information," in the *New England Journal of Medicine*, December 14, 1972, pp. 1238-1239.
3. Dickey either literally or figuratively puts on masks in any number of poems—notably "Armor," "Drinking from a Helmet," and "Approaching Prayer" (in which he puts on a "hollow hog's head").
4. Dickey's perfect vision singled him out for training in night fighters, in the Army Air Corps. Throughout his poetry there is a concern, not just imagistic or metaphorical, with vision—eyesight—which makes doubly poignant his conclusion in "False Youth: Two Seasons" (*Falling*) that his youth was "a lifetime search / For the blind." Also, the conclusion of "The Eye-Beaters" shows us the poet "in perversity and the sheer / Despair of invention" taking his "double-clear bifocals off"—then succumbing to a fantasy of regressive madness.
5. *The Suspect in Poetry,* p. 77. The word "helplessness" is repeated several times in connection with Jarrell, and in a very positive essay on Howard Nemerov (a review of Nemerov's *Selected Poems,* 1960), Dickey praises Nemerov for what seem to me the wrong reasons: ". . . the enveloping emotion that arises from his writing is helplessness: the helplessness we all feel in the face of the events of our time, and of life itself: the helplessness one feels as one's legitimate but chronically unfair portion in all the things that can't be assuaged or explained" (p. 67). Throughout *Self-Interviews,* which seems the work of a different James Dickey, one who cannot do justice to the excellence of the essential Dickey, there is a reliance upon an inner, moral "helplessness," as if certain emotional prejudices were *there,* in human nature, and one might as well acquiesce to them; though elsewhere Dickey takes on as rigorously combative a tone as Nietzsche, in feeling that the true artist would not tolerate the world as it is even for one instant.
6. From Dickey's account of his growth as a poet, in *Poets on Poetry* (1966), edited by Howard Nemerov. It is ironic that Dickey should so distrust and mock his own reflective, intellectual nature, since he knows himself a poet of the "Second Birth"— one who has worked hard at this craft. Yet his finest poems give the impression of having been written very quickly; one feels the strange compulsion to read them quickly, as if to keep pace with the language. Dickey's poems are structures that barely contain the energies they deal with. That "agent" in the poem known as the "I" is unpredictable, at times frightening, for he may lead us anywhere. Dickey may have written extraordinary short stories, had he not chosen to develop himself as a poet almost exclusively. In an excellent essay, "The Self as Agent," from *Sorties,* Dickey says that the chief glory and excitement of writing poetry is the chance it gives the poet to "confront and dramatize parts of himself that otherwise would not have surfaced. The poem is a window opening not on truth but on possibility" (p. 161).

7. Dickey's reviews of *Howl* and *Kaddish* are both negative. He says that Ginsberg's principal state of mind is "hallucination" and that the poetry is really "strewn, mishmash prose." Yet Dickey allows that, somewhere, in the Babel of undisciplined contemporary poets, "there might one day appear a writer to supply the in-touch-with-living authenticity which current American poetry so badly needs, grown as it has genteel and almost suffocatingly proper." From *The Suspect in Poetry*, pp. 16-19. When a poet-critic speaks in these terms one may always assume he is talking about himself, whether he knows it or not.

8. Raymond Smith, "The Poetic Faith of James Dickey," *Modern Poetry Studies*, 2 (1971), 259-272. Masculine response to Dickey's poetry probably differs inevitably from a woman's response.

9. Dickey has granted a number of interviews, all of them characterized by an extraordinary frankness. In a recent one, the poet William Heyen asks him to discuss the violent "morality" of *Deliverance*, and Dickey states that there is a kind of "absolutism" about country people in his part of the world: "Life and death . . . are very basic gut-type things, and if somebody does something that violates your code, you *kill* him, and you don't think twice about it. . . . The foremost fear of our time, especially with the growing crime rate, crime in the cities and so on, the thing we're most terrified of is being set upon by malicious strangers. . . ." He therefore agrees with the decisions his characters make in the novel, and it is clear from his discussion of Ed Gentry's decision to kill and Gentry's growing realization that he is a "born killer" (Dickey's words) that the novel, like much of the poetry, is an attempt to deal with an essentially mystical experience. That it is also brutal and dehumanizing is not Dickey's concern. Murder is a "quietly transfiguring influence" on the novel's hero. "A Conversation with James Dickey," edited by William Heyen, *The Southern Review,* 9 (Winter 1973), 135-156.

Stanley Plumly (review date July 1977)

SOURCE: Plumly, Stanley. A review of *The Zodiac*, by James Dickey. *American Poetry Review* 6, no. 4 (July 1977): 42-3.

[*In the following unfavorable review, Plumly asserts that* The Zodiac *is "overwhelmed by its own ambition."*]

James Dickey ends his twelve-part, twelve-tiered poem of *The Zodiac* with a kind of nautical prayer.

> Oh my own soul, put me in a solar boat.
> Come into one of these hands
> Bringing quietness and the rare belief
> That I can steer this strange craft to the morning
> Land that sleeps in the universe on all horizons
> And give this home-come man who listens in his room
> To the rush and flare of his father
> Drawn at the speed of light to Heaven
> Through the wrong end of his telescope, expanding the universe . . .

This moment, almost an interlude in spite of its conclusive position, suggests not only a rest from the labors of a long journey but an arrival at a place of reconciliation. This, for the poet and his poem, is the Land of Nod, the still-point in his ever-turning world. It is also the most believable writing in a book overwhelmed by its own ambition. Dickey has been among our most distinguished poets, unique, really, in terms of the energy, the emotional pile-drive of his work. ***Poems 1957-1967*** represents one of the best ten years out of any contemporary American writer's career. ***The Zodiac*** is his first volume of poetry since the success of ***Deliverance.*** The bitch-goddess cliche may be too handy, especially as the collection of poems immediately preceding the novel (***The Eye-Beaters,*** etc.) was decidedly uneven. But the new book, star-glazed and star-crossed, is a mistake in conception and execution. First of all, the book's, the poem's origins are borrowed. As Dickey explains it: "This poem is based on another of the same title. It was written by Hendrik Marsman, who was killed by a torpedo in the North Atlantic in 1940. It is in no sense a translation, for the liberties I have taken with Marsman's original poem are such that the poem I publish here, with the exception of a few lines, is completely my own. Its twelve sections are the story of a drunken and perhaps dying Dutch poet who returns to his home in Amsterdam after years of travel and tries desperately to relate himself, by means of stars, to the universe." Except for a few lines. No doubt the writing is all Dickey's. Yet why confuse the substance with the suggestion? Why be so literal-minded about the sources: by setting the poem in Amsterdam, by appropriating a Dutch sailor-poet? If the poem, "with the exception of a few lines," is completely Dickey's, why not complete the exchange—why not steal whole-heartedly and write directly out of the facts of one's own life, drunken and/or dying, instead of effecting an elliptical and artificial mode? The result of the borrowing is that Dickey is forced to create a character, to narrate a protagonist into the material, to speak of and through a third person that the poet, at critical junctures, absorbs into his own large voice. ***The Zodiac*** reads like a failed fiction, because it does not ring true. There are more than liberties at stake here; oddly enough, Dickey's poem has the feel of being made from whole cloth. As for the making of the poem, its imagination, its language, Dickey reaches beyond hyperbole to what, for want of a word, we must call *superbole*. For example:

When the tide turns
He turns left   his eyes back-swivel into his head
　In hangover-pain like the flu   the flu
　　Dizzy with tree tops
　　　all dead, but eye going
Barely getting   but getting you're damned right but
　still
　　Getting them.
　　　Trees, all right. No leaves. All right,
Trees, stand
　and deliver.   They stand and deliver
Not much . . .
　　　　． ． ． ． ．
　You son of a bitch, you! Don't try to get away
　　　from yourself!
I won't have it! You know God-damned well I mean
　you! And you too,
　　Pythagoras! Put down that guitar, lyre, whatever
　it is!
You've driven me nuts enough with your music of the
　spheres!
　　But I'll bet you know what to know:

　　Where God once stood in the stadium
Of European history, and battled mankind in the blue
　air
　　　Of manmade curses, under the exploding flags
Of dawn . . .

If it sounds like bombast it must be bombast. Dickey's rationalization for the compounding, ever-expanding rhetoric is to pass it off as the hallucinosis of a drunk—"Christ, would you tell me why my head / Keeps thinking up these nit-witted, useless images? // Whiskey helps." One of his chief means for illustrating that rhetoric is the famous Dickey-shift—that variable pause or parting in or around a line in which the white space and silence inveigh against the speech. The consequence is melodrama, as throughout the poem—the words spreading like star-charts across the page—the speaker indulges the imitative fallacy of *being* drunk, hung over. The art of the thing and the sobriety of the artist himself are continually called into question. Our ears almost numb, our eyes half-opened, the language demands, page after page, that we pay attention. All of the above aside, **The Zodiac** could have at least been a good story, but it has no plot, no vital cause-and-effect forward and inevitable motion to its "action." Except for being inside a drunk Dutch poet's hangover, inside the self-exile of his Amsterdam room, "over the broker's peaceful / Open-bay office at the corner of two canals," *except* for his short season in hell, we have too little to deal with—except Dickey's cosmic vision. And vision, of course, is what the zodiac is all about. A vision of destiny as well as design, a vision of omnipotence ("Religion, Europe, death, and the stars: / I'm holding them all in my balls, right now.") as well as impotence ("I've traveled and screwed too much."). A vision of the macro world in the mind of one man. Like a lot of beautiful ideas, without the complication of a story this vision rests in stasis: and without its working-out and working-through, it seems a gratuity. Ironically, for all his "polar-bearing" through his poem, there is not enough of Dickey in it—none of the particulars, none of the local terrors that might convince us that a poet of his stature stands behind it. These sixty-two pages were to be an ontological journey, and struggle, from a place of disaffection to a place of affection, out to the stars, out to those shapes that only seem to make sense, and back again, back home. **The Zodiac** suggests a man in real trouble, dumb drunk to the bone, shouting the walls down, writing it down.

James M. French (review date spring 1978)

SOURCE: French, James M. "A Horoscope Reading." *Prairie Schooner* 52, no. 1 (spring 1978): 113-15.

[*In the following review, French provides a negative assessment of* The Zodiac.]

James Dickey's reputation as a writer has grown in the past ten years. In fact, Dickey has lately become a highly visible public figure as well. Within the past two years his poetic productivity and presence has not diminished. In that period he has published **The Zodiac,** written the text to *In God's Image,* and graced the ritual occasion of Jimmy Carter's inauguration. As a poet, James Dickey is not undeserving of the recognition he has now achieved. Yet at least one of Dickey's latest offerings, **The Zodiac,** does not demonstrate the strength of much of the earlier verse.

The Zodiac is by far Dickey's most ambitious effort to compose a long and major poem. In the headnote he describes **Zodiac** as a poem "based on another by the same title" (p. 7) by the Dutch poet, Hendrik Marsman. Dickey discounts his work as translation; instead, "it is a story of a drunken and perhaps dying Dutch poet who returns to his home . . . and tries desperately to relate himself to the universe." It is in this mode that Dickey presents Marsman and transforms him into a symbolic vehicle. One is not surprised, then, to see Marsman's tragic life in terms of a self-conscious examination of the poetic process.

The Zodiac ends with a proclamation that the generative "tuning fork" of the universe

　　shall vibrate through the western world
So long as the hand can hold its island
　　Of blazing paper, and bleed for its images:
　　Make what it can of what is:

　　So long as the spirit hurls on space
　　The star-beasts of intellect and madness.

[P. 62]

For a poem that rarely breaks free of the tortured syntax of Dickey's insane and drunken protagonist, these last lines are amazingly coherent. It seems to be Dickey's point that while "bleeding . . . for images" one can gain eloquence as well as grace. The basic concept is a familiar one—the poet is akin to outcast, madman, or prophet. Ever since Coleridge, the literary world has seen an array of sensitive and suffering wanderers. Dickey maintains the image of the Mariner through Marsman, substitutes a "tuning fork" for the animating force of the Aeolian Harp, and an ambiguous sexual tragedy in Marsman's past takes the place of the murdered albatross (sec. 9). It would be unfair to condemn Dickey for the display of what may indeed be central mythic elements, but his use of Romantic themes and images is often cloyingly obvious. For example, Dickey represents Marsman's alcoholism and obsession with death in a descent motif. While Marsman is suffering from delirium tremens, the narrator states:

> —god-*damn* it, he *can't* quit,
> But—*listen* to me—how can he *rise*
>   When he's *digging?* Digging through the smoke
> Of distance, throwing columns around to find . . .
> He's drunk again.
>
> [P. 40]

This passage demonstrates the extent to which the "bleeding" poet can be reduced to cliché. For Dickey, Marsman's message was that one shouldn't "shack up with the intellect," yet to "conceive with meat / Alone" is to doom the "child" (p. 47). Thus the struggle for the marriage of heaven and hell, mind and heart continues. This modern sense of alienation is brought to a climax when, in the face of the "expanding Universe," Marsman "can't tell Europe / From his own Death" (p. 39). Like these examples, the language repeatedly strikes one as banal and unimaginative.

Obviously, Dickey had great ambitions in the creation of the poem. But for this reviewer the goals of the poem are never successfully realized. One is never sure whether the erratic syntax and abrupt alterations in speaker, time, and voice simply parallel and reflect the mental state of Marsman. There is the temptation to judge Dickey's verse as haphazardly constructed or flawed. It is also difficult to determine the correlation between the Zodiac and the structure of the poem. The poem's twelve sections seem more convenient than functional. As a type, *The Zodiac* does have precedents. Don Finkel's *Adequate Earth*, Warren's *Audubon: A Vision*, and Berryman's *Homage to Mistress Bradstreet* are all examples of successful mixtures of the historical, psychological, and mythic. Dickey's predicament in *The Zodiac*, though, may be a result of his own poetic theorizing. In *Babel to Byzantium*, Dickey wrote that he was gaining interest "in the conclusionless poem, the open or ungeneralizing poem, the unwell-made poem." While *The Zodiac* is neither "conclusionless" or "ungeneralizing," it is certainly "unwell-made."

If Dickey is now at the popular zenith of his career, his audience can expect his publishers to capitalize on the marketability of his name. I hope, though, that our unofficial poet laureate does not allow more works like *The Zodiac* to reach the public in third-rate condition.

Linda Mizejewski (essay date summer 1978)

SOURCE: Mizejewski, Linda. "Shamanism Toward Confessionalism: James Dickey, Poet." *Georgia Review* 32 (summer 1978): 409-19.

[*In the following essay, Mizejewski explores the confessional poetry of* The Zodiac, *focusing on Dickey's poetic persona.*]

Since the mid-sixties or so, one or two people at almost any English Department cocktail party have had a James Dickey story. Perhaps even more amazing than the stories themselves has been Dickey's mercurial quality that renders an anecdote from nearly every college reading and from so many personal encounters. After 1972, the stories became Jim Dickey-Burt Reynolds stories, and after January, 1977, there were tales from Carter's inaugural, but by then they were appearing in popular news magazines. Developing as a celebrity-poet, Dickey has broken from the university circuits of rumors and readings, and materialized in middle-class living rooms—in glossy coffeetable books and on the television screen, where he is likely to be reciting from his Biblical prose-poetry on a talk show.

President Carter certainly blessed an unusual inaugural poet. Unlike E. A. Robinson or Robert Frost, who had been nationally honored by Theodore Roosevelt and Kennedy, Dickey does not write an easily accessible "popular" poetry. His poems are certainly not academic, but the average reader who believes he can understand the somewhat deceptive simplicity of Frost or the small-town characters of Robinson might be confused by Dickey's elaborate sentence structures that snake like the Coosawattee and make breathtaking turns around tricky prepositional phrases. He might be disturbed by a poetry that, far from making Frost's humanizing inquiries into nature, sees man as an animal coded to hunt and survive by blood in the natural world, so that war, too, is a natural human activity. He might be disturbed by a poetry in which a middle-class, middle-aged man tries to reckon with how he had firebombed the Japanese by understanding his own sense of personal power as godlike destroyer and suburban builder—all this in semi-Biblical, Southern rhetoric.

This fine, complex poetry, in which the imagination is often the subject as well as the creator, is probably not the work of Dickey's that most Americans know. Far more have probably read his novel, **Deliverance,** and the fiction in *Esquire.* Even more than that identify him with the movie version of the novel, or know him as the publicized poet of inauguration week when Dickey, identified by the media as "the voice of the South," interpreted the election of a Southern administration as no less than a Biblical event. Dickey has promoted not just a Southern mystique, but a Dickey mystique, and has become not just a nationally known poet like Frost, but a personality as self-mythologizing as the President's own brother.

The showmanship of the yarn-spinning and rhetoric during inauguration week is a trademark of the poet whose best work has always been charged with the presence of the master performer. The best of his ***Poems 1957-1967*** work like an ideal, reversed ending of the Oz story: the curtain might be pulled aside for a glimpse of the professor working the levers to produce the sound effects and smoke, but the wizardry—contrived as it may be—continues anyway, and with a great deal of success. There is no demand for a return to the farm in Kansas—or Georgia—where real life is without magic and masks altogether. Instead, all sorts of bizarre and unlikely conjurings go on: a traffic jam becomes the Apocalyse, a military execution turns into an acrobatic stunt, a man's legs fall asleep and pick up the dream of the hunting dog sleeping on his feet. The artifices of showmanship and magic *save* us in poems such as **"The Hospital Window," "The Celebration," "Slave Quarters," "Power and Light."** They save us from sentimentality, pain, or self-pity. "Guilt is magical," says the speaker at the end of **"Adultery,"** because guilt has been *performed* in the poem, exorcised by a shaman-narrator who has dissolved the walls of a motel room and extended the risks of a love affair into all the open frontiers of American history.

The presence of the poet-performer in those poems is as intense as the personal presence by which Dickey has become nationally known in the media over the past year. However, the public personality—of shaman, storyteller, good ole boy—is always that of a man who knows he is onstage and who keeps an actor's distance between himself and his audience. In the earlier poems, Dickey did likewise, always avoiding the "confessional" sort of personality found in Lowell, Snodgrass, Berryman, or Sexton. Dickey was especially critical of Sexton's work, which he found indulgent and uncontrolled. But while the public Dickey was developing as a showman, the poet Dickey was experimenting with how loosely personal his act could become. **Eyebeaters** showed some of this experimentation, but his most recent poetry, the book-length poem **The Zodiac,** shows an actor-poet who has gone as far as he can, almost on a dare, into a painful, public exploration of trauma. While Snodgrass or Lowell would have written unabashedly personal accounts of the loneliness, fear of failure, terror of mortality, and struggle with language that haunt **Zodiac,** Dickey opts for the shaman's mask again—this time, the mask of an historical person far removed in location and time.

In this case, though, the mask is too flimsy and the role too superficial, so that not even Dickey can play it right. Juggling with materials that he does not want to play confessionally, Dickey slips in his act and is finally unable to achieve the distance of the public, acting figure. **Zodiac,** which awed and puzzled most of its critics, demonstrates enough of the old Dickey eloquence and power to make it worthwhile to ask what went wrong. More than that, it asks us to examine what is perhaps the real difference between confessional and nonconfessional poetry: the extent to which the speaker is onstage consciously enjoying his own performance as shaman, wizard, showman.

Zodiac has all the material for shamanistic transformations. The main character, Hendrick Marsman, is a hallucinating, half-mad poet-sailor who wants to "relate himself, by means of stars, to the universe," as Dickey explains in the introduction. The scene is Europe in the late thirties or early forties, just before Marsman's death. Like an epic poet-hero sailing into the stars, Marsman knows he is a man in the hands of patterns and monsters created by someone or something else in the sky, and he is trying to construct a fantastic sort of metaphysics of the constellations.

But this time Dickey's conjurings fail. The power behind the poetic machinery blinks off, and the transformations never occur. Because there is often very little distance between Dickey and his subject, Marsman never becomes as dramatic as the self-performing speakers of the earlier poems. Often the metaphors are not imaginative juxtapositions but attempts by a drunken narrator to relate himself to *anything.* And even though Marsman is attempting to recreate a zodiac, the zodiac never becomes a real structure for his personality or imagination. The twelve sections take different scenes in a four-day span, alluding randomly to some of the constellations and signs, giving brief vignettes, and always returning to Marsman's terror of and fascination with the night sky. But there is no sense of closure to this loose history except for Marsman's impending death. When last seen, Marsman is writing and/or being firebombed, and the final affirmation of the transcendence of his art seems tacked-on in relation to Marsman's miserable, drunken wanderings throughout the other sections. Nothing in those other scenes justifies a triumph of either Marsman or the universal artist suggested throughout. In general, without the transformative magic of drama and distance, there is a sad exposure of the poet stepping out to admit it's all been just levers and smoke, and willing to give us now an "honest" account of the impossible attempt to transcend pain through language.

The transformations that do go on in *Zodiac* are mostly those between drunkenness, sleep, and brief periods of sobriety. Using alcoholic spiels as frames for monologues, like using dreams, allows for repetition, illogical apposition, random imagery, and quick shifts of scene. But unlike the dreamer, the drunk is also subject to misinterpretation and misperception of what is really there. Like Lowry in *Under the Volcano*, Dickey is relying on a belief in moments of drunken clarity and even brilliance, the ability of the drunk to come to realizations he could not have made sober. In a novel the length and scope of Lowry's, it is possible to develop a character who is a lucid and magnificent drunk. But in Dickey's poem of less than sixty pages, no character equalling the magnificence of the Consul is developed, although Dickey clearly intends to suggest an experience much wider than the historical Marsman's. As critics have pointed out, this is Dickey's most ambitious work, the epic that summarizes the themes of all his early work: the poet as part of history, man as an alien to nature and able to enter it only through the moment of the imagination, and language as the shaman's power against mortality.

Marsman, then, is romanticized as the poet-sailor to the extent that his "craft"—poetry and ship—becomes in the end the death-ship similar to the Anglo-Saxon burial ships for kings. In the last stanzas, Marsman identifies his personal struggle and extinction with the tragedy of all mortal poets attempting immortal tasks. His dramatic directives—". . . put me in a solar boat . . . / That I can steer this strange craft to morning"—suggest the epic adventurer, too. But when Marsman hopes to "steer" to morning, he also simply wants to make it through another drunken night. So the question is whether Marsman's experience as presented by Dickey is, in fact, raised to such heroic stature—that is, if there is justification for such intimate and painful exploration of this speaker's psyche.

Facing the dilemma of how to give this kind of serious, even tragic stature to a character who is a personal and professional failure, Dickey attempts, like Lowry, to identify the "fall" of his character with the decline of western culture during the rise of Fascism and Nazism. But Dickey's background scenes, the European war setting, are only vaguely described. In most of the scenes, Marsman could actually be in any city in any historical period. We're told several times that Europe is itself at the edge of disaster, but in each instance this seems to be a momentary judgment made by Marsman in his own disastrous condition. At one point the comparison generalizes, "He goes on without anywhere to go. This is what you call Europe. / Right?" Marsman is wandering the city drunk, and we know *he* has no place to go, but there are no details given to suggest that all of Europe, too, is about to collapse. The observations about the historical situation seem oddly out of place, as in Part II when after telling us "His life is shot my life is shot," the narrating voice concludes that "The gods are in pieces / All over Europe," even though all we have seen up to that point is one of Marsman's hallucinations from the DT's. Marsman, we're told, has "been there / Among the columns:/ among Europe. He can't tell Europe / From his own death."

However, except that we know the general time period, the idea of European decline is never fully developed. We never get the impact of a landscape like Lowry's, which is made real *outside* of the Consul's perceptions of it through the reports of the Battle of the Ebro, the Day of the Dead, the oppressive heat and dust, the overpowering presence of the ravine or *barranca*. Dickey uses a ravine, too, in two different places, but we can't be certain either is real like the real ditches all over Lowry's Quauhnahuac. Once Marsman imagines the sky as full of "gullies" with the moon itself fallen into one. But the hallucination is not very convincing, since the image dissolves into undescribed "Realities." Marsman decides that "the key *image* / Tonight *tonight* / is the gully gullies: / Clouds make them, and other Realities / Are revealed in Heaven , / as clouds drift across." The problem is that the metaphor seems appended rather than conjured, especially since it is self-consciously labeled by the poet Marsman as "the key image."

As a poet, Marsman worries aloud frequently about this problem of his own perspective and "universality." He comes across the other ravine image when he wanders the city one morning, either drunk or very hungover, and finds "some kind of / Lit-ravine" which he can't cross and which seems to "move across" him. He asks quickly, "But is it universal?", using the word half-mockingly as he does on two previous occasions when he addresses God in poet-*vs.*-the-cosmos challenges. He taunts God in those earlier scenes as a "universal son of a bitch," the creator to whom the critics can't object, the poet who is *always* universal. But in the third reference at the ravine hallucination, the term actually raises a serious problem in Dickey's book. It begins a long description of the zodiac, explaining how the ravine—that is, Marsman's spiritual abyss and ruin—has "been lifted from the beginning / Into this night-black— / Into the Zodiac." Marsman's question here is significant: are his perceptions of himself in the gullies of the world and sky the hallucinations of one drunken artist, or are they symbols of a sustained tragic vision? Is Marsman's failure to "relate himself, through stars, to the universe" the failure of one mad poet or a symbol of what all artists attempt and fail to achieve?

This question is complicated by the dual nature of Marsman's crisis. His struggle for a metaphysical zodiac is therapeutic as well as artistic; he is seeking not just a spiritual framework, but a way to deal with his loneliness, alcoholism, sense of failure, and sense of his approaching death. One way to do this is to see an animistic universe which is dying *with* the personal self and which is full of symbols, signs, and some degree of empathy.

The constellations are the most obvious "signs," and Marsman is especially obsessed with how they are full of "beasts," animals and monsters that make a "scrambled zoo" similar to his personal zoo of hallucinations. Ironically, the only effective shamanistic move in the book occurs when Marsman decides to create a new constellation to fight Cancer or death: the Lobster, which sadly and comically turns into one of his creatures from the DT's and which turns on him and attacks him. The difference between this move and the metaphoric transformations in earlier Dickey poems is its self-consciousness. "Imagination and dissipation both fire at me," Marsman says, thereby stepping out of the role of shaman and pointing to what he's doing, identifying it as *just* metaphor, which can't help him personally. "I didn't mean it," he apologizes, at the mercy of his own hallucination. Unfortunately, the metaphors in *Zodiac* often really do control the poet rather than vice versa.

Essentially, they are personifications, attempts to identify with and humanize the world rather than transform it. The confessional poetry of Sexton uses this technique again and again as a desperate kind of therapy. In *Zodiac,* these metaphors are sometimes forced or heavyhanded in the struggle to appropriate the external world into the psyche of the speaker. Describing his rooms, Marsman asserts that "A flower couldn't make it in this place. / It couldn't live, or couldn't get here at all. / No flower could get up these steps, / It'd wither at the hollowness / Of these foot-stomping / failed creative-man's boards." This is an explanation that the "boards" of the artist-perhaps in the sense of the stage as well as of "drawing boards"—have failed, but the metaphor itself fails by getting out of control, switching contexts from creative survival to the more farfetched concept of the plant walking upstairs. Stranger things have happened in earlier Dickey poems—a man is hooked up to his own house wiring, or a shark gets loose in a living room—but only in a context that prepares us for the imaginative leap gradually through tone and narrative detail. That context is missing here, and we're left only with the desperate need to personify.

This happens several times in *Zodiac* when the appropriateness of the metaphor is clear only in relation to Marsman's undependable perception. We must take the word of the speaker that "The fish, too, / Are afraid of the sun," or that the "Innocence" of water is an "ultimate marigold horror." At one point a painting "squeezes art's blood out of the wallpaper," a bridge is a "slain canal," and the "gully of clouds" in the sky is "a shameless place" where "the rest of nature is." All these are equations of Marsman's misery with a more universal misery, but they are also flat assertions rather than conjurations of a credible animism. This kind of exaggerated, bombastic metaphor led Stanley Plumly to ask in a review if Dickey has perhaps gone beyond hyperbole into "superbole."

Wayne Shumaker suggests in *Literature and the Irrational* that all metaphor is essentially a belief in or hope for animism. But the personification used in *Zodiac* shows a shift in Dickey from magic to a kind of psychotherapy, or from lyric celebration to a thinly disguised confessional poetry. Part of this is the fault of the failed distancing device, which is an intermittent third-person narrator whose tone is never clear and who is rather extraneous to what is really Hendrik Marsman's poem. While Dickey at times seems to identify with Marsman wholly, at other times this third-person voice seems straining for objectivity, judgment, even reproach.

Zodiac opens with this narrator who is clearly outside the mind and situation of Marsman, "The man I'm telling you about," as he says in the first line. Sometimes the shift from this objective narrator to an interior monologue is obvious, as when the narrator is used to introduce a thought of Marsman's. But often the point of view is ambiguous enough to be either interior monologue or objective description, and this creates a problem in tone. We're sometimes not sure if the perceptions are the results of Marsman's limited vision or alcoholic fantasies, or are descriptions of a setting from a more removed and dependable narrator. This is actually the problem with some of the personification metaphors which might come from a paranoid Marsman or, more problematically, from the narrator who is in charge of Marsman's story.

Part of the problem is that the narrator sometimes uses the diction of Marsman, even the drunken diction, and this is a real shift from the historical voice of the opening. Before we get to the first interior monologue by Marsman, the third-person voice has already dropped such lines as "Hot damn, here they come!" to describe the DT's, and "You talk about *looking*: would you look at *that* / Electric page." In general, though there are first-person and third-person technical points of view, the voices are identical, and it is difficult to account for the presence of the outside narrator at all. Not only are they identical, but they are not very different in diction and sociology from the speakers in some of Dickey's earlier work. Drunk or sober, Marsman more often comes across as an out-of-shape Southern ex-football player than a Dutch sailor. He addresses Pythagoras as his "old lyre-picking buddy," and he later laments, "O flesh, that takes on any dirt / At all / I can't get you back in shape." Even some of the images are the same as those Dickey has used to describe other personas. When Marsman "polar-bears through the room," it's difficult not to remember the middle-aged teacher at the end of **"False Youth: Two Seasons"** who "skates like an out-of-shape bear" to his car.

In spite of this strained characterization of Marsman, the more important question in the end is whether the poem's form resolves the problems of the speaker. Although the twelve-part division suggests, like Lowry, a "twelfth hour" or end of a cycle, the structure of the poem is actually not a pattern of hours, months, or zodiac signs. It works instead as a looser pattern of drunkenness, ambition, self-reproach, and finally hope. While Marsman is obsessed with the zodiac, it is never actually materialized and never used as a means to structure his imagination. So the kind of resolution in the last section tries to be a closure to a structure and heroic pattern that is never really there. For the last lines of the book make a case for the triumph of Marsman, if not as an individual, then as symbol of a universal artist who might find the "instrument the tuning fork" that can create a music of the spheres which is possible "So long as the hand can hold its island / Of blazing paper, and bleed for its images."

Without the integrity of a justifiable character and a clear structure behind it, the entire last section seems somewhat overwritten. Poetry, or at least the nobility of the poet's struggle, is affirmed in a sort of revelation like a thunderbolt: "A day like that. But afterwards the fire / Comes straight down through the roof, white-lightning nightfall, / A face-up flash. Poetry." This also suggests a night bombing or even Marsman's death by torpedo which had been mentioned in the introduction. Throughout, Marsman asserts that poetry for him is a way of reading and writing in the night sky among the constellations. So having the sky literally fall on him can be either tragic or sadly and almost comically ironic. The problem is that the lines themselves become inflated at this point: "Poetry. Triangular eyesight. It draws his / fingers together at the edge / Around a pencil. He crouches bestially, / The darkness stretched out on the waters / Pulls back, humming Genesis." This carries mixed connotations of a football quarterback and an epic Biblical movie. Unfortunately, Marsman has done nothing to make himself godlike enough for Genesis. In fact, one of the better passages in the book shows Marsman as poet opposing God as creator, setting up a nice contrast between creation of the universe by God and transformation of the universe through the imagination of man. "I say right now," Marsman challenges at that point," . . . like a man / Bartending for God, / What'll it be? . . . my old man / Was an astronomer, of sorts, and didn't he say the whole night sky's / *invented*?" But the invention never materializes in the poem itself, neither in any poem by Marsman nor in Dickey's romanticization of Marsman.

It is sad that the poet who criticized Sexton for her lack of control should write a long work that Harold Bloom hesitantly calls "obsessive and perhaps even hysterical." Yet *Zodiac* illustrates all the hazards of confessionalism, despite its removed character and setting: the problem of justifying interest in the detailed personal problems of the speaker, the risks of using metaphor as a means of humanizing and appropriating a hostile world, and most of all, the problem of how to make the imagination transcend intense subjectivity so that there is a resolution in the art, if not in the troubled mind, of the poet.

Finally, it is ironic that the poem about poetry for which Dickey may be best remembered is in his very first volume of poetry—his elegy for Donald Armstrong, **"The Performance."** Here we find many of the themes later developed in *Zodiac*. It is about how the poet, the man who died, and all men who know they are playing temporary roles can use the imagination to make the final surprising gesture which is the only recourse we have against death, uncertainty, and "the great untrustworthy air" in which Donald Armstrong flies as a pilot in the war. Armstrong's real, faulty acrobatic act is finished and perfected in the poet's memory and in his acrobatics of the imagination. And like the acrobatics, the stanzas and syntax are orchestrated "under pressure" in long, dazzling sentences and in a breathtaking handstand that turns reality upside down and gives us the vision that is suddenly clear and perfect, the vision of a man whose blood has rushed to his head. The background and character are entirely credible—and entirely credible, too, is the sudden backflip from the actual experience into the poetic fantasy. This is the Dickey most of us love and remember, the man who loves to dazzle his readers, "Doing all his lean tricks to amaze them," like Armstrong's imaginary stunts. And this is the Dickey we hope to see again in his future work—for though Dickey is not a young poet anymore, he demonstrates the enormous amount of energy of the master performer who can avoid the confessional poet's trap of becoming too entangled in experience to use the magic and artifice of Prospero and Oz.

Turner Cassity (review date 1980)

SOURCE: Cassity, Turner. "Double Dutch." *Parnassus* 8, no. 2 (1980): 177-93.

[*In the following mixed review of* The Strength of Fields *and* The Zodiac, *Cassity questions stylistic elements of Dickey's poetry.*]

If you write in lines so long that your book has to be printed sideways, it seems to me you might well reconsider your methods. However, James Dickey has always been the least succinct of poets, and here, in a grand horizontal sprawl, is *The Strength of Fields,* a collection of lyrics and of adaptations from other languages. Dickey writes with undiminished vigor, but I am not sure I can say this as praise. Intellectually, he is so seldom on secure ground that he ought perhaps to proceed with caution.

His title poem, for example, is in direct contradiction to the Warren Court. It seems to say that politicians do represent trees and stones.

> Men are not where he is
>   Exactly now, but they are around him   around
> him like the strength
> Of fields . . .
>   The stars splinter, pointed and wild. The dead lie
> under
> The pastures. They look on and help.

Perhaps President Carter, for whose inauguration the poem was written, needs livelier helpers. One is reminded of those unreadable Scandinavian novels about "The Land." If Dickey covets a Nobel Prize, *The Strength of Fields,* as a title, should do it. For its purposes, it is the best since *The Good Earth.*

As a matter of fact, the poet's position is not vastly different from what Mrs. Buck's used to be. He has real talent, a wide public, a geographical area delineated for him by that public, and no serious critical appeal whatever. Buckhead, even when Dickey was living there, must have borne about the same resemblance to The South as the coastal treaty ports to China, or Pasadena to the Wild West. No Wonder his Buckhead Boys feel rather out of things.

Within his limits—one cannot really call them self-imposed; that would imply a sense of focus he does not have—he can be effective. "**Root-light, or The Lawyer's Daughter**" is a very amusing put-down of the idea of the Platonic Idea. Or would be if one could rescue it from its surrounding welter of verbiage. It is the dread Southern urge to use eight words wherever one will do. Surely it will be the punishment of the garrulous to sit in Hell at the knee of Edith Wharton's mother.

> She came flying
>   Down from Eugene Talmadge
> Bridge, just to long for . . .
>   If you asked me how to find the Image
>   Of Woman to last
>   All your life, I'd say go lie
>   Down underwater . . .
>   Be eight years old . . .
>   in the clean palmetto color
>   [and] naked with bubbles,
>   Head-down . . . there she is.

No Georgian, I least of all, would be willing to forsake Eugene Talmadge Bridge, but the rest of the detail in the full version adds nothing.

> That any just to long for
> The rest of my life, would come, diving like a lifetime
> Explosion in the juices
> Of palmettoes flowing
> Red in the St. Mary's River as it sets in the east
> Georgia from Florida off, makes whatever child
> I was lie still, dividing,
> Swampy states   watching
> The lawyer's daughter shocked
> With silver   and I wished for all holds
> On her like root-light. She came flying
> Down from Eugene Talmadge
> Bridge, just to long for as I burst with never
> Rising never
> Having seen her except where she worked
> For J.C. Penney in Folkston. Her regular hours
> Took fire, and God's burning bush of the morning
> Sermon was put on her; I had never seen it where
> It has to be. If you asked me how to find the Image
> Of Woman to last
> All your life, I'd say go lie
> Down underwater for nothing
> Under a bridge and hold Georgia
> And Florida from getting at each other   hold
> Like walls of wine. Be eight years old from Folkston
>   ten
> From Kingsland twelve miles in the clean palmetto
>   color
> Just as it blasts
> Down with a body   red and silver buck
> Naked with bubbles on Sunday   root
> light explodes
> head-down, and there she is.

Root-light is phosphorescence, one of many spooky Southern phenomena. What has phosphorescence to do with the lawyer's daughter? Nothing. That is why I left it out. "The clean palmetto color" is of course so attractive a phrase I should like to steal it, and may.

I do not understand why he sets up the poem typographically as he does. If there is any rhythmic measure, or any non-random relationship of sentence to line, I cannot discern it. I have heard him read the poem—most engagingly—and still cannot. As a lyric it is marred by a leering resemblance to a *Playboy* cartoon, but it does represent the poet at his least pretentious.

"**False Youth: Autumn: Clothes of the Age**" (even his titles are long) shows him at his most pretentious, but may nevertheless be the most successful poem in the book. It is worth quoting in full, because, unlike root-light, its details are relevant to its subject, and do not paralyze the narrative.

> Three red foxes on my head, come down
> There last Christmas from Brooks Brothers
> As a joke, I wander down Harden Street
> In Columbia, South Carolina, fur-haired and bald,
> Looking for impulse in camera stores and redneck greeting cards.
> A pole is spinning
> Colors I have little use for, but I go in
> Anyway, and take off my fox hat and jacket
> They have not seen from behind yet. The barber does what he can
> With what I have left, and I hear the end man say, as my own
> Hair-cutter turns my face
> To the floor, Jesus, if there's anything I hate
> It's a middle-aged hippie. Well, so do I, I swallow
> Back: so do I   so do I
> And to hell. I get up, and somebody else says
> When're you gonna put on that hat,
> Buddy? Right now. Another says softly,
> Goodbye, Fox. I arm my denim jacket
> On and walk to the door, stopping for the murmur of chairs,
> And there it is
> hand-stitched by the needles of the mother
> Of my grandson   eagle riding on his claws with a banner
> Outstretched as the wings of my shoulders,
> Coming after me with his flag
> Disintegrating, his one eye raveling
> Out, filthy strings flying
> From the white feathers, one wing nearly gone:
> Blind eagle, but flying
> Where I walk, where I stop with my fox
> Head at the glass to let the row of chairs spell it out
> And get a lifetime look at my bird's
> One word, raggedly blazing with extinction and soaring loose
> In red threads burning up white until I am shot in the back
> Through my wings   or ripped apart
> For rags:
> *Poetry*

Poetry is not so badly off as all that, Mr. Dickey; it needs only to be saved from its practitioners. One is tempted to say that Thom Gunn could have written the poem better, but since he hasn't, there is no point in withholding praise from the actual author. The barber pole is a real inspiration. Admittedly, I am predisposed to like any poem that savages Columbia, South Carolina. I went through basic training there. If the following line break is not random it is a stroke of genius, and the very last sort of effect one ordinarily expects to find in Dickey.

> I arm my denim jacket
> On and walk to the door

The defensiveness is gotten across with marvelous subtlety.

"The Rain Guitar" suffers from being a sequel to or trial run for the dueling banjos scene in ***Deliverance***—that abyss—and from our suspicion that what a man of Dickey's age should really be playing is a ukulele. The guitar reappears in **"Exchanges,"** a notably bad performance. The poet, with no hint of irony, is apparently going down a checklist of cocktail party chic: smog, offshore drilling, freeways, the quality of life, and the death of whales. All too appropriate, unfortunately, for a Phi Beta Kappa poem, "being in the form of a dead-living dialogue with Joseph Trumbull Stickney (1874-1904)—(Stickney's words are in italics)." Italicizing was not necessary. It is perfectly obvious which words are Stickney's: his are the ones that make sense. In the Dickey text nothing has anything to do with anything else. You cannot call it free association because there is no association. The narrator is sitting on a bluff above the Pacific Ocean outside Los Angeles (where else?) and playing Appalachian music to a companion while worrying about environmental pollution. "We sang and prayed for purity." A reader who will believe that will believe anything, although I should say in its defense that it is the most straightforward utterance in the poem. Compare it with this:

> Day-moon meant more
> Far from us   dazing the oil-slick with the untouched remainder
> Of the universe   spreading   contracting
> Catching fish at the living end
> In their last eye   the guitar rang moon and murder
> And Appalachian love, and sent them shimmering from the cliff

The operative phrase is living end. The girl, we learn presently, is now in Forest Lawn, and everything—astronauts have by now been added—is supposed to come together in an image of death. It doesn't. Nothing could get itself together after images like "birds black with corporations." It brings one solidly down on the side of Chevron. Well, if there is anything I hate it is a middle-aged hippie.

I take this opportunity to say I personally find offshore drilling platforms the most attractive thing in any seascape. They provide a middle distance. In the bay at Santa Barbara they are like great ideographs on the oriental haze of the islands.

It would be just as easy to hatchet **"For the Death of Lombardi,"** a maudlin threnody for the iconic coach. It would be easy but counter-productive. We should regret instead that someone who is uniquely qualified to give us a good poem on the world of the locker room has failed to do so. Very few writers play football, and we should have our understanding enlarged if a poet could convey to us what it is actually like. My interest in endangered species is in seeing that they do not disappear from the table, but I neither hunt nor fish. I therefore owe a particular debt to Ernest Hemingway, and come away from Dickey with a sense of waste and frustration, his as well as mine.

"**Lombardi**" confirms what one has suspected for years: Dickey thinks he is Paul Hornung (whose autobiography, incidentally, is not to be missed; its narcissism makes poets seem self-effacing).

> Yet running in my mind
> As Paul Hornung, I made it here
> With the others, sprinting down railroad tracks,
> Hurdling bushes and backyard Cyclone
> Fences, through city after city, to stand, at last, around
>   you

The debt to John Cheever is this side of plagiarism, but only just. The real trouble with the poem is that its details are predictable. The statement of them is furiously hyped, but they are themselves predictable without being inevitable. They are exactly what I should have used in writing a poem about locker rooms, and I never go close to locker rooms.

> Around your bed the knocked-out teeth like hail-
>   pebbles
> Rattle down   miles of adhesive tape from hands and
>   ankles
> Writhe in the room like vines   gallons of sweat
>   blaze in buckets
> In the corners   the blue and yellow of bruises
> Make one vast sunset around you.

To measure their failure you have only to think of the hyena in *Green Hills of Africa* "racing the little nickelled death inside him," or of the Kipling galley-slaves.

> We fainted with our chins on the oars and you did not
>   see that
> we were idle, for we still swung to and fro.

The sunset of bruises is wonderfully bad, the taste of the Easter show at Radio City Music Hall brought to literature, and it appears *twice*.

> the bruise-colors brighten   deepen
> On the wall   the last tooth spits itself free
> Of a line-backer's aging head

The tooth exemplifies the syntactical desperation to which Dickey has been reduced: something, anything, to make the obvious seem "poetic." There is no conceivable way in which a tooth can spit itself out. The meaningless reflexive makes one see why Freshman English instructors tell their students to avoid the passive. The writing in **"Lombardi,"** as writing, confronts us with what three generations of modern poets have been unwilling to face: no amount of talent is going to help if the rest of your mind is a mess. Common sense is as useful in poetry as it is elsewhere.

I do not want anyone to think I underrate Dickey's talent. The best phrase in the poem is very good indeed.

> the weekly, inescapable dance
> Of speed, deception, and pain

It is no accident that it consists of abstractions (you can be sure in any modern poem that dance does not actually refer to dancing).

The passage on the athletes grown middle-aged ought to work but doesn't.

> Paul Hornung has withdrawn
> From me [sic], and I am middle-aged and gray . . .
> We stand here among
> Discarded TV commercials:
> Among beer-cans and razor-blades and hair-tonic
>   bottles,
> Stinking with male deodorants: we stand here
> Among teeth and filthy miles
> Of unwound tapes, novocaine needles, contracts,
>   champagne
> Mixed with shower-water . . .

I have to say, however, the champagne mixed with shower water has exactly the unexpectedness whose absence I was deploring above. As for the deodorants, well, surely it is better to stink with them than without them.

I am not familiar with the originals of the translations in **Strength of Fields,** but I conclude either that the translator likes long-winded poets or that he can make anyone seem long-winded, even an oriental.

> But I remember, and I feel the grass and the fire
> Get together in April   with you and me, and that
> Is what I want   both age-gazing living and dead

Nothing could be further from an ideograph.

More Chinese than his Po Chu-yi is Dickey's own brilliantly observed image in **"The Rain Guitar."**

> eelgrass trying to go downstream with all the right
>   motions
> But one

A bit dynamic—fluid, if you like—for the oriental taste, but you will find no haiku nearly as good. Pound's *Cathay,* much of it, is static by comparison.

> the willows
> have overfilled the close garden

Alfred Jarry is here (*Ubu roi*; the guitar player is still going down that checklist). Octavio Paz is represented, as is Georg Heym. In English, the best of the lot is Vicente Aleixandre. I do not know him, but assume he is fashionable, as he is in the company of Evgeny Yevtushenko. I have a feeling I am using different systems of transliteration for the first and last names, but let it pass. The swordfish in **"Undersea Fragment in Colons"** is strikingly rendered.

> Swordfish, I know you are tired: tired out with the
>   sharpness of your face:

> Exhausted with the impossibility of ever
> Piercing the shade: with feeling the tunnel-breathing
>   streamline of your flesh
> Enter and depart

The Art Deco quality of the fish is perfectly captured.

It would be agreeable to say that in the translations we are at least freed of Dickey as a persona, but the voice of most of them is relentlessly first person, and we never get very far away from Paul Hornung. Still . . . Dickey's egoism has generated a thousand self-perpetuating anecdotes, yet the truth is, he is less imprisoned in his psyche than most poets. Whatever his poems are, they are not claustrophobic. Extroversion is an attractive thing about them, and may well account for their popularity. The poets he translates are, compared to him, closeted.

Speaking in his own voice he is a lyricist whose gift for the dramatic moment, for the accurate, vivid observation quickly rendered, is dissipated in non-structures enormously inflated. I seem to be describing Meyerbeer, and one could say that, like Meyerbeer, he will be immortal in his lifetime and for a few months after. The identification is not capricious: Meyerbeer may be said to have invented publicity—advertising—as we know it, and publicity has made Dickey one of the better poets who has ever been really popular.

Curious, therefore, that reviewers and public alike have by and large ignored *The Zodiac,* his magnum opus, if not his masterpiece. It appeared in 1976 in a trade edition from Doubleday and in a luxury edition from Bruccoli Clark. For the latter the author wrote an introduction that obscures as much as it reveals, and which I shall have to contradict from time to time.

I want to say at once **The Zodiac** is a work not just anyone could have written (so is *Les Huguenots*), and the question of indebtedness is to that extent moot. In basing it on "another of the same title," however, he invites speculation. That other is by Hendrik Marsman, a Dutch poet killed in World War II. In the introduction to the Doubleday edition Dickey says "This poem is in no sense a translation, for the liberties I have taken with Marsman's original poem are such that the poem I publish here, with the exception of a few lines, is completely my own." Prefacing the Bruccoli he says "Some thirty years ago, as a student at Vanderbilt, I read Hendrik Marsman's original." I think he did not. I think he read A. J. Barnouw's translation of it published in *The Sewanee Review* in 1947, and I think Barnouw, not Marsman, is due the disclaimer. Everyone who compares the two will have to decide for himself the degree of Dickey's indebtedness. The main difference, to put it bluntly, is that Dickey's protagonist is more of a drunkard.

One can see what attracted Dickey. If Barnouw has represented the original dependably, it is the most American poem ever written by a European. Of his own version Dickey writes "**The Zodiac** is at the same time a vindication of the drunken, demonic poet and the desperately serious artist." Although they were drunken and demonic respectively, there was nothing American about Verlaine or Rimbaud. Verlaine was too incompetent, and Rimbaud could have come only from the French bourgeoisie of the nineteenth century. At one point he wanted to work for the *Compagnie Universelle du Canal Interocéanique.* The presence of Arthur Rimbaud is perhaps the one thing that could have made the problems of the French in Panama worse than they were.

A strength of the Marsman-Barnouw is that in spite of manifold opportunities it at no point evokes Rimbaud. "Its twelve sections are the story of a drunken and perhaps dying Dutch poet who retires to his home in Amsterdam after years of travel and tries desperately, by means of stars, to relate himself to the universe." (Dickey, in his own version.)

I can spare scholars of those months of Dickey's posthumous immortality a great deal of trouble by telling them that the division into twelve sections does not mean a one to one relationship with the signs of the Zodiac. Cancer the Crab appears, but the divisions are purely arbitrary.

The Dickey gets off to an unpromising start, by sticking too close to the Marsman-Barnouw.

> The man I'm telling you about brought himself back
>   alive
> A couple of years ago. He's here,
> Making no trouble
> over the broker's peaceful
> Open-bay office at the corner of two canals
> That square off and starfish into four streets
> Stumbling like mine-tunnels all over town.
>
>   (Dickey)

> The man of whom I tell this narrative
> Returned, some time ago, to his native land.
> He has since lived, for nearly a full year,
> Over the peaceful broker's offices
> Which, at the corner between two canals,
> Front on the square that, starfish-shaped, ejects
> Its corridors into the city's mine.
>
>   (Barnouw)

The starfish is too ingenious by half, and doubly inappropriate to Amsterdam, which has neither beaches nor salt water. Nor do the tunnels improve things. Holland cannot even keep water out of its basements. Dickey had no reason to know better—except by checking his facts—but his mother lode had.

The real Amsterdam makes its appearance here:

> . . . houses whose thick basement-stones
> Turn water into cement inch by inch
> As the tide grovels down.
> (Dickey)

> . . . a row of mansions
> Whose cellars stand in water masonried
> (Barnouw)

One up for Dickey. It would be invidious to point out that the city is sealed off from the tide by locks, and as the canals are flushed artificially every now and then, I am prepared to give the benefit of the doubt. Most of the first section is devoted to the vagaries of the badly hungover protagonist, but the author announces his theme baldly.

> The Zodiac.
> He must solve it must believe it learn to read it
> No, wallow in it
> As poetry.

Here he does not follow the Barnouw closely enough. It says simply

> The puzzling palimpsest of the common life
> That he must solve and read as poetry

An attack of D.T.'s—he imagines an invasion of army ants [Author's Note: The ants are an expansion of Barnouw's "insect plague of his own thoughts."]—delays things, but soon he is drunk and writing, and the poem rises to a passage of genuine power. It is not parallelled in the original.

> Will the animals come back
> Gently, creatively open
> Like they were?
> Yes.
> The great, burning Beings   melt into place
> A few billion-lighted inept beasts
> Of God—

Embedded in the delirium is an article of faith any poet will have to respect.

> the poem is *in* there   out there
> Somewhere, the lines that will change
> Everything, like your squares and square roots
> Creating the heavenly music.

Section II is a meditation on the nature of time, precipitated by the striking of a clock.

> The whole time-thing: after all
> There's only this rosette of a great golden stylized asshole

The level of diction in this section, throughout, is the uneasiest in the poem, and owes nothing to Barnouw. To credit its force I shall say I can never look at the rose-window of a cathedral in quite the same way again. Another onslaught of the shakes ends the meditation, and this time the poet imagines that he is attacked by a giant lobster, whom he considers elevating to Zodiacal status. The passage may or may not be a parody of Eliot's pair of ragged claws. In any event, the lobster is in the Barnouw.

Section III, the least effective in the poem—Dickey's and his model—is a reminiscence of travel.

> That remembered Greek blue
> Is *fantastic*. That's all: no words
> But the ones anybody'd use: the ones from humanity's garbage can
> Of language.

"Anybody'd," I think, is a word practically nobody would use.

Section IV is a recovery. A poetic recovery; the narrator's liver is beyond recall. The section includes one of Dickey's more interesting conceits.

> Without that hugely mortal beast   that multi-animal animal
> There'd be no present time:
> Without the clock-dome, no city here,
> Without the axis and the poet's image   God's image
> No turning stars   no Zodiac   without God's conceiving
> Of Heaven as beast-infested   Of Heaven in terms of beasts
> There'd be no calendar   dates   seasons
> No Babylon   those abstractions that blitzed their numbers
> Into the Colosseum's crazy gates   and down down
> Into the woven beads that make the rosary
> Live sing and swirl like stars
> Of creatures

The train of associations, while quite free, can easily be followed. Of course, it has Barnouw to keep it on the track. "Blitzed" is a mistake. In a poem about the heavens the root meaning, lightning, will get in the way of the Panzer divisions. The fault is Dickey's. In Barnouw the verb is "struck."

We have in section V the first hint of reconciliation, of relating by means of stars to the universe. Barnouw's lines are quoted without alteration.

> The faster I sleep,
> The faster the universe sleeps

To seek in sex the meaning of the cosmos is about as intelligent as it would be to use an ephemeris as a sex manual, and I should like to dislike section VII on principle, but I cannot. I like it. The meaning could not be more clearly conveyed, and the sense of quiet at the end is very impressive.

> Don't shack up with the intellect:
> Don't put your prick in a cold womb.
> Nothing but walking snakes would come of *that*—
> but if you conceive with meat
> Alone,
> that child, too, is doomed.
>
> . . . . .
>
> Realities
> Are revealed in Heaven, as clouds drift across,
> Mysterious sperm-colored:
> Yes.
> There, the world is original, and the Zodiac shines
>   anew
> After every night-cloud. New
> With a nameless tiredness   a depth
> Of field I can't read an oblivion with no bottom

The Marsman-Barnouw, in the casting of old barren Reason from the house, is downright priggish.

> Do not sleep with the intellect,
> Do not couple with a cold womb.

I incline to a view that writing is one thing and sex is another, but whatever turns you on, as they used to say in my and Mr. Dickey's early middle age.

I do not know what to make of Section VIII, and I don't think Dickey does either. In the Barnouw it gives the impression of a lyric imported from somewhere else, from Heredia, or one of the later Parnassians (nothing American here).

> He goes along
> The dead canal that sleeps in its bronze bed
> Between the quays.

Dickey gives it the full treatment, to try to bring it in line with the rest of the poem, but nothing he does really works. First we have the Midnight Cowboy.

> Time
> To city-drift leg after leg, looking Peace
> In its empty eyes as things are beginning
> Already to go twelve hours
> Toward the other side of the clock

He takes on the canal as if he were Teddy Roosevelt.

> He moves along the slain canal
> Snoring in its bronze
> Between docks

In another line he big-sticks the Parnassians on their own ground.

> The trees are motionless, helping their leaves hold
>   back
> Breath

I can produce no hard evidence, but I have an impression section IX owes something to *Tonio Kröger,* in German-language courses in the Netherlands often a set piece.

> . . . the bitter right his shyness granted her
> To pass him in the street with a frigid look,
> Haughtily jesting with the sinister boy
> Who once had been his idol and his friend
> And who had taken her away from him
>
>   (Barnouw)

Again, Dickey's only response is to hype it up.

> Empty is the grave of youth
>
>   (Barnouw)

The grave of youth? HA! I told you: there's nobody *in* it.

                                       (Dickey)

One feels he has sat too long in creative writing classes where they tell you everything must be dramatized.

Section X is a love scene, and not at all interesting. Where a little sexiness would have helped, Dickey perversely adds none.

Section XI is the first intrusion of social life into the poem. The protagonist goes to a party. How he secured an invitation I find the most stimulating problem the work poses. Barnouw renders the arrival vividly, and Dickey wisely does not change it.

> He polar-bears through the room

But if, as Dickey claims, he completely re-worked the "original," why did he feel compelled to stick so close to it when no purpose is served? His worst enemy never said he did not know how to enjoy a party, and surely this is a scene in which we had rather have Dickey than Marsman. What, finally, did the Barnouw mean to Dickey? If it stuck in his mind for thirty years, and had enough force to make him compromise what is clearly intended as his artistic testament with the hint of plagiarism, it must have seemed to him a text brought down on stone tablets, but a text to be elaborated in art and lived out in life. I can think of no more convincing argument for keeping romantic poems out of the hands of the young, and for discharging agrarians who would put them there.

Easy to see that Dickey's idea of making something poetic is to add "intensity"—as if he went about with a hard gemlike Bunsen burner. In spite of his fondness for Appalachian stage effects (if one did not know Buckhead better, one would say he grew up waited on by White servants who sang a lot), it seldom occurs to him to use a homey image. The voltage would seem to him too low. On the rare occasion when he does use one, it is a disaster: the determination to say everything by way of images, be the image good, bad, or indifferent.

> The garden, he thinks, was here,
> Bald   a few sparse   elephant-head hairs

"Bald" is in the Barnouw, but for the elephant-head Dickey has no one but himself to blame. Nor was the bald itself necessary; I presume the Dutch word is *kaal*, which can also be translated as "bare." In the Transvaal, kaalveld is bare veldt.

The concluding section has been praised, and correctly so.

> Oh my own soul,   put me in a solar boat.
> Come into one of these hands
> Bringing quietness and the rare belief
> That I can steer this strange craft to the morning
> Land that sleeps   in the universe on all horizons
>   . . . . .
> So long as the hand can hold its island
> Of blazing paper, and bleed for its images:
> Make what it can of what is:
> So long as the spirit hurls on space
> The star-beasts of intellect and madness.

If we can have an elaborate statement of a simplistic notion, **Zodiac** is the most elaborate and the most explicit example we have of the idea of poetry as the unconsidered utterance of the bardic genius aided in his unreason, if need be, by drink and drugs. If we take Whitman and Sandburg seriously, we have to consider Dickey, because he has more specific literary talent than either, and is by no means the phoniest of the three. His poems compare poorly with those of Hart Crane, but who knows what Crane would have written like in his fifties. I for one doubt that he could have written at all. Appalachia knows what to call such transports—speaking in tongues—and what to think of them: they are in the same category as the handling of snakes. In secular and more pretentious guise they are endemic to American poetic thought, and are not likely to go away. My own feeling is that if you wanted to invent a method to get the least out of the most talent, you could hardly do better.

Richard J. Calhoun and Robert W. Hill (essay date 1983)

SOURCE: Calhoun, Richard J., and Robert W. Hill. "The Literary Criticism, Lately Neglected." In *James Dickey,* pp. 124-35. New York: Twayne Publishers, 1983.

[*In the following essay, Calhoun and Hill discuss Dickey's reputation and work as a literary critic.*]

THE "SUSPECT" IN POETRY

James Dickey's career as a literary critic began when he was poetry editor and reviewer for the *Sewanee Review.* There he developed something of a reputation as a "hatchet man" who deftly chopped down the reputations of poets he did not respect. Robert Penn Warren, later a friend and admirer, recalls: "When James Dickey came to my attention as a reviewer, I thought he was one of the roughest around."[1] This reputation was not quite deserved since Dickey's critical hatchet was reserved only for what he called in the first collection of his reviews the "suspect" in poetry. Dickey's reviews were perceived variously as entertaining, opinionated, sometimes harsh, displaying an excess of ego; but not, as they might well be regarded in retrospect, as important contributions to Dickey's own vision of a freer, personal, but still carefully crafted postmodernist poetry. Style and tone were admired more than substance.

There are other reasons for James Dickey's meager reputation as a literary critic. First of all, he began as a poetry reviewer, and he has continued to express his critical ideas outside formal critical performances—writing not essays but additional reviews, giving numerous interviews, and tape recording for publication one uniquely egocentric volume—*Self-Interviews.* Second, the personality of Dickey, his "unrepressed ego," was always much in evidence in what he wrote, to the annoyance of some of his reviewers; the consequence of Dickey's intense subjectivity has been to obscure the importance of his contributions as poet-critic as well as the relationship of intensely held critical ideas to his poetry. Finally, Dickey has also contributed to the critical disregard for his literary criticism through his own statements about what he has done. He has, for example, disavowed his first major collection of his reviews, **Babel to Byzantium,** as a "full-scale critical performance," modestly asserting that he knows "any reasonably good student of aesthetics could tear [my] 'ideas' apart with no trouble."[2] This pose of a dabbler has been held consistently in regard to his prose; Dickey's position has always been that his "preoccupation is with poetry, and everything else is a spin-off from that—novels, literary criticism, screen plays, whatever."[3]

The reviews reprinted from the *Sewanee Review* in **The Suspect in Poetry** and in **Babel to Byzantium** are much less polemic than their reputation would suggest. When told of Robert Penn Warren's impression of his roughness on poets in his early days as a poetry reviewer, Dickey demurred: "Well, I'm not all that rough. I have a very naive feeling as a reviewer. I don't believe that a reviewer or a critic can really criticize well unless he can praise well. I always liked that about Randall Jarrell. He praised well. James Agee praises well. You've got to be able to like the right things to be enabled to dislike the wrong things."[4] What Dickey's statement about Jarrell ignores is that Jarrell's reputation in his early days as a reviewer was much the same as Dickey's own for roughness. Dickey's harsh reputation may have resulted from his ability to express his negative judgments wittily and memorably: "[J. V.] Cunningham is a good, deliberately small and authentic poet, a man with tight lips, a good education, and his own agonies. His handsome little book should be read, and above all by future Traditionalists and Compressors; he is their man." (*BB* [*Babel to Byzantium*], 194).

Dickey is clearly not "their man" and he makes that abundantly clear. What he does like and praises well is less memorable, and his reasons are clear only when what he wrote then is read along with the essays in his later volume, *Sorties*. What he does not like in his early criticism is any kind of academicism, especially "the university-taught" garden variety poets or "the School of Charm" (*BB*, 10).

In his earliest *Sewanee Review* criticism Dickey stresses that the first step in restoring meaning to poetry is by compelling the reader's belief through establishing "the presence of a living being," creating "a distinctive poetic voice" (*BB*, 107). Two other requirements are made of the poets he reviews. The poet must also earn belief, establish a connection between poet and reader, by making "effective *statements,* ones you believe, and believe in, at first sight . . ." (*BB*, 151). Dickey also prefers "a basis of narrative," through describing or depicting "an action" in poetry, and regaining for poetry what it had lost to fiction (*BB*, 287).

BABEL TO BYZANTIUM: VISION AND FORM

The essays in **The Suspect in Poetry** and in **Babel to Byzantium** were written during the late 1950s and the early 1960s at a time when Randall Jarrell and Karl Shapiro were also in their different ways breaking with "new critical" formalism and the modernist tradition that had favored impersonality, mythology, and academicism in poetry. Dickey was in his own way nurturing the same seeds of change as Jarrell and Shapiro. Among the older generation of poets, William Carlos Williams, who had long had his differences with the Eliot brand of modernism, was an influence on the new directions being taken by Allen Ginsberg and Robert Lowell in the 1950s. Dickey also admired Williams at his best, but his view of Williams's poetry was somewhat different from theirs. Williams's best poems demonstrate how one can be close to the surfaces of life while avoiding the commonplace. The commonplace is clearly as foreign to Dickey's concept of good poetry as the university-oriented academicism of many modernist poets. Williams is better than his imitators because he transcends the commonplace by instant symbolization: his poetry has its magic "moments when a commonplace event or object is transfigured without warning . . ." (*BB*, 244).

Dickey not only demands that good poems of other poets be both nonacademic and nonliteral, but he also commends to his reader his own penchant for "'the big basic forms'—rivers, mountains, woods, clouds, oceans . . ." (*BB*, 291). For Dickey it is the commitment to both ". . . vision and to the backbreaking craft of verse" that makes the good poet. His exemplars in this respect are Roethke, Rilke, and D. H. Lawrence, who are, he declares, the "great empathizers" and "the awakeners," who can go beyond the commonplace and even "change your life" by compelling belief in what they write through "inducing you to believe that you were *meant* to perceive things" as they present them" (*BB*, 149). It is when poetry accomplishes this goal that it becomes the kind of magical thing Dickey believes it should be.

When Dickey attempts to describe the kind of substance he likes in poetry, he may owe something to the New Critics' praise of "tension" in poetry. Dickey's version is a preference for a tonal complexity that comes from a "sense of being glad to be alive to write that particular poem" but also from outrage at the possibility of the loss of all things that have meant much to him—a sense of "outrage that these personal, valuable things could ever be definitely lost for anyone" (*BB*, 281). In describing the poets he admires most, Dickey identifies his kind of tension. In Theodore Roethke the tension is the ability of Roethke to be "not far from total despair" but also "not far from total joy" (*BB*, 151); and in Edwin Arlington Robinson, the poet he admires almost equally with Roethke, it is his "desperately poised uncertainty" (*BB*, 223).

In a key essay in *Babel to Byzantium,* **"The Poet Turns on Himself,"** Dickey's concern is consistent with the emphasis in the essays in his later books, *Self-Interviews* and *Sorties*. It is in this essay that the significance of his title *Babel to Byzantium* becomes evident; each poet has his own vision, his vision of Byzantium. To actualize this vision he is dependent on a flow of images from the memory, even out of the subconscious, but it requires the right language and the proper form. Dickey clearly regards his own best poetic efforts and those of the poets he values the most as an attempt to find the language necessary to "incarnate" those moments which are "most persistent and obsessive" in the memory (*BB*, 292). Dickey was supportive of the new freedom in the poetry of the 1950s and the 1960s, but to earn his praise a poet must also be a craftsman who can maintain a proper balance between the passion of his visions and the formal demands of language. The poet must use his talent with language to find among the many tongues of Babel the right words for his Byzantium—the vision he desires to communicate. Unfortunately, as his brief reviews make clear, in his judgment, many contemporary poets fail at the one extreme or the other, producing either vision without the necessary craftsmanship or the craftsmanship without the vision. His reviews specify the failures.

Self-Interviews

The most representative essay in **Babel to Byzantium,** revealing Dickey as almost as much the subject of his essays as the poet he is reviewing, is Dickey's essay on Randall Jarrell. Dickey conducts a dialogue with himself as critic, who responds intellectually and judgmentally to Jarrell's poetry, and as a poet, who responds emotionally and empathetically to Jarrell's successes and failures as a fellow poet.

A reviewer who had taken careful note of Dickey's Jarrell dialogue would have been less surprised by Dickey's next book of criticism, *Self-Interviews* (1970), than most of his reviewers were. This book of tape talk was the product of Dickey's response via tape recorder to questions about himself and his poetry asked by co-editors James and Barbara Reiss. The volume is slender, but seldom has a contemporary poet told more about himself as author than Dickey has in this volume and in his next, *Sorties* (1971). The confessionalism that Dickey had denied the poet seems more acceptable to him in his own prose. The dialogue in the Jarrell essay has become monologue, the distinctive voice of James Dickey speaking on himself, occasionally at his best, but also at his worst. *Self-Interviews* is nevertheless valuable as a handbook of information on Dickey as poet and as repudiation of T. S. Eliot's formalism, both his doctrine of impersonality for modern poetry and his practice of expressing his critical ideas in carefully crafted essays that advance the art of that form. Dickey also seems bent on rejecting another formalist tenet, dear to the New Critics, the intentional fallacy, their exposure as a fallacy the belief that a writer's own statements about his works can exhaust the possible meanings of those works. To New Critics like Cleanth Brooks or Robert Penn Warren nothing except a close explication of the literary text by a critic can reveal the actual meaning as opposed to the intended meaning. *Self-Interviews* is Dickey's testimony to his belief that a poet's statements about origins and personal meanings of a work can be of value in understanding it.

Part one of *Self-Interviews,* "The Poet at Mid-Career," traces the development of Dickey's creative psyche from his earliest creative efforts to the publication of his first major collection, **Poems 1957-1967.** Part two, "The Poem as Something That Matters," is divided into five sections, one for each of his first five volumes of poetry. The coverage is extensive: practically every major poem Dickey has written is discussed. Dickey is descriptive of his intentions; but he is seldom prescriptive about meanings, since he is not trying to preclude anybody else's interpretation. His accounts of the origins of his poems are anecdotal and entertaining re-creations of the creative act, such as Allen Tate undertook in his classic essay on his poem "Ode to the Confederate Dead."

Self-Interviews is nevertheless a product of Dickey's staunch faith in his memory; it expresses his belief in the importance of drawing on and building on the best of his memories that come up from out of "that strange limbo between conscious memory and the unconscious, where remembered things have what physicists call a half-life" (*SI* [*Self-Interviews*], 55).

The informal autobiography of the mind of the poet that begins in *Self-Interviews* and continues in the "Journals" section of his next book, *Sorties,* is largely an account of the connections Dickey has made in his poetry and also of his convictions as poet-critic on how these connections are best made. He indicates that he has always desired to achieve "presentational immediacy" in his poetry in the belief that this quality would lead to the kind of reader involvement with poetry that good writers of prose fiction get. In his poetry the poet will be concerned with many disparate subjects, but he must present them concretely enough to communicate to his readers a convincing illusion that there is a connection among all the different strands of divergence.

Above all, Dickey stresses the importance of memory to the poet, and he unabashedly uses himself as his own exemplar. To Dickey the poet values "remembered things," and he cannot bear to believe that they will ever "be totally expunged" (*SI,* 57). He writes his poems with the intention of preserving both the memories and the passion that they occasion which permit the creation of the poem. The memories are subject to the changes that linguistic structure may necessitate, and the poet's "censor" should eliminate what might be aesthetically bad. Beyond this Dickey will not go. He is entirely opposed to T. S. Eliot's antiromantic dictum that the poet must find objective correlatives and transmute his personal emotions into impersonal artistic feelings. On the contrary, Dickey has a neoromantic faith that emotions can lead to creativity. He declares: "I want to try to conserve the passion, wind it up tight like a spring so that it always has that sense of energy and compression, that latency which is always available to anyone who looks for it" (*SI,* 65). He desires to preserve the instinctual life that is left to civilized man, and he envies in animals the "instinctual notion of how much energy to expend, the ability to do a thing thoughtlessly and do it right . . ." (*SI,* 60). Dickey is a neoromantic in his faith and in instinctual life and a post-Darwinian poet in his belief in the possibility of regressing and regaining temporarily the instincts and extrarational powers that man has just about evolved out of. He imagines this possibility in his poetry and in his novel **Deliverance.** In *Self-Interviews* he proclaims his faith in this resource for his creative imagination: "There's a part of me that has never heard of a telephone. By an act of will I can call up the whole past which includes telephones, but there is a half-dreaming, half-animal part of me that is fundamentally primitive. I really believe this, and I try to get it into poems; I don't think this quality should die out of people" (*SI,* 68-69).

One might say that James Dickey has his own version of the dissociation of sensibility between thought and feeling that preoccupied T. S. Eliot in his concern for the modern poet. Eliot saw a split between thought and feeling; Dickey sees modern man deprived of instinctual life. If this quality does die out of people, it will be a result of the premium contemporary society places on specialization. The price of specialization is "the loss of a sense of intimacy with the natural process" (*SI,* 68). For a more unified sensibility the poet must establish connections with the great mystery of process in nature, with "the great natural cycles of birth and death, the seasons, the growing up of plants and the dying of the leaves, the generations of animals and of men . . ." (*SI,* 68). It is this kind of connection that permits good poetry, in Dickey's view, to transcend the commonplace and become magical. Modernist poetry has been predominantly concerned with man in the modern wasteland, the city. The natural world is more important to Dickey than the man-made world. His Vanderbilt predecessors lamented the passing of an agrarian way of life in the South. Dickey laments with D. H. Lawrence that "as a result of our science and industrialization, we have lost the cosmos" (*SI,* 67).

SORTIES

The "Journals" section of Dickey's 1971 volume of essays, *Sorties,* is a continuation of the artistic self-analysis begun in *Self-Interviews.* There are, however, differences. The entries are in the form of scattered notes, and they are written at a time of actual engagement in creative work rather than in retrospect, as in *Self-Interviews.* The material is even more personal and intimate than in the previous volume, and as much as Dickey dislikes the term, even confessional.

Once more, Dickey deliberately avoids the formal critical performance, preferring to express his critical ideas in a more personal and intimate form than the formal critical essay permits. The form chosen is traditional, since notebooks and journals have always been an important part of a writer's creative activity even though not always intended for the public. It would not be accurate to say that Dickey does not write critical essays, for in *Sorties* he includes five essays written originally as lectures and for special occasions as well as a brief epilogue for the volume. Unfortunately, adverse critical responses to what seemed the deliberately egocentric presence of Dickey's own personality obscured for some reviewers the importance of the essays to an understanding of Dickey's intentions in his poetry and of his contributions to a postmodernist literary criticism. *Sorties* and *Self-Interviews* were seemingly just too much of a self-congratulatory ego trip through Dickey's own memories and critical prejudices to be taken seriously as literary criticism. The personality of Dickey in print had become almost as evident as in his enormously successful, though occasionally controversial, public readings. There was another reason for a definite note of hostility toward Dickey. As a southern poet who had not perceptibly participated in the protest movement against the war in Vietnam he had become suspect among liberals. The case against Dickey was presented by his former friend and the publisher of *The Suspect in Poetry,* Robert Bly.[5] According to Webster a "sortie" is "a sally of troops from a besieged place against the besiegers." Dickey had chosen the right title for another book of criticism. His new book and his reputation were both under minor siege. The quantity of Dickey's production of poetry, and in the view of some reviewers, the quality, too, had declined. Dickey was apparently giving too much of himself and writing too little of literary consequence. A judgment of contemporary criticism of poetry offered near the beginning of *Sorties* might be applied to his own work: "Contemporary criticism of poetry: far too much is made of far too little. The critic is attempting to be more ingenious and talented than the poem, and stands on his head to be original: that is, to *invent* an originality for the poems that can come to them only through him" (*S* [*Sorties*], 6).

The personal equation in *Sorties* is intentional, and it is of value for what it reveals about the relationship between Dickey and the critical personae that he has created. All the Dickey self-stances appear. There is the macho Dickey, who said that, if he is not an advocate of virility in contemporary literature, he would not object if assigned that role.[6] He occasionally sounds like his own fictional creation, Lewis Medlock: "The body is the one thing you cannot fake. It is what it is, and it does what it does. It also fails to do what it cannot do. It would seem to me that people would realize this, especially men" (*S,* 4). He also appears as a Whitmanesque, intensified man as poet who would change his reader and even a good bit of his world:

> What I want to do most as a poet is to charge the world with vitality: with the vitality that it already has, if we could rise to it. This vitality can be expressed in the smallest thing and in the largest; from the ant heaving at a grain of sand to the stars straining not to be extinguished.
>
> (*S,* 5)

Whitman could not have asked for much more.

In striking contrast, Dickey also gives his reader a brief glimpse of a self he usually tries to conceal, that of the university professor who as a poet avoids writing academic poetry but who enjoys the professorial life. He confesses: "It is a marvelous thing, this having a house full of books. Something crosses the mind—a flash of light, some connection, some recognition—and one simply rises from one's chair and goes, as though by predestination, to that book, to that poem" (*S,* 5-6).

More often Dickey appears as one of the "roughs," as a poet who prefers the open life and open forms in literature to the urban or academic life and to the closed forms preferred by modernists and formalists. He does not "like the locked-in quality of formalist verse." Formalists desire the impression of coming "at an effect of inevitability. There are lots of other kinds of inevitability than this, and the best of these do not have the sense of claustrophobia that formalist verse has" (*S,* 8-9). Formalists prefer compression. Dickey makes his preference clear. "I want, mainly, the kind of poetry that opens out, instead of closes down" (*S,* 9).

Dickey may prefer open forms, and he admires "power" and a sense of "abandon" in poetry; but he never advocates uncontrolled or critically uncensored spontaneity. The neoromantic in Dickey may advocate openness and freedom; but the formalist, the worker with language, counters with the case for artistic control and careful craftsmanship. He tells himself to play with "confidence, power, and relaxation" and to add "abandon." But then he adds as equally important: "To that, add precision" (*S,* 9). He urges himself to revise—to get it right: "*Phrase* it, *phrase* it. One cannot work too much on such a thing" (*S,* 10).

In still another Whitmanesque stance Dickey extols his own poetic sensibility, assuring himself that he has a greater "accessibility to experience" than even Henry James ever had and affirming his memory for those things which mean something to him. He offers himself as an example of what in the personality of a writer makes him a writer. He is his own representative poet, "born with some kind of extra sensitivity to things" and capacity "to receive impressions" and to retain them because "they *mean* something to him." Things "matter" to him; he feels for them and remembers them (*S,* 20-21).

Not all is egotism or egocentric. Dickey is aware of writing, after a period of critical formalism, on the personality of the poet in relation to his works in a great romantic tradition, part Wordsworthian self-analysis of the mind of the poet and part Whitmanesque assertion of the importance of the self in a poetry in which a celebration of life is still possible.

Part II of *Sorties* consists of Dickey's largest collection of critical essays so far, six in all, and a brief epilogue. Two essays were talks given while Dickey was poetry consultant at the Library of Congress—**"Metaphor as Pure Adventure"** and **"Spinning the Crystal Ball."** Two are reprints of reviews of biographies, of Louis Coxe's biography of Edwin Arlington Robinson,[7] and of Allen Seager's biography of Theodore Roethke.[8] These reviews are as much concerned with the poet as with poetry. The remaining two essays, **"The Self as Agent"** and **"The Son, the Cave, and the Burning Bush,"** were originally included in anthologies.[9] In all of these essays the approach is personal and subjective, with little or no objective explication of poetic texts. The reader is given instead Dickey's opinions, which come more from his interests as a poet than from his role as a literary critic. Dickey is obviously expanding on ideas and judgments he has made in his previous interviews and reviews. The difference in *Sorties* is his concern for the lives, the individual existential situations, of the poets he considers compared to their goals and accomplishments, a subject that had much personal meaning for Dickey himself in the 1970s as his poetic output began to slow down. He is struck by the contradictions between the affirmative in the poems and the destructiveness in the lives of the poets.

The final essay in *Sorties* is one of Dickey's best. **"The Self as Agent"** is a significant essay on a subject of great importance to Dickey as an opponent of impersonality in poetry—the role of the self in the poem. The view here is not exactly unbridled romanticism. Dickey's romantic tendencies are once more moderated by his Vanderbilt New Critical heritage. Form is important, as is content. The "I" in the poem is more than the ordinary self. The poet's obligation is not just to tell the literal truth but rather to "make" his truth so that "the vision of the poem will impose itself on the reader as more memorable and value-laden than the actuality it is taken from" (*S,* 156). The theme of participation in the poem by both poet and reader is restated. His emphasis here is on what the poem does for the poet more than for the reader. A good poem is also a participation in a self-discovery. "During the writing of the poem the poet comes to feel that he is releasing into its proper field of response a portion of himself he has never really understood" (*S,* 157). The self is essential in the poem because it is the agent that helps the poet to "discover" his poem. Dickey's preference is for the I-poem and the I-narration because the poet in Dickey's view "is capable of inventing or bringing to light out of himself a very large number of I-figures to serve in different poems . . ." (*S,* 161). For the poet "the chief glory and excitement of writing poetry" comes from this "chance to confront and dramatize parts of himself that otherwise would not have surfaced" (*S,* 161). The poet is providing for his reader, through participating in a self-discovery, a sensation of emotional truth. Poetry is a kind of experiential knowledge: the poet "has a new or insufficiently known part of himself released," and he is able to convey this knowledge convincingly to the reader as humanly important emotional truth (*S,* 161). If Dickey does not quite provide the rationale for such theories, appropriately for a critic who values personality, he does reiterate his personal beliefs with the conviction that comes from the experience of his own practice.

Dickey's literary criticism is a criticism of fragments—short reviews, brief introductions, public lectures, interviews, self-interviews tape recorded. He has expressed consistent attitudes, though he has not attempted to organize his critical essays as clearly around a theme, as Allen Tate, Karl Shapiro, and Randall Jarrell have done with a greater consistency. He does not rank poets though he gives candid judgments of individual poets; nor is Dickey the spokesman for any kind of great tradition in modern poetry as his Vanderbilt predecessors Tate, Brooks, and Warren were. A comparison with Randall Jarrell is apt because Dickey admired Jarrell and because, like Dickey, Jarrell broke with formalist theory and practice, restored the poet to the poem and the personality of the critic to literary criticism. Jarrell, in *Poetry and the Age,* and Dickey, consistently in his criticism, desire the readers to be participants in the poems they read.

Dickey's criticism is pertinent to postmodernism in poetry and to postformalism in criticism. His approach to criticism is subjective, not objective and hermeneutical, and his view of the poem is as a dramatization of unrealized aspects of the ego of the poet rather than as a self-contained or autotelic artifact. Dickey has been a determined spokesman for connections between the author and his poem without deteriorating into a poetry of literalism or of commonplaces. He seeks significant connections between persona of the poem and the reader that can compel belief in a transcendence of the ordinary limitations of the self. He is aware of the destructive forces in nature, but he regards himself as a poet like Theodore Roethke, as a celebrator of life. If Dickey is a believer in possibilities of meaning in art and in life, he is also aware of the dangers of a complete surrender to the instincts and to the emotions—of becoming like "unthinking nature." If he is neoromantic in his preference for open forms and in his penchant for personality, he is also an advocate of balance between the demands of form and the freedom required for inspiration. In short, Dickey is for Dionysian passion but also for Apollonian control.

James Dickey's favorite myth seems to be that of Orpheus. He has used it in his poetry and in his novel *Deliverance.* There is also a kind of orphic stance in his literary criticism. He has a strong sense of the mission of the poet as the one with the power to make things happen in the imagination of his readers. Yet his poet, and he is his own chief example, is a grateful survivor of chaos who can still be a celebrant of life in spite of the inevitable "dismemberments" of men, not by Thracian women but by war, age, and disease.

Dickey's poems of the 1970s, though few in number, suggest a change to more objective personae who are not Dickey himself but others who serve as surrogates. Because he has written very few critical essays in the 1970s, there is no comparable discernible shift from his consistent advocacy of the subjective in poetry to championing anything like "objective correlatives" for personal feelings, although the critical essays he has written recently are less personal, less controversial, and less significant than the earlier ones.

In 1979 Dickey gave a lecture at the University of Idaho on Ezra Pound. Earlier Dickey had tended to lump Pound with Eliot as a modernist who sought to give his readers not himself but *culture.* Dickey's revaluation is similar to the current revisionist view that sees Pound still as an influence on Eliot and on modernism but also as an influence on a much less impersonal and freer postmodernism. What he now finds valuable is not the "academic Pound of quotation and cultural cross-reference" but rather the Pound of "the amazing image," "the fresh clean language," and "the sound of a voice saying something simple and extraordinary" with the tone "of a delivered truth."[10] What Dickey finds of use in this Pound is not "the shock of recognition" but "the shock of possibility."

It is the tiny essay in the privately published ***Billy Goat*** that makes clear James Dickey's continuing commitment to his version of a Whitmanesque role for the poet, an intensified poet who establishes the necessary connections to make possible an intensified reader. There has been a slight change in terminology. He now desires an "energized man," nothing as sensational as a man "like a creature from another planet, giving off strange rays of solar energy," but simply "a human creature, like you, like me—like you *could be,* like I like to think I could be."[11]

The existential literature of three decades ago was once described as "the literature of possibility."[12] That phrase would be apt for a description of the kind of freedom that James Dickey desires for poets today, certainly for himself.

Notes

1. Warren's comment is discussed in Franklin Ashley, "James Dickey: The Art of Poetry," *Paris Review* 65 (Spring 1976):70.

2. James Dickey, *Babel to Byzantium* (New York, 1968), p. ix. Dickey has frequently repeated this comment. Neither in writings nor in public readings does he refer to himself as a critic.

3. Ashley, "James Dickey," p. 81.

4. Ibid., p. 170.

5. Bly, "The Collapse of James Dickey," pp. 70-79.

6. Kizer and Boatwright, "A Conversation with James Dickey," pp. 3-28.

7. James Dickey, "The Greatest American Poet," *Atlantic Monthly,* November 1968, pp. 53-58.

8. James Dickey, "The Poet of Secret Lives and Misspent Opportunities," *New York Times Book Review,* 18 May 1969, pp. 1, 10.

9. James Dickey, "The Self as Agent," in *The Great Ideas Today,* ed. Robert M. Hutchins and Mortimer J. Adler (Chicago: Encyclopaedia Britannica, 1968), pp. 91-97; James Dickey, "The Son, the Cave, and the Burning Bush," in *The Young American Poets,* ed. Paul Carroll (Chicago: Follett; Big Table, 1968), pp. 7-19.

10. James Dickey, *The Water-Bug's Mittens: Ezra Pound: What We Can Use* (Bloomfield Hills, Mich.; Columbia, S.C.: Bruccoli Clark, 1980), p. 15.

11. James Dickey, *Billy Goat 2* (Clemson, S.C.: Billy Goat Press, 1979), p. 3.

12. See Hazel Barnes, *Humanistic Existentialism: The Literature of Possibility* (Lincoln: University of Nebraska Press, 1959).

Ronald Baughman (essay date 1985)

SOURCE: Baughman, Ronald. "*Deliverance*." In *Understanding James Dickey,* pp. 109-21. Columbia: University of South Carolina Press, 1985.

[*In the following essay, Baughman explores the theme of renewal in* Deliverance.]

How Dickey changes and forms again is dramatically demonstrated in his only novel to date, **Deliverance.** In this work his protagonist achieves the renewal—the deliverance—for which the writer has struggled throughout his poetry. The speaker is able to find a new order, a new connection, a new sense of real well-being that becomes his passionate affirmation of life. Because the economy of language required in poetry does not allow for the expansive analysis that fiction provides, it is understandable that Dickey most fully develops this transforming function of survivor's guilt in his novel.

The ordeal shared by the four suburbanites who travel down the river in **Deliverance** clearly parallels that confronting the soldier in combat. In the first chapter of the novel, "Before," the suburbanites are revealed as quite ordinary men leading quite ordinary, inconsequential lives; they, like raw recruits, have not tested their courage or themselves. During the central three chapters—"September 14th," "September 15th," and "September 16th"—they are brutalized both by the wild river and by vicious mountain men; in order to survive they, like soldiers, must conquer and kill their enemies and must witness death in their own ranks. Finally, throughout the last chapter, "After," survivors of the trip must come to terms with their death encounters; they must, like combat veterans, weigh their responsibilities for the deaths they have caused and observed. Such is the process that protagonist Ed Gentry goes through as he seeks and ultimately attains deliverance.

The "Before" section of the novel establishes the individual characters and histories of the four suburbanites. Bobby Trippe, who works with mutual funds, is the figure most acclimated to city life. Popular and social, he is "a pleasant surface human being," though Ed has once seen him blow up at a party with "the rage of a weak king"[1]. Bobby is the least inclined of the four to take the canoe trip through the wilds. Drew Ballinger, who seems to regard nature as a picturesque location for mountain musicians, is a solid citizen and company man: "He worked as a sales supervisor for a big soft-drink company and he believed in it and the things it said it stood for with his very soul" (9). Drew also becomes a spokesman for the laws of civilization during the trip. That he has a son bearing "some kind of risen hornlike blood blister on his forehead that his eyebrow grew out of and around in a way to make you realize the true horrors of biology" (9) should warn him about nature's defiance of man's laws; yet Ballinger remains a naïve though well-intentioned man.

Lewis Medlock, who lives on the revenues of inherited rental properties, devotes himself wholeheartedly to fitness in order to be prepared for the time when "the whole thing is going to be reduced to the human body, once and for all" (42). He wishes to test himself to see if he is capable of withstanding or triumphing over the wilderness in its most primitive state: "You might say I've got the survival craze, the real bug" (43). What he prepares for is his own immortality, his victory over man and nature and death. He approaches the experience of the weekend trip armed with primitive weapons—a bow and arrow, a knife, and a canoe. But his most important weapon, he feels, is his "values" (48), his mental attitude, which earlier had enabled him to crawl unassisted out of the woods with a painfully broken ankle. Lewis admires the "dependability" (47) of the mountain people in equipping themselves for the rigors of a natural, primitive existence, even though they are "ignorant and full of superstition and bloodshed and murder and liquor and hookworm and ghosts and early deaths" (49). Lewis becomes Ed Gentry's primary instructor in the art of surviving nature's—and man's—violence.

Ed, the narrator-protagonist, is a "get-through-the-day-man" who is "mainly interested in sliding" (41). He has reduced his work, his relationships, and, indeed, his entire life to the "mechanical": "I was a mechanic of the graphic arts, and when I could get the problem to appear mechanical to me, and not the result of inspiration, I could do something with it. . . . And that, as far as art was concerned, was it" (26-27). He is pleased with the idea of the unpressured, "no-sweat shop" (13) that he and his partner run, yet the description suggests a place of little real commitment. And, in fact, he scorns would-be artists who, "like George Holley, my old Braque man," say, "I am with you but not of you" (15). Even with his wife, Martha, who believes more in his talent than he himself does, Ed responds primarily to her "normalcy"—her "toughness that got things done," her "practical approach to sex" (28)—rather than to the "absolutely personal connection" (26) that she has once offered. Like many of the figures in Dickey's war poetry Ed is imprisoned, but his primary cage is his sense of his life's worthlessness: "The feeling of the inconsequence of whatever I would do, of anything I would pick up or think about or turn to see was at that moment being set in the very bone marrow. . . . It was the old mortal, helpless, time-terrified human feeling" (18).

The nature of the wilderness that these four suburbanites enter is suggested by the mountain people they encounter in the town of Oree. Physically and mentally twisted by inter-marriage, inadequate health care, and the hardships of their lives, these inhabitants of "the country of nine-fingered people" (56) seem hostile toward the city dwellers. Drew shares a guitar-banjo duet with an albino boy who has "pink eyes like a white rabbit's; one of them stared off at a furious and complicated angle. That was the eye he looked at us with, with his face set in another direction. The sane, rational eye was fixed on something that wasn't there, somewhere in the dust of the road" (58-59). Although Ballinger and the boy make musical connection, no other sort is invited. Furthermore, as the suburbanites negotiate with—and antagonize—the Griner brothers, who reluctantly agree to deliver Lewis's car to Aintry, Ed notes the Hadeslike environment of the mountain men's garage:

> It was dark and iron-smelling, hot with the closed-in heat that brings the sweat out as though it had been waiting all over your body for the right signal. Anvils stood around or lay on their sides, and chains hung down, covered with coarse, deep grease. The air was full of hooks; there were sharp points everywhere—tools and nails and ripped-open rusty tin cans . . . and through everything, out of the high roof, mostly, came this clanging hammering, meant to deafen and even blind.
>
> (62)

The imagery of the description explicitly conveys the danger these men and others like them pose to intruders from another culture.

The river itself, the Cahulawassee, offers both threat and promise to the suburbanites. Like the rivers and streams of Dickey's poetry it functions as a pathway to death as well as to life. Entering the Cahulawassee, the four men note its pollution—a severed chicken's head reminds Ed of a human head—and throughout their trip the men are battered by its force. Yet when Gentry first steps into the water to free his canoe from rocks, he senses its positive power: "It felt profound, its motion built into it by the composition of the earth for hundreds of miles upstream and down, and by thousands of years. The standing there was so good, so fresh and various and continuous, so vital and uncaring around my genitals, that I hated to leave it" (75). Embracing his sexual-creative parts, the river provides his baptism into nature. This experience is confirmed by an encounter Ed has that night when an owl lands on his tent roof. He touches its talon, and he then imagines that he hunts with the bird as it repeatedly leaves and returns to his tent: "I hunted with him as well as I could, there in my weightlessness. The woods burned in my head. Toward morning I could reach up and touch the claw without turning on the light" (89).

The connections between man and river, man and bird, signal the beginning of Gentry's movement from the civilized world into the world of nature. As he awakens next morning and prepares to hunt while the others sleep, he realizes that in this place "none—or almost none—of my daily ways of living my life would work" (93). He begins to abandon his habit of sliding; and walking through a dense river fog "exactly to my teeth" (96), he seems to disappear and then reemerge into a new state of being. However, he badly misses his bow-and-arrow shot at a deer, revealing that he is still a novice, still only partially formed.

Later the same morning comes the encounter with nature—and with nature's men—that puts Ed and his friends to their first real test. Gentry and Bobby, who share a canoe, become separated from the other pair because of Bobby's ineptness. Growing tired of fighting the waters, of "learning the hard way" (107), they decide to rest in the apparent safety of the riverbank. They find there, instead, the real threat of two mountain men whose appearance and movements suggest Dickey's earlier descriptions of snakes and sharks, his embodiments of absolute but indifferent evil:

> One of them, the taller one, narrowed in the eyes and face. They came forward, moving in a kind of half circle as though they were stepping around something. The shorter one was older, with big white eyes and a half-white stubble that grew in whorls on his cheeks.

> His face seemed to spin in many directions. . . . The other was lean and tall, and peered as though out of a cave or some dim simple place far back in his yellow-tinged eyeballs.
>
> (108)

Nature's men in nature's setting sodomize Bobby and threaten Ed. But when one of the men tells Ed to "Fall down on your knees and pray, boy. And you better pray good" (116), Gentry's prayer is answered not by God but instead by Lewis, another of nature's creatures, who shoots the older man through the chest with his bow and arrow and frightens the other man into the woods. Clearly in this setting life is reduced to its simplest terms; in the wilderness, as in combat, man kills or is killed.

What action should follow, however, is not so easily resolved by the suburbanites, and each man's position indicates the degree to which he is bound by civilization's conventional beliefs. Drew, for example, says that they should "Listen to reason" (130), that they have committed "justified homicide" (121), and that the legal system will give them a fair trial if they tell "the whole story" (121). Lewis, at the other extreme, dismisses Drew's views as "boy scoutish" (123); he declares that the men themselves are the law, that "no body, no crime" (125), and that there is "not any right thing" (123) except what they determine is right. When asked for his opinion, Bobby fulfills Ed's earlier description of his having "the rage of a weak king" by repeatedly kicking the mountain man's corpse in the face.

While the others argue, Gentry tries to define his own position by turning to the river: "I tried to think ahead, and I couldn't see anything but desperate trouble, and for the rest of my life. . . . I could feel myself beginning to breathe fast in the stillness. . . . I listened to the woods and the river to see if I could get an answer" (123-24). Like the combat veteran, Ed realizes that this death encounter will stay with him forever, and his appeal to nature further confirms the transformation occurring within him. Finally the four agree to bury the dead man, conceal their actions, and live with the guilt they share. In killing the man they have done what they had to do, they decide, and only Drew believes that confession would save them. Yet like the combat-veteran speaker in **"The Firebombing,"** they are uncertain about whether ultimately they should be granted absolution or sentence for their actions.

After the men have buried the mountain man and started down the river again, Ed concedes that "something came to an edge in me. . . . A gigantic steadiness took me over . . . that added up to a kind of equilibrium" (139). This equilibrium is tested by disastrous events. The men are thrown into the river, and Ed feels the life-threatening nature of his second baptism: "I turned over and over. I rolled, I tried to crawl along the flying bottom. Nothing worked. I was dead. I felt myself fading out into the unbelievable violence and brutality of the river, joining it. . . . I got on my back and poured with the river, sliding over the stones like a creature I had always contained but never released" (144). This experience marks his full recognition of nature's power and of men's proper relationship with it: not to fight it but to merge with it, adopt its methods. Ed's realization comes at exactly the right moment, for Drew has been killed—possibly by a shot from the cliffs above the river—and Lewis, the group's leader, has broken his leg. Ed therefore must assume command, and he feels infused with a new inner power: "I liked hearing the sound of my voice in the mountain speech. . . . It sounded like somebody who knew where he was and knew what he was doing" (152-53).

That Gentry has achieved oneness with nature is revealed through his climb up a mountainside to hunt the surviving mountain man, who may or may not be stalking the suburbanites. Before he begins his ascent, Ed again approaches the river:

> Then for some reason I stepped into the edge of the river. In a way, I guess, I wanted to get a renewed feel of all the elements present. . . . I stood with the cold water flowing around my calves and my head back, watching the cliff slant up into the darkness. More stars had come out around the top of the gorge, a kind of river of them.
>
> (156)

His vision fuses river, mountain, and stars, and as he begins his ascent, he himself connects with the natural elements. In the darkness he finds himself in a dreamlike state, one in which he becomes a wary but sensitive lover of the mountainside: "With each shift to a newer and higher position I felt more and more tenderness toward the wall. . . . I turned back into the cliff and leaned my mouth against it, feeling all the way out through my nerves and muscles exactly how I had possession of the wall . . . in a way that held the whole thing together" (163). Ed's connection with the cliff is throughout expressed in sexual terms. Furthermore, several times during his ascent he has dangerous slips; "Often a hand or foot would slide and then catch on something I knew, without knowing, would be there, and I would go on up" (177). Because his instincts are now thoroughly those of nature, he can find the secure spots without actually seeing them. He had earlier evidenced some of this same ability by making contact with the owl and its talons, but here his sense is much more fully developed.

As he attains the summit, Gentry casts himself and the mountain man in nature's predator-prey relationship: "I'll make a circle inland, very quiet, and look for him like I'm some kind of animal. What kind? It doesn't matter, as long as I'm quiet and deadly. I could be a snake" (174). He thinks as the mountain man thinks—"our minds fuse" (180)—and adopts the cold "indifference" of both the man and nature. He predicts where his prey will emerge from the woods, climbs carrying bow and arrow into a tree, and, using his graphic designer's sense in a new way, creates a pattern which only the mountain man can complete. That the stranger does, in fact, enter that precise spot may at first seem an unconvincing manipulation of plot; yet Dickey clearly intends it to show how completely Ed has become nature's predator who is able to read the mind, foresee the actions, of his prey. And as the stranger steps into Ed's mechanical design, the picture becomes in a very real sense a work of art, allowing Ed to say, "I had never seen a more beautiful or convincing element of a design. I wanted to kill him just like that" (189). Gentry's shot is true, but with it he falls out of the tree and wounds himself in the side with his remaining arrow, and he has to track down the man, who has stumbled into the woods. Finding his prey dead, Ed declares, "His brain and mine unlocked and fell apart" (199); the protagonist is no longer exclusively a predator.

Whether he has killed the right man remains unclear. Ed cannot positively identify the man as his would-be sodomizer and murderer; nor can he be certain, later in the novel, that the man is the deputy sheriff's missing brother-in-law. Neither can he or the other survivors be sure, when they find Drew's body, that he has been killed by a rifle shot. Because they cannot know the truth, they decide to bury both bodies in the river and thereby avoid legal inquiries. The question of right and wrong remains, but Dickey purposely leaves it unanswered. **Deliverance** is not a simple morality tale of violation and revenge; it is a story of men who must learn to live with uncertainty about their own guilt or innocence. They, like the speaker in **"The Firebombing,"** cannot know whether they deserve absolution or sentence.

Yet in the novel, for the first time in his work, Dickey creates a figure who does achieve complete renewal. Ed Gentry outwits the authorities who await the men at the end of their canoe trip, and following a final drink of water from the river he returns to the family and the life that he feels are going to save him. However, the real salvation lies in his experiences on the river and his later appraisal of them. Ed has undergone the classic stages of survivor's guilt. He has confronted his enemy in a death encounter. He feels that he is alive because someone else has died in his place: "I had a friend there who in a way had died for me, and my enemy was there" (275). He has undergone a series of baptisms in the river and a series of exchanges helping him to merge with nature; such fusions have helped him to reorder his perspective on who and what he is. He has emerged from the fog into a renewal as a changed human being. Now he goes home to be healed and saved. Martha does help heal him physically, yet his real salvation lies within his own mind: "And so it ended, except in my mind, which changed the events more deeply into what they were, into what they meant to me alone" (274).

His deliverance alters Ed in his everyday life. He abandons his role as a "slider" and becomes instead a man with purpose. He now takes himself seriously as an artist, identifying with the office's one other serious artist: George Holley "has become my best friend, next to Lewis, and we do a lot of serious talking about art" (276). His office now displays the work of Braque as well as "headlines of war and student strikes" (276). And although Bobby returns unchanged to the "affable, faintly nasty manner he always had" (276), Lewis also learns an important lesson about himself. He discovers that "he can die now; he knows that dying is better than immortality. He is a human being, and a good one" (277). Lewis and Ed have learned how to gain real control over their lives; each now is able to become "the author of [his] own life story,"[2] as Lifton phrases it.

Lewis describes his archery as "passing over into Zen. . . . You shouldn't fight it. Better to cooperate with it. Then it'll take you there; take the arrow there" (278). His description applies also, of course, to the lives of these two men. Rather than wrestling with questions of their personal innocence or guilt, they submit to the flow of their lives as if carried by the river that now runs only in Ed's mind:

> The river and everything I remembered about it became a possession to me, a personal, private possession, as nothing else in my life ever had. Now it ran nowhere but in my head, but there it ran as though immortally. I could feel it—I can feel it. . . . In me it still is, and will be until I die, green, rocky, deep, fast, slow, and beautiful beyond reality.
>
> (275)

The river becomes a private, haunting emblem of experiences that have transformed Ed Gentry, have delivered him into a new life.

Notes

1. *Deliverance* (Boston: Houghton Mifflin, 1970) 9. The page references within the text are to this edition.
2. Lifton, *Home from the War* 393.

Paul Christensen (essay date spring-summer 1986)

SOURCE: Christensen, Paul. "Toward the Abyss: James Dickey at Middle Age." *Parnassus* 13 (spring-summer 1986): 202-19.

[*In the following essay, Christensen contends that the problem with* The Central Motion: Poems, 1968-1979 *is that Dickey "has tried to deal with middle age, his own, and fails to perceive in it value or meaning."*]

"The secret is that on whiteness you can release
The blackness . . ."

—*The Zodiac*

The psychological geography of America is familiar by now: the East and West form a significant polarity in culture—the one old and resolute, fixed by time; the other fluid and novel, sending back its innovations which ruffle and reconstitute American identity. East and West make up a sort of tectonic plate of crumbling and emerging reality. The Midwest is that drab emptiness no one can fill except with a certain malevolence of humor: it is the only place in America that never tempered its reality with a threatening frontier. As in the case of Indiana, the heartland of America until the 1950s, where no Indians (despite its name!) confronted the whites who settled it. Almost at the moment it was occupied, there ensued in the Midwest its tedious image of a placid, almost rancid domesticity, from which artists and thinkers of each generation have longed for and immortalized their dreams of escape—either to the East or to the West, depending on the sensibility of the escapee. But the South remains a puzzle, even to the most ardent Southern historians. The South is difficult from almost any perspective, but interesting in its opaqueness and mystique. It was an anomaly from the outset: half its states are named after English kings and queens, the other half have Indian names; its culture was derived from medieval Western Europe, and its aristocratic ways were cultivated in the teeth of a democratized, industrial North. The Civil War was, in some respects, a replay of the French Revolution, in which sansculotte Yankees destroyed an intransigent nobility. The emergence of a national corporate economy in America following the Civil War parallels the development of an industrial republic from the smoking buckets of the guillotine.

The identity of the South does not lie in its opposition to the North but in its opposition to itself, within itself, a whirligig of polarities that in their fury and violence forged the essential nature of the region. "Love-hate," James Dickey wrote, "is stronger than love or hate." The kudzu vine that conquers numberless pastures and meadows, barns and electric poles of the Deep South is a metaphor of the voluptuous fertility of the ground; but it is countered in the classic antebellum South by a sedate and exacting symmetry of nature on the plantation estates—a willful control of the green world brought over from neoclassical Europe. The image we have of the South, nationally, is of an unsynthesized state somewhere between kudzu and Monticello, between cypress swamps and lynch mobs and the pristine whiteness of a Greek-styled manor house, columned and domed, an emblem of human triumph over the powerful counterthrust of tropical abundance. The original polarity between human symmetry and nature's fertility has undergone constant revision, but it remains the key point of the South's psychic bearings. The vestiges of an old order's will are embodied in Blanche DuBois and in Stanley Kowalski's dark fertility, which longs to overtake her. The polarities within the Southern psyche are myriad, a Zen universe of poised and equal adversaries that constitute the yin and yang of its sensibility.

In a way, the South is the burial ground of the Western mind. The South was formed in the closing decades of the European Renaissance, in the era in which a state culture was being wrested from a sacred one, dooming Europe to decline from a civilization to an economic system. The Western mind, as Charles Olson has argued, began somewhere far back in time in a feud with nature. The axis of Western thought ever since had been toward the control of the realms of growth and decay, the domination of the natural order. It sought to protect itself from mutability through a faith in a heaven of immortal things, each perfect and unchanging; so long as it was able to aspire to such a realm of static bliss, the Western mind thrived in its conflict with all its earthly adversaries. But when the sacred and mundane were separated politically in the Protestant Reformation, the aspirations of the Western mind were thwarted and redirected to nurturing a secular state, with all its mundane responsibilities and repairs. The loss of heaven, as Georg Lukacs observed, was the loss of reality in European art and philosophy. The Renaissance separation of essence from substance closed the routes to heaven in Western ideology and aesthetics, and a kind of sorrowful dream was vented and driven off to the new Eden of the Southern United States. The South glowed like a dream for two centuries: wide fields of symmetrical cultivation, a code of chivalrous conduct, the naming of cities after those of Rome and Greece. The South was an ersatz European country, with the Negro essential to its pretensions: his servile role in the social order was the fulfillment of an old Western ambition: for the Negro was supremely the human extension of Africa's wild, undiluted nature.

The moment the South grasped its role as the inheritor of Europe's humanism, its mind was forged and its psychological conflicts were set in motion. It was an old order in a new country; it was a civilization thrust upon a wilderness; it was a regime of whites ruling over blacks. It was a culture of refinements that soon learned savage ways of punishment and internecine feuding. In every way, the South grappled with opposition and conflict, and its culture was oddly mute to the rest of the nation and the world. Its silence for two centuries was secretive, a brooding within itself that resembled the hard silence of a schizophrenic patient. The South had no way to grow or develop, no way to traffic with the world; it was captive to its own profound conflict and contradiction. In **"Notes on the Decline of Outrage"** (1961), Dickey describes the feelings of a white Southern male who has boarded a bus with blacks:

> At this moment he is very much aware of himself as a Southerner, and that he is in some way betraying someone or something, even though the impulse which brought him to his present seat on the bus may have been completely laudable, *sub specie aeternitatis*. Oddly enough, he cannot help feeling also a sharp upswing of defiant joy at remembering that he *is* a Southerner, a joy that in no way wishes to distinguish approval from disapproval, right from wrong, good from evil.

His memories of a Southern grandfather are "now intolerably confused," for his grandfather's life was "inextricably entangled with attitudes which, rightly seen, are and have always been indefensible, inhuman, corrupt, and corrupting."

> The young man understands himself as the victim of a cruel and fathomless paradox, a dilemma between the horns of which only a god could survive and still retain his identity.

Dickey has tried to make a poetry of that "mixed state" of mind which he argues, here and elsewhere in essays, *is* the Southern mind. In **"The Poet Turns on Himself,"** published in 1966, he set out this goal for himself:

> I should like now to develop a writing instrument which would be capable of embodying these [inseparably bound] moments and their attendant states of mind, and I would be most pleased if readers came away from my poems not at all sure as to where the danger and the repose separate, where joy ends and longing begins. Strongly mixed emotions are what I usually have and what I usually remember from the events of my life. Strongly mixed, but giving the impression of being one emotion—that is the condition I am seeking to impose on my readers, whoever they may be.

The South is where the European mind unraveled; the brittle culture that kept alive its separatist vision of things collapsed under the tread of another culture. What whelmed up from its ruins and smoking cinders is the *afterlife* of the Western mind—the imagination entangled in oppositions and paradoxes. The literal and material experience of Southern life is only a surface under which the depths of myth and mystery glitter; the Southern character is a mosaic of contending elements, bestial and human, dark and light, irrational and rational. Poe's voice rises out of the region to declare the start of this imagination, its erased borders and mazelike patterns of thought, its lurid and brilliant perceptions. He was the first anticipation of the breakdown of categorical logic; what rose to replace it was an odd fusion of Indian, African, and European dispositions, the slow and inexorable mixing of elements to create the jointed processes of Southern awareness—felt in its dialects, its rural architecture, its peculiar and contradictory jurisprudence, its paradoxic masculinity, which compresses myriad conflicting images of boy-men in the same youth; its sacred and desecrating values of the female, and so on. The Western mind thinned out into a delta here, a swampy mixture of elements that dissolved its original binary character. This Southern fusion is the point of Twain's *Huckleberry Finn,* whose plot shows the creation of the Southern mind—as tutored by a black surrogate father, whose spiritual advice is opposed to the literal, skeptical outlook Huck has inherited from Europe. Huck cannot affect the reality of the river settlements with mere logical powers; he learns to accept the paradoxes of human character through repeated trial and error, until he has achieved double-sightedness and can sympathize with the entangled elements composing human nature.

The writer who approaches the subject of the South must look for a graspable aspect of its paradox. For Faulkner, as for George Washington Cable and Kate Chopin, the essential paradox was time itself: the lingering insistence of a high European culture, the steady erosion of it by the present, between which dangled the helpless Southern soul. When Dickey emerged in the 1960s, he had been well schooled in the literature of the region. He had the good fortune to be born in Atlanta, perhaps the center of Southern paradox—destroyed by Sherman, rebuilt as the capital of the new South, it became the emblem of urban industrialism surrounded by the primitive culture thriving in its hills and river valleys. It is the seat of Emory University and of the Coca-Cola Company; it was to become in Dickey's mind the citadel of urban drudgery, from which the average Atlantan longed to escape—into the hillsides, where he could drink at the springs of its primitive counterpart once more. Dickey attended Clemson briefly, and after the war took degrees from Vanderbilt, where an aging fringe of the original agrarians still lingered on its faculty. Their work obliquely enters into Dickey's style and attitudes, but it was the paradox of Southern life itself that shaped even the earliest lyrics of Dickey's canon.

The rites of passage of Southern boyhood have been explored by every major writer of the region; they differ remarkably from female rites, particularly as noted in Eudora Welty's fiction, as in "Moon Lake," where mock intercourse is performed on a nearly drowned girl by a wiry, primal lifeguard. A Negro pushed her into the lake from her perch, and in her rescue, all the girls of the camp watch as a male ritually matures the frail form beneath his legs. But where the Southern female receives her lessons in life and life-bearing, the Southern male is taught the mysteries of death and violence, of the role of hunter in nature. He is raised to see himself as the destroyer of Otherness, a conqueror of the primal realm. But to kill the enemy requires that one perceive his affinity and kinship with the lower world. The growing up of the Southern boy requires a rebirth in nature, from which he emerges only after he has killed an animal and rubbed his face in the blood of his victory, as does "the boy" in Faulkner's "The Old

uninspired language; a breast-beating drunken hero, whose pains are monotonous, and a concern for failing health and an aging mind, at which he is vivid and dramatic.

The Strength of Fields (1979), the third and last book of *The Central Motion,* is a slight but fluid collection of original poems, with an appendix of fourteen translations. Dickey has made some adjustments to style in it—an emphasis on sound and the musically enriched phrase, and away from a crisp narrative focus. The poems seem reluctant to tell anything—an image will do, as in **"Root-Light, or the Lawyer's Daughter,"** with its rush of baroque imagery, its subject withheld until the final lines, when a naked girl dives from a bridge into a river as a lasting memory of youth and beauty. **"The Strength of Fields"** was commissioned for Carter's inauguration, and it is an elegant tribute to a new President. It explores the delicate sense of fealty between one isolated self and the lives that fill the surrounding cosmos as a low, baleful train whistle is heard in the distance to remind one of change and mortality. The poem's elegant sophistications of language are tempered a bit by the form they construct—an open-ended variation on the blues ballad of freight trains and lonely travel. **"The Rain Guitar"** is a silly bit of mythmaking, with Dickey as magic minstrel again, playing his regional music as an English fisherman helplessly dances in excitement. It is a throwback to the magical realism Dickey produced earlier, but its self-glorifications hardly seem naïve any longer.

Especially interesting is the poem **"For the Death of Lombardi,"** which is Dickey at his vintage best. In Lombardi Dickey finds a mystical Southern father—someone who drove the boys to manhood, who died and is lamented self-consciously in mythical terms as a source of Dickey's own manhood. His death by cancer is metaphorical of a terrible inexorability, which Dickey fears now that he is "middle-aged and gray." Other fathers are listed in the lament: Paul Hornung, who "has withdrawn from me," and George Patton, "who created armies" the way Lombardi "created us." Lombardi is the archetypal coach. His death spells death for all he raised—"We're with you all the way / You're going forever, Vince." It is followed, a bit too neatly, with **"False Youth: Autumn: Clothes of the Age,"** in which Dickey gets a haircut and is scorned by the barber as a "middle-aged hippie." Upon leaving, he notices a youth wearing an embroidered jacket with a portentous figure on it:

> eagle riding on his claws with a banner
> Outstretched as the wings of my shoulders
> Coming after me with his flag
> Disintegrating, his one eye raveling
> Out, filthy strings flying
> From the white feathers, one wing nearly gone:
> Blind eagle but flying
> Where I walk, where I stop with my fox

> Head at the glass to let the row of chairs spell it out
> And get a lifetime look at my bird's
> One word, raggedly blazing with extinction and soaring loose
> In red threads burning up white until I am shot in the back
> Through my wings or ripped apart
> For rags:
> *Poetry.*

Mortality, old age, and death are the terms of this poetry, but Dickey seems to have found peace with himself. The poems are less shrill and frenzied; they balance once more on their plumb lines, the lines tapering and expanding as he packs all the music he can into their lumpy, jarring phrases. Some of the language reads like tongue-twisting elocution drills, but there are also somber themes that buoy up the dizzying lyric spells. In the closing poem of Part One, **"Exchanges,"** Dickey merges his words with lines from Joseph Trumbull Stickney, as both describe the California coast. The Stickney lines are romantic and reverent, while Dickey's are sober and realistic: together they merge the two halves of history—the beautiful wilderness, the gloomy sea of oil rigs and pollution. It ends on Dickey's most persistent theme: the human curse upon nature:

> Nothing for me
> Was solved. I wandered the beach
> Mumbling to a dead poet
> In the key of A, looking for the rainbow
> Of oil, and the doomed
> Among fish.
> —*Let us speak softly of living.*

The group of translations which closes *The Central Motion* bears the nervous title **"Head-Deep in Strange Sounds: Free-Flight Improvisations from the un-English,"** and offers some loose renderings of various poems. "I chose them nearly at random," he tells us in his preface, but most are about old age, fate, a serene resignation to the way of things:

> I am of shadow and of sun of the sun
> Returning always,
> And I laugh, silently.

"O death so dear to me" opens another poem. Beyond the theme of aging, there is another, more subliminal one: a longing for the animal realm:

> I am tired of existing
> As an animal of intelligence—
> . . . Let us go back into the immense and soft-handed, double
> Fire-bringing ignorance.

But Dickey is clever by half. *He* hasn't made his peace; he has found it through others and only cosigns their counsels through his own boisterous, rowdy American versions. His tone almost contradicts *their* emotions: "I play the hell-game / That dances on the horizon," or "Raging with discovery like a prow / Into the oncoming Never." He tells us through a Yevtushenko poem, "I'm not a damn thing but old," but that "It's *horrible* to live / And even more horrible / not to live."

The Central Motion is the waffling poetry of a major writer of the 1970s. It's a slim volume with a few very good poems in it; the rest is confusion and ramblings, awkward experiments and grim failures. It comes after a decade of remarkable successes and awards and was perhaps an inevitable falling off. The seventies were themselves unheroic and inward-looking, and their atmosphere wears off in this work. The view is almost always within, at failing health and waning convictions; it is a book about struggle and grief, arguments with the self, a desire to go on as the feet grow leaden. It is partly about being caught in one's own confected image, the duties that it imposes, which are false and wearying. Americans took to Dickey, even non-readers, who flocked to his readings. Sporting-goods manufacturers plied him with canoes and power bows, hoping for his endorsements. The book seems to sigh under the load of that publicity and vanity, as real things ensue—mortality, death of loved ones, illnesses, qualms, and fears. It is a book of thrashings and throes by a man who cannot easily face his aging. Unlike Lear, who reached an epiphany of sorts—that man is a bare, forked animal gripped by change—Dickey's voice keeps arguing alone in the dark, in thickets of confusion and ill humor, trying to find the drama and the lyric ebullience to somehow get through it. But all Dickey can argue here is that youth is everything—and to lose it is the only tragedy.

Monroe K. Spears (essay date winter 1987)

SOURCE: Spears, Monroe K. "James Dickey as a Southern Visionary." *Virginia Quarterly Review* 63, no. 1 (winter 1987): 110-23.

[*In the following essay, Spears places Dickey and his work within the context of the Southern literary tradition.*]

Some years ago James Dickey, who will be 64 next month, responded to an interviewer's question about the sense in which he was a Southern writer with the ringing declaration that "the best thing that ever happened to me was to have been born a Southerner. First as a man and then as a writer." He would not want to feel that he was limited in any way by being a Southerner or was expected to "indulge in the kind of regional chauvinism that has sometimes been indulged in by Southern writers," he said, but the tragic history of the South gave him a set of values "some of which are deplorable, obviously, but also some of which are the best things that I have ever had as a human being." Southerners, he suggested, let their ancestors help: "I have only run-of-the-mill ancestors but they knew that one was supposed to do certain things. Even the sense of evil, which is very strong with me, would not exist if I had no sense of what evil was."

Dickey is convinced, then, that being Southern is central to the way he thinks and feels, but doesn't want to be thought of as *merely* regional; he suggests that the most valuable Southern quality is a special awareness of the personal past in the sense of inheriting traditions and codes of values from one's ancestors, and a special awareness of the regional past in its full tragic meaning, including the sense of evil. But rather than continue to depend on Dickey's own statements, now that I have used him to run interference for me, let me try to define more specifically just what kind of Southern writer he is and how he is related to other Southern writers.

The obvious starting-point is his relation to the Fugitive-Agrarian groups. Except for Donald Davidson, all the Fugitives and most of the Agrarians had left Vanderbilt long before Dickey arrived; so there was no possibility of personal influence. But Ransom, Tate, and Warren had become major figures in the literary world, and Brooks, Jarrell, and others were establishing high reputations. Vanderbilt students and faculty—most of them—were proud of the connection, and the campus was alive with legends of the days when giants had walked that very earth. In this context, creative writing seemed exciting and important to a good many students, and so did being a Southerner. It seems plain enough that Dickey's commitment to poetry and his awareness of his identity as Southerner owed much both to his reading of the Fugitive-Agrarian writers and to the Vanderbilt tradition of respect for serious writing. R. V. Cassill is amusing but, I think, quite wrong when he portrays Dickey as a rebellious Young Turk who refused to conform to the Southern ruling circles by speaking "smartly about Miss Eudora and Mr. Ransom" and being "reverent about Traveler" while snickering down Whitman and the Midwesterners. In the first place, the Southern literary establishment, insofar as there ever was one, was not reverential about Traveler; Tate abandoned his biography of Lee because he had ceased to believe in him, and *The Fugitive* announced early that it fled nothing so much as the genteel pieties of the Old South. In the second place, Dickey was recognized early by the Southerners and usually given whatever awards they had to offer. While he never had the rare good luck the Fugitives did of close association with a group of like-minded peers, the fact that the tradition of serious writing was still alive at Vanderbilt kept him from the near-total isolation of a writer like Faulkner. A few years ago Tate went on record with the opinion that Dickey is the best poet the South has produced since the heyday of the Fugitives, and Warren has said in the *South Carolina Review* that he is "among Jim's greatest admirers" and in the *New York Times Book Review* that **The Zodiac** is a major achievement, worthy of comparison to Hart Crane's *The Bridge*.

In recent years some nostalgic epigones of the Fugitive-Agrarians at Vanderbilt have written requiems for the Southern Literary Renascence, maintaining that it has suffered death by melancholy. Their thesis is that Southern literature has been dying since World War II, when modernism triumphed over the South; and any hope is illusory. I have never quite believed in the Southern Renascence, suspecting that it was created artificially, like Frankenstein's monster, in the laboratories of academic critics; and reports of the loss of such artificial life need not disturb us. At any rate, Dickey, thank God, like Madison Jones and others of his contemporaries at Vanderbilt, and like such older Southern writers as Robert Penn Warren, Walker Percy, and Eudora Welty, doesn't know he's dead and refuses to lie down. As stubbornly as the astronomical phenomena that Galileo saw through his telescope in spite of the irrefutable arguments of his learned opponents that they couldn't possibly be there, the works of these writers continue to exist and to grow, unquestionably alive. Most of us, however we may feel about the modern world, would rather have the poems and novels than have a thesis about it demonstrated; and our own Poe has taught us to beware of premature burial. So we will be grateful that some of our writers flourish, and we will refuse to abandon hope.

II

While Dickey seems to have no interest in Agrarianism as a political or economic program, he shares with the Agrarians a deep concern about man's relation to nature and the distortions produced in this relation by the increasing urbanism and commercialism of our society. Dickey's true subject, however, is neither rural nor urban, but *suburban*. Since Southern cities are smaller, their suburbs are not wholly distinct from nearby small towns, and both maintain more connection with the country than their Northern counterparts. Compare, in this respect, those Dickey represents with John Cheever's dormitory suburbs around New York, with swimming pools linked in one giant fantasy. But both writers describe the modern nuclear family—nuclear both in being small and without the connections families used to have and in being under the threat of nuclear war. In these respects there is little difference between North and South, though the South may be slightly less nuclear simply because it is less urban.

Dickey's remarkable achievement is that he has taken his subject seriously and redeemed the word *suburban* from its comic or pejorative overtones. Instead of describing bored wives at the country club, adulteries in Commuterdom, hysteria and desperation breaking out from the pressures of enforced uniformity, or the absurdities of Little League baseball, he shows us a suburban world that is still in touch with a nature that remains wild, not tamed or prettified. Dickey's suburbs have no cute ceramic animals, no dear little Bambis or gnomes on the lawns, but the call of the real wild, an inner nature answering to outer. ***Deliverance*** is the most extended example, with its gradual revelation that the wilderness has always been present in the suburbs, whose security is an illusion. On the other hand, **"The Firebombing"** treats the homeowner's longing for security sympathetically because of his vivid awareness of its precariousness in view of what he did to his Japanese counterparts. **"Dark Ones"** transmutes into poetry the evening ritual of the arrival home of the commuters.

To say that Dickey is a visionary poet is a paralyzingly obvious assertion: almost every poem he writes describes a vision of one kind or another, and in recent years he has dealt explicitly with the loss of physical vision in works such as the unfinished novel *Cahill is Blind*. Perhaps he will become the patron or mascot of the ophthalmologists, as Wallace Stevens was adopted by the ice-cream manufacturers after writing "The Emperor of Ice-Cream." Yet the truism is worth repeating, for it says something about his relation to Southern literature. Dickey belongs to the line of visionaries running from Blake through Rimbaud and Whitman to such modern exemplars as Hart Crane, George Barker, Dylan Thomas, and Theodore Roethke. It is noteworthy that there are no Southern names on this list, since as far as I know there are few Southern poets who could be called visionary. Tate and Warren, for example, are in their different ways primarily concerned with history, with attempting to relate the past to the present. Perhaps one reason good Southern poets have shied away from the visionary mode is that they remember how much older Southern poetry was emasculated by the necessity of avoiding politics and hence driven from reality into fake vision. The old Southern tradition of escapism and sentimentality—of high gutless swooning, to borrow a phrase from Faulkner—was certainly one thing the Fugitives were fleeing. South Carolinian Henry Timrod often exemplified this tradition, and Tate surely intended a contrast with Timrod's "Ode Sung at the Decoration of the Graves of the Confederate Dead at Magnolia Cemetery" when he wrote his own ironic "Ode to the Confederate Dead." Timrod's "Ethnogenesis" is a kind of vision, it is true, but appallingly detached from any sense of reality: in it the new Confederacy, with its economy based on cotton and slavery, is seen as bringing wealth, moral improvement, and a better climate to the whole world.

Before Dickey, the only Southern poet who was a true visionary was Poe; and his visions, as every schoolchild knows, were very peculiar indeed. Though one might argue that Dickey's poetic rhythms are often incantatory, and intended to put the reader into a kind of trance state, they are far more subtle than Poe's blatantly hypnagogic music; and though both poets are most interested in states of consciousness beyond normal waking life, they are not interested in the same states. Much as I would like to, I don't see how I can make a case for any resemblance beyond the fact that they are both visionaries. Dickey has none of Poe's morbid preoccupation with death, his concern being rather with new and different modes of life; you can't imagine his saying that the ideal poetic subject is the *death* of a beautiful woman. Poe strives obsessively to make the reader feel the horror of being a living soul in a dead body, of an irreparable crack or split in the edifice of the mind, of long-ago irremediable losses. Dickey, in contrast, produces in the reader a new awareness of nonhuman forms of life, from dogs on the feet to owls in the woods and panthers in the zoo; the poems seek new forms of union, wider possibilities of consciousness. Mind and body are not separated as they are in Poe, but totally fused. Finally, Dickey gets into his poems a solid feeling of everyday reality and normal experience before moving to transcend them. It is this feeling or rendering that distinguishes him not only from Poe but from the kind of fantasy that is now so enormously popular in movies and cheap fiction. Dickey's visions have nothing in common with these self-indulgent daydreams unrelated to any kind of reality.

III

Dickey's most ambitious visionary poem is certainly *The Zodiac,* which deals with nothing less than the meaning of the visible universe. Since it is based on a work by the Dutch poet Hendrik Marsman, whom Dickey retains as speaker and protagonist of the poem, it has nothing whatever to do with the South; the point of view is distinctively European when it is not cosmic. Why would Dickey choose to adopt a persona so different from his usual one? Partly, I would guess, because the difference was liberating: writing as Marsman, Dickey has a different mask of the self and different memories. Instead of the South or the wartime Pacific, he writes as a man of an earlier European generation about Amsterdam; instead of writing as a survivor, he is now one who will die early in the same war. Even the name *Marsman* may have reinforced this appeal: an author with a message from outer space. But on a deeper level, Marsman's poem expresses concerns and beliefs that Dickey shares. Dickey has always been moved by astronomy and by the religious sense of "how wild, inexplicable, marvelous, and endless creation is." His religion "involves myself and the universe, and it does not admit of any kind of intermediary, such as Jesus or the Bible." He would like to be reincarnated as a migratory sea bird like a tern or wandering albatross. The themes of the aging wanderer returning home and so finding his own identity and of the poet's reexamination and reaffirmation of his poetic faith and vocation—we might call them the *Ulysses* and *Lycidas* archetypes—must have appealed to Dickey with peculiar force in the Dutch poem. Imitating Marsman, then, frees Dickey from his usual self and gives him a fresh start at the same time that it provides him with a way of expressing some of his most deeply felt concerns and beliefs from a different perspective. By transforming the language, he makes Marsman's poem his own. Giving it a tone quite different from Marsman's and with far more dramatic power and variety, he makes it emphatically contemporary and personal. Through this process of expansion and dramatization, Dickey's poem becomes about twice as long as Marsman's.

The central fact about the protagonist is that he is a poet dedicated to the belief that poetry reveals ultimate truth and that it comes from sources above or beyond the rational intellect. Under the pressure of impending catastrophe—for he feels that he has wasted and misused his life, and he sees his world moving swiftly to destruction in World War II—he reexamines this visionary faith. The drama consists in his struggle to clarify and reaffirm it. Like all poets who conceive of their art as lamp rather than mirror, he worries that the light will die with the guttering lamp and vacillates about the reality of what it reveals; but he has the additional problems of distinguishing the hallucinations produced by delirium tremens from reality and of reconciling a knowledge of modern astronomy with belief in the significance of the zodiac. The zodiac may seem a curiously archaic and implausible locus of poetic faith; but it is its age and mythological richness that make it the supreme test case of the relation between man's imagination and God's. To believe in its significance is to believe that the universe is not meaningless, that there is a connection between the little world of man and the great world of the stars, between inside and outside.

To show the difference between Marsman's poem and Dickey's, let me quote the conclusion, in which the main themes are recapitulated. Here is Marsman (no doubt rather flatly translated):

> O spirit, grant to this small hand
> The calm and quiet resolution
> To steer the ship on to the morning land
> That slumbering waits and each horizon's bar.
> And give that he who listens to the swish
> That sweeps along the waving of the planets
> And through the whirling of the emerald sea
> May tune the instruments upon the fork
> Which at the touch reveals the structural form
> Of the immemorial European song
> That sounded at the dawn of cultured life,
> Whose course began upon the azure sea
> And shall still undulate through the west world

knows, were very peculiar indeed. Though one might argue that Dickey's poetic rhythms are often incantatory, and intended to put the reader into a kind of trance state, they are far more subtle than Poe's blatantly hypnagogic music; and though both poets are most interested in states of consciousness beyond normal waking life, they are not interested in the same states. Much as I would like to, I don't see how I can make a case for any resemblance beyond the fact that they are both visionaries. Dickey has none of Poe's morbid preoccupation with death, his concern being rather with new and different modes of life; you can't imagine his saying that the ideal poetic subject is the *death* of a beautiful woman. Poe strives obsessively to make the reader feel the horror of being a living soul in a dead body, of an irreparable crack or split in the edifice of the mind, of long-ago irremediable losses. Dickey, in contrast, produces in the reader a new awareness of nonhuman forms of life, from dogs on the feet to owls in the woods and panthers in the zoo; the poems seek new forms of union, wider possibilities of consciousness. Mind and body are not separated as they are in Poe, but totally fused. Finally, Dickey gets into his poems a solid feeling of everyday reality and normal experience before moving to transcend them. It is this feeling or rendering that distinguishes him not only from Poe but from the kind of fantasy that is now so enormously popular in movies and cheap fiction. Dickey's visions have nothing in common with these self-indulgent daydreams unrelated to any kind of reality.

III

Dickey's most ambitious visionary poem is certainly *The Zodiac,* which deals with nothing less than the meaning of the visible universe. Since it is based on a work by the Dutch poet Hendrik Marsman, whom Dickey retains as speaker and protagonist of the poem, it has nothing whatever to do with the South; the point of view is distinctively European when it is not cosmic. Why would Dickey choose to adopt a persona so different from his usual one? Partly, I would guess, because the difference was liberating: writing as Marsman, Dickey has a different mask of the self and different memories. Instead of the South or the wartime Pacific, he writes as a man of an earlier European generation about Amsterdam; instead of writing as a survivor, he is now one who will die early in the same war. Even the name *Marsman* may have reinforced this appeal: an author with a message from outer space. But on a deeper level, Marsman's poem expresses concerns and beliefs that Dickey shares. Dickey has always been moved by astronomy and by the religious sense of "how wild, inexplicable, marvelous, and endless creation is." His religion "involves myself and the universe, and it does not admit of any kind of intermediary, such as Jesus or the Bible." He would like to be reincarnated as a migratory sea bird like a tern or wandering albatross. The themes of the aging wanderer returning home and so finding his own identity and of the poet's reexamination and reaffirmation of his poetic faith and vocation—we might call them the *Ulysses* and *Lycidas* archetypes—must have appealed to Dickey with peculiar force in the Dutch poem. Imitating Marsman, then, frees Dickey from his usual self and gives him a fresh start at the same time that it provides him with a way of expressing some of his most deeply felt concerns and beliefs from a different perspective. By transforming the language, he makes Marsman's poem his own. Giving it a tone quite different from Marsman's and with far more dramatic power and variety, he makes it emphatically contemporary and personal. Through this process of expansion and dramatization, Dickey's poem becomes about twice as long as Marsman's.

The central fact about the protagonist is that he is a poet dedicated to the belief that poetry reveals ultimate truth and that it comes from sources above or beyond the rational intellect. Under the pressure of impending catastrophe—for he feels that he has wasted and misused his life, and he sees his world moving swiftly to destruction in World War II—he reexamines this visionary faith. The drama consists in his struggle to clarify and reaffirm it. Like all poets who conceive of their art as lamp rather than mirror, he worries that the light will die with the guttering lamp and vacillates about the reality of what it reveals; but he has the additional problems of distinguishing the hallucinations produced by delirium tremens from reality and of reconciling a knowledge of modern astronomy with belief in the significance of the zodiac. The zodiac may seem a curiously archaic and implausible locus of poetic faith; but it is its age and mythological richness that make it the supreme test case of the relation between man's imagination and God's. To believe in its significance is to believe that the universe is not meaningless, that there is a connection between the little world of man and the great world of the stars, between inside and outside.

To show the difference between Marsman's poem and Dickey's, let me quote the conclusion, in which the main themes are recapitulated. Here is Marsman (no doubt rather flatly translated):

> O spirit, grant to this small hand
> The calm and quiet resolution
> To steer the ship on to the morning land
> That slumbering waits and each horizon's bar.
> And give that he who listens to the swish
> That sweeps along the waving of the planets
> And through the whirling of the emerald sea
> May tune the instruments upon the fork
> Which at the touch reveals the structural form
> Of the immemorial European song
> That sounded at the dawn of cultured life,
> Whose course began upon the azure sea
> And shall still undulate through the west world

duced since the heyday of the Fugitives, and Warren has said in the *South Carolina Review* that he is "among Jim's greatest admirers" and in the *New York Times Book Review* that **The Zodiac** is a major achievement, worthy of comparison to Hart Crane's *The Bridge*.

In recent years some nostalgic epigones of the Fugitive-Agrarians at Vanderbilt have written requiems for the Southern Literary Renascence, maintaining that it has suffered death by melancholy. Their thesis is that Southern literature has been dying since World War II, when modernism triumphed over the South; and any hope is illusory. I have never quite believed in the Southern Renascence, suspecting that it was created artificially, like Frankenstein's monster, in the laboratories of academic critics; and reports of the loss of such artificial life need not disturb us. At any rate, Dickey, thank God, like Madison Jones and others of his contemporaries at Vanderbilt, and like such older Southern writers as Robert Penn Warren, Walker Percy, and Eudora Welty, doesn't know he's dead and refuses to lie down. As stubbornly as the astronomical phenomena that Galileo saw through his telescope in spite of the irrefutable arguments of his learned opponents that they couldn't possibly be there, the works of these writers continue to exist and to grow, unquestionably alive. Most of us, however we may feel about the modern world, would rather have the poems and novels than have a thesis about it demonstrated; and our own Poe has taught us to beware of premature burial. So we will be grateful that some of our writers flourish, and we will refuse to abandon hope.

II

While Dickey seems to have no interest in Agrarianism as a political or economic program, he shares with the Agrarians a deep concern about man's relation to nature and the distortions produced in this relation by the increasing urbanism and commercialism of our society. Dickey's true subject, however, is neither rural nor urban, but *suburban*. Since Southern cities are smaller, their suburbs are not wholly distinct from nearby small towns, and both maintain more connection with the country than their Northern counterparts. Compare, in this respect, those Dickey represents with John Cheever's dormitory suburbs around New York, with swimming pools linked in one giant fantasy. But both writers describe the modern nuclear family—nuclear both in being small and without the connections families used to have and in being under the threat of nuclear war. In these respects there is little difference between North and South, though the South may be slightly less nuclear simply because it is less urban.

Dickey's remarkable achievement is that he has taken his subject seriously and redeemed the word *suburban* from its comic or pejorative overtones. Instead of describing bored wives at the country club, adulteries in Commuterdom, hysteria and desperation breaking out from the pressures of enforced uniformity, or the absurdities of Little League baseball, he shows us a suburban world that is still in touch with a nature that remains wild, not tamed or prettified. Dickey's suburbs have no cute ceramic animals, no dear little Bambis or gnomes on the lawns, but the call of the real wild, an inner nature answering to outer. **Deliverance** is the most extended example, with its gradual revelation that the wilderness has always been present in the suburbs, whose security is an illusion. On the other hand, **"The Firebombing"** treats the homeowner's longing for security sympathetically because of his vivid awareness of its precariousness in view of what he did to his Japanese counterparts. **"Dark Ones"** transmutes into poetry the evening ritual of the arrival home of the commuters.

To say that Dickey is a visionary poet is a paralyzingly obvious assertion: almost every poem he writes describes a vision of one kind or another, and in recent years he has dealt explicitly with the loss of physical vision in works such as the unfinished novel *Cahill is Blind*. Perhaps he will become the patron or mascot of the ophthalmologists, as Wallace Stevens was adopted by the ice-cream manufacturers after writing "The Emperor of Ice-Cream." Yet the truism is worth repeating, for it says something about his relation to Southern literature. Dickey belongs to the line of visionaries running from Blake through Rimbaud and Whitman to such modern exemplars as Hart Crane, George Barker, Dylan Thomas, and Theodore Roethke. It is noteworthy that there are no Southern names on this list, since as far as I know there are few Southern poets who could be called visionary. Tate and Warren, for example, are in their different ways primarily concerned with history, with attempting to relate the past to the present. Perhaps one reason good Southern poets have shied away from the visionary mode is that they remember how much older Southern poetry was emasculated by the necessity of avoiding politics and hence driven from reality into fake vision. The old Southern tradition of escapism and sentimentality—of high gutless swooning, to borrow a phrase from Faulkner—was certainly one thing the Fugitives were fleeing. South Carolinian Henry Timrod often exemplified this tradition, and Tate surely intended a contrast with Timrod's "Ode Sung at the Decoration of the Graves of the Confederate Dead at Magnolia Cemetery" when he wrote his own ironic "Ode to the Confederate Dead." Timrod's "Ethnogenesis" is a kind of vision, it is true, but appallingly detached from any sense of reality: in it the new Confederacy, with its economy based on cotton and slavery, is seen as bringing wealth, moral improvement, and a better climate to the whole world.

Before Dickey, the only Southern poet who was a true visionary was Poe; and his visions, as every schoolchild

As long as the afflatus spans around space
A firmament of intellect and dream.

And here is Dickey's version, a triumph of what Lowell called imitation:

Oh my own soul, put me in a solar boat.
Come into one of these hands
Bringing quietness and the rare belief
That I can steer this strange craft to the morning
Land that sleeps   in the universe on all horizons
And give this home-come man who listens in his room

To the rush and flare of his father
Drawn at the speed of light to Heaven
Through the wrong end of his telescope, expanding the
universe,
The instrument   the tuning-fork—
He'll flick it with his bandless wedding-finger—
Which at a touch reveals the form
Of the time-loaded European music
That poetry has never really found,
Undecipherable as God's bad, Heavenly sketches,
Involving fortress and flower, vine and wine and bone,
And shall vibrate through the western world
So long as the hand can hold its island
Of blazing paper, and bleed for its images:
Make what it can of what is:

So long as the spirit hurls on space
The star-beasts of intellect and madness.

Poets of other persuasions do not seek meaning in the stars. Auden could say cheerfully, "Looking up at the stars, I know quite well / That for all they care, I can go to hell," and Warren that the stars "are only a backdrop for / The human condition" and the sky "has murder in the eye, and I / Have murder in the heart, for I / Am only human. We look at each other, the sky and I. / We understand each other. . . ." Visionary poets, however, affirm that there is a relation, that the stars are saying something to man. Just what they say is, naturally, impossible to state in cool discursive prose. But Dickey's essential affirmation would seem to be essentially the same as that made by his visionary predecessors, from Blake through Hart Crane and the Dylan Thomas of *Altarwise by Owllight*: the analogy, or identity, of the poetic imagination and the divine power that created the stars. For this symbolic affirmation, the zodiac works better than Brooklyn bridge.

IV

To say that visionary poets do not age well is an academic understatement or litotes. Rimbaud gave up poetry for gun-running at the age of 19, and Hart Crane leaped into the sea at 30; Dylan Thomas drank himself to death at 39, and Roethke, after increasingly harrowing bouts of mania and depression, in his fifties. Blake and Smart, under cover of madness, made it into their fifties. But except for Whitman, who was only in one sense a visionary poet, it is hard to think of any who attained the age of 60. Dickey's achievement in surviving not only two wars but the special hazards that beset his kind of poet is, then, a notable one: like Faulkner's Dilsey, he has endured.

Dickey has not only remained very much active, but he has continued to grow and develop. His latest volume, ***Puella***, seems to me to mark his entrance into a distinctive new stage. In ***Puella*** there is a shift from the cosmic vision of ***The Zodiac*** to a very different kind of vision that might be called domestic. The poet is not tamed but gentled as he lovingly describes what Hopkins called the *mundus muliebris,* the woman's world inhabited by the daughter-wife figure whose girlhood he relives. At the risk of embarrassing Dickey, I might suggest a large and vague parallel with the change in Shakespeare's career from tragedies like *Lear* to romances like *Cymbeline, The Winter's Tale,* and *The Tempest,* with their themes of reconciliation, fulfillment, the joy of recovering what was thought to be lost forever. Deborah in these poems has something in common with Marina, Perdita, Miranda, and other such young girls in these plays; with Yeats' Dancers and the daughter for whom he wrote the great prayer; and with the young girls in Hopkins—in "Margaret, are you grieving" and the "Echo" poems, for example. (I am beginning to sound like those 19th-century studies of the girlhood of Shakespeare's heroines; but that is the mood of the book, with its charming epigraph from T. Sturge Moore: "I lived in thee, and dreamed, and waked / Twice what I had been." If the word *mellow* had not been preempted by Doonesbury's Californians, it would be hard to avoid using it here. This is also the first time the word *charming* has been conceivable as a description of Dickey's poetry.)

The girl in the poems is intensely herself, yet she is also representative of all young girls, as the title ***Puella*** suggests. She is pictured in scenes that are archetypal, sometimes *rites de passage,* sometimes with mythical or historical contexts; sometimes heraldic as if in medieval tapestry, sometimes playfully absurd as if in a modern folk-naïve painting. While the poems are obviously very personal, they exhibit a new kind of formality, both in the speaker's attitude toward his subject—affection tinged with gentle humor, folk ceremoniousness, a degree of detachment making possible fresh appreciation of physical beauty—and in the verse itself. Dickey has always treasured the "wildness" aspect of Hopkins, as did Roethke—"Long live the weeds and the wildness yet!"—but these poems show a new sense of the beauty of formal sound-patterns that is often reminiscent of that poet. There is a tenderness, a delicacy, a fresh appreciation of the beauty of the visible universe that seem to owe something to Hopkins while being also strongly individual.

The beginning of **"Heraldic: Deborah and Horse in Morning Forest,"** has an epigraph from Hopkins and is a kind of homage to that poet:

> It could be that nothing you could do
> Could keep you from stepping out and blooding-in
> An all-out blinding heraldry for this:
> A blurred momentum-flag
> That must be seen sleep-weathered and six-legged,
> Brindling and throwing off limbo-light
> Of barns. . . .

In another, Hopkins' verse-techniques are used to describe Deborah's piano-playing:

> With a fresh, gangling resonance
> Truing handsomely, I draw on left-handed space
> For a brave ballast shelving and bracing, and from it, then, the light
> Prowling lift-off, the treble's strewn search and wide-angle glitter.

As for playful folk-ceremony poems—a world apart from what some critic calls the "country surrealism" of **"May Day Sermon"**—there are **"Deborah and Deirdre as Drunk Bridesmaids Foot-Racing at Daybreak"** and **"Veer-Voices: Two Sisters under Crows,"** in both of which the titles are enough for present purposes. But I cannot resist quoting the end of my favorite poem in the book, **"Deborah in Ancient Lingerie, in Thin Oak over Creek."** This is both a vision, at once tender and absurd, of Deborah in her "album bloomers" diving into the creek, and a ritual acted out in the poem itself:

> . . . snake-screaming,
> Withering, foster-parenting for animals
> I can do
> very gently from just about
> Right over you, I can do
> at no great height I can do
> and bear
> And counter-balance and do
> and half-sway and do
> and sway
> and outsway and
> do.

The poems move from the realism of **"Deborah as Scion,"** where she is seen **"In Lace and Whalebone"** thinking of the kind of looks she has inherited—"Bullheaded, big-busted . . . I am totally them in the / eyebrows, / Breasts, breath and butt"—to the visionary heights of **"The Lyric Beasts,"** where she speaks as **"Dancer to Audience"** and becomes a kind of goddess challenging the audience to "Rise and on faith / Follow." In a sense, I suppose the book is Dickey's reply to the radical feminists, for Deborah in it is both herself and Dickey's ideal modern woman, enacting her archetypal feminine role in full mythic resonance, but not enslaved or swallowed up by it. If so, Kate Millett and Adrienne Rich may eat their hearts out!

I have not mentioned many qualities in Dickey that might be called distinctively Southern, on the ground that they are large, vague, and obvious—more obvious in the novel ***Deliverance*** and the two books about the South, ***Jericho*** and ***God's Images,*** than in the poetry—but perhaps they should be summed up briefly. A strong sense of place is the first, as in the poems about Cherrylog Road, kudzu, chenille, the Buckhead boys, the woman preacher, and the lawyer's daughter whose dive from the Eugene Talmadge Bridge brought revelation from the burning bush. Love of story-telling, and hence of communal myth, is important, and from this it is a short step to love of ceremony and ritual both within the family and with other life-forms, from the Owl King to ***Puella.*** Dickey's humor is more frequently present than most people seem to realize, but its most characteristic form is the preposterous lie or grotesquely implausible vision which outrages the reader but then turns out to be, in a deeper sense, true. Like most Southerners, he has a strong religious sense: his poems are often sermons or prayers or invocations. But his creed might be called natural supernaturalism, or fundamentalism so fundamental that it concerns man's relation to all other life forms.

As we have seen, Dickey has little significant relation to earlier Southern writing; it would take a truly ingenious academic to show how he was influenced by Sidney Lanier! Poe seems to be his only Southern predecessor in being a genuine visionary; but he was a very different kind: whereas Poe's visions are of horror and death-in-life, Dickey's are of larger modes of life. Dickey is, in fact, so far from being a regionalist in any exclusive sense that the spiritual ancestors most prominent in his recent poetry are that New Englander of the New Englanders, Joseph Trumbull Stickney, who lies behind the wonderful poem **"Exchanges"**; the Dutch poet and sailor Hendrik Marsman, who lies behind ***The Zodiac***; and the English Jesuit G. M. Hopkins, who lies behind ***Puella.***

In contrast to more recent Southern poets like Tate and Warren, Dickey has not been interested in communion with other humans through acceptance of the human condition but in getting beyond ordinary humanity to participate in the life of nonhuman creatures and in more-than-human forces. His essential subject has been exchange or metamorphosis or *participation mystique* between man and wild animals, fish, or birds; or, in ***Zodiac,*** stars and the mysterious universe in general. Since the rational mind is a hindrance, or at best irrelevant, to this quest, his poems represent extreme states of consciousness: intoxication, terror, rage, lust, hallucination, somnambulism or mystical exaltation. His concern is not the limitations but the possibilities of human and nonhuman nature, not history but vision.

As I have tried to suggest, his latest book, ***Puella***, constitutes a new kind of vision, back from the cosmic extremities of *The Zodiac* to the human and domestic world. The figure of the daughter-wife is suffused with a new tenderness, gentleness, and humor, and the verse takes on a new formal musicality. A Jungian would say that the girl in these poems is an *anima*-figure; but whether the sense of fulfillment and joy in these poems comes from integration of the personality or from some deeper cause, I will not attempt to decide. Nor will I comment on the fact that Deborah is not only Southern but South Carolinian; Southern chivalry toward ladies who have the misfortune to be born elsewhere forbids it. But I will risk the charge of Southern chauvinism by saying that the book is a most notable contribution to Southern letters.

William W. Starr (essay date 1987)

SOURCE: Starr, William W. "*Alnilam*: James Dickey's Novel Explores Father and Son Relationships." In *The Voiced Connections of James Dickey: Interviews and Conversations,* edited by Ronald Baughman, pp. 258-62. Columbia: University of South Carolina Press, 1989.

[*In the following essay, which was initially published in 1987, Starr considers the major thematic concerns of Dickey's* Alnilam.]

James Dickey's second novel, **Alnilam,** is definitely not another **Deliverance,** which created a storm of acclaim and readership when it appeared seventeen years ago.

But that's just fine with Dickey, author of two dozen literary works and holder of a host of prizes to go with them.

. . . The University of South Carolina poet-in-residence and a Columbian for nearly two decades said, "This is no *Deliverance 2* or *Son of Deliverance.* I'm not going to do that kind of thing. People will just have to take it for what it is."

And what **Alnilam** is—once the reader gets by a title that catches in the mouth—is a massive, ambitious, seriously focused novel that at times soars with the majesty and power of Dickey's imaginative writing. It deals with "big" issues: the nature and sources of power, leadership, faith, and the relationship between fathers and sons.

"I'm sixty-four now, and I figure I don't have infinite time left to me, so I wanted to get these things out and deal with them in the novel," Dickey explained in an interview at his Lake Katherine home almost eleven months after a scary experience with brain surgery.

He had suffered severe headaches and vision problems for several months last year before doctors diagnosed a massive blood clot and ordered brain surgery. The June 30 operation followed within days of his becoming the first inductee in the new South Carolina Academy of Authors. Today, Dickey says his recovery is complete.

"I was going blind in my left eye," Dickey recalled, perhaps with a touch of irony. The principal character in *Alnilam*—Frank Cahill—is a man who goes blind early in the novel.

"Cahill is an inarticulate, redneck carpenter, who acts only for himself," Dickey said. And yet it is Cahill, and his determination to understand the son he never knew, who ultimately opens the doors for the exploration of large-scale, powerfully articulated themes in **Alnilam.**

Dickey's story is set in World War II. Cahill—who has become blind as a result of diabetes—and his ferocious dog, Zack, head for the small town of Peckover, N.C. That's the location of an Army Air Corps base where his son, Joel, apparently has died in a flight training accident.

Why Cahill is in Peckover is not clear—especially to him. For while Joel had listed him as next of kin, Cahill has never actually seen his son, having separated from the boy's mother at the time of Joel's birth.

Once at the base, Cahill talks with the officers and cadets who knew Joel. From them, he pieces together the story of his son's brilliant but oddly enigmatic and charismatic personality, and the mysterious and ultimately disturbing meaning of **Alnilam.**

The son's spellbinding, perhaps fanatical hold over his fellow cadets—even after his presumed death—is both puzzling and challenging to Cahill.

The father struggles to grasp the impact of Joel's continuing authority and relationship to his peers and those who commanded him. Readers who confront that same mystery may unravel the key to **Alnilam** as well, Dickey said.

"The nature of power, one man's power over another, is a very mysterious thing, and it has always fascinated me.

"It doesn't take a whole lot to exercise power over people. The leadership concept is varied, but there are certain similarities in all forms. One of those is that leaders possess a great deal of charisma, and the other is an enigmatic quality."

The question for readers is why these young cadets act the way they do, even to the extent of forming a secret society (named Alnilam, after the central star in the belt of the constellation Orion) that could undermine the chain of command.

And why would they do that with no more apparent reason than their relationship with the charismatic, enigmatic Joel?

"The answer, of course, is that's exactly why they behave the way they do. And that's the core of *Alnilam*. If readers can get that, they have the central point of the novel," said Dickey, who flew night fighter missions in the Pacific during World War II.

Many readers who come to *Alnilam* may not be prepared for what they find. The sprawling novel—nearly seven-hundred pages, more than twice as long as *Deliverance*—lacks that earlier work's sustained intensity. *Alnilam* is a "bigger" novel in every sense, however, in its heightened vision and profound thematic concepts.

It also features an audacious, dramatic typographical layout that may at once confuse, startle, and illuminate. Dickey calls it "my great experiment."

In *Alnilam,* Dickey seeks to combine the inner vision of the blind man with the visible world of those around him—a James Joyce-like attempt to embrace the seen and the felt simultaneously. To convey that, a number of pages are split in parallel columns, the bold words on the left side embodying Cahill's sensations and the right side depicting what is actually happening in the sighted world.

"It's a double point of observation, internal and external vision," Dickey said.

Some early readers of the novel have found it initially confusing but adapted to it. Others, including a reviewer in *Publishers Weekly*,[1] describe it as "merely awkward."

Regardless of the reaction to such techniques, the novel is getting a big publicity push from Doubleday. The huge New York-based publishing house is issuing *Alnilam* in a substantial first printing of 100,000 copies later this month, and reportedly is spending six figures for promotion.

There's plenty of talk, but no details, about movie rights.

And since Dickey is a national literary figure, he's in demand for interviews by major publications in advance of the book's official release date.

Dickey, who has seldom shied from publicity, seems to relish the experience and is eager to talk about the novel.

He said he isn't concerned that some readers will find *Alnilam* a little tougher going than *Deliverance*.

"A writer has to go with his imagination," he said. "You're not really an artist if you try to give the people what they want. Because most of the time they don't know what they want until they get it."

Sometimes that applies to the author as well, for Dickey has worked at the idea of *Alnilam* off and on for thirty-seven years, trying to get it in the shape he wanted.

"I wrote it at intermittent times going back to 1950. I started when I was teaching at Rice Institute (now Rice University) in Texas. I remember I went out on the grassy part of campus and opened a brand new notebooklike ledger because I once heard Thomas Wolfe wrote in those. I had bought one figuring what worked for him might work for me," Dickey told a Doubleday interviewer.

"I was writing a lot of poetry at that time, not very good poetry, so I put the novel aside. I took it up again when I lived in the south of France in 1954, but the story wasn't clear in my mind. I only knew it had to do with a man who lost his son in a training accident in the early days of World War II. But after I wrote about his journey to this small town where the air base was I didn't know what would happen. But I kept my notes, and eventually the story began to develop and I finished it in early 1986."

In its final form—incomplete portions were published twice in *Esquire*[2] magazine, the first in 1976—Dickey's novel examines the shape of relationships between fathers and sons, but with a twist.

Usually it is the son who comes to an understanding of himself through an exploration of the father's life. In *Alnilam,* the father discovers the truth about his son.

"But also I like to hint in a couple of places that the son is trying in his own way to bring his father to him. So the novel may be seen in some ways as a reciprocal search under the strangest of circumstances," Dickey said.

"Also, it's hinted that the son has been trying to figure out ways to come in contact with the father he has never seen, because, after all, the son might not be dead. He's been in a crash, but his body has never been found."

Early readers of the novel seem in agreement that *Alnilam* contains some of Dickey's finest prose ever.

Always a poet first, Dickey evokes his poetic foundations strongly throughout the novel, particularly in his writing about the blind man's world and the grandeur and heart-pounding excitement of flight.

"I have tried to give strong emphasis to the mystique of flying," he said. "I try to give the reader the physical sensation of flying on the human body. Being on a jet is like being in a hotel lobby twenty-thousand feet up. But in one of those small trainers you truly get a sense of being precariously sustained in another element, the air, that you're not supposed to be in, and yet one in which you have some kind of control over."

Dickey's editors at Doubleday—he's had seven during the creation of *Alnilam*—have been unstinting in their expressions of support and praise for the novel. And Dickey is grateful for their counsel in the editing process.

But he also made it clear that the direction and style is his and his alone—and it has always been that way.

He cited an incident in the late 1960s when he had completed the manuscript of *Deliverance,* and confronted the editor-in-chief at his publishing house, then Houghton Mifflin.

"He read the cliff-climbing episode in the novel and told me he thought it was entirely too long, that it shouldn't be more than one page. I said um-hum not very enthusiastically. And he said of course maybe I'd like to talk to another editor about it, although it's rare for a first-time novelist not to accept the advice of an editor-in-chief.

"Anyway, I went to see the other editor, who was younger, and he read it and told me the cliff-climbing scene couldn't possibly be cut, in fact it ought to be even longer. I told him 'Now you're talking!' and that's the way we left it."

Dickey said he is prepared for the public's and critics' verdicts on *Alnilam,* but he seems comfortable with his accomplishment. It is a work that extends his imaginative novelistic craft into new dimensions, and he's eager to get out and talk with readers about their reactions.

"I'm not going to tell people exactly what it means. I don't write deliberately to provoke mystery, but I do try to invest my stories and poems with many layers of meanings. Each reader can find his own, make his own interpretation. That's what's really important about a novel or a poem: what you can take from it."

Notes

1. 231 (17 April 1987), 65.
2. "Cahill Is Blind," *Esquire,* 85 (February 1976), 67-69, 139-144, 146; "The Captains," *Esquire,* 107 (April 1987), 176-178, 181-182, 185-186.

Angelin P. Brewer (essay date fall 1990)

SOURCE: Brewer, Angelin P. "'To Rise above Time': The Mythic Hero in Dickey's *Deliverance* and *Alnilam.*" *James Dickey Newsletter* 7, no. 1 (fall 1990): 9-14.

[*In the following essay, Brewer perceives the storylines of Dickey's two novels as interpretations of the passage of the mythical hero as detailed in Joseph Campbell's* The Hero with a Thousand Faces.]

Ed Gentry and Frank Cahill, protagonists in James Dickey's novels *Deliverance* (1970) and *Alnilam* (1987), are called to make a journey. The common pattern of these journeys depicts the three steps in the mythic hero's passage: a withdrawal from the real world, a penetration to a power source, and, finally, a life-enhancing return. Completion of the journey, with its psychological and physical dangers, renders the individual heroic. Chosen by men seemingly confident of their own immortality, Lewis Medlock and Joel Cahill, respectively, Gentry and Cahill initially appear as disciples of these self-styled Christ-figures who wish to transcend the physical. Medlock, who builds his body into an almost indestructible shield, excels as an outdoor sportsman, always in search of mental and physical perfection. Joel Cahill, on the other hand, achieves the immortal perfection by inhabiting the minds of others. His disappearance before *Alnilam* even opens secures his future existence in the memories of the other young airmen at the base.

Ed Gentry and Frank Cahill undergo changes through certain tests. To pass the attendant challenges of the river and the air, Gentry and Cahill must connect with living, natural forces that will alter their lives. Each man instinctively and purposely creates an emotional bridge between himself and nature that transcends reason, effecting a change in the two mythical heroes such that subsequently there is an appreciation of life. Finally, life has renewed consequence for each man.

Gentry's and Cahill's tests are phases of the mythic hero's passage detailed in Joseph Campbell's *The Hero With a Thousand Faces*. The hero's quest, the *rites de passage,* includes a departure, an initiation, and a return. In the departure, the hero abandons his membership in society and embarks on a journey that draws him into a relationship with mysterious forces: "No matter what the stage . . . of life, the call rings up the curtain, always on a mystery of transfiguration—a rite, or moment of spiritual passage, which, when complete, amounts to a dying and a rebirth" (Campbell 51). This summons may be denied originally; however, in order to complete his passage the hero must shed his ego, becoming newly available to the world. To avoid self-disintegration, the heroic figure responds to his calling by turning inside himself in order "to be born again" (Campbell 91), ultimately permitting renewed consequentiality into his life. Rebirth signals the crossing of the first threshold when "the hero moves in a dream landscape . . . where he must survive a succession of trials" (Campbell 97).

The initiation that both Gentry and Cahill undergo is a readjustment of the hero's emotions with a consequent gain of freedom over fear. As Campbell states, "This is the release potential . . . which anyone can attain—through herohood" (151). The hero, a potentially superior man, crosses many thresholds in order to transcend limitations, which restrain a character's development, and establish spiritual growth. In the tests that challenge the hero's temperament, timing is crucial because changes cannot occur until the individual has proven himself worthy.

The return of the hero "from the mystic realm into the land of common day" (Campbell 216) allows for renewed humanity. At times the hero finds leaving the bliss of his new-found world difficult; however, he soon discovers "the two worlds, the divine and the human . . . are actually one" (217). The mythological is merely an extension of the human realm and only those capable of such unity may touch the divine. By virtue of their survival, Gentry and Cahill are heroes who have discovered this sense of unification that allows for a redefined reality.

Gentry's heroic journey in **Deliverance,** for instance, details his passage from American suburbia to turbulent waters over a period of three days and depicts his rediscovery of self. Life has become routine, and he feels at times his job as art director at Emerson-Gentry has more control over him than he has over it: "It seemed like everything just went right by me," Gentry thinks, "nothing mattered at all. I couldn't have cared less about anything or anybody" (**Deliverance** 27). His existence lacks consequence; he is simply a "get-through-the-day man" (41). Medlock, who plays at being a survivalist and believes himself equal to if not stronger than anything, provides the break through the monotony in Gentry's life. He devises a canoe trip to test physical restrictions and Gentry, compliant, goes along.

On the morning of September 15, Gentry doubts his intentions of joining the trip, a condition typical of the mythic hero: "The routine I was used to pulled at me," he thinks; and yet, "something in me rose daringly above it, full of fear and feeling weak and incompetent but excited" (26). Medlock assures Gentry that his body has immeasurable power and that, when called upon, it will prove to be a great asset: "It's what you can make it do . . . and what it'll do for you when you don't even know what's needed" (29). By allowing Gentry into his confidence, Medlock has accepted him as a sort of personal disciple.

The hero myth stresses, as does **Deliverance,** the use of the body as a means toward survival. For Gentry, the river embodies such a test. In a canoe, however, Gentry is uncertain as to how to govern the river's current. He fumbles with his paddle and consequently loses the canoe's balance. Yet after several hours and a few beers, he develops a feel for the water and instinctively settles into a "good motion" (73). This feeling matures into a deeper understanding comparable to Frank Cahill's sixth sense regarding the air in **Alnilam.** For example, Gentry is able to forecast the river's lack of drive, patterns in speed, and the location of falls, rapids, and curves. This "terrifyingly enjoyable" (145) union with the river, that differentiates Gentry from Medlock because of the connection made with a living, natural force, qualifies him as a participant in the mythic hero's journey.

Gentry's designation as the hero in passage takes place as the men emerge from a canoe spill; Drew Ballinger, another participant on the journey, is found to be missing, and Medlock has fractured his leg. Recognizing Gentry's superiority as hero, Medlock whispers hoarsely to him: "It's you. It's got to be you" (150). As such, Gentry initiates an escape the next morning. Prior to departure, he will have climbed the gorge looming over them to abduct and kill Ballinger's murderer.

The cliff converts Gentry's trip into a passage of the hero. The juxtaposition of man and force, displayed by Gentry's connection with the gorge, is the second phase of the rites of passage. In order to determine the cliff's power, Gentry walks to its gorge side and places his hand onto the cliff's earth, believing, "I might be able to feel what the whole cliff was like, the whole problem, and hold it in my palm" (160-161). The climb lasts the entire night as Gentry journeys from one foothold to the next. Utterly uncovered to the night, he perceives his nakedness as an exposure to death, aware that his losing grip would signal a fall. Thus, he concentrates all his efforts into "becoming ultrasensitive to the cliff" (163). Knowing the rock wall as fervently as he knew the river is obligatory to Gentry's survival: "I turned back into the cliff and leaned my mouth against it, feeling all the way out through my nerves and muscles exactly how I had possession of the wall at four random points in a way that held the whole thing together" (163). This intimacy, almost sexual, Gentry shares with the cliff elates him: "My heart expanded with joy at the thought of where I was going and what I was doing" (161). Medlock's belief that the body, when summoned, will perform beyond ordinary expectations proves accurate, for Gentry is held "in the air by pure will" (165). Dickey has recently asserted, "I see illusion in the world as one of the basic motivating factors in it" (Letter). The illusion of Gentry's actual penetration with the cliff is necessary because it permits a sense of consequentiality.

The final section of **Deliverance,** entitled "After," presents Gentry's rebirth as a Christ-like hero rising again on the third day. With his beard, he appears haggard, but his emotions are enhanced due to his connection to death in the water and on the cliff. This connection has resulted in Gentry's appreciation for life: "The river underlies . . . everything I do. It is always finding a way to serve me, from my archery to some of my recent ads and to the new colleagues I have been attempting for my friends" (275-276). For Gentry, life has renewed consequence. He is the mythic hero of the story because of his departure from his home, his connection to an elemental force, and his return as an altered man. Commenting in an interview, Dickey notes: "If there's any literary or mythological precedent for **Deliverance,** it comes from a review . . . by Stanley Edgar Hyman on a number of books on myths and rituals, and he quotes Van Gennep's 'rites de passage' and cites 'a separation from the world, a penetration to some source of power, and a life-enhancing return'" (Arnett 295). Thus, Gentry's mythological passage to heroism seems reinforced.

Like **Deliverance, Alnilam** depicts a character's entrance into a new world where life-enhancing powers permit larger understanding. Frank Cahill's journey exemplifies the three steps in the mythic hero's passage in a more complex way than does Ed Gentry's journey. The three days of the canoe trip clearly define the hero's withdrawal, penetration, and return in **Deliverance**; however, the separation of these stages is less clear in **Alnilam.** Cahill's blindness, caused by diabetes, represents a new world, and the realm he eventually enters is the air. "The air itself," claims Dickey, is "the real protagonist" (Letter). Cahill's devotion to his swimming pool and its refinement, as later to his seeing-eye dog, Zack, provide him with a connection to the world, but they do not satisfy the need for meaning in his life.

Consequentiality, a vital part of the hero-myth, is necessary for Cahill to acquire a renewed existence. Capturing knowledge about the disappearance of his twenty year-old son, Joel, provides a purpose in the elder Cahill's life. After travelling to Peckover, North Carolina, he begins to perceive his son as an extraordinary individual through the eyes of others at the base where Joel trained. A navigator recalls Joel's characteristic instinctiveness: "When I came to this place a couple of months ago, . . . your boy . . . described the inner feeling of all things working for you, according to a mystery. . . . Cadet Cahill was not exactly on to something, but he was *getting* on to something. . . . Things seemed to come together for him" (**Alnilam** 153-154). Followers of the younger Cahill's beliefs, who refer to themselves as Alnilam, are distraught about Joel's untimely death; however, they perceive Cahill's blindness as a degree of instinct and decide to initiate him into their membership.

The initiation process, several tests that grade Cahill's intuition, are phases of the mythic hero's initiation. Alnilam's objective is to control the air surrounding an aircraft, to travel with the air. Knowledge of that element lends an understanding of the meaning of life for them: "Your principle of order comes back . . . and if you keep hold of yourself, the order holds up" (216). In **Alnilam,** Cahill must penetrate the air and make it move with him: "An airplane is . . . like . . . a bird, a big one. . . . You're ridin' it, and it feels everything, up, down, and to the sides. It feels everything that's in the *thing* it's in, the air, and you feel it through the plane. The air is different from the ground. The way you move is so different. . . . It's personal" (138). Connection is the second stage of the hero's rite of passage.

Cahill's nature, like Gentry's, enables him to enter the second passage of the mythic hero: Initiation. Cahill must connect with an element of power, in this instance, air. The Alnilam group realizes that air provides "complete knowledge" (311); to know air intimately offers a man superhuman characteristics. Thus, Cahill and the frenzied young men of Alnilam want to test this conclusion. In a Link Trainer, where simulation of an aircraft's flight patterns is provided, Cahill is instructed to act as pilot. The machine's illusion allows Cahill momentarily to touch the divine, as he feels himself "coming to a point, of penetrating, as if flowing upon some river" (337). Two pilots on the base, Captain Faulstick and Captain Whitehall, who flew in wars bringing each close to death, emphasize the all-powerful knowledge of air. Faulstick comments that, even in combat, one may experience an intimacy with the air: "It's private. . . . It stays with me. . . . I'm just left with it; that's all. I'll die seeing it" (211). Flight also alters Whitehall: "I don't feel closed in nearly so much anymore. . . . Maybe that's one reason you don't think about death when you're on a mission, except your own, and the main feeling when you're on the way back in life; it's a life feeling" (216-217).

The return of the mythic hero becomes a needed, culminating connection that alters him in some way, and it is predicted that Cahill will return rejuvenated: "And one big thing you're gonna get. . . . It'll come to you. . . . It'll go on with you, all the way till you die" (283). A part of this return is his final test, piloting an actual airplane called a Stearman. During the flight, kept secret by the Alnilam group, Cahill is given directions on how to fly by a civilian instructor, McClintock

McCaig. Anxious at first as to direction, eventually Cahill levels the Stearman accurately thousands of feet above the ground. He refers to his instinct to handle such power as "distance-hearing": "His distance-hearing—or instinct, sixth sense, or something else—developed further. . . . This was the thing he sought" (489-490). Almost instantly, however, the plane has possession of Cahill: "I've got this thing now," (492) he thinks; "Cahill started for the fire, calling. . . . [He] climbed and screamed . . . with tremendous muscular strength, and unguessed energy, a vision worth the pain" (495). After the penetration and recovery of the plane, Cahill is brought closer to death and, ironically, to life.

Leaving the experience, Cahill returns to his life as he knew it before the connection, the moment signifying the return of the mythic hero. Not surprisingly, he is now able to identify with people, despite the tragic death of his dog during a parade and air show. In contrast to Cahill's beginning journey, where his sole companion is Zack, he now innately needs people in his life. As Dickey notes, "Frank Cahill is different at the end of *Alnilam*; not greatly different—he still has his iron will and his truculence—but changed in some essential ways. This is partly shown by the fact that he does not plan to get another dog. . . . It is also signified by the fact that he wants to take Hannah with him, and establish some kind of life with her, though they are both seriously impaired. . . . He is a little more humanized, and less fanatical, and because of this he may possibly come to understand his enigmatic son in ways not possible before" (Letter). Cahill, like Gentry, transforms himself into a force as mysterious as the force made in his connection.

Dickey's heroes, Ed Gentry and Frank Cahill, surpass ordinary men because they have escaped ordinary life. Their lives are enriched from a sense of consequence, the establishment of significance and meaning. Beyond the boundaries of society and upon his return, a man's psychological make-up is transformed into that of an heroic individual. This journey marks the moment of deliverance for a man. And in that one moment lives possibility.

Works Cited

Arnett, David L. "An Interview With James Dickey." *Contemporary Literature* 16. Summer 1975: 286-300.

Campbell, Joseph. *The Hero With a Thousand Faces*. Princeton: Princeton UP, 1968.

Dickey, James. *Alnilam*. Garden City: Doubleday, 1987.

———. *Deliverance*. Boston: Houghton Mifflin, 1970.

———. Letter received by author. 26 October 1989.

Ronald Schmitt (essay date fall 1991)

SOURCE: Schmitt, Ronald. "Transformations of the Hero in James Dickey's *Deliverance*." *James Dickey Newsletter* 8, no. 1 (fall 1991): 9-16.

[*In the following essay, Schmitt maintains that Dickey provides an ironic treatment of the mythical hero in his novel* Deliverance.]

According to James Dickey himself, the source of the novel *Deliverance* was a 1949 review essay in the *Kenyon Review* by Stanley Edgar Hyman which mentions both Joseph Campbell's *Hero With a Thousand Faces* and Arnold Van Gennep's *Les Rites de Passage* (Eisiminger 53). According to Hyman, ". . . as students of myth we must separate from the world, penetrate to a source of knowledge, and return with whatever power of life-enhancement the truth may contain" (qtd. in Eisiminger 53). Dickey himself documents his interest in myth and its importance to modern man:

> The parts of the universe we can investigate by means of machinery and scientific empirical techniques we may understand better than our predecessors did, but we no longer know the universe emotionally. It's a great deal easier to relate to the moon emotionally if the moon figures in a kind of mythology which we have inherited, or maybe invented, than it is to relate to it as a collocation of chemical properties. There's no moon goddess now. But when we believed there was, then the moon was more important, maybe not scientifically, but more important emotionally. It was something a man had a personal relationship to, instead of its being simply a dead stone, a great ruined stone in the sky
>
> (*Self-Interviews* 67).

Such an interest in man's role in nature and identification with mythic concepts and patterns such as those outlined by Campbell can be seen throughout Dickey's poetry as well as in the novel *Deliverance*. Because of this fascination with nature in the midst of a technological world, many critics assume that Dickey starts from nineteenth-century transcendentalist/romantic concerns (Foust 201). His personal interests in camping and bowhunting also contribute to the notion that *Deliverance* is primarily a macho adventure novel which embraces such naive principles as noble savagery and heroic survivalism.

However, for a number of critics, including me, the ironic components of *Deliverance* emerge as clear indicators that, instead of creating a male fantasy of wilderness adventure, this novel is involved in questioning the applicability of romantic conceptions of man's relationship with nature in the modern world. Linda Wagner, recognizing the romantic relationship, says, "***Deliver-***

ance can be considered a kind of gothic, even bitter *Adventures of Huckleberry Finn*" (112). The idea that man can, as Lewis Medlock believes, return to some difficult but ultimately noble state of primitivism and again become one with nature is revealed as a lie in this novel. To Dickey, the lie is important. He says:

> But I really began to develop as a poet, at least according to my own particular way of looking at things, when I saw the creative possibilities of the lie. My parents were very much against lying in any form. But I think lying, with luck sublimely, is what the creative man does
>
> (*Self* 32).

As Chet Taylor points out, "deliverance is a lie; ***Deliverance*** is not" (63). What ***Deliverance*** (the novel) does do is to create an unresolved and unresolvable tension between the seductive myth of the heroic quest-romance to the cleansing and enlightening initiation of the wilderness, and modern man's irreversibly civilized and mechanized state of alienation from the wilderness.

Dickey's many ironic treatments and reversals of romantic notions of the wilderness have been observed by various critics. The notions of Nature as a "tender, feminine, submissive" force subjected to man's rape (Love 182), the "primitive" forest dweller as more noble and moral than civilized man (Taylor 59), and the survival of the fittest in nature (Davis 226) are all reversed in ***Deliverance***, thereby plunging the reader into a wilderness as fearsome as the one in the novel: the wilderness of moral relativity. Nature, despite our best attempts at myth-making, has no concern whatever with man's laws and moral principles. Man, now increasingly alienated from any but peripheral contact with nature, finds his constructed illusions of order and meaning shattered when he enters the wilderness. When man turns from the wasteland of his mechanization to the wilderness, he often finds only another wasteland, one with which he is now unfamiliar and in which he is even more alienated. While primal connections can be revitalized and result in growth, there is no deliverance: from the city, from the wilderness, or from ourselves. The myth of deliverance through wilderness adventure is, like the model which haunts Ed's thoughts, "a pleasant part of the world, but minor. She is imaginary" (235).

I would like to suggest another ironic treatment, not of romanticism in this case, but of Dickey's acknowledged source of ***Deliverance***, Campbell's *Hero With a Thousand Faces*. Specifically, I suggest that the characterizations of the four central figures in ***Deliverance***—Ed, Lewis, Bobby, and Drew—can be seen as ironic modern manifestations of Campbell's "transformations of the hero," namely, the hero as warrior, the hero as lover, the hero as emperor/tyrant, and the hero as world redeemer/saint (334-356). What is shown through these characterizations is the impossibility of modern man's achieving cultural initiation, much less archetypal heroic status, through the wilderness experience. The mythic rituals which modern technological man must devise to define manhood and heroic status are necessarily different from previous cultures, especially primitive, non-technological ones. We can no longer say that "the labyrinth is thoroughly known; we have only to follow the thread of the hero path" (*Hero* 25). Since our everyday survival no longer depends on skills involving an intimate understanding of nature and because our technological world grows ever more distant from the natural world, achieving an autonomy unimaginable even one hundred years ago, our mythic quests for identity no longer follow the path of the ancient monomyth.

Lewis Medlock, the survivalist of the group and initiator of the canoe trip in ***Deliverance***, indicates his awareness of the schism between modern man's experiences and experiences of a truly unadulterated wilderness:

> If everything wasn't dead [he says], you could make a kind of life that wasn't out of touch with everything, with the other forms of life. Where the seasons would mean something, would mean everything. Where you could hunt as you needed to, and maybe do a little light farming and get along. You'd die early, and you'd suffer, and your children would suffer, but you'd be in touch
>
> (42).

Ed Gentry, the narrator, on the other hand, sees Lewis' survivalist beliefs as a "fantasy life" (46), yet admits to being "so tanked up on your river-mystique that I'm sure I'll go through some fantastic change as soon as I dig the paddle in the first time" (49). The desire for technological man to "make a kind of life that [isn't] out of touch with everything" and renew the primal and mythic connections with nature described above by Dickey's statements about the moon, is an extremely seductive myth in its own right and one which he never discards in his writing as entirely fallacious. Indeed, Dickey's own feelings about the characterization of Lewis represent the simultaneous revulsion and attraction which Ed feels at the start of the novel. In an interview with Bill Moyers, Dickey describes Lewis as "full of philosophical platitudes" and agrees with Moyers that when Lewis says, "I think the machines are going to fail. I think the system is going to fail, and a few men are going to take to the woods and start over," this is a "wish" of shallow empowerment comparable to the violence perpetrated by "nothings" like Sarah Moore and Lee Harvey Oswald (Dickey, *Night* 95). Yet, in an address given at the University of Virginia in June 1973, Dickey indicates an ambivalence about Lewis' character:

> As I originally conceived him, I wanted to make him a figure both attractive and a little repellent, with his authoritarian manner and clear-cut bodily superiority to the other characters. But as I got more deeply into the character of Lewis, an odd thing began to happen to the author. I began to sympathize more and more with what Lewis was making me make him say. And what is even stranger, I began to admire him tremendously
>
> (Dickey, *Night* 180).

Clearly, the argumentation between Ed and Lewis is an ongoing argument within Dickey (and within many men in the modern world) between an attraction to the empowerment of the survivalist's "preparedness" (***Deliverance*** 44) and the intellectual realization of the elements of fantasy inherent in such a myth.

Lewis is clearly the hero as warrior in Campbell's schema. It is the quest of this type of hero to conquer the "tyrant" of the world which Campbell says represents the "status quo." Thus, "the ogre-tyrant is the champion of the prodigious fact, the hero the champion of creative life" (*Hero* 337). The prodigious fact in ***Deliverance*** is the death of the wilderness represented by the imminent flooding of the valley in which the Cahulawassee River runs, a flooding that will result in what in the movie is described as "one big, dead lake." It is also, ironically, a form of man's control and power over nature's forces. This control is clearly abhorrent to Lewis, despite the fact that he also seeks control and power. The image of the map at the start of the novel, and Ed's feeling that "all streams everywhere quit running" (7) when Lewis paused in explaining something, is a brilliant metaphor for the survivalist's armchair illusions of control and power. The brutal fact that all streams will soon quit flowing as a result of man's technology and not his personal will is more than Lewis can bear.

So, as Campbell describes, the hero's adventure begins "only when villages and cities have expanded over the land" and the monsters or tyrants which dwell beyond the village's outskirts and prohibit the community's growth must be "cleared away" by the hero (337). The irony and reversal in ***Deliverance***, of course, is that the status quo has already won; the human community has expanded so much that it eradicates the primal dangers which Lewis seeks out to test his manhood and establish his identity.

Despite Lewis' greatest attempts at preparedness, he is shattered by the wilderness experience he initiates. While it is true that his one act of heroism, the killing of the first mountain man, saves the lives of Ed and Bobby, the act, rather than establishing his heroic status, must be hidden and remain a perpetual secret among the men. Lewis returns to society "a great, broken thing" (182) with a permanent limp. Referring to the canoe in which he has lain, useless and a burden to the other men for half of the trip, he says, "I want to get out of my coffin, this fucking piece of tin junk" (195) which is modern technology, a coffin for men like Lewis. Ed says of Lewis at the end of the book, "He can die now; he knows that dying is better than immortality. He is a human being, and a good one" (235). No longer the mythic warrior hero in his own or the other's eyes, Lewis joins the "soft-jowled suburbanites" (Dickey, *Night* 95) to live out his life.

Bobby Trippe can be seen as an extremely ironic reversal of Campbell's hero as lover. The bride to which the hero is entitled after the slaying of the monster or tyrant is for Campbell the symbolic manifestation of life energy released from the tyrannical hold of the status quo: "She is the maiden of the innumerable dragon slayings, the bride abducted from the jealous father, the virgin rescued from the unholy lover" (342). Bobby, rather than being the hero who abducts the bride, is himself rescued from the unholy lover, but only after he is violated. This violation makes Bobby a pariah and an embarrassment for the remainder of the trip, especially to Ed who admits that "he felt tainted to me" (111).

In the clearest instance of gender typing in the book, Ed refuses to see any value whatever in Bobby's clear role as nurturer in the novel. Instead, Ed continually describes Bobby as "dead-weight" (234). When Ed goes up to kill the second mountain man he perceives Bobby as a coward because he "can't even shoot a bow" (132). He is even ready to kill Bobby for leaving later than he is supposed to. Bobby emerges from the novel as the male having the most traditionally "feminine" attributes: He is raped rather than being the rapist, he cares for Lewis while Ed goes off to do the "man's work" of killing, and he is physically weaker than the others. Thus, much to their disdain, while the men think that they have left the women behind to go on this quest, it is clear that they are wrong. As Campbell says of the woman the lover hero finds on his quest, "She is the other portion of the hero himself—for each is both" (342).

The image of what was traditionally the raper, man, being raped is also a powerful metaphor appropriate to our modern times. All the men in this novel are "raped" by the river in terms of physical violation and subjugation. They are also emasculated by the technological society from which they came. But, as Davis points out (226), the belief that the strongest will survive in nature is inverted in ***Deliverance.*** Bobby, the weakest, is the least hurt of the men at the end of the trip. Chet Taylor may be right in observing that "Perhaps he who submits to violation is the model of the modern survivor. We seem a long way from Darwin's survival of the fittest, or are we? Conditions for survival have changed with civilization. Perhaps Bobby is now the most fit" (62).

Ed Gentry emerges as an ironic modern version of Campbell's hero as emperor/tyrant. As Campbell points out, the heroic quest is an ongoing cycle, for as the hero vanquishes the status quo to liberate the society's life energy, he becomes the new status quo which must in turn be vanquished. The ways in which the hero chooses to represent his status as cultural symbol determine whether he is regarded as a benevolent emperor or a tyrant to be usurped. Yet, either way, the hero who returns to lead his people has made some atonement with the Father, who is "the invisible unknown"; thus, "The hero blessed by the father, returns to represent the father among men" (*Hero* 345, 347).

In *Deliverance,* the Father is clearly the wilderness itself, the river. It is also clear that Ed, especially in the pivotal cliff-climbing scene, attains the closest thing in the novel to a communion with the natural world. The overtly sexual language involved in Ed's climb up the cliff (151) perpetuates yet reverses the sense of physical violation which the river has accorded the men. Ed achieves a heightened consciousness (120, 157) as well as a temporary, primal, animal state (167-170) through his "fusion" with nature and the mountain man whom he kills. Ed seizes the scepter of control from Lewis and takes over as the leader of the men on the remainder of the trip as well as afterward, during the police investigation. But accompanying Ed's heroism are both a negative movement toward tyranny in his attitude toward Bobby and a barbarism to which he nearly succumbs after killing the mountain man. Still, when Ed says, at the close of the novel, that the river now "ran nowhere but in my head, but there it ran as though immortally" (234), he can be seen as the hero who returns to represent the Father among men and "Since he is now centered in the source, he makes visible the repose and harmony of the central place" (Campbell, *Hero* 347). His artistic creativity is revitalized upon his return for, as he says, "The river underlies, in one way or another, everything I do" (234).

But, of course, the irony of Ed's heroic status is that it must remain a secret to himself. There is no repose for him. The symbol of the emperor hero, Campbell says, is the "scepter of dominion, or the book of the law" (345), but the men must forever shrink from the law. Ed the hero, who should have returned to redefine the law as the men did after killing the first mountain man (108-110) says at the end: "There is still a special small fear in any strange automobile headlights near the house, or any phone call with an unfamiliar voice in it . . ." (233). The only control which Ed maintains is in the lie which he, Bobby, and Lewis must perpetuate about the events which have occurred: "My lies seemed better, more and more like truth; the bodies in the woods and in the river did not move" (215).

Finally, Drew Ballinger can be seen as both the hero as world redeemer and the hero as saint in an ironic sense.

Campbell notes that while some heroes might return to represent the Father as "emissary," the ultimate hero is the one who realizes that "I and the Father are one" (349). Thus, this hero reconciles the contradictions and dualities of the world knowing that "The hero of yesterday becomes the tyrant of tomorrow, unless he crucifies himself today" (*Hero* 353). Drew, described by Ed as "the best of us" and "the only decent one; the only sane one" (186), cannot accept the men's relativistic redefinition of the law. In answer to Lewis' statement—"There's not any right thing"—Drew says, "You bet there is. . . . There's only ONE thing" (107). In death, Drew's eyes are described as "seeming to see out of the open water, back into the mountains, around all the curves of the river, infinitely" (183). The other men, while they feel they need to know whether Drew's gunshot wound was fatal, can never be sure it was. There remains an indeterminacy in Drew's death, as much a suicide as a murder.

If the "repose and harmony of the central place" is made visible in any man, it is in Drew, whose guitar playing with the albino boy "emphasized nothing, but through everything he played there was a lovely unimpeded flowing that seemed endless" (55). Unable to reconcile the duplicity and non-harmony of this world and of the other men, and having given the world a glimpse of the harmony at the central place, Drew becomes the hero as Saint, described by Campbell:

> The pattern is that of going to the Father, but to the unmanifest rather than the manifest aspect: taking the step that the Bodhisattva renounced: that from which there is no return. Not the paradox of the dual perspective, but the ultimate claim of the unseen is here intended. The ego is burnt out. Like a dead leaf in a breeze, the body continues to move about the earth, but the soul has dissolved already into the ocean of bliss
>
> (*Hero* 354).

The irony of Drew's death is the reaction of his wife to his death. She says to Ed that "It's all so useless" (230), and indeed it is. No world redemption is achieved through the death of this good man, for all remains a secret. There are only Ed's "nightmares and night sweats to come" (187) in thinking of Drew's calloused fingers sinking into the river.

What these characterizations, and their sometimes bitterly ironic resemblance to heroic mythology like that described by Campbell, suggest is that modern, technological man cannot travel the same path as our ancestors in attempting to discover what it means to be a man (or woman). We must write new myths. Far from being a macho adventure novel, *Deliverance* calls into question the entire notion of heroism as it has been established through the centuries in the many manifestations of the initiating epic journey to the wilderness. As Campbell says at the end of *Myths To Live By,*

Our mythology now, therefore, is to be of infinite space and its light, which is without as well as within. Like moths, we are caught in the spell of its allure, flying to it outward, to the moon and beyond, and flying to it, also, inward

(274-275).

Perhaps, as with Ed, we must be content with the notion that now the rivers run nowhere but in our heads, but there they run as though immortally.

Works Cited

Campbell, Joseph. *The Hero With A Thousand Faces.* Princeton: Princeton UP, 1949.

———. *Myths to Live By.* New York: Bantam, 1972.

Davis, Charles. "The Wilderness Revisited—Irony in James Dickey's *Deliverance.*" *Studies in American Fiction* 4 (Autumn 1976): 223-230.

Dickey, James. *Deliverance.* New York: Dell, 1970.

———. *Night Hurdling.* Columbia and Bloomfield Hills: Bruccoli Clark, 1983.

———. *Self-Interviews.* Ed. Barbara & James Reiss. Garden City: Doubleday, 1970.

Eisiminger, Sterling. "James Dickey's *Deliverance*: A Source Note." *American Notes & Queries* 19 (Nov/Dec 1980): 53-54.

Foust, R. E. "*Tactus Eruditus*: Phenomenology as Method and Meaning of James Dickey's *Deliverance.*" *Studies in American Fiction* 9.2 (1981): 199-216.

Love, Glen. "Ecology in Arcadia." *Colorado Quarterly* 21 (1972): 182.

Taylor, Chet. "A Look into the Heart of Darkness: A View of *Deliverance.*" *James Dickey: Splintered Sunlight.* Ed. Patricia De La Fuente. Edinburgh, TX: Pan American University, 1979. 59-64.

Wagner, Linda. "*Deliverance*: Initiation and Possibility". *Modern Critical Views: James Dickey.* Ed. Harold Bloom. New York: Chelsea, 1987. 107-118.

Gordon Van Ness (essay date 1992)

SOURCE: Van Ness, Gordon. "Other Prose: *Jericho, God's Images, Wayfarer,* and *Southern Light.*" In *Outbelieving Existence: The Measured Motion of James Dickey,* pp. 101-11. Columbia, S.C.: Camden House. 1992.

[*In the following essay, Van Ness surveys the central thematic concerns of and the critical reaction to Dickey's nonfiction.*]

In a 1974 article discussing his efforts and those of painter Hubert Shuptrine to produce a major book about the South, Dickey declares,

I want to write *how it feels to be in this place, the South. The essence of it. The mood of it. How it feels to be there on the coast . . . to go there today and stand looking out over the marshes. And why it feels that way. Every place has its own quality of strangeness. Which is really uniqueness. That's what we want to capture. In paintings and words. The* feeling *of places.*

(Logue 186)

Jericho: The South Beheld (1974), the book that resulted from the project initiated by *Southern Living,* was a commercial success and a critical failure. Following the publication in 1970 of ***The Eye-Beaters, Deliverance,*** and ***Self-Interviews,*** a book where Dickey examines his own life and poetry, he issued ***Sorties*** the following year, which contains his journals and several essays. All were intended for a scholarly audience. Critics consider ***The Eye-Beaters,*** published by Doubleday, and ***Deliverance,*** issued by Houghton Mifflin, major works, and ***Self-Interviews*** and ***Sorties,*** both by Doubleday, significantly address Dickey's own career as well as the contemporary literary scene in general. However, ***Jericho*** and ***God's Images*** (1977), published by Oxmoor House, the book division of The Progressive Farmer Company, are oversized books in which Dickey combines his writing with illustrations for a collector's edition market. Later volumes in the seventies also reveal Dickey's interest in this specialized audience: ***The Enemy from Eden*** (Lord Jim Press), ***The Owl King*** (Red Angel Press), ***In Pursuit of the Grey Soul*** (Bruccoli-Clark Press), and ***Head-Deep in Strange Sounds*** (Palaemon Press). These small publishing companies, often concerned with luxury editions, appealed to a less scholarly market than Dickey's major works.

Bowers-Martin (1984) sees the books published in the mid-seventies as transitional in Dickey's career. ***The Zodiac*** (1976) culminates his exploration of "transcendence through the idiom of the creative lie" (144), which constitutes his central thematic concern. Its "exaggerated horizontal shape" (144) suggests the large coffee-table books that immediately precede and follow it. Moreover, like ***The Zodiac,*** based on Barnouw's translation, ***Jericho*** and ***God's Images*** derive from other sources, the former from traditional Southern culture and the latter from the Bible. Yet ***The Zodiac,*** while logically grouped with Dickey's serious poetry because of its theme, also evidences the poet's interest in a specialized market. The poem's working manuscript was sectioned and bound into special-edition volumes; these Bruccoli-Clark collector editions were then sold by private subscription at $400 per book. Bowers-Martin, noting the specialized market intended by ***Jericho*** and ***God's Images,*** declares that neither book denies Dickey's theme of transcendence, but they explain the drastic turn in his publishing history. During the seventies Dickey failed to discover subjects and themes around which to create a new experimental poetry. Because *The Zodiac* concludes the poetic idiom he had been exploring, his inability to depict transcendence through a new technique led to **Jericho** and **God's Images,** which are "attempts to get extra mileage from what has worked before" (145).

Yet **Jericho** is only partly successful because Dickey fails to use "the main sources of his power" (145), including his own artistic control of the transcendent experience. In the introduction the poet asks the reader to become a "beholder," someone who can

> enter into objects and people and places with the sense of these things entering into him. What starts out as a deliberate act of attention ends as though he were not so much performing a rendition of Reality, but that a living action were being perpetrated on him.

While this approach poetically succeeds with **"The Beholders"** in *Falling* by fusing the personae and their surroundings, the implication in **Jericho** is that Dickey himself cannot impart "that energy, that transcendence" (145), particularly when he asks the reader to provide the imaginative vision requisite for such a fusion of inner and outer states: "You, reader, must open up until you reach the point . . . of sensing your locality pour into you simultaneously through every sense." Dickey additionally eliminates the need for the creative lie, the very means by which he has previously provided transcendency and thereby given the reader, for example, a sheep child, two young lovers living in the mist around their wrecked motorcycle, a stewardess who lives only as she prepares to die, and blind children who attempt to see the origins of the race. In **Jericho** he takes traditional stories and asks the reader to view them in a heightened manner, an approach which undercuts his ability to lie creatively.

Dickey uses the persona of a seabird to view the South as the Promised Land. While hovering, swooping, or changing forms, the bird becomes whatever is necessary for each experience, but it always remains the same narrator, accompanying the reader in a series of "flickers." These experiences combine with actual landings as the bird touches Southern soil, a technique anticipated by the book's epigraph from Joshua: "Loose thy shoe from off thy foot; for the place whereon thou standest is holy." The first flicker occurs at St. Augustine, the South's oldest city, when the persona notices an oyster shell. Its condition, Bowers-Martin declares, establishes an important element in Dickey's fusion—the union of the natural and man-made worlds (146). Observing the shell, the bird says: "It is not lying on a beach, half-embedded in sand, but is jutting from a wall at an angle it never had in the sea." Such a conjunction is often repeated, as when the seabird flickers to Mobile's gardens: "No matter how close to them we are, no matter whether we help them grow or kill them, they are forever beyond us, these flowers." Southerners themselves exhibit this dichotomy in the way they lead their lives, partly grounded in their past dependence on the land and partly lived in an increasingly industrialized future.

Jericho concludes with a warning about the frailty of this fusion on which the new South rests. In Birmingham, Vulcan, the god of steel who provides the foundation for the Promised Land, says to the bird and the reader, "All this hardware I make: well, don't tell those new high-rising buildings of Jericho I told you; men used to call me Mulciber. You know what that means? The softener. They might get jittery. I might fall off this hill." Bowers-Martin believes this ending flicker reveals the elements of danger, repose, and joy that he also attempts to incarnate in his poems (147). Yet following these flickers, Dickey withdraws, leaving his audience to unify the experiences themselves: "Come down, reader, and be whole here."

Yardley's (1974) criticism seeks to define the larger nature of **Jericho,** asking whether the book is art or literature or "anything more than a colossal instrument" (43). Shuptrine's drawings are skillful, but they are also "imitative and sentimental" (43); Dickey's language "rolls" (43). Yet **Jericho** offers only a "sanitized and idealized" (43) South. Tailored to accommodate the readers of *Southern Living,* it is a book "for regional chauvinists to wallow in" (43), honoring only those qualities that affirm the Southern myth and ignoring those aspects that do not.

Critics quickly observed the extensive promotional campaign that accompanied the book's publication and which stressed not simply its size and Southern focus but also the magnitude of the sales effort. As Yardley does, they just as quickly faulted the content of **Jericho.** Evans (1975), for example, notes the book's big size (12 1/2 by 16 inches) and weight (7 pounds), its large first printing (150,000 numbered copies), and its extensive press release, which announced that the printing of **Jericho** required "28 carloads (one million pounds) of paper and 31 miles of cloth" (4). Such commercialism suggests "the poet decided to give himself over to the Alabama Chamber of Commerce" (4). Jones (1976) details the successful marketing strategy and campaign, arguing that the book's commercial popularity owes not only to the thorough testing and execution of a direct-mail campaign and the intense regional pride of Southerners but also to a national trend for nostalgia and a return to the land (250). Yet Evans, conceding that **Jericho** captures the South's haunted sense of pride and defeat, sees the failure to mention the Negro struggle for freedom as a major omission. Rather than presenting the civil rights movement, the book captures "the South that white Southerners think they live in" (4). Evans does acknowledge Dickey's awareness of the racial problem, citing his 1961 essay **"Notes on the Decline of Courage."** There he describes the black struggle as

> pointing up as nothing else in this country has ever done before, the fearful consequences of systematic and heedless oppression for both the oppressed and the oppressor, who cannot continue to bear such a burden without becoming himself diminished, and in the end debased, by such secret and cruel ways. . . . It is not too much to say that in the "Negro problem" lies the problem of the South itself.
>
> (*Babel* 258-59)

Later in *Self-Interviews* Dickey also states, "One must not be coerced . . . into writing about nothing but contemporary events; the larger forms of nature are still there. Not only the Watts and Washington riots exist, but the universe exists as well" (70). Dickey consequently is on "defensible ground" (5), Evans believes, when choosing those experiences that move or interest him, but *Jericho* is "an interpretative history" (5) whose announced theme is "The South Beheld." That such a book omits the civil rights movement, therefore, "shouts with Dickey's silence" (5). Furthermore, he omits discussion of the decline of Southern values and specifically the region's new homogeneity. The book's commercial success, despite these flaws, owes to the attitude it promulgates, a nostalgia that confirms the white Southerner's view of himself as a citizen in the Promised Land. It assures him that he lives in "a white paradise without any recognition of a paradise lost" (5).

Lacking such a pronounced political focus, Donald's (1975) lengthy review challenges the use of the word "collaboration" to describe the Shuptrine-Dickey relationship since each traveled his own way through the South by different means and recorded what each thought significant. As Dickey writes, "We have made no attempt in this book to have paintings and words coincide." Donald notes that, beside the obvious differences in their portrayals, one visual and the other verbal, Shuptrine views the heart of the South as the mountains, particularly those of North Carolina, since over one-third of his paintings derive from these and another one-third from the adjacent states of Virginia, Tennessee, Georgia, and South Carolina (185). Dickey's scope is larger, "fourteen or so states," he writes, asking the reader to follow in

> a gigantic spiral, going . . . first along the Gulf Coast, through the bayous and over the Delta and the Great River, then into the huge and bewildering and heartening blue of West Texas, then north to Arkansas, through Kentucky and West Virginia and Virginia, briefly down to the South Carolina coast . . . through Appalachia into Atlanta.

While Shuptrine's artistic focus is the countryside and country people, Dickey concentrates on small-town life. As Dickey himself remarks, Shuptrine is an artist "struck by *things*," while he himself excels not so much with the trees, dogs, and dwellings of the South as with its people—the faith healer, the bank robber, and the mill woman. Yet Donald believes both artists share a common vision of the South as the Promised Land. Within their respective mediums, what appears is their love of the land and the sense that the idealized Southern life they present is dying or already dead. While containing humor, Dickey's language is "elegiac" (186), and his rhetoric, while celebrating the South, has "a dying fall" (186). These characteristics appear, for example, when he depicts the owner of a garden of azaleas: "He stands with both hands in the time-shade, bowed down with his money, exhausted with the income and upkeep of ancient Jericho, with the expense, the overhead of flowers, of old ladies fainting with vegetative rapture." Dickey more directly suggests the decline of the Old South when he writes: "This is a land of ghosts, and we feel nowhere come-truer than in a cemetery." Shuptrine's paintings express the same mood, the same sense of "a world in its final autumn" (186). Therefore, *Jericho* is not so much "a preview of the Promised Land but a nostalgic glance at Paradise Lost" (187).

Steadman (1975) faults *Jericho* both for artistic reasons and for its overstated assertion. While the text exhibits virtues of vitality, strong imagery, and a "sensual immediacy" (9), it nevertheless reveals a lessening of the intensity and sense of abandon that characterizes Dickey's poetry. Though Shuptrine's watercolors remarkably mirror Dickey's style, their concentration and emphasis on detail occasionally resulting in realism or something beyond realism, his paintings "do not penetrate beneath the visual to provide any deeper meaning" (9). Yet the book's principal danger lies in the reader believing *Jericho* more than it is, a problem Dickey compounds in his introduction by calling it "two deep views of Jericho, that will not come—or come together—again." The title, together with his statement that he and Shuptrine have "beheld" the South and offerred it with a "Biblical intensity," suggests that *Jericho* mythologizes the region more than it actually does. Dickey writes that the "landscapes, seascapes, mountains, rivers and people . . . are our significance." However, the book fails both to depict the South's inextricable relationship with the past and, more importantly, to "cohere into a larger, expansive theme" (9).

More recent criticism, however, views *Jericho* as both a creative achievement and a product of Dickey's business acumen. Calhoun and Hill (1983) acknowledge Dickey's turn from his proclaimed mission as poet to a prose work intended for a popular audience and offerred by small publishing houses concentrating exclusively on luxury editions. The focus suggests either that Dickey was unable to explore familiar themes in creatively new poetry or that he could not finish **Alnilam**. The novel was finally published in 1987, but he had originally titled it *Death's Baby Machine* and detailed certain of its scenes as early as **Sorties** (1971). Yet this new direction also reveals Dickey's capacity "to 'make connections' with different kinds of readers" (121), showing many of the motifs previously apparent in his poetry, fiction, and criticism. **Jericho** depicts Dickey's Southern heritage, his ability to see clearly and poetically the details of the Southern landscape, and his "Agrarian love of the land" (121). The major change dictated by the new popular audience is Dickey's abandonment of "his role of poet of the expansive imagination" (121). No longer does he compel belief in situations and personae beyond the commonplace; rather, the reader assumes the imaginative task, instructed by Dickey to go "deeply into human life . . . of our particular segment of the world and what it offers . . . to those familiar with it by birth . . . and those who come to the South as strangers." Perhaps because of the reversal of previously expected poet-reader roles, as well as the absence of the usual Dickey persona, **Jericho** succeeds only in parts; good images and inescapable scenes occur only infrequently. Calhoun and Hill additionally note the quantity of literary allusions, including ones to John Crowe Ransom, Allen Tate, and Donald Davidson as well as echoes of Dickey's own poems, a fact especially surprising since Dickey remains critical of "academicism" (122).

Like *Jericho*, **God's Images** (1977) has attracted almost no lengthy, critical study. Reviews were mixed, and later critics compare it unfavorably to **Jericho**. Less ambitious in size, though not in artistic intent, it contains fifty-three prose-poems that not so much re-interpret as re-present particular Biblical texts from individual perspectives. A similar number of etchings by Marvin Hayes accompany these re-presentations. Marty (1977) believes Dickey's text faithful in intent to the Biblical motifs it depicts, but while some passages are rich, others become too poetically sensual. Hayes's drawings, at once technical and imaginative, combine the literal with the visionary. When both artists "aspire least they accomplish most" (13). DeCandido (1978), however, considers Dickey's passages "oddly secular" (154), stating that they lack a "palpable spirituality" (154) because the emphasis shifts from God to the figures that present the Biblical story, characters moreover that are "predominantly masculine" (154). Admitting the prose is crafted and deeply felt, the review strikes a feminist approach, noting the absence of Judith, Esther, and Mary Magdalene from the portrayals and observing that Ruth and Mary are only "shadow and symbol" (154). **God's Images** narrows the Bible to "the worldly visions of two men" (154), a comment which ignores Dickey's own statements in the book's foreword:

> To an artist such as Marvin Hayes, or to a poet, such as I hold myself to be, these images have unfolded in us by means of the arts we practice. These are *our* images of *God's Images*. . . . These then, in this book, are some of the images from the inner kingdoms of two men. . . . Hayes and I do not wish to supercede or in any way substitute our interpretations of the Bible for yours. These are crucial to you, and therefore vital and living. We should like to think, though, that we may be able to give an added dimension to your own inner Bible and enrich your personal kingdom of God, there where it lies forever . . . within you.

DeCandido fails to give Dickey the choice of his material.

Other reviews, however, were not influenced by political correctness. *Publishers Weekly* (1977), for example, states that Dickey's imaginatively subjective prose complements the etchings, which blend "realism with a disciplined sense of formal beauty" (Johnston 63). The reviewer notes the sincerity of both artists, particularly Dickey, whose effort was compelled by the death of his first wife, Maxine Syerson, a fact the poet acknowledges in the foreword: "She was all her life a devoted dweller in the Bible, and now, through the flowering tomb, she resides among the superhuman reality of God's images." *Booklist* (1977) and *American Artist* (1977) similarly see the collaborative interpretations of Dickey and Hayes as felicitous. The former asserts that Hayes's strength lies not only in his innovative approach to depicting well-known stories (the Crucifixion, for example, is shown as a reflection in Mary's tearing eye) but also in "the grace and economy of their realization" (344). Dickey lends this artistic interpretation an "emotional accompaniment" (344), often assuming the voice of the person he depicts, a technique which poetically reflects upon the visual meaning. This collaboration, *American Artist* observes, effects "a significant religious contribution for modern readers" (Preiss 26).

Oxmoor House, anticipating possible controversy from the book's unusual perspectives, established an advisory board of Biblical scholars, both Jewish and Christian, to assure that the portrayals were faithful to scriptural materials. Despite the offense taken by DeCandido, *Christian Century* (1977) sees **God's Images** favorably. Hayes's etchings bring a "new comprehension of biblical ideas" (1173), and Dickey's prose, "florid and reverent at once" (1173), reinforces the themes. Writing in *Theology Today*, Dillenberger (1979) raises questions about a literary work that depicts a religious subject. Hayes's etchings offer a series of select, dramatized vignettes, literally presented but without a comprehensive understanding of the Bible. Lacking such a unified overview, both artist and poet substitute piety. The illustrations sometimes evoke the theology of the sixties, as when in "Second Coming," Jesus becomes a tiny figure walking through a wide field of flowers. The "Crucifixion" has bathos, not pathos, although others like the "Death of Absalom" effectively present "the small, enclosed, compressed image which operates visually much as the epigram does verbally" (509). Many pictures, moreover, reveal an evasiveness about sexuality, with the figures seeming either castrated or purposely sexless, a troubling tendency since other sketches reflect the decade's more liberal attitudes. Too often, Dickey's prose passages must explain the disparity between the picture and the Scripture which accompanies it, breaching the incompatibility as if the poet's role were interpretive. Dillenberger questions the relevancy of the panel of church experts whose names and credentials are listed in the frontmatter, suggesting instead a group of advisors from art and literature, because *God's Images* is literary, not theological, in its focus.

Calhoun and Hill (1983) view *God's Images* as more academic than *Jericho* because within Dickey's text lie the voices of Milton, Blake, and the translators of the King James Bible, not just certain past and present Southern poets. However, the varied narrations undermine the "conversational vigor" (122) inherent in a work with only a single narrator. Moreover, unlike *Jericho, God's Images* has no unifying thesis. Rather than trying to justify the ways of God to man, Dickey attempts to rework the images in his own poetic idiom. Trying to recover the common, unrecognized culture within his readers, however, Dickey actualizes Biblical images that, as he writes in the foreword, are "buried and live in us." While the poet in *Jericho* seeks to establish a shared Southern connection between poet and painter on the one hand and artists and their readers on the other, he endeavors in *God's Images* to broaden this intent to include Protestantism. Because of such purposes, both books become more than mere commercial enterprises.

Bowers-Martin (1984) extensively examines *God's Images,* both as it compares specifically to *Jericho* and more generally to Dickey's major themes and artistic techniques. Unlike Calhoun and Hill, she sees these books as a decided retreat from previous efforts. Dickey eliminates the need for the creative lie by randomly presenting stories with which the reader already is familiar and admitting in the foreword: "We all have our images of God, given to us by the Bible, which is the Word of God. These images are ours, and in calling them up in our minds we are living witnesses of the fact that 'the kingdom of God is within you.'" Yet in believing that his interpretation of the reader's personal images will engender a heightened understanding of each Biblical story, Dickey relies not on his own creativity but rather these preexisting stories. The fusion of the reader's inner state with the larger Kingdom of God, therefore, lies not with the poet but with his audience. Moreover, unlike the earlier book, *God's Images* lacks a unifying narrative voice; the episodes remain fragmented. In such poems as **"The Sheep Child," "May Day Sermon," "Falling,"** and **"Madness,"** the strong narrative voice compels belief by combining first-person immediacy with third-person objectivity, but Dickey now resorts "to whatever voice strikes him" (148). Sixteen of the twenty-nine Old Testament scenes use the omniscient narrator, while only six of the twenty-three New Testament episodes do, a statistic accounting for the former being the weaker section because it fails to provide what Lieberman ("Notes on James Dickey's Style" 1968) calls the feeling of "heightened reportage" (63). While exceptions to this in the Old Testament do exist, such as the account of Jacob's wrestling with an angel or of Joseph and the coat of many colors, these episodes for the most part fail to depict the fusion of inner and outer states. Each scene seems isolated and still, as if constrained within its own boundaries, an immobility that "negates the motion, the energy, that allows Dickey's best ideas to work" (149). Though the Old Testament section exhibits his main theme of transcendence, it remains "a gathering of fragmented thoughts" (149). The New Testament stories, however, allow Dickey more latitude to create the fusion of forces because Christ embodies the union of God and man. Additionally, Jesus is the speaker in five of the episodes and the subject of most others, which enables the reader to know him through experiences related by other voices. For example, Mary comments on her son's birth: "He is mine, or at least half of him is mine. . . . I cannot understand any of this, but I do know I hold in my lap a child who comes from me. . . . God needs a human mate to bring forth a human child." Christ possesses a double vision, seeing both into the world and beyond it, allowing him a serenity derived from knowing what other men through God may become. This attitude of becoming is the foundation of Dickey's work. He alludes to this theme in the foreword when he notes "the fabulous world we all have fallen from, and toward which we are always falling, not backward in time, but forward toward that moment when each story, each image of God will be found, will happen again."

In an interview in the spring 1976 issue of the *Paris Review,* Dickey refers to any effort other than poetry as a "spin-off" (Ashley 81), adding: "The main thing in poetry is the discovery of an idiom and the exploitation of it over an area of thought for a long period of time" (81-82). Bowers-Martin sees Dickey as successful here because the creative lie has remained the idiom through which he has successfully explored transcendence (150). However, in the interview Dickey also declares, "A poet's pages are filled up with what he's done, that he can live on and trade on; but he has *got* to find some way to love that white empty page, those words he hasn't yet said" (76). Here, *God's Images* fails because it does not fulfill Dickey's stated hopes as a poet. The scenes are merely "his old pages repackaged, and the process diminishes their quality" (151).

Dickey returns to the South in **Wayfarer: A Voice from the Southern Mountains** (1988), the subtitle indicating the continued use of his cultural and family heritage. The unnamed narrator greets a wayfarer he encounters at the book's opening. Superstitious and wise, he has lived his life in the Appalachians. When the traveler becomes sick, the narrator uses mountain medicines to restore his health, taking the wayfarer on a figurative journey as he talks about the food, geography, customs, handiwork, folklore, and music. He asserts, "We ain't got everything, but we got somethin'." As with **Jericho** and **God's Images,** the book is a collaborative effort, with William Bake's photographs not so much adhering to the story as cohering. The 178 pictures, primarily from the Southern Appalachians and particularly that section of the range from North Carolina, also strangely includes photographs from Texas and Oklahoma.

Reviews are almost nonexistent and generally superficial. Adams (1989) briefly compliments Dickey's "charming text" and Bake's "fine photographs" (120) and observes that the setting is appropriately never identified. Starr (1988) also views the joint effort as beneficial, declaring that the pictures reveal "an explorer's sense and an artist's eye" (1F) and comparing Bake to Monet and Wyeth. The people he captures belong only to the mountains; they are "constant, sturdy, quietly dignified" (1F). The pictures, however, are rarely correlated to Dickey's prose passages, most being grouped at the book's conclusion where they serve as "a visual epiphany" (8F).

Van Ness's (1989) essay-review more substantially discusses the book's dramatic development, declaring that **Wayfarer** "is not, or at least not only or even principally" (31) a coffee-table book. Bake's photographs create "an emotional immediacy," while Dickey's understated language presents truth as "an imaginative connection" (31), linking the reader to what the Appalachians are in and of themselves, "their spacial and metaphoric fullness" (31). To do so, Dickey guides the reader on an heroic journey to recover what modern man has lost. As the narrator declares in **"Departure,"** for example, speaking of mountain people, "They got ways of knowin'."

Dickey has always celebrated the individual who either begins over or who returns to a source and who must therefore relate what he has learned. That voice often appears suddenly in the narrative as the poet follows his own personae. Chance occurrences begin a poetic search for the forces that govern life, a search revealing "man's awful responsibility to drive toward self-discovery and self-determination" (32). The encounter between the anonymous narrator and the wayfarer, therefore, presents a familiar Dickey concern—the confrontation between an individual and a force larger than himself. In **Wayfarer** that other is the Southern mountains. While Dickey has poetically treated aspects of this subject before (for example, foxhunting and quilting in **"Listening to Foxhounds"** and **"Chenille,"** respectively), the narrative framework of **Wayfarer** allows for greater breadth of treatment to depict what Van Ness calls "a larger natural inclusiveness in the world" (32). Consequently, when the speaker asserts, "It don't matter why it comes, but it does; it comes on through, and it's done been put into both of us, don't you see," Dickey moves beyond a discussion of family blood lines into "the lines of connection that link all men to the land and the natural impulses, the human need, to create and recreate what one sees and hears in the world" (32).

While **The Zodiac** and **Puella** also concern the artistic impulse and depict an individual seeking an exchange, **Wayfarer** differs in several respects. Not only does it attempt to have the visual and the verbal mediums interrelate, but its speaker also acts as an intermediary or guardian spirit, a guide who imparts to the adventurer certain protective amulets, as when the narrator gives the wayfarer a fairy stone shaped "like a cross" and which brings "good luck." As a result of his experiences, the traveler becomes "the new priest, a man who has been both outside and in" (32). His decision at the conclusion to speak for the first time, quoting Ransom's "Antique Harvesters," shows that he has undergone mythic rites of passage. Having crossed a threshold and penetrated forgotten truths, he poetically offers up what he has learned as he now prepares to return.

Southern Light (1991), Dickey's latest collaborative effort, attempts to capture through a poetic prose and the color photographs of James Valentine the distinctive qualities held in and projected by light. Valentine's 188 pictures dominate the book, which sections a day into dawn, morning, noon, afternoon, and evening and examines the world as light defines it during those times. In the introduction Dickey urges the reader to undertake the imaginative connection himself, a similar surrender critics like Bowers-Martin fault in his other oversized books. "Enter light," Dickey says,

> as though you were part of it, as though you were pure spirit—or pure beholding human creature, which is the same thing—to become part of light in many places and intensities, to make it something like a dream of itself with you in it; that way you will be seeing by human light, as well as by the light shining since Genesis.

Unlike his previous mixed-media works, the prose text does not complement but anticipates Valentine's photographs. Their subtle textures and startling vibrancy demand confrontation, while Dickey's description establishes the uniqueness of the respective moments captured by the camera. When at dawn, for example, light causes the things of the world to come into themselves, Dickey invites participation by singling out what one might personally hold in perspective: "In all remoteness you have a hand, as everything sharpens, attunes: sharpens *toward*. If you want more leaves, beckon, and they come." In evening, he asks how successful the encounters have been and reminds the reader of the special quality of what light makes possible: "Nothing like it ever given, except by means of Time. This time, this day." The artistic intent seeks to allow a physical and emotional confrontation by having the words defer to the photographs and yet prepare one to experience them. Dickey establishes this collaborative dependency when, speaking of the creative impulse present throughout all human history, he states in the introduction: "The cave artist and the photographer, standing for all others, want to see not through but into: want you to stay with and *in* the work, and for it to stay with you, for it is in its very essence a form of ritual magic." While Dickey guides the reader's journey through the twenty-four hours **Southern Light** captures in words and pictures, he paradoxically remains less tangible a presence than in **Wayfarer**, despite his use of the imperative and despite the latter's narrative, which often subsumes Dickey's voice. However, as in all his efforts, his principal concern is the sense of consequence derived from human communion with the world.

Dave Smith (essay date spring 1994)

SOURCE: Smith, Dave. "James Dickey's Motions." *South Carolina Review* 26, no. 2 (spring 1994): 41-60.

[*In the following essay, Smith views Dickey in the context of a Southern writer.*]

With the death of Robert Penn Warren, the mantle of preeminent Southern poet seems destined to fall to James Dickey. Wendell Berry, Donald Justice, Eleanor Ross Taylor, and A. R. Ammons are all worthy candidates, but each has deemphasized a Southern identity in ways Dickey has not. Much has been written about James Dickey that is misinformed, silly, or plainly wrong, especially in the latter half of his career. The critical profile ranges from a dismissive, apparently political, condescension to a sycophantic cheering. In *A History of Modern Poetry*, David Perkins writes tersely of Dickey's "Southern narratives" and implicitly of the facile local color some readers regard as characteristic of Dickey's poetry. Charles Molesworth and Neal Bowers are more expansive but, essentially, view Dickey as a charlatan and boor, extending Robert Bly's early attack on Dickey's poetry for what such critics oppose as socially and politically objectionable opinions. At the other extreme, Robert Kirschten ends his book *James Dickey and the Gentle Ecstasy of Earth: A Reading of the Poems* with an unbridled partisan cheer when he writes "Long may James Dickey be the slugger of creative daring and commitment to poetry so that we may continue our circle and sing."

Whatever the nature of critical response to Dickey, I think a predisposition to matters "Southern" plays a role. To outsiders, Southern culture, if those are not self-contradictory words, remains renegade, bogus, mysterious, often buffoonish. The South has long and variously paid the cost of its disjunction from other regions of the United States. Even the election of two presidents from the South does not easily convince the Southerner that equity or respect has arrived. Just as New Yorkers may imagine a South Carolinian to be fully a product of swamps and hokum, the South Carolinian—any Southerner—believes *plus ca change* to be the rule. His children, if possible, will be sent as far northward to college as money and ability permit. His novels will appear in New York. He will accept, reluctantly, the Northern standard as definitive.

The Southern poet, like the cottonmouth water moccasin, does not travel well and thrives mostly at home. James Dickey has often enough been treated by his press as exactly what Bly called him, a "great blubbery southern toad of a poet." Moreover, both in his poetry and out of it, he has confirmed the persistent view of the almost oxymoronic *Southern poet*, and not least by playing the role of the redneck sheriff in *Deliverance*. One has only to think of Donald Justice or Archie Ammons to note how different and how melodramatically poetic has been the role Dickey has played.

A Georgian who has lived most of his adult life in South Carolina, Dickey mounted his career in the 1960's and 70's, not merely upon rhythmically fresh and experientially different poems, but also on often corrosive opinions of the poets currently favored by one contingency or another. His success, and exuberant pleasure in his success, seemed unrestrained to many at his frequent stops along the poetry reading circuit. Indeed, Dickey's personal conduct on the circuit has generated an apocrypha about him not unlike that of Dylan Thomas. Dickey's advertising-man acumen rightly counted on notoriety to carry his poetry to an audience not often touched by academic meekness, but it may well be that his outlaw image among academics has underwritten the image of the Southern poet as inherently inferior and crude. Nevertheless, audiences that have turned out in hundreds to hear him from Portland, Maine, to Portland, Oregon, have found in Dickey a true grit not found in surreal fantasies, metric cosmologies, confession, therapy, or counter-culture meetings. Dickey's poetry seemed like life in the last half of the twentieth century—imperiled, dangerous, unprogrammed, abrupt.

Dickey speaks frankly from inside a male, individual, exuberant, and joyous experience. **"The Performance,"**

"Walking on Water," "At Darien Bridge," not his most celebrated poems but each standing as a chronological step in his art, are stations toward the roaring joyride of **"Cherrylog Road,"** a ride which reaches apotheosis in **"The May Day Sermon to the Women of Gilmer County, Georgia, By A Woman Preacher Leaving the Baptist Church."** The mystic lift-off from an apparently ordinary dramatic situation that might occur in any reader's life is a formidable trope employed by Dickey. Out of the ashes of momentary, mortal circumstance, Dickey offers the reader what religions have always offered, what **"The Salt Marsh"** shows: ". . . your supple inclusion / Among fields without promise of harvest, / In their marvelous, spiritual walking / Everywhere, anywhere." It is the joy of those who discover consequence in human connections such as the truckdrivers hymned in **"Them, Crying"** because they feel for *Those few who transcend themselves, / The superhuman tenderness of strangers.*"

Dickey's is a poetry far from ignorant of the dead, the hurt, the maligned, the abandoned peoples who are the common interest of lyric American poetry, but his investigation and his investment have nevertheless been in transcendent joy. His poems seek a good time, and they do it on middle-class terms. They are scarcely marked by the gloom of the American poet's self-conscious rehearsal of personal problems from Lowell's New England dance card to Sharon Olds's sexual abuses. *His* story is upper tier Southern, a bourgeois search for life after success: up from the fens of suburbia, to a university of modest name, discovery of imagination's life, a coven of writers, war and survival, a new and scrupulously-to-be-examined life, books published, a teaching eminence, more books. Had Randall Jarrell played football instead of tennis, he might have been this poet.

Until the publication of *The Whole Motion: Poems 1945-1992,* there was no abundant evidence in Dickey's books for what Emerson, in his note to Whitman, called a "foreground." The poems gathered under the title "Summons" now show how assiduously Dickey labored to present from his first published work a different sound in his poem. Yet even in the earliest poetry there is little of the historical Southern self-awareness and *mea culpa* whose breastbeating, in dark Faulknerian tones, constituted the "burden" of consciousness which would appeal, and does appeal, to generations of specialists. That it might not prove attractive to the educated, general reader, Dickey saw well enough. He set out to transform the pastoral lyric tradition by combining it with a heroic quest for a Southern self who would be, as Fred Hobson has described him, "the unburdened Southerner." Hobson, writing specifically of Barry Hannah and young Southern fictionists, might be saying of all Southern poets what Cleanth Brooks seemed to say in citing the disinclination of lyric to attach to a determinate landscape and purview—that there is no such cat. Hobson says in *The Postmodern Writer in the South* that "not only do family and past mean nothing to him, the South and his identity as Southerner, he insists, mean nothing to him either. The South of his remembrance . . . isn't mysterious, isn't violent, isn't savage, isn't racially benighted, isn't Gothic or grotesque, isn't even interesting."

The trajectory of Dickey's quest, as poems evolved structure, has moved from outside to inside, from emblematic anecdote treated narratively to experienced states of being, known lyrically. The scene, typical of the pastoral poem, has been the wood world or the sea world, nature, because it hosts the unknown and, traditionally, nurtures the spirit. Put bluntly, Dickey like Emerson, like Poe, like Keats has gone outside to find answers to questions echoing on the inside. As with all romantic and lyric poets, the problem was ever how to make intuited consolation, the joy of asserted consequence, credible to readers. What he has done, it now appears in his seventieth year, is to have commanded a formidable rhythmic shift whose expression has baffled as many of us as it may have dazzled.

Whether James Dickey is or is not a "Southern" poet may seem irrelevant to the matter of rhythm. The usual definition of the "Southern" is a historical consciousness aware of a great civil loss and a fearsomely burdened future; the location of story, as Flannery O'Connor put it, at the intersection of time and place where the clash and consequence of values may most effectively appear; the portrait of people unlikely to benefit from schemes of improvement but driven to suffer them; the environmental effects of rural reality, as the South has known it; the context of violence and violation—these are all to be found in Dickey's poetry. But so, too, is the presence of season, the confident cyclic regularity of living which suffers change and yet endures. The rhythmic nature of being Southern, though it may be something much older and deeper, is Dickey's subject and strategy in the work of his most recent decade.

Change continues to occur so fast we scarcely assimilate what it is. The physical landscape of the South has everywhere become an ugly memorial to greed and profit, every town and village marked at ingress and egress by the fecal-like stain of fast food dispensers, gas stations, auto lots, the Arabian knights of neon. Suburbs rise overnight to create instant slums which themselves breed every conceivable social ill. Yet the evidence of a past still alive is everywhere, too. There are living daughters of Confederate veterans in Richmond, the very last literal connection to that war. My own grandfather, who died at age eighty-eight this past winter, like many worked a lifetime without benefit of a formal education. He became an aeronautical engineer, who as a boy had hoboed a train to see the first automobiles. Sam Walton, an Arkansas man of the fields, transformed the South by harvesting Wal-Marts everywhere, creating appetites as well as an exchange of goods and ideas whose end we can't guess. The Agrarian ideal that early informed the classics-tutored imaginations of Southern poets has been lately expressed by Walter Sullivan who says, "Life lived on the farm is more authentic than life lived in the city, because the rural experience teaches the nature of reality." One end of change much observed by Dickey's poems is the waning of Walter Sullivan's reality.

Freb Hobson is probably correct that writers from the South increasingly attend to a new, urbanized experience, the life they are actually living. But that no South, remembered or lived, is of any interest to contemporary Southern writers seems hardly demonstrable in the work of the region's poets. Their South is more, not less, violent, broken, grotesque, disintegrating, *present,* and interesting. It may not even be inhabited as much by Southerners—people who want to know what they are, and why; people defined by the consequence of a place. The once stable culture Fugitives found so severely altered remains alongside, not instead of, the South that constituted the "burden." Southern poets, like writers of fiction, feel obligated to examine what is around them, what is inside them. Their interrogation takes a different path, but it remains an interrogation, even literally so in the voice of Robert Penn Warren. Ransom stroked and cooed. Tate fussed. Davidson nattered.

Dickey's voice, from his earliest poems, has possessed remarkable ventriloquial ability and is capable of calibration for effect, at times admonishing, assertive, but also evangelical with a range of wailing, crooning, wall-bursting rhetoric. The cast of characters through whom he has spoken, while not infinite, displays operatic range: a king, warrior, hunter, fisherman, fish, bird, wild boar, wolverine, leopard, quarterback, musician, woman preacher, womanchild, lifeguard, and others. Dickey's poems, being mysterious conduits for special speech, give back vital messages to the wobbling world, a message of solidarity and continuity from a scene of human engagement with natural force. Even the most patent "nature" reverie summons its authority for speech from an intuited scheme of order known both to Milton's "Lycidas" and to Poe, an order in jeopardy. This visionary role encourages Dickey in a self-appointed status as the civic voice of his tribe; he urges upon the people virtues to be celebrated for civilization and for vitality.

This twin-celebratory imperative has, I think, brought Dickey's poetry to a gulch it has not always transcended. The lyric hasn't the equipment or scope for a patient portrait of social ills and their remedies. Without being an epic chronicler of national states (one reason for the contemporary argument about whether lyric can be successfully political), the lyric poet feels he must contend against all risk for the biggest stakes. Dickey once told me he hadn't and wouldn't ever write "anything small." Although *small* may have meant physical length, I understood it to mean poems not adequately ambitious to speak of and for the soul of the tribal life. His specifically regional and "big" poems mark Dickey's "Southernness." **"Hunting Civil War Relics at Nimblewill Creek," "Snow on a Southern State,"** and, later, **"Sled Burial, Dream Ceremony," "Slave Quarters,"** and **"Two Poems of Going Home"** are variant examples.

The will to assume a civic voice characterizes a number of poems that began to appear with *The Eye-Beaters, Blood, Victory, Madness, Buckhead and Mercy* (1970) where the line-tempered and stanza-restrained form Dickey had refined to award-winning acuteness yielded to poems whose visual dimension is irregular and whose aural experience one must call, in general, loud. **"Apollo," "The Strength of Fields," "The Olympian,"** and **"For a Time and Place"** reveal Dickey assuming the venerable role of poet for the republic, broadcaster of answers. It is, I think, the wrong role for Dickey who seems here at his most bathetic and transparently bad. He is bad because he loses his skill for rhythmic delicacy, not because he abandons his narrative gift. He is bad because he fails to employ language as an act of discovery, a door into that wood world whose secrets the pastoral poet always unlocks. Dickey bangs dully, laboring more and more mightily, as if noise will overcome deafness, as in **"For the Running of the New York City Marathon":**

> I am second
> Wind and native muscle in the streets   my image lost
>   and discovered
> Among yours: lost and found in the endless panes
> Of a many-gestured bald-headed woman, caught between
> One set of clothes and tomorrow's: naked, pleading
>   in her wax
> For the right, silent words to praise
> The herd-hammering pulse of our sneakers,
> And the time gone by when we paced
> River-sided, close-packed in our jostled beginning,
> O my multitudes.

Whitman, of course, would have smiled at this.

Even here, however, is the gist of Dickey's greatness, the seed of "right, silent words to praise." Dickey is at his best when he abandons pretension to social and cohesive opinion, when he strikes off to find and celebrate the rural life which until his generation was dominant in the South. Indeed, Dickey's interest is most fervent for the pre-rural, wild landscape, the Adamic scene of long scars to our bodies and dark fears to our souls. This may well define the Southern poet, and Dickey in particular, as an American example of what Seamus

Heaney has called a "venerator." Dickey's quest has been to locate and report the sites of sacred energy which are the unploughed and unknown thickets our myths, legends, and souls regard as compelling, maternal, and tutorial.

The poet-venerator who praises the natural seems inevitably a pastoralist. More often an elegiac than an epic or dramatic writer, he means to concentrate emotive power to evoke immediate and strong response. It is a poetic attitude necessarily more backward-facing than forward, for it laments change that erodes the durable and the good by which we have so long flourished; yet it is also a poetic attitude whose interrogative aspect is less divorced from political and social engagement than we might suspect. To praise the past against a corrupted present is to lodge complaint against the causes and conditions of the corruption. As the portrait moves toward articulated vision, the transcendent and mythical scheme presses more vigorously into the receptive consciousness of the poet. The poem seeks to distill everything to essences beyond which no consciousness can go, the very process undertaken by Dickey's poems in books after the mid-1970's. Two possibilities open for the poet, one formal, one scenic. In evolving toward a poetic sound, Dickey found himself with gifts of the venerator but attracted by the imperatives of a republican voice, a divided duty as it were. The retraining needed to resolve that dilemma results in the characteristic (and not very Southern) sound of poetry Dickey has written in the 1980's and 1990's as collected in ***Head-Deep in Strange Sounds: Free-Flight Improvisations from the unEnglish*** (1979), ***Puella*** (1982), and ***The Eagle's Mile*** (1990).

Paul Ramsey, a Southern poet whose tastes tend toward the conventionally metric Anglo style, has written, provocatively, that "the metrical history of James Dickey can be put briefly and sadly: a great lyric rhythm found him; he varied it; loosened it; then left it, to try an inferior form." The rhythmic form Ramsey so admired was not found by Dickey so much as forged by him for his need. It flashes in the twenty-five poems of "Summons" with which Dickey opens ***The Whole Motion: Collected Poems 1945-1992.*** Stanzas from **"For Robert Bhain Campbell"** illustrate:

> I like him; I love him,
> I shall soon sit cold in an office,
> Hearing the sea swing, the dead man step:
> The sun at sunset in the mind
> Never falls, never fails.
>
> There is Berryman's poem, where you were a bird.
> And I, an unsocial man,
> Live working for some kind of living
> In a job where there is no light. But
> I can summon, can summon,
> And your face in my mind is hid
> By a beard I read you once grew.

An intense voice, wanting both intimate and chanting registers, swings through uncertain feet that sound at moments smooth and at moments about to collapse. But the last three lines display what Ramsey had in mind, a mesmerizing rhythm exactly embodied in the line statement, whether trimeter or tetrameter, syllables falling with firm yet delicate motion that is the anapestic shape for which Dickey's poetry would become known. Very shortly, one imagines, Dickey's sense for the line would have revised stanza one this way:

> In an office, hearing
> The sea swing, the dead man
> Step the sun at sunset
> In the mind, never failing.

Dickey's short line with a faintly incantatory quality has a talent for bodying drama *inside* the mind, a consciousness which moves easily backward and forward in time. Aggressive, sensitively receptive, it rocks with a feel of speed but also with grip and vision. By 1962, in ***Drowning With Others,*** Dickey had learned the subtleties inherent in this form, not least lean, agile stanzas in five and six lines, clusters of perception, and leaps from the real to the mystical, as in **"Fog Envelopes the Animals"**:

> Fog envelopes the animals.
> Not one can be seen, and they live.
> At my knees, a cloud wears slowly
> Up out of the buried earth.
> In a white suit I stand waiting.

While four of the five lines make bold statement, a firm sonic progression of tetrameter creates a background sense of reluctant movement common in confronting the unknown. Each line proceeds as a consequence of the factual line one, though nothing else appears factual because of the shimmery, slightly and oddly formal syntax which makes "and they live" a soft cry of discovery, makes the cloud out of the earth seem a spirit, and makes the white suit of the speaker the ritual dress of the about-to-be-changed. Here, Dickey's trademark anapests create the three-pace phrase which retards an energy always threatening to bolt. Thus "and they live" holds back momentum and permits discovery, as "At my knees" sets it up.

By the mid-1960's Dickey mastered variations of the anapestic rhythm. They were needed to avoid the inherent monotony of his stichic incantation, a weakness especially troublesome for one of the two kinds of poems he wanted to write. Dickey had from the start an exceptional narrative talent, an ability to bring life to a scene, to color it, expand it, and cinematically make it move. The short line enabled that feel of immersion, the stress pushing ahead and the double drag of anapest retarding.

The action of statement was realistic and external, assisting movement, and with it Dickey saw how to tap into moments of mythic reach. Here are two first stanzas that illustrate: "When the rattlesnake bit, I lay / In a dream of the country, and dreamed / Day after day of the river . . ." (**"The Poisoned Man"**). "Beginning to dangle beneath / The wind that blows from the undermined wood, / I feel the great pulley grind . . ." (**"In the Marble Quarry"**).

Dickey's ability to blow up ordinary scenes into posters of experience, an ability that would force his work farther from the domestic arena and into such wilderness as might be left to an urbanized South, created a need for a line form which did not risk monotony and did not delay progression through temporal and spatial levels. Dickey wanted form capable of what he called, after Whitehead, "presentational immediacy." The poems of **Buckdancer's Choice** (1965), widely seen as his best book, restlessly range through the irregular lines and stanzas (his gap space device appears) of **"The Firebombing"** to the long-line quintets of **"Reincarnation"** to the scrupulous sculpted quatrains reminiscent of Herbert in **"The War Wound"** to the wall of words in **"The Shark's Parlor"** and **"The Fiend."**

Dickey had worked himself into possession of many rhythms, none of which sufficed entirely for the tune he wanted to play. Nothing better illustrates Dickey's rhythmic hunt for the sound than his worksheets held by Washington University. Here are the first eight lines of **"The May Day Sermon to the Women of Gilmer County, Georgia, By A Woman Preacher Leaving the Baptist Church,"** in the first draft, then called **"Sears."**

> The wide-open dance of motes.
> The swinging sand of the motes.
> The wide-open dance,
> The swinging sand of dust.
> That other glory shall pass.
> The stable wanders over the earth.
> And at night, in the animal's sleep,
> The stable wanders over the earth.

The initial lines fumble with that peaceful image of dust as if Dickey can't find a way through tranquillity to his violent tale of paternal and religious abuse, and indeed the struggle lies between potentially soporific iambs and anapests, all jarred by trochees. But by line six a stability arrives as the anapests set a dominant pace, one Dickey will couch in longer lines only in the very last draft before publication. Buried in the lines which seem sculpted by a worshipper's intensifying in-breath and out-breath, the surge and drag of Dickey's old trimeter works into, parallels, sometimes counters an older tetrameter whose sound is a rhythmic composite of Anglo-Saxon beats and King James idiom. With this shift of form, of rhythm, Dickey explodes his poem toward a hybrid and mystical parable of joyful ascension:

> Open   to show you the dark where the one pole of
>   light is paid out
> In spring by the loft, and in it the croker sacks sprawl-
>   ing and
> shuttling
> Themselves into place as it comes   comes   through
>   spiders dead
> Drunk on their threads   the hog's fat bristling   the
>   milk
> Snake in the rafters unbending through gnats to touch
>   the last
> place
> Alive on the sun with his tongue   I shall flickering
>   from my mouth . . .

Ramsey was certainly correct in observing that Dickey had "loosened" the rhythm. He did so to liberate the poem from its own success, the solid "click" of the trimeter lyric as in **"The Heaven of Animals."** Doubtless, the gain for Dickey was simply pleasure in stepping outside reader expectations, his own included. This will to change and change again seems, in retrospect, characteristic of Dickey's writing, as it was of Robert Penn Warren's. Having disguised and modulated his initial rhythm with the new spread of lines, increasingly other aspects of Dickey's treatment of language became manifest. In some respects language became his primary subject. He cultivated syntactic reversals, suspensions, word-fusions, print gimmicks, clausal ambiguities, and enjambments that left comprehension hovering mid-margin like annotation. **"The Eye-Beaters,"** in fact, employed the poem's margins for authorial commentary. Dickey transformed verbs into nouns, nouns into adjectives, adjectives into phrases. He played loose with syllable counts; he truncated sentences to fragments; he made lines of single words. He generally abandoned stanzaic regularity, allowing the words to determine rhythm visually by sometimes sprawling, sometimes marching, always defining their function in their management of the white space of the page.

The result of Dickey's improvisations was to move his brand of poem visibly away—as it had already removed itself thematically—from the more conventional contemporary poem. It was not unusual to hear, even among Dickey's partisans in the late seventies, that he was becoming hermetic. In truth, because of their interiority, their will to shift inner and outer forums, Dickey's poems had never been very accessible, but they became ever more oblique as he cut the reader's connectors and transitions, offered few clues to relationships, or left unnamed what he was talking about. Still, his tales spoke more than ever in the voice of what he had called "the energized man," and nowhere more so than in **The Zodiac** (1976), a poem about poetry and language as much as it is about anything. The energized man, as far as Ramsey and traditional formalists were concerned, was a howler. And was passion enough to justify the willful obliquity of such lines as these from **"Root-light, or the Lawyer's Daughter"**?

> That any just to long for
> The rest of my life, would come, diving like a lifetime
> Explosion in the juices
> Of palmettoes flowing
> Red in the St. Mary's River as it sets in the east
> Georgia from Florida off, makes whatever child
> I was lie still, dividing . . .

Dickey made formal experiments jam more and more intense life into the poem, the poem as enactment. Desiring to wed fiction, poetry, and film, Dickey was reflecting a break between himself and his more traditional predecessors in Southern poetry. Only Warren evinced anything like the formal trials Dickey attempted, and Warren never escaped the critical estimate of being a fiction writer who traveled in the netherland of poetry. Dickey, with the publication of ***Deliverance, Alnilam,*** and now ***To the White Sea,*** runs a similar risk with the Southern literature industry. But it is his poetry, surely, and its innovative motions that make him important both as writer and Southerner.

Dickey, to use Fred Hobson's word again, is *unburdened* by any great sense of classical obligation. The pressure exerted upon his formal choices comes not from an antiquarian standard but from an attempt to accommodate contemporary experience in a living language. Allen Tate said the problem for the modern was not that he had no form, but that he had too many. Dickey's problem has obliged him to understand that his engendered form would have to avoid the monotony his early and middle lyrics seemed headed toward. But the new form must also enable clear shifts away from the direct narratives which undergirded his accomplishment and reputation.

The nature of what constitutes a Southern narrative may best be known to the person who receives it as such. If the benchmarks of Southern fiction are applied, then one supposes there must be violence, warfare, sexual encounters, pursuit of a wild creature in the wood with an accompanying recalibration of the spirit's experience. If the dominant subjects of the poems are family members, dysfunctional or otherwise, and if the stories invoke the memory that composes a sort of compound of law and expectation for the family, then the grid definition for Southern literature may qualify poems as Southern narratives. But I see no reason why "In the Waiting Room," Elizabeth Bishop's poem about a visit to the dentist, or Adrienne Rich's "Diving Into the Wreck," an undersea divagation, might not be equally Southern, excepting, of course, neither poet identifies the landscape employed as Southern and, in any regional sense, the landscapes do not function as actors. When there is nothing definitively Southern in subject matter, we may wonder to what extent rhythmic patterns define what is Southern. Poet James Applewhite has suggested (in "The Poet at Home and in the South") a relationship clearly Southern between tropical weather and slowed, indigenous poetic rhythm.

With landscape as rhythm and a form evolving to minimize the narrative, squeezing it between the lines, Dickey's most recent poetry arrives at a new phase. I mean by rhythm, now, what Warren meant in *Democracy & Poetry* when he wrote that rhythm is "not mere meter, but all the pulse of movement, density, and shadings of intensity of feeling." Dickey's reason for the change, insofar as it may be a personal choice, cannot be known; we can see, though, that his interest in peopled dramas has lessened (though it is not entirely abandoned) in favor of an interest in states of being realized through intense, and, after ***Puella,*** drastically shorter nodes of language. *Puella* is an odd interstice, as I think is ***The Zodiac,*** for its poems attempt to speak in the voice of Dickey's second wife, Deborah, hence as dramatic monologue, and they attempt the coherence of a bildungsroman or a portrait much like an autobiography, a fictive self self-made.

These poems are unsuccessful heroic quests, narratives of a speaker whose goal must be an emergence from darkness into a treasure-hoard of bright knowledge. For all of Dickey's story skills, neither ***Puella*** nor ***The Zodiac*** sustains a beginning-middle-end clarity and progress that we will pay to watch all the way through. I think neither voice is so credibly itself as it is Dickey's, pitched, squeaky, noddingly thrown. The life-plot in each poem is so subordinated to a massing of language appropriate to Dickey's interest in states of passionate being that confusion results. Nor does a lift-off occur, transporting us to revelation. Both poems are never "small" but they try too hard to be "big." In them may be seen the manner of Dickey's late poetry, its richness and a manner arguably Southern, observably a different rhythm, and yet visibly the result of a shift meant to realign Dickey's formal strategies with his continued search for an inwardly intensified consciousness and an outwardly pressurized rhythm.

Without study of his worksheets and drafts, no definite date can be assigned for the emergence of the lyric sound characteristic of everything Dickey has published since 1976. The poem of this sound shows a baffling, edged sense of incompleteness, arbitrariness, and rough-born form that some have regarded as proof of a failed talent. Although there is no doubt the late poems are tougher going, I think Dickey's last collections are no less and probably more referential, accessible, and reality-based than John Ashbery's. But the rhythmic pitch is different, as in this excerpt from ***Puella***:

> With a fresh, gangling resonance
> Truing handsomely. I draw on left-handed space
> For a brave ballast shelving and bracing, and from it, then, the light
> Prowling lift-off, the treble's strewn search and wide-angle
> glitter.

In this five-line passage from **"From Time,"** Dickey buries his statement ("I draw on left-handed space") in a haze of unpatterned syllables which make an appositional elaboration, a stretched and gliding poetic sound which features three suspensions or caesuric swirls. Dickey recognizes that his poem resists referential access, so he provides a subtitle ("Deborah for Years at the Piano"). The passage cited is, otherwise, unresolvably ambiguous—yet feels rhythmically persuasive as it works by accretion and momentum, prose principles, and alludes to carpentry, stress forces, and photographic effect all to reinforce a sense of "measuring" in the reader. The laid-in quality of language intense with intention but struggling to maintain movement explains the frequent verbals. To the extent that the lines exist to be commentary on what it *feels like to play piano,* they are registers of inward awareness, slowed thought imitating act and look.

The registration of states of being, of conditions of feeling, as the emphatic enactment of poems appears to migrate toward a form which employs greater ellipsis, compression, and density, all provided for not through symbol so much as through the word-function shifts which Dickey favors, a truncated and often spatially isolated or dramatically enjambed statement for which the usual expectations are frustrated, subverted, and altered. He removes the scaffolding of dramatic circumstance and blurs the occasion of speech, leaving primarily a language of emotive intensity, a sort of curriculum for the soul's exuberant epiphanies. *The Eagle's Mile* (1990) reads, even for a long-immersed Dickey partisan, with a difficulty unmatched by any previous work. But that difficulty has always been a part of Dickey's artistic project and it seems transient for steady readers.

Head-Deep in Strange Sounds: Free-Flight Improvisations From the unEnglish appeared in 1979, a baker's dozen poems, each carrying such handrails as "after Alfred Jarry," "near Eugenio Montale," and "from the Hungarian of Attila Joszef, head crushed between two boxcars." Are they translations? Imitations? Some sort of shared composition? I think it matters primarily that they are poems which seek a form-sound in the translation experience of European poets at the same time and in much the same way that James Wright and others did, and do so by breaking the chronological-anecdotal structure, linear and clear as ancestral verse, seeking a dream-fusion of states of being, a braiding in which the inhibitions of usual form and practice may be escaped, and in which looming death-shadows can be cheated by colloquy. It is also a form which permits Dickey to speak of emotion as well as of a citizen's public experiences, about, as he says "the evil / of just living . . ."; or of the magic of the language of numbers "from the frozen, radiant center / Of that ravishing clarity you give. . . ."

Double-Tongue: Collaborations and Rewrites, the final section of *The Eagle's Mile,* contains nine poems very similar to those of *Head-Deep,* each displaying the phrase-making power that has made Dickey a notably epigrammatic poet as well as an image creator with the skills of a jeweler, a power reenfranchised by the brevity, spatial sculpting, and concentration characteristic of this later work. With compressive form, Dickey has vitalized landscapes as historical and evolutionary witnesses. In **"Lakes of Värmland,"** he eulogizes and releases Viking warriors "in water turned to brass" by old wars, his precursors, of whom he says "I wish to gather near them . . . ," a discourse as doomed and moving as that of **"The Seafarer,"** that Anglo-Saxon call to the quest tinged and poignant with late-life's hard wisdom. Indeed, the common landscapes in these poems are rife with danger, with cold, height, inhospitable trials, the blank mercilessness of rooms of air a man comes to— "No side protected, at home, play-penned / With holocaust. . . ." Dickey's late season poetry has left him with a chilling view, sometimes *vistas,* of mortal experience, one which does not always offer consequence for the yearner, though it has cyclical inevitability, which Dickey seems to regard as a sort of master rhythm to which man must seek to fit himself. For that, the poet's pastoral yearning has never been quite enough to satisfy Dickey, though he has deep roots in the agrarian and Southern awareness of elemental cycles. Landscapes contain now, it would seem, the full evocation of final ends he wants. In the talky but, perhaps, undeniable **"Farmers"** he says:

> When love gives him back the rough red of his face
>   he dares
>
> To true-up the seasons of life with the raggedness of
>   earth,
> With the underground stream as it turns its water
> Into the free stand of the well: a language takes hold
>
> And keeps on, barely making it, made
> By pain: the pain that's had him ever since school,
> At the same time the indivisible common good
> Being shared among the family
> Came clear to him: he disappears into fog . . .

His old habit of conducting big matters from the civic podium forces Dickey to assert what he does not dramatize, the noble and exemplary synchronization of environment and manhood, deed and principle. The Southerner knows this ordinary farmer, praised into mystical junction with the elements, knows that language of pain and sacrifice; this is an old mainstay in the program of

At McLendon's table, Frank participates in his most important discussions, those with two war veterans, Captain Lennox Whitehall, who now teaches navigation at Peckham air base, and Captain Claude Faulstick, who instructs the cadets in the theory of flight. Whitehall, Faulstick, McLendon, and Frank form "a special group" (194) founded on mutual respect; yet this group supports and praises individuality, unlike the Alnilam cadets, who subjugate the individual to the group. Furthermore, Whitehall and Faulstick lament their present plight of "wandering-around among these boys" (196), drawing a clear distinction between themselves as seasoned veterans and the inexperienced novices they train; these mature men have developed their ideas about flying and the military through their combat experiences, their blood sacrifices; whereas the Alnilam cadets base their theories on pure intellectual and mystical speculations.

Moreover, Whitehall's most significant reflections are presented not to the cadets but rather to the other mature adults at McLendon's table. Unlike the young member of the Alnilam group, Whitehall tempers the solely intellectual by voicing the emotional center of his war experiences. Because of his navigational skills during a particularly bloody mission in the South Pacific, Whitehall has saved the lives of his crew members. When Faulstick comments that the saved men must have "loved you after that," Whitehall replies, "Love me? Do you think that really comes into it? Gratitude? Respect? Awe, maybe, even? You're kidding when you say love, Faulstick, but you may just be right" (214). Whitehall has saved the lives of his comrades by relying on himself, his intelligence, his skill; but he has not separated himself from—elevated himself above—the needs, of others. In a statement reminiscent of Whitman's "I was the man," Whitehall declares, "I was the guy, and they were the others, and we didn't die. We want out to kill people, and we must have killed a good bunch of them . . . and the main feeling when you're on your way back is life; it's a life feeling . . . you want to become a doctor, or a saint. You want to do good for little children. . . . You don't want anybody to be lonely or scared" (217). Whitehall's declaration illustrates that the Alnilam cadets have aspired to achieve but finally have failed to comprehend: that the individual can rise above the ordinary yet still have compassion for others, that the heart can be as important a source of power as the intellect, that the two finally cannot be separated if the individual is to survive.

Frank absorbs the lessons of this "special" society—the amenities McLendon offers, the message of comradeship Whitehall provides, and the compassionate understanding that Faulstick voices—and expresses it in terms of his own experience: "They had come here, to this hot room, this whiskey and meat, because of him. He rallied to himself as he had always done since the total of his blindness, as the center, the reason for the disembodied voices that called themselves humanity, wherever he was" (197). Through his new vision in blindness Frank encompasses their experience and their message and, in doing so, connects with them to discover both himself and the humanity he shares with them.

Initially, Frank's cold, distorted heart keeps him confined within his self-created prison / park. His distance from others marks his extreme position outside the community of man. In order to resurrect his dead son, at least in his own mind, Frank moves into the secretive world of an opposing yet equally extreme social unit. At the Peckover air base, Frank confronts a system that attempts to crush and subjugate the individual, primarily through an unfeeling, tyrannical intellect gone mad. Finally, the protagonist achieves a harmonious balance between these extremes at McLendon's Peckover Hotel. In this setting Frank Cahill experiences a renewal to life once he discovers a balance between the mind and the heart, between the individual and society; he thus reaches the center point that is his own Alnilam.

Work Cited

Dickey, James. *Alnilam*. Garden City, New York: Doubleday, 1987.

Ernest Suarez (essay date winter-summer 1994-1995)

SOURCE: Suarez, Ernest. "*Deliverance*: Dickey's Original Screenplay." *Southern Quarterly* 33, no. 2 (winter-summer 1994-1995): 161-69.

[*In the following essay, Suarez juxtaposes Dickey's novel with the film version of* Deliverance.]

James Dickey and director John Boorman battled over the making of **Deliverance** to the point that Dickey was asked to leave the set. To Dickey's chagrin, Boorman cut the original screenplay's first twenty-five pages, altered scenes and changed the film's ending in order to create a more commercially palatable product. After the film was finished, Boorman felt that he had influenced Dickey's product to the extent that he claimed co-authorship, which would have entitled Boorman to approximately $250,000. Though the Screen Writers' Guild eventually adjudicated in Dickey's favor, and though the film received much critical acclaim and generated Dickey a huge amount of publicity, Dickey has continued to express dissatisfaction with the movie. Dickey's primary objection resides in Boorman's handling of characterization, as the director's emphasis on creating a taut, thrilling adventure film left little room for what Dickey calls "the psychological orientation—the *being* of the characters, their interrelations, their talk with each other, the true dramatic progression . . . it is not the film as I would have it . . . though something which resembles the original story remains, the texture, the field of nuance, the details, characterizations, dramatic buildup and resolution as originally conceived are lost; nothing but the bones are left" (*Screenplay* 156-57).

Dickey's remarks are not surprising because of his longtime preoccupation with the psychological dimensions of primitivism, a phenomenon he has explored in **To the White Sea,** his screenplay of **Call of the Wild**, "**Reincarnation II**," "**Approaching Prayer**," "**The Fiend**" and many other poems. In **Deliverance,** Dickey creates four differing characters, all suburbanites, and plunges them into a situation in which they must battle nature (including primitive man) for survival. By emphasizing how each character behaves, Dickey demonstrates how returning to a primal condition can be simultaneously horrifying and enlivening. Unlike Boorman, who wanted to get the canoers on the water as quickly as possible in order to quicken the film's pace, Dickey desired to use the opening scenes to create a complex relationship between the characters and, particularly, *within* Ed.

Unlike the movie, which begins with shots of the flooded river and the dam's construction, highlighting the vanishing wilderness, the screenplay echoes the novel's opening scene, with the four main characters drinking beer in a tavern while looking over a topographical map. Dickey uses this scene, as well as others that Boorman cut, as a lens through which to interpret the wilderness episodes, especially those involving Ed's reversion to a feral state, a transformation which the film ignores. Whereas in the film the characters first appear fully outfitted, in the mountains and driving towards the river, the screenplay uses the tavern scene to distinguish between them, first through close-ups of Lewis's muscular hand pointing to coordinates on a map, followed by an emphasis on how his attire—"an expensive sport shirt"—differs from the others' business suits. Dickey also suggests that "one of the three men—anyone but LEWIS—occasionally glances at the behind of one of the waitresses in sheernet tights" (2). However, when "the waitresses pass the table, he (LEWIS) is the one they look at" (3). Lewis is clearly the center of attention, as well as in control:

ED:

I'll go along. For some reason I always do. But what are we proving, Lewis?

LEWIS:

Maybe nothing, maybe everything. Now tell me the truth, buddy. You ever regret going with me?

ED:

(hesitating just a little, but not much): No, but sometimes I've had the shit scared out of me. Like when it was your idea to put our lights out in that cave "to hear the very sound of the earth," as you said, and then couldn't get them back on.

LEWIS:

But we got them back on, didn't we?

ED:

Finally, but my God. . . . I'll take the river.

DREW:

Well, by damn, let's *do* take it! I need to get out some. I'm getting too soft. I can't even climb the steps to my office without worrying about a heart attack. I just stand at the top panting.

BOBBY:

They tell me that this is the kind of thing that gets hold of suburban dwellers once in a while. But most of them just lie down till the feeling passes.

LEWIS:

And when most of them lie down they're at Woodlawn before they think about getting up.

BOBBY:

I mean, the whole thing does seem kind of crazy.

LEWIS:

(looking down): All right. Let me demonstrate. What are you going to be doing this afternoon?

BOBBY:

Oh . . . most likely I'll see a couple of new people about mutual funds. I have to draw up some papers and get them notarized.

LEWIS:

How about you, Drew?

DREW:

Hire some more route salesmen. Our newest carbonated miracle is not selling like we want it to. The whole soft-drink market is in a slump now, especially our share of it. Somebody's got to find out why.

LEWIS:

Ed?

ED:

Take some photographs for Kitts Textile Mills. Kitt'n Britches. Cute girl in our britches stroking her pussy. A real cat, you understand.

LEWIS:

> (with a tolerant grin as he leans back): Too bad. But have I made my point?
>
> (3-4)

This exchange situates Ed between Lewis and the other two characters. Unlike Lewis, Ed and the others are "average" Americans, but Ed's relationship to Lewis implies that Ed possesses the desire to move beyond his current circumstance. However, for Ed the escapades with Lewis represent a diversion from daily monotony; for Lewis they also serve as preparations for a future in which "the machines are going to fail, the political systems are going to fail, and a few good men are going to take to the hills and start over" (19). Though Lewis is the scene's focal point, Dickey specifies that viewers should "see this scene as though . . . sitting in the position occupied by Ed" because he wants the audience to share Ed's fascination with—and difference from—Lewis (2). In this manner, Lewis functions to provide insight into Ed's psyche, setting the contours of the transformation Ed undergoes when he becomes both predator and prey.

The screenplay's next scenes continue to emphasize Ed's psychological state, as the description of Ed sauntering back to his advertising agency indicates:

> A full, middle-distance shot now as ED begins to walk, and we see him, occasionally pulling at the stickiness of his jacket, walk along in an unorganized but plentiful procession of secretaries of all ages, most of them with exaggerated hairdos and tasteless summer clothing. If desired, the camera can pick out some of these faces in close-ups, showing a gum-chewing young one, a middle-aged one with a toothpick in her mouth, and various other unimaginative, commonplace, hopeless everyday female human beings going back towards doing what they have to do.
>
> ED moves along in this procession, uncomfortable but resigned to it; but, though he goes along quietly, it should be obvious that, though he can stand it, he dislikes it.
>
> A closer shot as a large leaf comes down. He stops for a moment and looks up, and as another leaf falls, he catches it in his hand.
>
> Close-up on leaf, which is beginning to turn with autumn. ED's hand travels briefly around the edge of the leaf. He discards it and walks on.
>
> Long shot of ED in procession of women, which, it is now obvious, is heading for a big, modern office building. At the fountain in front of the building where one of the women tosses in a coin, the procession divides, and in this division there is something both comical and ceremonial. ED goes around the fountain in his part of the line and enters the building.
>
> (6-7)

Dickey accents Ed's relationship to the civilized, a circumstance that threatens Ed's masculinity. The women, costumed in "exaggerated hairdos and tasteless summer clothing," are used to represent society's artificiality. The series of adjectives—"unimaginative, commonplace, hopeless everyday"—employed to describe them provides a sharp contrast to the realm of masculine adventure that Lewis inhabits. Details ranging from the "stickiness" of Ed's jacket to the meditative moment of grasping the leaf, as well as his place in the "procession," suggest Ed's anxiety that he is wasting his life by becoming an automaton groveling for coins. When he enters the "antiseptic" building, he is told that "nothing interesting" has happened, and, glancing at advertising layouts, he experiences sensations of "disgust, boredom, fed-upness" and "simple ennui" that convey "futility, well-financed boredom, uselessness, unorganized tedium" (7-8).

However, in the midst of this suburban sterility Dickey interjects a moment used in later scenes to suggest Ed's desire for something beyond his present circumstance, as well as to indicate the illusory dimensions of his desires. When Ed enters the studio where the Kitt'n Britches advertisement is being shot, the young model

> manages to convey, through the way in which she gets up, that she is doing it for ED, and for no one else in the whole world. There should be no professionalism in this, no standard glamour, but just a simple and private act of giving.
>
> In close, very close on the girl's face, and then right into her right eye, where there is a curious-looking but unforgettable fleck of gold.
>
> (9)

Unlike the scene where he is walking to the office, here Ed is not just another body in a procession but the focus of someone's attention. In contrast to the secretarial horde, the model is pictured as genuine, with "no professionalism," "no artificiality." The "unforgettable fleck" in the woman's eye also establishes the moment's uniqueness for Ed, who responds to the robed woman's sexuality.

After several shots highlighting the model's eroticism and Ed's fascination with her, the script fades to a scene of "practical sexuality," Ed's and his wife's bedroom on the morning of the canoe trip. Dickey employs Martha's appearance and sex to further define Ed's emotional condition. In contrast to the model, "Martha moves towards" Ed in "a movement we can see is entirely habitual" and she "is definitely not glamorous," "her head wrapped in a towel" (10). As Martha reaches for a jar of vaseline, Ed grumbles.

ED:

> Do you always have to be so *surgical* about it? (But he likes this about her, and she knows it.)

MARTHA:

> (knowing this is something that she *can* do): What do you expect from an exsurgical nurse? Any nurse can tell you that sex is not romance. It's practice. Whatever helps, helps.

ED:

Ok. Ok. Do your thing.

MARTHA:

(after a short silence): Which way do you want it honey?

ED:

Why don't you turn over this time.

MARTHA:

Will do.

What follows now I will leave to the discretion and ingenuity of the director and the cameraman. There should be a confused but quite definite suggestion of sexual intercourse, not ecstatic but rhythmical and orderly. There might be a cut or two of MARTHA's bare back heaving and the sound of her muffled sexual voice coming from the pillow.

Out of this should come, as though called forth, an ectoplasmic image of the girl in the studio, and then a close-up of her face and then her eye, as she appears in Ed's mind. Through and beneath this might also still be suggested the heaving of Martha's back, as she dutifully labors.

(12)

Similar to the way that Dickey locates Ed between the adventurous Lewis and the more commonplace Bobby and Drew, he places Martha between the model and the secretarial mass. She is not "artificial," but neither is she exotic, a distinction stressed by her attitude towards sex and the description of the sex as "not ecstatic but rhythmical and orderly." But, like Dickey's use of Lewis, Bobby and Drew, the distinctions between the female characters are less revealing about them than about Ed. Ed's choice of having Martha "turn over" so that he cannot see her face during intercourse and his fantasy about the model as Martha "dutifully labors" reinforce how he feels about his own existence—he wants change—and foreshadow his eventual realization of Martha's value.

Having established Ed's psychological state, the scenes following the bedroom episode begin to illuminate the reversion motif. The characters (Ed and Lewis in one car with Drew and Bobby following in another) drive through suburbia, onto two-lane rural highways, and into the mountains, a sequence which Dickey uses to indicate "that they are moving towards more primitive people, wilder scenes" (18). As the cars climb up the narrow mountain roads, Ed, who has been "alternately sleeping, dozing, and waking," becomes increasingly aware of danger, a process described as "sinister but exciting," making Ed "wake up fully." When Lewis begins to espouse his survivalist philosophy, Ed "wakes up even more fully," indicating that, despite his cynicism, dormant aspects of his nature are beginning to stir:

ED:

Oh, I don't care anything about all that, Lewis. You ought to know that by now. I'm a get-through-the-day man. I'm not a great art director. I'm not a great archer. I like the way I live well enough.

LEWIS (CONFIDENTLY):

We'll see. (he pats the dashboard as though it represented all manmade things) You've had all that office furniture in front of you, all these years: desks and bookcases, and filing cabinets and the rest. You've been sitting in a chair that won't move. But when that river is under you, all that is going to change. There's nothing you do as vice-president of Emerson-Gentry that's going to make any difference at all, when the water starts to foam up. Then, it's not going to be what your title says you do, but what you end up doing. You know, *doing*. (19)

. . . . .

ED:

Oh, I don't know. If you wanted to, Lewis, you could go up in the hills and live right now. You could have all those same conditions. You could hunt. You could farm. You could suffer just as much as if they dropped the H-bomb. You could even start a colony.

LEWIS:

It's not the same. Don't you see? It would just be eccentric. Survival depends—well, it depends on *having* to survive. The kind of life I'm talking about depends on its being the last chance. The very last of all.

(21-22)

Lewis's claims intrigue and unsettle Ed, who goes on to question Lewis about life in the mountains. After their conversation Ed "shrugs, tries to relax again and doesn't succeed" because, in an indefinite manner, the survivalist scenarios that Lewis has posited, like his encounter with the model, speak to a fundamental part of his being. And, indeed, Lewis's observation that "when the river is under you, all that is going to change" is confirmed by an exhilarating first day of whitewater canoeing, as well as by the horrifying experiences of the second and third days in the wilderness.

Boorman's elimination of the screenplay's early scenes caused the suburbanites' encounters with the mountain people to lose subtlety and psychological impact. Though the screenplay and the movie employ the same basic cast of mountain characters, the film highlights these characters' grotesquery, whereas the screenplay *uses* their grotesquery to develop the reversion motif. As a result, in the film the implications for Ed's sense of himself and of his civilized existence are severely diminished. For instance, Dickey uses Ed's conversation with Lewis during the drive to suggest the nature of Ed's transformation in the rape scene, which Dickey asserts should "be filmed from" Ed's "point of view, with the camera reeling and tracking unexpectedly and violently" (63-64). After Lewis shoots the hillbilly with an arrow, Dickey calls for:

> Close-up of Ed as he rises, transfigured by terror and by the turn events have taken. He is beastlike with the power of having the gun. He wraps the string the gun uses for a trigger around his hand and swings the barrel to cover the woods and everything in it: to be able to blast whatever will come.
>
> Now we go back to a full shot of the man (the hillbilly that Lewis shot) as he falls to his knees and then to his side, rolling back and forth, spitting and gritting his teeth. Then he gets, with awful comic seriousness, back onto his feet again, this time with his lips red with blood and drooling saliva and blood. He turns towards the woods and takes a couple of halting steps toward them, and then seems to change his mind and turns back to ED, holding out one hand like an Old Testament prophet about to divulge a secret to one of the chosen.
>
> (66-67)

Lewis's claim that "survival . . . depends on *having* to survive" (22) resonates throughout the scene: the trip changes from a journey that enables Ed to fantasize about shedding suburban *angst* to a situation that genuinely awakens dormant energies, but at a substantial cost. The shock of Bobby's rape and of his own near-rape by truly primitive people "transfigures" Ed, making him "beastlike" by releasing his aggressive urges. Indeed, Dickey's description of the dying man moving towards Ed "like an Old Testament prophet" stresses that the suburbanite has been initiated into a new condition, for he has attained an awareness which will later enable him to kill.

The screenplay's early episodes also inform Dickey's treatment of the main characters after the canoers decide to conceal the hillbilly's body. Bobby and Drew, the two most contentedly civilized characters, are completely ineffectual in the wilderness, where civilized mores do not apply; Drew, who wants to call in the police and rely on the system, is murdered and Bobby is paralyzed by fear. By foregrounding Ed's initial differences from Bobby and Drew, as well as the changes in Ed that have taken place during the journey, the connection between Ed as a fantasizing, discontented city man and as a creature who is both predator and prey becomes apparent, a point suggested by Dickey's use of the model during the cliff climbing scene:

ED:

> (mumbling profoundly): What a view. *What* a view.
>
> He lies watching, and we watch with him. Nothing happens for a while. Then we might have a very brief, nearly subliminal image of the girl model in the studio: just her face, superimposed on the river. From the little we are able to tell, she is looking inviting and enigmatic, as mysterious as the river and the wilderness itself. Then she is gone, and we are not sure we have seen her at all.
>
> (97)

Dickey associates Ed's feeling towards the model with the river and the wilderness, implying that the same energy that caused Ed's discontent with social conformity feeds his instinctual urges. In the movie, Ed appears to be gambling out of desperation and succeeding through willpower and luck; there is no sense that his essential nature has changed. But in the screenplay, like the novel, Ed's experiences take on a mystical quality, a near-religious dimension, which is reflected by Dickey's instructions that Ed should appear "absolutely crucified on this cliff," and that when Ed reaches the top he seems "not completely mortal or even human" but "more Godlike, or demonic." The climb makes him "infinitely more sensitive to the *feel* of things than he's been before," resulting in "a profound sense of exaltation" (98).

Dickey's description of Ed as "Godlike, or demonic," and the terror and "exaltation" he senses, also reveal the paradoxical qualities of Ed's transformation. When Ed's mind merges ("I'm going to do just exactly what I would do if I was him.") with the hillbilly's, it becomes clear that he has shucked civilization's artificiality, but, again, with results that he never supposed. After Ed shoots the hillbilly through the throat with an arrow, the screenplay, unlike the movie, describes Ed hunting him down, following the "blood spoor like a dog would" (104). When he finds the body, he is "fascinated," as he takes his knife and issues a "low growl," indicating that he is on a predatory level. As he hovers over the dead man, "the audience cannot possibly know what Ed is going to do . . . he could do anything," but "shaken by his own incipient violence," a Beatles song and an advertising jingle pop into his mind, signaling the beginning of his return to a civilized condition (106).

The concluding scenes that Boorman excised return to the suburbs, starting with Ed's drive back from the mountains, a sequence that shows him moving "gradually back into his own territory, his own life." This continues until he pulls "into his own driveway," where he gets out of the car, "takes his knife and belt . . . slings them deep into the suburban woods behind the house, and takes Martha in his arms," indicating his awareness of his previous life's value (146). Dickey reinforces this through Martha's rebandaging of Ed's wounds:

ED:

> Is this what you call romance?

MARTHA:

> No. *I* never called it romance. I call it love, actually. It includes enemas and cleaning up after a man's vomit. (pointing to ED's side) Us wives and nurses know it includes *this*.

ED:

What about wine and roses?

MARTHA:

(smiling a tough, practical, loving smile): We get those, too.

ED:

Yes. That's the real thing I guess. *All* of it. (pause) Look, let me go see Drew's wife. Then I'm coming back to sleep for a week. Right with you. Right with you.

(149)

Ed's visit to Drew's wife underlines the tremendous cost of the knowledge Ed attains, but in contrast to Ed's fantasy about the model while he had sex with Martha, he now affirms her reality and importance. She is not a fantasy, but a "tough, practical, loving" part of his life, a realization brought about, at least subconsciously, by the rape, when he and Bobby were the victims of others' desires for sexual adventure. Indeed, the screenplay's closing scene, which shows Ed and Lewis shooting arrows at targets while Ed's son skis on the lake created by flooding the river, echoes Ed's assertion in the novel that the "river underlies, in one way or another, everything I do," a point the screenplay suggests by interjecting "an ear-splitting scream, a scream exactly like Bobby's in the forest when he was raped" into the work's closing moments (274-75, 151). The scream comes from Ed's son (though this is not immediately apparent), and "could be a terrible human cry of pain," but as the closing shot pulls away it becomes evident that the boy's cries are of "exultation," capturing the paradoxical nature of Ed's wilderness experience (151).

Dickey's screenplay, like his fiction and much of his poetry, reflects his tendency to explore situations that may positively enhance an individual's capacity for experience and/or lead to devastating consequences. Unlike Boorman's film, which concludes with Ed having a haunting nightmare, Dickey's concluding scenes focus on the ways that the weekend journey have altered Ed's relationship to himself and his surroundings. At the office Ed's creative energies are reignited, for he now works "busily . . . seems vigorous and very much in place," but he must live with the thought that Drew—"the best of us . . . the only decent one"—lies under the lake on which Ed's son skis (150).

Whether Dickey's version of the film would have been as successful as Boorman's depends on one's valuative criteria. Dickey's **Deliverance** would be much longer, not only because of the additions to the work's start and conclusion, but because scenes, such as Ed hunting the hillbilly, would be more detailed and complex. In an age of shortened attention spans, such demands would likely diminish the film's commercial appeal, as Boorman was no doubt aware. However, the original screenplay does more accurately reflect the Dickey ouevre, particularly its preoccupation with an individual's relationship to nature, humanity's potential for violence, and the connection between the instinctual and the imaginative, concerns that have made Dickey one of America's most compelling writers for four decades.

Works Cited

Dickey, James. *Deliverance.* Boston: Houghton, 1970.

———. *Deliverance* (Screenplay) with "Afterword." Carbondale: Southern Illinois UP, 1982.

Martin Bidney (essay date fall 1995)

SOURCE: Bidney, Martin. "Spirit-Bird, Bowshot, Water-Snake, Corpses, Cosmic Love: Reshaping the Coleridge Legacy in Dickey's *Deliverance*." *Papers on Language and Literature* 31, no. 4 (fall 1995): 389-405.

[*In the following essay, Bidney underscores the relationship between Dickey's* Deliverance *and the work of Samuel Taylor Coleridge.*]

> I'd like to be some sort of bird, a migratory seabird like a tern or a wandering albatross. But . . . I'll have to keep trying to do it, to die and fly, by words.
>
> —James Dickey, *Self-Interviews* 79

"I like to work my mind, such as it is," said James Dickey to Francis Roberts in 1968, "to see what I can get out of it and put into it. As John Livingston Lowes revealed in that wonderful book on Coleridge, *The Road to Xanadu,* if these things are in your mind, Lord knows what amalgams you can get out of it" (Baughman, *Voiced* 44). Two years later, in his 1970 novel **Deliverance,** Dickey demonstrated his capacity to produce not only a visionary "amalgam" of the sort he found laid out in Lowes but, more surprisingly, a richly suggestive pattern of allusions to the work of Coleridge himself. In what follows I would like to offer a brief "Road to *Deliverance,*" exploring that neo-Coleridgean pattern and its (re)visionary implications.

Dickey has elsewhere made clear his fondness for Coleridge. It has been noted (Baughman, *Understanding* 84) that the last line of the war poem **"Bread"** ("I ate the food I ne'er had eat" [Dickey, *Poems* 266]) varies "It ate the bread it ne'er had eat" from "The Rime of the Ancient Mariner" (l. 67 [text in *Poetical Works* 2: 186-209; hereafter *AM* referenced by line number]). And in 1965 Dickey expressed to an interviewer from *Eclipse* the ambition to produce in his own verse "a sense such as if you stumbled on the village idiot, and he began to mutter amazing things to you, and, like in 'The Ancient Mariner,' you could not help but hear . . ." (Baughman, *Voiced* 23).[1] ***Deliverance***, as the title of my essay implies, is firmly anchored in the thematic pattern of "Mariner." But "The Eolian Harp" and "Dejection" and "Kubla Khan" will be seen to play a role as well; Dickey has done many and varied things with the legacy of his wise but troubled mentor.

Daniel B. Marin, the one critic who refers explicitly to "Ancient Mariner" in the context of ***Deliverance***,[2] writes that the tone at the book's conclusion is "quiet and maybe even melancholy. I am reminded of Coleridge's Wedding Guest: 'A sadder and a wiser man / He rose the morrow morn,' though not exactly. Is it that the note of 'pure abandon' Dickey reaches so wonderfully in the poetry can never be sung here in the darklight, in the 'darkness visible' of ***Deliverance?***" (Calhoun 116-17). My own feeling about the contrast between the endings of "Mariner" and ***Deliverance*** is rather the opposite of Marin's: I find Dickey more disposed to conclude on a note of comradely reassurance. Coleridge's aged sailor must endlessly retell the tale of his crime in an immortal repetition compulsion that is rightly styled "Life-in-Death" (*AM* 193). By contrast, Dickey's narrator Ed Gentry is not possessed by the vision of his narrative; the story is *his* possession—not something he owns up to guiltily, but something he owns proudly: "The river and everything I remembered about it became a possession to me, a personal, private possession, as nothing else in my life ever had. Now it ran nowhere but in my head, but there it ran as though immortally" (***Deliverance*** [hereafter ***D***] 281).

This is no Life-in-Death but a far pleasanter kind of immortality. Ed Gentry tells us that his hero-friend, Medlock Lewis—likewise no guilt-ridden intrusive presence but comfortably called "a human being, and a good one"—refers to Ed confidentially as "U. C., which means—to him and me—'Unorganized Crime,' and this has become a kind of minor conversation piece at parties, and at lunch in the city with strangers" (***D*** 283). Unorganized Crime of this smoothed-over sort, when juxtaposed to the Mariner's paranoid guilt obsession, seems a fraternal joke, or a whimsical authorial wink at the visionary tradition: "U. C." = "You (and I) *see*."

Yet the sad wisdom invoked by Marin is deep-rooted in Dickey's book as well; indeed, the entire conflictual structure of the work is Coleridgean. Every reader of "Mariner" feels the unresolved tension between the explicit transcendent message of cosmic love and the punishing prophetic burden of the driven wanderer who is forced to preach it, the difficulty of separating divine revelation from cruel fate, heavenly truth from purgatorial reality. Dickey's two epigraphs epitomize a similar unresolved tension between metaphysical meaning and the sense of ungovernable chaos, as the biblical Obadiah reveals a meaningful moral order ("The pride of thine heart hath deceived thee") while the philosopher Georges Bataille blames the inescapable conditions of human life itself for our frustrations ("Il existe à la base de la vie humaine, un principe d'insuffisance").

This is the same tension or conflict that generally divides analyses of Dickey's book into two groups. Some critical accounts of ***Deliverance*** have emphasized the heartening messages apparently conveyed: "penetrating insights into the political values forged by the American experience" (Redenius 286), "the alleviation of fears associated with the omnipotence of thought by making restitution for hostile, destructive wishes" (Hamilton 404), or the "discovery, *in extremis*, that the sole means of controlling anxiety is through the imposition of aesthetic order" and "the maintenance of civilized values" (Glenday 156-57). Other analyses have just as emphatically portrayed the overwhelming power of evil or "darkness visible" in ***Deliverance***—the idea that the narrator's "being-beyond-himself is the result of an act of transgression" (Tschachler 87), or the analogous potentials for evil revealed in both heroes *and* villains ("The 'countrified jerk' in the city who wants a girl's buttocks in his ad is a part of Ed himself, and his domain is deep in Ed's unconscious"; "The cat that claws the girl's panties in Ed's dream and the owl that rips the canvas of Ed's tent anticipate the bestial man who commands Bobby to 'drop them panties'" in the scene of sexual violence [Endel 622]).[3]

What the pattern of Coleridgean allusion accomplishes is to dramatize all these conflicting tendencies and thereby to heighten the visionary drama of ***Deliverance***. We shall see that here, as in "Mariner," images of spirit-like bird and flashing water-snake each embody an ambivalence; juxtaposed, they create still further conflict. The motifs of multiple corpses and cosmic love, taken from Coleridge's enigmatic epos of terror and transcendence, are enlisted in the service of Dickey's equally vivid moral-metaphysical *chiaroscuro*. Additional themes—dulcimer and sacred circle from "Kubla Khan," wind-played musical instrument and dancing diamonds on the main from "The Eolian Harp," as well as the motifs of rottenness, water tracks, angels, firewater unity and the moving moon from "Mariner"—give ***Deliverance*** a pervasively Coleridgean ambiance and make it a major neo-Romantic re-envisioning and revision.

"Revision" is the key word here, for it is not only the reassuring tonality of the ending that (as I have suggested) distinguishes ***Deliverance*** from "Mariner." Rather, this changed conclusion indicates a noticeable shift in concern—from the psychodynamics of persecution to the ambivalences central to (human) nature. Only through the extremely risky unleashing of a desire for violent victory does Ed attain the transcendent insights of pantheistic oneness. As Heinz Tschachler has shown, this is a troublesome dialectic traceable in part to Georges Bataille: in *Deliverance* as in the thinking of Bataille, only when the "principle of individuation" is put at risk (as a result of the individual's risking his life) are hidden continuities exposed to view and feelings of sacred merger briefly attainable (Tschachler 83-85). By strategic alterations and re-orchestration of Coleridgean motifs Dickey makes this thesis vivid and its *exemplum* ineffaceably present to the imagination.

As Lewis, with evangelizing fervor, outlines to Ed his project for a canoeing venture, the latter worries at one point that "he's going to turn this into . . . A lesson. A Moral" (*D* 14); here Ed shows the same discomfort with "morals" that Coleridge showed when, responding to Anna Barbauld's complaint that "Ancient Mariner" lacked a moral, the poet famously countered that it had "too much" of one (*Table Talk* 31 May 1830 in *Works* 4:324). Ed buys into the trip, mainly out of boredom induced by routine; when his wife asks, "Is it my fault?" he says no but thinks to himself that "it partly was, just as it's any woman's fault who represents normalcy" (*D* 37). Ed likes his wife well enough; it's just that married life has the fault of being normal: in "Mariner" the Wedding Guest was obliged to direct his imaginative attention to something a good deal less normal than weddings, and in *Deliverance* the same priority is given to an extraordinary experience promised by a man. Lewis's surname, "Medlock," has in fact a striking resemblance to "wedlock," but what Lewis offers in proposing his expedition for a group of four men is a venture in platonic male bonding, a *m*ale adventure trip that will temporarily replace the routine life Ed leads in w*edlock* (an idea hideously parodied, of course, in the eventual rape committed by the rural stranger). One may find a bit of misogyny in this humdrum picture of marriage, but if so, it is a problem Dickey shares with Coleridge.

The chief attraction of the trip for Ed, as sportsman, is not canoeing but hunting with a bow; only in the film version is a crossbow used, certainly an additional contribution to "Mariner" thematics.[4] Allusions to the motif of the albatross are also oblique, but they are multiple, varied, and ingenious. The *alb*-syllable, an etymon for the whiteness of the white bird, appears, along with the birdlike motif of music, when the "*alb*ino boy" Lonnie plays banjo in a duet of magical beauty with Ed's and Lewis's co-traveler Drew (*D* 68). Playing with Lonnie makes even the back of Drew's neck express "sheer joy" (*D* 69): the albino conveys a sudden and profound inspiration, like that suggested by Coleridge's quasi-supernatural white bird.[5] Each of the albino's eyes is singular in its strange independence, as they focus in different directions; soon afterwards, another singular eye, the "glazed" and "half-open" eye of a chicken's head, appears to the travelers in a stagnant patch of river downstream from the poultry plant (*D* 86). So even if no albatross is killed in *Deliverance,* the singular eye of the bird-related albino appears to us soon in a metamorphosed form of death.

Bird allusions abound in the first part of *Deliverance*; for example, a certain Mr. Holley, Ed's subordinate in his design consulting firm, turns "one of Braque's birds into a Pegasus" (*D* 26), and Lewis Medlock himself rather strikingly resembles a bird, with his "face like a hawk," beakish "long-nosed" profile, and "whitish patch up toward the crown of his head" (*D* 20). C. Hines Edwards, Jr. has specifically studied the prominent and recurrent owl-theme, noting the contrasts it embodies: the owl is at once bird "of prey" and "bird of wisdom," conventionally an "ill omen" and yet used in the book to suggest both nature and—in the form of the owl-shaped wind chime—civilization (Edwards 96-97).

But two Coleridgean insights need to be added to this. First, the repeated mention of the "ringing of the owl on the other birds, in Martha's wind-toy at home" (*D* 269—and see *D* 35) brings the bird motif together with the Aeolian harp motif, betokening Coleridgean inspiration: wind chimes are modern suburbia's answer to the Aeolian harp. Second, the owl that repeatedly visits Ed during the night—and whose frightening "stony toe" Ed even learns to touch without fear—resembles a familiar spirit, a haunting presence familiar yet uncanny in its incessant departures and returns: "All night the owl kept coming back to hunt from the top of the tent" (*D* 98), just as the Coleridgean albatross, "every day, for food or play, / Came to the mariner's hollo!" (*AM* 73-74). In its quasi-supernatural uncanniness, in its friendly association with the wind-generated music favored by Coleridge, and in its ambivalent implications, Dickey's owl-symbol, like the musical albino, shares the enigmatic nature of the Coleridgean Mariner's albatross. Even in its size the owl is exceptional, closer to the ungainly dimensions of the Coleridgean bird—a "big night bird—surely it was very big, from the size of the nails and feet" (*D* 97).

The ambivalent implications of both albatross and owl are in part covert: the Mariner has no way of suspecting that if he kills the albatross 200 sailors' deaths will result; and Ed, who spends the night pleasantly imagining the owl's hunting feats on its various flights, does not imagine that the huge "talons" which had so terrifyingly punctured the roof of his tent (*D* 97) are foreshadowings of the *lex talionis,* the pitiless rule of retribution or Law of the Claw that will govern the latter part of the men's violent adventure. But in both the Coleridge and Dickey narratives, an atmosphere of nausea is quickly induced by the recurrent use of the theme of "rot" as the tales proceed. After the Mariner kills the bird, "The very deep did rot: O Christ! / That ever this should be!" (*AM* 123-24). After the rural villain commits his rape of Bobby, the adventurers find themselves "by a sump of some kind, a blue-black seepage of rotten water," and when Lewis kills the rapist and tries to bury the body, the earth has turned into sheer rot: "There was no earth; it was all leaves and rotten stuff. It had the smell of generations of mould" (*D* 141-42). In both stories, intimations of unfathomably deep corruption overwhelm the soul and body.

Yet it is not long before the moon provides, for both Coleridge's and Dickey's protagonists, a moving emblem of visionary hope. Life-in-Death has won the Mariner's soul; Drew has been murdered by the rapist's cohort. Yet the Mariner, at least, has triumphed over Death itself; and Lewis and Ed have worked out their plans for both defense and retribution—they, too, can somehow glory in "pure survival" (*D* 167). The moon, betokening hope, is evoked with strikingly similar language in the two works. Coleridge's marginal annotations describe a "silent *joy*" in the scene where "The moving Moon *went up* the sky, / And no where did abide: / Softly she *was going up* . . ." (*AM* 263-65; emphases added). And Ed tells us his "heart expanded with *joy*" as he watched while "the moon *was going up and up* . . ." (*D* 167; emphases added). It will only take another moment, in both narratives, for the climactic water-snake epiphany to arise in moonlit glory.

Let us look first at the Coleridgean precedent, which Dickey will vary in a composite epiphany consisting of four brief episodes. In the light of the just-ascended moon, says the Mariner,

> I watched the water-snakes:
> They moved in tracks of shining white,
> And when they reared, the elfish light
> Fell off in hoary flakes.
> . . . . .
> They coiled and swam; and every track
> Was a flash of golden fire.
> O happy living things! no tongue
> Their beauty might declare:
> A spring of love gushed from my heart,
> And I blessed them unaware. . . .
>
> (*AM* 273-76, 280-85)

Traditionally cursed, the seeming symbol of evil is revealed as in its unfamiliar way wholly divine. Serpentine horrors can now be seen as inseparable from the life-power, the fertility and wisdom and immortality, that mythic traditions world-wide have rightly credited to the coiled *ouroboros*.

In Dickey's four-phase moonlit epiphany all the appearances of the water-snake are metaphoric. But they are overpoweringly real. And note the evocative borrowings already in phase one:

> Despite everything, I looked down. The river had spread flat and *filled with moonlight*. It took up the whole of space under me, bearing in the center of itself a long *coiling image of light*, a chill, bending *flame*. I must have been seventy-five or a hundred feet above it, hanging poised over some kind of inescapable glory, a bright pit.
>
> (*D* 169; emphases added)

Coleridge's "fire" is Dickey's "flame"; the Mariner's snakes that flashingly "coiled" have become Ed's "coiling image of light"; moonlight fills the water in both scenes. Dickey wants no loss of symbolic ambivalence in the transfer: he insists on the image of the snaky abyss in his "bright pit." Inescapable glory is wedded to acceptance of the lowest.

In fact, a few pages later the light spreads out on the water "eternally, the moon so huge on it that it hurt the eyes" (*D* 178), just as the Mariner speaks soon afterward of the blinding lightning descending from moon-level as "a river steep and wide" (*AM* 326). And when "angelic spirits" (*AM* marg. to 346) come down instantly to enter the bodies of the dead and one of these spirits even helps the Mariner as they pull together "at one rope" (*AM* 343), a precedent is set for a vivid metaphoric wording in Dickey's analogous multiphase epiphany: "The thought struck me with my full adrenaline supply, all hitting the veins at once. Angelic. Angelic. Is that what it means? It very likely does. And I have a lot of nylon rope . . ." (*D* 176). Coleridge writes of water-snakes and heavenly angels in the literal language of suspended disbelief, of high gothic dreamwork; Dickey's snakes and angels are metaphoric, observing the conventions of lyrical-psychological prose. But it is still visionary prose—vatic, and Coleridgean.

The third phase of the metaphoric water-snake epiphany returns to Coleridge's original depiction of the snakes:

> What a view, I said again. The river was *blank* and *mindless* with beauty. It was the most glorious thing I have ever seen. But it was not seeing, really. For once it was not just seeing. It was beholding. I *beheld* the river in its icy pit of brightness, in its far-below sound and *indifference*, in its *large coil* and *tiny points and flashes of the moon*, in its *long sinuous form*, in its *uncomprehending* consequence.
>
> (*D* 177; emphases added, except for "beheld," italicized by Dickey)

Words like "mindless" and "indifference" and "uncomprehending" recall the Mariner's blessing the snakes "unaware"; the "large coil" and "long sinuous form" make the serpent-image gloriously present in an emphatically Coleridgean way; the "tiny points and flashes of the moon" on the water clearly recall the "hoary flakes" of moonlight and the multiform "flash" of reflected moon-fire from Coleridge's sacred scene. Ed's experience is a visionary triumph—an act of not mere seeing but beholding—in itself. But reading it with Coleridge in mind heightens its vibrancy and reveals it as a worthy homage to a suitably complex and many-sided master.

The fourth and final phase of the neo-Coleridgean epiphany repeats and underlines the main motifs—awe, the life-force, the moon, the metaphoric snake, the visionary light:

> Fear and a kind of enormous *moon-blazing sexuality* lifted me, millimeter by millimeter. . . . I looked for a slice of gold . . . in the river . . . something lovable, in the *huge serpent-shape of light.*
>
> Above me the darks changed, and in one of them was a star. On both sides of that small light the rocks went on up, black and solid as ever, but *their power was broken.* . . .
>
> I was crying. What reason? There was not any, for I was really not ashamed or terrified; I was just there. . . . Lord, Lord. The river hazed and danced into the sparkle of my eyelashes, the more wonderful for being unbearable.
>
> (***D*** 182-83; emphases added)

Ed's mysterious sense that the "power" of the rocks was "broken" by the visionary light makes us remember how "The spell begins to break" in Coleridge's marginal annotation to the line, after the water-snake epiphany, in which the Mariner finds himself finally able again to worship (*AM* marginalia to 288). "That selfsame moment I could pray," says the Mariner—the precedent for Ed's joyous, awed outcry, "Lord, Lord." The fact that the river "hazed and *danced* into the *sparkle*" of [Ed's] *eyelashes*" (emphases added) alludes to yet another epiphanic scene: recall the speaker in "The Eolian Harp," who stretches his limbs at noon "Whilst through my half-clos'd *eyelids* I behold / The sunbeams *dance,* like *diamonds,* on the main" ("The Eolian Harp" 36-37; emphases added). Dickey has conflated two scenarios of Coleridgean glory.

Coleridgean revelation also sheds a closely related light on Ed's foolhardy but heroic adventurer-mentor, Lewis Medlock. For all his miscalculations and improvidence, Medlock is deemed worthy of transfiguration for a moment in a clever variant of the Mariner's water-snake reverie. We remember that when the water-snakes glided through the moonlit waves, "every track / Was a flash of golden fire": the tracks of the glorious creatures seem wondrously to unite the incompatible elements of fire and water. The same word, "track," the same motif of tracks in the water, and the same quasi-miraculous union of the fiery and the liquid ("red" for fire and "blue" for water) are motifs reworked in Ed's wonderstruck portrait of his mentor:

> Everything he had done for himself for years paid off as he stood there in his *tracks in the water.* I could tell by the way he glanced at me; the payoff was in my eyes. . . . The muscles were bound up in him smoothly, and when he moved, the veins in the moving part would surface. If you looked at him that way, he seemed made out of well-matched *red*-brown chunks wrapped in *blue* wire.
>
> (***D*** 110; emphases added)

The "Mariner" variation is ingenious, unobtrusive, and effective. In the vivid and often coarse tale that constitutes ***Deliverance,*** Dickey has lost none of the delicate allusive subtlety that distinguishes him as lyric poet.

When Coleridge somewhat perversely insisted to Mrs. Barbauld that "Ancient Mariner" had too much of a moral—that it "ought to have had no more moral than the Arabian Nights' tale" of the merchant who, during a snack, tosses a nutshell aside and is accused of murder because a genie claims the shell has put out the eye of the genie's son (*Works* 4:324)—Coleridge was mistaken. The cosmic love moral, as we may call it—

> He prayeth well, who loveth well
> Both man and bird and beast.
>
> He prayeth best, who loveth best
> All things both great and small;
> For the dear God who loveth us,
> He made and loveth all
>
> (*AM* 612-17)

—is crucial to the poem's enduring fascination, which lies precisely in the tension between the Mariner's moment of transcendence and the immense, absurdly disproportionate price he has to pay for it. Such paradoxes afflict and bless and puzzle all of us. James Dickey's ***Deliverance*** likewise takes account of them, building on Coleridge's insights, not on his arbitrary or irked disclaimers.

There are many cosmic love or universal empathy passages in Dickey's narrative, suitably presented in the context of the four-phase water-snake epiphany: for example, as he moves up the steep escarpment, Ed begins, as it were, to "make love to the cliff"; as he inches upward he moves "with the most intimate motions of my body, motions I had never dared use with Martha, or with any other human woman" (***D*** 182-83).[6] But the central, most striking passage of paradoxical empathy is the one in which Ed opens up to a strange transpersonal oneness with his enemy, precisely the man on whom he will wreak revenge with a bowshot for the murder of Drew:

> I had thought so long and hard about him that to this day I still believe I felt, in the moonlight, our minds fuse. It was not that I felt myself turning evil, but that an enormous physical indifference, as vast as the whole abyss of light at my feet, came to me: an indifference not only to the other man's body scrambling and kicking on the ground with an arrow through it, but also to mine. If Lewis had not shot his companion, he and I would have made a kind of love, painful and terrifying to me, in some dreadful way pleasurable to him, but we would have been together in the flesh, there on the floor of the woods, and it was strange to think of it.
>
> (***D*** 186)

This cosmic empathy feeling recurs repeatedly in ever-changing forms: a few pages later we read, for example,

The needles were filling slowly with the beginnings of daylight, and the tree began to flow softly, shining the frail light held by the needles inward on me, and I felt as though I were giving it back outward.

(*D* 193)[7]

Even after he has killed the offender, Ed feels that "His brain and mine unlocked and fell apart, and in a way I was sorry to see it go. I never had thought with another man's mind on matters of life and death, and would never think that way again" (*D* 205). The precedent for these seemingly inconceivable unities disclosed in existential crisis may be found in "Mariner," but the Coleridgean revelation is elaborated and multiply varied in **Deliverance.**

It would not be easy—to say the least of it—for Ed "to get used to the idea that I had buried three men [the rapist killed by Lewis, then Drew, and finally Drew's murderer] in two days, and that I had killed one of them" (*D* 237). But the neo-Coleridgean fascination of Ed's narrative would not exert its hypnotic force without both of the factors that constitute the book's reason-challenging antinomy, its tragic enlightenment: multiple corpses *and* cosmic empathy; deadly peril and lifegiving love—a quasi-mystical or pantheist transcendence that arises from an existential test, pushing aside the principle of individuation to reveal unimaginable continuities, unsuspected and not always gratifying oneness.

It is in the light of this antinomy, finally, that we should read the "Kubla Khan" and "Dejection" allusions in the earlier part of **Deliverance**—which I have postponed for separate treatment for that reason. These unmistakable allusions begin when Lewis tries to interest Ed in the folkloric riches of mountain music: "there are songs in those hills that collectors have never put on tape. And I've seen one family with a dulcimer" (*D* 50). "If those people in the hills," retorts Ed skeptically, "the ones with the folk songs and *dulcimers,* came out of the hills and led us all toward *a new heaven and a new earth,* it would not make a particle of difference to me" (*D* 50; emphases added). In this wittily allusive interchange we not only hear an echo of Coleridge's "damsel with a dulcimer" ("Kubla Khan" 37) but also an ironic reference to the "new Earth and new Heaven" which Imagination gives us by "wedding Nature to us" ("Dejection: An Ode" 68-69)—as it does when Aeolian harps (which are wind-dulcimers, emblems of the harmonious unity of spirit/breath and world) function properly.

The Coleridgean irony grows into a dreadful grotesquerie after the villainous rapist, mortally wounded by Lewis's avenging arrow, goes into "convulsions" that resemble the visionary seizure of the shaman-figure depicted in "Kubla Khan":

> He took a couple of strides toward the woods and then seemed to change his mind and *danced* back to me, *lurching* and clog-stepping in a *secret circle.* He held out a hand to me, like a *prophet.* . . .

(*D* 125; emphases added)

The verb "danced" and the "secret circle" make us think of Coleridge's "Weave a circle round him thrice"—a circle woven precisely through ritual dance; the "lurching" and "convulsions" of the dizzily dancing victim recall the "flashing eyes and floating hair" of the shamanistic seer in "Kubla Khan," his being possessed in a state of seizure, a fit—precisely the mad ecstasy of a "prophet," as Dickey says (see "Kubla Khan" 51, 50). All this relates with horrific irony but all-too-evident appropriateness—via the mountain "dulcimer" motif—to the evil archetype of the "demon-lover" ("Kubla Khan" 16).

Yet there is a Coleridgean tragic tenderness, as well, in Dickey's final symbolic depiction of the criminal-victim's farewell: "He held out a hand to me, like a prophet. . . ." In a context of Coleridgean allusion, the word "prophecy" refers to no specific predictions or forecasts; rather, it points to some transcendent insight or awareness of ultimate value: here, the prophetic insight acquired—even by a bestial villain—at the threshold of death is unspoken, perhaps unspeakable. The Ancient Mariner, too, was a prophet, though a reluctant one, like Jonah, or like Paul. It may, indeed, be best to end our comparative journey with this final instance of an epitomizing symbol of deep kinships that can never be fully articulated, a symbolic gesture that serves as testimony to a neo-Coleridgean seed of enlightenment arising from crisis and trial, a "bright pit."

Notes

1. Interestingly, in Dickey's "The Eye-Beaters," "The dramatic situation is indicated in the first of the marginalia of the poem (a technique recalling 'The Rime of the Ancient Mariner,' by Coleridge)" (Calhoun and Will 96).

2. Though I find no Coleridgean studies of *Deliverance,* a Wordsworthian one is Guttenberg *passim.* Guttenberg, however, does not adduce specific detailed verbal allusions to Wordsworth as I have attempted to do for Coleridge; such minute particulars are important if one wishes to establish a pattern of influence and appropriation. I also think Coleridge's gothic dream-poem is more relevant than Wordsworth to the ambivalences in Dickey's narrative; as important as the "pattern of redemption" are the terrors, the grotesqueness, the psychological price.

3. Another useful pair of complementary contrasts is that between Robert Armour's depiction of the four men in *Deliverance* as archetypical American Adams (after the model of the well-known book

by R. W. B. Lewis—see Armour *passim*) and Ronald Schmitt's presentation of the men as ironic reflections on Joseph Campbell's four hero-types, with which Dickey was demonstrably familiar: the hero as warrior, lover, emperor/tyrant, and redeemer/saint (Schmitt 10).

4. It is worth noting here that in R. Barton Palmer's analysis of both book and film, the latter appears significantly more "pessimistic" (Palmer 10).

5. It bears emphasizing that there is nothing merely casual or contingent in Dickey's choice of an *albino* as emblem of inspiration; he calls the symbol to our minds again later in the adventure: "I thought of Drew and the albino boy picking and singing in the filling station" (*D* 159). Apropos of specifically musical inspiration, John Jolly calls attention to some fascinating phrasings that suggest Drew's own typological relation to Orpheus (Jolly 103-05 and *passim*).

6. Foust's phenomenological essay on the primacy of touch in *Deliverance* is valuable (*passim*), but his polemic against any idea of Romanticist "merger" (see especially 200-03) as in any respect relevant to the novel is unjustified. A subjective experience of imaginative merger may be phenomenologically described; Foust's approach and the neo-Coleridgean one employed in my essay are quite compatible.

7. The dizzying paradoxicality of the experience, however, includes not only Ed's unity with the killer-enemy but a kind of artistic pride. When Ed, describing how he felt when aiming his bow, says, "We were closed together, and the feeling of a peculiar kind of intimacy increased, for he was shut within a frame within a frame, all of my making" (*D* 197) one feels that Ed, as artist (he is an advertising designer by profession), savors the power and pleasure of framing some truly fearful symmetry. The Ancient Mariner, of course, is prophet of God's love, a teacher of empathy, but as compulsive narrator he is also self-obsessed, a trapped, obsessive visionary narcissist. Other modern American prose refashioners of "Ancient Mariner" (Sherwood Anderson, Harold Brodkey) have chosen to intensify and grotesquely parody this component in the Coleridgean protagonist's mentality (see Bidney 1990, 1994). Dickey is exceptional in not playing up the aspect of narcissism.

Works Cited

"An Interview with James Dickey." *Eclipse* 5 (1965-66): 5-20. Rpt. Ronald Baughman, ed. *The Voiced Connections of James Dickey: Interviews and Conversations.* Columbia: U of South Carolina P, 1989, 12-27.

Armour, Robert. "*Deliverance*: Four Variations on the American Adam." *Literature/Film Quarterly* 1 (1973): 280-85.

Baughman, Ronald. *Understanding James Dickey.* Columbia: U of South Carolina P, 1985.

———, ed. *The Voiced Connections of James Dickey: Interviews and Conversations.* Columbia: U of South Carolina P, 1989.

Bidney, Martin. "An Unreliable Modern 'Mariner': Rewriting Coleridge in Harold Brodkey's 'The State of Grace.'" *Studies in Short Fiction* 31 (1994): 47-55.

———. "Refashioning Coleridge's Supernatural Trilogy: Sherwood Anderson's 'A Man of Ideas' and 'Respectability.'" *Studies in Short Fiction* 27 (1990): 221-35.

Calhoun, Richard J., ed. *James Dickey: The Expansive Imagination.* Deland, FL: Everett/Edwards, 1973.

Calhoun, Richard J. and Robert W. Hill. *James Dickey.* Boston: Hall, 1983.

Coleridge, Samuel Taylor. *The Complete Poetical Works of Samuel Taylor Coleridge.* 2 vols. Volume I: Poetry. Ed. E. H. Coleridge. Oxford: Oxford UP, 1912.

———. *Complete Works of Samuel Taylor Coleridge.* 7 vols. New York: Harper, 1856. Dickey, James. *Deliverance.* Boston: Houghton, 1970.

———. *Poems 1957-1967.* New York: Macmillan, 1958.

———. *Self-Interviews.* Recorded and ed. Barbara and James Reiss. New York: Dell, 1970.

Edwards, C. Hines, Jr. "Dickey's *Deliverance*: The Owl and the Eye." *Critique: Studies in Modern Fiction* 15 (1973): 95-101.

Endel, Peggy Goodman. "Dickey, Dante, and the Demonic: Reassessing *Deliverance*." *American Literature* 60 (1988): 611-24.

Foust, R. E. "*Tactus Eruditus*: Phenomenology as Method and Meaning of James Dickey's *Deliverance.*" *Studies in American Fiction* 9 (1981): 199-216.

Glenday, Michael K. "*Deliverance* and the Aesthetics of Survival." *American Literature* 56 (1984): 149-61.

Guttenberg, Barnett. "The Pattern of Redemption in Dickey's *Deliverance*." *Critique: Studies in Modern Fiction* 18 (1977): 83-91.

Hamilton, James W. "James Dickey's *Deliverance*: Midlife and the Creative Process." *American Imago* 38.4 (1981): 389-405.

Jolly, John. "Drew Ballinger as 'Sacrificial God' in James Dickey's *Deliverance*." *The South Carolina Review* 17 (1985): 102-08.

Marin, Daniel B. "James Dickey's *Deliverance*: Darkness Visible." In Richard J. Calhoun, ed. *James Dickey: The Expansive Imagination.* Deland FL: Everett/Edwards, 1973, 105-17.

Palmer, R. Barton. "Narration, Text, Intertext: The Two Versions of *Deliverance*." *The James Dickey Newsletter* 2.2 (1986): 1-11.

Redenius, Charles M. "Recreating the Social Contract: James Dickey's *Deliverance*." *The Canadian Review of American Studies* 17 (1986): 285-99.

Roberts, Francis. "James Dickey: An Interview." *Per/Se* 3 (1968): 8-12. Rpt. Ronald Baughman, ed. *The Voiced Connections of James Dickey: Interviews and Conversations.* Columbia: U of South Carolina P, 1989, 41-49.

Schmitt, Ronald. "Transformations of the Hero in James Dickey's *Deliverance*." *The James Dickey Newsletter* 8 (1991): 9-16.

Tschachler, Heinz. "*Un principe d'insuffisance*: Dickey's Dialogue with Bataille." *Mosaic* 20 (1987): 81-93.

Ihab Hassan (essay date 1995)

SOURCE: Hassan, Ihab. "The Spirit of Quest in Contemporary American Letters." In *Rumors of Change: Essays of Five Decades,* pp. 187-207. Tuscaloosa: University of Alabama Press, 1995.

[*In the following excerpt, Hassan contrasts the two main characters—Ed and Lewis—in Dickey's novel* Deliverance.]

In contrast to Bellow's and Mailer's fictions, James Dickey's ***Deliverance*** (1970) seems less a quest than a brutal tale of survival. The reader may wonder: deliverance from what? From moral complacencies, social pieties, perhaps from civilization itself? The clues are scattered, and in one place they become nearly explicit. Making love to his wife on the morning of his fateful adventure, the narrator, Ed Gentry, imagines—he is on the whole steady, unimaginative—the golden eye of a girl, a studio model: "The gold eye shone, not with the practicality of sex, so necessary to its survival, but the promise of it that promised other things, another life, deliverance." Another life, deliverance: there lies the book's knot, which links its two heroes, Ed Gentry and Lewis Medlock, doubles.

Ed—all are called by their first names—is practical and forthright, given to the task at hand; Lewis is visionary. Lewis seeks immortality and learns finally to settle for death. In the interim, he trains himself implacably, trains his instincts, will, and powerful body, to survive an atomic holocaust in the Georgia woods. He insists on turning the canoe trip of four urban businessmen into a moral, a life principle, a way, a provocation to everything Western civilization has achieved in three thousand years. He wants to recover something absolutely essential and in doing so to perform some superhuman feat that beggars eternity. But Lewis breaks his leg early on the trip—again that wound—and Ed pulls the survivors through after two murders and one death by drowning.

The scene is perfectly set for the encounter between nature and civilization, instinct and law, within the West itself. An entire region of the north Georgia wilderness is about to drown, turned into a serviceable lake. The Cahulawassee River, with its horrendously beautiful whitewater rapids, must vanish. Ageless hillbilly cemeteries must be moved to higher ground. Marinas and real estate developments will appear on the dammed lake. On the eve of their departure, the four white, married, middle-class men pore over a colored map of the region, intuiting the secret harmonies of the land, thinking that, henceforth, a fragment of the American wilderness will survive only in archives and the failing memories of old woodsmen.

Excepting Lewis, though, these businessmen are unfit to venture; they have learned to meet existence mainly on legal, domestic, or social terms. Still, they sense obscurely an alternative to their humdrum lives. "Up yonder," Lewis tells them, life demands to be taken on other terms, as they discover in scene after harrowing scene, in encounters with the stupendous force of nature (the rapids) and malevolence of man (hillbilly outlaws). Yet, too, they experience a strange happiness at the heart of violence. Three of them survive, irrevocably altered.

Dickey's novel is a masterpiece in the poetry of action and menace. Relentlessly, it renders, in a prose at once tight, elusive, and earthy, the atavism and terror of two autumn days in the Georgia woods. The book spares no detail in the struggle of life for itself. But the book also reveals instants of subtle intimacy, moments of pure being. Having climbed, with bare hands, the sheer face of a gorge to kill a man at daybreak, Ed suddenly exclaims:

> What a view. *What* a view. But I had my eyes closed. The river was running in my mind, and I raised my lids and saw exactly what had been the image of my thought. For a second I did not know what I was seeing and what I was imagining; there was such an utter sameness that it didn't matter; both were the river. It spread there eternally, the moon so huge on it that it hurt the eyes, and the mind, too, flinched like an eye. What? I said. Where? There was nowhere but here. Who, though? Unknown. Where can I start? . . . What a view I said again. The river was blank and mindless with beauty. It was the most glorious thing I had ever

seen. But it was not seeing, really. For once it was not just seeing. It was beholding. I *beheld* the river in its icy pit of brightness, in its far-below sound and indifference, in its large coil and tiny points and flashes of the moon, in its long sinuous form, in its uncomprehending consequence. What was there?

Perhaps this is the selflessness of every mountaineer, every adventurer, at his moment of truth, healing all wounds.

Dickey prefixes an epitaph from Georges Bataille that proposes a "principle of insufficiency" at the base of human existence. The radical lack may underlie all life as perceived by human beings. Something is always buried, hidden, lost to us: murdered bodies lying under forest leaves, the forest itself flooded beneath a lake, hillbillies invisible, colonized within their own state, some part of our own nature, concealed and irreclaimable. Ed and Lewis—Ed becomes Lewis—manage to discover this perilous part of existence and manage through great pain to reclaim it. But they must also face the ordinary world again, which Ed sees, at the end, in the image of a policeman: "When we reached town [the policeman] went into a cafe and made a couple of calls. It frightened me some to watch him talk through the tripled glass—windshield, plate glass, and phone booth—for it made me feel caught in the whole vast, inexorable web of modern communication." The feeling passes, for Ed possesses the river permanently: "Now it ran nowhere but in my head, but there it ran as though immortally." So ends his quest.

Keen Butterworth (essay date spring 1996)

SOURCE: Butterworth, Keen. "The Savage Mind: James Dickey's *Deliverance*." *Southern Literary Journal* 28, no. 2 (spring 1996): 69-78.

[*In the following essay, Butterworth provides an interpretation of the psychological aspects of* Deliverance.]

On the dust jacket of the first edition of James Dickey's ***Deliverance*** an eye peers out through a surrounding cluster of hemlock fronds. It is not the poison hemlock shrub of Socrates, but the benign water-loving hemlock tree (*Tsuga canadensis*) of our Appalachian forests. It would grow in abundance, probably in virgin stands, along the Cahulawassee, the fictional river on which most of the story of ***Deliverance*** takes place. The fronds provide the screen of Nature from which the eye looks out. The eye's blue iris is the color of the sky—or of clear deep pools of water. The white ball is the color of clouds—or of turbid falling waters. The skin around the eye has the green cast of deep forests. Is it the eye of the murderous mountaineer? The eye of the narrator Ed Gentry? Of some Nature spirit or pantheistic god? Is it the eye of the author? Probably it is all of these, for it is the eye of the book itself.

In lectures and readings Dickey often quotes the final statement of Rilke's poem "Archaic Torso of Apollo": "You must change your life." (*Du muss dein leben andern.*) This, says Dickey, is what all important art demands, and certainly this is the effect that Dickey wants his work—poems and novels—to have on his readers. I am reminded of the warning Boehme gives at the outset of one of his books: he asks his readers to go no further unless they are willing to make changes in their lives that the book will call for; if they are not, then reading the book might be bad for them, even dangerous. Readers of ***Deliverance*** might heed a similar warning, for the novel records a harrowing descent into the abyss, the dark chasm of our own psyches; and the change Dickey calls for is in our understanding of ourselves as human animals whose genetic origins lie in a dark but certain past. Unless the reader understands the violence of the story as it relates to his own psyche, then the effect of the novel might indeed be dangerous.

"*Denn da ist keine Stelle, die dich nicht sieht.*" This assertion which precedes the final statement of Rilke's poem seems even more to the point: "There is no part that does not see you." We stand naked before the naked work of art. It sees us—and if we have the stomach for it, we see ourselves, through reflection and contrast—for what we are: flawed, incomplete creatures; and we must change, or, at least, accept the imperative to change.

Flawed certainly, but to say we are *incomplete* may be misleading: our incompleteness often results from our refusal to accept a part of ourselves, an innate part of our psyches, which we are afraid to claim. Under the intimidating light of modern civilization, we hide our shadow, our instinctual selves, not only because we distrust it, but also because John Locke and the Enlightenment have convinced us that it does not exist. The Puritan/Manichean ethos has taught us to project it conveniently elsewhere—as the devil, or on some darker complexioned race. Yet from time to time we feel the Aurignacian Man lurking just beneath our skins, and that scares the devil out of us; so we turn him out, or push him back deep into the recesses of our psyches, where we will not have to face his reality at close hand. To that subterfuge of modern man Dickey says his No—not in Thunder, but to the roar of mountain water. In the poem **"Falling"** the protagonist strips away her clothes, the integuments of civilization, to the roar of wind, as she falls from womb to grave, discovering—or inventing—in the process who she is. In ***Deliverance*** Dickey strips himself bare by breaking the psyche down into its component parts and testing them in a baptism, a trial by water, original water, near the source, not yet damped by the controls of civilization: the uterine font, launching the quartet of characters forth into a new life where only the fittest will prevail.

And so the eye of Dickey's book sees us: subdued creatures of an urban-industrial civilization, separated from Nature—save our own; and that nature-in-ourselves we cannot understand because of our isolation from the natural world which could furnish the analogies necessary for understanding. The rise of civilization, Carl Jung tells us, has been the history of the rational mind's successive gains against the instinctual, until we scarcely recognize ourselves as part of the natural world at all, but rather, in the Christian redaction, as separate creations altogether. The problems caused by this sublimation have been enumerated and analyzed by modern psychology. In *Deliverance* those problems, and perhaps a solution, have been dramatized.

Deliverance. From what? From the murderous mountain men? From the primordial dangers of the river? Certainly these are the most obvious referents of the title. But there is also the implication of a deliverance from the enslaving monotony of modern urban life. And, beyond that, to a deliverance from the parts of ourselves which also hold us in a kind of bondage, which thwart self-knowledge and consequently hinder our pursuit of vitality itself.

Dickey has discouraged symbolic readings of his novels and poems because he wants to emphasize the importance of story and storytelling, which he feels are too often devalued by modern theory and practice. Whatever meaning, in the abstract sense, his work might suggest has grown out of narrative action. This is certainly a healthy corrective to synthetic theories deriving from Poe and tracing their development through the symbolists, T. S. Eliot's objective correlative, to the postmodern practices of the anti-novel, where effect (or idea) is the first consideration and the synthesis of materials to produce that effect second: narrative thus becomes tertiary—a means of effecting the synthesis, often by inventive but unnatural means. Dickey opts for Nature. He would agree, I think, with Landor's old philosopher: "Nature I loved, and next to Nature Art." For Dickey empirical experience is authentic, salutary. His mode is thus mimetic, but informed by the esemplastic imagination.

Form and metaphor, Dickey says, must grow out of the material. But then, too, we know that the imagination of the artist is attracted to those materials in which form and metaphor inhere. First, the basic structure of *Deliverance* is archetypal: Descent and Return—as old at least as *The Gilgamesh,* and tracing its lineage upward through *The Odyssey, The Divine Comedy, King Lear, Faust, Moby-Dick.* There are some who hold that it is the basic structure of all great narrative. It is certainly the emphasized structure of *Deliverance.* Then, there is the river—the great mystery and power of water: life-giving but dangerous, vitalizing, primarily feminine in its associations. American literature is obsessed with water, whether it be Cooper's and Poe's and Melville's oceanic expanses, or Twain's and Faulkner's rivers. Water is life—vast and deep in the collective oceans, flowing and inexorable in its journey from highlands to estuary. But Dickey's Cahulawassee differs significantly from Twain's and Faulkner's Mississippi. It is the river of origins, chaotic and primitive. The Mississippi has tremendous power, but it is a gathered power, belied by its placid surface. The Cahulawassee is anything but placid; it is too original and unsophisticated to disguise its energy as it plunges through the rapids and gorges of North Georgia. It represents life untouched by the civilizing hand of man, or even by the tempering forces of Nature itself. The river is raw and wild.

On the other hand, there is the opposing metaphor of the dam being built at Aintry, which will cause the submersion of the river as it floods the valleys and gorges through which the characters of the novel travel. The dam is a symbol of man's abstractions, of Bergson's geometric order. As an architectural structure, it is like man's laws, his mores, his religions, his arts, which he uses to subdue and control the wild and primitive vitality in himself. As the waters rise behind the dam, they will subdue the wild river, diffuse its power, and cover over the rugged landscape it has wrought. Finally, it will create a placid, monotonous surface, and the wild river will be only a personal memory of those who have experienced it, or a cultural memory of those who have heard or read the stories told by their forebears. Like the dam, the shaping forms of civilization do not so much create order as they effect a monotonous peace which allows man to go about his daily business without threat of disruption. Instinct and passion are sublimated for the sake of society and progress.

Dickey illustrates this monotonous peace in the first section of the novel. In this prologue entitled "Before," Ed Gentry, the narrator, goes through his daily routines as an advertising executive and suburban family man in Atlanta. By the standards of modern society, it is a good life, but dull and feminized: when Ed returns to his office from lunch, he realizes there is not a man, save himself, on the street, only a bevy of women. His business, though prosperous, is mediocre: it cannot even strive for excellence, lest it out-class the market and thus lose accounts. His wife Martha is a generous, sympathetic woman, but their sexual coupling indicates that romance and adventure have long since departed their marriage. The only excitement Ed experiences is caused by the gold fleck in the eye of a nearly nude model his agency has employed. The eye is different, mysterious—it seems to represent the flaw in humanity, in the human condition, which can be beautiful and fascinating, particularly when found in an object or person approximating perfection. It is a symbol of mystery and exotic possibility. Her eye seizes Ed's imagination, and its image comes back to him several times during the course of the novel; but it offers only a temporary relief from the general boredom of his life.

At an unconscious level, Ed seeks deliverance from the monotony and tedium of this urban-suburban life. Yet he hesitates to go on the trip his friend Lewis Medlock has planned down the Cahulawassee. Adventure seems hardly worth the trouble of disrupting the comfortable apathy of his life, just as a passionate pursuit of the girl with the golden eye would disrupt his impersonal business relations. But he goes nevertheless because of the contagious enthusiasm of Lewis: psychologically, it would be more difficult for Ed to refuse Lewis than to go along with him. Thus, in a way, even here, Ed is choosing a path of least resistance. He is seduced by Lewis's enthusiasm: when Lewis rolls the topographical map out on the table for Drew, Bobby, and Ed to see, he makes the trip sound like pure romance. The map, however, gives no more idea of what the actual terrain is like than a textbook in anthropology allows us to understand the life of an ice-age hunter. It is an abstraction, another of the reductions by which we separate ourselves from the concrete reality of things and events. There are only two ways of confronting and understanding that reality. Direct experience: the way of Ed Gentry. Or by an act of the imagination: the way of Dickey, the poet-novelist.

What happens to the characters during their ordeal on the Cahulawassee, and what they learn from that experience, is directly related to the personalities they reveal during the course of the narrative. Drew is a corporate executive with a highly developed sense of social and moral order. He is an organization man, but in the best, not the pejorative, sense of the term. He is also a family man with a strong sense of duty. His love of music, which has a mathematical order and logic, but also an emotional warmth, reflects these qualities in him. Even his last name, Ballenger, might suggest balance. Because of this highly developed sense of order and social morality, Drew is not able to cope with the chaos of the primitive drama in which he is forced to participate. Consequently, he is destroyed.

Bobby, on the other hand, is violated, but not destroyed. He is a social being also, but without the ideals of Drew. Whereas Drew is an executive with responsibility and position, Bobby is the salesman who has to sell himself, to please and win others, at whatever cost to his own integrity and pride. He also lacks discipline, as revealed by Ed's memory of his blowing up at a party. He is the softest, effeminate and porcine, and the quickest to complain. Thus, Bobby cannot protect himself from the violation of his being by gratuitous evil, represented by the two mountaineers, Stovall and Benson. But he does survive that violation, because his moral lassitude (some might call it flexibility) allows him to.

Lewis Medlock, the enthusiast and instigator of the trip, is quite different from either Drew or Bobby. He is a man of independent means, directly indebted to no one. He can develop his individuality at will—which he does, and thus comes to believe in his own invincibility. He has become expert at every athletic activity he pursues—archery, fly-casting, weight-lifting—and insists on doing everything his own way. He even believes that he can survive a nuclear holocaust, if it comes. As Ed says, Lewis thinks he is immortal. Perhaps Lewis is weakened by his overspecialization and hubris. In the course of the ordeal he is humbled by his experience and forced to realize his vulnerability and mortality. He is a changed and wiser man when he returns to Atlanta.

Ed is the most successful of the four men in coping with his experience, probably because he is the best all around, and the least specialized. He also has more imagination, more of a power of empathy or negative capability, than the other three. He is able to understand moral relativity and adapt to the unexpected very quickly. He also establishes a rapport with nature in a short time, even though almost totally ignorant of her ways before this adventure. His flexibility allows him to enter into the drama of survival of the fittest and call on reserves deep inside himself to predict and destroy his enemy. As a result of his experience he realizes the violence that man, himself included, is capable of committing, but he can also take pride in his ability to enter the primitive world on its own terms and survive if not triumph over it. "Deliverance" at this level takes on a new meaning: it suggests that Ed has been delivered from the terror of his primitive ordeal and the realized savage in himself. When he returns to Atlanta, he has a new understanding of himself and an appreciation of the values and amenities of civilized life. His experience has indeed been a "recreation," in a way he could not have suspected when he drove north out of Atlanta with Lewis: it has been a "re-creation" of the life of his distant ancestry—tribal, or even pretribal, man. The routines, the manners, the trivialized human encounters of modern life—these are the price we pay for our deliverance from the terrors of primal chaos. But our realization and memory of that terror can give meaning, and poignancy, to the tedium of our daily lives. This is the lesson Ed Gentry has learned, and his memory will keep that lesson alive. Ed has, indeed, "changed his life."

Dickey's use of characterization to structure and inform *Deliverance* suggests other possibilities of interpretation as well. From a certain angle of vision, the four main characters appear to be four aspects of the author's own personality. In fact, they might be classified in psychoanalytic terms. Bobby has certain characteristics of the id: he is concerned with his own immediate comfort and gratification; he is impulsive, almost totally lacking in self-control; he is androgynous, undifferentiated, social without a social conscience. Because he lacks anything like a "higher" consciousness, we might say that he lives on an animal level, the level of instinct, much as the id operates within the psychic totality. (In this regard, the mountaineers, Benson and Stovall, who rape Bobby, probably murder Drew, and threaten to kill Lewis and Ed, might be seen as elements of the libido, an unchecked and undifferentiated sexual energy which is frightening and destructive until brought under control by the psyche.)

Lewis, on the other hand, can be seen as the ego: he is concerned with his own survival as an individual, not with the survival of society; he values his relative independence from the economic institutions of society; of all the characters he is the most in touch with external (physical) reality; he is disciplined, but only in activities related to his personal fitness for survival. Before the ordeal on the Cahulawassee he believes, as Freud said of the ego, that he is "immortal."

Drew is like the superego: he is social-institutional man; his values are the internalized codes of his civilization; his reactions are not instinctive, but they are reflexive, because in him the internalization of values is so complete that they operate on an unconscious level. (I am avoiding here the question of how much of social consciousness is innate and how much learned. The modern science of ethology has indeed shown that a large part of what we might call "superego" is instinctual and present in many of the mammalian species. But for the purposes of the analysis here I am assuming that consideration irrelevant.) Drew places more value on corporate and social well-being than on his own. His highest allegiance is to the articulated principles, such as law, that make civilization possible. His love of music might seem an anomaly, but it is not. Music mediates and formalizes the instincts and passions through the orderly arrangement of tone and rhythm, and thus allows "civil" communication. It expresses our human interrelatedness: like the other arts it is one of the highest expressions of our sense of community.

Ed Gentry is the psyche: he takes charge over the other components of the personality, because none of them, by themselves, is adequate to meet the demands of the ordeal, which require the totality of self for survival. As narrator, Ed is the mediator between the other characters and the external world (represented by the reading public), just as the psyche must be the mediator between the various components of the personality and its environment. Ed is adequate to the task; thus, the self, though much battered and altered, prevails. An interesting development, however, is that Bobby (the id) disappears: although the id survives, the ordeal has dispatched it so that the psyche no longer has to deal with it directly. The id has been chastened and brought under control; it is sufficient only that the psyche remember that the id still exists.

On the other hand, Drew, the superego, does not survive. The implication here is that an automatic, reflexive code based on societal values cannot survive when it ventures beyond the protective boundaries of the civilization that evolved those values for its own preservation. In the primal chaos outside those boundaries, the superego is not only irrelevant; it is also a hindrance to survival. Thus it is destroyed. This does not mean that the superego is without value. As Ed says at the end of the novel, Drew was the "best" of the bunch of them. Because of the psychic violence of the ordeal, the superego cannot survive as an autonomous component of the self, but it can be valued in memory as a valuable principle.

Although this Freudian structure may not be immediately obvious, once discovered it seems too precise not to have been a consideration during composition. In my own conversations with Dickey, however, he has denied that he was conscious of this division of the Freudian paradigm among the four characters of the novel. If this is so, an interesting possibility is raised: Freudian metaphor has become so imbedded in modern thought that it often functions today at a subliminal level.

An indication that Dickey consciously intended the four major characters to represent aspects of himself is the distribution of his vocations and hobbies among them. The narrator Ed Gentry is an advertising executive in Atlanta: Dickey had been a highly successful advertising executive in Atlanta and New York during the late 1950s. Lewis Medlock lifts weights and is an expert archer: Dickey was an athlete who took his weightlifting seriously, and during the 1950s and 60s he became an expert field archer—an accomplishment he has been quite proud of. Drew Ballenger is a guitarist: Dickey's house is filled with guitars, both 6- and 12-stringed varieties; during the 1960s he practiced on the instrument religiously and became a technically proficient musician, and he still plays with much enjoyment today.

That leaves only Bobby Trippe to account for: he has no talents except his sociability; his name suggests the porcine and unsavory; his behavior is childish, cowardly, and embarrassing. It seems that Bobby represents that undisciplined and sometimes ludicrous part of the self that we all wish to be rid of. And that is just what Dickey does in the course of the novel: dispatch Bobby to regions where he will not be an embarrassment to Ed and Lewis.

If the four characters represent aspects of the author, the novel can then be seen as metaphor for Dickey's own life. He leaves the security of a good position in advertising and a comfortable middle-class family existence to enter the imaginative life of the poet. That life requires a descent into the abyss of being to find the sources of imaginative energy. Horrors lurk there, but discovery of the hidden self can be exhilarating. The poet finds in the depths and recesses of the conscious and unconscious mind the primitive well-springs of the poetic imagination. Support for this interpretation can be found in the sleep-dream motif of the novel. Before the adventure, Ed plunged deeply into sleep each night, probably to renew contact with the unconscious sources of vitality. But something has always kept him from remembering what he dreamed; his internal censor will not allow the dreams' contents to rise to consciousness. On the trip with Lewis to the Cahulawassee, Ed moves in and out of sleep, as though he is about to enter a dream. And indeed he does—a nightmare out of man's primitive past, violent and lawless. And this time he brings the dream back into the light of consciousness by telling us about it, just as the poet Dickey is objectifying and dramatizing, through metaphor, his descent into his own elemental self.

Deliverance is not an American *Heart of Darkness.* Unlike Marlow, the American hero does not beat a paranoiac retreat when he encounters the primitive aspects of his own psyche; rather he approaches those manifestations, with trepidation perhaps, but also with fascination and a desire to understand their meaning and value. Natty Bumppo, Ishmael, Huck Finn, Isaac McCaslin, R. P. McMurphy, all embrace their shadows. (Both Hawthorne and Henry James are primarily European in their attitudes toward the shadow, and are thus exceptions to the generalizations I am making here.) The instinctual self turns out to be a source not only of vitality but also of some of man's most admirable traits. In ***Deliverance,*** however, there is no Chingachgook, Queequeg, Jim, Sam Fathers, or Bromden, because Dickey's vision has passed beyond the Puritan/Manichean psychology that begot the shadow. Dickey's psychology is more modern, more complex, for the instinctual self rises from within when called upon to meet the challenge of survival. Projection is evident only in Ed's mildly paranoiac attitude toward mountain people in general, and in the symbolic projection of evil onto Benson and Stovall, in particular. Nonetheless, ***Deliverance*** stands in the tradition of Cooper, Melville, Twain, Hemingway, and Faulkner. It is also indebted to the primitivism of Jack London, particularly to *The Call of the Wild,* for which Dickey wrote the screenplay of a 1975 television production. The American work that ***Deliverance*** stands closest to, however, is Poe's *The Narrative of Arthur Gordon Pym.* Both are explorations of the modern psyche in similar motival and symbolic terms. The major difference between the two works lies in the authors' attitudes toward knowledge. Poe's residual transcendentalism takes for granted that ultimate knowledge lies outside the self, in a realm whose shadowy existence can be sensed only through the intuition. If for Dickey transcendental knowledge exists, it is not a concern of either his poetry or fiction. Knowledge in ***Deliverance*** comes from within, from the shadowy regions deep in the individual psyche. For Dickey, it would seem, the only access to that knowledge is through action, the recreation of archetypal experience, the realization of dream. The act may entail actual participation—or it may be realized in the creation of art. In both, the archetypal is externalized and made concrete.

For many of us, an opportunity to participate in archetypal experience like that described in ***Deliverance*** is unavailable or improbable. And if it were available, most of us would be unequal to the ordeal of confronting and absorbing its terror. Furthermore, unless we are writers of the order of Melville or Faulkner or Dickey, we shall never realize such experience effectively through imagination. That is why the artist is of extraordinary value to our modern culture: he has the imaginative power and will to break through the conventions that blind us to the nature of reality outside those conventions—and to the darker regions of our own psyche, which, again, convention urges us to suppress or ignore. The great writer is our Perseus who confronts and overcomes the bright Medusa of existence, the Gorgon which we all contain within ourselves—for the Medusa is the consummate Anima figure, in all her beauty and hideousness. The writer's mirror-shield is his art. In it he sees Life, he sees Us—thus inviting us to see ourselves. He also invites us to grasp, with him, the Sickle of Knowledge and slay the Gorgon. If we have the courage to accept that invitation and sever the petrifying head, then Pegasus flies free and our lives are changed. That is the only kind of knowledge that gives meaning to the tedium of our daily existence, and allows us to rise occasionally above it to perform a heroic action—or at least to understand the nature of heroism.

Terry Thompson (essay date December 1998)

SOURCE: Thompson, Terry. "Cahulawassee: The Bend Sinister River in *Deliverance.*" *English Language Notes* 36, no. 2 (December 1998): 44-8.

[*In the following essay, Thompson considers the "heraldic symbolism" found in Dickey's* Deliverance.]

Originally published in 1970, ***Deliverance,*** James Dickey's first and most popular novel, has been much lauded for its poetic description of nature and for its vivid narration of a harrowing canoe trip down a wild Georgia river by four would-be outdoorsmen from Atlanta whose adventurous weekend getaway quickly turns into a bloody nightmare once they discover "the primordial dangers of the river."[1] Their overly romanticized view of nature—and what might lurk in it—is shattered by their encounter with human savagery and depravity, including torture, rape, and murder. The naive quartet of urban Nimrods learn through blood trial that, as D. H. Lawrence once argued, "The essential American soul is hard, isolate, stoic, and a killer."[2]

Although lambasted in the early seventies by numerous social and political critics for its machismo and violence, *Deliverance* became a huge best-seller since "The plot had the ingredients for a surefire success, the old adventure story of hunter and hunted in a modern setting, with urban men forced to regain primitive instincts in order to kill and survive."[3] Furthermore, the many "Mythological and archetypal readings, even Jungian interpretations, suggest that Dickey . . . caught in this novel something far more than the average adventure story" (Calhoun and Hill 118). This wild river journey is "as old at least as *The Gilgamesh*," and its literary lineage extends "through *The Odyssey, The Divine Comedy, King Lear, Faust, Moby-Dick*," and well beyond (Butterworth 71). It is a riveting tale of personal growth gained by meeting challenge, of great wisdom earned by spilling blood. In short, "*Deliverance* provides an initiation which . . . is brutal and adolescent. . . ."[4] The three suburbanites who survive the ordeal, much like Gilgamesh, Odysseus, Aeneas, Ishmael, et al., will be forever changed by their frightening journey; they will never again view the world or their fellow man with the same dull eyes.

Just as in so many memorable novels, such as *A Tale of Two Cities, Pride and Prejudice, The Portrait of a Lady*, and *Moby-Dick*, the opening lines of *Deliverance* provide important background information as well as foreshadow what the plot holds for the reader; the first person narrator, Ed Gentry, describes an uncooperative topographical map of north Georgia spread out on a bar room table:

> It unrolled slowly, forced to show its colors, curling and snapping back whenever one of us turned loose. The whole land was very tense until we put four steins on its corners and laid the river out to run for us through the mountains 150 miles north. Lewis' hand took a pencil and marked out a small strong X in a place where some of the green bled away and the paper changed with high ground, and began to work downstream, northeast to southwest through the printed woods.[5]

Although the topography of this "map anticipates the land's and the river's energy," the wild waterway is quite unremarkable; the Cahulawassee will, like all streams, eventually find its way to the sea or some other large body of open water.[6] However, there is a very subtle bit of heraldic symbolism in the compass directions provided in the narrator's description: the fifty-mile stretch of river chosen for the ill-starred canoe trip runs precisely *bend sinister*—from upper left to lower right—on the colorful map the four men study so carefully in the opening scene. This subtle allusion, so very early in the novel, to medieval heraldic devices dovetails elegantly with the idea, suggested by numerous critics, that *Deliverance* offers a modernized, urbanized treatment of the archetypal male quest story, a journey tale as old as Moses, as violent as Beowulf, as noble as Arthur.

The beginnings of heraldry as we know it are relatively well documented: it "originated independently in western Europe and in Japan, in each case in the twelfth century."[7] Although modern day heraldry is seen by some as merely an affectation of the idle rich or an arcane hobby, it actually developed from military necessity: "When body armour prevented recognition of leaders, the need arose for signs by which to distinguish them" (Pine 31). According to Bruno Bernard Heim, a noted authority on coats of arms and their history, "The supreme law of heraldic design is visibility, arising from the need to see clearly the charges on the shield and helmet in order to recognize their bearer even from a distance and in the heat of battle."[8] However, because of the proclivity of some European kings and princes to "scatter their seed," as it were, "the arms of the illegitimate sons [who often far outnumbered the legitimate heirs] were made to carry some charge or alteration to show that there was some reason which debarred inheritance by their users, whilst there remained those entitled to bear arms without the mark of distinction.'"[9] In other words, bastard sons had to add to their family crests the bend sinister device—two parallel lines drawn from the upper left to the lower right—to symbolize their illegitimacy.

However, the association of the bend sinister with bastardy's taint is not especially germane to Dickey's tale; it is not the main reason for the subtle reference. Rather, there is another meaning inherent in the left-to-right and downward-flowing stretch of the Cahulawassee River, a meaning that is much more symbolically pertinent to the novel; in many ancient cultures—and a few modern ones—the whole left half of the body was considered unclean, was, in fact, the side of the Devil. Hence, it was labeled the "sinister" side in heraldic language, deriving from the Latin for "on the left." Today, however, the word "sinister" has expanded in meaning to include anything frightening, threatening, evil, wicked, or foreboding. It is to this dark and ominous meaning that the map directions in the opening paragraph so obliquely allude.

Many early cultures believed that Satan lurked—quite literally—just behind a person's left shoulder; from there, he constantly observed human behavior to detect a sin or transgression or moment of weakness. The old superstition that the spilling of salt was horribly unlucky—because of salt's great value to early cultures—led to the practice of tossing a pinch of the spilled condiment over the left shoulder and directly into Satan's eyes. The resulting temporary blindness would enable the person to escape the Evil One and avoid a sure spell of bad luck. Even today, in some societies, children who appear to be born left-handed are forced to become right-handed—occasionally by having their "wrong" hands bound up as tightly as a Chinese maiden's feet. The belief that the left side of the body harbors wickedness is nothing if not persistent.

For over eight centuries—from King Richard the Lion Hearted[10] to Sir Winston Churchill, from dispossessed Scottish lairds to the latest nouveau riche Londoners, from country club crests to blazer buttons—formal heraldry has continued to play an important role in Western life, albeit an increasingly smaller one: "Thanks to its brilliant colors, its power of suggestion, and the rich store of symbols it has accumulated, the noble art of heraldry has been a source of deep and mysterious enchantment for many people down the ages" (Heim 9).

Given James Dickey's detailed description of the segment of the river selected by the four Atlantans for their amateurish and bloody fling with the north Georgia wilderness, the novelist's cryptic allusion to a medieval heraldic device adds an extra touch of meaning to an introductory paragraph that is already richly layered with subtle irony and careful inference. The overconfident quartet of urban knights-errant do not understand the veiled warning in their chosen topography; thus, they suffer the terrible consequences of uneducated and unskilled questing along the Cahulawassee, a left-handed and sinister river.

Notes

1. Keen Butterworth, "The Savage Mind: James Dickey's *Deliverance*," *The Southern Literary Journal* 28.2 (1996): 71. All subsequent references to these sources will be documented parenthetically within the text.
2. D. H. Lawrence, *Studies in Classic American Literature* (New York: Viking, 1964) 62.
3. Richard J. Calhoun and Robert W. Hill, *James Dickey* (Boston: Twayne, 1983) 108.
4. Henry J. Lindborg, "James Dickey's *Deliverance*: The Ritual of Art," *The Southern Literary Journal* 6.2 (1974): 90.
5. James Dickey, *Deliverance* (Boston: Houghton, 1970) 13.
6. Daniel B. Marin, "James Dickey's *Deliverance*: Darkness Visible," *James Dickey: The Expansive Imagination: A Collection of Critical Essays*, ed. Richard J. Calhoun (Deland, FL: Everett/Edwards, 1973) 108.
7. L. G. Pine, *International Heraldry* (Rutland, VT: Charles E. Tuttle, 1970) 20.
8. Bruno Bernard Heim, *Heraldry in the Catholic Church: Its Origins, Customs, and Laws* (Gerrards Cross, Buckinghamshire, UK: Van Duren, 1978) 12.
9. Arthur Charles Fox-Davies, *The Complete Guide to Heraldry* (New York: Bonanza, 1978) 509.
10. Reverend Charles Boutell, *Boutell's Heraldry*, revised by C. W. Scott and J. P. Brooke-Little (London: Frederick Warne, 1963) 121-22. This book was originally published in 1863.

R. S. Gwynn (essay date summer 1999)

SOURCE: Gwynn, R. S. "Subject Matters." *Hudson Review* 52, no. 2 (summer 1999): 323-31.

[*In the following excerpt, Gwynn compares Dickey's work and declining critical reputation to that of the Georgian poets, especially Rupert Brooke.*]

No group of poets has suffered worse at the hands of posterity than the Georgians, whose poems were collected in five eponymous semiannual anthologies. The last of these had the misfortune to appear in the same year as *The Waste Land,* and after Eliot, Edith Sitwell, and Middleton Murry had finished mopping the floor with it, the Georgians were consigned to the back matter of the history of modernism. Of their number, none has been devalued more than Rupert Brooke, who is remembered chiefly as the poster boy for British army recruitment, the result of the great popularity of "1914," the sonnet sequence he wrote in the last year of his life. Brooke, who by all accounts was intelligent, handsome, charming, a bit facetious, and a fearlessly outspoken Fabian in matters political, would doubtless have been appalled by the reasons for his posthumous fame. But, to readers familiar with Sassoon, Graves, and Owen, his lines comparing a foredoomed generation's call to the trenches to "swimmers into cleanness leaping" seem hopelessly, even criminally naive.

A shame in a way, for the poetry on which Brooke built a not inconsiderable reputation accurately captures that lulling decade before the Great War, an era which, if the huge success of *Titanic* is any measure, large numbers of us still privately embrace (Those tea dances! Those great hats!). It must have been an auspicious time for a rising young poet, especially if, like Brooke, one had the necessary prerequisites of social standing, the right school ties, a bit of money, and rather more of talent. The typical Brookean/Georgian poem celebrates the long mornings at the country house, mowed lawns and overgrown gardens, the declamation of one's latest strophes over crumpets and croquet balls with even the fish "fly-replete, in depth of June, / Dawdling away their wat'ry noon." Even what Brooke later called "all the little emptiness of love" rarely breaks the calm; one's most fervent passions are reserved for "the cool kindliness of sheets, that soon / Smooth away trouble," and no matter seems more pressing than that notorious closing question, "And is there honey still for tea?" Reading the Georgian anthologies provides quick transport into the servants-at-the-ready realm of Merchant-Ivory—sans conflict, bad weather, and the Great War lurking in the shadows.

I dredge up this ancient matter for a reason: if the work of many contemporary poets is any indication, we are in the midst of a Georgian revival. The weekend has become the setting in which our poets thrive. Who can blame them? They live in comfortable times; the issues that impelled them thirty years ago to take to the barricades lie far behind. They are loath to resurrect their checkered pasts or to jeopardize their futures by confessing present sins. They may have lived through the whirlwind but now seem content to cultivate their gardens—not imaginary ones with real toads in them but real ones flourishing with everything but imagination. They desperately need the challenge of urgent subjects but cannot urge themselves to look for them outside their own privacy fences. We have slipped from the Age of Causes to the Age of Cozy; if Thoreau were to survey the current scene, he might be forced to conclude that the mass of men lead lives of quiet.

If James Dickey, whose selected poems [*The Selected Poems*] have recently appeared, is to have any lasting legacy, it strikes me that it will lie in the way he was able to infuse our suburban humdrum with an energy that is well nigh sacramental. Rereading early poems like **"Sleeping Out on Easter," "The Vegetable King"** or **"The Mountain Tent,"** I *know* that this is just Everyguy camping out in a state park on the fringes of urban Atlanta, but a palpable shiver still comes with lines like

> I am hearing the shape of the rain
> Take the shape of the tent and believe it,
> Laying down all around where I lie
> A profound, unspeakable law.

Those incantatory trimeters contribute to the effect, true, but I can never hear them without feeling a little smaller and weaker, without wishing my inadequate sleeping bag could hide me completely. As stagey and predictable as many of Dickey's performances seem when we revisit them, they were, and *are,* capable of generating an awe that none of his contemporaries ever quite managed. If I am not quite struck with it on reading **"Falling"** for the umpteenth time, I can at least honestly recall that I *was* the first five or six.

Rupert Brooke's reputation has declined mightily, but that falling off seems less precipitous than the collapse of Dickey's, the fault less of the poems that made his name than of the noisy celebrity and weak books of his last two decades. His work has all but disappeared from the anthologies of American literature, and even in Norton's recent *The Literature of the American South* he is allotted only the same number of pages as nikki giovanni! His son's widely read memoir and the inevitable biographies will doubtless spur reassessments; thus, it is good to have Robert Kirschten's portable volume at hand. That said, I can't help but have several regrets about the editor's initial assumptions and the choices that result. In an attempt to define Dickey's best qualities, Kirschten outlines Dickey's "four major poetic modes": his natural mysticism, his Pythagorean reverence for music, his romanticism, and his primitivism. These are valid enough, perhaps, but they ignore the solid grounding in his generation's realities that gave Dickey's early work such resonance. First, there are the war poems. Kirschten includes **"The Performance,"** with its curious syntax brilliantly mimicking the unsteady acrobatics of its doomed protagonist, but he excludes **"Between Two Prisoners,"** in which two captured Americans await execution in an island schoolroom, and the spooky **"The Driver,"** where Dickey (as always, a problematical assumption) dives into a Pacific lagoon and sits in the driver's seat of a sunken half-track.

Further, I miss many of Dickey's best poems of postwar civilized discontent: **"The Leap,"** a narrative about the suicide of a woman remembered from childhood; **"On the Coosawattee,"** which contains the probable (and certainly less melodramatic) genesis of *Deliverance*; **"Power and Light,"** a brutal blue-collar dramatic monologue; and **"Adultery,"** which is bracketed by the best opening and closing lines of any Dickey poem: "We have all been in rooms / We cannot die in, and they are odd places, and sad" and

> We have done it again   we are
> Still living. Sit up and smile,
> God bless you. Guilt is magical.

I would have preferred more guilty magic like this (and where is the marvelous **"Kudzu"**?) to reprinting the ten-page **"Reincarnation (II)"** or more than the briefest sample from Dickey's last book, the inscrutable *The Eagle's Mile.*

Kirschten states that his aim is "to gather and showcase [Dickey's] very best material" and in doing so has to admit that Dickey's collected poems, *The Whole Motion,* is a bit *too* whole for most tastes (even Dickey excluded portions of the slack *Puella*). Kirschten does get a fair portion of the best ones in his limited space (the book is over a hundred pages shorter than *Poems 1957-*

1967), but it is probably a sign of the times that in introducing Dickey's four "politically controversial" poems—**"Slave Quarters," "The Fiend," "The Sheep Child,"** and **"The Firebombing"**—he feels it necessary to attach a disclaimer (his italics): "Further, *representation is not recommendation.*" Now we can all sleep better. One wonders how this editor would preface a selection from the works of Robert Browning.

Dickey once said, "The whole tragedy of the American poets of my generation is that they were afraid to change. . . ." Dickey's own example provides one effective counterargument to that, for his changes in retrospect seem invariably for the worst.

Denis Donoghue (review date 18 November 1999)

SOURCE: Donoghue, Denis. "Lives of a Poet." *New York Review of Books* 46, no. 18 (18 November 1999): 55-7.

[*In the following review, Donoghue discusses Dickey's public persona as well as poets that influenced his writing, particularly Theodore Roethke.*]

In November 1968 James Dickey told readers of the *Atlantic Monthly* that Theodore Roethke (1908-1963) was "in my opinion the greatest poet this country has yet produced." He also took the opportunity to rebuke Beatrice Roethke for allegedly setting a limit on Allan Seager's disclosures in *The Glass House,* his biography of her husband:

> It may be that she has come to regard herself as the sole repository of the "truth" of Roethke, which is understandable as a human—particularly a wifely—attitude, but is not pardonable in one who commissions a biography from a serious writer.

In the December issue of the magazine several prominent poets and critics replied to Dickey's essay. While they rejected his nomination of Roethke as the greatest American poet, none of them wondered aloud how he had disposed of Whitman, Dickinson, Frost, and Stevens before awarding the prize. Nor did any of them remark that Dickey seemed to be claiming Roethke for himself and fending off rival suitors, even the poet's widow. That the Consultant in Poetry to the Library of Congress should be handing out the grand rosette to Roethke or any other poet didn't strike the poets and critics as inappropriate. In the December issue, too, Beatrice Roethke corrected Dickey's factual errors and said that "with one exception, a matter in which I had no selfish interest, Seager was free to say anything he could substantiate with honest evidence." There the matter ended, so far as I know.

It was a minor episode, but it marked a new, vulgar phase of Dickey's career, the years in which, not content to be a mere poet, he turned himself by force of will into a public presence, a mythic figure, laureate of John Wayne's America.

James Lafayette Dickey was born on February 2, 1923, to Eugene Dickey and Maibelle Swift Dickey in Buckhead, a neighborhood of Atlanta, Georgia. His mother came from an established and well-to-do family. His father was, as the poet's son Christopher describes him in his memoir, a "dilettante lawyer and devoted gambler who took his son with him to cockfights, or to watch raccoons chained to floating logs fighting off packs of hounds, or to just about anything else where blood and death had money riding on them."[1] James Dickey read indiscriminately—pulp fiction, Southern novels, bits of philosophy—and gave his spare hours to weightlifting and bodybuilding, inspired by Mr. Universe, Charles Atlas. In 1942 he enrolled at Clemson Agricultural College, did pretty well in football there, and enlisted in the Army Air Corps. In February 1943 he started basic training as a pilot, but failed the course and had to settle for the smaller thrill of becoming a radar observer, an "intercept officer."

After the war, he entered Vanderbilt University and started writing poems and critical essays, some of which were published in *Sewanee Review.* In 1950 he took a teaching job at Rice Institute in Houston, Texas, until he was called up during the Korean War and assigned to teach radar at bases in Mississippi and Texas. Returned to civilian life, he set about making a career in poetry, reviewing, and teaching, helped along by the novelist Andrew Nelson Lytle and the critic Monroe K. Spears.

Dickey's early work in criticism, collected in **The Suspect in Poetry** (1964) and **Babel to Byzantium** (1968), was remarkably pugnacious. He was willing to praise a few English poets, especially dead ones—Christopher Smart, Blake, Hopkins—and with reservations a few living ones, including Dylan Thomas, W.S. Graham, Philip Larkin, Jon Silkin, and Geoffrey Hill. European poets sent him into hyperboles: Char, Supervielle ("the best poet of the twentieth century," "my all-time favorite poet in any and all languages"), and Montale, "in my opinion the greatest living poet." But he dismissed nearly every American poet who might appear to be a competitor. He derided "the overrefined, university-pale subtleties" of the genteel tradition of American poetry, which was content with the "well-meaning, mannered management of nothing." He regarded Ginsberg's *Howl* as "the conventional maunderings of one type of American adolescent, who has discovered that machine civilization has no interest in his having read Blake." William Carlos Williams was "a poet of no merit whatsoever." Charles Olson was "congenitally unable to say one memorable thing." Dickey deplored the influence of Wallace Stevens, "whose mannered artificiality and poetry-about-writing-poetry-about-poetry have driven large numbers of writers delightedly back into their shimmering, wordy sensibilities and buried them there." He sympathized with Anne Sexton and other "confessional" poets in their tragic lives, but could not take their poems seriously. He told Donald Hall:

> I want a poetry that illuminates my experience. I want a poetry that gives me some of my life, over again; that restores something to me, or creates a need for more life, more feeling; something that gets me closer to the world: that gets me *inside* the world, in a new way, or in a way older than the world.

Roethke and Robert Penn Warren were the American poets Dickey praised most consistently:

> The powerful, almost somnambulistic statements of [Roethke's] observations and accountings come to us as from the bottom of the "deep well of unconscious cerebration" itself, from a Delphic trance where everything one says is the right, undreamed-of, and known-by-the-gods-all-the-time thing that should be and never is said.

Warren was of the true visionary company, because his poetry was "so deeply and compellingly linked to man's ageless, age-old drive toward self-discovery, self-determination." "I think of you as the best of all of us," Dickey told him.

But Warren was an exception in one respect. He was a visionary in the sense that his poems gave feelings and intimations every privilege over the authority of mere events, but he was also sane. Most of the writers Dickey cared about were post-Romantic figures, men ruined in their lives but recovered in their Orphic, Delphic words—Hart Crane, James Agee, Malcolm Lowry, Roethke. In a note on Smart's "A Song to David," Dickey asked:

> How shall we deal with the mad in their perfect disguises? From the beginning we have suspected them of magic and have wanted what they have, the revelations. But how may we come by these and still retain our own sanity? What must *we* do in order to connect safely with the insane at their clairvoyant and dangerous levels?

"What we have always wanted from the insane," he said, is "the life-extending, life-deepening insight, the ultimate symbolic sanity."

In this respect, Roethke was Dickey's exemplar: he had manic phases, and then he could not write, but when he was sane, he remained at one with his visions, and spoke with their authority. Before and after the manic episodes, he was the strange, childlike poet whom Kenneth Burke described in "The Vegetal Radicalism of Theodore Roethke." In an early notebook Dickey transcribed sentences from Burke's essay. Examining Roethke's *The Lost Son* and "The Visitant," Burke said that this poet "goes as far as is humanly possible in quest of a speech wholly devoid of abstractions." Using Kant's distinction, in the *Critique of Pure Reason,* between the three phases of knowledge—intuitions of sensibility, concepts of the understanding, and ideas of reason—Burke asked:

> Do not these distinctions of Kant's indicate the direction which poetry might take, in looking for a notable purification of language? If one could avoid the terms for "ideas," and could use "concepts" only insofar as they are needed to unify the manifold of "intuitions," the resultant vocabulary would move toward childlike simplicity.

Roethke's aesthetic, and Dickey's to a degree, could then be summed up as a minimum of "ideas," and a maximum of "intuitions," "concepts" being admitted as a regrettable necessity. But Dickey was more willing than Roethke to add conceptual notes to his intuitions, as in **"Power and Light"** he refers to "the red-veined eyeball of a bulb," and in **"False Youth: Two Seasons"** he writes of "the tight belt of time." Roethke would have stopped at "eyeball" and "belt"; he would not have added the conceptual explanations.

In "The Visitant," to stay with Burke's instance, Roethke begins with a natural scene, conveyed as fully as possible by intuitions of sensibility:

> A cloud moved close. The bulk of
> the wind shifted.
> A tree swayed over water.
> A voice said:
> Stay. Stay by the slip-ooze. Stay.
>
> Dearest tree, I said, may I rest here?
> A ripple made a soft reply.
> I waited, alert as a dog.
> The leech clinging to a stone waited;
> And the crab, the quiet breather.

It is "such a natural scene," Burke said, "as would require a local deity, a *genius loci,* to make it complete." Hence as the poem begins, "the place described is infused with a *numen* or *pneuma,* a concentration of spirit just on the verge of apparition." Dickey's note reads:

> K. Burke: "begins with such a natural scene as would require a genius loci to make it complete." Idea of a "completing" or "fulfilling" presence. "As would require" here the suggestive phrase. Scene which you set up during which the audience waits for an unknown inevitability to be fulfilled, to complete the scene which requires it. Sense of presence. Might be fruitful. Can be terribly hammed up.

It is a sensitive note, up to a point, indicating that Dickey started out as an artist, however careless he became in that capacity during the later years. The *genius loci*, the spirit of the place, is implicit in the way its different parts cohere; it has nothing to do with an audience waiting for something to happen. But Dickey saw in Roethke's poems, and clearly in Burke's account of them, a direction of energy eminently congenial to his own talent: to endow a landscape, a scene, with the spirit of the place, and to constitute himself as that spirit. Corresponding to the imagery of Roethke's "vegetal radicalism," which features roses, orchids, and weeds, Dickey had his own geological and animal images of rivers, mountains, forests, deer, snakes, wolves. He becomes the *genius loci* by being attentive to the peremptory radiance of the natural world.

One of the poems in **Helmets** (1964), **"In the Marble Quarry,"** has Dickey descending to a quarry in North Georgia and rising with a block of marble on a pulley:

> To feel sadness fall off as though
> I myself
> Were rising from stone
>
> Held by a thread in midair,
> Badly cut, local-looking, and
> totally uninspired,
> Not a masterwork
>
> Or even worth seeing at all
> But the spirit of this place just the
> same,
> Felt here as joy.

"As joy," because if Dickey feels himself to be the spirit of the place, nothing more is needed to authenticate the experience. If he wants to round out the experience further, he appeals to astronomy, the largest natural perspective that displaces metaphysics as the grammar of Being.

This explains, I think, why Dickey's poems take their bearings from the natural world to the extent of regarding the acculturated world as an aberration, however insistent. As a young man he read Alfred North Whitehead's *Process and Reality* and was impressed by Whitehead's emphasis on "presentational immediacy"—"our perception of the contemporary world by means of the senses"—and on the assumption that "actual entities in the contemporary universe are causally independent of each other." That seemed as close to the beginnings of knowledge as Dickey could come. Until forced by circumstances, he gave little credence to the world in its "later" cultural, domestic, social, political, and moral manifestations—the world in which each thing seems rigid to him and resists being transformed. "The natural world seems infinitely more important to me than the man-made world," Dickey said. "There's a part of me that has never heard of a telephone." His chosen poetic place is the natural scene, mostly Georgia, the back woods, and South Carolina, where some terrain, even yet, is untamed, and therefore susceptible to his mythic desires, processes of transfiguration. In return for such attention, the natural world gives him the conviction that he is flying upon wings other than his own; it seems to take the harm out of dying by assimilating it to larger sequences and continuities.

But Dickey did not long remain content with the decorum of poetry and the *genius loci*. He got going as a writer after the war and started being noticed in 1954. He published his best poems in **Into the Stone and Other Poems** (1960), **Drowning with Others** (1962), **Helmets** (1964), and **Buckdancer's Choice** (1965). When Roethke died on August 1, 1963, Dickey thought that he was now king of the cats and should step forward to claim the privilege. When he took up his appointment as Consultant in Poetry to the Library of Congress in September 1966 and moved to Washington, he entered on a period of his life and work that was to be personally and poetically disastrous, though it must have seemed, in a material sense, a triumph. Sounding off on the poetry circuit, money, fast cars, women, drunkenness—"I like it like Patton liked war," he told Gordon Lish—added up to his becoming a star.

Crux: The Letters of James Dickey tells the wretched story, mainly because the editors decided to make the letters annotate Dickey's career:

> The letters assembled in this volume represent perhaps twenty percent of James Dickey's located correspondence. The double rationale for selection was first to document the growth of a major writer—how a scarcely educated jock discovered that he possessed genius and that writing was the only thing that counted—then, second, to document the ways he fulfilled his genius and advanced his career. Jim was unabashedly a careerist. He had a clear understanding of the odds against any poet, no matter how gifted, and he recognized that his poetry did not exist if it was not read. He deliberately promoted and exaggerated his several reputations—genius, drinker, woodsman, athlete—until the legends took over after **Deliverance**.

Most of the letters were written to other writers, and there are memorable details, as in a letter to Robert Fagles:

> Poetry makes plenty happen; it can change your life. My whole existence has proceeded from one *word* in a poem, which I read in an anthology on Okinawa during the last weeks of the second War.

The editors of ***Crux*** tell us that the word was "shivered," in these lines from Trumbull Stickney's "Live Blindly and Upon the Hour":

> Thou art divine, thou livest,—as
> of old
> Apollo springing naked to the
> light,

> And all his island shivered into
> flowers.

But what many of the letters reveal is Dickey's myth-making vanity. The materials include true statements, bombast, improprieties, and lies. I suppose it is true that he hunted deer with bow and arrow and diamondbacks with a blowgun. He canoed the rapids of the Coosawattee River. Did he, at the age of eighteen, marry a woman in Australia, as he claimed, before he married Maxine Syerson? No. In a letter to John Berryman he referred to meeting someone in Waco, Texas, "where I was in the Air Force for the second time, and just back from Korea." He was never in Korea. Nor was he a fighter pilot, though he allowed Bill Moyers to say on WNET on January 25, 1976, that he was, and he let the *Atlantic Monthly* call him "a former star athlete, fighter pilot with more than 100 missions on his record in World War II and the Korean conflict." Did he really attend a lecture by Camus at the Sorbonne—"and he was talking about the Existentialist proposition that we no longer have any supernatural sanctions"? I don't believe it.

The letters indicate that Dickey's life from 1967 on belongs to the history of publicity and legend-making. "I am at a stage now," he told Richard Wilbur on September 16, 1968, "where I can reach a really *mass* audience." The only thing he could not do was stay quiet. He was so compulsively accessible that an editor at *Esquire* thought he would pose nude for the magazine. He had the grace to decline: "Please tell Jill Goldstein that I have decided not to pose nude; that, really, is not for me." *Deliverance* appeared on March 23, 1970, and became a best seller, second to Erich Segal's *Love Story*. The book was Dickey's dream of immortality, man and the natural world, two forces nearly equal. His hero Lewis Medlock "could do with his life exactly what he wanted to," challenging the river, the rocks and falls: "My God, those falls must have been something, back there," Lewis says to Ed Gentry.

Dickey's career was now a triumph of visibility. "I am shaking the great man's throne," Dickey said of Robert Lowell on November 19, 1970. Filming of **Deliverance** started in May 1971, and Dickey had a minor part as Sheriff Bullard. Meanwhile he abandoned scruple and delicacy. He was out of control. **Sorties,** a ragbag of critical pieces, was one of the ten books nominated in the Arts and Letters section of the National Book Award in 1971. In a string of calumnies, Dickey urged Stanley Burnshaw, one of the three judges for the award, not to give it to Edmund Wilson, "the most over-rated literary critic I have ever read":

> His work is one long tissue of self-indulgent clichés and self-aggrandizement. And when I read the Lowells in the *New York Review of Books* talk about what a "great writer" he is, I feel the sudden cold touch which indicates the prevalence of literary log-rolling in this country. Edmund Wilson is a great writer to the Lowells and to the *New York Review of Books* simply because he endorses Lowell as a poet.

The award went to Charles Rosen for *The Classical Style*.

The Selected Poems and **The James Dickey Reader** serve different purposes. The **Reader** gives samples of every phase of his work, good and bad. It is niggardly on the early poems, but it includes nine pages of **The Zodiac** (1976), a poem I could barely force myself to read. It is ostensibly the soliloquy of a drunken Dutch poet, Hendrik Marsman, forcing the stars to deliver the meaning of life:

> You son of a bitch, you!
> Don't try to get away from
> yourself!
> I won't have it! You know God-
> damned well I mean you! And
> you too,
> Pythagoras! Put down that
> guitar, lyre, whatever it is!

The poems account for less than half of the **Reader,** the rest is taken up with excerpts from the novels **Deliverance, Alnilam** (1987), **To the White Sea** (1993), and **Crux,** an unpublished and indeed barely begun novel. (Crux is a constellation in the southern hemisphere near Centaurus and Musca; it is also called the Southern Cross.) The **Reader** also includes essays from **Babel to Byzantium, Sorties** (1971), and **Night Hurdling** (1983). **The Selected Poems** does not cover the scene; it intends to present the best of Dickey and to draw poems from all the books except **The Zodiac.** But again the early books, which contain his best work, get short measure; only three poems from **Into the Stone,** five from **Drowning with Others,** six from **Helmets,** and seven from **Buckdancer's Choice.**

Comparing both books with **The Whole Motion: Collected Poems 1945-1992,**[2] I find that the editors, while often disagreeing in their selections, are at one in emphasizing the social, domestic poems at the expense of the visionary or planetary ones. Most of the chosen poems are those in which an actual event has taken place and seized Dickey's attention, and he makes the most of it. **"The Hospital Window"**—it's in the **Reader,** not in **The Selected Poems**—begins, "I have just come down from my father," and I assume it started from such a visit. It may be that the visionary poems have not attracted many readers, and that the circumstantial poems are easier to hold in mind. But it is unfortunate that the poems of natural magic, such as **"Inside the River,"** have not been selected from **The Whole Motion.** Only a determined reader will go to that book now that the **Reader** and **The Selected Poems** are available. Here is a passage from **"Inside the River"**:

> Let flowing create
> A new, inner being:
> As the source in the mountain
> Gives water in pulses,
> These can be felt at
> The heart of the current.
> And here it is only
> One wandering step
> Forth, to the sea.
> Your freed hair floating
> Out of your brain.

Here, as throughout the poem, intuitions of sensibility survive their passage through the imperative phrases. The poem is unlikely to win as many readers as **"The Hospital Visit," "The Fiend,"** and the celebrated piece of magical realism, **"Falling,"** do, but it embodies a distinctive part of Dickey's talent, the neo-Roethkean part, which produced some of his finest and least flamboyant work.

Notes

1. Christopher Dickey, *Summer of Deliverance: A Memoir of Father and Son* (Simon and Schuster, 1998), p. 30.

2. Wesleyan University Press/University Press of New England, 1992.

Henry Hart (essay date winter 2000)

SOURCE: Hart, Henry. "James Dickey: The World as a Lie." *Sewanee Review* 108, no. 1 (winter 2000): 93-106.

[*In the following essay, Hart addresses the problems in researching Dickey's life story, asserting that "nearly everything Dickey said about his life was an embroidery of fiction and fact."*]

When James Dickey died on January 19, 1997, most of the obituaries—from the six-column one in the *New York Times* to the shorter ones in *Time* and *Newsweek*—paid tribute to the big, life-loving, hard-drinking bard who had written the best-selling novel ***Deliverance***. The eulogists pointed out that he had been a star college football player, a combat pilot with one hundred missions during World War II and the Korean War, an advertising executive for the Coca-Cola company, a tournament archer and expert bow-hunter, a National Book Award-winning poet, a poetry consultant at the Library of Congress, a popular professor, and an author of poetry books, coffee-table books, literary criticism, novels, and children's books. In Dickey's hometown newspaper, the *Atlanta Journal and Constitution*, David Kirby announced that "A boozy, bold 'Dylan Thomas of the South,'" had died, and that Dickey had "staked out the position of premier tough-guy writer that Ernest Hemingway had held in the previous generation." Kirby also contended that Dickey was an aesthete and impersonator in the tradition of Oscar Wilde.

During a memorial service at the University of South Carolina, the novelist Pat Conroy remarked on Dickey's personae and impersonations as well: "He tried to live a hundred lives and succeeded in living about 95 of them. No American life has been so restless in its pursuit of expertise in so many fields. A whole city of men lived in that vivid, restless country behind James Dickey's transfixing eyes." Because Dickey aspired to be a Jeffersonian Renaissance man as much as a Rabelaisian hell-raiser, Conroy expressed sympathy for the recorder of his life: "Pity the biographer of James Dickey. If this biographer . . . gets all of the far-flung outrageous stories on paper, then the life of James Dickey will make Ernest Hemingway look like a florist from the Midwest. This is a promise, not a premise, a certainty, not a guess." If Dickey had modeled his life on Hemingway's, he had also sought to outperform the great performer.

By the time of Dickey's death, at least six writers had proposed gathering "the far-flung outrageous stories" into a biography, but Dickey had declared as early as 1980 that he would authorize no biography. In interviews he allied himself with T. S. Eliot and Matthew Arnold in opposing such a book, and in private he did what he could to keep the biographical hounds off his trail. "No one will ever be able to reconstruct my life. It is more complicated and more unknowable than of Lawrence of Arabia," he wrote in a journal published in 1971. If Dickey confounded researchers, he also courted them by saving almost every scrap of paper he wrote on and every scrap that was ever written to him. To make them accessible to the public, he began selling his papers to Washington University in 1964. In 1993 he sold so many letters, manuscripts, notebooks, military documents, teaching materials, appointment books, financial statements, and other records to Emory University that it took 233 boxes and about 100 feet of shelf space to contain all the material. About five years later, Emory bought many more papers that had been stored in Dickey's house when he died. Hundreds of his letters had already made their way to other archives around the country. In these various havens I have found lines of poetry Dickey scribbled on Applebee's napkins, a little book about toothpaste and toothbrushing he assembled when he was five years old, love letters he received from Atlanta girls when he was a teenager, his international Playboy key, and even a sixteen-ounce can of Budweiser beer.

For all his half-hearted objections to potential biographers, Dickey loved to read biographies, and in his essays, most notably those he wrote on Lawrance Thompson's *Robert Frost: The Early Years* and Allan Seager's

The Glass House: The Life of Theodore Roethke, he laid out a blueprint of the kind he most admired. In his review of Thompson's book, focusing on Frost the man versus Frost the myth, Dickey could have been addressing his own hagiographers when he cautioned Frost's: "'Beloved' is a term that must always be mistrusted when applied to artists, and particularly to poets. Poets are likely to be beloved for only a few of the right reasons, and for almost all the wrong ones: for saying things we want to hear, for furnishing us with an image of ourselves that we enjoy believing in, even for living for a long time in the public eye." He praised Thompson for scrutinizing Frost with both approbation and disapproval: "As partial as it is [toward Frost], Dr. Thompson's account is yet the fully documented record of what Frost was like when he was not beloved: when he was, in fact, a fanatically selfish, egocentric, and at times dangerous man; was from the evidence, one of the least lovable figures in American literature. What we get from Dr. Thompson is the . . . construction of a complex mask, a *persona,* an invented personality that the world, following the man, was pleased, was overjoyed, finally, to take as an authentic identity, and whose main interest, biographically and humanly, comes from the fact that the mask is almost the diametrical opposite of the personality that lived in and motivated the man all his life." Dickey concluded: "Looking back on Frost through the lens of Dr. Thompson's book, one finds it obvious that the mode, the manner in which a man lies, and what he lies about—these things and the *form* of his lies—are the main things to investigate in a poet's life and work."

In reviewing Seager's biography Dickey restated his position. Although he entitled his review "Roethke: The Greatest American Poet," he was anything but fawning. He drew attention to Roethke's egotism, drinking, violence, and insanity; but his worst offense, according to Dickey, was his pathetically unbelievable lying, which Dickey witnessed on a trip to Seattle in 1963:

> [Roethke] would enter into a long involved story about himself. "I used to spar with Steve Hamas," he would say. I remember trying to remember who Steve Hamas was, and by the time I had faintly conjured up an American heavyweight who was knocked out by Max Schmeling, Roethke was glaring at me anxiously. "What the hell's wrong?" he said. "You think I'm a damned liar?"
>
> I did indeed, but until he asked me, I thought he was just rambling on in the way of a man who did not intend for others to take him seriously. He *seemed* serious enough, for he developed the stories at great length, as though he had told them, to others or to himself, a good many times before.

Dickey fell into a bitter silence as he listened to Roethke's long-winded, self-centered tales. Although Roethke wanted him to corroborate the lies in order "to help protect him from his sense of inadequacy, his dissatisfaction with what he was as a man," Dickey refused. "My own disappointment," he remembered, "was not at all in the *fact* that Roethke lied, but in the obviousness and uncreativeness of the manner in which he did it. Lying of an inspired, habitual, inventive kind, given a personality, a form, and a rhythm, is mainly what poetry *is,* I have always believed. All art, as Picasso is reported to have said, is a lie that makes us see the truth."

For Dickey, Roethke embodied his masterly lies in his poems, and while he commended Seager for explaining the biographical context—the "glass house"—in which the poems grew, he attacked those responsible for imposing limits on Seager's book. "Something is wrong here," Dickey commented. "One senses too much of an effort to mitigate certain traits of Roethke's, particularly in regard to his relations with women. It may be argued that a number of people's feelings and privacy are being spared." Because of Seager's reticence Dickey believed that "a whole—and very important—dimension of the subject has thereby been left out of account." For those who preferred a whitewashed, mythic Roethke, Dickey had harsh words: "It is no good to assert, as some have done, that Roethke was a big lovable clumsy affectionate bear who just incidentally wrote wonderful poems. It is no good to insist that Seager show 'the good times as well as the bad' in anything like equal proportions; these are not the proportions of the man's life. The driving force of him was agony, and to know him we must know all the forms it took." Dickey blamed Seager's reluctance to tell the whole truth on Roethke's wife, Beatrice, and attacked her for placing obstacles in Seager's way.

Writing a biography is a complex business, especially when your subject or your subject's family and friends are still alive. It was Oscar Wilde who noted that the biographer added one more fear to the prospect of death. Wilde also said that the great writer has many apostles, and usually it's Judas who writes the biography. In her book about the numerous problems facing Sylvia Plath's biographers, Janet Malcolm called the biographer a professional burglar. I would add to the list of epithets the name of Adam. Many biographers begin their perilous adventures in relative innocence—in an adorational Eden. Out of a fascination with their subject's writings, they want to pluck the apple that contains the secrets, or seeds, of their subject's life and art. Biographers quickly realize that there are some people who would rather they left the apple alone. Much biographical information, after all, is private knowledge, forbidden knowledge, harmful knowledge.

Out of my own enchantment with Dickey's early work and curiosity about his life, I wrote Dickey around 1992 that I planned to write his biography. He never responded, but mutual friends told me of his dismay.

Over the next four years, partly because he realized I was persevering with my research, he warmed to the project. About a year before he died, a Dickey scholar, Gordon Van Ness, told me that Dickey wanted to speak to me. Since I had been working on the book for several years, and since I feared he might try to restrict or block it, I made my first phone call to his house with great trepidation. When I told him my name and where I was calling from, there was a pause, and then he nearly shrieked: "Henry Hart! That's not your name!" He made up a menacing name that sounded like a character's in *The Godfather*: "You're not Henry Hart. You're Henrico Corleone! You're a hit-man for the mafia!" (In two months, after telling me that he read Edgar Rice Burroughs's *Tarzan* books as a boy, he signed some of his letters to me "Bolgani, the Gorilla," presumably because Tarzan had killed the gorilla.) To my great relief, despite his discombobulating jokes that portrayed me as his executioner, Dickey expressed little animosity toward my project. But he obviously had worries, the main one being the way I would address the romanticized versions of his life that he had aired so free-spiritedly in conversations and publications.

Although Dickey liked to ridicule T. S. Eliot's self-conscious aesthete, J. Alfred Prufrock, he shared Prufrock's need to "prepare a face to meet the faces that you meet." In an anecdote about his first poetry reading, which he said he had approached with diffidence and fear, he admitted in 1989: "The public image, whatever that may be, notwithstanding, I'm really a rather shy person. It made me very nervous to get up in front of even as few as ten or fifteen people. My wife noticed how nervous it was making me. We were on a relatively modest salary at the time at a small West Coast experimental school [Reed College, where he taught in 1963], and even though I got a couple of hundred dollars that we very much needed for a week's work, I just didn't know if it was worth what I was going through to get it." Dickey finally told his wife that he would decline the offer to read at Oregon State. When she advised him to relax and just be himself on stage, he responded: "But what self, which one?" To mask his insecurities, he confessed that he "had to invent a self" and chose for his model the "big, strong, hard drinking, hard fighting" Ernest Hemingway. He added: "Nothing could be less characteristic of the true James Dickey, who is a timid, cowardly person."

Right after telling this story to the interviewer, Ernest Suarez (and it *was* a story; he had given numerous poetry readings before teaching at Reed), he named Hemingway and T. E. Lawrence as the twentieth century's "two great invented selves, people who wished to become other than they really were and who wrote and acted out of the assumed personality." He could also have included William Butler Yeats, who once argued: "All happiness depends on the energy to assume the mask of some other life, on a rebirth as something not one's self, something created in a moment and perpetually renewed. . . . The poet finds and makes his mask in disappointment, the hero in defeat." Like his self-conscious and self-inventing forebears, Dickey regularly chose to overcome disappointment and defeat by creating and then flaunting heroic masks. When he wrote that no biographer could do justice to his life because he was more complicated than Lawrence of Arabia, what he meant was that he wore more masks and played more roles than Lawrence. To close friends like Paula Goff he confided that he was "the sum of all the roles he played"—a sum that, presumably, no one would ever be able to tally.

On July 15, 1996, during my second phone conversation with Dickey, he again brought up the matter of lying. He wanted to know what I planned to call my biography. I said I might call it *James Dickey: A Rage to Live* after a couplet from Alexander Pope's "Epistle to a Lady" that he greatly admired: "You purchase Pain with all that Joy can give, / And die of nothing but a Rage to live." He thought for a moment, and then said: "No. Henry, we've got to shake them up out there. We've got to call it: *James Dickey: The World as a Lie*." The title reminded me of a line from Schopenhauer quoted by one of Dickey's favorite writers, Joseph Campbell, in *The Mythic Image*. (I learned later that he had borrowed the phrase from the title of a poem by Paula Goff.) The world of time and space, Schopenhauer proposed, was "a vast dream, dreamed by a single being, in such a way that all the dream characters dream too." What Dickey meant was what Schopenhauer meant: the world could be viewed as a dream or lie or invention—something created mysteriously and majestically out of the void—in which all the characters dreamed or lied, too. The Greek word behind poetry is *poesis*, "a making," and Dickey implied that we all are poets or artist-gods making or "making-up" the world. With a childlike sense of wonder, as well as with the many sextants he bought as an adult, he obsessively contemplated the stars and cosmic origins. With his head in the heavens, he laughed like a mystic comedian at the mundane facts at his feet.

Nearly everything Dickey said about his life was an embroidery of fiction and fact. Trying to comprehend his penchant for tall tales and cavalier behavior, friends and foes alike attributed it to his southernness. "Most Southern literature comes right off the front porch," Dickey once said. "[It arises from] people sitting and talking, long-windedly, but always willing to listen to each others' stories because they've all got good ones to tell." Dickey's conviction that he was free to invent his past and future as he chose also had foreign sources—the existential writings of Albert Camus and Jean-Paul Sartre. In a televised conversation with Bill Moyers, Dickey once recalled listening with rapt atten-

with William the Conqueror" and assumes all his (often self-serving) informants have told him the truth. Dickey, who was not on oath and preferred the imagined to the real, exclaimed: "I'm an artist. I make the truth." Despite his considerable achievements (he wasn't a pilot but did fly 120 combat hours in the Pacific and won five Bronze Battle Stars), his ego demanded the creation of a mythical life, a Hemingway-like legend and a series of invented selves that attracted readers and sold books. Refusing to distinguish between fact and fiction, history and fantasy, for his imagination sparked all of them, he liked to make up stories to hoodwink and entertain. The humorless Hart ignores Dickey's deliberate outrageousness and desire to shock. Impatient with his civilized self as well as with his repressed and respectable audience, Dickey often thought: "What is the worst thing I can say or do at the moment?"

Such a complicated character, however appalling his behavior, cries out for understanding and elucidation. Instead, Hart solemnly and inexorably lists his deceits. Dickey's lies spring from deeper motives than the desire to scandalize. Like so many American writers, he had a strong mother and weak (or absent) father. He called his wealthy father, who raised fighting cocks and owned a lot of real estate in Georgia, an "unsuccessful lawyer, a born loser." But he desperately wanted to impress his father, who disdained poetry, with his own outdoorsmanship and military prowess. Dickey also had to compete with his dead—and therefore perfect—older brother as well as with a younger brother who was a much better athlete. When reality was insufficient, as it usually was, Dickey—like Hemingway and Malraux—created myths. As Dickey wrote of his semblable et frere Theodore Roethke, his favorite American poet,

> these lures and ruses and deceptions did enable him to exist, though painfully, and to write; they were the paraphernalia of the wounded artist who cannot survive without them.

In one agonizing scene, witnessed by an artist who illustrated Dickey's extremely lucrative coffee-table books,

> Dickey was lying on the floor, cursing, and banging his fists up and down, and the girl [in his bed] was saying, "That's all right, Jim. I know you can do it."

Dickey once told me that a biographer should be "an investigative reporter of the spirit." But Hart, ignoring the spiritual element, is as heartless as a cosmetic mortician. Describing this scene, he merely concludes, without a trace of sympathy or compassion: "Exhaustion and alcohol had once again rendered Dickey impotent." I hope Hart will never have to confront the demons of drink, marital strife, and disease that destroyed Dickey, but if he has to, I doubt that he could face them with Dickey's stoicism and courage.

In his self-reflective essay on Roethke, Dickey asked:

> Why all this insistence on being the best, the acknowledged best, the written-up best? . . . And why the really appalling pettiness about other writers like Lowell, who were not poets to him, but rivals merely? . . . His broad, boyish face had an expression of constant bewilderment and betrayal, a continual agony of doubt.

Yet Dickey himself, creating a Roethkean persona of a poet who hung around with tough guys and was pretty tough himself, brought his aggressive and competitive instincts, reinforced by sports and business, into the world of poetry. Like a cornered buccaneer, he angrily cut and slashed a path through his rivals.

Like Yeats, who on Swinburne's death confidently declared himself "king of the cats" or John Berryman who uneasily asked, when Frost died, "It's scary. Who's number one? Cal [Lowell] is number one, isn't he?" Dickey proclaimed himself *capo di tutti capi* after Berryman threw himself off a cold Yankee bridge and Lowell became crackers. But Dickey was not, despite his ungenerous letters, entirely negative. He could bless as well as blast and admired his early masters: Hopkins, Crane, Tate, and Dylan Thomas. As Hart concedes, Dickey praised "Geoffrey Hill, Philip Larkin, W. S. Graham, and Jon Silkin among the British; John Berryman, Howard Nemerov, and Theodore Roethke among the Americans." His critical missiles, though ungracious, were devastatingly on target. Jarrell was sentimental, self-indulgent, and self-pitying; James Merrill, with whom Dickey maintained an uneasy truce, often was a "chocolate-frosting of a poet"; Anthony Hecht was tiresome in his empty elegance. Anne Sexton, obsessed with "the pathetic and disgusting aspects of bodily experience," he wittily lampooned as "Ragtime Annie." John Updike was (and is) superficial, unoriginal, and too negative—slick and prolific, but devoid of content.

Hart gives endlessly repetitive, mind-numbing accounts of how Dickey, living up to his reputation as a hell-raising poet, became drunk, lecherous, out of control—breaking up furniture, parties, and marriages while reaping the sexual rewards of poetic fame. When, by force of will, he suddenly stopped drinking but refused to take drugs to ease his withdrawal, he suffered a seizure, bit off part of his tongue and nearly bled to death. Incisive about his own failings but unable to help himself, Dickey observed:

> People say that the good feeling that alcohol gives you is false—but all you have to do is live a human life to know that, in many instances, a false good feeling is better than none at all.

Hart doesn't explain that when Dickey's later poetry failed to correspond to his self-generated hype and the burden of honors he'd received, the old navigator lost his bearings and tried to obliterate his sense of unworthiness with alcohol.

Dickey's two marriages were disastrous, but Hart does little to explain his powerful bond with these two most important women in his life. His first wife, in Maxine Syerson, was the illegitimate child of a Danish immigrant, who abandoned her mother just after she was born. Hart vaguely describes her as "gracious, funloving, and capable of running the practical business of a household," and cryptically adds that her "efficiency was evident in her 'practical approach to sex.'"

After Maxine bore two sons, began to drink heavily (partly because of Dickey's adultery), and gained a lot of weight ("Hast thou seen the white whale?" Moby-Dickey would ask when she entered the room), she had for him "the sex appeal of a walrus." She became frigid; he became impotent with her and continued to consort with other women. But, completely dependent on her, he always came back. She was "the last of the poet's wives who could stick it out," and preferred to be Mrs. James Dickey than Ms. Nobody. In 1976, after twenty-eight years of marriage, Maxine suffered a massive internal hemorrhage (there was so much blood on the floor that Dickey first thought she'd been attacked by a burglar) and died at the age of fifty.

Dickey's marriage two months later to the beautiful Deborah Dodson (she was twenty-five and he was fifty-three) was even more of a nightmare. Deborah became a heroin addict, pawned Dickey's possessions, stole his medicines, and was violently threatened by her criminal suppliers. She had drug-induced seizures to match his alcoholic ones. After smashing Dickey on the head with a heavy frying pan and causing a massive blood clot that needed an emergency operation, Deborah had to be committed to a mental institution to save her own life—and his. Despite the traumatic marriages, Dickey's children turned out remarkably well. Christopher became a successful author and the Paris bureau chief for *Newsweek,* Kevin, a professor at Yale Medical School. Bronwen, abandoned by Deborah and brought up by Dickey, went to Choate and published a touching obituary of her father in *Newsweek.*

After teaching brilliantly at Rice, Florida, Reed, and San Fernando State, in 1968 Dickey finally got a permanent post at the University of South Carolina—another third-rate university in an extremely dreary town. His precipitous decline began right after the astonishing success of his novel ***Deliverance,*** which had sold 1.8 million copies by 1973, and of the superb film (for which Dickey wrote the script and played the redneck Sheriff Bullard) based on his book. Hart fails to note that Dickey's deterioration coincided with his long, tedious years in South Carolina.

Dickey's serious health problems began in 1980 with a major operation for a hiatus hernia. His intestine had strangled his esophagus, which made it much easier to drink than to eat. After the doctors "challenged the Dark Man with their short knives" his weight suddenly dropped from 250 to 190 pounds. His blood clot operation was followed in 1994 by a severe case of hepatitis, which attacked his liver and nearly killed him. After a long struggle, he was finally finished off by fibrosis of the lung.

Hart does not ask, let alone answer, the big questions about Dickey's life. What accounts for his self-destructive streak and sharp decline? Pride, arrogance, egoism, vanity, and perhaps some hidden tragic flaw certainly contributed to his demise. Perhaps, in America, the rewards for success are too sudden and too ample, the penalties for failure too great. As Hemingway, a negative model for Dickey, bitterly observed in *Green Hills of Africa,* nearly everything can hurt a vulnerable writer: "Politics, women, drink, money, ambition. And the lack of politics, women, drink, money, and ambition."

Finally, we must ask, how good is Dickey's best work? Two of his novels are first-rate. William Styron, who says more in a sentence than Hart does in fifteen pages, wrote, "[I] began to see how ***Deliverance,*** which I had so admired as a novel, was in a sense an allegory of fear and survival"—a *Heart of Darkness* for our time. Hart misses the point of the greatly underrated ***To the White Sea*** when he claims that its "puerile machismo soon turns pathological." On the contrary, the hero of Dickey's intensely lyrical and dramatic novel achieves transcendence through a mystical identification with nature. He is not meant to be a pleasant fellow or a virtuous man. Shot down in wartime Japan, he is—like the hero of *The Call of the Wild*—an expertly trained, self-reliant, and necessarily ruthless survivor.

Dickey's best poems, published in his first five volumes between 1957 and 1967, include **"May Day Sermon," "The Performance"** (about the beheading by the Japanese of a captured American airman), **"The Firebombing," "The Sheep Child," "Adultery," "Encounter in the Cage Country"** (inspired by Rilke's "The Panther"), and **"Falling"** (about a stewardess who was sucked out of a plane). These deeply moving poems express Dickey's transfiguring imagination, delicate sense of music, courageous tenderness, and capacity for wonder. They "strike the reader," as he said, "down through the more obvious levels of his being into the hidden and essential ones." Dickey's reputation, battered by his letters and biography, now seems at a low ebb. But, ten years from now, we may come to appreciate him more. The greatest postwar American poets may not be the manic confessionalists, Lowell and Berryman, but the more joyous and affirmative Roethke and Dickey.

Notes

1. *Crux: The Letters of James Dickey,* edited by Matthew Bruccoli and Judith Baughman; Alfred A. Knopf, 574 pages.

2. *James Dickey: The World as a Lie,* by Henry Hart; Picador, 811 pages.

Henry Hart (essay date spring 2000)

SOURCE: Hart, Henry. "James Dickey: Journey to War." *Southern Review* 36, no. 2 (spring 2000): 348-77.

[*In the following essay, Hart investigates the ways in which Dickey's wartime experiences affected his poetic sensibility.*]

During the spring of 1945, Radar Officer James Dickey was hard at work composing poems and reading Louis Untermeyer's poetry anthology and Shakespeare's sonnets. He paid particular attention to Untermeyer's selection of Ernest Dowson's delicate, antiquated lyrics, and tried to imitate them in his own poems. He liked Dowson so much that he asked his mother on May 29 to find his Dowson collection, copy out several poems, and send them to him. He also asked her to send a biography of Dowson by Mark Longaker, and grew furious when she suggested, after having bought the book, that she might return it to the store. To show Dowson's beneficial effects on his style, he mailed her one of his imitations:

> I having found in you more than dreams
> more sunlight than pride or wine
> huddles in the heart, now sanction,
> before diaphanous memories bequeath us
> to nothingness effete—
>
> the sun winking
> the slow radiance
> fading
> dissolving the lean shadows—
> all glorious things
> in utter loveliness stand
> held in an instant fleeting to darkness

It was Dowson's sentimental melancholia and his gift for phrase-making that made him attractive. "It's funny," Dickey remarked after the war, "that a minor 1890s versifier could have been such a phrase-maker such as everybody and his brother could have picked up on. 'Gone with the wind' comes from Ernest Dowson. 'Wine and woman and song' and 'days of wine and roses' come from him. 'Faithful . . . in my fashion' comes from him." During the war, the nostalgia for wine, women, and song gripped Dickey's emerging poetic sensibility.

Few would have expected Dickey to feel kinship with the sickly, hashish-smoking esthete who had read Latin poetry at Oxford, dissipated the rest of his short life in seedy taverns near the London docks and Paris markets, and written a few quaint poems about girls he dared not touch. Dickey seemed surprised by his Dowson infatuation, and in his sonnet **"Dedication, To Ernest Dowson,"** which began a pamphlet of poems he wrote in the Philippines, he tried to analyze the Victorian poet's spell on him:

> No mighty invocation, this, O weary singer
> Who had no thundrous tongue to hurl
> Defiance at Time, only one song to linger
> After you, treader backward from the world
> Toward oblivion, what then, have you left us
> We who lift our lyres to Milton's praise
> In smoky halls, why in lowered tones discuss
> One who only sang of listless days,
> Of weakened waters, of virginal devotion
> And unrequited love; a young French girl.—
> Why this, O weary, why this forward seeking motion
> And the quiet-frenzied nostalgia in one loose curl?
> This, Ernest, in thy song shares memory
> Who ever lost his love, who lost her not like thee?

Dickey admits to sharing Dowson's idealization of purity, an idealization that leads, paradoxically, to decadence. He may have been thinking of his asexual love for Gwen Leege, and how his nostalgia for her overshadowed his desire for other, more sexually inclined women. The poem also evinces a longing for the archaic diction of poets like Milton. Dickey's later scorn of Milton as one of the great "stuffed goats" of English departments derived from a need to dispel his early influence.

Dickey's *Poetical Remains,* as he humbly called his pamphlet, was little more than juvenilia. Awash with sentimental pining and sententious philosophizing, the poems are interesting mainly for the light they throw on Dickey's emotional state—his homesickness, his sorrow over lost loves, his disillusionment with the military, his morbid cynicism, and his yearning for "easeful Death" and other forms of oblivion. A poem titled **"Dirge"** typifies his angry brooding:

> So much have I been lined, tagged, asked questions to
> Preceded by one, followed by another, that I am past
> Sickness or indignation, and apathetically acquiesce.
> In much
> The same manner shall I die, shoved unquestioningly
>   into line
> Awaiting my turn.
> Through dull eyes, I have seen, however
> That life is no better or worse than war; the only dif-
>   ference being
> That life makes no pretense of heroics over death, is
>   not methodical
> And takes longer.

To the jaded poet, life, war, and death all seem to partake of the same mechanical futility. Before long,

Dickey renounced Dowson's hackneyed diction and aimed for a vivid, visceral way of addressing the war.

To gain practice in a more empirical style of writing, in March 1945 Dickey volunteered to replace Philip Porter as squadron historian. Until late May, Dickey kept track of the 418th's activities and also typed orders for citations and awards bestowed by General George Kenney, who commanded the Far East air forces. As might be expected, Dickey's prose in the squadron history has an elegance and Gothic tinge absent in chapters by his predecessors, but there is little remarkable about his accounts of combat missions and camp life until March 16, when a calamity occurred that resonated in Dickey's imagination for the rest of his life. He wrote:

> A most unexpected and tragic occurrence befell the Squadron when 2nd Lt. DONALD H. ARMSTRONG . . . and his observer F/O JAMES J. LALLY . . . high-speed-stalled close to the ground over the Jap strip at St. Jose, Panay, and crashed northwest of the field. . . . [The plane] was found to be almost completely demolished except for a small portion of the crew nacelle. The entire Squadron awaited apprehensively the guerrilla radio operating near San Jose, for the plane had gone down between Japanese and Filipino-held positions. Finally the guerrillas informed us that Armstrong had been killed and Lally, badly injured, was in the hands of the enemy. There has been no further news to date.

The accident happened on a daylight flight back to Mindoro after the squadron had flown night cover for a convoy making its way to Panay, an island about a hundred miles southeast of their base. Relieved by day fighters, Armstrong decided to buzz the runway on Panay. One of the only eyewitness reports of the accident came from Herbert Vaughn, radar operator for Second Lieutenant Spencer Porter, who had been flying alongside Armstrong. In his diary Vaughn recorded how both crews had flown over Panay to look at some bombed Japanese airplanes:

> Both planes went down to buzz and get a better look. Lt. Armstrong and F/O Lally made a sharp turn and crashed into a bunch of coconut trees. We circled and saw that the plane didn't burn. We could see that it was torn all to pieces and could see no sign of life. I don't know if they landed in Jap or Guerrilla territory as they are fighting around there.

As it turned out, they had landed in Japanese territory.

Though Dickey remained aloof from many of the night fighters, he identified with Armstrong's offbeat ways and usually insisted that Armstrong was his best friend in the squadron. "He was an enthusiast," Dickey said—like Lewis Medlock. He was particularly saddened by Armstrong's death because only a few nights before, the lieutenant had invited him to watch the film *Laura*. To Dickey, the gesture proved that Armstrong cared for him. Others in the squadron remembered Armstrong as a kind of free-spirited "nut" whose marital turmoil in the States contributed to his erratic behavior. If he planned to strafe the Panay airstrip, he did so without orders, since that job was usually delegated to day fighters. In any case, the strip was insignificant; only a small enemy force inhabited the area. Harold Whittern, who was with the 418th at the time, had a different explanation for Armstrong's decision. Armstrong, he said, had an attack of diarrhea in the air, tried unsuccessfully to relieve himself out the plane's window, and then decided to land: "He called control tower giving his reasons for landing. He was totally unaware that it was held by Japanese." He didn't live long enough to find out whether the strip was safe.

After the war Dickey again and again transformed his original report of Armstrong and Lally's plane crash, all the while pretending he was repeating the facts. In 1984 he told an interviewer that Armstrong was "making a raid on the islands south of us called Panay. . . . He misjudged the distance. He hit the ground and tore up the airplane. He and an observer were taken out and kept prisoner for a night and beheaded the next morning. The Filipino guerrilla forces on the island radioed almost a blow-by-blow description of the whole proceedings. We knew almost exactly what happened." On September 19, 1945, six months after the crash, Spencer Porter and Herbert Vaughn returned to Panay on a fact-finding mission. The Army Air Corps wanted to declare the two men officially dead. At first failing to uncover any new information, Vaughn and Porter finally located, in the town of Iloilo, American intelligence reports based on interrogations of the captured Japanese who had participated in or witnessed the executions. Vaughn said the reports "described how [the Japanese] found the crashed airplane with the pilot dead. Lally was hurt but alive. They took him to their camp but would only doctor his wounds when told to do so by an officer." The Japanese subsequently beheaded Lally.

According to Darrell Campbell, who was also privy to the reports, the Japanese suspected Lally of belonging to a secret intelligence outfit: "When the Japanese became aware that the Americans were invading Panay, they decided to execute however many prisoners they were holding. According to their records, they dug a long trench, bound all of the prisoners, blindfolded them, forced them to kneel on the edge of the trench, & then beheaded them one by one with a Samurai sword." George Kamajian recalled grislier details of Lally's and Armstrong's fate. "Their remains," he said, had been "buried to their shoulders," and their "heads had been used for bayonet practice." Besides Armstrong and Lally, the 418th lost no crews to crashes or executions during Dickey's tenure. Because of its uniqueness, the

track vehicles. If Dickey needed Gothic subjects for his writing, there were plenty here. One of the first papers he wrote at Vanderbilt described the carnage of Okinawa.

To make the situation worse, forty-mile-an-hour winds soon assailed the campsite and toppled the soldiers' tents. The inclement weather and ghastly locale exacerbated Dickey's ill temper. In letters home he fired salvos at his parents, as if hoping they would join him in his misery. "If I was religious I could not stand this life here. Don't ever talk to me again about 'God's justice,'" he wrote his devout mother. On July 28, Dickey and Bradley left their hellish surroundings on their first "night intruder" bombing and strafing mission over Japan. The target was Kanoya, on the southern coast of Kyushu. According to Dickey, these missions were the result of a new policy conceived by Commander Sellers, whom he called "an alcoholic guy . . . ambitious for himself and for the squadron." Dickey added:

> A lot of people . . . didn't like that because they were used to things being the way they were under Carroll Smith. But Sellers wanted us to go out. He wanted us to take it to them. I was not at all averse to that. . . . In fact, I wanted to do it. I took every mission I could find, with Bradley or with anybody else. If they wanted to fly I went with them. I had twice as much time as any R.O. in the outfit.

In fact, Sellers was not an alcoholic, no major shift in strategy had occurred, few in the 418th complained about the intruder work, and Dickey did not compile twice as much flight time as the other R.O.'s. A slight change in tactics did occur, however, in which Dickey played a small part. Sellers wanted to keep Japanese planes on the ground rather than risk fatalities in dogfights, and he had Bradley and Dickey deliver this plan to the one-star general at Okinawa's wing headquarters. The general approved it. As a result, the 418th spent a good deal of time circling Japanese airfields and then strafing targets on the way home.

In July, Dickey had a relatively easy schedule, with only twenty-two hours in the air. He flew routine convoy covers and patrols as well as intruder missions to Kyushu. In early August, as Dickey and his squadronmates scrounged lumber to build two houses over the rain-soaked earth and fretted about numerous Japanese planes flying over their camp at night, they did so with the conviction that the war would soon end. Rumors of a surrender increased after President Truman, Winston Churchill, and other leaders met at Potsdam on July 26 and issued an ultimatum: Japan must agree to a unilateral surrender or face complete destruction. Fearing the zealous militarists surrounding him, the Japanese premier, Suzuki, refused to respond. On the morning of August 6, 1945, Colonel Paul Tibbets flew the *Enola Gay* over Hiroshima, a city known for its shipbuilding factories, electrical works, and other industries. His bombardier dropped the first atomic device—a uranium bomb named Little Boy. The ensuing inferno killed about seventy thousand civilians and soldiers, wounded about eighty thousand more, and incinerated roughly 80 percent of the city's buildings. Thousands later died from radiation. With a mixture of dread and relief, the 418th listened to radio news about the blast. Years after the cataclysmic event, Dickey said: "I remember coming in from a mission and somebody telling me that the United States had just dropped a bomb on Japan that was the equivalent of twenty thousand tons of TNT. We thought it was just some sort of extra-powerful type of dynamite. We didn't know. Everybody was mystified by it. I don't think we knew it was an atomic bomb for several days." Dickey and his fellow aviators gazed in disbelief at newspaper pictures of Hiroshima's charred rubble.

Despite this lethal blow, the war continued. On August 7, the 418th registered a rare "kill." As Vaughn noted in his diary, a pilot "reported that he had shot down a Jap plane as it was about to land at Kumamoto. That was the first plane that our squadron has gotten in eight months." Dickey's stories of knocking planes from the sky like the Red Baron were just that—stories. Three days after the bomb fell on Hiroshima, a plutonium bomb named Fat Man, which had also been flown from Tinian, fell on Nagasaki, killing about thirty-five thousand and wounding thousands more. Dickey recalled, "We were all up that night. They told us not to go over there, on the west side [of Kyushu]. We just thought maybe the third fleet was up there and they were afraid of us tangling with some of their night fighters or something. But really they were keeping us away because they dropped the atomic bomb on Nagasaki."

The 418th had been bombing the city of Kumamoto, sixty miles from Nagasaki, and on the night of August 9 some of the men decided to fly over there to see if the fires were still visible. According to Bradley, "Jim and I were over Fuchu the night after Nagasaki was bombed and we were very careful not to go into any clouds in the area. I couldn't at that time believe that it would have been that dangerous." Dickey could see smoke over Nagasaki from the plane.

In a 1978 interview with a veterans' newsletter, Dickey placed himself closer to the blast: "I was flying above Nagasaki when they dropped the second atomic bomb. Nobody knew exactly what had been going on. . . . We didn't know that the secret of the universe was involved." Dickey gave his imaginary flights over conflagrations a more permanent form in his novels—in Joel Cahill's disastrous flight over a fire at his Air Corps base and in Muldrow's similarly ill-fated sortie over the flames of Tokyo. In fact, Dickey kept his distance from all such infernos.

Dickey may have had another reason for associating plane crashes with enormous fires. Close to the time of the explosions in Hiroshima and Nagasaki, he and Bradley, on a routine mission, nearly collided with a Japanese plane. The near miss had more to do with an argument between Dickey and his pilot than with hostile intent. Such embarrassing events always provoked colorful accounts from Dickey, who said that he and Bradley had an opportunity to shoot down two enemy planes:

> Bradley told me that he had a visual on the aircraft. They were in . . . night formation and they had wing lights on. They were not showing any IFF [Identification: Friend or Foe]. So they were either Allies or they were Japanese, and we were going to fire. . . . I had run a real good interception on them, real good, the best I ever did. Bradley said, "I got them; I got them." But he didn't want to fire the gun because it might mess it up and we were way out, a thousand miles from home base. We didn't want anything happening. So we navigated with the air-to-air radar, which you have to do in a special way. And so Bradley had miscalculated the closure rate and he went right in between them. Next thing, I looked around and they were behind us and they could've shot us right out of the sky. . . . Bradley screwed it up. We could have had two kills right there; they were sitting right there. Minimum range, attack position, everything, and he just went right through them. . . . Bradley panicked. . . . He took evasive action. . . . I regret that to this day.

After the near miss, Dickey expressed his disgust to Robert Herzberger and other squadron members. The memory still rankled years later, when he incorporated the incident in *Crux*.

Stanley Logan, who flew on the same mission and spoke to Dickey right after they landed, recalled a very different sequence of events:

> After Dickey picked up a radar blip, he kept telling Bradley to "throttle back" again and again as he recognized a continuously high overtaking speed. Because they didn't cooperate well, Bradley discounted the commands ("You're crazy; they can't be going that slow!") and was slow in throttling back. They had slowed to 100 mph or less when they overtook and flew between two Jap biplanes, assumed later to be Jap Air Cadets up for night training.

The "enemies," Logan said, were unarmed. Bradley was similarly dismissive of Dickey's version of the botched dogfight:

> I looked down below me to the right and saw a single plane with running lights on. I was sure that it was a Black Cat [a top-secret B-24 used for Allied night work], but we went in on it anyway. The plane turned out its lights but Jim had locked onto it. He kept telling me that we were closing too fast—I had my throttles all the way back and had dropped flaps but just as I got a good visual we whizzed by him just a few inches below him, it seemed, and instantly the tail warning device went off, set off by the plane that we had just shot past. The plane was a very slow biplane with floats that couldn't have been traveling over 90 miles an hour. I took some evasive action but when we turned back to pick him up again we couldn't do it so we finished our mission and came home. I was so sure that the plane would be a Black Cat that I possibly waited too long for a more perfect visual. I did see the exhaust earlier and he would have been a sitting duck had I fired—I guess I was too cautious because some Allied planes had been attacked by our own planes and I didn't want to make that mistake.

By his testimony, then, Dickey was impetuous, overeager to register a "kill."

The mission report filed with the squadron clarifies some details that Dickey later embellished. On August 8, Bradley and Dickey had strafed and bombed Kumamoto, with "nil observed results." While over Shiraiwa Yama they saw two enemy aircraft flying at four thousand feet:

> Upon obtaining visual, pilot immediately closed in with throttles clear closed and overshot as he held fire in attempt to identify the planes. As pilot passed the bogeys, he recognized them as bi-planes. Upon completing first pass, P-61 sighted another bogey passing head-on off his port wing. Pilot then started to make 360 degree turn to second pass on the bogeys, but discovered another plane, believed to be an enemy night fighter, was on his tail. P-61 took 20 minutes of evasive action and the bogeys were gone when P-61 shook enemy plane off tail.

In the official report, Dickey's plane was more pursued than pursuing. His imagination, however, refused to accept the unflattering truth.

During the last few days of the war, Dickey practiced some small-scale firebombing that would lead to one of his most controversial poems. Until then, Dickey's grandiose claims notwithstanding, he and his squad-mates had done little bombing of any kind. Most of this work was done by B-24s, which were flying from a strip not far from Dickey's base, and by the B-29 "Superforts," which in the spring and summer were flying from Tinian and adjacent islands. General Curtis LeMay had decided in the late winter of 1945 to load B-29s with oil-and-napalm incendiaries, and to alter conventional policy by attacking Japanese cities at night. The raids were devastating. On the night of March 9, 334 B-29s lifted off from Tinian and other islands in the Marianas and flew to Tokyo. The napalm bombs and resultant fires killed more than 83,000 people and wounded 41,000 others. A quarter of the city's buildings—nearly 267,000—went up in flames. One million civilians were left homeless. During March, LeMay ordered four more night raids, on the cities of Osaka, Kobe, and Nagoya. Between June and August he ordered sixteen more on fifty smaller industrial towns. In *To the White Sea*, Dickey bore witness to the holocaust created by these bombs.

In his poem **"The Firebombing"**—famous partly because it elicited a vociferous attack from the writer Robert Bly—Dickey pretends to be one of the pilots who took part in LeMay's raids. Though he stipulates that he flies from Okinawa, which is in the Ryukyu and not the Mariana Islands, his detractors took his narrative to be largely autobiographical. Dickey encouraged this by presenting his account as a confession: "One is cool and enthralled in the cockpit, / Turned blue by the power of beauty, / In a pale treasure-hole of soft light / Deep in aesthetic contemplation, / Seeing the ponds catch fire." Bly and like-minded critics in the '60s condemned Dickey for shamelessly committing and then glamorizing atrocities.

When interviewed about his poem, Dickey spoke of "the sense of power one has as a pilot of an aircrew dropping bombs," a "sensation [that] is humanly reprehensible" in hindsight but, in the context of war, is necessary. He intended his poem to express

> the guilt at the inability to feel guilty because you have not only proved yourself a patriot but something of a hero. You've been given medals for doing this. Your country has honored you—but there are those doubts that stay with you. You feel as a family man what all those unseen, forever unseen, people felt that you dropped those bombs on. You did it. The detachment one senses when dropping the bombs is the worst evil of all—yet it doesn't seem so at the time.

If Dickey felt little guilt, one reason was that he never participated in the sort of massive attacks **"Firebombing"** describes. His poem, however, is full of the empathy that makes guilt possible. He depicts the bombed Japanese "homeowners" as no different from his American neighbors. He is keenly aware of Japanese suffering, as his graphic images of their plight attest. His pilot-narrator, like so many Dickey characters, is a projection rather than a mirror image of his actual self.

Dickey's response to the firebombing of Japan, which killed more civilians than the atomic bombs, was complex. In a biographical statement he sent to *Contemporary Authors* on April 11, 1983, he repeated his desire to take responsibility for the firebombing by claiming—falsely—that he had dropped napalm on the Japanese as a pilot. To the end of his life he maintained, "We carried two thousand-pound bombs and three-hundred-gallon gasoline tanks full of napalm. We carried as much payload as a B-25, but we had to put them on wing shackles . . . instead of having them in the bomb-bay. . . . We did a lot of bombing, firebombing, napalm, phosphorus." His pilot confirmed that during the four days between the bombing of Nagasaki and the surrender, "We . . . used fire bombs twice . . . on the Japanese. These flights were mainly for us to learn some of the techniques involved so we could pass the information along. The war ended before we ever got into full swing." In preparation for the "scorched-earth" policy of the invasion of Japan, Dickey and Bradley tested their firebombing capabilities on the port city of Fuchu. A mission report filed on August 11 substantiates Bradley's claims, revealing that he and Dickey, along with three other crews, dropped eight one-thousand-pound "demos," which were firebombs.

As Bradley explained, the Japanese had moved many manufacturing operations from factories into homes or other shelters in rural areas:

> Because of this we stopped bombing factories; everything was open for attack. Many people lived on boats along a riverfront. These boats were production lines also. It was efficient in that the boats could be moved to different locations as the need dictated. The sad part of this was that the families lived in the houses and boats. Jim and I would usually announce our departure from an area by strafing these boats, so it seemed natural that we would do the same with the napalm, which we did on these two trial missions. I always maintained a detached state of mind when we did things like this, but Jim . . . placed himself, mentally, into the scene . . . [and] imagined what it must have been like to have been on those boats or in those houses when they were attacked. . . . All I remember were huge fires behind us as we sped away at low altitude. These happened just before daylight—we had some light, enough to get fairly low, but not as low as the dayfighters because of the visibility problem. At that time . . . [the Japanese] were saving their planes, gas and everything else as a final defense so we were not challenged on these two missions except perhaps from small arm fire.

The bombs they dropped near Fuchu on these two occasions burned one-hundred-yard swaths. They dropped no phosphorus bombs, as Dickey claimed (only the igniting devices were made of phosphorus).

In his story **"The Eye of the Fire,"** Dickey collapses these two fire-bombing missions into one:

> The mission was an important one; if successful it would do much to establish the P-61 as an offensive weapon. . . . [Nettles's] ship and White's were equipped for the first time with napalm bombs: three-hundred-gallon drop tanks which, upon impact, would scatter jellied gasoline over a wide area, to cling, burning, to whatever it struck.

Nettles, who resembles Dickey, describes how he and White, who stands in for Bradley, fly at night to a group of small houses that supposedly contain ammunition. They drop their bombs, but Nettles reflects that he "was not at all certain that he had hit the right group of huts." After the war, when Dickey claimed he had participated in the firebombings of Japanese cities, his squadron-mates reacted with incredulity. In his fantasies he seemed determined to play the role of Dr. Strangelove, raining bombs on the enemy so he could confess, enigmatically, that he had little guilt to confess.

It was not until 10:00 P.M. on August 14 that Dickey and the rest of the 418th heard that the beleaguered Japanese emperor had accepted the Potsdam terms. The squadron history recalls:

> On the night of 14 August the 418th was torn away from "Two Girls and a Sailor" by a most unprecedented demonstration of fire from practically every gun on the island. At first everyone ran for cover, thinking the Nips were making final kamikaze charges on all installations on Okinawa. Soon, however, rumors swept across the island that the Japs had sued for peace. Everyone became violently excited with every news report on the radio or with liquor laid away against VJ Day. As each outfit heard a fresh rumor, there were new outbursts of hilarity and fireworks until there was a greater display of ack ack in the sky than there had been for any Nip bomb raid. The celebration came to a sudden halt when the island commander ordered a red alert as a safety precaution against wild shooting and falling flak.

Though sporadic fighting would continue, the war had finally come to an end.

Several days later, Dickey received instructions regarding the imminent occupation of Japan. Yen were distributed, and the commanding officer, General Ennis Whitehead, circulated a letter that mingled contempt for the Japanese with calls for forgiveness and civility. Dickey found it hard to forgive his wartime enemies, then and later:

> We hated the Japanese so much. They beheaded Armstrong and Lally, tortured them and beheaded them in the Philippines. We hated them. Boy, I would have done anything against the Japanese. If there were any creatures on this earth that I would want to drop an atomic bomb on, it would have been them. And it still would. I've never forgotten it.

Many of the antagonists in his novels and poems are based on the Japanese.

On August 28, after delivering a lengthy lecture on what to expect over the next few months, Major Sellers told his squadron they would settle in the Tokyo area between September 1 and 15. He also declared that the lackadaisical lifestyle of the Mindoro and Okinawa camps would change. The men would have to obey military dress codes, salute officers, and wear standard uniforms. Officers would inspect to make sure clean clothes and clean shaves were the rule rather than the exception. Calisthenics and close-order drills would be mandatory. Used to a more relaxed regimen, Dickey found the new rules a nuisance. He made no attempt to hide his antipathy when, on August 31, he told his mother he would rather fight than put up with all the peacetime army's "crap."

To lay the groundwork for the invasion, General MacArthur and Admiral Nimitz sent an advance group to Atsugi airfield, where Dickey would shortly be stationed. Ships from the American and British fleets entered Tokyo Bay, and on September 2, 1945, MacArthur, the Japanese foreign minister, and representatives from eight Allied countries signed the surrender agreement on the battleship *Missouri*. As was his style, MacArthur made a dramatic broadcast to Americans from the ship: "Today the guns are silent. A great tragedy has ended. A great victory has been won." With the horrendous destructiveness so recently displayed, he warned that "the survival of civilization" was in the balance: "If we do not devise some greater and more equitable system, Armageddon will be at our door." The Pandora's box of the nuclear age had been opened, and like MacArthur, Dickey viewed it with both trepidation and relief. In his 1978 interview with the journal *Vetletter*, Dickey acknowledged that he and many of his compatriots owed their lives to the atomic bombs. Yet like millions of others, Dickey feared the possibility of nuclear annihilation. In **Deliverance**, he projected those fears onto Lewis Medlock, who builds a well-stocked shelter to survive a nuclear holocaust.

Though impatient with the new regulations, Dickey had more pressing concerns in September when a typhoon with seventy-mile-per-hour winds struck Okinawa. On September 17 he woke in the middle of the night to find that the wind, having changed direction and accelerated, had blown down many of the tents. The only relief from the chores of nailing down equipment and cleaning up debris came on September 22 in the form of an officers' dance that two hundred nurses attended. The weather taxed the equanimity of even the most patient air crews, as did the crowded quarters and the declining quality of food. As another typhoon advanced in mid-October, winds gusted to 120 miles per hour, leveling all rather than just some of the tents. A Quonset hut was uprooted and bent into an L shape. Only Major Sellers's shack remained intact.

To escape the storm's fury, some of the men hid in tombs in the hills, tossing urns filled with ashes out the narrow doorways to create more space. Because the tombs were holy sites, the Okinawans vehemently protested. Dickey later told of escaping into the tombs on October 7 with a first edition of Conrad Aiken's collected poems (his mother had mailed him a copy, which he supposedly brought home after the war and, years later, gave to Aiken when he met him in Savannah, Georgia). In fact, Dickey and most of the other men found protection in less controversial, if less comfortable, settings. They stayed in their aircraft. In mid-October Dickey wrote his father that the wind had blown so hard it was almost impossible to stand up: "Finally we went down to the airstrip and spent the night in B-25s."

One of the benefits of the typhoon, Dickey later pointed out, was the multitude of "armed service edition" books blown from a destroyed library at ISCOM—Island

Command. For the bibliophile, this was paradise regained from pandemonium. Dickey said that he recovered from the mud a rain-sodden copy of Yeats's collected poems; the famous textbook by Robert Penn Warren and Cleanth Brooks, *Understanding Poetry*; J. B. Priestley's *Midnight on the Desert*; and novels by Melville, Faulkner, Thomas Wolfe, James Agee, and Somerset Maugham (some but not all of these were armed-service editions). The storm undoubtedly scattered books, but probably rendered them unreadable as well (in his tellings, Dickey often changed the date of the storm and titles of the books). Though Dickey's claim about the Pacific typhoon educating him had the rugged glamor of Ishmael's declaration in *Moby-Dick* that a whaling ship had been his Harvard and Yale, Dickey's mother was the more likely source of his growing library.

If the effect of the typhoon on Dickey's scholarship was questionable, there was nothing uncertain about its effect on the planes. They were battered. The crews worked for a week repairing them before flying, on October 25, to Atsugi, about ten miles from Yokohama. Here Dickey and his squad-mates stayed in large, cold, rickety wooden barracks formerly occupied by kamikaze pilots. The air inside was stifling. The oil stoves used for heat were dangerous and smoky, and one barracks burned down as a result. The toilets were primitive. Beds were too small to accommodate taller men like Dickey, but the officers did enjoy certain privileges, like personal valets. American cooks supervised the Japanese cooks, ensuring that the food was better than usual. Dickey was glad to have fresh eggs, fruit, vegetables, and meats like ham, steak, and lamb. The men made their quarters more pleasant by installing Ping-Pong and pool tables. From his new domicile, Dickey could see Mount Fujiyama's snow-glazed summit, though the constant rains usually obscured it.

Newly released from combat, the soldiers tried to acquaint themselves with their enemy's territory. As tourists, they visited sites in Tokyo like the Dai Itchi Building, the Palace, the Imperial Hotel, and the open-air markets. They fraternized with Japanese girls, who, like the rest of the population, had been ordered by Emperor Hirohito to treat the invaders as royal guests. Some visited families in their homes, toured a plane-assembly plant that was partly underground, warmed their cold bodies in hot tubs, and explored miles of tunnels the Japanese had wired with lights and stocked with food to survive Allied bombardments. Dickey made note of many such places for his later poems and for his novel **To the White Sea**.

As October waned and many of the men, including Dickey's pilot and his commander, returned to the States, Dickey once again slumped into a melancholic funk. In November he complained to his father, "I am pretty well shot as far as nerves go." Having received his orders to return home, he was anxious to leave. Yet thoughts of his future in the U.S. depressed him. He was disheartened to learn that Peg Roney, the Atlanta girl he contemplated marrying, had chosen a navy pilot. Dickey told his mother that he might marry Gwen Leege. Because she was "really loaded down with dough," as he put it, he wouldn't have to worry about being a destitute student. Then, with Hamlet-like vacillation, he reported: "I probably won't do any of this. All the nice things I imagine for myself always seem to remain exclusively in my mind. But I'll have to see how everything works out when I get back." He vented his frustrations by accusing his mother of refusing to send more books. In the absence of typhoons, he depended on her largesse, and refused to accept her explanation that a paper shortage made some of his desired books hard to find and expensive.

Acclimated to the tropical Philippines, Dickey began to think of Japan as a gigantic refrigerator, a fit locale for his cold-hearted enemies. On November 9 the temperature hovered around thirty-one degrees during the day and sank to twenty-three at night. The men had to drain water from their Jeep radiators. The cold dried the muddy roads. Dust blew relentlessly and stuck to the men, making them look ghostly. To keep warm at night, some wore their flying suits. It got so frigid in mid-November that many of the men couldn't sleep. Dickey woke on December 4 to find the ground white with frost and ice, and on December 18 it snowed for the first time at the Atsugi base. Japan's snowy desolation would be featured, hauntingly, in **To the White Sea,** where it represented, among other things, the cold-blooded predator/prey relationship between all creatures.

Dickey no doubt read the front page story in the December 6 *Stars and Stripes* about a Japanese sergeant who had used a sharp sword to behead two American airmen on Cebu Island on March 26. The revelation came in one of the war-crimes trials proceeding in Manila. The executioner, Takeo Kawaii, described the atrocity with chilling sangfroid:

> I was sitting on a bench in the normal school yard . . . watching Sgt. Maj. Higashi . . . execute a prisoner in a very unskillful manner. My captain, Tsurayama, said: "Go over and give him a hand." . . . I had a dull sword, so I borrowed the sword of Lt. Seijiro Sakai . . . because I thought it brutal to kill a prisoner with a dull sword. Then . . . I replaced Higashi and he made the American sit near a foxhole with his hands behind him. I stood behind him, lopped off his head with one stroke, and he fell into the hole.

Kawaii argued with his commander against beheading the second airman, to no avail. The fact that the captives were kept in a Cebu schoolhouse must have given

Dickey the idea to place Lally and Armstrong in a schoolhouse in **"Between Two Prisoners."** Proximity of time and place probably touched off Dickey's associations: the incident reported in *Stars and Stripes* occurred ten days after Armstrong's fateful crash on an island almost adjacent to Cebu. The next day, under the headline "'Bataan Butcher' Must Hang," an article described the conviction and sentencing of the first Japanese war criminal, General Yamashita, for condoning sixty thousand atrocities during the Bataan Death March. This trial, too, took place in Manila, and though the Japanese general appealed to both the American and Philippine supreme courts, he was hanged on February 23, 1946. Fifteen years later, these or similar accounts of war trials helped shape Dickey's poems about Armstrong and Lally.

Having once scoffed at his pilot's eagerness for combat, Dickey was pleased to take some of the credit for defeating Japan once the war was over. "Well, it has been quite a war and I am sure glad I was in it," he told his mother. "I don't think I would have felt quite right about it if I hadn't come overseas." He was also pleased by the decorations he received on October 27, 1945: an Air Medal for operational flight missions from January 31 to August 11, an Asiatic Theater Ribbon, a Philippines Liberation Ribbon, several Overseas Service Bars, a Battle Star for the Southern Philippines Campaign, a Battle Star for the Air Offensive in the Japanese Campaign, an American Theater Ribbon, and a World War II victory medal. His Report of Separation indicated that he earned a total of five Bronze Battle Stars for his role in the air offensives over the Philippines, Japan, and Borneo.

Though Dickey struck some colleagues as a sloppy, aloof intellectual "with his nose forever in a book," he made a better impression on others. On December 15, 1945, First Lieutenant Paul Fridley wrote to the commanding general about Dickey's eight-hour missions during the Borneo campaign. Fridley praised Dickey and his pilot for flying out of Sanga Sanga to provide cover to the invasion forces off Balikpapan when other crews refused to go up because of bad weather. With regard to "intruder work against the Japanese homeland," Dickey's missions were laudable "because they involved low level strafing and bombing at night over unfamiliar terrain." Friendly fire, apparently, was a constant threat: "Many times, because of lack of fuel, it was necessary to land at the home base on Okinawa during red alerts and air raids; and therefore he was fired upon several times by friendly ack-ack and night fighters, who were too eager to check for proper identification." And he had witnessed horrendous devastation when he flew to Hiroshima in November. According to Fridley, during twelve months of overseas duty and eight months of combat, Dickey never received a rest leave. He now deserved one.

Later in life Dickey would provide friends with similarly inflated data and cajole them into writing letters on his behalf, usually to encourage prominent magazines such as the *Atlantic Monthly, Poetry,* and *Harper's* to publish his poems, college adminstrations to give him honorary degrees, or prize committees to grant him awards. Could Dickey have pressured Fridley into writing a flattering recommendation to the general? At least one of his comrades, Stanley Logan, thought so:

> I don't know why Fridley wrote the alleged letter unless it was a blanket letter covering a number of crews. Many of us endured the long gruelling missions to Borneo. I never heard of any night fighter pilot who "refused to go up because of bad weather." We cut our eye teeth on such weather. This sounds like more B.S. Similarly with Kyushu missions. Following the friendly fire incident that Maj. Smith related in January, before we joined the squadron, the only incident of friendly fire that I knew about was when Frumer (an R.O.) bailed out over a naval unit near Okinawa they made the mistake of flying over unannounced.

Logan also pointed out that most flyers never received rest leave.

However he procured Fridley's testimonial, Dickey got approval from army headquarters in Atsugi for a six-day leave. He and Herbert Vaughn packed their clothes early on Christmas Day, then drove their Jeep four hours through little villages covered with snow to the Fuji-View Hotel at the foot of Mount Fujiyama. They relaxed in the hotel's steam heat, bath, and soft beds; dallied with two Red Cross women (one of whom they knew from New Guinea); consumed sandwiches and coffee all day in the snack bar; and at night dined by candlelight on steak, French fries, and ice cream. Two days after they arrived, it began to snow. Feeling adventurous, Dickey experimented with skis. He also rowed on the lake, attended a Japanese stage show, sampled a sukiyaki dinner with hot sake in a Japanese home, and watched a kimono demonstration before driving back to Atsugi on the last day of the year. Years later he planned to end ***Crux*** the way he ended his war year, with the main character, Harbelis, on rest leave at a Mount Fujiyama hotel, drinking whiskey or martinis, visiting the Japanese, and mumbling the secret language of the Alnilam cabal to the mountain.

Dickey's most significant year had begun on New Year's Eve of 1944, so it was fitting that he began his return to civilian life on the same day a year later. For the rest of his life, the plot that gripped his imagination most consistently was that of the circular journey in which beginnings and ends coincide. After his heroes survive their ordeals, they compulsively return home. Gazing at the mountain beyond his hotel, as his poem **"A View of Fujiyama after the War"** bears out, Dickey felt the tremors of war in the tremors of earth (in the form of a slight earthquake); he also felt a survivor's sense of blissful release. The volcanic mountain, beautiful in its dormancy, was a fit symbol for his sense of transcendence and tranquility. "Overcome by the enemy's peace," he pledges to "live at the heart / Of his saved, shaken life," and write from a sense of hard-won triumph.

Dickey's return home on the USS *Sea Devil,* which commenced on January 10, 1946, took approximately the same time as his journey to the war—about two weeks—and he passed the time in much the same way—by reading books. He told the poet Frederick Turner years later that he devoted many happy hours to reading J. B. Priestley's book on time theory, *Midnight on the Desert.* He also thought about his future: "I still couldn't get used to the idea that I was going to live. I didn't have any plans. I sort of thought about going back and playing [foot]ball again, but I didn't really want to do that. I thought that maybe I could go to another school and further my literary interests. I had no idea that I would be a writer. That was too ambitious for me." But his writerly ambitions had already incubated and hatched in the heat of the Pacific islands. He docked in Seattle on January 23, made his way back to Atlanta, and from there traveled to Vanderbilt to become a writer.

A form filled out by air-crew personnel upon returning to the States outlined Dickey's war service. His official position was listed as "radar observer," his total combat hours 119.10, and total combat missions 38 (any assigned flight in a combat zone, with the exception of training flights and DC-3 supply flights, was considered a combat flight). Dickey's Separation Qualification Record, issued at Fort McPherson, just south of Atlanta, on March 1, 1946, confirmed these numbers. A brief account of his service appeared under the heading "Summary of Military Occupations":

> [James Lafayette Dickey] flew long range night strafing and bombing missions. Acted as bomber escort on night missions and provided cover for landing forces and convoy attacks. Tracked and bombed seaborne and land targets by means of synchronized radar methods, using designated radar bombing equipment. Operated and performed first echelon maintenance on radio and radar sets and equipment. Completed 38 combat missions. Total flying time 403 hours, of which 120 were combat hours.

Upon these bare bones Dickey fleshed out his myth of piloting, dog-fighting, firebombing, and crashing in P-61 Black Widows. Apprised of his inventions, some squadron-mates wondered if he had simply forgotten his activities in the war. Since he carried a photostat of his discharge papers in his wallet for the rest of his life, he obviously had not.

Dickey's exaggerations would be accepted readily by a postwar audience eager to believe that American soldiers had acted daringly in vanquishing an evil empire. Like the character played by William Holden in *The Bridge on the River Kwai,* a movie he loved, Dickey prevaricated about his status as a combat pilot to impress men and women alike. And like his movie counterpart, he admitted the facts only when pressed by those who knew or suspected the truth.

Only the well-informed knew the extent to which Dickey embellished. As his career as poet and novelist flourished, so did his military tales, becoming so ingrained that even a scholar like Richard Calhoun mistakenly affirmed in a critical study that "Dickey was in the Air Force from 1942 to 1946, heavily involved in combat, flying nearly one hundred combat missions in the Pacific campaign in the Philippines, at Okinawa, and participating in the firebombings of major Japanese cities." When asked by John Kelly, who was writing *Night Fighters to the Sea,* to give specifics of his record as a pilot, Dickey pretended to be too busy to answer. On the same day he refused Kelly, August 4, 1982, he requested from Prosper Rufur, one of his old night-fighter cohorts, a copy of the squadron history for use in his burgeoning novel, **Alnilam.** He told Rufur, who was in charge of squadron records, that he had refrained from attending reunions in the past but might go to an upcoming one in Orlando. Perhaps out of fear of having his invented war record questioned, he never went to a reunion.

Dickey was as deeply ambivalent about his military service as he was about his lies. In the early '50s he proposed to write a short story that would evince some of his feelings regarding the Army Air Corps. The narrator would visit a deserted base where he had once trained and say, "I was glad to see it standing deserted, for I had always hated military life, with the really profound hatred of uninterrupted irritation and interference, though I had nothing better, or other, to do." He never expressed his ambivalence better than when he told his friend Ernest Suarez, who watched with him as a group of ROTC students jogged across the University of South Carolina campus several weeks before Dickey died, "There's nothing that attracts and horrifies me more than people marching and chanting. The rhythm is extraordinary; it makes you want to be part of it, to get up and join them. But for all we know they're the next Hitler Youth." Despite his harsh remarks, Dickey always acknowledged that his World War II experience was the catalyst for his literary career. The war purged many of the superficial values of his Atlanta upbringing, made him more aware of the fragility of life, and convinced him of the subversive and ultimately redemptive powers of the imagination.

About a decade after he left Japan, Dickey hailed his decision to become a writer to the novelist Andrew Lytle:

> To be of the same variety, the same profession, or calling, as the writers I like (or love) is quite sufficient compensation for my life. I have never valued life greatly, since I was in the war so young. It seemed then that most of the things I had been told about human life were false, constructions, rationalizations only, which would not stand up against any kind of forceful reality. But the artist is after another kind of reality: the underlying, the typical, the profound, the symbolic, the substructure of reality, the hidden anatomy.

In becoming a writer, Dickey substituted "symbolic" fictions, which revealed the truth of his feelings and ideas, for the "false constructions" of his youth, as well as for the "realities" he found arrayed against him. He began to live more consistently in an "invented world," a "supreme fiction"—as Wallace Stevens would say—of his own making, and he persuaded others to do the same.

FURTHER READING

Bibliography

Glancy, Eileen. *James Dickey: The Critic as Poet, An Annotated Bibliography with An Introductory Essay.* Troy, NY: Whitston Publishing Co., 1971, 107 p.
  Primary and secondary bibliography.

Biographies

Calhoun, Richard J., and Robert W. Hill. *James Dickey.* Boston: Twayne Publishers, 1983, 156 p.
  Biographical and critical study.

Hart, Henry. *James Dickey: The World as a Lie.* New York: Picador, 2000, 811 p.
  Biographical study of Dickey.

Criticism

Alexander, George L. "A Psychoanalytic Observation on the Scopophilic Imagery in James Dickey's *Deliverance.*" *James Dickey Newsletter,* 11, no. 1 (fall 1994): 2-11.
  Traces the scopophilic theme in Dickey's novel.

Baughman, Ronald. *Understanding James Dickey.* Columbia: University of South Carolina Press, 1985, 174 p.
  Full-length critical study of Dickey's poetry, novels, and literary criticism.

———, ed. *The Voiced Connections of James Dickey: Interviews and Conversations.* Columbia: University of South Carolina Press, 1989, 281 p.
  Collection of interviews with and essays on Dickey.

Bowers, Neal. *James Dickey: The Poet as Pitchman.* Columbia: University of Missouri Press, 1985, 86 p.
  Investigates Dickey's penchant for publicity and its impact on his work.

Calhoun, Richard J. *James Dickey: The Expansive Imagination, A Collection of Critical Essays.* Deland, Fla.: Everett/Edwards, 1973, 231 p.
  Collection of interviews and critical essays.

Gleason, Judith. "That Lingering Child of Air." *Parnassus* 8 (1980): 63-82.
  Derogatory review of *Tucky the Hunter.*

Howard, Richard. "James Dickey." *Alone with America: Essays on the Art of Poetry in the United States since 1950,* pp. 75-98. New York: Atheneum, 1969.
  Traces Dickey's poetic development.

Kellman, Steven G. "All the World's a Movie Set: Dickey's *Deliverance.* *South Carolina Review* 26, No. 2 (spring 1994): 155-61.
  Asserts that "many elements in Dickey's novel facilitated translation from the medium of prose fiction to that of cinema."

Kirschten, Robert. *James Dickey and the Gentle Ecstasy of Earth: A Reading of the Poems.* Baton Rouge: Louisiana State University Press, 1988, 218 p.
  Analyzes stylistic and thematic elements of Dickey's poetry.

Kuehl, John R., and Linda K. Kuehl. "'The Principle of Uncertainty' in *Deliverance.*" *South Carolina Press* 26, no. 2 (spring 1994): 162-72.
  Surveys critical perspectives on Dickey's novel.

Moorhead, Michael. "Dickey's *Deliverance.*" *Explicator* 51, no. 4 (summer 1993): 247-48.
  Examines the conclusion of Dickey's novel.

Spears, Monroe K. "James Dickey's Poetry." *Southern Review* 30, no. 4 (autumn 1994): 751-60.
  Explores the defining characteristics of Dickey's poetry.

Suarez, Ernest. *James Dickey and the Politics of Canon: Assessing the Savage Ideal.* Columbia: University of Missouri Press, 1993, 170 p.

    Investigates Dickey's development as writer and celebrity within the context of contemporary poetry and late twentieth-century American culture.

———. "James Dickey's Literary Reputation: Romanticism and Hedonism in *To the White Sea* and *Deliverance.*" *South Carolina Review* 26, no. 2 (sSpring 1994): 141-54.

    Discusses parallels between Dickey's *To the White Sea* and *Deliverance.*

Van Ness, Gordon. *Outbelieving Existence: The Measured Motion of James Dickey.* Columbia, S.C.: Camden House, 1992, 139 p.

    Explores critical reaction to Dickey's work and reputation.

Additional coverage of Dickey's life and career is contained in the following sources published by the Gale Group: *American Writers Supplement*, Vol. 4; *Authors and Artists for Young Adults*, Vol. 50; *Authors in the News*, Vols. 1, 2; *Beacham's Encyclopedia of Popular Fiction: Biography & Resources*, Vol. 1; *Concise Dictionary of American Literary Biography*, Vols. 1968-1988; *Contemporary Authors*, Vols. 9-12R; *Contemporary Authors Bibliographical Series*, Vol. 2; *Contemporary Authors New Revision Series*, Vols. 10, 48, 61, 105; *Contemporary Authors—Obituary*, Vol. 156; *Contemporary Literary Criticism*, Vols. 1, 2, 4, 7, 10, 15, 47, 109; *Contemporary Poets* Ed. 7; *Contemporary Popular Writers*; *Contemporary Southern Writers*; *Dictionary of Literary Biography*, Vols. 5, 193; *Dictionary of Literary Biography Documentary Series*, Vol. 7; *Dictionary of Literary Biography Yearbook*, 1982, 1993, 1996, 1997, 1998; *DISCovering Authors 3.0*; *DISCovering Authors Modules: Novelists, Poets* and *Popular Fiction*; *Encyclopedia of World Literature in the 20th Century*, Ed. 3; *Literature Resource Center*; *Major 20th-Century Writers*, Eds. 1, 2; *Novels for Students*, Vol. 9; *Poetry Criticism*, Vol. 40; *Poetry for Students*, Vols. 6, 11; *Reference Guide to American Literature*, Ed. 4; and *Twayne's United States Authors.*

Hunger

Knut Hamsun

Sult (1890; *Hunger*) is Hamsun's breakthrough novel about a young writer struggling to maintain his dignity while trying to survive in a desolate and lonely world.

INTRODUCTION

Published in 1890, *Hunger* was a literary breakthrough for Hamsun, establishing him as one of the most important writers of his time. Written from the perspective of a struggling writer living in the city of Christiania, near Oslo, Norway, the story is somewhat autobiographical, reflecting Hamsun's own struggle as he worked to establish his literary reputation. Today, the work is acknowledged as a work of powerful originality, infused with Hamsun's unique writing style, and a premier example of the psychological novel. Following the publication of *Hunger*, Hamsun went on to write several other novels, including *Mysteries* (1892), *Pan* (1894), and *Growth of the Soil* (1917). The last earned Hamsun a Nobel Prize in Literature in 1920, thus paving the way for his work to be translated into other languages, and becoming accessible to larger audiences.

Hamsun was born in 1859 in Lom, Gudbrandsdal in central Norway. His parents, Peder and Tora Pederson, were farmers forced to move the family to the town of Hamaroey for financial reasons. There, a wealthy uncle had acquired a farm called Hamsund, which they were to farm. Hamsun was separated from his family at the age of nine to go and work for his uncle, who also owned and ran the town post office. The young Hamsun was ill-treated by his uncle, who often starved and beat him. Years later, Hamsun would continue to refer to the abuse he suffered at the hands of his uncle, which he believed, was responsible for many of his chronic nervous illnesses. In 1874, Hamsun managed to escape from Hamaroey. He lived itinerantly for the next few years, working various petty jobs. Simultaneously, he also published several books, even presenting literary lectures for interested audiences. However, he was unable to interest a major publisher in his work. Disappointed with the failure, Hamsun moved to the United States in 1882. Once again, Hamsun was faced with a life of labor, with little literary success. He returned to Norway in 1884, publishing an article on Mark Twain under the name of Knut Pederson Hamsund. Hamsun returned to the United States in 1886, moving back to Norway permanently in 1888. It is believed that his harsh experiences in America influenced his political views deeply and were partly responsible for his reactionary politics later in life. Hamsun continued to write and lecture, publishing the first few chapters on *Hunger* anonymously. When the novel was published in its entirety, it finally brought with it the literary success Hamsun had been seeking for many years.

PLOT AND MAJOR CHARACTERS

Hunger is a monologue related by a struggling artist and is considered one of Hamsun's most autobiographical works. Regarded as one of the first examples of psychological literature and the stream-of-consciousness technique later developed by writers such as James Joyce, the novel is largely devoid of plot and character development. Instead, the narrative focuses on the thoughts and actions of the first-person narrator, a struggling artist, who lives in Christiania, Oslo, hoping to strike success. Divided into four parts that are very similar in form, content, and style, the book follows an unnamed narrator as he attempts to find food, lodging, and work while dreaming of making it as a writer. Instead, he finds himself alone, with nowhere to live, and nothing to eat. Alone in the big city, the protagonist reaches catastrophe in each section of the book, saved at the last minute by random events, such as the sale of an article, help from an old friend, and eventually at the end of the book, a job on a ship that takes him away from the desolation of the city.

MAJOR THEMES

Many critics consider *Hunger* an illustration of the literary views Hamsun had expressed in his other early works. Although *Hunger* is very autobiographical, drawing deeply on Hamsun's years of suffering, loneliness, and struggle both as a child and later, as an artist, it is also a literary experiment. As such, it describes an artist-hero struggling to survive while trying to maintain the purity of his artistic thoughts and inspiration: "Nothing escaped my eyes. I was sharp and my brain was very much alive, everything poured in toward me with a staggering distinctness." The novel is very different from Hamsun's other works, in that it focuses its attention solely on a single character—characterized by many critics as a Dostoievskian hero, sick in body, suffering from physical depravity that forces him to have hallucinations and paranormal ideas. The entire narrative, thus, focuses on the effects of an intense physical condition—hunger—on the psyche of one man. In addition to a study of the psychological effects of hunger, Hamsun's novel is also a work of protest. His focus on the protagonist is also interpreted as an act of resistance on the part of Hamsun, who reacted strongly to the realistic, socially-focused novels of nineteenth-century Scandinavian literature, especially the works of such writers as Henrik Ibsen. In fact, Hamsun's literary lectures shortly before the publication of *Hunger* focused often on his opposition to a theory and practice of literature that advocated the highlighting of social problems. Thus, the action and focus of this book is particularly significant in the way it focuses entirely on the protagonist and his thoughts, with no concern for any issues of social injustice or politics.

CRITICAL RECEPTION

Hunger was published to great critical success in Norway in 1890, and Hamsun was hailed as one of the most significant Norwegian writers by many. International recognition followed later, once he received the Nobel Prize in 1920. Although much attention is paid to Hamsun's controversial political and social views, he also is acknowledged as one of the most significant precursors of stream-of-consciousness literature, and writing focused on the subjective, mostly due to his work on *Hunger*. In many ways, this novel exemplifies the contrasts that characterized Hamsun himself, notes Edwin Björkman in his introduction to George Egerton's translation of that work. Lauding him as "the foremost creative writer of the Scandinavian countries" after Ibsen and Strindberg, Björkman writes that *Hunger* is a novel about an unusual theme, told in a strikingly different format, heralding the neo-romantic movement in Scandinavia. In his biography of Hamsun, Robert Ferguson notes that the writer himself considered *Hunger* a work representative of his own perspective on the role of the writer. According to Ferguson, the novel remains largely undated except for a few minor details because of Hamsun's complete focus on the inner workings of an individual mind—for the first time in literature, writes Ferguson, consciousness itself is a hero. According to Paul Auster's analysis of *Hunger*, the radically subjective viewpoint expressed in the work immediately eliminates any connection with traditional narratives. Instead, writes Auster, *Hunger* is a work of existential art, a story in which a human being looks into the face of death, with no hope of salvation.

PRINCIPAL WORKS

Fra det moderne Amerikas aandsliv [*On the Cultural Life of Modern America*] (essays) 1888

Sult [*Hunger*] (novel) 1890

Mysterier [*Mysteries*] (novel) 1892

Pan, af Løitnant Thomas Glahns papirer [*Pan*] (novel) 1894

Victoria: En kaerligheds historie [*Victoria*] (novel) 1898

Rosa: Af student Parelius' papirer [*Rosa*] (novel) 1908

Livet ivold [*In the Grip of Life*] (novel) 1910

Markens Grøde [*Growth of the Soil*] (novel) 1917

Konerne ved Vandposten [*The Women at the Pump*] (novel) 1920

Siste kapitel [*Chapter the Last*] (novel) 1923

Landstrykere [*Vagabonds*] (novel) 1927

August (novel) 1930

Men livet lever [*The Road Leads On*] (novel) 1933

Ringen sluttet [*The Ring is Closed*] (novel) 1936

Paa gjengrodde stier [*On Overgrown Paths*] (memoirs) 1949

CRITICISM

Hunter T. Stagg (review date 15 February 1921)

SOURCE: Stagg, Hunter T. Review of *Hunger*, by Knut Hamsun. *Reviewer* 1, no. 1 (15 February, 1921): 23-4.

[*In the following review of* Hunger, *Stagg lauds Hamsun's powerful and vivid writing style.*]

It seems inevitable that the conspicuous success in this country of a foreign writer hitherto unknown to us should be followed by an influx of other translations from distant and little exploited pastures of literary endeavor. Upon the heels of Blasco Ibanez's financially triumphant introduction to the American public came other Spanish authors, whose bids for favor proved less ingratiating. Then Latin America was raked—is still being raked—for material offering the elements of popularity.

France, of course, we knew, and Russia. Scandinavia, too, but not so well, and chiefly through the theater at that, so the publishers turned northward and presently Johan Bojer burst upon us to be accorded without delay a prominent place in our list of novelists no one can afford to neglect. Now, through the doors of Alfred A. Knopf, comes another welcome addition, Knut Hamsun, whose first work to reach us inspires only wonder that it was so long in finding its way across the Atlantic. This writer, a Norwegian, has been awarded the Nobel Prize for literature for 1920. He is sixty years old, and his works have been famous in European countries for at least a quarter of a century, being translated, it is said, into seventeen languages. And at last they are being brought to America, a country in which, as a poverty stricken young man, the author twice sought without success a place in the sun.

So few of Hamsun's writings have been rendered into English, and those few at such long intervals and with so little enterprise, that one is justified in calling ***Hunger*** the first to reach us. That it will not be the last seems guaranteed by the widespread interest the book has awakened. It is in many ways a distressing, and in no way a pleasant book, for the hunger that is its theme is not that of the spirit but of the flesh, a plain unvarnished craving for bread with which to keep life in the body. Knowledge that the story is, as Edwin Bjorkman tells us in his introduction, largely autobiographical, was not needed to give it that vividness which makes for actual pain in the reader's own breast as he watches the bitter struggle for existence of one poor journalist in the city of Christiana. Vividness is, indeed, the essence of Knut Hamsun's style. If hunger ever took a visible, touchable form it does in this book.

And if vividness is the essence of his manner, violence, often to the point of brutality, is the outstanding characteristic of his method. In unfolding his story Hamsun spares us not one significant detail of the hero's terrible degradation through starvation. He has subtlety, too, for he has known how to enhance the awfulness of that degradation through the upspringing now and then of a little hope. He has, finally, deep artistry; for while the reader sometimes revolts from the harshness of the scenes depicted, as a psychological study of a proud, sensitive nature in the grip of the most primitive of all forces, hunger, the book would not be complete without, say, the pitiful passage where the hero is reduced to childish wailings: "Lord God, I feel so wretched!"—or the later ironic touch when, after a period of delirium, he secures a bit of food and finds his stomach too weak to retain it. There are other scenes of which one can only say they are very nearly appalling in their frankness, but it is these, and others such as these, which for their humanness one remembers longest.

If crudities of style and construction be noted in the book it must be remembered that ***Hunger*** is Hamsun's first novel, first published in 1890. In spite of them it is a gripping work, hard to leave unfinished. It marks Hamsun, moreover, a valuable addition to the imported literature of our own land, and the sizeable list of books to his credit with which Mr. Knopf has promised to follow up the present volume will be greeted with interest by every reader of ***Hunger***.

Robert Coles (essay date 23 September 1967)

SOURCE: Coles, Robert. "Knut Hamsun: The Beginning and the End." *New Republic* 157, no. 13 (23 September 1967): 21-4.

[*In the following essay, Coles summarizes the major action and themes in* Hunger, *concluding with a short history of Hamsun's literary career and political struggles.*]

On February 19, 1952 a man of 93 died near Grimstad, Norway. He was a writer, indeed one who had won the Nobel Prize for Literature in 1920. He was also at the time of his death an officially recognized traitor, allowed by his nation to live out his last years at home only because of the "permanently impaired faculties" that advanced age was supposed to have caused. Now, fifteen years later, Knut Hamsun's first novel, ***Hunger***, has been translated into English by the American poet Robert Bly; and at the same time we are offered a translation by Carl Anderson of the last writing Hamsun did, while a prisoner and forced inmate of a mental hospital between 1945 and 1948.

Some lives are themselves epics, and Hamsun's was an epic life, as long and rich and defiantly unique as anything he wrote. He was born Knut Petersen, the son of a faintly aristocratic mother and a father who farmed for a living, but loved to recite legends and walk endlessly in the woods. When the boy was four his parents took him north, from a valley in central Norway to the region near Bodö, way up the coast, in *true* Nordland, where a growing child must come to terms with nights that last a month and summers that must seem like much more than a prize, or even a form of reparation and reconciliation—perhaps like a passionate act of atonement by a God who can stay sullen and aloof only so long. Hamsun's family settled on another farm called Hamsund, hence the name Knut Petersen later assumed. Neither the mother nor the father was anxious to send their son to school. Instead, he worked on the land, worked with a shoemaker, and began to write.

At twenty Hamsun had finished a short novel called *Frida.* He took it to Oslo—then called Christiana—and failed to secure a publisher. He returned to a rooming house in the capital city, and nearly starved to death. Eventually he left for the countryside. He spent what seemed like his last bit of energy looking for anything "physical" to do. He had had enough of thinking and putting ideas to word. He worked as a farm hand and he worked on the roads. At twenty-three he left for America, where like many of his countrymen he sought out the plains of the middle west. He lived in Wisconsin, in Minnesota, worked in lumberyards, became an auctioneer. He was always on the move, and never with much money. In time he became desperately ill with tuberculosis, and returned to Norway, supposedly to die. He recovered and resumed his marginal existence in Oslo.

Still thinking of himself as a writer, still unable to write, still a proud, eccentric, willfully isolated young man he returned to America in 1886, at twenty-seven. I suppose it can be said that his mind was unsettled; certainly his body was incredibly restless. He made for Chicago, where he worked as a streetcar conductor. He went to North Dakota and harvested wheat. For a while he was a barber. In 1888 he thought of working as a fisherman on the Newfoundland Banks, something he had once before done for three years; but he was homesick at last and that year returned to Europe—first to Copenhagen, then Oslo. In Denmark he began working on *Hunger.* In Norway he wrote—apparently in a frenzy—a book called *The Cultural Life of Modern America.* In some respects it is like Kafka's *Amerika,* full of sly, humorous irony, and at heart a fanciful, extravagant work of the imagination rather than a literal description of anything "American" that Hamsun experienced. He had lived close to our soil, and came to know our late 19th-century life very intimately and concretely; yet the New World seemed to stir his mind in the direction of private imagery and extraordinary metaphor.

In 1890, when Hamsun was thirty-one, *Hunger* was published. He would never again be unknown. Robert Bly tells us that Hamsun's style in his first novel was somewhat similar to Hemingway's—curt, almost severe, and to the point. Others have claimed that America's raw, nervous and informal life comes across almost miraculously in Hamsun's Norwegian prose. Yet the novel's plot and its central character also manage to evoke Russians like Gogol and Dostoevsky, and such contemporary European ("existentialist") writers as Camus and Sartre. Hamsun seems to have drawn upon the best of two continents, and the result is a work of art that is still forceful, still provocative, and not in the slightest "out of date." In point of fact, *Hunger* is a "fashionable" novel, all taken up with "our" concerns and discoveries—the world's injustice as it affects the individual, the unconscious and its various workings, the question of what is psychologically "normal" and what is socially permissible.

Hunger is one nameless man's narrative, his description of what it is like to live on the extreme edge of life, without a supply of food that can be taken for granted, and without the friendship or love of anyone. Right off, the suffering man announces that "all of this happened while I was walking around starving in Christiania"; and much later, when he has had enough of both starvation and the city, he takes a job on a ship and describes himself as he "straightened up, wet from fever and exertion, looked in toward land and said goodbye for now to the city, to Christiania, where the windows of the homes all shone with such brightness." The hero is apart at the beginning. He continues to keep people at arm's length, no matter how closely he watches them. At the end he goes away, out of the way, a long way off.

Hamsun was always an uncompromising outsider. In *Hunger* he showed he could even stand outside himself. If the city is full of the comic, the preposterous and the fake, the mind of its half-wretched, half-indulgent observer emerges as no less ridiculous and pitiable. Though the narrator of *Hunger* reminds one of Raskolnikov or even Kafka's K, Hamsun is neither as strict and serious as Dostoevsky nor as incurably forlorn as Kafka. He does seem to have a pilgrimage in mind for his hero, or at the very least some serious travelling. Perhaps it is a mistake to try to find in *Hunger* the quests *we* have made. The Hamsun who wrote *Hunger* might have had *Piers Plowman* in mind, or the strange and bizarre events that can be found in almost any medieval chronicle of a soul's "way."

In 1893 Hamsun published *Mysteries,* in many respects a sequel to *Hunger.* (Farrar, Straus and Giroux have announced that an English translation of *Mysteries* is on the way.) Again there is a stranger, now given the name of Nagel. Again he observes everything, particularly himself. Again the reader is forcibly confronted with a character's resourceful capacity to deceive both himself and the "outside" world. Before Pirandello, before Freud, before the self-conscious 20th century began, Hamsun was obsessed—and systematically so—with the nature of illusion. He did not take man's psychological life for granted, nor did he simply allude to the terror, the vagaries and the caprices of the mind's daily life. Deliberately and carefully—as if he were one of today's psychologists or psychiatrists—Hamsun examines (through Nagel and the people he manages to confuse, puzzle and torment) all sorts of familiar subjects: the child in man; the motive that hides other motives; the power of a shrewd and willing observer both to anger a person and lay bare his most ingrained and self-sustaining conceits.

In 1894 the Norwegian public had to deal with an avalanche of Hamsun. *New Ground* and *Editor Lynge* were published, neither of them "great" books, and both of them totally unlike the two novels that had previously appeared. From portraits of very particular, very unusual and very inward individuals Hamsun turned to devastating and scornful descriptions of social cliques. In *Editor Lynge,* Oslo's politicians are relentlessly exposed as mean, calculating, dishonest. In *New Ground* the city's literary "set" is subject to withering ridicule. Hamsun fixes upon "artists" and "thinkers" every stereotype they so often use to brand businessmen or members of the "petit bourgeoisie." Fake, pretentious, calculating, and self-serving "intellectuals" are contrasted with mere workers, mere shopkeepers. Let other authors turn their biting satire on the greedy, hypo-critical mercantile class, and the aspirants who serve it. Hamsun scorned the scornful, the nervously "aware" and the proudly "enlightened"—who score points on one another rather than make money, and who can be as showy and snobbish and fiercely competitive as the most successful of burghers. These two books ordinarily might be ignored, certainly in any account of Hamsun's significant artistic successes. Yet they give an important clue to his way of looking at politics and society, and if they do not "explain" his later pro-Nazi statements, they at least show how uncongenial his mind was to a rising "liberal" or "progressive" intellectual and political tradition—and therefore how susceptible he might have logically become in later years to the powerful military alternative of Nazi fascism. A man who at 35 saw rot and scandal in the "best" of the Western world, and who even then was living his own, proud and intensely private life, could much later flinch not at all when Hitler called for more purges and bloodbaths.

Also published in 1894 was *Pan*, a contrast to Hamsun's twin effort at social criticism. (An excellent English translation by James McFarlane was made available ten years ago.) *Pan* is a love story in the Nordic tradition, full of sadness and tenderness, passion and disappointment—and finally, that threesome of separation, search and death. Hamsun is done with Oslo. He places his heroes up North, in a fishing village. The sea, the forest, the weather figure prominently. The movement is away from the inward, the private, and toward Nature. At the same time there is an ironic new interest in groups of people, in contrast to *a* person. I suppose one can say the hero of *Pan* is a "repressed" Victorian; he takes women for granted, seems to want to use them rather than respect their particular desires and needs. They are "objects," a term still used by some psychiatrists to describe a person who is wanted and sought.

In *Victoria,* his next novel and a companion piece to *Pan,* Hamsun also describes a youthful love affair. Johannes, the suitor, is again brusque, uncouth and distant—but poetic. He desires a rich man's daughter—perhaps to marry his native poetry to some firmly established way of life. What Johannes wanted, Hamsun achieved. He gradually became a well-to-do, insistently private man whose lyric inspiration was to be shared with the world only out of a writer's need. No longer was he hungry or jobless, and if he remembered the wild sea and the inviting forests of his youth, he largely forgot the social and economic injustice he had occasion to see firsthand for so long. Now the odd spirit moved and the cloistered pen obliged. "Causes" were ignored—and with them all of Norway's intellectuals. Plays appeared and a number of short stories and poems were written. He travelled all over the world and described what he saw and felt while living in various places. He wrote several gentle and witty novels, and it has to be noted that their characters are no longer poor, hungry, desperate or even very young and uncertain about life. Indeed, by 1915, he had completed a two-volume portrayal of a rich and powerful family whose rural, aristocratic ways can no longer survive modern, technological society. Hamsun feared what would happen when the various "classes" of people are less firmly ordered and separated. With *Growth of the Soil* (1917) he even gave up trying to understand that kind of "social change." His concern is now with the land, with man the tiller and lonely pioneer who lives in an essentially timeless and constant world. Factories, political upheavals, scientific achievements for the good and the bad—none of them has anything to do with the bleak, inhospitable and unpeopled terrain described by the increasingly patrician man-of-letters.

Hamsun's chief public was in Germany. He was relatively ignored in England and America. Unlike Strindberg he payed little attention to contemporary events, and unlike Munch he lost his early interest in the mind's hard and sometimes terrible struggle for day-to-day coherence and "sanity"—though Munch's barren landscapes are perhaps parallels to Hamsun's later works. Germans responded to his unashamed romanticism, more than his own countrymen did. In Norway he was admired and respected as a world-famous writer; but he made no effort to be loved by his fellow citizens, who reportedly found him personally austere and in a flash capable of being pitilessly derisive.

Like Ezra Pound he became a traitor, though for different reasons and in a very different way. He committed himself briefly and severely to "the new order." There was none of Pound's furious, apocalyptic writing. Certainly he did not share Pound's economic and ideological "justifications" of fascism. He welcomed Hitler, but he constantly interceded with him for captured members of the Norwegian resistance. He was over eighty when the Nazis came—and a famous man quietly living out his last few years. To many Norwegians his words of support for the Germans were but a final proof of his "reactionary" style of life and his "irrelevant" books. When the war ended he was arrested, jailed, and in keeping with our century's enlightenment, sent off to be queried and observed by a collection of nurses, social workers and, of course, psychiatrists.

All the while—from 1945 to 1948—he wrote down his thoughts and experiences. He was nearing 90, and eventually the doctors would tell a court that he should be let go because he was a "person with permanently impaired faculties." He was found guilty, heavily fined, and sent home to die. He lived on, though; and in 1949 published what he modestly called "trifles," all of them written by a man under the constant "examination" of doctors. We now have those trifles in English; they are a series of vivid, keen reflections, and they have been translated with real tenderness by Carl Anderson. Hamsun's title for this last book is **On Overgrown Paths,** and its haunting self-scrutiny justifies the author's right to claim that not only was he always "sane," but considerably more intelligent and subtle of mind than his observers. Of course Hamsun never cares to argue with his jailors or doctors. He lets his words show his moods, his sadness, his detachment, his occasional wry humor, his open conversational intimacy with Death. One sees again how stupid, vulgar or evasive it is possible for doctors and lawyers and judges to be. Hamsun wants justice, and certainly preferred explicit condemnation to the humiliating and absurd treatment he received at the hands of his psychiatrists—who took "four months to affix learned labels to every conceivable state of mind I might have been in." In this, his last testament, he resumes a long abandoned self; once again he is pointing out how insulting and humiliating people can be to other people. No one has done a better job of documenting the simple-minded, abusive and condescending questions a breed of psychiatrists can ask and inflict on their patients.

To the very end Hamsun could recognize banality, and he described it effortlessly but pointedly: "The professor required me to explain my 'two marriages' as he put it." Well, eventually the doctors "explained" more than his marriages. They brushed aside with medical and psychiatric jargon a complicated, defiant man who right under their eyes wrote mournful, cheerful and loving words. At all times he comes across clear and unafraid. He does not deny his past, or even try to excuse it. The paths he took were overgrown—certainly not as clear-cut as those who "evaluated" and judged him. Long before the Nazis arrived to make murder a "civilized" nation's chief purpose, Hamsun had withdrawn from the world—out of choice, not because his mind was "impaired." He lived long enough to see his personal prejudices and social fears become accessories to a much larger enterprise—the Nazi armies and crematoria. He died late enough to know that even the valleys and fjords he sought in sanctuary were of no avail. The inner and near-mad world that he first described in **Hunger** came back to plague him in the late evening of his life. Now madness was fantastically institutionalized; it was everywhere and into everything. Yet, the Hamsun who as a youth virtually made a study of madness, of all that is weird and bizarre, was destined to be unprepared for what happened to Norway and to the world from 1940 to 1945. By the end of the war even Quisling and the Nazis ridiculed him. He was a tragic, broken and discredited man who had not an ounce of dignity left. It seems that it was his accusers and his keepers who gave him back his dignity.

Alex Bolckmans (November 1975)

SOURCE: Bolckmans, Alex. "Henry Miller's *Tropic of Cancer* and Knut Hamsun's *Sult*." *Scandinavica: An International Journal of Scandinavian Studies* 14, no. 2 (November 1975): 115-26.

[*In the following essay, Bolckmans focuses on the similarities between* Tropic of Cancer *and* Hunger, *contending that Hamsun's work served as a model for Miller's novel.*]

About Henry Miller's attitude to Knut Hamsun there can be no two opinions. Miller is a great admirer of the Norwegian. Again and again he has made the point.

In *The Books in My Life* (1952) he appends a list of "The Hundred books Which Influenced Me Most"—a list which had already been published in French in *Pour Une Bibliothèque Idéale* (1951)—and Knut Hamsun is listed there with the entry "His works in general". In the introduction to the book, Hamsun is included among those five authors of whom Miller says: "I know I shall never say my last word about them" (p. 15). The others are Emerson, Dostoievsky, Maeterlinck and G. A. Henty. In the body of the book Hamsun's name again occurs several times. When, for example, Miller speaks of his earliest reading, he says emphatically: "Hamsun, as I have often said, is one of the authors who vitally affected me *as writer*" (p. 40). When he draws up a list of the names of authors who "influenced me as a man and as a writer" (p. 124), Hamsun is one of the select company of twenty-eight names. When he writes there of friends and acquaintances, Hamsun is frequently a point of reference: for example p. 172, or p. 259 where one of his friends mentions certain Hamsun books Miller is unfamiliar with. This prompts him to speak of "a pang of regret", followed by "a touch of joy" at the thought that there was still so much awaiting him "even if I have to read them in Norwegian!" (As far as I know, Miller's knowledge of Norwegian is minimal, perhaps even non-existent.)

Miller also speaks of Hamsun in his essays. At two points in "Reflections on Writing", where Miller is attempting an explanation of his own style and technique, one finds Hamsun standing in the company of Nietzsche, Dostoievsky and Thomas Mann (a less motley group, indeed, than that which appears in *The Books in My Life*):

> I began assiduously examining the style and technique of those whom I once admired and worshipped: Nietzsche, Dostoievski, Hamsun, even Thomas Mann, whom today I discard as being a skilful fabricator, a brickmaker, an inspired jackass or draught horse. I imitated every style in the hope of finding the clue to the gnawing secret of how to write. Finally I came to a dead end, to a despair and desperation which few men have known, because there was no divorce between myself as a writer and myself as man: to fail as a writer meant to fail as a man.[1]

References to Hamsun are also to be found in Miller's letters. In, for example, *Letters to Anaïs Nin* (1965)—a 379-page selection of his letters to her between 1931 and 1946—Hamsun is mentioned five times, and not merely in passing (pp. 35, 156, 158, 159, and 194). In his correspondence with Durrell, however, Hamsun's name seems not to occur, at least to judge by the index.

Finally, there are the novels themselves, where among the wealth of references to authors' names in general, Hamsun's is also frequently to be found.

It is altogether beyond doubt that Henry Miller is deeply interested in Hamsun, and knows the works well. Doubtless he read Hamsun in German. His upbringing was in German and English, and the general atmosphere—if one accepts the testimony of William A. Gordon[2]—was German. In any case there were few English translations of Hamsun available in Miller's early years: up to the year 1920 when an English translation of **Markens Grøde** appeared—Hamsun was awarded the Nobel Prize in 1919—only **Sult** and **Ny Jord** had been translated, in 1899 and 1914 respectively.[3] By contrast, all his books were available in German.

Miller's enthusiasm for Hamsun centres chiefly on **Mysterier**. In *The Books in My Life* he writes: 'I can recall with accuracy the first books I singled out to reread" (p. 40). And **Mysterier** is one of the five he mentions: "Hamsun, as I have often said, is one of the authors who vitally affected me *as writer*. None of his books intrigued me as much as **Mysteries**." Nor does his estimate change in the course of time; later in the same book he says in reference to **Mysterier**:

> Even if, as a writer, I am aware with each rereading of the "defects" or, to be more kind, "the weaknesses" of my favourite author, the man in me still responds to him, to his language, to his temperament, just as warmly.
>
> (p. 212.)

In Miller's letters to Anaïs Nin, three of the five references to Hamsun relate to **Mysterier**, the most important of which reveals that he had borrowed a copy for her:

> Meanwhile, riding the subway, I reread **Mysteries** which I am holding for you. It swept me off my feet again. And what resemblances there are between Hamsun and myself, *His* dreams, his crazy stories, his buffoonishness. It's a *deceptive* book! If you were to pick it up all by yourself and *skim* thru it, you would probably say it was *trash*. But believe me, it isn't. And you *can't*, or *mustn't* skim it through (sic). He was and still remains one of my idols. I wanted to get **Wanderers** for you but this is equally representative—if not quite so poetic. But all his force, his passion, his whimsicality, are here. You ought to adore it.[4]

Miller does not speak in detail of Hamsun's other books. He mentions certain titles in passing, e.g. in *The Books in My Life* where "**Pan, Hunger, Victoria, Wanderers, Segelfoss Town, Women at the Pump** . . ." (p. 259) are mentioned; or further on in the book, **Sult** is again mentioned, but not in relation to the novel itself but Jean-Louis Barrault's dramatization of it.

I do not doubt that—as Gregory Nybø puts it—"Henry Millers beundring for **Mysterier** værmer et norsk hjerte";[5] but it is nevertheless somewhat strange to see the American praising Hamsun's *second* novel so fulsomely whilst hardly mentioning at all the novel with which Hamsun made his debut: **Sult**. A more detailed comparison of these books with which Miller and Hamsun made their respective breakthroughs throws up so many parallels that it is difficult to believe that there was not some more causal connection.

One might begin with the genesis of the two works and with a number of external biographical correspondences. Both *Tropic of Cancer* and **Sult** are debut novels which established their authors as writers of the first rank in the literary world of the day. Neither men were any longer exactly young when the books appeared: Hamsun was 31, Miller 33. On the other hand, this was for neither man the first entry into literature. Hamsun had already published quite a number of articles, a few short stories, and one or two essay-type publications,[6] without however establishing for himself a place on the Parnassus of the day. Henry Miller had also previously published a number of articles, had written some prose poems and a novel or two for which he had been unable to find a publisher (e.g. "Clipped Wings", "This Gentile World"). It was then that the Obelisk Press in Paris, run by an expatriate American Jack Kahane, showed interest in the manuscript of *Tropic of Cancer*, mainly on account of its more scandalous passages. In a letter to Durrell, Miller himself said about Kahane: "He won't publish a thing unless it has a sensational quality, unless it might be banned in England and America. . . . He hasn't much taste either I can tell you."[7]

A further similarity between the two authors relates to the singlemindedness of their determination to be a writer, and the persistence which they brought to the task. Hamsun first tried in Norway, then went to America, then returned to try anew, until at length he succeeded and was able to bid farewell to all those little odd jobs he had taken to keep body and soul together. Similarly Henry Miller had had all sorts of jobs, as is reported in the various "chronologies" in the books about him: "Worked at a great variety of jobs, ranging from father's tailor shop to employment manager of messenger department, Western Union Telegraph Company, 1909-1924."[8] Then he determined to become a writer, tried without success in America, came to Europe, returned to America, then back again to Europe where he eventually succeeded in having *Tropic of Cancer* published. Thus they both found themselves in existential situations of some similarity.

Too much emphasis should not be placed on these details. They relate only to external matters, and may simply be coincidental. In truth, in these two sets of preparatory experiences for authorship there is much that is almost cliché-like: a desperate desire to be a writer, a period travelling abroad to improve one's fortunes, the early hack writing, the readiness to endure economic and social privation in order to reach one's goal, and so on. Other parallels would not be difficult to find.

Two things nevertheless, in my view, lend a certain extra significance to these outward events. In the first place there is the element of social revolt which manifests itself in both their attitudes. They both crave recognition as great writers, but they resist submitting themselves to the literary modes of the day. On the contrary, they conduct themselves like real Bohemians; they set out to "épater le bourgeois", indeed to create scandal, and make their way into the world of literature by writing scandalous books. In Hamsun's case, this is to some extent true of **Sult**; and alongside it one thinks also of his lecture tour where he turned fiercely on the older generation of writers. In Miller's case, it was rather the challenging sexual descriptions which he later rationalized in Freudian and Jungian terms, e.g. in "Utinerine Hunger" in the essay collection *The Wisdom of the Heart* (1941), but which equally led to a considerable "succès de scandale".

The second thing is that, running like a scarlet thread through many of Miller's comments about himself and his work, is his insistence that the man and the artist must in his case be seen as a unity, and that his books are to be read as explorations of the man and the artist. The books are about the man, he says, and about how the man became what he is. If one combines these comments with the many literary influences on him—which Miller in no way plays down, rather the reverse—there are good reasons for thinking that the man whose experience of life was so similar, i.e. Hamsun, played an important part at the formative stage.

Clearly decisive here is the question of how far Miller was familiar with the details of Hamsun's life, and whether he was himself conscious of any parallel. I have not come across any clear evidence concerning this; and it is unclear to what extent Miller read *about* the authors he admired. There is nothing on this subject in *The Books in My Life*, apart from the fact that he also read essayists and critics. The most one can say is that he had opportunities for acquainting himself with the facts of Hamsun's life. In the absence of any conclusive evidence, it is perhaps best not to press these external similarities too far.

But there are other things. There are many inner correspondences between *Tropic of Cancer* and **Sult** which make it seem likely that Hamsun's book played a part, consciously or unconsciously, in the emergence of Miller's first novel. Hamsun always insisted that **Sult** was no novel. What he probably meant by this was that the book had nothing in common with the "usual" kind of realistic novel which was being written at the time, with the sort of wideranging descriptions of men and society which were to be found in Lie, Kielland, Garborg and others. He wanted to make clear that he was offering something new, also on the level of technique. In the same way, Henry Miller writes on the first page of his debut novel:

> This is not a book. This is libel, slander, defamation of character. This is not a book, in the ordinary sense of the word. No, this is a prolonged insult, a gob of spit in the face of Art, a kick in the pants to God, Man, Destiny, Time, Love, Beauty . . . what you will.[9]

He too is concerned to emphasize that he is coming with something new. He goes even further than Hamsun: it is not a novel, not even a book; it is purely invective.

Both pronouncements are open to dispute. There is no real reason to prevent one characterizing both books as novels. The pronouncements in each case are declarations of literary intent and say nothing about the structural unity found in the books.

In the case of **Sult** one might define the theme of the novel as being that of the struggle of the artist's "jeg" for moral self-assertion; this struggle leads to defeat in the field of practical living; the "jeg" takes to flight, but has preserved its integrity. *Tropic of Cancer* treats of the emergence of an artist in the midst of life's chaos; it does not lead to defeat, but the conclusion is nevertheless characterized by ambivalence; the artist's "I" is content where he is, but one of the hero's alter-ego figures, Fillmore, is forced into hasty flight which the hero has arranged. The two novels have identical frameworks of plot and action. Both are urban novels, both treat of man and the big city, of the city's fascination, and of the main character's progression through it. In both instances, the action consists in the hunt for jobs and in erotic adventures.

The organization of the plot on the other hand varies. The structuralizing element in Hamsun's novel is the hero's relationship with the girl called Ylajali; and the four sections may be termed encounter, dreams, association and departure. All the while the hero is job-hunting. All the time he is starving, but is repeatedly saved: in the first place by his fee for a story, in the second by a helping hand, and in the third by an advance which the newspaper editor gives him. Only when the girl he loves sends him charity does he give up and flee. Three times he is able to let himself be rescued without moral compromise. To accept charity from a woman on the other hand would be moral degradation, would turn him into a kind of Irgens figure (from **Ny Jord**) and this he finds impossible. The hero's erotic adventures are the thin connecting thread in a book of fragmentary scenes which illustrate the twists and turns of starvation fantasy and of his attempts to find a job.

The reverse is the case in *Tropic of Cancer*. The structuralizing element here is the repeated attempt to find a job. The book consists of fifteen sections of varying length; the sections are untitled and are marked only by the fact that the text starts a new page. The central section is the eighth (pp. 91-150). It tells of Van Norden and his friend Carl and his history with "the rich cunt, Irene" (p. 97) and of the book's first-person hero who gets a regular job as a proof-reader (p. 131). Apart from the teaching job he gets in Dijon and which is recorded in the penultimate section, this is the one real job he gets.

The section can be called central for several reasons. The characters Van Norden and Carl make it clear that they represent different sides of the novel's first-person hero. The story of Irene is a kind of résumé of the book's stories about women. The story about the job is a conflation of the colourful *vie de bohème* which was lived in those circles. Added to this is the fact that the seven preceding sections deal in large measure with fantasies—fantasies about the books he is going to write, about how one gets hold of something to eat, about the women in his life. The most important are those fantasies about food and how one acquires it (sects. 5 and 6, for example, pp. 49-71). In the last seven sections, on the other hand, it is the stories about women which acquire the greatest importance: the revels in Le Havre (sect. 10), the story of the two streetwalkers who are after his money (sect. 11), and about Fillmore and his Russian princess who suffers from gonorrhea (sect. 12).

One can therefore go much further than Kingsley Widmer who claims that "what unity the book has must be discovered mostly in its metaphors".[10] I would say that the novel has a distinct if not entirely stringent composition. This is perhaps not immediately apparent at first reading, when the likelihood is that one gains a chaotic impression of a collection of anecdotes with no inherent unity apart from the fact that they represent the hero's experiences. The same impression is created by an unsuspecting first reading of Hamsun's **Sult**. The linking thread of the hero's relationship to Ylajali is not so immediate as to present an initial impression that this is little more than a collection of anecdotes.

In terms of composition, therefore, the two novels have much in common: an anecdotal, apparently chaotic unity with a less than obvious structure, but with similar components: starvation fantasies, erotic adventures, and the artist's need for self-assertion.

The similarity in the choice of motif is also conspicuous—not so much, perhaps, in the main elements, but very strongly marked when it comes to the dreams of becoming a writer. The hero of **Sult** writes articles, stories, a big drama ("Korsets Tegn" about "en herlig, fanatisk Skjøge", SV, I, p. 151). The hero of *Tropic of Cancer* is often described as sitting at his typewriter (pp. 4, 21, 44, etc.); he has "manuscripts, pages scrawled with revisions" (p. 8); he speaks about "my manuscript" (p. 26); he writes articles, and so on.

In the matter of the erotic experiences it is hardly possible to make comparison between Hamsun's highly allusive art and Miller's frequently provocative formulations and overt sexual descriptions. One might point to elements of Eighties bohemianism in **Sult**: "den sortklædte Dame" (SV, I, p. 104), a demimondaine who takes the hero back home, the whore-romanticism of the planned drama, etc. There is in any case a fair amount of challenging eroticism in Hamsun's novel. Miller's sexual abandonment fits appropriately into the post-war atmosphere of "the gay twenties" and surrealism's "écriture automatique". Miller does not wish to write "literature"; he simply wishes to talk about himself, and his imagination is fed by the unconscious.[11] One can see a parallel here to Hamsun who, shortly after his first novel, published his article on "Om det ubevidste Sjæleliv" in the new periodical *Samtiden*. Both authors are fundamentally doing the same thing. Here possibly lies the explanation for Miller's lavish praise of **Mysterier**. Nagel's way of life and his fantasies are perhaps closer to Miller's than those of **Sult**'s hero, even though in essence in the latter case they are the same.

The starvation fantasies on the other hand are much more readily comparable. Both men live in a large city without regular income; they starve, and this leads to fantasies. Hamsun's hero is clearly worse off than Miller's, who occasionally has money sent to him by his wife in America. The more important passages dealing with hunger and food in Miller come in sections 3, 5 and 6, and also in 9. The difference between Hamsun's and Miller's accounts might be summarized by saying that Hamsun writes more about the psychological effects of hunger, whilst Miller's fantasies dwell more on food and on ways of getting free meals.

Alongside these main motifs there are a number of minor ones that show marked similarities. The motif of the attraction of the big city plays an important role in both books. It is with this that Hamsun begins his book: ". . . i Kristiania, denne forunderlige By som ingen forlater før han har faat Mærker av den . . . (SV, I, p. 7). He moves around the city; street names are mentioned, and one can often follow the hero in his movements (e.g. SV, I, p. 41). The book ends with his saying "Farvel for denne Gang til Byen, til Kristiania hvor Vinduerne lyste saa blankt fra alle Hjem" (SV, I, p. 177). The city has provided a constant background, has been witness to the hero's despairing struggle and ultimate defeat.

So it is also in *Tropic of Cancer*. Paris is the background the whole time for the hero's experiences. He moves about the city; street and other names are mentioned which locate the action. On the opening page is the sentence: "It is now the fall of my second year in Paris. I was sent here for a reason I have not yet been able to fathom" (p. 1). Miller was not sent to Paris; he was there by chance. He means: it must surely have been some higher power which directed me.

Later, in section 9, there is clear reference to the mysterious attraction and charm exerted by the city: "When you've suffered and endured things here it's then that Paris takes hold of you, grabs you by the balls, you might say, . . ." (p. 155). And later: "An eternal city, Paris . . . The very navel of the world . . . And like a cork . . . one floats here in the scum and wrack of the seas, listless, hopeless. . . . The streets were my refuge. And no man can understand the glamour of the streets until he is obliged to take refuge in them . . ." (p. 164). And a little later, section 11 begins: "Paris is like a whore. From a distance she seems ravishing, you can't wait until you have her in your arms. And five minutes later you feel empty, disgusted with yourself. You feel tricked" (p. 188). The book ends with the hero sending his friend Fillmore away; he sits over a beer and deliberates whether or not he should leave the city. But the river Seine which "gently winds through the girdle of hills" (p. 286) gives him a "wonderful peace" (p. 287). He feels he must stay where he is.

The main difference is that Miller is much more explicit than Hamsun in the working out of his motifs. But this is a permanent feature of his style. He says what he means in obvious words, whilst Hamsun is content with hints.

Another side motif is the playing with words. In **Sult** there is the name Ylajali, and the section with the paper cone and the constable (SV, I, p. 54); and the even better known example of the invention of the new word "kuboaa" (SV, I, p. 62). In *Tropic of Cancer* one finds a similar situation: "I'm lying there on the iron bed . . . when bango: out pops the word: NONENTITY!" (p. 72). In the section on the Hindu Nanantatee there is also a fragment where the author plays with words:

> "The fucking business is bad, Endree," he says. "But I will give you a word that will always make you lucky; you must say it everyday, over and over, a million times you must say it. It is the best word there is Endree . . . say it now . . . OOMAHARUMOOMA!"
>
> "OOMARABOO . . ."
>
> "No, Endree . . . like this . . . OOMAHARUMOOMA!"
>
> "OOMAMABOOMBA . . ."
>
> "No, Endree . . . like this . . ."
>
> (p. 82).

A further side motif—carelessness about money—is one that I would call a typical Hamsun motif: the man who throws his money about, despite the fact that he only came by it through some lucky chance and needs it himself. In **Sult** at one point the hero is given too much change; he eats a large steak which makes him sick, and then gives the remainder to a woman selling cakes on the street (SV, I, pp. 100-13). There is a similar incident in Miller, where the hero acquires some money, squanders rather too much on a meal and then gives the money to two street girls (sect. 11, pp. 188-97).

Also reminiscent of Hamsun is the story in Miller of Carl who, with a full bladder, pays court to a lady: "He imagines, the cute little prick that he is, that the situation calls for delicacy" (p. 102). This prompts one to recall the incident in *Mysterier* where Nagel tells of the lady in London whose company he was enjoying, and whom he did not wish to leave even though "Naturens krav" began to assert itself; he finally sees no other solution than to wet his trousers (SV, I, pp. 135-6).

In the light of these examples I think it is not unreasonable to establish a connection between these two novels, and to assume that *Sult* played a significant part in Miller's writing of *Tropic of Cancer*.

When one looks at the characters in the two books, one's initial impressions are not immediately similar. *Sult* treats essentially of *one* character, the young would-be author who speaks in the first person. None of the other characters in the book is anything much more than a shadow. The black-clad lady is the only one we hear very much about, yet even she is little more than sketched in. All the others glide past; we catch a glimpse of them without learning a great deal about them. In a compositional sense, this is entirely appropriate to the first-person narrative; the reader learns only what the hero experiences.

Tropic of Cancer is also a first-person narrative, in which the "I" is occasionally identified as Henry Miller (e.g. p. 99). But the book is not simply about this man Miller's life in Paris, but also about Van Norden, about Carl, and about Fillmore's. In general terms, they all four of them lead the same bohemian life. Fillmore is the only one with a steady job; the other three write books and live from free-lance journalism. They go out drinking together, and fill their leisure moments with wine and women. It is often difficult to distinguish clearly among the different characters. One might go seeking for small differences, as William A. Gordon does in his book;[12] but my feeling is that it is unnecessary. Miller writes about various characters and apparently divided up his portrayals, but it is clear that the whole book treats of himself and his own experiences in Paris. The other characters in fact illustrate various sides of his own individuality: Van Norden sexuality, Carl authorship, and Fillmore the regularity of work.

Support for this interpretation is to be found on p. 93: "I call him [Van Norden] Joe because he calls me Joe. When Carl is with us he is Joe too. Everybody is Joe because it's easier that way. It's also a pleasant reminder not to take yourself too seriously." The identities of the different characters are blurred; they are all put on the same basis. When one remembers moreover how preoccupied with self the whole book is, there are quite strong arguments for assuming that in the various characters the author is describing himself.

If one is prepared to acknowledge this, then the ending might also be interpreted rather differently. The 15th and final section treats Fillmore's foolish betrothal to Ginette and his flight to America. Miller actively helps him. I believe one must be allowed to interpret this ending as an expression of the hero's ambivalence in respect of this flight: he can contemplate leaving, but at the same time wishes to remain in Paris. The latter feeling finally conquers.

Such an interpretation comes very close to the conclusion of *Sult*: the hero has suffered defeat and escapes from the city by ship. Miller's first-person hero does not have to accept actual defeat, but neither has he won; he merely comes to accept the situation. One has to remember that throughout the entire book America is there as a last possibility, e.g. p. 187: "It's best to keep America just like that, always in the background, a sort of picture post card which you look at in a weak moment." The same thing occurs in *Sult* where several times ships appear in the background as though to indicate the possibility of flights. (SV, I, pp. 63, 71, 89, etc.)

Finally a word must be said about the style. Miller has himself admitted his debt to Hamsun in the matter of style. This is doubtless meant generally. To demonstrate similarities in detail would require a much more extensive investigation than is possible here. I limit myself to adducing one passage from Miller and a similar one from Hamsun where it seems to me certain parallels are obvious.

The hero of *Tropic of Cancer* goes on an empty stomach to a concert in Salle Gaveau and reports his experiences:

> My mind is curiously alert; it's as though my skull had a thousand mirrors inside it. My nerves are taut, vibrant! The notes are like glass balls dancing on a million jets of water. I've never been to a concert before on such an empty belly. Nothing escapes me, not even the tiniest pin falling. It's as though I had no clothes on and every pore of my body was a window and all the windows open and the light flooding my gizzards. I can feel the light curving under the vault of my ribs and my ribs hang there over a hollow nave trembling with reverberations.

(pp. 87-8)

This passage can be compared with the following passage in Hamsun where the hero of *Sult* first meets Ylajali:

> Saa fremmed som jeg i dette Øieblikk var for mig selv, saa fuldstændig et Bytte for usynlige Indflytelser, foregik intet omkring mig uten at jeg la Mærke til det. En stor brun Hund sprang tværs over Gaten, henimot Lunden og ned til Tivoli; den hadde et smalt Halsbaand av Nysølv. Høiere op i Gaten aapnedes et Vindu i anden Etage og en Pike la sig ut av det med opbrættede Ærmer og gav sig til at pusse Ruterne paa Yttersiden. Intet undgik min Opmærksomhet, jeg var klar og aand-

expressed fears of incipient lunacy, his prodigious industry ('he makes Balzac look like a dwarf'). He had already sent to Strindberg an article written on him in America and published in English on 20 December 1888 in the magazine *America*, though the text had been so mutilated and 'edited' that he half-expected an angry reply from Strindberg. When now he came across **On the Cultural Life of Modern America,** Strindberg was impressed. He was another like Hamsun, a man willing to express his opinion on anything under the sun—and in his case, on most of the things beyond it—and the book's violent subjectivity appealed to him. In April 1890 he wrote to Brandes that 'all the opinions I've suffered half to death for over the last five years' were 'openly and frankly expressed' in Hamsun's book.[8]

Hamsun was already very conscious of the fact and form of his growing fame. He wanted to meet the writers he admired, and had written to Arne Garborg asking him to put him in touch with Strindberg's friend and ally in Nietzsche, Ola Hansson. He was also keen to meet Strindberg himself—but not yet. He wrote to Victor Nilsson in January 1889:

> I look forward to meeting Strindberg one day. I was invited to a party one evening at which he was to be present, but I did not go. I am proud, in my way.

Hamsun realised that **Hunger** was the key to his whole future. He wanted fame, and the respect of the Strindbergs and Ola Hanssons; but only the deserved fame, the warranted respect, that the writing of an exceptional novel would bring him. His wish to be famous, though compulsive to the point of obsession, was nevertheless not the desire for fame at any price, and he was not deluded by the intense local fame created in Copenhagen and Christiania by his magazine and newspaper articles, and his hastily written demolition job on American civilisation, into thinking that he was now worthy of Strindberg's attention.[9]

In the Spring of 1889 Hamsun returned to Norway. Johan Sørensen had prepared a room for him at his house in Fagerstrand where he could write in peace, and sent his assistant Olaf Huseby to meet Hamsun off the Copenhagen train at Christiania station on Good Friday. Sørensen took his duties as patron seriously, and when Hamsun arrived was able to inform him that he had arranged a house-party consisting of the historian Ernst Sars, and the newspapermen Lars Holst and Ola Thommessen, three of the most influential names in contemporary Norwegian cultural life. Hamsun and Sørensen talked alone for a while, and suddenly a full-scale quarrel erupted: Hamsun had dared to speak his mind about Sørensen's household gods, Bjørnson and a language reformer named Knud Knudsen. Hamsun admired and respected Bjørnson, but was never guilty of the idolatry so many of his fellow countrymen practised towards him; it was typical of Hamsun's courage, and his almost fanatical insistence on independence, that instead of retreating when he saw that he was treading on his benefactor's toes, he trod all the harder. Sørensen was not a man used to being crossed, and the two men argued long into the night and Hamsun eventually left the house rather than sleep the night there. He returned the next day to collect his suitcase, and that was the end of the association with Sørensen.[10]

In June he moved into a flat on the fourth floor at Number 18 Torvgaden, just around the corner from the Grand Hotel on Karl Johans gate, the 'Bernina' of the Norwegian capital, where famous and would-be famous artists met to drink and talk. Still he did not finish **Hunger.** The lure of controversy proved too great for him, and over the next few months he produced a number of newspaper articles, most of them on non-literary topics, which performed the undeniably useful function of making his name better known and providing him with a small independent income.

The first of these was an article for *Dagbladet* on Fridtjof Nansen, whose achievement in walking east to west across Greenland had made him a national hero in Norway. Nansen's popularity never penetrated to the Christiania smart-set; they felt that his habit of going about the streets of the capital ostentatiously wearing his 'famous explorer's clothes' was in poor taste. Hamsun's attitude to what he called the 'hysteria' surrounding Nansen was also one of superior disapproval. For him, the writers were the aristocrats of a society, the natural recipients of its highest forms of praise, status and attention. He did not so much begrudge the explorer his fame as find it incomprehensible and slightly ridiculous. The fame of sportsmen affected him in the same way. He called the whole business 'humbug', a word that was to whizz around his own head like a boomerang over the next few years.[11]

His next target was Ibsen. In August 1889 Hamsun reviewed August Lindberg's production of *Ghosts* at the Christiania National Theatre for *Dagbladet,* and the article appeared on the front page—as indeed everything he wrote appeared on the the front page in the year of his Norwegian breakthrough. Here he voiced for the first time—at least publicly—the aesthetic and artistic doubts about Ibsen which he developed as the subject of one of the lectures he was to deliver on his sensational national tour of 1891. This early attack on a man who was already, like Bjørnson, a demi-god among his countrymen, was controlled. He praised some of the acting, shook his head over Fru Alving's relentless capability, and questioned some of Ibsen's dialogue:

> There are one or two lines in the last Act that I do not quite understand, although they apparently went down very well in England and Germany. To mention but one, Osvald's line 'Mother, give me the sun'.[12]

Hamsun was being ironic: he understood the lines only too well. He found Ibsen simplistic and obvious, and was baffled and irritated by his reputation as a difficult writer. He felt that Ibsen had betrayed his talent in switching from the verse-dramas of his early period like *Brand* and *Peer Gynt* to the dogged prose realism of plays like *Ghosts,* a possibility that Ibsen himself hinted at in his last play, *When We Dead Awaken.*[13]

Next up: Lars Oftedal. Oftedal was a pietist politician, editor, and moral agitator, one of the most feared men in Norwegian politics. Hamsun had an old score to settle with him: he was the man whose teachings had captured the dark imagination of his uncle Hans Olsen up in Hamarøy in the 1860s. Now, with re-elections to the Norwegian parliament looming, Hamsun produced a series of articles for *Dagbladet* which he hoped would destroy Oftedal's chances. 'I shall make Oftedollops of the man', he wrote gleefully to Erik Frydenlund.

The eleven articles[14] appeared throughout October 1889, and they gave Hamsun a taste of something that was to be rare for him in the coming decade—widespread public popularity. He fully expected—perhaps even hoped—to be sued by Oftedal, for the style was as ever personal and unashamedly subjective. But Oftedal did not. Instead, the articles were read with approval, and his name noted in circles which would not normally have cared about a writer. It was also one of the few times in his life in which he publicly and unequivocally stood on the Left.

The amount of attention the articles attracted induced a small publisher in Bergen, Mons Litleré, to publish them in book form in December. Hamsun received a further 250 kroner for this, and the number of works published before the full version of *Hunger* appeared now rises to five. *Lars Oftedal* continued to have a local, Scandinavian reputation: the Danish writer Jeppe Aajaer recalled[15] that in the 1890s it came 'crashing like a rock through the windows of the mission houses', and, in writing his own *Master and Mission* against pietism in 1897, used Hamsun's book as his model.[16]

In September Hamsun took a short holiday in Valdres. He warned Erik that he would be bearing with him a number of eccentric gifts—hats 'the like of which you have never seen—one for each of us. Individually styled to accommodate the unique architecture of our heads to my express specifications.' He must have enjoyed himself up there—he managed to lose a short story about 'an extremely unusual horse' which he wrote in the Valdres cariole.[17] It turned up in time to make the Christmas Eve number of *Dagbladet,* a marvellous comic vignette about a horse making a fool of a man.

Back in the capital he moved again, in November, to a fourth-floor apartment at Number 3 Waldemar Thranes gate. The flat cost him forty kroner a month, and was a decent distance from the centre of town and the attractions of the Grand Café; he was now quite determined to get **Hunger** finished. Bjørnson had offered him free board and lodging at his house at Aulestad for a year, but he turned it down, knowing that with a human whirlwind like Bjørnson around he would never get his writing done. He was also receiving repeated offers of the job of theatre director at Bergen's National Stage, the second-most important theatre in Norway after Christiania's National Theatre. This was a post both Ibsen and Bjørnson had occupied in their time, and the temptation must have been considerable. And at 4000 kroner a year, the money was tremendous. Nevertheless, he appears to have turned it down with a minimum of soul-searching, explaining to friends that he did not know enough about the theatre to take it on. Another reason may have been that he feared further postponements on **Hunger.**

Hamsun worked hard throughout the winter, putting together the scraps of the novel he had been assembling ever since the autumn of 1888. Finally, in the spring of 1890, with the end of the book in sight, he moved back to Copenhagen, and just as he had done with **On the Cultural Life of Modern America,** wrote the final sections of it while the earlier parts were already going through the printers. The full version finally appeared on 5 June 1890.

Hunger is one of the great novels of urban alienation, on a par with Kafka's *Castle,* Dostoevsky's *Notes from the Underground,* and Rilke's *Notebook of Malte Laurids Brigge,* and what gives it its peculiar authority is that it was in many ways Hamsun's own story. In writing it he drew on the experiences he underwent during his two most desperate periods in Christiania in the winters of 1880-81 and 1885-86, and probably also drew on the experiences of his winter in Chicago in 1886-87. The many small correspondences of fact and fiction—the narrator's visit to the castle, for example, and his address at Tomtegaten II—as well as the autobiographical details that crop up in letters to Erik Frydenlund and Johan Sørensen, indicate that the book is Hamsun's self-portrait in fiction. From America Victor Nilsson wrote asking him whether the events described in **Hunger** had really happened to him: 'Yes, all of it, and much more, right here at home', replied Hamsun.

The novel describes a period of months in the life of a young stranger who lives in Christiania while trying to make a name for himself as a writer. The absurdly ambitious nature of the subjects he writes about—appreciations of Correggio, denunciations of Kant, a verse drama set in the Middle Ages—means that he is rarely in luck with the editors of the newspapers where he tries to sell his stuff. Most of his time is spent in the effort to keep body and soul together. Always hungry, often homeless, he wanders the streets of Christiania, an emaciated human consciousness in rags, looking for work, begging for food, becoming involved in a series of preposterous encounters with policemen, tramps and whores, strange beings who are nevertheless not half so strange as he. Like the protagonist of **"On Tour,"** he is pitifully and absurdly keen to keep from a surrounding world always perceived as hostile the catastrophic extent of the gap between the pretensions and the realities of his life. It's a grim theme, but the novel's great triumph is that in Hamsun's careful hands, it doesn't finally seem grim at all. As the hero's vivid torments continue, we begin gradually to suspect something that Hamsun undoubtedly wanted us to suspect; namely that what looks at first like a dogged *inability* to do anything about his plight is in reality a dogged *refusal* to act. He does not in actual fact want release, and is in some perverse way enjoying his predicament, savouring to the full the bizarre sensations of homelessness, hunger, insecurity, and the attendant forms of isolation, social, cultural, sexual, economic. We get the curious feeling that the whole thing is willed; a life-game that the hero is playing, to see how far it can go, how far he can let it go, how low he can sink, how long suffer. It is a prolonged flirtation with death and madness which the narrator can indulge in only because he knows he has the strength to withdraw from the game before it claims him. The novel has no plot—plot is replaced by this tension created by the struggle between the narrator's strong mind and the attracting forces of total personal annihilation. Few things are better suited to break down and render anonymous a human personality than prolonged want of the most primitive kind—want of love, money, warmth, food, a place of one's own—and the narrator's secret victory, always achieved, is that he remains hugely and quixotically himself through the worst deprivations and humiliations that befall him. When on the last pages he joins a ship bound for England, and sails away both from the novel and the city with which he has wrestled so desperately, it is clearly no retreat, but only a temporary withdrawal.

Hamsun was proud of the book. Fifteen years and a great deal more disillusionment later, he described it with a wry fondness as 'My first book, written in the days when the way of the writer seemed to me the most honourable in the world.'[18] Yet even at the time, he was aware that the book had faults—eight of them, 'or rather, lacks',[19] as he specified on more than one occasion, leaving one with the curious impression that he had worked from some kind of list of psychological states to be described. We get the same impression from a comment to Georg Brandes which also shows again how extremely competitive Hamsun's attitude towards literature was: 'If we were to count them', he wrote, 'I do not think that we would find a greater number of spiritual fluctuations in for example *Raskolnikov*[20] or in *Germinie Lacerteux* than in my book.'[21] On several occasions he protested vigorously that **Hunger** was 'not a novel', and ought not to be treated as such. 'The book plays on just one string', he pointed out, 'but tries to draw hundreds of notes from it—no doubt with a varying degree of success, naturally.'[22]

The book's fame and its status as one of the central texts of modern European and American literature confirm that he achieved in fact a consistently high degree of success. Save for a few external details, such as the presence of horse-drawn carriages in the streets, **Hunger** remains eerily and thrillingly undated. Hamsun's concern, after all, was with the workings of his mind, and in **Hunger** he produced perhaps the first novel to make consciousness itself a hero. In so doing he signalled the voyage inwards towards introspection which in our century probably reaches its furthest point in Samuel Beckett's work, via Kafka, Joyce, and Virginia Woolf.[23] The achievement was largely the result of his own talent and genius; yet a look at the literary background in Europe against which Hamsun produced his novel indicates that he was also, inevitably, a child of his own time.

The sensation created by **Hunger** on its publication—and its enthusiastic critical reception among writers rather than critics—reflects a literary world in a process of dramatic change affecting every artistic capital of Europe, and the figure of Georg Brandes was central to this process of change and development. A Dane who was also a European, he made it his business to introduce the most important European thinkers to Danish minds. In his *Main Currents in 19th Century Literature,* published through the 1870s, he had written on Taine, Renan, John Stuart Mill, and called for a utilitarian literature of social debate. The rise of Ibsen and Bjørnson was closely connected with his championing of them, and especially with the spread of their reputation and influence across northern Europe. Then in the 1880s Brandes came across Nietzsche. The two corresponded, and Brandes became convinced of Nietzsche's genius. The series of lectures he delivered on him in Copenhagen in May 1888 effectively signalled Nietzsche's 'breakthrough' as a major philosophical and literary influence on the younger generation of European writers. These lectures served in a sense to crystallise for literature a host of large and small indices which had been confusedly abroad in European literary circles since the middle of the century. This was the sense that somehow, somewhere, something had been shattered. Between them, Darwin and Nietzsche put an end to God and the old certainties. This 'shattering' of the soul in a curious way echoes the shattering of the atom by physicists, and Strindberg was one of the first to try to accept and reflect and live out these new understandings. His preface to the published version of his play *Miss Julie* in 1888 sounded the keynote of the new vision. In it, he wrote of 'modern characters, living in an age of transition more urgently hysterical at any rate than the age which preceded it', and as a response to this claimed to have created in his play characters who were 'split and vacillating'. He described the human soul as something 'patched together'. This essay had a particularly strong effect on Hamsun, whose own theoretical justifications for his writing often make points similar to those made here, notably in the aversion to the idea of 'characters', whether on stage or in a novel, who are in fact merely clichés, exhibiting Taine's 'dominant characteristic', and repeating at regular intervals short catch-phrases or exclamations by means of which audiences and readers might readily recognise them.

'Aristocratic radicalism' was Brandes' term for the new stance, a term embraced by Nietzsche himself. It struck a chord at once among his audience of young poets and novelists bored by the fustian literature of naturalism and social utilitarianism, and ushered in a decade of proudly individualistic and defiantly 'useless' writing. Hamsun arrived back from America just too late to hear Brandes' lectures in May 1888, but Nietzsche continued to be the talk of the Bernina in Copenhagen and the Grand in Christiania. He was 'in the air', as Dostoevsky was in the air, and Hamsun could not have failed to pick up the ideas. In view of his sympathies for Fascist regimes in the 1930s and during the Second World War, it is natural to wonder to what extent he was influenced by Nietzsche in his youth, and whether this influence was decisive. Certainly the concept of 'aristocratic radicalism' must have appealed to him; deprived of the satisfaction of being a 'real' aristocrat by reason of his social background, his own unusually strong personality, and not least his achievement in writing a masterpiece like **Hunger** seemed to demand some sort of explanation. The kind of problems Hamsun had to face merely in being Hamsun were probably unusual: physically strong, brave, handsome, clever and quick of mind—the possession of such qualities can easily destroy a person. Where one is always effortlessly superior, the fun disappears; one ceases to bother to compete at all, but rests in the certain knowledge of one's mere superiority. These problems of the laxness of arrogance were something Hamsun had successfully surmounted. In seeking therefore to understand his own personality and success, the idea of the 'born' or 'natural' aristocrat implicit in Nietzsche's teaching, the concept of the 'spiritual aristocrat' must have seemed to provide an ideal explanation. Or perhaps more correctly, an ideal intellectual justification for something he had known instinctively all along—that in terms of the game of life, in terms of the rat race of society, he was born 'better' than the others. There were few, after all, who could have made the journey—largely unaided—from a dirty little farm in Hamarøy to the lecture hall at the Students' Union in Copenhagen. Nietzsche did matter to him, but hardly taught him anything he didn't already know.

When the novel was published, Hamsun set about its energetic defence and promotion. Reviews by Irgens Hansen in Bergen, and Carl Ewald and Edward Brandes in Copenhagen pleased him, and his friend Erik Skram, in the Bergen magazine *Samtiden* and the Danish *Tilskueren,* wrote enthusiastic appreciations of the book. But the one review he would really have liked—Georg Brandes'—he did not get. He presented Brandes with a copy, and perhaps rushed him for a response—'you cannot have read enough of the book yesterday afternoon, and not enough in context', he retorted when Brandes described the book as 'monotonous'. The long letter of defence which this criticism fired off tells us a lot about what Hamsun was trying to do as a writer:

> I have been thinking about what you said about my book. I had not expected such a view from *you.* In the first place, the action takes place in the space of just a few months, and in such a limited space of time not a great deal more usually happens than that which I have described; secondly, I have avoided all the usual stuff about suicidal thoughts, weddings, trips to the country and dances up at the mansion house. This is too cheap for me. What fascinates me is the endless motion of my own mind, and I thought I had described in ***Hunger*** moods whose very strangeness should strike one as being precisely not monotonous. . . .
>
> My book must not be considered as a novel. There are enough authors who write novels when they write about hunger—from Zola to Kielland. They all do it. And if it is a lack of the 'novelistic' that possibly makes my book monotonous, then that is in fact a recommendation, since I had made up my mind quite simply not to write a novel.[24]

Hamsun was noticeably more guardedly technical in his discussions of the book with literary men like Brandes, and in contrast to his attitude towards friends like Frydenlund and Nilsson seemed anxious to play down the autobiographical element. In letters to the Swedish critic Gustaf af Geijerstam he carefully distanced himself from 'the man in the book' and 'the I of the book'. The general reaction of shocked excitement which **Hunger** created among the reading public at home in Norway must have confirmed him in his belief that he had succeeded at last in his ambition to produce something startlingly new and unusual in literature. Technically he had achieved this by his artful confusion of two forms, the autobiography and the novel. In succeeding experiments with the new genre over the course of the next ten years he was to discover that the public found this deliberate confusion of fact and fiction teasing, not a little disorienting, at times downright enraging, but always—fortunately for him—fascinating.

He was nervous and overworked after the last strenuous spurt on **Hunger**. and with the anodyne of hard work removed he felt loneliness keenly. Half-jokingly he asked Erik Frydenlund to look out for a woman for him, complaining that he was tired of travelling around without a single person he could turn to, without a home or any permanent place, from hotel to hotel, from country to country. He knew that he should rest, but felt that he could not afford it. He had received 2100 kroner for *Hunger*, but was spending money 'like a pig'. As he turns over in his mind the possibilities for the summer, for the first time the idea of a trip to the near East comes up; he wanted to travel to Constantinople, a two-month sea voyage via Antwerp, Tunisia, Piraeus, Salonika and Odessa.[25] This is the first direct expression of a more than passing interest in the Orient—which in those days meant the near East—an interest that was probably fostered by his reading of Confucius and certain Buddhist scriptures which he would have found in Kristofer Janson's library in the course of his energetic progress towards self-education. Hamsun writes of this trip as though it had been firmly planned in his mind, and only circumstances had contrived to put it off for what he described as 'at least a couple of months'. In fact, he had to wait another ten years before he made it. He lived on the wing during these days, constantly changing his address, making and abandoning plans with a bewildering, whimsical rapidity in which we recognise again the character portrayed in *Hunger*.

He looked round for a small place where he could settle down for a few months quite anonymously and work; he had a collection of 'curious short stories' which he was hoping to add to and publish in time to catch the Christmas book market in Christiania. Sometime in June he moved into a hotel room in the small Norwegian coastal town of Lillesand,[26] on the south coast between Kristiansand and Grimstad. From here he continued his efforts to promote *Hunger*; the first edition of 2000 was selling poorly after the original sensation, and his publisher Philipsen was only 'reasonably pleased'. He quickly abandoned his idea for a shortstory collection and thought of another novel: 'I'll write a new book which will stir things up for the four prophets here at home, so help me God I will', he wrote to Erik Skram in Denmark.[27] It was the idea of the competition that thrilled and inspired Hamsun most in the early days, the thought of killing kings and capturing citadels. It was not enough for him just to write and be published—nothing short of a complete victory over all other writers, sealed by some kind of crowning ceremony, was going to be enough for him.

His room had a large balcony overlooking the sea and the Saltholmen lighthouse,[28] with numerous potted plants and creepers, and he spent hours walking back and forth here trying to get started on the new book. A neighbour whom he described as a 'mad musician' disturbed his concentration with his violin playing. Hamsun soon found that he did not like the town. 'Fillesand' he called it punningly—Ragtown—and complained that it was a wretched little town whose only inhabitants were one priest and a lame tailor. The pleasures of the graveyard, which had brought him such comfort when a boy in Uncle Hans' house, and which had often soothed him during his worst times in Christiania,[29] exerted their old attraction on him here in Lillesand, and he frequently took the walk to Molands Church where he would 'amuse himself' by reading the different inscriptions on the gravestones, counting them, and sorting them by motto.

A distraction of a different kind was the visit of a young Englishwoman named Mary Dunne, a writer herself and already at twenty-nine a rich widow. Having come across Hamsun's *Hunger* in a bookshop, she had become infatuated with him, and wrote to him suggesting that she translate the book into English. What correspondence the two may have had has been lost, but from references Hamsun makes to Mary Dunne in letters to friends, and using Mary Dunne's own lightly fictionalised account of their relationship in her short story "Now Spring Has Gone,"[30] it seems clear that when she visited him that summer in order to discuss the translation, she fell in love with him. Hamsun was slightly flattered, slightly amused, and—apart from the possibility of being translated into English—distinctly not interested: early in September she visited him at Arendal and presented him with a photograph of herself which he carefully wrapped in a handkerchief and placed in the bottom of his yellow leather suitcase.[31] According to Hamsun she actually proposed to him,[32] an assertion that the tone of her story of the meeting lends credibility to. Clearly he wanted *Hunger* to appear in English, and occasionally permitted himself to dream of the riches an appearance in what he called the 'beef-language' would bring him; but Mary Dunne had difficulty in finding a publisher for her work, and his interest in the project soon disappeared.

Unable to get on with his novel, Hamsun eventually did the next best thing and produced a statement of intention for it which he called **"From the Unconscious Life of the Mind,"** published in the Bergen literary magazine *Samtiden*. It provides an interesting footnote not only to *Hunger*, but to all the fiction he was to produce throughout the 1890s:

> We have an old proverb: There are many things hidden in Nature. For the attentive, searching man of today, fewer and fewer of these secrets remain hidden. One after another they are being brought forth for observation and identification. An increasing number of people who lead mental lives of great intensity, people who are sensitive by nature, notice the steadily more frequent appearance in them of mental states of great strangeness. It might be something completely inexplicable—a wordless and irrational feeling of ecstasy; or a breath of psychic pain; a sense of being spoken to from afar, from the sky, or the sea; an agonisingly developed sense of hearing which can cause one to wince at the murmuring of unseen atoms; an unnatural staring into the heart of some closed kingdom suddenly and briefly

revealed; an intuition of some approaching danger in the midst of a carefree hour . . .

It was this vision of the unguessed-at complexity of the human mind—or at least, its under-representation in literature—that concerned Hamsun. He wanted a literature that would redefine normality and abnormality, that would in effect expand the known territory of consciousness and give a more vivid and accurate picture of what it's really like to be a human being.

Hamsun was proud of his article. To a friend he wrote that he felt he had gone 'as far as a sane man can go—except the Russians, who can go as far again'.[33] But if we ignore for a moment the chirpiness and look at the article itself, we find that it casts interesting and probably unintentional light on the author's personal life at this time, confirming his essential loneliness, his sense of isolation, and indeed his slight paranoia. Describing his walk home from the Molands Church one day, he writes that he 'met a number of people walking in the town . . . It interested me that all these good people I met glared so indignantly at me, as if the mere fact that also I was walking there was the height of impudence. I was used to these looks and scowls. I recognised them all again.'[34] He also mentions how he looked through an old newspaper trying to trace the source of an image that cropped up in his dreams; finding it, he realises that he did not register it consciously on the earlier reading because he was on that occasion searching its pages for something else, namely an attack on him which he 'assumed' the paper would contain—he apparently regularly received from America copies of any newspapers which contained attacks on him for his book *On the Cultural Life of Modern America*. He also mentions five anonymous, threatening letters received from America in connection with the book.

Later in the year the novel began to move a little. Nevertheless he knew that it was going to be a large book, and that he could not expect to see money for it for some time yet. He simply had to find a way to finance himself. One of the most important results of the publication of **Hunger** in June was the speed with which the book was taken up in Germany. Within one month of publication in Norway the book was being translated into German for the Berlin publishing house of S. Fischer. Although it did not relieve his immediate financial needs, the importance of this for Hamsun's career as a writer, for his economic future, and for his future attitude towards Germany cannot be overestimated. Without it, Hamsun might have gone the way of many another author from a small linguistic community, and simply disappeared along with all his works. And this goes not merely for authors, but for all artists: it is hard to think of a single known Norwegian artist from this period—or indeed from succeeding periods—who did not come to European prominence through German enthusiasm. The most well-known examples are the most obvious—Ibsen, Grieg, Edvard Munch and Hamsun himself.

The traditional links between the lands were strong: Germany gave Denmark-Norway her religion, her kings, her aristocracy, her military, her schooling. And just as there was an intellectual cult of 'Norwegianness' prevailing in Copenhagen which helped to make **Hunger** such an immediate critical success, so there was a corresponding cult of Scandinavianism in Germany around the year 1890 which ensured that the book received immediate attention, and subsequent translation. Ibsen and Bjørnson were the founders of this cult of Scandinavianism, but as the influence of Nietzsche and Dostoevsky spread among the younger writers it was names like Strindberg and Hamsun that came to the fore. The cult reached its heights in Berlin, where a group led by the Polish writer and musician Stanislaw Przybyszewski and his Norwegian wife Dagny Juel, Ola Hansson and Strindberg, and including Edvard Munch and the writers Arne Garborg and Andreas Aubert, set a frantic intellectual and social pace which only the most dedicated of romantics could follow. Hamsun was never a member of this group—he visited Germany only once, and briefly, in the early part of his life—but he profited by its existence. Ola Hansson wrote a critical study of him in German, and Harald Hansen reviewed **Hunger** for the influential magazine *Freie Buhne*. The magazine also printed **Hunger** prior to its publication in book form in 1891. Hamsun was of course delighted at this response to what was effectively his first novel. He could also inform Erik Skram that he had received further requests for authorisation to translate the book from Proznan in Poland, from Marienbad, from Vienna, as well as from England.

For the most part, however, this impressive list of successes was a matter of prestige and status rather than money. Hamsun corresponded energetically with a German translator named Marie Herzfeld throughout his stay in Lillesand, sending her short stories as well as his programme article **"From The Unconscious Life of the Mind."** He exhorted her to read an imminent German translation of his American book by a Dr Hans Kurella (it never materialised), and enquired about the quality of the translation her colleague Maria von Borsch had produced of **Hunger** for *Freie Buhne*. He was particularly pleased with the violence of the blasphemous outburst that appears in the last part of the novel, and when Fischer's edition appeared, wrote anxiously to Marie Herzfeld asking her to check that it had been included. He sent her a long short-story **"Chance,"** written in the summer of 1889 though not published in Norway until Christmas Eve. Apparently she had trouble placing her German translation of it. He wrote to her on 26 November 1890:

I am sorry you have had such problems with **"Chance"**; it was wrong of me to send it. Next time you must simply refuse me when I send you poor quality stuff. In any case, I do not write like that any more; it does not interest me.

Nevertheless, she eventually managed to persuade *Freie Buhne* to take it in 1891. It was a small success, and one which Hamsun may later have wished undone in view of the storm which broke out over the story in 1892.

With the money earned from **Hunger** Hamsun was now able to start repaying some of the debts he had amassed in the course of the previous few years. He was particularly pleased to be able to pay off Nils Frydenlund the 200 kroner outstanding from 1886, plus a payment for interest on the money. But typically, no sooner had he repaid it than he had to start borrowing again. A man from his home county of Nordland had written to him describing the hard time he was having looking after his family of five children and wife. Hamsun knew the couple—had even been in love with the girl once himself—but this man had won her. Now he found that he had written promising the man 100 kroner in October, money which he no longer had, having just lent 100 kroner to a schoolteacher in Lillesand. This money, he was informed locally, he was unlikely to see again. He wrote in some embarrassment explaining the problem to Erik Frydenlund and, as usual, Frydenlund did not let him down.[35]

Money, the new novel, and how to make sure that the new 'psychological' literature continued to make progress, and did not wither in the shadow of Norway's ageing 'great men'—Ibsen, Bjørnson, Kielland and Lie; these were the three problems uppermost in Hamsun's mind during his six months' stay at Lillesand. And at some point he hit upon an idea which seemed to offer a partial solution to all three: a lecture tour of Norway's major cities in which he would both promote the new literature and explicitly condemn the old. The controversy would ensure the financial success of such an undertaking, and between lectures he would be able to continue work on the new book. By September 1890 he was already wholly committed to the idea, and had ceased work on the novel in order to prepare the lectures. In December he returned to Christiania to put the finishing touches to them, and in February 1891 took them with him to Bergen to begin one of the most controversial years of his long life of controversy.

Notes

1. *EKF* p233
2. *Herman Bang Vol 3* H Jacobsen p58
3. *KHSHV* TH p55
4. Ibid p48
5. Emerson had been a Unitarian minister at Boston from 1829 to 1832.
6. Letter to Langens of 25.4.1914, for example, in OUB
7. *KHSHV* TH p97
8. Letter to Georg Brandes of April 1890 in *Strindberg—Brev* Stockholm 1965 p123
9. Their meeting, when it did take place in Paris some five years later, was electric with misunderstandings, with Strindberg at the height of his inferno crisis, and Hamsun doing his best to help him.
10. *KHSHV* TH p58
11. *Olaf Norli—Et Festskrift* Article by Olaf Huseby, Oslo 1933 p27-28
12. Quoted in Øyvind Anker *Boken om Karoline* Oslo 1982 p193
13. Characteristic of the terms of opposition in which Hamsun conceived even literary reputations was an elevation of Bjørnson at the expense of Ibsen. 'How refreshing to read Bjørnson again', he wrote in 1890. 'We have had enough, thank you, of the supremely enigmatic writing that began with *The Wild Duck* and has lately reached new heights of lunacy with *The Lady from the Sea*.'[12]
14. The first of them is reprinted in *Artikler 1889-1928*
15. *Før det dages*—Jeppe Aakjær, Copenhagen 1929 p184
16. Oftedal did take a tumble—in 1891—but not as a result of Hamsun's book. He was involved in a scandal that also involved several young women which effectively ruined him as a church figure. Even so, there were loyal parishioners who refused to believe the stories, and his career as a politician continued.
17. *EKF* p236
18. *Kringsjaa* Christiania 1904 p500
19. *KHSHV* TH p99, p116
20. The title by which *Crime And Punishment* is traditionally known in Norway.
21. *KHSHV* p75
22. Ibid p72
23. Beckett's short story "The End" has striking parallels with *Hunger*. A tramp wanders pointlessly round a city, alternately comforted and tormented by the voice in his own head. He has the same

fleeting, slightly ridiculous contact with people as the narrator of *Hunger,* and the story ends in his taking to a boat just as Hamsun's tormented hero does.

24. Ibid p75

25. *EKF* p238. Also *Hvad jeg har oplevet* Kristofer Janson p225

26. *KHSHV* TH p98

27. *Artikler 1889-1928* p34

28. *Norske Intelligenssedler* 13.6.1890

29. The narrator of *Hunger* is often to be found sitting on benches in the cemetery at Our Saviour's Church.

30. In the collection *Keynotes,* London 1894, under the *nom de plume* she also used for her translation of *Hunger,* George Egerton. The collection carries a dedication to Knut Hamsun.

31. Letter to Bolette Pavels Larsen (no date) OUB

32. Letter to Arne Garborg 10.9. (no year) OUB

33. Letter to Bolette Pavels Larsen (no date) OUB

34. *Artikler 1889-1928* p33

35. *EKF* p241

Donald C. Riechel (essay date May 1989)

SOURCE: Riechel, Donald C. "Knut Hamsun's 'Imp of the Perverse': Calculation and Contradiction in *Sult* and *Mysterier.*" *Scandinavica: An International Journal of Scandinavian Studies* 28, no. 1 (May 1989): 29-53.

[*In the following essay, Riechel studies two of Hamsun's early novels, noting that the narrative effects in both* Hunger *and* Mysteries *are achieved from a combination of ambiguity, irony, and self-contradiction.*]

Nietzsche once wrote that becoming accustomed to irony and sarcasm spoils one's character: in the end one resembles a snapping dog that besides knowing how to bite has learned how to laugh[1]. Perhaps such habituation spoiled Knut Hamsun, who in his life and in his art always seems to have manoeuvred for the last laugh, to the fascinated discomfort of his readers. Hamsun's 'insistence on ambiguity', to use Robert Ferguson's words, 'his rejection of certainty, his juggling with lies that turn out to be true, and truths that turn out to be lies, his recognition and reproduction of the calculating nature of the mind's voice'[2] identify him as a Modernist in Nietzsche's wake. Neither Hamsun's ironic habits nor Nietzsche's profoundly ironic mind are measured in the least by the philosopher's early admonition, and definition, in *Menschliches Allzumenschliches,* that irony is appropriate only as a pedagogical method.

Hamsun was admired by Franz Kafka, Thomas Mann, and Robert Musil, yet no one has suggested calling him 'the Ironic Norwegian'. Ferguson, author of the first full-length biography of Hamsun in English, calls him 'a multiple paradox; a living riddle; a human question-mark' (p. 3), whose unrepentant support of the Quisling government and of Hitler's Germany at the end of his life compromises even his earliest works, *Sult* (*Hunger,* 1890), *Mysterier* (*Mysteries,* 1892), *Pan* (1894), the novels that established his international reputation. The critical attempt to uncover a proto-fascist ideology in them can be just as disagreeably inadequate as an apologia; in each case interpretation loses sight of Hamsun's horizon of irony. A Norwegian commentator, in an analysis of the first of the Segelfoss novels, *Børn av Tiden* (*Children of the Age,* 1913), regards irony as the essential element of Hamsun's art, perhaps the very element that lures the reader into adopting the authorial bias against social change. According to this Marxist argument irony veils ideology, seduces rather than liberates[3].

Irony is always in some way a 'fencing' strategy, either as parry or thrust, evasion or penetration; it is invariably thought of as a sophisticated intellectual attitude and manner, requiring mental agility, wit, to hover between incompatibilities, irreconcilable opposites[4]. Ironies are not usually shouted. Hamsun's style, in apparent contrast, especially in *Sult* and *Mysterier,* (the novels to be considered in the following), has a vehemence and haste about it, a paratactical, often hyperbolic abruptness, and an insistent hypnotic rhythm that suggest the opposite of ironic utterance. In literary irony the reader is also usually initiated into the ironic game of meaning and shares the narrator's superior perspectives. But in *Sult* and *Mysterier* particularly the narrator is completely unreliable, and authenticates nothing, for Hamsun writes in the Nietzschean conviction that objectivity is nothing more than a bias, and that no individual has a privileged access to his or her innermost self.[5] If 'irony is the art of saying something without really saying it' (Muecke, p. 5), what is it that Hamsun is not saying, about himself, and in his fiction?

The narrative effects in *Sult* and *Mysterier* derive from countless ambiguities, but the polarities of ironic structure seem peculiarly energized not by intellect but by elemental aggression. These stories are driven by an irresolvable compulsion both to assert and to contradict the self, by self-betrayal and self-destruction, or by what Edgar Allan Poe, nearly a half-century before *Sult,* called 'the imp of the perverse'. There is no evidence that Hamsun discovered Poe during his American years, when he read Twain, Emerson and Whitman. Poe is nevertheless an uncanny presence in Hamsun's early fiction, as Nietzsche, the Poe- and Baudelaire-reader, would very likely have recognized, had *Sult* and *Mysterier* been published and translated into German or French before Nietzsche's correspondence with Georg Brandes began in 1887. Nietzsche read Strindberg, as he did Dostoevsky, in French[6]. Brandes, through his lectures on Nietzsche in Copenhagen in the spring of 1888, introduced the philosopher's thought not only to Strindberg and Hamsun, but to all Scandinavia, and with that, to Europe[7]. In the view of most Hamsun critics, the title of Brandes's essay on Nietzsche, '*Aristocratic Radicalism*', published 1889, defines the philosophical limits of the connection between Hamsun and Nietzsche: anti-democratic elitism. But Hamsun was a 'disciple' of the philosopher not so much in the narrow terms of direct intellectual encounter as in the wide sense of the genealogy of Modernism. The connections Poe—Baudelaire—Dostoevsky—Strindberg—Nietzsche represent the formula for Hamsun's Modernist breakthrough as well as for his self-understanding as a writer even in his last years. (One cannot say, as does Frederick R. Karl, that 'Modernism bypassed Hamsun' or that he is 'a now forgotten author'[8]).

Hamsun seems to have depended on literary models, as did Nietzsche, for his view of self and world, as though leading 'life as literature', to borrow the title of Alexander Nehamas's study of Nietzsche. Harald Næss has noted that even the written statements Hamsun made to the psychiatrist who was to determine Hamsun's fitness to stand trial for treason after 1945 were in essence reflections on his earliest literary identity[9]. The psychiatrist included Hamsun's fiction as a matter of course in the analysis of the writer's personality, and the artist-patient-prisoner explained himself as a matter of course in terms of his books, in which there are 'several hundred different characters, every one of them spun from myself, with faults and virtues such as all created characters have' (Ferguson, p. 398). The depiction of character was a matter at the heart of Hamsun's rebellion against literary tradition in 1890. The octogenarian skips over a half-century of life and work and returns to his lectures repudiating Kielland, Lie, Zola, the Naturalists who 'wrote about people with dominant characteristics. They had no use for the more subtle psychology, people all had this "dominant characteristic" which ordained their actions' (Ferguson, p. 398). Hamsun then names Dostoevsky as a writer from whom he had learned, and continues: 'From the time I began I do not think that in my entire output you will find a character with a single dominant characteristic. They are all without so-called "character". They are split and fragmented, not good and not bad, but both at once, and changeable in their attitudes and in their deeds. No doubt I am also like this myself.' (ibid.)

Hamsun is in effect one of his own characters, or several of his characters; his multiple self-inventions entangle us in the contradictions that to him denoted the truth about life and literature and that continued the polemics of his aesthetic breakthrough, when he began as a Strindberg-disciple by vehemently attacking the literary establishment, only to represent himself in later years as the spokesman and preceptor of his nation, in the manner of Bjørnstjerne Bjørnson. Hamsun has been described both as a 'Scandinavian Rousseau'[10], an anti-intellectual vitalist who celebrated the fertile earth, and as an intellectual who read widely[11]. He bought a farm in Norway in 1911, but we learn that he was only a 'gentleman farmer' and that he 'continued to stay for longer or shorter periods away from home' (Næss, p. 19). In his last days, this farmer who was no farmer sat 'most of the time in an old wicker chair in his room' with 'no other company than two portraits of Goethe and Dostoevsky looking down at him from the walls' (Næss, p. 26). Goethe *and* Dostoevsky is the same order of contradiction as Rousseau and Nietzsche or Strindberg and Bjørnson; nothing about Hamsun allows of an either-or, in his life or in his fiction. Contradiction is the basic structure of Hamsun's narrative art, which from the beginning was curiously preoccupied with time. It is a pre-occupation which by itself identifies Hamsun as a pioneer of the modern novel, which is a riot of discordant clocks, to borrow from Theodor Ziolkowski,[12] of clocks indicating the conflict between the individual experience of duration, the longing for redemption from the natural progression of time toward death through the timelessness of myth, and the perception of the cold rigidity of public measurements, of an oppressive society. The epiphanies of a Joyce or Proust or Musil pierce 'through all deceptive appearances to the timeless core of things' (Ziolkowski, p. 84), and redeem the self from the pain of contemplating the clock as Baudelaire expressed it in 'L'Horloge' ('The Clock') in *Les Fleurs du Mal*: 'Trois mille six cents fois par heure, la Seconde / —Chuchote: *Souviens-toi!*: —Rapide, avec sa voix / D'insecte, Maintenant dit: Je suis Autrefois, / Et j'ai pompé ta vie avec ma trompe immonde!' ('Thirty-six hundred times in every hour / the Second whispers: *Remember*! and Now replies / in its maddening mosquito hum: I am Past, / who passing lit and sucked your life and left!')[13].

Ferguson remarks that Hamsun all his life was 'very particular about knowing what time of day it was. During the last two years his sight failed, so that he could no longer see his watch. [His wife] bought him a large, round red wall-clock, and he would sit in his armchair with this in his lap. It had no glass in the face, so that he could feel the fingers with his hands' [*sic*] (Ferguson, p. 420). It is a scene Hamsun might have written himself. His kindred creatures, the vagabond souls of *Landstrykere* (*Wayfarers*, 1927), buy, sell, trade, lend, lose and find watches—watch and chain are badges of importance and success—and periodically encounter the itinerant old Jewish watch dealer, Papst, who has many mysterious pockets, like E. T. A. Hoffmann's Coppelius, with his eyeglasses, in *The Sandman,* but nothing of the romantic-demonic about him. He is the paradigmatic time-keeping wayfarer, neither good nor bad, whose life and death demonstrate both the relevance and the irrelevance of time. 'All life goes on'[14].

It has been noted that **Sult,** is full of clocks, and that the first event in the novel is: 'a clock struck six somewhere below'[15]. Such a sentence seldom detains the reader; whether it is six o'clock in the novel or ten has no bearing on the experience of reading and holds no interest as a realistic-naturalistic detail. But in **Sult,** 'a pure narrative present, a sense of time continuously billowing and literally getting nowhere, for the first time fully occupies fiction'[16]. Time-keeping here is not a realistic device, and the public time of clocks and calendars, of churches and city halls is a provocation the starving narrator in **Sult,** challenges with a wilful time-keeping of his own. Roaming the streets of Christiania (Oslo, after 1924), he once sidles up to a policeman and says that it is ten o'clock. 'Nei den er to, svarte han forundret. Nei den er ti, sa jeg, Klokken er ti. Og stønnende av Sinne traadte jeg endnu et Par Skridt frem, knyttet min Haand og sa: Hør, vet De hvad—Klokken er ti' (**Sult,** p. 45). ('No, it's two,' he answered surprised. 'No, it's ten,' I said. 'It's ten o'clock'. Growling with anger, I went two steps nearer, clenched my fist, and said, 'Listen, take my word for it, it's ten o'clock.' **Hunger,** pp. 72f.). This bizarre insistence on the correctness of an intensely private, subjectively experienced time, or a fiction, a lie, anticipates the narrator's desperate re-definition of reality near the end of the novel, where a grocer's cart comes by '. . . og jeg ser at det er Poteter i den Kjærre, men av Raseri, av Halsstarrighet finder jeg paa at si at det slet ikke er Poteter, det var Kaalhoder, og jeg bandte grusomt paa at det var Kaalhoder. Jeg hørte godt hvad jeg selv sa og jeg svor bevisst Gang efter Gang paa denne Løgn bare for at ha den morsomme Tilfredsstillelse at jeg begik en stiv Mened' (p. 140). ('and I saw it was filled with potatoes, but out of fury, from sheer obstinacy, I decided that they were not potatoes at all, they were cabbages, and I swore violent oaths that they were cabbages. I heard my own words very well, and I took the oath again and again on this lie and swore deliberately just to have the delightful satisfaction of committing such clear perjury'). (p. 181).

In his hunger-induced hallucinations trivial objects, coat buttons, seem to return the wild stares of an imagination that belongs to a writer[17]. If the narrator is an artist-figure, then his 'perjuries', his whirling spontaneous fictions take on the aesthetic dimension that Nietzsche first articulated: '*Nur* Narr! *Nur* Dichter!' ('*Merely* fool! *Merely* poet!'). 'Und die Dichter lügen zuviel!' ('And the poets lie too much!'; from *Zarathustra, Werke,* II, 534; II, 345). Hamsun's distrust of artists becomes a principal theme in **Mysterier,** but it is also an aspect of his self-understanding, and one pole of another contradiction: the artist, the writer, as clown—and as great man. In a lecture to students at Christiania University, Hamsun warned against overestimating writers and writing, saying that writers 'had the souls of wandering tramps' and were akin to 'travelling organ-grinders' (Ferguson, p. 166-167). The protagonist of **Sult** is an unfathomable liar. He invents and re-invents himself, as a journalist, as a member of a distinguished aristocratic family, as a proper middle-class citizen, while being unable to escape his beggar's appearance. The creative imagination asserts its fictions as the only reality, and this is part of Hamsun's aesthetic program in the 1890s. What is reality? he asked in a lecture: 'er da en faktisk foregaaet Fantasi mindre virkelig end en faktisk eksisterende Ytterfrakke eller en Ildtang?' ('Is an actually experienced fantasy less real than an actually existing overcoat or a pair of firetongs?')[18]

Nothing less than salvation is at stake, redemption from the confinement by the maps and clocks of the world. Time is told again and again in **Sult** by the clock of the Church of Our Saviour. The building is a Christiania landmark the narrator passes and circles repeatedly, and like the city hall it represents public authority whose grace is extended only on condition of conformity, or of self-effacement, and in their function they anticipate the public edifices in Kafka's works. At one point in **Sult** the narrator decides to seek the help of a pastor, but first must convince himself that he has not lost his faith. Somehow he arrives too late, after the minister's office hours: 'Naadens Tid var omme!'(p. 63; 'grace hour is over!' p. 92). His own counting of hours has gone awry; the 'imp of the perverse' arranges a missed opportunity. Redemption comes not from religion, however, but from a ship in the harbour. The narrator alternately prays to and rails against God, but his only piety is toward his hunger. God is dead, and there is no discoverable metaphysical shelter. At the same time, the narrator's hunger has been real, and not a metaphor. Why then did he starve, when there are always ships to work on? (**Sult,** p. 103).

Perversely too, despite his hunger, Hamsun's protagonist insists on writing the unreadable, instead of the popular material the newspaper editor requires (**Sult,** p. 105). He is a Modernist insisting on difficulty and protest, on a revaluation of values, and prefers to offer essays on 'Crimes of the Future', 'Freedom of the Will' (p. 25) or 'Philosophical Consciousness' (p. 27), or a sketch on Correggio (p. 104). Later he turns against himself as a potential producer of books with a plan of an allegory about a fire in a bookstore (p. 156), but soon it is brains, not books, that are in flames (p. 162)[19]. Aggression inward is followed by aggression outward, with an attempt at a one-act play called 'The Sign of the Cross', in which a 'fiery prostitute' sins at the foot of the altar, 'bare av deilig Foragt for Himlen', p. 126, ('simply out of a delicious contempt for eternity' (p. 164), which is a phrase comparable to 'the delightful satisfaction of committing such clear perjury' (p. 181) in swearing potatoes are cabbages.

Aggression toward the self, in imagination and in actual hunger, and aggression toward the world are again the whirling poles of contradiction, the fundamental structure of **Sult**. **Sult** by that token has been interpreted as the single model for all Hamsun's writings[20]. The narrator is the prototypical Hamsun-character, caught between affirming the inner world of imagination and negating the external world, while still seeking acceptance in that public world. He must affirm society's values, out of hunger, but by attempting to force acceptance of his own values at the same time, he provokes the world's rejection (Masát, pp. 322-325). The Kafkaesque conflict is insoluble, and in essence suicidal[21]. The protagonist of **Mysterier**, Johan Nilsen Nagel, and the protagonist of **Pan**, Lieutenant Glahn, will actually kill themselves. **Sult** ends when the narrator steps out of the conflict by joining a ship's crew, a non-solution that compels the ship to return, as it were, in **Mysterier**, with Nagel on board.

As Ferguson comments, the reader of **Sult** soon comes to suspect that the narrator's sufferings result not from an inability but from a refusal to act. 'He . . . is in some perverse way enjoying his predicament', he wills it, as though to see 'how low he can sink, how much he can endure' (Ferguson, p. 111), as though hunger were a stimulus to life—which is an idea to be found in Nietzsche's unpublished notes from the 1880s (*Werke*, III, 682). The most basic activity in living things, Nietzsche argues, is not a will to self-preservation, but the desire to experience an expansion, intensification of the organism, to experience power. Man does not seek pleasure and avoid pain; that is merely consequence, interpretation. Hamsun's hunger is perverse only by the measure of the church clock, only in terms of the antithetical thinking that divides experience and behaviour into discrete opposites, good and evil, cause and effect, subject-object, love-hate (see particularly *Beyond Good and Evil*, Part I). **Sult**, Hamsun's first successful novel, is by that token a wildly Nietzschean experiment, as plotless as its narrator is literally hungry. The counting of the hours and days marks the boldness of a radical emptiness, of an 'ironic leisure' (Vernon, p. 167) in which dire need masquerades as grandeur. The narrator is a caricature of the flaneur and dandy, always concerned with interpretations of his appearance. He needs audiences, and wanting to be seen and heard, he risks self-prostitution[22].

In structure and theme **Sult** is the equivalent of Nietzsche's notion of 'the perfect book': in an unpublished note the philosopher once imagined that such a work should be 'an ideal monologue', 'a kind of memoir' ('eine Art mémoires'), relating 'die abstraktesten Dinge am leibhaftesten und blutigsten; die ganze Geschichte wie *persönlich erlebt und erlitten* . . . nicht "Beschreibung"; alle Probleme ins Gefühl übersetzt, bis zur Passion' ('the most abstract things at their most corporeal, at their bloodiest; the whole story as *personally experienced and endured* . . . not "description"; all problems translated into feeling, even unto passion').[23] **Sult** is a personal reminiscence, told after the experiment was abandoned.

By way of the genealogy of Modernism, Hamsun's first-person narrator in **Sult** also has an antecedent in Poe's narrative voices, as in three stories that are particularly relevant to a reading of **Sult** and **Mysterier**: *The Man of the Crowd* (1840), *A Descent into the Maelström* (1841) and *The Imp of the Perverse* (1845). The latter opens reflectively, philosophically, as an essay, only to end in the panic of the murderer-narrator who unaccountably betrayed himself. The spirit of the perverse impels us to a deed precisely because we should not do it; it is as self-destructive as Hamsun's voluntary hunger and deliberate delaying and evasion of solutions. This perverseness is 'a *mobile* without motive, a motive not *motiviert*'[24]. It is striking that Poe anticipates Nietzsche here in rejecting the conventional interpretations of human behaviour in terms of cause and effect or God's will, locating the promptings of our actions in our physiology: 'I am not more certain that I breathe, than that the assurance of the wrong or error of any action is often the one unconquerable *force* which impels us, and alone impels us to its prosecution. Nor will this overwhelming tendency to do wrong for wrong's sake admit of analysis, or resolution into ulterior elements. It is a radical, a primitive impulse—elementary' (Poe, *The Imp of the Perverse*, p. 281).

Poe, and his European discoverer Baudelaire, share with Nietzsche and the first Modernist generation the nineteenth-century anti-metaphysical interest in explaining emotional, psychological, sociological, moral phenomena in terms of natural science[25]. Long before Nietzsche described art as the expression of the processes of life, Stendhal, who was among the writers Nietzsche most admired, published the essay *De l'Amour* (1822), which he intended as a 'physiology of love'[26]. There were physiologies of the flaneur, the grisette, the proper lady, the English tourist (Pfotenhauer, p. 1). Among the notable titles are Brillat-Savarin's *Physiologie du goût* (1825), Balzac's *Physiologie du mariage* (1829), and Paul Bourget's *Physiologie de l'amour moderne* (1891). Baudelaire first had planned to publish his *De l'essence du Rire* as a *Physiologie du Rire* (Pfotenhauer, p. 204). For Nietzsche physiological urges and needs are the motives that our moralities, logical systems, our language, our 'objectivity' mask (e.g. in *Werke*, I, 1261; II,

11; II, 569; III, 710). Art as physiology means Dionysian affirmation of the tragic experience of our physical vulnerability and mortality (Pfotenhauer, p. 170).

Hamsun's 'hunger artist' does not deny life, as Kafka's does, but is himself a predator loose in the city streets, affirming the primacy of an uninhibited imagination. The self-destructive, suicidal aspect of the experiment will become explicit in the second novel, **Mysterier,** but both **Sult** and **Mysterier** are demonstrations of an aesthetic program that is also a physiology of art. The new psychology Hamsun advocated in his essays and lectures of 1890-1891 is in essence a Nietzschean probing into the mind as body, into blood and bone as thought and feeling. He was preceded in this by Strindberg, who in his preface to the play *Fröken Julie,* 1888, disputed the '*bourgeois* conception of the immutability of the soul'. His characters will lack character, and their behaviour will not be reducible to single motives; they are self-contradictory beings[27]. For Strindberg and Hamsun self-contradiction is the dramatic form of the soul's incalculability. Both concluded, with Nietzsche, that intention and action are not separable, that the content of a thought or desire cannot be isolated from the content of other thoughts and desires, that the doer cannot be separated from the deed. The self 'is constituted not simply by the fact *that* it thinks, wants and acts but also by precisely *what* it thinks, wants and does . . . What we think, want and do is seldom if ever a coherent collection. Our thoughts contradict one another and contrast with our desires, which are themselves inconsistent and are in turn belied by our actions' (Nehamas, p. 180).

In the essay **"Fra det ubevidste Sjæleliv"**("**From the Unconscious Life of the Mind**"), published in 1890 in the new journal *Samtiden,* Hamsun repudiates types in literature as he would deny decades later that he was a type, a definable—hence punishable?—character. If literature were to explore psychological states,

> Vi fik erfare lidt om de hemmelige Bevægelser, som bedrives upaaagtet paa de afsides Steder i Sjælen, den Fornemmelsernes uberegnelige Uorden, det delikate Fantasiliv holdt under Luppen, disse Tankens og Følelsens Vandringer i det blaa, skridtløse, sporløse Rejser med Hjærnen og Hjærtet, sælsomme Nervevirksomheder, Blodets Hvisken, Benpibernes Bøn, hele det ubevidste Sjæleliv.
>
> (We would get to know a little about the secret stirrings that go on unnoticed in the remote parts of the mind, the incalculable chaos of impressions, the delicate life of the imagination seen under the magnifying glass; the random wanderings of those thoughts and feelings; untrodden trackless journeyings by brain and heart, strange workings of the nerves, the whisper of the blood, the entreaty of the bone, all the unconscious life of the mind.[28].

The structure of this essay is itself an argument for the subjectivity, the incalculability of all structures, whether narrative or psychological, and is by that token an anticipation of the structural hoax that is the novel *Mysterier*. **"Fra det ubevidste Sjæleliv"** offers no science, but the abstract as the personal, a monologue with reminiscences and witty, seemingly improvised variations of its theme[29].

At the same time as Hamsun's physiology of literature is Nietzschean, it has, like Nietzsche's own uses of physiology, general nineteenth-century, and in this case, also quite native, roots. The Christiania of **Sult** is, for example, the same city whose bohemian circle inspired the artist Edvard Munch to his own Modernist breakthrough, and to a manifesto that is a remarkably close counterpart to Hamsun's program in **From the Unconscious Life of the Mind**[30]. While living in St. Cloud (a suburb of Paris) in 1889, Munch jotted down for himself the conviction that painting needed the authenticity of personal emotion, needed to abandon traditional genres for the direct expression of thoughts and feelings (Reinhold Heller, p. 64). In the following year he wrote of his critics: 'De kan inte få in i huvudet att dessa bilder är gjorda på allvar—med lidelse—att de är en produkt av vakna nätter—ak de har kostat ens blod—ens nerver'('They will not get it into their heads that these paintings were created in all seriousness and in suffering, that they are products of sleepless nights, that they have cost me blood and weakened my nerves'; Heller, p. 65 and p. 230 no. 39). To paint 'with blood' (Heller, p. 50) is to practise Nietzsche's physiology of art; Munch transforms nature according to his own subjective disposition (ibid., p. 66), as he does in *The Scream* (1893), a hallucinatory vision that captures an intense experience of loneliness and despair, which can be understood here as forms of hunger. Munch's ideas, as he acknowledged years later, ripened in the Christiania Bohème (ibid., p. 21) in the late 1880s. Christiania, 'denne forunderlige By som ingen forlater før han har faat Mærker av den' ('that strange city no one escapes from until it has left its mark on him'; *Sult,* p. 21), small as it was, felt the same winds of cultural change that were stirring through Copenhagen, Berlin, Vienna, and Paris. Its artists, led by the writer Hans Jæger, were participants in the earliest phase of Modernism, while Hamsun was in America (1886-1888), and nevertheless well informed, as Næss (pp. 10-16) and Ferguson (pp. 87-95) have shown. Nietzsche, 'the single most significant figure' in the Modernist revolution, who dramatized his philosophy through different voices (Karl, pp. 81 ff.), was discussed everywhere after 1888, and Hamsun regarded him as a mentor, for Nietzsche both confirmed him in ideas he had already formed and served him in his strategy for success. With his essays and lectures, and particularly with the publication of **Sult** and **Mysterier,** Hamsun positioned himself skilfully and conspicuously in the literary avant garde and with that in the literary market place (Kirkegaard, p. 150). His insistence upon the incalculability of motivation was itself well calculated. It seems permissible to surmise that a similar opportunism prompted Hamsun to alter the subject matter and style of his fiction after 1900. It does not therefore matter, in a discussion of Hamsun as Modernist, that Hamsun very likely read more about Nietzsche before 1900 than he did Nietzsche's writings, or that Christiania was not a major city in the 1880s. The Modernist experience of the city is a theme already in Poe's *The Man of the Crowd* (1840), in which the narrator follows someone through the dark streets of London to discover the secret of his behaviour, but the man of the crowd, like the narrator of *Sult,* is a book 'that does not permit itself to be read' (Poe, p. 75).

Sult, which Hamsun began writing in a cheap hotel room in a working-class district of Copenhagen (Ferguson, p. 97), was conceived as the expression of modern, urban, existential urgency, and can well be called 'a textbook on the stigmata of modernism' (Kirkegaard, p. 42), 'the first modern text' (Vernon, p. 144), 'one of the great novels of urban alienation' (Ferguson, p. 110). In the next novel, ***Mysterier,*** Hamsun, the denier of calculability and master calculator, turns calculation and incalculability into a diabolical mockery of both writing and reading, of text and interpretation.

Mysterier was not well received when it appeared in 1892, and it has confounded critics ever since. At the same time it seems to attract more critical attention than any other novel by Hamsun[31], and just as ***Sult*** has been described as the single model for all Hamsun's writings (Masát, above), ***Mysterier*** has been considered the one theme of which the entire subsequent work is the endless series of variations[32]. It has also been called Hamsun's 'first and only complete masterpiece' (De Mendelssohn), 'formless', 'disjointed'[33]; 'a rather unsuccessful novel' (Kirkegaard, p. 197), and as 'an act of literary improvisation' (Ferguson, pp. 129 and 132). Few commentators have shared Næss's observation that 'As a prose writer Hamsun was the most meticulous craftsman in Norwegian literature' (p. 72). He was a meticulous craftsman at least with ***Mysterier,*** as I intend to show. The novel has also been read as a detective story[34], but there is no agreement about whether there was a murder, or some other crime, or about who did it. The protagonist, Johan Nilsen Nagel, behaves like a private detective who suspects the character known as the Midget of the murder of a theology student named Karlsen—or perhaps of yet another crime. Perhaps the 'detective' himself, Nagel, is the murderer[35]. Ferguson finds it reasonable to suspect that the Midget raped the spinster Martha Gude (p. 127), but Walter Baumgartner considers that unlikely, since the Midget, Johannes Grøgaard, and Martha Gude were overheard using their first names on saying goodbye[36]. Næss concludes that 'as a detective story ***Mysterier*** is unsatisfactory, not only because symbolism and depth psychology take the place of simple induction, but more particularly because the reader is provided with no solutions' (p. 41).

Yet the title itself suggests the genre 'detective story' and the thought of the genre naturally leads the reader to the pursuit of relevant structural clues, despite any concession that the mysteries here may well be the kind that transcend rational explanation. But such a concession still operates in the hope of a satisfying structure. At first the novel seems to present the familiar pattern of detective fiction in which the crime has already been committed before the story begins, and in which the detective, in solving the crime, restores order to the world. The expectation that the detective will redeem a violated reality is all the greater because of the peculiar intensity of the reader's engagement with the text. Ferguson recalls in the Introduction to his biography of Hamsun that his interest in the writer began with his reading of ***Pan*** and the experience of a 'hypnotic intensity about the prose style, even in translation' (pp. 2-3). The composer Edvard Grieg once wrote of the hypnotic effect of Hamsun's style, in a letter to Bjørnson, 7 December 1904 (Popperwell, p. 11), and Walter Benjamin noted to himself after reading ***Landstrykere*** that Hamsun's storytelling was like incantation, that he narrated 'als ob er der Wirklichkeit kein Wort glaubt' ('as though he doesn't believe a word in reality')[37].

If anywhere, it is in ***Mysterier*** where Hamsun is an 'author-hypnotist'—Strindberg used the term in his Preface to *Miss Julie,* 1888, and it suggests a narrative art that works with the most elemental, primitive effects. John Vernon's speculation (in *Money and Fiction*) that storytelling may have its origins in telling secrets about a third person is useful here (p. 85-86). 'Through secrets, characters gain control over each other and begin the process of plotting. . . . If novels reveal secrets, what else is a reader but a kind of eavesdropper? Eavesdropping, exchanged confidences, intercepted mail, confessions, and even their opposites, concealed information or disguises, are all transformations of secrets and secret telling' (p. 87). The narrator in ***Mysterier*** is himself an eavesdropper and quickly implicates the reader in eavesdropping, and in voyeurism, so that reading simultaneously enchants and disenchants; a vague guilt shadows the act. Nagel stands in his room, lost in thought, and awakes 'med et stærkt rykk, så stærkt at det kunde være påtat, ret som om han længe hadde ståt og studeret paa gjøre dette rykk skjønt han var alene i værelset ('with a violent start, so exaggerated that it didn't seem genuine; it was as if the gesture had been made for effect, even though he was alone in the room', p. 7)[38]. The reader must now feel observed, and become peculiarly self-conscious, all the more because the narrator is not to be trusted. He is not in full possession of the facts, may be biased, and is given to speculation. 'Vilde han ved denne bemærkning gjøre en liten jeip til sig selv og sin rolle?' (p. 60; 'Was [Nagel] laughing at himself and the role he was playing?' p. 65), the narrator wonders. And on another occasion: 'Var det spil eller oprigtighet?' (p. 66; 'Was he acting or was it real?' p. 72). The narrator, in Baumgartner's view, practises disloyalty toward the reader and employs the same strategies of bluff and dissembling as does Nagel (p. 266). The novel is full of examples of disturbed, perverted communication (p. 261), not only among the various characters, but between the author and his readership. Baumgartner's eminently useful analysis of *Mysterier*, based on communication theory, ends in a condemnation of Hamsun himself. The basic principle of the novelist's relation to the reader is mystification (p. 266); Hamsun has a need to make fools of his readers as well as of his characters, and therefore practises a nihilistic narrative strategy (p. 269). The novels betray 'eine immoralistische und irrationalistische Geisteshaltung und eine destruktive soziale Praxis . . .' ('an immoral and irrational mentality and a destructive social practice' *ibid.*).

Baumgartner's indictment of Hamsun is tantamount to a repudiation of irony wherever it does not serve the critic's cause, whether it is instruction, reform or revolution (see Muecke, p. 232ff.) Irony is irresponsibility, or worse, where there is no reliable communication between the ironist and his audience. The irritated sensibility expressed in Baumgartner's argument may also have to do with the particular history of Hamsun's reception in Germany[39]. In any case, *Mysterier* is a disquieting text. One may be tempted in the end to attribute a certain malevolence to its design.

The first mystery in *Mysterier* is Johan Nilsen Nagel, who acts as though he knew he was being watched even when alone in his hotel room, and whose private behaviour is as calculated for effect as his public displays. He sends himself telegrams, wears a conspicuous yellow suit, and a ring of iron, and carries a vial of prussic acid in his pocket. 'Hvorfor bærer jeg den da og hvorfor har jeg anskaffet den? Humbug det også, bare humbug, moderne dekadence-humbug, reklame og snobberi' (p. 31) (But why do I carry it around, and why did I get it in the first place? Hypocrisy again, nothing but a sham; the decadence, phoneyness, self-adulation, and snobbery of our times!, p. 34). Nagel's monologues are gestures of self-deception; here he avoids saying what soon becomes clear: the vial of poison is a token of his long preoccupation with suicide[40]. It is also clear that Nagel already read about Karlsen's death before his arrival; like Sherlock Holmes he scours the newspapers for information and wanders the town's streets at all hours, collects gossip, notes details. The reader thus becomes a detective following a narrator-detective who observes the detective Nagel in pursuit of the suspect, the misshapen dwarf Grøgaard, whom Hamsun once referred to as Nagel's alter ego (Ferguson, p. 133), and each seems aware of the other, as a parody is always aware of its model. But the ratiocination of Poe's or Conan Doyle's detectives is repudiated in *Mysterier*, not only, and not merely, by the suicide of the detective, but by a plot against us that is hidden in trivialities, in numbers, time-telling, quantifications, measurements, in the daily domestic science of counting to establish order. No one has yet shown that the structure of *Mysterier*, the outer organization of its narrative material as well as its inner weave of motifs, is a compulsive and scrupulous numerological arrangement, the precise counterpart to the protagonist's manifestly 'schizoid organization of mind'[41]. The programmatic irrationality of the outsider Nagel has a direct equivalent in an obsessive, asymmetrical design that invites and then baffles calculation, the detection of meaning.

I have suggested that the Nagel who arrives by ship in *Mysterier*, at six in the evening on 12 June (p. 5), is the narrator of *Sult*, a figure both artist and clown, a 'poseur, a pathological phenomenon who is part madman and part genius', as Hamsun once characterized Nagel (Ferguson, p. 126)—and perhaps himself. The enigma that was Knut Hamsun may be that he was literally the masks he invented; behind one mask was another mask. The artist is the confidence man. Hamsun would have recognized his own fantasies, like the charlatan Nagel, in a peculiar case of literature as life that the historian Bernard Wasserstein describes in *The Secret Lives of Trebitsch Lincoln* (1988)[42], the story of a Hungarian Jew (born 1879) whose career of endless masks went through innumerable aliases, passports, and professions including most naturally that of a spy for both sides in the First World War.

Nagel's claim that he is an agronomist may be as false, as devious, as K.'s claim, in Kafka's *Das Schloss*, that he is a land surveyor (in German 'Vermesser', 'surveyor', 'measurer', is related to 'vermessen': 'daring, presumptuous, insolent')[43]. Kamma, the Danish woman who visits Nagel on his birthday, suggests as much. Her arrival in the twelfth chapter has been traced to the inspiration of an actual occasion in Hamsun's wanderings while he was writing *Mysterier*, but that does not explain her role[44]. With the twelfth chapter the reader joins the narrator as it were at the keyhole, as a pure eavesdropper, overhearing emotional intimacies from a woman whose own 'sensibilité nerveuse' (to quote Bourget on Baudelaire; Pfotenhauer, p. 104) makes her a particularly keen observer of Nagel's behaviour. Kamma's visit is a scene and a chapter that dramatizes the unbridgeable gap between inside and outside worlds, between the reader and the creator of this fiction, and between the narrator and the characters in it. Nothing is verifiable. 'Deres passiar blev avbrutt og dunkel, med halve ord som bare de selv forstod meningen av og med mange hentydninger til fortiden.

De hadde truffet hverandre før og kjendte hverandre' (p. 121f.; 'Their conversation was disconnected; they made many elliptical allusions to the past and used words and phrases that had meaning only for them. They obviously knew each other well', p. 132). At one point Kamma says: 'Og hvorfor kan jeg aldri slippe dig? Jeg vet at du er gal, at dine øine er aldeles forrykte . . . Dr. Nissen har sagt at du er gal, og Gud skal vite du må være meget gal når du har kunnet slå dig ned på et slikt sted som dette og kalde dig agronom' (p. 124; 'Why can't I let you go? I know you're crazy; your eyes are the eyes of a madman . . . Dr. Nissen said that you're mad, and God knows it must be true, if you can bury yourself in a hole like this and call yourself an agronomist . . . p. 134). He has played his game before, with the same iron ring and yellow suit.

Nagel's name may also be false. Kamma calls him Simonsen (p. 35), but that may be only a pet name (p. 132). Readers have found other mischief in the syllables Na-gel. Ferguson sees in them 'an anagram in Norwegian of "en gal" (a madman) and in English of "angel"' (p. 133), but the name is also nearly an anagram of Glahn, whose story is told in **Pan**.[45] Næss has pointed out that Nagel was the middle name of Kristofer Janson, Unitarian minister in Minnesota and poet who aided and encouraged Hamsun and whose 'Christian kindliness' is mocked and reversed in the Nietzschean elitism of the protagonist of **Mysterier** (Næss, pp. 44-46). The self-styled agronomist Nagel has nothing but contempt for the humble Norwegian farmer. At the same time, as we will see, there is mischief by association in Nagel's first name as well.

Like Odin in the Icelandic sagas, Hamsun's hero is a shape-changer. Næss refers to a comment Hamsun once made, in a letter from 1890, that it had always been his ambition to appear somewhere suddenly, stay for a time incognito, and then disappear just as suddenly as he came, which, as Næss concludes, reflects an ambition 'to become a myth' (p. 41-42), to be a god, beyond the time that is so relentlessly counted in **Sult** and **Mysterier.** It is curious too that Nagel has androgynous features: broad shoulders, but small stature, 'and a soft, rather feminine mouth' (**Mysterier,** p. 7)[46]. Nagel is a bringer of myths and fairy tales, who relates, or invents, elaborate dreams and visions, offering them as a more valuable alternative to the science and rational liberalism espoused by the town physician. 'Hvad vinding er det i grunden endog rent praktisk talt at man ribber livet for al poesi, al drøm, al skjøn mystik, al løgn? Hvad er sandhet, vet De det? Vi bevæger os jo frem bare gjennem symboler, og disse symboler skifter vi efterhvert som vi skrider frem' (p. 136;'. . . what are we gaining by a pragmatism that robs our life of poetry, dreams, mysticism—are these all lies? What is truth?

Can you tell me that? We can only struggle along by using symbols, and we change them as we alter our views', p. 148).

Nagel's mythopoesis aggressively affirms the logic in his blood (p. 38) in defying conventional assumptions about greatness and virtue in life and in art, and it is striking how often the mythmaker uses literature as a foil. In preferring the fairy tales of the Orient to 'Disse æventyr fra Gudbrandsdalen, dens såre bondefulde poesi . . . Vor helt var ikke en pragtfuld prins, men en snedig klokker' (p. 83; 'the rustic, earthbound poetry of the tales from Gudbrandsdal', in which the hero is not 'a handsome prince but a village bumpkin', p. 91), Nagel expresses his anti-democratic, anti-Christian elitism while also attacking Ibsen: Peer Gynt is a bumpkin from Gudbrandsdal. But with the mention of the valley in the heart of Norway, the possibility arises that Hamsun is engaging in self-irony, for his own roots are in the Gudbrandsdal (Næss, p. 1). The literary allusiveness of **Mysterier** and Nagel's symbolic and mythic inventions may in the end be elements of a strategy that intends **Mysterier** as a parody of **Sult,** and by that token as a demonstration of the artist's suspicion of all art: '*Nur* Narr! *Nur* Dichter!'

The characters in **Mysterier** read and lend each other books. Alfred de Musset and Victor Hugo are mentioned (p. 36), as well as Turgenev (p. 25), Garborg (p. 25), Tolstoi (p. 91), Bjørnson (p. 151), Maupassant ('that crude hack'; p. 150), Ibsen (p. 150), and Skram (p. 155). Shakespeare and Nietzsche are mentioned in the same paragraph, dismissively, for Nagel is arguing that it is far better to be handsome, and illiterate, than to be intelligent (p. 70), as though suggesting Thomas Mann's biological-mythic alternatives. The three principal characters Nagel encounters also bear the names of actual prominent Norwegians: Grøgaard, and the two women Nagel attempts to seduce, the attractive young Dagny Kielland and the spinster Martha Gude[47]. Kielland was a novelist whom Hamsun had once faulted in a lecture for his simple, one-dimensional characters (Beyer, I, 248). Meanwhile Jacobsen, the name Nagel gives to a puppy (p. 8), was a major Danish writer. **Mysterier** plays incessantly with public and literary indiscretions and outrageous opinions, as though the entire novel were clothed in the yellow of Nagel's suit. It merits noting here that yellow, in the Scandinavian tradition, is the colour of deceit, falsehood. Næss prefers to read it as representing 'a poet's dream of freedom and beauty' (p. 47)[48]. But dreaming and lying are Nietzschean equivalents. A question-mark pursues the mythmaker Nagel, who in a sense sacrifices himself to his own creative imagination. During an evening party at the physician's home, he attributes magic powers to his ordinary iron ring. 'Her skulde man for eksempel se at han bar en ring, en unanselig ring av jærn, men med den underbareste ævne. Skulde man tro det når man så den? Men mistet han den ring en kvæld klokken ti, måtte han lete den op igjen inden tolv, ellers gik det ham galt' (p. 68; 'No one would believe it by looking at it! But if he should lose the ring—at ten o'clock, say—he would have to find it by midnight, or something dreadful would happen', p. 74). Later he deliberately throws the ring into the sea, and drowns trying to find it before the stroke of twelve (p. 251). In order to commit suicide, however, he must overcome his other self, Grøgaard, the dwarf, who seeks to thwart him.

Næss describes Nagel's relationship to the Midget as 'the most interesting and most intriguing aspect of *Mysterier*' (p. 44). To Edvard Beyer the close relationship between them is the key to the novel (Beyer, p. 255). Nagel becomes obsessed with 'den lille gråhårete nar' (p. 17; 'the little grey jester', p. 19) from the time he first sees him, no doubt in part because the Midget represents repressed aspects of his own soul, but also because the Midget has a mythic identity that Nagel detects and that links the shabby, grey, limping figure with his own dandified appearance in yellow. Nagel senses 'mystically', intuits Grøgaard's first name, Johannes, which is his own (pp. 122, 169, 234). Crippled and shy, the Midget is the embodiment of the dwarf of European myth, the personification of archaic fears and guilt[49]. The dwarf is usually described as being poorly dressed, or in rags; the colour grey predominates; he walks with a limp or a shuffle; tends to be shy, because of his ugliness but also because he can be invisible, or because as a night spirit he shuns the light. Nagel tells him once: 'De stod pludselig midt ute i gaten, uten at jeg hadde set hvor De kom fra' (p. 217; 'You suddenly appeared in the middle of the street and I had no idea where you came from', p. 234). Dwarfs were believed to be abductors of children and women. Nagel relates two dreams he had (or composed) about a dwarfed madman, a poeticized Johannes Grøgaard in each case, first on Midsummer Eve, 23 June (pp. 56-57) and then on the following night, and in the only chapter with a title, 'White Nights' (pp. 85-90; in the Norwegian edition, 'lyse nætter', and without chapter number, p. 72). On Midsummer or St. John's Eve, 'Johannisnacht', bonfires are lit on the hillsides, and the ashes and coals from such fires were thought to have magical power to protect the home—a power relativized here by the presence of the dwarf: the Midget, who is mocked and bullied in the town, earns his living by carrying coal. Reinhard H. Friederich has speculated, in his article 'Kafka and Hamsun's *Mysterier*', that there may be significance in the coincidence of Nagel's arrival and Dagny Kielland's engagement on 12 June, following the feastday of St. Barnabas, 11 June[50]. Like John, Barnabas became associated with Midsummer rites; his day in the Julian calendar had been 22 June. Nagel notices bonfires on the hills surrounding the town and learns to his delight that it is Midsummer Eve (p. 52), but does not know of Barnabas, whose protection he will need: Barnabas is mentioned in a ninth-century magic formula against being possessed (*Handwörterbuch des deutschen Aberglaubens,* IX, 927). The Barnabas figure in *Mysterier,* however, the messenger and companion, seems to be the Midget Johannes, the constant observer of Nagel's efforts to bring the message of myth to the unbelievers. It is interesting too that the dwarf suffers his own kind of 'Johanniskrankheit', 'Johannistanz', an epileptic or St. Vitus dance, for he is forced to dance barefoot in the streets[51]. With his suspicions, fantasies and dread, Nagel links the action of the novel with the unconscious. The realm of myth and dream, the realm of primal experience, threatens the integrity of the conscious mind, which is structured as a defence against the shocks of sudden, involuntary self-knowledge, traumatic memories of recurring elemental impressions[52]. The Midget haunts Nagel in the way the figure of the hunchbacked dwarf, Benjamin's 'das bucklige Männlein', haunts Kafka's work[53]. The greatest danger for Nagel emerges precisely from the myths he opposes to the rational world. He must therefore constantly be on his guard against himself, must constantly calculate (see Benjamin on Baudelaire, pp. 111ff.) and contradict himself, which Dagny Kielland, in the chapter 'White Nights', cannot understand. 'Når De nu beregner at slik og slik vil det gå og De lægger det hele tilrette og De opnår hvad De ønsker, hvorfor går De så nu bakefter og spolerer alting ig jen ved å bekjende— som De kalder det—Deres bedrageri?' (p. 75; 'When you make such careful calculations and fabricate your story to suit your ends, and then undo everything by confessing your deviousness—or deceit, as you call it— what am I to think?', p. 82).

Nagel is a Baudelairean character, an artist figure, with no occupation, part dandy, part flaneur, part detective, whose strategy is to shock, and change course suddenly (Kirkegaard, *Hamsun som modernist,* p. 199). He is a creature of hotel rooms, cafés, streets, skilled in lightning reactions and feigned nonchalance (Benjamin, *Charles Baudelaire,* p. 38ff.). Like Kafka's K. a tireless and incessant calculator, Nagel calls attention to the 'utmost importance' of trifles (p. 115) and is himself amazed at his power to record 'the most insignificant detail' (p. 114). Nagel's behaviour closely resembles that of Axel Borg, the elegantly dressed scientific Inspector of Fisheries in Strindberg's *I havsbandet,* (*By the Open Sea,* 1890; Penguin edition translated by Mary Sandbach, 1987), a novel that has a striking structural kinship with *Mysterier* (Baumgartner, p. 270 n. 1). He can calculate and foretell the migration of fishes from his sofa (p. 94), and on the basis of psychological observation of people assign them their equations (p. 47). But he also wears a magic gold bracelet, in the form of a serpent biting its tail, and in the derangement of his last days—Borg drowns himself—he wants to hear fairy tales (p. 180). The calculator abandons calculation, while Nagel drowns in a frenzy of it. Above all, like his predecessor in **Sult,** Nagel records the time, sometimes to kill time, as in the fourth chapter, when he stays in bed until ten in the morning (p. 31) and delivers an interior monologue for two hours until noon, the hour of Karlsen's funeral. Ten and twelve, as we have seen, measure the time his myth allots him to find his ring and live.

The principal keeper of time is not Nagel, however, but the narrator, who follows his subject with watch in hand. He times the length of sleep and of conversation (a three-hour talk with the Midget, p. 13), times arrivals and departures, notes ages (the Midget is forty-three, Dagny is twenty-three, and Nagel between twenty-eight and thirty), and marks the calendar so consistently that the reader is able to calculate the duration of the action: some six weeks elapse between Nagel's arrival on 12 June and his drowning on 18 July at midnight, in the year 1891. Karlsen was killed, or killed himself, on 6 June. It would have been a remarkable suicide, since both wrists were cut, with Dagny Kielland's dull knife: a piece of paper was found with the words 'Would that thy knife were as sharp as thy final no' (p. 11). That is not mystery but hilarity over the impending defeat of all our reader-expectations.

The narrator's clock and calendar suggest that reality is orderly and legible, but we have before us a text that aims at being unreadable, contradictory. Among Nietzsche's unpublished notes from the 1880s there is a passage that could have served as Hamsun's credo: 'Um die Welt zu begreifen, müssen wir sie berechnen können . . . Die Berechenbarkeit der Welt, die Ausdrückbarkeit alles Geschehens in Formeln—ist das wirklich ein "Begreifen"?' (In order to understand the world, we have to be able to calculate it . . . The calculability of the world, the expressibility of all events in formulas—is that really an "understanding"?' III, 896). In 1888 Hamsun delivered a comparable opinion, in a critique of the literary tradition and its miserable traffic in 'types', in characters whose intellectual or emotional life was expressible in whole numbers[54]. In a diatribe against an admired 'great man', the British prime minister Gladstone, Nagel voices his contempt for conventionally accepted virtue and the righteous arithmetic of optimistic reason and problem-solving:

> Jeg har hørt ham i en budgetdebat på vise at sytten ganger tre og tyve er tre hundrede og en og niti, og han seiret knusende, seiret enormt, han hadde atter ret . . . Men nu stanset jeg virkelig op og så på manden . . . Jeg står der og tænker over hans tre hundrede og en og niti og jeg finder at det er ret, men jeg smaker desuagtet litt på det og sier så til mig selv: Nei stop! sytten ganger tre og tyve er tre hundrede og *syv* og niti! Jed vet vel at det er én og niti, men jeg sier allikevel mot bedre vidende syv og niti, for å være på en anden side end dette menneske, denne rettens professionist.
>
> (p. 61)

> (. . . I have heard him [Gladstone] claim, in a budget debate, that seventeen times twenty-three is three hundred ninety-one, and he came off with a smashing . . . victory. Again, right was on his side . . . But at that point I had to stop, look, query . . . I stood there checking his arithmetic—three hundred ninety-one—and it was correct, yet I turned it over and over again in my mind, saying to myself: Wait a minute. Seventeen times twenty-three is three-hundred ninety-*seven*! I knew very well that it was ninety-one, but against all logic I decided on ninety-seven, just to oppose this man, the man who makes it his business to be in the right!
>
> (p. 67).

Throughout this novel of twenty-three chapters Nagel pits his own savage arithmetic of the soul against the formidable virtue of the world's public computations.

Nagel's hypnotic arithmology has a curious counterpart in Arthur Conan Doyle's singular revenge upon the confident Darwinist science of the early twentieth century. The authors of an article entitled 'The Perpetrator at Piltdown', in the magazine *Science 83,* argue that it may well have been Doyle who arranged the famous Piltdown hoax[55]. Hamsun's **Mysterier** proves itself by the numbers to be that kind of hoax. It is also interesting that Doyle had hoped to rid himself of the burden of Holmesian cerebration and all its imitators by having the detective drown in Reichenbach Falls, in the clutches of the villain Moriarty (*The Final Problem* was published in *The Strand,* Dec. 1893). Hamsun of course has his detective drown himself in an unnamed Norwegian harbour.

Certain numbers begin to emerge in the novel and suggest pattern, order, structure, solution to the mystery, and among them is the number three with its multiples, as in 6 June, 12 June, 18 July. We read for example that Nagel arrives by steamer at six pm and appears on deck as one of three passengers. But even when the ship's bell rings for the third time, he fails to disembark for some reason, and then re-arrives on 13 June. Nagel goes to a party at the physician's home, on 24 June, at 6; he buys one of three chairs from Martha Gude, who is twelve years older than he (p. 191), on 6 July (p. 173); he leaves town for three days, without explanation (p. 182); attends a bazaar on 9 July at 9 pm and plays a violin, handed down through three generations, with three initials on it (p. 188), and so on. We have already noted the calendar of the novel: a six-week period from 12 June to 18 July, and the midnight drowning. After dinner on the first day Nagel goes out and does not return to the hotel until 'før klokken slog tre' (p. 6) 'before the clock struck three', p. 6). It is on the third morning when he first sees the Midget, with his fateful three-syllable name Johannes; Nagel's full name contains six syllables. In his room are the three telegrams he sent himself, and a picture of Napoleon III on his wall. But the enigmatic self-propagandist, man of fashion, master calculator and master of the *coup d'état* evidently reminds Nagel too much of himself. He asks the maid to remove the picture, confirming the genealogy of the Hamsun hero, and with that, in advance, all the connections Walter Benjamin found between the political methods of Napoleon III and Baudelaire's style in his theoretical writings (*Charles Baudelaire,* p. 9-10).

The reader-detective could continue to decode the text of ***Mysterier*** for further components of what appears to be a meaningful narrative arithmetic, but would find only that in one combination or another the number three bedevils the novel's twenty-three chapters and frustrates any multiplication or division to discover the expected principle of integration, the expected solution to 'mysteries'.

Nagel himself, watch in hand, counting minutes, rushes outside to the docks to drown himself at midnight. Earlier he had thought of buying a pistol (Norwegian 'Seksløper', 'six-shooter') to commit suicide, to pay for his behaviour 'i tidens fylde, når klokken slog' (p. 192; 'with my soul when the time comes, when the clock strikes', p. 207). The novel culminates then in Nagel's obsessive counting of hours and midnight panic, but all the numbers in all the twenty-three chapters do not yield a pattern divisible by three, which is all the more baffling inasmuch as the number three suggests itself again and again as a reliable clue and principle of order and sanity.

It is possible to define two kinds of three in ***Mysterier.*** There are threes that 'rhyme' with multiples of three, and there are threes that mock the rhyme-scheme by participating in combinations that are always one short of being a multiple of three, as twenty-three chapters are one short of twenty-four and twenty-nine short of thirty. However one divides, there are always remainders in fractions. There is 6 June (Karlsen's death) and 12 June, 24 June ('White Nights') and 9 July (the bazaar); but there is also 13 June, Nagel's actual arrival, and 29 June, his 29th birthday, and of course 23 June, Midsummer or St. John's Eve. At one point Nagel tells Dagny a story about an eccentric friend who once organized an excursion. 'Engang hadde han fåt i sinde å foranstalte en uhyre kjøretur. Han hadde ingen bekjendtskaper, han leiet derfor alene for sig selv fire og tyve vogner som han satte i gang en efter en. De tre og tyve kjører aldeles tomme og i den fire og tyvende—den siste—der sitter så han selv, skuende ned på de spaserende, stolt som en gud over det svære optog han hadde fåt istand' (p. 144; 'He didn't have any companions, but he hired twenty-four carriages, which he dispatched one by one. Twenty-three of them were empty, and in the last one, the twenty-fourth, he sat alone, looking down at the pedestrians, elated at the sensation he was creating', p. 156). The arbiter and principle of order, the one who counts the twenty-three empty carriages, sits in the twenty-fourth, alone with his attempt to create meaning, or mock it. In the structure of the novel the meaning of Nagel's life and death, Karlsen's fate, and the Midget's transgression, are contained in the uneven number of twenty-three chapters, and the twenty-fourth, which would have provided structural symmetry, balance, and resolution, a correspondence between public and private, reader and narrator, reader and author, is withheld.

Chapter twenty-three is the shortest of all the chapters of ***Mysterier,*** little more than a half-page of text, and as such a stark contrast to Nagel's elaborate monologues, harangues, and visions. Goethe had ended *Werther* in a similar fashion, with bare reportage, sober registration of facts and events that return the reader of Werther's ecstasies and terrors of imagination to hard reality. But the reader of ***Mysterier*** is an eavesdropper who can only speculate about the Midget's bad end, and about what the Midget did to Martha Gude, who in this final scene walks home from a party with Dagny, late one night in the April following Nagel's death, nine months after the six-month calendar of the action, in other words. As the two women help one another over icy patches on the dark road, the reader overhears sentences that conceal rather than reveal and witnesses gestures referring to a story that has not been told. Dagny and Martha, arm in arm, avoid, as it were, the reader's inquiry.

If Nagel's relationship to Johannes Grøgaard began as an attempt to rescue the Midget from the town's abuse, began, in other words, as a social or political project to rescue the downtrodden, aid the poor, and besides that to advocate mythic thinking over scientific logic, charisma over democracy[56], and if Nagel fails, as he does, in these projects, then ***Mysterier*** cannot be said to represent a proto-fascist ideology. Everything Nagel represents is scrupulously cancelled by an ironic narrative structure that denies coherence, that calculates with contradictions, and parodies the function and meaning of the smallest mythic ingredient in storytelling, the number three, the three of fairy tales, of 'knock three times' and 'say it thrice'. Sequence of number for Nagel is not a progression but an insistent, inexplicable refrain, as when he meets a small girl awkwardly holding a cat: 'Er det din kat? Ja. To fire seks syv. Jaså, du kan tælle også? Ja. Syv otte elleve to fire seks syv', (p. 45; 'Is that your cat?' 'Yes. Two - four - six - seven'. 'So you already know how to count?' 'Yes. Seven - eight - eleven - two - four -six - seven', p. 49; the Norwegian 'tælle' calls attention to the etymological relationship between counting, in the Germanic language family, and telling: German 'erzählen' and 'zählen', which is what the bankteller does). Nagel's calculation is a desperate alertness in a state of dread, an attempt at control and delay at the brink of a terrifying abyss, such as is experienced by the narrator in Poe's "A Descent into the Maelström": 'six hours of deadly terror' (p. 127), at a specific longitude and latitude, on a specific day, 10 July, beginning when the narrator's watch stopped at seven. His 'unnatural curiosity', as his boat begins its 'sickening sweep of the descent' (p. 136) leads him to speculate 'upon the relative velocities' of objects caught in the maelstrom. Analysis and horror are inseparable.

While Nagel counts in desperation, the narrator of *Mysterier* counts to frustrate interpretation, especially by way of the number three. The number three, the first real number to the Pythagoreans, the number representing the union of opposites (in Böhme's mysticism as well as to the Romantics) is mocked in Hamsun's *Mysterier,* and with it not only all the clocks and calendars of civilized order but traditional myths and modern detection as well. Narrative structure is a matter of spurious arrangements, a Piltdown hoax on behalf of the mysteries of imagination and the sovereign ego of the storyteller who cannot free himself from the suspicion that fiction is also fraud, that 'jedes Wort eine Maske [ist]' ('every word is a mask', Nietzsche, *Werke,* II, 752), that farming is perhaps better than writing. In the later novels, such as *Markens grøde* (*Growth of the Soil* 1917) and *Landstrykere,* Hamsun no longer calculates his irony and contradicts narrative structures, but simplifies storytelling in order to locate irony in life itself. 'De var Menneske og kravlet, de gik frem efter sine Kaar og de levet til de døde' (p. 26; 'They were human beings', he writes in *Landstrykere,* 'stumbling on, carrying on as circumstances permitted; and they lived until they died'). Time-telling now becomes the registration of eternal, inevitable rhythms: 'Men det gik ogsaa paa den Maaten, alting gaar' (*Landstrykere,* p. 453; 'All life goes on . . .'). But Hamsun prefers irony to inevitability and either-or; irony is life. One can imagine the aged Hamsun sitting with his glassless red kitchen clock in his lap, feeling the minute and hour hands with his fingertips, and now and then, perhaps, holding the hands, pushing them back a little, toying with their inevitable progression.

Notes

1. Friedrich Nietzsche, *Werke in drei Bänden,* edited by Karl Schlechta (Munich, 1960), I, 642. All further references to this edition are given after quotations in the text.

2. Robert Ferguson, *Enigma. The Life of Knut Hamsun* (New York, 1987), p. 100. All further references given after quotations in the text.

3. Rakel Christina Granaas, 'Ironie und Ideologie. Eine Analyse von Knut Hamsuns *Kinder der Zeit,* in *Auf alten und neuen Pfaden. Eine Dokumentation zur Hamsun-Forschung,* edited by Heiko Uecker, Texte und Untersuchungen zur Germanistik und Skandinavistik, 2 vols. (Frankfurt am Main, 1983), II, 295-318 (303).

4. See D. C. Muecke, *The Compass of Irony* (London, 1969). Remarkably, Muecke manages a study of irony without once mentioning Nietzsche.

5. In interpreting Nietzsche on the self I follow Alexander Nehamas, *Nietzsche. Life as Literature* (Cambridge, MA. 1985). See Part II, 'The Self', pp. 141-234 (p. 186).

6. Curt Paul Janz, *Friedrich Nietzsche. Biographie,* 3 vols. (Munich, 1981), II, 637; on Dostoevsky, II, 505-507.

7. Janz, II, 584-590.

8. Frederick R. Karl, *Modern and Modernism. The Sovereignty of the Artist 1885-1925* (New York, 1988), p. 185, footnote.

9. Harald Næss, *Knut Hamsun,* Twayne's World Author Series, 715 (Boston, 1984), p. 30. All further references given in parentheses in the text.

10. Dolores Buttry, 'Knut Hamsun: A Scandinavian Rousseau'. Ph.D. Dissertation, University of Illinois at Urbana-Champaign, 1978. See also *Scandinavica,* 19 (1980), pp. 121-150.

11. Anni Carlsson, *Ibsen. Strindberg. Hamsun. Essays zur skandinavischen Literatur* (Kronberg, 1978), p. 87. See also Klaus von See, 'Knut Hamsun—Naturschwärmer, Herrenmensch, Faschist? Eine Auseinandersetzung mit seinen Verehrern und seinen Kritikern', in *Auf alten und neuen Pfaden. Eine Dokumentation zur Hamsun-Forschung,* II, 237-243.

12. Theodor Ziolkowski, *Dimensions of the Modern Novel. German Texts and European Contexts* (Princeton, 1969), pp. 183-214. See also Walter Jens, *Statt einer Literaturgeschichte* (Pfullingen, 1957), pp. 23-58, and Stephen Kern, *The Culture of Time and Space 1880-1918* (Cambridge, MA, 1983), pp. 1-130.

13. Charles Baudelaire, *Les Fleurs du Mal,* translated by Richard Howard (Boston, 1983), p. 82.

14. Knut Hamsun, *Wayfarers,* translated by James McFarlane, Berkley Books (New York, 1985), p. 453.

15. Michael Hofmann, 'Without fear or shame', review of Robert Ferguson's *Enigma. The Life of Knut Hamsun,* in *TLS,* Oct. 2-8, 1987, p. 1081. References to Hamsun's *Hunger* are to the translation by Robert Bly, Bard Books/Avon (New York, 1975), and will henceforth appear in the text after quotations. References to the Norwegian edition of *Sult* in *Samlede Verker* (Kristiania, 1921), I Bind, will likewise appear in the text.

16. John Vernon, *Money and Fiction. Literary Realism in the Nineteenth and Early Twentieth Centuries.* (Ithaca, 1984), p. 117.

17. For a Marxist interpretation of hallucination in *Hunger*, see John Vernon, *Money and Fiction*, pp. 142-170.

18. Knut Hamsun, *Paa Turné: Tre Foredrag om Litteratur* (Oslo, 1960), p. 69.

19. See Dolores Buttry, 'A Thirst for Intimacy: Knut Hamsun's Pyromania', *Scandinavica*, 26 (1987), pp. 129-139.

20. András Masát, 'Handlungs- und Wertstrukturen in Hamsuns *Hunger* und *Pan*. Modell und Interpretation', in *Auf alten und neuen Pfaden*, II, 319-336.

21. See Walter H. Sokel, *Franz Kafka. Tragik und Ironie* (Frankfurt am Main, 1964), pp. 30-31.

22. Nietzsche's insight into the character of the dandy, as discussed by Helmut Pfotenhauer, *Die Kunst als Physiologie. Nietzsches ästhetische Theorie und literarische Produktion* (Stuttgart, 1985), p. 108.

23. Nietzsche, *Werke, Kritische Gesamtausgabe*, edited by Giorgio Colli and Mazzino Montinari, 30 vols (Berlin, 1967-1978), VIII/2, p. 64f.

24. Edgar Allan Poe, *The Complete Tales and Poems*, the Modern Library (New York, 1938), p. 281. All further references to this edition will appear in the text after quotations.

25. See Helmut Pfotenhauer, *Die Kunst als Physiologie*, p. 1.

26. Peter Gay, *The Bourgeois Experience: Victoria to Freud*. Vol. II: *The Tender Passion* (New York, 1986), p. 60.

27. August Strindberg, *Plays* Vol. I., translated by Michael Meyer (New York, 1964), p. 102.

28. As translated by James W. McFarlane in his 'The Whisper of the Blood. A Study of Knut Hamsun's Early Novels', *PMLA*, 71 (1956), p. 568. The essay is printed in Knut Hamsun, *Artikler 1889-1928*, Fakkel-bøkene F73 (Oslo, 1968), pp. 33-44.

29. Peter Kirkegaard, *Knut Hamsun som modernist* (Copenhagen, 1975), p. 182. Further references to this study will appear in the text.

30. The parallels in the early work of Hamsun and Munch have been noted by Wilhelm Friese, 'Hamsun und der Jugendstil', in *Auf alten und neuen Pfaden*, II, 78; Harald Næss, *Knut Hamsun*, Preface, and pp. 18;38;61; by Ferguson, p. 131, and by Reinhold Heller, *Munch: His Life and Work* (Chicago, 1984), pp. 43 and 70.

31. Ronald G. Popperwell noted this already nearly twenty years ago in 'Critical Attitudes to Knut Hamsun, 1890-1969', *Scandinavica*, 9 (1970), pp. 13-14.

32. Peter De Mendelssohn, *Der Geist in der Despotie. Versuche über die moralischen Möglichkeiten des Intellektuellen in der totalitären Gesellschaft* (Berlin-Grunewald, 1953), p. 78.

33. Sven H. Rossel, *A History of Scandinavian Literature 1870-1980*, translated by Anne C. Ulmer (Minneapolis, 1982), p. 100; Trygve Braatøy, *Livets Cirkel* (1929), p. 77, quoted in Edvard Beyer, 'Knut Hamsuns *Mysterien*', in *Auf alten und neuen Pfaden*, p. 252; also Baumgartner, p. 269, has the same opinion (see note 36).

34. Gregory Nybø, *Knut Hamsuns 'Mysterier'* (Oslo, 1969).

35. Ronald G. Popperwell, 'Critical Attitudes to Knut Hamsun, 1890-1969', *Scandinavica* 9. (1970), p. 13.

36. Walter Baumgartner, 'Nagel und Minute im kommunikativen Clinch. Vorschlag zu einer entmystifizierenden Lektüre von Knut Hamsuns *Mysterier*' (1982), in *Der Nahe Norden. Otto Oberholzer zum 65. Geburtstag. Eine Festschrift*, edited by Wolfgang Butt and Bernhard Glienke (Frankfurt am Main, 1985), p. 265.

37. Walter Benjamin, *Gesammelte Schriften*, edited by Rolf Tiedemann and Hermann Schweppenhäuser (Frankfurt am Main, 1974), VI, 143.

38. Knut Hamsun, *Mysteries*, translated by Gerry Bothmer, Bard Books/-Avon (New York, 1975), p. 7. Knut Hamsun, *Mysterier*, Lanternebøkene L 147 (Oslo, 1978), p. 7. All further references to these editions will follow quotations in the text.

39. See Fritz Paul, 'Hamsun und der Faschismus', in *Wege der Literaturwissenschaft* (Bonn, 1985), pp. 303-314. See also Gabriele Schulte, *Hamsun im Spiegel der deutschen Literaturkritik 1890 bis 1975* (Frankfurt am Main, 1986).

40. See Edvard Beyer, 'Knut Hamsuns *Mysterien*, in *Auf alten und neuen Pfaden*, I, 254.

41. To borrow from R. D. Laing, *The Divided Self* (New York, 1960), pp. 78ff.

42. Bernard Wasserstein, *The Secret Lives of Trebitsch Lincoln* (New Haven, 1988).

43. Noted by Erich Heller in his *The Disinherited Mind* (New York, 1959), p. 216, and Walter Sokel, *Franz Kafka. Tragik und Ironie*, p. 451. See also Jürgen Born, 'Kafkas unermüdliche Rechner', *Euphorion*, 64 (1970), p. 409.

44. Harald S. Næss, 'A Strange Meeting and Hamsun's *Mysteries*', *Scandinavian Studies*, 36 (1964), pp. 48-58.

45. Alfred Turco, 'Hamsun's *Pan* and the Riddle of Glahn's Death', *Scandinavica*, 19 (1980), p. 14.

46. Harald Næss, 'Who was Hamsun's Hero?' in *The Hero in Scandinavian Literature from Peer Gynt to the Present,* edited by John M. Weinstock and Robert T. Rovinsky (Austin, 1975), p. 67.

47. Ronald G. Popperwell, 'Interrelatedness in Hamsun's *Mysteries*', *Scandinavian Studies,* 38 (1966), p. 297.

48. Rolf Nyboe Nettum disagrees with Næss on this point, in his review of Næss's *Knut Hamsun, Scandinavica,* 24 (1985), pp. 233-235.

49. *Handwörterbuch des deutschen Aberglaubens* (Berlin, 1938-41), IX, pp. 1008-1032.

50. Reinhard H. Friederich, 'Kafka and Hamsun's *Mysteries*', *Comparative Studies,* 28 (1976), p. 48, note 20.

51. *Kulturhistorik Leksikon for nordisk middelalder fra vikingstid til reformationstid* (Copenhagen, 1966), XI, 612-613.

52. See Walter Benjamin's discussion of Freud's *Jenseits des Lustprinzips* in Walter Benjamin, *Charles Baudelaire. Ein Lyriker im Zeitalter des Hochkapitalismus,* Suhrkamp Taschenbuch Wissenschaft, 47 (Frankfurt am Main: 1980), pp. 108-111.

53. Benjamin, *Gesammelte Schriften,* II/2, 431.

54. In the essay 'Kristofer Janson', published in *Ny Jord,* Copenhagen, Oct. 1888, pp. 371ff, quoted in McFarlane, 'The Whisper of the Blood', p. 567.

55. John Hathaway Winslow and Alfred Meyer, 'The Perpetrator at Piltdown', *Science 83,* Number 7 (1983), pp. 32-43.

56. On 'Fascist Modernism' see Russell A. Berman's argument in his *The Rise of The Modern German Novel. Crisis and Charisma* (Cambridge, MA, 1986), Chapter 9.

Paul Auster (essay date 1992)

SOURCE: Auster, Paul. "The Art of *Hunger.*" In *The Art of Hunger: Essays, Prefaces, Interviews and The Red Notebook*, pp. 9-20. New York: Penguin, 1992.

[*In the following essay, Auster offers a thematic analysis of* Hunger, *characterizing the work as a pioneering text about artistic achievement.*]

> What is important, it seems to me, is not so much to defend a culture whose existence has never kept a man from going hungry, as to extract, from what is called culture, ideas whose compelling force is identical with that of hunger.
>
> —Antonin Artaud

A young man comes to a city. He has no name, no home, no work: he has come to the city to write. He writes. Or, more exactly, he does not write. He starves to the point of death.

The city is Christiania (Oslo); the year is 1890. The young man wanders through the streets: the city is a labyrinth of hunger, and all his days are the same. He writes unsolicited articles for a local paper. He worries about his rent, his disintegrating clothes, the difficulty of finding his next meal. He suffers. He nearly goes mad. He is never more than one step from collapse.

Still, he writes. Now and then he manages to sell an article, to find a temporary reprieve from his misery. But he is too weak to write steadily and can rarely finish the pieces he has begun. Among his abortive works are an essay entitled "Crimes of the Future," a philosophical tract on the freedom of the will, an allegory about a bookstore fire (the books are brains), and a play set in the Middle Ages, "The Sign of the Cross." The process is inescapable: he must eat in order to write. But if he does not write, he will not eat. And if he cannot eat, he cannot write. He cannot write.

He writes. He does not write. He wanders through the streets of the city. He talks to himself in public. He frightens people away from him. When, by chance, he comes into some money, he gives it away. He is evicted from his room. He eats, and then throws everything up. At one point, he has a brief flirtation with a girl, but nothing comes of it except humiliation. He hungers. He curses the world. He does not die. In the end, for no apparent reason, he signs on board a ship and leaves the city.

These are the bare bones of Knut Hamsun's first novel, **Hunger.** It is a work devoid of plot, action, and—but for the narrator—character. By nineteenth-century standards, it is a work in which nothing happens. The radical subjectivity of the narrator effectively eliminates the basic concerns of the traditional novel. Similar to the hero's plan to make an "invisible detour" when he came to the problem of space and time in one of his essays, Hamsun manages to dispense with historical time, the basic organizing principle of nineteenth-century fiction. He gives us an account only of the hero's worst struggles with hunger. Other, less difficult times, in which his hunger has been appeased—even though they might last as long as a week—are passed off in one or two sentences. Historical time is obliterated in favor of inner duration. With only an arbitrary beginning and an arbitrary ending, the novel faithfully records the vagaries of the narrator's mind, following each thought from its mysterious inception through all its meanderings, until it dissipates and the next thought begins. What happens is allowed to happen.

This novel cannot even claim to have a redeeming social value. Although **Hunger** puts us in the jaws of misery, it offers no analysis of that misery, contains no call to political action. Hamsun, who turned fascist in his old age during the Second World War, never concerned himself with the problems of class injustice, and his narrator-hero, like Dostoevsky's Raskolnikov, is not so much an underdog as a monster of intellectual arrogance. Pity plays no part in *Hunger*. The hero suffers, but only because he has chosen to suffer. Hamsun's art is such that he rigorously prevents us from feeling any compassion for his character. From the very beginning, it is made clear that the hero need not starve. Solutions exist, if not in the city, then at least in departure. But buoyed by an obsessive, suicidal pride, the young man's actions continually betray a scorn for his own best interests.

> I began running so as to punish myself, left street after street behind me, pushed myself on with inward jeers, and screeched silently and furiously at myself whenever I felt like stopping. With the help of these exertions I ended up along Pile Street. When I finally did stop, almost weeping with anger that I couldn't run any farther, my whole body trembled, and I threw myself down on a house stoop. "Not so fast!" I said. And to torture myself right, I stood up again and forced myself to stand there, laughing at myself and gloating over my own fatigue. Finally, after a few minutes I nodded and so gave myself permission to sit down; however, I chose the most uncomfortable spot on the stoop.[1]

He seeks out what is most difficult in himself, courting pain and adversity in the same way other men seek out pleasure. He goes hungry, not because he has to, but from some inner compulsion, as if to wage a hunger strike against himself. Before the book begins, before the reader has been made the privileged witness of his fate, the hero's course of action has been fixed. A process is already in motion, and although the hero cannot control it, that does not mean he is unaware of what he is doing.

> I was conscious all the time that I was following mad whims without being able to do anything about it . . . Despite my alienation from myself at that moment, and even though I was nothing but a battleground for invisible forces, I was aware of every detail of what was going on around me.

Having withdrawn into a nearly perfect solitude, he has become both the subject and object of his own experiment. Hunger is the means by which this split takes place, the catalyst, so to speak, of altered consciousness.

> I had noticed very clearly that every time I went hungry a little too long it was as though my brains simply ran quietly out of my head and left me empty. My head became light and floating, I could no longer feel its weight upon my shoulders . . .

If it is an experiment, however, it has nothing to do with the scientific method. There are no controls, no stable points of reference—only variables. Nor can this separation of mind and body be reduced to a philosophical abstraction. We are not in the realm of ideas here. It is a physical state, brought into being under conditions of extreme duress. Mind and body have been weakened; the hero has lost control over both his thoughts and actions. And yet he persists in trying to control his destiny. This is the paradox, the game of circular logic that is played out through the pages of the book. It is an impossible situation for the hero. For he has willfully brought himself to the brink of danger. To give up starving would not mean victory, it would simply mean that the game was over. He wants to survive, but only on his own terms: survival that will bring him face to face with death.

He fasts. But not in the way a Christian would fast. He is not denying earthly life in anticipation of heavenly life; he is simply refusing to live the life he has been given. And the longer he goes on with his fast, the more death intrudes itself upon his life. He approaches death, creeps toward the edge of the abyss, and once there, clings to it, unable to move either forward or backward. Hunger, which opens the void, does not have the power to seal it up. A brief moment of Pascalian terror has been transformed into a permanent condition.

His fast, then, is a contradiction. To persist in it would mean death, and with death the fast would end. He must therefore stay alive, but only to the extent that it keeps him on the point of death. The idea of ending is resisted in the interests of maintaining the constant possibility of the end. Because his fasting neither posits a goal nor offers a promise of redemption, its contradiction must remain unresolved. As such, it is an image of despair, generated by the same self-consuming passion as the sickness unto death. The soul, in its despair, seeks to devour itself, and because it cannot—precisely because it despairs—sinks further into despair.

Unlike a religious art, in which self-debasement can play an ultimately cleansing role (the meditative poetry of the seventeenth century, for example), hunger only simulates the dialectic of salvation. In Fulke Greville's poem, "Down in the depth of mine iniquity," the poet is able to look into a "fatal mirror of transgression" which "shows man as fruit of his degeneration," but he knows that this is only the first step in a two-fold process, for it is in this mirror that Christ is revealed "for the same sins dying / And from that hell I feared, to free me, come . . ." In Hamsun's novel, however, once the depths have been sounded, the mirror of meditation remains empty.

He remains at the bottom, and no God will come to rescue the young man. He cannot even depend on the props of social convention to keep him standing. He is rootless, without friends, denuded of objects. Order has disappeared for him; everything has become random. His actions are inspired by nothing but whim and ungovernable urge, the weary frustration of anarchic discontent. He pawns his waistcoat in order to give alms to a beggar, hires a carriage in search of a fictitious acquaintance, knocks on strangers' doors, and repeatedly asks the time of passing policemen, for the single reason that he fancies to do so. He does not revel in these actions, however. They remain profoundly disquieting for him. Furiously trying to stabilize his life, to put an end to his wanderings, find a room, and settle down to his writing, he is thwarted by the fast he has set in motion. Once it starts, hunger does not release its progenitor-victim until its lesson has been made unforgettable. The hero is seized against his will by a force of his own making and is compelled to respond to its demands.

He loses everything—even himself. Reach the bottom of a Godless hell, and identity disappears. It is no accident that Hamsun's hero has no name: as time goes on, he is truly shorn of his self. What names he chooses to give himself are all inventions, summoned forth on the spur of the moment. He cannot say who he is because he does not know. His name is a lie, and with this lie the reality of his world vanishes.

He peers into the darkness hunger has created for him, and what he finds is a void of language. Reality has become a confusion of thingless names and nameless things for him. The connection between self and world has been broken.

> I remained for a while looking into the dark—this dense substance of darkness that had no bottom, which I couldn't understand. My thoughts could not grasp such a thing. It seemed to be a dark beyond all measurement, and I felt its presence weigh me down. I closed my eyes and took to singing half aloud and rocking myself back and forth on the cot to amuse myself, but it did no good. The dark had captured my brain and gave me not an instant of peace. What if I myself became dissolved into the dark, turned into it?

At the precise moment that he is in the greatest fear of losing possession of himself, he suddenly imagines that he has invented a new word: *Kubooa*—a word in no language, a word with no meaning.

> I had arrived at the joyful insanity hunger was: I was empty and free of pain, and my thoughts no longer had any check.

He tries to think of a meaning for his word but can only come up with what it doesn't mean, which is neither "God," nor the "Tivoli Gardens," nor "cattle show," nor "padlock," nor "sunrise," nor "emigration," nor "tobacco factory," nor "yarn."

> No, the word was actually intended to mean something spiritual, a feeling, a state of mind—if only I could understand it? And I thought and thought to find something spiritual.

But he does not succeed. Voices, not his own, begin to intrude, to confuse him, and he sinks deeper into chaos. After a violent fit, in which he imagines himself to be dying, all goes still, with no sounds but those of his own voice, rolling back from the wall.

This episode is perhaps the most painful in the book. But it is only one of many examples of the hero's language disease. Throughout the narrative, his pranks most often take the form of lies. Retrieving his lost pencil from a pawn shop (he had accidentally left it in the pocket of a vest he had sold), he tells the proprietor that it was with this very pencil that he had written his three-volume treatise on Philosophical Consciousness. An insignificant pencil, he admits, but he has a sentimental attachment to it. To an old man on a park bench he recites the fantastic story of a Mr. Happolati, the inventor of the electric prayer book. Asking a store clerk to wrap his last possession, a tattered green blanket that he is too ashamed to carry around exposed to view, he explains that it is not really the blanket he wants wrapped, but the pair of priceless vases he has folded inside the blanket. Not even the girl he courts is immune from this sort of fiction. He invents a name for her, a name that pleases him for its beauty, and he refuses to call her by anything else.

These lies have a meaning beyond the jests of the moment. In the realm of language the lie has the same relationship to truth that evil has to good in the realm of morals. That is the convention, and it works if we believe in it. But Hamsun's hero no longer believes in anything. Lies and truths are as one to him. Hunger has led him into the darkness, and there is no turning back.

This equation of language and morals becomes the gist of the final episode in ***Hunger***.

> My brain grew clearer, I understood that I was close to total collapse. I put my hands against the wall and shoved to push myself away from it. The street was still dancing around. I began to hiccup from fury, and struggled with every bit of energy against my collapse, fought a really stout battle not to fall down. I didn't want to fall, I wanted to die standing. A wholesale grocer's cart came by and I saw it was filled with potatoes, but out of fury, from sheer obstinacy, I decided that they were not potatoes at all, they were cabbages, and I swore violent oaths that they were cabbages. I heard my own words very well, and I took the oath again and again on this lie, and swore deliberately just to have the delightful satisfaction of committing such clear perjury. I became drunk over this superb sin, I lifted three fingers in the air and swore with trembling lips in the name of the Father, the Son, and the Holy Ghost that they were cabbages.

And that is the end of it. There are only two possibilities left for the hero now: live or die; and he chooses to live. He has said no to society, no to God, no to his own words. Later that same day he leaves the city. There is no longer any need to continue the fast. Its work has been done.

Hunger: or a portrait of the artist as a young man. But it is an apprenticeship that has little in common with the early struggles of other writers. Hamsun's hero is no Stephen Dedalus, and there is hardly a word in *Hunger* about aesthetic theory. The world of art has been translated into the world of the body—and the original text has been abandoned. Hunger is not a metaphor; it is the very crux of the problem itself. If others, such as Rimbaud, with his program for the voluntary derangement of the senses, have turned the body into an aesthetic principle in its own right, Hamsun's hero steadfastly rejects the opportunity to use his deficiencies to his own advantage. He is weak, he has lost control over his thoughts, and yet he continues to strive for lucidity in his writing. But hunger affects his prose in the same way it affects his life. Although he is willing to sacrifice everything for his art, even submit to the worst forms of debasement and misery, all he has really done is make it impossible for himself to write. You cannot write on an empty stomach, no matter how hard you try. But it would be wrong to dismiss the hero of *Hunger* as a fool or a madman. In spite of the evidence, he knows what he is doing. He does not want to succeed. He wants to fail.

Something new is happening here, some new thought about the nature of art is being proposed in *Hunger*. It is first of all an art that is indistinguishable from the life of the artist who makes it. That is not to say an art of autobiographical excess, but rather, an art that is the direct expression of the effort to express itself. In other words, an art of hunger: an art of need, of necessity, of desire. Certainty yields to doubt, form gives way to process. There can be no arbitrary imposition of order, and yet, more than ever, there is the obligation to achieve clarity. It is an art that begins with the knowledge that there are no right answers. For that reason, it becomes essential to ask the right questions. One finds them by living them. To quote Samuel Beckett:

> What I am saying does not mean that there will henceforth be no form in art. It only means that there will be a new form, and that this form will be of such a type that it admits the chaos and does not try to say that the chaos is really something else . . . To find a form that accommodates the mess, that is the task of the artist now.[2]

Hamsun gives the portrait of this artist in the first stages of his development. But it is in Kafka's story, *A Hunger Artist,* that the aesthetics of hunger receives its most meticulous elaboration. Here the contradictions of the fast conducted by Hamsun's hero—and the artistic impasse it leads to—are joined in a parable that deals with an artist whose art consists in fasting. The hunger artist is at once an artist and not an artist. Though he wants his performances to be admired, he insists that they shouldn't be admired, because they have nothing to do with art. He has chosen to fast only because he could never find any food that he liked. His performances are therefore not spectacles for the amusement of others, but the unravelling of a private despair that he has permitted others to watch.

Like Hamsun's hero, the hunger artist has lost control over himself. Beyond the theatrical device of sitting in his cage, his art in no way differs from his life, even what his life would have been had he not become a performer. He is not trying to please anyone. In fact, his performances cannot even be understood or appreciated.

> No one could possibly watch the hunger artist continuously, day and night, and so no one could produce firsthand evidence that the fast had really been rigorous and continuous; only the artist himself could know that; he was therefore bound to be the sole completely satisfied spectator of his own fast.

This is not the classic story of the misunderstood artist, however. For the very nature of the fast resists comprehension. Knowing itself from the outset to be an impossibility, and condemning itself to certain failure, it is a process that moves asymptotically toward death, destined to reach neither fruition nor destruction. In Kafka's story, the hunger artist dies, but only because he forsakes his art, abandoning the restrictions that had been imposed on him by his manager. The hunger artist goes too far. But that is the risk, the danger inherent in any act of art: you must be willing to give your life.

In the end, the art of hunger can be described as an existential art. It is a way of looking death in the face, and by death I mean death as we live it today: without God, without hope of salvation. Death as the abrupt and absurd end of life.

I do not believe that we have come any farther than this. It is even possible that we have been here much longer than we are willing to admit. In all this time, however, only a few artists have been able to recognize it. It takes courage, and not many of us would be willing to risk everything for nothing. But that is what happens in *Hunger,* a novel written in 1890. Hamsun's character systematically unburdens himself of every belief in every system, and in the end, by means of the hunger he has inflicted upon himself, he arrives at nothing. There is nothing to keep him going—and yet he keeps on going. He walks straight into the twentieth century.

Notes

1. All quotations are from the Robert Bly translation, Farrar, Straus, and Giroux, 1967.

2. From an interview with Tom Driver, "Beckett at the Madeleine," in *The Columbia University Forum,* Summer 1961.

Mark B. Sandberg (essay date fall 1999)

SOURCE: Sandberg, Mark B. "Writing on the Wall: The Language of Advertising in Knut Hamsun's *Sult*." *Scandinavian Studies* 71, no. 3 (fall 1999): 265-96.

[*In the following essay, Sandberg proposes that although* Hunger *is often regarded as a subjective novel of private literary expression, it is equally valid as a text that links itself, via its language, to the public world of news, economics, and advertising.*]

Here is an opening scene: the unnamed main character of *Sult* [*Hunger*] awakens in his rented room. He hears the bells outside ringing six o'clock and people beginning to walk up and down the stairs. The walls of his room, papered with old issues of the newspaper *Morgenbladet,* provide him with his first reading material as he comes to consciousness. He notices in order, over by the door, "en bekjendtgjørelse fra fyrdirektøren" [an announcement from the lighthouse director] and then "et fett, bugnende avertissement fra baker Fabian Olsen om nybakt brød" [a fat, bulging advertisement from Baker Fabian Olsen for newly baked bread] and finally, as it grows lighter and lighter in the room, he sees "de magre, grinende bokstaver om 'Liksvøp hos jomfru Andersen, tilhøire i porten'" (7) [the lean, grimacing letters of "Burial shrouds at Miss Andersen's, through the gate to the right"]. He continues reading these advertisements—for two whole hours, we are left to conclude from the fact that the bells soon ring eight o'clock.

The scene, of course, comes at the first shift to present-tense narration after the narrator's famous retrospective opening statement, "Det var i den tid jeg gik omkring og sultet i Kristiania, denne forunderlige by som ingen forlater før han har fåt mærker av den. . . ." (7) [It was back when I went around starving in Christiania, that strange city that no one leaves before being branded by it . . .]. The first page of the novel moves between the world of literature and the world of advertisements, between *mærker* [brands, marks] and *varemærker* [brand names]. In this attic room, wallpapered with words and images from old newspapers, the novel's protagonist comes into being and enters into language. As Atle Kittang has put it, "*Sult*-heltens medvit konstituerer seg med andre ord som eit medvit om språk, i denne overgangen frå ikkje-være til være" (38) [The consciousness of *Hunger*'s protagonist constitutes itself in other words as a consciousness of language, in this transition from non-being to being]. I would revise Kittang's important insight slightly: this is not simply entry into language in the abstract—since that is never the case—but into a specific language system, with historical dimensions and social horizons: here, the discourse of advertising.

This will turn out to be a crucial shift of emphasis, since if one leaves language in the abstract, as Kittang does, one will be more inclined to draw conclusions of a broadly literary or psychoanalytic nature. In Kittang's reading, *Sult* is thus ultimately about the possibilities of the novel as a genre, about modernist literary consciousness, and about narcissism. The perspective I am proposing here is that the language system surrounding the narrator in this opening scene is also a quite particular one, a *kind* of language. The subject that enters this particular language system is in important ways *not* the same as every other subject that enters into language, precisely because he is called into being by a late-nineteenth century advertisement. Although his "hunger" has important literary and linguistic dimensions, the opening scene of *Sult* begins not with a literary reader, but a newspaper reader, and the model of writing, reading, and consumption developed throughout the novel should take that into account. This famously subjective novel, this novel about the inner world, the whisper of the blood, and small psychic tremors begins with a prominently placed description of a newspaper, where the private world of the reader intersects with the public world of news, economy, and advertising.

Theoretical approaches to Hamsun's novel have tended to emphasize the former; that is, its subjectivity as a form of private literary expression. When linked to the concerns of European literary modernism, its possible relationship to a cultural-historical setting does indeed drop out fairly quickly. It becomes a "timeless" novel, allowing Hamsun biographer Robert Ferguson, for instance, to characterize *Sult* enthusiastically as "eerily and thrillingly undated" (112). Interestingly, it sometimes becomes "spaceless" as well as "timeless" in standard literary histories. Literary scholars eager to overcome Hamsun's exclusion from the literary modernist mainstream are perhaps most willing to sacrifice the Norwegian cultural setting as too "small" for such a great novel and quickly promote Christiania to the ranks of interchangeable European metropolises. It is the *idea* of the city that is at stake, they might claim, not the Norwegian capital itself.

Scholars may just be following Hamsun's lead in this regard; after all, when *Sult* came out, he himself wrote to Scandinavian critics like Georg Brandes of his disdain for social novels: "Jeg har gjort et Forsøg paa at skrive—ikke en Roman, men en Bog, uden Giftermaal, Landture og Bal hos Grossereren, en Bog om en ømtaalig Menneskesjæls fine Svingninger, det sære, ejendommelige Sindsliv, Nervernes Mysterier in en udsultet Krop" (*Knut Hamsuns Brev* 161-2) [I have made an attempt to write not a novel, but a book—without marriages, trips to the countryside, and dances at the merchant's house—a book about a sensitive human soul's delicate oscillations, the peculiar, strange life of the mind, the mysteries of the nerves in a starved body]. And while working on the first fragment of *Sult,* he also wrote this to Brandes's brother Edvard:

> *Den Bog, jeg arbejder paa, er desperat lidet norsk, og jeg er ikke ligegyldig for dens Skjæbne. Jeg havde ikke villet skrive for Nordmænd—der er ikke et Stednavn i den hele Bog—jeg har villet skrive for* Mennesker *hvorsomhelst de fandtes.*
>
> (*Brev* 81, original emphasis)

(The book I am working on is desperately un-Norwegian, and I am not disinterested in its fate. I didn't want to write for Norwegians—there is not a place name in the whole book—I have wanted to write for *human beings* wherever they might be found.)

Even a casual reader of ***Sult*** might smile about this last claim—as is often remarked, the finished novel is on the contrary full of place names and urban geographic detail. Now one might simply claim, as does Einar Eggen in his well-known article from 1966, that the book's geography is a bit of a sham, that it does not lead anywhere and is only in the novel to be discredited (71-2). Peter Kirkegaard makes a similar point:

> *Med stor nøjagtighed registrerer han gadenavne og steder, og man kan more sig med at finde hans 'yndlingsruter' på et Kristianiakort, men blot for derved at konstatere, at denne præcision er uden betydning. Forf. vandrer de samme veje igen og igen, men stedsfæstelsen er arbitrær, ikke tilknyttet ham på andet end negativ absurdistisk måde; han går i kreds, i en labyrint.*
>
> (154)

(With great precision he makes note of street names and places, and one can have fun finding his "favorite routes" on a map of Christiania, but only in order to prove that this precision is meaningless. The author wanders the same paths over and over again, but the spatial location is arbitrary, not linked to him except in a negative, absurdist way; he walks in circles, in a labyrinth.)

Even if absurd in effect, the geographic specificity of the novel seems to be part of a strategy, a system of reference to time and place that seems all the more deliberate since Hamsun apparently played up the geographic specificity as the project progressed. ***Sult*** does have a relationship to its historical setting. What *kind* of relationship is what needs sorting out.

I emphasize this because my own interest in the novel is decidedly cultural historical. This is not to say that the literary-theoretical and the socio-historical aspects of Hamsun's work are necessarily at odds. Part of the intention here is in fact to demonstrate their intimate connection by examining Hamsun's novel together with historical developments in the practice of advertising. The argument will be that the discourse of advertising and the discourse of Hamsun's novel are part of the same cultural production of space at the end of the nineteenth century. The relevant term of the relationship is the intersection between *modernity*—the social conditions of the turn of the twentieth century—and *modernism*—the literary and artistic movement of the same period.

THIS SPACE FOR HIRE

The treatment of advertising space here will draw on two urban geographies: that of the capital city, Christiania, since Hamsun's novel is set there, but also that of Chicago, where Hamsun had perhaps his most modern, urban experience the year before he began writing the novel. In part, the aim is to outline the historical horizon of advertising to show its potential meanings in these two late nineteenth-century cities, especially as they meet in the personal experience of Knut Hamsun. Closely tied to that, however, is a particular theoretical interest in advertising space, especially the changing relationship between language and place as played out in cityscapes of the 1880s and '90s. This theoretical interest, in other words, is also historical since it explores a moment of transition in a representational system and cultural since it depends on comparative trajectories in two different cultural spheres.

The best way to begin this discussion is perhaps in terms of circulation. Crudely put, the claim is that the processes of modernity and urbanization involved an ungrounding of space.[1] Not in any absolute sense—the world was not simply "rooted" before nor wholly "mobile" after—but as an effect of acceleration, which encouraged those experiencing rapid social change to view the traditional world left behind as stable and unchanging. Shifts in everyday experience required new conceptualizations of space, especially in relation to the objects of labor and consumption that are so crucial to redefining social life in the latter part of the century. The movement of people and goods made possible by new forms of transportation, for example, meant that work and home could be farther apart. So could the sites of production and consumption, since both goods and people began to travel in ever-widening circuits. And accompanying the actual circulation of physical objects and bodies was the proliferation and movement of images that came with the revolutions in technologies of visual reproduction.

Jorunn Veiteberg and Einar Økland claim that this multiplication and mobility was actually a necessity given new modes of factory production for consumer goods. They begin their history of Norwegian advertising images by describing a pre-modern stage of advertising that was closely tied to the tradition of the simple shop sign:

Likevel er dette uskuldige kunngjeringsformer som berre skulle gjere folk merksame på dei varer og tenester som fanst i eit distrikt, og få dei omsett. Det var reklame til bruk i nærmiljøet. Lokale produsentar søkte kontakt med lokale kundar. Det var klare grenser for kor mykje ein kunne vone å få omsett, liksom det var grenser for kor mykje ein kunne produsere.

(8)

(At the same time, these are innocent forms of notification that were only intended to make people aware of the goods and services that could be found in a single district and to get them sold. It was advertising for local use. Local producers sought contact with local customers. There were clear limits to how much one could hope to sell, just as there were limits to how much one could produce.)

If this local form of advertising was "innocent," then the "fallen" state of advertising, one can assume, would be when the advertising sign leaves the proximity of its referent. Veiteberg and Økland link this development to the factory mass-production of goods, which introduced both the ability and the need to reach a larger group of consumers. Products needed to circulate more widely in order to find an audience that corresponded in size to the expanding potential for rapid production, and advertising helped that process along by establishing new patterns of circulation.

The idea of the advertising sign contains this tension between stasis and movement. Today, of course, the advertising sign can be found anywhere, far away from the product it promotes, because the paths back to the product are so extensively developed: highways, telephones, electronic media, and the postal service. When one saw an advertising sign in the mid-nineteenth century or before, however, the assumption would likely have been exactly the opposite, namely that the sign's referent would be found in the immediate vicinity. Especially if traditional shop signs are understood as an early form of advertising, the starting point for the development of modern advertising would involve a necessarily close connection between place, name, and product. The street sign was in other words strongly indexical—it said, in effect, *"Here* is where you will find both the baker and his bread."

Not so, once advertising became more common in the print medium—an early development in the US and Britain, but delayed until the 1870s and '80s in Norway. The advertising sign began to circulate and did so in multiple copies. An advertisement could now go wherever a newspaper might go, even into private spaces. To choose a particularly relevant example, one might even read about Baker Fabian Olsen and his bread on the wallpaper of an attic room, as does Hamsun's narrator. This mobility meant a shift in the semiotic status of advertising: now it referred not to what was present, but what was absent. To find the bread and the baker one had to make one's way through the city streets until the sign and the place came back together.

An even more radical change came with the advent of brand-name, factory-made products, which with the explosive growth of the patent-medicine industry had become widespread in America and England by the 1880s, but not in Scandinavia until the end of the century.[2] A brand-name advertisement did not need to mention the name of Baker Fabian Olsen at all, because the product was no longer connected either to a personal producer or to a particular place. Factory-made products could float throughout the city in identical copies, and one store became as good as the next for buying it. (Interestingly, the development of brand-name products was a spatial consideration from the start, since it was motivated initially by the export business, and its need to keep proprietary control of products that entered into very wide circulation abroad.)[3]

Histories generally locate the first important stage of modern advertising in the period between 1880 and 1920, when the concentration on the product made existing goods available to ever-expanding groups of consumers. Gunhild Agger's analysis of advertising historiography claims the general consensus to be that advertising language before 1880 was straightforwardly informative, not persuasive in intent. The important implication here is that before advertising became a rhetorical project, it was essentially geographic: one of the initial goals was to conquer spatial barriers that made buying a local activity and hindered the development of a mass market. It involved getting that information to the expanding number of middle-class consumers and getting them in turn transported to the store. This problem could be solved on the one hand with the help of new technologies of visual representation and the proliferating print media, especially the newspaper, and on the other by systems of public transportation that gave consumers greater geographic range.

America and England led the way in most of these developments, especially in the aggressivity of their advertising culture. By the 1870s, outdoor advertising in both countries had become so extensive that it began to attract notice. One example is this trade card for the New York Advertising Sign Co. [not reproduced here —ed.], which as shown also had affiliates in Philadelphia, Chicago, and San Francisco. Along the left side of the card is the claim, "Signs Painted Anywhere," with the joke at the bottom ("our artist at Niagara Falls") making the tongue-in-cheek claim that they could even paint a sign on a waterfall if paid to do so. . . . The free-ranging American advertising sign was promoted as radically disassociated from its referent already by the mid-1870s. It could potentially show up anywhere.[4]

For most of the nineteenth century, the Scandinavian cityscapes were relatively "clean" of advertising in comparison to Chicago, New York, or London, a fact that emerged when Scandinavians traveled to those destinations. Danish satirist and illustrator Storm P. emphasized the contrast in 1901 in this excerpt from his travel diary during a trip to Newcastle, here quoted by Søholm:

> Reklamen *er overordentlig fremtrædende og storstilet i England—overalt hvor man sender Øjet ser man Plakater og Skilte—paa Gavle—Plankeværker—Skorstene—Vogne osv. osv.—Plakaterne ere tit saa store at en enkelt optager en hel Husgavl—og de ere alle kunstnerisk udførte—smagfulde saa vel i Stil—som i Farve—den overvejende Del er dog Humoristiske—ja man kan more sig en hel Dag—blot med at iagttage hele den Mængde af brogede Billeder som dækker enhver bar Plet i Newcastle.*
>
> (15, original emphasis; also cited in Agger 132)

(*Advertising* is unusually conspicuous and large-scale in England—everywhere one sends one's eyes one sees posters and signs—on gables—wooden fences—chimneys—carriages, etc. etc. The posters are often so large that a single one takes up the whole gable of a house—and they are all artistically done—tasteful in style and color—the great majority of them are humorous—yes, one can amuse oneself for an entire day—just by observing the whole mass of motley pictures that cover every bare spot in Newcastle.)

Perhaps because he was a humorist, Storm P. finds great appeal in the advertising-dominated cityscape. He likes the idea that the modern city is one that can be read, one that is decorated visually with words, signs, and pictures.

The gap between the advertising practices in American and Scandinavian cityscapes at the end of the nineteenth century was of course destined to narrow with time, and with the professionalization of advertising internationally in the 1920s, the two systems increasingly converged. For this reason, while looking at Christiania photographs of the 1880s and '90s, one gets the impression that one is seeing the moment before the flood. The *date* is late enough in the century that many photographic documents are available, but the *place*, Christiania, still lags enough behind the developments in other European and American metropolises that only the first hints of what we might call modern advertising's system of displacement are apparent. More common in these photographs is a relatively grounded system of reference—those with a secure link between name, place, and product. Christiania in 1880s was for the most part apparently still a city with secure signs.

Other photographs of the city also illustrate this point. The first is a photograph from the late 1860s, a view from the railway station up Karl Johans gate [not reproduced here —ed.].[5] This relatively cluttered streetscape, which is actually unusual for photographs from that early date, nevertheless show what Veiteberg and Økland would call "innocent" advertising (in my analysis, "grounded" signs). Each shows the name of the person found in the shop, and the goods mentioned in lettering on the walls and windows are described generally, not by brand name. More typical of Christiania streets before the turn of the century is this photograph of Karl Johans gate in the early 1890s taken by the renowned Swedish photographer Axel Lindahl [not reproduced here —ed.].[6] The street is relatively free of signs but the signs that can be seen show the names of hotels and restaurants. Even in newspaper advertisements from the period, this sense of grounding was invoked by some advertisements that showed pictures not of the product, but of the factory where it was produced or the store in which it could be purchased, as one sees in this advertising page [not reproduced here —ed.] from *Ny Illustreret Tidende* in 1888.

When outdoor advertising signs begin to "drift" in Christiania toward the end of the century, it is interesting that it does so in connection with expanding circuits of transportation. One of the earliest examples (1899) of brand-name advertising in the Christiania street photographs, for instance, is found on a streetcar [not reproduced here —ed.].[7] The product is Pellerins Margarin, one of the few trademarks with any visual presence in Christiania before the turn of the century. By attaching the advertisement to the system of transportation itself, the sign, like the streetcar, becomes unmoored and without place. We might take this for granted today, since public transportation has become one of the most typical advertising spaces. But here in the historical moment of the 1890s, we can catch the shift toward greater advertising mobility just as it begins to happen.

Another streetcar photograph from around 1910 shows what must have been one of the most "decorated" Norwegian buildings from the turn of the century [not reproduced here —ed.].[8] This is the administration building for Christiania Elektriske Sporvei, which introduced the first electric streetcar line to the city in the 1890s. Located at the Majorstuen station, somewhat outside the city center, this building had as early as 1898 become a magnet for the kind of advertising shown here (even though this particular photo is of later date). A close look at the same building's advertisements in other photographs taken from different angles further reveals some crucial shifts in advertising practice. For one, there is a brand-name sign for Pellerins Margarin on the roof of the station and an advertisement for *Morgenbladet* on the building's façade, another obvious choice since the newspaper, like the streetcar and the brand name, could circulate freely throughout the city. Finally, there are ads for two stores, one selling sporting goods and the other machine oil, stores located on

good sentences pop into my mind that could be used in a sketch or a serial, refined linguistic strokes of luck unlike anything I had found before.)

These bits and pieces of newspaper-like collage, these word coincidences, assemble themselves into a narrative, which quickly floods out to fill twenty pages: "Det var som en åre var sprunget i mig" (26) [It was as if an artery had burst in me]. As Kittang points out, this is in fact the only truly successful writing experience in the series of dismal failures depicted in the novel (50).

In many ways, this second awakening is an inversion of the book's opening scene. Here the narrator *writes* for the newspaper instead of simply reading it, and just to strengthen the connection, he repeats the reference to the advertisements. First he says, "Det lysner mere og mere, jeg kan halvveis skjælne fyrdirektørens bekjendtgjørelse nede ved døren, og ved vinduet er det allerede så lyst at jeg til nød kunde se å skrive" (27) [It gets gradually lighter, I can half-way make out the lighthouse director's announcement down by the door, and at the window it is already so light that in a pinch I could see enough to write]. Two things stand out in this passage: first, that the legibility of the advertisements is, as in the first scene, once again used to measure progression through the stages of visibility and consciousness. Second, that the novel's most successful writing experience has apparently taken place in the dark, since only after he is done can he "halfway make out" the ads on the wall, and "in a pinch" ("til nød") could see enough to write if he sat over by the window, he says. As it gets lighter, the narrator switches roles again, turning back from writer into reader as he reviews what he has written: "Jeg steiler overrasket foran den ene gode ting efter den andre og sier til mig selv at det var det bedste jeg nogensinde hadde læst" (27) [I was startled by one good thing after the other and say to myself that it was the best thing I had ever read]—*read*, not written. As he estimates the article's value, he mentions again off-handedly, "det blev lysere og lysere i værelset, jeg kastet et blik ned mot døren og kunde uden synderlig møie læse de fine, skeletagtige bokstaver om jomfru Andersens liksvøp tilhøire i porten" (27) [It got lighter and lighter in the room; I cast a glance down at the door and could without much effort read the delicate skeleton-like typeface about Miss Andersen's burial shrouds, through the gate to the right]. That same morning, he leaves the rented room for good, but not before he bows in front of both advertisements as he leaves (28).

There are elements of automatic writing in this episode quite similar in kind to the one Hamsun describes in the essay "Fra det ubevidste sjæleliv" (From the unconscious life of the soul), which he wrote for the journal *Samtiden* later in 1890. There Hamsun describes how suggestions picked up from reading a newspaper article make their way into his unconscious and resurface in two short sketches that he apparently writes in his sleep and then tries to decipher the next morning. The stylistic characteristics of the narrator's successful newspaper piece in *Sult* are left unspecified, but if it is anything like the strange, absurdist stories produced by the automatic writing in "Fra det ubevidste sjæleliv," then the model of writing produced in this second morning scene is very modern indeed.

Most striking is the way the protagonist keeps checking in with the advertisements as the scene progresses, returning to notice them at different stages of waking as he writes and reads. The ads almost seem to be involved in the production of writing, as if the miscellaneous juxtaposition of an announcement from the lighthouse director, the ad for Baker Olsen's bread, and funeral shrouds together suggest the form of the written text that emerges from the narrator's hand. Like the subliminal suggestion of the newspaper article read half-consciously, the ads are linked to both reading and writing in these two morning scenes. Reading and writing are shown to be part of the same process. I should emphasize again that for me the ads ask to be read for their form rather than their content—not necessarily for thematic clues, but for the kind of writing they imply. In other words, they may "mean" *miscellany* and *juxtaposition,* as much as they do *bureaucracy, food,* and *death,* as Kittang has suggested (38). Like the journalistic sketch the narrator produces half consciously, the ads gather themselves into a whole—such as that of the newspaper's advertising page—by "fine, sproglige lykketræf."

It might be useful here to make a link to the episode in the jail cell when the protagonist invents his new word, *kuboå.* He says, "Med de mest forunderlige spring i min tankegang søker jeg å utgranske betydningen av det nye ord. Det behøvet ikke å bety hverken Gud eller tivoli, og hvem hade sagt at det skulde bety dyrskue?" (50) [With the most amazing jumps in thought I try to examine the meaning of the new word. It did not necessarily mean God or tivoli, and who says that it should mean animal show?]. As he continues through the list of things the word should *not* mean, there emerges an effect of radically random juxtaposition such as one might encounter in a newspaper, between its various articles and its advertising pages: *Gud, tivoli, dyrskue, hengelås, soloppgang, emigration, tobakksfabrikk, strikkegarn* [God, amusement park, padlock, sunrise, emigration, tobacco factory, knitting yarn]. He rejects all of these because he wants the new word to mean something more refined: "Nei egentlig var ordet egnet til å bety noget *sjælelig,* en følelse, en tilstand" (51, original emphasis) [No, actually the word was suited to mean something *spiritual,* a feeling, a condition]. Here again we might observe a dialectic between modernity and literary modernism with the rejected meanings for *kuboå* together forming a collage of sensory impressions from modern life and the elusive, sought-after meaning ("something spiritual"), the literary modernist transformation of those impressions. In other words, the newspaper's form may again be complimentary to the writing project conducted by both Hamsun and his narrator, providing the principle of juxtaposition that becomes the key to a new writing style.

Closely related to this idea is the spatial aspect of new advertising media in the 1880s and '90s, especially in Norway. Juxtaposition, that is, implies the adjacency of things that do not seem naturally to belong together, things that have been willfully taken from their expected contexts and put arbitrarily side by side in a new one [not reproduced here —ed.]. The typical advertising page of a newspaper would certainly fulfill that definition, with its references to stores and goods from all over the city, all brought together in the advertising page, a context lacking any single spatial referent. Especially when one considers that the advertising page in Norwegian newspapers had only recently become a standard feature in the 1880s and that the means of shop signage prior to that development had been strongly rooted to geographic place, the juxtaposition of advertisements raises important questions about the ability of language to point reliably to a location.

As noted earlier, several commentators in the Hamsun criticism have discussed the loss of a secure geography in **Sult**—the addresses lead nowhere, the people he tries to visit are not home, he himself wanders aimlessly through the city following small hunches that rarely pan out. The narrator is not so much tormented by this geographic nonreferentiality as he is complicit in it. Think for example of the episode in which he hires the coachman, even though he has no money, to drive him wildly from false address to false address in search of the fictional Kjerulf. "Ullevålsveien numer 37," he calls out first, then "Tomtegaten numer 11" (91-2). He even goes in to find the man he knows is not there and is amused when the coachman contributes to the fictional development of this invented character by asking about details of his personal appearance. This *gatespill,* if we want to call it that, suggests that the possession of an address is no guarantee of a successful search.

The connection of the search with new systems of advertising is made at the end of this episode and is worth careful attention. After abandoning the coachman without an explanation, Hamsun's protagonist makes his way through the courtyard, a hallway, and then emerges out onto the street on the next block—Vognmandsgaten [Coachman Street]—an appropriate name, as it turns out, given who has been left waiting for him a block away. The name of the building itself is significant: "Jeg ser opover huset som jeg just har passert igjennem og læser over døren: Beværtning & logi for reisende" (93) [I look up at the building I have just passed through and read over the door: Food and Lodging for travelers]. The condition of constant motion is the one that he has just acted out with the coachman, the journey with only a fictional hope of a destination.

He then sits on a bench and takes stock of his physical condition, noticing especially the skeleton-like effect of his hands: "Jeg føler mig ved synet av mine magre fingrer råt påvirket, jeg hater hele mit slunkne legeme og gyser ved å bære på det, føle det om mig" (94) [The sight of my emaciated fingers has a raw effect on me, I hate my whole collapsed body and shudder to have to carry it, to feel it around me]. At that moment, he stands up and reads another bit of writing on the wall:

> *Underveis kom jeg forbi en port hvor det stod følgende å læse: "Liksvøp hos jomfru Andersen, tilhøire i porten."—Gamle minder! sa jeg og husket mit forrige rum på Hammersborg, den lille gyngestol, avisbetrækket nede ved døren, fyrdirektørens avertissement og baker Fabian Olsens nybakte brød.*
>
> (94)

(On the way, I passed a gate where the following could be read: "Burial shrouds at Miss Andersen's, through the gate to the right."—Old memories! I said and remembered my previous room at Hammersborg, the little rocking chair, the newspaper wallpaper near the door, the lighthouse director's announcement and Baker Fabian Olsen's newly-baked bread.)

The entire episode of the chase after Joachim Kjerulf is full of these "linguistic strokes of luck": the name of the street referring coincidentally back to the waiting coachman, the name of the building referring similarly to the wandering protagonist, and Jomfru Andersen's "magre, grinende bokstaver" [lean, grinning letters] mirroring the skeleton-like fingers of the protagonist. But the play with urban geography in this passage seems intent on building up to the moment when the advertisement from the apartment's wallpaper and its referent come together again. The distance between the wandering advertising sign and its referent is now so great that the original sign is now only "et gammelt minde" [an old memory]. Not only that, but the system of reference is reversed: now the *place* refers back to the advertisement, which has semiotic priority because it has been introduced first in the novel. The effect seems not so much emphatic of a connection between sign and physical place, as it is of the enormous psychological distance between them—such a chasm, that to find that the shop-owner referred to previously in the ad (*the* Miss Andersen!) actually has a real referent in a physical location has an uncanny effect.

Furthermore, the insistent indexicality of the Andersen ad ("through the gate to the right") invokes an adjacency that only now gets a physical context, one referred to but literally out of place in the newspaper format. A similar effect occurs at another moment in the text, one that I will juxtapose with a final Christiania photograph. The episode comes at one of the many moments when the protagonist is desperate for food and ransacks the possibilities that lie open to him. Suddenly he hits on something:

> *Det var nu for eksempel musikhandler Cisler, ham hadde jeg slet ikke været hos. Der blev nok en råd. . . . Således gik jeg og talte til jeg igjen fik mig selv til å gråte av rørelse. Bare ikke bli anholdt! Cisler? Var det kanske et høiere fingerpek? Hans navn hadde faldt mig ind uten grund og han bodde så langt borte; men jeg vilde dog opsøke ham, gå sakte og hvile iblandt. Jeg kjente stedet, jeg hadde været der ofte, kjøpt litt noter i de gode dager.*
>
> (66)

(There was for example the music-seller Cisler, I had not been to see him. That was an idea. . . . In this way I went around talking until I once again got myself to cry with emotion. Just do not get arrested! Cisler? Was that perhaps a finger pointing from on high? His name had occurred to me for no reason and he lived so far away; but I wanted to look him up anyway, go slowly and rest in between. I knew the place, I had been there often, purchased a bit of music in better days.)

After making his way there, he asks for money, but Cisler turns him down without explanation. He searches his mind for an explanation: "Hvorfor skulde netop hans navn falde mig ind da jeg stod langt nede i Vaterland?" (67) [Why would precisely his name occur to me when I stood far away down in Vaterland]. Why indeed, unless perhaps that the spatial effects of advertising are beginning to make that kind of long-distance suggestion more common. Or to use an earlier example from one of the photographs, why would the name of a sporting goods store in Kirkeveien suddenly occur to a person boarding a streetcar out at Majorstuen? Was that perhaps a finger pointing from on high?

One of the most common graphic icons of late nineteenth-century advertising was of course the pointing finger, so common internationally that in some senses it could be said to "mean" advertising in general. . . . The pointing finger was an icon that could be found adorning the sides of buildings as well, increasingly common in the visual cityscapes of both Christiania and Chicago before the turn of the century. Here, for example, is one of those fingers pointing insistently to an underwear shop on Stortorvet around the turn of the century [not reproduced here —ed.]. In this photograph the icon makes an insistent claim of physical reference: *here* is where you will find the shop, the owner, and the advertised goods. Was *that* perhaps a finger pointing from on high?

As should be evident from the preceding discussion, nothing could be more complicated than this pointing finger. It implies both a secure system of reference and its undoing. Perhaps because of his position between cultures in the late 1880s, Hamsun experiences that pointing finger mainly as a tease: it is both the finger of God and the mocking finger of media advertising, which leads and misleads at the same time. The "finger pointing from on high" in his novel holds no guarantee of special meaning, nor of finding the promised goods. When *Sult*'s protagonist follows the pointing finger, it sends him on a path of circulation as meaningless as the one that leads the coachman in search of Joachim Kjerulf. Perhaps it turns out that after all, the pointing finger of the new advertising points not to place, but only to more text.

Notes

1. For a book-length treatment of modernity's transformations of the perception of time and space, see Kern, *The Culture of Time and Space, 1880-1918.*

2. For a discussion of early Norwegian brand-name products around the turn of the century, see Jørstad, *Reklamebyen Bergen,* 18-20.

3. Veiteberg and Økland make this point about the sardine industry's use of labels, 14.

4. Margolin, et al. give this description of the American advertising landscape: "Patent medicine manufacturers were the greatest despoilers of the landscape. From the 1860s to the 1880s, painted letters from six inches to two feet high advertised home remedies on rocks and cliffs, barns, abandoned structures, and any other available service" (36).

5. The dating of photographs in the following analysis is in some cases a best guess based on visual clues within the photographs and a comparison of shop signs with the entries in the Christiania address books for the years in question. In this case, for example, there is only one year's address book (1866) in which all of the shopkeeper names visible in this photograph are listed together in the same part of the city.

6. My choice of which photographs to emphasize out of the hundreds available at the Oslo City Museum and the University Library cannot help but be arbitrary, but I have tried to choose photos that are representative of the available street images, or to give some indication of how they compare to other photographs.

7. The given date is that deduced by historian Thorlief Strandholt, based on when this particular car (nr. 29) was entered into service. See Strandholt 15.

8. Again, the date of this and an earlier picture of the same building come from Strandholt's history, 14, 22.

9. For an historical overview of Norwegian newspapers, see Gunnar Christie Wasberg, *Norsk presse i hundre år, 1820-1920*.

Works Cited

Agger, Gunhild. "Fra Fabrik til forførelse—om dansk reklames udvikling i perioden 1880-1920." *Reklame-Kultur*. Eds. Jens F. Jensen, et al. FISK-serien I. Aalborg, Denmark: Aalborg Universitetsforlag, 1993. 129-64.

Cease, Julie. "Semiotics, City, *Sult*: Hamsun's text of 'hunger.'" *Edda* (1992): 136-46.

Eggen, Einar. "Mennesket og tingene: Hamsun's *Sult* og 'den nye roman.'" *Søkelys på Knut Hamsuns 90-års Diktning*. Ed. Øystein Rottem. Oslo: Universitetsforlaget, 1979. 55-76.

Ferguson, Robert. *Enigma: The Life of Knut Hamsun*. London: Hutchinson, 1987.

Fritzsche, Peter. *Reading Berlin 1900*. Cambridge, MA: Harvard UP, 1996.

Hamsun, Knut. *Fra det Moderne Amerikas Aandsliv*. Copenhagen: P. G. Philipsens Forlag, 1889.

———. "Fra det ubevidste Sjæleliv." *Samtiden* (1890): 325-34.

———. *Knut Hamsuns Brev*. Ed. Harald Næss. Olso: Gyldendal Norsk Forlag, 1994.

———. *Sult. Samlede Verker*. Vol. 1. Oslo: Gyldendal, 1954.

Jørstad, Finn R. *Reklamebyen Bergen*. Bergen: Stiftelsen Norsk Handelsmuseum/Norsk Reklamemuseum, 1995.

Kern, Stephen. *The Culture of Time and Space, 1880-1918*. Cambridge, MA: Harvard UP, 1983.

Kirkegaard, Peter. *Knut Hamsun som modernist*. Copenhagen: Medusa, 1975.

Kittang, Atle. *Luft, vind, ingenting: Hamsuns desillusionsromaner frå* Sult *til* Ringen Sluttet. Oslo: Gyldendal Norsk Forlag, 1984.

Larsen, Lars Frode. *Den unge Knut Hamsun (1859-1888): En studie i hans personlige og idémessige utvikling*. Diss., University of Oslo, 1998.

Margolin, Victor, Ira Brichta, and Vivian Brichta. *The Promise and the Product: 200 Years of American Advertising Posters*. New York: Macmillan, 1979.

Næss, Harald. *Knut Hamsun og Amerika*. Oslo: Gyldendal Norsk Forlag, 1969.

Strandholt, Thorleif. *A/S Kristiania Elektriske Sporvei, 1892-1924*. Oslo: Sporvejshistorisk Selskab, 1983.

Søholm, Eigil. *Storm P. før Ping, Bladvid og satire 1902-20*. Copenhagen: Haase, 1986.

Veiteberg, Jorunn and Einar Økland. *Reklamebildet: Norske annonsar og plakatar frå århundreskiftet til i dag*. Oslo: Det Norske Samlaget, 1986.

Wasberg, Gunnar Christie. *Norsk presse i hundre år, 1820-1920*. Oslo: Gyldendal Norsk Forlag, 1969.

Mark Axelrod (essay date 1999)

SOURCE: Axelrod, Mark. "The Poetics of Peripatetics and Peripety in Hamsun's *Hunger*." In *The Poetics of Novels: Fiction and Its Execution*, pp. 140-70. London: Macmillan, 1999.

[*In the following essay, Axelrod examines the use of space, travel, movement, and change in* Hunger.]

Published in 1890, **Hunger** is probably Hamsun's best known and, arguably, his best written novel. Sizeably autobiographical, it deals with the time Hamsun existed in Kristiania (Oslo) and is extraordinary in terms of psychological depth and poetic temperament. But one cannot easily dismiss the effect starvation had on Hamsun and to that extent one cannot discount intentionality. As Robert Ferguson writes of **Hunger** in his biography, *Enigma: The Life of Knut Hamsun*: 'In writing it he drew on the experiences he underwent during his two most desperate periods in Kristiania in the winters of 1880-81 and 1885-86, and probably, also drew on the experiences of his winter in Chicago in 1886-87. The many small correspondences of fact and fiction—the narrator's visit to the castle, for example, and his address at Tomtegaten II—as well as the autobiographical details that crop up in letters to Erik Frydenlund and Johan Sørensen, indicate that the book is Hamsun's self-portrait in fiction' (Ferguson, p. 110). Implicit in that notion is that the voice of the protagonist is often the voice of Hamsun not only in terms of content, 'The things I have written about in **Hunger** I have experienced here—and many more worse things besides. God how I have suffered. But I live . . .' (Hamsun, Naess and McFarlane [hereafter *Letters*], 97), but in terms of poetics, 'My book! My book! About these delicate nuances. I would want to sift through the remotest nuances of the mind—I would let them listen to the mimosa's breathing—every word like brilliantly white wings—movements on the shining surface of language' (Hamsun, *Letters*, p. 88).

The course of the novel follows the nameless protagonist as he virtually wanders throughout the city while dwelling on the notions of life, death, homelessness, hunger and art all within the confines of the city's ethos. What one discovers about the character, if not with all people who are homeless, impoverished, and hungry, is that their *raison d'être* is a kind of survival, contingent on mobility. That is, without mobility they are effectively doomed to perish, death being the virtue of stasis. It is only this ability to move, to push a shopping cart, or carry a knapsack, or just be able to walk, that enables them to survive. In that course of that mobilization, at least in the protagonist's case, one sees two distinct features at work—peripatetics and peripety—since both notions are clearly formulated in Hamsun's **Hunger** and in his nameless hero.

What one knows of things peripatetic, (from the Greek *peripatetikos,* given to walking about), relate, of course, to Aristotle and to the school of the same name. The legend, fictional as it must be, registers that Aristotle taught and walked through the loggia of the school and hence the school became known as the Peripatos. But 'the extant "lives" are without exception late; they were written, or rather compiled, many centuries after Aristotle's death, in the late Roman period; their sources are uncertain and, at best, even these go back to Hellenistic times' (Grayeff, p. 13). But in a curious way there is a distinct relationship between the things peripatetic and with peripety (Greek *peripeteia,* a sudden change esp. that on which the plot of a tragedy hinges), and their connection between wandering and philosophizing. One discovers that the notion of things peripatetic, of things itinerant, applies with extended regularity to Hamsun's urban alienated protagonist who does, in fact, tend to philosophize whether hungry or temporarily sated. Likewise, he experiences peripety with a certain amount of regularity and the peripety sustains him in order that he may carry on with his work.

What is significant about the title of the novel is that the word, *hunger,* operates on several levels: hunger is obviously the physiologically painful sensation caused by lack of food, but it can also be strong desire or craving. So is the hunger a craving for food only or for something else? If the former, the food sates the hunger, but the hero is not satisfied with merely being sated. If the latter, what else is it? A hunger for death? Spirituality? Art? There is something to say for all of these things in **Hunger,** for all of them are attributable to it.

The novel begins as a memoir: 'It was in those days when I wandered about hungry in Kristiania, that strange city which no one leaves before it has set its mark upon him . . .' (Hamsun, p. 3). And the ellipsis, the leap or sudden passage from one topic to another, lets the reader know that the hero has not succumbed to starvation. From the opening lines one realizes that although it is a memoir, a recollection, the past events are revivified by the way Hamsun records them: 'Lying awake in my attic room, I hear a clock strike six downstairs' (Hamsun, p. 3). Even though this is a recollection of past events, the experience lingers on in the present. The relationship between past and present, between the events of the past and the re-experiencing of those events in the present is crucial in Hamsun's poetics. For in addition to the preoccupation the protagonist has with 'space' (he constantly tells us where he is going) he is also preoccupied with 'time' (he constantly informs us of the time of day) for in the daily exercise of someone who is homeless there are three main constituents: where one is, what time of day it is, and what one is thinking during the day. One's thoughts can be as desultory as one's movements and are as varied as the vagabond himself. But if one's thoughts revolve around one's station and how one got to be in that station, then the thoughts can be as varied as one's attitude towards philosophy or death or the absence of God. Perhaps one has a daily route one follows or perhaps one merely moves vagrantly, as one might expect from a wanderer. In any case, what is established is the necessity to establish cause and to dwell on one's reason for being.

As the novel opens, it is six in the morning. Our hero's wall is papered with old issues of the *Morning Times* and ads from both the Director of Lighthouses and Fabian Olsen, Baker as well as from 'Shrouds at Madam Andersen's'. Certainly the juxtaposition of these four items has not been made precipitously and the connection among 'light' and 'bread' and 'death' is not a serendipitous one on Hamsun's part. As a matter of fact, the foundation for the entire novel rests on the notions of light and bread and death since they are part of the wandering process that the protagonist experiences. 'Autumn had arrived, that lovely cool time of year when everything turns colour and dies . . . This empty room, where the floor rocked up and down at every step I took, was like a horrible, broken-down coffin' (Hamsun, p. 4). It is also early in the novel that the protagonist's appeals to the divine begin. These are appeals for either divine intervention or divine understanding or divine apprehension as in: 'God knows, I thought, if there is any point to my looking for work anymore!' (Hamsun, p. 4) and as the novel proceeds the supplications often become invectives though the protagonist never entirely loses faith even while he is in the process of denouncing it.

The conflicting notions of life and death persist as one also discovers that, 'All summer long I had haunted the cemeteries and Palace Park, where I would sit and prepare articles for the newspapers, column after column about all sorts of things—strange whimsies, moods, caprices of my restless brain' (Hamsun, p. 5). At this point one discovers that the act of writing is not peripheral to the protagonist's hunger. As a matter of fact, the act of writing, the art of writing, is fundamental to the novel since the novel is not only about hunger, spiritual and physical, but about the art of writing.

Then it is nine o'clock in the morning. Three hours have passed and 'Nothing was further from my mind than just taking a morning walk in the fresh air' (Hamsun, p. 5). At this point the wandering begins in earnest. Only capable of thinking about his hunger 'If only one had a bite to eat on such a clear day!' (Hamsun, p. 6) he 'looked up—the clock in the tower of Our Saviour's showed ten. Continuing through the streets, I roamed about without a care in the world, stopped at a corner without having to, turned and went down a side street without an errand there. I went with the flow, borne from place to place this happy morning, rocking serenely to and fro among other happy people' (Hamsun, p. 6). The protagonist is very specific about where he goes and what he is doing there. Whether it be trailing a cripple or hastening to a pawnbroker, each movement is a calculated movement; each movement is done with some measure of purpose; each movement is not done for the simple sake of moving, but to accomplish some daily task and at the same time to think about the measure of what one has accomplished. Yet as one reads on, the deleterious effects of hunger affect him: aches in his ribs, pelvis, lower extremities; he is consumed by nervous excitement, extreme irritability, there is the loosening of social bonds, the lessening of morale; apathy appears, mental depression, nausea, lack of concentration, lack of ambition, melancholy, submissiveness, all exhibit themselves as being directly influenced by hunger. Curiously, sexual indifference is not included. But one sees influences in the manner in which Hamsun alters the focus of the paragraph:

> Once I had pulled through, I certainly didn't want to owe anybody a blanket; I might start an article this very day about the crimes of the future or the freedom of the will, anything whatever, something worth reading, something I would get at least ten kroner for . . . And at the thought of this article I instantly felt an onrush of desire to begin right away, tapping my chock-full brain. I would find myself a suitable place in Palace Park and not rest till it was finished.
>
> (Hamsun, p. 7)

There is absolutely no causal connection between the blanket and the article, nothing to stimulate the thought of it and just as quickly the thought is dispelled. After finally getting a bite to eat at Palace Hill 'my courage rose markedly; I was no longer satisfied with writing an article about something so elementary and straightforward as crimes of the future, which anybody could guess, or simply learn by reading history. I felt capable of a greater effort and, being in the mood to surmount difficulties, decided upon a three-part monograph about philosophical cognition' (Hamsun, p. 9). After he eats, he discards the idea of 'crimes of the future' for a more difficult enterprise dealing with Kant and Renan. Naturally, he says, he would 'deal a deathblow to Kant's sophistries' (Hamsun, p. 10) though one might be hard-pressed to decipher what sophistries he is talking about; however, one may speculate that the link between Kant and Renan appears to be their representative positions on the existence of God and how those philosophies relate to the protagonist. Then, with another ellipsis, he discovers that his pencil is gone. He pleads to God again, 'God, how everything I touched seemed bent on going wrong' (Hamsun, p. 10) and he attempts to recover the pencil forgotten at the pawn shop. As he does, he decides not to attack Kant, and says 'I just had to make an imperceptible detour when I came to the problem of time and space' (Hamsun, p. 10), but he 'wouldn't have to answer for Renan, that old parson' (Hamsun, p. 10). Hamsun's choice is not serendipitous. Of course, the peripatetic hero not only philosophizes, but intends to write on philosophical issues (clearly an un-commercial exercise) and the issues he chooses to write about are integral to the hero's character and his journey. Hamsun's choices here beg a kind of decomposition.

Certainly one of the things that brings both Kant and Renan together are their approaches to the existence of God. Kant's *Der einzig mögliche Beweisgrun* (*The One Possible Basis for a Demonstration of the Existence of God*), is the fundamental underpinning of the *Critique of Pure Reason* published two decades later. Simply formulated, the work consists of three sections which put forward the ground of proof, the utility of the proof and the reasons which demonstrate the existence of God, but Kant also leads with a disclaimer that 'The rule of thoroughness does not always require that every concept, in even the most profound essay, be developed or defined; particularly if one may be assured that the clear, common concept can cause no misunderstanding where it is used' (Kant, p. 53). But Kant's 'strategy is to show that God is necessary because some things are possible' (Kant, p. 14). To that end, 'it is not possible for there to be nothing, for the very possibility of total non-being would itself have to be at least a possibility. If sheer non-being is impossible, whatever is requisite as ground for even the possibility of anything is necessary' (Kant, p. 14). That the protagonist talks about Kant's sophisms can only be taken in the context in which he is referring to Kant (that is, in relation to God). If Kant speaks in sophisms it is purely in relation to the existence of God and since God is fundamentally indifferent to the protagonist's welfare, the existence of Kant's God is not co-existent with the protagonist's notions of God. What is curious is that the protagonist eventually recants and decides not to 'deal a deathblow to Kant's sophisms' since it could be avoided by an imperceptible detour 'when I came to the problem of time and space'. One might ask why he would avoid dealing with issues of time and space since time and space are all he owns. In terms of pure reason, philosophers in Kant's time (Descartes, Spinoza, Leibniz) agreed that pure reason could prove the existence of God and the nature of the soul. With Kant's *Critique of Pure Reason* all Rational sciences came under scrutiny.

Perhaps the answer comes from Kant himself. In the *Critique of Pure Reason, First Section of the Transcendental Aesthetic, §2. Of Space,* he writes: 'Space is represented as an infinite given quantity. Now it is quite true that every concept is to be thought as a representation, which is contained in an infinite number of different possible representations (as their common characteristic), and therefore comprehends them: but no concept, as such, can be thought as if it contained in itself an infinite number of representations. Nevertheless, space is so thought (for all parts of infinite space exist simultaneously). Consequently, the original representation of space is an *intuition a priori,* and not a concept' (Kant, p. 63). In the *Second Section of the Transcendental Aesthetic, §4. Of Time,* Kant writes: 'Time is not an empirical concept deduced from any experience, for neither coexistence nor succession would enter into our perception, if the representation of time were not given *a priori.* Only when this representation *a priori* is given, can we imagine that certain things happen at the same time (simultaneously) or at different times (successively)' (Kant, p. 67). Clearly both of these examples indicate why Hamsun's protagonist (or anyone else starving to death) would indeed make a detour around Kant's notions of space and time especially in how it relates to notions of the divine; however, Renan is another story.

Renan did not believe in a transcendent and personal God. Borrowing the 'three age' theory from Cousin, Renan believed in the final age of man to be both scientific and religious and believed in the clear scientific action of a universe in which there was no perceptible action of a free will superior to man. According to Renan, mankind 'had been pictured by classical historians in terms of an absolute, fixed, static being, the great advance of the nineteenth-century historical thought lies in "substituting the category of *becoming* (*devenir*) for that of *being* (*être*), the conception of the *relative* (*relatif*) for that of the *absolute* (*absolu*), and movement for immobility"' (Chadbourne, p. 50). Renan 'conceives of God no longer as a personal being, absolute and eternal, but as a spiritual reality emerging from human history. "What else is God for humanity except the transcendent sum of its spiritual needs, the category of the ideal, the form under which we conceive the ideal, just as space and time are categories or forms under which we conceive physical bodies"' (Chadbourne, p. 50). Renan objected to the transcendental because, for him, knowledge of reality was obtained through observation and the verification of empirical hypotheses. Positive knowledge of reality must have an experimental basis and that was why the enlightened man could not believe in God since a being who does not reveal himself by any act is for science a being that does not exist. The occurrence of divine intervention has never been proved yet the empirical evidence does not preclude the act of faith and this is exactly the conundrum the character is faced with and that is why he decides to avoid dealing with Kant and take issue with Renan. On the face of it the selection appears quite arbitrary, but subsequently the true significance of choosing these two philosophers becomes quite clear.

But whatever the choice, 'what had to be done was to write an article filling so and so many columns; the unpaid rent and my landlady's long looks when I met her on the stairs in the morning, tormented me all day and popped up even in my happy moments, when there wasn't another dark thought in my head' (Hamsun; p. 10).

In order to finish his article he needs the pencil and with that pencil he had 'written my monograph about philosophical cognition in three volumes' (Hamsun, p. 14). Hadn't the pawnbroker heard of it? So not only does the 'lie' establish the protagonist as a kind of literary provocateur, it also establishes the need, the hunger, he has to write. By now it is twelve noon and as he walks down Karl Johan Street, by the University, and wanders up Palace Hill he begins to think about his present circumstances in relation to the 'happy' people he sees on the street. At this point the apparent philosophical digression becomes specific and the ambivalence comes to fruition.

> Coddling myself with this thought I found that a terrible injustice had been done to me. Why had these last few months been so exceedingly rough on me? . . . What was the matter with me? Had the Lord's finger pointed at me? But why exactly me? . . . why precisely I should have been chosen as a guinea pig for a caprice of divine grace . . . I wandered about debating this matter, unable to get it out of my mind; I discovered the weightiest objections to the Lord's arbitrariness in letting me suffer for everybody else's sake . . . What if God simply intended to annihilate me? I stood up and paced back and forth in front of my bench . . . The thought of God began to occupy me again. It seemed to me quite inexcusable of him to meddle every time I applied for a job and thus upset everything, since all I was asking for was my daily bread . . . I felt increasingly bitter toward God for his continual oppressions. If he meant to draw me closer to himself and make me better by torturing me and casting adversity in my way, he was simply mistaken, that I could vouch for. *And* nearly crying with defiance, I looked up toward heaven and told him so once and for all, inwardly . . . Had not my heavenly Father provided for me as he had for the sparrows of the air, *and* had he not shown me the grace of pointing at his humble servant? God had stuck his finger down into the network of my nerves *and* gently, quite casually, brought a little confusion among the threads. *And* God had withdrawn his finger *and* behold! there were fibres *and* delicate filaments on his finger from the threads of my nerves. *And*

there was a gaping hole after his finger, which was God's finger, *and* wounds in my brain from the track of his finger. But where God had touched me with the finger of his hand he let me be *and* touched me no more, *and* allowed no evil to befall me. He let me go in peace, *and* he let me go with that gaping hole. *And no evil shall befall me from God, who is the Lord through all eternity* . . . (my emphasis)

(Hamsun, pp. 16-17)

The paragraph is noteworthy in that there is a subtle shift from being divinely accusative, filled with imprecations, to being divinely contrite which is totally consistent with his own moral ambivalence. In other words, ultimately he embraces Kant and dismisses Renan since he initially refuses to take personal responsibility, but, rather, blames his condition on the Lord. But the blame does not last. Soon the Lord gains a 'reprieve', hostage as the protagonist is to his childhood and the 'cadences' of the Bible, and the protagonist assumes some kind of personal responsibility for his actions.

But, stylistically, the paragraph is unique in that what Hamsun is attempting to achieve here through the use of *polysyndeton* is a kind of Biblical rhythm and in the poetics of that Biblical rhythm there is a clear valorization not only of the Biblical discourse itself, but the subject of the Biblical discourse. The use of *polysyndeton* is equivalent to the *leitwort* that Robert Alter speaks of in *The Art of Biblical Narrative*. 'A *leitwort* is a word or a word- root that recurs significantly in a text, in a continuum of texts, or in a configuration of texts: by following these repetitions, one is able to decipher or grasp a meaning of the text, or at any rate, the meaning will be revealed more strikingly . . . The measured repetition that matches the inner rhythm of the text, or rather, that wells up from it, is one of the most powerful means for conveying meaning without expressing it' (Alter, p. 93). Hence the shift in style from the accusative to the contrite; from the implied acceptance of Kant to the implied condemnation of Renan and all of this is done peripatetically. By now, it is two o'clock in the afternoon.

But it is not only the relationship of the protagonist to his God that is significant, but the relationship of the writer to his work. In that sense he is to his work what God is to him. One cannot easily attribute his rapid digressions to the fact he is starving since the narrator is not starving. The narrator is recalling what it was like to starve which is a completely different version of starvation indeed. Hamsun clearly captures the physiological and psychological privation inherent in the condition, but precisely because it is a reconstruction of the incidents makes it such a unique work especially when one considers that he was completing the novel in Copenhagen where he was often not lacking. But woven within the fabric of the novel one clearly distinguishes that it is, as in the works of Austen or Smart or Lispector, a novel about writing as well. The entire Happolati incident is just such an example in which lies appear 'full-fledged in my head on the spur of the moment' (Hamsun, p. 20) and as he continues fabricating the tale of the fictitious Happolati he himself becomes carried away with the fiction. 'This was beginning to get interesting. The situation was running away with me, and one lie after another sprang up in my head . . . The little dwarf's gullibility made me reckless, I felt like stuffing full of lies come what may, driving him from the field in grand style. Had he heard about the electric hymn book that Happolati had invented?' . . . I was completely taken up with my own tales, wonderful visions hovered before my eyes, the blood rushed to my head and I lied like a trooper' (Hamsun, pp. 21-3). These are not the thoughts of a 'madman'; they are the thoughts of a fiction writer absorbed in the details of his fabrication as the fabrication takes over the writer and, in a way, the writing itself. The passage: 'Quite instinctively, I had gotten paper and pencil into my hands, and I sat and wrote mechanically the date 1848 in every corner of the page. If only a single scintillating thought would come, grip me utterly, and put words in my mouth! It had happened before after all, it had really happened that such moments came over me, so that I could write a long piece without effort and get it wonderfully right. I sit there on the bench and write 1848 dozens of times; I write this number crisscross in all possible shapes and wait for a usable idea to occur to me. A swarm of loose thoughts is fluttering about in my head' (Hamsun, p. 25), is clearly and precisely a summary of the entire writing process.

What is significant about this passage is that it begins talking about writing and segue-ways into writing about autumn and death then shifts back to writing:

And I sat down again, picked up my pencil once more and was ready to attack my article in earnest. It would never do to give up when the unpaid rent was staring me in the face. My thoughts gradually began to compose themselves. Taking great care I wrote slowly a couple of well-considered pages, an introduction to something; it could serve as the beginning to almost anything, whether a travelogue or a political article, depending on what I felt like doing. It was an excellent beginning to something or other.

(Hamsun, pp. 25-6)

Then, he perceives a 'gaping emptiness' followed by '"Lord, my God and Father!" I cried in agony, and I repeated this cry several times in succession without adding a word' (Hamsun, p. 26). With one last appeal to God he prays 'silently to God for this job' (Hamsun, p. 27) he has discovered. 'Then I went back up to my room and sat down to think in my rocking chair, while the darkness grew more and more impenetrable. It was beginning to be difficult to stay up now' (Hamsun, p. 27). And so ends the first day.

The second day begins much as the first. Time, as well as space, continues to be of critical concern. He notes that it is five o'clock. What he is preoccupied with at that time of day is neither physical hunger nor the existence of God, but writing:

> Suddenly one or two good sentences occur to me, suitable for a sketch or story, nice linguistic flukes the likes of which I had never experienced before. I lie there repeating these words to myself and find that they are excellent. Presently they are joined by others, I'm at once wide-awake, sit up and grab paper and pencil from the table behind my bed. It was as though a vein had burst inside me—one word follows another, they connect with one another and turn into situations; scenes pile on top of other scenes, actions and dialogue well up in my brain, and a wonderful sense of pleasure takes hold of me. I write as if possessed, filling one page after another without a moment's pause. My thoughts strike me so suddenly and continue to pour out so abundantly that I lose a lot of minor details I'm not able to write down fast enough, though I am working at full blast. They continue to crowd in on me, I am full of my subject, and every word I write is put in my mouth.
>
> (Hamsun, p. 28)

Hamsun continues in this fashion for several more paragraphs as if possessed by the writing process until 'Elated with a sense of fulfillment and puffed up with joy, I feel on top of the world' (Hamsun, p. 28) and reckons the piece to be worth at least five, maybe ten kroner. Coterminous with the completion of the story, 'it was growing lighter and lighter in the room' (Hamsun, p. 28) even though he could read 'the fine, skeleton-like letters concerning Madam Andersen's shrouds' (Hamsun, p. 28). By now it is past seven, but not quite eight. And as he leaves his room with a 'glorious feeling' making me thankful to God and everyone, and I

> kneeled down by the bed and thanked God in a loud voice, for his goodness toward me this morning. I knew—oh yes, I knew that the exalted moment and the inspiration I had just experienced and written down was a wonderful work of heaven in my soul, an answer to my cry of distress yesterday. 'It's God! It's God!' I cried to myself and I wept from enthusiasm over my own words . . .
>
> (Hamsun, p. 30)

There is, of course, the relationship between God and inspiration and when the protagonist is 'inspired' to produce he thanks God in the same way he blasphemes against God when he is not inspired. The word 'enthusiasm' means 'to be filled with God' and the relationship is clear. This attitude is a bit understated by Hamsun himself when he was asked to describe his attitude towards religion and he replied 'Almost indifferent. I am not godless, but like all my friends and acquaintances, indifferent to questions of religion. No, no change whatsoever. I am not much good at praying to God, but warmly grateful to him when he has been merciful, and saved me from something or other' (Ferguson, p. 399). His letters as well as his novel belie that attitude.

At ten o'clock he drops off the manuscript he has been toiling over. The editor is not there. He must return at four. He begins to walk. Then the doubts begin to enter. He walks to Our Saviour's Church and daydreams. Time passes. He reconsiders the manuscript, questions his ability; his hope moves to despair: 'Could I be absolutely certain that my story was truly inspired, a little artistic masterpiece? God knows it might have some faults here and there . . . What if it was quite mediocre or perhaps downright bad; what guarantee did I have that it wasn't at this very moment lying in the wastepaper basket already?' (Hamsun, p. 33). It is now twelve. He continues to walk and to ponder. Suddenly he realizes it is past four and returns, sees the editor who says he will be in touch. The piece has not been rejected. 'My hopes are fired up again, nothing was lost yet—on the contrary, I could still win everything, for that matter. And my brain began to fantasize about a great council in heaven where it had just been decided that I should win, win capitally, ten kroner for a story . . . (Hamsun, p. 35). He walks to the harbour and ponders. It is nine. He falls asleep, awakes. He walks some more. It is ten when he finally reaches the Bogstad Woods and so ends the second day.

When the third day begins there is no sun when he awakes at about three in the afternoon. He continues to walk and as he walks, as he ponders his condition, he says 'All in all, it was simply absurd to live like this. Holy Christ, what had I done to deserve this special persecution anyway! I simply couldn't understand' (Hamsun, p. 39). The rest of the day is spent in idle wandering moving from one venue to another, thinking the same, yet different, thoughts. At seven he goes to the Oplandske Café waiting for someone from whom he can borrow money. At eight the person arrives, but he has nothing to lend. 'Oh God, I'm so miserable! Oh God, I'm so miserable' (Hamsun, p. 46) and he continues walking again. He finally returns to his room, to the place he'd never return to and discovers a letter:

> A stream of light seems to surge through my breast, and I hear myself giving a little cry, a meaningless sound of joy: the letter was from the editor, my story was accepted, it had gone directly to the composing room! A few minor changes . . . corrected a few slips of the pen . . . promising work . . . to be printed tomorrow . . . ten kroner. Laughing and crying, I made a running start and raced down the street, stopped to slap my thighs and flung a solemn oath into space for no particular reason. And time passed.
>
> (Hamsun, p. 48)

At the conjunction of depression and wandering, peripeteia appears: the ten kroner. By the end of Part I, the protagonist has been on a perpipatetic journey that has taken him at least one time to the following places: Our Saviour's Church, Grænsen Street, Palace Park, Palace Hill, Pascha's Bookstore, Pilestrædet Lane, Cisler's Music store, University Street, St. Olaf Place, Karl Johan Street, the Students' Promenade, Stortorvet Square, Aker Street, Ullevaal Road, St. Hanshaugen, Kirke Street, Haegdenhaugen district, Majorstuen, Bogstad Woods, Jærnbanetorvet Square, the Steam Kitchen, Grønlandsleret Street, Møller Street, Christ's Cemetery, Oplandske Café, Torv Street, the Arcades. But it has also taken him on a peripatetic journey as well since his situation has been changed by virtue of selling an article. Hence this is how the protagonist survives: the peripatetic wanderer dependent on the peripeteic investment of others.

As part two begins, a fortnight has passed and the narrator is back in the cemetery again, before leaving for Jærnbane Pier. It is ten at night, he is disconsolate and he is broke again, but what is of interest here is the relationship between his hunger and his art. As he attempts to 'kill time' at the pier he is also in the process of creating fiction. 'I sat there with tears in my eyes gasping for breath, quite beside myself with feverish merriment. I began to talk aloud, told myself the story of the cornet, aped the poor policeman's movements, peeped into the hollow of my hand and repeated over and over to myself: He coughed when he threw it away! He coughed when he threw it away! I added new words, with titillating supplements, changed the whole sentence and made it more pointed' (Hamsun, p. 53). In this feverish excitement of the 'revisionary' process, the protagonist segue-ways into the relationship between ships and voyages before the transition into the discourse on Ylajali, the fictional name of a woman he meets on the street. But the poetics of the mental journey take him via the 'silent monsters' and their 'black hulls', resting in the harbour, across the sea to Ylajali's castle in which he writes in detail how both she and the space appear as he employs such figurative language as: a sparkling hall (light); amethyst walls (blue); a throne of yellow roses (light); twenty summers (light); every white night (light); bright orchards (light); brilliant emerald hall (sparkling green); sun shines (light); choral music (harmony); waves of fragrance (sweetness); wild beauty of enchantment; red hall of rubies; and among all this light, they kiss. When he thinks of love, he thinks in images of brilliance, of light. She is a fictional redeemer. She and her love redeem him (at least at the fictive level) from the darkness associated with death. He comments on his blood perceiving a subtle greeting from her (Hamsun, p. 13) and feels 'the wild beauty of enchantment race through my blood' (Hamsun, p. 54). She becomes, in effect, the queen goddess of the world for the woman is life who saves him from the darkness. It is not coincidental that in describing his meeting with Ylajali in the castle, the protagonist begins in the yellow chamber, progresses through a corridor to another, green chamber, then through another corridor to the innermost recesses of the red chamber before he is thrust back into a 'hurricane of light' after which he returns to wakefulness 'mercilessly called back to life and my misery' (Hamsun, p. 54). But, of course, the image of the woman is not the woman and the fictive quality of woman is much greater than her presence in the flesh.

Whereas the Ylajali Episode is almost totally contingent on notions of light, the Tangen Episode is almost totally contingent on darkness. The Tangen Episode (so called because the protagonist when offered by the police a place to spend the night because of his 'homelessness' uses the pseudonym, Andreas Tangen, journalist) works as a counterpoint to the Ylajali Episode. He thinks spending the night as an indigent in the warm confines of the police station is a good idea since it will afford him a place to rest. But what happens during the night is he becomes captive to his own fear and that is reflected in his language. After the lights are turned out he says:

> But I wasn't sleepy and couldn't fall asleep. I lay awhile looking into the darkness, a thick massive darkness, without end that I wasn't able to fathom. My thoughts couldn't grasp it. It struck me as excessively dark and I felt its presence as oppressive. I closed my eyes, began to sing in an undertone, and tossed back and forth in the bunk to distract myself, but it was no use. The darkness had taken possession of my thoughts and didn't leave me alone for a moment. What if myself were to be dissolved into darkness, made one with it? I sit up in bed and flail my arms.
>
> (Hamsun, p. 60)

'Darkness' of various intensity seems to be the operative word here as Tangen struggles against it. And in his battle against the darkness he suddenly chances upon a word—*Kuboaa*.

> The word stood out sharply against the darkness before me. I sit with open eyes, amazed at my find and laughing for joy. Then I start whispering: they might be spying on me, and I intended to keep my invention a secret.
>
> (Hamsun, p. 61)

He struggles to make some sense of the word.

> No, the word was really suited to mean something *spiritual*, a feeling, a state of mind—couldn't I understand that? And I try to jog my memory to come up with something spiritual. Then it seems to me someone is speaking, sticking his nose into my chat, and I answer angrily, What was that? Oh my, you'll get the prize for biggest idiot! Knitting yarn? Go to hell! Why should I be under an obligation to let it mean knitting yarn when I was particularly opposed to its meaning knitting yarn?
>
> (Hamsun, p. 61-2)

But then the darkness returns but with more intensity and he uses such phrases as 'brooding darkness', 'the same unfathomable black eternity', both of which lead him into thoughts of dying. 'This is what it's like to die, I said to myself, and now you're going to die!' (Hamsun, p. 63) until he spots a 'grayish square in the wall, a whitish tone, a hint of something—it was the daylight' (Hamsun, p. 63) and it is only then that he 'returns to his senses' and falls asleep from exhaustion. Not coincidentally, it is the manifestation of the word Kuboaa and its sundry meanings that rescues him from the darkness and sustains him until the first meagre morning light as it has been the word that has sustained him throughout the course of the novel when he has been on the brink of starvation.

The remainder of Part II continues in much the same way as it has up to Part II consisting of: his imprecations to God; his wanderings (especially to the harbour); his chats with himself; his acts of self-torture and persecution; his acknowledgement of the powers of darkness; his suffering from the ache of honour all of which lead eventually to Part III which opens with 'a week went by in joy and gladness' (Hamsun, p. 91). After which the narrator talks of two specific items: his writing and *The Nun,* which was ready to sail from Kristiania. The allusion to the ship and to sailing has already been established and essentially has laid the groundwork for the narrator's imminent departure which one reads at the conclusion of Part IV. But the major portion of the opening pages of Part III is devoted exclusively to his writing. 'I toiled at my work day after day, barely allowing myself time to gulp down my food before going on with my writing again' (Hamsun, p. 91). He finishes an article and takes it to the Editor and while he is there he looked about me in the small office: busts, lithographs, clippings, and an immense wastebasket that looked as though it could swallow a man whole. I felt sad at the sight of this huge maw, these dragon's jaws which were always open, always ready to receive fresh scrapped writings—fresh blasted hopes' (Hamsun, p. 92). Of course his article, on Correggio, is politely rejected by the editor with the statement, 'Everything we can use must be so popular . . . You know the sort of public we have. Couldn't you try to make it a bit simpler? Or else come up with something that people will understand better?' (Hamsun, p. 93), but he refuses to take an advance and decries his 'unlucky stars' (dis/aster) before he meets a young woman, Marie, and the narrative shifts to sexually explicit events, yet he is presumably impotent. 'Alas, I had no real bounce in me these days. Women had become almost like men to me. Want had dried me up. But I felt I was cutting a sorry figure vis-à-vis this strange tart and wanted to save face' (Hamsun, p. 98). He preaches to her under the pseudonym of Pastor such and such then sends her off in favour of his writing, of revising. Standing outside of his room, in the lamplight he tries to write, 'But the words wouldn't come. I read through the entire piece from the beginning, read each sentence aloud, but I just couldn't collect my thoughts for this crashing climax' (Hamsun, p. 99).

What is of significance here is the relationship the narrator has with writing and how the act of writing sustains him. From the Tangen Episode one recalls that it was the 'word' that kept the oppressive darkness from consuming him; in the Marie Episode, he dispatches the woman in favor of his writing. Clearly, there is a relationship between what the novel is about and the writing of the novel itself. What the novel is about is hunger, but it is also about the act and process of writing. Writing under the influence of hunger, writing and the writing process. There are several levels of writing at work. On one level it is the narrator talking about his own writing, but it is also Hamsun writing about the narrator writing as well. So we have the narrator writing about his trials as a writer under the influence of hunger and of Hamsun's writing of **Hunger** under the influence of hunger. Which brings up the experience of hunger and its psychology. The cumulative effects of hunger inevitably lead to emotional instability. There are protracted periods of depression; the inability to sustain mental or physical effort; the discouragement due to one's relative inability to cope with daily life; there is increased irritability; a lack of self-discipline and self-control; an increased sensitivity to noise; marked nervousness; and personal neglect. Hamsun himself writes in a letter dated 2 December 88:

> I cannot work—not well, not with the right touch. I am sitting here in a garret with the wind blowing through the walls. There is no stove, almost no light, only one small pane in the roof . . . The food situation has also been quite desperate; many times last summer it seemed all up with me. Edvard Brandes saved me several times; so I used what I got from Brandes to write a little for *Politiken,* but in the meantime the money has gone and my position is no different from what it was. In the end you really become quite wretched, quite faint. Then you can't write; and you just start crying when you can't get things to go
>
> (Naess & McFarlane, p. 71).

One finds that the presumed 'madness' experienced by the narrator is often the same as the presumed 'madness' of his creator. From the Tangen Episode one reads:

> I had passed over into the sheer madness of hunger; I was empty and without pain and my thoughts were running riot. I debate with myself in silence. With the oddest jumps in my line of thought, I try to ascertain the meaning of my "new word".
>
> (Hamsun, p. 61)

And from a letter dated 1888 one reads:

> I cannot get away from it. My book! my book! About these delicate nuances. I would want to sift through the remotest nuances of the mind—I would let them listen

to the mimosa's breathing—every word like brilliantly white wings—movements of the shining surface of language. My mind cries out in its longing to begin! I haven't time to wait—the devils of my work will not leave me in peace! Now is the fullness of time! Now my book should be out!

(Naess and McFarlane, p. 88)

Certainly, the relationship between narrator and creator is there in the language, in the structure of the language and in the passion of the language. Just as the language is there to help sustain the narrator in times of financial and physical crisis, the language is there for Hamsun to sustain him in the same dilemma. Women do not sustain him. The image of Ylajali he has in Part II is not the same as his eventual 'revelation' of her, which concludes in Part III with:

> She came quickly over to me and held out her hand. I looked at her full of distrust. Was she doing this freely, with a light heart? Or was she doing it just to get rid of me? She put her arm around my neck, tears in her eyes. I just stood and looked at her. She offered me her mouth but I couldn't believe her, it was bound to be a sacrifice on her part, a means of getting it over with.

(Hamsun, p. 143)

Certainly the realization of the woman is not the same as the fascination of the woman and the subject of one's desires cannot in any meaningful way sustain in the narrator the same way the fascination of the subject can. In other words, any realization of an event cannot be as redeeming as the fictionalizing of the event. The realization of the event is purely in the power of the manifested word and not in the manifestation of the event. That is the reason why the narrator constantly returns to his writing, to the manuscript at hand, to the words. And with the conclusion of the 'amorous affair' with Ylajali in both mind and matter, the narrator returns to his writing in Part IV.

As Part IV opens, winter has arrived. The narrator has been living in Vaterland district for several weeks attempting to avoid the landlady over the rent. Though he is out of money, his situation has improved somewhat and he continues to pursue his writing though he has reached a kind of 'writer's block' on a piece he started that was supposed to be 'an allegory abut a fire in a bookstore'. At that time there comes a confrontation with the landlady in which the following dialogue ensues:

> 'I'm working on an article, as I mentioned to you before,' I said, 'and as soon as it's finished you'll get your money. There's no need to worry.'
>
> 'But you won't ever finish that article, will you?'
>
> 'You think so? I may feel inspired to write tomorrow, or maybe even tonight; it's not all impossible that the inspiration will come sometime tonight, and then my article will be finished in a quarter of an hour, at the most. You see, it's not the same with *my work* (my emphasis) as with other people's; I can't just sit down and get so much done every day, I have to wait for the right moment. And nobody can tell the day or the hour when the spirit will come upon him. It must take its course.

(Hamsun, p. 150)

The admission is not convincing and not only does the landlady walk away, but later in the chapter she tells him it will be his last night there. But what is different about this part of the novel is that the narrator has made an admission that heretofore has not been admitted; namely, he is a writer. He establishes that it is his work and that admission focalizes the chapter in a significant way, a significant writerly way, since he now associates himself with his writing. The difficulties arise when the landlady and her tenants give the narrator a difficult time by not allowing him to 'write in peace'.

> 'While I think of it, I must tell you that I simply can't afford to let people have board and room on credit,' she said. 'I have told you this before, remember.'
>
> 'But please, it's only a matter of a couple of days, till my article gets finished,' I answered. 'Then I'll gladly give you an extra five-krone bill, yes, very gladly.'
>
> But she obviously had no faith in my article, I could see that.

(Hamsun, p. 156)

What one finds in this section of the fourth part is that the narrator does not wander. In previous sections, he has wandered about, often aimlessly, in search of something to quell his 'hunger'. But in this section his needs have been sated, at least for the short term, and he is able to devote his attention, albeit divided, to writing. Except for several excursions from his room, the narrator is constantly absorbed with two things: paying his rent and finishing the article which is eventually abandoned in favour of a drama titled "The Sign of the Cross" with a theme from the Middle Ages. It is with the play that the narrator deals with a number of aspects of the writing process and it is well to quote in full what he says:

> In particular, the central character was fully worked out in my mind—a gorgeous fanatical whore who had sinned in the temple, not out of weakness or lust, but from a hatred of heaven, had sinned at the very foot of the altar with the altar cloth under her head, simply from a voluptuous contempt of heaven.
>
> 'I became more an more obsessed by this character as the hours went by. She stood vividly alive before my eyes at last, exactly the way I wanted to portray her. Her body was to be misshapen and repulsive: tall, very skinny and rather dark, with long legs that showed through her skirts at every step she took. She would also have big, protruding ears. In short, she would not be easy on the eyes, barely tolerable to look at. What

interested me about her was her wonderful shamelessness, the desperate excess of pre-meditated sin that she had committed. I was actually too much taken up with her, my brain was downright swollen with this queer monstrosity of a human being. I worked for two whole hours at a stretch on my play.

When I had done about ten pages, or perhaps twelve, often with great difficulty, at times with long intervals during which I wrote to no avail and to tear up my sheets, I was tired, quite numb with cold and weariness, and I got up and went out into the street.

(Hamsun, p. 157)

The narrator has exercised his mind and his creative skill to the limit and only when he has finished does he leave his room and even then he still thinks about the work he has to finish. The focus of Part IV vacillates between the two conditions of revising the work-in-progress and the inability to work without interruption, the latter of which constantly impinges on the former. If it is not the landlady who interrupts him, then it is the noise and agitation of the other residents. Frustrated with the attempt, he leaves the house again and returns to the docks a venue which works on two levels: first, the docks are a kind of 'refrain' in the storyline since the narrator is constantly returning to the docks as if it will be his final salvation; and two, it offers him a place to continue his writing, albeit for a short period of time.

I came down to the docks. A big barque with a Russian flag was unloading coal; I read its name, *Copégoro,* on the ship's side . . . The sun, the light, the salty breath from the ocean, all this lively, bustling activity stiffened my backbone and set my heart throbbing. All at once it occurred to me that I might do a couple of scenes of my play while sitting here. I took my sheets of paper from my pocket.

I tried to shape up some line from the lips of the monk, lines that ought to swell with intolerance and power, but I didn't succeed. So I skipped the monk and tried to work out a speech, that which the judge addressed to the desecrator of the temple, and I wrote half a page of this speech, whereupon I stopped. My words just wouldn't evoke the right atmosphere. The bustling activity around me, the sea shanties, the noise of the capstans, and the incessant clanking of the railcar couplings agreed poorly with that thick, musty air of mediaevalism which was to envelop my play, like fog. I gathered up my papers and got up.

(Hamsun, p. 168)

It is not surprising that Hamsun has set up the narrator for his inevitable departure in this way. There is the relationship between the departure from Kristiania (the return) and the satiation of the narrator's hunger (his writing). The narrator has often come to the docks before, but the docks had a distinctly onerous and oneiric quality to them distinct from the rather exhuberant quality he experiences in Part IV. The reason for the change is apparent: he has found his work. Once he has found his work, the reason for staying in Kristiania is over. Just as Hamsun had to experience hunger to write about it, so too does his narrator need to experience hunger to write about it.

He returns to his room and, as in previous parts, a peripety awaits when 'A few steps outside the entrance the messenger catches up with me, says hello once more and stops me. He hands me a letter. Angry and reluctant, I tear it open—a ten-krone bill falls out of the envelope, but no letter, not a word' (Hamsun, p. 173). Saved once again, the narrator pays off his debt to his landlady and strikes off again knowing that he has no money to eat on. But the physical hunger is displaced as he once again turns his attention to his work:

It was probably around four by now, in a couple of hours I might get to see the theatre manager if my play had been finished. I take out the manuscript on the spot and try to put together the three or four last scenes, by hook or by crook. I think and sweat and read it through from the beginning but can't get anywhere. No nonsense, now! I say, no bullheadedness there! And so I work for dear life on my play, writing down everything that comes to mind just to finish quickly and be off. I tried to convince myself I was having another big moment, lying to my face and openly deceiving myself while scribbling away as though there was no need to look for the right words. That's good! That's a real find! I whispered every so often, just get it down! Eventually, however, my most recent lines of dialogue began to sound suspicious to me: they contrasted too sharply with the dialogue in the early scenes. Besides, there wasn't the slightest tinge of the Middle Ages about the monk's words. I break my pencil between my teeth, jump up, tear my manuscript to bits, every single sheet, toss my hat in the gutter and trample it. 'I'm lost,' I whisper to myself. 'Ladies and gentlemen, I'm lost!' I say nothing except these words as I stand there trampling my hat.

(Hamsun, p. 175-6)

The passage expresses the anguish which accompanies the revisionary process, but the narrator has achieved what he set out to achieve in the opening movements of the novel: the journey has taken him from a non-committed space to a committed one. Regardless of what he has done to the manuscript, he has finally entered the terrain of the writer and the experiences coterminous with it. It is not unusual, then, for his last wandering to be towards the pier where he asks the captain of the *Copégoro* if he can use a deck-hand. The captain says yes, yet another peripety, and the novel ends with 'Once out in the fjord I straightened up, wet with fever and fatigue, looked in toward the shore and said goodbye for now to the city, to Kristiania, where the windows shone so brightly in every home' (Hamsun, p. 182).

The discussion of the novel has revolved around the notions of peripatetics and peripety; however, there are some very interesting things about this co-mingling of

Aristotelian philosophizing, the manner of its presentation and the way in which we find the narrator wandering in philosophical, spiritual and topographic ways. In a sense, the whole notion of peripatus, even beginning with Aristotle, deals with 'quest' and quests, all quests, have a number of things in common all of which pertain to the notion of movement, of wandering: that is, the movements of separation, initiation, and return. These movements can be seen in **Hunger** as well as in other rites of passage on both spiritual and intellectual levels. Though there are certain places the narrator visits more frequently than others, he is on a journey, a peripatetic journey, and, like all homeless people, exists for the purpose of walking. Being ambulatory gives them some significance. They have a purpose for being since they are walking to somewhere, purposefully. Their days are measured by their walking and in that walking there is some substance to their lives. Like Aristotle, 'Tangen,' constantly philosophizes while he walks, while he sits, while he wanders. His thoughts are truly philosophical thoughts, thoughts that often escape the boundaries of logical, reasonable thoughts, but are none the less philosophical. It is only when he rests and writes that he can synthesize what he has been thinking about. Though Hamsun declines to acknowledge the work is 'a novel', it is, arguably, one of his best works since it deals forthrightly with the demonic nature of writing, the writing process, the 'hunger' of writing and the anguish of writing under duress.

The peripatetic and peripeteic nature of the narrator's quest can best be seen in relation to the routes taken and the reward given for such. By the beginning of Part III one sees how Hamsun has 'intentionally' fashioned the narrative as being 'not a novel'. Part I deals primarily with the narrator's wanderings ending with the peripety of ten kroner; Part II continues, after a two-week respite, with the peripatetic hero essentially repeating the same yet different experiences he had in Part I with the peripety of five kroner; Part III begins in an iterative manner with 'a week went by in joy and gladness' (Hamsun, p. 91) and continues in the fashion established in Parts I and II (i.e. wandering, philosophizing, wandering, writing, wandering) the main difference being he spends considerably more time writing. 'I toiled . . . left' (pp. 91-2). In Part IV the narrator continues his writing as his situation has improved. The financial problems with his landlady are alleviated with a peripety of ten kroner which allows him to settle up with the landlady, end the journey and begin another. Even when he has given up his ten kroner to his landlady, he is saved again at the end of the novel by the captain, thus closing the quest. From the initial separation in which we find the narrator, through the initiation which constitutes the novel itself, to his final departure and return, the narrator has experienced the suffering of growth through the prevailing notions of peripatetics and peripety finally resulting in the recognition that his life's work is his words and the facilitation of them.

ADDENDUM

The addendum gives a detailed account of the narrator's peripatetic movements and the accompanying peripety.

PART I

As the quest commences, the 'separation' has already been established as the journey begins in a place other than his home. The entire novel deals with his 'initiation' into the role of 'writer'.

PERIPATETIC JOURNEY—DAY ONE

Point of Departure: His attic room
    Wanders a nameless street
    Arcades
    Wanders nameless streets
    Grænsen Street
    Palace Park
    Pilestrædet Lane
    Palace Hill
    Pascha's Bookstore
    Cisler's Music Store
    University Street
    St Olaf Place
    Side street
    Karl Johan Street
    University
    Palace Hill
    The Students' Promenade
    Wanders down nameless streets
    Returns to his room

PERIPATETIC JOURNEY—DAY TWO

Point of Departure: His attic room
    Wanders nameless streets
    Semb's
    Stortorvet Square
    Newspaper office
    Grænsen Street
    Karl Johan Street
    Our Saviour's Cemetery near the chapel
    Aker Street
    Ullevaal Road
    St. Hanshaugen
    Sagene section
    Empty lots and cultivated fields
    Wanders a nameless country road
    St. Hanshaugen
    Newspaper office
    Semb's
    Kirke Street
    Ingebret's
    Nameless theatre
    Lodge Building
    Water and the Fortress
    Haegdehaugen section (in memory)
    Karl Johan Street

Storting
Tordenskjold Street
Wanders nameless streets
University clock
Haegdehaugen area
Majorstuen
Bogstad Woods
Falls asleep there

PERIPATETIC JOURNEY—DAY THREE

Point of Departure: Bogstad Woods
The Steam Kitchen
Jærnbanetorvet Square
Grønlandsleret Street
Møller Street
Stortorvet Square
Newspaper office
The Arcades
Christ's Cemetery
Oplandske Café
Torv Street
Between the church and the Arcades
Attic room

PERIPETY: TEN KRONER

END PART I

PART II

PERIPATETIC JOURNEY:—TWO WEEKS LATER

Point of Departure: Cemetery
Wanders aimlessly
City Jail
Harbour
Jærnbane Pier
Nameless streets
City Jail

PERIPATETIC JOURNEY—NEXT DAY

Point of Departure: City Jail
Youngstorvet Square
Home
Newspaper office
Homansbyen section
Toldbod Street
Bernt Anker Street No. 10
Wanders nameless streets
Jærnbanetorvet Square/Clock at Our Saviour's
Jaernbane Pier
Newspaper office
Pilestaedet Lane
Fire station
Pascha's Bookstore
Pastor Levion's
Stortorvet Square
Home
Stener Street
Wanders nameless streets
Church of Our Saviour
Wanders nameless streets
Bakery
Ropewalk

Cisler's Music Store
Wanders nameless streets
Yarn Store
Wanders nameless streets
Church of Our Saviour
Wanders nameless streets
Pawnbroker

PERIPETY: TEN KRONER

END PART II

PART III

PERIPATETIC JOURNEY—A WEEK WENT BY

Point of Departure: His room
Newspaper office
Several evenings pass
Room
Wanders nameless streets
Oplandske Café
Palace
Karl Johan Street
Grand Hotel
Blomquist's entranceway
Storting Place
Returns home
Wanders nameless streets
Dry goods store

PERIPETY: FIVE KRONER

Storgaten Way; eats
Wanders nameless streets; vomits
Café
Home
Walks woman home
St. Olaf Place

PERIPATETIC JOURNEY—NEXT DAY

POINT OF DEPARTURE: HIS ROOM
Clothing stalls
Stortorvet Square
Elephant Pharmacy
Grænsen Street
Storting Place
37 Ullevaal Road
11 Tomte Street
Vognmand Street
Grønland section
Wanders nameless streets
His room

PERIPATETIC JOURNEY—NEXT DAY

POINT OF DEPARTURE: HIS ROOM
Torv Street
Arcades
Smiths' Passage
Youngsbakken Lane
Jaernbane Pier
Jaernbanetorvet Square
Havn Street

PERIPETY: TEN KRONER
Wanders nameless streets
11 Tomte Street

PERIPATETIC JOURNEY—TUESDAY

POINT OF DEPARTURE: TOMTE STREET
2 St Olaf Place
Karl Johan Street
University Street
2 St Olaf Place

END PART III

PART IV

PERIPATETIC JOURNEY—MANY WEEKS LATER

POINT OF DEPARTURE: ROOM IN VATERLAN
Stays in his room

PERIPATETIC JOURNEY—A FEW DAYS WENT BY

POINT OF DEPARTURE: HIS ROOM
Drammen Road
Karl Johan Street near Jaernbanetorvet Square
His room

PERIPATETIC JOURNEY—NEXT DAY

POINT OF DEPARTURE: HIS ROOM
Kirke Street
Fortress
Docks
His room
Peripety: Ten kroner
Tomte St and Jaernbanetorvet Square
Wanders nameless streets
Royal Hotel
Arcades
Our Saviour's
Vognmand Street
Jaernbane Pier

PERIPETY: JOB ABOARD THE COPÉGORO

When one breaks down the parts into their individual journeys, one finds the following:
Part I 56 areas mentioned plus nameless streets
Part II 27 areas mentioned plus nameless streets
Part III 39 areas mentioned plus nameless streets
Part IV 13 areas mentioned plus nameless streets

One might think that as the novel progresses, the narrator would minimize his wanderings and, in fact, the numbers do decrease from Part I to Part II, increase slightly in Part III and dramatically decrease by Part IV. By Part IV, the narrator has, in a way, become initiated into that 'writer's space' which he has longed to find throughout the novel. By virtue of finding that space, the need to wander diminishes. Once he has found his 'calling', the narrator can then embark on another journey, hence the decrease in interest in the surroundings and the eventual departure from Kristiania. But be that as it may, the narrator rarely wanders far from the centre of the city. The included map (*circa* 1909) of Kristiania, indicates that the narrator's wanderings were well within a defined area of circumscription. The geometric space within which the narrator chooses to isolate himself, is not unlike the geometric space of the novel. Just as the narrator wanders from place to place within the city, apparently with no other motive but to wander, the narrative displaces a linear kind of narrative in favour of a kind of narrative that, too, wanders.

Works Cited

Chadbourne, Richard M., *Ernest Renan*. New York: Twayne Publishers, 1968.

Ferguson, Robert, *Enigma: The Life of Knut Hamsun*. New York: Farrar, Straus & Giroux, 1987.

Grayeff, Felix, *Aristotle and His School*. London: Gerald Duckworth & Company, 1974.

Hamsun, Knut, *Hunger*. Trans. Sverre Lyngstad. Edinburgh: Rebel, Canongate Books Ltd, 1996.

Kant, Immanuel, *The One Possible Basis for a Demonstration of the Existence of God*. Trans. and Introduction by Gordon Treash. New York: Abaris Books, 1979.

Kant, Immanuel, *The Essential Kant*. Introduction by Arnulf Zweig (ed.). New York: New American Library, 1970.

Naess, Harald and McFarlane, James, *Knut Hamsun: Selected Letters, Volume I, 1879-98*. Norwich: Norvik Press, 1990.

FURTHER READING

Criticism

Blythe, Ronald. "Starving Differently." *Listener* 91, no. 2344 (28 February 1974): 281.
   Brief, positive review of Robert Bly's translation of *Hunger*.

Cahill, Edgar H. "Purity in the Sixth Printing." *Nation* 113, no. 2928 (1921): 181.
   Reviews the sixth printing of *Hunger* by Alfred A. Knopf, faulting the publisher for censoring the work.

Gustafson, Alrik. "*Man and the Soil*, Knut Hamsun." In *Six Scandinavian Novelists: Lie, Jacobsen, Heidenstam, Selma Lagerlöf, Hamsun, Sigrid Undset*, pp. 226-85. Princeton, N.J.: Princeton University Press, 1940.

Detailed analysis of *Man and the Soil,* including information on Hamsun's personal life and literary career.

Keates, Jonathan. "Through Starving Eyes." *Times Literary Supplement*, no. 3760 (29 March 1974): 313.
Brief review of Robert Bly's translation of *Hunger.*

McFarlane, James Walter. "Knut Hamsun." In *Ibsen and the Temper of Norwegian Literature*, pp. 114-57. London: Oxford University Press, 1960.
Critical evaluation of Hamsun's major works, including *Hunger.*

Næss, Harald. "Vagabond." In *Knut Hamsun*, pp. 128-57. Boston, Mass.: Twayne, 1984.
Critical evaluation of Hamsun's later works, while also providing an overview of the author's final years.

Additional information on Hamsun's life and career is published in the following sources by the Gale Group: *Encyclopedia of World Literature in the 20th Century,* **Ed. 3;** *European Writers,* **Vol. 8;** *Literature Resource Center*; *Reference Guide to World Literature,* **Eds. 2, 3; and** *Twentieth-Century Literary Criticism,* **Vols. 2, 14, 49.**

Joseph Heller
1923-1999

American novelist, playwright, and autobiographer.

The following entry presents criticism of Heller's works from 1990 through 2000. For further information on his life and career, see *CLC*, Volumes 1, 3, 5, 8, 11, 36, and 63; for a discussion of his novel *Catch-22* (1961), see *TCLC*, Volume 131.

INTRODUCTION

Heller is remembered as a popular and respected writer whose first and best-known novel, *Catch-22* (1961), is considered a classic of the post-World War II era. Heller's tragicomic vision of modern life, found in all of his novels, focused on the erosion of humanistic values and the ways in which language obscures and confuses reality. In addition, Heller's use of anachronism reflected the disordered nature of contemporary existence. His protagonists are antiheroes who search for meaning in their lives and struggle to avoid being overwhelmed by such institutions as the military, big business, government, and religion.

BIOGRAPHICAL INFORMATION

Heller was born May 1, 1923, in Brooklyn, New York, to first-generation Russian-Jewish immigrants. His father, a bakery truck driver, died after a bungled operation when Heller was only five years old. Many critics believe that Heller developed the sardonic, wisecracking humor that marked his writing style while growing up in the Coney Island section of Brooklyn. After graduating from high school in 1941, he worked briefly in an insurance office, an experience he later drew upon for the novel *Something Happened* (1974). In 1942 Heller enlisted in the Army Air Corps. Two years later he was sent to Corsica, where he flew sixty combat missions as a wing bombardier, earning an Air Medal and a Presidential Unit Citation. Discharged from the military in 1945, Heller married Shirley Held and began his college education. He obtained a B.A. in English from New York University and an M.A. from Columbia University. He then attended Oxford University as a Fulbright Scholar for a year before becoming an English instructor at Pennsylvania State University. Two years later Heller began working as an advertising copywriter, securing positions at such magazines as *Time, Look,* and *McCall's* from 1952 to 1961. The office settings of these companies also yielded material for *Something Happened*. During this time Heller was writing short stories and scripts for film and television as well as working on *Catch-22*. Although his stories easily found publication, Heller considered them insubstantial and derivative of Ernest Hemingway's works. After the phenomenal success of *Catch-22*, Heller quit his job at *McCall's* and concentrated exclusively on writing fiction and plays. In December of 1981 he contracted Guillain-Barre syndrome, a rare type of polyneuritis that afflicts the peripheral nervous system. Heller chronicled his medical problems and difficult recovery in *No Laughing Matter* (1986) with Speed Vogel, a friend who helped him during his illness. He died of a heart attack in 1999.

MAJOR WORKS

Catch-22 concerns a World War II bombardier named Yossarian who believes his foolish, ambitious, mean-spirited commanding officers are more dangerous than the enemy. In order to avoid flying more missions, Yossarian retreats to a hospital with a mysterious liver complaint, sabotages his plane, and tries to get himself declared insane. Variously defined throughout the novel, the term "Catch-22" refers to the ways in which bureaucracies control the people who work for them. Many critics contend that while *Catch-22* is ostensibly a war novel, World War II and the Air Force base where most of the novel's action takes place function primarily as a microcosm that demonstrates the disintegration of language and human value in a bureaucratic state. *Catch-22* enjoyed enormous success during the Vietnam War, when many soldiers strongly identified with Yossarian's plight. Heller's second novel, *Something Happened*, centers on Bob Slocum, a middle-aged businessman who has a large, successful company but who feels emotionally empty. Narrating in a drab, spiritless tone, Slocum attempts to find the source of his malaise and his belief that modern American bourgeois life has lost meaning, by probing into his past and exploring his relationships with his wife, children, and coworkers. Although critics consider Slocum a generally unlikable character, he ultimately achieves sympathy because he has so thoroughly assimilated the values of his business that he has lost his own identity. *Good as Gold* (1979) marks Heller's first fictional use of his Jewish heritage and childhood experiences in Coney Island. The protagonist of this novel, Bruce Gold, is an unfulfilled college professor who is writing a book about "the Jewish experience," but he also harbors political ambitions. Offered a high government position after giving a positive review of a book written by the president, Gold accepts, leaves his wife and children, and finds himself immersed in a farcical bureaucracy in which officials speak in a confusing, contradictory language. In this novel Heller harshly satirized former Secretary of State Henry Kissinger as a Jew who has essentially forsaken his Jewishness. In so doing, the author draws an analogy between the themes of political lust for power and Jewish identity. Similarly, Gold's motives for entering politics are strictly self-aggrandizing, as he seeks financial, sexual, and social rewards. Throughout the novel, Heller alternates the narrative between scenes of Gold's large, garrulous Jewish family and the mostly gentile milieu of Washington, employing realism to depict the former and parody to portray the latter. Heller's next novel, *God Knows* (1984), is a retelling of the biblical story of King David, the psalmist of the Old Testament. A memoir in the form of a monologue by David, the text abounds with anachronistic speech, combining the Bible's lyricism with a Jewish-American dialect reminiscent of the comic routines of such humorists as Lenny Bruce, Mel Brooks, and Woody Allen. In an attempt to determine the origin of his despondency near the end of his life, David ruminates on the widespread loss of faith and sense of community, the uses of art, and the seeming absence of God. In *Picture This* (1988) Heller used Rembrandt's painting *Aristotle Contemplating the Bust of Homer* to draw parallels between ancient Greece, seventeenth-century Holland, and contemporary America. Moving backward and forward among these eras, this novel meditates on art, money, injustice, the folly of war, and the failures of democracy. Many critics questioned whether *Picture This* should be considered a novel, a work of history, or a political tract. *No Laughing Matter*, written with his friend Speed Vogel, is a work that can be loosely termed nonfiction concerning Heller's experiences suffering from Guillain-Barre syndrome. With Heller's chapters interspersed between Vogel's, the book resembles an often humorous and deadpan dialogue between friends who experience Heller's illness in very different ways. *Closing Time* (1994), considered a sequel to *Catch-22*, revisits characters from that novel, including some who appeared only peripherally or in discussion; the tone of *Closing Time*, however, unlike that of *Catch-22*, is uniformly absurdist rather than a mix of absurdism and realism. *Now and Then: From Coney Island to Here* (1998) is an autobiographical account of Heller's childhood and young adulthood in and around Coney Island. A more extended self-examination than any of the autobiographical passages in his novels, *Now and Then* serves to fill in the gaps and explain Heller's lifelong sardonic world view. At his death Heller left a finished novel, *Portrait of the Artist, as an Old Man* (2000), about a writer attempting to maintain his talents and abilities in the face of rapidly encroaching age and death.

CRITICAL RECEPTION

While Heller's place in twentieth-century letters is assured with *Catch-22*, he is also highly regarded for his other works, which present a comic vision of modern society with serious moral implications. A major theme throughout his writing is the conflict that occurs when individuals interact with such powerful institutions as corporations, the military, and the federal government. Over the course of his career, Heller's novels displayed increasing pessimism over the inability of individuals to reverse society's slide toward corruption and degeneration. Heller repeatedly rendered the chaos and absurdity of contemporary existence through disjointed chronology, anachronistic and oxymoronic language, and repetition of events while emphasizing the necessity of identifying and accepting responsibility social and personal evils and, as individuals, adopting beneficial behavioral changes. Some critics claim that Heller's later work pales in comparison with *Catch-22* and *Something Happened*, but others maintain that his canon viewed as a whole displays his continued evolution as a writer.

PRINCIPAL WORKS

Catch-22 (novel) 1961
We Bombed in New Haven (drama) 1967
Catch-22 (drama) 1971
Clevinger's Trial (drama) 1973
Something Happened (novel) 1974
Good as Gold (novel) 1979
God Knows (novel) 1984
No Laughing Matter (autobiography) 1986
Picture This (novel) 1988
Closing Time: A Novel (novel) 1994
Now and Then: From Coney Island to Here (autobiography) 1998
Portrait of the Artist, as an Old Man (novel) 2000

CRITICISM

Marshall Toman (essay date 1990)

SOURCE: Toman, Marshall. "The Political Satire in Joseph Heller's *Good as Gold*." *Studies in Contemporary Satire* 17 (1990): 6-14.

[*In the following essay, Toman examines Heller's satirical treatment of the American neoconservative political program in* Good as Gold.]

Stephen W. Potts says of Joseph Heller's ***Good as Gold*** that "this satire shoots very wide, as with birdshot, aiming broadly at politics as an institution rather than at particular practices of the near past or the present."[1] The criticism itself shoots wide, for neoconservative thought as it developed in the United States through the 1960s and 70s is the specific target. In *The Neoconservatives,* Peter Steinfels identifies important principles, at least four of which are objects of Heller's satire: (1) "*neoconservatives refuse to put responsibility for the present situation heavily on the shoulders of governing elites*"; (2) they view government as "*the victim of 'overload.' Attempting too much, it has naturally failed*"; (3) they tend to feel that, since incessant, impossible demands upon the government doom it to repeated failure and consequent loss of authority, "*the authority of government should be shielded by dispersing responsibility for this failure as much as possible*"; and (4) they espouse "*the theory of unanticipated consequences.*"[2]

Let us briefly examine each of the four points with respect to the novel. While Heller may agree with the neoconservatives that there is a failure of authority, he does not exonerate the ruling elite. In ***Good as Gold,*** the president naps and writes his book. The members of the Committee on Education do not even attempt to accomplish anything. Though Gold's morality leaves much to be desired, that of Kissinger, Andrea (in her capacity as government official), and Ralph leave more. In a further elaboration of this first principle, neoconservatives believe the loss of faith in institutional structures "*is primarily a cultural crisis, a matter of values, morals, and manners*" (p. 55) and not something spawned by the behavior of men in power. But, as can be shown, the Gold family, a constituent part of the culture neoconservatives blame, has a firmer grasp upon socially beneficial values and morals, if not manners, than any of the novel's governing elite.

Secondly, in Heller's view, rather than being burdened by overload, the government is remiss in accepting too few responsibilities, as is suggested by the satirical presentation of a state legislator's attempt to withdraw aid from education.[3]

On the third point, Steinfels quotes Daniel Moynihan: "Diffusing responsibility for social outcomes tends to retard the rise of social distrust when the promised or presumed outcome does not occur" (p. 64). Heller does not enter into the specifics of the neoconservative program here. (One technique neoconservatives suggested was the interposition of a market system between government policy and its actual implementation so the market could absorb the blame in the event of failure and add credence to government excuses.) But he does capture the essence of the evasive maneuvers in Ralph's tactics. Evasions on the part of government officials are not new, yet the public discussion of effective techniques (Moynihan's comment appears in his 1973 volume, *The Politics of a Guaranteed Income*) tends to legitimize as a worthwhile government attitude what ordinarily would be viewed as irresponsibility.

The notion alluded to under point four was argued forcefully by Irving Kristol in the introduction to *On the Democratic Idea in America*: "The unanticipated consequences of social action are always more important, and usually less agreeable, than the intended consequences" (quoted in Steinfels, p. 99). The position provides neoconservatives with a theoretical basis from which they respond to opponents' humanistic demands. In effect, the argument runs as follows: "In the first place, things won't work out the way that you liberal reformers envision them so, since you may even realize this, you had better inquire into your own motives [understood: "which are either naively impractical or self-interested"]; and, secondly, since the results of government intervention are counterintuitive, you had best leave matters to experts." When Bruce Gold, abandoning his former liberal beliefs and adopting neoconservative opinions for the power their espousal will bring him, writes "Nothing Succeeds as Planned," he contributes precisely the intellectual support that the conservative government needs to justify its lack of social involvement.[4]

Heller not only disparages the neoconservative program but also attacks the tendentious motives of the neoconservatives themselves, particularly, it would seem, those of Irving Kristol. Heller's ever-inspiring, Presidential-dinner-remembering Lieberman resembles Kristol, whose efforts as a publicist cause Steinfels to dub him the neoconservative "standard-bearer." "If Horatio Alger had written about intellectuals instead of newsboys, Kristol could have been one of his heroes. *Irving, the Editor; or From Alcove No. 1 to the President's Dinner Table*" (Steinfels, p. 81).[5] Like Kristol, and like many of the New York Jewish neoconservatives (see Steinfels, pp. 25-30), Lieberman began his political life with socialist ideas. Lieberman is implicated in a scandal involving government support for the supposedly independent journal he edits, and the background of a similar episode from Kristol's career provides a prototype. Kristol had been the founding editor of *Encounter*, one of the journals sponsored by the Paris-based Congress for Cultural Freedom and dedicated to counteracting "'mendacious Communist propaganda'" (Steinfels, p. 29). In the mid-60s, a scandal erupted when it was discovered that the Congress, and in turn the journals, was supported by the CIA. In Heller's novel, Lieberman defends his acceptance of dubious funding by claiming that he changed his political position before governmental backing. (Steinfels, too, acknowledges that this order of events may have been the case with formerly Marxist neoconservatives.) But Heller's point, demonstrated by Lieberman's intellectual drooling over his past closeness to the centers of power (symbolized in his oft remembered dinner at the White House), is that having once fed at the public trough, it is difficult to assume again the diet necessitated by independence. And there are further similarities between Lieberman and the neoconservative "standard-bearer." Kristol, like Lieberman, is capable of changing his mind (against Nixon in 1968, for him in 1972) and, like Lieberman, was rewarded for his support with a White House dinner invitation. In 1972, a report circulated that Kristol was being considered for an appointment as "'a broad gauge advisor on domestic policy'" (quoted in Steinfels, p. 89), a position that Lieberman hopes for. Lieberman is in favor of "repressive police actions when necessary" (p. 44). During the campus unrest of the 60s Kristol advocated restructuring universities along principles of riot control: "It is clearly foolish to assemble huge and potentially riotous mobs in one place . . . We should aim at the 'scatteration' of the student population, so as to decrease their capacity to cause significant trouble" (quoted in Steinfels, pp. 88-89). Especially interesting from a literary standpoint are the excesses of thought and language shared by Kristol and the fictional Lieberman. Steinfels describes a sampling of Kristol's assertions as simplified versions of complexities, exaggerated, unqualified (p. 100); Gold and Pomoroy often deprecate Lieberman's ideas (especially pp. 162-64, 167-68). And Kristol's use of language can be comically inaccurate, as Steinfels' "*sic*" indicates: "The corporation is 'an utterly defenseless institution . . . literally [*sic*] up the creek without a paddle, alienated and friendless . . . the essence of flabbiness . . . picked on and bullied so easily'" (p. 95; Steinfels is quoting from *On the Democratic Idea*). Compare this use of "literally" with one of Lieberman's during a lunch with Gold and Pomoroy:

> "I know how flexible you can be," Pomoroy accused sardonically, and Lieberman colored. "I saw your name in the papers again at another one of your fucking fascist dinners. My imagination fails me," Pomoroy went on with as much wonder as reproof. "What goes through your mind when you sit there listening to those anti-Semitic speakers. What do you think of?"
>
> Lieberman lowered his eyes. "I do my multiplication tables," he answered shyly.
>
> "Do you applaud?" asked Gold.
>
> "No," answered Lieberman. "I swear, I literally sit on my hands through the whole meal."
>
> "How do you eat?" inquired Gold.
>
> "I was speaking figuratively."
>
> "Then why did you say literally?" said Pomoroy.
>
> "Don't words mean anything to you?" said Gold.
>
> [p. 164]

Another prominent neoconservative who helped to shape the cultural style Heller attacks is New York Senator Daniel Patrick Moynihan, whom Steinfels characterizes as the "professorial politician."[6] His glibness has similarities to Gold's. "The careful reader of Moynihan's published essays is always stumbling across instances of deft evasion, retouched shading, and personal promotion that clash disturbingly with the image of the man of knowledge in politics he has projected for himself and others" (Steinfels, pp. 115-16). This description of Moynihan's writing recalls Gold's ability to slant the same speech toward either a liberal or a conservative audience (p. 43).

The Neoconservatives, brought out in the same year and by the same publisher as Heller's novel, reads almost like *A Reader's Guide to the Satire in* **Good as Gold.** Steinfels' book could not have influenced Heller, but both authors drew on similar sources. Heller had a file of clippings from the *New York Times* relating to the neoconservatives.[7] Heller has said that his political ideas are developed through informal discussion and newspaper reading (not through doctrinaire political essays),[8] and he had ample opportunity to follow the careers of prominent neoconservatives in the *Times.* Kristol published his "Memoirs of a Trotskyist" in the January 23, 1977, issue of the *New York Times Magazine.* His article, "Basic Principles of Riot Control," also originally appeared there on December 8, 1968. Moynihan was profiled five times in this same magazine between 1965 and the publication of **Good as Gold** (and appeared on *Time*'s cover twice). Kristol's public support for Nixon and his dinners at the White House were prominently reported in the daily *Times* (29 Jan. 1972; 5 Sept. 1973). Another of Heller's and Steinfels' common sources was *Commentary,* where, for example, a symposium, "What Is a Liberal—Who Is a Conservative?" was published in September of 1976. Kristol's "Why I am for Humphrey" appeared in the *New Republic,* 8 June 1968. And Heller could easily reach back into his political memory to events such as the scandal involving CIA financing of journals like *Encounter* (reported in the *Times* in 1966 and confirmed by an ex-CIA agent in *The Saturday Evening Post,* 20 May 1967).

Two examples can serve to emphasize the way in which Steinfels' careful discussion helps clarify the satire in **Good as Gold.** The first involves Steinfels' analysis of a Moynihan rationalization, similar to some of Gold's and to some that Ralph offers to Gold. When Moynihan, a Democrat, joined the Nixon Administration, he countered public surprise by the following statement:

> When the only President we have asks me to come work for him, I am pretty much disposed, on the terms he asked it, to do anything he asks. . . . I was doing what any person ought to do. You don't decline to serve the President of the United States in an advisory capacity, under almost any circumstances—that is, if you've got the internal fortitude to advise him as you really see it. On what grounds would you say, "No, I will not advise the President"?
>
> [quoted in Steinfels, p. 131]

Until Gold realizes that achieving his aspirations will not be worth the personal cost and does turn down a presidential appointment, Moynihan's statement represents arguments that Gold has been advancing to himself. Steinfels almost-New-Critical analysis of Moynihan's statement allows us to understand Gold's justifications as only rationalizations.

> The question is put as though, barring the case of Nazism, there is no reply. Yet Moynihan must know that the answer is not at all obscure, though it might require some distinctions in that easy glide from "advise" (the occasional trip to Washington, the drafting of a position paper) to "work for" (full-time identification with the Administration) to "do anything he asks" (John Dean? or merely promising not to resign over disagreements). If one estimates that an Administration for whatever reason, is unlikely to enact the policies one favors, and is in fact apt to strengthen the policies one abhors, then one lends one's talents and energies to the opposition, one retains the privilege of criticizing freely, and one builds the foundation for the election of a different Administration more likely to enact the desired measures.
>
> [p. 131]

The politics of Ralph Newsome and the president are not what Gold's have been, yet Gold's rationalizations can seem as convincing as Moynihan's. Steinfels' criticism gives us a firmer perspective on Gold's reasoning.[9]

A second example can be pointed to in Steinfels' criticism of Kristol's "law." Steinfels argues from the authority of the Ford Foundation that the theory of unanticipated consequences is bunk. The Foundation proceedings were reported in a special issue of *The Public Interest* (Winter 1974) for which conference directors Eli Ginzberg and Robert M. Solow served as guest editors. They reproduce the following conclusion.

> There are sometimes unintended and unwanted side effects; and some public programs simply don't work. But there is nothing in the history of the 1960's to suggest that it is a law of nature that social legislation cannot deal effectively with social problems.
>
> [quoted in Steinfels, p. 224]

The dismissal places Gold's "Nothing Succeeds As Planned" (Heller's parody of the theory) into perspective.

Both Steinfels' and Heller's critiques are self-contained, but while the analysis supports the fiction, the fiction reciprocally illumines the analysis. Steinfels notes the opportunism and self-promotion of neoconservatives. Such attributes are difficult to demonstrate though because they involve personal motives for which there is ordinarily only circumstantial evidence. In addition, while such basically ad hominem arguments may be effective rhetorically they do not promote the tone of objective analysis that Steinfels cultivates. Heller's novel does perform a convincing job of exposing the presumed self-interest of neoconservatives.[10]

Notes

1. *From Here to Absurdity: The Moral Battlefields of Joseph Heller* (San Bernadino: Borgo Press, 1982), p. 58.

2. *The Neoconservatives: The Men Who are Changing America's Politics* (New York: Simon and Schuster, 1979), pp. 55, 58, 64, 65. I am grateful to Christopher P. Wilson for directing my attention to sources that have broadened my understanding of *Good as Gold*'s satire.

3. *Good as Gold* (New York: Pocket Books, 1980), p. 154. All further page references are to this edition.

4. See two passages from *Good as Gold*: "'God, Bruce,' Ralph began, 'I can't tell you how you're boggling our minds. If nothing succeeds as planned and you really present such a strong argument—then the President has just the excuse he needs for not doing anything'" (p. 76); and "Ralph was in earnest. 'I'm told [the President] already has a blowup of your proverb "Nothing Succeeds as Planned" on a wall of his breakfast room right beside a quotation from Pliny. It's a daily reminder not to attempt to do too much'" (p. 121).

5. Steinfels explains that "Alcove No. 1 was the bit of 'turf' in the City College of New York cafeteria that tradition had assigned to the non-Communist socialists. The Communists and their friends exercised their territorial imperative over Alcove No. 2" (p. 81).

6. Moynihan is one of many neoconservatives who have held positions at prestigious universities. Gold is not drawn from any one in particular any more than Lieberman is a "portrait" of Kristol. To the extent that the characters have prototypes, their characterization is a composite of them. Both the public sphere and Heller's private acquaintance contributed to the development, and the book's dedication to "several gallant families and numerous unwitting friends whose help, conversations, and experiences play so large a part" indicates a variety of inspirations. Among the many who contributed to the characterization of Gold (including Heller himself, who like his protagonist has been a professor of English), Kristol, as well as Moynihan, is a possibility, at least for a minor detail. Gold aspires to an academic sinecure, an endowed chair in the Urban Studies Program (p. 144). By 1970, Irving Kristol was "Professor of Urban Values" at New York University (Steinfels, p. 88).

7. Kristol, for instance, appears in one such clipping:

> Office buildings rose as spectacles where there was no lack of office space, and organizations with Brobdingnagian names were sprouting like unmanageable vines and spreading like mold with sinecures and conferments for people of limited mentality and unconvincing motive. Gold knew several by heart from pieces he had clipped:
>
> Irving Kristol is Resident
> Scholar at the American
> Enterprise Institute for
> Public Policy Research. . . .
>
> [p. 355]

The newspaper quotations in *Good as Gold* are verbatim, according to Heller's statement to Charlie Reilly, "Talking with Joseph Heller," rpt. in James Nagel's *Critical Essays on Joseph Heller* (Boston: G.K. Hall, 1984), p. 180.

8. Dale Gold, "Portrait of a Man Reading" (*Washington Post Book World*, 20 July 1969), p. 2.

9. In his being willing to support those in power regardless of their party affiliation, Gold has turned his back to his previous beliefs, as an exchange with his family in which Gold must lie demonstrates:

> "Bruce," Esther found nerve enough to ask at the door, while the others waited with glummest concern, "if you go to Washington, you wouldn't ever do anything to make us ashamed, would you?"
>
> Gold was almost afraid to inquire. "Like what?"
>
> Here Esther's courage failed, and others took over.
>
> "Like ever vote Republican?"
>
> "Never," he answered.
>
> "Or help one get elected?"
>
> "Of course not!"
>
> "Not even if he was Jewish?"
>
> "Especially."
>
> "Thank God," said his stepmother.
>
> [pp. 118-19]

Gold is able to justify his actions to himself, though others see his motives clearly. A boyhood friend of Gold's comments,"'So you're going into politics in Washington and cash in big, huh?' . . . 'I look at it,' said Gold, 'as performing a useful service to society.' 'That's what I'm laughing about,' said Spotty Weinrock" (p. 199). And when the presidential summons does arrive, Ralph uses arguments like Moynihan's to persuade Gold:

> "You have to, Bruce. You can't say no to the President."
>
> "Why not?"
>
> "Because nobody does. You have to say yes when your President asks."
>
> "Who does?"
>
> "Everybody, Bruce. You can't say no when your President asks. . . . Your President needs you. He often says you're the only person in the country with whom he feels completely comfortable."
>
> [pp. 479, 482]

10. Satiric comments that are plausible in the novel include those by or about the following characters: (Lieberman) "'I would support a war every day in the week if I knew I could eat at the White House again'" (p. 59); (Ralph) "'In government, Bruce, experience doesn't count and knowledge isn't important. If there's one lesson of value to

be learned from the past, Bruce, it's to grab what you want when the chance comes to get it'" (p. 124); (Gold) "'Power. Raw power. Brute, illegal power. I'll misuse it to ruin [Conover] and make his life miserable. I'll tap his telephones. I'll have the FBI ask insinuating questions about him'" (p. 267); (and Harris Rosenblatt, Secretary of the Treasury, who reassures the business community and "'promises to hold down deficits.'") "'He doesn't actually hold them down, you understand, but merely promises to. He also looks after the financial interests of himself and his friends so they can continue to live on the level they're used to'" (p. 222).

John Clark Pratt (essay date 1991)

SOURCE: Pratt, John Clark. "Yossarian's Legacy: *Catch-22* and the Vietnam War." In *Fourteen Landing Zones: Approaches to Vietnam War Literature,* edited by Philip K. Jason, pp. 88-110. Iowa City: University of Iowa Press, 1991.

[*In the following essay, Pratt explores parallels between* Catch-22 *and the experience of fighting in the Vietnam War.*]

At the outset, I must confess to some unintentional skullduggery. When going to Vietnam in the summer of 1969, I took with me a copy of *Catch-22.* From what I knew then about the war, I suspected that reviewing the plight of Yossarian from time to time might provide some continued reassurance that my world at war would not really be any more insane than Joseph Heller's.

I could not know, of course, that the colonel seated next to me throughout that long, ominous flight would comment on my choice of fiction and provide me with some early material for my novel, *The Laotian Fragments.* In *Fragments,* Major Bill Blake also reads *Catch-22* on the flight over, and when the colonel asks about the book (obviously not having heard of it), Blake tells him only that it is "a novel about World War II." Returning for his second tour, the colonel observes, "That was a real war . . . not like this one" (9). Later, Blake signs many of his official memos "Love, Yossarian."

Naturally, those of us who knew *Catch-22* could not help but see some obvious parallels to Vietnam, and almost all of them involved the fact of conflicting realities that lie at the core of Heller's vision of the modern world. Vietnam was a "conflict" that was neither a war nor a Korean "police action." In Vietnam, many of us became involved in operations that we could not talk about, even to people who were also involved in often contiguous operations that they couldn't talk about either. We discovered that the war had been going on longer than even many of the senior commanders knew and that it was being fought in and by countries that professed neutrality and noninvolvement. What FNG (Fucking New Guy) who knew *Catch-22* could help but wonder, when visiting either the Saigon exchanges or the stalls in Cholon, where Milo Minderbinder might be? And who of us can ever forget the sense of incredible irony when we exited the aircraft that had brought us to Vietnam and heard the phrase that only Heller could have written, spoken perfunctorily by an obviously veteran stewardess: "Hope you enjoyed your flight. See you in a year."

General comparisons are one thing, but the unreal reality, the actuality of *Catch-22* provided specifics as well to all of us who knew the novel—so many, so often, and so incredibly true that the book should properly be seen as a paradigm for the Vietnam War itself. When looking at the "facts" as well as at the fiction written about the war, to ignore what Heller has written is to obfuscate, misunderstand, and more dangerously, I think, distort what the Vietnam experience really was.

Let us look first at the "fact," then at the fiction. In *Dispatches,* Michael Herr said it best: "You couldn't avoid the way in which things got mixed, the war itself with those parts of the war that were just like the movies, just like *The Quiet American* or *Catch-22* (a Nam standard because it said that in a war everybody thinks that everybody else is crazy) . . ." (210). It's Yossarian, of course, who tells the chaplain, "Everybody is crazy but us" (14), a feeling that I know was held by many of the pilots who flew north from Thailand (a country *not* at war) into the Red River Valley or against the Thanh Hoa bridge, taking the same routes at the same times day after day, experiencing ever-increasing flak from antiaircraft artillery and surface-to-air missile sites that had been off-limits for enough time to allow the North Vietnamese to make them operational. Still classified, for instance, are the details about a senior officer's being relieved of command because he authorized and planned an attack against SAM sites under construction, but just as the armed aircraft were readying for takeoff, the mission was canceled from Washington. In all this, one recalls Milo's having alerted the German antiaircraft artillery in order to "be fair to both sides" during the attack on the highway bridge at Orvieto (261).

There were the medals, too. In *Catch-22,* "men went mad and were rewarded with medals" (16), often for deeds they never did. So too in Vietnam, where a Bronze Star was practically assured, especially to Saigon desk soldiers who had typewriters, and many of the medals, even though deserved, were awarded for fictional heroics because the actual sites of the events were not officially admitted to be in the war zone. Even today, many heroes cannot reveal that the citations on their truly deserved awards are invented. Similarly, and more paradoxical, is the fact of the missing names from the Vietnam War Memorial, names of those Americans killed in action while in combat against the VC, North Vietnamese, or Pathet Lao before the "official" date of U.S. involvement in Vietnam. Any one of these men would have made a fitting tentmate for Yossarian, like "Mudd the unknown soldier who had never had a chance." As was Mudd, these men are "really unknown" (112) and should be recognized.

The parallels continue. Although few pilots were privy to the facts of the regular "Tuesday lunch" in Washington where all missions into North Vietnam were approved personally by the president, some of the fighter pilots' songs such as "Mañana" showed that someone, at least, understood:

> Before we fly a mission
> And everything's o.k.
> Mac[namara] has to get permission from
> Flight Leader LBJ.
>
> (Pratt, *Voices* 248)

One is reminded of Clevinger's quivering rationalization, "But it's not for us to determine what targets must be destroyed or who's to destroy them. . . . There are men entrusted with winning the war who are in a much better position than we are to decide what targets have to be bombed" (127). A major target in North Vietnam was, of course, the Thanh Hoa bridge, which was not destroyed until the last days of the war despite ingenious attempts such as Project "Carolina Moon" on May 30, 1966. A specially modified C-130 was to drop 5,000-pound "pancake" bombs about 8 feet in diameter. At night, at 400 feet and 150 knots, the C-130 delivered five bombs near the bridge, then returned to base despite heavy groundfire. The next day's reconnaissance revealed no sign of damage or exploded bombs. One wonders if Yossarian would have returned to the target that night, as another C-130 did "with only slight modification in its route of flight." This aircraft disappeared and was never heard from again (LaValle 52-55). Yossarian made his second bombing run over the bridge on the river Po, and when asked why, he replies, "We'd have had to go back there again. . . . And maybe there would have been more losses, with the bridge still left standing" (142).

Not only bridges but mountain passes too provide irony for both *Catch-22* and the Vietnam War. In *Catch-22*, an attempt is made to interdict a road in order to block two armored divisions coming down from Austria. The plan is to destroy a small mountain village that "will certainly tumble right down and pile up on the road." Dunbar objects: "What the hell difference will it make? . . . It will only take them a couple of days to clear it" (335). Colonel Korn refuses to listen. "We don't care about the roadblock," he says. "Colonel Cathcart wants to come out of this mission with a good, clean aerial photograph he won't be ashamed to send through channels" (337). The hundreds of air force and navy pilots who flew missions against Vietnam's Mu Gia or Ban Karai passes may see some real truth here.

There are many more episodes in *Catch-22* that seemed to prefigure the facts of aerial combat in Vietnam, not the least of which is the question of the number of missions, the basis of the concept of the phrase "Catch-22" itself. To document the various Vietnam War mission requirements for awards and decorations and for rotation home would require a book-length computer printout; it is enough to say that some missions counted, others did not, depending upon the dates they were flown, the country to which they were directed, and the Rules of Engagement at the time. I often heard pilots say "Catch-22" when these rules were changed, but thanks to their understanding of Heller's concept, most of them accepted with grace what they knew was craziness. As one F-4 pilot put it:

> Flew on Dave Connett's wing on his final mission. It was a spectacular display for his finale. The night was moonless and we were using napalm and CBU's on a storage area. The above mission turned out to be my final one also. I completed 102 in all but, because of a ruling halfway through the tour, some of the missions into Laos didn't count after 1 February 1966.
>
> (Pratt, *Voices* 239)

Other events of note are the sad prefiguring of fragging in the plot to kill Colonel Cathcart, and the unpublicized, but severe infighting among and within the Central Intelligence Agency, State Department, and Department of Defense as well as among the services, as can be seen in General Peckem's plan to grab control of all commands. There is also the frightening rationality of Ex-PFC Wintergreen when we first meet him in the novel. He has no objection to digging holes at Lowry field "as long as there was a war going on." His reason: "It's a matter of duty, . . . and we each have our own to perform. My duty is to keep digging these holes, and I've been doing such a good job of it that I've just been recommended for the Good Conduct Medal. Your duty is to screw around in cadet school and hope the war ends before you get out" (108-109). It is a recorded fact that candidates for admission to the service academies presented higher and higher test scores as the Vietnam War progressed, and that when the draft was rescinded in 1972, resignations of cadets suddenly increased. While teaching *Catch-22* during this period at the United States Air Force Academy, I heard many slightly embarrassed laughs from my draft-exempt students when I highlighted Wintergreen's credo. One cannot argue with reason—or with Ex-PFC Wintergreen, wherever he may be today.

It's quite apparent, then, that in both general and specific areas, *Catch-22* did indeed provide a paradigm for many aspects of the Vietnam War. And as those just starting in the military during the mid-1950s snidely called some commanders Captain Queeg, so did the names Colonel Cathcart and Major Major pass often from the lips of the Vietnam-era military men. *Catch-22* as novel had influenced our thinking, but Vietnam as *Catch-22* itself affected our immediate existence.

I believe, too, that knowing Heller's work, seeing such irony and paradox come alive, made many of us more able to cope with the unreal reality of Vietnam. Nothing but *Catch-22* could have prepared us, for instance, for the initially unreported firing of General John D. LaVelle, Commander of Seventh Air Force, Saigon. His testimony before Congress in June 1972 has dialogue that could have been written by Heller himself. Having authorized "protective reaction" (a Helleresque term) air strikes against a buildup of North Vietnamese missiles and equipment in an area near the Laos-North Vietnam border, LaVelle explained his actions. A questioner (Mr. Pike) asked:

> Were you concerned that the bomb damage report showed damage to trucks or a SAM transporter or to POL, rather than to something [the missiles themselves] that you were allowed to hit?

GENERAL LAVELLE:

> No, Sir.

MR. PIKE:

> Tell us why. You said they were missile-related equipment. Is that it?

GENERAL LAVELLE:

> Yes, sir.

MR. PIKE:

> Did you feel that under the rules of engagement, as you interpreted them, your right to attack missiles would include a missile on a transporter?

GENERAL LAVELLE:

> Yes, sir.

MR. PIKE:

> When you say these trucks were missile-related equipment, how were they missile-related equipment?

GENERAL LAVELLE:

> We had picked up, or identified by reconnaissance, missiles on transporters parked along-side the road, waiting for the bad weather, to come through the pass, to come into Laos. They were never alone. The missiles had associated equipment, generator, vans, fuel, or just equipment for the personnel. But we never found a missile on a transporter by itself. We found missiles and trucks with them. . . .

MR. PIKE:

> Would it have been permissible for you to have hit those targets between the 26th and the 31st of December?

GENERAL LAVELLE:

> 26th and 31st; yes, sir.

MR. PIKE:

> Would it have been permissible for you to have hit those targets on the 17th and 18th of February?

GENERAL LAVELLE:

> No, sir, because of their location.

> (Pratt, *Voices* 521-522)

These incidents, taken primarily from air force experiences, show the pervasive quality of Catch-22ness in Vietnam, but there are so many more examples. Perhaps some future article will portray the colonel, in charge of a classified research project in Saigon, who would stride like Cathcart up and down the aisle between two rows of diligent writers, screaming, "Do not say that an F-4 cannot hit a truck. Do not say . . ." I hope, too, that someone, sometime will find, declassify, and write the story about the discovery during the height of the bombing of a yacht being transported down the Ho Chi Minh trail as a gift from the Chinese government to the leader of Cambodia, Prince Sihanouk, or about the episode of the seeding of a wetting agent on the same trail complex to create continuous mud, leading one high official to comment that it was "better to make mud, not war." Unfortunately, the rains washed out the experiment. Or the time a pilot who was not supposed to be stationed in Vientiane, Laos, had an affair with the daughter of the North Vietnamese ambassador. There are so many of these stories, and they are all sadly and wonderfully ironic. So Catch-22.

Many fiction writers have, however, attempted to apply *Catch-22* to the Vietnam War by direct reference, analogy, echo, and in a few instances parody. In the vast literature of the war (more than four hundred novels, hundreds of poems, short stories, and plays), the existence of *Catch-22* appears to be a given, but some writers believe that Heller did not go far enough. In Charles Durden's *No Bugles, No Drums,* for example, PFC Jamie Hawkins begins to feel "like I was ODing on absurdity. . . . Things get so outa hand that nothin' makes sense. . . . Alice in Wonderland was gettin' to be timid shit next to this." He remembers "readin' a book called *Catch-22*" and believing that "this dude's gotta be crazy. He was. But he wasn't crazy enough" (207). Similarly, Ward Just, in *To What End,* reflects on "the similarity of the soldier and the war correspondent, the basic text for which comes from Joseph Heller's novel, *Catch-22*. On the one hand, no one wants to get ambushed or to be where bullets are fired in anger. On the other, if nothing happens there is no story. If the patrol does meet the enemy you are likely to be killed or wounded, or at the very least scared to death. Catch-23" (181).

Critic and veteran Philip Beidler (who first identified the above *Catch-22* references) believes that writers had difficulty portraying post-*Catch-22* Vietnam because they could not write "a *Catch-22* about Catch-22." "At best," Beidler says, "*Catch-22*, with its almost sublime spirit of absurd apocalypse, seemed to bear on the attempt to make literary sense of Vietnam only insofar as it suggested something like a set of mathematical upper limits" (11). Because Vietnam became "*Catch-22* come giddily real" (145), Beidler feels that those who wrote about the war as Heller had done for World War II produced works that were only "Catch-21 1/2 or 3/4 or 7/8" (63).

It is certainly true that Heller's chaplain had already seemed to set the Vietnam experience in concrete: "So many monstrous events were occurring that he was no longer positive which events *were* monstrous and which *were* really taking place" (287). But I think that Beidler's assessment needs emending. Many writers did try to equal Heller, and some, I think, succeeded, simply by writing about the war as they saw it. Of the nine major novels that would probably not have been written without *Catch-22* as a model, five are essentially realistic (with *Catch-22* situations, characters, and overtones), while only four use Pianosalike settings and characters that, in Heller's words, "could obviously not accommodate all of the actions described" (5). These four are the fanciful *Ears of the Jungle*, 1972, by Pierre Boule; *Gangland*, 1982, by David Winn; *Brandywine's War*, 1971, by Robert Vaughn and Monroe Lynch; and the remarkable novel *Bridge Fall Down*, 1985, by Nicholas Rinaldi. The other novels, listed in order of their internally dateable realism, are *The Land of a Million Elephants*, 1970, by Asa Baber (1960-1961); *Parthian Shot*, 1975, by Lloyd Little (1964); *Incident at Muc Wa*, 1967, by Daniel Ford (1964), *The Only War We've Got*, 1970, by Derek Maitland (1967); and *The Bamboo Bed*, 1969, by William Eastlake (1967-1968). Each of these novels moves so deftly from the real to the surreal and back again that a reader not versed in many of the facts of the Vietnam War does not know when he or she is reading fiction or when the events are real—an effect the writers intended. As a result, these books succeed differently than does *Catch-22* and become particularly representative of the real unreality of the Vietnam War.

In any of these nine novels, however, one needs only to meet the characters to recognize whose world—Joseph Heller's—they are entering. In Baber's *The Land of a Million Elephants,* for instance, a U.S. colonel spends most of his time in Chanda (Laos) on a roof watching the beautiful Wampoon, mistress to the king; Nadolsky, the Russian agent, gets excited by listening on his electronic device to his CIA counterpart make love; M/Sgt Campo keeps looking for the nonexistent PX; and Coakley, the effeminate State Department clerk, prances throughout the novel. There are also Indian, North Vietnamese, American, and Laotian characters who constantly protest each other's truce violations. Many of these characters, however, are thinly veiled satires of actual participants in the unbelievable events of 1960-1961 Laos, and if one knows the history, one will recognize the little Captain Kong Le playing himself.

Parthian Shot begins with Special Forces Team A-376 being notified that it has been shipped home two weeks earlier; thus it is no longer in Vietnam. The team contains a second lieutenant who can't be promoted, he suspects, because his voice is too high and a sergeant who starts Hoa Hoa Unlimited, Ltd., first to make VC flags, then to manufacture fake AK-47s. Hoa Hoa Unlimited, Ltd., later branches out into brassieres and blouses, sells stock, receives a Small Business Administration loan, and finally commissions a RAND Corporation study that advises them to cooperate with both the VC and the U.S. commands. Eventually, their enterprise becomes international in scope.

Similarly, *Incident at Muc Wa,* a novel that was billed as "The *Catch-22* of the War in Southeast Asia," introduces a general who has no unit patch on his shoulder but who chews everyone out for not wearing one, a Christian Scientist medic who juices vegetables and even field grass for his health, and a captain who will do anything to get a combat infantryman's badge. In this novel, the Americans shoot most of the Vietnamese they encounter, in part because the major has ordered them to report two enemy casualties for every one of their own, while in sector headquarters everyone keeps watching the "master mosquito-control chart."

Although called by the *Times Literary Supplement* "The *Catch-22* of the 1970's," Maitland's *The Only War We've Got* becomes Helleresque more from its selection of fact-based targets of satire than from the inventiveness of its author. Commanding General Windy asks his secretary to spy on his second-in-command, General Cretan, "to find out what he's plot . . . I mean thinking" (34), while General Cretan's secretary is doing the same thing to him. There are two U.S. ambassadors to Saigon, each of whom thinks he is in charge. One of them devises a plan to dress everyone in VC pajamas for security reasons and trumpets his intention to defoliate the entire country. Also appearing are an NVA unit that loves the Hershey bars left behind by Americans; a soldier named Leaping Prick Smith who, because of his few drops of Sioux blood, keeps cheering the outcome of Custer movie reruns; and the great "Happy Hour Shutdown" when no American aircraft are available for combat.

Of these realistically centered novels, Eastlake's *The Bamboo Bed* is probably the most like **Catch-22**. The title refers both to the underground love nest of the mysterious and beautiful Madame Dieudonné and to the helicopter in which Captain Knightbridge and the nurse keep setting altitude records for having sex. Captain Clancy goes into battle wearing a plumed helmet and sword, marching to the beat of his drummerboy. B-52 crews drink martinis on their way to a mission, while below, the hippies Bethany and Pike are on their "way to the front to give flowers to the troops" (73-74). There is also a black sergeant who wants to surrender all the white men in his company to the VC; and Captain Knightbridge's crew consists of men named Disraeli Pong, Lavender the Purple Negro, and Ozz, his copilot, who like his **Catch-22** namesake Orr, has a "secret dream." Only the location is different. Ozz wants "to fly to Katmandu and declare himself neutral" (132).

Although the fanciful **Catch-22** follow-on novels are patently unrealistic in setting as well as character, each shares a common subject: the use and impact of U.S. technology not only in the war but also (often by not too subtle association) on the future of the world as well. These novels are all darkly prophetic, and each is really a warning more about the future (as is **Catch-22** itself) than it is about the war in which it is supposedly set.

Pierre Boule's *Ears of the Jungle,* for instance, while probably the most simplistic, inaccurate, and juvenile of any of the novels, does offer an apocalyptic vision of technology defeating itself. Based loosely on Task Force Alpha, the electronic nerve center of the Air Force's Laotian bombing efforts, Boule's novel shows what can happen when a beautiful NVA spy manages to compromise the electronic targeting system by placing audiotapes beside truck-spotting sensors. Madame Ngha also manages to reprogram the center's computer to call in airstrikes on itself, but she manages to get herself blown up as well. In this novel, U.S. air raids kill enough water buffalo to feed the North Vietnamese, an American officer waits to destroy a hamlet until his tanks can have their carburetors adjusted to reduce air pollution, and Air Force pilots read detective stories while flying missions.

Much more incisive (although patently derivative) is Vaughn and Lynch's *Brandywine's War,* which is really **Catch-22** set in Vietnam and which perfectly exemplifies what Beidler has cited as the difficulty of writing **Catch-22** about Catch-22. CWO Brandywine, a helicopter pilot, generates insane memos and telephone calls that everyone believes. Characters include Sgt. Percival, NCOIC of Defecation Elimination, and the hippie "unsoldier" who is in Vietnam by mistake and has an "unfile" that he can't inspect. The "unsoldier" eventually expands his marijuana business into an international cartel, but can never be sent home because he's not officially assigned to Vietnam. There are also General Deegle, who is obsessed with his rashes and keeps sprinkling baby powder in his crotch, and Lt. Soverign, the chaplain misassigned as a helicopter pilot who, like Yossarian, runs away in the end. An indictment of practically everything about the Vietnam War, this novel lacks **Catch-22**'s overwhelming sense of humanity and merely stops, implying the endlessness of the war and the authors' conviction that nothing will change.

The last two novels to be noted here go far beyond the Vietnam War. They are to the war what the war was to **Catch-22**; in other words, they show that the absurdity and craziness seen in Vietnam have become a part of the present and, alarmingly, the future as well. Most of Winn's *Gangland* takes place in post-Vietnam War California, where the Women's Defense League patrols the streets with M-16s, the Fast-food Marxists are everywhere, and the lotzl's (young female medical students) give the men backrubs and, flaunting their sexuality, live chaste lives while eating only health food. As it conducted (rather imperfectly) the Vietnam War, so does the master computer ANIMA still control the present as it sends personal LED messages to Dunkle, the protagonist, on any available video screen. No one except Dunkle appreciates what the Vietnam experience, referred to again and again as "the greatest adventure of our generation," really means. In the Vietnam scenes, ANIMA is linked with the Weary Weasel box in the company compound, and because of this black box, the men are able to take pictures and "interpret" the meaning of the war's development. Unfortunately, power outages and faulty data predominate, so no one really knows anything, not even how Dunkle's friend has died. Two of the significant characters are Madame Verrukteswerke, who is in Vietnam writing a "series on the children of the Americans left in the military" (104), and the Green Man, "who looks like a disease-wasted gas station mechanic." Everyone knows, however, that he is really a colonel (99). By the end of the novel, Dunkle has admitted that "things are hopeless" and that any change will "probably be for the worse, so the best thing to do is mind your own business as best you can" (221).

Finally, it seems entirely appropriate that the ultimate **Catch-22** novel about the Vietnam War is actually, despite many reviewers' attributions, not about the Vietnam War at all—but it has to be, even if it isn't. *Bridge Fall Down,* author Rinaldi tells us carefully in phrases scattered throughout the novel, is *not* set in Africa, but it does take place somewhere near the equator in a tropical, Asiatic country where the "monkeys from the North" are trying, with the help of all Communist countries, to conquer the "monkeys from the South," assisted by the Americans. One character mentions that some time ago, "the French were here" (92), and the mad general who leads the patrol is about fifty and had served during the Korean War when he was twenty-seven years old. Nowhere is Vietnam ever mentioned—but the subject is really the Vietnam War made timeless, much like Joe Haldeman's use of Vietnam as paradigm in his futuristic novel *The Forever War*, published in 1974.

In *Bridge Fall Down*, a patrol that includes two women, one of whom is the group's sharpshooter, is on a mission to blow up a vital enemy bridge (one immediately thinks of Thanh Hoa). Their meals are delivered by air, cooked by the pilot-chef Sugarman who apologizes for not bringing caviar to supplement his gourmet offerings of steak, swordfish, or scallopini. Under continual but sporadic attack from friend and foe, the patrol is being constantly filmed by Meyerbeer, who many suspect is actually running the war from his rainbow-painted helicopter. More randomly than in *Incident at Muc Wa*, these American soldiers kill even the friendly "monkeys" indiscriminately, and every time they pass a village, the brutal Sugg rapes someone. Central to their mission is the "black box," a small computer carried by a man known only as Merlin, who uses it to communicate with headquarters, to navigate, to forecast the weather, to spot the enemy (but like the Weary Weasel box of *Gangland* this one doesn't always work), and to carry on a running chess game with a Russian master. When Merlin is killed, no one else knows how to use the box—so the patrol is forced to complete its mission on its own. During a journey that often resembles a mad *Odyssey* set in Wonderland, the patrol passes a symbolic tree covered with hanging skeletons, meets the Queen of Skulls, escapes from the Falling Down disease, is tracked by a UFO, and has a battle at the Resort on the Lake, where vacationers from all parts of the world have come to swim, sunbathe, water ski, and relax. One might say that *Bridge Fall Down*, like *The Forever War*, concerns what might have happened if the U.S. had remained in Vietnam—but unlike Haldeman's book, Rinaldi's novel contains all the ingredients of both **Catch-22** and the Vietnam War and also presents characters (like Heller's) who really matter.

Other Vietnam novels also contain references to and echoes of **Catch-22**, but these nine seem to me to be the most obvious in their derivation. The first five differ most, though, in their realistic bases. Often, such as in Baber's *The Land of a Million Elephants* or in Maitland's *The Only War We've Got*, one can recognize the real people being satirized. In *Elephants*, for instance, Colonel Kelly is based on Colonel "Bull" Simons who commanded the clandestine "White Star" teams in Laos, whose mission was to train the Lao against the North Vietnamese and Pathet Lao. Also, much of the apparent madness such as Russians and Americans both training the same people or Kong Le's vacillating politics and actions actually did happen. Maitland's General Windy is based on General "Westy" Westmoreland, and Windy's deputy and successor, General Cretan, is a parody of General Creighton Abrams, who succeeded Westmoreland as commander of U.S. forces in Vietnam. Also, there actually were two U.S. ambassadors in Saigon, and Maitland's portrait of Ambassador Risher satirizes Special Ambassador Komer who initiated and directed the controversial CORDS project for revolutionary development. Likewise in *Parthian Shot*, the base camp in the delta is entirely realistic, and many of the unit's activities ring true. The camp at Muc Wa, too, derives from actual plans for such outposts, and the relationships between the American advisers and their Montagnard raiders are poignantly accurate. Even in *The Bamboo Bed*, as many Vietnam veterans will attest, much of the apparent madness is real, especially the ground combat scenes.

What one sees, I think, in the best Vietnam novels is precisely what Beidler identifies as "**Catch-22** come giddily real." Consider this interchange in *Incident at Muc Wa*. Two officers are discussing the impending attack against the recently built outpost. Says Major Barber, "Charlie's thrown a whole battalion against Muc Wa—would he be doing that if it wasn't important to him?" Captain Olivetti replies, "Well, sir, maybe he's thinking the same thing. Maybe he's throwing men in there because he thinks it's important to us" (146). As in an earlier novel, Jonathan Rubin's *The Barking Deer* (1974), one side is reacting to what it sees the other side doing—the effect becomes the cause—and the real reason for the action does not exist. Catch-22, verily.

There are many other examples of **Catch-22** dilemmas in the fiction, usually expressed in equally authentic **Catch-22** dialogue. In *The Land of a Million Elephants*, as they watch the entire population of the capital of Chanda (Laos) flee to the countryside, the king, U.S. Colonel Kelly, and the Russian Nadolsky reflect on their respective predicaments. Says the king, "How can I be king without my people?" Complains Colonel Kelly, "How can we advise an army we haven't got?" Reflects Nadolsky, "How can the confrontation of the Twentieth Century be brought to conclusion in dialectical terms, if we have no people to sway?" (208). The answers are identical, of course, but each will continue trying to succeed, even if he knows he can't.

Beidler notes one of the most obvious examples of **Catch-22** dialogue in *The Bamboo Bed*. Two characters talk:

> "Why are you shooting at them?"
> "Because they are shooting at us."

"Who is shooting at whom?"

"Everyone is shooting at each other."

"Why?"

"War."

(Beidler 54)

My favorite passage in the same novel is this interchange which, like so many of Heller's, sets up a comic perspective, develops it, and then abruptly presents a horrible resolution. Two soldiers discuss the news:

> "I heard on the radio transmitter this morning that Clancy's outfit got wiped out," Oliver said.
>
> "You mean all killed? Not Clancy too?"
>
> "We reckon."
>
> "Did you report this to Captain Knightbridge?"
>
> "No."
>
> "That's supposed to be our job."
>
> "I didn't want him to feel bad," Oliver said.
>
> "Our job is to report what we hear on the transmitter."
>
> "I didn't want to make the captain feel bad," Oliver said.
>
> "How is Search and Rescue going to rescue people if you don't report who needs to be rescued?"
>
> "They don't need to be rescued."
>
> "Explain. Explain."
>
> "They're all dead," Oliver said.

(Eastlake 41)

Likewise in *Brandywine's War*, the following discussion involves Lt. Soverign, the chaplain who has been mistakenly sent to Vietnam as a pilot:

> "I'm not a pilot," Soverign told the check-out pilot that afternoon as they started their ascent.
>
> "He's not a pilot," the check-out pilot told Major Casey after he had barely managed to recover the aircraft from a near-crash landing.
>
> "He's not a pilot," Major Casey told General Deegle after he had talked to the check-out pilot.
>
> General Deegle had the Department of the Army TWX'd. They pulled Soverign's data card . . . and inserted it into their UNIVAC.
>
> "He's a pilot," DA told General Deegle.
>
> "You will fly," Major Casey told Lieutenant Soverign.
>
> "*I'll get killed!*" Soverign protested.
>
> "A lot of pilots are getting killed," Major Casey said. . . .
>
> "I'm afraid to fly."
>
> "A lot of pilots are afraid to fly."

(22-23)

Hardly afraid, but just as derivative, is North Vietnamese Colonel Khanh in Maitland's *The Only War We've Got*. Having been smuggled into Saigon in a coffin, Khanh is told by his local cadre commander, "We read in the newspaper that your regiment had been wiped out in the Central Highlands." Khanh replies:

> "My dear sir . . . If we took the time to add up all the Communists the Americans claimed to have killed so far in this war, South Vietnam would be a nation of ghosts."
>
> "Colonel," said Tran, "I would like to introduce you to Nguyen Hue, who is directing the funerals. Nguyen Hue's various, er enterprises in Saigon have served us well." Nguyen Hue stepped forward and bowed low.
>
> "It is an honor to . . ."
>
> "Shoot him," Colonel Khanh snapped.
>
> "What?"
>
> "Shoot him. He knows too much. We cannot risk jeopardizing our mission."
>
> "But we cannot shoot him," Tran protested. "Not yet. . . ."
>
> "Hmmmmmmmmmmmmmm," Khanh breathed. "O.K. We'll shoot him in the morning."

(233)

In the same novel, General Windy is upset when two American platoons are wiped out by the enemy while only four NVA are reported killed. He is relieved, however, when he is told:

> "It's like this, sir. The official body count was only four, the intelligence officer said that unofficially it could be as high as four hundred and seventy-five—you know, blood trails, fire ratio, allowances for wounded and all that."
>
> The General's color rushed back into his cheeks, and he sighed with relief. "Phew. That's better. Then it's not really a defeat, is it?"
>
> "I guess not, sir."
>
> "And if it's not really a defeat, it must be victory."
>
> "I guess you're right, sir."

(79)

Such conflicting realities are seen often in the **Catch-22**-influenced fiction. Perhaps the most ironic occurs in *Parthian Shot*, where an American general meets a North Vietnamese general at the invitation of Hoa Hoa Unlimited, Ltd. Both generals are interested in investing in the enterprise, and both have been told that the other is a defector to his cause. They talk about the "enemy," and NVA General Phat asks, "Between us, Arlington [a rather funereal name], how soon do you think we can defeat them?" The American replies, "To be honest, Phat, I don't know. We can win, but the enemy is tough. And persistent. They're a lot tougher than we figured." Thinking that Arlington the "defector" is on his side, General Phat replies, "You're right there. Our original timetable to win this war was five years. We never thought they would commit as many men and supplies as they have" (270). The bottom line, however, turns out to be profit when the Communist and capitalist generals both buy stock in Hoa Hoa Unlimited, Ltd., because of the same, convincingly apolitical sales pitch: "All of this . . . was built and paid for by the people themselves. And the people get the profits" (268). Everybody, as Milo Minderbinder would say, gets a share.

Similarly, in *Bridge Fall Down,* Meyerbeer is officially filming the attempt to blow up the bridge for the Corps and has established interlocking corporations in Hollywood, West Berlin, and Tokyo to produce and distribute his movie. He sells stock to everyone but plans to liquidate the companies at the war's end and force his stockholders into bankruptcy. His sales pitch: "When you get back to the states, you can retire and live off the dividends" (45).

Likewise in *Brandywine's War,* Sergeant Coty, who has requisitioned thousands of yards of Astroturf for one of his ventures, trades his Vietnamese real-estate holdings for a half share of the "unsoldier's" marijuana business, and together they form the Greater East Asian Company Prosperity Sphere conglomerate, which rents a Saigon villa to the local VC commander. And like the business ventures of *Parthian Shot,* one unit in this novel also makes VC flags for extra money.

At least one outfit has problems that even Milo Minderbinder might not be able to solve. In *The Bamboo Bed,* the SAR unit has been issued two bridges for one river, so it sells one to the VC, who have none. Because of political considerations, the VC want to sell their bridge back to the Americans so that they can have a bridge to blow up, because they've blown up all the other ones around.

As did the real war, the fiction of the U.S. involvement in Vietnam presents startling individual echoes of **Catch-22**. In addition to the dialogue, the emphasis on "business," and the obvious character echoes, one should consider the following parallels. On the war in general: "The problem with this war is that it is out of human control" (Eastlake 251). On the bombing of one's own troops, like Milo's attack on his own base: in *Incident at Muc Wa,* Corporal Conney leads his Montagnard raiders on a fake attack against Muc Wa in order to impress the visiting U.S. General Hardnetz, but they find themselves a part of a real NVA attack on the base, thus disrupting the statistics of the Saigon-based "Incident-Flow-Priority-Indicator." In *Bridge Fall Down,* even General Trask cannot call off a programmed B-52 strike (which Meyerbeer films) against his own troops. The only casualty—reminding one of Elpenor, the lost sailor in the *Odyssey*—is a man named Polymer, from Plastic, Idaho.

As for promotion problems similar to those of Major Major, that of the tenor lieutenant in *Parthian Shot* has already been noted. In addition, Captain Carmondy in *Brandywine's War* will never make major because General Deegle likes "the alliteration of the phrase. . . . Captain Carmondy was doomed to remain a captain forever, trapped by the poetry of his name" (49).

Echoing the old Italian's view in **Catch-22** of eventual victory by losing is the village chief in *Bridge Fall Down,* who claims that his people are "friendly with anybody who's willing to be friends. They're even friendly with their enemies [the northern 'monkeys']. They have no guns and know they'd lose any war they got involved in, so for them . . . war is a bad idea" (93).

Even the inquisition of **Catch-22**'s chaplain is echoed in the trial of *Brandywine's War*'s B. Dowling Mudd (one suspects dual derivation here), and what Heller presents as one naked man at war becomes a full-scale battle in *Parthian Shot* when a VC unit strips in order better to be able to identify its enemy, but then the South Vietnamese unit does likewise. *Brandywine's War,* too, has an important PFC, but unlike Ex-PFC Wintergreen, PFC Hill operates in the foreground and, claiming to be the son of the secretary of defense, controls General Deegle and as result the whole Vietnam War.

What permeates all of these Vietnam novels is the **Catch-22** concept of craziness, mentioned earlier as Yossarian's belief that "everyone is crazy but us." To Simon in *Bridge Fall Down,* the war becomes a "madness, a wild, blistering insanity that he didn't understand, and wanted desperately to get away from" (104). In *The Bamboo Bed,* Captain Knightbridge thinks "he must be going crazy." Except for the Asians in his helicopter unit (all of whom are actually VC agents), he believes that "all the rest are after me. Picture a naked man being chased by seventy-eight million Asians" (147). Yossarian, at least, could take refuge in a tree. Most derivative, however, is the craziness of Weintraub, the former war protester in the same novel, who says that he feels "fine" after dropping napalm:

> "That is why I want to check and see if I'm going crazy," Weintraub said.
>
> "You're not going crazy, Weintraub," Appelfinger said.
>
> "Sure?"

"Yes. I know enough about evolution to know that man adapts."

"You mean that if he adapts to insanity he's not going crazy?"

"Yes," Appelfinger said.

"But he's crazy if he doesn't become crazy? If everyone else is crazy?"

"Yes."

"Why is that?"

"Because we have to set a norm," Appelfinger said.

"Even if that norm is crazy, it's called a mean. . . ."

"It's an interesting theory. That I am not crazy."

"It's not a theory, it's a fact. . . . I promise you it's a fact."

"Why did everybody laugh when I said the Bamboo Bed was our conscience?"

"Because," Appelfinger said, "those guys in the Bamboo Bed are crazy. They are against both sides and they are for both sides. In any book, that's crazy."

"Yes, I guess it is," Weintraub said.

(296)

Says Philip Beidler, writing about Ward Just's "real" vision of the Vietnam War as expressed in *To What End*, "Joseph Heller could have written it, but he could not have written it better, because it was already true" (62). Well, Heller did foresee the major contradictions of the Vietnam War, but he built better than perhaps he knew, and he also presented a protagonist, Yossarian, with a final choice that is denied his fictional legatees. In the majority of the novels not mentioned in this essay, many of the characters do embark on a quest similar to Yossarian's—and for much the same reason—"to survive" (Heller 30). In Tim O'Brien's *Going after Cacciato*, for instance, Private Paul Berlin has but one goal: "to live long enough to establish goals worth living still longer for" (27); and in many of the Vietnam War novels that do *not* use **Catch-22** as a point of departure, the major characters engage in the same quest for survival as does Yossarian.

Not so in the novels discussed above. If any of the characters survive, they do so by chance, and their main objectives are to exist *within* the madness, not escape it. Even if they do survive the war, they will encounter a similar environment at home. For them, no Swedish sanctuary exists. Although Yossarian's initial goal is only to get to Rome, he like his alter ego Chief Bromden in Ken Kesey's *One Flew over the Cuckoo's Nest*, still is able to get *out*. Not so fortunate are their fictional heirs.

One need only to compare the endings of the novels discussed in this essay to see how different their authors' visions are from Heller's vision. In *The Bamboo Bed*, for instance, everyone dies in a surrealistic assimilation of the helicopter with nature: "When the Bamboo Bed came out on the other side there was nothing left . . . forever lost, disappeared, eaten by tigers, enveloped in the gentle, tomblike Asian night" (350). In *Parthian Shot*, the entire village, including the Americans who have stayed to run Hoa Hoa Unlimited, Ltd., which has so improved the local conditions, is obliterated by a misdirected American bombing strike. *Brandywine's War*, as noted earlier, merely stops, its truncated ending showing that nothing will change. In the final scene of *Incident at Muc Wa*, all die, including the American adviser who might have escaped but chooses to return to see if any of his indigenous friends are still alive. In *The Land of a Million Elephants*, the American solution, a nuclear airstrike, is thwarted only by the local "phi," the spirits of the land and the country, and instead of destruction, the bombs create only flowers and little mushrooms. The people of *Ears of the Jungle* destroy themselves, and the protagonist of *Gangland*, one of the few survivors in these apocalyptic novels, wants only to be let alone in a crazy world that is bound to get even worse.

Another main character survives, too, but at tremendous cost. Jonathan Wilkinson of *The Only War We've Got* leaves Vietnam for his native England (note that he is not an American), but the horror of the war has come home:

> Where was the rabid Socialist who'd stomped up and down the country, wild-eyed and frothing forth dissent, disgust, revulsion at what the Americans were doing? Where was the brave soul who'd stood by the strength of his own convictions at the point of Capt. Beau Hinkle's pistol? Wilkinson could summon up many reasons for leaving—disgust, revulsion, extreme cynicism, escapism, were some of them. But his real nemesis was fear, Wilkinson was scared; and he was scared because on the night of Chua Ben, war had suddenly become real—as real as the crimson tracers that poured into the rice paddy; as real as the horrible death dance of the trapped Viet Cong; the artillery blasts and boiling napalm that all but leveled the little hamlet of Chua Ben. All that had gone before now meant nothing. War meant death and destruction, and no amount of brave moral argument could change that. Words went in one ear and out the other, but bullets killed and shrapnel maimed and napalm left hideous burns. And there was no room for talk.

(261)

The two "lovers," Tess and Simon, of *Bridge Fall Down* also survive the massacre of their patrol after first blowing up the bridge, then discovering that their entire mission has been a diversionary action for another attack on a munitions factory. It is Meyerbeer the filmmaker who rescues them, and in an ending similar to but more hopeless than that of *Gangland*, Simon realizes that the madness will continue: he understands at last that Meyerbeer "wasn't just filming the war, recording it, but inventing it, creating it, or at least co-creating it with the ones who had the detonators and knew how to blow things up" (275). A few moments later, Meyerbeer speaks:

> I'll give it to you straight. It's film, folks. Film and videotape are remaking the world. Haven't you simpletons noticed? Image. Appearance. What you see. It's here to stay, so you might as well get used to it. . . . It makes and remakes, twists and turns, shapes and reshapes. It's the divine energy—pulse and power. It gives life and takes it away. Film is God.
>
> (277)

Ex-PFC Wintergreen has indeed left a legacy to Meyerbeer, but the latter's control is much more inclusive. Accordingly, close inspection of the Vietnam War fiction that evolved from *Catch-22* does indeed show a darkening vision and growing despair over the progress of the modern world. Primarily, I think, the authors despair in our ability to perceive what we are doing to ourselves, especially with our dependence upon technology and media. Like Heller, these novelists point toward a future that is indeed *Catch-22* come real. In almost everything that has happened in the past twenty-five years, Heller was really quite prophetic, even to his remarkable insight (developed in greater depth by Rinaldi) into why Americans in particular elevate people to higher office. One has only to look at 1980s' politics from Carmel, California, to the highest office in Washington, D.C., and remember that Major Major is promoted in *Catch-22* only because he either looks like or actually is—movie star Henry Fonda. Nurtured by, derived from, and dependent upon the greatness of *Catch-22,* the subsequent fiction about the Vietnam War shows that there is no longer an equivalent to Yossarian and Orr's World War II Sweden, no place left for Americans to escape even from themselves.

Works Cited

Baber, Asa. *The Land of a Million Elephants.* New York: Morrow, 1970.

Beidler, Philip. *American Literature and the Experience of Vietnam.* Athens: University of Georgia Press, 1982.

Boule, Pierre. *Ears of the Jungle.* New York: Vanguard, 1972.

Durden, Charles. *No Bugles, No Drums.* New York: Viking, 1976.

Eastlake, William. *The Bamboo Bed.* New York: Simon, 1969.

Ford, Daniel. *Incident at Muc Wa.* 1967. New York: Pyramid, 1968.

Haldeman, Joe. *The Forever War.* New York: Ballantine, 1974.

Heller, Joseph. *Catch-22.* 1961. New York: Dell, 1974.

Herr, Michael. *Dispatches.* New York: Knopf, 1977.

Just, Ward. *To What End.* Boston: Houghton, 1968.

LaValle, Major A. J. C., ed. *The Tale of Two Bridges.* Vol. 1, USAF Southeast Asia Monograph Series. Washington, D.C.: U.S. Government Printing Office, 1976.

Little, Lloyd. *Parthian Shot.* New York: Viking, 1975.

Maitland, Derek. *The Only War We've Got.* New York: Morrow, 1970.

O'Brien, Tim. *Going after Cacciato.* New York: Delacorte, 1978.

Pratt, John Clark. *The Laotian Fragments.* 1974. New York: Avon, 1985.

———. *Vietnam Voices.* New York: Viking, 1984.

Rinaldi, Nicholas. *Bridge Fall Down.* New York: Marek-St. Martins, 1985.

Rubin, Jonathan. *The Barking Deer.* New York: Braziller, 1974.

Vaughn, Robert, and Monroe Lynch. *Brandywine's War.* New York: Bartholomew House, 1971.

Winn, David. *Gangland.* New York: Knopf, 1982.

David M. Craig (essay date fall-winter 1994)

SOURCE: Craig, David M. "From Avignon to *Catch-22.*" *War, Literature, and the Arts* 6, no. 2 (fall-winter 1994): 27-54.

[*In the following essay, Craig discusses the influence of Heller's World War II experience as a pilot over Avignon on the writing of* Catch-22.]

> Rage, rage against the dying of the light.
>
> —Dylan Thomas

Joseph Heller's experiences as a bombardier over Avignon during World War II were catalytic to his career as a writer. In the experiences over Avignon, *Catch-22* begins. These experiences did not spark Heller's desire to be an author, for that had burned unabated since childhood.[1] Nor did the reaction the Avignon experiences occasioned occur quickly, regularly, or consciously. Rather, Avignon provided in highly compressed from Heller's essential subject—human mortality—and Avignon engaged his imagination in a way that this subject could eventually be given expression. No *Catch-22* reader is likely to forget the result, the Snowden death scene over Avignon or the secret of Snowden's entrails: "Man was matter . . . Drop him out a window and he'll fall. Set fire to him and he'll burn. Bury him and he'll rot like other kinds of garbage" (429-430). While the evidence for the importance of Avignon is unmistakable, many pieces of the story are unknown or missing today. Heller's public accounts of these experiences come long after he has begun to feature Avignon in his writing, and, predictably, these accounts partake of the persona of Joseph Heller, the author of *Catch-22*.[2] The accounts are couched in jokes that distance the experience from the man.

Heller's early writing furnishes some of the links between his real-life experience and *Catch-22,* and these early fictional versions of Avignon illuminate the novel (and, for that matter, Heller's subsequent writing) as if by ultraviolet light, defamiliarizing the familiar. Avignon serves as the setting for two unpublished stories, **"The Miracle of Danrossane"** and **"Crippled Phoenix,"** Heller's only short stories about the war.[3] Avignon also figures prominently in the planning material for *Catch-22,* most notably in an early draft of the Snowden death scene.[4] In this material, not in the published stories that preceded *Catch-22,* one first discovers Heller's masterplot, the core narrative that propels each of his novels. This masterplot—what I call the "dead child story"—consists of the same constellation of narrative elements: guilt, secret knowledge, bad faith, and the death of children (or, alternatively, of wounded innocents). The thrust and destination of this narrative is death, a death that serves, as does Snowden's in *Catch-22,* as the occasion for narrative clarification.[5] The narrative's import is as humanly simple and as humanly complex as mortality itself: humans are matter. With this masterplot, Heller seeks to do what Tolstoy does in *The Death of Ivan Ilych,* to have character and reader alike experience the immanence and imminence of death. Like Ivan Ilych, we are apt to be resisting readers, able to acknowledge, as Ivan does, the rightness of the syllogistic reasoning that says "Caius (or Snowden) is a man; men are mortal"; but not wanting, as Ivan and Yossarian do not want, to apply this abstraction to ourselves. Heller's early writing about Avignon, then, allows exploration of the process by which he draws upon and gains control over personal experience and documents its "increasingly conscious transformation into writing" (Said 196).[6]

Each of the accounts of Avignon—**"The Miracle of Danrossane," "Crippled Phoenix,"** the early manuscript, the published one, and, as I discuss elsewhere, **"Catch-22** Revisited"—has an aspect of meta-narration entailing a struggle of how to locate and voice the story. In **"The Miracle of Danrossane,"** the Avignon story—that is, the dead child story—is a secret known only by the local residents, and Heller's plot unfolds his American protagonist's efforts to find someone who will disclose the secret. In **"Crippled Phoenix,"** the story resides within the principal characters themselves, in the guilty pasts of Dan Cramer, an American pilot, and Morain, a member of the French underground. The plots of both stories depend upon working out what can and cannot be told as well as what can and cannot be confronted. In an early manuscript version of the Snowden death scene, Yossarian endeavors to have the chaplain understand his own reactions to what happened over Avignon, not the event itself. Finally, in *Catch-22,* Yossarian endeavors to unlock the significance of Snowden's dying words and, in so doing, to plumb the meaning of death. As in the previous versions, Yossarian's understanding hinges upon telling the story of what happened, albeit to himself. In each story of Avignon, Heller makes the telling of the story as important as the having told, as if the repeated tellings will help the author himself understand what happened.

During the war, Heller flew two missions to Avignon. Before the Avignon missions, he had, by his own account, romanticized war: "I wanted action, not security. I wanted a sky full of dogfights, daredevils and billowing parachutes. I was twenty-one years old. I was dumb" ("Revisited" 51). Avignon shatters his romantic wishes, for as he remarks in "*Catch-22* Revisited": "There was the war, in Avignon, not in Rome or Ile Rousse or Poggibonsi or even Ferrara" (141).[7] On the August 8, 1944 mission to bomb a railroad bridge, Heller for the first time saw a plane shot down.[8] As a bombardier on one of the lead planes, which had been assigned to drop metallic paper to disrupt the radar for the anti-aircraft guns, Heller could look back on what was happening to the rest of the squadron. He saw a burning plane fall into an uncontrollable spin. Parachutes billowed and opened: he would later learn that three men had gotten out, while three others were killed in the crash. One of the three survivors was found by members of the Avignon underground, hidden and eventually smuggled back across enemy lines. This mission provides the basis for the "Crippled Phoenix" and, presumably, the inspiration for the survivor's guilt that its protagonist Dan Cramer experiences.

On August 15, 1944, Heller's squadron returned to Avignon to bomb another railroad bridge over the Rhone, and this mission would provide the model for the Snowden death scene. For both Heller and Yossarian, it was their 37th mission. In notes Heller made in 1966 about the mission, he records: "Man wounded in leg. Wohlstein and Moon killed" ("Chronology 2/13/66," Heller papers, Brandeis University). According to Heller, the details from the novel correspond

> . . . perhaps ninety percent to what I did experience. I did have a co-pilot go berserk and grab the controls. The earphones did pull out. I did think I was dying for what seemed like thirty minutes but was actually three-hundredths of a second. When I did plug my earphones in, there was a guy sobbing on the intercom, "Help the bombardier, but the gunner was only shot in the leg."
>
> (Heller, **"Translating"** 357)

In recounting the experience, Heller confines the correspondences between the actual and the novelistic Avignon missions to "physical details" and denies any similarity between Yossarian's emotional reactions and his own.[9]

Heller's own explanations as well as his fictional use of Avignon indicate that more than physical details are at play. Whether factual or fictional, each account that Heller gives of Avignon contains an Ur-plot that turns upon an intense experience of personal mortality. In answering interviewers' questions about his own experience, Heller repeatedly dwells on his sensation that he had died in the air above Avignon. He remembers pressing the talk button of his head set, hearing nothing, and thinking he was already dead. Heller stresses his sense of distorted time, of events that unfolded in microseconds seeming to last much longer.[10] His change of habits after this Avignon mission also testifies to the mission's effects; from then on, Heller carried a personal first-aid kit and vowed never to fly once his combat missions were over (a vow kept until 1960 when a 24-hour train ride convinced him to reassess the dangers of flying). The comic "*Catch-22* Revisited" retelling provides a perspective on Heller's reactions in that he makes himself, not the wounded airman, the victim. "I went to the hospital the next day. He looked fine. They had given him blood, and he was going to be all right. But I was in terrible shape, and I had twenty-three more missions to fly" ("Revisited" 142). Of course, the wound becomes mortal in *Catch-22,* or as Heller laconically describes the wound's change: "He was shot through the leg . . . But I added to it and had him shot in the middle" (Barnard 298).

"The Miracle of Danrossane" and "Crippled Phoenix" mark the artistic steps by which the wound gets relocated. Together with the early draft of the Snowden death scene and *Catch-22* itself, the stories offer a complex range of reactions to death: denial, confusion, immersion, and understanding. While all of these reactions figure in each work, one predominates in each, as if designating stages in Heller's thinking, from denial in **"The Miracle of Danrossane"** to understanding in *Catch-22*. As this progression indicates, the stories and manuscript draft of the death scene provided the vehicle by which Heller worked out his master plot, and determined that *death* could serve as thrust and destination for his narratives. In the stories, the journey toward this death is spatial and temporal, a visit to Avignon in **"Danrossane"** and a return to it in **"Crippled Phoenix."** In *Catch-22* and the novels that follow, the journey becomes psychological and emotional, one culminating in a death that surfaces, like Snowden's does, as if from the protagonist's subconscious.

"The Miracle of Danrossane," the slighter of the two unpublished war stories, recounts a correspondent's visit to the village outside Avignon where his father was born. This story's plot turns upon a father's denying his sons' deaths. The correspondent is intrigued by the name of the inn in which he stays, *L'Auberge des Sept Fils* [Inn of the Seven Sons]. While Durland, the innkeeper, will not talk about the name, the mayor tells the correspondent Durland's story. This telling provides the principal plot of Heller's story. Even though Durland had been a Nazi collaborator during the war, his seven sons had been killed by the Nazis as a reprisal for the death of two German soldiers. Durland himself bears responsibility for his sons' deaths because he neglected to protect them. The story is irony-laden: the Nazis' random selection of reprisal victims results in the deaths of Durland's sons (hence the darkly ironic title); although the Nazis think their selection random, one of Durland's sons has, in fact, been involved in killing the Nazi soldiers as revenge for the rape of a village girl by the soldiers; one of the actual killers goes free even though he volunteers to turn himself over to the Nazis and despite the mayor's informing on him. Durland himself never comes to terms with his sons' deaths; in fact, he tells the correspondent that his sons are out working in the fields.

In this earliest Avignon story, Heller announces the concerns that will characterize his subsequent accounts, as well as provide the principal concerns of his novels: guilt, secret knowledge, bad faith, and, most crucially, the death of children. **"The Miracle of Danrossane"**'s underlying structure has the primitive, evocative force of a folk tale. A young man, who is looking symbolically for his father (and thus for his own origins), finds a surrogate whose act of paternal bad faith has caused his own sons' deaths. Refusing to acknowledge their deaths or his own complicity in them, this father lives "respectably" in a house memorializing the dead sons. When the correspondent discovers the father's secret, he returns home and, as artist, transforms the secret into story. Thus conceived, the story the reader has just read originates in guilty, concealed knowledge—a conception that aligns it with such myths as those of Prometheus and the Garden of Eden, myths which Heller explicitly draws upon in *Catch-22*. The architecture of **"Danrossane,"** particularly the crucial element of the sons' deaths, is striking for the way that it anticipates the design of Heller's novels. Later characterizing this design, Heller says:

> Death is always present as a climactic event that never happens to the protagonist but affects him profoundly. I think I'm drawing unconsciously from experience for inspiration. The child, the dependent child or sacrificed child is always there. I would think that the death of my father when I was about five years old had much to do with that. There was almost no conversation about it . . . Indeed, the traumatized child denies death very successfully, and then sublimates it, which I think is the process that went on in me. But it leaves me very sensitive to the helplessness of children and the ease

with which they can be destroyed or betrayed deliberately or otherwise.[11]

(Flippo 60)

Whether one accepts Heller's psychological explanation for the phenomenon or not, one cannot escape the way in which death serves as climactic event and as catalyst for narrative clarification in his writing and does so from the onset of his career.

"Crippled Phoenix" marks another step on Heller's journey toward *Catch-22.* Guilt-caused confusion characterizes the story's account of death, and, like the novel, this story features a protagonist who has been wounded in the leg. As its title signifies, the life after the Avignon death is crippling; there is no phoenix-like resurrection. Evidently, Heller spent considerable time on the story, for there are three versions of it in the Brandeis collection and he tried placing it with different literary agents. Possessing clear affinities with *Catch-22,* as well as with *Something Happened,* "Crippled Phoenix" tells a double story of conscience: that of Dan Cramer, an American pilot who feels guilty for surviving the crash in which he was the only survivor, and of Morain, a French peasant who aided with Cramer's escape after the crash. Cramer has returned to Avignon to see Morain, to whom he feels grateful and about whom he feels guilty because Morain's son had been killed when a bombardier with one mission left to fly dropped his bombs too early. Cramer has an additional reason for guilt in that he has been unfaithful to his wife during a recent stay in London, and, even in bed with his wife in Avignon, he finds his mind wandering back to Luciana, a wartime liaison in Rome.[12]

More crucial to the action of the story, Cramer fails to come to terms with all this guilt. First, although Cramer goes to see Morain with the intention "of help[ing] him in some way," he cannot provide the support that Morain wants, for Morain suffers from his own wartime guilt. To Cramer, Morain confesses that he was afraid his daughter would be taken away to a Nazi work camp and so he forced her to become the mistress of a German official (which ruins her life and that of her child born of the relationship). Although Morain explicitly asks him to return to visit, Cramer, even after agreeing to, cannot bring himself to do so. Second, he fails to come to terms with his wife, although he shares some of the details with her about the wartime plane crash, which he alone survived. Convinced that his wife is too superficial to understand his feelings, especially about the war, he allows her to believe that their marital difficulties have been reconciled, all the while despising her.

Significantly, Cramer, who stands in Yossarian's position as participant in events of the past, cannot fully disclose his story to anyone; he thus remains isolated and tormented. In a symbolically resonant moment, Heller communicates the moral wilderness that Cramer has brought himself into because he is unable to confront his guilt; he also conveys the way in which Cramer has deliberately estranged himself from his wife.

> Suddenly, though, [Cramer] was frightened. The forest was immediately before them (his guide, his wife, and himself), and he realized that Katherine belonged only to the fringe of his emotions, on that their endless surface of amiability and routine, and that everything might still be all right if he kept her there. But they were already between the trees.

This passage forecasts the role that Avignon will play in *Catch-22* (as well as anticipates Slocum's marriage in *Something Happened*). The passage locates the wilderness within the self, that wilderness which, as Conrad demonstrates in *Heart of Darkness,* is the territory of the modern condition. While the same elements—dead children, secret knowledge, guilt, and bad faith—constitute the story, Heller relocates them. In **"Danrossane,"** Durland's history was part of public discourse, unknown only to the correspondent, the outsider. In **"Crippled Phoenix,"** Cramer's and Morain's pasts are secret—in particular, the responsibility that each feels for a death. Each discloses his guilty past in the vain hope of confessional relief. However, both disclosures fail because the two men look to others to assuage their own inner guilt: Morain to Cramer when the injured party is his daughter and Cramer to his wife when he cannot accept his own actions. The guilty knowledge of what happened at Avignon isolates and estranges, at least until what happened there can be fully confronted and related. As the early manuscript version of the Snowden death scene powerfully suggests, this is what *Catch-22* is about.

An early draft of the Snowden scene documents Heller's evolving conception of Avignon and dramatizes the imperative for reporting what happened there. Snowden represents the death at a distance—Yossarian recounts the experience to the chaplain. Yet, this early version is raw and, in some ways, more emotionally charged than the novel. While the Snowden scene plays off the bloody hands scene in *Macbeth,* the literary allusion seems like a patina over what Heller will call in *God Knows* the "stink of mortality and reek of mankind" (107). In Heller's early rendering, Yossarian not only sees death, but also immerses himself in it.

> "Dirty hands," Yossarian said. "Yesterday they touched a dead man's flesh."

The chaplain attempts to comfort him, but Yossarian continues:

> "A dead man's private parts. I spoke to Doc Daneeker. Probably his lungs, his pancreas, his liver, his stomach, and some canned tomatoes that he had for breakfast. I hate canned tomatoes . . ."

The chaplain tries again.

> "But you don't understand. I enjoyed it. I actually enjoyed touching the graying flesh, the clotting blood. I actually enjoyed touching his lungs, his pancreas, his liver, his stomach and some canned tomatoes from his breakfast, even though I hate canned tomatoes. I made excuses to myself to touch every shriveling shred."

The chaplain tries one final time to console Yossarian.

> "But even that's not the worst of it. I rubbed blood all over myself. And do you know why I rubbed blood all over myself? To impress people. To impress those God damned Red Cross biddies with the smiles and doughnuts . . . and by God, it impressed, even Doc Daneeker, who broke down and gave me some codeine and told me about Cathcart and a tour of duty."
>
> (Heller papers, Brandeis University)

There are many noteworthy differences between this early version and the published one. Snowden's mortal wound is open, displaying what Heller will call in the novel "God's plenty" (429). Yossarian is compelled to touch the viscera, then compelled to relate to the chaplain his enjoyment of doing so. He has previously told Doc Daneeker about his experience. In *Catch-22,* Yossarian tells no one, although his recollections have the quality of telling the story to himself. Time works differently as well. In the manuscript, the experience, only a day old, has the immediacy of the here and now, while in the novel version, it emerges as if from Yossarian's subconsciousness. In *Catch-22,* the intensity of Yossarian's remembrance erupts into the present: "liver, lungs, kidneys, ribs, stomach, and bits of . . . stewed tomatoes" (429). The same message is embedded in both—*man is matter*—but in the manuscript, Yossarian, and perhaps Heller, has not yet apprehended its significance.

The unpublished early version is, at once, more public and more private than the Avignon of the *Catch-22.* The appropriation of the dirty hands motif from *Macbeth* dissociates this version from Heller himself, connecting it to a literary past rather than a personal one.[13] Also by having Yossarian report the story, Heller publicizes Avignon in a way that third-person narration would not. This recounting of Avignon proclaims Yossarian's guilty consciousness, whereas the novel displaces it into the tree-of-life episode, in which Yossarian's nakedness reveals his guilt (likewise triggered by Snowden's blood).[14] Simultaneously, this early version is more private, more evocative of the Heller who experienced Avignon and of the author who repeatedly sets key scenes there. The confessional quality of the incident, with Yossarian trying to make the chaplain understand what he has done, directs attention to the personal reaction to the experience. Finally, Yossarian's revelation that, on one level, he enjoyed the experience points to the complexity of Heller's own experience over Avignon. This early version illustrates the attraction of the horrifying—an attraction that Heller seems compelled to specify.

Significantly, before the idea for *Catch-22* came to him, Heller had virtually given up writing. Of the time between the short stories that he wrote in the forties and the novel which he began in 1953, Heller later said, "I wanted to write something that was very good and I had nothing good to write. So I wrote nothing" (Sam Merrill 68). Out of the silence—a silence that he partially filled with reading—came a new method of writing, anti-realist and comic in orientation. Reading

> the comic novels of Evelyn Waugh and Celine's *Journey to the End of the Night* . . . Nathanael West's *Miss Lonelyhearts,* and . . . Nabokov's *Laughter in the Dark* particularly, I was comprehending for the first time that there were different ways to tell a story, and the methods these people used were much more compatible with my own technical ability . . . with my own imagination.
>
> (Ruas 151)

The realization that there are many ways to tell a story is what Heller's evolving use of the Avignon experiences documents.[15] The discovery was long in coming, though, for he did not publish *Catch-22* until 1961, sixteen years after the publication of his first story. By this time, he was 38, the same age as two other late-blooming, first-time novelists, George Eliot and Willa Cather.

Heller's key discovery involves discourse, not story, the *how* of narrative rather than the *what*.[16] His Avignon short stories (as did most of his other short stories) had linear plots that unfolded on a single narrative level. In each, characters journeyed to Avignon (or nearby Danrossane) to learn something from the past. Heller's narrative method was straightforward, the plots proceeding until access was gained to characters who disclose crucial, secret knowledge from the past. In *Catch-22,* Heller makes discourse—the narrative act itself—part of the story as well as its means of transmission. The Avignon mission on which Snowden dies illustrates this. As is well-known, Heller's narrator distributes references to the mission throughout the novel; sometimes cryptically as in the first reference: "Where are the Snowdens of yesteryear?" (35); sometimes explicitly as in: "the way Snowden had frozen to death after spilling his secret to Yossarian in the back of the plane" (170). In effect, the narrator dissects the Avignon plot as if performing a narrative autopsy on Snowden. This dissection creates a much richer narrative progression than that of the Avignon stories, one that depends upon discourse (the vertical narrative axis) as well as upon story (the horizontal axis).[17] Three effects follow from this: first, the meaning of Snowden's secret depends upon the interplay among narrative levels and involves the contrast of tragic and comic perspectives; second, Heller uses the synthetic dimension of narrative to complicate the narrative progression so that the authorial reader must participate in the unraveling of Snowden's secret;

and third, Heller can make the text the verbal embodiment of Snowden's secret, that is, mortality exists in the conjunction of mind and matter.[18]

Heller's first reference to Avignon typifies the way he takes advantage of the interplay among the narrative levels. Yossarian's question about the Snowdens of yesteryear has complementary roles in the novel's story and discourse, in each case providing the pathway to who Snowden is and what his secret entails. For Yossarian, the question speaks to both an actual and a linguistic quest; he wants to know "why so many people were trying so hard to kill him" (34). To gain the knowledge he seeks, Yossarian, like the protagonists of the Avignon stories, must unlock a secret from the past, a secret of which Snowden is the embodiment (potentially, this knowledge is already available to him because he has already ministered to the dying Snowden). But the question is also about language as well as about history, as becomes clear when Yossarian translates it into French: "*Ou sont les Neigedens d'antan?*" [Where are the Snowdens of yesteryear?] (35). Heller underscores the seriousness of this linguistic dimension with the narrator's comment about Yossarian's willingness "to pursue [the corporal of whom he asked his question] through all the words of the world" (35). The narrator, of course, knows the answer to Yossarian's question, but instead of relating it, explains to the narrative audience why the question is so upsetting.[19] In doing so, the narrator also makes this query part of another narrative, that of the Fall. "Group Headquarters was alarmed, for there was no telling what people might find out once they were free to ask whatever questions they wanted to"—a concern for which Colonel Korn devises the ingenious solution of permitting only those people to ask questions who never asked any (35). At this moment, the story is simultaneously proceeding on different narrative planes, its comedy, in part, stemming from the resulting incongruity. Heller's discourse takes Yossarian's question to a higher level where Group Headquarters' response echoes the fears of the God from Genesis, who worries that Adam and Eve, possessing the knowledge of good and evil, may now be tempted to eat from the tree of life. The mythic echoes refigure Yossarian's Avignon experience as a fall into mortality and mortal knowledge, a point that Heller makes more forcefully in the subsequent tree-of-life scene.

The reference to "the secret Snowden had spilled to Yossarian" exemplifies the synthetic narrative progression of *Catch-22*, the progression implied by the novel's language. The episode advances the plot: for Yossarian, being in the hospital is better than flying over Avignon with Snowden dying (164). As the narrator formulates the matter, it is not just because the hospital is safer, protecting Yossarian from war, but also because people "couldn't dominate Death inside the hospital, but they certainly made her behave" (164). Death has become a character and its plot is the Lisa Doolittle story: "They had taught her manners. They couldn't keep Death out, but while she was in she had to act like a lady" (164). With this conception, Yossarian and the narrator seek to control death. Of course, their plotting undoes them. In Heller's mordant, novel-long joke, death is no lady, although this metaphor does, for Heller, speak to its nature.[20] As with the many euphemisms for death, this reference makes dying seem familiar, comfortable, and acceptable.

As novelist, Heller knows better, representing death as violent, certain, and inevitable; and yet, he rages against its sway. In *Catch-22,* unlike his Avignon stories, he finds a form to express his outrage, the humor of the novel's discourse being its expression. His handling of "the secret Snowden had spilled to Yossarian" reference can illustrate this: his mixing comic and tragic perspectives; his verbal pyrotechnics, his delight in language as language; and his presentation of crucial narrative information (i.e. what exactly the secret entails) in a way that resists understanding. The passage itself iconically embodies Snowden's secret, the coded message encased by and hidden among the myriad external and internal threats to one's life.

> There were too many dangers for Yossarian to keep track of. There was Hitler, Mussolini, and Tojo, for example, and they were all out to kill him. There was Lieutenant Scheisskopf with his fanaticism for parades and there was the bloated colonel with his fat mustache and his fanaticism for retribution, and they wanted to kill him. There was Appleby, Havermeyer, Black, and Korn . . . There were bartenders, bricklayers and bus conductors all over the world who wanted him dead, landlords and tenants, traitors and patriots, lynchers, leeches and lackeys, and they were all out to bump him off. *That was the secret Snowden had spilled to him on the mission to Avignon . . .*
>
> There were lymph glands that might do him in. There were kidneys, nerve sheaths and corpuscles. There were tumors of the brain. There was Hodgkin's disease, leukemia, amyotrophic lateral sclerosis. There were fertile red meadows of epithelial tissue to catch and coddle a cancer cell. There were diseases of the skin, diseases of the bone, diseases of the lung, diseases of the stomach, diseases of the heart, blood and arteries . . .
>
> (170-71)

Heller is in high comic form here. Repetition, alliteration and pseudo-classification schemes, among other things, control the sequencing of details, and the details themselves multiply, even as I truncate them with ellipses, as if the details were cancer cells. The nonsense of this—"the many diseases . . . [of] a truly diseased mind"—has, of course, a deadly seriousness, although neither Yossarian, nor the narrative or authorial audiences can entirely understand this yet (171). It is easier to proclaim human mortality than to understand it, easier to catalog external and internal threats to one's life than to comprehend them. This is what *Catch-22* is about; this is what readers along with Yossarian must be educated to. As the **"The Miracle of Danrossane," "Crippled Phoenix,"** and the early version of the Snowden death scene demonstrate, here is also the journey that Heller himself has made from Avignon to *Catch-22*.

The second Avignon mission serves further to educate Yossarian and the authorial audience, and Heller's handling of it illumines the way in which he has transmuted experience into art. The mission is largely non-narrated, because Yossarian does not fly on it, having been previously wounded in the leg over Leghorn. Nevertheless, the mission provides an essential gateway to apprehending Snowden's secret and to Sweden, where Yossarian can indeed "live forever or die in the attempt" (29). In his notes to the novel, Heller describes how Yossarian's squadron comes to return to Avignon, and this description highlights another interpretation of Snowden's death, that of the army bureaucracy. "In the Chaplain's presence, Colonel Cathcart volunteers the Group for another mission to Avignon: he is instituting the procedure of having form letters sent to the families of casualties, and he wants to obtain a large number of casualties quickly enough to be written up in the Christmas issue of the *Saturday Evening Post*" (Heller papers, Brandeis University). In fact, however, no one is killed on the mission, although Orr, Yossarian's bunkmate and guide to Sweden is shot down. Orr seizes the opportunity to test all the equipment and supplies on his life raft in preparation for his journey to Sweden. After the mission, Yossarian leaves the hospital only to learn that the number of mandatory flying missions has been raised once more. At this news, he agrees to enlist in Dobbs' plot to assassinate Colonel Cathcart. If Yossarian would instead listen to Orr, who wants Yossarian to fly with him, Yossarian would have taken the direct route to Sweden, for Orr is shot down on his next mission, only to resurface in Sweden at novel's end. However, Yossarian would have not learned what he needs to, nor would Heller's readers.

In narrative terms, this Avignon mission operates according to the principle of substitution. The premises of the Snowden scene are reversed, with Yossarian himself playing the part of injured airman. For example, when Yossarian is wounded in the leg, he immediately overestimates the seriousness of the wound, immediately believing it to be life-denying, albeit sexually so. "I have lost my balls! Aarfy, I lost my balls! . . . I said I lost my balls! Can't you hear me? I'm wounded in the groin!" (283-284). In Heller's notes to the novel, the wound was, in fact, intended as a castration, a conception that lends further evidence to the importance Avignon holds to Heller (Nagel, "The *Catch-22* Note Cards" 52-53). During the mission itself, Yossarian safely resides in the hospital recuperating, a proleptic version of the stay during which he finally cracks Snowden's secret. The danger of the mission also constitutes a substitution, the ambitious colonels who need casualties causing the real peril, rather than the Germans. This Avignon episode underscores what Yossarian has yet to learn: the significance of the threat posed by living in society, confirmed when Yossarian subsequently agrees to be the colonels' pal and to say nice things about them. At novel's end, thinking about this deal, he allows himself to remember Snowden and for first time meditates on his own experience over Avignon. Examining the entrails, albeit in memory, Yossarian confronts what he has previously refused to acknowledge.

With the design of the Snowden death scene, Heller expects the authorial audience to return to Avignon with Yossarian, demanding that they too inspect Snowden's exposed vital organs and understand the message those organs contain. The narrative approach is erratic, recapitulating the comi-tragic rhythms of the novel as a whole.[21] Yossarian is in the hospital recovering from the side wound that the knife-wielding Nately's whore inflicts on him. Predictably, the danger that the wound occasions results from the doctors who want to treat him by operating on his liver, not from treating the wound itself.[22] Heller's method is comic, but his point is serious:

"Where were you born?" [asks a fat, gruff colonel with a mustache.]

"On a battlefield," [Yossarian] answers.

"No, no. In what state were you born?"

"In a state of innocence."

(420)

The meaning and humor of this exchange depend upon the interplay between discourse and story. The incongruity of meanings that results alerts the authorial audience to what Yossarian must still learn. He does not yet realize the deal that he has just accepted from Colonels Cathcart and Korn to "[s]ay nice things about [them]" (416) is "a way to lose [him]self" (456). To discover this and to learn Snowden's secret, Yossarian must first unravel the message of the strange man who keeps repeating, "we've got your pal, buddy. We've got your pal" (422). At this point in the novel, Colonel Korn, the chaplain, and Aarfy all fit the message, for each could be the pal: Korn because he knows what the deal demands, Aarfy because he has been the navigator on so many of Yossarian's "missions," and the chaplain because he has indeed been Yossarian's friend. Instinctively, Yossarian realizes that each of the obvious possibilities is wrong, and in "the sleepless bedridden nights that take an eternity to dissolve into dawn" (426), he resolves the riddle. In the perverse logic of riddles,

Snowden "had never been his pal" but was "a vaguely familiar kid who was badly wounded and freezing to death" (426). If Snowden was only vaguely familiar in life, he will become, through the power of recollection, intimately known in death. In death, he is Yossarian's pal and catalyst for his essential discovery of self.[23]

The death scene is so frequently analyzed that it needs little further examination here. I want, however, briefly to consider a passage from earlier in the novel which sets up this inspection. Its progression is reminiscent of Heller's own artistic journey toward Avignon: slow, hesitant, made in uncertain steps. The passage speaks to the problem at the heart of *Catch-22,* that of locating the wound and telling its story.

> And Yossarian crawled slowly out of the nose and up on the top of the bomb bay and wriggled back into the rear section of the plane—passing the first-aid kit on the way that he had to return for—to treat Snowden for the wrong wound, the yawning, raw, melon-shaped hole as big as a football in the outside of his thigh, the unsevered, blood-soaked muscle fibers inside pulsating weirdly like blind things with lives of their own, the oval naked wound that was almost a foot long and made Yossarian moan in shock and sympathy the instant he spied it and nearly made him vomit. And the small, slight tail gunner was lying on the floor beside Snowden in a dead faint, his face as white as a handkerchief, so that Yossarian sprang forward with revulsion to help him first.
>
> (341)

Yossarian crawls back through the plane, as if moving back in time as well as in space. He mislocates the wound and even then cannot immediately bring himself to treat it, choosing instead to aid the tail gunner. The essential story, human mortality, is reified in Snowden's flesh. In his revulsion, Yossarian can better deal with the gunner's "dead faint" than with Snowden's living wound. The simile, "like blind things with lives of their own," renders mortality as a mysterious otherness, not just Snowden's but also, implicitly, Yossarian's own.

Eventually, Yossarian traces the wound with his fingers, just as he did in the manuscript version, and when he does, he unwittingly begins to explore his own mortality as well as Snowden's deadly wound. Yossarian finds "[t]he actual contact with the dead flesh . . . not nearly as repulsive as he had anticipated, and excuse to caress the wound with his fingers again and again to convince himself of his own courage" (428). The reworking of these details from the manuscript confirms their importance, but significantly shifts the emphasis and meaning of the scene. In the manuscript, Yossarian caresses the viscera, in the novel the fleshy leg wound. In the manuscript, Yossarian attempts to "impress" others with actions as if this will authenticate his courage, while in the novel he wants to ascertain his own courage. But, in both cases, he initially touches without understanding. In fact, after fingering and then treating Snowden's leg wound, Yossarian can assure him confidently, "You're going to be all right, kid . . . Everything is under control" (429). Of course, it isn't. What Yossarian needs to understand lies open before him, signified by the blood "*dripping . . . like snow melting on the eaves, but viscous and red, already thickening as it dropped*" (emphasis added, 427). For Heller, the mystery of mortality lies in human embodiment—in the flesh, not in the spirit. Life begins and ends with the body. With his hands inside Snowden's wound, Yossarian experiences this, feels what he does not yet understand. However, his physical grasp anticipates and makes possible apprehension of the message of Snowden's entrails.

In Yossarian's famous insight, Heller defines mortality as a fusion of mind and matter, Yossarian's conceptualization of man enduring even as Snowden's body dissolves into bloody inert matter. Reflecting upon Snowden's death, Yossarian comes to understand his own mortality. As Denis de Rougement observes, "Suffering and understanding are deeply connected; death and self-awareness are in league" (51). Heller insists that Yossarian trace the contours of Snowden's and thus his own mortality: "liver, lungs, kidneys, ribs, stomach, and bits of stewed tomatoes Snowden had eaten that day for lunch" (429). The prose is hard and violent, as hard and violent as Snowden's wounds; its violence partakes of the violence of Heller's experience of treating a wounded colleague. The viscera of humans tether them to the material world. The viscera also take in the material world, digesting it like Snowden's stewed tomatoes. When the digestive process is viewed as Snowden's is, it becomes ugly and repulsive. But Heller believes these entrails also allow the viewer, as prophets have long believed, to detect the secrets of human existence: "Man was matter, that was Snowden's secret. Ripeness was all" (429-430).[24] Finally, Yossarian deciphers the message that has been available to him all along. The message identifies the two components of humanity: the material that inexorably leads to death, and the spiritual that Heller leaves deliberately ambiguous. In formulating the spiritual element, Heller omits the verb, so that the statement reads "the spirit gone." This formulation neither affirms nor denies the existence of spirit; it simply announces the concept. Without predication, the concept cannot be completed or brought to fulfillment. As deconstructionists would argue, the verb's absence only can be noted.

Heller's insistence that his authorial audience inspect Snowden's viscera also accomplishes quite a different end, what Bakhtin calls the "familiarization of the world through laughter" (23). "In this plane (the plane of laughter) one can disrespectfully walk around whole objects; therefore, the back and rear portions of an object (and also its innards, not normally accessible for viewing) assume special prominence" (23). Death, of course, is the object that Heller wants to inspect. By means of such elements as "the Snowdens of yesteryear," the Death that behaves, and the litany of threats to Yossarian's life, Heller has taken his authorial audience on this kind of narrative walk in his peripatetic approach to Avignon. In the catalog of Snowden's vital organs, Yossarian, the narrator, and Heller act out the imperatives for Bakhtin's comic formula. Having already familiarized the reader with the elements of this catalog, especially the liver and the tomatoes, the beginning and ending of the catalog, Heller allows the reality of mortality to be known, familiarized in a laughter that ridicules. Death, as well as life, is stripped in Heller's catalog, his comic dismemberment destroying the power that death had when it was unknown.

In retracing some of Heller's steps to the Snowden death scene, one is reminded of the blacking factory sections of David Copperfield and how they have helped to explain so much of Charles Dickens's life and art. Like Dickens, Heller uses his art to digest personal shocks, to explain them to himself, and to give an intelligible picture of the world in which such things occur.[25] So too like Dickens, Heller is a great humorist, and the acuity of his social vision frequently has been missed, as was Dickens's, in the laughter his fiction occasions. This laughter offers an escape from social institutions whose grip on the individual seems as intractable as that of **Catch-22** on Yossarian. While providing the pathway and accommodation for Snowden's secret, this laughter is begotten by pain. Heller's early representations of Avignon instance this; there is no humor in **"The Miracle of Danrossane"** or **"Crippled Phoenix."** For Heller, the painful recognition of Snowden's secret generates anger, anger usually expressed by black humor and unleashed by the genius of his novelistic discourse. He rages against the dying of the light.[26]

Notes

1. Since childhood, Heller wrote stories and submitted them for publication, sending them to places like the *New York Daily News, Liberty,* and *Collier's*. He also dreamed of becoming a dramatist and in high school aspired to writing comedies like those of Moss Hart and George S. Kaufmann.

2. Heller's interviews continually address the issue of correspondence between his life and fiction, with Heller giving a variety of answers, sometimes contradictorily so. For a representative selection of interviews treating his war experience, see: Heller, "Translating," *Gentlemen's Quarterly,* Sam Merrill, Weatherby, Barnard, and Flippo.

3. "The Miracle of Danrossane," "Crippled Phoenix," and all other unpublished material to which I refer are part of a collection of Heller's papers that Brandeis University Library holds. In addition to these stories, Heller also worked on a novel about the war as early as 1945, which involved a flier nearing the end of his required quota of bombing missions and thinking about the meaning of the war.

4. James Nagel has done the seminal work on the manuscript and other working papers for *Catch-22*, but much more study remains to be done. Nagel isolates interesting and important changes between Heller's early plans and published novel, arguing that this material documents the author's "meticulous planning and analysis of his novel at each state of composition" ("Note Cards" 404); see Nagel.

5. While the Snowden death scene in *Catch-22* provides the most memorable formulation of such a death, variants on this story reappear at the end of the rest of Heller's work. In the novels, the crucial death always occurs in the penultimate chapter, with the exception of *Good as Gold* in which the funeral occurs in the penultimate chapter. In *We Bombed in New Haven,* Captain Starkey must tell and retell each newly named version of his son that he will die on the next bombing mission. In the ending of *Something Happened,* Slocum finally calls back to memory the details of the accident in which he killed his son, the spurting blood and twisted arms and legs. But he resists the knowledge available in this recollection, concluding it instead with the plea, "Don't tell my wife" (562). In a reversal of the pattern, *Good as Gold* closes with Bruce Gold standing at his mother's grave hoping for a message that does not come. The death of another "child," his brother Sid, has brought him to the cemetery. *God Knows* concludes with King David yearning for a God who will understand and make understandable the grief he feels for his dead sons: "I feel nearer to God when I am deepest in anguish" (338). In *Picture This,* Heller revises one of history's most famous death scenes, that of Socrates, so that he dies with the retching and convulsions caused by ingesting hemlock. Finally, in *Closing Time,* Heller uses Kilroy's death to mourn the passing of the World War II generation, to parody the dead child story, and to cast a retrospective light upon *Catch-22* in general and Snowden's death in particular.

6. Said makes a larger point about the relationship between certain writers' careers and the texts produced by them that can usefully be applied to Heller and, by extension, to his authorial returns to Avignon: "the text is a multidimensional structure extending from the beginning to the end of the writer's career. A text is the source and aim of a man's desire to be an author, it is the form of

7. Each of these sites has personal significance to Heller: Rome, which Heller visited shortly after it was liberated, afforded him his most memorable wartime leave (see Note 12); Il Rousse was an army rest camp on Corsica near where he was based; Poggibonsi was the destination for his first bombing mission, a mission on which he got bored and dropped his bombs too late; and Ferrara was the first mission on which Heller's squadron lost a plane.

8. There is a discrepancy in Heller's dating of this first Avignon mission; he lists it as August 8 in the "Chronology 2/13/66" and as August 3 in "*Catch-22* Revisited." In the "Chronology," Heller describes the mission as follows: "Rail Road bridge. Hirsch shot down, Burrhus, Yellon killed. First plane I saw shot down" (Heller papers, Brandeis University).

9. Notably, Robert Merrill, among others, agrees with Heller: "the fact that *Catch-22* appeared sixteen years after the end of World War II suggests that its author was not primarily interested in recapturing the intensity of his own experiences" (4).

10. See, for example, Sam Merrill 68 and Barnard 298.

11. In recounting a letter that his editor received from Bruno Bettelheim, Heller extends the implication of this narrative pattern, admitting in the case of *Something Happened* that the protagonist may be complicit in the child's death: "Now it could be that in terms of drawing on recesses of my mind, with which I'm not in touch, what Bruno Bettelheim said was there [i.e., the validity of a death in which a father deliberately kills his son]. I was not aware that I was aware of it"(Ruas 164).

12. Luciana apparently is an early version of the Luciana of *Catch-22*. As Cramer remembers her: "Luciana was best. Tall, young, and graceful, she was a novice at love, and he remembered her smile as she came to him, her ingenuous astonishment at the sudden force of her passion, and the fumbling manner." This early appearance of Luciana is also interesting for the light that it sheds on Heller's artistic recycling of personal experience. As he tells interviewer Sam Merrill, "[Yossarian's] encounter with Luciana, the Roman whore, corresponds exactly with an experience I had. He sleeps with her, she refuses money and suggests that he keep her address on a slip of paper . . . That's exactly what happened to me in Rome. Luciana was Yossarian's vision of a perfect relationship. That's why he saw her only once, and perhaps that's why I saw her only once. If he examined perfection too closely, imperfections would show up" (64). As *Catch-22* reveals though, the Luciana plot is more closely tied to Heller's core authorial concerns than his remarks about his own personal experience would indicate. In the novel, Luciana's "perfection" is already impaired, for she has been wounded in an air raid and wears a pink chemise to hide her scar even while making love with Yossarian. Yossarian, however, is fascinated by it, runs his hands over it, and insists that she relate its story. Later after he has torn up the slip of paper with her address on it, Yossarian's search for her leads him into symbolic encounters with death: death in his nightmares about the Bologna mission and proleptic death he looks for her in Snowden's room.

13. While the allusion to *Macbeth* dissociates the experience from Heller's own, it also represents a connection, for Heller studied Shakespeare at Oxford while on a Fulbright Fellowship between writing his Avignon stories and planning *Catch-22*. This study may well provide another pathway between Heller's personal experience and the novel. The planning material to *Catch-22* reveals the extensive role literary allusions played in Heller's conception of the novel, especially Shakespearean allusions. For studies of these allusions in *Catch-22,* see Larson, and Aubrey and McCarron.

14. The importance of these elements—death, blood, guilt, and touch—is confirmed by the way that Heller reworks them in *Something Happened*. In its climactic episode, Slocum responds to the "streams of blood spurting from holes in his [son's] face and head and pouring down over one hand from inside a sleeve" by clutching him to his chest and in the process accidentally suffocating him (562). Unlike Yossarian, Slocum resists recounting the event, instead refiguring it, as Heller's chapter title tells us, into how "My boy has stopped talking to me."

15. David Seed shows how war novels like James Jones's From *Here to Eternity* and Norman Mailer's *The Naked and the Dead* also contributed to Heller's evolving conception of *Catch-22*; see 23-33.

16. Extending structuralist thought, Seymour Chatman uses the distinction, story and discourse, to differ-

entiate between narrative content and the means by which this content is transmitted.

17. Patrick O'Neill insightfully demonstrates the way in which humor in modern and postmodern texts depends upon privileging discourse over story. In particular, he is interested in what he calls entropic comedy, comedy that is aware of the fictionality of all discourse and "of the element of play" that is involved in the production of any meaning (23). O'Neill's discussion of *Catch-22* as an example of entropic satire is also valuable, although I disagree with his conclusion that the novel's discourse undercuts the implications of its story.

18. I borrow the notion of a synthetic element of narrative from James Phelan, although I am modifying his definition. Phelan explores the relationship between character and narrative progression, and he conceives of three aspects of character, which in turn contribute to narrative progression: thematic (as conveyer of narrative and authorial meaning), mimetic (as designation for a "person," albeit a textual one), and synthetic (as linguistic construct). I use the concept of synthetic component of narrative progression, without attaching it to character.

19. Peter Rabinowitz distinguishes between narrative and authorial audiences. The authorial audience is the ideal reader posited by an author, the reader who completely attends to authorial intentionality. By contrast, the narrative audience is the reader implied by the text itself, by its narrative and rhetorical structure; this reader participates in the illusion that the text is real, that it constitutes a world.

20. There are several ways in which Heller's imagination links death and women. In the short stories, women frequently occasion symbolic, if not literal deaths. For example, in the unpublished "The Death of the Dying Swan," when Sidney Cooper returns home, he gives up his quest for life and, in effect, accepts death: "He longed for people who were real, people who lived with honest passions and found vigorous pleasure in the mere event of existing, people for whom death came too soon" (Heller papers, Brandeis University). *Something Happened* and *Good as Gold* work variations on this pattern. But Heller also associates women with insensate death, that in which senility (the death of the mind) precedes physical demise. The most noteworthy example of this occurs when Slocum believes his mother's senility and death foretell his own: "I can see myself all mapped out inanimately in stages around that dining room table, from mute beginning (Derek) to mute, fatal, bovine end (Mother), passive and submissive as a cow, and even beyond through my missing father (Dad)" (401). Finally, Heller connects passion with death, as when he uses Yossarian's love-making with Nurse Duckett on the beach to set up the scene in which McWatt's plane hits Kid Sampson, thereby turning the ocean red with blood and severed limbs. Similarly, Yossarian's passion for Luciana leads to death, albeit via memory and dreams.

21. Heller's comic strategies depend upon continually negating or reversing expectations. Typically, Heller's scenes suddenly darken in mood, as he reveals that what the reader has just been laughing at begets violence, death, or the morally outrageous; or similarly, dark scenes beget comic ones, dramatically changing the character of the text. Thus, the comic and the tragic function both as figure and ground in much the way they do in an Escher drawing. They constitute a pattern in which the relationship between figure and ground constantly reverses itself, so that first one element then another assumes the foreground.

22. The threat to operate on Yossarian's liver extends a novel-long joke and set of allusions to the Prometheus myth. As in this instance, the effect is usually double-edged, occasioning laughter and signifying mortality. The motif culminates, of course, in the Snowden death scene when Yossarian inspects the wounded airman's liver along with the other viscera. Heller uses tomatoes to a similar end, especially all the jokes about the chaplain's hot plum tomato. The stewed tomatoes that spill out of Snowden's stomach take part of their meaning from the tomato jokes that preceded them.

23. Heller reprises this conception in his conclusions to *God Knows* and *Closing Time*. In *God Knows,* the image of David's youthful self provides the catalyst for self-discovery. Lying on his deathbed, David serves as his own Snowden. In *Closing Time,* Yossarian and Sammy Singer, a narrator and Heller figure, talk about how Snowden, scarcely an acquaintance in life, becomes the closest of friends in death and the source for what they want to talk about for the rest of their lives.

24. This inspection accomplishes another kind of education as well, one that undercuts the typical military education and that reproduces the experience of combat veterans. As an aside, it bears attention that Heller satirically treats military education throughout *Catch-22*; for example, in such episodes as Lieutenant Scheisskopf's parades and the many briefing sessions. As described by John Keegan in his classic study *The Face of Battle*, the aim of such an education "is to reduce war to a set of rules and a system of procedures—and thereby to make orderly and rational what is es-

sentially chaotic and instinctive. It is an aim analogous to that . . . pursued by medical schools in their fostering among their students a detached attitude to pain and distress in their patients, particularly victims of accidents" (20). Yossarian has long recognized the insanity of war, but he has not, even while treating the wounded Snowden, taken the next step of recognizing his complicity in this insanity. Nor has he yet comprehended the effects of a "military" education. As his subsequent actions demonstrate, his studied recollection of Snowden's death occasions these recognitions. The death scene also serves as a brilliant representation of the sensations of the combat veteran. Again to draw upon John Keegan, in battle the combatants experience a "sense of littleness, almost of nothingness, of their abandonment in a physical wilderness, dominated by vast impersonal forces, from which even the passage of time had been eliminated. The dimensions of the battlefield (in this instance the inside of combat aircraft) . . . reduced [the combatant's] subjective role, objectively vital though it was, to that of a mere victim" (322). Keegan's account closely parallels Yossarian's sensations in the Snowden scene and defines what Yossarian—and by extension the reader—must be reeducated to reject.

25. Edmund Wilson provides the classic formulation of the effects of childhood trauma on Dickens's subsequent career in "Dickens: The Two Scrooges." In part, I have adapted Wilson's argument to discuss the effects Avignon have on Heller's fiction and to draw my characterization of Dickens's comic art.

26. I have greatly benefited from the suggestions of Linda Van Buskirk, Randall Craig, Donald Purcell, John Serio, and Peter Freitag.

Works Cited

Aubrey, James R., and William E. McCarron. "More Shakespearean Echoes in *Catch-22*." *American Notes & Queries*. 3 (January 1990): 25-27.

Bakhtin, M. M. "Epic and Novel." *The Dialogic Imagination,* ed. Michael Holquist, trans. Carl Emerson and Michael Holquist. Austin: U of Texas, 1981.

Barnard, Ken. "Interview with Joseph Heller." *A Catch-22 Casebook,* eds. Frederick Kiley and Walter McDonald. New York: Crowell, 1973. 294-301.

Chatman, Seymour. *Story and Discourse*. Ithaca: Cornell UP, 1978.

Craig, David M. "Joseph Heller's *Catch-22* Revisited." *War, Literature, and the Arts*. 1.2 (1989-90): 33-43.

Flippo, Chet. "Checking in with Joseph Heller." *Rolling Stone*. 16 April 1981: 50 +.

Heller, Joseph. *Catch-22*. New York: Simon and Schuster, 1961.

———. "*Catch-22* and After." *Gentleman's Quarterly*. March 1963, 95 +.

———. "*Catch-22* Revisited." *Holiday* April 1967: 44 +.

———. "On Translating *Catch-22* into a Movie." *A Catch-22 Casebook,* eds. Frederick Kiley and Walter McDonald. New York: Crowell, 1973.

———. *Something Happened*. New York: Knopf, 1974.

———. *Good as Gold*. New York: Simon and Schuster, 1979.

———. *God Knows*. New York: Knopf, 1984.

———. *Picture This*. New York: Putnam, 1988.

———. *Closing Time*. New York: Simon and Schuster, 1994.

Keegan, John. *The Face of Battle*. New York: Viking, 1976.

Larson, Michael. "Shakespearean Echoes in *Catch-22*." *American Notes & Queries*. 17 (1979): 76-78.

Merrill, Robert. *Joseph Heller*. Boston: Twayne, 1987.

Merrill, Sam. "*Playboy* Interview: Joseph Heller." June 1975: 59 +.

Nagel, James. "The *Catch-22* Note Cards." *Studies in the Novel*. 8 (1976): 394-405.

———. "Two Brief Manuscript Sketches." *Modern Fiction Studies*. 20 (1974): 221-224.

O'Neill, Patrick. *The Comedy of Entropy: Humour/Narrative/Reading*. Toronto: U of Toronto P, 1990.

Phelan, James. *Reading People, Reading Plots*. Chicago: U of Chicago P, 1989.

Rabinowitz, Peter. "Truth in Fiction: A Reexamination of Audiences." *Critical Inquiry*. 4 (1977): 121-141.

Rougement, Denis de. *Love in the Western World,* trans. Montgomery Belgion. New York: Pantheon, 1956.

Ruas, Charles. "Joseph Heller." *Conversation with American Writers*. New York: Knopf, 1984.

Said, Edward. *Beginnings: Intention and Method*. New York: Basic Books, 1975.

Seed, David. *The Fiction of Joseph Heller*. New York: St. Martin's, 1989.

Tolstoy, Leo. *The Death of Ivan Ilych and Other Stories*. New York: Signet, 1960.

Weatherby, W. J. "The Joy Catcher." *Guardian*. 20 November 1962: 7.

Wilson, Edmund. *The Wound and the Bow.* New York: Oxford UP, 1947.

Daniel M. Murtaugh (review date 24 February 1995)

SOURCE: Murtaugh, Daniel M. Review of *Closing Time,* by Joseph Heller. *Commonweal* 122, no. 4 (24 February 1995): 57-58.

[*In the following review, Murtaugh finds* Closing Time *to be ultimately disappointing in its "central organizing idea."*]

In Joseph Heller's two best novels, **Catch-22** and **Something Happened,** the narrative circles obsessively around a repressed memory that it is the stories' business finally to confront. We feel the tremors of its eventual eruption in each book even as the narrator frantically distracts us with slapstick improvisation. In his newest novel, **Closing Time,** Heller brings back the (anti-) hero of **Catch 22,** John Yossarian, and once again something horrific is building beneath his life and those of his generation and their century as they all draw to a close.

But this time it is not a brute fact lodged in memory, the something that draws its power simply from having happened. It is instead something that is going to happen—we're going to die—and it draws its power from—well—how we feel about that. The problem is that we may not all feel the same way about our approaching death, as we cannot fail to do about Howie Snowden bleeding to death on the floor of the bomber in **Catch 22.** We cannot really imagine our death. On the other hand, try as we might, we cannot help imagining Snowden. It comes down to a question of authority, the authority of an author's claim on our imagination. There is less of it in **Closing Time.**

It reaches for such authority by reading into the passing of the World War II generation a paranoid apocalypse in the manner of Thomas Pynchon and Don DeLillo. Yossarian's life goes into and out of a kind of virtual reality involving a Dantesque underworld entered through the false back of a basement tool locker in the New York Port Authority Bus Terminal. Beneath this underworld runs an underground railroad meant to provide indefinite protection for the elite of the military/industrial/political complex chosen by triage to survive the coming nuclear holocaust. As catalyst for that holocaust we are given a mentally challenged president known to us only by his affectionate nickname, the Little Prick, who is enthralled by the video games that fill a room just off the Oval Office, especially the game called Triage which enables him eventually to trip the wire on the conclusive Big Bang.

Heller's underworld has some fetching attributes. It is managed by George C. Tilyou, the Coney Island entrepreneur who ran the Steeplechase amusement park before World War I. Tilyou died before any of the novel's protagonists was born, but the remembered stories about him and his slowly sinking house with the family name on the front step qualify him as a jolly major domo of hell, a man whose love for his fellows sincerely expressed itself in fleecing them. Now, below the sub-sub-basement of the bus terminal, he rejoices in having taken it with him, for his house and eventually his whole amusement park sank down around him. Rockefeller and Morgan come by and panhandle miserably for his wealth, having learned too late that their more conventional philanthropy could not sanctify their plunder or secure their grasp on it.

Other aspects of Heller's grand scheme are less successful. Two characters from **Catch 22,** Milo Minderbinder and ex-Pfc. Wintergreen, are strawmen representatives of the military-industrial complex, peddling a nonexistent clone of the Stealth bomber to a succession of big-brass boobies with names like Colonel Pickering and Major Bowes. Much of this is the sort of thing that killed vaudeville and is now killing *Saturday Night Live.*

Against these gathering forces of death, Yossarian asserts his allegiance to life in a way that is by now a reflex of the Norman Mailer generation: he has an affair with and impregnates a younger woman, a nurse whom he meets in a hospitalization of doubtful purpose at the opening of the novel. Thank heavens, I thought as I read, that I belong to the only sex capable of such late and surprising assertions. But, as the euphoria ebbed, I had to admit that Yossarian's amatory exertions were more than faintly repulsive.

So the novel is disappointing where it hurts the most, in its central organizing idea. Why, after all, does Yossarian's generation get to take the whole world down with it? Well, it doesn't, really, and yet the veterans of World War II do have a special claim on us as they pass from our sight. This claim is more convincingly urged by the long first-person narratives of two characters who, we learn, moved invisibly on the periphery of events in **Catch-22.**

Lew Rabinowitz and Sammy Singer are non-neurotics whose stories reveal their limitations and, at the same time, allow us to see around and beyond them. This is harder to do with normal people, and Heller brings it off beautifully. Rabinowitz is an aggressive giant, the son of a Coney Island junk dealer, an instinctively successful businessman who lacked the patience for the college education offered him by the G.I. Bill, and who never comprehended as we do his own delicacy of feeling. Singer, a writer of promotional and ad copy for

Times, is, by his own account, a bit of a pedant given to correcting Rabinowitz's grammar. Heller sometimes allows Singer's prose style to stiffen in a way that is entirely in character and that gives an unexpected dignity and pathos to passages like those that describe his wife's last illness.

Rabinowitz and Singer basically get more respect from their author than Yossarian and the characters who figure in his story. The two new characters tell us stories embued with an unforced humor and with the sort of gravity that attends good people as they come to terms with their mortality. And this goes for their wives as well, for both men make good and entirely credible marriages that last a lifetime. Yossarian should have been so lucky.

Joseph Heller and Charlie Reilly (interview date 24 October 1996)

SOURCE: Heller, Joseph, and Charlie Reilly. "An Interview with Joseph Heller." *Contemporary Literature* 39, no. 4 (winter 1998): 507-22.

[*In the following interview, which took place on October 24, 1996, Heller discusses his themes, influences, and techniques for writing his novels.*]

Despite the fact that he has also composed two memoirs (***No Laughing Matter*** [1986] and ***Now and Then*** [1998]) and a drama (***We Bombed in New Haven*** [1967]), Joseph Heller's reputation rests, in general, upon his six novels, and in particular upon the first of those six, ***Catch-22*** (1961). Although ***Catch-22*** remains his most celebrated work, each of Heller's novels was written and has been received as a work of literary fiction, and each has been praised in that special context. His rich humor, high satire, and relentless experimentation have earned him professorships (at Oxford, Yale, and Penn, to name a few), honors, and literally millions of readers during his four and one-half decades of writing.

Though laced with humor, Heller's novels are fiercely critical of his times. As is often the case with satire, again and again his works involve a startling confrontation with the reader. The world of Heller's fiction is an eerily insane one—perhaps an eerily sane one—filled with preposterous characters mired in outrageous circumstances. But long before each novel's end, the reader recognizes the connections between Heller's apparent absurdity and the target of his satire. Though speaking about ***Catch-22,*** Heller described his overall modus operandi when he said to me, "My objective is not merely to tell the reader a story but to make him a participant—to have him experience the book rather than read it" (*Delaware Literary Review* Spring 1975).

With more than ten million copies sold, ***Catch-22*** remains one of modern literature's most admired novels. Drawing upon his World War II experiences as a bombardier, Heller plunges the reader into a world in which generals cheerfully send men to be slaughtered, officers lie and steal, whores become heroines, and, as Falstaff puts it in a similar context, "Honor is a mere scutcheon." Time has been turned upside down in the world of ***Catch-22.*** Characters killed off in early passages pop up noisily in later chapters; dead men live on in empty tents; living men are "disappeared." Some characters get rich selling chocolate-covered cotton; others vault hundreds of miles in apparent seconds. When all is said and done, Heller composed a brilliant attack not only upon the horror and lunacy of a just-completed war but upon the hypocrisy and savagery of the ongoing McCarthy witch-hunts. In addition, as he explains in this interview, his work was closely entwined with Homer's Iliad. And, with "Catch-22" itself, he added a phrase to the language.

Conscious of his first novel's extraordinary success, Heller spent thirteen years "doing something different." The result, ***Something Happened*** (1974), is a chilling description of the deterioration and breakdown of a Manhattan business executive. Again, Heller's work operates in the worlds of literature and satire. The author does not hesitate to credit Samuel Beckett's *Molloy, Malone Dies,* and *The Unnamable* for the book's most striking feature: the forlorn, almost detached voice of its first-person narrator. Heller's attack on the aridity and agonies of corporate existence is superbly handled, but more than anything else it is the narrator's description of his own dissolution which makes the novel so arresting.

Each of the next three works reflects Heller's determination not to repeat himself and his continued use of satire and literature. ***Good as Gold*** (1979) ferociously criticizes modern politics in general and Henry Kissinger in particular. Its method of narration is reminiscent of a Barth-like postmodernism: the unnamed third-person narrator plays an important role in the tale and at one point butts in to concede that he could have better served the protagonist. But Heller's inspiration predates postmodernism: much of his manipulation of point of view, he has said, derived from Laurence Sterne's *Tristram Shandy* ("Talking with Joseph Heller," *Critical Essays on Joseph Heller* [Hall, 1984] 178-79).

God Knows (1984) continues the march. Again, the work is filled with satiric humor. Again, it is rich in literary allusions. ***God Knows*** is a lengthy deathbed monologue by the Bible's King David. On the one hand, David seems like a stand-up comedian, railing against a God who owes him an apology, deploring the thickwittedness of his son Solomon, and shaking his head over Michelangelo's depiction of an uncircumcised member. On the other hand, Heller comments tellingly about the misapprehensions and misery that have followed in the wake of far too many Biblical passages.

Picture This (1988) raises Heller's fascination with narrative point of view to new heights. Reduced to its simplest terms, the book considers Rembrandt's famous painting *Aristotle Contemplating the Bust of Homer.* But the novel is really a satire on war and politics—in ancient Athens and Sparta, in seventeenth-century Holland and Vietnam, and in twentieth-century America and Vietnam. Heller's use of point of view in ***Picture This*** is his most ambitious to date, with his tale alternately "told" by Rembrandt, Aristotle, and Homer, each brilliantly re-created.

Closing Time (1994), the subject of this interview, reflects a startling change for Joseph Heller. For the first time in his fiction, he comes face to face with the legacy of ***Catch-22***—and does so in a sequel which resurrects some of the more memorable creations of that legendary first novel. In the interview, Heller speaks tenderly of the "real life" characters in his book, the most realistic he has ever created, and describes the intricate and carefully planned method he uses to create his novels. In addition, he speaks at length about his use of a dual point of view, the relationships between ***Catch-22*** and ***Closing Time,*** and the connections between ***Catch-22*** and the *Iliad.*

This interview took place on October 24, 1996, at Joseph Heller's home in East Hampton, New York. Words cannot express my gratitude for Mr. Heller's generosity, his hospitality, and his wise responses to my often fumbling questions. To make a splendid day perfect, Mr. Heller took me for a post-interview stroll on a windswept beach, then led the way to "the Hamptons' best tomato stand."

And there was no catch.

[Reilly]: *A few years ago Mordecai Richler wrote that the Brooklyn passages in* **Something Happened** *contained some of best writing you have ever done.* **Closing Time** *spends a lot of time in Brooklyn, especially in your old Coney Island section, and it contains some of the most grippingly realistic characters you have ever created. Did they play an important role in the original plan of the novel?*

[Heller]: My ambitions lay elsewhere. To one degree or another, the characters you are describing were based on people who have been on my mind for a long time—maybe it has something to do with being in my seventies. I never wanted to write an autobiography, but part of my plan was to write a novel which contained autobiographical elements. The structure of ***Closing Time*** was very carefully planned; everything in there was intended to be in there. It was a different matter with ***Catch-22,*** where some of the characters, like Milo and Major Major, had a far greater effect than I had originally intended.

My original plan, and I can't think of a good word for it, was more literary than anything else. I knew from the start I wanted to develop a sharp contrast between realistic and surrealistic techniques, and I wanted to keep two sets of characters and styles apart for most of the novel. With one exception, when Sammy visits Lew in the hospital and sees Yossarian, the scenes with the Brooklyn characters were consciously written in a realistic style.

That hospital scene, by the way, illustrates another difference between ***Closing Time*** and the other novels. In ***Catch-22*** I probably would have further developed the discussion about the extent to which modern medicine has become unnatural, the extent to which it interferes with the natural direction of biology.

Those scenes seemed different from ones in your other novels. Certainly Bob Slocum is realistically portrayed in **Something Happened,** *but Lew, Sammy, Claire, and Glenda seemed so real that I feel I could drive over to Coney Island today and bump into them. Are they based on real people?*

Glenda Singer is a combination of three people, one of them my ex-wife, but she is mostly based on an old friend. When I was at *Time* magazine, I became close to a guy named Jerry Broidy and his wife, and she died of ovarian cancer pretty much the way Glenda did. At times Sammy Singer is me, but only at times; ultimately he's a literary character. The story of Claire Rabinowitz is no story; it actually happened: when they met, how they married, even the business about her virginity. Lew is a very real figure. We met in elementary school and remained close friends until the day he died. You could call us disease-ridden pals: he lived fourteen years with Hodgkin's disease and I've been living with the residual weaknesses of Guillain-Barre Syndrome since 1981.

I've never talked about it much, but I have a very special memory of Lew and ***Catch-22.*** When the book came out and got that terrible review in the *Times* book review section, my first wife and I got out of town. We went up to Middletown to spend the weekend with Lew and his wife. To this day I don't know how he managed it, but he arranged for the one bookstore in town to fill the window with copies of ***Catch-22.*** It was the perfect gesture at a time when I would have been grateful for any gesture. You know, despite our lifelong friendship, I have no idea whether he ever read the book. Or any of my books. It didn't matter; he was a friend, not a reader.

Claire Rabinowitz and Glenda Singer were so vivid, so convincing. They are beautiful creations.

Thank you; they were intended to be. I'm happy to hear your response to them, and I think I know the reason why. **Closing Time** is the first time in my work, and, I think, the first time in the work of any American male novelist in this century, where women are consistently treated with respect and where marriage is consistently described as a desirable condition. Three strong influences on me when I was younger were Ernest Hemingway, Irwin Shaw, and John O'Hara. I don't think you can find a woman in any of their works who is treated with sympathy of a marriage which is described as nourishing.

Closing Time *is not all about disease and death, but there is a lot of disease and death in it.*

You're right: there is a recurrent theme of cancer, of malignance, and, I hope, a not too obvious attempt to link that malignance with imperialism and social behavior. If you read the book again, you'll find there are remarks linking the way cancer cells spread to the way imperialist nations colonize and destroy. I didn't want to beat the point to death because at this stage of the history of novels, and at my own stage in my small history of novels, it would be emphasizing what is fairly obvious. Nor am I the first one to compare certain industrialists of the past to malignant forces. The unfortunate difference is, unlike empires, they don't wind up destroying themselves. They wind up getting rich.

When I contemplated the death and destruction in **Closing Time,** *I found myself thinking about Swift's epitaph, about his savage indignation. I wonder what the effect was of writing about the deaths of characters who were part of your own life, and about the deteriorating condition of the planet. Did it take its toll? Did you find yourself savagely indignant?*

No, no. It's something I discovered while writing what became the first draft of **Catch-22**. The attitude of the writer is very much different from that of the reader—at least I hope it is. Writing is a ruthless process, a detached process. I can be furious about a subject before or after writing, I can be furious during research. But during the act of writing, if it's done well, I'm happy. Elmer Edgar Stoll once made a very wise comment about Shakespeare. He said it was ridiculous to assume Shakespeare was depressed when he wrote *Hamlet* and *Lear*. Depressed people, Stoll said, don't write.

The way Snowden's death is, ultimately, described in **Catch-22** is a good example. I wrote it in longhand—I still write my first drafts in longhand—and I deliberately described it in a traditional manner: precise details, normal time sequence, and so forth. I've reread it on a number of occasions, and, even though I knew what was going to happen, it had an extremely powerful effect on me. But at the time I wrote the scene it took me two, maybe three, nights to get it right, and when I finished I knew it was good. I'll never forget it: at that moment I had an impulse to laugh out loud. Giddy, triumphant, relieved? But certainly the effect it was intended to have on the reader was profoundly different from the feelings I was experiencing. I had a similar detachment with those realistic scenes in **Closing Time**.

I suspect this is true of all the arts. It became clear to me while writing **Picture This** that, while Rembrandt was working on *The Crucifixion,* he was at least as concerned with the painting as with the crucifixion. Certainly he didn't break down and start praying to the image he was creating. Probably the most moving of the literary arts is the theater because it's actually taking place in front of you. But if you stop to think of the process of putting on a play—all the rewriting, all the rehearsals—you can see the subject matter becomes increasingly less important. And, when it's done, the experience of watching it in the audience is not the experience of putting it together.

I do an enormous amount of planning, of prewriting, so in the process of writing I always know what the next chapter will be about and where the book is going. Emotionally, the writing is not difficult. What takes its toll is the act of writing, the struggling for the right word or sentence or image. And, of course, the revision; I cut more than two hundred typed pages from **Closing Time.** So any time I find the fight word for a sentence or get an idea which I know is the right one, I am exhilarated. I am tempted to say that's probably true for all novelists, but "exhilarated" might not be the right word to describe Samuel Beckett. He always seemed depressed.

I guess I'm headed for another "No" because I was deeply touched by **No Laughing Matter** *and wondered if you were using all you went through with Guillain-Barre Syndrome when writing about the suffering in* **Closing Time.**

How about, You're right in that you're not right? In **Closing Time** you'll find the emphasis is on the natural deterioration of the human being. What you have with Sammy, Glenda, and Lew are natural processes. Sammy's wife gets cancer and dies; Lew gets Hodgkin's disease and lives—lives well, in fact—until his time runs out. By the end, the emphasis is on the inevitability of death. Yossarian and Sammy are in their seventies. Each of them knows he is not going to have much more time. Sammy's resigned to it; he doesn't expect anything surprising or important to happen to him. Yossarian is the eternal optimist. He's falling in love again and he's going to live for the day.

Something that fascinated me about **Closing Time** *was its dual nature. There were times with Milo and Yossarian when I was almost helpless with laughter, the satire was so biting.*

Yes, good.

And then, all of a sudden, wham! The scenes with Lew and Sammy were so riveting. With Lew you can see him slipping, you can feel the pain, and you get to like him so much. Did you write the two "halves" of the novel the way I read them, or were they written as separate pieces?

I wrote the chapters consecutively—in other words, just as you read them—and I had that dualism in mind from the very beginning. I was consciously working with two different forms of fiction: realism and something which is at least analogous to surrealism. I wanted to write a novel which was consistent with the way the human mind works. It works consciously, it works unconsciously, and it very much deals with memory. George C. Tilyou is literally a fantastic figure, and yet there is a scene where he shows up with Lew and with a couple of "real" characters from *Catch-22*. I was dealing there with what we might call consciousness and the part of the human mind that remembers.

I'm not sure I follow that.

Think about the idea of an afterlife and the existence of a fantasy life. At one time or another, everyone speculates about some form of afterlife, whether we believe in it or not. In *Closing Time* there is an afterlife of sorts—I'm thinking of J. P. Morgan, Henry Ford, George C. Tilyou, and the other dead characters who seem to return to the world of the living. With Tilyou, you are aware you're dealing with fantasy, and, within the context of the novel, you know Chaplain Tappman is a real person. When the two almost meet, there is a fusion, a fusion between the real and the fantastic. Again, think of the way the human mind works.

How long did **Closing Time** *take?*

The usual, between four and five years.

And right from the start did you know where you were going?

Oh yes. With all of my novels, by the time I really start writing I know where it's going and how it will end. In fact, with almost every one I had a precise opening sentence in mind before I began. Sometimes that particular sentence didn't wind up at the beginning of page 1, it wound up somewhere else in an early passage. But from the very beginning of *Closing Time,* I had that sentence: "When people our age speak of the war it is not of Vietnam but of the one that broke out more than half a century ago and swept in almost all the world." That sentence was the genesis of the novel. Then I decided, if I'm going to do a work about the war, it's got to be somewhat autobiographical in nature, and then I decided it made sense to work in my own novel, *Catch-22,* in some way or another.

Had something like **Closing Time** *been in the back of your mind for a long time?*

No, it hadn't; it was a sudden thing.

Do you think somewhere in the back of your mind you were avoiding a return to **Catch-22**?

No, I neither consciously avoided it nor sought to improve upon it. I have enough trouble coming up with an idea for a novel, so I certainly wouldn't be inclined to avoid anything. Throughout my career I've always had only one idea for a novel at a time. This one started out as a wish to write about the war and a subsequent wish to include autobiographical materials. If I had begun by thinking about a sequel to *Catch-22*, I probably would have rejected the idea out of hand. Although *Closing Time* is a sequel.

At the same time, so much of it was inspired by current events. With the wedding in the Port Authority bus terminal, I know I had *The Great Gatsby* somewhere in my mind, and I know I had been struck by a social event in East Hampton where the hostess put together living tableaux of her favorite paintings. But once I decided to include the wedding scene, my real inspiration was newspaper and magazine clippings about real, spectacular weddings. It was fascinating reading, and by the time I started to write that chapter, I had quite a portfolio. Then it was largely a matter of exaggeration.

It was a wonderful touch to use the Port Authority bus terminal. I've been in and out of it since I was a kid and was always struck by the way it seemed a cross between a bustling urban transportation center and, well, a zoo.

It was just what I had in mind. You'll find just about every level of American society there except the very wealthy—who don't take buses and who give their galas in places like the Metropolitan Museum of Art or the New York Public Library. *Closing Time* reflects the fact that, even in the best neighborhoods, homeless people and beggars can no longer be hidden. At least I was trying to make that statement.

Could we talk about the climax of **Closing Time**?

I'd be happy to. I worked hard on it, and while I won't say it's even better than the ending of *Catch-22*, I wouldn't want to choose between them. *Closing Time* began with Sammy, and I knew I wanted to end with Sammy. As a rule I have the final chapter of a book at least in rough draft, sometimes in finished prose, very early in the writing process. With **Closing Time** I had those last pages written before I was halfway through the book. The same thing was true of **Catch-22**.

When I finished the novel I was deeply stirred and quite confused. Characters are descending forty miles below the ground, dead people are walking around, Gaffney says we don't need the wedding now that we have it on tape, Yossarian goes back up the escalator, apparently convinced he and Melissa and the baby will survive. And, at the same time, the sun is an ashen gray, Mc-Watt and Kid Sampson, the "ghost riders in the sky," have to go in again for yet another bombing mission, and the radio system on Sammy's airplane seems to have failed. The book ends from Sammy's point of view, and he reports, "the yellow moon turned orange and soon was as red as a setting sun." I don't know quite how to ask this question, but it seems clear the world is about to be blown up.

Exactly.

To be honest, I had been counting on the reviewers to help me out, but with two exceptions they all but ignored the approaching apocalypse. Would you comment on the ending?

Either the world is ending or it's not. Yossarian doesn't know what he'll find when he goes outside, and I don't know either. Whether the end is taking place fight there on that page, or whether it will take place in a week or two when the missiles come back, or whether it will take place in a billion years when the sun explodes, it's going to take place. Some of the imagery in the final pages comes from Revelation—for example, the comments about the ships being turned over and the moon being red.

I deliberately included contradictions between what Sammy and Yossarian see and think. I don't know the answer. The people you want to ask are Yossarian, Sammy, and Claire. Me, I have no idea, and I don't want the reader to have any idea. They asked me the same question about the ending to **Catch-22,** and I have the same answer: I really don't know.

*Fair enough; you're the author. But after all the uproar about the "fairy-tale" ending of **Catch-22**, the critics went back to what you wrote and decided what you had in mind made sense. And I think you cleared matters up in **Closing Time**.*

Good. I guess some critics didn't want **Catch-22** to end the way it did. I suppose it could be called a fantasy ending.

*But in fairness to you, at the end of **Catch-22** your text makes it clear that Yossarian isn't doing anything fantastic. As he says, the point is he is trying, and someone's got to break the chain.*

That's correct. Yossarian is running into danger, not away from it. He says there's a little girl in Rome whom he might be able to save. It's ironic that, after all the discussion about the ending of the novel, the film depicts Yossarian trying to row to Sweden. Nothing could have been farther from the case in the novel.

*I loved the way in **Closing Time** someone asks Yossarian, Didn't you get away on a little yellow raft? and he replies, That only happens in the movies.*

A couple of people who have written about the book, especially after the film came out, seem to think the book ends that way.

Catch-22 doesn't end that way, and neither does Homer's Iliad. *You've said there are connections.*

Conscious ones. **Catch-22** was not an imitation of the *Iliad*—for example, there is so much fantasy and humor in my novel. But I was very conscious of Homer's epic when writing the novel, and at one point, late in the book, I directly compare Yossarian to Achilles. At the same time, I'd be the first to agree that, as a hero, Yossarian is different from most heroes of antiquity. From most heroes, period.

My ending had the same problem the Trojans had, that damned horse. Most people think the *Iliad* ends with the Trojan horse, but Homer's work, and mine, stop long before. Just as the *Iliad* is ending, there's that magnificent scene when Achilles meets with Priam and his sympathy and emotions finally come pouring out. The ending of **Catch-22** shows Yossarian going through a similar experience.

*Were you thinking of Homer's ending when you wrote the conclusion to **Catch-22**?*

Very much so. The *Iliad* was one of the first books I read and enjoyed as a child. The first version I read was a children's version, and it came "complete" with the horse and the fall of Troy. I recall that the first time I read the real *Iliad* I was shocked; I thought I had stumbled upon a corrupt edition. But the more I thought about "Homer's ending," the more I admired it.

The opening lines of an epic are so important. The *Iliad*'s very first line talks about "the dreadful anger of Achilles"—not about the fall of Troy or the Trojan horse or anything else. And the final scene with Priam shows Achilles' nobler side overcoming that wrath. **Catch-22** went beyond that, of course; it was very much concerned with attitudes toward war, attitudes toward bureaucracy. It occurred to me at one point that I could draw an analogy between Yossarian and Colonel Cathcart, on one hand, and Achilles and Agamemnon on the other. But it wouldn't have worked. Agamemnon and Cathcart are completely different people.

There is another echo of the *Iliad* insofar as the hierarchy of power is concerned. At the beginning Homer makes it clear Achilles isn't interested in acquiring another concubine; he wants Agamemnon to return the priest's daughter. When Agamemnon returns the girl and then steals Briseis, Achilles finds himself powerless. He broods in his tent until Patroclus is killed and then he finally takes action. Yossarian is faced with a similar problem. He is powerless until, after Nately's death, he is driven to break the chain.

And yet in **Closing Time** *some of the chain seems unbroken. I thought one passage in the conclusion was heartbreaking: when two characters who were killed in* **Catch-22,** *McWatt and Kid Sampson, almost sigh as they realize they'll "have to go in again."*

It is heartbreaking. Since I began **Closing Time,** we've had Grenada, Panama, and the Gulf War. They'll find a reason to go in again, and again, and again.

In **Closing Time** *you provide some fascinating information about what happens "after"* **Catch-22.** *For example, you have someone explain to Yossarian that "they sent us home as soon as they caught you."*

I've been asked that question by so many readers: what happened to the rest of them after Yossarian broke the chain? It was a case of feeling that anyone who read *Catch-22* with some respect was entitled to an explanation.

Dante's and Thomas Mann's works play very important roles in **Closing Time.** *Were they on your mind from the start?*

Death in Venice was there almost from the start. The scene when Yossarian was in the hospital seemed a good place to make a literary analogy between Yossarian and Aschenbach, although it didn't occur to me at the time that Yossarian was a good deal older. I especially had Dante in mind in the final chapters. The references to a sea of ice and lake of blood are from the *Inferno*. In the scene where Yossarian is walking with his son, the images of blood under the wheels of the limousine and the cartridges that look like arrows are from Dante.

At the risk of going too far, why?

You might ask the same question about the literary allusions in *Catch-22,* and the answer would be the same: I don't know why. It seemed appropriate to me in those books to make use of them. Now I'll say this: **Closing Time** is very much about literature, contemporary literature, as expressed in its various literary styles.

I didn't mean it to be a smart-aleck question.

I didn't take it that way. I took it as an effort, like Einstein's, to get a unified theory. It was important to me that **Closing Time** maintain a literary approach and not be unduly concerned with physics and quantum mechanics and atomic bombs. The potential of nuclear destruction is such an important issue, and so often it's treated the way they treat Chaplain Tappman when he starts passing heavy water: "He's a big problem and we're kind of sorry we discovered him."

Closing Time *contains some gripping descriptions of the fire-bombing of Dresden, and Kurt Vonnegut appears in the novel. What were your descriptions based on?*

I did some research—a book which very much impressed me was an autobiography of a woman who had lived through it as a girl—and many of the details came from Kurt Vonnegut himself. My wife and I have gotten to know him and his wife. They're very nice people.

It occurs to me for the first time that you were a bombardier and Vonnegut was bombed on. Did you ever talk about it?

No, never together.

Are you ever haunted by the memory of the bombs you dropped?

No. Remember the first line of **Closing Time**: "When people my age speak of the war. . . ." It was a different time. If I had had orders to bomb Dresden, I would have bombed Dresden. At the same time, most of our sixty missions were directed at bridges, and I know I concentrated on the bridges, not the people who might be nearby. There was one mission, though—it found its way into *Catch-22*—where we had to bomb a village into a road. We had to destroy it, in other words, in such a manner so it would become a roadblock.

Yes. That's where Dunbar deliberately misses the target, and Yossarian reaches a point where he is able to say he no longer cares where his bombs fall. That really happened?

It happened. That time I was aware we were bombing civilians, but I can't say it had much of an effect on me. Even when I got to that part of *Catch-22*—it was almost ten years to the day—the writing didn't affect me. But thinking about it did. Thinking about it certainly affects me now.

You know, I have often thought about the differences between a German soldier and an American soldier back then. I can't carry the idea too far myself since, if I had been a German, they would have put me into an oven instead of an airplane. But I guess while I lasted I would have been as patriotic a German as I was an American. Which is not that patriotic. You do what you're told, to become socially acceptable.

I guess anyone who didn't live through it can only imagine what it was like.

I can't say I lived through "it." I've talked to some of the people in the infantry and read about what was going on in Eighth Air Force, and I feel I was not in that war. They had a totally different experience. Paul Fussell has a new book out—its title, *Doing Battle: The Making of a Skeptic,* says so much—and his description of combat is harrowing.

This is my "Say it ain't so, Joe" question. **Closing Time** *closes down so many things . . .*

Oh no, it's not my last book—if for no other reason than I'd have nothing else to do all day out here in East Hampton. I enjoy writing more than anything else. I enjoy spending two or more hours a day being lost in it, being absorbed by it. It's not that simple, of course. A problem I always have is, What do I write next? I don't want to imitate myself, ever.

I think of **Catch-22** *and* **Something Happened** *and* **Picture This** *and* **Closing Time.** *You'd have a hard time imitating. . . .*

Actually it would be easy, but I would never be what I call absorbed in such a project, and it would not be successful. I've often been asked to describe my "literary talent," and when you get asked that enough, you get to thinking. As a rule the basic story line, the sequence of action, plays a minor role in my books. It's the texture, the approach, which makes them distinctive. I don't deal with conventional plots, most of my novels don't even follow chronological sequence. To write, I need a new idea, a complicated idea—not an imitation of something I've already done.

For a time I toyed with another biblical book but it wasn't right for me. I had the first line, though: "God's wife had been against the idea from the start." It's a good beginning, and if I had been younger, if I had thought of it after *Catch-22,* I might have done that book. But it would take me a year just for the planning, and I've done too much of it already—the biblical humor, the feminism, God's life.

I guess part of the fun with Joseph Heller is that the reader has no idea what the next book will be about.

Joseph Heller doesn't know either. He puts together a vision of a novel that he feels ought to be written, a novel that he, that I, can write. Imitation has nothing to do with it. There are some authors whom I find delightful, but I know I would be foolish even to attempt to imitate them. Right now I am fascinated with John Barth's latest book, *On with the Story.* I read it once and was so intrigued I sat down and read it again. It's a collection of short stories, but I found myself reading it as a novel. There are connecting episodes which I suspect deal with the same couple, and I feel there is a good deal of autobiographical material too. It's a terrific book—well conceived, well executed. Now I could never write like John Barth, and I'd be foolish to try. He has such an impressive mind and such an array of literary techniques. Right from the start, from *Floating Opera* and *End of the Road,* you could see how talented he was. And he wrote them both in a very short period of time, some say in a year.

In any case, no, it's not closing time for me. I am working on something new, but I try never to talk about works in progress.

James Nagel (essay date 1996)

SOURCE: Nagel, James. "The Early Composition History of *Catch-22*." In *Biographies of Books: The Compositional Histories of Notable American Writings,* edited by James Barbour and Tom Quirk, pp. 262-90. Columbia: University of Missouri Press, 1996.

[*In the following essay, Nagel explores Heller's writing process for* Catch-22, *finding the early draft manuscripts rich with implications for the final published version of the novel.*]

In 1978, the *Wilson Quarterly* conducted a survey of professors of American literature to determine the most important novels published after World War II. To be sure, the result was a most impressive list, but Joseph Heller's *Catch-22* was ranked first.[1] Its position in this survey indicates the esteem and seriousness with which literary scholars have come to regard Heller's first novel since it appeared in October 1961. Only two months later, on December 7, 1961, Heller took obvious pleasure in writing to the dean of the College of Arts and Letters at the University of Notre Dame that "*Catch-22* is already being discussed in literature courses at Harvard, Brown, and two universities here in New York City."[2] Since Heller had taught for two years in the Department of English at Pennsylvania State University, he was fully conversant with the academy, with both its genuine intellectual stimulation and its professional excesses. Indeed, in the early stages of planning *Catch-22,* Heller had planned a satiric scene in which Major

Major "meets an old drunk at an MLA convention who was ruined by a man who said he liked Henry James."[3] In another section Major Major "was from the winter wheat fields of Vermont and a former teacher of English. Made the mistake of stating publicly that he did not like Henry James," and there is a suggestion that Major Major "never realized that Proust and Henry James were the same man." Although these comments did not survive to the final version of the novel, no one would have enjoyed the satire more than Heller's former colleagues in the academy.

Beyond its high regard in universities throughout the world, *Catch-22* has become an enormous commercial success as well, selling well over ten million copies in just the first two decades after it was published. Such enormous popularity seems to have come as something of a surprise to both author and publisher, since Simon and Schuster is reported to have ordered a first printing of only 4,000 copies. The financial arrangements, too, suggest modest expectations for all concerned; Heller's advance for the novel was only $1,500, $750 upon signing the contract and another $750 when the manuscript was delivered.[4] Nor did the novel enjoy immediate success: it did not make the best-seller list in hardbound and did not become an international sensation until the paperback edition was released. Some of the attention paid to the novel was surely due to its satiric treatment of war and to the escalating antiwar feeling throughout the 1960s, what Pearl K. Bell labeled "that passionately antiwar decade and its nay-saying, antinomian, black-comic Zeitgeist."[5]

It was a fortuitous coincidence, for nowhere in the *Catch-22* materials is there any reference to the Vietnam War or anything like it, although the novel and the manuscripts resonate with antiwar sentiments, including a notation Heller recorded in 1955 that Douglas MacArthur, in his seventy-fifth-birthday speech, urged "people to let their leaders know that they will refuse to fight wars."[6] But even without the Vietnam War, *Catch-22* would have been notable on purely artistic grounds, for writers and literary scholars quickly responded to its robust wit, devastating satire, and complex satiric method that hearkened to the eighteenth century as well as to the twentieth. John Steinbeck, for example, wrote to Heller in July of 1963 to say that he felt peace had become as ridiculous as war and that he found the novel "great" for both its attitude and its writing. Among others, James Jones, himself the author of a highly regarded war novel, wrote to Simon and Schuster to express his sense of awe at the conflict of tragedy and comedy in the book, finding it "delightful" and "disturbing." Perhaps illustrative of the broad appeal of the novel, actor Tony Curtis wrote to Heller as early as 1962 expressing an interest in doing the movie and calling himself Yossarian.[7]

Despite the enormous popularity of Heller's first novel, and the volume of critical attention it has received in the three decades since it was published, relatively little attention has been paid to the composition history of *Catch-22,* even though the record of the growth of the manuscripts reveals a great deal about the development of the central themes and devices as the concept grew over the years.[8] Of particular importance are the early notes and drafts of the manuscript, for they are enormously detailed and complex, often direct in stating Heller's objectives and reservations about what he was doing with his material. Heller's memories of the beginning of his first novel have been recorded many times in interviews, always with the same basic story:

> I was lying in bed in my four room apartment on the West Side when suddenly this line came to me: "It was love at first sight. The first time he saw the chaplain 'Someone' fell madly in love with him." I didn't have the name Yossarian. The chaplain wasn't necessarily an army chaplain—he could have been a *prison* chaplain. But as soon as the opening sentence was available, the book began to evolve clearly in my mind, even most of the particulars—the tone, the form, many of the characters, including some I eventually couldn't use. All of this took place within an hour and a half. It got me so excited that I did what the cliché says you're supposed to do: I jumped out of bed and paced the floor. That morning I went to my job at the advertising agency and wrote out the first chapter in long hand. Before the end of the week, I had typed it out and sent it to Candida Donadio, my agent. One year later, after much planning, I began chapter two.[9]

The idea was to offer it as the first chapter of a book, and, as a result, it appeared as "Catch-18" in *New World Writing* later that year.[10]

Precisely when the original composition of the novel began has been a matter of some confusion, since Heller has indicated both 1953 and 1955 as the starting dates for the novel, probably referring to different stages in the development of the concept. There are indications in the manuscript, however, that Heller started working on the idea in 1953, trying out many different approaches to the novel before he arrived at the strategy used in the first chapter that was published two years later. By this time Heller had drafted hundreds of note cards outlining virtually every character and incident in the novel along with pages of sketches, conversations, time schemes, and the development of various themes.[11] It is clear that by 1955 he had a first chapter to publish but did not have a major section of the novel completed until 1957, when he submitted it to Robert Gottlieb at Simon and Schuster. Gottlieb was only twenty-six at the time, and a junior editor, but he expressed his interest in the project, made some suggestions, and Heller signed a contract the following year. It took him three more years to complete work on the novel. After publication in late 1961, Heller became an international sensation, and Robert Gottlieb became editor-in-chief of Alfred A. Knopf.

The initial composition of **Catch-22** is important in several senses. On the simplest, perhaps the most important, level, it records the process of invention of one of the most remarkable novels of the twentieth century. It is no inconsequential body of papers that will reveal the process of significant creation at work, and the manuscripts clearly show Heller suggesting ideas to himself, discarding them, outlining possible structures for the shape of his narrative, trying out absurd conversations that underscore important themes. There is much to be learned about both characters and themes in material that was never published, for the manuscripts often are clear about motivations for various actions that are unclear in the novel, why Yossarian went into the hospital with a false liver ailment, for example. In many instances scenes and speeches in the manuscripts elucidate an episode in the published novel. A world of biographical reference in the manuscripts is largely lost in the published novel (in which the setting and the names of characters were changed): references to the places and people Heller knew during his service in the Army Air Corps in World War II, depictions of some of the men in his unit, some of the notable events that preoccupied them during the summer of 1944. These various documents, written in Heller's hand, provide an invaluable guide to understanding the composition and meaning of a monumental contemporary novel.

One point that should be made at the inception of any discussion of the stages of composition of Heller's first novel is that from beginning to end the title of the book was "Catch-18," a title with somewhat richer thematic overtones than "Catch-22." The early drafts of the novel, particularly the sketches and note cards, have a somewhat more "Jewish" emphasis than does the published novel. In Judaism, "eighteen" is a significant number in that the eighteenth letter of the Hebrew alphabet, "chai," means "living" or "life." Eighteen thus has a meaning for Jews that it does not have for other people: the *Mishnah* promotes eighteen as the ideal age for men to marry, and Jews often give personal gifts or charitable contributions in units of eighteen. Thematically, the title "Catch-18" would thus contain a subtle reference to the injunction in the *Torah* to choose life, a principle endorsed by Yossarian at the end of the novel when he deserts.[12]

It is also clear that the title was changed not because Heller had second thoughts but because a few weeks before the scheduled printing of the novel, Heller's publisher learned that Leon Uris, who had earlier written *Exodus,* was coming out with a novel entitled *Mila-18.* A change had to be made, and there was discussion of using "Catch-11" in that the duplication of the digit 1 would parallel the structural use of the repetition of scenes. But "11" was rejected because of the movie *Ocean's Eleven* and the now familiar concern for using a number already current in the public imagination.[13] Then Heller found a new title he liked, "Catch-14," and on January 29, 1961, he wrote to his publisher in defense of it: "The name of the book is now CATCH-14. (Forty-eight hours after you resign yourself to the change, you'll find yourself almost preferring this new number. It has the same bland and nondescript significance of the original. It is far enough away from Uris for the book to establish an identity of its own, I believe, yet close enough to the original title to still benefit from the word of mouth publicity we have been giving it.)" For whatever reason, and legend has it that Robert Gottlieb did not find "14" to be a funny number, the title was finally changed once again, this time to "Catch-22," recapturing the concept of repetition. Since the central device of the novel is *déjà vu,* with nearly every crucial scene, until the conclusion, coming back a second time, the title was once again coordinate with the organizational schema of the narrative. As Heller remarked, "the soldier in white comes back a second time, the dying soldier sees everything twice, the chaplain thinks that everything that happens has happened once before. For that reason the two 2's struck me as being very appropriate to the novel."[14] On this logic, and a decidedly accidental series of events, the phrase "catch-22," rather than "catch-18," became the term for bureaucratic impasse the world over.

It did so, however, only because readers found in the novel something they felt was important, a level of humor that was painfully resonant of their own experience, a grim reality that, in the 1960s, seemed all too close to current events. But even these aspects of the novel would not have had much impact were it not for the craft of the book, an artistry won through years of Heller's meticulous attention to the details of his novel. Indeed, one of the remarkable aspects of the writing of **Catch-22** is that Heller seems not to have discarded anything from the very beginning of composition, as though he somehow knew even from the start what a sensation his first attempt at extended fiction would be. As a result, the **Catch-22** manuscripts contain literally thousands of pages of materials, note cards, early sketches, drafts of scenes, outlines of chapters, detailed lists of the appearance of each character in each chapter, outlines of thematic progressions, chronologies in which the events of the novel are measured against actual events in 1944, and hundreds of other pages dealing with proposed scenes and characters. They constitute a truly remarkable creative record, one unmatched in the papers of any other important American novel.

One of the most fascinating stages in the growth of the manuscript is a collection of note cards on which Heller, writing at his desk at work, planned the structure of the novel before composition and then analyzed its contents after the first complete draft.[15] The most important of these is a group of thirty-seven cards, written in Heller's hand, headed "CHAPTER CARDS (outlines for chapters before they were written.)" Based on what Heller has said in a letter, these cards would have been assembled in 1953, at the earliest stage of composition, two years before the "sudden inspiration" that resulted in "Catch-18."[16]

Perhaps the most striking feature of these cards, especially in light of the frequent charges that the novel is "unstructured," "disorganized," or even "chaotic," is the detail of the initial plan. Not only are the main events in each chapter suggested, but characters are named and described, and such matters as structure, chronology, and various themes (including sex and "catch-18") are set into a complex pattern. Other cards indicate the relationships among events, with key sentences written in. A typical card, about twelfth from the beginning,[17] treats the characters and events for what was projected to be a single chapter:

1. Cathcart's background & ambition. Puzzled by _____ de Coverley.

2. Hasn't a chance of becoming a general. Ex-corporal Wintergreen, who evaluates his work, also wants to be a general.

3. For another, there already was a general, Dreedle.

4. ↑Tries to have Chaplain say prayer at briefing.↑

5. Description of General Dreedle. His Nurse.

6. Dreedle's quarrel with Moodis [sic].

7. Snowden's secret revealed in argument with Davis.

8. Dreedle brings girl to briefing.

9. Groaning. Dreedle orders Korf shot.

10. That was the mission in which Yossarian lost his balls.

The section of the published novel that relates to these items now comprises much of chapters 19 ("Colonel Cathcart") and 21 ("General Dreedle"), with chapter 20 ("Corporal Whitcomb"), unrelated to these matters, interspersed between them. Thus the ten items on the card resulted in roughly twenty-one pages of the novel.[18]

The business of Colonel Cathcart's background and ambition now begins in chapter 19 with a description of him as a "slick, successful, slipshod, unhappy man of thirty-six who lumbered when he walked and wanted to be a general" (*Catch*, 185). These matters cover a bit over two pages and then give way to item 4 on the card, "Tries to have Chaplain say prayer at briefing." To demonstrate how closely Heller worked with the note cards, this item had directional arrows pointing up on both sides of it, and, indeed, in execution the matter listed was moved forward in the chapter. This move underscores the logical relationship between the two concerns: "Colonel Cathcart wanted to be a general so desperately he was willing to try anything, even religion . . ." (*Catch*, 187). The idea develops systematically: Cathcart is impressed by a photograph in *The Saturday Evening Post* of a colonel who has his chaplain conduct prayers before each mission and he reasons, "maybe if we say prayers, they'll put my picture in *The Saturday Evening Post*" (*Catch*, 188). The humor of the situation progresses as Cathcart's thinking begins to take shape in his conversation with the chaplain:

> "Now, I want you to give a lot of thought to the kind of prayers we're going to say. . . . I don't want any of this kingdom of God or Valley of Death stuff. That's all too negative. What are you making such a sour face for?"
>
> "I'm sorry, sir," the chaplain stammered. "I happened to be thinking of the Twenty-third Psalm just as you said that."
>
> "How does that one go?"
>
> "That's the one you were just referring to, sir. 'The Lord is my shepherd I—.'"
>
> "That's the one I was just referring to. It's out. What else have you got?"
>
> (*Catch*, 189)

Cathcart's logic leads him to an admission that "I'd like to keep away from the subject of religion altogether if we can" and to the true object of his desires: "Why can't we all pray for something good, like a tighter bomb pattern?" (*Catch*, 190). But the plan for prayers is abandoned altogether when the chaplain reveals that the enlisted men do not have a separate God, as Cathcart had assumed, and that excluding them from prayer meetings might antagonize God and result in even looser bomb patterns. Cathcart concludes "the hell with it, then" (*Catch*, 193). Thus the first item on Heller's note card and the elevated matter regarding prayer grew to make up all of chapter 19. The secondary notions of each of these items were moved: Cathcart's puzzlement at _____ de Coverley was delayed to chapter 21, and the revelation that Milo is now the mess officer was placed earlier, in chapter 13, when Major _____ de Coverley promotes him out of a desire for fresh eggs.

The remaining items on the card became chapter 21, "General Dreedle." This chapter presents two main issues: the first is the string of obstructions to Cathcart's promotion to general, one of which is General Dreedle; the second is General Dreedle himself. In the novel, the chapter develops the topics equally. The balance is enriching: the ambitious colonel trying to get promoted contrasts the entrenched general trying to preserve what he has. Cathcart's problems in the novel reflect precisely what Heller listed as items 2 and 3 on his note card:

> Actually, Colonel Cathcart did not have a chance in hell of becoming a general. For one thing, there was ex-P.F.C. Wintergreen, who also wanted to be a general and who always distorted, destroyed, rejected or misdirected any correspondence by, for, or about Colonel Cathcart that might do him credit. For another, there already was a general, General Dreedle, who knew that General Peckem was after his job but did not know how to stop him.
>
> (*Catch*, 212)

Heller demoted Wintergreen from "ex-corporal" in the notes to "ex-P.F.C." in the novel. General Peckem, called P. P. Peckenhammer throughout the note cards and the manuscript, has been added as a further complication.

The business of General Dreedle, note card items 5 through 9, now occupies the last half of the chapter (*Catch*, 212-20) with only minor alterations from the notes. "Moodis" is changed to "Moodus"; in the incident of the "groaning" at the staff meeting, Dreedle orders Major Danby, not "Korf," shot for "moaning" (*Catch*, 218). Two items are not treated: the business of Snowden's secret was saved for the conclusion of the novel (*Catch*, 430), where it becomes climactic of the *déjà vu* technique and the most powerful scene in the novel. Placed where it is now, the further revelation of Snowden's secret, that man is matter, emphasizes the theme of mortality just when Yossarian is most concerned with death and survival.

The second idea not treated, relating to Yossarian's castration, Heller later rejected in manuscript revision. The incident of Yossarian's wound was ultimately moved to chapter 26: Aarfy, called "Aarky" throughout the note cards, gets lost on the mission to Ferrara and, before McWatt can seize control of the plane, flies back into the flak and the plane is hit. Yossarian's wound in the novel is in his thigh, but his first assessment follows the suggestion of the note card:

> He was unable to move. Then he realized he was sopping wet. He looked down at his crotch with a sinking, sick sensation. A wild crimson blot was crawling rapidly along his shirt front like an enormous sea monster rising to devour him. He was hit! . . . A second solid jolt struck the plane. Yossarian shuddered with revulsion at the queer sight of his wound and screamed at Aarfy for help.
>
> "I lost my balls! I lost my balls! . . . I said I lost my balls! Can't you hear me? I'm wounded in the groin!"
>
> (*Catch*, 283-84)

Heller changed a terrible reality to an understandable confusion that represents a normal fear in war. In its revised state the idea unites the sexual theme with the dangers of war and the destructive insensitivity of Aarfy. Yossarian's wound also serves the plot in getting him back into the hospital, where the themes of absurdity, bureaucracy, and insanity are explored: Nurse Cramer insists to Yossarian that his leg is "certainly . . . not your leg! . . . That leg belongs to the U.S. government" (*Catch*, 286). It would have been difficult to make this conversation humorous if Yossarian had been castrated. Nonetheless, the relationship of the published novel to the suggestions on the note card reveals that although Heller continued the creative process throughout the composition and revision of his book, the final product is remarkably consistent with his initial conception. The central tone, the key events, the characters (although often with changed names), and the underlying themes are essentially what Heller recorded on a note card eight years prior to the publication of the novel.

Another note card of particular interest is one entitled "Night of Horrors" in the notes and the manuscript chapter derived from it but "The Eternal City" in the published novel. The card contains seven entries, the first four of which concern matters not eventually made part of the chapter. These have to do with the discovery of penicillin (which Yossarian apparently needs for syphilis), Yossarian's attempts to get the drug through Nurse Duckett, and the acquisition of it by "Aarky." The discovery by Yossarian that the old man in the whorehouse is dead, and that the girls have been driven out of the apartment by the vagaries of "catch-18," thus would have been the result of his search for a cure. He has come to the apartment in Rome to see Aarky. The villain in this episode turns out to be Milo, as item 7 explains: "Milo is exposed as the source of penicillin [*sic*], tricking both Aarky & Yossarian, and as the man who infected the girl to create a demand for his new wonder drug. Yossarian breaks with him." This concept, finally rejected, would have been an interesting but perhaps unnecessary further development of Milo's corruption. It would also have been an overt expression of Yossarian's underlying values, one not in the novel because Milo simply leaves Yossarian in Rome out of a desire to make money from the traffic in illegal tobacco.

This idea and all but one of the other suggestions on the card were finally abandoned or subordinated to what appears as item 5: "Yossarian finally walks through the streets of Rome witnessing various horrors, among them the maid, who has been thrown from the window by Aarky." It is this concept that ultimately became the heart of "The Eternal City" (*Catch*, 396-410). Yossarian, in Rome to look for Nately's whore's kid sister, in an attempt to keep her from a life of prostitution, discovers a nightmare world. In the novel Milo shares these generous motives until he learns of the smuggling of illegal tobacco (*Catch*, 402). What emerges in the chapter is Yossarian's "night of horrors," his surrealistic walk through Rome at night, in which greed, violence, corruption, insanity, and death, prime themes throughout the novel, converge on his consciousness from all sides, and he is arrested for being AWOL.

There are numerous other note cards as intriguing and significant as these two and several individual ideas that were developed or abandoned after their first conception in the notes. That Snowden will be killed on the mission to Avignon, that in response Yossarian will parade in the nude and sit naked in a tree during the funeral, are all established on a card entitled "Ferrara." An example of the kind of minor detail that Heller frequently changed is the suggestion on this card that when Yossarian is awarded his medal, still standing naked in formation, "Dreedle orders a zoot suit for him." Another such revision concerns what is finally chapter 30, "Dunbar" (*Catch*, 324-33), but is called "McAdam" in the notes. (The name "McAdam," of course, was later changed to "McWatt.") The two most dramatic events of the chapter are here suggested: McAdam dives low over the beach, slicing Kid Sampson in half, and then commits suicide. The note card indicates an indefinite "man" as the victim and also suggests that "McAdam kills himself & Daneeker," which was revised, but the main focus of the published chapter is all there. This card also contains a fascinating suggestion: "Nurse Cramer's family tree traced back to include all known villains in History. She completes the line by being a registered Republican who doesn't drink, smoke, fornicate, or lust consciously & [is] guiltless of similar crimes."

An entry for chapter 40, entitled "Catch-18" in the notes, reads "in the morning, Cathcart sends for Yossarian and offers him his deal. Big Brother has been watching Yossarian." The concluding phrase makes explicit an underlying thematic allusion to George Orwell's *1984,* one now more subtly beneath the action of the novel. The same card contains the suggestion that Nately's whore will stab Yossarian as he leaves Cathcart's office, which occurs in the novel, and that she will shout "olé" as she plunges the knife in, which does not.

The note for the final chapter, "Yossarian," contains not only plot suggestions but some interpretive remarks as well. There is a good deal of interest in Yossarian's mortality: "Yossarian is dying, true, but he has about 35 years to live." Another provocative entry, one rejected, suggests that "Among other things, he really does have chronic liver trouble. Condition is malignant & would have killed him if it had not been discovered." It is fortuitous that this idea was changed, for Yossarian's trips to the hospital are now linked to his protest against the absurdity of the war and his personal quest for survival; to add to those ideas the serendipitous saving of his life through the discovery of his cancer in a military hospital he has falsely entered would have been to compound too many levels of irony. Perhaps the most important comments on this note card are those relating to the thematic significance of Yossarian's refusal of Cathcart's deal. In the note card, Yossarian discusses the ethics of the deal and his alternatives with an English deserter: "Easiest would be to go home or fly more missions. Hardest would be for him to fight for identity without sacrificing moral responsibility." The following entry reads "He chooses the last, after all dangers are pointed out to him."

In the novel, the English deserter has been replaced by Major Danby, who, since he does not appear in the preliminary notes, would seem to be a late invention. The conception of the "fight for identity" has been altered: Yossarian says, "I've been fighting all along to save my country. Now I'm going to fight a little to save myself. The country's not in danger any more, but I am" (*Catch,* 435). The "identity" motif has been submerged into the "survival" theme, one centered on Yossarian's physical and moral survival. Thus Yossarian can now claim, "I'm not running away from my responsibilities. I'm running to them" (*Catch,* 440). In thematic terms, this change is among the most important ideas in the preliminary note cards. What is remarkable about them as a group, however, is how closely they correspond to what Heller eventually published some eight years later. It is a dramatic testimony to the clarity of his initial conception, for, although there were many early changes and deletions, along with alterations in the final version of the manuscript, the finished product is well described by the note cards Heller developed in his advertising office, shaping and defining and trying out his idea in miniature before he actually wrote the first draft.

In addition to the note cards, Heller also worked on a number of other documents prior to writing the first full draft of his novel. One group of these that is particularly important is composed of "plans," outlines, sketches, brief exchanges of dialogue, summaries of the role of a character, ideas for plot developments, checklists on which Heller indicated that a certain idea had or had not been included in the first draft. These pages, somewhat more than a hundred, allowed Heller more room than did the note cards to expand on concepts and outlines, although to some extent they serve the same function. For example, on the sheet for "Catch-18" Heller recorded his ideas for the permutations of that concept:

A. Censoring letters

B. Increases Wintergreen's punishment

C. Colonel must request transfer

D. Sanity in soldier

E. Drives girls out

F. Will send Nately Back

G. Deal With Yossarian.[19]

Heller had thus decided before he began writing that the matter of "catch-18" would occur at least seven times in the novel. Further, as the outline indicates, the general direction of the recurrence progresses from humor to tragedy, from the business of having Wintergreen dig holes to contain the dirt created from previous holes to the final matter of Yossarian's being trapped in a moral dilemma in which his self-respect and his very life are seriously threatened.

Some of Heller's notations to himself reveal a considerable interpretive intelligence. On a page about Corporal Snark, Milo's first chef in the novel and the character who poisons the squadron with soap in the mashed potatoes to prove that the men have no taste (*Catch,* 63), Heller records his comments about this relatively minor character. It is clear that Snark is to be thematically opposed to Milo in that Snark cooks for the "art" of his craft and Milo is interested only in the commercial aspects of food. Heller wrote that Snark "would like to forge within the smithy of his soul the uncreated soufflés of the world." Another entry is particularly ironic: "Spots the significance of Milo's enterprises. An egg, in case the critics have missed it, is a symbol of creation. A hard-boiled egg is the symbol of the creative process frozen. A scrambled egg is the symbol of creation scrambled. A powdered egg is the symbol of the creative process pulverized—destroyed." No one reading through Heller's plans would doubt that he gave extraordinary attention to every detail of his novel, including the role and thematic impact of every character in every scene. This pertains even in instances in which Heller did not follow his suggestions, as with some of his ideas for Snowden: "Snowden's innards are loathsome things brought up through a crack in the earth. . . . Snowden's luggage in the bedroom at the enlisted men's apartment . . . Snowden's secret is that they are out to kill Yossarian." These ideas, particularly the last, are not implemented in the novel, nor are such related plans as the notion that General Eisenhower and Harry Truman want Yossarian dead.

One of the documents deals with the war novel that Yossarian and Dunbar struggle to write, a matter suggested on a note card and developed in Heller's plans but not incorporated into the final novel. The note cards contained two suggestions that relate to this document: one entry, item 7, suggests that "Yossarian & Dunbar write novel, although Jew won't conform & they still lack a radical" and the second, item 10, indicates a "parody of Hemingway in introduction of attempt to assemble cast for war novel." In the brief sketches derived from the note-card entries, Heller wrote a half-page developing each idea, the first of which, entitled "Perfect Plot," begins

> now they had just about everything to make a perfect plot for a best selling war novel. They had a fairy, they had a slav named Florik from the slums, an Irishman, a thinker with a Phd, a cynic who believed in nothing, a husband who's [sic] wife had sent him a Dear John letter, a clean-cut young lad who was doomed to die. They had everything there but the sensitive Jew, and that was enough to turn them against the whole race. They had a Jew but there was just nothing they could do with him. He was healthy, handsome, rugged, and strong, and if anybody else in the ward wanted to make something out of anything he could have taken them in turn, anybody but Yossarian, who didn't want to make anything out of anything. All he cared about was women and there was just nothing in the world you could do with a Jew like that.[20]

Several matters are of interest in the paragraph, including the suggestion that Yossarian is Jewish, an idea buttressed by Heller's comments in a letter in 1974.[21] That Yossarian and Dunbar would be writing a novel about war would be thematically awkward in the context of the progressive immediacy of danger and death. The writing of fiction implies remoteness, the vantage of the observer, more than direct involvement. Heller's idea that an outfit with an ethnic distribution would somehow parody Hemingway seems confused, since Hemingway never wrote any novels along those lines. The parody would seem better directed at some of the popular war movies that circulated in the 1950s. Another important dimension to this scene is that Yossarian and Dunbar are in the hospital, implying either that they are ill or wounded or, more likely, that they are feigning illness to escape hazardous duty, a ruse that runs throughout the novel.

Another Heller document, however, explores alternative reasons why Yossarian wants to go into the hospital. On a page entitled "Conspiracy to Murder Him," Heller outlined some thoughts about Yossarian's growing preoccupation with death:

> Grows aware of it with Snowden's death. They were all shooting at him, and when they hit someone else it was a case of mistaken identity. They wanted him dead, there was no doubt about it and there was no doubt that it was all part of a gigantic conspiracy. . . . Colonel Cathcart wanted him dead. General Dreedle wanted him dead. . . . Eisenhower and Harry S Truman wanted him dead. It was the one thing upon which even the enemies were agreed. Hitler wanted him dead because he was Assyrian, Stalin wanted him dead because he wasn't. Mussolini wanted him dead because he was Mussolini, and Tojo wanted him dead because he was short and far away and couldn't make himself understood. . . . The only safe place for him in the whole world was in the hospital, because in the hospital nobody seemed to care whether he lived or died.

This material has genuine comic potential, even in Heller's brief outline of it, although it makes Yossarian's fear of death somewhat more paranoiac than in the novel, where his continuous proximity to death is a matter of circumstance rather than malevolence. Heller's decision not to develop this idea was part of a general pattern of excision of references to real persons. Without the resonance of the names, the humor of the passage is greatly diminished.

Several of the other sketches Heller worked on are also intriguing documents, including a page on which Yossarian, Orr, and Hungry Joe all move the bomb line before the mission to Bologna. This page, entitled "Rebukes Yossarian for moving bomb line," contains dialogue in which Clevinger argues with his obtuse good sense that Yossarian was unfair to the others in moving the line on the map. In the following paragraph the plot thickened in a way it does not in the novel:

> It was another clear night filled with bright yellow stars he knew he might never see again. Moving the bomb line was not fair to the other men in the squadron, men like Orr, who tiptoed out into the darkness and moved the bomb line up an inch, and like Hungry Joe, who moved it up another inch, and the steady stream of all the others, each one moving it one inch so that it was up over Sweden when daylight glowed.

Yossarian alone is culpable in the novel, but this passage establishes the universality of his apprehension in a manner that may have enriched this motif. On the other hand, Heller's ultimate rejection of a scene in which Yossarian explains to the chaplain how much he enjoyed touching Snowden's torn flesh and organs, and how he rubbed blood over himself to impress everyone back at the base, was wisely deleted. In this sketch Heller seems to have been exploring the possibilities of his material, developing ideas before discarding them. The obvious thematic incongruence of Yossarian being pleased by the very death that transforms him would have considerably weakened the Snowden scenes.

There are other related documents that seem to have been written at this stage, after the note cards but before the first draft of the novel. Heller was obviously very concerned about the chronology of the action, not only that it progress in accord with certain key scenes but that these events be consistent with the history of the actual war. At one point he constructed a detailed outline of events in the European theater from 1943 to 1945. He begins in 1943 with the landings in Sicily on June 11 and follows with the Anzio landings in January of 1944, the Normandy invasion on June 6, and the stabilization of German forces in Italy (which necessitated the bombing of transportation lines). He did a separate page on events in Italy between May and August of 1944 (the period of his own bombing missions), outlining the objective of the Italian campaign ("tie down Germans; gain air bases near S. Germany") and the stalemate in southern Italy that delayed the Allied advance. He particularly notes the taking of Rome on June 4, 1944, D-Day two days later, and the victories in Pisa and Florence. His broad outline continues through 1945 and the Battle of the Bulge, the advance of the Russians on the eastern front, the execution of Mussolini, the crossing of the Po, and the fall of Berlin on May 3.

With the historical facts clear, he worked on the chronological outline of his own narrative, using the closest paper large enough to contain his detailed notations, the blotter on his desk. On this document Heller recorded not only the general events of the novel but, within a grid crossing time values with characters, the action for each character at the time of the central events. Heller's chart would then tell him, as he worked on a given scene, what all of the characters were doing. For example, the entries indicate that when Yossarian is wounded he comes into contact with Nurse Duckett and gets psychoanalyzed by Major Sanderson, Dunbar cracks his head in the hospital, Nately refuses to enter the hospital, Aarky gets lost on the mission, Orr has a flat tire, the Soldier in White reappears, and the old man of the Roman brothel continues to be a mystery. Reading the chart down, Heller could follow the activities of any character he chose; reading it across, he could coordinate their activities and keep a complex chronology straight. In this he did not entirely succeed, but, given the intricate time structure of the novel, he needed a method of organizing the complex events.[22]

At some point Heller constructed other documents that also clarify the actions of the characters and the key themes of the novel. Taking their interaction in the plot apart, he meticulously recorded the progression of events involving each character. These documents cover nearly a hundred pages and reveal the painstaking care and detailed attention that Heller gave to the structure of his fiction. Many of these entries contain humorous ideas not in, or submerged in, the novel, one being that Major Major "was from the winter wheat fields of Vermont and a former teacher of English. Made the mistake of stating publicly that he did not like Henry James." Another entry explores the idea that "Rome was a sort of school for sexual experience." Other entries explore the "Night of Horrors," later changed to "The Eternal City," and others the concept of free enterprise. One outline reveals Heller's plan for the ending, which begins "Yossarian is wounded, recovers, and continues flying combat missions until he completes seventy." The emphasis is on Nately's whore, how she tries to stab him when he tells her of Nately's death. That sketch takes him through to the end:

> Yossarian can lend himself obediently to all Colonel Cathcart's designs and lose his life; he can accept Colonel Cathcart's proposition and lose his character. Or, he can desert, and risk losing both when he is eventually apprehended, as he knows he will probably be. There is no way he can remain a citizen in good standing without falling victim to one dishonorable scheme or another of his legal superior.

> In the end, he runs off, closely pursued by Nately's mistress, the embodiment of danger and of a violent conscience that will never leave him in peace.

As these comments indicate, Heller often gave his ideas critical substance even before he wrote the scenes, acting as creative writer and interpreter simultaneously in a manner rarely equaled for detail and insight in American fiction.

The most important manuscript of *Catch-22* is a handwritten draft a good deal longer than, but essentially the same as, the published novel. It is complete save for the first chapter, which was published separately as "Catch-18" in *New World Writing* in 1955, and for chapter 9, which is simply missing from this draft although present in the typescript. This manuscript displays the additions, deletions, insertions, typeovers, misspellings, and informal punctuation of the type normally found in first drafts.[23] It is essentially handwritten, although there are paragraphs and occasionally pages that are typed, indicating, perhaps, some revision simultaneous to the initial composition. Two chapters of the manuscript do not appear in the novel (as a result the numbers of the chapters are different in each case) and hundreds of brief passages were deleted. Indeed, Heller's revisions consisted more of deletion and addition than of alterations in scenes. The pages are numbered sequentially by chapter, although as other pages were inserted, varying numbering and lettering schemes were used to keep order so that pages frequently have several numbers or letters on them. As was true on the note cards, many of the names of characters differ in the manuscript from the novel: Aarfy appears consistently as Aarky; Peckem is known throughout the manuscript as P. P. Peckenhammer. Nately is a more important character in the manuscript than in the novel, and an entire chapter about his family was deleted. One important character in the manuscript, Rosoff, does not appear at all in the novel. But the central point is that Heller's first draft remains remarkably close to what he outlined in his note cards and to the published novel.

There are other matters in the early composition stages that are significant. One of them is that the location of Yossarian's base throughout the note cards and manuscript is Corsica, where Heller himself had been stationed. Pianosa was not introduced until the manuscript and even the typescript had been completed. The manuscript is more detailed than the novel in describing features of the setting, since Heller had been to Corsica himself and knew the topography intimately; there is no evidence that he ever visited Pianosa. Yossarian's unit in the manuscript is also Heller's old outfit, the Twelfth Air Force, whereas in the novel it is the Twenty-seventh, a nonexistent unit. In the manuscript there is a much more "literary" frame of reference than in the final novel, and Yossarian is compared to Ahasuerus, Gulliver, and Samson Agonistes, reflecting Heller's graduate training in literature. The manuscript is also somewhat more sexually explicit than the published version, as in the scene in which Daneeka shows the newlyweds how to make love. In the manuscript Daneeka says, "I showed them how penetration was accomplished and explained its importance to impregnation." This reference was dropped in the final draft. In a similar vein, the manuscript has more scatological dialogue, so that when Milo maneuvers a package of dates away from his friend, "Yossarian always did things properly, too, and he gave Milo the package of pitted dates and told him to shove his personal note up his ass." This passage, and this tone, did not survive to publication (*Catch,* 64).

Another area of frequent revision is the final paragraphs of the chapters, which show a great deal of revision, more than any other section of the manuscript. For example, in the first draft the last paragraph of chapter 7, which concludes a section on Milo's complex investment schemes, reads

> the only one complaining was Milo. And the only ones who were happy, as it turned out, were Milo and the grinning thief, for by the time McWatt returned to his tent another bedsheet was gone, along with the sweet tooth and a brand new pair of red polka dot pajamas sent him with love by a wealthy sister-in-law who despised him for what he had been told was his birthday.

Heller crossed all of that out in his manuscript and substituted "but Yossarian still didn't understand." By the time the novel appeared the passage had become

> but Yossarian still didn't understand either how Milo could buy eggs in Malta for seven cents apiece and sell them at a profit in Pianosa for five cents,
>
> (*Catch,* 66)

which better conveys the absurd humor.

One way in which the manuscript differs from the novel is that there are more passages of interpretive comment in the first draft, such as a comment in chapter 2 about the Texan. In the manuscript the narrator says

> that's what was wrong with the Texan, not that he never ended kneeding [his jowls], but that he overflowed with goodwill and brought the whole ward down trying to cheer it up. He was depressing. He was worse than a missionary or an uncle. <The Texan> [He] wanted <everybody in the ward> to be happy. He was really very sick.

In the novel this passage has been reduced in a manner typical of Heller's changes:

> The Texan wanted everybody in the ward to be happy but Yossarian and Dunbar. He was really very sick.
>
> (*Catch,* 16)

Heller," *Pages* 1 (1976): 77. My comments here closely follow those in "The *Catch-22* Note Cards," 51-61. The note cards are lined, 5" × 8" Kardex cards of a type used by the Remington Rand office Heller worked in during the composition of the novel. Heller's comments on the cards are variously in blue, red, and black ink, with occasional pencil notations. The variations in ink would suggest that the planning progressed slowly, during which the implements on Heller's desk changed. The cards might also suggest that some of the planning work was done in the office, whereas Heller has indicated that the writing of the novel was done at home, in the evenings, whenever he felt like it. He did not rush, and the development of the novel was stretched over eight years.

16. Joseph Heller, letter to author, March 13, 1974, p. 2, Heller Manuscripts.

17. Given the disorganized state of the Heller manuscripts, it is difficult now to determine the precise order of the cards and even, in some cases, whether a given card was written before or after the initial draft. All references to the numbers and groups of cards are therefore based on my own judgment of the most likely function of the cards when they were written. Heller's comments to me in conversation about the manuscripts has guided my judgment, but even he was unable to remember precise details after a lapse of many years.

18. Joseph Heller, *Catch-22* (New York: Simon and Schuster, 1961), 185-92, 206-20. Hereafter cited parenthetically in the text as *Catch*.

19. These sheets are not organized or numbered in any coherent fashion, suggesting that they were written at various times and not as a discrete stage of composition. Some pages are not numbered, while others begin the numbering or lettering scheme all over again. The "Catch-18" sheet is numbered 17, which is crossed out, and renumbered 15. The letters on the outline are enclosed in circles, which I do not indicate in my text.

20. This entry is on a sheet entitled "Hospital." For a more detailed transcription of Heller's paragraphs, see James Nagel, "Two Brief Manuscript Sketches: Heller's *Catch-22*," *Modern Fiction Studies* 20 (1974): 221-24.

21. Joseph Heller, letter to Daniel Walden. I have read this letter but do not have a copy. In it Heller says that he always thought of Yossarian as Jewish. However, in other places Heller has said directly that he wanted Yossarian to be without ethnic identity.

22. For copies of Heller's blotter, I am indebted to Colonel Frederick Kiley of the United States Air Force, who was generous with both his time and materials when I spoke with him in Washington, D.C. Kiley used the blotter for the cover of his book *A 'Catch-22' Casebook,* ed. Frederick Kiley and Walter McDonald (New York: Crowell, 1973).

23. I will use the term *manuscript* to designate the handwritten draft of the novel, distinct from the *typescript*. Some of the pages of the manuscript have been typed and inserted; some paragraphs were typed with handwriting following, suggesting a revision during the process of composition. In my quotations I will attempt to represent the manuscript accurately, adding only periods to end sentences (sometimes on the manuscript it is not clear if there is a period or not). Throughout my transcriptions, [ ] will be used for editorial interpolations, <X> to indicate additions made to the text, and to denote deletions by Heller.

24. There is a suggestion in the deleted dialogue that Havermeyer and Appleby discuss the incident and agree that Yossarian shot the gun on purpose, which would change the attitude of Appleby.

Charles Glass (review date 20 March 1998)

SOURCE: Glass, Charles. "Shy Raconteur." *New Statesman* (20 March 1998): 54.

[*In the following review, Glass finds* Now and Then *lacking as autobiography.*]

Now and Then is a detailed guide to subway travel and cheap food in 1930s Coney Island, New York. It begins in Coney Island, lingers in Coney Island and, somehow, ends in Coney Island. Its title could have been *No Escape from Coney Island* or—because the author also wrote **Catch-22**—*Catch a Life in Here if You Can.* Or, as writer of that other masterpiece, **Something Happened,** Joseph Heller might have called this *Nothing Happened.* Nothing much does.

You can almost hear the rocking chair creaking on the front porch as Old Joe Heller recalls, to anyone who will listen, the childhood of Little Joey Heller. He grew up with his widowed mother, his half-brother and half-sister in "four rooms, looking out on West 31st Street near Surf Avenue", near Coney's giant amusement parks.

He knew where to find the best hot dogs and ice cream, but no one told him his brother and sister had a different mother. She had died in Russia before his father emigrated. When he learnt this from a toast at the wedding of his brother, Lee, "I felt victimised, disgraced. My response to rage then, as it chiefly is still, was to break off speaking to the person offending me."

The person was his father, who was already dead.

Although Joey was five when Heller *père* died, Heller did not discover the cause was a bleeding ulcer until he himself was in his thirties. Everyone assumed, as with the maternity of his siblings, that someone else had told him. Old Joe writes: "If anything, the passing away of Mr Isaac Daniel Heller was for me more a matter of embarrassment than anything else."

And later: "But not only did we not complain much in my family, we didn't talk much about anything deeply felt. We didn't ask for much either."

None of the three grown children would care for the mother when she grew old, and they deposited her in a "Hebrew home for the aged". Heller's only reflection is: "The subject never arose, but I would guess that each of us secretly suffered at least some remorse. In our family, we did not talk about sad things."

When he left for training in the army air corps that he would satirise mercilessly in *Catch-22*, his mother sobbed only after his trolley car had carried him away. "My mother never mentioned the occasion to me, and I never brought it up with her. Our family tendency to keep disturbing emotions to ourselves has lasted as long as we have."

He evokes a time when, he writes, the poor didn't know they were poor, no one locked a door, Italian and Jewish immigrant neighbourhoods overlapped and no whites thought about black people. Much of it is tedious: "The summer would begin officially for us, I suppose, on that day in late June we called 'promotion', when we would come running jubilantly home on that last day of school, waving our report cards, me with my A in classwork and B+ in deportment, calling out to everyone who flew by that we had been promoted. 'Over the ocean / tomorrow's promotion' was a refrain we chanted. Another was 'No more classes / no more books / no more teachers' dirty looks'."

He mentions in passing that he took the name of the main character of *Catch-22* and *Closing Time,* Yossarian, from a fellow airman named Yohannon. He does not say why. Other *Catch-22* characters—Orr, Major _____ de Coverley, Hungry Joe—were in the same unit, but he keeps to himself the secret of how and why they evolved into fiction.

There are brief references, no more, to the Guillain-Barré syndrome that nearly crippled him for life and to the nurse for whom he left his wife of 35 years. Again and again he steps towards the brink of some revelation and withdraws. If he wanted to maintain the family tradition of silence, why did he write his memoirs? He admits: "I am walking proof of at least part of Freud's theories of repression and the domain of the unconscious, and perhaps, in writing this way here and in other things I've published, of denial and sublimation, too."

You want to listen to the old man in the rocker, repeating himself, recalling unrelated incidents and people from childhood, because he is Joseph Heller. And Joseph Heller, one of the great postwar American novelists, deserves respect. "In my book *Closing Time* I say of a character, Yossarian, that he couldn't learn to make a bed and would sooner starve than cook," he tells you in *Now and Then.* "*That* is autobiography."

This isn't.

Publishers Weekly (review date 29 May 2000)

SOURCE: Review of *Portrait of the Artist, as an Old Man,* by Joseph Heller. *Publishers Weekly* 247, no. 22 (29 May 2000): 52.

[*In the following review, the anonymous critic finds* Portrait of the Artist, as an Old Man *lacking in profundity but worth reading for the insight it provides into Heller's reaction to his own aging.*]

This slim posthumous novel [*Portrait of the Artist, as an Old Man*], playing blithely with the idea of an elderly novelist in search of a subject, is the last thing the author of *Catch-22* left us. Although not a profound leave-taking, it is nonetheless a pleasant reminder of the author's great charm and fluency. Eugene Pota, Heller's alter ego here, rifles the back corners of his mind for a new novel that will restore to him some of the luster that shone from his earlier efforts. In the beginning he tries to do something with Tom Sawyer, first with a postmodernist Tom on Wall Street, then as a character determined to run down the secrets of success for an American writer. But Pota discovers, in his wry researches into the lives of Tom's own creator, Jack London, Bret Harte, Ambrose Bierce, Herman Melville, Henry James and many others, that a combination of prosperity and cheerfulness are profoundly elusive for an author. This segues into a speech Heller himself used to make about the many afflictions, particularly alcoholism, of noted American writers. Pota toys with the idea of a book to be called *The Sexual Biography of My Wife,* then realizes he doesn't know enough about women's sexuality, and doesn't like to ask his wife, so he calls on some old flames, and begins a few cautious, elderly flirtations. He plays, too, with the idea of the Creation from God's point of view, has some fun with Hera and Zeus, and engages in regular, despondent talks about his lack of progress with his editor (who is unfortunately about to retire). Some of this is familiar, some is simply rambling, but it is all done with a spirit of faintly irritated self-reproach that is endearing. At the very least, this is a frank and at times funny look at how a legendary American novelist coped with the onset of old age.

Robert L. McLaughlin (review date fall 2000)

SOURCE: McLaughlin, Robert L. Review of *Portrait of the Artist, as an Old Man,* by Joseph Heller. *Review of Contemporary Fiction* 20, no. 3 (fall 2000): 144-45.

[*In the following review, McLaughlin considers* Portrait of the Artist, as an Old Man *a bittersweet and satisfying final work.*]

Joseph Heller's posthumous *Portrait of an Artist, as an Old Man* is a more fitting and satisfying final work than either his ill-considered *Catch-22* sequel, *Closing Time,* or his been-there-done-that memoir, *Now and Then.* Seemingly autobiographical, the novel focuses on Eugene Pota, an aging writer who has never been able to match the success of his first big novel and who is desperately trying to find an idea for a final masterpiece. This situation allows for meditations on the effects of old age, a dissection of writer's block, an examination of the despair that has historically beset writers near the ends of their lives, and the presentation of scraps of Pota's aborted attempts at that final novel, some of which are so funny, one wishes they went on longer. Heller, through Pota, wrestles here in a thought-provoking way with the challenges of creation: he can find nothing to write about in his own experiences that won't repeat his earlier books, yet he can't summon the energy to do the research necessary to write outside of his experiences; he is also paralyzed by the literature-of-exhaustionish discovery that everything he attempts has already been done by someone else. Thus his false starts are all self-conscious reworkings of other texts, from Classical mythology to the Bible to *The Metamorphosis* to *The Adventures of Tom Sawyer.* If Heller didn't give us a final masterpiece, he has given us a smart, funny, bittersweet, personal novel about writing novels as a farewell gift.

FURTHER READING

Criticism

Kiley, Frederick T., and Walter McDonald. A *Catch-22* Casebook. New York: Crowell, 1973, 403 p.
Selection of representative criticism including early reviews and analyses of form, structure, theme, and the relationship of *Catch-22* to Absurdist literature.

Nagel, James. *Critical Essays on Joseph Heller.* Boston: G. K. Hall, 1984, 253 p.
Anthology of criticism including essays by Kurt Vonnegut, Jr., Clive Barnes, and John W. Aldridge.

Additional information on Heller's life and career is published in the following sources published by the Gale Group: *American Writers,* **Vol. 4;** *Authors and Artists for Young Adults,* **Vol. 24;** *Authors in the News,* **Vol. 1;** *Beacham's Encyclopedia of Popular Fiction: Biography and Resources,* **Vol. 2;** *Beacham's Guide to Literature for Young Adults,* **Vol. 1;** *Contemporary Authors,* **Vol. 5-8R, 187;** *Contemporary Authors Bibliographical Series,* **Vol. 1;** *Contemporary Authors New Revision Series,* **Vols. 8, 42, 66;** *Contemporary Literary Criticism,* **Vols. 1, 3, 5, 8, 11, 36, 63;** *Contemporary Novelists,* **Ed. 7;** *Contemporary Popular Writers;* *Dictionary of Literary Biography,* **Vols. 2, 28, 227;** *Dictionary of Literary Biography Yearbook,* **1980, 1999;** *DISCovering Authors: British Edition;* *DISCovering Authors: Canadian Edition;* *DISCovering Authors Modules: Most-studied Authors,* *Novelists,* **and** *Popular Fiction;* *DISCovering Authors 3.0;* *Encyclopedia of World Literature in the 20th Century,* **Ed. 3;** *Exploring Novels;* *Literature and Its Times,* **Vol. 4;** *Literature Resource Center;* *Major 20th-Century Writers,* **Eds. 1, 2;** *Novels for Students,* **Vol. 1;** *Reference Guide to American Literature,* **Ed. 4;** *St. James Guide to Young Adult Writers;* *Twayne's United States Authors;* *Twentieth-Century Literary Criticism,* **Vol. 131; and** *World Literature Criticism.*

How to Use This Index

The main references

> Calvino, Italo
> 1923-1985 .... CLC 5, 8, 11, 22, 33, 39,
> 73; SSC 3, 48

list all author entries in the following Gale Literary Criticism series:

AAL = Asian American Literature
BG = The Beat Generation: A Gale Critical Companion
BLC = Black Literature Criticism
BLCS = Black Literature Criticism Supplement
CLC = Contemporary Literary Criticism
CLR = Children's Literature Review
CMLC = Classical and Medieval Literature Criticism
DC = Drama Criticism
HLC = Hispanic Literature Criticism
HLCS = Hispanic Literature Criticism Supplement
HR = Harlem Renaissance: A Gale Critical Companion
LC = Literature Criticism from 1400 to 1800
NCLC = Nineteenth-Century Literature Criticism
NNAL = Native North American Literature
PC = Poetry Criticism
SSC = Short Story Criticism
TCLC = Twentieth-Century Literary Criticism
WLC = World Literature Criticism, 1500 to the Present
WLCS = World Literature Criticism Supplement

The cross-references

> See also CA 85-88, 116; CANR 23, 61;
> DAM NOV; DLB 196; EW 13; MTCW 1, 2;
> RGSF 2; RGWL 2; SFW 4; SSFS 12

list all author entries in the following Gale biographical and literary sources:

AAYA = Authors & Artists for Young Adults
AFAW = African American Writers
AFW = African Writers
AITN = Authors in the News
AMW = American Writers
AMWR = American Writers Retrospective Supplement
AMWS = American Writers Supplement
ANW = American Nature Writers
AW = Ancient Writers
BEST = Bestsellers
BPFB = Beacham's Encyclopedia of Popular Fiction: Biography and Resources
BRW = British Writers
BRWS = British Writers Supplement
BW = Black Writers
BYA = Beacham's Guide to Literature for Young Adults
CA = Contemporary Authors
CAAS = Contemporary Authors Autobiography Series
CABS = Contemporary Authors Bibliographical Series
CAD = Contemporary American Dramatists
CANR = Contemporary Authors New Revision Series
CAP = Contemporary Authors Permanent Series
CBD = Contemporary British Dramatists
CCA = Contemporary Canadian Authors
CD = Contemporary Dramatists
CDALB = Concise Dictionary of American Literary Biography
CDALBS = Concise Dictionary of American Literary Biography Supplement
CDBLB = Concise Dictionary of British Literary Biography

CMW = *St. James Guide to Crime & Mystery Writers*
CN = *Contemporary Novelists*
CP = *Contemporary Poets*
CPW = *Contemporary Popular Writers*
CSW = *Contemporary Southern Writers*
CWD = *Contemporary Women Dramatists*
CWP = *Contemporary Women Poets*
CWRI = *St. James Guide to Children's Writers*
CWW = *Contemporary World Writers*
DA = *DISCovering Authors*
DA3 = *DISCovering Authors 3.0*
DAB = *DISCovering Authors: British Edition*
DAC = *DISCovering Authors: Canadian Edition*
DAM = *DISCovering Authors: Modules*
    DRAM: *Dramatists Module;* **MST:** *Most-studied Authors Module;*
    MULT: *Multicultural Authors Module;* **NOV:** *Novelists Module;*
    POET: *Poets Module;* **POP:** *Popular Fiction and Genre Authors Module*
DFS = *Drama for Students*
DLB = *Dictionary of Literary Biography*
DLBD = *Dictionary of Literary Biography Documentary Series*
DLBY = *Dictionary of Literary Biography Yearbook*
DNFS = *Literature of Developing Nations for Students*
EFS = *Epics for Students*
EXPN = *Exploring Novels*
EXPP = *Exploring Poetry*
EXPS = *Exploring Short Stories*
EW = *European Writers*
FANT = *St. James Guide to Fantasy Writers*
FW = *Feminist Writers*
GFL = *Guide to French Literature,* Beginnings to 1789, 1798 to the Present
GLL = *Gay and Lesbian Literature*
HGG = *St. James Guide to Horror, Ghost & Gothic Writers*
HW = *Hispanic Writers*
IDFW = *International Dictionary of Films and Filmmakers: Writers and Production Artists*
IDTP = *International Dictionary of Theatre: Playwrights*
LAIT = *Literature and Its Times*
LAW = *Latin American Writers*
JRDA = *Junior DISCovering Authors*
MAICYA = *Major Authors and Illustrators for Children and Young Adults*
MAICYAS = *Major Authors and Illustrators for Children and Young Adults Supplement*
MAWW = *Modern American Women Writers*
MJW = *Modern Japanese Writers*
MTCW = *Major 20th-Century Writers*
NCFS = *Nonfiction Classics for Students*
NFS = *Novels for Students*
PAB = *Poets: American and British*
PFS = *Poetry for Students*
RGAL = *Reference Guide to American Literature*
RGEL = *Reference Guide to English Literature*
RGSF = *Reference Guide to Short Fiction*
RGWL = *Reference Guide to World Literature*
RHW = *Twentieth-Century Romance and Historical Writers*
SAAS = *Something about the Author Autobiography Series*
SATA = *Something about the Author*
SFW = *St. James Guide to Science Fiction Writers*
SSFS = *Short Stories for Students*
TCWW = *Twentieth-Century Western Writers*
WLIT = *World Literature and Its Times*
WP = *World Poets*
YABC = *Yesterday's Authors of Books for Children*
YAW = *St. James Guide to Young Adult Writers*

Literary Criticism Series
Cumulative Author Index

20/1631
See Upward, Allen

A/C Cross
See Lawrence, T(homas) E(dward)

Abasiyanik, Sait Faik 1906-1954
See Sait Faik
See also CA 123

Abbey, Edward 1927-1989 .... **CLC 36, 59**
See also AMWS 13; ANW; CA 45-48; 128; CANR 2, 41; DA3; DLB 256, 275; LATS 1; MTCW 2; TCWW 2

Abbott, Edwin A. 1838-1926 .... **TCLC 139**
See also DLB 178

Abbott, Lee K(ittredge) 1947- .... **CLC 48**
See also CA 124; CANR 51, 101; DLB 130

Abe, Kobo 1924-1993 ...... **CLC 8, 22, 53, 81; SSC 61; TCLC 131**
See also CA 65-68; 140; CANR 24, 60; DAM NOV; DFS 14; DLB 182; EWL 3; MJW; MTCW 1, 2; RGWL 3; SFW 4

Abe Kobo
See Abe, Kobo

Abelard, Peter c. 1079-c. 1142 ...... **CMLC 11**
See also DLB 115, 208

Abell, Kjeld 1901-1961 .... **CLC 15**
See also CA 191; 111; DLB 214; EWL 3

Abercrombie, Lascelles
1881-1938 .... **TCLC 141**
See also CA 112; DLB 19; RGEL 2

Abish, Walter 1931- .... **CLC 22; SSC 44**
See also CA 101; CANR 37, 114; CN 7; DLB 130, 227

Abrahams, Peter (Henry) 1919- .... **CLC 4**
See also AFW; BW 1; CA 57-60; CANR 26, 125; CDWLB 3; CN 7; DLB 117, 225; EWL 3; MTCW 1, 2; RGEL 2; WLIT 2

Abrams, M(eyer) H(oward) 1912- ... **CLC 24**
See also CA 57-60; CANR 13, 33; DLB 67

Abse, Dannie 1923- .... **CLC 7, 29; PC 41**
See also CA 53-56; CAAS 1; CANR 4, 46, 74, 124; CBD; CP 7; DAB; DAM POET; DLB 27, 245; MTCW 1

Abutsu 1222(?)-1283 .... **CMLC 46**
See Abutsu-ni

Abutsu-ni
See Abutsu
See also DLB 203

Achebe, (Albert) Chinua(lumogu)
1930- ...... **BLC 1; CLC 1, 3, 5, 7, 11, 26, 51, 75, 127, 152; WLC**
See also AAYA 15; AFW; BPFB 1; BRWC 2; BW 2, 3; CA 1-4R; CANR 6, 26, 47, 124; CDWLB 3; CLR 20; CN 7; CP 7; CWRI 5; DA; DA3; DAB; DAC; DAM MST, MULT, NOV; DLB 117; DNFS 1; EWL 3; EXPN; EXPS; LAIT 2; LATS 1; MAICYA 1, 2; MTCW 1, 2; NFS 2; RGEL 2; RGSF 2; SATA 38, 40; SATA-Brief 38; SSFS 3, 13; TWA; WLIT 2; WWE 1

Acker, Kathy 1948-1997 .... **CLC 45, 111**
See also AMWS 12; CA 117; 122; 162; CANR 55; CN 7

Ackroyd, Peter 1949- .... **CLC 34, 52, 140**
See also BRWS 6; CA 123; 127; CANR 51, 74, 99; CN 7; DLB 155, 231; HGG; INT CA-127; MTCW 1; RHW; SUFW 2

Acorn, Milton 1923-1986 .... **CLC 15**
See also CA 103; CCA 1; DAC; DLB 53; INT CA-103

Adamov, Arthur 1908-1970 .... **CLC 4, 25**
See also CA 17-18; 25-28R; CAP 2; DAM DRAM; EWL 3; GFL 1789 to the Present; MTCW 1; RGWL 2, 3

Adams, Alice (Boyd) 1926-1999 .. **CLC 6, 13, 46; SSC 24**
See also CA 81-84; 179; CANR 26, 53, 75, 88; CN 7; CSW; DLB 234; DLBY 1986; INT CANR-26; MTCW 1, 2; SSFS 14

Adams, Andy 1859-1935 .... **TCLC 56**
See also TCWW 2; YABC 1

Adams, (Henry) Brooks
1848-1927 .... **TCLC 80**
See also CA 123; 193; DLB 47

Adams, Douglas (Noel) 1952-2001 .. **CLC 27, 60**
See also AAYA 4, 33; BEST 89:3; BYA 14; CA 106; 197; CANR 34, 64, 124; CPW; DA3; DAM POP; DLB 261; DLBY 1983; JRDA; MTCW 1; NFS 7; SATA 116; SATA-Obit 128; SFW 4

Adams, Francis 1862-1893 .... **NCLC 33**

Adams, Henry (Brooks)
1838-1918 .... **TCLC 4, 52**
See also AMW; CA 104; 133; CANR 77; DA; DAB; DAC; DAM MST; DLB 12, 47, 189, 284; EWL 3; MTCW 1; NCFS 1; RGAL 4; TUS

Adams, John 1735-1826 .... **NCLC 106**
See also DLB 31, 183

Adams, Richard (George) 1920- ... **CLC 4, 5, 18**
See also AAYA 16; AITN 1, 2; BPFB 1; BYA 5; CA 49-52; CANR 3, 35, 128; CLR 20; CN 7; DAM NOV; DLB 261; FANT; JRDA; LAIT 5; MAICYA 1, 2; MTCW 1, 2; NFS 11; SATA 7, 69; YAW

Adamson, Joy(-Friederike Victoria)
1910-1980 .... **CLC 17**
See also CA 69-72; 93-96; CANR 22; MTCW 1; SATA 11; SATA-Obit 22

Adcock, Fleur 1934- .... **CLC 41**
See also CA 25-28R, 182; CAAE 182; CAAS 23; CANR 11, 34, 69, 101; CP 7; CWP; DLB 40; FW; WWE 1

Addams, Charles (Samuel)
1912-1988 .... **CLC 30**
See also CA 61-64; 126; CANR 12, 79

Addams, Jane 1860-1935 .... **TCLC 76**
See also AMWS 1; FW

Addams, (Laura) Jane 1860-1935 . **TCLC 76**
See also AMWS 1; CA 194; FW

Addison, Joseph 1672-1719 .... **LC 18**
See also BRW 3; CDBLB 1660-1789; DLB 101; RGEL 2; WLIT 3

Adler, Alfred (F.) 1870-1937 .... **TCLC 61**
See also CA 119; 159

Adler, C(arole) S(chwerdtfeger)
1932- .... **CLC 35**
See also AAYA 4, 41; CA 89-92; CANR 19, 40, 101; CLR 78; JRDA; MAICYA 1, 2; SAAS 15; SATA 26, 63, 102, 126; YAW

Adler, Renata 1938- .... **CLC 8, 31**
See also CA 49-52; CANR 95; CN 7; MTCW 1

Adorno, Theodor W(iesengrund)
1903-1969 .... **TCLC 111**
See also CA 89-92; 25-28R; CANR 89; DLB 242; EWL 3

Ady, Endre 1877-1919 .... **TCLC 11**
See also CA 107; CDWLB 4; DLB 215; EW 9; EWL 3

A.E. .... **TCLC 3, 10**
See Russell, George William
See also DLB 19

Aelfric c. 955-c. 1010 .... **CMLC 46**
See also DLB 146

Aeschines c. 390B.C.-c. 320B.C. .... **CMLC 47**
See also DLB 176

Aeschylus 525(?)B.C.-456(?)B.C. .. **CMLC 11, 51; DC 8; WLCS**
See also AW 1; CDWLB 1; DA; DAB; DAC; DAM DRAM, MST; DFS 5, 10; DLB 176; LMFS 1; RGWL 2, 3; TWA

Aesop 620(?)B.C.-560(?)B.C. .... **CMLC 24**
See also CLR 14; MAICYA 1, 2; SATA 64

Affable Hawk
See MacCarthy, Sir (Charles Otto) Desmond

Africa, Ben
See Bosman, Herman Charles

Afton, Effie
See Harper, Frances Ellen Watkins

Agapida, Fray Antonio
See Irving, Washington

Agee, James (Rufus) 1909-1955 ...... **TCLC 1, 19**
See also AAYA 44; AITN 1; AMW; CA 108; 148; CDALB 1941-1968; DAM NOV; DLB 2, 26, 152; DLBY 1989; EWL 3; LAIT 3; LATS 1; MTCW 1; RGAL 4; TUS

345

Aghill, Gordon
See Silverberg, Robert

Agnon, S(hmuel) Y(osef Halevi)
1888-1970 .... **CLC 4, 8, 14; SSC 30, TCLC 151**
See also CA 17-18; 25-28R; CANR 60, 102; CAP 2; EWL 3; MTCW 1, 2; RGSF 2; RGWL 2, 3

Agrippa von Nettesheim, Henry Cornelius
1486-1535 .... **LC 27**

Aguilera Malta, Demetrio
1909-1981 .... **HLCS 1**
See also CA 111; 124; CANR 87; DAM MULT, NOV; DLB 145; EWL 3; HW 1; RGWL 3

Agustini, Delmira 1886-1914 .... **HLCS 1**
See also CA 166; DLB 290; HW 1, 2; LAW

Aherne, Owen
See Cassill, R(onald) V(erlin)

Ai 1947- .... **CLC 4, 14, 69**
See also CA 85-88; CAAS 13; CANR 70; DLB 120; PFS 16

Aickman, Robert (Fordyce)
1914-1981 .... **CLC 57**
See also CA 5-8R; CANR 3, 72, 100; DLB 261; HGG; SUFW 1, 2

Aidoo, (Christina) Ama Ata
1942- .... **BLCS; CLC 177**
See also AFW; BW 1; CA 101; CANR 62; CD 5; CDWLB 3; CN 7; CWD; CWP; DLB 117; DNFS 1, 2; EWL 3; FW; WLIT 2

Aiken, Conrad (Potter) 1889-1973 .... **CLC 1, 3, 5, 10, 52; PC 26; SSC 9**
See also AMW; CA 5-8R; 45-48; CANR 4, 60; CDALB 1929-1941; DAM NOV, POET; DLB 9, 45, 102; EWL 3; EXPS; HGG; MTCW 1, 2; RGAL 4; RGSF 2; SATA 3, 30; SSFS 8; TUS

Aiken, Joan (Delano) 1924-2004 ...... **CLC 35**
See also AAYA 1, 25; CA 9-12R, 182; CAAE 182; CANR 4, 23, 34, 64, 121; CLR 1, 19, 90; DLB 161; FANT; HGG; JRDA; MAICYA 1, 2; MTCW 1; RHW; SAAS 1; SATA 2, 30, 73; SATA-Essay 109; SUFW 2; WYA; YAW

Ainsworth, William Harrison
1805-1882 .... **NCLC 13**
See also DLB 21; HGG; RGEL 2; SATA 24; SUFW 1

Aitmatov, Chingiz (Torekulovich)
1928- .... **CLC 71**
See Aytmatov, Chingiz
See also CA 103; CANR 38; CWW 2; MTCW 1; RGSF 2; SATA 56

Akers, Floyd
See Baum, L(yman) Frank

Akhmadulina, Bella Akhatovna
1937- .... **CLC 53; PC 43**
See also CA 65-68; CWP; CWW 2; DAM POET; EWL 3

Akhmatova, Anna 1888-1966 ..... **CLC 11, 25, 64, 126; PC 2, 55**
See also CA 19-20; 25-28R; CANR 35; CAP 1; DA3; DAM POET; DLB 295; EW 10; EWL 3; MTCW 1, 2; RGWL 2, 3

Aksakov, Sergei Timofeyvich
1791-1859 .... **NCLC 2**
See also DLB 198

Aksenov, Vasilii (Pavlovich)
See Aksyonov, Vassily (Pavlovich)
See also CWW 2

Aksenov, Vassily
See Aksyonov, Vassily (Pavlovich)

Akst, Daniel 1956- .... **CLC 109**
See also CA 161; CANR 110

Aksyonov, Vassily (Pavlovich)
1932- .... **CLC 22, 37, 101**
See Aksenov, Vasilii (Pavlovich)
See also CA 53-56; CANR 12, 48, 77; EWL 3

Akutagawa Ryunosuke 1892-1927 ... **SSC 44; TCLC 16**
See also CA 117; 154; DLB 180; EWL 3; MJW; RGSF 2; RGWL 2, 3

Alabaster, William 1568-1640 .... **LC 90**
See also DLB 132; RGEL 2

Alain 1868-1951 .... **TCLC 41**
See also CA 163; EWL 3; GFL 1789 to the Present

Alain de Lille c. 1116-c. 1203 .... **CMLC 53**
See also DLB 208

Alain-Fournier .... **TCLC 6**
See Fournier, Henri-Alban
See also DLB 65; EWL 3; GFL 1789 to the Present; RGWL 2, 3

Al-Amin, Jamil Abdullah 1943- .... **BLC 1**
See also BW 1, 3; CA 112; 125; CANR 82; DAM MULT

Alanus de Insluis
See Alain de Lille

Alarcon, Pedro Antonio de
1833-1891 .... **NCLC 1; SSC 64**

Alas (y Urena), Leopoldo (Enrique Garcia)
1852-1901 .... **TCLC 29**
See also CA 113; 131; HW 1; RGSF 2

Albee, Edward (Franklin) (III)
1928- .. **CLC 1, 2, 3, 5, 9, 11, 13, 25, 53, 86, 113; DC 11; WLC**
See also AAYA 51; AITN 1; AMW; CA 5-8R; CABS 3; CAD; CANR 8, 54, 74, 124; CD 5; CDALB 1941-1968; DA; DA3; DAB; DAC; DAM DRAM, MST; DFS 2, 3, 8, 10, 13, 14; DLB 7, 266; EWL 3; INT CANR-8; LAIT 1; LMFS 1; MTCW 1, 2; RGAL 4; TUS

Alberti (Merello), Rafael
See Alberti, Rafael
See also CWW 2

Alberti, Rafael 1902-1999 .... **CLC 7**
See Alberti (Merello), Rafael
See also CA 85-88; 185; CANR 81; DLB 108; EWL 3; HW 2; RGWL 2, 3

Albert the Great 1193(?)-1280 .... **CMLC 16**
See also DLB 115

Alcaeus c. 620B.C.- .... **CMLC 65**
See also DLB 176

Alcala-Galiano, Juan Valera y
See Valera y Alcala-Galiano, Juan

Alcayaga, Lucila Godoy
See Godoy Alcayaga, Lucila

Alcott, Amos Bronson 1799-1888 .... **NCLC 1**
See also DLB 1, 223

Alcott, Louisa May 1832-1888 . **NCLC 6, 58, 83; SSC 27; WLC**
See also AAYA 20; AMWS 1; BPFB 1; BYA 2; CDALB 1865-1917; CLR 1, 38; DA; DA3; DAB; DAC; DAM MST, NOV; DLB 1, 42, 79, 223, 239, 242; DLBD 14; FW; JRDA; LAIT 2; MAICYA 1, 2; NFS 12; RGAL 4; SATA 100; TUS; WCH; WYA; YABC 1; YAW

Aldanov, M. A.
See Aldanov, Mark (Alexandrovich)

Aldanov, Mark (Alexandrovich)
1886(?)-1957 .... **TCLC 23**
See also CA 118; 181

Aldington, Richard 1892-1962 .... **CLC 49**
See also CA 85-88; CANR 45; DLB 20, 36, 100, 149; LMFS 2; RGEL 2

Aldiss, Brian W(ilson) 1925- . **CLC 5, 14, 40; SSC 36**
See also AAYA 42; CA 5-8R, 190; CAAE 190; CAAS 2; CANR 5, 28, 64, 121; CN 7; DAM NOV; DLB 14, 261, 271; MTCW 1, 2; SATA 34; SFW 4

Aldrich, Bess Streeter
1881-1954 .... **TCLC 125**
See also CLR 70

Alegria, Claribel
See Alegria, Claribel
See also CWW 2; DLB 145, 283

Alegria, Claribel 1924- .... **CLC 75; HLCS 1; PC 26**
See Alegria, Claribel
See also CA 131; CAAS 15; CANR 66, 94; DAM MULT; EWL 3; HW 1; MTCW 1

Alegria, Fernando 1918- .... **CLC 57**
See also CA 9-12R; CANR 5, 32, 72; EWL 3; HW 1, 2

Aleichem, Sholom .... **SSC 33; TCLC 1, 35**
See Rabinovitch, Sholem
See also TWA

Aleixandre, Vicente 1898-1984 .... **HLCS 1; TCLC 113**
See also CANR 81; DLB 108; EWL 3; HW 2; RGWL 2, 3

Aleman, Mateo 1547-1615(?) .... **LC 81**

Alencon, Marguerite d'
See de Navarre, Marguerite

Alepoudelis, Odysseus
See Elytis, Odysseus
See also CWW 2

Aleshkovsky, Joseph 1929-
See Aleshkovsky, Yuz
See also CA 121; 128

Aleshkovsky, Yuz .... **CLC 44**
See Aleshkovsky, Joseph

Alexander, Lloyd (Chudley) 1924- ... **CLC 35**
See also AAYA 1, 27; BPFB 1; BYA 5, 6, 7, 9, 10, 11; CA 1-4R; CANR 1, 24, 38, 55, 113; CLR 1, 5, 48; CWRI 5; DLB 52; FANT; JRDA; MAICYA 1, 2; MAICYAS 1; MTCW 1; SAAS 19; SATA 3, 49, 81, 129, 135; SUFW; TUS; WYA; YAW

Alexander, Meena 1951- .... **CLC 121**
See also CA 115; CANR 38, 70; CP 7; CWP; FW

Alexander, Samuel 1859-1938 .... **TCLC 77**

Alexie, Sherman (Joseph, Jr.)
1966- .... **CLC 96, 154; NNAL; PC 53**
See also AAYA 28; BYA 15; CA 138; CANR 65, 95; DA3; DAM MULT; DLB 175, 206, 278; LATS 1; MTCW 1; NFS 17; SSFS 18

al-Farabi 870(?)-950 .... **CMLC 58**
See also DLB 115

Alfau, Felipe 1902-1999 .... **CLC 66**
See also CA 137

Alfieri, Vittorio 1749-1803 .... **NCLC 101**
See also EW 4; RGWL 2, 3

Alfred, Jean Gaston
See Ponge, Francis

Alger, Horatio, Jr. 1832-1899 .... **NCLC 8, 83**
See also CLR 87; DLB 42; LAIT 2; RGAL 4; SATA 16; TUS

Al-Ghazali, Muhammad ibn Muhammad
1058-1111 .... **CMLC 50**
See also DLB 115

Algren, Nelson 1909-1981 ..... **CLC 4, 10, 33; SSC 33**
See also AMWS 9; BPFB 1; CA 13-16R; 103; CANR 20, 61; CDALB 1941-1968; DLB 9; DLBY 1981, 1982, 2000; EWL 3; MTCW 1, 2; RGAL 4; RGSF 2

al-Hariri, al-Qasim ibn 'Ali Abu Muhammad al-Basri
1054-1122 .... **CMLC 63**
See also RGWL 3

Ali, Ahmed 1908-1998 .... **CLC 69**
See also CA 25-28R; CANR 15, 34; EWL 3

Ali, Tariq 1943- .... **CLC 173**
See also CA 25-28R; CANR 10, 99

Alighieri, Dante
See Dante

Allan, John B.
See Westlake, Donald E(dwin)

Allan, Sidney
See Hartmann, Sadakichi

Allan, Sydney
See Hartmann, Sadakichi

Allard, Janet .... **CLC 59**

Allen, Edward 1948- .... **CLC 59**

Allen, Fred 1894-1956 .... **TCLC 87**

Allen, Paula Gunn 1939- ..... **CLC 84; NNAL**
See also AMWS 4; CA 112; 143; CANR 63; CWP; DA3; DAM MULT; DLB 175; FW; MTCW 1; RGAL 4

Allen, Roland
See Ayckbourn, Alan

Allen, Sarah A.
See Hopkins, Pauline Elizabeth

Allen, Sidney H.
See Hartmann, Sadakichi

Allen, Woody 1935- .... **CLC 16, 52**
See also AAYA 10, 51; CA 33-36R; CANR 27, 38, 63, 128; DAM POP; DLB 44; MTCW 1

Allende, Isabel 1942- ... **CLC 39, 57, 97, 170; HLC 1; SSC 65; WLCS**
See also AAYA 18; CA 125; 130; CANR 51, 74, 129; CDWLB 3; CWW 2; DA3; DAM MULT, NOV; DLB 145; DNFS 1; EWL 3; FW; HW 1; INT CA-130; LAIT 5; LAWS 1; LMFS 2; MTCW 1, 2; NCFS 1; NFS 6, 18; RGSF 2; RGWL 3; SSFS 11, 16; WLIT 1

Alleyn, Ellen
See Rossetti, Christina (Georgina)

Alleyne, Carla D. .... **CLC 65**

Allingham, Margery (Louise)
1904-1966 .... **CLC 19**
See also CA 5-8R; 25-28R; CANR 4, 58; CMW 4; DLB 77; MSW; MTCW 1, 2

Allingham, William 1824-1889 ...... **NCLC 25**
See also DLB 35; RGEL 2

Allison, Dorothy E. 1949- .... **CLC 78, 153**
See also AAYA 53; CA 140; CANR 66, 107; CSW; DA3; FW; MTCW 1; NFS 11; RGAL 4

Alloula, Malek .... **CLC 65**

Allston, Washington 1779-1843 .... **NCLC 2**
See also DLB 1, 235

Almedingen, E. M. .... **CLC 12**
See Almedingen, Martha Edith von
See also SATA 3

Almedingen, Martha Edith von 1898-1971
See Almedingen, E. M.
See also CA 1-4R; CANR 1

Almodovar, Pedro 1949(?)- .... **CLC 114; HLCS 1**
See also CA 133; CANR 72; HW 2

Almqvist, Carl Jonas Love
1793-1866 .... **NCLC 42**

al-Mutanabbi, Ahmad ibn al-Husayn Abu al-Tayyib al-Jufi al-Kindi
915-965 .... **CMLC 66**
See also RGWL 3

Alonso, Damaso 1898-1990 .... **CLC 14**
See also CA 110; 131; 130; CANR 72; DLB 108; EWL 3; HW 1, 2

Alov
See Gogol, Nikolai (Vasilyevich)

Al Siddik
See Rolfe, Frederick (William Serafino Austin Lewis Mary)
See also GLL 1; RGEL 2

Alta 1942- .... **CLC 19**
See also CA 57-60

Alter, Robert B(ernard) 1935- .... **CLC 34**
See also CA 49-52; CANR 1, 47, 100

Alther, Lisa 1944- .... **CLC 7, 41**
See also BPFB 1; CA 65-68; CAAS 30; CANR 12, 30, 51; CN 7; CSW; GLL 2; MTCW 1

Althusser, L.
See Althusser, Louis

Althusser, Louis 1918-1990 .... **CLC 106**
See also CA 131; 132; CANR 102; DLB 242

Altman, Robert 1925- .... **CLC 16, 116**
See also CA 73-76; CANR 43

Alurista .... **HLCS 1**
See Urista (Heredia), Alberto (Baltazar)
See also DLB 82; LLW 1

Alvarez, A(lfred) 1929- .... **CLC 5, 13**
See also CA 1-4R; CANR 3, 33, 63, 101; CN 7; CP 7; DLB 14, 40

Alvarez, Alejandro Rodriguez 1903-1965
See Casona, Alejandro
See also CA 131; 93-96; HW 1

Alvarez, Julia 1950- .... **CLC 93; HLCS 1**
See also AAYA 25; AMWS 7; CA 147; CANR 69, 101; DA3; DLB 282; LATS 1; LLW 1; MTCW 1; NFS 5, 9; SATA 129; WLIT 1

Alvaro, Corrado 1896-1956 .... **TCLC 60**
See also CA 163; DLB 264; EWL 3

Amado, Jorge 1912-2001 ... **CLC 13, 40, 106; HLC 1**
See also CA 77-80; 201; CANR 35, 74; CWW 2; DAM MULT, NOV; DLB 113; EWL 3; HW 2; LAW; LAWS 1; MTCW 1, 2; RGSF 2; RGWL 2, 3; TWA; WLIT 1

Ambler, Eric 1909-1998 .... **CLC 4, 6, 9**
See also BRWS 4; CA 9-12R; 171; CANR 7, 38, 74; CMW 4; CN 7; DLB 77; MSW; MTCW 1, 2; TEA

Ambrose, Stephen E(dward)
1936-2002 .... **CLC 145**
See also AAYA 44; CA 1-4R; 209; CANR 3, 43, 57, 83, 105; NCFS 2; SATA 40, 138

Amichai, Yehuda 1924-2000 .. **CLC 9, 22, 57, 116; PC 38**
See also CA 85-88; 189; CANR 46, 60, 99; CWW 2; EWL 3; MTCW 1

Amichai, Yehudah
See Amichai, Yehuda

Amiel, Henri Frederic 1821-1881 .... **NCLC 4**
See also DLB 217

Amis, Kingsley (William)
1922-1995 ...... **CLC 1, 2, 3, 5, 8, 13, 40, 44, 129**
See also AITN 2; BPFB 1; BRWS 2; CA 9-12R; 150; CANR 8, 28, 54; CDBLB 1945-1960; CN 7; CP 7; DA; DA3; DAB; DAC; DAM MST, NOV; DLB 15, 27, 100, 139; DLBY 1996; EWL 3; HGG; INT CANR-8; MTCW 1, 2; RGEL 2; RGSF 2; SFW 4

Amis, Martin (Louis) 1949- .... **CLC 4, 9, 38, 62, 101**
See also BEST 90:3; BRWS 4; CA 65-68; CANR 8, 27, 54, 73, 95; CN 7; DA3; DLB 14, 194; EWL 3; INT CANR-27; MTCW 1

Ammianus Marcellinus c. 330-c.
395 .... **CMLC 60**
See also AW 2; DLB 211

Ammons, A(rchie) R(andolph)
1926-2001 ...... **CLC 2, 3, 5, 8, 9, 25, 57, 108; PC 16**
See also AITN 1; AMWS 7; CA 9-12R; 193; CANR 6, 36, 51, 73, 107; CP 7; CSW; DAM POET; DLB 5, 165; EWL 3; MTCW 1, 2; PFS 19; RGAL 4

Amo, Tauraatua i
See Adams, Henry (Brooks)

Amory, Thomas 1691(?)-1788 .... **LC 48**
See also DLB 39

Anand, Mulk Raj 1905- .... **CLC 23, 93**
See also CA 65-68; CANR 32, 64; CN 7; DAM NOV; EWL 3; MTCW 1, 2; RGSF 2

Anatol
See Schnitzler, Arthur

Anaximander c. 611B.C.-c.
546B.C. .... **CMLC 22**

Anaya, Rudolfo A(lfonso) 1937- ...... **CLC 23, 148; HLC 1**
See also AAYA 20; BYA 13; CA 45-48; CAAS 4; CANR 1, 32, 51, 124; CN 7; DAM MULT, NOV; DLB 82, 206, 278; HW 1; LAIT 4; LLW 1; MTCW 1, 2; NFS 12; RGAL 4; RGSF 2; WLIT 1

Andersen, Hans Christian
1805-1875 .... **NCLC 7, 79; SSC 6, 56; WLC**
See also CLR 6; DA; DA3; DAB; DAC; DAM MST, POP; EW 6; MAICYA 1, 2; RGSF 2; RGWL 2, 3; SATA 100; TWA; WCH; YABC 1

Anderson, C. Farley
See Mencken, H(enry) L(ouis); Nathan, George Jean

Anderson, Jessica (Margaret) Queale
1916- .... **CLC 37**
See also CA 9-12R; CANR 4, 62; CN 7

Anderson, Jon (Victor) 1940- .... **CLC 9**
See also CA 25-28R; CANR 20; DAM POET

Anderson, Lindsay (Gordon)
1923-1994 .... **CLC 20**
See also CA 125; 128; 146; CANR 77

Anderson, Maxwell 1888-1959 .... **TCLC 2, 144**
See also CA 105; 152; DAM DRAM; DFS 16; DLB 7, 228; MTCW 2; RGAL 4

Anderson, Poul (William)
1926-2001 .... **CLC 15**
See also AAYA 5, 34; BPFB 1; BYA 6, 8, 9; CA 1-4R, 181; 199; CAAE 181; CAAS 2; CANR 2, 15, 34, 64, 110; CLR 58; DLB 8; FANT; INT CANR-15; MTCW 1, 2; SATA 90; SATA-Brief 39; SATA-Essay 106; SCFW 2; SFW 4; SUFW 1, 2

Anderson, Robert (Woodruff)
1917- .... **CLC 23**
See also AITN 1; CA 21-24R; CANR 32; DAM DRAM; DLB 7; LAIT 5

Anderson, Roberta Joan
See Mitchell, Joni

Anderson, Sherwood 1876-1941 .. **SSC 1, 46; TCLC 1, 10, 24, 123; WLC**
See also AAYA 30; AMW; AMWC 2; BPFB 1; CA 104; 121; CANR 61; CDALB 1917-1929; DA; DA3; DAB; DAC; DAM MST, NOV; DLB 4, 9, 86; DLBD 1; EWL 3; EXPS; GLL 2; MTCW 1, 2; NFS 4; RGAL 4; RGSF 2; SSFS 4, 10, 11; TUS

Andier, Pierre
See Desnos, Robert

Andouard
See Giraudoux, Jean(-Hippolyte)

Andrade, Carlos Drummond de ...... **CLC 18**
See Drummond de Andrade, Carlos
See also EWL 3; RGWL 2, 3

Andrade, Mario de .... **TCLC 43**
See de Andrade, Mario
See also EWL 3; LAW; RGWL 2, 3; WLIT 1

Andreae, Johann V(alentin)
1586-1654 .... **LC 32**
See also DLB 164

Andreas Capellanus fl. c. 1185- .... **CMLC 45**
See also DLB 208

Andreas-Salome, Lou 1861-1937 ... **TCLC 56**
See also CA 178; DLB 66

Andreev, Leonid
See Andreyev, Leonid (Nikolaevich)
See also DLB 295; EWL 3

Andress, Lesley
See Sanders, Lawrence

Andrewes, Lancelot 1555-1626 .... **LC 5**
See also DLB 151, 172

Andrews, Cicily Fairfield
See West, Rebecca

Andrews, Elton V.
See Pohl, Frederik

Andreyev, Leonid (Nikolaevich)
1871-1919 .... **TCLC 3**
See Andreev, Leonid
See also CA 104; 185

Andric, Ivo 1892-1975 .... **CLC 8; SSC 36; TCLC 135**
See also CA 81-84; 57-60; CANR 43, 60; CDWLB 4; DLB 147; EW 11; EWL 3; MTCW 1; RGSF 2; RGWL 2, 3

Androvar
See Prado (Calvo), Pedro

Angelique, Pierre
See Bataille, Georges

Angell, Roger 1920- .... **CLC 26**
See also CA 57-60; CANR 13, 44, 70; DLB 171, 185

Angelou, Maya 1928- ... **BLC 1; CLC 12, 35, 64, 77, 155; PC 32; WLCS**
See also AAYA 7, 20; AMWS 4; BPFB 1; BW 2, 3; BYA 2; CA 65-68; CANR 19, 42, 65, 111; CDALBS; CLR 53; CP 7; CPW; CSW; CWP; DA; DA3; DAB; DAC; DAM MST, MULT, POET, POP; DLB 38; EWL 3; EXPN; EXPP; LAIT 4; MAICYA 2; MAICYAS 1; MAWW; MTCW 1, 2; NCFS 2; NFS 2; PFS 2, 3; RGAL 4; SATA 49, 136; WYA; YAW

Angouleme, Marguerite d'
See de Navarre, Marguerite

Anna Comnena 1083-1153 .... **CMLC 25**

Annensky, Innokentii Fedorovich
See Annensky, Innokenty (Fyodorovich)
See also DLB 295

Annensky, Innokenty (Fyodorovich)
1856-1909 .... **TCLC 14**
See also CA 110; 155; EWL 3

Annunzio, Gabriele d'
See D'Annunzio, Gabriele

Anodos
See Coleridge, Mary E(lizabeth)

Anon, Charles Robert
See Pessoa, Fernando (Antonio Nogueira)

Anouilh, Jean (Marie Lucien Pierre)
1910-1987 . **CLC 1, 3, 8, 13, 40, 50; DC 8, 21**
See also CA 17-20R; 123; CANR 32; DAM DRAM; DFS 9, 10; EW 13; EWL 3; GFL 1789 to the Present; MTCW 1, 2; RGWL 2, 3; TWA

Anselm of Canterbury
1033(?)-1109 .... **CMLC 67**
See also DLB 115

Anthony, Florence
See Ai

Anthony, John
See Ciardi, John (Anthony)

Anthony, Peter
See Shaffer, Anthony (Joshua); Shaffer, Peter (Levin)

Anthony, Piers 1934- .... **CLC 35**
See also AAYA 11, 48; BYA 7; CA 200; CAAE 200; CANR 28, 56, 73, 102; CPW; DAM POP; DLB 8; FANT; MAICYA 2; MAICYAS 1; MTCW 1, 2; SAAS 22; SATA 84, 129; SATA-Essay 129; SFW 4; SUFW 1, 2; YAW

Anthony, Susan B(rownell)
1820-1906 .... **TCLC 84**
See also CA 211; FW

Antiphon c. 480B.C.-c. 411B.C. .... **CMLC 55**

Antoine, Marc
See Proust, (Valentin-Louis-George-Eugene) Marcel

Antoninus, Brother
See Everson, William (Oliver)

Antonioni, Michelangelo 1912- .... **CLC 20, 144**
See also CA 73-76; CANR 45, 77

Antschel, Paul 1920-1970
See Celan, Paul
See also CA 85-88; CANR 33, 61; MTCW 1

Anwar, Chairil 1922-1949 .... **TCLC 22**
See Chairil Anwar
See also CA 121; 219; RGWL 3

Anzaldua, Gloria (Evanjelina)
1942- .... **HLCS 1**
See also CA 175; CSW; CWP; DLB 122; FW; LLW 1; RGAL 4

Apess, William 1798-1839(?) .... **NCLC 73; NNAL**
See also DAM MULT; DLB 175, 243

Apollinaire, Guillaume 1880-1918 .... **PC 7; TCLC 3, 8, 51**
See Kostrowitzki, Wilhelm Apollinaris de
See also CA 152; DAM POET; DLB 258; EW 9; EWL 3; GFL 1789 to the Present; MTCW 1; RGWL 2, 3; TWA; WP

Apollonius of Rhodes
See Apollonius Rhodius
See also AW 1; RGWL 2, 3

Apollonius Rhodius c. 300B.C.-c. 220B.C. .... **CMLC 28**
See Apollonius of Rhodes
See also DLB 176

Appelfeld, Aharon 1932- ... **CLC 23, 47; SSC 42**
See also CA 112; 133; CANR 86; CWW 2; EWL 3; RGSF 2

Apple, Max (Isaac) 1941- .... **CLC 9, 33; SSC 50**
See also CA 81-84; CANR 19, 54; DLB 130

Appleman, Philip (Dean) 1926- .... **CLC 51**
See also CA 13-16R; CAAS 18; CANR 6, 29, 56

Appleton, Lawrence
See Lovecraft, H(oward) P(hillips)

Apteryx
See Eliot, T(homas) S(tearns)

Apuleius, (Lucius Madaurensis)
125(?)-175(?) .... **CMLC 1**
See also AW 2; CDWLB 1; DLB 211; RGWL 2, 3; SUFW

Aquin, Hubert 1929-1977 .... **CLC 15**
See also CA 105; DLB 53; EWL 3

Aquinas, Thomas 1224(?)-1274 .... **CMLC 33**
See also DLB 115; EW 1; TWA

Aragon, Louis 1897-1982 .... **CLC 3, 22; TCLC 123**
See also CA 69-72; 108; CANR 28, 71; DAM NOV, POET; DLB 72, 258; EW 11; EWL 3; GFL 1789 to the Present; GLL 2; LMFS 2; MTCW 1, 2; RGWL 2, 3

Arany, Janos 1817-1882 .... **NCLC 34**

Aranyos, Kakay 1847-1910
See Mikszath, Kalman

Aratus of Soli c. 315B.C.-c. 240B.C. .... **CMLC 64**
See also DLB 176

Arbuthnot, John 1667-1735 .... **LC 1**
See also DLB 101

Archer, Herbert Winslow
See Mencken, H(enry) L(ouis)

Archer, Jeffrey (Howard) 1940- .... **CLC 28**
See also AAYA 16; BEST 89:3; BPFB 1; CA 77-80; CANR 22, 52, 95; CPW; DA3; DAM POP; INT CANR-22

Archer, Jules 1915- .... **CLC 12**
See also CA 9-12R; CANR 6, 69; SAAS 5; SATA 4, 85

Archer, Lee
See Ellison, Harlan (Jay)

Archilochus c. 7th cent. B.C.- .... **CMLC 44**
See also DLB 176

Arden, John 1930- .... **CLC 6, 13, 15**
See also BRWS 2; CA 13-16R; CAAS 4; CANR 31, 65, 67, 124; CBD; CD 5; DAM DRAM; DFS 9; DLB 13, 245; EWL 3; MTCW 1

Arenas, Reinaldo 1943-1990 .. **CLC 41; HLC 1**
See also CA 124; 128; 133; CANR 73, 106; DAM MULT; DLB 145; EWL 3; GLL 2; HW 1; LAW; LAWS 1; MTCW 1; RGSF 2; RGWL 3; WLIT 1

Arendt, Hannah 1906-1975 .... **CLC 66, 98**
See also CA 17-20R; 61-64; CANR 26, 60; DLB 242; MTCW 1, 2

Aretino, Pietro 1492-1556 .... **LC 12**
See also RGWL 2, 3

Arghezi, Tudor .... **CLC 80**
See Theodorescu, Ion N.
See also CA 167; CDWLB 4; DLB 220; EWL 3

Arguedas, Jose Maria 1911-1969 .... **CLC 10, 18; HLCS 1; TCLC 147**
See also CA 89-92; CANR 73; DLB 113; EWL 3; HW 1; LAW; RGWL 2, 3; WLIT 1

Argueta, Manlio 1936- .... **CLC 31**
See also CA 131; CANR 73; CWW 2; DLB 145; EWL 3; HW 1; RGWL 3

Arias, Ron(ald Francis) 1941- .... **HLC 1**
See also CA 131; CANR 81; DAM MULT; DLB 82; HW 1, 2; MTCW 2

Ariosto, Ludovico 1474-1533 ... **LC 6, 87; PC 42**
See also EW 2; RGWL 2, 3

Aristides
See Epstein, Joseph

Aristophanes 450B.C.-385B.C. .... **CMLC 4, 51; DC 2; WLCS**
See also AW 1; CDWLB 1; DA; DA3; DAB; DAC; DAM DRAM, MST; DFS 10; DLB 176; LMFS 1; RGWL 2, 3; TWA

Aristotle 384B.C.-322B.C. .... **CMLC 31; WLCS**
See also AW 1; CDWLB 1; DA; DA3; DAB; DAC; DAM MST; DLB 176; RGWL 2, 3; TWA

Arlt, Roberto (Godofredo Christophersen)
1900-1942 .... **HLC 1; TCLC 29**
See also CA 123; 131; CANR 67; DAM MULT; EWL 3; HW 1, 2; LAW

Armah, Ayi Kwei 1939- . **BLC 1; CLC 5, 33, 136**
See also AFW; BW 1; CA 61-64; CANR 21, 64; CDWLB 3; CN 7; DAM MULT, POET; DLB 117; EWL 3; MTCW 1; WLIT 2

Armatrading, Joan 1950- .... **CLC 17**
See also CA 114; 186

Armitage, Frank
See Carpenter, John (Howard)

Armstrong, Jeannette (C.) 1948- .... **NNAL**
See also CA 149; CCA 1; CN 7; DAC; SATA 102

Arnette, Robert
See Silverberg, Robert

Arnim, Achim von (Ludwig Joachim von Arnim) 1781-1831 ..... **NCLC 5; SSC 29**
See also DLB 90

Arnim, Bettina von 1785-1859 ...... **NCLC 38, 123**
See also DLB 90; RGWL 2, 3

Arnold, Matthew 1822-1888 ..... **NCLC 6, 29, 89, 126; PC 5; WLC**
See also BRW 5; CDBLB 1832 1890; DA; DAB; DAC; DAM MST, POET; DLB 32, 57; EXPP; PAB; PFS 2; TEA; WP

Arnold, Thomas 1795-1842 .... **NCLC 18**
See also DLB 55

Arnow, Harriette (Louisa) Simpson 1908-1986 .... **CLC 2, 7, 18**
See also BPFB 1; CA 9-12R; 118; CANR 14; DLB 6; FW; MTCW 1, 2; RHW; SATA 42; SATA-Obit 47

Arouet, Francois-Marie
See Voltaire

Arp, Hans
See Arp, Jean

Arp, Jean 1887-1966 .... **CLC 5; TCLC 115**
See also CA 81-84; 25-28R; CANR 42, 77; EW 10

Arrabal
See Arrabal, Fernando

Arrabal, Fernando 1932- ... **CLC 2, 9, 18, 58**
See Arrabal (Teran), Fernando
See also CA 9-12R; CANR 15; EWL 3; LMFS 2

Arrabal (Teran), Fernando 1932-
See Arrabal, Fernando
See also CWW 2

Arreola, Juan Jose 1918-2001 .... **CLC 147; HLC 1; SSC 38**
See also CA 113; 131; 200; CANR 81; CWW 2; DAM MULT; DLB 113; DNFS 2; EWL 3; HW 1, 2; LAW; RGSF 2

Arrian c. 89(?)-c. 155(?) .... **CMLC 43**
See also DLB 176

Arrick, Fran .... **CLC 30**
See Gaberman, Judie Angell
See also BYA 6

Arriey, Richmond
See Delany, Samuel R(ay), Jr.

Artaud, Antonin (Marie Joseph) 1896-1948 .... **DC 14; TCLC 3, 36**
See also CA 104; 149; DA3; DAM DRAM; DLB 258; EW 11; EWL 3; GFL 1789 to the Present; MTCW 1; RGWL 2, 3

Arthur, Ruth M(abel) 1905-1979 ..... **CLC 12**
See also CA 9-12R; 85-88; CANR 4; CWRI 5; SATA 7, 26

Artsybashev, Mikhail (Petrovich) 1878-1927 .... **TCLC 31**
See also CA 170; DLB 295

Arundel, Honor (Morfydd) 1919-1973 .... **CLC 17**
See also CA 21-22; 41-44R; CAP 2; CLR 35; CWRI 5; SATA 4; SATA-Obit 24

Arzner, Dorothy 1900-1979 .... **CLC 98**

Asch, Sholem 1880-1957 .... **TCLC 3**
See also CA 105; EWL 3; GLL 2

Ascham, Roger 1516(?)-1568 .... **LC 101**
See also DLB 236

Ash, Shalom
See Asch, Sholem

Ashbery, John (Lawrence) 1927- .. **CLC 2, 3, 4, 6, 9, 13, 15, 25, 41, 77, 125; PC 26**
See Berry, Jonas
See also AMWS 3; CA 5-8R; CANR 9, 37, 66, 102; CP 7; DA3; DAM POET; DLB 5, 165; DLBY 1981; EWL 3; INT CANR-9; MTCW 1, 2; PAB; PFS 11; RGAL 4; WP

Ashdown, Clifford
See Freeman, R(ichard) Austin

Ashe, Gordon
See Creasey, John

Ashton-Warner, Sylvia (Constance) 1908-1984 .... **CLC 19**
See also CA 69-72; 112; CANR 29; MTCW 1, 2

Asimov, Isaac 1920-1992 ..... **CLC 1, 3, 9, 19, 26, 76, 92**
See also AAYA 13; BEST 90:2; BPFB 1; BYA 4, 6, 7, 9; CA 1-4R; 137; CANR 2, 19, 36, 60, 125; CLR 12, 79; CMW 4; CPW; DA3; DAM POP; DLB 8; DLBY 1992; INT CANR-19; JRDA; LAIT 5; LMFS 2; MAICYA 1, 2; MTCW 1, 2; RGAL 4; SATA 1, 26, 74; SCFW 2; SFW 4; SSFS 17; TUS; YAW

Askew, Anne 1521(?)-1546 .... **LC 81**
See also DLB 136

Assis, Joaquim Maria Machado de
See Machado de Assis, Joaquim Maria

Astell, Mary 1666-1731 .... **LC 68**
See also DLB 252; FW

Astley, Thea (Beatrice May) 1925- .. **CLC 41**
See also CA 65-68; CANR 11, 43, 78; CN 7; DLB 289; EWL 3

Astley, William 1855-1911
See Warung, Price

Aston, James
See White, T(erence) H(anbury)

Asturias, Miguel Angel 1899-1974 .... **CLC 3, 8, 13; HLC 1**
See also CA 25-28; 49-52; CANR 32; CAP 2; CDWLB 3; DA3; DAM MULT, NOV; DLB 113, 290; EWL 3; HW 1; LAW; LMFS 2; MTCW 1, 2; RGWL 2, 3; WLIT 1

Atares, Carlos Saura
See Saura (Atares), Carlos

Athanasius c. 295-c. 373 .... **CMLC 48**

Atheling, William
See Pound, Ezra (Weston Loomis)

Atheling, William, Jr.
See Blish, James (Benjamin)

Atherton, Gertrude (Franklin Horn) 1857-1948 .... **TCLC 2**
See also CA 104; 155; DLB 9, 78, 186; HGG; RGAL 4; SUFW 1; TCWW 2

Atherton, Lucius
See Masters, Edgar Lee

Atkins, Jack
See Harris, Mark

Atkinson, Kate 1951- .... **CLC 99**
See also CA 166; CANR 101; DLB 267

Attaway, William (Alexander) 1911-1986 .... **BLC 1; CLC 92**
See also BW 2, 3; CA 143; CANR 82; DAM MULT; DLB 76

Atticus
See Fleming, Ian (Lancaster); Wilson, (Thomas) Woodrow

Atwood, Margaret (Eleanor) 1939- ... **CLC 2, 3, 4, 8, 13, 15, 25, 44, 84, 135; PC 8; SSC 2, 46; WLC**
See also AAYA 12, 47; AMWS 13; BEST 89:2; BPFB 1; CA 49-52; CANR 3, 24, 33, 59, 95; CN 7; CP 7; CPW; CWP; DA; DA3; DAB; DAC; DAM MST, NOV, POET; DLB 53, 251; EWL 3; EXPN; FW; INT CANR-24; LAIT 5; MTCW 1, 2; NFS 4, 12, 13, 14; PFS 7; RGSF 2; SATA 50; SSFS 3, 13; TWA; WWE 1; YAW

Aubigny, Pierre d'
See Mencken, H(enry) L(ouis)

Aubin, Penelope 1685-1731(?) .... **LC 9**
See also DLB 39

Auchincloss, Louis (Stanton) 1917- .. **CLC 4, 6, 9, 18, 45; SSC 22**
See also AMWS 4; CA 1-4R; CANR 6, 29, 55, 87; CN 7; DAM NOV; DLB 2, 244; DLBY 1980; EWL 3; INT CANR-29; MTCW 1; RGAL 4

Auden, W(ystan) H(ugh) 1907-1973 . **CLC 1, 2, 3, 4, 6, 9, 11, 14, 43, 123; PC 1; WLC**
See also AAYA 18; AMWS 2; BRW 7; BRWR 1; CA 9-12R; 45-48; CANR 5, 61, 105; CDBLB 1914-1945; DA; DA3; DAB; DAC; DAM DRAM, MST, POET; DLB 10, 20; EWL 3; EXPP; MTCW 1, 2; PAB; PFS 1, 3, 4, 10; TUS; WP

Audiberti, Jacques 1900-1965 .... **CLC 38**
See also CA 25-28R; DAM DRAM; EWL 3

Audubon, John James 1785-1851 . **NCLC 47**
See also ANW; DLB 248

Auel, Jean M(arie) 1936- .... **CLC 31, 107**
See also AAYA 7, 51; BEST 90:4; BPFB 1; CA 103; CANR 21, 64, 115; CPW; DA3; DAM POP; INT CANR-21; NFS 11; RHW; SATA 91

Auerbach, Erich 1892-1957 .... **TCLC 43**
See also CA 118; 155; EWL 3

Augier, Emile 1820-1889 .... **NCLC 31**
See also DLB 192; GFL 1789 to the Present

August, John
See De Voto, Bernard (Augustine)

Augustine, St. 354-430 .... **CMLC 6; WLCS**
See also DA; DA3; DAB; DAC; DAM MST; DLB 115; EW 1; RGWL 2, 3

Aunt Belinda
See Braddon, Mary Elizabeth

Aunt Weedy
See Alcott, Louisa May

Aurelius
See Bourne, Randolph S(illiman)

Aurelius, Marcus 121-180 .... **CMLC 45**
See Marcus Aurelius
See also RGWL 2, 3

Aurobindo, Sri
See Ghose, Aurabinda

Aurobindo Ghose
See Ghose, Aurabinda

Austen, Jane 1775-1817 ...... **NCLC 1, 13, 19, 33, 51, 81, 95, 119; WLC**
See also AAYA 19; BRW 4; BRWC 1; BRWR 2; BYA 3; CDBLB 1789-1832; DA; DA3; DAB; DAC; DAM MST, NOV; DLB 116; EXPN; LAIT 2; LATS 1; LMFS 1; NFS 1, 14, 18; TEA; WLIT 3; WYAS 1

Auster, Paul 1947- .... **CLC 47, 131**
See also AMWS 12; CA 69-72; CANR 23, 52, 75, 129; CMW 4; CN 7; DA3; DLB 227; MTCW 1; SUFW 2

Austin, Frank
See Faust, Frederick (Schiller)
See also TCWW 2

Austin, Mary (Hunter) 1868-1934 . **TCLC 25**
See Stairs, Gordon
See also ANW; CA 109; 178; DLB 9, 78, 206, 221, 275; FW; TCWW 2

Averroes 1126-1198 .... **CMLC 7**
See also DLB 115

Avicenna 980-1037 .... **CMLC 16**
See also DLB 115

Avison, Margaret 1918- .... **CLC 2, 4, 97**
See also CA 17-20R; CP 7; DAC; DAM POET; DLB 53; MTCW 1

Axton, David
See Koontz, Dean R(ay)

Ayckbourn, Alan 1939- ...... **CLC 5, 8, 18, 33, 74; DC 13**
See also BRWS 5; CA 21-24R; CANR 31, 59, 118; CBD; CD 5; DAB; DAM DRAM; DFS 7; DLB 13, 245; EWL 3; MTCW 1, 2

Aydy, Catherine
See Tennant, Emma (Christina)

Ayme, Marcel (Andre) 1902-1967 ... **CLC 11; SSC 41**
See also CA 89-92; CANR 67; CLR 25; DLB 72; EW 12; EWL 3; GFL 1789 to the Present; RGSF 2; RGWL 2, 3; SATA 91

Ayrton, Michael 1921-1975 .... **CLC 7**
See also CA 5-8R; 61-64; CANR 9, 21

Aytmatov, Chingiz
See Aitmatov, Chingiz (Torekulovich)
See also EWL 3

Azorin .... **CLC 11**
See Martinez Ruiz, Jose
See also EW 9; EWL 3

Azuela, Mariano 1873-1952 .. **HLC 1; TCLC 3, 145**
See also CA 104; 131; CANR 81; DAM MULT; EWL 3; HW 1, 2; LAW; MTCW 1, 2

Ba, Mariama 1929-1981 .... **BLCS**
See also AFW; BW 2; CA 141; CANR 87; DNFS 2; WLIT 2

Baastad, Babbis Friis
See Friis-Baastad, Babbis Ellinor

Bab
See Gilbert, W(illiam) S(chwenck)

Babbis, Eleanor
See Friis-Baastad, Babbis Ellinor

Babel, Isaac
See Babel, Isaak (Emmanuilovich)
See also EW 11; SSFS 10

Babel, Isaak (Emmanuilovich)
1894-1941(?) .... **SSC 16; TCLC 2, 13**
See Babel, Isaac
See also CA 104; 155; CANR 113; DLB 272; EWL 3; MTCW 1; RGSF 2; RGWL 2, 3; TWA

Babits, Mihaly 1883-1941 .... **TCLC 14**
See also CA 114; CDWLB 4; DLB 215; EWL 3

Babur 1483-1530 .... **LC 18**

Babylas 1898-1962
See Ghelderode, Michel de

Baca, Jimmy Santiago 1952- . **HLC 1; PC 41**
See also CA 131; CANR 81, 90; CP 7; DAM MULT; DLB 122; HW 1, 2; LLW 1

Baca, Jose Santiago
See Baca, Jimmy Santiago

Bacchelli, Riccardo 1891-1985 .... **CLC 19**
See also CA 29-32R; 117; DLB 264; EWL 3

Bach, Richard (David) 1936- .... **CLC 14**
See also AITN 1; BEST 89:2; BPFB 1; BYA 5; CA 9-12R; CANR 18, 93; CPW; DAM NOV, POP; FANT; MTCW 1; SATA 13

Bache, Benjamin Franklin
1769-1798 .... **LC 74**
See also DLB 43

Bachelard, Gaston 1884-1962 ...... **TCLC 128**
See also CA 97-100; 89-92; DLB 296; GFL 1789 to the Present

Bachman, Richard
See King, Stephen (Edwin)

Bachmann, Ingeborg 1926-1973 .... **CLC 69**
See also CA 93-96; 45-48; CANR 69; DLB 85; EWL 3; RGWL 2, 3

Bacon, Francis 1561-1626 .... **LC 18, 32**
See also BRW 1; CDBLB Before 1660; DLB 151, 236, 252; RGEL 2; TEA

Bacon, Roger 1214(?)-1294 .... **CMLC 14**
See also DLB 115

Bacovia, George 1881-1957 .... **TCLC 24**
See Vasiliu, Gheorghe
See also CDWLB 4; DLB 220; EWL 3

Badanes, Jerome 1937- .... **CLC 59**

Bagehot, Walter 1826-1877 .... **NCLC 10**
See also DLB 55

Bagnold, Enid 1889-1981 .... **CLC 25**
See also BYA 2; CA 5-8R; 103; CANR 5, 40; CBD; CWD; CWRI 5; DAM DRAM; DLB 13, 160, 191, 245; FW; MAICYA 1, 2; RGEL 2; SATA 1, 25

Bagritsky, Eduard .... **TCLC 60**
See Dzyubin, Eduard Georgievich

Bagrjana, Elisaveta
See Belcheva, Elisaveta Lyubomirova

Bagryana, Elisaveta .... **CLC 10**
See Belcheva, Elisaveta Lyubomirova
See also CA 178; CDWLB 4; DLB 147; EWL 3

Bailey, Paul 1937- .... **CLC 45**
See also CA 21-24R; CANR 16, 62, 124; CN 7; DLB 14, 271; GLL 2

Baillie, Joanna 1762-1851 .... **NCLC 71**
See also DLB 93; RGEL 2

Bainbridge, Beryl (Margaret) 1934- . **CLC 4, 5, 8, 10, 14, 18, 22, 62, 130**
See also BRWS 6; CA 21-24R; CANR 24, 55, 75, 88, 128; CN 7; DAM NOV; DLB 14, 231; EWL 3; MTCW 1, 2

Baker, Carlos (Heard)
1909-1987 .... **TCLC 119**
See also CA 5-8R; 122; CANR 3, 63; DLB 103

Baker, Elliott 1922- .... **CLC 8**
See also CA 45-48; CANR 2, 63; CN 7

Baker, Jean H. .... **TCLC 3, 10**
See Russell, George William

Baker, Nicholson 1957- .... **CLC 61, 165**
See also AMWS 13; CA 135; CANR 63, 120; CN 7; CPW; DA3; DAM POP; DLB 227

Baker, Ray Stannard 1870-1946 .... **TCLC 47**
See also CA 118

Baker, Russell (Wayne) 1925- .... **CLC 31**
See also BEST 89:4; CA 57-60; CANR 11, 41, 59; MTCW 1, 2

Bakhtin, M.
See Bakhtin, Mikhail Mikhailovich

Bakhtin, M. M.
See Bakhtin, Mikhail Mikhailovich

Bakhtin, Mikhail
See Bakhtin, Mikhail Mikhailovich

Bakhtin, Mikhail Mikhailovich
1895-1975 .... **CLC 83**
See also CA 128; 113; DLB 242; EWL 3

Bakshi, Ralph 1938(?)- .... **CLC 26**
See also CA 112; 138; IDFW 3

Bakunin, Mikhail (Alexandrovich)
1814-1876 .... **NCLC 25, 58**
See also DLB 277

Baldwin, James (Arthur) 1924-1987 . **BLC 1; CLC 1, 2, 3, 4, 5, 8, 13, 15, 17, 42, 50, 67, 90, 127; DC 1; SSC 10, 33; WLC**
See also AAYA 4, 34; AFAW 1, 2; AMWR 2; AMWS 1; BPFB 1; BW 1; CA 1-4R; 124; CABS 1; CAD; CANR 3, 24; CDALB 1941-1968; CPW; DA; DA3; DAB; DAC; DAM MST, MULT, NOV, POP; DFS 11, 15; DLB 2, 7, 33, 249, 278; DLBY 1987; EWL 3; EXPS; LAIT 5; MTCW 1, 2; NCFS 4; NFS 4; RGAL 4; RGSF 2; SATA 9; SATA-Obit 54; SSFS 2, 18; TUS

Bale, John 1495-1563 .... **LC 62**
See also DLB 132; RGEL 2; TEA

Ball, Hugo 1886-1927 .... **TCLC 104**

Ballard, J(ames) G(raham) 1930- . **CLC 3, 6, 14, 36, 137; SSC 1, 53**
See also AAYA 3, 52; BRWS 5; CA 5-8R; CANR 15, 39, 65, 107; CN 7; DA3; DAM NOV, POP; DLB 14, 207, 261; EWL 3; HGG; MTCW 1, 2; NFS 8; RGEL 2; RGSF 2; SATA 93; SFW 4

Balmont, Konstantin (Dmitriyevich)
1867-1943 .... **TCLC 11**
See also CA 109; 155; DLB 295; EWL 3

Baltausis, Vincas 1847-1910
See Mikszath, Kalman

Balzac, Honore de 1799-1850 ... **NCLC 5, 35, 53; SSC 5, 59; WLC**
See also DA; DA3; DAB; DAC; DAM MST, NOV; DLB 119; EW 5; GFL 1789 to the Present; LMFS 1; RGSF 2; RGWL 2, 3; SSFS 10; SUFW; TWA

Bambara, Toni Cade 1939-1995 .... **BLC 1; CLC 19, 88; SSC 35; TCLC 116; WLCS**
See also AAYA 5, 49; AFAW 2; AMWS 11; BW 2, 3; BYA 12, 14; CA 29-32R; 150; CANR 24, 49, 81; CDALBS; DA; DA3; DAC; DAM MST, MULT; DLB 38, 218; EXPS; MTCW 1, 2; RGAL 4; RGSF 2; SATA 112; SSFS 4, 7, 12

Bamdad, A.
See Shamlu, Ahmad

Bamdad, Alef
See Shamlu, Ahmad

Banat, D. R.
See Bradbury, Ray (Douglas)

Bancroft, Laura
See Baum, L(yman) Frank

Banim, John 1798-1842 .... **NCLC 13**
See also DLB 116, 158, 159; RGEL 2

Banim, Michael 1796-1874 .... **NCLC 13**
See also DLB 158, 159

Banjo, The
See Paterson, A(ndrew) B(arton)

Banks, Iain
See Banks, Iain M(enzies)

Banks, Iain M(enzies) 1954- .... **CLC 34**
See also CA 123; 128; CANR 61, 106; DLB 194; 261; EWL 3; HGG; INT CA-128; SFW 4

Banks, Lynne Reid .... **CLC 23**
See Reid Banks, Lynne
See also AAYA 6; BYA 7; CLR 86

Banks, Russell (Earl) 1940- .... **CLC 37, 72, 187; SSC 42**
See also AAYA 45; AMWS 5; CA 65-68; CAAS 15; CANR 19, 52, 73, 118; CN 7; DLB 130, 278; EWL 3; NFS 13

Banville, John 1945- .... **CLC 46, 118**
See also CA 117; 128; CANR 104; CN 7; DLB 14, 271; INT CA-128

Banville, Theodore (Faullain) de
1832-1891 .... **NCLC 9**
See also DLB 217; GFL 1789 to the Present

Baraka, Amiri 1934- .... **BLC 1; CLC 1, 2, 3, 5, 10, 14, 33, 115; DC 6; PC 4; WLCS**
See Jones, LeRoi
See also AFAW 1, 2; AMWS 2; BW 2, 3; CA 21-24R; CABS 3; CAD; CANR 27, 38, 61; CD 5; CDALB 1941-1968; CP 7; CPW; DA; DA3; DAC; DAM MST, MULT, POET, POP; DFS 3, 11, 16; DLB 5, 7, 16, 38; DLBD 8; EWL 3; MTCW 1, 2; PFS 9; RGAL 4; TUS; WP

Baratynsky, Evgenii Abramovich
1800-1844 .... **NCLC 103**
See also DLB 205

Barbauld, Anna Laetitia
1743-1825 .... **NCLC 50**
See also DLB 107, 109, 142, 158; RGEL 2

Barbellion, W. N. P. .... **TCLC 24**
See Cummings, Bruce F(rederick)

Barber, Benjamin R. 1939- .... **CLC 141**
See also CA 29-32R; CANR 12, 32, 64, 119

Barbera, Jack (Vincent) 1945- .... **CLC 44**
See also CA 110; CANR 45

Barbey d'Aurevilly, Jules-Amedee
1808-1889 .... **NCLC 1; SSC 17**
See also DLB 119; GFL 1789 to the Present

Barbour, John c. 1316-1395 .... **CMLC 33**
See also DLB 146
Barbusse, Henri 1873-1935 .... **TCLC 5**
See also CA 105; 154; DLB 65; EWL 3; RGWL 2, 3
Barclay, Bill
See Moorcock, Michael (John)
Barclay, William Ewert
See Moorcock, Michael (John)
Barea, Arturo 1897-1957 .... **TCLC 14**
See also CA 111; 201
Barfoot, Joan 1946- .... **CLC 18**
See also CA 105
Barham, Richard Harris
1788-1845 .... **NCLC 77**
See also DLB 159
Baring, Maurice 1874-1945 .... **TCLC 8**
See also CA 105; 168; DLB 34; HGG
Baring-Gould, Sabine 1834-1924 ... **TCLC 88**
See also DLB 156, 190
Barker, Clive 1952- .... **CLC 52; SSC 53**
See also AAYA 10, 54; BEST 90:3; BPFB 1; CA 121; 129; CANR 71, 111; CPW; DA3; DAM POP; DLB 261; HGG; INT CA-129; MTCW 1, 2; SUFW 2
Barker, George Granville
1913-1991 .... **CLC 8, 48**
See also CA 9-12R; 135; CANR 7, 38; DAM POET; DLB 20; EWL 3; MTCW 1
Barker, Harley Granville
See Granville-Barker, Harley
See also DLB 10
Barker, Howard 1946- .... **CLC 37**
See also CA 102; CBD; CD 5; DLB 13, 233
Barker, Jane 1652-1732 .... **LC 42, 82**
See also DLB 39, 131
Barker, Pat(ricia) 1943- ...... **CLC 32, 94, 146**
See also BRWS 4; CA 117; 122; CANR 50, 101; CN 7; DLB 271; INT CA-122
Barlach, Ernst (Heinrich)
1870-1938 .... **TCLC 84**
See also CA 178; DLB 56, 118; EWL 3
Barlow, Joel 1754-1812 .... **NCLC 23**
See also AMWS 2; DLB 37; RGAL 4
Barnard, Mary (Ethel) 1909- .... **CLC 48**
See also CA 21-22; CAP 2
Barnes, Djuna 1892-1982 .... **CLC 3, 4, 8, 11, 29, 127; SSC 3**
See Steptoe, Lydia
See also AMWS 3; CA 9-12R; 107; CAD; CANR 16, 55; CWD; DLB 4, 9, 45; EWL 3; GLL 1; MTCW 1, 2; RGAL 4; TUS
Barnes, Jim 1933- .... **NNAL**
See also CA 108, 175; CAAE 175; CAAS 28; DLB 175
Barnes, Julian (Patrick) 1946- . **CLC 42, 141**
See also BRWS 4; CA 102; CANR 19, 54, 115; CN 7; DAB; DLB 194; DLBY 1993; EWL 3; MTCW 1
Barnes, Peter 1931- .... **CLC 5, 56**
See also CA 65-68; CAAS 12; CANR 33, 34, 64, 113; CBD; CD 5; DFS 6; DLB 13, 233; MTCW 1
Barnes, William 1801-1886 .... **NCLC 75**
See also DLB 32
Baroja (y Nessi), Pio 1872-1956 .... **HLC 1; TCLC 8**
See also CA 104; EW 9
Baron, David
See Pinter, Harold
Baron Corvo
See Rolfe, Frederick (William Serafino Austin Lewis Mary)
Barondess, Sue K(aufman)
1926-1977 .... **CLC 8**
See Kaufman, Sue
See also CA 1-4R; 69-72; CANR 1

Baron de Teive
See Pessoa, Fernando (Antonio Nogueira)
Baroness Von S.
See Zangwill, Israel
Barres, (Auguste-)Maurice
1862-1923 .... **TCLC 47**
See also CA 164; DLB 123; GFL 1789 to the Present
Barreto, Afonso Henrique de Lima
See Lima Barreto, Afonso Henrique de
Barrett, Andrea 1954- .... **CLC 150**
See also CA 156; CANR 92
Barrett, Michele .... **CLC 65**
Barrett, (Roger) Syd 1946- .... **CLC 35**
Barrett, William (Christopher)
1913-1992 .... **CLC 27**
See also CA 13-16R; 139; CANR 11, 67; INT CANR-11
Barrie, J(ames) M(atthew)
1860-1937 .... **TCLC 2**
See also BRWS 3; BYA 4, 5; CA 104; 136; CANR 77; CDBLB 1890-1914; CLR 16; CWRI 5; DA3; DAB; DAM DRAM; DFS 7; DLB 10, 141, 156; EWL 3; FANT; MAICYA 1, 2; MTCW 1; SATA 100; SUFW; WCH; WLIT 4; YABC 1
Barrington, Michael
See Moorcock, Michael (John)
Barrol, Grady
See Bograd, Larry
Barry, Mike
See Malzberg, Barry N(athaniel)
Barry, Philip 1896-1949 .... **TCLC 11**
See also CA 109; 199; DFS 9; DLB 7, 228; RGAL 4
Bart, Andre Schwarz
See Schwarz-Bart, Andre
Barth, John (Simmons) 1930- ... **CLC 1, 2, 3, 5, 7, 9, 10, 14, 27, 51, 89; SSC 10**
See also AITN 1, 2; AMW; BPFB 1; CA 1-4R; CABS 1; CANR 5, 23, 49, 64, 113; CN 7; DAM NOV; DLB 2, 227; EWL 3; FANT; MTCW 1; RGAL 4; RGSF 2; RHW; SSFS 6; TUS
Barthelme, Donald 1931-1989 ... **CLC 1, 2, 3, 5, 6, 8, 13, 23, 46, 59, 115; SSC 2, 55**
See also AMWS 4; BPFB 1; CA 21-24R; 129; CANR 20, 58; DA3; DAM NOV; DLB 2, 234; DLBY 1980, 1989; EWL 3; FANT; LMFS 2; MTCW 1, 2; RGAL 4; RGSF 2; SATA 7; SATA-Obit 62; SSFS 17
Barthelme, Frederick 1943- ...... **CLC 36, 117**
See also AMWS 11; CA 114; 122; CANR 77; CN 7; CSW; DLB 244; DLBY 1985; EWL 3; INT CA-122
Barthes, Roland (Gerard)
1915-1980 .... **CLC 24, 83; TCLC 135**
See also CA 130; 97-100; CANR 66; DLB 296; EW 13; EWL 3; GFL 1789 to the Present; MTCW 1, 2; TWA
Barzun, Jacques (Martin) 1907- ..... **CLC 51, 145**
See also CA 61-64; CANR 22, 95
Bashevis, Isaac
See Singer, Isaac Bashevis
Bashkirtseff, Marie 1859-1884 .... **NCLC 27**
Basho, Matsuo
See Matsuo Basho
See also PFS 18; RGWL 2, 3; WP
Basil of Caesaria c. 330-379 .... **CMLC 35**
Basket, Raney
See Edgerton, Clyde (Carlyle)
Bass, Kingsley B., Jr.
See Bullins, Ed
Bass, Rick 1958- .... **CLC 79, 143; SSC 60**
See also ANW; CA 126; CANR 53, 93; CSW; DLB 212, 275

Bassani, Giorgio 1916-2000 .... **CLC 9**
See also CA 65-68; 190; CANR 33; CWW 2; DLB 128, 177; EWL 3; MTCW 1; RGWL 2, 3
Bastian, Ann .... **CLC 70**
Bastos, Augusto (Antonio) Roa
See Roa Bastos, Augusto (Antonio)
Bataille, Georges 1897-1962 .... **CLC 29**
See also CA 101; 89-92; EWL 3
Bates, H(erbert) E(rnest)
1905-1974 .... **CLC 46; SSC 10**
See also CA 93-96; 45-48; CANR 34; DA3; DAB; DAM POP; DLB 162, 191; EWL 3; EXPS; MTCW 1, 2; RGSF 2; SSFS 7
Bauchart
See Camus, Albert
Baudelaire, Charles 1821-1867 . **NCLC 6, 29, 55; PC 1; SSC 18; WLC**
See also DA; DA3; DAB; DAC; DAM MST, POET; DLB 217; EW 7; GFL 1789 to the Present; LMFS 2; RGWL 2, 3; TWA
Baudouin, Marcel
See Peguy, Charles (Pierre)
Baudouin, Pierre
See Peguy, Charles (Pierre)
Baudrillard, Jean 1929- .... **CLC 60**
See also DLB 296
Baum, L(yman) Frank 1856-1919 .. **TCLC 7, 132**
See also AAYA 46; BYA 16; CA 108; 133; CLR 15; CWRI 5; DLB 22; FANT; JRDA; MAICYA 1, 2; MTCW 1, 2; NFS 13; RGAL 4; SATA 18, 100; WCH
Baum, Louis F.
See Baum, L(yman) Frank
Baumbach, Jonathan 1933- .... **CLC 6, 23**
See also CA 13-16R; CAAS 5; CANR 12, 66; CN 7; DLBY 1980; INT CANR-12; MTCW 1
Bausch, Richard (Carl) 1945- .... **CLC 51**
See also AMWS 7; CA 101; CAAS 14; CANR 43, 61, 87; CSW; DLB 130
Baxter, Charles (Morley) 1947- . **CLC 45, 78**
See also CA 57-60; CANR 40, 64, 104; CPW; DAM POP; DLB 130; MTCW 2
Baxter, George Owen
See Faust, Frederick (Schiller)
Baxter, James K(eir) 1926-1972 .... **CLC 14**
See also CA 77-80; EWL 3
Baxter, John
See Hunt, E(verette) Howard, (Jr.)
Bayer, Sylvia
See Glassco, John
Baynton, Barbara 1857-1929 .... **TCLC 57**
See also DLB 230; RGSF 2
Beagle, Peter S(oyer) 1939- .... **CLC 7, 104**
See also AAYA 47; BPFB 1; BYA 9, 10, 16; CA 9-12R; CANR 4, 51, 73, 110; DA3; DLBY 1980; FANT; INT CANR-4; MTCW 1; SATA 60, 130; SUFW 1, 2; YAW
Bean, Normal
See Burroughs, Edgar Rice
Beard, Charles A(ustin)
1874-1948 .... **TCLC 15**
See also CA 115; 189; DLB 17; SATA 18
Beardsley, Aubrey 1872-1898 .... **NCLC 6**
Beattie, Ann 1947- ..... **CLC 8, 13, 18, 40, 63, 146; SSC 11**
See also AMWS 5; BEST 90:2; BPFB 1; CA 81-84; CANR 53, 73, 128; CN 7; CPW; DA3; DAM NOV, POP; DLB 218, 278; DLBY 1982; EWL 3; MTCW 1, 2; RGAL 4; RGSF 2; SSFS 9; TUS
Beattie, James 1735-1803 .... **NCLC 25**
See also DLB 109

Beauchamp, Kathleen Mansfield 1888-1923
See Mansfield, Katherine
See also CA 104; 134; DA; DA3; DAC; DAM MST; MTCW 2; TEA

Beaumarchais, Pierre-Augustin Caron de 1732-1799 .... **DC 4; LC 61**
See also DAM DRAM; DFS 14, 16; EW 4; GFL Beginnings to 1789; RGWL 2, 3

Beaumont, Francis 1584(?)-1616 .. **DC 6; LC 33**
See also BRW 2; CDBLB Before 1660; DLB 58; TEA

Beauvoir, Simone (Lucie Ernestine Marie Bertrand) de 1908-1986 .... **CLC 1, 2, 4, 8, 14, 31, 44, 50, 71, 124; SSC 35; WLC**
See also BPFB 1; CA 9-12R; 118; CANR 28, 61; DA; DA3; DAB; DAC; DAM MST, NOV; DLB 72; DLBY 1986; EW 12; EWL 3; FW; GFL 1789 to the Present; LMFS 2; MTCW 1, 2; RGSF 2; RGWL 2, 3; TWA

Becker, Carl (Lotus) 1873-1945 ..... **TCLC 63**
See also CA 157; DLB 17

Becker, Jurek 1937-1997 .... **CLC 7, 19**
See also CA 85-88; 157; CANR 60, 117; CWW 2; DLB 75; EWL 3

Becker, Walter 1950- .... **CLC 26**

Beckett, Samuel (Barclay) 1906-1989 .. **CLC 1, 2, 3, 4, 6, 9, 10, 11, 14, 18, 29, 57, 59, 83; DC 22; SSC 16; TCLC 145; WLC**
See also BRWC 2; BRWR 1; BRWS 1; CA 5-8R; 130; CANR 33, 61; CBD; CDBLB 1945-1960; DA; DA3; DAB; DAC; DAM DRAM, MST, NOV; DFS 2, 7, 18; DLB 13, 15, 233; DLBY 1990; EWL 3; GFL 1789 to the Present; LATS 1; LMFS 2; MTCW 1, 2; RGSF 2; RGWL 2, 3; SSFS 15; TEA; WLIT 4

Beckford, William 1760-1844 .... **NCLC 16**
See also BRW 3; DLB 39, 213; HGG; LMFS 1; SUFW

Beckham, Barry (Earl) 1944- .... **BLC 1**
See also BW 1; CA 29-32R; CANR 26, 62; CN 7; DAM MULT; DLB 33

Beckman, Gunnel 1910- .... **CLC 26**
See also CA 33-36R; CANR 15, 114; CLR 25; MAICYA 1, 2; SAAS 9; SATA 6

Becque, Henri 1837-1899 .... **DC 21; NCLC 3**
See also DLB 192; GFL 1789 to the Present

Becquer, Gustavo Adolfo 1836-1870 .... **HLCS 1; NCLC 106**
See also DAM MULT

Beddoes, Thomas Lovell 1803-1849 .. **DC 15; NCLC 3**
See also DLB 96

Bede c. 673-735 .... **CMLC 20**
See also DLB 146; TEA

Bedford, Denton R. 1907-(?) .... **NNAL**

Bedford, Donald F.
See Fearing, Kenneth (Flexner)

Beecher, Catharine Esther 1800-1878 .... **NCLC 30**
See also DLB 1, 243

Beecher, John 1904-1980 .... **CLC 6**
See also AITN 1; CA 5-8R; 105; CANR 8

Beer, Johann 1655-1700 .... **LC 5**
See also DLB 168

Beer, Patricia 1924- .... **CLC 58**
See also CA 61-64; 183; CANR 13, 46; CP 7; CWP; DLB 40; FW

Beerbohm, Max
See Beerbohm, (Henry) Max(imilian)

Beerbohm, (Henry) Max(imilian) 1872-1956 .... **TCLC 1, 24**
See also BRWS 2; CA 104; 154; CANR 79; DLB 34, 100; FANT

Beer-Hofmann, Richard 1866-1945 .... **TCLC 60**
See also CA 160; DLB 81

Beg, Shemus
See Stephens, James

Begiebing, Robert J(ohn) 1946- .... **CLC 70**
See also CA 122; CANR 40, 88

Behan, Brendan (Francis) 1923-1964 .... **CLC 1, 8, 11, 15, 79**
See also BRWS 2; CA 73-76; CANR 33, 121; CBD; CDBLB 1945-1960; DAM DRAM; DFS 7; DLB 13, 233; EWL 3; MTCW 1, 2

Behn, Aphra 1640(?)-1689 .. **DC 4; LC 1, 30, 42; PC 13; WLC**
See also BRWS 3; DA; DA3; DAB; DAC; DAM DRAM, MST, NOV, POET; DFS 16; DLB 39, 80, 131; FW; TEA; WLIT 3

Behrman, S(amuel) N(athaniel) 1893-1973 .... **CLC 40**
See also CA 13-16; 45-48; CAD; CAP 1; DLB 7, 44; IDFW 3; RGAL 4

Belasco, David 1853-1931 .... **TCLC 3**
See also CA 104; 168; DLB 7; RGAL 4

Belcheva, Elisaveta Lyubomirova 1893-1991 .... **CLC 10**
See Bagryana, Elisaveta

Beldone, Phil "Cheech"
See Ellison, Harlan (Jay)

Beleno
See Azuela, Mariano

Belinski, Vissarion Grigoryevich 1811-1848 .... **NCLC 5**
See also DLB 198

Belitt, Ben 1911- .... **CLC 22**
See also CA 13-16R; CAAS 4; CANR 7, 77; CP 7; DLB 5

Bell, Gertrude (Margaret Lowthian) 1868-1926 .... **TCLC 67**
See also CA 167; CANR 110; DLB 174

Bell, J. Freeman
See Zangwill, Israel

Bell, James Madison 1826-1902 .... **BLC 1; TCLC 43**
See also BW 1; CA 122; 124; DAM MULT; DLB 50

Bell, Madison Smartt 1957- ...... **CLC 41, 102**
See also AMWS 10; BPFB 1; CA 111, 183; CAAE 183; CANR 28, 54, 73; CN 7; CSW; DLB 218, 278; MTCW 1

Bell, Marvin (Hartley) 1937- .... **CLC 8, 31**
See also CA 21-24R; CAAS 14; CANR 59, 102; CP 7; DAM POET; DLB 5; MTCW 1

Bell, W. L. D.
See Mencken, H(enry) L(ouis)

Bellamy, Atwood C.
See Mencken, H(enry) L(ouis)

Bellamy, Edward 1850-1898 ...... **NCLC 4, 86**
See also DLB 12; NFS 15; RGAL 4; SFW 4

Belli, Gioconda 1949- .... **HLCS 1**
See also CA 152; CWW 2; DLB 290; EWL 3; RGWL 3

Bellin, Edward J.
See Kuttner, Henry

Bello, Andres 1781-1865 .... **NCLC 131**
See also LAW

Belloc, (Joseph) Hilaire (Pierre Sebastien Rene Swanton) 1870-1953 .... **PC 24; TCLC 7, 18**
See also CA 106; 152; CWRI 5; DAM POET; DLB 19, 100, 141, 174; EWL 3; MTCW 1; SATA 112; WCH; YABC 1

Belloc, Joseph Peter Rene Hilaire
See Belloc, (Joseph) Hilaire (Pierre Sebastien Rene Swanton)

Belloc, Joseph Pierre Hilaire
See Belloc, (Joseph) Hilaire (Pierre Sebastien Rene Swanton)

Belloc, M. A.
See Lowndes, Marie Adelaide (Belloc)

Belloc-Lowndes, Mrs.
See Lowndes, Marie Adelaide (Belloc)

Bellow, Saul 1915- . **CLC 1, 2, 3, 6, 8, 10, 13, 15, 25, 33, 34, 63, 79, 190; SSC 14; WLC**
See also AITN 2; AMW; AMWC 2; AMWR 2; BEST 89:3; BPFB 1; CA 5-8R; CABS 1; CANR 29, 53, 95; CDALB 1941-1968; CN 7; DA; DA3; DAB; DAC; DAM MST, NOV, POP; DLB 2, 28; DLBD 3; DLBY 1982; EWL 3; MTCW 1, 2; NFS 4, 14; RGAL 4; RGSF 2; SSFS 12; TUS

Belser, Reimond Karel Maria de 1929-
See Ruyslinck, Ward
See also CA 152

Bely, Andrey .... **PC 11; TCLC 7**
See Bugayev, Boris Nikolayevich
See also DLB 295; EW 9; EWL 3; MTCW 1

Belyi, Andrei
See Bugayev, Boris Nikolayevich
See also RGWL 2, 3

Bembo, Pietro 1470-1547 .... **LC 79**
See also RGWL 2, 3

Benary, Margot
See Benary-Isbert, Margot

Benary-Isbert, Margot 1889-1979 .... **CLC 12**
See also CA 5-8R; 89-92; CANR 4, 72; CLR 12; MAICYA 1, 2; SATA 2; SATA-Obit 21

Benavente (y Martinez), Jacinto 1866-1954 .... **HLCS 1; TCLC 3**
See also CA 106; 131; CANR 81; DAM DRAM, MULT; EWL 3; GLL 2; HW 1, 2; MTCW 1, 2

Benchley, Peter (Bradford) 1940- .. **CLC 4, 8**
See also AAYA 14; AITN 2; BPFB 1; CA 17-20R; CANR 12, 35, 66, 115; CPW; DAM NOV, POP; HGG; MTCW 1, 2; SATA 3, 89

Benchley, Robert (Charles) 1889-1945 .... **TCLC 1, 55**
See also CA 105; 153; DLB 11; RGAL 4

Benda, Julien 1867-1956 .... **TCLC 60**
See also CA 120; 154; GFL 1789 to the Present

Benedict, Ruth (Fulton) 1887-1948 .... **TCLC 60**
See also CA 158; DLB 246

Benedikt, Michael 1935- .... **CLC 4, 14**
See also CA 13-16R; CANR 7; CP 7; DLB 5

Benet, Juan 1927-1993 .... **CLC 28**
See also CA 143; EWL 3

Benet, Stephen Vincent 1898-1943 ... **SSC 10; TCLC 7**
See also AMWS 11; CA 104; 152; DA3; DAM POET; DLB 4, 48, 102, 249, 284; DLBY 1997; EWL 3; HGG; MTCW 1; RGAL 4; RGSF 2; SUFW; WP; YABC 1

Benet, William Rose 1886-1950 ..... **TCLC 28**
See also CA 118; 152; DAM POET; DLB 45; RGAL 4

Benford, Gregory (Albert) 1941- ..... **CLC 52**
See also BPFB 1; CA 69-72, 175; CAAE 175; CAAS 27; CANR 12, 24, 49, 95; CSW; DLBY 1982; SCFW 2; SFW 4

Bengtsson, Frans (Gunnar) 1894-1954 .... **TCLC 48**
See also CA 170; EWL 3

Benjamin, David
See Slavitt, David R(ytman)

Benjamin, Lois
See Gould, Lois

Benjamin, Walter 1892-1940 .... **TCLC 39**
See also CA 164; DLB 242; EW 11; EWL 3

Ben Jelloun, Tahar 1944-
See Jelloun, Tahar ben
See also CA 135; CWW 2; EWL 3; RGWL 3; WLIT 2

Benn, Gottfried 1886-1956 .. **PC 35; TCLC 3**
See also CA 106; 153; DLB 56; EWL 3; RGWL 2, 3

Bennett, Alan 1934- .... **CLC 45, 77**
See also BRWS 8; CA 103; CANR 35, 55, 106; CBD; CD 5; DAB; DAM MST; MTCW 1, 2

Bennett, (Enoch) Arnold
1867-1931 .... **TCLC 5, 20**
See also BRW 6; CA 106; 155; CDBLB 1890-1914; DLB 10, 34, 98, 135; EWL 3; MTCW 2

Bennett, Elizabeth
See Mitchell, Margaret (Munnerlyn)

Bennett, George Harold 1930-
See Bennett, Hal
See also BW 1; CA 97-100; CANR 87

Bennett, Gwendolyn B. 1902-1981 .... **HR 2**
See also BW 1; CA 125; DLB 51; WP

Bennett, Hal .... **CLC 5**
See Bennett, George Harold
See also DLB 33

Bennett, Jay 1912- .... **CLC 35**
See also AAYA 10; CA 69-72; CANR 11, 42, 79; JRDA; SAAS 4; SATA 41, 87; SATA-Brief 27; WYA; YAW

Bennett, Louise (Simone) 1919- .... **BLC 1; CLC 28**
See also BW 2, 3; CA 151; CDWLB 3; CP 7; DAM MULT; DLB 117; EWL 3

Benson, A. C. 1862-1925 .... **TCLC 123**
See also DLB 98

Benson, E(dward) F(rederic)
1867-1940 .... **TCLC 27**
See also CA 114; 157; DLB 135, 153; HGG; SUFW 1

Benson, Jackson J. 1930- .... **CLC 34**
See also CA 25-28R; DLB 111

Benson, Sally 1900-1972 .... **CLC 17**
See also CA 19-20; 37-40R; CAP 1; SATA 1, 35; SATA-Obit 27

Benson, Stella 1892-1933 .... **TCLC 17**
See also CA 117; 154; 155; DLB 36, 162; FANT; TEA

Bentham, Jeremy 1748-1832 .... **NCLC 38**
See also DLB 107, 158, 252

Bentley, E(dmund) C(lerihew)
1875-1956 .... **TCLC 12**
See also CA 108; DLB 70; MSW

Bentley, Eric (Russell) 1916- .... **CLC 24**
See also CA 5-8R; CAD; CANR 6, 67; CBD; CD 5; INT CANR-6

ben Uzair, Salem
See Horne, Richard Henry Hengist

Beranger, Pierre Jean de
1780-1857 .... **NCLC 34**

Berdyaev, Nicolas
See Berdyaev, Nikolai (Aleksandrovich)

Berdyaev, Nikolai (Aleksandrovich)
1874-1948 .... **TCLC 67**
See also CA 120; 157

Berdyayev, Nikolai (Aleksandrovich)
See Berdyaev, Nikolai (Aleksandrovich)

Berendt, John (Lawrence) 1939- ...... **CLC 86**
See also CA 146; CANR 75, 93; DA3; MTCW 1

Beresford, J(ohn) D(avys)
1873-1947 .... **TCLC 81**
See also CA 112; 155; DLB 162, 178, 197; SFW 4; SUFW 1

Bergelson, David (Rafailovich)
1884-1952 .... **TCLC 81**
See Bergelson, Dovid
See also CA 220

Bergelson, Dovid
See Bergelson, David (Rafailovich)
See also EWL 3

Berger, Colonel
See Malraux, (Georges-)Andre

Berger, John (Peter) 1926- .... **CLC 2, 19**
See also BRWS 4; CA 81-84; CANR 51, 78, 117; CN 7; DLB 14, 207

Berger, Melvin H. 1927- .... **CLC 12**
See also CA 5-8R; CANR 4; CLR 32; SAAS 2; SATA 5, 88; SATA-Essay 124

Berger, Thomas (Louis) 1924- .. **CLC 3, 5, 8, 11, 18, 38**
See also BPFB 1; CA 1-4R; CANR 5, 28, 51, 128; CN 7; DAM NOV; DLB 2; DLBY 1980; EWL 3; FANT; INT CANR-28; MTCW 1, 2; RHW; TCWW 2

Bergman, (Ernst) Ingmar 1918- ...... **CLC 16, 72**
See also CA 81-84; CANR 33, 70; CWW 2; DLB 257; MTCW 2

Bergson, Henri(-Louis) 1859-1941 . **TCLC 32**
See also CA 164; EW 8; EWL 3; GFL 1789 to the Present

Bergstein, Eleanor 1938- .... **CLC 4**
See also CA 53-56; CANR 5

Berkeley, George 1685-1753 .... **LC 65**
See also DLB 31, 101, 252

Berkoff, Steven 1937- .... **CLC 56**
See also CA 104; CANR 72; CBD; CD 5

Berlin, Isaiah 1909-1997 .... **TCLC 105**
See also CA 85-88; 162

Bermant, Chaim (Icyk) 1929-1998 ... **CLC 40**
See also CA 57-60; CANR 6, 31, 57, 105; CN 7

Bern, Victoria
See Fisher, M(ary) F(rances) K(ennedy)

Bernanos, (Paul Louis) Georges
1888-1948 .... **TCLC 3**
See also CA 104; 130; CANR 94; DLB 72; EWL 3; GFL 1789 to the Present; RGWL 2, 3

Bernard, April 1956- .... **CLC 59**
See also CA 131

Berne, Victoria
See Fisher, M(ary) F(rances) K(ennedy)

Bernhard, Thomas 1931-1989 ..... **CLC 3, 32, 61; DC 14**
See also CA 85-88; 127; CANR 32, 57; CDWLB 2; DLB 85, 124; EWL 3; MTCW 1; RGWL 2, 3

Bernhardt, Sarah (Henriette Rosine)
1844-1923 .... **TCLC 75**
See also CA 157

Bernstein, Charles 1950- .... **CLC 142**
See also CA 129; CAAS 24; CANR 90; CP 7; DLB 169

Bernstein, Ingrid
See Kirsch, Sarah

Berriault, Gina 1926-1999 .... **CLC 54, 109; SSC 30**
See also CA 116; 129; 185; CANR 66; DLB 130; SSFS 7,11

Berrigan, Daniel 1921- .... **CLC 4**
See also CA 33-36R; 187; CAAE 187; CAAS 1; CANR 11, 43, 78; CP 7; DLB 5

Berrigan, Edmund Joseph Michael, Jr.
1934-1983
See Berrigan, Ted
See also CA 61-64; 110; CANR 14, 102

Berrigan, Ted .... **CLC 37**
See Berrigan, Edmund Joseph Michael, Jr.
See also DLB 5, 169; WP

Berry, Charles Edward Anderson 1931-
See Berry, Chuck
See also CA 115

Berry, Chuck .... **CLC 17**
See Berry, Charles Edward Anderson

Berry, Jonas
See Ashbery, John (Lawrence)
See also GLL 1

Berry, Wendell (Erdman) 1934- ... **CLC 4, 6, 8, 27, 46; PC 28**
See also AITN 1; AMWS 10; ANW; CA 73-76; CANR 50, 73, 101; CP 7; CSW; DAM POET; DLB 5, 6, 234, 275; MTCW 1

Berryman, John 1914-1972 ... **CLC 1, 2, 3, 4, 6, 8, 10, 13, 25, 62**
See also AMW; CA 13-16; 33-36R; CABS 2; CANR 35; CAP 1; CDALB 1941-1968; DAM POET; DLB 48; EWL 3; MTCW 1, 2; PAB; RGAL 4; WP

Bertolucci, Bernardo 1940- ...... **CLC 16, 157**
See also CA 106; CANR 125

Berton, Pierre (Francis Demarigny)
1920- .... **CLC 104**
See also CA 1-4R; CANR 2, 56; CPW; DLB 68; SATA 99

Bertrand, Aloysius 1807-1841 .... **NCLC 31**
See Bertrand, Louis oAloysiusc

Bertrand, Louis oAloysiusc
See Bertrand, Aloysius
See also DLB 217

Bertran de Born c. 1140-1215 .... **CMLC 5**

Besant, Annie (Wood) 1847-1933 ..... **TCLC 9**
See also CA 105; 185

Bessie, Alvah 1904-1985 .... **CLC 23**
See also CA 5-8R; 116; CANR 2, 80; DLB 26

Bestuzhev, Aleksandr Aleksandrovich
1797-1837 .... **NCLC 131**
See also DLB 198

Bethlen, T. D.
See Silverberg, Robert

Beti, Mongo .... **BLC 1; CLC 27**
See Biyidi, Alexandre
See also AFW; CANR 79; DAM MULT; EWL 3; WLIT 2

Betjeman, John 1906-1984 ...... **CLC 2, 6, 10, 34, 43**
See also BRW 7; CA 9-12R; 112; CANR 33, 56; CDBLB 1945-1960; DA3; DAB; DAM MST; POET; DLB 20; DLBY 1984; EWL 3; MTCW 1, 2

Bettelheim, Bruno 1903-1990 .... **CLC 79; TCLC 143**
See also CA 81-84; 131; CANR 23, 61; DA3; MTCW 1, 2

Betti, Ugo 1892-1953 .... **TCLC 5**
See also CA 104; 155; EWL 3; RGWL 2, 3

Betts, Doris (Waugh) 1932- ..... **CLC 3, 6, 28; SSC 45**
See also CA 13-16R; CANR 9, 66, 77; CN 7; CSW; DLB 218; DLBY 1982; INT CANR-9; RGAL 4

Bevan, Alistair
See Roberts, Keith (John Kingston)

Bey, Pilaff
See Douglas, (George) Norman

Bialik, Chaim Nachman
1873-1934 .... **TCLC 25**
See also CA 170; EWL 3

Bickerstaff, Isaac
See Swift, Jonathan

Bidart, Frank 1939- .... **CLC 33**
See also CA 140; CANR 106; CP 7

Bienek, Horst 1930- .... **CLC 7, 11**
See also CA 73-76; DLB 75

Bierce, Ambrose (Gwinett)
1842-1914(?) ..... **SSC 9; TCLC 1, 7, 44; WLC**
See also AAYA 55; AMW; BYA 11; CA 104; 139; CANR 78; CDALB 1865-1917; DA; DA3; DAC; DAM MST; DLB 11, 12, 23, 71, 74, 186; EWL 3; EXPS; HGG; LAIT 2; RGAL 4; RGSF 2; SSFS 9; SUFW 1

Biggers, Earl Derr 1884-1933 .... **TCLC 65**
See also CA 108; 153

Billiken, Bud
See Motley, Willard (Francis)

Billings, Josh
See Shaw, Henry Wheeler

Billington, (Lady) Rachel (Mary)
1942- .... **CLC 43**
See also AITN 2; CA 33-36R; CANR 44; CN 7

Binchy, Maeve 1940- .... **CLC 153**
See also BEST 90:1; BPFB 1; CA 127; 134; CANR 50, 96; CN 7; CPW; DA3; DAM POP; INT CA-134; MTCW 1; RHW

Binyon, T(imothy) J(ohn) 1936- .... **CLC 34**
See also CA 111; CANR 28

Bion 335B.C.-245B.C. .... **CMLC 39**

Bioy Casares, Adolfo 1914-1999 ... **CLC 4, 8, 13, 88; HLC 1; SSC 17**
See Casares, Adolfo Bioy; Miranda, Javier; Sacastru, Martin
See also CA 29-32R; 177; CANR 19, 43, 66; CWW 2; DAM MULT; DLB 113; EWL 3; HW 1, 2; LAW; MTCW 1, 2

Birch, Allison .... **CLC 65**

Bird, Cordwainer
See Ellison, Harlan (Jay)

Bird, Robert Montgomery
1806-1854 .... **NCLC 1**
See also DLB 202; RGAL 4

Birkerts, Sven 1951- .... **CLC 116**
See also CA 128; 133, 176; CAAE 176; CAAS 29; INT CA-133

Birney, (Alfred) Earle 1904-1995 .. **CLC 1, 4, 6, 11; PC 52**
See also CA 1-4R; CANR 5, 20; CP 7; DAC; DAM MST, POET; DLB 88; MTCW 1; PFS 8; RGEL 2

Biruni, al 973-1048(?) .... **CMLC 28**

Bishop, Elizabeth 1911-1979 ..... **CLC 1, 4, 9, 13, 15, 32; PC 3, 34; TCLC 121**
See also AMWR 2; AMWS 1; CA 5-8R; 89-92; CABS 2; CANR 26, 61, 108; CDALB 1968-1988; DA; DA3; DAC; DAM MST, POET; DLB 5, 169; EWL 3; GLL 2; MAWW; MTCW 1, 2; PAB; PFS 6, 12; RGAL 4; SATA-Obit 24; TUS; WP

Bishop, John 1935- .... **CLC 10**
See also CA 105

Bishop, John Peale 1892-1944 ..... **TCLC 103**
See also CA 107; 155; DLB 4, 9, 45; RGAL 4

Bissett, Bill 1939- .... **CLC 18; PC 14**
See also CA 69-72; CAAS 19; CANR 15; CCA 1; CP 7; DLB 53; MTCW 1

Bissoondath, Neil (Devindra)
1955- .... **CLC 120**
See also CA 136; CANR 123; CN 7; DAC

Bitov, Andrei (Georgievich) 1937- ... **CLC 57**
See also CA 142

Biyidi, Alexandre 1932-
See Beti, Mongo
See also BW 1, 3; CA 114; 124; CANR 81; DA3; MTCW 1, 2

Bjarme, Brynjolf
See Ibsen, Henrik (Johan)

Bjoernson, Bjoernstjerne (Martinius)
1832-1910 .... **TCLC 7, 37**
See also CA 104

Black, Robert
See Holdstock, Robert P.

Blackburn, Paul 1926-1971 .... **CLC 9, 43**
See also BG 2; CA 81-84; 33-36R; CANR 34; DLB 16; DLBY 1981

Black Elk 1863-1950 .... **NNAL; TCLC 33**
See also CA 144; DAM MULT; MTCW 1; WP

Black Hawk 1767-1838 .... **NNAL**

Black Hobart
See Sanders, (James) Ed(ward)

Blacklin, Malcolm
See Chambers, Aidan

Blackmore, R(ichard) D(oddridge)
1825-1900 .... **TCLC 27**
See also CA 120; DLB 18; RGEL 2

Blackmur, R(ichard) P(almer)
1904-1965 .... **CLC 2, 24**
See also AMWS 2; CA 11-12; 25-28R; CANR 71; CAP 1; DLB 63; EWL 3

Black Tarantula
See Acker, Kathy

Blackwood, Algernon (Henry)
1869-1951 .... **TCLC 5**
See also CA 105; 150; DLB 153, 156, 178; HGG; SUFW 1

Blackwood, Caroline 1931-1996 .... **CLC 6, 9, 100**
See also BRWS 9; CA 85-88; 151; CANR 32, 61, 65; CN 7; DLB 14, 207; HGG; MTCW 1

Blade, Alexander
See Hamilton, Edmond; Silverberg, Robert

Blaga, Lucian 1895-1961 .... **CLC 75**
See also CA 157; DLB 220; EWL 3

Blair, Eric (Arthur) 1903-1950 .... **TCLC 123**
See Orwell, George
See also CA 104; 132; DA; DA3; DAB; DAC; DAM MST, NOV; MTCW 1, 2; SATA 29

Blair, Hugh 1718-1800 .... **NCLC 75**

Blais, Marie-Claire 1939- .... **CLC 2, 4, 6, 13, 22**
See also CA 21-24R; CAAS 4; CANR 38, 75, 93; CWW 2; DAC; DAM MST; DLB 53; EWL 3; FW; MTCW 1, 2; TWA

Blaise, Clark 1940- .... **CLC 29**
See also AITN 2; CA 53-56; CAAS 3; CANR 5, 66, 106; CN 7; DLB 53; RGSF 2

Blake, Fairley
See De Voto, Bernard (Augustine)

Blake, Nicholas
See Day Lewis, C(ecil)
See also DLB 77; MSW

Blake, Sterling
See Benford, Gregory (Albert)

Blake, William 1757-1827 . **NCLC 13, 37, 57, 127; PC 12; WLC**
See also AAYA 47; BRW 3; BRWR 1; CDBLB 1789-1832; CLR 52; DA; DA3; DAB; DAC; DAM MST, POET; DLB 93, 163; EXPP; LATS 1; LMFS 1; MAICYA 1, 2; PAB; PFS 2, 12; SATA 30; TEA; WCH; WLIT 3; WP

Blanchot, Maurice 1907-2003 .... **CLC 135**
See also CA 117; 144; 213; DLB 72, 296; EWL 3

Blasco Ibanez, Vicente 1867-1928 . **TCLC 12**
See also BPFB 1; CA 110; 131; CANR 81; DA3; DAM NOV; EW 8; EWL 3; HW 1, 2; MTCW 1

Blatty, William Peter 1928- .... **CLC 2**
See also CA 5-8R; CANR 9, 124; DAM POP; HGG

Bleeck, Oliver
See Thomas, Ross (Elmore)

Blessing, Lee 1949- .... **CLC 54**
See also CAD; CD 5

Blight, Rose
See Greer, Germaine

Blish, James (Benjamin) 1921-1975 . **CLC 14**
See also BPFB 1; CA 1-4R; 57-60; CANR 3; DLB 8; MTCW 1; SATA 66; SCFW 2; SFW 4

Bliss, Reginald
See Wells, H(erbert) G(eorge)

Blixen, Karen (Christentze Dinesen)
1885-1962
See Dinesen, Isak
See also CA 25-28; CANR 22, 50; CAP 2; DA3; DLB 214; LMFS 1; MTCW 1, 2; SATA 44

Bloch, Robert (Albert) 1917-1994 .... **CLC 33**
See also AAYA 29; CA 5-8R, 179; 146; CAAE 179; CAAS 20; CANR 5, 78; DA3; DLB 44; HGG; INT CANR-5; MTCW 1; SATA 12; SATA-Obit 82; SFW 4; SUFW 1, 2

Blok, Alexander (Alexandrovich)
1880-1921 .... **PC 21; TCLC 5**
See also CA 104; 183; DLB 295; EW 9; EWL 3; LMFS 2; RGWL 2, 3

Blom, Jan
See Breytenbach, Breyten

Bloom, Harold 1930- .... **CLC 24, 103**
See also CA 13-16R; CANR 39, 75, 92; DLB 67; EWL 3; MTCW 1; RGAL 4

Bloomfield, Aurelius
See Bourne, Randolph S(illiman)

Blount, Roy (Alton), Jr. 1941- .... **CLC 38**
See also CA 53-56; CANR 10, 28, 61, 125; CSW; INT CANR-28; MTCW 1, 2

Blowsnake, Sam 1875-(?) .... **NNAL**

Bloy, Leon 1846-1917 .... **TCLC 22**
See also CA 121; 183; DLB 123; GFL 1789 to the Present

Blue Cloud, Peter (Aroniawenrate)
1933- .... **NNAL**
See also CA 117; CANR 40; DAM MULT

Bluggage, Oranthy
See Alcott, Louisa May

Blume, Judy (Sussman) 1938- ..... **CLC 12, 30**
See also AAYA 3, 26; BYA 1, 8, 12; CA 29-32R; CANR 13, 37, 66, 124; CLR 2, 15, 69; CPW; DA3; DAM NOV, POP; DLB 52; JRDA; MAICYA 1, 2; MAICYAS 1; MTCW 1, 2; SATA 2, 31, 79, 142; WYA; YAW

Blunden, Edmund (Charles)
1896-1974 .... **CLC 2, 56**
See also BRW 6; CA 17-18; 45-48; CANR 54; CAP 2; DLB 20, 100, 155; MTCW 1; PAB

Bly, Robert (Elwood) 1926- .... **CLC 1, 2, 5, 10, 15, 38, 128; PC 39**
See also AMWS 4; CA 5-8R; CANR 41, 73, 125; CP 7; DA3; DAM POET; DLB 5; EWL 3; MTCW 1, 2; PFS 6, 17; RGAL 4

Boas, Franz 1858-1942 .... **TCLC 56**
See also CA 115; 181

Bobette
See Simenon, Georges (Jacques Christian)

Boccaccio, Giovanni 1313-1375 ... **CMLC 13, 57; SSC 10**
See also EW 2; RGSF 2; RGWL 2, 3; TWA

Bochco, Steven 1943- .... **CLC 35**
See also AAYA 11; CA 124; 138

Bode, Sigmund
See O'Doherty, Brian

Bodel, Jean 1167(?)-1210 .... **CMLC 28**

Bodenheim, Maxwell 1892-1954 .... **TCLC 44**
See also CA 110; 187; DLB 9, 45; RGAL 4

Bodenheimer, Maxwell
See Bodenheim, Maxwell

Bodker, Cecil 1927-
See Bodker, Cecil

Bodker, Cecil 1927- .... **CLC 21**
See also CA 73-76; CANR 13, 44, 111; CLR 23; MAICYA 1, 2; SATA 14, 133

Boell, Heinrich (Theodor)
1917-1985 ..... **CLC 2, 3, 6, 9, 11, 15, 27, 32, 72; SSC 23; WLC**
See Boll, Heinrich
See also CA 21-24R; 116; CANR 24; DA; DA3; DAB; DAC; DAM MST, NOV; DLB 69; DLBY 1985; MTCW 1, 2; TWA

Boerne, Alfred
See Doeblin, Alfred

Boethius c. 480-c. 524 .... **CMLC 15**
See also DLB 115; RGWL 2, 3

Boff, Leonardo (Genezio Darci)
1938- .... **CLC 70; HLC 1**
See also CA 150; DAM MULT; HW 2

Bogan, Louise 1897-1970 .... **CLC 4, 39, 46, 93; PC 12**
See also AMWS 3; CA 73-76; 25-28R; CANR 33, 82; DAM POET; DLB 45, 169; EWL 3; MAWW; MTCW 1, 2; RGAL 4

Bogarde, Dirk
See Van Den Bogarde, Derek Jules Gaspard Ulric Niven
See also DLB 14

Bogosian, Eric 1953- .... **CLC 45, 141**
See also CA 138; CAD; CANR 102; CD 5

Bograd, Larry 1953- .... **CLC 35**
See also CA 93-96; CANR 57; SAAS 21; SATA 33, 89; WYA

Boiardo, Matteo Maria 1441-1494 .... **LC 6**

Boileau-Despreaux, Nicolas 1636-1711 . **LC 3**
See also DLB 268; EW 3; GFL Beginnings to 1789; RGWL 2, 3

Boissard, Maurice
See Leautaud, Paul

Bojer, Johan 1872-1959 .... **TCLC 64**
See also CA 189; EWL 3

Bok, Edward W(illiam)
1863-1930 .... **TCLC 101**
See also CA 217; DLB 91; DLBD 16

Boker, George Henry 1823-1890 . **NCLC 125**
See also RGAL 4

Boland, Eavan (Aisling) 1944- .. **CLC 40, 67, 113**
See also BRWS 5; CA 143, 207; CAAE 207; CANR 61; CP 7; CWP; DAM POET; DLB 40; FW; MTCW 2; PFS 12

Boll, Heinrich
See Boell, Heinrich (Theodor)
See also BPFB 1; CDWLB 2; EW 13; EWL 3; RGSF 2; RGWL 2, 3

Bolt, Lee
See Faust, Frederick (Schiller)

Bolt, Robert (Oxton) 1924-1995 .... **CLC 14**
See also CA 17-20R; 147; CANR 35, 67; CBD; DAM DRAM; DFS 2; DLB 13, 233; EWL 3; LAIT 1; MTCW 1

Bombal, Maria Luisa 1910-1980 .... **HLCS 1; SSC 37**
See also CA 127; CANR 72; EWL 3; HW 1; LAW; RGSF 2

Bombet, Louis-Alexandre-Cesar
See Stendhal

Bomkauf
See Kaufman, Bob (Garnell)

Bonaventura .... **NCLC 35**
See also DLB 90

Bond, Edward 1934- .... **CLC 4, 6, 13, 23**
See also AAYA 50; BRWS 1; CA 25-28R; CANR 38, 67, 106; CBD; CD 5; DAM DRAM; DFS 3, 8; DLB 13; EWL 3; MTCW 1

Bonham, Frank 1914-1989 .... **CLC 12**
See also AAYA 1; BYA 1, 3; CA 9-12R; CANR 4, 36; JRDA; MAICYA 1, 2; SAAS 3; SATA 1, 49; SATA-Obit 62; TCWW 2; YAW

Bonnefoy, Yves 1923- .... **CLC 9, 15, 58**
See also CA 85-88; CANR 33, 75, 97; CWW 2; DAM MST, POET; DLB 258; EWL 3; GFL 1789 to the Present; MTCW 1, 2

Bonner, Marita .... **HR 2**
See Occomy, Marita (Odette) Bonner

Bonnin, Gertrude 1876-1938 .... **NNAL**
See Zitkala-Sa
See also CA 150; DAM MULT

Bontemps, Arna(ud Wendell)
1902-1973 ..... **BLC 1; CLC 1, 18; HR 2**
See also BW 1; CA 1-4R; 41-44R; CANR 4, 35; CLR 6; CWRI 5; DA3; DAM MULT, NOV, POET; DLB 48, 51; JRDA; MAICYA 1, 2; MTCW 1, 2; SATA 2, 44; SATA-Obit 24; WCH; WP

Boot, William
See Stoppard, Tom

Booth, Martin 1944-2004 .... **CLC 13**
See also CA 93-96, 188; CAAE 188; CAAS 2; CANR 92

Booth, Philip 1925- .... **CLC 23**
See also CA 5-8R; CANR 5, 88; CP 7; DLBY 1982

Booth, Wayne C(layson) 1921- .... **CLC 24**
See also CA 1-4R; CAAS 5; CANR 3, 43, 117; DLB 67

Borchert, Wolfgang 1921-1947 .... **TCLC 5**
See also CA 104; 188; DLB 69, 124; EWL 3

Borel, Petrus 1809-1859 .... **NCLC 41**
See also DLB 119; GFL 1789 to the Present

Borges, Jorge Luis 1899-1986 ... **CLC 1, 2, 3, 4, 6, 8, 9, 10, 13, 19, 44, 48, 83; HLC 1; PC 22, 32; SSC 4, 41; TCLC 109; WLC**
See also AAYA 26; BPFB 1; CA 21-24R; CANR 19, 33, 75, 105; CDWLB 3; DA; DA3; DAB; DAC; DAM MST, MULT; DLB 113, 283; DLBY 1986; DNFS 1, 2; EWL 3; HW 1, 2; LAW; LMFS 2; MSW; MTCW 1, 2; RGSF 2; RGWL 2, 3; SFW 4; SSFS 17; TWA; WLIT 1

Borowski, Tadeusz 1922-1951 .... **SSC 48; TCLC 9**
See also CA 106; 154; CDWLB 4; DLB 215; EWL 3; RGSF 2; RGWL 3; SSFS 13

Borrow, George (Henry)
1803-1881 .... **NCLC 9**
See also DLB 21, 55, 166

Bosch (Gavino), Juan 1909-2001 ..... **HLCS 1**
See also CA 151; 204; DAM MST, MULT; DLB 145; HW 1, 2

Bosman, Herman Charles
1905-1951 .... **TCLC 49**
See Malan, Herman
See also CA 160; DLB 225; RGSF 2

Bosschere, Jean de 1878(?)-1953 ... **TCLC 19**
See also CA 115; 186

Boswell, James 1740-1795 ... **LC 4, 50; WLC**
See also BRW 3; CDBLB 1660-1789; DA; DAB; DAC; DAM MST; DLB 104, 142; TEA; WLIT 3

Bottomley, Gordon 1874-1948 ..... **TCLC 107**
See also CA 120; 192; DLB 10

Bottoms, David 1949- .... **CLC 53**
See also CA 105; CANR 22; CSW; DLB 120; DLBY 1983

Boucicault, Dion 1820-1890 .... **NCLC 41**

Boucolon, Maryse
See Conde, Maryse

Bourget, Paul (Charles Joseph)
1852-1935 .... **TCLC 12**
See also CA 107; 196; DLB 123; GFL 1789 to the Present

Bourjaily, Vance (Nye) 1922- .... **CLC 8, 62**
See also CA 1-4R; CAAS 1; CANR 2, 72; CN 7; DLB 2, 143

Bourne, Randolph S(illiman)
1886-1918 .... **TCLC 16**
See also AMW; CA 117; 155; DLB 63

Bova, Ben(jamin William) 1932- ...... **CLC 45**
See also AAYA 16; CA 5-8R; CAAS 18; CANR 11, 56, 94, 111; CLR 3, 96; DLB 1981; INT CANR-11; MAICYA 1, 2; MTCW 1; SATA 6, 68, 133; SFW 4

Bowen, Elizabeth (Dorothea Cole)
1899-1973 . **CLC 1, 3, 6, 11, 15, 22, 118; SSC 3, 28, 66; TCLC 148**
See also BRWS 2; CA 17-18; 41-44R; CANR 35, 105; CAP 2; CDBLB 1945-1960; DA3; DAM NOV; DLB 15, 162; EWL 3; EXPS; FW; HGG; MTCW 1, 2; NFS 13; RGSF 2; SSFS 5; SUFW 1; TEA; WLIT 4

Bowering, George 1935- .... **CLC 15, 47**
See also CA 21-24R; CAAS 16; CANR 10; CP 7; DLB 53

Bowering, Marilyn R(uthe) 1949- .... **CLC 32**
See also CA 101; CANR 49; CP 7; CWP

Bowers, Edgar 1924-2000 .... **CLC 9**
See also CA 5-8R; 188; CANR 24; CP 7; CSW; DLB 5

Bowers, Mrs. J. Milton 1842-1914
See Bierce, Ambrose (Gwinett)

Bowie, David .... **CLC 17**
See Jones, David Robert

Bowles, Jane (Sydney) 1917-1973 ..... **CLC 3, 68**
See Bowles, Jane Auer
See also CA 19-20; 41-44R; CAP 2

Bowles, Jane Auer
See Bowles, Jane (Sydney)
See also EWL 3

Bowles, Paul (Frederick) 1910-1999 . **CLC 1, 2, 19, 53; SSC 3**
See also AMWS 4; CA 1-4R; 186; CAAS 1; CANR 1, 19, 50, 75; CN 7; DA3; DLB 5, 6, 218; EWL 3; MTCW 1, 2; RGAL 4; SSFS 17

Bowles, William Lisle 1762-1850 . **NCLC 103**
See also DLB 93

Box, Edgar
See Vidal, Gore
See also GLL 1

Boyd, James 1888-1944 .... **TCLC 115**
See also CA 186; DLB 9; DLBD 16; RGAL 4; RHW

Boyd, Nancy
See Millay, Edna St. Vincent
See also GLL 1

Boyd, Thomas (Alexander)
1898-1935 .... **TCLC 111**
See also CA 111; 183; DLB 9; DLBD 16

Boyd, William 1952- .... **CLC 28, 53, 70**
See also CA 114; 120; CANR 51, 71; CN 7; DLB 231

Boyesen, Hjalmar Hjorth
1848-1895 .... **NCLC 135**
See also DLB 12, 71; DLBD 13; RGAL 4

Boyle, Kay 1902-1992 .... **CLC 1, 5, 19, 58, 121; SSC 5**
See also CA 13-16R; 140; CAAS 1; CANR 29, 61, 110; DLB 4, 9, 48, 86; DLBY 1993; EWL 3; MTCW 1, 2; RGAL 4; RGSF 2; SSFS 10, 13, 14

Boyle, Mark
See Kienzle, William X(avier)

Boyle, Patrick 1905-1982 .... **CLC 19**
See also CA 127

Boyle, T. C.
See Boyle, T(homas) Coraghessan
See also AMWS 8

Boyle, T(homas) Coraghessan
1948- .... CLC 36, 55, 90; SSC 16
See Boyle, T. C.
See also AAYA 47; BEST 90:4; BPFB 1;
CA 120; CANR 44, 76, 89; CN 7; CPW;
DA3; DAM POP; DLB 218, 278; DLBY
1986; EWL 3; MTCW 2; SSFS 13, 19

Boz
See Dickens, Charles (John Huffam)

Brackenridge, Hugh Henry
1748-1816 .... NCLC 7
See also DLB 11, 37; RGAL 4

Bradbury, Edward P.
See Moorcock, Michael (John)
See also MTCW 2

Bradbury, Malcolm (Stanley)
1932-2000 .... CLC 32, 61
See also CA 1-4R; CANR 1, 33, 91, 98;
CN 7; DA3; DAM NOV; DLB 14, 207;
EWL 3; MTCW 1, 2

Bradbury, Ray (Douglas) 1920- .... CLC 1, 3,
10, 15, 42, 98; SSC 29, 53; WLC
See also AAYA 15; AITN 1; AMWS 4;
BPFB 1; BYA 4, 5, 11; CA 1-4R; CANR
2, 30, 75, 125; CDALB 1968-1988; CN
7; CPW; DA; DA3; DAB; DAC; DAM
MST, NOV, POP; DLB 2, 8; EXPN;
EXPS; HGG; LAIT 3, 5; LATS 1; LMFS
2; MTCW 1, 2; NFS 1; RGAL 4; RGSF
2; SATA 11, 64, 123; SCFW 2; SFW 4;
SSFS 1; SUFW 1, 2; TUS; YAW

Braddon, Mary Elizabeth
1837-1915 .... TCLC 111
See also BRWS 8; CA 108; 179; CMW 4;
DLB 18, 70, 156; HGG

Bradfield, Scott (Michael) 1955- .... SSC 65
See also CA 147; CANR 90; HGG; SUFW
2

Bradford, Gamaliel 1863-1932 .... TCLC 36
See also CA 160; DLB 17

Bradford, William 1590-1657 .... LC 64
See also DLB 24, 30; RGAL 4

Bradley, David (Henry), Jr. 1950- .... BLC 1;
CLC 23, 118
See also BW 1, 3; CA 104; CANR 26, 81;
CN 7; DAM MULT; DLB 33

Bradley, John Ed(mund, Jr.) 1958- . CLC 55
See also CA 139; CANR 99; CN 7; CSW

Bradley, Marion Zimmer
1930-1999 .... CLC 30
See Chapman, Lee; Dexter, John; Gardner,
Miriam; Ives, Morgan; Rivers, Elfrida
See also AAYA 40; BPFB 1; CA 57-60; 185;
CAAS 10; CANR 7, 31, 51, 75, 107;
CPW; DA3; DAM POP; DLB 8; FANT;
FW; MTCW 1, 2; SATA 90, 139; SATA-
Obit 116; SFW 4; SUFW 2; YAW

Bradshaw, John 1933- .... CLC 70
See also CA 138; CANR 61

Bradstreet, Anne 1612(?)-1672 .... LC 4, 30;
PC 10
See also AMWS 1; CDALB 1640-1865;
DA; DA3; DAC; DAM MST, POET; DLB
24; EXPP; FW; PFS 6; RGAL 4; TUS;
WP

Brady, Joan 1939- .... CLC 86
See also CA 141

Bragg, Melvyn 1939- .... CLC 10
See also BEST 89:3; CA 57-60; CANR 10,
48, 89; CN 7; DLB 14, 271; RHW

Brahe, Tycho 1546-1601 .... LC 45

Braine, John (Gerard) 1922-1986 . CLC 1, 3,
41
See also CA 1-4R; 120; CANR 1, 33; CD-
BLB 1945-1960; DLB 15; DLBY 1986;
EWL 3; MTCW 1

Braithwaite, William Stanley (Beaumont)
1878-1962 .... BLC 1; HR 2; PC 52
See also BW 1; CA 125; DAM MULT; DLB
50, 54

Bramah, Ernest 1868-1942 .... TCLC 72
See also CA 156; CMW 4; DLB 70; FANT

Brammer, William 1930(?)-1978 ...... CLC 31
See also CA 77-80

Brancati, Vitaliano 1907-1954 .... TCLC 12
See also CA 109; DLB 264; EWL 3

Brancato, Robin F(idler) 1936- .... CLC 35
See also AAYA 9; BYA 6; CA 69-72; CANR
11, 45; CLR 32; JRDA; MAICYA 2;
MAICYAS 1; SAAS 9; SATA 97; WYA;
YAW

Brand, Max
See Faust, Frederick (Schiller)
See also BPFB 1; TCWW 2

Brand, Millen 1906-1980 .... CLC 7
See also CA 21-24R; 97-100; CANR 72

Branden, Barbara .... CLC 44
See also CA 148

Brandes, Georg (Morris Cohen)
1842-1927 .... TCLC 10
See also CA 105; 189

Brandys, Kazimierz 1916-2000 .... CLC 62
See also EWL 3

Branley, Franklyn M(ansfield)
1915-2002 .... CLC 21
See also CA 33-36R; 207; CANR 14, 39;
CLR 13; MAICYA 1, 2; SAAS 16; SATA
4, 68, 136

Brant, Beth (E.) 1941- .... NNAL
See also CA 144; FW

Brathwaite, Edward Kamau
1930- .... BLCS; CLC 11; PC 56
See also BW 2, 3; CA 25-28R; CANR 11,
26, 47, 107; CDWLB 3; CP 7; DAM
POET; DLB 125; EWL 3

Brathwaite, Kamau
See Brathwaite, Edward Kamau

Brautigan, Richard (Gary)
1935-1984 .... CLC 1, 3, 5, 9, 12, 34, 42;
TCLC 133
See also BPFB 1; CA 53-56; 113; CANR
34; DA3; DAM NOV; DLB 2, 5, 206;
DLBY 1980, 1984; FANT; MTCW 1;
RGAL 4; SATA 56

Brave Bird, Mary .... NNAL
See Crow Dog, Mary (Ellen)

Braverman, Kate 1950- .... CLC 67
See also CA 89-92

Brecht, (Eugen) Bertolt (Friedrich)
1898-1956 ..... DC 3; TCLC 1, 6, 13, 35;
WLC
See also CA 104; 133; CANR 62; CDWLB
2; DA; DA3; DAB; DAC; DAM DRAM,
MST; DFS 4, 5, 9; DLB 56, 124; EW 11;
EWL 3; IDTP; MTCW 1, 2; RGWL 2, 3;
TWA

Brecht, Eugen Berthold Friedrich
See Brecht, (Eugen) Bertolt (Friedrich)

Bremer, Fredrika 1801-1865 .... NCLC 11
See also DLB 254

Brennan, Christopher John
1870-1932 .... TCLC 17
See also CA 117; 188; DLB 230; EWL 3

Brennan, Maeve 1917-1993 ... CLC 5; TCLC
124
See also CA 81-84; CANR 72, 100

Brent, Linda
See Jacobs, Harriet A(nn)

Brentano, Clemens (Maria)
1778-1842 .... NCLC 1
See also DLB 90; RGWL 2, 3

Brent of Bin Bin
See Franklin, (Stella Maria Sarah) Miles
(Lampe)

Brenton, Howard 1942- .... CLC 31
See also CA 69-72; CANR 33, 67; CBD;
CD 5; DLB 13; MTCW 1

Breslin, James 1930-
See Breslin, Jimmy
See also CA 73-76; CANR 31, 75; DAM
NOV; MTCW 1, 2

Breslin, Jimmy .... CLC 4, 43
See Breslin, James
See also AITN 1; DLB 185; MTCW 2

Bresson, Robert 1901(?)-1999 .... CLC 16
See also CA 110; 187; CANR 49

Breton, Andre 1896-1966 .. CLC 2, 9, 15, 54;
PC 15
See also CA 19-20; 25-28R; CANR 40, 60;
CAP 2; DLB 65, 258; EW 11; EWL 3;
GFL 1789 to the Present; LMFS 2;
MTCW 1, 2; RGWL 2, 3; TWA; WP

Breytenbach, Breyten 1939(?)- .. CLC 23, 37,
126
See also CA 113; 129; CANR 61, 122;
CWW 2; DAM POET; DLB 225; EWL 3

Bridgers, Sue Ellen 1942- .... CLC 26
See also AAYA 8, 49; BYA 7, 8; CA 65-68;
CANR 11, 36; CLR 18; DLB 52; JRDA;
MAICYA 1, 2; SAAS 1; SATA 22, 90;
SATA-Essay 109; WYA; YAW

Bridges, Robert (Seymour)
1844-1930 .... PC 28; TCLC 1
See also BRW 6; CA 104; 152; CDBLB
1890-1914; DAM POET; DLB 19, 98

Bridie, James .... TCLC 3
See Mavor, Osborne Henry
See also DLB 10; EWL 3

Brin, David 1950- .... CLC 34
See also AAYA 21; CA 102; CANR 24, 70,
125, 127; INT CANR-24; SATA 65;
SCFW 2; SFW 4

Brink, Andre (Philippus) 1935- . CLC 18, 36,
106
See also AFW; BRWS 6; CA 104; CANR
39, 62, 109; CN 7; DLB 225; EWL 3; INT
CA-103; LATS 1; MTCW 1, 2; WLIT 2

Brinsmead, H. F(ay)
See Brinsmead, H(esba) F(ay)

Brinsmead, H. F.
See Brinsmead, H(esba) F(ay)

Brinsmead, H(esba) F(ay) 1922- .... CLC 21
See also CA 21-24R; CANR 10; CLR 47;
CWRI 5; MAICYA 1, 2; SAAS 5; SATA
18, 78

Brittain, Vera (Mary) 1893(?)-1970 . CLC 23
See also CA 13-16; 25-28R; CANR 58;
CAP 1; DLB 191; FW; MTCW 1, 2

Broch, Hermann 1886-1951 .... TCLC 20
See also CA 117; 211; CDWLB 2; DLB 85,
124; EW 10; EWL 3; RGWL 2, 3

Brock, Rose
See Hansen, Joseph
See also GLL 1

Brod, Max 1884-1968 .... TCLC 115
See also CA 5-8R; 25-28R; CANR 7; DLB
81; EWL 3

Brodkey, Harold (Roy) 1930-1996 .. CLC 56;
TCLC 123
See also CA 111; 151; CANR 71; CN 7;
DLB 130

Brodsky, Iosif Alexandrovich 1940-1996
See Brodsky, Joseph
See also AITN 1; CA 41-44R; 151; CANR
37, 106; DA3; DAM POET; MTCW 1, 2;
RGWL 2, 3

Brodsky, Joseph . CLC 4, 6, 13, 36, 100; PC
9
See Brodsky, Iosif Alexandrovich
See also AMWS 8; CWW 2; DLB 285;
EWL 3; MTCW 1

Brodsky, Michael (Mark) 1948- .... CLC 19
See also CA 102; CANR 18, 41, 58; DLB
244

Brodzki, Bella ed. .... **CLC 65**
Brome, Richard 1590(?)-1652 .... **LC 61**
See also DLB 58
Bromell, Henry 1947- .... **CLC 5**
See also CA 53-56; CANR 9, 115, 116
Bromfield, Louis (Brucker)
1896-1956 .... **TCLC 11**
See also CA 107; 155; DLB 4, 9, 86; RGAL 4; RHW
Broner, E(sther) M(asserman)
1930- .... **CLC 19**
See also CA 17-20R; CANR 8, 25, 72; CN 7; DLB 28
Bronk, William (M.) 1918-1999 .... **CLC 10**
See also CA 89-92; 177; CANR 23; CP 7; DLB 165
Bronstein, Lev Davidovich
See Trotsky, Leon
Bronte, Anne 1820-1849 ..... **NCLC 4, 71, 102**
See also BRW 5; BRWR 1; DA3; DLB 21, 199; TEA
Bronte, (Patrick) Branwell
1817-1848 .... **NCLC 109**
Bronte, Charlotte 1816-1855 ...... **NCLC 3, 8, 33, 58, 105; WLC**
See also AAYA 17; BRW 5; BRWC 2; BRWR 1; BYA 2; CDBLB 1832-1890; DA; DA3; DAB; DAC; DAM MST, NOV; DLB 21, 159, 199; EXPN; LAIT 2; NFS 4; TEA; WLIT 4
Bronte, Emily (Jane) 1818-1848 ... **NCLC 16, 35; PC 8; WLC**
See also AAYA 17; BPFB 1; BRW 5; BRWC 1; BRWR 1; BYA 3; CDBLB 1832-1890; DA; DA3; DAB; DAC; DAM MST, NOV, POET; DLB 21, 32, 199; EXPN; LAIT 1; TEA; WLIT 3
Brontes
See Bronte, Anne; Bronte, Charlotte; Bronte, Emily (Jane)
Brooke, Frances 1724-1789 .... **LC 6, 48**
See also DLB 39, 99
Brooke, Henry 1703(?)-1783 .... **LC 1**
See also DLB 39
Brooke, Rupert (Chawner)
1887-1915 ..... **PC 24; TCLC 2, 7; WLC**
See also BRWS 3; CA 104; 132; CANR 61; CDBLB 1914-1945; DA; DAB; DAC; DAM MST, POET; DLB 19, 216; EXPP; GLL 2; MTCW 1, 2; PFS 7; TEA
Brooke-Haven, P.
See Wodehouse, P(elham) G(renville)
Brooke-Rose, Christine 1926(?)- ..... **CLC 40, 184**
See also BRWS 4; CA 13-16R; CANR 58, 118; CN 7; DLB 14, 231; EWL 3; SFW 4
Brookner, Anita 1928- .. **CLC 32, 34, 51, 136**
See also BRWS 4; CA 114; 120; CANR 37, 56, 87; CN 7; CPW; DA3; DAB; DAM POP; DLB 194; DLBY 1987; EWL 3; MTCW 1, 2; TEA
Brooks, Cleanth 1906-1994 . **CLC 24, 86, 110**
See also CA 17-20R; 145; CANR 33, 35; CSW; DLB 63; DLBY 1994; EWL 3; INT CANR-35; MTCW 1, 2
Brooks, George
See Baum, L(yman) Frank
Brooks, Gwendolyn (Elizabeth)
1917-2000 ... **BLC 1; CLC 1, 2, 4, 5, 15, 49, 125; PC 7; WLC**
See also AAYA 20; AFAW 1, 2; AITN 1; AMWS 3; BW 2, 3; CA 1-4R; 190; CANR 1, 27, 52, 75; CDALB 1941-1968; CLR 27; CP 7; CWP; DA; DA3; DAC; DAM MST, MULT, POET; DLB 5, 76, 165; EWL 3; EXPP; MAWW; MTCW 1, 2; PFS 1, 2, 4, 6; RGAL 4; SATA 6; SATA-Obit 123; TUS; WP

Brooks, Mel .... **CLC 12**
See Kaminsky, Melvin
See also AAYA 13, 48; DLB 26
Brooks, Peter (Preston) 1938- .... **CLC 34**
See also CA 45-48; CANR 1, 107
Brooks, Van Wyck 1886-1963 .... **CLC 29**
See also AMW; CA 1-4R; CANR 6; DLB 45, 63, 103; TUS
Brophy, Brigid (Antonia)
1929-1995 .... **CLC 6, 11, 29, 105**
See also CA 5-8R; 149; CAAS 4; CANR 25, 53; CBD; CN 7; CWD; DA3; DLB 14, 271; EWL 3; MTCW 1, 2
Brosman, Catharine Savage 1934- ..... **CLC 9**
See also CA 61-64; CANR 21, 46
Brossard, Nicole 1943- .... **CLC 115, 169**
See also CA 122; CAAS 16; CCA 1; CWP; CWW 2; DLB 53; EWL 3; FW; GLL 2; RGWL 3
Brother Antoninus
See Everson, William (Oliver)
The Brothers Quay
See Quay, Stephen; Quay, Timothy
Broughton, T(homas) Alan 1936- ..... **CLC 19**
See also CA 45-48; CANR 2, 23, 48, 111
Broumas, Olga 1949- .... **CLC 10, 73**
See also CA 85-88; CANR 20, 69, 110; CP 7; CWP; GLL 2
Broun, Heywood 1888-1939 .... **TCLC 104**
See also DLB 29, 171
Brown, Alan 1950- .... **CLC 99**
See also CA 156
Brown, Charles Brockden
1771-1810 .... **NCLC 22, 74, 122**
See also AMWS 1; CDALB 1640-1865; DLB 37, 59, 73; FW; HGG; LMFS 1; RGAL 4; TUS
Brown, Christy 1932-1981 .... **CLC 63**
See also BYA 13; CA 105; 104; CANR 72; DLB 14
Brown, Claude 1937-2002 ... **BLC 1; CLC 30**
See also AAYA 7; BW 1, 3; CA 73-76; 205; CANR 81; DAM MULT
Brown, Dee (Alexander)
1908-2002 .... **CLC 18, 47**
See also AAYA 30; CA 13-16R; 212; CAAS 6; CANR 11, 45, 60; CPW; CSW; DA3; DAM POP; DLBY 1980; LAIT 2; MTCW 1, 2; NCFS 5; SATA 5, 110; SATA-Obit 141; TCWW 2
Brown, George
See Wertmueller, Lina
Brown, George Douglas
1869-1902 .... **TCLC 28**
See Douglas, George
See also CA 162
Brown, George Mackay 1921-1996 ... **CLC 5, 48, 100**
See also BRWS 6; CA 21-24R; 151; CAAS 6; CANR 12, 37, 67; CN 7; CP 7; DLB 14, 27, 139, 271; MTCW 1; RGSF 2; SATA 35
Brown, (William) Larry 1951- .... **CLC 73**
See also CA 130; 134; CANR 117; CSW; DLB 234; INT CA-134
Brown, Moses
See Barrett, William (Christopher)
Brown, Rita Mae 1944- .... **CLC 18, 43, 79**
See also BPFB 1; CA 45-48; CANR 2, 11, 35, 62, 95; CN 7; CPW; CSW; DA3; DAM NOV, POP; FW; INT CANR-11; MTCW 1, 2; NFS 9; RGAL 4; TUS
Brown, Roderick (Langmere) Haig-
See Haig-Brown, Roderick (Langmere)
Brown, Rosellen 1939- .... **CLC 32, 170**
See also CA 77-80; CAAS 10; CANR 14, 44, 98; CN 7

Brown, Sterling Allen 1901-1989 ...... **BLC 1; CLC 1, 23, 59; HR 2; PC 55**
See also AFAW 1, 2; BW 1, 3; CA 85-88; 127; CANR 26; DA3; DAM MULT, POET; DLB 48, 51, 63; MTCW 1, 2; RGAL 4; WP
Brown, Will
See Ainsworth, William Harrison
Brown, William Hill 1765-1793 .... **LC 93**
See also DLB 37
Brown, William Wells 1815-1884 ...... **BLC 1; DC 1; NCLC 2, 89**
See also DAM MULT; DLB 3, 50, 183, 248; RGAL 4
Browne, (Clyde) Jackson 1948(?)- ... **CLC 21**
See also CA 120
Browning, Elizabeth Barrett
1806-1861 ... **NCLC 1, 16, 61, 66; PC 6; WLC**
See also BRW 4; CDBLB 1832-1890; DA; DA3; DAB; DAC; DAM MST, POET; DLB 32, 199; EXPP; PAB; PFS 2, 16; TEA; WLIT 4; WP
Browning, Robert 1812-1889 . **NCLC 19, 79; PC 2; WLCS**
See also BRW 4; BRWC 2; BRWR 2; CDBLB 1832-1890; CLR 97; DA; DA3; DAB; DAC; DAM MST, POET; DLB 32, 163; EXPP; LATS 1; PAB; PFS 1, 15; RGEL 2; TEA; WLIT 4; WP; YABC 1
Browning, Tod 1882-1962 .... **CLC 16**
See also CA 141; 117
Brownmiller, Susan 1935- .... **CLC 159**
See also CA 103; CANR 35, 75; DAM NOV; FW; MTCW 1, 2
Brownson, Orestes Augustus
1803-1876 .... **NCLC 50**
See also DLB 1, 59, 73, 243
Bruccoli, Matthew J(oseph) 1931- ... **CLC 34**
See also CA 9-12R; CANR 7, 87; DLB 103
Bruce, Lenny .... **CLC 21**
See Schneider, Leonard Alfred
Bruchac, Joseph III 1942- .... **NNAL**
See also AAYA 19; CA 33-36R; CANR 13, 47, 75, 94; CLR 46; CWRI 5; DAM MULT; JRDA; MAICYA 2; MAICYAS 1; MTCW 1; SATA 42, 89, 131
Bruin, John
See Brutus, Dennis
Brulard, Henri
See Stendhal
Brulls, Christian
See Simenon, Georges (Jacques Christian)
Brunner, John (Kilian Houston)
1934-1995 .... **CLC 8, 10**
See also CA 1-4R; 149; CAAS 8; CANR 2, 37; CPW; DAM POP; DLB 261, MTCW 1, 2; SCFW 2; SFW 4
Bruno, Giordano 1548-1600 .... **LC 27**
See also RGWL 2, 3
Brutus, Dennis 1924- ... **BLC 1; CLC 43; PC 24**
See also AFW; BW 2, 3; CA 49-52; CAAS 14; CANR 2, 27, 42, 81; CDWLB 3; CP 7; DAM MULT, POET; DLB 117, 225; EWL 3
Bryan, C(ourtlandt) D(ixon) B(arnes)
1936- .... **CLC 29**
See also CA 73-76; CANR 13, 68; DLB 185; INT CANR-13
Bryan, Michael
See Moore, Brian
See also CCA 1
Bryan, William Jennings
1860-1925 .... **TCLC 99**
Bryant, William Cullen 1794-1878 . **NCLC 6, 46; PC 20**
See also AMWS 1; CDALB 1640-1865; DA; DAB; DAC; DAM MST, POET; DLB 3, 43, 59, 189, 250; EXPP; PAB; RGAL 4; TUS

Bryusov, Valery Yakovlevich
1873-1924 .... **TCLC 10**
See also CA 107; 155; EWL 3; SFW 4

Buchan, John 1875-1940 .... **TCLC 41**
See also CA 108; 145; CMW 4; DAB; DAM POP; DLB 34, 70, 156; HGG; MSW; MTCW 1; RGEL 2; RHW; YABC 2

Buchanan, George 1506-1582 .... **LC 4**
See also DLB 132

Buchanan, Robert 1841-1901 .... **TCLC 107**
See also CA 179; DLB 18, 35

Buchheim, Lothar-Guenther 1918- .... **CLC 6**
See also CA 85-88

Buchner, (Karl) Georg 1813-1837 . **NCLC 26**
See also CDWLB 2; DLB 133; EW 6; RGSF 2; RGWL 2, 3; TWA

Buchwald, Art(hur) 1925- .... **CLC 33**
See also AITN 1; CA 5-8R; CANR 21, 67, 107; MTCW 1, 2; SATA 10

Buck, Pearl S(ydenstricker)
1892-1973 .... **CLC 7, 11, 18, 127**
See also AAYA 42; AITN 1; AMWS 2; BPFB 1; CA 1-4R; 41-44R; CANR 1, 34; CDALBS; DA; DA3; DAB; DAC; DAM MST, NOV; DLB 9, 102; EWL 3; LAIT 3; MTCW 1, 2; RGAL 4; RHW; SATA 1, 25; TUS

Buckler, Ernest 1908-1984 .... **CLC 13**
See also CA 11-12; 114; CAP 1; CCA 1; DAC; DAM MST; DLB 68; SATA 47

Buckley, Christopher (Taylor)
1952- .... **CLC 165**
See also CA 139; CANR 119

Buckley, Vincent (Thomas)
1925-1988 .... **CLC 57**
See also CA 101; DLB 289

Buckley, William F(rank), Jr. 1925- . **CLC 7, 18, 37**
See also AITN 1; BPFB 1; CA 1-4R; CANR 1, 24, 53, 93; CMW 4; CPW; DA3; DAM POP; DLB 137; DLBY 1980; INT CANR-24; MTCW 1, 2; TUS

Buechner, (Carl) Frederick 1926- . **CLC 2, 4, 6, 9**
See also AMWS 12; BPFB 1; CA 13-16R; CANR 11, 39, 64; CN 7; DAM NOV; DLBY 1980; INT CANR-11; MTCW 1, 2

Buell, John (Edward) 1927- .... **CLC 10**
See also CA 1-4R; CANR 71; DLB 53

Buero Vallejo, Antonio 1916-2000 ... **CLC 15, 46, 139; DC 18**
See also CA 106; 189; CANR 24, 49, 75; CWW 2; DFS 11; EWL 3; HW 1; MTCW 1, 2

Bufalino, Gesualdo 1920-1996 .... **CLC 74**
See also CWW 2; DLB 196

Bugayev, Boris Nikolayevich
1880-1934 .... **PC 11; TCLC 7**
See Bely, Andrey; Belyi, Andrei
See also CA 104; 165; MTCW 1

Bukowski, Charles 1920-1994 ... **CLC 2, 5, 9, 41, 82, 108; PC 18; SSC 45**
See also CA 17-20R; 144; CANR 40, 62, 105; CPW; DA3; DAM NOV, POET; DLB 5, 130, 169; EWL 3; MTCW 1, 2

Bulgakov, Mikhail (Afanas'evich)
1891-1940 .... **SSC 18; TCLC 2, 16**
See also BPFB 1; CA 105; 152; DAM DRAM, NOV; DLB 272; EWL 3; NFS 8; RGSF 2; RGWL 2, 3; SFW 4; TWA

Bulgya, Alexander Alexandrovich
1901-1956 .... **TCLC 53**
See Fadeev, Aleksandr Aleksandrovich; Fadeev, Alexandr Alexandrovich; Fadeyev, Alexander
See also CA 117; 181

Bullins, Ed 1935- ... **BLC 1; CLC 1, 5, 7; DC 6**
See also BW 2, 3; CA 49-52; CAAS 16; CAD; CANR 24, 46, 73; CD 5; DAM DRAM, MULT; DLB 7, 38, 249; EWL 3; MTCW 1, 2; RGAL 4

Bulosan, Carlos 1911-1956 .... **AAL**
See also CA 216; RGAL 4

Bulwer-Lytton, Edward (George Earle Lytton) 1803-1873 .... **NCLC 1, 45**
See also DLB 21; RGEL 2; SFW 4; SUFW 1; TEA

Bunin, Ivan Alexeyevich 1870-1953 ... **SSC 5; TCLC 6**
See also CA 104; EWL 3; RGSF 2; RGWL 2, 3; TWA

Bunting, Basil 1900-1985 ...... **CLC 10, 39, 47**
See also BRWS 7; CA 53-56; 115; CANR 7; DAM POET; DLB 20; EWL 3; RGEL 2

Bunuel, Luis 1900-1983 ... **CLC 16, 80; HLC 1**
See also CA 101; 110; CANR 32, 77; DAM MULT; HW 1

Bunyan, John 1628-1688 ..... **LC 4, 69; WLC**
See also BRW 2; BYA 5; CDBLB 1660-1789; DA; DAB; DAC; DAM MST; DLB 39; RGEL 2; TEA; WCH; WLIT 3

Buravsky, Alexandr .... **CLC 59**

Burckhardt, Jacob (Christoph)
1818-1897 .... **NCLC 49**
See also EW 6

Burford, Eleanor
See Hibbert, Eleanor Alice Burford

Burgess, Anthony . **CLC 1, 2, 4, 5, 8, 10, 13, 15, 22, 40, 62, 81, 94**
See Wilson, John (Anthony) Burgess
See also AAYA 25; AITN 1; BRWS 1; CDBLB 1960 to Present; DAB; DLB 14, 194, 261; DLBY 1998; EWL 3; MTCW 1; RGEL 2; RHW; SFW 4; YAW

Burke, Edmund 1729(?)-1797 .... **LC 7, 36; WLC**
See also BRW 3; DA; DA3; DAB; DAC; DAM MST; DLB 104, 252; RGEL 2; TEA

Burke, Kenneth (Duva) 1897-1993 ... **CLC 2, 24**
See also AMW; CA 5-8R; 143; CANR 39, 74; DLB 45, 63; EWL 3; MTCW 1, 2; RGAL 4

Burke, Leda
See Garnett, David

Burke, Ralph
See Silverberg, Robert

Burke, Thomas 1886-1945 .... **TCLC 63**
See also CA 113; 155; CMW 4; DLB 197

Burney, Fanny 1752-1840 .... **NCLC 12, 54, 107**
See also BRWS 3; DLB 39; NFS 16; RGEL 2; TEA

Burney, Frances
See Burney, Fanny

Burns, Robert 1759-1796 ... **LC 3, 29, 40; PC 6; WLC**
See also AAYA 51; BRW 3; CDBLB 1789-1832; DA; DA3; DAB; DAC; DAM MST, POET; DLB 109; EXPP; PAB; RGEL 2; TEA; WP

Burns, Tex
See L'Amour, Louis (Dearborn)
See also TCWW 2

Burnshaw, Stanley 1906- .... **CLC 3, 13, 44**
See also CA 9-12R; CP 7; DLB 48; DLBY 1997

Burr, Anne 1937- .... **CLC 6**
See also CA 25-28R

Burroughs, Edgar Rice 1875-1950 . **TCLC 2, 32**
See also AAYA 11; BPFB 1; BYA 4, 9; CA 104; 132; DA3; DAM NOV; DLB 8; FANT; MTCW 1, 2; RGAL 4; SATA 41; SCFW 2; SFW 4; TUS; YAW

Burroughs, William S(eward)
1914-1997 .. **CLC 1, 2, 5, 15, 22, 42, 75, 109; TCLC 121; WLC**
See Lee, William; Lee, Willy
See also AITN 2; AMWS 3; BG 2; BPFB 1; CA 9-12R; 160; CANR 20, 52, 104; CN 7; CPW; DA; DA3; DAB; DAC; DAM MST, NOV, POP; DLB 2, 8, 16, 152, 237; DLBY 1981, 1997; EWL 3; HGG; LMFS 2; MTCW 1, 2; RGAL 4; SFW 4

Burton, Sir Richard F(rancis)
1821-1890 .... **NCLC 42**
See also DLB 55, 166, 184

Burton, Robert 1577-1640 .... **LC 74**
See also DLB 151; RGEL 2

Buruma, Ian 1951- .... **CLC 163**
See also CA 128; CANR 65

Busch, Frederick 1941- ... **CLC 7, 10, 18, 47, 166**
See also CA 33-36R; CAAS 1; CANR 45, 73, 92; CN 7; DLB 6, 218

Bush, Barney (Furman) 1946- .... **NNAL**
See also CA 145

Bush, Ronald 1946- .... **CLC 34**
See also CA 136

Bustos, F(rancisco)
See Borges, Jorge Luis

Bustos Domecq, H(onorio)
See Bioy Casares, Adolfo; Borges, Jorge Luis

Butler, Octavia E(stelle) 1947- .. **BLCS; CLC 38, 121**
See also AAYA 18, 48; AFAW 2; AMWS 13; BPFB 1; BW 2, 3; CA 73-76; CANR 12, 24, 38, 73; CLR 65; CPW; CSW; DA3; DAM MULT, POP; DLB 33; LATS 1; MTCW 1, 2; NFS 8; SATA 84; SCFW 2; SFW 4; SSFS 6; YAW

Butler, Robert Olen, (Jr.) 1945- ...... **CLC 81, 162**
See also AMWS 12; BPFB 1; CA 112; CANR 66; CSW; DAM POP; DLB 173; INT CA-112; MTCW 1; SSFS 11

Butler, Samuel 1612-1680 .... **LC 16, 43**
See also DLB 101, 126; RGEL 2

Butler, Samuel 1835-1902 .... **TCLC 1, 33; WLC**
See also BRWS 2; CA 143; CDBLB 1890-1914; DA; DA3; DAB; DAC; DAM MST, NOV; DLB 18, 57, 174; RGEL 2; SFW 4; TEA

Butler, Walter C.
See Faust, Frederick (Schiller)

Butor, Michel (Marie Francois)
1926- .... **CLC 1, 3, 8, 11, 15, 161**
See also CA 9-12R; CANR 33, 66; CWW 2; DLB 83; EW 13; EWL 3; GFL 1789 to the Present; MTCW 1, 2

Butts, Mary 1890(?)-1937 .... **TCLC 77**
See also CA 148; DLB 240

Buxton, Ralph
See Silverstein, Alvin; Silverstein, Virginia B(arbara Opshelor)

Buzo, Alex
See Buzo, Alexander (John)
See also DLB 289

Buzo, Alexander (John) 1944- .... **CLC 61**
See also CA 97-100; CANR 17, 39, 69; CD 5

Buzzati, Dino 1906-1972 .... **CLC 36**
See also CA 160; 33-36R; DLB 177; RGWL 2, 3; SFW 4

Byars, Betsy (Cromer) 1928- .... **CLC 35**
See also AAYA 19; BYA 3; CA 33-36R, 183; CAAE 183; CANR 18, 36, 57, 102; CLR 1, 16, 72; DLB 52; INT CANR-18; JRDA; MAICYA 1, 2; MAICYAS 1; MTCW 1; SAAS 1; SATA 4, 46, 80; SATA-Essay 108; WYA; YAW

Byatt, A(ntonia) S(usan Drabble) 1936- .... **CLC 19, 65, 136**
See also BPFB 1; BRWC 2; BRWS 4; CA 13-16R; CANR 13, 33, 50, 75, 96; DA3; DAM NOV, POP; DLB 14, 194; EWL 3; MTCW 1, 2; RGSF 2; RHW; TEA

Byrne, David 1952- .... **CLC 26**
See also CA 127

Byrne, John Keyes 1926-
See Leonard, Hugh
See also CA 102; CANR 78; INT CA-102

Byron, George Gordon (Noel) 1788-1824 ..... **NCLC 2, 12, 109; PC 16; WLC**
See also BRW 4; BRWC 2; CDBLB 1789-1832; DA; DA3; DAB; DAC; DAM MST, POET; DLB 96, 110; EXPP; LMFS 1; PAB; PFS 1, 14; RGEL 2; TEA; WLIT 3; WP

Byron, Robert 1905-1941 .... **TCLC 67**
See also CA 160; DLB 195

C. 3. 3.
See Wilde, Oscar (Fingal O'Flahertie Wills)

Caballero, Fernan 1796-1877 .... **NCLC 10**

Cabell, Branch
See Cabell, James Branch

Cabell, James Branch 1879-1958 .... **TCLC 6**
See also CA 105; 152; DLB 9, 78; FANT; MTCW 1; RGAL 4; SUFW 1

Cabeza de Vaca, Alvar Nunez 1490-1557(?) .... **LC 61**

Cable, George Washington 1844-1925 .... **SSC 4; TCLC 4**
See also CA 104; 155; DLB 12, 74; DLBD 13; RGAL 4; TUS

Cabral de Melo Neto, Joao 1920-1999 .... **CLC 76**
See Melo Neto, Joao Cabral de
See also CA 151; DAM MULT; LAW; LAWS 1

Cabrera Infante, G(uillermo) 1929- . **CLC 5, 25, 45, 120; HLC 1; SSC 39**
See also CA 85-88; CANR 29, 65, 110; CDWLB 3; CWW 2; DA3; DAM MULT; DLB 113; EWL 3; HW 1, 2; LAW; LAWS 1; MTCW 1, 2; RGSF 2; WLIT 1

Cade, Toni
See Bambara, Toni Cade

Cadmus and Harmonia
See Buchan, John

Caedmon fl. 658-680 .... **CMLC 7**
See also DLB 146

Caeiro, Alberto
See Pessoa, Fernando (Antonio Nogueira)

Caesar, Julius .... **CMLC 47**
See Julius Caesar
See also AW 1; RGWL 2, 3

Cage, John (Milton, Jr.) 1912-1992 . **CLC 41**
See also CA 13-16R; 169; CANR 9, 78; DLB 193; INT CANR-9

Cahan, Abraham 1860-1951 .... **TCLC 71**
See also CA 108; 154; DLB 9, 25, 28; RGAL 4

Cain, G.
See Cabrera Infante, G(uillermo)

Cain, Guillermo
See Cabrera Infante, G(uillermo)

Cain, James M(allahan) 1892-1977 .. **CLC 3, 11, 28**
See also AITN 1; BPFB 1; CA 17-20R; 73-76; CANR 8, 34, 61; CMW 4; DLB 226; EWL 3; MSW; MTCW 1; RGAL 4

Caine, Hall 1853-1931 .... **TCLC 97**
See also RHW

Caine, Mark
See Raphael, Frederic (Michael)

Calasso, Roberto 1941- .... **CLC 81**
See also CA 143; CANR 89

Calderon de la Barca, Pedro 1600-1681 .... **DC 3; HLCS 1; LC 23**
See also EW 2; RGWL 2, 3; TWA

Caldwell, Erskine (Preston) 1903-1987 .... **CLC 1, 8, 14, 50, 60; SSC 19; TCLC 117**
See also AITN 1; AMW; BPFB 1; CA 1-4R; 121; CAAS 1; CANR 2, 33; DA3; DAM NOV; DLB 9, 86; EWL 3; MTCW 1, 2; RGAL 4; RGSF 2; TUS

Caldwell, (Janet Miriam) Taylor (Holland) 1900-1985 .... **CLC 2, 28, 39**
See also BPFB 1; CA 5-8R; 116; CANR 5; DA3; DAM NOV, POP; DLBD 17; RHW

Calhoun, John Caldwell 1782-1850 .... **NCLC 15**
See also DLB 3, 248

Calisher, Hortense 1911- ..... **CLC 2, 4, 8, 38, 134; SSC 15**
See also CA 1-4R; CANR 1, 22, 117; CN 7; DA3; DAM NOV; DLB 2, 218; INT CANR-22; MTCW 1, 2; RGAL 4; RGSF 2

Callaghan, Morley Edward 1903-1990 ..... **CLC 3, 14, 41, 65; TCLC 145**
See also CA 9-12R; 132; CANR 33, 73; DAC; DAM MST; DLB 68; EWL 3; MTCW 1, 2; RGEL 2; RGSF 2; SSFS 19

Callimachus c. 305B.C.-c. 240B.C. .... **CMLC 18**
See also AW 1; DLB 176; RGWL 2, 3

Calvin, Jean
See Calvin, John
See also GFL Beginnings to 1789

Calvin, John 1509-1564 .... **LC 37**
See Calvin, Jean

Calvino, Italo 1923-1985 .... **CLC 5, 8, 11, 22, 33, 39, 73; SSC 3, 48**
See also CA 85-88; 116; CANR 23, 61; DAM NOV; DLB 196; EW 13; EWL 3; MTCW 1, 2; RGSF 2; RGWL 2, 3; SFW 4; SSFS 12

Camara Laye
See Laye, Camara
See also EWL 3

Camden, William 1551-1623 .... **LC 77**
See also DLB 172

Cameron, Carey 1952- .... **CLC 59**
See also CA 135

Cameron, Peter 1959- .... **CLC 44**
See also AMWS 12; CA 125; CANR 50, 117; DLB 234; GLL 2

Camoens, Luis Vaz de 1524(?)-1580
See Camoes, Luis de
See also EW 2

Camoes, Luis de 1524(?)-1580 . **HLCS 1; LC 62; PC 31**
See Camoens, Luis Vaz de
See also DLB 287; RGWL 2, 3

Campana, Dino 1885-1932 .... **TCLC 20**
See also CA 117; DLB 114; EWL 3

Campanella, Tommaso 1568-1639 .... **LC 32**
See also RGWL 2, 3

Campbell, John W(ood, Jr.) 1910-1971 .... **CLC 32**
See also CA 21-22; 29-32R; CANR 34; CAP 2; DLB 8; MTCW 1; SCFW; SFW 4

Campbell, Joseph 1904-1987 .... **CLC 69; TCLC 140**
See also AAYA 3; BEST 89:2; CA 1-4R; 124; CANR 3, 28, 61, 107; DA3; MTCW 1, 2

Campbell, Maria 1940- .... **CLC 85; NNAL**
See also CA 102; CANR 54; CCA 1; DAC

Campbell, (John) Ramsey 1946- ..... **CLC 42; SSC 19**
See also AAYA 51; CA 57-60; CANR 7, 102; DLB 261; HGG; INT CANR 7; SUFW 1, 2

Campbell, (Ignatius) Roy (Dunnachie) 1901-1957 .... **TCLC 5**
See also AFW; CA 104; 155; DLB 20, 225; EWL 3; MTCW 2; RGEL 2

Campbell, Thomas 1777-1844 .... **NCLC 19**
See also DLB 93, 144; RGEL 2

Campbell, Wilfred .... **TCLC 9**
See Campbell, William

Campbell, William 1858(?)-1918
See Campbell, Wilfred
See also CA 106; DLB 92

Campion, Jane 1954- .... **CLC 95**
See also AAYA 33; CA 138; CANR 87

Campion, Thomas 1567-1620 .... **LC 78**
See also CDBLB Before 1660; DAM POET; DLB 58, 172; RGEL 2

Camus, Albert 1913-1960 .... **CLC 1, 2, 4, 9, 11, 14, 32, 63, 69, 124; DC 2; SSC 9; WLC**
See also AAYA 36; AFW; BPFB 1; CA 89-92; DA; DA3; DAB; DAC; DAM DRAM, MST, NOV; DLB 72; EW 13; EWL 3; EXPN; EXPS; GFL 1789 to the Present; LATS 1; LMFS 2; MTCW 1, 2; NFS 6, 16; RGSF 2; RGWL 2, 3; SSFS 4; TWA

Canby, Vincent 1924-2000 .... **CLC 13**
See also CA 81-84; 191

Cancale
See Desnos, Robert

Canetti, Elias 1905-1994 .. **CLC 3, 14, 25, 75, 86**
See also CA 21-24R; 146; CANR 23, 61, 79; CDWLB 2; CWW 2; DA3; DLB 85, 124; EW 12; EWL 3; MTCW 1, 2; RGWL 2, 3; TWA

Canfield, Dorothea F.
See Fisher, Dorothy (Frances) Canfield

Canfield, Dorothea Frances
See Fisher, Dorothy (Frances) Canfield

Canfield, Dorothy
See Fisher, Dorothy (Frances) Canfield

Canin, Ethan 1960- .... **CLC 55; SSC 70**
See also CA 131; 135

Cankar, Ivan 1876-1918 .... **TCLC 105**
See also CDWLB 4; DLB 147; EWL 3

Cannon, Curt
See Hunter, Evan

Cao, Lan 1961- .... **CLC 109**
See also CA 165

Cape, Judith
See Page, P(atricia) K(athleen)
See also CCA 1

Capek, Karel 1890-1938 .... **DC 1; SSC 36; TCLC 6, 37; WLC**
See also CA 104; 140; CDWLB 4; DA; DA3; DAB; DAC; DAM DRAM, MST, NOV; DFS 7, 11; DLB 215; EW 10; EWL 3; MTCW 1; RGSF 2; RGWL 2, 3; SCFW 2; SFW 4

Capote, Truman 1924-1984 . **CLC 1, 3, 8, 13, 19, 34, 38, 58; SSC 2, 47; WLC**
See also AMWS 3; BPFB 1; CA 5-8R; 113; CANR 18, 62; CDALB 1941-1968; CPW; DA; DA3; DAB; DAC; DAM MST, NOV, POP; DLB 2, 185, 227; DLBY 1980, 1984; EWL 3; EXPS; GLL 1; LAIT 3; MTCW 1, 2; NCFS 1; RGAL 4; RGSF 2; SATA 91; SSFS 2; TUS

Capra, Frank 1897-1991 .... **CLC 16**
See also AAYA 52; CA 61-64; 135

Caputo, Philip 1941- .... **CLC 32**
See also CA 73-76; CANR 40; YAW

Caragiale, Ion Luca 1852-1912 ...... **TCLC 76**
See also CA 157

Card, Orson Scott 1951- .... **CLC 44, 47, 50**
See also AAYA 11, 42; BPFB 1; BYA 5, 8; CA 102; CANR 27, 47, 73, 102, 106; CPW; DA3; DAM POP; FANT; INT CANR-27; MTCW 1, 2; NFS 5; SATA 83, 127; SCFW 2; SFW 4; SUFW 2; YAW

Cardenal, Ernesto 1925- .... **CLC 31, 161; HLC 1; PC 22**
See also CA 49-52; CANR 2, 32, 66; CWW 2; DAM MULT, POET; DLB 290; EWL 3; HW 1, 2; LAWS 1; MTCW 1, 2; RGWL 2, 3

Cardinal, Marie 1929-2001 .... **CLC 189**
See also CA 177; CWW 2; DLB 83; FW

Cardozo, Benjamin N(athan) 1870-1938 .... **TCLC 65**
See also CA 117; 164

Carducci, Giosue (Alessandro Giuseppe) 1835-1907 .... **PC 46; TCLC 32**
See also CA 163; EW 7; RGWL 2, 3

Carew, Thomas 1595(?)-1640 . **LC 13; PC 29**
See also BRW 2; DLB 126; PAB; RGEL 2

Carey, Ernestine Gilbreth 1908- .... **CLC 17**
See also CA 5-8R; CANR 71; SATA 2

Carey, Peter 1943- .... **CLC 40, 55, 96, 183**
See also CA 123; 127; CANR 53, 76, 117; CN 7; DLB 289; EWL 3; INT CA-127; MTCW 1, 2; RGSF 2; SATA 94

Carleton, William 1794-1869 .... **NCLC 3**
See also DLB 159; RGEL 2; RGSF 2

Carlisle, Henry (Coffin) 1926- .... **CLC 33**
See also CA 13-16R; CANR 15, 85

Carlsen, Chris
See Holdstock, Robert P.

Carlson, Ron(ald F.) 1947- .... **CLC 54**
See also CA 105, 189; CAAE 189; CANR 27; DLB 244

Carlyle, Thomas 1795-1881 ..... **NCLC 22, 70**
See also BRW 4; CDBLB 1789-1832; DA; DAB; DAC; DAM MST; DLB 55, 144, 254; RGEL 2; TEA

Carman, (William) Bliss 1861-1929 ... **PC 34; TCLC 7**
See also CA 104; 152; DAC; DLB 92; RGEL 2

Carnegie, Dale 1888-1955 .... **TCLC 53**
See also CA 218

Carossa, Hans 1878-1956 .... **TCLC 48**
See also CA 170; DLB 66; EWL 3

Carpenter, Don(ald Richard) 1931-1995 .... **CLC 41**
See also CA 45-48; 149; CANR 1, 71

Carpenter, Edward 1844-1929 .... **TCLC 88**
See also CA 163; GLL 1

Carpenter, John (Howard) 1948- ... **CLC 161**
See also AAYA 2; CA 134; SATA 58

Carpenter, Johnny
See Carpenter, John (Howard)

Carpentier (y Valmont), Alejo 1904-1980 . **CLC 8, 11, 38, 110; HLC 1; SSC 35**
See also CA 65-68; 97-100; CANR 11, 70; CDWLB 3; DAM MULT; DLB 113; EWL 3; HW 1, 2; LAW; LMFS 2; RGSF 2; RGWL 2, 3; WLIT 1

Carr, Caleb 1955- .... **CLC 86**
See also CA 147; CANR 73; DA3

Carr, Emily 1871-1945 .... **TCLC 32**
See also CA 159; DLB 68; FW; GLL 2

Carr, John Dickson 1906-1977 .... **CLC 3**
See Fairbairn, Roger
See also CA 49-52; 69-72; CANR 3, 33, 60; CMW 4; MSW; MTCW 1, 2

Carr, Philippa
See Hibbert, Eleanor Alice Burford

Carr, Virginia Spencer 1929- .... **CLC 34**
See also CA 61-64; DLB 111

Carrere, Emmanuel 1957- .... **CLC 89**
See also CA 200

Carrier, Roch 1937- .... **CLC 13, 78**
See also CA 130; CANR 61; CCA 1; DAC; DAM MST; DLB 53; SATA 105

Carroll, James Dennis
See Carroll, Jim

Carroll, James P. 1943(?)- .... **CLC 38**
See also CA 81-84; CANR 73; MTCW 1

Carroll, Jim 1951- .... **CLC 35, 143**
See Carroll, James Dennis
See also AAYA 17; CA 45-48; CANR 42, 115; NCFS 5

Carroll, Lewis ..... **NCLC 2, 53, 139; PC 18; WLC**
See Dodgson, Charles L(utwidge)
See also AAYA 39; BRW 5; BYA 5, 13; CDBLB 1832-1890; CLR 2, 18; DLB 18, 163, 178; DLBY 1998; EXPN; EXPP; FANT; JRDA; LAIT 1; NFS 7; PFS 11; RGEL 2; SUFW 1; TEA; WCH

Carroll, Paul Vincent 1900-1968 ...... **CLC 10**
See also CA 9-12R; 25-28R; DLB 10; EWL 3; RGEL 2

Carruth, Hayden 1921- ..... **CLC 4, 7, 10, 18, 84; PC 10**
See also CA 9-12R; CANR 4, 38, 59, 110; CP 7; DLB 5, 165; INT CANR-4; MTCW 1, 2; SATA 47

Carson, Anne 1950- .... **CLC 185**
See also AMWS 12; CA 203; DLB 193; PFS 18

Carson, Rachel
See Carson, Rachel Louise
See also AAYA 49; DLB 275

Carson, Rachel Louise 1907-1964 .... **CLC 71**
See Carson, Rachel
See also AMWS 9; ANW; CA 77-80; CANR 35; DA3; DAM POP; FW; LAIT 4; MTCW 1, 2; NCFS 1; SATA 23

Carter, Angela (Olive) 1940-1992 ...... **CLC 5, 41, 76; SSC 13; TCLC 139**
See also BRWS 3; CA 53-56; 136; CANR 12, 36, 61, 106; DA3; DLB 14, 207, 261; EXPS; FANT; FW; MTCW 1, 2; RGSF 2; SATA 66; SATA-Obit 70; SFW 4; SSFS 4, 12; SUFW 2; WLIT 4

Carter, Nick
See Smith, Martin Cruz

Carver, Raymond 1938-1988 ..... **CLC 22, 36, 53, 55, 126; PC 54; SSC 8, 51**
See also AAYA 44; AMWS 3; BPFB 1; CA 33-36R; 126; CANR 17, 34, 61, 103; CPW; DA3; DAM NOV; DLB 130; DLBY 1984, 1988; EWL 3; MTCW 1, 2; PFS 17; RGAL 4; RGSF 2; SSFS 3, 6, 12, 13; TCWW 2; TUS

Cary, Elizabeth, Lady Falkland 1585-1639 .... **LC 30**

Cary, (Arthur) Joyce (Lunel) 1888-1957 .... **TCLC 1, 29**
See also BRW 7; CA 104; 164; CDBLB 1914-1945; DLB 15, 100; EWL 3; MTCW 2; RGEL 2; TEA

Casal, Julian del 1863-1893 .... **NCLC 131**
See also DLB 283; LAW

Casanova de Seingalt, Giovanni Jacopo 1725-1798 .... **LC 13**

Casares, Adolfo Bioy
See Bioy Casares, Adolfo
See also RGSF 2

Casas, Bartolome de las 1474-1566
See Las Casas, Bartolome de
See also WLIT 1

Casely-Hayford, J(oseph) E(phraim) 1866-1903 .... **BLC 1; TCLC 24**
See also BW 2; CA 123; 152; DAM MULT

Casey, John (Dudley) 1939- .... **CLC 59**
See also BEST 90:2; CA 69-72; CANR 23, 100

Casey, Michael 1947- .... **CLC 2**
See also CA 65-68; CANR 109; DLB 5

Casey, Patrick
See Thurman, Wallace (Henry)

Casey, Warren (Peter) 1935-1988 .... **CLC 12**
See also CA 101; 127; INT CA-101

Casona, Alejandro .... **CLC 49**
See Alvarez, Alejandro Rodriguez
See also EWL 3

Cassavetes, John 1929-1989 .... **CLC 20**
See also CA 85-88; 127; CANR 82

Cassian, Nina 1924- .... **PC 17**
See also CWP; CWW 2

Cassill, R(onald) V(erlin) 1919-2002 .... **CLC 4, 23**
See also CA 9-12R; 208; CAAS 1; CANR 7, 45; CN 7; DLB 6, 218; DLBY 2002

Cassiodorus, Flavius Magnus c. 490(?)-c. 583(?) .... **CMLC 43**

Cassirer, Ernst 1874-1945 .... **TCLC 61**
See also CA 157

Cassity, (Allen) Turner 1929- .... **CLC 6, 42**
See also CA 17-20R; CAAS 8; CANR 11; CSW; DLB 105

Castaneda, Carlos (Cesar Aranha) 1931(?)-1998 .... **CLC 12, 119**
See also CA 25-28R; CANR 32, 66, 105; DNFS 1; HW 1; MTCW 1

Castedo, Elena 1937- .... **CLC 65**
See also CA 132

Castedo-Ellerman, Elena
See Castedo, Elena

Castellanos, Rosario 1925-1974 .... **CLC 66; HLC 1; SSC 39, 68**
See also CA 131; 53-56; CANR 58; CDWLB 3; DAM MULT; DLB 113, 290; EWL 3; FW; HW 1; LAW; MTCW 1; RGSF 2; RGWL 2, 3

Castelvetro, Lodovico 1505-1571 .... **LC 12**

Castiglione, Baldassare 1478-1529 ...... **LC 12**
See Castiglione, Baldesar
See also LMFS 1; RGWL 2, 3

Castiglione, Baldesar
See Castiglione, Baldassare
See also EW 2

Castillo, Ana (Hernandez Del) 1953- .... **CLC 151**
See also AAYA 42; CA 131; CANR 51, 86, 128; CWP; DLB 122, 227; DNFS 2; FW; HW 1; LLW 1

Castle, Robert
See Hamilton, Edmond

Castro (Ruz), Fidel 1926(?)- .... **HLC 1**
See also CA 110; 129; CANR 81; DAM MULT; HW 2

Castro, Guillen de 1569-1631 .... **LC 19**

Castro, Rosalia de 1837-1885 ... **NCLC 3, 78; PC 41**
See also DAM MULT

Cather, Willa (Sibert) 1873-1947 . **SSC 2, 50; TCLC 1, 11, 31, 99, 132; WLC**
See also AAYA 24; AMW; AMWC 1; AMWR 1; BPFB 1; CA 104; 128; CDALB 1865-1917; DA; DA3; DAB; DAC; DAM MST, NOV; DLB 9, 54, 78, 256; DLBD 1; EWL 3; EXPN; EXPS; LAIT 3; LATS 1; MAWW; MTCW 1, 2; NFS 2; RGAL 4; RGSF 2; RHW; SATA 30; SSFS 2, 7, 16; TCWW 2; TUS

Catherine II
See Catherine the Great
See also DLB 150

Catherine the Great 1729-1796 .... **LC 69**
See Catherine II

Cato, Marcus Porcius
234B.C.-149B.C. .... **CMLC 21**
See Cato the Elder
Cato, Marcus Porcius, the Elder
See Cato, Marcus Porcius
Cato the Elder
See Cato, Marcus Porcius
See also DLB 211
Catton, (Charles) Bruce 1899-1978 . **CLC 35**
See also AITN 1; CA 5-8R; 81-84; CANR 7, 74; DLB 17; SATA 2; SATA-Obit 24
Catullus c. 84B.C.-54B.C. .... **CMLC 18**
See also AW 2; CDWLB 1; DLB 211; RGWL 2, 3
Cauldwell, Frank
See King, Francis (Henry)
Caunitz, William J. 1933-1996 .... **CLC 34**
See also BEST 89:3; CA 125; 130; 152; CANR 73; INT CA-130
Causley, Charles (Stanley)
1917-2003 .... **CLC 7**
See also CA 9-12R; CANR 5, 35, 94; CLR 30; CWRI 5; DLB 27; MTCW 1; SATA 3, 66; SATA-Obit 149
Caute, (John) David 1936- .... **CLC 29**
See also CA 1-4R; CAAS 4; CANR 1, 33, 64, 120; CBD; CD 5; CN 7; DAM NOV; DLB 14, 231
Cavafy, C(onstantine) P(eter) .... **PC 36; TCLC 2, 7**
See Kavafis, Konstantinos Petrou
See also CA 148; DA3; DAM POET; EW 8; EWL 3; MTCW 1; PFS 19; RGWL 2, 3; WP
Cavalcanti, Guido c. 1250-c. 1300 .... **CMLC 54**
Cavallo, Evelyn
See Spark, Muriel (Sarah)
Cavanna, Betty .... **CLC 12**
See Harrison, Elizabeth (Allen) Cavanna
See also JRDA; MAICYA 1; SAAS 4; SATA 1, 30
Cavendish, Margaret Lucas
1623-1673 .... **LC 30**
See also DLB 131, 252, 281; RGEL 2
Caxton, William 1421(?)-1491(?) .... **LC 17**
See also DLB 170
Cayer, D. M.
See Duffy, Maureen
Cayrol, Jean 1911- .... **CLC 11**
See also CA 89-92; DLB 83; EWL 3
Cela (y Trulock), Camilo Jose
See Cela, Camilo Jose
See also CWW 2
Cela, Camilo Jose 1916-2002 .... **CLC 4, 13, 59, 122; HLC 1; SSC 71**
See Cela (y Trulock), Camilo Jose
See also BEST 90:2; CA 21-24R; 206; CAAS 10; CANR 21, 32, 76; DAM MULT; DLBY 1989; EW 13; EWL 3; HW 1; MTCW 1, 2; RGSF 2; RGWL 2, 3
Celan, Paul .... **CLC 10, 19, 53, 82; PC 10**
See Antschel, Paul
See also CDWLB 2; DLB 69; EWL 3; RGWL 2, 3
Celine, Louis-Ferdinand .. **CLC 1, 3, 4, 7, 9, 15, 47, 124**
See Destouches, Louis-Ferdinand
See also DLB 72; EW 11; EWL 3; GFL 1789 to the Present; RGWL 2, 3
Cellini, Benvenuto 1500-1571 .... **LC 7**
Cendrars, Blaise .... **CLC 18, 106**
See Sauser-Hall, Frederic
See also DLB 258; EWL 3; GFL 1789 to the Present; RGWL 2, 3; WP
Centlivre, Susanna 1669(?)-1723 .... **LC 65**
See also DLB 84; RGEL 2

Cernuda (y Bidon), Luis 1902-1963 . **CLC 54**
See also CA 131; 89-92; DAM POET; DLB 134; EWL 3; GLL 1; HW 1; RGWL 2, 3
Cervantes, Lorna Dee 1954- ..... **HLCS 1; PC 35**
See also CA 131; CANR 80; CWP; DLB 82; EXPP; HW 1; LLW 1
Cervantes (Saavedra), Miguel de
1547-1616 .... **HLCS 1; LC 6, 23, 93; SSC 12; WLC**
See also BYA 1, 14; DA; DAB; DAC; DAM MST, NOV; EW 2; LAIT 1; LATS 1; LMFS 1; NFS 8; RGSF 2; RGWL 2, 3; TWA
Cesaire, Aime (Fernand) 1913- .... **BLC 1; CLC 19, 32, 112; DC 22; PC 25**
See also BW 2, 3; CA 65-68; CANR 24, 43, 81; CWW 2; DA3; DAM MULT, POET; EWL 3; GFL 1789 to the Present; MTCW 1, 2; WP
Chabon, Michael 1963- ... **CLC 55, 149; SSC 59**
See also AAYA 45; AMWS 11; CA 139; CANR 57, 96, 127; DLB 278; SATA 145
Chabrol, Claude 1930- .... **CLC 16**
See also CA 110
Chairil Anwar
See Anwar, Chairil
See also EWL 3
Challans, Mary 1905-1983
See Renault, Mary
See also CA 81-84; 111; CANR 74; DA3; MTCW 2; SATA 23; SATA-Obit 36; TEA
Challis, George
See Faust, Frederick (Schiller)
See also TCWW 2
Chambers, Aidan 1934- .... **CLC 35**
See also AAYA 27; CA 25-28R; CANR 12, 31, 58, 116; JRDA; MAICYA 1, 2; SAAS 12; SATA 1, 69, 108; WYA; YAW
Chambers, James 1948-
See Cliff, Jimmy
See also CA 124
Chambers, Jessie
See Lawrence, D(avid) H(erbert Richards)
See also GLL 1
Chambers, Robert W(illiam)
1865-1933 .... **TCLC 41**
See also CA 165; DLB 202; HGG; SATA 107; SUFW 1
Chambers, (David) Whittaker
1901-1961 .... **TCLC 129**
See also CA 89-92
Chamisso, Adelbert von
1781-1838 .... **NCLC 82**
See also DLB 90; RGWL 2, 3; SUFW 1
Chance, James T.
See Carpenter, John (Howard)
Chance, John T.
See Carpenter, John (Howard)
Chandler, Raymond (Thornton)
1888-1959 .... **SSC 23; TCLC 1, 7**
See also AAYA 25; AMWC 2; AMWS 4; BPFB 1; CA 104; 129; CANR 60, 107; CDALB 1929-1941; CMW 4; DA3; DLB 226, 253; DLBD 6; EWL 3; MSW; MTCW 1, 2; NFS 17; RGAL 4; TUS
Chang, Diana 1934- .... **AAL**
See also CWP; EXPP
Chang, Eileen 1921-1995 .... **AAL; SSC 28**
See Chang Ai-Ling; Zhang Ailing
See also CA 166
Chang, Jung 1952- .... **CLC 71**
See also CA 142
Chang Ai-Ling
See Chang, Eileen
See also EWL 3

Channing, William Ellery
1780-1842 .... **NCLC 17**
See also DLB 1, 59, 235; RGAL 4
Chao, Patricia 1955- .... **CLC 119**
See also CA 163
Chaplin, Charles Spencer
1889-1977 .... **CLC 16**
See Chaplin, Charlie
See also CA 81-84; 73-76
Chaplin, Charlie
See Chaplin, Charles Spencer
See also DLB 44
Chapman, George 1559(?)-1634 . **DC 19; LC 22**
See also BRW 1; DAM DRAM; DLB 62, 121; LMFS 1; RGEL 2
Chapman, Graham 1941-1989 .... **CLC 21**
See Monty Python
See also CA 116; 129; CANR 35, 95
Chapman, John Jay 1862-1933 .... **TCLC 7**
See also CA 104; 191
Chapman, Lee
See Bradley, Marion Zimmer
See also GLL 1
Chapman, Walker
See Silverberg, Robert
Chappell, Fred (Davis) 1936- .... **CLC 40, 78, 162**
See also CA 5-8R, 198; CAAE 198; CAAS 4; CANR 8, 33, 67, 110; CN 7; CP 7; CSW; DLB 6, 105; HGG
Char, Rene(-Emile) 1907-1988 .... **CLC 9, 11, 14, 55; PC 56**
See also CA 13-16R; 124; CANR 32; DAM POET; DLB 258; EWL 3; GFL 1789 to the Present; MTCW 1, 2; RGWL 2, 3
Charby, Jay
See Ellison, Harlan (Jay)
Chardin, Pierre Teilhard de
See Teilhard de Chardin, (Marie Joseph) Pierre
Chariton fl. 1st cent. (?)- .... **CMLC 49**
Charlemagne 742-814 .... **CMLC 37**
Charles I 1600-1649 .... **LC 13**
Charriere, Isabelle de 1740-1805 .. **NCLC 66**
Chartier, Alain c. 1392-1430 .... **LC 94**
See also DLB 208
Chartier, Emile-Auguste
See Alain
Charyn, Jerome 1937- .... **CLC 5, 8, 18**
See also CA 5-8R; CAAS 1; CANR 7, 61, 101; CMW 4; CN 7; DLBY 1983; MTCW 1
Chase, Adam
See Marlowe, Stephen
Chase, Mary (Coyle) 1907-1981 .... **DC 1**
See also CA 77-80; 105; CAD; CWD; DFS 11; DLB 228; SATA 17; SATA-Obit 29
Chase, Mary Ellen 1887-1973 .... **CLC 2; TCLC 124**
See also CA 13-16; 41-44R; CAP 1; SATA 10
Chase, Nicholas
See Hyde, Anthony
See also CCA 1
Chateaubriand, Francois Rene de
1768-1848 .... **NCLC 3, 134**
See also DLB 119; EW 5; GFL 1789 to the Present; RGWL 2, 3; TWA
Chatterje, Sarat Chandra 1876-1936(?)
See Chatterji, Saratchandra
See also CA 109
Chatterji, Bankim Chandra
1838-1894 .... **NCLC 19**
Chatterji, Saratchandra .... **TCLC 13**
See Chatterje, Sarat Chandra
See also CA 186; EWL 3
Chatterton, Thomas 1752-1770 .... **LC 3, 54**
See also DAM POET; DLB 109; RGEL 2

Chatwin, (Charles) Bruce
1940-1989 .... **CLC 28, 57, 59**
See also AAYA 4; BEST 90:1; BRWS 4;
CA 85-88; 127; CPW; DAM POP; DLB
194, 204; EWL 3

Chaucer, Daniel
See Ford, Ford Madox
See also RHW

Chaucer, Geoffrey 1340(?)-1400 .. **LC 17, 56;
PC 19; WLCS**
See also BRW 1; BRWC 1; BRWR 2; CDBLB Before 1660; DA; DA3; DAB;
DAC; DAM MST, POET; DLB 146;
LAIT 1; PAB; PFS 14; RGEL 2; TEA;
WLIT 3; WP

Chavez, Denise (Elia) 1948- .... **HLC 1**
See also CA 131; CANR 56, 81; DAM
MULT; DLB 122; FW; HW 1, 2; LLW 1;
MTCW 2

Chaviaras, Strates 1935-
See Haviaras, Stratis
See also CA 105

Chayefsky, Paddy .... **CLC 23**
See Chayefsky, Sidney
See also CAD; DLB 7, 44; DLBY 1981;
RGAL 4

Chayefsky, Sidney 1923-1981
See Chayefsky, Paddy
See also CA 9-12R; 104; CANR 18; DAM
DRAM

Chedid, Andree 1920- .... **CLC 47**
See also CA 145; CANR 95; EWL 3

Cheever, John 1912-1982 ..... **CLC 3, 7, 8, 11,
15, 25, 64; SSC 1, 38, 57; WLC**
See also AMWS 1; BPFB 1; CA 5-8R; 106;
CABS 1; CANR 5, 27, 76; CDALB 1941-
1968; CPW; DA; DA3; DAB; DAC;
DAM MST, NOV, POP; DLB 2, 102, 227;
DLBY 1980, 1982; EWL 3; EXPS; INT
CANR-5; MTCW 1, 2; RGAL 4; RGSF
2; SSFS 2, 14; TUS

Cheever, Susan 1943- .... **CLC 18, 48**
See also CA 103; CANR 27, 51, 92; DLBY
1982; INT CANR-27

Chekhonte, Antosha
See Chekhov, Anton (Pavlovich)

Chekhov, Anton (Pavlovich)
1860-1904 ...... **DC 9; SSC 2, 28, 41, 51;
TCLC 3, 10, 31, 55, 96; WLC**
See also BYA 14; CA 104; 124; DA; DA3;
DAB; DAC; DAM DRAM, MST; DFS 1,
5, 10, 12; DLB 277; EW 7; EWL 3;
EXPS; LAIT 3; LATS 1; RGSF 2; RGWL
2, 3; SATA 90; SSFS 5, 13, 14; TWA

Cheney, Lynne V. 1941- .... **CLC 70**
See also CA 89-92; CANR 58, 117

Chernyshevsky, Nikolai Gavrilovich
See Chernyshevsky, Nikolay Gavrilovich
See also DLB 238

Chernyshevsky, Nikolay Gavrilovich
1828-1889 .... **NCLC 1**
See Chernyshevsky, Nikolai Gavrilovich

Cherry, Carolyn Janice 1942-
See Cherryh, C. J.
See also CA 65-68; CANR 10

Cherryh, C. J. .... **CLC 35**
See Cherry, Carolyn Janice
See also AAYA 24; BPFB 1; DLBY 1980;
FANT; SATA 93; SCFW 2; SFW 4; YAW

Chesnutt, Charles W(addell)
1858-1932 .... **BLC 1; SSC 7, 54; TCLC
5, 39**
See also AFAW 1, 2; BW 1, 3; CA 106;
125; CANR 76; DAM MULT; DLB 12,
50, 78; EWL 3; MTCW 1, 2; RGAL 4;
RGSF 2; SSFS 11

Chester, Alfred 1929(?)-1971 .... **CLC 49**
See also CA 196; 33-36R; DLB 130

Chesterton, G(ilbert) K(eith)
1874-1936 . **PC 28; SSC 1, 46; TCLC 1,
6, 64**
See also BRW 6; CA 104; 132; CANR 73;
CDBLB 1914-1945; CMW 4; DAM NOV,
POET; DLB 10, 19, 34, 70, 98, 149, 178;
EWL 3; FANT; MSW; MTCW 1, 2;
RGEL 2; RGSF 2; SATA 27; SUFW 1

Chiang, Pin-chin 1904-1986
See Ding Ling
See also CA 118

Chief Joseph 1840-1904 .... **NNAL**
See also CA 152; DA3; DAM MULT

Chief Seattle 1786(?)-1866 .... **NNAL**
See also DA3; DAM MULT

Ch'ien, Chung-shu 1910-1998 .... **CLC 22**
See Qian Zhongshu
See also CA 130; CANR 73; MTCW 1, 2

Chikamatsu Monzaemon 1653-1724 ... **LC 66**
See also RGWL 2, 3

Child, L. Maria
See Child, Lydia Maria

Child, Lydia Maria 1802-1880 .. **NCLC 6, 73**
See also DLB 1, 74, 243; RGAL 4; SATA
67

Child, Mrs.
See Child, Lydia Maria

Child, Philip 1898-1978 .... **CLC 19, 68**
See also CA 13-14; CAP 1; DLB 68; RHW;
SATA 47

Childers, (Robert) Erskine
1870-1922 .... **TCLC 65**
See also CA 113; 153; DLB 70

Childress, Alice 1920-1994 .... **BLC 1; CLC 12,
15, 86, 96; DC 4; TCLC 116**
See also AAYA 8; BW 2, 3; BYA 2; CA 45-
48; 146; CAD; CANR 3, 27, 50, 74; CLR
14; CWD; DA3; DAM DRAM, MULT,
NOV; DFS 2, 8, 14; DLB 7, 38, 249;
JRDA; LAIT 5; MAICYA 1, 2; MAICYAS 1; MTCW 1, 2; RGAL 4; SATA 7,
48, 81; TUS; WYA; YAW

Chin, Frank (Chew, Jr.) 1940- ...... **CLC 135;
DC 7**
See also CA 33-36R; CANR 71; CD 5;
DAM MULT; DLB 206; LAIT 5; RGAL
4

Chin, Marilyn (Mei Ling) 1955- .... **PC 40**
See also CA 129; CANR 70, 113; CWP

Chislett, (Margaret) Anne 1943- .... **CLC 34**
See also CA 151

Chitty, Thomas Willes 1926- .... **CLC 11**
See Hinde, Thomas
See also CA 5-8R; CANR 3, 10, 132; CN 7

Chivers, Thomas Holley
1809-1858 .... **NCLC 49**
See also DLB 3, 248; RGAL 4

Choi, Susan 1969- .... **CLC 119**

Chomette, Rene Lucien 1898-1981
See Clair, Rene
See also CA 103

Chomsky, (Avram) Noam 1928- ..... **CLC 132**
See also CA 17-20R; CANR 28, 62, 110;
DA3; DLB 246; MTCW 1, 2

Chona, Maria 1845(?)-1936 .... **NNAL**
See also CA 144

Chopin, Kate .... **SSC 8, 68; TCLC 127;
WLCS**
See Chopin, Katherine
See also AAYA 33; AMWR 2; AMWS 1;
BYA 11, 15; CDALB 1865-1917; DA;
DAB; DLB 12, 78; EXPN; EXPS; FW;
LAIT 3; MAWW; NFS 3; RGAL 4; RGSF
2; SSFS 17; TUS

Chopin, Katherine 1851-1904
See Chopin, Kate
See also CA 104; 122; DA3; DAC; DAM
MST, NOV

Chretien de Troyes c. 12th cent. - . **CMLC 10**
See also DLB 208; EW 1; RGWL 2, 3;
TWA

Christie
See Ichikawa, Kon

Christie, Agatha (Mary Clarissa)
1890-1976 .. **CLC 1, 6, 8, 12, 39, 48, 110**
See also AAYA 9; AITN 1, 2; BPFB 1;
BRWS 2; CA 17-20R; 61-64; CANR 10,
37, 108; CBD; CDBLB 1914-1945; CMW
4; CPW; CWD; DA3; DAB; DAC; DAM
NOV; DFS 2; DLB 13, 77, 245; MSW;
MTCW 1, 2; NFS 8; RGEL 2; RHW;
SATA 36; TEA; YAW

Christie, Philippa .... **CLC 21**
See Pearce, Philippa
See also BYA 5; CANR 109; CLR 9; DLB
161; MAICYA 1; SATA 1, 67, 129

Christine de Pizan 1365(?)-1431(?) .... **LC 9**
See also DLB 208; RGWL 2, 3

Chuang Tzu c. 369B.C.-c.
286B.C. .... **CMLC 57**

Chubb, Elmer
See Masters, Edgar Lee

Chulkov, Mikhail Dmitrievich
1743-1792 .... **LC 2**
See also DLB 150

Churchill, Caryl 1938- .... **CLC 31, 55, 157;
DC 5**
See Churchill, Chick
See also BRWS 4; CA 102; CANR 22, 46,
108; CBD; CWD; DFS 12, 16; DLB 13;
EWL 3; FW; MTCW 1; RGEL 2

Churchill, Charles 1731-1764 .... **LC 3**
See also DLB 109; RGEL 2

Churchill, Chick 1938-
See Churchill, Caryl
See also CD 5

Churchill, Sir Winston (Leonard Spencer)
1874-1965 .... **TCLC 113**
See also BRW 6; CA 97-100; CDBLB
1890-1914; DA3; DLB 100; DLBD 16;
LAIT 4; MTCW 1, 2

Chute, Carolyn 1947- .... **CLC 39**
See also CA 123

Ciardi, John (Anthony) 1916-1986 . **CLC 10,
40, 44, 129**
See also CA 5-8R; 118; CAAS 2; CANR 5,
33; CLR 19; CWRI 5; DAM POET; DLB
5; DLBY 1986; INT CANR-5; MAICYA
1, 2; MTCW 1, 2; RGAL 4; SAAS 26;
SATA 1, 65; SATA-Obit 46

Cibber, Colley 1671-1757 .... **LC 66**
See also DLB 84; RGEL 2

Cicero, Marcus Tullius
106B.C.-43B.C. .... **CMLC 3**
See also AW 1; CDWLB 1; DLB 211;
RGWL 2, 3

Cimino, Michael 1943- .... **CLC 16**
See also CA 105

Cioran, E(mil) M. 1911-1995 .... **CLC 64**
See also CA 25-28R; 149; CANR 91; DLB
220; EWL 3

Cisneros, Sandra 1954- .. **CLC 69, 118; HLC
1; PC 52; SSC 32**
See also AAYA 9, 53; AMWS 7; CA 131;
CANR 64, 118; CWP; DA3; DAM MULT;
DLB 122, 152; EWL 3; EXPN; FW; HW
1, 2; LAIT 5; LATS 1; LLW 1; MAICYA
2; MTCW 2; NFS 2; PFS 19; RGAL 4;
RGSF 2; SSFS 3, 13; WLIT 1; YAW

Cixous, Helene 1937- .... **CLC 92**
See also CA 126; CANR 55, 123; CWW 2;
DLB 83, 242; EWL 3; FW; GLL 2;
MTCW 1, 2; TWA

Clair, Rene .... **CLC 20**
See Chomette, Rene Lucien

Clampitt, Amy 1920-1994 .... **CLC 32; PC 19**
See also AMWS 9; CA 110; 146; CANR 29, 79; DLB 105

Clancy, Thomas L., Jr. 1947-
See Clancy, Tom
See also CA 125; 131; CANR 62, 105; DA3; INT CA-131; MTCW 1, 2

Clancy, Tom .... **CLC 45, 112**
See Clancy, Thomas L., Jr.
See also AAYA 9, 51; BEST 89:1, 90:1; BPFB 1; BYA 10, 11; CMW 4; CPW; DAM NOV, POP; DLB 227

Clare, John 1793-1864 .. **NCLC 9, 86; PC 23**
See also DAB; DAM POET; DLB 55, 96; RGEL 2

Clarin
See Alas (y Urena), Leopoldo (Enrique Garcia)

Clark, Al C.
See Goines, Donald

Clark, (Robert) Brian 1932- .... **CLC 29**
See also CA 41-44R; CANR 67; CBD; CD 5

Clark, Curt
See Westlake, Donald E(dwin)

Clark, Eleanor 1913-1996 .... **CLC 5, 19**
See also CA 9-12R; 151; CANR 41; CN 7; DLB 6

Clark, J. P.
See Clark Bekederemo, J(ohnson) P(epper)
See also CDWLB 3; DLB 117

Clark, John Pepper
See Clark Bekederemo, J(ohnson) P(epper)
See also AFW; CD 5; CP 7; RGEL 2

Clark, Kenneth (Mackenzie)
1903-1983 .... **TCLC 147**
See also CA 93-96; 109; CANR 36; MTCW 1, 2

Clark, M. R.
See Clark, Mavis Thorpe

Clark, Mavis Thorpe 1909-1999 ...... **CLC 12**
See also CA 57-60; CANR 8, 37, 107; CLR 30; CWRI 5; MAICYA 1, 2; SAAS 5; SATA 8, 74

Clark, Walter Van Tilburg
1909-1971 .... **CLC 28**
See also CA 9-12R; 33-36R; CANR 63, 113; DLB 9, 206; LAIT 2; RGAL 4; SATA 8

Clark Bekederemo, J(ohnson) P(epper)
1935- .... **BLC 1; CLC 38; DC 5**
See Clark, J. P.; Clark, John Pepper
See also BW 1; CA 65-68; CANR 16, 72; DAM DRAM, MULT; DFS 13; EWL 3; MTCW 1

Clarke, Arthur C(harles) 1917- .... **CLC 1, 4, 13, 18, 35, 136; SSC 3**
See also AAYA 4, 33; BPFB 1; BYA 13; CA 1-4R; CANR 2, 28, 55, 74; CN 7; CPW; DA3; DAM POP; DLB 261; JRDA; LAIT 5; MAICYA 1, 2; MTCW 1, 2; SATA 13, 70, 115; SCFW; SFW 4; SSFS 4, 18; YAW

Clarke, Austin 1896-1974 .... **CLC 6, 9**
See also CA 29-32; 49-52; CAP 2; DAM POET; DLB 10, 20; EWL 3; RGEL 2

Clarke, Austin C(hesterfield) 1934- .. **BLC 1; CLC 8, 53; SSC 45**
See also BW 1; CA 25-28R; CAAS 16; CANR 14, 32, 68; CN 7; DAC; DAM MULT; DLB 53, 125; DNFS 2; RGSF 2

Clarke, Gillian 1937- .... **CLC 61**
See also CA 106; CP 7; CWP; DLB 40

Clarke, Marcus (Andrew Hislop)
1846-1881 .... **NCLC 19**
See also DLB 230; RGEL 2; RGSF 2

Clarke, Shirley 1925-1997 .... **CLC 16**
See also CA 189

Clash, The
See Headon, (Nicky) Topper; Jones, Mick; Simonon, Paul; Strummer, Joe

Claudel, Paul (Louis Charles Marie)
1868-1955 .... **TCLC 2, 10**
See also CA 104; 165; DLB 192, 258; EW 8; EWL 3; GFL 1789 to the Present; RGWL 2, 3; TWA

Claudian 370(?)-404(?) .... **CMLC 46**
See also RGWL 2, 3

Claudius, Matthias 1740-1815 .... **NCLC 75**
See also DLB 97

Clavell, James (duMaresq)
1925-1994 .... **CLC 6, 25, 87**
See also BPFB 1; CA 25-28R; 146; CANR 26, 48; CPW; DA3; DAM NOV, POP; MTCW 1, 2; NFS 10; RHW

Clayman, Gregory .... **CLC 65**

Cleaver, (Leroy) Eldridge
1935-1998 .... **BLC 1; CLC 30, 119**
See also BW 1, 3; CA 21-24R; 167; CANR 16, 75; DA3; DAM MULT; MTCW 2; YAW

Cleese, John (Marwood) 1939- .... **CLC 21**
See Monty Python
See also CA 112; 116; CANR 35; MTCW 1

Cleishbotham, Jebediah
See Scott, Sir Walter

Cleland, John 1710-1789 .... **LC 2, 48**
See also DLB 39; RGEL 2

Clemens, Samuel Langhorne 1835-1910
See Twain, Mark
See also CA 104; 135; CDALB 1865-1917; DA; DA3; DAB; DAC; DAM MST, NOV; DLB 12, 23, 64, 74, 186, 189; JRDA; LMFS 1; MAICYA 1, 2; NCFS 4; SATA 100; SSFS 16; YABC 2

Clement of Alexandria
150(?)-215(?) .... **CMLC 41**

Cleophil
See Congreve, William

Clerihew, E.
See Bentley, E(dmund) C(lerihew)

Clerk, N. W.
See Lewis, C(live) S(taples)

Cliff, Jimmy .... **CLC 21**
See Chambers, James
See also CA 193

Cliff, Michelle 1946- .... **BLCS; CLC 120**
See also BW 2; CA 116; CANR 39, 72; CDWLB 3; DLB 157; FW; GLL 2

Clifford, Lady Anne 1590-1676 .... **LC 76**
See also DLB 151

Clifton, (Thelma) Lucille 1936- .... **BLC 1; CLC 19, 66, 162; PC 17**
See also AFAW 2; BW 2, 3; CA 49-52; CANR 2, 24, 42, 76, 97; CLR 5; CP 7; CSW; CWP; CWRI 5; DA3; DAM MULT, POET; DLB 5, 41; EXPP; MAICYA 1, 2; MTCW 1, 2; PFS 1, 14; SATA 20, 69, 128; WP

Clinton, Dirk
See Silverberg, Robert

Clough, Arthur Hugh 1819-1861 ... **NCLC 27**
See also BRW 5; DLB 32; RGEL 2

Clutha, Janet Paterson Frame 1924-2004
See Frame, Janet
See also CA 1-4R; CANR 2, 36, 76; MTCW 1, 2; SATA 119

Clyne, Terence
See Blatty, William Peter

Cobalt, Martin
See Mayne, William (James Carter)

Cobb, Irvin S(hrewsbury)
1876-1944 .... **TCLC 77**
See also CA 175; DLB 11, 25, 86

Cobbett, William 1763-1835 .... **NCLC 49**
See also DLB 43, 107, 158; RGEL 2

Coburn, D(onald) L(ee) 1938- .... **CLC 10**
See also CA 89-92

Cocteau, Jean (Maurice Eugene Clement)
1889-1963 ...... **CLC 1, 8, 15, 16, 43; DC 17; TCLC 119; WLC**
See also CA 25-28; CANR 40; CAP 2; DA; DA3; DAB; DAC; DAM DRAM, MST, NOV; DLB 65, 258; EW 10; EWL 3; GFL 1789 to the Present; MTCW 1, 2; RGWL 2, 3; TWA

Codrescu, Andrei 1946- .... **CLC 46, 121**
See also CA 33-36R; CAAS 19; CANR 13, 34, 53, 76, 125; DA3; DAM POET; MTCW 2

Coe, Max
See Bourne, Randolph S(illiman)

Coe, Tucker
See Westlake, Donald E(dwin)

Coen, Ethan 1958- .... **CLC 108**
See also AAYA 54; CA 126; CANR 85

Coen, Joel 1955- .... **CLC 108**
See also AAYA 54; CA 126; CANR 119

The Coen Brothers
See Coen, Ethan; Coen, Joel

Coetzee, J(ohn) M(axwell) 1940- ..... **CLC 23, 33, 66, 117, 161, 162**
See also AAYA 37; AFW; BRWS 6; CA 77-80; CANR 41, 54, 74, 114; CN 7; DA3; DAM NOV; DLB 225; EWL 3; LMFS 2; MTCW 1, 2; WLIT 2; WWE 1

Coffey, Brian
See Koontz, Dean R(ay)

Coffin, Robert P(eter) Tristram
1892-1955 .... **TCLC 95**
See also CA 123; 169; DLB 45

Cohan, George M(ichael)
1878-1942 .... **TCLC 60**
See also CA 157; DLB 249; RGAL 4

Cohen, Arthur A(llen) 1928-1986 ...... **CLC 7, 31**
See also CA 1-4R; 120; CANR 1, 17, 42; DLB 28

Cohen, Leonard (Norman) 1934- ...... **CLC 3, 38**
See also CA 21-24R; CANR 14, 69; CN 7; CP 7; DAC; DAM MST; DLB 53; EWL 3; MTCW 1

Cohen, Matt(hew) 1942-1999 .... **CLC 19**
See also CA 61-64; 187; CAAS 18; CANR 40; CN 7; DAC; DLB 53

Cohen-Solal, Annie 19(?)- .... **CLC 50**

Colegate, Isabel 1931- .... **CLC 36**
See also CA 17-20R; CANR 8, 22, 74; CN 7; DLB 14, 231; INT CANR-22; MTCW 1

Coleman, Emmett
See Reed, Ishmael

Coleridge, Hartley 1796-1849 .... **NCLC 90**
See also DLB 96

Coleridge, M. E.
See Coleridge, Mary E(lizabeth)

Coleridge, Mary E(lizabeth)
1861-1907 .... **TCLC 73**
See also CA 116; 166; DLB 19, 98

Coleridge, Samuel Taylor
1772-1834 ...... **NCLC 9, 54, 99, 111; PC 11, 39; WLC**
See also BRW 4; BRWR 2; BYA 4; CD-BLB 1789-1832; DA; DA3; DAB; DAC; DAM MST, POET; DLB 93, 107; EXPP; LATS 1; LMFS 1; PAB; PFS 4, 5; RGEL 2; TEA; WLIT 3; WP

Coleridge, Sara 1802-1852 .... **NCLC 31**
See also DLB 199

Coles, Don 1928- .... **CLC 46**
See also CA 115; CANR 38; CP 7

Coles, Robert (Martin) 1929- .... **CLC 108**
See also CA 45-48; CANR 3, 32, 66, 70; INT CANR-32; SATA 23

Colette, (Sidonie-Gabrielle)
1873-1954 .... **SSC 10; TCLC 1, 5, 16**
See Willy, Colette
See also CA 104; 131; DA3; DAM NOV; DLB 65; EW 9; EWL 3; GFL 1789 to the Present; MTCW 1, 2; RGWL 2, 3; TWA

Collett, (Jacobine) Camilla (Wergeland)
1813-1895 .... **NCLC 22**

Collier, Christopher 1930- .... **CLC 30**
See also AAYA 13; BYA 2; CA 33-36R; CANR 13, 33, 102; JRDA; MAICYA 1, 2; SATA 16, 70; WYA; YAW 1

Collier, James Lincoln 1928- .... **CLC 30**
See also AAYA 13; BYA 2; CA 9-12R; CANR 4, 33, 60, 102; CLR 3; DAM POP; JRDA; MAICYA 1, 2; SAAS 21; SATA 8, 70; WYA; YAW 1

Collier, Jeremy 1650-1726 .... **LC 6**

Collier, John 1901-1980 . **SSC 19; TCLC 127**
See also CA 65-68; 97-100; CANR 10; DLB 77, 255; FANT; SUFW 1

Collier, Mary 1690-1762 .... **LC 86**
See also DLB 95

Collingwood, R(obin) G(eorge)
1889(?)-1943 .... **TCLC 67**
See also CA 117; 155; DLB 262

Collins, Hunt
See Hunter, Evan

Collins, Linda 1931- .... **CLC 44**
See also CA 125

Collins, Tom
See Furphy, Joseph
See also RGEL 2

Collins, (William) Wilkie
1824-1889 .... **NCLC 1, 18, 93**
See also BRWS 6; CDBLB 1832-1890; CMW 4; DLB 18, 70, 159; MSW; RGEL 2; RGSF 2; SUFW 1; WLIT 4

Collins, William 1721-1759 .... **LC 4, 40**
See also BRW 3; DAM POET; DLB 109; RGEL 2

Collodi, Carlo .... **NCLC 54**
See Lorenzini, Carlo
See also CLR 5; WCH

Colman, George
See Glassco, John

Colman, George, the Elder
1732-1794 .... **LC 98**
See also RGEL 2

Colonna, Vittoria 1492-1547 .... **LC 71**
See also RGWL 2, 3

Colt, Winchester Remington
See Hubbard, L(afayette) Ron(ald)

Colter, Cyrus J. 1910-2002 .... **CLC 58**
See also BW 1; CA 65-68; 205; CANR 10, 66; CN 7; DLB 33

Colton, James
See Hansen, Joseph
See also GLL 1

Colum, Padraic 1881-1972 .... **CLC 28**
See also BYA 4; CA 73-76; 33-36R; CANR 35; CLR 36; CWRI 5; DLB 19; MAICYA 1, 2; MTCW 1; RGEL 2; SATA 15; WCH

Colvin, James
See Moorcock, Michael (John)

Colwin, Laurie (E.) 1944-1992 .... **CLC 5, 13, 23, 84**
See also CA 89-92; 139; CANR 20, 46; DLB 218; DLBY 1980; MTCW 1

Comfort, Alex(ander) 1920-2000 .... **CLC 7**
See also CA 1-4R; 190; CANR 1, 45; CP 7; DAM POP; MTCW 1

Comfort, Montgomery
See Campbell, (John) Ramsey

Compton-Burnett, I(vy)
1892(?)-1969 .... **CLC 1, 3, 10, 15, 34**
See also BRW 7; CA 1-4R; 25-28R; CANR 4; DAM NOV; DLB 36; EWL 3; MTCW 1; RGEL 2

Comstock, Anthony 1844-1915 ...... **TCLC 13**
See also CA 110; 169

Comte, Auguste 1798-1857 .... **NCLC 54**

Conan Doyle, Arthur
See Doyle, Sir Arthur Conan
See also BPFB 1; BYA 4, 5, 11

Conde (Abellan), Carmen
1901-1996 .... **HLCS 1**
See also CA 177; CWW 2; DLB 108; EWL 3; HW 2

Conde, Maryse 1937- ..... **BLCS; CLC 52, 92**
See also BW 2, 3; CA 110, 190; CAAE 190; CANR 30, 53, 76; CWW 2; DAM MULT; EWL 3; MTCW 1

Condillac, Etienne Bonnot de
1714-1780 .... **LC 26**

Condon, Richard (Thomas)
1915-1996 .... **CLC 4, 6, 8, 10, 45, 100**
See also BEST 90:3; BPFB 1; CA 1-4R; 151; CAAS 1; CANR 2, 23; CMW 4; CN 7; DAM NOV; INT CANR-23; MTCW 1, 2

Confucius 551B.C.-479B.C. .... **CMLC 19, 65; WLCS**
See also DA; DA3; DAB; DAC; DAM MST

Congreve, William 1670-1729 ... **DC 2; LC 5, 21; WLC**
See also BRW 2; CDBLB 1660-1789; DA; DAB; DAC; DAM DRAM, MST, POET; DFS 15; DLB 39, 84; RGEL 2; WLIT 3

Conley, Robert J(ackson) 1940- .... **NNAL**
See also CA 41-44R; CANR 15, 34, 45, 96; DAM MULT

Connell, Evan S(helby), Jr. 1924- . **CLC 4, 6, 45**
See also AAYA 7; CA 1-4R; CAAS 2; CANR 2, 39, 76, 97; CN 7; DAM NOV; DLB 2; DLBY 1981; MTCW 1, 2

Connelly, Marc(us Cook) 1890-1980 . **CLC 7**
See also CA 85-88; 102; CANR 30; DFS 12; DLB 7; DLBY 1980; RGAL 4; SATA-Obit 25

Connor, Ralph .... **TCLC 31**
See Gordon, Charles William
See also DLB 92; TCWW 2

Conrad, Joseph 1857-1924 ..... **SSC 9, 67, 69, 71; TCLC 1, 6, 13, 25, 43, 57; WLC**
See also AAYA 26; BPFB 1; BRW 6; BRWC 1; BRWR 1; BYA 2; CA 104; 131; CANR 60; CDBLB 1890-1914; DA; DA3; DAB; DAC; DAM MST, NOV; DLB 10, 34, 98, 156; EWL 3; EXPN; EXPS; LAIT 2; LATS 1; LMFS 1; MTCW 1, 2; NFS 2, 16; RGEL 2; RGSF 2; SATA 27; SSFS 1, 12; TEA; WLIT 4

Conrad, Robert Arnold
See Hart, Moss

Conroy, (Donald) Pat(rick) 1945- ... **CLC 30, 74**
See also AAYA 8, 52; AITN 1; BPFB 1; CA 85-88; CANR 24, 53, 129; CPW; CSW; DA3; DAM NOV, POP; DLB 6; LAIT 5; MTCW 1, 2

Constant, (de Rebecque), (Henri) Benjamin
1767-1830 .... **NCLC 6**
See also DLB 119; EW 4; GFL 1789 to the Present

Conway, Jill K(er) 1934- .... **CLC 152**
See also CA 130; CANR 94

Conybeare, Charles Augustus
See Eliot, T(homas) S(tearns)

Cook, Michael 1933-1994 .... **CLC 58**
See also CA 93-96; CANR 68; DLB 53

Cook, Robin 1940- .... **CLC 14**
See also AAYA 32; BEST 90:2; BPFB 1; CA 108; 111; CANR 41, 90, 109; CPW; DA3; DAM POP; HGG; INT CA-111

Cook, Roy
See Silverberg, Robert

Cooke, Elizabeth 1948- .... **CLC 55**
See also CA 129

Cooke, John Esten 1830-1886 .... **NCLC 5**
See also DLB 3, 248; RGAL 4

Cooke, John Estes
See Baum, L(yman) Frank

Cooke, M. E.
See Creasey, John

Cooke, Margaret
See Creasey, John

Cooke, Rose Terry 1827-1892 ...... **NCLC 110**
See also DLB 12, 74

Cook-Lynn, Elizabeth 1930- .... **CLC 93; NNAL**
See also CA 133; DAM MULT; DLB 175

Cooney, Ray .... **CLC 62**
See also CBD

Cooper, Douglas 1960- .... **CLC 86**

Cooper, Henry St. John
See Creasey, John

Cooper, J(oan) California (?)- .... **CLC 56**
See also AAYA 12; BW 1; CA 125; CANR 55; DAM MULT; DLB 212

Cooper, James Fenimore
1789-1851 .... **NCLC 1, 27, 54**
See also AAYA 22; AMW; BPFB 1; CDALB 1640-1865; DA3; DLB 3, 183, 250, 254; LAIT 1; NFS 9; RGAL 4; SATA 19; TUS; WCH

Cooper, Susan Fenimore
1813-1894 .... **NCLC 129**
See also ANW; DLB 239, 254

Coover, Robert (Lowell) 1932- ...... **CLC 3, 7, 15, 32, 46, 87, 161; SSC 15**
See also AMWS 5; BPFB 1; CA 45-48; CANR 3, 37, 58, 115; CN 7; DAM NOV; DLB 2, 227; DLBY 1981; EWL 3; MTCW 1, 2; RGAL 4; RGSF 2

Copeland, Stewart (Armstrong)
1952- .... **CLC 26**

Copernicus, Nicolaus 1473-1543 ...... **LC 45**

Coppard, A(lfred) E(dgar)
1878-1957 .... **SSC 21; TCLC 5**
See also BRWS 8; CA 114; 167; DLB 162; EWL 3; HGG; RGEL 2; RGSF 2; SUFW 1; YABC 1

Coppee, Francois 1842-1908 .... **TCLC 25**
See also CA 170; DLB 217

Coppola, Francis Ford 1939- ... **CLC 16, 126**
See also AAYA 39; CA 77-80; CANR 40, 78; DLB 44

Copway, George 1818-1869 .... **NNAL**
See also DAM MULT; DLB 175, 183

Corbiere, Tristan 1845-1875 .... **NCLC 43**
See also DLB 217; GFL 1789 to the Present

Corcoran, Barbara (Asenath)
1911- .... **CLC 17**
See also AAYA 14; CA 21-24R, 191; CAAE 191; CAAS 2; CANR 11, 28, 48; CLR 50; DLB 52; JRDA; MAICYA 2; MAICYAS 1; RHW; SAAS 20; SATA 3, 77; SATA-Essay 125

Cordelier, Maurice
See Giraudoux, Jean(-Hippolyte)

Corelli, Marie .... **TCLC 51**
See Mackay, Mary
See also DLB 34, 156; RGEL 2; SUFW 1

Corman, Cid .... **CLC 9**
See Corman, Sidney
See also CAAS 2; DLB 5, 193

Corman, Sidney 1924-2004
See Corman, Cid
See also CA 85-88; CANR 44; CP 7; DAM POET

Cormier, Robert (Edmund)
1925-2000 .... **CLC 12, 30**
See also AAYA 3, 19; BYA 1, 2, 6, 8, 9; CA 1-4R; CANR 5, 23, 76, 93; CDALB 1968-1988; CLR 12, 55; DA; DAB; DAC; DAM MST, NOV; DLB 52; EXPN; INT CANR-23; JRDA; LAIT 5; MAICYA 1, 2; MTCW 1, 2; NFS 2, 18; SATA 10, 45, 83; SATA-Obit 122; WYA; YAW

Corn, Alfred (DeWitt III) 1943- .... **CLC 33**
See also CA 179; CAAE 179; CAAS 25; CANR 44; CP 7; CSW; DLB 120, 282; DLBY 1980

Corneille, Pierre 1606-1684 ... **DC 21; LC 28**
See also DAB; DAM MST; DLB 268; EW 3; GFL Beginnings to 1789; RGWL 2, 3; TWA

Cornwell, David (John Moore)
1931- .... **CLC 9, 15**
See le Carre, John
See also CA 5-8R; CANR 13, 33, 59, 107; DA3; DAM POP; MTCW 1, 2

Cornwell, Patricia (Daniels) 1956- . **CLC 155**
See also AAYA 16; BPFB 1; CA 134; CANR 53; CMW 4; CPW; CSW; DAM POP; MSW; MTCW 1

Corso, (Nunzio) Gregory 1930-2001 . **CLC 1, 11; PC 33**
See also AMWS 12; BG 2; CA 5-8R; 193; CANR 41, 76; CP 7; DA3; DLB 5, 16, 237; LMFS 2; MTCW 1, 2; WP

Cortazar, Julio 1914-1984 ... **CLC 2, 3, 5, 10, 13, 15, 33, 34, 92; HLC 1; SSC 7**
See also BPFB 1; CA 21-24R; CANR 12, 32, 81; CDWLB 3; DA3; DAM MULT, NOV; DLB 113; EWL 3; EXPS; HW 1, 2; LAW; MTCW 1, 2; RGSF 2; RGWL 2, 3; SSFS 3; TWA; WLIT 1

Cortes, Hernan 1485-1547 .... **LC 31**

Corvinus, Jakob
See Raabe, Wilhelm (Karl)

Corwin, Cecil
See Kornbluth, C(yril) M.

Cosic, Dobrica 1921- .... **CLC 14**
See also CA 122; 138; CDWLB 4; CWW 2; DLB 181; EWL 3

Costain, Thomas B(ertram)
1885-1965 .... **CLC 30**
See also BYA 3; CA 5-8R; 25-28R; DLB 9; RHW

Costantini, Humberto 1924(?)-1987 . **CLC 49**
See also CA 131; 122; EWL 3; HW 1

Costello, Elvis 1954- .... **CLC 21**
See also CA 204

Costenoble, Philostene
See Ghelderode, Michel de

Cotes, Cecil V.
See Duncan, Sara Jeannette

Cotter, Joseph Seamon Sr.
1861-1949 .... **BLC 1; TCLC 28**
See also BW 1; CA 124; DAM MULT; DLB 50

Couch, Arthur Thomas Quiller
See Quiller-Couch, Sir Arthur (Thomas)

Coulton, James
See Hansen, Joseph

Couperus, Louis (Marie Anne)
1863-1923 .... **TCLC 15**
See also CA 115; EWL 3; RGWL 2, 3

Coupland, Douglas 1961- .... **CLC 85, 133**
See also AAYA 34; CA 142; CANR 57, 90; CCA 1; CPW; DAC; DAM POP

Court, Wesli
See Turco, Lewis (Putnam)

Courtenay, Bryce 1933- .... **CLC 59**
See also CA 138; CPW

Courtney, Robert
See Ellison, Harlan (Jay)

Cousteau, Jacques-Yves 1910-1997 .. **CLC 30**
See also CA 65-68; 159; CANR 15, 67; MTCW 1; SATA 38, 98

Coventry, Francis 1725-1754 .... **LC 46**

Coverdale, Miles c. 1487-1569 .... **LC 77**
See also DLB 167

Cowan, Peter (Walkinshaw)
1914-2002 .... **SSC 28**
See also CA 21-24R; CANR 9, 25, 50, 83; CN 7; DLB 260; RGSF 2

Coward, Noel (Peirce) 1899-1973 . **CLC 1, 9, 29, 51**
See also AITN 1; BRWS 2; CA 17-18; 41-44R; CANR 35; CAP 2; CDBLB 1914-1945; DA3; DAM DRAM; DFS 3, 6; DLB 10, 245; EWL 3; IDFW 3, 4; MTCW 1, 2; RGEL 2; TEA

Cowley, Abraham 1618-1667 .... **LC 43**
See also BRW 2; DLB 131, 151; PAB; RGEL 2

Cowley, Malcolm 1898-1989 .... **CLC 39**
See also AMWS 2; CA 5-8R; 128; CANR 3, 55; DLB 4, 48; DLBY 1981, 1989; EWL 3; MTCW 1, 2

Cowper, William 1731-1800 ..... **NCLC 8, 94; PC 40**
See also BRW 3; DA3; DAM POET; DLB 104, 109; RGEL 2

Cox, William Trevor 1928-
See Trevor, William
See also CA 9-12R; CANR 4, 37, 55, 76, 102; DAM NOV; INT CANR-37; MTCW 1, 2; TEA

Coyne, P. J.
See Masters, Hilary

Cozzens, James Gould 1903-1978 . **CLC 1, 4, 11, 92**
See also AMW; BPFB 1; CA 9-12R; 81-84; CANR 19; CDALB 1941-1968; DLB 9, 294; DLBD 2; DLBY 1984, 1997; EWL 3; MTCW 1, 2; RGAL 4

Crabbe, George 1754-1832 .... **NCLC 26, 121**
See also BRW 3; DLB 93; RGEL 2

Crace, Jim 1946- .... **CLC 157; SSC 61**
See also CA 128; 135; CANR 55, 70, 123; CN 7; DLB 231; INT CA-135

Craddock, Charles Egbert
See Murfree, Mary Noailles

Craig, A. A.
See Anderson, Poul (William)

Craik, Mrs.
See Craik, Dinah Maria (Mulock)
See also RGEL 2

Craik, Dinah Maria (Mulock)
1826-1887 .... **NCLC 38**
See Craik, Mrs.; Mulock, Dinah Maria
See also DLB 35, 163; MAICYA 1, 2; SATA 34

Cram, Ralph Adams 1863-1942 ..... **TCLC 45**
See also CA 160

Cranch, Christopher Pearse
1813-1892 .... **NCLC 115**
See also DLB 1, 42, 243

Crane, (Harold) Hart 1899-1932 .... **PC 3; TCLC 2, 5, 80; WLC**
See also AMW; AMWR 2; CA 104; 127; CDALB 1917-1929; DA; DA3; DAB; DAC; DAM MST, POET; DLB 4, 48; EWL 3; MTCW 1, 2; RGAL 4; TUS

Crane, R(onald) S(almon)
1886-1967 .... **CLC 27**
See also CA 85-88; DLB 63

Crane, Stephen (Townley)
1871-1900 .... **SSC 7, 56, 70; TCLC 11, 17, 32; WLC**
See also AAYA 21; AMW; AMWC 1; BPFB 1; BYA 3; CA 109; 140; CANR 84; CDALB 1865-1917; DA; DA3; DAB; DAC; DAM MST, NOV, POET; DLB 12, 54, 78; EXPN; EXPS; LAIT 2; LMFS 2; NFS 4; PFS 9; RGAL 4; RGSF 2; SSFS 4; TUS; WYA; YABC 2

Cranmer, Thomas 1489-1556 .... **LC 95**
See also DLB 132, 213

Cranshaw, Stanley
See Fisher, Dorothy (Frances) Canfield

Crase, Douglas 1944- .... **CLC 58**
See also CA 106

Crashaw, Richard 1612(?)-1649 .... **LC 24**
See also BRW 2; DLB 126; PAB; RGEL 2

Cratinus c. 519B.C.-c. 422B.C. ..... **CMLC 54**
See also LMFS 1

Craven, Margaret 1901-1980 .... **CLC 17**
See also BYA 2; CA 103; CCA 1; DAC; LAIT 5

Crawford, F(rancis) Marion
1854-1909 .... **TCLC 10**
See also CA 107; 168; DLB 71; HGG; RGAL 4; SUFW 1

Crawford, Isabella Valancy
1850-1887 .... **NCLC 12, 127**
See also DLB 92; RGEL 2

Crayon, Geoffrey
See Irving, Washington

Creasey, John 1908-1973 .... **CLC 11**
See Marric, J. J.
See also CA 5-8R; 41-44R; CANR 8, 59; CMW 4; DLB 77; MTCW 1

Crebillon, Claude Prosper Jolyot de (fils)
1707-1777 .... **LC 1, 28**
See also GFL Beginnings to 1789

Credo
See Creasey, John

Credo, Alvaro J. de
See Prado (Calvo), Pedro

Creeley, Robert (White) 1926- ... **CLC 1, 2, 4, 8, 11, 15, 36, 78**
See also AMWS 4; CA 1-4R; CAAS 10; CANR 23, 43, 89; CP 7; DA3; DAM POET; DLB 5, 16, 169; DLBD 17; EWL 3; MTCW 1, 2; RGAL 4; WP

Crevecoeur, Hector St. John de
See Crevecoeur, Michel Guillaume Jean de
See also ANW

Crevecoeur, Michel Guillaume Jean de
1735-1813 .... **NCLC 105**
See Crevecoeur, Hector St. John de
See also AMWS 1; DLB 37

Crevel, Rene 1900-1935 .... **TCLC 112**
See also GLL 2

Crews, Harry (Eugene) 1935- ..... **CLC 6, 23, 49**
See also AITN 1; AMWS 11; BPFB 1; CA 25-28R; CANR 20, 57; CN 7; CSW; DA3; DLB 6, 143, 185; MTCW 1, 2; RGAL 4

Crichton, (John) Michael 1942- .... **CLC 2, 6, 54, 90**
See also AAYA 10, 49; AITN 2; BPFB 1; CA 25-28R; CANR 13, 40, 54, 76, 127; CMW 4; CN 7; CPW; DA3; DAM NOV, POP; DLB 292; DLBY 1981; INT CANR-13; JRDA; MTCW 1, 2; SATA 9, 88; SFW 4; YAW

Crispin, Edmund .... **CLC 22**
See Montgomery, (Robert) Bruce
See also DLB 87; MSW

Cristofer, Michael 1945(?)- .... **CLC 28**
See also CA 110; 152; CAD; CD 5; DAM DRAM; DFS 15; DLB 7

Criton
See Alain

Croce, Benedetto 1866-1952 .... **TCLC 37**
See also CA 120; 155; EW 8; EWL 3

Crockett, David 1786-1836 .... **NCLC 8**
See also DLB 3, 11, 183, 248

Crockett, Davy
See Crockett, David

Crofts, Freeman Wills 1879-1957 .. **TCLC 55**
See also CA 115; 195; CMW 4; DLB 77; MSW

Croker, John Wilson 1780-1857 .... **NCLC 10**
See also DLB 110

Crommelynck, Fernand 1885-1970 .. **CLC 75**
See also CA 189; 89-92; EWL 3

Cromwell, Oliver 1599-1658 .... **LC 43**

Cronenberg, David 1943- .... **CLC 143**
See also CA 138; CCA 1

Cronin, A(rchibald) J(oseph)
1896-1981 .... **CLC 32**
See also BPFB 1; CA 1-4R; 102; CANR 5; DLB 191; SATA 47; SATA-Obit 25

Cross, Amanda
See Heilbrun, Carolyn G(old)
See also BPFB 1; CMW; CPW; MSW

Crothers, Rachel 1878-1958 .... **TCLC 19**
See also CA 113; 194; CAD; CWD; DLB 7, 266; RGAL 4

Croves, Hal
See Traven, B.

Crow Dog, Mary (Ellen) (?)- .... **CLC 93**
See Brave Bird, Mary
See also CA 154

Crowfield, Christopher
See Stowe, Harriet (Elizabeth) Beecher

Crowley, Aleister .... **TCLC 7**
See Crowley, Edward Alexander
See also GLL 1

Crowley, Edward Alexander 1875-1947
See Crowley, Aleister
See also CA 104; HGG

Crowley, John 1942- .... **CLC 57**
See also BPFB 1; CA 61-64; CANR 43, 98; DLBY 1982; FANT; SATA 65, 140; SFW 4; SUFW 2

Crud
See Crumb, R(obert)

Crumarums
See Crumb, R(obert)

Crumb, R(obert) 1943- .... **CLC 17**
See also CA 106; CANR 107

Crumbum
See Crumb, R(obert)

Crumski
See Crumb, R(obert)

Crum the Bum
See Crumb, R(obert)

Crunk
See Crumb, R(obert)

Crustt
See Crumb, R(obert)

Crutchfield, Les
See Trumbo, Dalton

Cruz, Victor Hernandez 1949- ... **HLC 1; PC 37**
See also BW 2; CA 65-68; CAAS 17; CANR 14, 32, 74; CP 7; DAM MULT, POET; DLB 41; DNFS 1; EXPP; HW 1, 2; LLW 1; MTCW 1; PFS 16; WP

Cryer, Gretchen (Kiger) 1935- .... **CLC 21**
See also CA 114; 123

Csath, Geza 1887-1919 .... **TCLC 13**
See also CA 111

Cudlip, David R(ockwell) 1933- .... **CLC 34**
See also CA 177

Cullen, Countee 1903-1946 .... **BLC 1; HR 2; PC 20; TCLC 4, 37; WLCS**
See also AFAW 2; AMWS 4; BW 1; CA 108; 124; CDALB 1917-1929; DA; DA3; DAC; DAM MST, MULT, POET; DLB 4, 48, 51; EWL 3; EXPP; LMFS 2; MTCW 1, 2; PFS 3; RGAL 4; SATA 18; WP

Culleton, Beatrice 1949- .... **NNAL**
See also CA 120; CANR 83; DAC

Cum, R.
See Crumb, R(obert)

Cummings, Bruce F(rederick) 1889-1919
See Barbellion, W. N. P.
See also CA 123

Cummings, E(dward) E(stlin)
1894-1962 .. **CLC 1, 3, 8, 12, 15, 68; PC 5; TCLC 137; WLC**
See also AAYA 41; AMW; CA 73-76; CANR 31; CDALB 1929-1941; DA; DA3; DAB; DAC; DAM MST, POET; DLB 4, 48; EWL 3; EXPP; MTCW 1, 2; PAB; PFS 1, 3, 12, 13, 19; RGAL 4; TUS; WP

Cummins, Maria Susanna
1827-1866 .... **NCLC 139**
See also DLB 42; YABC 1

Cunha, Euclides (Rodrigues Pimenta) da
1866-1909 .... **TCLC 24**
See also CA 123; 219; LAW; WLIT 1

Cunningham, E. V.
See Fast, Howard (Melvin)

Cunningham, J(ames) V(incent)
1911-1985 .... **CLC 3, 31**
See also CA 1-4R; 115; CANR 1, 72; DLB 5

Cunningham, Julia (Woolfolk)
1916- .... **CLC 12**
See also CA 9-12R; CANR 4, 19, 36; CWRI 5; JRDA; MAICYA 1, 2; SAAS 2; SATA 1, 26, 132

Cunningham, Michael 1952- .... **CLC 34**
See also CA 136; CANR 96; DLB 292; GLL 2

Cunninghame Graham, R. B.
See Cunninghame Graham, Robert (Gallnigad) Bontine

Cunninghame Graham, Robert (Gallnigad) Bontine 1852-1936 .... **TCLC 19**
See Graham, R(obert) B(ontine) Cunninghame
See also CA 119; 184

Curnow, (Thomas) Allen (Monro)
1911-2001 .... **PC 48**
See also CA 69-72; 202; CANR 48, 99; CP 7; EWL 3; RGEL 2

Currie, Ellen 19(?)- .... **CLC 44**

Curtin, Philip
See Lowndes, Marie Adelaide (Belloc)

Curtin, Phillip
See Lowndes, Marie Adelaide (Belloc)

Curtis, Price
See Ellison, Harlan (Jay)

Cusanus, Nicolaus 1401-1464 .... **LC 80**
See Nicholas of Cusa

Cutrate, Joe
See Spiegelman, Art

Cynewulf c. 770- .... **CMLC 23**
See also DLB 146; RGEL 2

Cyrano de Bergerac, Savinien de
1619-1655 .... **LC 65**
See also DLB 268; GFL Beginnings to 1789; RGWL 2, 3

Cyril of Alexandria c. 375-c. 430 . **CMLC 59**

Czaczkes, Shmuel Yosef Halevi
See Agnon, S(hmuel) Y(osef Halevi)

Dabrowska, Maria (Szumska)
1889-1965 .... **CLC 15**
See also CA 106; CDWLB 4; DLB 215; EWL 3

Dabydeen, David 1955- .... **CLC 34**
See also BW 1; CA 125; CANR 56, 92; CN 7; CP 7

Dacey, Philip 1939- .... **CLC 51**
See also CA 37-40R; CAAS 17; CANR 14, 32, 64; CP 7; DLB 105

Dafydd ap Gwilym c. 1320-c. 1380 ..... **PC 56**

Dagerman, Stig (Halvard)
1923-1954 .... **TCLC 17**
See also CA 117; 155; DLB 259; EWL 3

D'Aguiar, Fred 1960- .... **CLC 145**
See also CA 148; CANR 83, 101; CP 7; DLB 157; EWL 3

Dahl, Roald 1916-1990 .... **CLC 1, 6, 18, 79**
See also AAYA 15; BPFB 1; BRWS 4; BYA 5; CA 1-4R; 133; CANR 6, 32, 37, 62; CLR 1, 7, 41; CPW; DA3; DAB; DAC; DAM MST, NOV, POP; DLB 139, 255; HGG; JRDA; MAICYA 1, 2; MTCW 1, 2; RGSF 2; SATA 1, 26, 73; SATA-Obit 65; SSFS 4; TEA; YAW

Dahlberg, Edward 1900-1977 .. **CLC 1, 7, 14**
See also CA 9-12R; 69-72; CANR 31, 62; DLB 48; MTCW 1; RGAL 4

Daitch, Susan 1954- .... **CLC 103**
See also CA 161

Dale, Colin .... **TCLC 18**
See Lawrence, T(homas) E(dward)

Dale, George E.
See Asimov, Isaac

Dalton, Roque 1935-1975(?) ..... **HLCS 1; PC 36**
See also CA 176; DLB 283; HW 2

Daly, Elizabeth 1878-1967 .... **CLC 52**
See also CA 23-24; 25-28R; CANR 60; CAP 2; CMW 4

Daly, Mary 1928- .... **CLC 173**
See also CA 25-28R; CANR 30, 62; FW; GLL 1; MTCW 1

Daly, Maureen 1921- .... **CLC 17**
See also AAYA 5; BYA 6; CANR 37, 83, 108; CLR 96; JRDA; MAICYA 1, 2; SAAS 1; SATA 2, 129; WYA; YAW

Damas, Leon-Gontran 1912-1978 .... **CLC 84**
See also BW 1; CA 125; 73-76; EWL 3

Dana, Richard Henry Sr.
1787-1879 .... **NCLC 53**

Daniel, Samuel 1562(?)-1619 .... **LC 24**
See also DLB 62; RGEL 2

Daniels, Brett
See Adler, Renata

Dannay, Frederic 1905-1982 .... **CLC 11**
See Queen, Ellery
See also CA 1-4R; 107; CANR 1, 39; CMW 4; DAM POP; DLB 137; MTCW 1

D'Annunzio, Gabriele 1863-1938 ... **TCLC 6, 40**
See also CA 104; 155; EW 8; EWL 3; RGWL 2, 3; TWA

Danois, N. le
See Gourmont, Remy(-Marie-Charles) de

Dante 1265-1321 .... **CMLC 3, 18, 39; PC 21; WLCS**
See also DA; DA3; DAB; DAC; DAM MST, POET; EFS 1; EW 1; LAIT 1; RGWL 2, 3; TWA; WP

d'Antibes, Germain
See Simenon, Georges (Jacques Christian)

Danticat, Edwidge 1969- .... **CLC 94, 139**
See also AAYA 29; CA 152, 192; CAAE 192; CANR 73, 129; DNFS 1; EXPS; LATS 1; MTCW 1; SSFS 1; YAW

Danvers, Dennis 1947- .... **CLC 70**

Danziger, Paula 1944- .... **CLC 21**
See also AAYA 4, 36; BYA 6, 7, 14; CA 112; 115; CANR 37; CLR 20; JRDA; MAICYA 1, 2; SATA 36, 63, 102, 149; SATA-Brief 30; WYA; YAW

Da Ponte, Lorenzo 1749-1838 .... **NCLC 50**

Dario, Ruben 1867-1916 .... **HLC 1; PC 15; TCLC 4**
See also CA 131; CANR 81; DAM MULT; DLB 290; EWL 3; HW 1, 2; LAW; MTCW 1, 2; RGWL 2, 3

Darley, George 1795-1846 .... **NCLC 2**
See also DLB 96; RGEL 2

Darrow, Clarence (Seward)
1857-1938 .... **TCLC 81**
See also CA 164

Cormier, Robert (Edmund)
1925-2000 .... **CLC 12, 30**
See also AAYA 3, 19; BYA 1, 2, 6, 8, 9; CA 1-4R; CANR 5, 23, 76, 93; CDALB 1968-1988; CLR 12, 55; DA; DAB; DAC; DAM MST, NOV; DLB 52; EXPN; INT CANR-23; JRDA; LAIT 5; MAICYA 1, 2; MTCW 1, 2; NFS 2, 18; SATA 10, 45, 83; SATA-Obit 122; WYA; YAW

Corn, Alfred (DeWitt III) 1943- .... **CLC 33**
See also CA 179; CAAE 179; CAAS 25; CANR 44; CP 7; CSW; DLB 120, 282; DLBY 1980

Corneille, Pierre 1606-1684 ... **DC 21; LC 28**
See also DAB; DAM MST; DLB 268; EW 3; GFL Beginnings to 1789; RGWL 2, 3; TWA

Cornwell, David (John Moore)
1931- .... **CLC 9, 15**
See le Carre, John
See also CA 5-8R; CANR 13, 33, 59, 107; DA3; DAM POP; MTCW 1, 2

Cornwell, Patricia (Daniels) 1956- . **CLC 155**
See also AAYA 16; BPFB 1; CA 134; CANR 53; CMW 4; CPW; CSW; DAM POP; MSW; MTCW 1

Corso, (Nunzio) Gregory 1930-2001 . **CLC 1, 11; PC 33**
See also AMWS 12; BG 2; CA 5-8R; 193; CANR 41, 76; CP 7; DA3; DLB 5, 16, 237; LMFS 2; MTCW 1, 2; WP

Cortazar, Julio 1914-1984 ... **CLC 2, 3, 5, 10, 13, 15, 33, 34, 92; HLC 1; SSC 7**
See also BPFB 1; CA 21-24R; CANR 12, 32, 81; CDWLB 3; DA3; DAM MULT, NOV; DLB 113; EWL 3; EXPS; HW 1, 2; LAW; MTCW 1, 2; RGSF 2; RGWL 2, 3; SSFS 3; TWA; WLIT 1

Cortes, Hernan 1485-1547 .... **LC 31**

Corvinus, Jakob
See Raabe, Wilhelm (Karl)

Corwin, Cecil
See Kornbluth, C(yril) M.

Cosic, Dobrica 1921- .... **CLC 14**
See also CA 122; 138; CDWLB 4; CWW 2; DLB 181; EWL 3

Costain, Thomas B(ertram)
1885-1965 .... **CLC 30**
See also BYA 3; CA 5-8R; 25-28R; DLB 9; RHW

Costantini, Humberto 1924(?)-1987 . **CLC 49**
See also CA 131; 122; EWL 3; HW 1

Costello, Elvis 1954- .... **CLC 21**
See also CA 204

Costenoble, Philostene
See Ghelderode, Michel de

Cotes, Cecil V.
See Duncan, Sara Jeannette

Cotter, Joseph Seamon Sr.
1861-1949 .... **BLC 1; TCLC 28**
See also BW 1; CA 124; DAM MULT; DLB 50

Couch, Arthur Thomas Quiller
See Quiller-Couch, Sir Arthur (Thomas)

Coulton, James
See Hansen, Joseph

Couperus, Louis (Marie Anne)
1863-1923 .... **TCLC 15**
See also CA 115; EWL 3; RGWL 2, 3

Coupland, Douglas 1961- .... **CLC 85, 133**
See also AAYA 34; CA 142; CANR 57, 90; CCA 1; CPW; DAC; DAM POP

Court, Wesli
See Turco, Lewis (Putnam)

Courtenay, Bryce 1933- .... **CLC 59**
See also CA 138; CPW

Courtney, Robert
See Ellison, Harlan (Jay)

Cousteau, Jacques-Yves 1910-1997 .. **CLC 30**
See also CA 65-68; 159; CANR 15, 67; MTCW 1; SATA 38, 98

Coventry, Francis 1725-1754 .... **LC 46**

Coverdale, Miles c. 1487-1569 .... **LC 77**
See also DLB 167

Cowan, Peter (Walkinshaw)
1914-2002 .... **SSC 28**
See also CA 21-24R; CANR 9, 25, 50, 83; CN 7; DLB 260; RGSF 2

Coward, Noel (Peirce) 1899-1973 . **CLC 1, 9, 29, 51**
See also AITN 1; BRWS 2; CA 17-18; 41-44R; CANR 35; CAP 2; CDBLB 1914-1945; DA3; DAM DRAM; DFS 3, 6; DLB 10, 245; EWL 3; IDFW 3, 4; MTCW 1, 2; RGEL 2; TEA

Cowley, Abraham 1618-1667 .... **LC 43**
See also BRW 2; DLB 131, 151; PAB; RGEL 2

Cowley, Malcolm 1898-1989 .... **CLC 39**
See also AMWS 2; CA 5-8R; 128; CANR 3, 55; DLB 4, 48; DLBY 1981, 1989; EWL 3; MTCW 1, 2

Cowper, William 1731-1800 ..... **NCLC 8, 94; PC 40**
See also BRW 3; DA3; DAM POET; DLB 104, 109; RGEL 2

Cox, William Trevor 1928-
See Trevor, William
See also CA 9-12R; CANR 4, 37, 55, 76, 102; DAM NOV; INT CANR-37; MTCW 1, 2; TEA

Coyne, P. J.
See Masters, Hilary

Cozzens, James Gould 1903-1978 . **CLC 1, 4, 11, 92**
See also AMW; BPFB 1; CA 9-12R; 81-84; CANR 19; CDALB 1941-1968; DLB 9, 294; DLBD 2; DLBY 1984, 1997; EWL 3; MTCW 1, 2; RGAL 4

Crabbe, George 1754-1832 .... **NCLC 26, 121**
See also BRW 3; DLB 93; RGEL 2

Crace, Jim 1946- .... **CLC 157; SSC 61**
See also CA 128; 135; CANR 55, 70, 123; CN 7; DLB 231; INT CA-135

Craddock, Charles Egbert
See Murfree, Mary Noailles

Craig, A. A.
See Anderson, Poul (William)

Craik, Mrs.
See Craik, Dinah Maria (Mulock)
See also RGEL 2

Craik, Dinah Maria (Mulock)
1826-1887 .... **NCLC 38**
See Craik, Mrs.; Mulock, Dinah Maria
See also DLB 35, 163; MAICYA 1, 2; SATA 34

Cram, Ralph Adams 1863-1942 ..... **TCLC 45**
See also CA 160

Cranch, Christopher Pearse
1813-1892 .... **NCLC 115**
See also DLB 1, 42, 243

Crane, (Harold) Hart 1899-1932 .... **PC 3; TCLC 2, 5, 80; WLC**
See also AMW; AMWR 2; CA 104; 127; CDALB 1917-1929; DA; DA3; DAB; DAC; DAM MST, POET; DLB 4, 48; EWL 3; MTCW 1, 2; RGAL 4; TUS

Crane, R(onald) S(almon)
1886-1967 .... **CLC 27**
See also CA 85-88; DLB 63

Crane, Stephen (Townley)
1871-1900 .... **SSC 7, 56, 70; TCLC 11, 17, 32; WLC**
See also AAYA 21; AMW; AMWC 1; BPFB 1; BYA 3; CA 109; 140; CANR 84; CDALB 1865-1917; DA; DA3; DAB; DAC; DAM MST, NOV, POET; DLB 12, 54, 78; EXPN; EXPS; LAIT 2; LMFS 2; NFS 4; PFS 9; RGAL 4; RGSF 2; SSFS 4; TUS; WYA; YABC 2

Cranmer, Thomas 1489-1556 .... **LC 95**
See also DLB 132, 213

Cranshaw, Stanley
See Fisher, Dorothy (Frances) Canfield

Crase, Douglas 1944- .... **CLC 58**
See also CA 106

Crashaw, Richard 1612(?)-1649 .... **LC 24**
See also BRW 2; DLB 126; PAB; RGEL 2

Cratinus c. 519B.C.-c. 422B.C. ..... **CMLC 54**
See also LMFS 1

Craven, Margaret 1901-1980 .... **CLC 17**
See also BYA 2; CA 103; CCA 1; DAC; LAIT 5

Crawford, F(rancis) Marion
1854-1909 .... **TCLC 10**
See also CA 107; 168; DLB 71; HGG; RGAL 4; SUFW 1

Crawford, Isabella Valancy
1850-1887 .... **NCLC 12, 127**
See also DLB 92; RGEL 2

Crayon, Geoffrey
See Irving, Washington

Creasey, John 1908-1973 .... **CLC 11**
See Marric, J. J.
See also CA 5-8R; 41-44R; CANR 8, 59; CMW 4; DLB 77; MTCW 1

Crebillon, Claude Prosper Jolyot de (fils)
1707-1777 .... **LC 1, 28**
See also GFL Beginnings to 1789

Credo
See Creasey, John

Credo, Alvaro J. de
See Prado (Calvo), Pedro

Creeley, Robert (White) 1926- .. **CLC 1, 2, 4, 8, 11, 15, 36, 78**
See also AMWS 4; CA 1-4R; CAAS 10; CANR 23, 43, 89; CP 7; DA3; DAM POET; DLB 5, 16, 169; DLBD 17; EWL 3; MTCW 1, 2; RGAL 4; WP

Crevecoeur, Hector St. John de
See Crevecoeur, Michel Guillaume Jean de
See also ANW

Crevecoeur, Michel Guillaume Jean de
1735-1813 .... **NCLC 105**
See Crevecoeur, Hector St. John de
See also AMWS 1; DLB 37

Crevel, Rene 1900-1935 .... **TCLC 112**
See also GLL 2

Crews, Harry (Eugene) 1935- ...... **CLC 6, 23, 49**
See also AITN 1; AMWS 11; BPFB 1; CA 25-28R; CANR 20, 57; CN 7; CSW; DLB 6, 143, 185; MTCW 1, 2; RGAL 4

Crichton, (John) Michael 1942- .... **CLC 2, 6, 54, 90**
See also AAYA 10, 49; AITN 2; BPFB 1; CA 25-28R; CANR 13, 40, 54, 76, 127; CMW 4; CN 7; CPW; DA3; DAM NOV, POP; DLB 292; DLBY 1981; INT CANR-13; JRDA; MTCW 1, 2; SATA 9, 88; SFW 4; YAW

Crispin, Edmund .... **CLC 22**
See Montgomery, (Robert) Bruce
See also DLB 87; MSW

Cristofer, Michael 1945(?)- .... **CLC 28**
See also CA 110; 152; CAD; CD 5; DAM DRAM; DFS 15; DLB 7

Criton
See Alain

Croce, Benedetto 1866-1952 .... **TCLC 37**
See also CA 120; 155; EW 8; EWL 3

Crockett, David 1786-1836 .... **NCLC 8**
See also DLB 3, 11, 183, 248

Crockett, Davy
See Crockett, David

Darwin, Charles 1809-1882 .... **NCLC 57**
See also BRWS 7; DLB 57, 166; LATS 1; RGEL 2; TEA; WLIT 4
Darwin, Erasmus 1731-1802 .... **NCLC 106**
See also DLB 93; RGEL 2
Daryush, Elizabeth 1887-1977 ...... **CLC 6, 19**
See also CA 49-52; CANR 3, 81; DLB 20
Das, Kamala 1934- .... **PC 43**
See also CA 101; CANR 27, 59; CP 7; CWP; FW
Dasgupta, Surendranath 1887-1952 .... **TCLC 81**
See also CA 157
Dashwood, Edmee Elizabeth Monica de la Pasture 1890-1943
See Delafield, E. M.
See also CA 119; 154
da Silva, Antonio Jose 1705-1739 .... **NCLC 114**
Daudet, (Louis Marie) Alphonse 1840-1897 .... **NCLC 1**
See also DLB 123; GFL 1789 to the Present; RGSF 2
d'Aulnoy, Marie-Catherine c. 1650-1705 .... **LC 100**
Daumal, Rene 1908-1944 .... **TCLC 14**
See also CA 114; EWL 3
Davenant, William 1606-1668 .... **LC 13**
See also DLB 58, 126; RGEL 2
Davenport, Guy (Mattison, Jr.) 1927- .... **CLC 6, 14, 38; SSC 16**
See also CA 33-36R; CANR 23, 73; CN 7; CSW; DLB 130
David, Robert
See Nezval, Vitezslav
Davidson, Avram (James) 1923-1993
See Queen, Ellery
See also CA 101; 171; CANR 26; DLB 8; FANT; SFW 4; SUFW 1, 2
Davidson, Donald (Grady) 1893-1968 .... **CLC 2, 13, 19**
See also CA 5-8R; 25-28R; CANR 4, 84; DLB 45
Davidson, Hugh
See Hamilton, Edmond
Davidson, John 1857-1909 .... **TCLC 24**
See also CA 118; 217; DLB 19; RGEL 2
Davidson, Sara 1943- .... **CLC 9**
See also CA 81-84; CANR 44, 68; DLB 185
Davie, Donald (Alfred) 1922-1995 .... **CLC 5, 8, 10, 31; PC 29**
See also BRWS 6; CA 1-4R; 149; CAAS 3; CANR 1, 44; CP 7; DLB 27; MTCW 1; RGEL 2
Davie, Elspeth 1919-1995 .... **SSC 52**
See also CA 120; 126; 150; DLB 139
Davies, Ray(mond Douglas) 1944- ... **CLC 21**
See also CA 116; 146; CANR 92
Davies, Rhys 1901-1978 .... **CLC 23**
See also CA 9-12R; 81-84; CANR 4; DLB 139, 191
Davies, (William) Robertson 1913-1995 .... **CLC 2, 7, 13, 25, 42, 75, 91; WLC**
See Marchbanks, Samuel
See also BEST 89:2; BPFB 1; CA 33-36R; 150; CANR 17, 42, 103; CN 7; CPW; DA; DA3; DAB; DAC; DAM MST, NOV, POP; DLB 68; EWL 3; HGG; INT CANR-17; MTCW 1, 2; RGEL 2; TWA
Davies, Sir John 1569-1626 .... **LC 85**
See also DLB 172
Davies, Walter C.
See Kornbluth, C(yril) M.
Davies, William Henry 1871-1940 ... **TCLC 5**
See also CA 104; 179; DLB 19, 174; EWL 3; RGEL 2

Da Vinci, Leonardo 1452-1519 ..... **LC 12, 57, 60**
See also AAYA 40
Davis, Angela (Yvonne) 1944- .... **CLC 77**
See also BW 2, 3; CA 57-60; CANR 10, 81; CSW; DA3; DAM MULT; FW
Davis, B. Lynch
See Bioy Casares, Adolfo; Borges, Jorge Luis
Davis, Frank Marshall 1905-1987 ...... **BLC 1**
See also BW 2, 3; CA 125; 123; CANR 42, 80; DAM MULT; DLB 51
Davis, Gordon
See Hunt, E(verette) Howard, (Jr.)
Davis, H(arold) L(enoir) 1896-1960 . **CLC 49**
See also ANW; CA 178; 89-92; DLB 9, 206; SATA 114
Davis, Rebecca (Blaine) Harding 1831-1910 .... **SSC 38; TCLC 6**
See also CA 104; 179; DLB 74, 239; FW; NFS 14; RGAL 4; TUS
Davis, Richard Harding 1864-1916 .... **TCLC 24**
See also CA 114; 179; DLB 12, 23, 78, 79, 189; DLBD 13; RGAL 4
Davison, Frank Dalby 1893-1970 ..... **CLC 15**
See also CA 217; 116; DLB 260
Davison, Lawrence H.
See Lawrence, D(avid) H(erbert Richards)
Davison, Peter (Hubert) 1928- .... **CLC 28**
See also CA 9-12R; CAAS 4; CANR 3, 43, 84; CP 7; DLB 5
Davys, Mary 1674-1732 .... **LC 1, 46**
See also DLB 39
Dawson, (Guy) Fielding (Lewis) 1930-2002 .... **CLC 6**
See also CA 85-88; 202; CANR 108; DLB 130; DLBY 2002
Dawson, Peter
See Faust, Frederick (Schiller)
See also TCWW 2, 2
Day, Clarence (Shepard, Jr.) 1874-1935 .... **TCLC 25**
See also CA 108; 199; DLB 11
Day, John 1574(?)-1640(?) .... **LC 70**
See also DLB 62, 170; RGEL 2
Day, Thomas 1748-1789 .... **LC 1**
See also DLB 39; YABC 1
Day Lewis, C(ecil) 1904-1972 . **CLC 1, 6, 10; PC 11**
See Blake, Nicholas
See also BRWS 3; CA 13-16; 33-36R; CANR 34; CAP 1; CWRI 5; DAM POET; DLB 15, 20; EWL 3; MTCW 1, 2; RGEL 2
Dazai Osamu .... **SSC 41; TCLC 11**
See Tsushima, Shuji
See also CA 164; DLB 182; EWL 3; MJW; RGSF 2; RGWL 2, 3; TWA
de Andrade, Carlos Drummond
See Drummond de Andrade, Carlos
de Andrade, Mario 1892-1945
See Andrade, Mario de
See also CA 178; HW 2
Deane, Norman
See Creasey, John
Deane, Seamus (Francis) 1940- ...... **CLC 122**
See also CA 118; CANR 42
de Beauvoir, Simone (Lucie Ernestine Marie Bertrand)
See Beauvoir, Simone (Lucie Ernestine Marie Bertrand) de
de Beer, P.
See Bosman, Herman Charles
de Brissac, Malcolm
See Dickinson, Peter (Malcolm)
de Campos, Alvaro
See Pessoa, Fernando (Antonio Nogueira)

de Chardin, Pierre Teilhard
See Teilhard de Chardin, (Marie Joseph) Pierre
Dee, John 1527-1608 .... **LC 20**
See also DLB 136, 213
Deer, Sandra 1940- .... **CLC 45**
See also CA 186
De Ferrari, Gabriella 1941- .... **CLC 65**
See also CA 146
de Filippo, Eduardo 1900-1984 ... **TCLC 127**
See also CA 132; 114; EWL 3; MTCW 1; RGWL 2, 3
Defoe, Daniel 1660(?)-1731 .. **LC 1, 42; WLC**
See also AAYA 27; BRW 3; BRWR 1; BYA 4; CDBLB 1660-1789; CLR 61; DA; DA3; DAB; DAC; DAM MST, NOV; DLB 39, 95, 101; JRDA; LAIT 1; LMFS 1; MAICYA 1, 2; NFS 9, 13; RGEL 2; SATA 22; TEA; WCH; WLIT 3
de Gourmont, Remy(-Marie-Charles)
See Gourmont, Remy(-Marie-Charles) de
de Gournay, Marie le Jars 1566-1645 .... **LC 98**
See also FW
de Hartog, Jan 1914-2002 .... **CLC 19**
See also CA 1-4R; 210; CANR 1; DFS 12
de Hostos, E. M.
See Hostos (y Bonilla), Eugenio Maria de
de Hostos, Eugenio M.
See Hostos (y Bonilla), Eugenio Maria de
Deighton, Len .... **CLC 4, 7, 22, 46**
See Deighton, Leonard Cyril
See also AAYA 6; BEST 89:2; BPFB 1; CDBLB 1960 to Present; CMW 4; CN 7; CPW; DLB 87
Deighton, Leonard Cyril 1929-
See Deighton, Len
See also CA 9-12R; CANR 19, 33, 68; DA3; DAM NOV, POP; MTCW 1, 2
Dekker, Thomas 1572(?)-1632 ..... **DC 12; LC 22**
See also CDBLB Before 1660; DAM DRAM; DLB 62, 172; LMFS 1; RGEL 2
de Laclos, Pierre Ambroise Franois
See Laclos, Pierre Ambroise Francois
Delacroix, (Ferdinand-Victor-)Eugene 1798-1863 .... **NCLC 133**
See also EW 5
Delafield, E. M. .... **TCLC 61**
See Dashwood, Edmee Elizabeth Monica de la Pasture
See also DLB 34; RHW
de la Mare, Walter (John) 1873-1956 .. **SSC 14; TCLC 4, 53; WLC**
See also CA 163; CDBLB 1914-1945; CLR 23; CWRI 5; DA3; DAB; DAC; DAM MST, POET; DLB 19, 153, 162, 255, 284; EWL 3; EXPP; HGG; MAICYA 1, 2; MTCW 1; RGEL 2; RGSF 2; SATA 16; SUFW 1; TEA; WCH
de Lamartine, Alphonse (Marie Louis Prat)
See Lamartine, Alphonse (Marie Louis Prat) de
Delaney, Franey
See O'Hara, John (Henry)
Delaney, Shelagh 1939- .... **CLC 29**
See also CA 17-20R; CANR 30, 67; CBD; CD 5; CDBLB 1960 to Present; CWD; DAM DRAM; DFS 7; DLB 13; MTCW 1
Delany, Martin Robison 1812-1885 .... **NCLC 93**
See also DLB 50; RGAL 4
Delany, Mary (Granville Pendarves) 1700-1788 .... **LC 12**
Delany, Samuel R(ay), Jr. 1942- .... **BLC 1; CLC 8, 14, 38, 141**
See also AAYA 24; AFAW 2; BPFB 1; BW 2, 3; CA 81-84; CANR 27, 43, 115, 116; CN 7; DAM MULT; DLB 8, 33; FANT; MTCW 1, 2; RGAL 4; SATA 92; SCFW 4; SFW 4; SUFW 2

De la Ramee, Marie Louise (Ouida)
1839-1908
See Ouida
See also CA 204; SATA 20
de la Roche, Mazo 1879-1961 .... **CLC 14**
See also CA 85-88; CANR 30; DLB 68; RGEL 2; RHW; SATA 64
De La Salle, Innocent
See Hartmann, Sadakichi
de Laureamont, Comte
See Lautreamont
Delbanco, Nicholas (Franklin)
1942- .... **CLC 6, 13, 167**
See also CA 17-20R, 189; CAAE 189; CAAS 2; CANR 29, 55, 116; DLB 6, 234
del Castillo, Michel 1933- .... **CLC 38**
See also CA 109; CANR 77
Deledda, Grazia (Cosima)
1875(?)-1936 .... **TCLC 23**
See also CA 123; 205; DLB 264; EWL 3; RGWL 2, 3
Deleuze, Gilles 1925-1995 .... **TCLC 116**
See also DLB 296
Delgado, Abelardo (Lalo) B(arrientos)
1930- .... **HLC 1**
See also CA 131; CAAS 15; CANR 90; DAM MST, MULT; DLB 82; HW 1, 2
Delibes, Miguel .... **CLC 8, 18**
See Delibes Setien, Miguel
See also EWL 3
Delibes Setien, Miguel 1920-
See Delibes, Miguel
See also CA 45-48; CANR 1, 32; CWW 2; HW 1; MTCW 1
DeLillo, Don 1936- ..... **CLC 8, 10, 13, 27, 39, 54, 76, 143**
See also AMWC 2; AMWS 6; BEST 89:1; BPFB 1; CA 81-84; CANR 21, 76, 92; CN 7; CPW; DA3; DAM NOV, POP; DLB 6, 173; EWL 3; MTCW 1, 2; RGAL 4; TUS
de Lisser, H. G.
See De Lisser, H(erbert) G(eorge)
See also DLB 117
De Lisser, H(erbert) G(eorge)
1878-1944 .... **TCLC 12**
See de Lisser, H. G.
See also BW 2; CA 109; 152
Deloire, Pierre
See Peguy, Charles (Pierre)
Deloney, Thomas 1543(?)-1600 .... **LC 41**
See also DLB 167; RGEL 2
Deloria, Ella (Cara) 1889-1971(?) ..... **NNAL**
See also CA 152; DAM MULT; DLB 175
Deloria, Vine (Victor), Jr. 1933- ...... **CLC 21, 122; NNAL**
See also CA 53-56; CANR 5, 20, 48, 98; DAM MULT; DLB 175; MTCW 1; SATA 21
del Valle-Inclan, Ramon (Maria)
See Valle-Inclan, Ramon (Maria) del
Del Vecchio, John M(ichael) 1947- .. **CLC 29**
See also CA 110; DLBD 9
de Man, Paul (Adolph Michel)
1919-1983 .... **CLC 55**
See also CA 128; 111; CANR 61; DLB 67; MTCW 1, 2
DeMarinis, Rick 1934- .... **CLC 54**
See also CA 57-60, 184; CAAE 184; CAAS 24; CANR 9, 25, 50; DLB 218
de Maupassant, (Henri Rene Albert) Guy
See Maupassant, (Henri Rene Albert) Guy de
Dembry, R. Emmet
See Murfree, Mary Noailles
Demby, William 1922- .... **BLC 1; CLC 53**
See also BW 1, 3; CA 81-84; CANR 81; DAM MULT; DLB 33

de Menton, Francisco
See Chin, Frank (Chew, Jr.)
Demetrius of Phalerum c.
307B.C.- .... **CMLC 34**
Demijohn, Thom
See Disch, Thomas M(ichael)
De Mille, James 1833-1880 .... **NCLC 123**
See also DLB 99, 251
Deming, Richard 1915-1983
See Queen, Ellery
See also CA 9-12R; CANR 3, 94; SATA 24
Democritus c. 460B.C.-c. 370B.C. .. **CMLC 47**
de Montaigne, Michel (Eyquem)
See Montaigne, Michel (Eyquem) de
de Montherlant, Henry (Milon)
See Montherlant, Henry (Milon) de
Demosthenes 384B.C.-322B.C. ...... **CMLC 13**
See also AW 1; DLB 176; RGWL 2, 3
de Musset, (Louis Charles) Alfred
See Musset, (Louis Charles) Alfred de
de Natale, Francine
See Malzberg, Barry N(athaniel)
de Navarre, Marguerite 1492-1549 ..... **LC 61**
See Marguerite d'Angouleme; Marguerite de Navarre
Denby, Edwin (Orr) 1903-1983 .... **CLC 48**
See also CA 138; 110
de Nerval, Gerard
See Nerval, Gerard de
Denham, John 1615-1669 .... **LC 73**
See also DLB 58, 126; RGEL 2
Denis, Julio
See Cortazar, Julio
Denmark, Harrison
See Zelazny, Roger (Joseph)
Dennis, John 1658-1734 .... **LC 11**
See also DLB 101; RGEL 2
Dennis, Nigel (Forbes) 1912-1989 ...... **CLC 8**
See also CA 25-28R; 129; DLB 13, 15, 233; EWL 3; MTCW 1
Dent, Lester 1904(?)-1959 .... **TCLC 72**
See also CA 112; 161; CMW 4; SFW 4
De Palma, Brian (Russell) 1940- ...... **CLC 20**
See also CA 109
De Quincey, Thomas 1785-1859 ..... **NCLC 4, 87**
See also BRW 4; CDBLB 1789-1832; DLB 110, 144; RGEL 2
Deren, Eleanora 1908(?)-1961
See Deren, Maya
See also CA 192; 111
Deren, Maya .... **CLC 16, 102**
See Deren, Eleanora
Derleth, August (William)
1909-1971 .... **CLC 31**
See also BPFB 1; BYA 9, 10; CA 1-4R; 29-32R; CANR 4; CMW 4; DLB 9; DLBD 17; HGG; SATA 5; SUFW 1
Der Nister 1884-1950 .... **TCLC 56**
See Nister, Der
de Routisie, Albert
See Aragon, Louis
Derrida, Jacques 1930- .... **CLC 24, 87**
See also CA 124; 127; CANR 76, 98; DLB 242; EWL 3; LMFS 2; MTCW 1; TWA
Derry Down Derry
See Lear, Edward
Dersonnes, Jacques
See Simenon, Georges (Jacques Christian)
Desai, Anita 1937- .... **CLC 19, 37, 97, 175**
See also BRWS 5; CA 81-84; CANR 33, 53, 95; CN 7; CWRI 5; DA3; DAB; DAM NOV; DLB 271; DNFS 2; EWL 3; FW; MTCW 1, 2; SATA 63, 126
Desai, Kiran 1971- .... **CLC 119**
See also BYA 16; CA 171; CANR 127
de Saint-Luc, Jean
See Glassco, John

de Saint Roman, Arnaud
See Aragon, Louis
Desbordes-Valmore, Marceline
1786-1859 .... **NCLC 97**
See also DLB 217
Descartes, Rene 1596-1650 .... **LC 20, 35**
See also DLB 268; EW 3; GFL Beginnings to 1789
De Sica, Vittorio 1901(?)-1974 .... **CLC 20**
See also CA 117
Desnos, Robert 1900-1945 .... **TCLC 22**
See also CA 121; 151; CANR 107; DLB 258; EWL 3; LMFS 2
Destouches, Louis-Ferdinand
1894-1961 .... **CLC 9, 15**
See Celine, Louis-Ferdinand
See also CA 85-88; CANR 28; MTCW 1
de Tolignac, Gaston
See Griffith, D(avid Lewelyn) W(ark)
Deutsch, Babette 1895-1982 .... **CLC 18**
See also BYA 3; CA 1-4R; 108; CANR 4, 79; DLB 45; SATA 1; SATA-Obit 33
Devenant, William 1606-1649 .... **LC 13**
Devkota, Laxmiprasad 1909-1959 . **TCLC 23**
See also CA 123
De Voto, Bernard (Augustine)
1897-1955 .... **TCLC 29**
See also CA 113; 160; DLB 9, 256
De Vries, Peter 1910-1993 ..... **CLC 1, 2, 3, 7, 10, 28, 46**
See also CA 17-20R; 142; CANR 41; DAM NOV; DLB 6; DLBY 1982; MTCW 1, 2
Dewey, John 1859-1952 .... **TCLC 95**
See also CA 114; 170; DLB 246, 270; RGAL 4
Dexter, John
See Bradley, Marion Zimmer
See also GLL 1
Dexter, Martin
See Faust, Frederick (Schiller)
See also TCWW 2
Dexter, Pete 1943- .... **CLC 34, 55**
See also BEST 89:2; CA 127; 131; CANR 129; CPW; DAM POP; INT CA-131; MTCW 1
Diamano, Silmang
See Senghor, Leopold Sedar
Diamond, Neil 1941- .... **CLC 30**
See also CA 108
Diaz del Castillo, Bernal
1496-1584 .... **HLCS 1; LC 31**
See also LAW
di Bassetto, Corno
See Shaw, George Bernard
Dick, Philip K(indred) 1928-1982 ... **CLC 10, 30, 72; SSC 57**
See also AAYA 24; BPFB 1; BYA 11; CA 49-52; 106; CANR 2, 16; CPW; DA3; DAM NOV, POP; DLB 8; MTCW 1, 2; NFS 5; SCFW; SFW 4
Dickens, Charles (John Huffam)
1812-1870 .... **NCLC 3, 8, 18, 26, 37, 50, 86, 105, 113; SSC 17, 49; WLC**
See also AAYA 23; BRW 5; BRWC 1, 2; BYA 1, 2, 3, 13, 14; CDBLB 1832-1890; CLR 95; CMW 4; DA; DA3; DAB; DAC; DAM MST, NOV; DLB 21, 55, 70, 159, 166; EXPN; HGG; JRDA; LAIT 1, 2; LATS 1; LMFS 1; MAICYA 1, 2; NFS 4, 5, 10, 14; RGEL 2; RGSF 2; SATA 15; SUFW 1; TEA; WCH; WLIT 4; WYA
Dickey, James (Lafayette)
1923-1997 ... **CLC 1, 2, 4, 7, 10, 15, 47, 109; PC 40, TCLC 151**
See also AAYA 50; AITN 1, 2; AMWS 4; BPFB 1; CA 9-12R; 156; CABS 2; CANR 10, 48, 61, 105; CDALB 1968-1988; CP 7; CPW; CSW; DA3; DAM NOV, POET,

Dickey, William 1928-1994 .... **CLC 3, 28**
See also CA 9-12R; 145; CANR 24, 79; DLB 5

Dickinson, Charles 1951- .... **CLC 49**
See also CA 128

Dickinson, Emily (Elizabeth)
1830-1886 ... **NCLC 21, 77; PC 1; WLC**
See also AAYA 22; AMW; AMWR 1; CDALB 1865-1917; DA; DA3; DAB; DAC; DAM MST, POET; DLB 1, 243; EXPP; MAWW; PAB; PFS 1, 2, 3, 4, 5, 6, 8, 10, 11, 13, 16; RGAL 4; SATA 29; TUS; WP; WYA

Dickinson, Mrs. Herbert Ward
See Phelps, Elizabeth Stuart

Dickinson, Peter (Malcolm) 1927- .. **CLC 12, 35**
See also AAYA 9, 49; BYA 5; CA 41-44R; CANR 31, 58, 88; CLR 29; CMW 4; DLB 87, 161, 276; JRDA; MAICYA 1, 2; SATA 5, 62, 95, 150; SFW 4; WYA; YAW

Dickson, Carr
See Carr, John Dickson

Dickson, Carter
See Carr, John Dickson

Diderot, Denis 1713-1784 .... **LC 26**
See also EW 4; GFL Beginnings to 1789; LMFS 1; RGWL 2, 3

Didion, Joan 1934- . **CLC 1, 3, 8, 14, 32, 129**
See also AITN 1; AMWS 4; CA 5-8R; CANR 14, 52, 76, 128; CDALB 1968-1988; CN 7; DA3; DAM NOV; DLB 2, 173, 185; DLBY 1981, 1986; EWL 3; MAWW; MTCW 1, 2; NFS 3; RGAL 4; TCWW 2; TUS

Dietrich, Robert
See Hunt, E(verette) Howard, (Jr.)

Difusa, Pati
See Almodovar, Pedro

Dillard, Annie 1945- .... **CLC 9, 60, 115**
See also AAYA 6, 43; AMWS 6; ANW; CA 49-52; CANR 3, 43, 62, 90, 125; DA3; DAM NOV; DLB 275, 278; DLBY 1980; LAIT 4, 5; MTCW 1, 2; NCFS 1; RGAL 4; SATA 10, 140; TUS

Dillard, R(ichard) H(enry) W(ilde)
1937- .... **CLC 5**
See also CA 21-24R; CAAS 7; CANR 10; CP 7; CSW; DLB 5, 244

Dillon, Eilis 1920-1994 .... **CLC 17**
See also CA 9-12R, 182; 147; CAAE 182; CAAS 3; CANR 4, 38, 78; CLR 26; MAICYA 1, 2; MAICYAS 1; SATA 2, 74; SATA-Essay 105; SATA-Obit 83; YAW

Dimont, Penelope
See Mortimer, Penelope (Ruth)

Dinesen, Isak .... **CLC 10, 29, 95; SSC 7**
See Blixen, Karen (Christentze Dinesen)
See also EW 10; EWL 3; EXPS; FW; HGG; LAIT 3; MTCW 1; NCFS 2; NFS 9; RGSF 2; RGWL 2, 3; SSFS 3, 6, 13; WLIT 2

Ding Ling .... **CLC 68**
See Chiang, Pin-chin
See also RGWL 3

Diphusa, Patty
See Almodovar, Pedro

Disch, Thomas M(ichael) 1940- ... **CLC 7, 36**
See Disch, Tom
See also AAYA 17; BPFB 1; CA 21-24R; CAAS 4; CANR 17, 36, 54, 89; CLR 18; CP 7; DA3; DLB 8; HGG; MAICYA 1, 2; MTCW 1, 2; SAAS 15; SATA 92; SCFW; SFW 4; SUFW 2

Disch, Tom
See Disch, Thomas M(ichael)
See also DLB 282

d'Isly, Georges
See Simenon, Georges (Jacques Christian)

Disraeli, Benjamin 1804-1881 ... **NCLC 2, 39, 79**
See also BRW 4; DLB 21, 55; RGEL 2

Ditcum, Steve
See Crumb, R(obert)

Dixon, Paige
See Corcoran, Barbara (Asenath)

Dixon, Stephen 1936- .... **CLC 52; SSC 16**
See also AMWS 12; CA 89-92; CANR 17, 40, 54, 91; CN 7; DLB 130

Djebar, Assia 1936- .... **CLC 182**
See also CA 188; EWL 3; RGWL 3; WLIT 2

Doak, Annie
See Dillard, Annie

Dobell, Sydney Thompson
1824-1874 .... **NCLC 43**
See also DLB 32; RGEL 2

Doblin, Alfred .... **TCLC 13**
See Doeblin, Alfred
See also CDWLB 2; EWL 3; RGWL 2, 3

Dobroliubov, Nikolai Aleksandrovich
See Dobrolyubov, Nikolai Alexandrovich
See also DLB 277

Dobrolyubov, Nikolai Alexandrovich
1836-1861 .... **NCLC 5**
See Dobroliubov, Nikolai Aleksandrovich

Dobson, Austin 1840-1921 .... **TCLC 79**
See also DLB 35, 144

Dobyns, Stephen 1941- .... **CLC 37**
See also AMWS 13; CA 45-48; CANR 2, 18, 99; CMW 4; CP 7

Doctorow, E(dgar) L(aurence)
1931- .... **CLC 6, 11, 15, 18, 37, 44, 65, 113**
See also AAYA 22; AITN 2; AMWS 4; BEST 89:3; BPFB 1; CA 45-48; CANR 2, 33, 51, 76, 97; CDALB 1968-1988; CN 7; CPW; DA3; DAM NOV, POP; DLB 2, 28, 173; DLBY 1980; EWL 3; LAIT 3; MTCW 1, 2; NFS 6; RGAL 4; RHW; TUS

Dodgson, Charles L(utwidge) 1832-1898
See Carroll, Lewis
See also CLR 2; DA; DA3; DAB; DAC; DAM MST, NOV, POET; MAICYA 1, 2; SATA 100; YABC 2

Dodsley, Robert 1703-1764 .... **LC 97**
See also DLB 95; RGEL 2

Dodson, Owen (Vincent) 1914-1983 .. **BLC 1; CLC 79**
See also BW 1; CA 65-68; 110; CANR 24; DAM MULT; DLB 76

Doeblin, Alfred 1878-1957 .... **TCLC 13**
See Doblin, Alfred
See also CA 110; 141; DLB 66

Doerr, Harriet 1910-2002 .... **CLC 34**
See also CA 117; 122; 213; CANR 47; INT CA-122; LATS 1

Domecq, H(onorio Bustos)
See Bioy Casares, Adolfo

Domecq, H(onorio) Bustos
See Bioy Casares, Adolfo; Borges, Jorge Luis

Domini, Rey
See Lorde, Audre (Geraldine)
See also GLL 1

Dominique
See Proust, (Valentin-Louis-George-Eugene) Marcel

Don, A
See Stephen, Sir Leslie

Donaldson, Stephen R(eeder)
1947- .... **CLC 46, 138**
See also AAYA 36; BPFB 1; CA 89-92; CANR 13, 55, 99; CPW; DAM POP; FANT; INT CANR-13; SATA 121; SFW 4; SUFW 1, 2

Donleavy, J(ames) P(atrick) 1926- .... **CLC 1, 4, 6, 10, 45**
See also AITN 2; BPFB 1; CA 9-12R; CANR 24, 49, 62, 80, 124; CBD; CD 5; CN 7; DLB 6, 173; INT CANR-24; MTCW 1, 2; RGAL 4

Donnadieu, Marguerite
See Duras, Marguerite
See also CWW 2

Donne, John 1572-1631 ... **LC 10, 24, 91; PC 1, 43; WLC**
See also BRW 1; BRWC 1; BRWR 2; CD-BLB Before 1660; DA; DAB; DAC; DAM MST, POET; DLB 121, 151; EXPP; PAB; PFS 2, 11; RGEL 3; TEA; WLIT 3; WP

Donnell, David 1939(?)- .... **CLC 34**
See also CA 197

Donoghue, P. S.
See Hunt, E(verette) Howard, (Jr.)

Donoso (Yanez), Jose 1924-1996 ... **CLC 4, 8, 11, 32, 99; HLC 1; SSC 34; TCLC 133**
See also CA 81-84; 155; CANR 32, 73; CD-WLB 3; DAM MULT; DLB 113; EWL 3; HW 1, 2; LAW; LAWS 1; MTCW 1, 2; RGSF 2; WLIT 1

Donovan, John 1928-1992 .... **CLC 35**
See also AAYA 20; CA 97-100; 137; CLR 3; MAICYA 1, 2; SATA 72; SATA-Brief 29; YAW

Don Roberto
See Cunninghame Graham, Robert (Gallnigad) Bontine

Doolittle, Hilda 1886-1961 . **CLC 3, 8, 14, 31, 34, 73; PC 5; WLC**
See H. D.
See also AMWS 1; CA 97-100; CANR 35; DA; DAC; DAM MST, POET; DLB 4, 45; EWL 3; FW; GLL 1; LMFS 2; MAWW; MTCW 1, 2; PFS 6; RGAL 4

Doppo, Kunikida .... **TCLC 99**
See Kunikida Doppo

Dorfman, Ariel 1942- .... **CLC 48, 77, 189; HLC 1**
See also CA 124; 130; CANR 67, 70; CWW 2; DAM MULT; DFS 4; EWL 3; HW 1, 2; INT CA-130; WLIT 1

Dorn, Edward (Merton)
1929-1999 .... **CLC 10, 18**
See also CA 93-96; 187; CANR 42, 79; CP 7; DLD 5; INT CA-93-96; WP

Dor-Ner, Zvi .... **CLC 70**

Dorris, Michael (Anthony)
1945-1997 .... **CLC 109; NNAL**
See also AAYA 20; BEST 90:1; BYA 12; CA 102; 157; CANR 19, 46, 75; CLR 58; DA3; DAM MULT, NOV; DLB 175; LAIT 5; MTCW 2; NFS 3; RGAL 4; SATA 75; SATA-Obit 94; TCWW 2; YAW

Dorris, Michael A.
See Dorris, Michael (Anthony)

Dorsan, Luc
See Simenon, Georges (Jacques Christian)

Dorsange, Jean
See Simenon, Georges (Jacques Christian)

Dorset
See Sackville, Thomas

Dos Passos, John (Roderigo)
1896-1970 ... **CLC 1, 4, 8, 11, 15, 25, 34, 82; WLC**
See also AMW; BPFB 1; CA 1-4R; 29-32R; CANR 3; CDALB 1929-1941; DA; DA3; DAB; DAC; DAM MST, NOV; DLB 4, 9, 274; DLBD 1, 15; DLBY 1996; EWL 3; MTCW 1, 2; NFS 14; RGAL 4; TUS

Dossage, Jean
See Simenon, Georges (Jacques Christian)
Dostoevsky, Fedor Mikhailovich
1821-1881 .. **NCLC 2, 7, 21, 33, 43, 119; SSC 2, 33, 44; WLC**
See Dostoevsky, Fyodor
See also AAYA 40; DA; DA3; DAB; DAC; DAM MST, NOV; EW 7; EXPN; NFS 3, 8; RGSF 2; RGWL 2, 3; SSFS 8; TWA
Dostoevsky, Fyodor
See Dostoevsky, Fedor Mikhailovich
See also DLB 238; LATS 1; LMFS 1, 2
Doty, M. R.
See Doty, Mark (Alan)
Doty, Mark
See Doty, Mark (Alan)
Doty, Mark (Alan) 1953(?)- .... **CLC 176; PC 53**
See also AMWS 11; CA 161, 183; CAAE 183; CANR 110
Doty, Mark A.
See Doty, Mark (Alan)
Doughty, Charles M(ontagu)
1843-1926 .... **TCLC 27**
See also CA 115; 178; DLB 19, 57, 174
Douglas, Ellen .... **CLC 73**
See Haxton, Josephine Ayres; Williamson, Ellen Douglas
See also CN 7; CSW; DLB 292
Douglas, Gavin 1475(?)-1522 .... **LC 20**
See also DLB 132; RGEL 2
Douglas, George
See Brown, George Douglas
See also RGEL 2
Douglas, Keith (Castellain)
1920-1944 .... **TCLC 40**
See also BRW 7; CA 160; DLB 27; EWL 3; PAB; RGEL 2
Douglas, Leonard
See Bradbury, Ray (Douglas)
Douglas, Michael
See Crichton, (John) Michael
Douglas, (George) Norman
1868-1952 .... **TCLC 68**
See also BRW 6; CA 119; 157; DLB 34, 195; RGEL 2
Douglas, William
See Brown, George Douglas
Douglass, Frederick 1817(?)-1895 ..... **BLC 1; NCLC 7, 55; WLC**
See also AAYA 48; AFAW 1, 2; AMWC 1; AMWS 3; CDALB 1640-1865; DA; DA3; DAC; DAM MST, MULT; DLB 1, 43, 50, 79, 243; FW; LAIT 2; NCFS 2; RGAL 4; SATA 29
Dourado, (Waldomiro Freitas) Autran
1926- .... **CLC 23, 60**
See also CA 25-28R; 179; CANR 34, 81; DLB 145; HW 2
Dourado, Waldomiro Autran
See Dourado, (Waldomiro Freitas) Autran
See also CA 179
Dove, Rita (Frances) 1952- . **BLCS; CLC 50, 81; PC 6**
See also AAYA 46; AMWS 4; BW 2; CA 109; CAAS 19; CANR 27, 42, 68, 76, 97; CDALBS; CP 7; CSW; CWP; DA3; DAM MULT, POET; DLB 120; EWL 3; EXPP; MTCW 1; PFS 1, 15; RGAL 4
Doveglion
See Villa, Jose Garcia
Dowell, Coleman 1925-1985 .... **CLC 60**
See also CA 25-28R; 117; CANR 10; DLB 130; GLL 2
Dowson, Ernest (Christopher)
1867-1900 .... **TCLC 4**
See also CA 105; 150; DLB 19, 135; RGEL 2

Doyle, A. Conan
See Doyle, Sir Arthur Conan
Doyle, Sir Arthur Conan
1859-1930 .... **SSC 12; TCLC 7; WLC**
See Conan Doyle, Arthur
See also AAYA 14; BRWS 2; CA 104; 122; CDBLB 1890-1914; CMW 4; DA; DA3; DAB; DAC; DAM MST, NOV; DLB 18, 70, 156, 178; EXPS; HGG; LAIT 2; MSW; MTCW 1, 2; RGEL 2; RGSF 2; RHW; SATA 24; SCFW 2; SFW 4; SSFS 2; TEA; WCH; WLIT 4; WYA; YAW
Doyle, Conan
See Doyle, Sir Arthur Conan
Doyle, John
See Graves, Robert (von Ranke)
Doyle, Roddy 1958(?)- .... **CLC 81, 178**
See also AAYA 14; BRWS 5; CA 143; CANR 73, 128; CN 7; DA3; DLB 194
Doyle, Sir A. Conan
See Doyle, Sir Arthur Conan
Dr. A
See Asimov, Isaac; Silverstein, Alvin; Silverstein, Virginia B(arbara Opshelor)
Drabble, Margaret 1939- ...... **CLC 2, 3, 5, 8, 10, 22, 53, 129**
See also BRWS 4; CA 13-16R; CANR 18, 35, 63, 112; CDBLB 1960 to Present; CN 7; CPW; DA3; DAB; DAC; DAM MST, NOV, POP; DLB 14, 155, 231; EWL 3; FW; MTCW 1, 2; RGEL 2; SATA 48; TEA
Drakulic, Slavenka 1949- .... **CLC 173**
See also CA 144; CANR 92
Drakulic-Ilic, Slavenka
See Drakulic, Slavenka
Drapier, M. B.
See Swift, Jonathan
Drayham, James
See Mencken, H(enry) L(ouis)
Drayton, Michael 1563-1631 .... **LC 8**
See also DAM POET; DLB 121; RGEL 2
Dreadstone, Carl
See Campbell, (John) Ramsey
Dreiser, Theodore (Herman Albert)
1871-1945 .... **SSC 30; TCLC 10, 18, 35, 83; WLC**
See also AMW; AMWC 2; AMWR 2; BYA 15, 16; CA 106; 132; CDALB 1865-1917; DA; DA3; DAC; DAM MST, NOV; DLB 9, 12, 102, 137; DLBD 1; EWL 3; LAIT 2; LMFS 2; MTCW 1, 2; NFS 8, 17; RGAL 4; TUS
Drexler, Rosalyn 1926- .... **CLC 2, 6**
See also CA 81-84; CAD; CANR 68, 124; CD 5; CWD
Dreyer, Carl Theodor 1889-1968 ...... **CLC 16**
See also CA 116
Drieu la Rochelle, Pierre(-Eugene)
1893-1945 .... **TCLC 21**
See also CA 117; DLB 72; EWL 3; GFL 1789 to the Present
Drinkwater, John 1882-1937 .... **TCLC 57**
See also CA 109; 149; DLB 10, 19, 149; RGEL 2
Drop Shot
See Cable, George Washington
Droste-Hulshoff, Annette Freiin von
1797-1848 .... **NCLC 3, 133**
See also CDWLB 2; DLB 133; RGSF 2; RGWL 2, 3
Drummond, Walter
See Silverberg, Robert
Drummond, William Henry
1854-1907 .... **TCLC 25**
See also CA 160; DLB 92

Drummond de Andrade, Carlos
1902-1987 .... **CLC 18; TCLC 139**
See Andrade, Carlos Drummond de
See also CA 132; 123; LAW
Drummond of Hawthornden, William
1585-1649 .... **LC 83**
See also DLB 121, 213; RGEL 2
Drury, Allen (Stuart) 1918-1998 .... **CLC 37**
See also CA 57-60; 170; CANR 18, 52; CN 7; INT CANR-18
Dryden, John 1631-1700 ..... **DC 3; LC 3, 21; PC 25; WLC**
See also BRW 2; CDBLB 1660-1789; DA; DAB; DAC; DAM DRAM, MST, POET; DLB 80, 101, 131; EXPP; IDTP; LMFS 1; RGEL 2; TEA; WLIT 3
du Bellay, Joachim 1524-1560 .... **LC 92**
See also GFL Beginnings to 1789; RGWL 2, 3
Duberman, Martin (Bauml) 1930- ..... **CLC 8**
See also CA 1-4R; CAD; CANR 2, 63; CD 5
Dubie, Norman (Evans) 1945- .... **CLC 36**
See also CA 69-72; CANR 12, 115; CP 7; DLB 120; PFS 12
Du Bois, W(illiam) E(dward) B(urghardt)
1868-1963 ..... **BLC 1; CLC 1, 2, 13, 64, 96; HR 2; WLC**
See also AAYA 40; AFAW 1, 2; AMWC 1; AMWS 2; BW 1, 3; CA 85-88; CANR 34, 82; CDALB 1865-1917; DA; DA3; DAC; DAM MST, MULT, NOV; DLB 47, 50, 91, 246, 284; EWL 3; EXPP; LAIT 2; LMFS 2; MTCW 1, 2; NCFS 1; PFS 13; RGAL 4; SATA 42
Dubus, Andre 1936-1999 ..... **CLC 13, 36, 97; SSC 15**
See also AMWS 7; CA 21-24R; 177; CANR 17; CN 7; CSW; DLB 130; INT CANR-17; RGAL 4; SSFS 10
Duca Minimo
See D'Annunzio, Gabriele
Ducharme, Rejean 1941- .... **CLC 74**
See also CA 165; DLB 60
du Chatelet, Emilie 1706-1749 .... **LC 96**
Duchen, Claire .... **CLC 65**
Duclos, Charles Pinot- 1704-1772 .... **LC 1**
See also GFL Beginnings to 1789
Dudek, Louis 1918-2001 .... **CLC 11, 19**
See also CA 45-48; 215; CAAS 14; CANR 1; CP 7; DLB 88
Duerrenmatt, Friedrich 1921-1990 ... **CLC 1, 4, 8, 11, 15, 43, 102**
See Durrenmatt, Friedrich
See also CA 17-20R; CANR 33; CMW 4; DAM DRAM; DLB 69, 124; MTCW 1, 2
Duffy, Bruce 1953(?)- .... **CLC 50**
See also CA 172
Duffy, Maureen 1933- .... **CLC 37**
See also CA 25-28R; CANR 33, 68; CBD; CN 7; CP 7; CWD; CWP; DFS 15; DLB 14; FW; MTCW 1
Du Fu
See Tu Fu
See also RGWL 2, 3
Dugan, Alan 1923-2003 .... **CLC 2, 6**
See also CA 81-84; 220; CANR 119; CP 7; DLB 5; PFS 10
du Gard, Roger Martin
See Martin du Gard, Roger
Duhamel, Georges 1884-1966 .... **CLC 8**
See also CA 81-84; 25-28R; CANR 35; DLB 65; EWL 3; GFL 1789 to the Present; MTCW 1
Dujardin, Edouard (Emile Louis)
1861-1949 .... **TCLC 13**
See also CA 109; DLB 123
Duke, Raoul
See Thompson, Hunter S(tockton)

Dulles, John Foster 1888-1959 .... **TCLC 72**
See also CA 115; 149

Dumas, Alexandre (pere)
1802-1870 .... **NCLC 11, 71; WLC**
See also AAYA 22; BYA 3; DA; DA3; DAB; DAC; DAM MST, NOV; DLB 119, 192; EW 6; GFL 1789 to the Present; LAIT 1, 2; NFS 14; RGWL 2, 3; SATA 18; TWA; WCH

Dumas, Alexandre (fils) 1824-1895 ...... **DC 1; NCLC 9**
See also DLB 192; GFL 1789 to the Present; RGWL 2, 3

Dumas, Claudine
See Malzberg, Barry N(athaniel)

Dumas, Henry L. 1934-1968 .... **CLC 6, 62**
See also BW 1; CA 85-88; DLB 41; RGAL 4

du Maurier, Daphne 1907-1989 .. **CLC 6, 11, 59; SSC 18**
See also AAYA 37; BPFB 1; BRWS 3; CA 5-8R; 128; CANR 6, 55; CMW 4; CPW; DA3; DAB; DAC; DAM MST, POP; DLB 191; HGG; LAIT 3; MSW; MTCW 1, 2; NFS 12; RGEL 2; RGSF 2; RHW; SATA 27; SATA-Obit 60; SSFS 14, 16; TEA

Du Maurier, George 1834-1896 ..... **NCLC 86**
See also DLB 153, 178; RGEL 2

Dunbar, Paul Laurence 1872-1906 ... **BLC 1; PC 5; SSC 8; TCLC 2, 12; WLC**
See also AFAW 1, 2; AMWS 2; BW 1, 3; CA 104; 124; CANR 79; CDALB 1865-1917; DA; DA3; DAC; DAM MST, MULT, POET; DLB 50, 54, 78; EXPP; RGAL 4; SATA 34

Dunbar, William 1460(?)-1520(?) .... **LC 20**
See also BRWS 8; DLB 132, 146; RGEL 2

Dunbar-Nelson, Alice .... **HR 2**
See Nelson, Alice Ruth Moore Dunbar

Duncan, Dora Angela
See Duncan, Isadora

Duncan, Isadora 1877(?)-1927 .... **TCLC 68**
See also CA 118; 149

Duncan, Lois 1934- .... **CLC 26**
See also AAYA 4, 34; BYA 6, 8; CA 1-4R; CANR 2, 23, 36, 111; CLR 29; JRDA; MAICYA 1, 2; MAICYAS 1; SAAS 2; SATA 1, 36, 75, 133, 141; SATA-Essay 141; WYA; YAW

Duncan, Robert (Edward)
1919-1988 .... **CLC 1, 2, 4, 7, 15, 41, 55; PC 2**
See also BG 2; CA 9-12R; 124; CANR 28, 62; DAM POET; DLB 5, 16, 193; EWL 3; MTCW 1, 2; PFS 13; RGAL 4; WP

Duncan, Sara Jeannette
1861-1922 .... **TCLC 60**
See also CA 157; DLB 92

Dunlap, William 1766-1839 .... **NCLC 2**
See also DLB 30, 37, 59; RGAL 4

Dunn, Douglas (Eaglesham) 1942- .... **CLC 6, 40**
See also CA 45-48; CANR 2, 33, 126; CP 7; DLB 40; MTCW 1

Dunn, Katherine (Karen) 1945- .... **CLC 71**
See also CA 33-36R; CANR 72; HGG; MTCW 1

Dunn, Stephen (Elliott) 1939- .... **CLC 36**
See also AMWS 11; CA 33-36R; CANR 12, 48, 53, 105; CP 7; DLB 105

Dunne, Finley Peter 1867-1936 ...... **TCLC 28**
See also CA 108; 178; DLB 11, 23; RGAL 4

Dunne, John Gregory 1932-2003 ..... **CLC 28**
See also CA 25-28R; 222; CANR 14, 50; CN 7; DLBY 1980

Dunsany, Lord .... **TCLC 2, 59**
See Dunsany, Edward John Moreton Drax Plunkett
See also DLB 77, 153, 156, 255; FANT; IDTP; RGEL 2; SFW 4; SUFW 1

Dunsany, Edward John Moreton Drax Plunkett 1878-1957
See Dunsany, Lord
See also CA 104; 148; DLB 10; MTCW 1

Duns Scotus, John 1266(?)-1308 ... **CMLC 59**
See also DLB 115

du Perry, Jean
See Simenon, Georges (Jacques Christian)

Durang, Christopher (Ferdinand)
1949- .... **CLC 27, 38**
See also CA 105; CAD; CANR 50, 76; CD 5; MTCW 1

Duras, Marguerite 1914-1996 . **CLC 3, 6, 11, 20, 34, 40, 68, 100; SSC 40**
See Donnadieu, Marguerite
See also BPFB 1; CA 25-28R; 151; CANR 50; CWW 2; DLB 83; EWL 3; GFL 1789 to the Present; IDFW 4; MTCW 1, 2; RGWL 2, 3; TWA

Durban, (Rosa) Pam 1947- .... **CLC 39**
See also CA 123; CANR 98; CSW

Durcan, Paul 1944- .... **CLC 43, 70**
See also CA 134; CANR 123; CP 7; DAM POET; EWL 3

Durfey, Thomas 1653-1723 .... **LC 94**
See also DLB 80; RGEL 2

Durkheim, Emile 1858-1917 .... **TCLC 55**

Durrell, Lawrence (George)
1912-1990 ..... **CLC 1, 4, 6, 8, 13, 27, 41**
See also BPFB 1; BRWS 1; CA 9-12R; 132; CANR 40, 77; CDBLB 1945-1960; DAM NOV; DLB 15, 27, 204; DLBY 1990; EWL 3; MTCW 1, 2; RGEL 2; SFW 4; TEA

Durrenmatt, Friedrich
See Duerrenmatt, Friedrich
See also CDWLB 2; EW 13; EWL 3; RGWL 2, 3

Dutt, Michael Madhusudan
1824-1873 .... **NCLC 118**

Dutt, Toru 1856-1877 .... **NCLC 29**
See also DLB 240

Dwight, Timothy 1752-1817 .... **NCLC 13**
See also DLB 37; RGAL 4

Dworkin, Andrea 1946- .... **CLC 43, 123**
See also CA 77-80; CAAS 21; CANR 16, 39, 76, 96; FW; GLL 1; INT CANR-16; MTCW 1, 2

Dwyer, Deanna
See Koontz, Dean R(ay)

Dwyer, K. R.
See Koontz, Dean R(ay)

Dybek, Stuart 1942- .... **CLC 114; SSC 55**
See also CA 97-100; CANR 39; DLB 130

Dye, Richard
See De Voto, Bernard (Augustine)

Dyer, Geoff 1958- .... **CLC 149**
See also CA 125; CANR 88

Dyer, George 1755-1841 .... **NCLC 129**
See also DLB 93

Dylan, Bob 1941- .... **CLC 3, 4, 6, 12, 77; PC 37**
See also CA 41-44R; CANR 108; CP 7; DLB 16

Dyson, John 1943- .... **CLC 70**
See also CA 144

Dzyubin, Eduard Georgievich 1895-1934
See Bagritsky, Eduard
See also CA 170

E. V. L.
See Lucas, E(dward) V(errall)

Eagleton, Terence (Francis) 1943- .. **CLC 63, 132**
See also CA 57-60; CANR 7, 23, 68, 115; DLB 242; LMFS 2; MTCW 1, 2

Eagleton, Terry
See Eagleton, Terence (Francis)

Early, Jack
See Scoppettone, Sandra
See also GLL 1

East, Michael
See West, Morris L(anglo)

Eastaway, Edward
See Thomas, (Philip) Edward

Eastlake, William (Derry)
1917-1997 .... **CLC 8**
See also CA 5-8R; 158; CAAS 1; CANR 5, 63; CN 7; DLB 6, 206; INT CANR-5; TCWW 2

Eastman, Charles A(lexander)
1858-1939 .... **NNAL; TCLC 55**
See also CA 179; CANR 91; DAM MULT; DLB 175; YABC 1

Eaton, Edith Maude 1865-1914 .... **AAL**
See Far, Sui Sin
See also CA 154; DLB 221; FW

Eaton, (Lillie) Winnifred 1875-1954 .... **AAL**
See also CA 217; DLB 221; RGAL 4

Eberhart, Richard (Ghormley)
1904- .... **CLC 3, 11, 19, 56**
See also AMW; CA 1-4R; CANR 2, 125; CDALB 1941-1968; CP 7; DAM POET; DLB 48; MTCW 1; RGAL 4

Eberstadt, Fernanda 1960- .... **CLC 39**
See also CA 136; CANR 69, 128

Echegaray (y Eizaguirre), Jose (Maria Waldo) 1832-1916 .... **HLCS 1; TCLC 4**
See also CA 104; CANR 32; EWL 3; HW 1; MTCW 1

Echeverria, (Jose) Esteban (Antonino)
1805-1851 .... **NCLC 18**
See also LAW

Echo
See Proust, (Valentin-Louis-George-Eugene) Marcel

Eckert, Allan W. 1931- .... **CLC 17**
See also AAYA 18; BYA 2; CA 13-16R; CANR 14, 45; INT CANR-14; MAICYA 2; MAICYAS 1; SAAS 21; SATA 29, 91; SATA-Brief 27

Eckhart, Meister 1260(?)-1327(?) ... **CMLC 9**
See also DLB 115; LMFS 1

Eckmar, F. R.
See de Hartog, Jan

Eco, Umberto 1932- .... **CLC 28, 60, 142**
See also BEST 90:1; BPFB 1; CA 77-80; CANR 12, 33, 55, 110; CPW; CWW 2; DA3; DAM NOV, POP; DLB 196, 242; EWL 3; MSW; MTCW 1, 2; RGWL 3

Eddison, E(ric) R(ucker)
1882-1945 .... **TCLC 15**
See also CA 109; 156; DLB 255; FANT; SFW 4; SUFW 1

Eddy, Mary (Ann Morse) Baker
1821-1910 .... **TCLC 71**
See also CA 113; 174

Edel, (Joseph) Leon 1907-1997 .. **CLC 29, 34**
See also CA 1-4R; 161; CANR 1, 22, 112; DLB 103; INT CANR-22

Eden, Emily 1797-1869 .... **NCLC 10**

Edgar, David 1948- .... **CLC 42**
See also CA 57-60; CANR 12, 61, 112; CBD; CD 5; DAM DRAM; DFS 15; DLB 13, 233; MTCW 1

Edgerton, Clyde (Carlyle) 1944- ...... **CLC 39**
See also AAYA 17; CA 118; 134; CANR 64, 125; CSW; DLB 278; INT CA-134; YAW

Edgeworth, Maria 1768-1849 .... **NCLC 1, 51**
See also BRWS 3; DLB 116, 159, 163; FW; RGEL 2; SATA 21; TEA; WLIT 3

Edmonds, Paul
See Kuttner, Henry

Edmonds, Walter D(umaux)
1903-1998 .... **CLC 35**
See also BYA 2; CA 5-8R; CANR 2; CWRI 5; DLB 9; LAIT 1; MAICYA 1, 2; RHW; SAAS 4; SATA 1, 27; SATA-Obit 99

Edmondson, Wallace
See Ellison, Harlan (Jay)

Edson, Russell 1935- .... **CLC 13**
See also CA 33-36R; CANR 115; DLB 244; WP

Edwards, Bronwen Elizabeth
See Rose, Wendy

Edwards, G(erald) B(asil)
1899-1976 .... **CLC 25**
See also CA 201; 110

Edwards, Gus 1939- .... **CLC 43**
See also CA 108; INT CA-108

Edwards, Jonathan 1703-1758 .... **LC 7, 54**
See also AMW; DA; DAC; DAM MST; DLB 24, 270; RGAL 4; TUS

Edwards, Sarah Pierpont 1710-1758 .. **LC 87**
See also DLB 200

Efron, Marina Ivanovna Tsvetaeva
See Tsvetaeva (Efron), Marina (Ivanovna)

Egoyan, Atom 1960- .... **CLC 151**
See also CA 157

Ehle, John (Marsden, Jr.) 1925- ...... **CLC 27**
See also CA 9-12R; CSW

Ehrenbourg, Ilya (Grigoryevich)
See Ehrenburg, Ilya (Grigoryevich)

Ehrenburg, Ilya (Grigoryevich)
1891-1967 .... **CLC 18, 34, 62**
See also Erenburg, Il'ia Grigor'evich
See also CA 102; 25-28R; EWL 3

Ehrenburg, Ilyo (Grigoryevich)
See Ehrenburg, Ilya (Grigoryevich)

Ehrenreich, Barbara 1941- .... **CLC 110**
See also BEST 90:4; CA 73-76; CANR 16, 37, 62, 117; DLB 246; FW; MTCW 1, 2

Eich, Gunter
See Eich, Gunter
See also RGWL 2, 3

Eich, Gunter 1907-1972 .... **CLC 15**
See Eich, Gunter
See also CA 111; 93-96; DLB 69, 124; EWL 3

Eichendorff, Joseph 1788-1857 .... **NCLC 8**
See also DLB 90; RGWL 2, 3

Eigner, Larry .... **CLC 9**
See Eigner, Laurence (Joel)
See also CAAS 23; DLB 5; WP

Eigner, Laurence (Joel) 1927-1996
See Eigner, Larry
See also CA 9-12R; 151; CANR 6, 84; CP 7; DLB 193

Eilhart von Oberge c. 1140-c.
1195 .... **CMLC 67**
See also DLB 148

Einhard c. 770-840 .... **CMLC 50**
See also DLB 148

Einstein, Albert 1879-1955 .... **TCLC 65**
See also CA 121; 133; MTCW 1, 2

Eiseley, Loren
See Eiseley, Loren Corey
See also DLB 275

Eiseley, Loren Corey 1907-1977 .... **CLC 7**
See Eiseley, Loren
See also AAYA 5; ANW; CA 1-4R; 73-76; CANR 6; DLBD 17

Eisenstadt, Jill 1963- .... **CLC 50**
See also CA 140

Eisenstein, Sergei (Mikhailovich)
1898-1948 .... **TCLC 57**
See also CA 114; 149

Eisner, Simon
See Kornbluth, C(yril) M.

Ekeloef, (Bengt) Gunnar
1907-1968 .... **CLC 27; PC 23**
See Ekelof, (Bengt) Gunnar
See also CA 123; 25-28R; DAM POET

Ekelof, (Bengt) Gunnar 1907-1968
See Ekeloef, (Bengt) Gunnar
See also DLB 259; EW 12; EWL 3

Ekelund, Vilhelm 1880-1949 .... **TCLC 75**
See also CA 189; EWL 3

Ekwensi, C. O. D.
See Ekwensi, Cyprian (Odiatu Duaka)

Ekwensi, Cyprian (Odiatu Duaka)
1921- .... **BLC 1; CLC 4**
See also AFW; BW 2, 3; CA 29-32R; CANR 18, 42, 74, 125; CDWLB 3; CN 7; CWRI 5; DAM MULT; DLB 117; EWL 3; MTCW 1, 2; RGEL 2; SATA 66; WLIT 2

Elaine .... **TCLC 18**
See Leverson, Ada Esther

El Crummo
See Crumb, R(obert)

Elder, Lonne III 1931-1996 ..... **BLC 1; DC 8**
See also BW 1, 3; CA 81-84; 152; CAD; CANR 25; DAM MULT; DLB 7, 38, 44

Eleanor of Aquitaine 1122-1204 ... **CMLC 39**

Elia
See Lamb, Charles

Eliade, Mircea 1907-1986 .... **CLC 19**
See also CA 65-68; 119; CANR 30, 62; CDWLB 4; DLB 220; EWL 3; MTCW 1; RGWL 3; SFW 4

Eliot, A. D.
See Jewett, (Theodora) Sarah Orne

Eliot, Alice
See Jewett, (Theodora) Sarah Orne

Eliot, Dan
See Silverberg, Robert

Eliot, George 1819-1880 ...... **NCLC 4, 13, 23, 41, 49, 89, 118; PC 20; WLC**
See also BRW 5; BRWC 1, 2; BRWR 2; CDBLB 1832-1890; CN 7; CPW; DA; DA3; DAB; DAC; DAM MST, NOV; DLB 21, 35, 55; LATS 1; LMFS 1; NFS 17; RGEL 2; RGSF 2; SSFS 8; TEA; WLIT 3

Eliot, John 1604-1690 .... **LC 5**
See also DLB 24

Eliot, T(homas) S(tearns)
1888-1965 ...... **CLC 1, 2, 3, 6, 9, 10, 13, 15, 24, 34, 41, 55, 57, 113; PC 5, 31; WLC**
See also AAYA 28; AMW; AMWC 1; AMWR 1; BRW 7; BRWR 2; CA 5-8R; 25-28R; CANR 41; CDALB 1929-1941; DA; DA3; DAB; DAC; DAM DRAM, MST, POET; DFS 4, 13; DLB 7, 10, 45, 63, 245; DLBY 1988; EWL 3; EXPP; LAIT 3; LATS 1; LMFS 2; MTCW 1, 2; NCFS 5; PAB; PFS 1, 7; RGAL 4; RGEL 2; TUS; WLIT 4; WP

Elizabeth 1866-1941 .... **TCLC 41**

Elkin, Stanley L(awrence)
1930-1995 .. **CLC 4, 6, 9, 14, 27, 51, 91; SSC 12**
See also AMWS 6; BPFB 1; CA 9-12R; 148; CANR 8, 46; CN 7; CPW; DAM NOV, POP; DLB 2, 28, 218, 278; DLBY 1980; EWL 3; INT CANR-8; MTCW 1, 2; RGAL 4

Elledge, Scott .... **CLC 34**

Elliott, Don
See Silverberg, Robert

Elliott, George P(aul) 1918-1980 .... **CLC 2**
See also CA 1-4R; 97-100; CANR 2; DLB 244

Elliott, Janice 1931-1995 .... **CLC 47**
See also CA 13-16R; CANR 8, 29, 84; CN 7; DLB 14; SATA 119

Elliott, Sumner Locke 1917-1991 ..... **CLC 38**
See also CA 5-8R; 134; CANR 2, 21; DLB 289

Elliott, William
See Bradbury, Ray (Douglas)

Ellis, A. E. .... **CLC 7**

Ellis, Alice Thomas .... **CLC 40**
See Haycraft, Anna (Margaret)
See also DLB 194; MTCW 1

Ellis, Bret Easton 1964- ...... **CLC 39, 71, 117**
See also AAYA 2, 43; CA 118; 123; CANR 51, 74, 126; CN 7; CPW; DA3; DAM POP; DLB 292; HGG; INT CA-123; MTCW 1; NFS 11

Ellis, (Henry) Havelock
1859-1939 .... **TCLC 14**
See also CA 109; 169; DLB 190

Ellis, Landon
See Ellison, Harlan (Jay)

Ellis, Trey 1962- .... **CLC 55**
See also CA 146; CANR 92

Ellison, Harlan (Jay) 1934- ... **CLC 1, 13, 42, 139; SSC 14**
See also AAYA 29; BPFB 1; BYA 14; CA 5-8R; CANR 5, 46, 115; CPW; DAM POP; DLB 8; HGG; INT CANR-5; MTCW 1, 2; SCFW 2; SFW 4; SSFS 13, 14, 15; SUFW 1, 2

Ellison, Ralph (Waldo) 1914-1994 .... **BLC 1; CLC 1, 3, 11, 54, 86, 114; SSC 26; WLC**
See also AAYA 19; AFAW 1, 2; AMWC 2; AMWR 2; AMWS 2; BPFB 1; BW 1, 3; BYA 2; CA 9-12R; 145; CANR 24, 53; CDALB 1941-1968; CSW; DA; DA3; DAB; DAC; DAM MST, MULT, NOV; DLB 2, 76, 227; DLBY 1994; EWL 3; EXPN; EXPS; LAIT 4; MTCW 1, 2; NCFS 3; NFS 2; RGAL 4; RGSF 2; SSFS 1, 11; YAW

Ellmann, Lucy (Elizabeth) 1956- ..... **CLC 61**
See also CA 128

Ellmann, Richard (David)
1918-1987 .... **CLC 50**
See also BEST 89:2; CA 1-4R; 122; CANR 2, 28, 61; DLB 103; DLBY 1987; MTCW 1, 2

Elman, Richard (Martin)
1934-1997 .... **CLC 19**
See also CA 17-20R; 163; CAAS 3; CANR 47

Elron
See Hubbard, L(afayette) Ron(ald)

Eluard, Paul .... **PC 38; TCLC 7, 41**
See Grindel, Eugene
See also EWL 3; GFL 1789 to the Present; RGWL 2, 3

Elyot, Thomas 1490(?)-1546 .... **LC 11**
See also DLB 136; RGEL 2

Elytis, Odysseus 1911-1996 .... **CLC 15, 49, 100; PC 21**
See Alepoudelis, Odysseus
See also CA 102; 151; CANR 94; CWW 2; DAM POET; EW 13; EWL 3; MTCW 1, 2; RGWL 2, 3

Emecheta, (Florence Onye) Buchi
1944- .... **BLC 2; CLC 14, 48, 128**
See also AFW; BW 2, 3; CA 81-84; CANR 27, 81, 126; CDWLB 3; CN 7; CWRI 5; DA3; DAM MULT; DLB 117; EWL 3; FW; MTCW 1, 2; NFS 12, 14; SATA 66; WLIT 2

Emerson, Mary Moody
1774-1863 .... **NCLC 66**

Emerson, Ralph Waldo 1803-1882 . **NCLC 1, 38, 98; PC 18; WLC**
See also AMW; ANW; CDALB 1640-1865; DA; DA3; DAB; DAC; DAM MST,

POET; DLB 1, 59, 73, 183, 223, 270; EXPP; LAIT 2; LMFS 1; NCFS 3; PFS 4, 17; RGAL 4; TUS; WP

Eminescu, Mihail 1850-1889 .. **NCLC 33, 131**

Empedocles 5th cent. B.C.- .... **CMLC 50**
See also DLB 176

Empson, William 1906-1984 ... **CLC 3, 8, 19, 33, 34**
See also BRWS 2; CA 17-20R; 112; CANR 31, 61; DLB 20; EWL 3; MTCW 1, 2; RGEL 2

Enchi, Fumiko (Ueda) 1905-1986 ..... **CLC 31**
See Enchi Fumiko
See also CA 129; 121; FW; MJW

Enchi Fumiko
See Enchi, Fumiko (Ueda)
See also DLB 182; EWL 3

Ende, Michael (Andreas Helmuth) 1929-1995 .... **CLC 31**
See also BYA 5; CA 118; 124; 149; CANR 36, 110; CLR 14; DLB 75; MAICYA 1, 2; MAICYAS 1; SATA 61, 130; SATA-Brief 42; SATA-Obit 86

Endo, Shusaku 1923-1996 ..... **CLC 7, 14, 19, 54, 99; SSC 48**
See Endo Shusaku
See also CA 29-32R; 153; CANR 21, 54; DA3; DAM NOV; MTCW 1, 2; RGSF 2; RGWL 2, 3

Endo Shusaku
See Endo, Shusaku
See also DLB 182; EWL 3

Engel, Marian 1933-1985 .... **CLC 36; TCLC 137**
See also CA 25-28R; CANR 12; DLB 53; FW; INT CANR-12

Engelhardt, Frederick
See Hubbard, L(afayette) Ron(ald)

Engels, Friedrich 1820-1895 .. **NCLC 85, 114**
See also DLB 129; LATS 1

Enright, D(ennis) J(oseph) 1920-2002 .... **CLC 4, 8, 31**
See also CA 1-4R; 211; CANR 1, 42, 83; CP 7; DLB 27; EWL 3; SATA 25; SATA-Obit 140

Enzensberger, Hans Magnus 1929- .... **CLC 43; PC 28**
See also CA 116; 119; CANR 103; EWL 3

Ephron, Nora 1941- .... **CLC 17, 31**
See also AAYA 35; AITN 2; CA 65-68; CANR 12, 39, 83

Epicurus 341B.C.-270B.C. .... **CMLC 21**
See also DLB 176

Epsilon
See Betjeman, John

Epstein, Daniel Mark 1948- .... **CLC 7**
See also CA 49-52; CANR 2, 53, 90

Epstein, Jacob 1956- .... **CLC 19**
See also CA 114

Epstein, Jean 1897-1953 .... **TCLC 92**

Epstein, Joseph 1937- .... **CLC 39**
See also CA 112; 119; CANR 50, 65, 117

Epstein, Leslie 1938- .... **CLC 27**
See also AMWS 12; CA 73-76; 215; CAAE 215; CAAS 12; CANR 23, 69

Equiano, Olaudah 1745(?)-1797 . **BLC 2; LC 16**
See also AFAW 1, 2; CDWLB 3; DAM MULT; DLB 37, 50; WLIT 2

Erasmus, Desiderius 1469(?)-1536 ..... **LC 16, 93**
See also DLB 136; EW 2; LMFS 1; RGWL 2, 3; TWA

Erdman, Paul E(mil) 1932- .... **CLC 25**
See also AITN 1; CA 61-64; CANR 13, 43, 84

Erdrich, Louise 1954- .... **CLC 39, 54, 120, 176; NNAL; PC 52**
See also AAYA 10, 47; AMWS 4; BEST 89:1; BPFB 1; CA 114; CANR 41, 62, 118; CDALBS; CN 7; CP 7; CPW; CWP; DA3; DAM MULT, NOV, POP, DLB 152, 175, 206; EWL 3; EXPP; LAIT 5; LATS 1; MTCW 1; NFS 5; PFS 14; RGAL 4; SATA 94, 141; SSFS 14; TCWW 2

Erenburg, Ilya (Grigoryevich)
See Ehrenburg, Ilya (Grigoryevich)

Erickson, Stephen Michael 1950-
See Erickson, Steve
See also CA 129; SFW 4

Erickson, Steve .... **CLC 64**
See Erickson, Stephen Michael
See also CANR 60, 68; SUFW 2

Erickson, Walter
See Fast, Howard (Melvin)

Ericson, Walter
See Fast, Howard (Melvin)

Eriksson, Buntel
See Bergman, (Ernst) Ingmar

Eriugena, John Scottus c. 810-877 .... **CMLC 65**
See also DLB 115

Ernaux, Annie 1940- .... **CLC 88, 184**
See also CA 147; CANR 93; NCFS 3, 5

Erskine, John 1879-1951 .... **TCLC 84**
See also CA 112; 159; DLB 9, 102; FANT

Eschenbach, Wolfram von
See Wolfram von Eschenbach
See also RGWL 3

Eseki, Bruno
See Mphahlele, Ezekiel

Esenin, Sergei (Alexandrovich) 1895-1925 .... **TCLC 4**
See Yesenin, Sergey
See also CA 104; RGWL 2, 3

Eshleman, Clayton 1935- .... **CLC 7**
See also CA 33-36R, 212; CAAE 212; CAAS 6; CANR 93; CP 7; DLB 5

Espriella, Don Manuel Alvarez
See Southey, Robert

Espriu, Salvador 1913-1985 .... **CLC 9**
See also CA 154; 115; DLB 134; EWL 3

Espronceda, Jose de 1808-1842 ..... **NCLC 39**

Esquivel, Laura 1951(?)- ... **CLC 141; HLCS 1**
See also AAYA 29; CA 143; CANR 68, 113; DA3; DNFS 2; LAIT 3; LMFS 2; MTCW 1; NFS 5; WLIT 1

Esse, James
See Stephens, James

Esterbrook, Tom
See Hubbard, L(afayette) Ron(ald)

Estleman, Loren D. 1952- .... **CLC 48**
See also AAYA 27; CA 85-88; CANR 27, 74; CMW 4; CPW; DA3; DAM NOV, POP; DLB 226; INT CANR-27; MTCW 1, 2

Etherege, Sir George 1636-1692 . **DC 23; LC 78**
See also BRW 2; DAM DRAM; DLB 80; PAB; RGEL 2

Euclid 306B.C.-283B.C. .... **CMLC 25**

Eugenides, Jeffrey 1960(?)- .... **CLC 81**
See also AAYA 51; CA 144; CANR 120

Euripides c. 484B.C.-406B.C. .... **CMLC 23, 51; DC 4; WLCS**
See also AW 1; CDWLB 1; DA; DA3; DAB; DAC; DAM DRAM; MST; DFS 1, 4, 6; DLB 176; LAIT 1; LMFS 1; RGWL 2, 3

Evan, Evin
See Faust, Frederick (Schiller)

Evans, Caradoc 1878-1945 ... **SSC 43; TCLC 85**
See also DLB 162

Evans, Evan
See Faust, Frederick (Schiller)
See also TCWW 2

Evans, Marian
See Eliot, George

Evans, Mary Ann
See Eliot, George

Evarts, Esther
See Benson, Sally

Everett, Percival
See Everett, Percival L.
See also CSW

Everett, Percival L. 1956- .... **CLC 57**
See Everett, Percival
See also BW 2; CA 129; CANR 94

Everson, R(onald) G(ilmour) 1903-1992 .... **CLC 27**
See also CA 17-20R; DLB 88

Everson, William (Oliver) 1912-1994 .... **CLC 1, 5, 14**
See also BG 2; CA 9-12R; 145; CANR 20; DLB 5, 16, 212; MTCW 1

Evtushenko, Evgenii Aleksandrovich
See Yevtushenko, Yevgeny (Alexandrovich)
See also RGWL 2, 3

Ewart, Gavin (Buchanan) 1916-1995 .... **CLC 13, 46**
See also BRWS 7; CA 89-92; 150; CANR 17, 46; CP 7; DLB 40; MTCW 1

Ewers, Hanns Heinz 1871-1943 ..... **TCLC 12**
See also CA 109; 149

Ewing, Frederick R.
See Sturgeon, Theodore (Hamilton)

Exley, Frederick (Earl) 1929-1992 .... **CLC 6, 11**
See also AITN 2; BPFB 1; CA 81-84; 138; CANR 117; DLB 143; DLBY 1981

Eynhardt, Guillermo
See Quiroga, Horacio (Sylvestre)

Ezekiel, Nissim (Moses) 1924-2004 .. **CLC 61**
See also CA 61-64; CP 7; EWL 3

Ezekiel, Tish O'Dowd 1943- .... **CLC 34**
See also CA 129

Fadeev, Aleksandr Aleksandrovich
See Bulgya, Alexander Alexandrovich
See also DLB 272

Fadeev, Alexandr Alexandrovich
See Bulgya, Alexander Alexandrovich
See also EWL 3

Fadeyev, A.
See Bulgya, Alexander Alexandrovich

Fadeyev, Alexander .... **TCLC 53**
See Bulgya, Alexander Alexandrovich

Fagen, Donald 1948- .... **CLC 26**

Fainzilberg, Ilya Arnoldovich 1897-1937
See Ilf, Ilya
See also CA 120; 165

Fair, Ronald L. 1932- .... **CLC 18**
See also BW 1; CA 69-72; CANR 25; DLB 33

Fairbairn, Roger
See Carr, John Dickson

Fairbairns, Zoe (Ann) 1948- .... **CLC 32**
See also CA 103; CANR 21, 85; CN 7

Fairfield, Flora
See Alcott, Louisa May

Fairman, Paul W. 1916-1977
See Queen, Ellery
See also CA 114; SFW 4

Falco, Gian
See Papini, Giovanni

Falconer, James
See Kirkup, James

Falconer, Kenneth
See Kornbluth, C(yril) M.

Falkland, Samuel
See Heijermans, Herman

Fallaci, Oriana 1930- .... **CLC 11, 110**
See also CA 77-80; CANR 15, 58; FW; MTCW 1

Faludi, Susan 1959- .... **CLC 140**
See also CA 138; CANR 126; FW; MTCW 1; NCFS 3

Faludy, George 1913- .... **CLC 42**
See also CA 21-24R

Faludy, Gyoergy
See Faludy, George

Fanon, Frantz 1925-1961 .... **BLC 2; CLC 74**
See also BW 1; CA 116; 89-92; DAM MULT; DLB 296; LMFS 2; WLIT 2

Fanshawe, Ann 1625-1680 .... **LC 11**

Fante, John (Thomas) 1911-1983 .... **CLC 60; SSC 65**
See also AMWS 11; CA 69-72; 109; CANR 23, 104; DLB 130; DLBY 1983

Far, Sui Sin .... **SSC 62**
See Eaton, Edith Maude
See also SSFS 4

Farah, Nuruddin 1945- ...... **BLC 2; CLC 53, 137**
See also AFW; BW 2, 3; CA 106; CANR 81; CDWLB 3; CN 7; DAM MULT; DLB 125; EWL 3; WLIT 2

Fargue, Leon-Paul 1876(?)-1947 .... **TCLC 11**
See also CA 109; CANR 107; DLB 258; EWL 3

Farigoule, Louis
See Romains, Jules

Farina, Richard 1936(?)-1966 .... **CLC 9**
See also CA 81-84; 25-28R

Farley, Walter (Lorimer) 1915-1989 .... **CLC 17**
See also BYA 14; CA 17-20R; CANR 8, 29, 84; DLB 22; JRDA; MAICYA 1, 2; SATA 2, 43, 132; YAW

Farmer, Philip Jose 1918- .... **CLC 1, 19**
See also AAYA 28; BPFB 1; CA 1-4R; CANR 4, 35, 111; DLB 8; MTCW 1; SATA 93; SCFW 2; SFW 4

Farquhar, George 1677-1707 .... **LC 21**
See also BRW 2; DAM DRAM; DLB 84; RGEL 2

Farrell, J(ames) G(ordon) 1935-1979 .... **CLC 6**
See also CA 73-76; 89-92; CANR 36; DLB 14, 271; MTCW 1; RGEL 2; RHW; WLIT 4

Farrell, James T(homas) 1904-1979 . **CLC 1, 4, 8, 11, 66; SSC 28**
See also AMW; BPFB 1; CA 5-8R; 89-92; CANR 9, 61; DLB 4, 9, 86; DLBD 2; EWL 3; MTCW 1, 2; RGAL 4

Farrell, Warren (Thomas) 1943- ...... **CLC 70**
See also CA 146; CANR 120

Farren, Richard J.
See Betjeman, John

Farren, Richard M.
See Betjeman, John

Fassbinder, Rainer Werner 1946-1982 .... **CLC 20**
See also CA 93-96; 106; CANR 31

Fast, Howard (Melvin) 1914-2003 .. **CLC 23, 131**
See also AAYA 16; BPFB 1; CA 1-4R, 181; 214; CAAE 181; CAAS 18; CANR 1, 33, 54, 75, 98; CMW 4; CN 7; CPW; DAM NOV; DLB 9; INT CANR-33; LATS 1; MTCW 1; RHW; SATA 7; SATA-Essay 107; TCWW 2; YAW

Faulcon, Robert
See Holdstock, Robert P.

Faulkner, William (Cuthbert) 1897-1962 .... **CLC 1, 3, 6, 8, 9, 11, 14, 18, 28, 52, 68; SSC 1, 35, 42; TCLC 141; WLC**
See also AAYA 7; AMW; AMWR 1; BPFB 1; BYA 5, 15; CA 81-84; CANR 33; CDALB 1929-1941; DA; DA3; DAB; DAC; DAM MST, NOV; DLB 9, 11, 44, 102; DLBD 2; DLBY 1986, 1997; EWL 3; EXPN; EXPS; LAIT 2; LATS 1; LMFS 2; MTCW 1, 2; NFS 4, 8, 13; RGAL 4; RGSF 2; SSFS 2, 5, 6, 12; TUS

Fauset, Jessie Redmon 1882(?)-1961 .. **BLC 2; CLC 19, 54; HR 2**
See also AFAW 2; BW 1; CA 109; CANR 83; DAM MULT; DLB 51; FW; LMFS 2; MAWW

Faust, Frederick (Schiller) 1892-1944(?) .... **TCLC 49**
See Austin, Frank; Brand, Max; Challis, George; Dawson, Peter; Dexter, Martin; Evans, Evan; Frederick, John; Frost, Frederick; Manning, David; Silver, Nicholas
See also CA 108; 152; DAM POP; DLB 256; TUS

Faust, Irvin 1924- .... **CLC 8**
See also CA 33-36R; CANR 28, 67; CN 7; DLB 2, 28, 218, 278; DLBY 1980

Faustino, Domingo 1811-1888 ...... **NCLC 123**

Fawkes, Guy
See Benchley, Robert (Charles)

Fearing, Kenneth (Flexner) 1902-1961 .... **CLC 51**
See also CA 93-96; CANR 59; CMW 4; DLB 9; RGAL 4

Fecamps, Elise
See Creasey, John

Federman, Raymond 1928- .... **CLC 6, 47**
See also CA 17-20R, 208; CAAE 208; CAAS 8; CANR 10, 43, 83, 108; CN 7; DLBY 1980

Federspiel, J(uerg) F. 1931- .... **CLC 42**
See also CA 146

Feiffer, Jules (Ralph) 1929- ...... **CLC 2, 8, 64**
See also AAYA 3; CA 17-20R; CAD; CANR 30, 59, 129; CD 5; DAM DRAM; DLB 7, 44; INT CANR-30; MTCW 1; SATA 8, 61, 111

Feige, Hermann Albert Otto Maximilian
See Traven, B.

Feinberg, David B. 1956-1994 .... **CLC 59**
See also CA 135; 147

Feinstein, Elaine 1930- .... **CLC 36**
See also CA 69-72; CAAS 1; CANR 31, 68, 121; CN 7; CP 7; CWP; DLB 14, 40; MTCW 1

Feke, Gilbert David .... **CLC 65**

Feldman, Irving (Mordecai) 1928- ..... **CLC 7**
See also CA 1-4R; CANR 1; CP 7; DLB 169

Felix-Tchicaya, Gerald
See Tchicaya, Gerald Felix

Fellini, Federico 1920-1993 .... **CLC 16, 85**
See also CA 65-68; 143; CANR 33

Felltham, Owen 1602(?)-1668 .... **LC 92**
See also DLB 126, 151

Felsen, Henry Gregor 1916-1995 ..... **CLC 17**
See also CA 1-4R; 180; CANR 1; SAAS 2; SATA 1

Felski, Rita .... **CLC 65**

Fenno, Jack
See Calisher, Hortense

Fenollosa, Ernest (Francisco) 1853-1908 .... **TCLC 91**

Fenton, James Martin 1949- .... **CLC 32**
See also CA 102; CANR 108; CP 7; DLB 40; PFS 11

Ferber, Edna 1887-1968 .... **CLC 18, 93**
See also AITN 1; CA 5-8R; 25-28R; CANR 68, 105; DLB 9, 28, 86, 266; MTCW 1, 2; RGAL 4; RHW; SATA 7; TCWW 2

Ferdowsi, Abu'l Qasem 940-1020 . **CMLC 43**
See also RGWL 2, 3

Ferguson, Helen
See Kavan, Anna

Ferguson, Niall 1964- .... **CLC 134**
See also CA 190

Ferguson, Samuel 1810-1886 .... **NCLC 33**
See also DLB 32; RGEL 2

Fergusson, Robert 1750-1774 .... **LC 29**
See also DLB 109; RGEL 2

Ferling, Lawrence
See Ferlinghetti, Lawrence (Monsanto)

Ferlinghetti, Lawrence (Monsanto) 1919(?)- ..... **CLC 2, 6, 10, 27, 111; PC 1**
See also CA 5-8R; CANR 3, 41, 73, 125; CDALB 1941-1968; CP 7; DA3; DAM POET; DLB 5, 16; MTCW 1, 2; RGAL 4; WP

Fern, Fanny
See Parton, Sara Payson Willis

Fernandez, Vicente Garcia Huidobro
See Huidobro Fernandez, Vicente Garcia

Fernandez-Armesto, Felipe .... **CLC 70**

Fernandez de Lizardi, Jose Joaquin
See Lizardi, Jose Joaquin Fernandez de

Ferre, Rosario 1938- .... **CLC 139; HLCS 1; SSC 36**
See also CA 131; CANR 55, 81; CWW 2; DLB 145; EWL 3; HW 1, 2; LAWS 1; MTCW 1; WLIT 1

Ferrer, Gabriel (Francisco Victor) Miro
See Miro (Ferrer), Gabriel (Francisco Victor)

Ferrier, Susan (Edmonstone) 1782-1854 .... **NCLC 8**
See also DLB 116; RGEL 2

Ferrigno, Robert 1948(?)- .... **CLC 65**
See also CA 140; CANR 125

Ferron, Jacques 1921-1985 .... **CLC 94**
See also CA 117; 129; CCA 1; DAC; DLB 60; EWL 3

Feuchtwanger, Lion 1884-1958 .... **TCLC 3**
See also CA 104; 187; DLB 66; EWL 3

Feuerbach, Ludwig 1804-1872 ..... **NCLC 139**
See also DLB 133

Feuillet, Octave 1821-1890 .... **NCLC 45**
See also DLB 192

Feydeau, Georges (Leon Jules Marie) 1862-1921 .... **TCLC 22**
See also CA 113; 152; CANR 84; DAM DRAM; DLB 192; EWL 3; GFL 1789 to the Present; RGWL 2, 3

Fichte, Johann Gottlieb 1762-1814 .... **NCLC 62**
See also DLB 90

Ficino, Marsilio 1433-1499 .... **LC 12**
See also LMFS 1

Fiedeler, Hans
See Doeblin, Alfred

Fiedler, Leslie A(aron) 1917-2003 ..... **CLC 4, 13, 24**
See also AMWS 13; CA 9-12R; 212; CANR 7, 63; CN 7; DLB 28, 67; EWL 3; MTCW 1, 2; RGAL 4; TUS

Field, Andrew 1938- .... **CLC 44**
See also CA 97-100; CANR 25

Field, Eugene 1850-1895 .... **NCLC 3**
See also DLB 23, 42, 140; DLBD 13; MAICYA 1, 2; RGAL 4; SATA 16

Field, Gans T.
See Wellman, Manly Wade

Field, Michael 1915-1971 .... **TCLC 43**
See also CA 29-32R

Field, Peter
See Hobson, Laura Z(ametkin)
See also TCWW 2

Fielding, Helen 1958- .... **CLC 146**
See also CA 172; CANR 127; DLB 231

Fielding, Henry 1707-1754 .... **LC 1, 46, 85; WLC**
See also BRW 3; BRWR 1; CDBLB 1660-1789; DA; DA3; DAB; DAC; DAM DRAM, MST, NOV; DLB 39, 84, 101; NFS 18; RGEL 2; TEA; WLIT 3

Fielding, Sarah 1710-1768 .... **LC 1, 44**
See also DLB 39; RGEL 2; TEA

Fields, W. C. 1880-1946 .... **TCLC 80**
See also DLB 44

Fierstein, Harvey (Forbes) 1954- ..... **CLC 33**
See also CA 123; 129; CAD; CD 5; CPW; DA3; DAM DRAM, POP; DFS 6; DLB 266; GLL

Figes, Eva 1932- .... **CLC 31**
See also CA 53-56; CANR 4, 44, 83; CN 7; DLB 14, 271; FW

Filippo, Eduardo de
See de Filippo, Eduardo

Finch, Anne 1661-1720 .... **LC 3; PC 21**
See also BRWS 9; DLB 95

Finch, Robert (Duer Claydon) 1900-1995 .... **CLC 18**
See also CA 57-60; CANR 9, 24, 49; CP 7; DLB 88

Findley, Timothy (Irving Frederick) 1930-2002 .... **CLC 27, 102**
See also CA 25-28R; 206; CANR 12, 42, 69, 109; CCA 1; CN 7; DAC; DAM MST; DLB 53; FANT; RHW

Fink, William
See Mencken, H(enry) L(ouis)

Firbank, Louis 1942-
See Reed, Lou
See also CA 117

Firbank, (Arthur Annesley) Ronald 1886-1926 .... **TCLC 1**
See also BRWS 2; CA 104; 177; DLB 36; EWL 3; RGEL 2

Fish, Stanley
See Fish, Stanley Eugene

Fish, Stanley E.
See Fish, Stanley Eugene

Fish, Stanley Eugene 1938- .... **CLC 142**
See also CA 112; 132; CANR 90; DLB 67

Fisher, Dorothy (Frances) Canfield 1879-1958 .... **TCLC 87**
See also CA 114; 136; CANR 80; CLR 71,; CWRI 5; DLB 9, 102, 284; MAICYA 1, 2; YABC 1

Fisher, M(ary) F(rances) K(ennedy) 1908-1992 .... **CLC 76, 87**
See also CA 77-80; 138; CANR 44; MTCW 1

Fisher, Roy 1930- .... **CLC 25**
See also CA 81-84; CAAS 10; CANR 16; CP 7; DLB 40

Fisher, Rudolph 1897-1934 .... **BLC 2; HR 2; SSC 25; TCLC 11**
See also BW 1, 3; CA 107; 124; CANR 80; DAM MULT; DLB 51, 102

Fisher, Vardis (Alvero) 1895-1968 .... **CLC 7; TCLC 140**
See also CA 5-8R; 25-28R; CANR 68; DLB 9, 206; RGAL 4; TCWW 2

Fiske, Tarleton
See Bloch, Robert (Albert)

Fitch, Clarke
See Sinclair, Upton (Beall)

Fitch, John IV
See Cormier, Robert (Edmund)

Fitzgerald, Captain Hugh
See Baum, L(yman) Frank

FitzGerald, Edward 1809-1883 .... **NCLC 9**
See also BRW 4; DLB 32; RGEL 2

Fitzgerald, F(rancis) Scott (Key) 1896-1940 ... **SSC 6, 31; TCLC 1, 6, 14, 28, 55; WLC**
See also AAYA 24; AITN 1; AMW; AMWC 2; AMWR 1; BPFB 1; CA 110; 123; CDALB 1917-1929; DA; DA3; DAB; DAC; DAM MST, NOV; DLB 4, 9, 86, 219, 273; DLBD 1, 15, 16; DLBY 1981, 1996; EWL 3; EXPN; EXPS; LAIT 3; MTCW 1, 2; NFS 2; RGAL 4; RGSF 2; SSFS 4, 15; TUS

Fitzgerald, Penelope 1916-2000 . **CLC 19, 51, 61, 143**
See also BRWS 5; CA 85-88; 190; CAAS 10; CANR 56, 86; CN 7; DLB 14, 194; EWL 3; MTCW 2

Fitzgerald, Robert (Stuart) 1910-1985 .... **CLC 39**
See also CA 1-4R; 114; CANR 1; DLBY 1980

FitzGerald, Robert D(avid) 1902-1987 .... **CLC 19**
See also CA 17-20R; DLB 260; RGEL 2

Fitzgerald, Zelda (Sayre) 1900-1948 .... **TCLC 52**
See also AMWS 9; CA 117; 126; DLBY 1984

Flanagan, Thomas (James Bonner) 1923-2002 .... **CLC 25, 52**
See also CA 108; 206; CANR 55; CN 7; DLBY 1980; INT CA-108; MTCW 1; RHW

Flaubert, Gustave 1821-1880 .... **NCLC 2, 10, 19, 62, 66, 135; SSC 11, 60; WLC**
See also DA; DA3; DAB; DAC; DAM MST, NOV; DLB 119; EW 7; EXPS; GFL 1789 to the Present; LAIT 2; LMFS 1; NFS 14; RGSF 2; RGWL 2, 3; SSFS 6; TWA

Flavius Josephus
See Josephus, Flavius

Flecker, Herman Elroy
See Flecker, (Herman) James Elroy

Flecker, (Herman) James Elroy 1884-1915 .... **TCLC 43**
See also CA 109; 150; DLB 10, 19; RGEL 2

Fleming, Ian (Lancaster) 1908-1964 . **CLC 3, 30**
See also AAYA 26; BPFB 1; CA 5-8R; CANR 59; CDBLB 1945-1960; CMW 4; CPW; DA3; DAM POP; DLB 87, 201; MSW; MTCW 1, 2; RGEL 2; SATA 9; TEA; YAW

Fleming, Thomas (James) 1927- .... **CLC 37**
See also CA 5-8R; CANR 10, 102; INT CANR-10; SATA 8

Fletcher, John 1579-1625 .... **DC 6; LC 33**
See also BRW 2; CDBLB Before 1660; DLB 58; RGEL 2; TEA

Fletcher, John Gould 1886-1950 .... **TCLC 35**
See also CA 107; 167; DLB 4, 45; LMFS 2; RGAL 4

Fleur, Paul
See Pohl, Frederik

Flooglebuckle, Al
See Spiegelman, Art

Flora, Fletcher 1914-1969
See Queen, Ellery
See also CA 1-4R; CANR 3, 85

Flying Officer X
See Bates, H(erbert) E(rnest)

Fo, Dario 1926- .... **CLC 32, 109; DC 10**
See also CA 116; 128; CANR 68, 114; CWW 2; DA3; DAM DRAM; DLBY 1997; EWL 3; MTCW 1, 2

Fogarty, Jonathan Titulescu Esq.
See Farrell, James T(homas)

Follett, Ken(neth Martin) 1949- .... **CLC 18**
See also AAYA 6, 50; BEST 89:4; BPFB 1; CA 81-84; CANR 13, 33, 54, 102; CMW 4; CPW; DA3; DAM NOV, POP; DLB 87; DLBY 1981; INT CANR-33; MTCW 1

Fontane, Theodor 1819-1898 .... **NCLC 26**
See also CDWLB 2; DLB 129; EW 6; RGWL 2, 3; TWA

Fontenot, Chester .... **CLC 65**

Fonvizin, Denis Ivanovich 1744(?)-1792 .... **LC 81**
See also DLB 150; RGWL 2, 3

Foote, Horton 1916- .... **CLC 51, 91**
See also CA 73-76; CANR 34, 51, 110; CD 5; CSW; DA3; DAM DRAM; DLB 26, 266; EWL 3; INT CANR-34

Foote, Mary Hallock 1847-1938 .. **TCLC 108**
See also DLB 186, 188, 202, 221

Foote, Shelby 1916- .... **CLC 75**
See also AAYA 40; CA 5-8R; CANR 3, 45, 74; CN 7; CPW; CSW; DA3; DAM NOV, POP; DLB 2, 17; MTCW 2; RHW

Forbes, Cosmo
See Lewton, Val

Forbes, Esther 1891-1967 .... **CLC 12**
See also AAYA 17; BYA 2; CA 13-14; 25-28R; CAP 1; CLR 27; DLB 22; JRDA; MAICYA 1, 2; RHW; SATA 2, 100; YAW

Forche, Carolyn (Louise) 1950- .... **CLC 25, 83, 86; PC 10**
See also CA 109; 117; CANR 50, 74; CP 7; CWP; DA3; DAM POET; DLB 5, 193; INT CA-117; MTCW 1; PFS 18; RGAL 4

Ford, Elbur
See Hibbert, Eleanor Alice Burford

Ford, Ford Madox 1873-1939 ... **TCLC 1, 15, 39, 57**
See Chaucer, Daniel
See also BRW 6; CA 104; 132; CANR 74; CDBLB 1914-1945; DA3; DAM NOV; DLB 34, 98, 162; EWL 3; MTCW 1, 2; RGEL 2; TEA

Ford, Henry 1863-1947 .... **TCLC 73**
See also CA 115; 148

Ford, Jack
See Ford, John

Ford, John 1586-1639 .... **DC 8; LC 68**
See also BRW 2; CDBLB Before 1660; DA3; DAM DRAM; DFS 7; DLB 58; IDTP; RGEL 2

Ford, John 1895-1973 .... **CLC 16**
See also CA 187; 45-48

Ford, Richard 1944- .... **CLC 46, 99**
See also AMWS 5; CA 69-72; CANR 11, 47, 86, 128; CN 7; CSW; DLB 227; EWL 3; MTCW 1; RGAL 4; RGSF 2

Ford, Webster
See Masters, Edgar Lee

Foreman, Richard 1937- .... **CLC 50**
See also CA 65-68; CAD; CANR 32, 63; CD 5

Forester, C(ecil) S(cott) 1899-1966 ... **CLC 35**
See also CA 73-76; 25-28R; CANR 83; DLB 191; RGEL 2; RHW; SATA 13

Forez
See Mauriac, Francois (Charles)

Forman, James
See Forman, James D(ouglas)

Forman, James D(ouglas) 1932- .... **CLC 21**
See also AAYA 17; CA 9-12R; CANR 4, 19, 42; JRDA; MAICYA 1, 2; SATA 8, 70; YAW

Forman, Milos 1932- .... **CLC 164**
See also CA 109

Fornes, Maria Irene 1930- .... **CLC 39, 61, 187; DC 10; HLCS 1**
See also CA 25-28R; CAD; CANR 28, 81; CD 5; CWD; DLB 7; HW 1, 2; INT CANR-28; LLW 1; MTCW 1; RGAL 4

Forrest, Leon (Richard) 1937-1997 .... **BLCS; CLC 4**
See also AFAW 2; BW 2; CA 89-92; 162; CAAS 7; CANR 25, 52, 87; CN 7; DLB 33

Forster, E(dward) M(organ) 1879-1970 ...... **CLC 1, 2, 3, 4, 9, 10, 13, 15, 22, 45, 77; SSC 27; TCLC 125; WLC**
See also AAYA 2, 37; BRW 6; BRWR 2; BYA 12; CA 13-14; 25-28R; CANR 45; CAP 1; CDBLB 1914-1945; DA; DA3; DAB; DAC; DAM MST, NOV; DLB 34, 98, 162, 178, 195; DLBD 10; EWL 3; EXPN; LAIT 3; LMFS 1; MTCW 1, 2; NCFS 1; NFS 3, 10, 11; RGEL 2; RGSF 2; SATA 57; SUFW 1; TEA; WLIT 4

Forster, John 1812-1876 .... **NCLC 11**
See also DLB 144, 184

Forster, Margaret 1938- .... **CLC 149**
See also CA 133; CANR 62, 115; CN 7; DLB 155, 271

Forsyth, Frederick 1938- .... **CLC 2, 5, 36**
See also BEST 89:4; CA 85-88; CANR 38, 62, 115; CMW 4; CN 7; CPW; DAM NOV, POP; DLB 87; MTCW 1, 2

Forten, Charlotte L. 1837-1914 .... **BLC 2; TCLC 16**
See Grimke, Charlotte L(ottie) Forten
See also DLB 50, 239

Fortinbras
See Grieg, (Johan) Nordahl (Brun)

Foscolo, Ugo 1778-1827 .... **NCLC 8, 97**
See also EW 5

Fosse, Bob .... **CLC 20**
See Fosse, Robert Louis

Fosse, Robert Louis 1927-1987
See Fosse, Bob
See also CA 110; 123

Foster, Hannah Webster 1758-1840 .... **NCLC 99**
See also DLB 37, 200; RGAL 4

Foster, Stephen Collins 1826-1864 .... **NCLC 26**
See also RGAL 4

Foucault, Michel 1926-1984 . **CLC 31, 34, 69**
See also CA 105; 113; CANR 34; DLB 242; EW 13; EWL 3; GFL 1789 to the Present; GLL 1; LMFS 2; MTCW 1, 2; TWA

Fouque, Friedrich (Heinrich Karl) de la Motte 1777-1843 .... **NCLC 2**
See also DLB 90; RGWL 2, 3; SUFW 1

Fourier, Charles 1772-1837 .... **NCLC 51**

Fournier, Henri-Alban 1886-1914
See Alain-Fournier
See also CA 104; 179

Fournier, Pierre 1916- .... **CLC 11**
See Gascar, Pierre
See also CA 89-92; CANR 16, 40

Fowles, John (Robert) 1926- . **CLC 1, 2, 3, 4, 6, 9, 10, 15, 33, 87; SSC 33**
See also BPFB 1; BRWS 1; CA 5-8R; CANR 25, 71, 103; CDBLB 1960 to Present; CN 7; DA3; DAB; DAC; DAM MST; DLB 14, 139, 207; EWL 3; HGG; MTCW 1, 2; RGEL 2; RHW; SATA 22; TEA; WLIT 4

Fox, Paula 1923- .... **CLC 2, 8, 121**
See also AAYA 3, 37; BYA 3, 8; CA 73-76; CANR 20, 36, 62, 105; CLR 1, 44, 96; DLB 52; JRDA; MAICYA 1, 2; MTCW 1; NFS 12; SATA 17, 60, 120; WYA; YAW

Fox, William Price (Jr.) 1926- .... **CLC 22**
See also CA 17-20R; CAAS 19; CANR 11; CSW; DLB 2; DLBY 1981

Foxe, John 1517(?)-1587 .... **LC 14**
See also DLB 132

Frame, Janet .. **CLC 2, 3, 6, 22, 66, 96; SSC 29**
See Clutha, Janet Paterson Frame
See also CN 7; CWP; EWL 3; RGEL 2; RGSF 2; TWA

France, Anatole .... **TCLC 9**
See Thibault, Jacques Anatole Francois
See also DLB 123; EWL 3; GFL 1789 to the Present; MTCW 1; RGWL 2, 3; SUFW 1

Francis, Claude .... **CLC 50**
See also CA 192

Francis, Dick 1920- .... **CLC 2, 22, 42, 102**
See also AAYA 5, 21; BEST 89:3; BPFB 1; CA 5-8R; CANR 9, 42, 68, 100; CDBLB 1960 to Present; CMW 4; CN 7; DA3; DAM POP; DLB 87; INT CANR-9; MSW; MTCW 1, 2

Francis, Robert (Churchill) 1901-1987 .... **CLC 15; PC 34**
See also AMWS 9; CA 1-4R; 123; CANR 1; EXPP; PFS 12

Francis, Lord Jeffrey
See Jeffrey, Francis
See also DLB 107

Frank, Anne(lies Marie) 1929-1945 .... **TCLC 17; WLC**
See also AAYA 12; BYA 1; CA 113; 133; CANR 68; DA; DA3; DAB; DAC; DAM MST; LAIT 4; MAICYA 2; MAICYAS 1; MTCW 1, 2; NCFS 2; SATA 87; SATA-Brief 42; WYA; YAW

Frank, Bruno 1887-1945 .... **TCLC 81**
See also CA 189; DLB 118; EWL 3

Frank, Elizabeth 1945- .... **CLC 39**
See also CA 121; 126; CANR 78; INT CA-126

Frankl, Viktor E(mil) 1905-1997 ...... **CLC 93**
See also CA 65-68; 161

Franklin, Benjamin
See Hasek, Jaroslav (Matej Frantisek)

Franklin, Benjamin 1706-1790 .... **LC 25; WLCS**
See also AMW; CDALB 1640-1865; DA; DA3; DAB; DAC; DAM MST; DLB 24, 43, 73, 183; LAIT 1; RGAL 4; TUS

Franklin, (Stella Maria Sarah) Miles (Lampe) 1879-1954 .... **TCLC 7**
See also CA 104; 164; DLB 230; FW; MTCW 2; RGEL 2; TWA

Fraser, Antonia (Pakenham) 1932- . **CLC 32, 107**
See also CA 85-88; CANR 44, 65, 119; CMW; DLB 276; MTCW 1, 2; SATA-Brief 32

Fraser, George MacDonald 1925- ...... **CLC 7**
See also AAYA 48; CA 45-48, 180; CAAE 180; CANR 2, 48, 74; MTCW 1; RHW

Fraser, Sylvia 1935- .... **CLC 64**
See also CA 45-48; CANR 1, 16, 60; CCA 1

Frayn, Michael 1933- . **CLC 3, 7, 31, 47, 176**
See also BRWC 2; BRWS 7; CA 5-8R; CANR 30, 69, 114; CBD; CD 5; CN 7; DAM DRAM, NOV; DLB 13, 14, 194, 245; FANT; MTCW 1, 2; SFW 4

Fraze, Candida (Merrill) 1945- .... **CLC 50**
See also CA 126

Frazer, Andrew
See Marlowe, Stephen

Frazer, J(ames) G(eorge) 1854-1941 .... **TCLC 32**
See also BRWS 3; CA 118; NCFS 5

Frazer, Robert Caine
See Creasey, John

Frazer, Sir James George
See Frazer, J(ames) G(eorge)

Frazier, Charles 1950- .... **CLC 109**
See also AAYA 34; CA 161; CANR 126; CSW; DLB 292

Frazier, Ian 1951- .... **CLC 46**
See also CA 130; CANR 54, 93

Frederic, Harold 1856-1898 .... **NCLC 10**
See also AMW; DLB 12, 23; DLBD 13; RGAL 4

Frederick, John
See Faust, Frederick (Schiller)
See also TCWW 2

Frederick the Great 1712-1786 .... **LC 14**

Fredro, Aleksander 1793-1876 .... **NCLC 8**

Freeling, Nicolas 1927-2003 .... **CLC 38**
See also CA 49-52; 218; CAAS 12; CANR 1, 17, 50, 84; CMW 4; CN 7; DLB 87

Freeman, Douglas Southall 1886-1953 .... **TCLC 11**
See also CA 109; 195; DLB 17; DLBD 17

Freeman, Judith 1946- .... **CLC 55**
See also CA 148; CANR 120; DLB 256

Freeman, Mary E(leanor) Wilkins 1852-1930 .... **SSC 1, 47; TCLC 9**
See also CA 106; 177; DLB 12, 78, 221; EXPS; FW; HGG; MAWW; RGAL 4; RGSF 2; SSFS 4, 8; SUFW 1; TUS

Freeman, R(ichard) Austin 1862-1943 .... **TCLC 21**
See also CA 113; CANR 84; CMW 4; DLB 70

French, Albert 1943- .... **CLC 86**
See also BW 3; CA 167

French, Antonia
See Kureishi, Hanif

French, Marilyn 1929- .. **CLC 10, 18, 60, 177**
See also BPFB 1; CA 69-72; CANR 3, 31; CN 7; CPW; DAM DRAM, NOV, POP; FW; INT CANR-31; MTCW 1, 2

French, Paul
See Asimov, Isaac

Freneau, Philip Morin 1752-1832 .. **NCLC 1, 111**
See also AMWS 2; DLB 37, 43; RGAL 4

Freud, Sigmund 1856-1939 .... **TCLC 52**
See also CA 115; 133; CANR 69; DLB 296; EW 8; EWL 3; LATS 1; MTCW 1, 2; NCFS 3; TWA

Freytag, Gustav 1816-1895 .... **NCLC 109**
See also DLB 129

Friedan, Betty (Naomi) 1921- .... **CLC 74**
See also CA 65-68; CANR 18, 45, 74; DLB 246; FW; MTCW 1, 2; NCFS 5

Friedlander, Saul 1932- .... **CLC 90**
See also CA 117; 130; CANR 72

Friedman, B(ernard) H(arper) 1926- .... **CLC 7**
See also CA 1-4R; CANR 3, 48

Friedman, Bruce Jay 1930- ...... **CLC 3, 5, 56**
See also CA 9-12R; CAD; CANR 25, 52, 101; CD 5; CN 7; DLB 2, 28, 244; INT CANR-25; SSFS 18

Friel, Brian 1929- .... **CLC 5, 42, 59, 115; DC 8**
See also BRWS 5; CA 21-24R; CANR 33, 69; CBD; CD 5; DFS 11; DLB 13; EWL 3; MTCW 1; RGEL 2; TEA

Friis-Baastad, Babbis Ellinor 1921-1970 .... **CLC 12**
See also CA 17-20R; 134; SATA 7

Frisch, Max (Rudolf) 1911-1991 ... **CLC 3, 9, 14, 18, 32, 44; TCLC 121**
See also CA 85-88; 134; CANR 32, 74; CD-WLB 2; DAM DRAM, NOV; DLB 69, 124; EW 13; EWL 3; MTCW 1, 2; RGWL 2, 3

Fromentin, Eugene (Samuel Auguste)
1820-1876 .... **NCLC 10, 125**
See also DLB 123; GFL 1789 to the Present

Frost, Frederick
See Faust, Frederick (Schiller)
See also TCWW 2

Frost, Robert (Lee) 1874-1963 .. **CLC 1, 3, 4, 9, 10, 13, 15, 26, 34, 44; PC 1, 39; WLC**
See also AAYA 21; AMW; AMWR 1; CA 89-92; CANR 33; CDALB 1917-1929; CLR 67; DA; DA3; DAB; DAC; DAM MST, POET; DLB 54, 284; DLBD 7; EWL 3; EXPP; MTCW 1, 2; PAB; PFS 1, 2, 3, 4, 5, 6, 7, 10, 13; RGAL 4; SATA 14; TUS; WP; WYA

Froude, James Anthony
1818-1894 .... **NCLC 43**
See also DLB 18, 57, 144

Froy, Herald
See Waterhouse, Keith (Spencer)

Fry, Christopher 1907- .... **CLC 2, 10, 14**
See also BRWS 3; CA 17-20R; CAAS 23; CANR 9, 30, 74; CBD; CD 5; CP 7; DAM DRAM; DLB 13; EWL 3; MTCW 1, 2; RGEL 2; SATA 66; TEA

Frye, (Herman) Northrop
1912-1991 .... **CLC 24, 70**
See also CA 5-8R; 133; CANR 8, 37; DLB 67, 68, 246; EWL 3; MTCW 1, 2; RGAL 4; TWA

Fuchs, Daniel 1909-1993 .... **CLC 8, 22**
See also CA 81-84; 142; CAAS 5; CANR 40; DLB 9, 26, 28; DLBY 1993

Fuchs, Daniel 1934- .... **CLC 34**
See also CA 37-40R; CANR 14, 48

Fuentes, Carlos 1928- .. **CLC 3, 8, 10, 13, 22, 41, 60, 113; HLC 1; SSC 24; WLC**
See also AAYA 4, 45; AITN 2; BPFB 1; CA 69-72; CANR 10, 32, 68, 104; CDWLB 3; CWW 2; DA; DA3; DAB; DAC; DAM MST, MULT, NOV; DLB 113; DNFS 2; EWL 3; HW 1, 2; LAIT 3; LATS 1; LAW; LAWS 1; LMFS 2; MTCW 1, 2; NFS 8; RGSF 2; RGWL 2, 3; TWA; WLIT 1

Fuentes, Gregorio Lopez y
See Lopez y Fuentes, Gregorio

Fuertes, Gloria 1918-1998 .... **PC 27**
See also CA 178, 180; DLB 108; HW 2; SATA 115

Fugard, (Harold) Athol 1932- . **CLC 5, 9, 14, 25, 40, 80; DC 3**
See also AAYA 17; AFW; CA 85-88; CANR 32, 54, 118; CD 5; DAM DRAM; DFS 3, 6, 10; DLB 225; DNFS 1, 2; EWL 3; LATS 1; MTCW 1; RGEL 2; WLIT 2

Fugard, Sheila 1932- .... **CLC 48**
See also CA 125

Fukuyama, Francis 1952- .... **CLC 131**
See also CA 140; CANR 72, 125

Fuller, Charles (H.), (Jr.) 1939- .... **BLC 2; CLC 25; DC 1**
See also BW 2; CA 108; 112; CAD; CANR 87; CD 5; DAM DRAM, MULT; DFS 8; DLB 38, 266; EWL 3; INT CA-112; MTCW 1

Fuller, Henry Blake 1857-1929 .... **TCLC 103**
See also CA 108; 177; DLB 12; RGAL 4

Fuller, John (Leopold) 1937- .... **CLC 62**
See also CA 21-24R; CANR 9, 44; CP 7; DLB 40

Fuller, Margaret
See Ossoli, Sarah Margaret (Fuller)
See also AMWS 2; DLB 183, 223, 239

Fuller, Roy (Broadbent) 1912-1991 ... **CLC 4, 28**
See also BRWS 7; CA 5-8R; 135; CAAS 10; CANR 53, 83; CWRI 5; DLB 15, 20; EWL 3; RGEL 2; SATA 87

Fuller, Sarah Margaret
See Ossoli, Sarah Margaret (Fuller)

Fuller, Sarah Margaret
See Ossoli, Sarah Margaret (Fuller)
See also DLB 1, 59, 73

Fulton, Alice 1952- .... **CLC 52**
See also CA 116; CANR 57, 88; CP 7; CWP; DLB 193

Furphy, Joseph 1843-1912 .... **TCLC 25**
See Collins, Tom
See also CA 163; DLB 230; EWL 3; RGEL 2

Fuson, Robert H(enderson) 1927- .... **CLC 70**
See also CA 89-92; CANR 103

Fussell, Paul 1924- .... **CLC 74**
See also BEST 90:1; CA 17-20R; CANR 8, 21, 35, 69; INT CANR-21; MTCW 1, 2

Futabatei, Shimei 1864-1909 .... **TCLC 44**
See Futabatei Shimei
See also CA 162; MJW

Futabatei Shimei
See Futabatei, Shimei
See also DLB 180; EWL 3

Futrelle, Jacques 1875-1912 .... **TCLC 19**
See also CA 113; 155; CMW 4

Gaboriau, Emile 1835-1873 .... **NCLC 14**
See also CMW 4; MSW

Gadda, Carlo Emilio 1893-1973 ...... **CLC 11; TCLC 144**
See also CA 89-92; DLB 177; EWL 3

Gaddis, William 1922-1998 ... **CLC 1, 3, 6, 8, 10, 19, 43, 86**
See also AMWS 4; BPFB 1; CA 17-20R; 172; CANR 21, 48; CN 7; DLB 2, 278; EWL 3; MTCW 1, 2; RGAL 4

Gaelique, Moruen le
See Jacob, (Cyprien-)Max

Gage, Walter
See Inge, William (Motter)

Gaines, Ernest J(ames) 1933- .. **BLC 2; CLC 3, 11, 18, 86, 181; SSC 68**
See also AAYA 18; AFAW 1, 2; AITN 1; BPFB 2; BW 2, 3; BYA 6; CA 9-12R; CANR 6, 24, 42, 75, 126; CDALB 1968-1988; CLR 62; CN 7; CSW; DA3; DAM MULT; DLB 2, 33, 152; DLBY 1980; EWL 3; EXPN; LAIT 5; LATS 1; MTCW 1, 2; NFS 5, 7, 16; RGAL 4; RGSF 2; RHW; SATA 86; SSFS 5; YAW

Gaitskill, Mary (Lawrence) 1954- .... **CLC 69**
See also CA 128; CANR 61; DLB 244

Gaius Suetonius Tranquillus c. 70-c. 130
See Suetonius

Galdos, Benito Perez
See Perez Galdos, Benito
See also EW 7

Gale, Zona 1874-1938 .... **TCLC 7**
See also CA 105; 153; CANR 84; DAM DRAM; DFS 17; DLB 9, 78, 228; RGAL 4

Galeano, Eduardo (Hughes) 1940- . **CLC 72; HLCS 1**
See also CA 29-32R; CANR 13, 32, 100; HW 1

Galiano, Juan Valera y Alcala
See Valera y Alcala-Galiano, Juan

Galilei, Galileo 1564-1642 .... **LC 45**

Gallagher, Tess 1943- .... **CLC 18, 63; PC 9**
See also CA 106; CP 7; CWP; DAM POET; DLB 120, 212, 244; PFS 16

Gallant, Mavis 1922- ...... **CLC 7, 18, 38, 172; SSC 5**
See also CA 69-72; CANR 29, 69, 117; CCA 1; CN 7; DAC; DAM MST; DLB 53; EWL 3; MTCW 1, 2; RGEL 2; RGSF 2

Gallant, Roy A(rthur) 1924- .... **CLC 17**
See also CA 5-8R; CANR 4, 29, 54, 117; CLR 30; MAICYA 1, 2; SATA 4, 68, 110

Gallico, Paul (William) 1897-1976 ..... **CLC 2**
See also AITN 1; CA 5-8R; 69-72; CANR 23; DLB 9, 171; FANT; MAICYA 1, 2; SATA 13

Gallo, Max Louis 1932- .... **CLC 95**
See also CA 85-88

Gallois, Lucien
See Desnos, Robert

Gallup, Ralph
See Whitemore, Hugh (John)

Galsworthy, John 1867-1933 .... **SSC 22; TCLC 1, 45; WLC**
See also BRW 6; CA 104; 141; CANR 75; CDBLB 1890-1914; DA; DA3; DAB; DAC; DAM DRAM, MST, NOV; DLB 10, 34, 98, 162; DLBD 16; EWL 3; MTCW 1; RGEL 2; SSFS 3; TEA

Galt, John 1779-1839 .... **NCLC 1, 110**
See also DLB 99, 116, 159; RGEL 2; RGSF 2

Galvin, James 1951- .... **CLC 38**
See also CA 108; CANR 26

Gamboa, Federico 1864-1939 .... **TCLC 36**
See also CA 167; HW 2; LAW

Gandhi, M. K.
See Gandhi, Mohandas Karamchand

Gandhi, Mahatma
See Gandhi, Mohandas Karamchand

Gandhi, Mohandas Karamchand
1869-1948 .... **TCLC 59**
See also CA 121; 132; DA3; DAM MULT; MTCW 1, 2

Gann, Ernest Kellogg 1910-1991 ..... **CLC 23**
See also AITN 1; BPFB 2; CA 1-4R; 136; CANR 1, 83; RHW

Gao Xingjian 1940- .... **CLC 167**
See Xingjian, Gao

Garber, Eric 1943(?)-
See Holleran, Andrew
See also CANR 89

Garcia, Cristina 1958- .... **CLC 76**
See also AMWS 11; CA 141; CANR 73; DLB 292; DNFS 1; EWL 3; HW 2; LLW 1

Garcia Lorca, Federico 1898-1936 .... **DC 2; HLC 2; PC 3; TCLC 1, 7, 49; WLC**
See Lorca, Federico Garcia
See also AAYA 46; CA 104; 131; CANR 81; DA; DA3; DAB; DAC; DAM DRAM, MST, MULT, POET; DFS 4, 10; DLB 108; EWL 3; HW 1, 2; LATS 1; MTCW 1, 2; TWA

Garcia Marquez, Gabriel (Jose)
1928- ..... **CLC 2, 3, 8, 10, 15, 27, 47, 55, 68, 170; HLC 1; SSC 8; WLC**
See also AAYA 3, 33; BEST 89:1, 90:4; BPFB 2; BYA 12, 16; CA 33-36R; CANR 10, 28, 50, 75, 82, 128; CDWLB 3; CPW; DA; DA3; DAB; DAC; DAM MST, MULT, NOV, POP; DLB 113; DNFS 1, 2; EWL 3; EXPN; EXPS; HW 1, 2; LAIT 2; LATS 1; LAW; LAWS 1; LMFS 2; MTCW 1, 2; NCFS 3; NFS 1, 5, 10; RGSF 2; RGWL 2, 3; SSFS 1, 6, 16; TWA; WLIT 1

Garcilaso de la Vega, El Inca
1503-1536 .... **HLCS 1**
See also LAW

Gard, Janice
See Latham, Jean Lee

Gard, Roger Martin du
See Martin du Gard, Roger

Gardam, Jane (Mary) 1928- .... **CLC 43**
See also CA 49-52; CANR 2, 18, 33, 54, 106; CLR 12; DLB 14, 161, 231; MAICYA 1, 2; MTCW 1; SAAS 9; SATA 39, 76, 130; SATA-Brief 28; YAW

Gardner, Herb(ert George)
1934-2003 .... CLC 44
See also CA 149; 220; CAD; CANR 119; CD 5; DFS 18

Gardner, John (Champlin), Jr.
1933-1982 .... CLC 2, 3, 5, 7, 8, 10, 18, 28, 34; SSC 7
See also AAYA 45; AITN 1; AMWS 6; BPFB 2; CA 65-68; 107; CANR 33, 73; CDALBS; CPW; DA3; DAM NOV, POP; DLB 2; DLBY 1982; EWL 3; FANT; LATS 1; MTCW 1; NFS 3; RGAL 4; RGSF 2; SATA 40; SATA-Obit 31; SSFS 8

Gardner, John (Edmund) 1926- .... CLC 30
See also CA 103; CANR 15, 69, 127; CMW 4; CPW; DAM POP; MTCW 1

Gardner, Miriam
See Bradley, Marion Zimmer
See also GLL 1

Gardner, Noel
See Kuttner, Henry

Gardons, S. S.
See Snodgrass, W(illiam) D(e Witt)

Garfield, Leon 1921-1996 .... CLC 12
See also AAYA 8; BYA 1, 3; CA 17-20R; 152; CANR 38, 41, 78; CLR 21; DLB 161; JRDA; MAICYA 1, 2; MAICYAS 1; SATA 1, 32, 76; SATA-Obit 90; TEA; WYA; YAW

Garland, (Hannibal) Hamlin
1860-1940 .... SSC 18; TCLC 3
See also CA 104; DLB 12, 71, 78, 186; RGAL 4; RGSF 2; TCWW 2

Garneau, (Hector de) Saint-Denys
1912-1943 .... TCLC 13
See also CA 111; DLB 88

Garner, Alan 1934- .... CLC 17
See also AAYA 18; BYA 3, 5; CA 73-76; 178; CAAE 178; CANR 15, 64; CLR 20; CPW; DAB; DAM POP; DLB 161, 261; FANT; MAICYA 1, 2; MTCW 1, 2; SATA 18, 69; SATA-Essay 108; SUFW 1, 2; YAW

Garner, Hugh 1913-1979 .... CLC 13
See Warwick, Jarvis
See also CA 69-72; CANR 31; CCA 1; DLB 68

Garnett, David 1892-1981 .... CLC 3
See also CA 5-8R; 103; CANR 17, 79; DLB 34; FANT; MTCW 2; RGEL 2; SFW 4; SUFW 1

Garos, Stephanie
See Katz, Steve

Garrett, George (Palmer) 1929- .. CLC 3, 11, 51; SSC 30
See also AMWS 7; BPFB 2; CA 1-4R, 202; CAAE 202; CAAS 5; CANR 1, 42, 67, 109; CN 7; CP 7; CSW; DLB 2, 5, 130, 152; DLBY 1983

Garrick, David 1717-1779 .... LC 15
See also DAM DRAM; DLB 84, 213; RGEL 2

Garrigue, Jean 1914-1972 .... CLC 2, 8
See also CA 5-8R; 37-40R; CANR 20

Garrison, Frederick
See Sinclair, Upton (Beall)

Garro, Elena 1920(?)-1998 .... HLCS 1
See also CA 131; 169; CWW 2; DLB 145; EWL 3; HW 1; LAWS 1; WLIT 1

Garth, Will
See Hamilton, Edmond; Kuttner, Henry

Garvey, Marcus (Moziah, Jr.)
1887-1940 .... BLC 2; HR 2; TCLC 41
See also BW 1; CA 120; 124; CANR 79; DAM MULT

Gary, Romain .... CLC 25
See Kacew, Romain
See also DLB 83

Gascar, Pierre .... CLC 11
See Fournier, Pierre
See also EWL 3

Gascoyne, David (Emery)
1916-2001 .... CLC 45
See also CA 65-68; 200; CANR 10, 28, 54; CP 7; DLB 20; MTCW 1; RGEL 2

Gaskell, Elizabeth Cleghorn
1810-1865 .... NCLC 5, 70, 97, 137; SSC 25
See also BRW 5; CDBLB 1832-1890; DAB; DAM MST; DLB 21, 144, 159; RGEL 2; RGSF 2; TEA

Gass, William H(oward) 1924- . CLC 1, 2, 8, 11, 15, 39, 132; SSC 12
See also AMWS 6; CA 17-20R; CANR 30, 71, 100; CN 7; DLB 2, 227; EWL 3; MTCW 1, 2; RGAL 4

Gassendi, Pierre 1592-1655 .... LC 54
See also GFL Beginnings to 1789

Gasset, Jose Ortega y
See Ortega y Gasset, Jose

Gates, Henry Louis, Jr. 1950- ... BLCS; CLC 65
See also BW 2, 3; CA 109; CANR 25, 53, 75, 125; CSW; DA3; DAM MULT; DLB 67; EWL 3; MTCW 1; RGAL 4

Gautier, Theophile 1811-1872 .. NCLC 1, 59; PC 18; SSC 20
See also DAM POET; DLB 119; EW 6; GFL 1789 to the Present; RGWL 2, 3; SUFW; TWA

Gawsworth, John
See Bates, H(erbert) E(rnest)

Gay, John 1685-1732 .... LC 49
See also BRW 3; DAM DRAM; DLB 84, 95; RGEL 2; WLIT 3

Gay, Oliver
See Gogarty, Oliver St. John

Gay, Peter (Jack) 1923- .... CLC 158
See also CA 13-16R; CANR 18, 41, 77; INT CANR-18

Gaye, Marvin (Pentz, Jr.)
1939-1984 .... CLC 26
See also CA 195; 112

Gebler, Carlo (Ernest) 1954- .... CLC 39
See also CA 119; 133; CANR 96; DLB 271

Gee, Maggie (Mary) 1948- .... CLC 57
See also CA 130; CANR 125; CN 7; DLB 207

Gee, Maurice (Gough) 1931- .... CLC 29
See also AAYA 42; CA 97-100; CANR 67, 123; CLR 56; CN 7; CWRI 5; EWL 3; MAICYA 2; RGSF 2; SATA 46, 101

Geiogamah, Hanay 1945- .... NNAL
See also CA 153; DAM MULT; DLB 175

Gelbart, Larry (Simon) 1928- .... CLC 21, 61
See Gelbart, Larry
See also CA 73-76; CANR 45, 94

Gelbart, Larry 1928-
See Gelbart, Larry (Simon)
See also CAD; CD 5

Gelber, Jack 1932-2003 ...... CLC 1, 6, 14, 79
See also CA 1-4R; 216; CAD; CANR 2; DLB 7, 228

Gellhorn, Martha (Ellis)
1908-1998 .... CLC 14, 60
See also CA 77-80; 164; CANR 44; CN 7; DLBY 1982, 1998

Genet, Jean 1910-1986 .. CLC 1, 2, 5, 10, 14, 44, 46; TCLC 128
See also CA 13-16R; CANR 18; DA3; DAM DRAM; DFS 10; DLB 72; DLBY 1986; EW 13; EWL 3; GFL 1789 to the Present; GLL 1; LMFS 2; MTCW 1, 2; RGWL 2, 3; TWA

Gent, Peter 1942- .... CLC 29
See also AITN 1; CA 89-92; DLBY 1982

Gentile, Giovanni 1875-1944 .... TCLC 96
See also CA 119

Gentlewoman in New England, A
See Bradstreet, Anne

Gentlewoman in Those Parts, A
See Bradstreet, Anne

Geoffrey of Monmouth c.
1100-1155 .... CMLC 44
See also DLB 146; TEA

George, Jean
See George, Jean Craighead

George, Jean Craighead 1919- .... CLC 35
See also AAYA 8; BYA 2, 4; CA 5-8R; CANR 25; CLR 1; 80; DLB 52; JRDA; MAICYA 1, 2; SATA 2, 68, 124; WYA; YAW

George, Stefan (Anton) 1868-1933 . TCLC 2, 14
See also CA 104; 193; EW 8; EWL 3

Georges, Georges Martin
See Simenon, Georges (Jacques Christian)

Gerald of Wales c. 1146-c. 1223 ... CMLC 60

Gerhardi, William Alexander
See Gerhardie, William Alexander

Gerhardie, William Alexander
1895-1977 .... CLC 5
See also CA 25-28R; 73-76; CANR 18; DLB 36; RGEL 2

Gerson, Jean 1363-1429 .... LC 77
See also DLB 208

Gersonides 1288-1344 .... CMLC 49
See also DLB 115

Gerstler, Amy 1956- .... CLC 70
See also CA 146; CANR 99

Gertler, T. .... CLC 34
See also CA 116; 121

Gertsen, Aleksandr Ivanovich
See Herzen, Aleksandr Ivanovich

Ghalib .... NCLC 39, 78
See Ghalib, Asadullah Khan

Ghalib, Asadullah Khan 1797-1869
See Ghalib
See also DAM POET; RGWL 2, 3

Ghelderode, Michel de 1898-1962 ..... CLC 6, 11; DC 15
See also CA 85-88; CANR 40, 77; DAM DRAM; EW 11; EWL 3; TWA

Ghiselin, Brewster 1903-2001 .... CLC 23
See also CA 13-16R; CAAS 10; CANR 13; CP 7

Ghose, Aurabinda 1872-1950 .... TCLC 63
See Ghose, Aurobindo
See also CA 163

Ghose, Aurobindo
See Ghose, Aurabinda
See also EWL 3

Ghose, Zulfikar 1935- .... CLC 42
See also CA 65-68; CANR 67; CN 7; CP 7; EWL 3

Ghosh, Amitav 1956- .... CLC 44, 153
See also CA 147; CANR 80; CN 7; WWE 1

Giacosa, Giuseppe 1847-1906 .... TCLC 7
See also CA 104

Gibb, Lee
See Waterhouse, Keith (Spencer)

Gibbon, Edward 1737-1794 .... LC 97
See also BRW 3; DLB 104; RGEL 2

Gibbon, Lewis Grassic .... TCLC 4
See Mitchell, James Leslie
See also RGEL 2

Gibbons, Kaye 1960- .... CLC 50, 88, 145
See also AAYA 34; AMWS 10; CA 151; CANR 75, 127; CSW; DA3; DAM POP; DLB 292; MTCW 1; NFS 3; RGAL 4; SATA 117

Gibran, Kahlil 1883-1931 . **PC 9; TCLC 1, 9**
See also CA 104; 150; DA3; DAM POET, POP; EWL 3; MTCW 2

Gibran, Khalil
See Gibran, Kahlil

Gibson, William 1914- .... **CLC 23**
See also CA 9-12R; CAD 2; CANR 9, 42, 75, 125; CD 5; DA; DAB; DAC; DAM DRAM, MST; DFS 2; DLB 7; LAIT 2; MTCW 2; SATA 66; YAW

Gibson, William (Ford) 1948- ... **CLC 39, 63, 186; SSC 52**
See also AAYA 12; BPFB 2; CA 126; 133; CANR 52, 90, 106; CN 7; CPW; DA3; DAM POP; DLB 251; MTCW 2; SCFW 2; SFW 4

Gide, Andre (Paul Guillaume)
1869-1951 ..... **SSC 13; TCLC 5, 12, 36; WLC**
See also CA 104; 124; DA; DA3; DAB; DAC; DAM MST, NOV; DLB 65; EW 8; EWL 3; GFL 1789 to the Present; MTCW 1, 2; RGSF 2; RGWL 2, 3; TWA

Gifford, Barry (Colby) 1946- .... **CLC 34**
See also CA 65-68; CANR 9, 30, 40, 90

Gilbert, Frank
See De Voto, Bernard (Augustine)

Gilbert, W(illiam) S(chwenck)
1836-1911 .... **TCLC 3**
See also CA 104; 173; DAM DRAM, POET; RGEL 2; SATA 36

Gilbreth, Frank B(unker), Jr.
1911-2001 .... **CLC 17**
See also CA 9-12R; SATA 2

Gilchrist, Ellen (Louise) 1935- .. **CLC 34, 48, 143; SSC 14, 63**
See also BPFB 2; CA 113; 116; CANR 41, 61, 104; CN 7; CPW; CSW; DAM POP; DLB 130; EWL 3; EXPS; MTCW 1, 2; RGAL 4; RGSF 2; SSFS 9

Giles, Molly 1942- .... **CLC 39**
See also CA 126; CANR 98

Gill, Eric 1882-1940 .... **TCLC 85**
See Gill, (Arthur) Eric (Rowton Peter Joseph)

Gill, (Arthur) Eric (Rowton Peter Joseph)
1882-1940
See Gill, Eric
See also CA 120; DLB 98

Gill, Patrick
See Creasey, John

Gillette, Douglas .... **CLC 70**

Gilliam, Terry (Vance) 1940- .... **CLC 21, 141**
See Monty Python
See also AAYA 19; CA 108; 113; CANR 35; INT CA-113

Gillian, Jerry
See Gilliam, Terry (Vance)

Gilliatt, Penelope (Ann Douglass)
1932-1993 .... **CLC 2, 10, 13, 53**
See also AITN 2; CA 13-16R; 141; CANR 49; DLB 14

Gilman, Charlotte (Anna) Perkins (Stetson)
1860-1935 ...... **SSC 13, 62; TCLC 9, 37, 117**
See also AMWS 11; BYA 11; CA 106; 150; DLB 221; EXPS; FW; HGG; LAIT 2; MAWW; MTCW 1; RGAL 4; RGSF 2; SFW 4; SSFS 1, 18

Gilmour, David 1946- .... **CLC 35**

Gilpin, William 1724-1804 .... **NCLC 30**

Gilray, J. D.
See Mencken, H(enry) L(ouis)

Gilroy, Frank D(aniel) 1925- .... **CLC 2**
See also CA 81-84; CAD; CANR 32, 64, 86; CD 5; DFS 17; DLB 7

Gilstrap, John 1957(?)- .... **CLC 99**
See also CA 160; CANR 101

Ginsberg, Allen 1926-1997 .... **CLC 1, 2, 3, 4, 6, 13, 36, 69, 109; PC 4, 47; TCLC 120; WLC**
See also AAYA 33; AITN 1; AMWC 1; AMWS 2; BG 2; CA 1-4R; 157; CANR 2, 41, 63, 95; CDALB 1941-1968; CP 7; DA; DA3; DAB; DAC; DAM MST, POET; DLB 5, 16, 169, 237; EWL 3; GLL 1; LMFS 2; MTCW 1, 2; PAB; PFS 5; RGAL 4; TUS; WP

Ginzburg, Eugenia .... **CLC 59**

Ginzburg, Natalia 1916-1991 .... **CLC 5, 11, 54, 70; SSC 65**
See also CA 85-88; 135; CANR 33; DFS 14; DLB 177; EW 13; EWL 3; MTCW 1, 2; RGWL 2, 3

Giono, Jean 1895-1970 .... **CLC 4, 11; TCLC 124**
See also CA 45-48; 29-32R; CANR 2, 35; DLB 72; EWL 3; GFL 1789 to the Present; MTCW 1; RGWL 2, 3

Giovanni, Nikki 1943- ...... **BLC 2; CLC 2, 4, 19, 64, 117; PC 19; WLCS**
See also AAYA 22; AITN 1; BW 2, 3; CA 29-32R; CAAS 6; CANR 18, 41, 60, 91; CDALBS; CLR 6, 73; CP 7; CSW; CWP; CWRI 5; DA; DA3; DAB; DAC; DAM MST, MULT, POET; DLB 5, 41; EWL 3; EXPP; INT CANR-18; MAICYA 1, 2; MTCW 1, 2; PFS 17; RGAL 4; SATA 24, 107; TUS; YAW

Giovene, Andrea 1904-1998 .... **CLC 7**
See also CA 85-88

Gippius, Zinaida (Nikolaevna) 1869-1945
See Hippius, Zinaida (Nikolaevna)
See also CA 106; 212

Giraudoux, Jean(-Hippolyte)
1882-1944 .... **TCLC 2, 7**
See also CA 104; 196; DAM DRAM; DLB 65; EW 9; EWL 3; GFL 1789 to the Present; RGWL 2, 3; TWA

Gironella, Jose Maria (Pous)
1917-2003 .... **CLC 11**
See also CA 101; 212; EWL 3; RGWL 2, 3

Gissing, George (Robert)
1857-1903 .... **SSC 37; TCLC 3, 24, 47**
See also BRW 5; CA 105; 167; DLB 18, 135, 184; RGEL 2; TEA

Giurlani, Aldo
See Palazzeschi, Aldo

Gladkov, Fedor Vasil'evich
See Gladkov, Fyodor (Vasilyevich)
See also DLB 272

Gladkov, Fyodor (Vasilyevich)
1883-1958 .... **TCLC 27**
See Gladkov, Fedor Vasil'evich
See also CA 170; EWL 3

Glancy, Diane 1941- .... **NNAL**
See also CA 136; CAAS 24; CANR 87; DLB 175

Glanville, Brian (Lester) 1931- .... **CLC 6**
See also CA 5-8R; CAAS 9; CANR 3, 70; CN 7; DLB 15, 139; SATA 42

Glasgow, Ellen (Anderson Gholson)
1873-1945 .... **SSC 34; TCLC 2, 7**
See also AMW; CA 104; 164; DLB 9, 12; MAWW; MTCW 2; RGAL 4; RHW; SSFS 9; TUS

Glaspell, Susan 1882(?)-1948 ..... **DC 10; SSC 41; TCLC 55**
See also AMWS 3; CA 110; 154; DFS 8, 18; DLB 7, 9, 78, 228; MAWW; RGAL 4; SSFS 3; TCWW 2; TUS; YABC 2

Glassco, John 1909-1981 .... **CLC 9**
See also CA 13-16R; 102; CANR 15; DLB 68

Glasscock, Amnesia
See Steinbeck, John (Ernst)

Glasser, Ronald J. 1940(?)- .... **CLC 37**
See also CA 209

Glassman, Joyce
See Johnson, Joyce

Gleick, James (W.) 1954- .... **CLC 147**
See also CA 131; 137; CANR 97; INT CA-137

Glendinning, Victoria 1937- .... **CLC 50**
See also CA 120; 127; CANR 59, 89; DLB 155

Glissant, Edouard (Mathieu)
1928- .... **CLC 10, 68**
See also CA 153; CANR 111; CWW 2; DAM MULT; EWL 3; RGWL 3

Gloag, Julian 1930- .... **CLC 40**
See also AITN 1; CA 65-68; CANR 10, 70; CN 7

Glowacki, Aleksander
See Prus, Boleslaw

Gluck, Louise (Elisabeth) 1943- .. **CLC 7, 22, 44, 81, 160; PC 16**
See also AMWS 5; CA 33-36R; CANR 40, 69, 108; CP 7; CWP; DA3; DAM POET; DLB 5; MTCW 2; PFS 5, 15; RGAL 4

Glyn, Elinor 1864-1943 .... **TCLC 72**
See also DLB 153; RHW

Gobineau, Joseph-Arthur
1816-1882 .... **NCLC 17**
See also DLB 123; GFL 1789 to the Present

Godard, Jean-Luc 1930- .... **CLC 20**
See also CA 93-96

Godden, (Margaret) Rumer
1907-1998 .... **CLC 53**
See also AAYA 6; BPFB 2; BYA 2, 5; CA 5-8R; 172; CANR 4, 27, 36, 55, 80; CLR 20; CN 7; CWRI 5; DLB 161; MAICYA 1, 2; RHW; SAAS 12; SATA 3, 36; SATA-Obit 109; TEA

Godoy Alcayaga, Lucila 1899-1957 .. **HLC 2; PC 32; TCLC 2**
See Mistral, Gabriela
See also BW 2; CA 104; 131; CANR 81; DAM MULT; DNFS 1; HW 1, 2; MTCW 1, 2

Godwin, Gail (Kathleen) 1937- ...... **CLC 5, 8, 22, 31, 69, 125**
See also BPFB 2; CA 29-32R; CANR 15, 43, 69; CN 7; CPW; CSW; DA3; DAM POP; DLB 6, 234; INT CANR-15; MTCW 1, 2

Godwin, William 1756-1836 .. **NCLC 14, 130**
See also CDBLB 1789-1832; CMW 4; DLB 39, 104, 142, 158, 163, 262; HGG; RGEL 2

Goebbels, Josef
See Goebbels, (Paul) Joseph

Goebbels, (Paul) Joseph
1897-1945 .... **TCLC 68**
See also CA 115; 148

Goebbels, Joseph Paul
See Goebbels, (Paul) Joseph

Goethe, Johann Wolfgang von
1749-1832 .... **DC 20; NCLC 4, 22, 34, 90; PC 5; SSC 38; WLC**
See also CDWLB 2; DA; DA3; DAB; DAC; DAM DRAM, MST, POET; DLB 94; EW 5; LATS 1; LMFS 1; RGWL 2, 3; TWA

Gogarty, Oliver St. John
1878-1957 .... **TCLC 15**
See also CA 109; 150; DLB 15, 19; RGEL 2

Gogol, Nikolai (Vasilyevich)
1809-1852 .... **DC 1; NCLC 5, 15, 31; SSC 4, 29, 52; WLC**
See also DA; DAB; DAC; DAM DRAM, MST; DFS 12; DLB 198; EW 6; EXPS; RGSF 2; RGWL 2, 3; SSFS 7; TWA

Goines, Donald 1937(?)-1974 ... **BLC 2; CLC 80**
See also AITN 1; BW 1, 3; CA 124; 114; CANR 82; CMW 4; DA3; DAM MULT, POP; DLB 33

Gold, Herbert 1924- ... **CLC 4, 7, 14, 42, 152**
See also CA 9-12R; CANR 17, 45, 125; CN 7; DLB 2; DLBY 1981

Goldbarth, Albert 1948- .... **CLC 5, 38**
See also AMWS 12; CA 53-56; CANR 6, 40; CP 7; DLB 120

Goldberg, Anatol 1910-1982 .... **CLC 34**
See also CA 131; 117

Goldemberg, Isaac 1945- .... **CLC 52**
See also CA 69-72; CAAS 12; CANR 11, 32; EWL 3; HW 1; WLIT 1

Golding, Arthur 1536-1606 .... **LC 101**
See also DLB 136

Golding, William (Gerald)
1911-1993 ..... **CLC 1, 2, 3, 8, 10, 17, 27, 58, 81; WLC**
See also AAYA 5, 44; BPFB 2; BRWR 1; BRWS 1; BYA 2; CA 5-8R; 141; CANR 13, 33, 54; CDBLB 1945-1960; CLR 94; DA; DA3; DAB; DAC; DAM MST, NOV; DLB 15, 100, 255; EWL 3; EXPN; HGG; LAIT 4; MTCW 1, 2; NFS 2; RGEL 2; RHW; SFW 4; TEA; WLIT 4; YAW

Goldman, Emma 1869-1940 .... **TCLC 13**
See also CA 110; 150; DLB 221; FW; RGAL 4; TUS

Goldman, Francisco 1954- .... **CLC 76**
See also CA 162

Goldman, William (W.) 1931- ...... **CLC 1, 48**
See also BPFB 2; CA 9-12R; CANR 29, 69, 106; CN 7; DLB 44; FANT; IDFW 3, 4

Goldmann, Lucien 1913-1970 .... **CLC 24**
See also CA 25-28; CAP 2

Goldoni, Carlo 1707-1793 .... **LC 4**
See also DAM DRAM; EW 4; RGWL 2, 3

Goldsberry, Steven 1949- .... **CLC 34**
See also CA 131

Goldsmith, Oliver 1730-1774 .... **DC 8; LC 2, 48; WLC**
See also BRW 3; CDBLB 1660-1789; DA; DAB; DAC; DAM DRAM, MST, NOV, POET; DFS 1; DLB 39, 89, 104, 109, 142; IDTP; RGEL 2; SATA 26; TEA; WLIT 3

Goldsmith, Peter
See Priestley, J(ohn) B(oynton)

Gombrowicz, Witold 1904-1969 .... **CLC 4, 7, 11, 49**
See also CA 19-20; 25-28R; CANR 105; CAP 2; CDWLB 4; DAM DRAM; DLB 215; EW 12; EWL 3; RGWL 2, 3; TWA

Gomez de Avellaneda, Gertrudis
1814-1873 .... **NCLC 111**
See also LAW

Gomez de la Serna, Ramon
1888-1963 .... **CLC 9**
See also CA 153; 116; CANR 79; EWL 3; HW 1, 2

Goncharov, Ivan Alexandrovich
1812-1891 .... **NCLC 1, 63**
See also DLB 238; EW 6; RGWL 2, 3

Goncourt, Edmond (Louis Antoine Huot) de
1822-1896 .... **NCLC 7**
See also DLB 123; EW 7; GFL 1789 to the Present; RGWL 2, 3

Goncourt, Jules (Alfred Huot) de
1830-1870 .... **NCLC 7**
See also DLB 123; EW 7; GFL 1789 to the Present; RGWL 2, 3

Gongora (y Argote), Luis de
1561-1627 .... **LC 72**
See also RGWL 2, 3

Gontier, Fernande 19(?)- .... **CLC 50**

Gonzalez Martinez, Enrique
See Gonzalez Martinez, Enrique
See also DLB 290

Gonzalez Martinez, Enrique
1871-1952 .... **TCLC 72**
See Gonzalez Martinez, Enrique
See also CA 166; CANR 81; EWL 3; HW 1, 2

Goodison, Lorna 1947- .... **PC 36**
See also CA 142; CANR 88; CP 7; CWP; DLB 157; EWL 3

Goodman, Paul 1911-1972 ..... **CLC 1, 2, 4, 7**
See also CA 19-20; 37-40R; CAD; CANR 34; CAP 2; DLB 130, 246; MTCW 1; RGAL 4

GoodWeather, Harley
See King, Thomas

Googe, Barnabe 1540-1594 .... **LC 94**
See also DLB 132; RGEL 2

Gordimer, Nadine 1923- ...... **CLC 3, 5, 7, 10, 18, 33, 51, 70, 123, 160, 161; SSC 17; WLCS**
See also AAYA 39; AFW; BRWS 2; CA 5-8R; CANR 3, 28, 56, 88; CN 7; DA; DA3; DAB; DAC; DAM MST, NOV; DLB 225; EWL 3; EXPS; INT CANR-28; LATS 1; MTCW 1, 2; NFS 4; RGEL 2; RGSF 2; SSFS 2, 14, 19; TWA; WLIT 2; YAW

Gordon, Adam Lindsay
1833-1870 .... **NCLC 21**
See also DLB 230

Gordon, Caroline 1895-1981 . **CLC 6, 13, 29, 83; SSC 15**
See also AMW; CA 11-12; 103; CANR 36; CAP 1; DLB 4, 9, 102; DLBD 17; DLBY 1981; EWL 3; MTCW 1, 2; RGAL 4; RGSF 2

Gordon, Charles William 1860-1937
See Connor, Ralph
See also CA 109

Gordon, Mary (Catherine) 1949- .... **CLC 13, 22, 128; SSC 59**
See also AMWS 4; BPFB 2; CA 102; CANR 44, 92; CN 7; DLB 6; DLBY 1981; FW; INT CA-102; MTCW 1

Gordon, N. J.
See Bosman, Herman Charles

Gordon, Sol 1923- .... **CLC 26**
See also CA 53-56; CANR 4; SATA 11

Gordone, Charles 1925-1995 .. **CLC 1, 4; DC 8**
See also BW 1, 3; CA 93-96; 180; 150; CAAE 180; CAD; CANR 55; DAM DRAM; DLB 7; INT CA-93-96; MTCW 1

Gore, Catherine 1800-1861 .... **NCLC 65**
See also DLB 116; RGEL 2

Gorenko, Anna Andreevna
See Akhmatova, Anna

Gorky, Maxim .... **SSC 28; TCLC 8; WLC**
See Peshkov, Alexei Maximovich
See also DAB; DFS 9; DLB 295; EW 8; EWL 3; MTCW 2; TWA

Goryan, Sirak
See Saroyan, William

Gosse, Edmund (William)
1849-1928 .... **TCLC 28**
See also CA 117; DLB 57, 144, 184; RGEL 2

Gotlieb, Phyllis (Fay Bloom) 1926- .. **CLC 18**
See also CA 13-16R; CANR 7; DLB 88, 251; SFW 4

Gottesman, S. D.
See Kornbluth, C(yril) M.; Pohl, Frederik

Gottfried von Strassburg fl. c.
1170-1215 .... **CMLC 10**
See also CDWLB 2; DLB 138; EW 1; RGWL 2, 3

Gotthelf, Jeremias 1797-1854 .... **NCLC 117**
See also DLB 133; RGWL 2, 3

Gottschalk, Laura Riding
See Jackson, Laura (Riding)

Gould, Lois 1932(?)-2002 .... **CLC 4, 10**
See also CA 77-80; 208; CANR 29; MTCW 1

Gould, Stephen Jay 1941-2002 .... **CLC 163**
See also AAYA 26; BEST 90:2; CA 77-80; 205; CANR 10, 27, 56, 75, 125; CPW; INT CANR-27; MTCW 1, 2

Gourmont, Remy(-Marie-Charles) de
1858-1915 .... **TCLC 17**
See also CA 109; 150; GFL 1789 to the Present; MTCW 2

Gournay, Marie le Jars de
See de Gournay, Marie le Jars

Govier, Katherine 1948- .... **CLC 51**
See also CA 101; CANR 18, 40, 128; CCA 1

Gower, John c. 1330-1408 .... **LC 76**
See also BRW 1; DLB 146; RGEL 2

Goyen, (Charles) William
1915-1983 .... **CLC 5, 8, 14, 40**
See also AITN 2; CA 5-8R; 110; CANR 6, 71; DLB 2, 218; DLBY 1983; EWL 3; INT CANR-6

Goytisolo, Juan 1931- .... **CLC 5, 10, 23, 133; HLC 1**
See also CA 85-88; CANR 32, 61; CWW 2; DAM MULT; EWL 3; GLL 2; HW 1, 2; MTCW 1, 2

Gozzano, Guido 1883-1916 .... **PC 10**
See also CA 154; DLB 114; EWL 3

Gozzi, (Conte) Carlo 1720-1806 .... **NCLC 23**

Grabbe, Christian Dietrich
1801-1836 .... **NCLC 2**
See also DLB 133; RGWL 2, 3

Grace, Patricia Frances 1937- .... **CLC 56**
See also CA 176; CANR 118; CN 7; EWL 3; RGSF 2

Gracian y Morales, Baltasar
1601-1658 .... **LC 15**

Gracq, Julien .... **CLC 11, 48**
See Poirier, Louis
See also CWW 2; DLB 83; GFL 1789 to the Present

Grade, Chaim 1910-1982 .... **CLC 10**
See also CA 93-96; 107; EWL 3

Graduate of Oxford, A
See Ruskin, John

Grafton, Garth
See Duncan, Sara Jeannette

Grafton, Sue 1940- .... **CLC 163**
See also AAYA 11, 49; BEST 90:3; CA 108; CANR 31, 55, 111; CMW 4; CPW; CSW; DA3; DAM POP; DLB 226; FW; MSW

Graham, John
See Phillips, David Graham

Graham, Jorie 1950- .... **CLC 48, 118**
See also CA 111; CANR 63, 118; CP 7; CWP; DLB 120; EWL 3; PFS 10, 17

Graham, R(obert) B(ontine) Cunninghame
See Cunninghame Graham, Robert (Gallnigad) Bontine
See also DLB 98, 135, 174; RGEL 2; RGSF 2

Graham, Robert
See Haldeman, Joe (William)

Graham, Tom
See Lewis, (Harry) Sinclair

Graham, W(illiam) S(idney)
1918-1986 .... **CLC 29**
See also BRWS 7; CA 73-76; 118; DLB 20; RGEL 2

Graham, Winston (Mawdsley)
1910-2003 .... CLC 23
See also CA 49-52; 218; CANR 2, 22, 45, 66; CMW 4; CN 7; DLB 77; RHW

Grahame, Kenneth 1859-1932 ...... TCLC 64, 136
See also BYA 5; CA 108; 136; CANR 80; CLR 5; CWRI 5; DA3; DAB; DLB 34, 141, 178; FANT; MAICYA 1, 2; MTCW 2; RGEL 2; SATA 100; TEA; WCH; YABC 1

Granger, Darius John
See Marlowe, Stephen

Granin, Daniil .... CLC 59

Granovsky, Timofei Nikolaevich
1813-1855 .... NCLC 75
See also DLB 198

Grant, Skeeter
See Spiegelman, Art

Granville-Barker, Harley
1877-1946 .... TCLC 2
See Barker, Harley Granville
See also CA 104; 204; DAM DRAM; RGEL 2

Granzotto, Gianni
See Granzotto, Giovanni Battista

Granzotto, Giovanni Battista
1914-1985 .... CLC 70
See also CA 166

Grass, Guenter (Wilhelm) 1927- ... CLC 1, 2, 4, 6, 11, 15, 22, 32, 49, 88; WLC
See also BPFB 2; CA 13-16R; CANR 20, 75, 93; CDWLB 2; DA; DA3; DAB; DAC; DAM MST, NOV; DLB 75, 124; EW 13; EWL 3; MTCW 1, 2; RGWL 2, 3; TWA

Gratton, Thomas
See Hulme, T(homas) E(rnest)

Grau, Shirley Ann 1929- .... CLC 4, 9, 146; SSC 15
See also CA 89-92; CANR 22, 69; CN 7; CSW; DLB 2, 218; INT CA-89-92, CANR-22; MTCW 1

Gravel, Fern
See Hall, James Norman

Graver, Elizabeth 1964- .... CLC 70
See also CA 135; CANR 71, 129

Graves, Richard Perceval
1895-1985 .... CLC 44
See also CA 65-68; CANR 9, 26, 51

Graves, Robert (von Ranke)
1895-1985 .. CLC 1, 2, 6, 11, 39, 44, 45; PC 6
See also BPFB 2; BRW 7; BYA 4; CA 5-8R; 117; CANR 5, 36; CDBLB 1914-1945; DA3; DAB; DAC; DAM MST, POET; DLB 20, 100, 191; DLBD 18; DLBY 1985; EWL 3; LATS 1; MTCW 1, 2; NCFS 2; RGEL 2; RHW; SATA 45; TEA

Graves, Valerie
See Bradley, Marion Zimmer

Gray, Alasdair (James) 1934- .... CLC 41
See also BRWS 9; CA 126; CANR 47, 69, 106; CN 7; DLB 194, 261; HGG; INT CA-126; MTCW 1, 2; RGSF 2; SUFW 2

Gray, Amlin 1946- .... CLC 29
See also CA 138

Gray, Francine du Plessix 1930- ...... CLC 22, 153
See also BEST 90:3; CA 61-64; CAAS 2; CANR 11, 33, 75, 81; DAM NOV; INT CANR-11; MTCW 1, 2

Gray, John (Henry) 1866-1934 ...... TCLC 19
See also CA 119; 162; RGEL 2

Gray, Simon (James Holliday)
1936- .... CLC 9, 14, 36
See also AITN 1; CA 21-24R; CAAS 3; CANR 32, 69; CD 5; DLB 13; EWL 3; MTCW 1; RGEL 2

Gray, Spalding 1941-2004 .... CLC 49, 112; DC 7
See also CA 128; CAD; CANR 74; CD 5; CPW; DAM POP; MTCW 2

Gray, Thomas 1716-1771 .... LC 4, 40; PC 2; WLC
See also BRW 3; CDBLB 1660-1789; DA; DA3; DAB; DAC; DAM MST; DLB 109; EXPP; PAB; PFS 9; RGEL 2; TEA; WP

Grayson, David
See Baker, Ray Stannard

Grayson, Richard (A.) 1951- .... CLC 38
See also CA 85-88; 210; CAAE 210; CANR 14, 31, 57; DLB 234

Greeley, Andrew M(oran) 1928- ...... CLC 28
See also BPFB 2; CA 5-8R; CAAS 7; CANR 7, 43, 69, 104; CMW 4; CPW; DA3; DAM POP; MTCW 1, 2

Green, Anna Katharine
1846-1935 .... TCLC 63
See also CA 112; 159; CMW 4; DLB 202, 221; MSW

Green, Brian
See Card, Orson Scott

Green, Hannah
See Greenberg, Joanne (Goldenberg)

Green, Hannah 1927(?)-1996 .... CLC 3
See also CA 73-76; CANR 59, 93; NFS 10

Green, Henry .... CLC 2, 13, 97
See Yorke, Henry Vincent
See also BRWS 2; CA 175; DLB 15; EWL 3; RGEL 2

Green, Julian (Hartridge) 1900-1998
See Green, Julien
See also CA 21-24R; 169; CANR 33, 87; DLB 4, 72; MTCW 1

Green, Julien .... CLC 3, 11, 77
See Green, Julian (Hartridge)
See also EWL 3; GFL 1789 to the Present; MTCW 2

Green, Paul (Eliot) 1894-1981 .... CLC 25
See also AITN 1; CA 5-8R; 103; CANR 3; DAM DRAM; DLB 7, 9, 249; DLBY 1981; RGAL 4

Greenaway, Peter 1942- .... CLC 159
See also CA 127

Greenberg, Ivan 1908-1973
See Rahv, Philip
See also CA 85-88

Greenberg, Joanne (Goldenberg)
1932- .... CLC 7, 30
See also AAYA 12; CA 5-8R; CANR 14, 32, 69; CN 7; SATA 25; YAW

Greenberg, Richard 1959(?)- .... CLC 57
See also CA 138; CAD; CD 5

Greenblatt, Stephen J(ay) 1943- ...... CLC 70
See also CA 49-52; CANR 115

Greene, Bette 1934- .... CLC 30
See also AAYA 7; BYA 3; CA 53-56; CANR 4; CLR 2; CWRI 5; JRDA; LAIT 4; MAICYA 1, 2; NFS 10; SAAS 16; SATA 8, 102; WYA; YAW

Greene, Gael .... CLC 8
See also CA 13-16R; CANR 10

Greene, Graham (Henry)
1904-1991 .... CLC 1, 3, 6, 9, 14, 18, 27, 37, 70, 72, 125; SSC 29; WLC
See also AITN 2; BPFB 2; BRWR 2; BRWS 1; BYA 3; CA 13-16R; 133; CANR 35, 61; CBD; CDBLB 1945-1960; CMW 4; DA; DA3; DAB; DAC; DAM MST, NOV; DLB 13, 15, 77, 100, 162, 201, 204; DLBY 1991; EWL 3; MSW; MTCW 1, 2; NFS 16; RGEL 2; SATA 20; SSFS 14; TEA; WLIT 4

Greene, Robert 1558-1592 .... LC 41
See also BRWS 8; DLB 62, 167; IDTP; RGEL 2; TEA

Greer, Germaine 1939- .... CLC 131
See also AITN 1; CA 81-84; CANR 33, 70, 115; FW; MTCW 1, 2

Greer, Richard
See Silverberg, Robert

Gregor, Arthur 1923- .... CLC 9
See also CA 25-28R; CAAS 10; CANR 11; CP 7; SATA 36

Gregor, Lee
See Pohl, Frederik

Gregory, Lady Isabella Augusta (Persse)
1852-1932 .... TCLC 1
See also BRW 6; CA 104; 184; DLB 10; IDTP; RGEL 2

Gregory, J. Dennis
See Williams, John A(lfred)

Grekova, I. .... CLC 59
See Ventsel, Elena Sergeevna
See also CWW 2

Grendon, Stephen
See Derleth, August (William)

Grenville, Kate 1950- .... CLC 61
See also CA 118; CANR 53, 93

Grenville, Pelham
See Wodehouse, P(elham) G(renville)

Greve, Felix Paul (Berthold Friedrich)
1879-1948
See Grove, Frederick Philip
See also CA 104; 141, 175; CANR 79; DAC; DAM MST

Greville, Fulke 1554-1628 .... LC 79
See also DLB 62, 172; RGEL 2

Grey, Lady Jane 1537-1554 .... LC 93
See also DLB 132

Grey, Zane 1872-1939 .... TCLC 6
See also BPFB 2; CA 104; 132; DA3; DAM POP; DLB 9, 212; MTCW 1, 2; RGAL 4; TCWW 2; TUS

Griboedov, Aleksandr Sergeevich
1795(?)-1829 .... NCLC 129
See also DLB 205; RGWL 2, 3

Grieg, (Johan) Nordahl (Brun)
1902-1943 .... TCLC 10
See also CA 107; 189; EWL 3

Grieve, C(hristopher) M(urray)
1892-1978 .... CLC 11, 19
See MacDiarmid, Hugh; Pteleon
See also CA 5-8R; 85-88; CANR 33, 107; DAM POET; MTCW 1; RGEL 2

Griffin, Gerald 1803-1840 .... NCLC 7
See also DLB 159; RGEL 2

Griffin, John Howard 1920-1980 ..... CLC 68
See also AITN 1; CA 1-4R; 101; CANR 2

Griffin, Peter 1942- .... CLC 39
See also CA 136

Griffith, D(avid Lewelyn) W(ark)
1875(?)-1948 .... TCLC 68
See also CA 119; 150; CANR 80

Griffith, Lawrence
See Griffith, D(avid Lewelyn) W(ark)

Griffiths, Trevor 1935- .... CLC 13, 52
See also CA 97-100; CANR 45; CBD; CD 5; DLB 13, 245

Griggs, Sutton (Elbert)
1872-1930 .... TCLC 77
See also CA 123; 186; DLB 50

Grigson, Geoffrey (Edward Harvey)
1905-1985 .... CLC 7, 39
See also CA 25-28R; 118; CANR 20, 33; DLB 27; MTCW 1, 2

Grile, Dod
See Bierce, Ambrose (Gwinett)

Grillparzer, Franz 1791-1872 .... DC 14; NCLC 1, 102; SSC 37
See also CDWLB 2; DLB 133; EW 5; RGWL 2, 3; TWA

Grimble, Reverend Charles James
See Eliot, T(homas) S(tearns)

Grimke, Angelina (Emily) Weld
1880-1958 .... **HR 2**
See Weld, Angelina (Emily) Grimke
See also BW 1; CA 124; DAM POET; DLB 50, 54

Grimke, Charlotte L(ottie) Forten
1837(?)-1914
See Forten, Charlotte L.
See also BW 1; CA 117; 124; DAM MULT, POET

Grimm, Jacob Ludwig Karl
1785-1863 .... **NCLC 3, 77; SSC 36**
See also DLB 90; MAICYA 1, 2; RGSF 2; RGWL 2, 3; SATA 22; WCH

Grimm, Wilhelm Karl 1786-1859 .. **NCLC 3, 77; SSC 36**
See also CDWLB 2; DLB 90; MAICYA 1, 2; RGSF 2; RGWL 2, 3; SATA 22; WCH

Grimmelshausen, Hans Jakob Christoffel von
See Grimmelshausen, Johann Jakob Christoffel von
See also RGWL 2, 3

Grimmelshausen, Johann Jakob Christoffel von 1621-1676 .... **LC 6**
See Grimmelshausen, Hans Jakob Christoffel von
See also CDWLB 2; DLB 168

Grindel, Eugene 1895-1952
See Eluard, Paul
See also CA 104; 193; LMFS 2

Grisham, John 1955- .... **CLC 84**
See also AAYA 14, 47; BPFB 2; CA 138; CANR 47, 69, 114; CMW 4; CN 7; CPW; CSW; DA3; DAM POP; MSW; MTCW 2

Grosseteste, Robert 1175(?)-1253 . **CMLC 62**
See also DLB 115

Grossman, David 1954- .... **CLC 67**
See also CA 138; CANR 114; CWW 2; EWL 3

Grossman, Vasilii Semenovich
See Grossman, Vasily (Semenovich)
See also DLB 272

Grossman, Vasily (Semenovich)
1905-1964 .... **CLC 41**
See Grossman, Vasilii Semenovich
See also CA 124; 130; MTCW 1

Grove, Frederick Philip .... **TCLC 4**
See Greve, Felix Paul (Berthold Friedrich)
See also DLB 92; RGEL 2

Grubb
See Crumb, R(obert)

Grumbach, Doris (Isaac) 1918- . **CLC 13, 22, 64**
See also CA 5-8R; CAAS 2; CANR 9, 42, 70, 127; CN 7; INT CANR-9; MTCW 2

Grundtvig, Nicolai Frederik Severin
1783-1872 .... **NCLC 1**

Grunge
See Crumb, R(obert)

Grunwald, Lisa 1959- .... **CLC 44**
See also CA 120

Gryphius, Andreas 1616-1664 .... **LC 89**
See also CDWLB 2; DLB 164; RGWL 2, 3

Guare, John 1938- .... **CLC 8, 14, 29, 67; DC 20**
See also CA 73-76; CAD; CANR 21, 69, 118; CD 5; DAM DRAM; DFS 8, 13; DLB 7, 249; EWL 3; MTCW 1, 2; RGAL 4

Guarini, Battista 1537-1612 .... **LC 102**

Gubar, Susan (David) 1944- .... **CLC 145**
See also CA 108; CANR 45, 70; FW; MTCW 1; RGAL 4

Guenter, Erich
See Eich, Gunter

Guest, Barbara 1920- .... **CLC 34; PC 55**
See also BG 2; CA 25-28R; CANR 11, 44, 84; CP 7; CWP; DLB 5, 193

Guest, Edgar A(lbert) 1881-1959 ... **TCLC 95**
See also CA 112; 168

Guest, Judith (Ann) 1936- .... **CLC 8, 30**
See also AAYA 7; CA 77-80; CANR 15, 75; DA3; DAM NOV, POP; EXPN; INT CANR-15; LAIT 5; MTCW 1, 2; NFS 1

Guevara, Che .... **CLC 87; HLC 1**
See Guevara (Serna), Ernesto

Guevara (Serna), Ernesto
1928-1967 .... **CLC 87; HLC 1**
See Guevara, Che
See also CA 127; 111; CANR 56; DAM MULT; HW 1

Guicciardini, Francesco 1483-1540 ..... **LC 49**

Guild, Nicholas M. 1944- .... **CLC 33**
See also CA 93-96

Guillemin, Jacques
See Sartre, Jean-Paul

Guillen, Jorge 1893-1984 . **CLC 11; HLCS 1; PC 35**
See also CA 89-92; 112; DAM MULT, POET; DLB 108; EWL 3; HW 1; RGWL 2, 3

Guillen, Nicolas (Cristobal)
1902-1989 .... **BLC 2; CLC 48, 79; HLC 1; PC 23**
See also BW 2; CA 116; 125; 129; CANR 84; DAM MST, MULT, POET; DLB 283; EWL 3; HW 1; LAW; RGWL 2, 3; WP

Guillen y Alvarez, Jorge
See Guillen, Jorge

Guillevic, (Eugene) 1907-1997 .... **CLC 33**
See also CA 93-96; CWW 2

Guillois
See Desnos, Robert

Guillois, Valentin
See Desnos, Robert

Guimaraes Rosa, Joao 1908-1967 .... **HLCS 2**
See Rosa, Joao Guimaraes
See also CA 175; LAW; RGSF 2; RGWL 2, 3

Guiney, Louise Imogen
1861-1920 .... **TCLC 41**
See also CA 160; DLB 54; RGAL 4

Guinizelli, Guido c. 1230-1276 .... **CMLC 49**

Guiraldes, Ricardo (Guillermo)
1886-1927 .... **TCLC 39**
See also CA 131; EWL 3; HW 1; LAW; MTCW 1

Gumilev, Nikolai (Stepanovich)
1886-1921 .... **TCLC 60**
See Gumilyov, Nikolay Stepanovich
See also CA 165; DLB 295

Gumilyov, Nikolay Stepanovich
See Gumilev, Nikolai (Stepanovich)
See also EWL 3

Gunesekera, Romesh 1954- .... **CLC 91**
See also CA 159; CN 7; DLB 267

Gunn, Bill .... **CLC 5**
See Gunn, William Harrison
See also DLB 38

Gunn, Thom(son William)
1929-2004 . **CLC 3, 6, 18, 32, 81; PC 26**
See also BRWS 4; CA 17-20R; CANR 9, 33, 116; CDBLB 1960 to Present; CP 7; DAM POET; DLB 27; INT CANR-33; MTCW 1; PFS 9; RGEL 2

Gunn, William Harrison 1934(?)-1989
See Gunn, Bill
See also AITN 1; BW 1, 3; CA 13-16R; 128; CANR 12, 25, 76

Gunn Allen, Paula
See Allen, Paula Gunn

Gunnars, Kristjana 1948- .... **CLC 69**
See also CA 113; CCA 1; CP 7; CWP; DLB 60

Gunter, Erich
See Eich, Gunter

Gurdjieff, G(eorgei) I(vanovich)
1877(?)-1949 .... **TCLC 71**
See also CA 157

Gurganus, Allan 1947- .... **CLC 70**
See also BEST 90:1; CA 135; CANR 114; CN 7; CPW; CSW; DAM POP; GLL 1

Gurney, A. R.
See Gurney, A(lbert) R(amsdell), Jr.
See also DLB 266

Gurney, A(lbert) R(amsdell), Jr.
1930- .... **CLC 32, 50, 54**
See Gurney, A. R.
See also AMWS 5; CA 77-80; CAD; CANR 32, 64, 121; CD 5; DAM DRAM; EWL 3

Gurney, Ivor (Bertie) 1890-1937 ... **TCLC 33**
See also BRW 6; CA 167; DLBY 2002; PAB; RGEL 2

Gurney, Peter
See Gurney, A(lbert) R(amsdell), Jr.

Guro, Elena (Genrikhovna)
1877-1913 .... **TCLC 56**
See also DLB 295

Gustafson, James M(oody) 1925- ... **CLC 100**
See also CA 25-28R; CANR 37

Gustafson, Ralph (Barker)
1909-1995 .... **CLC 36**
See also CA 21-24R; CANR 8, 45, 84; CP 7; DLB 88; RGEL 2

Gut, Gom
See Simenon, Georges (Jacques Christian)

Guterson, David 1956- .... **CLC 91**
See also CA 132; CANR 73, 126; DLB 292; MTCW 2; NFS 13

Guthrie, A(lfred) B(ertram), Jr.
1901-1991 .... **CLC 23**
See also CA 57-60; 134; CANR 24; DLB 6, 212; SATA 62; SATA-Obit 67

Guthrie, Isobel
See Grieve, C(hristopher) M(urray)

Guthrie, Woodrow Wilson 1912-1967
See Guthrie, Woody
See also CA 113; 93-96

Guthrie, Woody .... **CLC 35**
See Guthrie, Woodrow Wilson
See also LAIT 3

Gutierrez Najera, Manuel
1859-1895 .... **HLCS 2; NCLC 133**
See also DLB 290; LAW

Guy, Rosa (Cuthbert) 1925- .... **CLC 26**
See also AAYA 4, 37; BW 2; CA 17-20R; CANR 14, 34, 83; CLR 13; DLB 33; DNFS 1; JRDA; MAICYA 1, 2; SATA 14, 62, 122; YAW

Gwendolyn
See Bennett, (Enoch) Arnold

H. D. .... **CLC 3, 8, 14, 31, 34, 73; PC 5**
See Doolittle, Hilda

H. de V.
See Buchan, John

Haavikko, Paavo Juhani 1931- .. **CLC 18, 34**
See also CA 106; EWL 3

Habbema, Koos
See Heijermans, Herman

Habermas, Juergen 1929- .... **CLC 104**
See also CA 109; CANR 85; DLB 242

Habermas, Jurgen
See Habermas, Juergen

Hacker, Marilyn 1942- ...... **CLC 5, 9, 23, 72, 91; PC 47**
See also CA 77-80; CANR 68, 129; CP 7; CWP; DAM POET; DLB 120, 282; FW; GLL 2; PFS 19

Hadewijch of Antwerp fl. 1250- ... **CMLC 61**
See also RGWL 3

Hadrian 76-138 .... **CMLC 52**

Haeckel, Ernst Heinrich (Philipp August)
1834-1919 .... **TCLC 83**
See also CA 157

Hafiz c. 1326-1389(?) .... **CMLC 34**
See also RGWL 2, 3
Hagedorn, Jessica T(arahata)
1949- .... **CLC 185**
See also CA 139; CANR 69; CWP; RGAL 4
Haggard, H(enry) Rider
1856-1925 .... **TCLC 11**
See also BRWS 3; BYA 4, 5; CA 108; 148; CANR 112; DLB 70, 156, 174, 178; FANT; LMFS 1; MTCW 2; RGEL 2; RHW; SATA 16; SCFW; SFW 4; SUFW 1; WLIT 4
Hagiosy, L.
See Larbaud, Valery (Nicolas)
Hagiwara, Sakutaro 1886-1942 .... **PC 18; TCLC 60**
See Hagiwara Sakutaro
See also CA 154; RGWL 3
Hagiwara Sakutaro
See Hagiwara, Sakutaro
See also EWL 3
Haig, Fenil
See Ford, Ford Madox
Haig-Brown, Roderick (Langmere)
1908-1976 .... **CLC 21**
See also CA 5-8R; 69-72; CANR 4, 38, 83; CLR 31; CWRI 5; DLB 88; MAICYA 1, 2; SATA 12
Haight, Rip
See Carpenter, John (Howard)
Hailey, Arthur 1920- .... **CLC 5**
See also AITN 2; BEST 90:3; BPFB 2; CA 1-4R; CANR 2, 36, 75; CCA 1; CN 7; CPW; DAM NOV, POP; DLB 88; DLBY 1982; MTCW 1, 2
Hailey, Elizabeth Forsythe 1938- ...... **CLC 40**
See also CA 93-96, 188; CAAE 188; CAAS 1; CANR 15, 48; INT CANR-15
Haines, John (Meade) 1924- .... **CLC 58**
See also AMWS 12; CA 17-20R; CANR 13, 34; CSW; DLB 5, 212
Hakluyt, Richard 1552-1616 .... **LC 31**
See also DLB 136; RGEL 2
Haldeman, Joe (William) 1943- .... **CLC 61**
See Graham, Robert
See also AAYA 38; CA 53-56, 179; CAAE 179; CANR 6, 70, 72; DLB 8; INT CANR-6; SCFW 2; SFW 4
Hale, Janet Campbell 1947- .... **NNAL**
See also CA 49-52; CANR 45, 75; DAM MULT; DLB 175; MTCW 2
Hale, Sarah Josepha (Buell)
1788-1879 .... **NCLC 75**
See also DLB 1, 42, 73, 243
Halevy, Elie 1870-1937 .... **TCLC 104**
Haley, Alex(ander Murray Palmer)
1921-1992 .... **BLC 2; CLC 8, 12, 76; TCLC 147**
See also AAYA 26; BPFB 2; BW 2, 3; CA 77-80; 136; CANR 61; CDALBS; CPW; CSW; DA; DA3; DAB; DAC; DAM MST, MULT, POP; DLB 38; LAIT 5; MTCW 1, 2; NFS 9
Haliburton, Thomas Chandler
1796-1865 .... **NCLC 15**
See also DLB 11, 99; RGEL 2; RGSF 2
Hall, Donald (Andrew, Jr.) 1928- ...... **CLC 1, 13, 37, 59, 151**
See also CA 5-8R; CAAS 7; CANR 2, 44, 64, 106; CP 7; DAM POET; DLB 5; MTCW 1; RGAL 4; SATA 23, 97
Hall, Frederic Sauser
See Sauser-Hall, Frederic
Hall, James
See Kuttner, Henry
Hall, James Norman 1887-1951 ..... **TCLC 23**
See also CA 123; 173; LAIT 1; RHW 1; SATA 21

Hall, Joseph 1574-1656 .... **LC 91**
See also DLB 121, 151; RGEL 2
Hall, (Marguerite) Radclyffe
1880-1943 .... **TCLC 12**
See also BRWS 6; CA 110; 150; CANR 83; DLB 191; MTCW 2; RGEL 2; RHW
Hall, Rodney 1935- .... **CLC 51**
See also CA 109; CANR 69; CN 7; CP 7; DLB 289
Hallam, Arthur Henry
1811-1833 .... **NCLC 110**
See also DLB 32
Halldor Kiljan Gudjonsson 1902-1998
See Halldor Laxness
See also CA 103; 164; CWW 2
Halldor Laxness .... **CLC 25**
See Halldor Kiljan Gudjonsson
See also DLB 293; EW 12; EWL 3; RGWL 2, 3
Halleck, Fitz-Greene 1790-1867 .... **NCLC 47**
See also DLB 3, 250; RGAL 4
Halliday, Michael
See Creasey, John
Halpern, Daniel 1945- .... **CLC 14**
See also CA 33-36R; CANR 93; CP 7
Hamburger, Michael (Peter Leopold)
1924- .... **CLC 5, 14**
See also CA 5-8R, 196; CAAE 196; CAAS 4; CANR 2, 47; CP 7; DLB 27
Hamill, Pete 1935- .... **CLC 10**
See also CA 25-28R; CANR 18, 71, 127
Hamilton, Alexander
1755(?)-1804 .... **NCLC 49**
See also DLB 37
Hamilton, Clive
See Lewis, C(live) S(taples)
Hamilton, Edmond 1904-1977 .... **CLC 1**
See also CA 1-4R; CANR 3, 84; DLB 8; SATA 118; SFW 4
Hamilton, Eugene (Jacob) Lee
See Lee-Hamilton, Eugene (Jacob)
Hamilton, Franklin
See Silverberg, Robert
Hamilton, Gail
See Corcoran, Barbara (Asenath)
Hamilton, Jane 1957- .... **CLC 179**
See also CA 147; CANR 85, 128
Hamilton, Mollie
See Kaye, M(ary) M(argaret)
Hamilton, (Anthony Walter) Patrick
1904-1962 .... **CLC 51**
See also CA 176; 113; DLB 10, 191
Hamilton, Virginia (Esther)
1936-2002 .... **CLC 26**
See also AAYA 2, 21; BW 2, 3; BYA 1, 2, 8; CA 25-28R; 206; CANR 20, 37, 73, 126; CLR 1, 11, 40; DAM MULT; DLB 33, 52; DLBY 01; INT CANR-20; JRDA; LAIT 5; MAICYA 1, 2; MAICYAS 1; MTCW 1, 2; SATA 4, 56, 79, 123; SATA-Obit 132; WYA; YAW
Hammett, (Samuel) Dashiell
1894-1961 .... **CLC 3, 5, 10, 19, 47; SSC 17**
See also AITN 1; AMWS 4; BPFB 2; CA 81-84; CANR 42; CDALB 1929-1941; CMW 4; DA3; DLB 226, 280; DLBD 6; DLBY 1996; EWL 3; LAIT 3; MSW; MTCW 1, 2; RGAL 4; RGSF 2; TUS
Hammon, Jupiter 1720(?)-1800(?) .... **BLC 2; NCLC 5; PC 16**
See also DAM MULT, POET; DLB 31, 50
Hammond, Keith
See Kuttner, Henry
Hamner, Earl (Henry), Jr. 1923- .... **CLC 12**
See also AITN 2; CA 73-76; DLB 6

Hampton, Christopher (James)
1946- .... **CLC 4**
See also CA 25-28R; CD 5; DLB 13; MTCW 1
Hamsun, Knut .... **TCLC 2, 14, 49, 151**
See Pedersen, Knut
See also DLB 297; EW 8; EWL 3; RGWL 2, 3
Handke, Peter 1942- .... **CLC 5, 8, 10, 15, 38, 134; DC 17**
See also CA 77-80; CANR 33, 75, 104; CWW 2; DAM DRAM, NOV; DLB 85, 124; EWL 3; MTCW 1, 2; TWA
Handy, W(illiam) C(hristopher)
1873-1958 .... **TCLC 97**
See also BW 3; CA 121; 167
Hanley, James 1901-1985 ..... **CLC 3, 5, 8, 13**
See also CA 73-76; 117; CANR 36; CBD; DLB 191; EWL 3; MTCW 1; RGEL 2
Hannah, Barry 1942- .... **CLC 23, 38, 90**
See also BPFB 2; CA 108; 110; CANR 43, 68, 113; CN 7; CSW; DLB 6, 234; INT CA-110; MTCW 1; RGSF 2
Hannon, Ezra
See Hunter, Evan
Hansberry, Lorraine (Vivian)
1930-1965 ... **BLC 2; CLC 17, 62; DC 2**
See also AAYA 25; AFAW 1, 2; AMWS 4; BW 1, 3; CA 109; 25-28R; CABS 3; CAD; CANR 58; CDALB 1941-1968; CWD; DA; DA3; DAB; DAC; DAM DRAM, MST, MULT; DFS 2; DLB 7, 38; EWL 3; FW; LAIT 4; MTCW 1, 2; RGAL 4; TUS
Hansen, Joseph 1923- .... **CLC 38**
See Brock, Rose; Colton, James
See also BPFB 2; CA 29-32R; CAAS 17; CANR 16, 44, 66, 125; CMW 4; DLB 226; GLL 1; INT CANR-16
Hansen, Martin A(lfred)
1909-1955 .... **TCLC 32**
See also CA 167; DLB 214; EWL 3
Hansen and Philipson eds. .... **CLC 65**
Hanson, Kenneth O(stlin) 1922- .... **CLC 13**
See also CA 53-56; CANR 7
Hardwick, Elizabeth (Bruce) 1916- . **CLC 13**
See also AMWS 3; CA 5-8R; CANR 3, 32, 70, 100; CN 7; CSW; DA3; DAM NOV; DLB 6; MAWW; MTCW 1, 2
Hardy, Thomas 1840-1928 .... **PC 8; SSC 2, 60; TCLC 4, 10, 18, 32, 48, 53, 72, 143; WLC**
See also BRW 6; BRWC 1, 2; BRWR 1; CA 104; 123; CDBLB 1890-1914; DA; DA3; DAB; DAC; DAM MST, NOV, POET; DLB 18, 19, 135, 284; EWL 3; EXPN; EXPP; LAIT 2; MTCW 1, 2; NFS 3, 11, 15; PFS 3, 4, 18; RGEL 2; RGSF 2; TEA; WLIT 4
Hare, David 1947- .... **CLC 29, 58, 136**
See also BRWS 4; CA 97-100; CANR 39, 91; CBD; CD 5; DFS 4, 7, 16; DLB 13; MTCW 1; TEA
Harewood, John
See Van Druten, John (William)
Harford, Henry
See Hudson, W(illiam) H(enry)
Hargrave, Leonie
See Disch, Thomas M(ichael)
Hariri, Al- al-Qasim ibn 'Ali Abu Muhammad al-Basri
See al-Hariri, al-Qasim ibn 'Ali Abu Muhammad al-Basri
Harjo, Joy 1951- ..... **CLC 83; NNAL; PC 27**
See also AMWS 12; CA 114; CANR 35, 67, 91, 129; CP 7; CWP; DAM MULT; DLB 120, 175; EWL 3; MTCW 2; PFS 15; RGAL 4
Harlan, Louis R(udolph) 1922- .... **CLC 34**
See also CA 21-24R; CANR 25, 55, 80

Harling, Robert 1951(?)- .... **CLC 53**
See also CA 147

Harmon, William (Ruth) 1938- .... **CLC 38**
See also CA 33-36R; CANR 14, 32, 35; SATA 65

Harper, F. E. W.
See Harper, Frances Ellen Watkins

Harper, Frances E. W.
See Harper, Frances Ellen Watkins

Harper, Frances E. Watkins
See Harper, Frances Ellen Watkins

Harper, Frances Ellen
See Harper, Frances Ellen Watkins

Harper, Frances Ellen Watkins
1825-1911 ..... **BLC 2; PC 21; TCLC 14**
See also AFAW 1, 2; BW 1, 3; CA 111; 125; CANR 79; DAM MULT, POET; DLB 50, 221; MAWW; RGAL 4

Harper, Michael S(teven) 1938- ... **CLC 7, 22**
See also AFAW 2; BW 1; CA 33-36R; CANR 24, 108; CP 7; DLB 41; RGAL 4

Harper, Mrs. F. E. W.
See Harper, Frances Ellen Watkins

Harpur, Charles 1813-1868 .... **NCLC 114**
See also DLB 230; RGEL 2

Harris, Christie
See Harris, Christie (Lucy) Irwin

Harris, Christie (Lucy) Irwin
1907-2002 .... **CLC 12**
See also CA 5-8R; CANR 6, 83; CLR 47; DLB 88; JRDA; MAICYA 1, 2; SAAS 10; SATA 6, 74; SATA-Essay 116

Harris, Frank 1856-1931 .... **TCLC 24**
See also CA 109; 150; CANR 80; DLB 156, 197; RGEL 2

Harris, George Washington
1814-1869 .... **NCLC 23**
See also DLB 3, 11, 248; RGAL 4

Harris, Joel Chandler 1848-1908 ..... **SSC 19; TCLC 2**
See also CA 104; 137; CANR 80; CLR 49; DLB 11, 23, 42, 78, 91; LAIT 2; MAICYA 1, 2; RGSF 2; SATA 100; WCH; YABC 1

Harris, John (Wyndham Parkes Lucas) Beynon 1903-1969
See Wyndham, John
See also CA 102; 89-92; CANR 84; SATA 118; SFW 4

Harris, MacDonald .... **CLC 9**
See Heiney, Donald (William)

Harris, Mark 1922- .... **CLC 19**
See also CA 5-8R; CAAS 3; CANR 2, 55, 83; CN 7; DLB 2; DLBY 1980

Harris, Norman .... **CLC 65**

Harris, (Theodore) Wilson 1921- .... **CLC 25, 159**
See also BRWS 5; BW 2, 3; CA 65-68; CAAS 16; CANR 11, 27, 69, 114; CDWLB 3; CN 7; CP 7; DLB 117; EWL 3; MTCW 1; RGEL 2

Harrison, Barbara Grizzuti
1934-2002 .... **CLC 144**
See also CA 77-80; 205; CANR 15, 48; INT CANR-15

Harrison, Elizabeth (Allen) Cavanna
1909-2001
See Cavanna, Betty
See also CA 9-12R; 200; CANR 6, 27, 85, 104, 121; MAICYA 2; SATA 142; YAW

Harrison, Harry (Max) 1925- .... **CLC 42**
See also CA 1-4R; CANR 5, 21, 84; DLB 8; SATA 4; SCFW 2; SFW 4

Harrison, James (Thomas) 1937- ..... **CLC 6, 14, 33, 66, 143; SSC 19**
See Harrison, Jim
See also CA 13-16R; CANR 8, 51, 79; CN 7; CP 7; DLBY 1982; INT CANR-8

Harrison, Jim
See Harrison, James (Thomas)
See also AMWS 8; RGAL 4; TCWW 2; TUS

Harrison, Kathryn 1961- .... **CLC 70, 151**
See also CA 144; CANR 68, 122

Harrison, Tony 1937- .... **CLC 43, 129**
See also BRWS 5; CA 65-68; CANR 44, 98; CBD; CD 5; CP 7; DLB 40, 245; MTCW 1; RGEL 2

Harriss, Will(ard Irvin) 1922- .... **CLC 34**
See also CA 111

Hart, Ellis
See Ellison, Harlan (Jay)

Hart, Josephine 1942(?)- .... **CLC 70**
See also CA 138; CANR 70; CPW; DAM POP

Hart, Moss 1904-1961 .... **CLC 66**
See also CA 109; 89-92; CANR 84; DAM DRAM; DFS 1; DLB 7, 266; RGAL 4

Harte, (Francis) Bret(t)
1836(?)-1902 ... **SSC 8, 59; TCLC 1, 25; WLC**
See also AMWS 2; CA 104; 140; CANR 80; CDALB 1865-1917; DA; DA3; DAC; DAM MST; DLB 12, 64, 74, 79, 186; EXPS; LAIT 2; RGAL 4; RGSF 2; SATA 26; SSFS 3; TUS

Hartley, L(eslie) P(oles) 1895-1972 ... **CLC 2, 22**
See also BRWS 7; CA 45-48; 37-40R; CANR 33; DLB 15, 139; EWL 3; HGG; MTCW 1, 2; RGEL 2; RGSF 2; SUFW 1

Hartman, Geoffrey H. 1929- .... **CLC 27**
See also CA 117; 125; CANR 79; DLB 67

Hartmann, Sadakichi 1869-1944 ... **TCLC 73**
See also CA 157; DLB 54

Hartmann von Aue c. 1170-c. 1210 .... **CMLC 15**
See also CDWLB 2; DLB 138; RGWL 2, 3

Hartog, Jan de
See de Hartog, Jan

Haruf, Kent 1943- .... **CLC 34**
See also AAYA 44; CA 149; CANR 91

Harvey, Caroline
See Trollope, Joanna

Harvey, Gabriel 1550(?)-1631 .... **LC 88**
See also DLB 167, 213, 281

Harwood, Ronald 1934- .... **CLC 32**
See also CA 1-4R; CANR 4, 55; CBD; CD 5; DAM DRAM, MST; DLB 13

Hasegawa Tatsunosuke
See Futabatei, Shimei

Hasek, Jaroslav (Matej Frantisek)
1883-1923 .... **SSC 69; TCLC 4**
See also CA 104; 129; CDWLB 4; DLB 215; EW 9; EWL 3; MTCW 1, 2; RGSF 2; RGWL 2, 3

Hass, Robert 1941- ... **CLC 18, 39, 99; PC 16**
See also AMWS 6; CA 111; CANR 30, 50, 71; CP 7; DLB 105, 206; EWL 3; RGAL 4; SATA 94

Hastings, Hudson
See Kuttner, Henry

Hastings, Selina .... **CLC 44**

Hathorne, John 1641-1717 .... **LC 38**

Hatteras, Amelia
See Mencken, H(enry) L(ouis)

Hatteras, Owen .... **TCLC 18**
See Mencken, H(enry) L(ouis); Nathan, George Jean

Hauptmann, Gerhart (Johann Robert)
1862-1946 .... **SSC 37; TCLC 4**
See also CA 104; 153; CDWLB 2; DAM DRAM; DLB 66, 118; EW 8; EWL 3; RGSF 2; RGWL 2, 3; TWA

Havel, Vaclav 1936- ..... **CLC 25, 58, 65, 123; DC 6**
See also CA 104; CANR 36, 63, 124; CDWLB 4; CWW 2; DA3; DAM DRAM; DFS 10; DLB 232; EWL 3; LMFS 2; MTCW 1, 2; RGWL 3

Haviaras, Stratis .... **CLC 33**
See Chaviaras, Strates

Hawes, Stephen 1475(?)-1529(?) .... **LC 17**
See also DLB 132; RGEL 2

Hawkes, John (Clendennin Burne, Jr.)
1925-1998 .. **CLC 1, 2, 3, 4, 7, 9, 14, 15, 27, 49**
See also BPFB 2; CA 1-4R; 167; CANR 2, 47, 64; CN 7; DLB 2, 7, 227; DLBY 1980, 1998; EWL 3; MTCW 1, 2; RGAL 4

Hawking, S. W.
See Hawking, Stephen W(illiam)

Hawking, Stephen W(illiam) 1942- . **CLC 63, 105**
See also AAYA 13; BEST 89:1; CA 126; 129; CANR 48, 115; CPW; DA3; MTCW 2

Hawkins, Anthony Hope
See Hope, Anthony

Hawthorne, Julian 1846-1934 .... **TCLC 25**
See also CA 165; HGG

Hawthorne, Nathaniel 1804-1864 ... **NCLC 2, 10, 17, 23, 39, 79, 95; SSC 3, 29, 39; WLC**
See also AAYA 18; AMW; AMWC 1; AMWR 1; BPFB 2; BYA 3; CDALB 1640-1865; DA; DA3; DAB; DAC; DAM MST, NOV; DLB 1, 74, 183, 223, 269; EXPN; EXPS; HGG; LAIT 1; NFS 1; RGAL 4; RGSF 2; SSFS 1, 7, 11, 15; SUFW 1; TUS; WCH; YABC 2

Haxton, Josephine Ayres 1921-
See Douglas, Ellen
See also CA 115; CANR 41, 83

Hayaseca y Eizaguirre, Jorge
See Echegaray (y Eizaguirre), Jose (Maria Waldo)

Hayashi, Fumiko 1904-1951 .... **TCLC 27**
See Hayashi Fumiko
See also CA 161

Hayashi Fumiko
See Hayashi, Fumiko
See also DLB 180; EWL 3

Haycraft, Anna (Margaret) 1932-
See Ellis, Alice Thomas
See also CA 122; CANR 85, 90; MTCW 2

Hayden, Robert E(arl) 1913-1980 ..... **BLC 2; CLC 5, 9, 14, 37; PC 6**
See also AFAW 1, 2; AMWS 2; BW 1, 3; CA 69-72; 97-100; CABS 2; CANR 24, 75, 82; CDALB 1941-1968; DA; DAC; DAM MST, MULT, POET; DLB 5, 76; EWL 3; EXPP; MTCW 1, 2; PFS 1; RGAL 4; SATA 19; SATA-Obit 26; WP

Hayek, F(riedrich) A(ugust von)
1899-1992 .... **TCLC 109**
See also CA 93-96; 137; CANR 20; MTCW 1, 2

Hayford, J(oseph) E(phraim) Casely
See Casely-Hayford, J(oseph) E(phraim)

Hayman, Ronald 1932- .... **CLC 44**
See also CA 25-28R; CANR 18, 50, 88; CD 5; DLB 155

Hayne, Paul Hamilton 1830-1886 . **NCLC 94**
See also DLB 3, 64, 79, 248; RGAL 4

Hays, Mary 1760-1843 .... **NCLC 114**
See also DLB 142, 158; RGEL 2

Haywood, Eliza (Fowler)
1693(?)-1756 .... **LC 1, 44**
See also DLB 39; RGEL 2

Hazlitt, William 1778-1830 ...... **NCLC 29, 82**
See also BRW 4; DLB 110, 158; RGEL 2; TEA

Hazzard, Shirley 1931- .... **CLC 18**
See also CA 9-12R; CANR 4, 70, 127; CN 7; DLB 289; DLBY 1982; MTCW 1

Head, Bessie 1937-1986 ...... **BLC 2; CLC 25, 67; SSC 52**
See also AFW; BW 2, 3; CA 29-32R; 119; CANR 25, 82; CDWLB 3; DA3; DAM MULT; DLB 117, 225; EWL 3; EXPS; FW; MTCW 1, 2; RGSF 2; SSFS 5, 13; WLIT 2; WWE 1

Headon, (Nicky) Topper 1956(?)- ...... **CLC 30**

Heaney, Seamus (Justin) 1939- ...... **CLC 5, 7, 14, 25, 37, 74, 91, 171; PC 18; WLCS**
See also BRWR 1; BRWS 2; CA 85-88; CANR 25, 48, 75, 91, 128; CDBLB 1960 to Present; CP 7; DA3; DAB; DAM POET; DLB 40; DLBY 1995; EWL 3; EXPP; MTCW 1, 2; PAB; PFS 2, 5, 8, 17; RGEL 2; TEA; WLIT 4

Hearn, (Patricio) Lafcadio (Tessima Carlos) 1850-1904 .... **TCLC 9**
See also CA 105; 166; DLB 12, 78, 189; HGG; RGAL 4

Hearne, Samuel 1745-1792 .... **LC 95**
See also DLB 99

Hearne, Vicki 1946-2001 .... **CLC 56**
See also CA 139; 201

Hearon, Shelby 1931- .... **CLC 63**
See also AITN 2; AMWS 8; CA 25-28R; CANR 18, 48, 103; CSW

Heat-Moon, William Least .... **CLC 29**
See Trogdon, William (Lewis)
See also AAYA 9

Hebbel, Friedrich 1813-1863 . **DC 21; NCLC 43**
See also CDWLB 2; DAM DRAM; DLB 129; EW 6; RGWL 2, 3

Hebert, Anne 1916-2000 .... **CLC 4, 13, 29**
See also CA 85-88; 187; CANR 69, 126; CCA 1; CWP; CWW 2; DA3; DAC; DAM MST, POET; DLB 68; EWL 3; GFL 1789 to the Present; MTCW 1, 2

Hecht, Anthony (Evan) 1923- ...... **CLC 8, 13, 19**
See also AMWS 10; CA 9-12R; CANR 6, 108; CP 7; DAM POET; DLB 5, 169; EWL 3; PFS 6; WP

Hecht, Ben 1894-1964 ..... **CLC 8; TCLC 101**
See also CA 85-88; DFS 9; DLB 7, 9, 25, 26, 28, 86; FANT; IDFW 3, 4; RGAL 4

Hedayat, Sadeq 1903-1951 .... **TCLC 21**
See also CA 120; EWL 3; RGSF 2

Hegel, Georg Wilhelm Friedrich 1770-1831 .... **NCLC 46**
See also DLB 90; TWA

Heidegger, Martin 1889-1976 .... **CLC 24**
See also CA 81-84; 65-68; CANR 34; DLB 296; MTCW 1, 2

Heidenstam, (Carl Gustaf) Verner von 1859-1940 .... **TCLC 5**
See also CA 104

Heidi Louise
See Erdrich, Louise

Heifner, Jack 1946- .... **CLC 11**
See also CA 105; CANR 47

Heijermans, Herman 1864-1924 .... **TCLC 24**
See also CA 123; EWL 3

Heilbrun, Carolyn G(old) 1926-2003 .... **CLC 25, 173**
See Cross, Amanda
See also CA 45-48; 220; CANR 1, 28, 58, 94; FW

Hein, Christoph 1944- .... **CLC 154**
See also CA 158; CANR 108; CDWLB 2; CWW 2; DLB 124

Heine, Heinrich 1797-1856 .... **NCLC 4, 54; PC 25**
See also CDWLB 2; DLB 90; EW 5; RGWL 2, 3; TWA

Heinemann, Larry (Curtiss) 1944- .. **CLC 50**
See also CA 110; CAAS 21; CANR 31, 81; DLBD 9; INT CANR-31

Heiney, Donald (William) 1921-1993
See Harris, MacDonald
See also CA 1-4R; 142; CANR 3, 58; FANT

Heinlein, Robert A(nson) 1907-1988 . **CLC 1, 3, 8, 14, 26, 55; SSC 55**
See also AAYA 17; BPFB 2; BYA 4, 13; CA 1-4R; 125; CANR 1, 20, 53; CLR 75; CPW; DA3; DAM POP; DLB 8; EXPS; JRDA; LAIT 5; LMFS 2; MAICYA 1, 2; MTCW 1, 2; RGAL 4; SATA 9, 69; SATA-Obit 56; SCFW; SFW 4; SSFS 7; YAW

Helforth, John
See Doolittle, Hilda

Heliodorus fl. 3rd cent. - .... **CMLC 52**

Hellenhofferu, Vojtech Kapristian z
See Hasek, Jaroslav (Matej Frantisek)

Heller, Joseph 1923-1999 .. **CLC 1, 3, 5, 8, 11, 36, 63; TCLC 131, 151; WLC**
See also AAYA 24; AITN 1; AMWS 4; BPFB 2; BYA 1; CA 5-8R; 187; CABS 1; CANR 8, 42, 66, 126; CN 7; CPW; DA; DA3; DAB; DAC; DAM MST, NOV, POP; DLB 2, 28, 227; DLBY 1980, 2002; EWL 3; EXPN; INT CANR-8; LAIT 4; MTCW 1, 2; NFS 1; RGAL 4; TUS; YAW

Hellman, Lillian (Florence) 1906-1984 .. **CLC 2, 4, 8, 14, 18, 34, 44, 52; DC 1; TCLC 119**
See also AAYA 47; AITN 1, 2; AMWS 1; CA 13-16R; 112; CAD; CANR 33; CWD; DA3; DAM DRAM; DFS 1, 3, 14; DLB 7, 228; DLBY 1984; EWL 3; FW; LAIT 3; MAWW; MTCW 1, 2; RGAL 4; TUS

Helprin, Mark 1947- .... **CLC 7, 10, 22, 32**
See also CA 81-84; CANR 47, 64, 124; CDALBS; CPW; DA3; DAM NOV, POP; DLBY 1985; FANT; MTCW 1, 2; SUFW 2

Helvetius, Claude-Adrien 1715-1771 .. **LC 26**

Helyar, Jane Penelope Josephine 1933-
See Poole, Josephine
See also CA 21-24R; CANR 10, 26; CWRI 5; SATA 82, 138; SATA-Essay 138

Hemans, Felicia 1793-1835 .... **NCLC 29, 71**
See also DLB 96; RGEL 2

Hemingway, Ernest (Miller) 1899-1961 ... **CLC 1, 3, 6, 8, 10, 13, 19, 30, 34, 39, 41, 44, 50, 61, 80; SSC 1, 25, 36, 40, 63; TCLC 115; WLC**
See also AAYA 19; AMW; AMWC 1; AMWR 1; BPFB 2; BYA 2, 3, 13, 15; CA 77-80; CANR 34; CDALB 1917-1929; DA; DA3; DAB; DAC; DAM MST, NOV; DLB 4, 9, 102, 210; DLBD 1, 15, 16; DLBY 1981, 1987, 1996, 1998; EWL 3; EXPN; EXPS; LAIT 3, 4; LATS 1; MTCW 1, 2; NFS 1, 5, 6, 14; RGAL 4; RGSF 2; SSFS 17; TUS; WYA

Hempel, Amy 1951- .... **CLC 39**
See also CA 118; 137; CANR 70; DA3; DLB 218; EXPS; MTCW 2; SSFS 2

Henderson, F. C.
See Mencken, H(enry) L(ouis)

Henderson, Sylvia
See Ashton-Warner, Sylvia (Constance)

Henderson, Zenna (Chlarson) 1917-1983 .... **SSC 29**
See also CA 1-4R; 133; CANR 1, 84; DLB 8; SATA 5; SFW 4

Henkin, Joshua .... **CLC 119**
See also CA 161

Henley, Beth .... **CLC 23; DC 6, 14**
See Henley, Elizabeth Becker
See also CABS 3; CAD; CD 5; CSW; CWD; DFS 2; DLBY 1986; FW

Henley, Elizabeth Becker 1952-
See Henley, Beth
See also CA 107; CANR 32, 73; DA3; DAM DRAM, MST; MTCW 1, 2

Henley, William Ernest 1849-1903 .. **TCLC 8**
See also CA 105; DLB 19; RGEL 2

Hennissart, Martha
See Lathen, Emma
See also CA 85-88; CANR 64

Henry VIII 1491-1547 .... **LC 10**
See also DLB 132

Henry, O. ..... **SSC 5, 49; TCLC 1, 19; WLC**
See Porter, William Sydney
See also AAYA 41; AMWS 2; EXPS; RGAL 4; RGSF 2; SSFS 2, 18

Henry, Patrick 1736-1799 .... **LC 25**
See also LAIT 1

Henryson, Robert 1430(?)-1506(?) .... **LC 20**
See also BRWS 7; DLB 146; RGEL 2

Henschke, Alfred
See Klabund

Henson, Lance 1944- .... **NNAL**
See also CA 146; DLB 175

Hentoff, Nat(han Irving) 1925- .... **CLC 26**
See also AAYA 4, 42; BYA 6; CA 1-4R; CAAS 6; CANR 5, 25, 77, 114; CLR 1, 52; INT CANR-25; JRDA; MAICYA 1, 2; SATA 42, 69, 133; SATA-Brief 27; WYA; YAW

Heppenstall, (John) Rayner 1911-1981 .... **CLC 10**
See also CA 1-4R; 103; CANR 29; EWL 3

Heraclitus c. 540B.C.-c. 450B.C. ... **CMLC 22**
See also DLB 176

Herbert, Frank (Patrick) 1920-1986 .... **CLC 12, 23, 35, 44, 85**
See also AAYA 21; BPFB 2; BYA 4, 14; CA 53-56; 118; CANR 5, 43; CDALBS; CPW; DAM POP; DLB 8; INT CANR-5; LAIT 5; MTCW 1, 2; NFS 17; SATA 9, 37; SATA-Obit 47; SCFW 2; SFW 4; YAW

Herbert, George 1593-1633 .... **LC 24; PC 4**
See also BRW 2; BRWR 2; CDBLB Before 1660; DAB; DAM POET; DLB 126; EXPP; RGEL 2; TEA; WP

Herbert, Zbigniew 1924-1998 ..... **CLC 9, 43; PC 50**
See also CA 89-92; 169; CANR 36, 74; CDWLB 4; CWW 2; DAM POET; DLB 232; EWL 3; MTCW 1

Herbst, Josephine (Frey) 1897-1969 .... **CLC 34**
See also CA 5-8R; 25-28R; DLB 9

Herder, Johann Gottfried von 1744-1803 .... **NCLC 8**
See also DLB 97; EW 4; TWA

Heredia, Jose Maria 1803-1839 .... **HLCS 2**
See also LAW

Hergesheimer, Joseph 1880-1954 ... **TCLC 11**
See also CA 109; 194; DLB 102, 9; RGAL 4

Herlihy, James Leo 1927-1993 .... **CLC 6**
See also CA 1-4R; 143; CAD; CANR 2

Herman, William
See Bierce, Ambrose (Gwinett)

Hermogenes fl. c. 175- .... **CMLC 6**

Hernandez, Jose 1834-1886 .... **NCLC 17**
See also LAW; RGWL 2, 3; WLIT 1

Herodotus c. 484B.C.-c. 420B.C. ... **CMLC 17**
See also AW 1; CDWLB 1; DLB 176; RGWL 2, 3; TWA

Herrick, Robert 1591-1674 .... **LC 13; PC 9**
See also BRW 2; BRWC 2; DA; DAB; DAC; DAM MST, POP; DLB 126; EXPP; PFS 13; RGAL 4; RGEL 2; TEA; WP

Herring, Guilles
See Somerville, Edith Oenone

Herriot, James 1916-1995 .... **CLC 12**
See Wight, James Alfred
See also AAYA 1, 54; BPFB 2; CA 148; CANR 40; CLR 80; CPW; DAM POP; LAIT 3; MAICYA 2; MAICYAS 1; MTCW 2; SATA 86, 135; TEA; YAW

Herris, Violet
See Hunt, Violet

Herrmann, Dorothy 1941- .... **CLC 44**
See also CA 107

Herrmann, Taffy
See Herrmann, Dorothy

Hersey, John (Richard) 1914-1993 .... **CLC 1, 2, 7, 9, 40, 81, 97**
See also AAYA 29; BPFB 2; CA 17-20R; 140; CANR 33; CDALBS; CPW; DAM POP; DLB 6, 185, 278; MTCW 1, 2; SATA 25; SATA-Obit 76; TUS

Herzen, Aleksandr Ivanovich
1812-1870 .... **NCLC 10, 61**
See Herzen, Alexander

Herzen, Alexander
See Herzen, Aleksandr Ivanovich
See also DLB 277

Herzl, Theodor 1860-1904 .... **TCLC 36**
See also CA 168

Herzog, Werner 1942- .... **CLC 16**
See also CA 89-92

Hesiod c. 8th cent. B.C.- .... **CMLC 5**
See also AW 1; DLB 176; RGWL 2, 3

Hesse, Hermann 1877-1962 ... **CLC 1, 2, 3, 6, 11, 17, 25, 69; SSC 9, 49; TCLC 148; WLC**
See also AAYA 43; BPFB 2; CA 17-18; CAP 2; CDWLB 2; DA; DA3; DAB; DAC; DAM MST, NOV; DLB 66; EW 9; EWL 3; EXPN; LAIT 1; MTCW 1, 2; NFS 6, 15; RGWL 2, 3; SATA 50; TWA

Hewes, Cady
See De Voto, Bernard (Augustine)

Heyen, William 1940- .... **CLC 13, 18**
See also CA 33-36R; 220; CAAE 220; CAAS 9; CANR 98; CP 7; DLB 5

Heyerdahl, Thor 1914-2002 .... **CLC 26**
See also CA 5-8R; 207; CANR 5, 22, 66, 73; LAIT 4; MTCW 1, 2; SATA 2, 52

Heym, Georg (Theodor Franz Arthur)
1887-1912 .... **TCLC 9**
See also CA 106; 181

Heym, Stefan 1913-2001 .... **CLC 41**
See also CA 9-12R; 203; CANR 4; CWW 2; DLB 69; EWL 3

Heyse, Paul (Johann Ludwig von)
1830-1914 .... **TCLC 8**
See also CA 104; 209; DLB 129

Heyward, (Edwin) DuBose
1885-1940 .... **HR 2; TCLC 59**
See also CA 108; 157; DLB 7, 9, 45, 249; SATA 21

Heywood, John 1497(?)-1580(?) .... **LC 65**
See also DLB 136; RGEL 2

Hibbert, Eleanor Alice Burford
1906-1993 .... **CLC 7**
See Holt, Victoria
See also BEST 90:4; CA 17-20R; 140; CANR 9, 28, 59; CMW 4; CPW; DAM POP; MTCW 2; RHW; SATA 2; SATA-Obit 74

Hichens, Robert (Smythe)
1864-1950 .... **TCLC 64**
See also CA 162; DLB 153; HGG; RHW; SUFW

Higgins, Aidan 1927- .... **SSC 68**
See also CA 9-12R; CANR 70, 115; CN 7; DLB 14

Higgins, George V(incent)
1939-1999 .... **CLC 4, 7, 10, 18**
See also BPFB 2; CA 77-80; 186; CAAS 5; CANR 17, 51, 89, 96; CMW 4; CN 7; DLB 2; DLBY 1981, 1998; INT CANR-17; MSW; MTCW 1

Higginson, Thomas Wentworth
1823-1911 .... **TCLC 36**
See also CA 162; DLB 1, 64, 243

Higgonet, Margaret ed. .... **CLC 65**

Highet, Helen
See MacInnes, Helen (Clark)

Highsmith, (Mary) Patricia
1921-1995 .... **CLC 2, 4, 14, 42, 102**
See Morgan, Claire
See also AAYA 48; BRWS 5; CA 1-4R; 147; CANR 1, 20, 48, 62, 108; CMW 4; CPW; DA3; DAM NOV, POP; MSW; MTCW 1, 2

Highwater, Jamake (Mamake)
1942(?)-2001 .... **CLC 12**
See also AAYA 7; BPFB 2; BYA 4; CA 65-68; 199; CAAS 7; CANR 10, 34, 84; CLR 17; CWRI 5; DLB 52; DLBY 1985; JRDA; MAICYA 1, 2; SATA 32, 69; SATA-Brief 30

Highway, Tomson 1951- ...... **CLC 92; NNAL**
See also CA 151; CANR 75; CCA 1; CD 5; DAC; DAM MULT; DFS 2; MTCW 2

Hijuelos, Oscar 1951- .... **CLC 65; HLC 1**
See also AAYA 25; AMWS 8; BEST 90:1; CA 123; CANR 50, 75, 125; CPW; DA3; DAM MULT, POP; DLB 145; HW 1, 2; LLW 1; MTCW 2; NFS 17; RGAL 4; WLIT 1

Hikmet, Nazim 1902(?)-1963 .... **CLC 40**
See also CA 141; 93-96; EWL 3

Hildegard von Bingen 1098-1179 . **CMLC 20**
See also DLB 148

Hildesheimer, Wolfgang 1916-1991 .. **CLC 49**
See also CA 101; 135; DLB 69, 124; EWL 3

Hill, Geoffrey (William) 1932- ...... **CLC 5, 8, 18, 45**
See also BRWS 5; CA 81-84; CANR 21, 89; CDBLB 1960 to Present; CP 7; DAM POET; DLB 40; EWL 3; MTCW 1; RGEL 2

Hill, George Roy 1921-2002 .... **CLC 26**
See also CA 110; 122; 213

Hill, John
See Koontz, Dean R(ay)

Hill, Susan (Elizabeth) 1942- ...... **CLC 4, 113**
See also CA 33-36R; CANR 29, 69, 129; CN 7; DAB; DAM MST, NOV; DLB 14, 139; HGG; MTCW 1; RHW

Hillard, Asa G. III .... **CLC 70**

Hillerman, Tony 1925- .... **CLC 62, 170**
See also AAYA 40; BEST 89:1; BPFB 2; CA 29-32R; CANR 21, 42, 65, 97; CMW 4; CPW; DA3; DAM POP; DLB 206; MSW; RGAL 4; SATA 6; TCWW 2; YAW

Hillesum, Etty 1914-1943 .... **TCLC 49**
See also CA 137

Hilliard, Noel (Harvey) 1929-1996 ... **CLC 15**
See also CA 9-12R; CANR 7, 69; CN 7

Hillis, Rick 1956- .... **CLC 66**
See also CA 134

Hilton, James 1900-1954 .... **TCLC 21**
See also CA 108; 169; DLB 34, 77; FANT; SATA 34

Hilton, Walter (?)-1396 .... **CMLC 58**
See also DLB 146; RGEL 2

Himes, Chester (Bomar) 1909-1984 .. **BLC 2; CLC 2, 4, 7, 18, 58, 108; TCLC 139**
See also AFAW 2; BPFB 2; BW 2; CA 25-28R; 114; CANR 22, 89; CMW 4; DAM MULT; DLB 2, 76, 143, 226; EWL 3; MSW; MTCW 1, 2; RGAL 4

Hinde, Thomas .... **CLC 6, 11**
See Chitty, Thomas Willes
See also EWL 3

Hine, (William) Daryl 1936- .... **CLC 15**
See also CA 1-4R; CAAS 15; CANR 1, 20; CP 7; DLB 60

Hinkson, Katharine Tynan
See Tynan, Katharine

Hinojosa(-Smith), Rolando (R.)
1929- .... **HLC 1**
See Hinojosa-Smith, Rolando
See also CA 131; CAAS 16; CANR 62; DAM MULT; DLB 82; HW 1, 2; LLW 1; MTCW 2; RGAL 4

Hinton, S(usan) E(loise) 1950- .. **CLC 30, 111**
See also AAYA 2, 33; BPFB 2; BYA 2, 3; CA 81-84; CANR 32, 62, 92; CDALBS; CLR 3, 23; CPW; DA; DA3; DAB; DAC; DAM MST, NOV; JRDA; LAIT 5; MAICYA 1, 2; MTCW 1, 2; NFS 5, 9, 15, 16; SATA 19, 58, 115; WYA; YAW

Hippius, Zinaida (Nikolaevna) .... **TCLC 9**
See Gippius, Zinaida (Nikolaevna)
See also DLB 295; EWL 3

Hiraoka, Kimitake 1925-1970
See Mishima, Yukio
See also CA 97-100; 29-32R; DA3; DAM DRAM; GLL 1; MTCW 1, 2

Hirsch, E(ric) D(onald), Jr. 1928- .... **CLC 79**
See also CA 25-28R; CANR 27, 51; DLB 67; INT CANR-27; MTCW 1

Hirsch, Edward 1950- .... **CLC 31, 50**
See also CA 104; CANR 20, 42, 102; CP 7; DLB 120

Hitchcock, Alfred (Joseph)
1899-1980 .... **CLC 16**
See also AAYA 22; CA 159; 97-100; SATA 27; SATA-Obit 24

Hitchens, Christopher (Eric)
1949- .... **CLC 157**
See also CA 152; CANR 89

Hitler, Adolf 1889-1945 .... **TCLC 53**
See also CA 117; 147

Hoagland, Edward 1932- .... **CLC 28**
See also ANW; CA 1-4R; CANR 2, 31, 57, 107; CN 7; DLB 6; SATA 51; TCWW 2

Hoban, Russell (Conwell) 1925- ...... **CLC 7, 25**
See also BPFB 2; CA 5-8R; CANR 23, 37, 66, 114; CLR 3, 69; CN 7; CWRI 5; DAM NOV; DLB 52; FANT; MAICYA 1, 2; MTCW 1, 2; SATA 1, 40, 78, 136; SFW 4; SUFW 2

Hobbes, Thomas 1588-1679 .... **LC 36**
See also DLB 151, 252, 281; RGEL 2

Hobbs, Perry
See Blackmur, R(ichard) P(almer)

Hobson, Laura Z(ametkin)
1900-1986 .... **CLC 7, 25**
See Field, Peter
See also BPFB 2; CA 17-20R; 118; CANR 55; DLB 28; SATA 52

Hoccleve, Thomas c. 1368-c. 1437 ...... **LC 75**
See also DLB 146; RGEL 2

Hoch, Edward D(entinger) 1930-
See Queen, Ellery
See also CA 29-32R; CANR 11, 27, 51, 97; CMW 4; SFW 4

Hochhuth, Rolf 1931- .... **CLC 4, 11, 18**
See also CA 5-8R; CANR 33, 75; CWW 2; DAM DRAM; DLB 124; EWL 3; MTCW 1, 2

Hochman, Sandra 1936- .... **CLC 3, 8**
See also CA 5-8R; DLB 5

Hochwaelder, Fritz 1911-1986 .... **CLC 36**
See Hochwalder, Fritz
See also CA 29-32R; 120; CANR 42; DAM DRAM; MTCW 1; RGWL 3

Hochwalder, Fritz
See Hochwaelder, Fritz
See also EWL 3; RGWL 2

Hocking, Mary (Eunice) 1921- .... **CLC 13**
See also CA 101; CANR 18, 40

Hodgins, Jack 1938- .... **CLC 23**
See also CA 93-96; CN 7; DLB 60

Hodgson, William Hope
1877(?)-1918 .... **TCLC 13**
See also CA 111; 164; CMW 4; DLB 70, 153, 156, 178; HGG; MTCW 2; SFW 4; SUFW 1

Hoeg, Peter 1957- .... **CLC 95, 156**
See also CA 151; CANR 75; CMW 4; DA3; DLB 214; EWL 3; MTCW 2; NFS 17; RGWL 3; SSFS 18

Hoffman, Alice 1952- .... **CLC 51**
See also AAYA 37; AMWS 10; CA 77-80; CANR 34, 66, 100; CN 7; CPW; DAM NOV; DLB 292; MTCW 1, 2

Hoffman, Daniel (Gerard) 1923- . **CLC 6, 13, 23**
See also CA 1-4R; CANR 4; CP 7; DLB 5

Hoffman, Eva 1945- .... **CLC 182**
See also CA 132

Hoffman, Stanley 1944- .... **CLC 5**
See also CA 77-80

Hoffman, William 1925- .... **CLC 141**
See also CA 21-24R; CANR 9, 103; CSW; DLB 234

Hoffman, William M(oses) 1939- ..... **CLC 40**
See Hoffman, William M.
See also CA 57-60; CANR 11, 71

Hoffmann, E(rnst) T(heodor) A(madeus)
1776-1822 .... **NCLC 2; SSC 13**
See also CDWLB 2; DLB 90; EW 5; RGSF 2; RGWL 2, 3; SATA 27; SUFW 1; WCH

Hofmann, Gert 1931- .... **CLC 54**
See also CA 128; EWL 3

Hofmannsthal, Hugo von 1874-1929 ... **DC 4; TCLC 11**
See also CA 106; 153; CDWLB 2; DAM DRAM; DFS 17; DLB 81, 118; EW 9; EWL 3; RGWL 2, 3

Hogan, Linda 1947- ..... **CLC 73; NNAL; PC 35**
See also AMWS 4; ANW; BYA 12; CA 120; CANR 45, 73, 129; CWP; DAM MULT; DLB 175; SATA 132; TCWW 2

Hogarth, Charles
See Creasey, John

Hogarth, Emmett
See Polonsky, Abraham (Lincoln)

Hogg, James 1770-1835 .... **NCLC 4, 109**
See also DLB 93, 116, 159; HGG; RGEL 2; SUFW 1

Holbach, Paul Henri Thiry Baron
1723-1789 .... **LC 14**

Holberg, Ludvig 1684-1754 .... **LC 6**
See also RGWL 2, 3

Holcroft, Thomas 1745-1809 .... **NCLC 85**
See also DLB 39, 89, 158; RGEL 2

Holden, Ursula 1921- .... **CLC 18**
See also CA 101; CAAS 8; CANR 22

Holderlin, (Johann Christian) Friedrich
1770-1843 .... **NCLC 16; PC 4**
See also CDWLB 2; DLB 90; EW 5; RGWL 2, 3

Holdstock, Robert
See Holdstock, Robert P.

Holdstock, Robert P. 1948- .... **CLC 39**
See also CA 131; CANR 81; DLB 261; FANT; HGG; SFW 4; SUFW 2

Holinshed, Raphael fl. 1580- .... **LC 69**
See also DLB 167; RGEL 2

Holland, Isabelle (Christian)
1920-2002 .... **CLC 21**
See also AAYA 11; CA 21-24R; 205; CAAE 181; CANR 10, 25, 47; CLR 57; CWRI 5; JRDA; LAIT 4; MAICYA 1, 2; SATA 8, 70; SATA-Essay 103; SATA-Obit 132; WYA

Holland, Marcus
See Caldwell, (Janet Miriam) Taylor (Holland)

Hollander, John 1929- .... **CLC 2, 5, 8, 14**
See also CA 1-4R; CANR 1, 52; CP 7; DLB 5; SATA 13

Hollander, Paul
See Silverberg, Robert

Holleran, Andrew 1943(?)- .... **CLC 38**
See Garber, Eric
See also CA 144; GLL 1

Holley, Marietta 1836(?)-1926 .... **TCLC 99**
See also CA 118; DLB 11

Hollinghurst, Alan 1954- .... **CLC 55, 91**
See also CA 114; CN 7; DLB 207; GLL 1

Hollis, Jim
See Summers, Hollis (Spurgeon, Jr.)

Holly, Buddy 1936-1959 .... **TCLC 65**
See also CA 213

Holmes, Gordon
See Shiel, M(atthew) P(hipps)

Holmes, John
See Souster, (Holmes) Raymond

Holmes, John Clellon 1926-1988 .... **CLC 56**
See also BG 2; CA 9-12R; 125; CANR 4; DLB 16, 237

Holmes, Oliver Wendell, Jr.
1841-1935 .... **TCLC 77**
See also CA 114; 186

Holmes, Oliver Wendell
1809-1894 .... **NCLC 14, 81**
See also AMWS 1; CDALB 1640-1865; DLB 1, 189, 235; EXPP; RGAL 4; SATA 34

Holmes, Raymond
See Souster, (Holmes) Raymond

Holt, Victoria
See Hibbert, Eleanor Alice Burford
See also BPFB 2

Holub, Miroslav 1923-1998 .... **CLC 4**
See also CA 21-24R; 169; CANR 10; CDWLB 4; CWW 2; DLB 232; EWL 3; RGWL 3

Holz, Detlev
See Benjamin, Walter

Homer c. 8th cent. B.C.- .... **CMLC 1, 16, 61; PC 23; WLCS**
See also AW 1; CDWLB 1; DA, DA3; DAB; DAC; DAM MST, POET; DLB 176; EFS 1; LAIT 1; LMFS 1; RGWL 2, 3; TWA; WP

Hongo, Garrett Kaoru 1951- .... **PC 23**
See also CA 133; CAAS 22; CP 7; DLB 120; EWL 3; EXPP; RGAL 4

Honig, Edwin 1919- .... **CLC 33**
See also CA 5-8R; CAAS 8; CANR 4, 45; CP 7; DLB 5

Hood, Hugh (John Blagdon) 1928- . **CLC 15, 28; SSC 42**
See also CA 49-52; CAAS 17; CANR 1, 33, 87; CN 7; DLB 53; RGSF 2

Hood, Thomas 1799-1845 .... **NCLC 16**
See also BRW 4; DLB 96; RGEL 2

Hooker, (Peter) Jeremy 1941- .... **CLC 43**
See also CA 77-80; CANR 22; CP 7; DLB 40

Hooker, Richard 1554-1600 .... **LC 95**
See also BRW 1; DLB 132; RGEL 2

hooks, bell
See Watkins, Gloria Jean

Hope, A(lec) D(erwent) 1907-2000 .... **CLC 3, 51; PC 56**
See also BRWS 7; CA 21-24R; 188; CANR 33, 74; DLB 289; EWL 3; MTCW 1, 2; PFS 8; RGEL 2

Hope, Anthony 1863-1933 .... **TCLC 83**
See also CA 157; DLB 153, 156; RGEL 2; RHW

Hope, Brian
See Creasey, John

Hope, Christopher (David Tully)
1944- .... **CLC 52**
See also AFW; CA 106; CANR 47, 101; CN 7; DLB 225; SATA 62

Hopkins, Gerard Manley
1844-1889 .... **NCLC 17; PC 15; WLC**
See also BRW 5; BRWR 2; CDBLB 1890-1914; DA; DA3; DAB; DAC; DAM MST, POET; DLB 35, 57; EXPP; PAB; RGEL 2; TEA; WP

Hopkins, John (Richard) 1931-1998 .. **CLC 4**
See also CA 85-88; 169; CBD; CD 5

Hopkins, Pauline Elizabeth
1859-1930 .... **BLC 2; TCLC 28**
See also AFAW 2; BW 2, 3; CA 141; CANR 82; DAM MULT; DLB 50

Hopkinson, Francis 1737-1791 .... **LC 25**
See also DLB 31; RGAL 4

Hopley-Woolrich, Cornell George 1903-1968
See Woolrich, Cornell
See also CA 13-14; CANR 58; CAP 1; CMW 4; DLB 226; MTCW 2

Horace 65B.C.-8B.C. .... **CMLC 39; PC 46**
See also AW 2; CDWLB 1; DLB 211; RGWL 2, 3

Horatio
See Proust, (Valentin-Louis-George-Eugene) Marcel

Horgan, Paul (George Vincent O'Shaughnessy) 1903-1995 .. **CLC 9, 53**
See also BPFB 2; CA 13-16R; 147; CANR 9, 35; DAM NOV; DLB 102, 212; DLBY 1985; INT CANR-9; MTCW 1, 2; SATA 13; SATA-Obit 84; TCWW 2

Horkheimer, Max 1895-1973 .... **TCLC 132**
See also CA 216; 41-44R; DLB 296

Horn, Peter
See Kuttner, Henry

Horne, Frank (Smith) 1899-1974 .... **HR 2**
See also BW 1; CA 125; 53-56; DLB 51; WP

Horne, Richard Henry Hengist
1802(?)-1884 .... **NCLC 127**
See also DLB 32; SATA 29

Hornem, Horace Esq.
See Byron, George Gordon (Noel)

Horney, Karen (Clementine Theodore Danielsen) 1885-1952 .... **TCLC 71**
See also CA 114; 165; DLB 246; FW

Hornung, E(rnest) W(illiam)
1866-1921 .... **TCLC 59**
See also CA 108; 160; CMW 4; DLB 70

Horovitz, Israel (Arthur) 1939- .... **CLC 56**
See also CA 33-36R; CAD; CANR 46, 59; CD 5; DAM DRAM; DLB 7

Horton, George Moses
1797(?)-1883(?) .... **NCLC 87**
See also DLB 50

Horvath, odon von 1901-1938
See von Horvath, Odon
See also EWL 3

Horvath, Oedoen von -1938
See von Horvath, Odon

Horwitz, Julius 1920-1986 .... **CLC 14**
See also CA 9-12R; 119; CANR 12

Hospital, Janette Turner 1942- .... **CLC 42, 145**
See also CA 108; CANR 48; CN 7; DLBY 2002; RGSF 2

Hostos, E. M. de
See Hostos (y Bonilla), Eugenio Maria de
Hostos, Eugenio M. de
See Hostos (y Bonilla), Eugenio Maria de
Hostos, Eugenio Maria
See Hostos (y Bonilla), Eugenio Maria de
Hostos (y Bonilla), Eugenio Maria de
1839-1903 .... **TCLC 24**
See also CA 123; 131; HW 1
Houdini
See Lovecraft, H(oward) P(hillips)
Houellebecq, Michel 1958- .... **CLC 179**
See also CA 185
Hougan, Carolyn 1943- .... **CLC 34**
See also CA 139
Household, Geoffrey (Edward West)
1900-1988 .... **CLC 11**
See also CA 77-80; 126; CANR 58; CMW 4; DLB 87; SATA 14; SATA-Obit 59
Housman, A(lfred) E(dward)
1859-1936 .... **PC 2, 43; TCLC 1, 10; WLCS**
See also BRW 6; CA 104; 125; DA; DA3; DAB; DAC; DAM MST, POET; DLB 19, 284; EWL 3; EXPP; MTCW 1, 2; PAB; PFS 4, 7; RGEL 2; TEA; WP
Housman, Laurence 1865-1959 .... **TCLC 7**
See also CA 106; 155; DLB 10; FANT; RGEL 2; SATA 25
Houston, Jeanne (Toyo) Wakatsuki
1934- .... **AAL**
See also AAYA 49; CA 103; CAAS 16; CANR 29, 123; LAIT 4; SATA 78
Howard, Elizabeth Jane 1923- ..... **CLC 7, 29**
See also CA 5-8R; CANR 8, 62; CN 7
Howard, Maureen 1930- .... **CLC 5, 14, 46, 151**
See also CA 53-56; CANR 31, 75; CN 7; DLBY 1983; INT CANR-31; MTCW 1, 2
Howard, Richard 1929- .... **CLC 7, 10, 47**
See also AITN 1; CA 85-88; CANR 25, 80; CP 7; DLB 5; INT CANR-25
Howard, Robert E(rvin)
1906-1936 .... **TCLC 8**
See also BPFB 2; BYA 5; CA 105; 157; FANT; SUFW 1
Howard, Warren F.
See Pohl, Frederik
Howe, Fanny (Quincy) 1940- .... **CLC 47**
See also CA 117; 187; CAAE 187; CAAS 27; CANR 70, 116; CP 7; CWP; SATA-Brief 52
Howe, Irving 1920-1993 .... **CLC 85**
See also AMWS 6; CA 9-12R; 141; CANR 21, 50; DLB 67; EWL 3; MTCW 1, 2
Howe, Julia Ward 1819-1910 .... **TCLC 21**
See also CA 117; 191; DLB 1, 189, 235; FW
Howe, Susan 1937- .... **CLC 72, 152; PC 54**
See also AMWS 4; CA 160; CP 7; CWP; DLB 120; FW; RGAL 4
Howe, Tina 1937- .... **CLC 48**
See also CA 109; CAD; CANR 125; CD 5; CWD
Howell, James 1594(?)-1666 .... **LC 13**
See also DLB 151
Howells, W. D.
See Howells, William Dean
Howells, William D.
See Howells, William Dean
Howells, William Dean 1837-1920 ... **SSC 36; TCLC 7, 17, 41**
See also AMW; CA 104; 134; CDALB 1865-1917; DLB 12, 64, 74, 79, 189; LMFS 1; MTCW 2; RGAL 4; TUS
Howes, Barbara 1914-1996 .... **CLC 15**
See also CA 9-12R; 151; CAAS 3; CANR 53; CP 7; SATA 5

Hrabal, Bohumil 1914-1997 .... **CLC 13, 67**
See also CA 106; 156; CAAS 12; CANR 57; CWW 2; DLB 232; EWL 3; RGSF 2
Hrotsvit of Gandersheim c. 935-c.
1000 .... **CMLC 29**
See also DLB 148
Hsi, Chu 1130-1200 .... **CMLC 42**
Hsun, Lu
See Lu Hsun
Hubbard, L(afayette) Ron(ald)
1911-1986 .... **CLC 43**
See also CA 77-80; 118; CANR 52; CPW; DA3; DAM POP; FANT; MTCW 2; SFW 4
Huch, Ricarda (Octavia)
1864-1947 .... **TCLC 13**
See also CA 111; 189; DLB 66; EWL 3
Huddle, David 1942- .... **CLC 49**
See also CA 57-60; CAAS 20; CANR 89; DLB 130
Hudson, Jeffrey
See Crichton, (John) Michael
Hudson, W(illiam) H(enry)
1841-1922 .... **TCLC 29**
See also CA 115; 190; DLB 98, 153, 174; RGEL 2; SATA 35
Hueffer, Ford Madox
See Ford, Ford Madox
Hughart, Barry 1934- .... **CLC 39**
See also CA 137; FANT; SFW 4; SUFW 2
Hughes, Colin
See Creasey, John
Hughes, David (John) 1930- .... **CLC 48**
See also CA 116; 129; CN 7; DLB 14
Hughes, Edward James
See Hughes, Ted
See also DA3; DAM MST, POET
Hughes, (James Mercer) Langston
1902-1967 ..... **BLC 2; CLC 1, 5, 10, 15, 35, 44, 108; DC 3; HR 2; PC 1, 53; SSC 6; WLC**
See also AAYA 12; AFAW 1, 2; AMWR 1; AMWS 1; BW 1, 3; CA 1-4R; 25-28R; CANR 1, 34, 82; CDALB 1929-1941; CLR 17; DA; DA3; DAB; DAC; DAM DRAM, MST, MULT, POET; DFS 6, 18; DLB 4, 7, 48, 51, 86, 228; EWL 3; EXPP; EXPS; JRDA; LAIT 3; LMFS 2; MAI-CYA 1, 2; MTCW 1, 2; PAB; PFS 1, 3, 6, 10, 15; RGAL 4; RGSF 2; SATA 4, 33; SSFS 4, 7; TUS; WCH; WP; YAW
Hughes, Richard (Arthur Warren)
1900-1976 .... **CLC 1, 11**
See also CA 5-8R; 65-68; CANR 4; DAM NOV; DLB 15, 161; EWL 3; MTCW 1; RGEL 2; SATA 8; SATA-Obit 25
Hughes, Ted 1930-1998 . **CLC 2, 4, 9, 14, 37, 119; PC 7**
See Hughes, Edward James
See also BRWC 2; BRWR 2; BRWS 1; CA 1-4R; 171; CANR 1, 33, 66, 108; CLR 3; CP 7; DAB; DAC; DLB 40, 161; EWL 3; EXPP; MAICYA 1, 2; MTCW 1, 2; PAB; PFS 4, 19; RGEL 2; SATA 49; SATA-Brief 27; SATA-Obit 107; TEA; YAW
Hugo, Richard
See Huch, Ricarda (Octavia)
Hugo, Richard F(ranklin)
1923-1982 .... **CLC 6, 18, 32**
See also AMWS 6; CA 49-52; 108; CANR 3; DAM POET; DLB 5, 206; EWL 3; PFS 17; RGAL 4
Hugo, Victor (Marie) 1802-1885 .... **NCLC 3, 10, 21; PC 17; WLC**
See also AAYA 28; DA; DA3; DAB; DAC; DAM DRAM, MST, NOV, POET; DLB 119, 192, 217; EFS 2; EW 6; EXPN; GFL 1789 to the Present; LAIT 1, 2; NFS 5; RGWL 2, 3; SATA 47; TWA

Huidobro, Vicente
See Huidobro Fernandez, Vicente Garcia
See also DLB 283; EWL 3; LAW
Huidobro Fernandez, Vicente Garcia
1893-1948 .... **TCLC 31**
See Huidobro, Vicente
See also CA 131; HW 1
Hulme, Keri 1947- .... **CLC 39, 130**
See also CA 125; CANR 69; CN 7; CP 7; CWP; EWL 3; FW; INT CA-125
Hulme, T(homas) E(rnest)
1883-1917 .... **TCLC 21**
See also BRWS 6; CA 117; 203; DLB 19
Humboldt, Wilhelm von
1767-1835 .... **NCLC 134**
See also DLB 90
Hume, David 1711-1776 .... **LC 7, 56**
See also BRWS 3; DLB 104, 252; LMFS 1; TEA
Humphrey, William 1924-1997 .... **CLC 45**
See also AMWS 9; CA 77-80; 160; CANR 68; CN 7; CSW; DLB 6, 212, 234, 278; TCWW 2
Humphreys, Emyr Owen 1919- .... **CLC 47**
See also CA 5-8R; CANR 3, 24; CN 7; DLB 15
Humphreys, Josephine 1945- ..... **CLC 34, 57**
See also CA 121; 127; CANR 97; CSW; DLB 292; INT CA-127
Huneker, James Gibbons
1860-1921 .... **TCLC 65**
See also CA 193; DLB 71; RGAL 4
Hungerford, Hesba Fay
See Brinsmead, H(esba) F(ay)
Hungerford, Pixie
See Brinsmead, H(esba) F(ay)
Hunt, E(verette) Howard, (Jr.)
1918- .... **CLC 3**
See also AITN 1; CA 45-48; CANR 2, 47, 103; CMW 4
Hunt, Francesca
See Holland, Isabelle (Christian)
Hunt, Howard
See Hunt, E(verette) Howard, (Jr.)
Hunt, Kyle
See Creasey, John
Hunt, (James Henry) Leigh
1784-1859 .... **NCLC 1, 70**
See also DAM POET; DLB 96, 110, 144; RGEL 2; TEA
Hunt, Marsha 1946- .... **CLC 70**
See also BW 2, 3; CA 143; CANR 79
Hunt, Violet 1866(?)-1942 .... **TCLC 53**
See also CA 184; DLB 162, 197
Hunter, E. Waldo
See Sturgeon, Theodore (Hamilton)
Hunter, Evan 1926- .... **CLC 11, 31**
See McBain, Ed
See also AAYA 39; BPFB 2; CA 5-8R; CANR 5, 38, 62, 97; CMW 4; CN 7; CPW; DAM POP; DLBY 1982; INT CANR-5; MSW; MTCW 1; SATA 25; SFW 4
Hunter, Kristin 1931-
See Lattany, Kristin (Elaine Eggleston) Hunter
Hunter, Mary
See Austin, Mary (Hunter)
Hunter, Mollie 1922- .... **CLC 21**
See McIlwraith, Maureen Mollie Hunter
See also AAYA 13; BYA 6; CANR 37, 78; CLR 25; DLB 161; JRDA; MAICYA 1, 2; SAAS 7; SATA 54, 106, 139; SATA-Essay 139; WYA; YAW

Hunter, Robert (?)-1734 .... **LC 7**
Hurston, Zora Neale 1891-1960 .... **BLC 2; CLC 7, 30, 61; DC 12; HR 2; SSC 4; TCLC 121, 131; WLCS**
See also AAYA 15; AFAW 1, 2; AMWS 6; BW 1, 3; BYA 12; CA 85-88; CANR 61; CDALBS; DA; DA3; DAC; DAM MST, MULT, NOV; DFS 6; DLB 51, 86; EWL 3; EXPN; EXPS; FW; LAIT 3; LATS 1; LMFS 2; MAWW; MTCW 1, 2; NFS 3; RGAL 4; RGSF 2; SSFS 1, 6, 11, 19; TUS; YAW
Husserl, E. G.
See Husserl, Edmund (Gustav Albrecht)
Husserl, Edmund (Gustav Albrecht) 1859-1938 .... **TCLC 100**
See also CA 116; 133; DLB 296
Huston, John (Marcellus) 1906-1987 .... **CLC 20**
See also CA 73-76; 123; CANR 34; DLB 26
Hustvedt, Siri 1955- .... **CLC 76**
See also CA 137
Hutten, Ulrich von 1488-1523 .... **LC 16**
See also DLB 179
Huxley, Aldous (Leonard) 1894-1963 .... **CLC 1, 3, 4, 5, 8, 11, 18, 35, 79; SSC 39; WLC**
See also AAYA 11; BPFB 2; BRW 7; CA 85-88; CANR 44, 99; CDBLB 1914-1945; DA; DA3; DAB; DAC; DAM MST, NOV; DLB 36, 100, 162, 195, 255; EWL 3; EXPN; LAIT 5; LMFS 2; MTCW 1, 2; NFS 6; RGEL 2; SATA 63; SCFW 2; SFW 4; TEA; YAW
Huxley, T(homas) H(enry) 1825-1895 .... **NCLC 67**
See also DLB 57; TEA
Huysmans, Joris-Karl 1848-1907 ... **TCLC 7, 69**
See also CA 104; 165; DLB 123; EW 7; GFL 1789 to the Present; LMFS 2; RGWL 2, 3
Hwang, David Henry 1957- . **CLC 55; DC 4, 23**
See also CA 127; 132; CAD; CANR 76, 124; CD 5; DA3; DAM DRAM; DFS 11, 18; DLB 212, 228; INT CA-132; MTCW 2; RGAL 4
Hyde, Anthony 1946- .... **CLC 42**
See Chase, Nicholas
See also CA 136; CCA 1
Hyde, Margaret O(ldroyd) 1917- ..... **CLC 21**
See also CA 1-4R; CANR 1, 36; CLR 23; JRDA; MAICYA 1, 2; SAAS 8; SATA 1, 42, 76, 139
Hynes, James 1956(?)- .... **CLC 65**
See also CA 164; CANR 105
Hypatia c. 370-415 .... **CMLC 35**
Ian, Janis 1951- .... **CLC 21**
See also CA 105; 187
Ibanez, Vicente Blasco
See Blasco Ibanez, Vicente
Ibarbourou, Juana de 1895-1979 ..... **HLCS 2**
See also DLB 290; HW 1; LAW
Ibarguengoitia, Jorge 1928-1983 ..... **CLC 37; TCLC 148**
See also CA 124; 113; EWL 3; HW 1
Ibn Battuta, Abu Abdalla 1304-1368(?) .... **CMLC 57**
See also WLIT 2
Ibn Hazm 994-1064 .... **CMLC 64**
Ibsen, Henrik (Johan) 1828-1906 .... **DC 2; TCLC 2, 8, 16, 37, 52; WLC**
See also AAYA 46; CA 104; 141; DA; DA3; DAB; DAC; DAM DRAM, MST; DFS 1, 6, 8, 10, 11, 15, 16; EW 7; LAIT 2; LATS 1; RGWL 2, 3

Ibuse, Masuji 1898-1993 .... **CLC 22**
See Ibuse Masuji
See also CA 127; 141; MJW; RGWL 3
Ibuse Masuji
See Ibuse, Masuji
See also DLB 180; EWL 3
Ichikawa, Kon 1915- .... **CLC 20**
See also CA 121
Ichiyo, Higuchi 1872-1896 .... **NCLC 49**
See also MJW
Idle, Eric 1943- .... **CLC 21**
See Monty Python
See also CA 116; CANR 35, 91
Ignatow, David 1914-1997 .... **CLC 4, 7, 14, 40; PC 34**
See also CA 9-12R; 162; CAAS 3; CANR 31, 57, 96; CP 7; DLB 5; EWL 3
Ignotus
See Strachey, (Giles) Lytton
Ihimaera, Witi (Tame) 1944- .... **CLC 46**
See also CA 77-80; CN 7; RGSF 2; SATA 148
Ilf, Ilya .... **TCLC 21**
See Fainzilberg, Ilya Arnoldovich
See also EWL 3
Illyes, Gyula 1902-1983 .... **PC 16**
See also CA 114; 109; CDWLB 4; DLB 215; EWL 3; RGWL 2, 3
Imalayen, Fatima-Zohra
See Djebar, Assia
Immermann, Karl (Lebrecht) 1796-1840 .... **NCLC 4, 49**
See also DLB 133
Ince, Thomas H. 1882-1924 .... **TCLC 89**
See also IDFW 3, 4
Inchbald, Elizabeth 1753-1821 .... **NCLC 62**
See also DLB 39, 89; RGEL 2
Inclan, Ramon (Maria) del Valle
See Valle-Inclan, Ramon (Maria) del
Infante, G(uillermo) Cabrera
See Cabrera Infante, G(uillermo)
Ingalls, Rachel (Holmes) 1940- .... **CLC 42**
See also CA 123; 127
Ingamells, Reginald Charles
See Ingamells, Rex
Ingamells, Rex 1913-1955 .... **TCLC 35**
See also CA 167; DLB 260
Inge, William (Motter) 1913-1973 ..... **CLC 1, 8, 19**
See also CA 9-12R; CDALB 1941-1968; DA3; DAM DRAM; DFS 1, 3, 5, 8; DLB 7, 249; EWL 3; MTCW 1, 2; RGAL 4; TUS
Ingelow, Jean 1820-1897 .... **NCLC 39, 107**
See also DLB 35, 163; FANT; SATA 33
Ingram, Willis J.
See Harris, Mark
Innaurato, Albert (F.) 1948(?)- ... **CLC 21, 60**
See also CA 115; 122; CAD; CANR 78; CD 5; INT CA-122
Innes, Michael
See Stewart, J(ohn) I(nnes) M(ackintosh)
See also DLB 276; MSW
Innis, Harold Adams 1894-1952 .... **TCLC 77**
See also CA 181; DLB 88
Insluis, Alanus de
See Alain de Lille
Iola
See Wells-Barnett, Ida B(ell)
Ionesco, Eugene 1912-1994 ... **CLC 1, 4, 6, 9, 11, 15, 41, 86; DC 12; WLC**
See also CA 9-12R; 144; CANR 55; CWW 2; DA; DA3; DAB; DAC; DAM DRAM, MST; DFS 4, 9; EW 13; EWL 3; GFL 1789 to the Present; LMFS 2; MTCW 1, 2; RGWL 2, 3; SATA 7; SATA-Obit 79; TWA
Iqbal, Muhammad 1877-1938 .... **TCLC 28**
See also CA 215; EWL 3

Ireland, Patrick
See O'Doherty, Brian
Irenaeus St. 130- .... **CMLC 42**
Irigaray, Luce 1930- .... **CLC 164**
See also CA 154; CANR 121; FW
Iron, Ralph
See Schreiner, Olive (Emilie Albertina)
Irving, John (Winslow) 1942- ... **CLC 13, 23, 38, 112, 175**
See also AAYA 8; AMWS 6; BEST 89:3; BPFB 2; CA 25-28R; CANR 28, 73, 112; CN 7; CPW; DA3; DAM NOV, POP; DLB 6, 278; DLBY 1982; EWL 3; MTCW 1, 2; NFS 12, 14; RGAL 4; TUS
Irving, Washington 1783-1859 . **NCLC 2, 19, 95; SSC 2, 37; WLC**
See also AMW; CDALB 1640-1865; CLR 97; DA; DA3; DAB; DAC; DAM MST; DLB 3, 11, 30, 59, 73, 74, 183, 186, 250, 254; EXPS; LAIT 1; RGAL 4; RGSF 2; SSFS 1, 8, 16; SUFW 1; TUS; WCH; YABC 2
Irwin, P. K.
See Page, P(atricia) K(athleen)
Isaacs, Jorge Ricardo 1837-1895 ... **NCLC 70**
See also LAW
Isaacs, Susan 1943- .... **CLC 32**
See also BEST 89:1; BPFB 2; CA 89-92; CANR 20, 41, 65, 112; CPW; DA3; DAM POP; INT CANR-20; MTCW 1, 2
Isherwood, Christopher (William Bradshaw) 1904-1986 .... **CLC 1, 9, 11, 14, 44; SSC 56**
See also BRW 7; CA 13-16R; 117; CANR 35, 97; DA3; DAM DRAM, NOV; DLB 15, 195; DLBY 1986; EWL 3; IDTP; MTCW 1, 2; RGAL 4; RGEL 2; TUS; WLIT 4
Ishiguro, Kazuo 1954- .. **CLC 27, 56, 59, 110**
See also BEST 90:2; BPFB 2; BRWS 4; CA 120; CANR 49, 95; CN 7; DA3; DAM NOV; DLB 194; EWL 3; MTCW 1, 2; NFS 13; WLIT 4; WWE 1
Ishikawa, Hakuhin
See Ishikawa, Takuboku
Ishikawa, Takuboku 1886(?)-1912 ..... **PC 10; TCLC 15**
See Ishikawa Takuboku
See also CA 113; 153; DAM POET
Iskander, Fazil (Abdulovich) 1929- .. **CLC 47**
See also CA 102; EWL 3
Isler, Alan (David) 1934- .... **CLC 91**
See also CA 156; CANR 105
Ivan IV 1530-1584 .... **LC 17**
Ivanov, Vyacheslav Ivanovich 1866-1949 .... **TCLC 33**
See also CA 122; EWL 3
Ivask, Ivar Vidrik 1927-1992 .... **CLC 14**
See also CA 37-40R; 139; CANR 24
Ives, Morgan
See Bradley, Marion Zimmer
See also GLL 1
Izumi Shikibu c. 973-c. 1034 .... **CMLC 33**
J. R. S.
See Gogarty, Oliver St. John
Jabran, Kahlil
See Gibran, Kahlil
Jabran, Khalil
See Gibran, Kahlil
Jackson, Daniel
See Wingrove, David (John)
Jackson, Helen Hunt 1830-1885 .... **NCLC 90**
See also DLB 42, 47, 186, 189; RGAL 4
Jackson, Jesse 1908-1983 .... **CLC 12**
See also BW 1; CA 25-28R; 109; CANR 27; CLR 28; CWRI 5; MAICYA 1, 2; SATA 2, 29; SATA-Obit 48

Jackson, Laura (Riding) 1901-1991 .... **PC 44**
See Riding, Laura
See also CA 65-68; 135; CANR 28, 89; DLB 48

Jackson, Sam
See Trumbo, Dalton

Jackson, Sara
See Wingrove, David (John)

Jackson, Shirley 1919-1965 . **CLC 11, 60, 87; SSC 9, 39; WLC**
See also AAYA 9; AMWS 9; BPFB 2; CA 1-4R; 25-28R; CANR 4, 52; CDALB 1941-1968; DA; DA3; DAC; DAM MST; DLB 6, 234; EXPS; HGG; LAIT 4; MTCW 2; RGAL 4; RGSF 2; SATA 2; SSFS 1; SUFW 1, 2

Jacob, (Cyprien-)Max 1876-1944 .... **TCLC 6**
See also CA 104; 193; DLB 258; EWL 3; GFL 1789 to the Present; GLL 2; RGWL 2, 3

Jacobs, Harriet A(nn)
1813(?)-1897 .... **NCLC 67**
See also AFAW 1, 2; DLB 239; FW; LAIT 2; RGAL 4

Jacobs, Jim 1942- .... **CLC 12**
See also CA 97-100; INT CA-97-100

Jacobs, W(illiam) W(ymark)
1863-1943 .... **TCLC 22**
See also CA 121; 167; DLB 135; EXPS; HGG; RGEL 2; RGSF 2; SSFS 2; SUFW 1

Jacobsen, Jens Peter 1847-1885 .... **NCLC 34**

Jacobsen, Josephine (Winder)
1908-2003 .... **CLC 48, 102**
See also CA 33-36R; 218; CAAS 18; CANR 23, 48; CCA 1; CP 7; DLB 244

Jacobson, Dan 1929- .... **CLC 4, 14**
See also AFW; CA 1-4R; CANR 2, 25, 66; CN 7; DLB 14, 207, 225; EWL 3; MTCW 1; RGSF 2

Jacqueline
See Carpentier (y Valmont), Alejo

Jacques de Vitry c. 1160-1240 ...... **CMLC 63**
See also DLB 208

Jagger, Mick 1944- .... **CLC 17**

Jahiz, al- c. 780-c. 869 .... **CMLC 25**

Jakes, John (William) 1932- .... **CLC 29**
See also AAYA 32; BEST 89:4; BPFB 2; CA 57-60, 214; CAAE 214; CANR 10, 43, 66, 111; CPW; CSW; DA3; DAM NOV, POP; DLB 278; DLBY 1983; FANT; INT CANR-10; MTCW 1, 2; RHW; SATA 62; SFW 4; TCWW 2

James I 1394-1437 .... **LC 20**
See also RGEL 2

James, Andrew
See Kirkup, James

James, C(yril) L(ionel) R(obert)
1901-1989 .... **BLCS; CLC 33**
See also BW 2; CA 117; 125; 128; CANR 62; DLB 125; MTCW 1

James, Daniel (Lewis) 1911-1988
See Santiago, Danny
See also CA 174; 125

James, Dynely
See Mayne, William (James Carter)

James, Henry Sr. 1811-1882 .... **NCLC 53**

James, Henry 1843-1916 .... **SSC 8, 32, 47; TCLC 2, 11, 24, 40, 47, 64; WLC**
See also AMW; AMWC 1; AMWR 1; BPFB 2; BRW 6; CA 104; 132; CDALB 1865-1917; DA; DA3; DAB; DAC; DAM MST, NOV; DLB 12, 71, 74, 189; DLBD 13; EWL 3; EXPS; HGG; LAIT 2; MTCW 1, 2; NFS 12, 16; RGAL 4; RGEL 2; RGSF 2; SSFS 9; SUFW 1; TUS

James, M. R.
See James, Montague (Rhodes)
See also DLB 156, 201

James, Montague (Rhodes)
1862-1936 .... **SSC 16; TCLC 6**
See James, M. R.
See also CA 104; 203; HGG; RGEL 2; RGSF 2; SUFW 1

James, P. D. .... **CLC 18, 46, 122**
See White, Phyllis Dorothy James
See also BEST 90:2; BPFB 2; BRWS 4; CDBLB 1960 to Present; DLB 87, 276; DLBD 17; MSW

James, Philip
See Moorcock, Michael (John)

James, Samuel
See Stephens, James

James, Seumas
See Stephens, James

James, Stephen
See Stephens, James

James, William 1842-1910 .... **TCLC 15, 32**
See also AMW; CA 109; 193; DLB 270, 284; NCFS 5; RGAL 4

Jameson, Anna 1794-1860 .... **NCLC 43**
See also DLB 99, 166

Jameson, Fredric (R.) 1934- .... **CLC 142**
See also CA 196; DLB 67; LMFS 2

Jami, Nur al-Din 'Abd al-Rahman
1414-1492 .... **LC 9**

Jammes, Francis 1868-1938 .... **TCLC 75**
See also CA 198; EWL 3; GFL 1789 to the Present

Jandl, Ernst 1925-2000 .... **CLC 34**
See also CA 200; EWL 3

Janowitz, Tama 1957- .... **CLC 43, 145**
See also CA 106; CANR 52, 89, 129; CN 7; CPW; DAM POP; DLB 292

Japrisot, Sebastien 1931- .... **CLC 90**
See Rossi, Jean-Baptiste
See also CMW 4; NFS 18

Jarrell, Randall 1914-1965 .... **CLC 1, 2, 6, 9, 13, 49; PC 41**
See also AMW; BYA 5; CA 5-8R; 25-28R; CABS 2; CANR 6, 34; CDALB 1941-1968; CLR 6; CWRI 5; DAM POET; DLB 48, 52; EWL 3; EXPP; MAICYA 1, 2; MTCW 1, 2; PAB; PFS 2; RGAL 4; SATA 7

Jarry, Alfred 1873-1907 .... **SSC 20; TCLC 2, 14, 147**
See also CA 104; 153; DA3; DAM DRAM; DFS 8; DLB 192, 258; EW 9; EWL 3; GFL 1789 to the Present; RGWL 2, 3; TWA

Jarvis, E. K.
See Ellison, Harlan (Jay)

Jawien, Andrzej
See John Paul II, Pope

Jaynes, Roderick
See Coen, Ethan

Jeake, Samuel, Jr.
See Aiken, Conrad (Potter)

Jean Paul 1763-1825 .... **NCLC 7**

Jefferies, (John) Richard
1848-1887 .... **NCLC 47**
See also DLB 98, 141; RGEL 2; SATA 16; SFW 4

Jeffers, (John) Robinson 1887-1962 .. **CLC 2, 3, 11, 15, 54; PC 17; WLC**
See also AMWS 2; CA 85-88; CANR 35; CDALB 1917-1929; DA; DAC; DAM MST, POET; DLB 45, 212; EWL 3; MTCW 1, 2; PAB; PFS 3, 4; RGAL 4

Jefferson, Janet
See Mencken, H(enry) L(ouis)

Jefferson, Thomas 1743-1826 . **NCLC 11, 103**
See also AAYA 54; ANW; CDALB 1640-1865; DA3; DLB 31, 183; LAIT 1; RGAL 4

Jeffrey, Francis 1773-1850 .... **NCLC 33**
See Francis, Lord Jeffrey

Jelakowitch, Ivan
See Heijermans, Herman

Jelinek, Elfriede 1946- .... **CLC 169**
See also CA 154; DLB 85; FW

Jellicoe, (Patricia) Ann 1927- .... **CLC 27**
See also CA 85-88; CBD; CD 5; CWD; CWRI 5; DLB 13, 233; FW

Jelloun, Tahar ben 1944- .... **CLC 180**
See Ben Jelloun, Tahar
See also CA 162; CANR 100

Jemyma
See Holley, Marietta

Jen, Gish .... **AAL; CLC 70**
See Jen, Lillian
See also AMWC 2

Jen, Lillian 1956(?)-
See Jen, Gish
See also CA 135; CANR 89

Jenkins, (John) Robin 1912- .... **CLC 52**
See also CA 1-4R; CANR 1; CN 7; DLB 14, 271

Jennings, Elizabeth (Joan)
1926-2001 .... **CLC 5, 14, 131**
See also BRWS 5; CA 61-64; 200; CAAS 5; CANR 8, 39, 66, 127; CP 7; CWP; DLB 27; EWL 3; MTCW 1; SATA 66

Jennings, Waylon 1937- .... **CLC 21**

Jensen, Johannes V(ilhelm)
1873-1950 .... **TCLC 41**
See also CA 170; DLB 214; EWL 3; RGWL 3

Jensen, Laura (Linnea) 1948- .... **CLC 37**
See also CA 103

Jerome, Saint 345-420 .... **CMLC 30**
See also RGWL 3

Jerome, Jerome K(lapka)
1859-1927 .... **TCLC 23**
See also CA 119; 177; DLB 10, 34, 135; RGEL 2

Jerrold, Douglas William
1803-1857 .... **NCLC 2**
See also DLB 158, 159; RGEL 2

Jewett, (Theodora) Sarah Orne
1849-1909 .... **SSC 6, 44; TCLC 1, 22**
See also AMW; AMWC 2; AMWR 2; CA 108; 127; CANR 71; DLB 12, 74, 221; EXPS; FW; MAWW; NFS 15; RGAL 4; RGSF 2; SATA 15; SSFS 4

Jewsbury, Geraldine (Endsor)
1812-1880 .... **NCLC 22**
See also DLB 21

Jhabvala, Ruth Prawer 1927- . **CLC 4, 8, 29, 94, 138**
See also BRWS 5; CA 1-4R; CANR 2, 29, 51, 74, 91, 128; CN 7; DAB; DAM NOV; DLB 139, 194; EWL 3; IDFW 3, 4; INT CANR-29; MTCW 1, 2; RGSF 2; RGWL 2; RHW; TEA

Jibran, Kahlil
See Gibran, Kahlil

Jibran, Khalil
See Gibran, Kahlil

Jiles, Paulette 1943- .... **CLC 13, 58**
See also CA 101; CANR 70, 124; CWP

Jimenez (Mantecon), Juan Ramon
1881-1958 .... **HLC 1; PC 7; TCLC 4**
See also CA 104; 131; CANR 74; DAM MULT, POET; DLB 134; EW 9; EWL 3; HW 1; MTCW 1, 2; RGWL 2, 3

Jimenez, Ramon
See Jimenez (Mantecon), Juan Ramon

Jimenez Mantecon, Juan
See Jimenez (Mantecon), Juan Ramon

Jin, Ha .... **CLC 109**
See Jin, Xuefei
See also CA 152; DLB 244, 292; SSFS 17

Jin, Xuefei 1956-
See Jin, Ha
See also CANR 91; SSFS 17

Joel, Billy .... **CLC 26**
See Joel, William Martin
Joel, William Martin 1949-
See Joel, Billy
See also CA 108
Johann Sigurjonsson 1880-1919 .... **TCLC 27**
See also CA 170; DLB 293; EWL 3
John, Saint 10(?)-100 .... **CMLC 27, 63**
John of Salisbury c. 1115-1180 ..... **CMLC 63**
John of the Cross, St. 1542-1591 .... **LC 18**
See also RGWL 2, 3
John Paul II, Pope 1920- .... **CLC 128**
See also CA 106; 133
Johnson, B(ryan) S(tanley William)
1933-1973 .... **CLC 6, 9**
See also CA 9-12R; 53-56; CANR 9; DLB 14, 40; EWL 3; RGEL 2
Johnson, Benjamin F., of Boone
See Riley, James Whitcomb
Johnson, Charles (Richard) 1948- .... **BLC 2; CLC 7, 51, 65, 163**
See also AFAW 2; AMWS 6; BW 2, 3; CA 116; CAAS 18; CANR 42, 66, 82, 129; CN 7; DAM MULT; DLB 33, 278; MTCW 2; RGAL 4; SSFS 16
Johnson, Charles S(purgeon)
1893-1956 .... **HR 3**
See also BW 1, 3; CA 125; CANR 82; DLB 51, 91
Johnson, Denis 1949- . **CLC 52, 160; SSC 56**
See also CA 117; 121; CANR 71, 99; CN 7; DLB 120
Johnson, Diane 1934- .... **CLC 5, 13, 48**
See also BPFB 2; CA 41-44R; CANR 17, 40, 62, 95; CN 7; DLBY 1980; INT CANR-17; MTCW 1
Johnson, E. Pauline 1861-1913 .... **NNAL**
See also CA 150; DAC; DAM MULT; DLB 92, 175
Johnson, Eyvind (Olof Verner)
1900-1976 .... **CLC 14**
See also CA 73-76; 69-72; CANR 34, 101; DLB 259; EW 12; EWL 3
Johnson, Fenton 1888-1958 .... **BLC 2**
See also BW 1; CA 118; 124; DAM MULT; DLB 45, 50
Johnson, Georgia Douglas (Camp)
1880-1966 .... **HR 3**
See also BW 1; CA 125; DLB 51, 249; WP
Johnson, Helene 1907-1995 .... **HR 3**
See also CA 181; DLB 51; WP
Johnson, J. R.
See James, C(yril) L(ionel) R(obert)
Johnson, James Weldon 1871-1938 .. **BLC 2; HR 3; PC 24; TCLC 3, 19**
See also AFAW 1; BW 1, 3; CA 104; 125; CANR 82; CDALB 1917-1929; CLR 32; DA3; DAM MULT, POET; DLB 51; EWL 3; EXPP; LMFS 2; MTCW 1, 2; PFS 1; RGAL 4; SATA 31; TUS
Johnson, Joyce 1935- .... **CLC 58**
See also BG 3; CA 125; 129; CANR 102
Johnson, Judith (Emlyn) 1936- .... **CLC 7, 15**
See Sherwin, Judith Johnson
See also CA 25-28R; 153; CANR 34
Johnson, Lionel (Pigot)
1867-1902 .... **TCLC 19**
See also CA 117; 209; DLB 19; RGEL 2
Johnson, Marguerite Annie
See Angelou, Maya
Johnson, Mel
See Malzberg, Barry N(athaniel)
Johnson, Pamela Hansford
1912-1981 .... **CLC 1, 7, 27**
See also CA 1-4R; 104; CANR 2, 28; DLB 15; MTCW 1, 2; RGEL 2
Johnson, Paul (Bede) 1928- .... **CLC 147**
See also BEST 89:4; CA 17-20R; CANR 34, 62, 100

Johnson, Robert .... **CLC 70**
Johnson, Robert 1911(?)-1938 .... **TCLC 69**
See also BW 3; CA 174
Johnson, Samuel 1709-1784 .... **LC 15, 52; WLC**
See also BRW 3; BRWR 1; CDBLB 1660-1789; DA; DAB; DAC; DAM MST; DLB 39, 95, 104, 142, 213; LMFS 1; RGEL 2; TEA
Johnson, Uwe 1934-1984 .. **CLC 5, 10, 15, 40**
See also CA 1-4R; 112; CANR 1, 39; CDWLB 2; DLB 75; EWL 3; MTCW 1; RGWL 2, 3
Johnston, Basil H. 1929- .... **NNAL**
See also CA 69-72; CANR 11, 28, 66; DAC; DAM MULT; DLB 60
Johnston, George (Benson) 1913- ...... **CLC 51**
See also CA 1-4R; CANR 5, 20; CP 7; DLB 88
Johnston, Jennifer (Prudence)
1930- .... **CLC 7, 150**
See also CA 85-88; CANR 92; CN 7; DLB 14
Joinville, Jean de 1224(?)-1317 ..... **CMLC 38**
Jolley, (Monica) Elizabeth 1923- ..... **CLC 46; SSC 19**
See also CA 127; CAAS 13; CANR 59; CN 7; EWL 3; RGSF 2
Jones, Arthur Llewellyn 1863-1947
See Machen, Arthur
See also CA 104; 179; HGG
Jones, D(ouglas) G(ordon) 1929- ..... **CLC 10**
See also CA 29-32R; CANR 13, 90; CP 7; DLB 53
Jones, David (Michael) 1895-1974 .... **CLC 2, 4, 7, 13, 42**
See also BRW 6; BRWS 7; CA 9-12R; 53-56; CANR 28; CDBLB 1945-1960; DLB 20, 100; EWL 3; MTCW 1; PAB; RGEL 2
Jones, David Robert 1947-
See Bowie, David
See also CA 103; CANR 104
Jones, Diana Wynne 1934- .... **CLC 26**
See also AAYA 12; BYA 6, 7, 9, 11, 13, 16; CA 49-52; CANR 4, 26, 56, 120; CLR 23; DLB 161; FANT; JRDA; MAICYA 1, 2; SAAS 7; SATA 9, 70, 108; SFW 4; SUFW 2; YAW
Jones, Edward P. 1950- .... **CLC 76**
See also BW 2, 3; CA 142; CANR 79; CSW
Jones, Gayl 1949- .... **BLC 2; CLC 6, 9, 131**
See also AFAW 1, 2; BW 2, 3; CA 77-80; CANR 27, 66, 122; CN 7; CSW; DA3; DAM MULT; DLB 33, 278; MTCW 1, 2; RGAL 4
Jones, James 1921-1977 ...... **CLC 1, 3, 10, 39**
See also AITN 1, 2; AMWS 11; BPFB 2; CA 1-4R; 69-72; CANR 6; DLB 2, 143; DLBD 17; DLBY 1998; EWL 3; MTCW 1; RGAL 4
Jones, John J.
See Lovecraft, H(oward) P(hillips)
Jones, LeRoi .... **CLC 1, 2, 3, 5, 10, 14**
See Baraka, Amiri
See also MTCW 2
Jones, Louis B. 1953- .... **CLC 65**
See also CA 141; CANR 73
Jones, Madison (Percy, Jr.) 1925- ...... **CLC 4**
See also CA 13-16R; CAAS 11; CANR 7, 54, 83; CN 7; CSW; DLB 152
Jones, Mervyn 1922- .... **CLC 10, 52**
See also CA 45-48; CAAS 5; CANR 1, 91; CN 7; MTCW 1
Jones, Mick 1956(?)- .... **CLC 30**
Jones, Nettie (Pearl) 1941- .... **CLC 34**
See also BW 2; CA 137; CAAS 20; CANR 88**

Jones, Peter 1802-1856 .... **NNAL**
Jones, Preston 1936-1979 .... **CLC 10**
See also CA 73-76; 89-92; DLB 7
Jones, Robert F(rancis) 1934-2003 .... **CLC 7**
See also CA 49-52; CANR 2, 61, 118
Jones, Rod 1953- .... **CLC 50**
See also CA 128
Jones, Terence Graham Parry
1942- .... **CLC 21**
See Jones, Terry; Monty Python
See also CA 112; 116; CANR 35, 93; INT CA-116; SATA 127
Jones, Terry
See Jones, Terence Graham Parry
See also SATA 67; SATA-Brief 51
Jones, Thom (Douglas) 1945(?)- ..... **CLC 81; SSC 56**
See also CA 157; CANR 88; DLB 244
Jong, Erica 1942- .... **CLC 4, 6, 8, 18, 83**
See also AITN 1; AMWS 5; BEST 90:2; BPFB 2; CA 73-76; CANR 26, 52, 75; CN 7; CP 7; CPW; DA3; DAM NOV, POP; DLB 2, 5, 28, 152; FW; INT CANR-26; MTCW 1, 2
Jonson, Ben(jamin) 1572(?)-1637 . **DC 4; LC 6, 33; PC 17; WLC**
See also BRW 1; BRWC 1; BRWR 1; CDBLB Before 1660; DA; DAB; DAC; DAM DRAM, MST, POET; DFS 4, 10; DLB 62, 121; LMFS 1; RGEL 2; TEA; WLIT 3
Jordan, June (Meyer)
1936-2002 .. **BLCS; CLC 5, 11, 23, 114; PC 38**
See also AAYA 2; AFAW 1, 2; BW 2, 3; CA 33-36R; 206; CANR 25, 70, 114; CLR 10; CP 7; CWP; DAM MULT, POET; DLB 38; GLL 2; LAIT 5; MAICYA 1, 2; MTCW 1; SATA 4, 136; YAW
Jordan, Neil (Patrick) 1950- .... **CLC 110**
See also CA 124; 130; CANR 54; CN 7; GLL 2; INT CA-130
Jordan, Pat(rick M.) 1941- .... **CLC 37**
See also CA 33-36R; CANR 121
Jorgensen, Ivar
See Ellison, Harlan (Jay)
Jorgenson, Ivar
See Silverberg, Robert
Joseph, George Ghevarughese .... **CLC 70**
Josephson, Mary
See O'Doherty, Brian
Josephus, Flavius c. 37-100 .... **CMLC 13**
See also AW 2; DLB 176
Josiah Allen's Wife
See Holley, Marietta
Josipovici, Gabriel (David) 1940- ...... **CLC 6, 43, 153**
See also CA 37-40R; CAAS 8; CANR 47, 84; CN 7; DLB 14
Joubert, Joseph 1754-1824 .... **NCLC 9**
Jouve, Pierre Jean 1887-1976 .... **CLC 47**
See also CA 65-68; DLB 258; EWL 3
Jovine, Francesco 1902-1950 .... **TCLC 79**
See also DLB 264; EWL 3
Joyce, James (Augustine Aloysius)
1882-1941 .... **DC 16; PC 22; SSC 3, 26, 44, 64; TCLC 3, 8, 16, 35, 52; WLC**
See also AAYA 42; BRW 7; BRWC 1; BRWR 1; BYA 11, 13; CA 104; 126; CDBLB 1914-1945; DA; DA3; DAB; DAC; DAM MST, NOV, POET; DLB 10, 19, 36, 162, 247; EWL 3; EXPN; EXPS; LAIT 3; LMFS 1, 2; MTCW 1, 2; NFS 7; RGSF 2; SSFS 1, 19; TEA; WLIT 4
Jozsef, Attila 1905-1937 .... **TCLC 22**
See also CA 116; CDWLB 4; DLB 215; EWL 3

Juana Ines de la Cruz, Sor
1651(?)-1695 ...... **HLCS 1; LC 5; PC 24**
See also FW; LAW; RGWL 2, 3; WLIT 1
Juana Inez de La Cruz, Sor
See Juana Ines de la Cruz, Sor
Judd, Cyril
See Kornbluth, C(yril) M.; Pohl, Frederik
Juenger, Ernst 1895-1998 .... **CLC 125**
See Junger, Ernst
See also CA 101; 167; CANR 21, 47, 106; DLB 56
Julian of Norwich 1342(?)-1416(?) . **LC 6, 52**
See also DLB 146; LMFS 1
Julius Caesar 100B.C.-44B.C.
See Caesar, Julius
See also CDWLB 1; DLB 211
Junger, Ernst
See Juenger, Ernst
See also CDWLB 2; EWL 3; RGWL 2, 3
Junger, Sebastian 1962- .... **CLC 109**
See also AAYA 28; CA 165
Juniper, Alex
See Hospital, Janette Turner
Junius
See Luxemburg, Rosa
Just, Ward (Swift) 1935- .... **CLC 4, 27**
See also CA 25-28R; CANR 32, 87; CN 7; INT CANR-32
Justice, Donald (Rodney) 1925- .. **CLC 6, 19, 102**
See also AMWS 7; CA 5-8R; CANR 26, 54, 74, 121, 122; CP 7; CSW; DAM POET; DLBY 1983; EWL 3; INT CANR-26; MTCW 2; PFS 14
Juvenal c. 60-c. 130 .... **CMLC 8**
See also AW 2; CDWLB 1; DLB 211; RGWL 2, 3
Juvenis
See Bourne, Randolph S(illiman)
K., Alice
See Knapp, Caroline
Kabakov, Sasha .... **CLC 59**
Kabir 1398(?)-1448(?) .... **PC 56**
See also RGWL 2, 3
Kacew, Romain 1914-1980
See Gary, Romain
See also CA 108; 102
Kadare, Ismail 1936- .... **CLC 52, 190**
See also CA 161; EWL 3; RGWL 3
Kadohata, Cynthia 1956(?)- ...... **CLC 59, 122**
See also CA 140; CANR 124
Kafka, Franz 1883-1924 ... **SSC 5, 29, 35, 60; TCLC 2, 6, 13, 29, 47, 53, 112; WLC**
See also AAYA 31; BPFB 2; CA 105; 126; CDWLB 2; DA; DA3; DAB; DAC; DAM MST, NOV; DLB 81; EW 9; EWL 3; EXPS; LATS 1; LMFS 2; MTCW 1, 2; NFS 7; RGSF 2; RGWL 2, 3; SFW 4; SSFS 3, 7, 12; TWA
Kahanovitsch, Pinkhes
See Der Nister
Kahn, Roger 1927- .... **CLC 30**
See also CA 25-28R; CANR 44, 69; DLB 171; SATA 37
Kain, Saul
See Sassoon, Siegfried (Lorraine)
Kaiser, Georg 1878-1945 .... **TCLC 9**
See also CA 106; 190; CDWLB 2; DLB 124; EWL 3; LMFS 2; RGWL 2, 3
Kaledin, Sergei .... **CLC 59**
Kaletski, Alexander 1946- .... **CLC 39**
See also CA 118; 143
Kalidasa fl. c. 400-455 .... **CMLC 9; PC 22**
See also RGWL 2, 3
Kallman, Chester (Simon)
1921-1975 .... **CLC 2**
See also CA 45-48; 53-56; CANR 3

Kaminsky, Melvin 1926-
See Brooks, Mel
See also CA 65-68; CANR 16
Kaminsky, Stuart M(elvin) 1934- ..... **CLC 59**
See also CA 73-76; CANR 29, 53, 89; CMW 4
Kamo no Chomei 1153(?)-1216 .... **CMLC 66**
See also DLB 203
Kamo no Nagaakira
See Kamo no Chomei
Kandinsky, Wassily 1866-1944 .... **TCLC 92**
See also CA 118; 155
Kane, Francis
See Robbins, Harold
Kane, Henry 1918-
See Queen, Ellery
See also CA 156; CMW 4
Kane, Paul
See Simon, Paul (Frederick)
Kanin, Garson 1912-1999 .... **CLC 22**
See also AITN 1; CA 5-8R; 177; CAD; CANR 7, 78; DLB 7; IDFW 3, 4
Kaniuk, Yoram 1930- .... **CLC 19**
See also CA 134
Kant, Immanuel 1724-1804 ..... **NCLC 27, 67**
See also DLB 94
Kantor, MacKinlay 1904-1977 .... **CLC 7**
See also CA 61-64; 73-76; CANR 60, 63; DLB 9, 102; MTCW 2; RHW; TCWW 2
Kanze Motokiyo
See Zeami
Kaplan, David Michael 1946- .... **CLC 50**
See also CA 187
Kaplan, James 1951- .... **CLC 59**
See also CA 135; CANR 121
Karadzic, Vuk Stefanovic
1787-1864 .... **NCLC 115**
See also CDWLB 4; DLB 147
Karageorge, Michael
See Anderson, Poul (William)
Karamzin, Nikolai Mikhailovich
1766-1826 .... **NCLC 3**
See also DLB 150; RGSF 2
Karapanou, Margarita 1946- .... **CLC 13**
See also CA 101
Karinthy, Frigyes 1887-1938 .... **TCLC 47**
See also CA 170; DLB 215; EWL 3
Karl, Frederick R(obert)
1927-2004 .... **CLC 34**
See also CA 5-8R; CANR 3, 44
Karr, Mary 1955- .... **CLC 188**
See also AMWS 11; CA 151; CANR 100; NCFS 5
Kastel, Warren
See Silverberg, Robert
Kataev, Evgeny Petrovich 1903-1942
See Petrov, Evgeny
See also CA 120
Kataphusin
See Ruskin, John
Katz, Steve 1935- .... **CLC 47**
See also CA 25-28R; CAAS 14, 64; CANR 12; CN 7; DLBY 1983
Kauffman, Janet 1945- .... **CLC 42**
See also CA 117; CANR 43, 84; DLB 218; DLBY 1986
Kaufman, Bob (Garnell) 1925-1986 . **CLC 49**
See also BG 3; BW 1; CA 41-44R; 118; CANR 22; DLB 16, 41
Kaufman, George S. 1889-1961 .... **CLC 38; DC 17**
See also CA 108; 93-96; DAM DRAM; DFS 1, 10; DLB 7; INT CA-108; MTCW 2; RGAL 4; TUS
Kaufman, Sue .... **CLC 3, 8**
See Barondess, Sue K(aufman)

Kavafis, Konstantinos Petrou 1863-1933
See Cavafy, C(onstantine) P(eter)
See also CA 104
Kavan, Anna 1901-1968 .... **CLC 5, 13, 82**
See also BRWS 7; CA 5-8R; CANR 6, 57; DLB 255; MTCW 1; RGEL 2; SFW 4
Kavanagh, Dan
See Barnes, Julian (Patrick)
Kavanagh, Julie 1952- .... **CLC 119**
See also CA 163
Kavanagh, Patrick (Joseph)
1904-1967 .... **CLC 22; PC 33**
See also BRWS 7; CA 123; 25-28R; DLB 15, 20; EWL 3; MTCW 1; RGEL 2
Kawabata, Yasunari 1899-1972 ..... **CLC 2, 5, 9, 18, 107; SSC 17**
See Kawabata Yasunari
See also CA 93-96; 33-36R; CANR 88; DAM MULT; MJW; MTCW 2; RGSF 2; RGWL 2, 3
Kawabata Yasunari
See Kawabata, Yasunari
See also DLB 180; EWL 3
Kaye, M(ary) M(argaret)
1908-2004 .... **CLC 28**
See also CA 89-92; CANR 24, 60, 102; MTCW 1, 2; RHW; SATA 62
Kaye, Mollie
See Kaye, M(ary) M(argaret)
Kaye-Smith, Sheila 1887-1956 .... **TCLC 20**
See also CA 118; 203; DLB 36
Kaymor, Patrice Maguilene
See Senghor, Leopold Sedar
Kazakov, Yuri Pavlovich 1927-1982 . **SSC 43**
See Kazakov, Yury
See also CA 5-8R; CANR 36; MTCW 1; RGSF 2
Kazakov, Yury
See Kazakov, Yuri Pavlovich
See also EWL 3
Kazan, Elia 1909-2003 .... **CLC 6, 16, 63**
See also CA 21-24R; 220; CANR 32, 78
Kazantzakis, Nikos 1883(?)-1957 .... **TCLC 2, 5, 33**
See also BPFB 2; CA 105; 132; DA3; EW 9; EWL 3; MTCW 1, 2; RGWL 2, 3
Kazin, Alfred 1915-1998 ..... **CLC 34, 38, 119**
See also AMWS 8; CA 1-4R; CAAS 7; CANR 1, 45, 79; DLB 67; EWL 3
Keane, Mary Nesta (Skrine) 1904-1996
See Keane, Molly
See also CA 108; 114; 151; CN 7; RHW
Keane, Molly .... **CLC 31**
See Keane, Mary Nesta (Skrine)
See also INT CA-114
Keates, Jonathan 1946(?)- .... **CLC 34**
See also CA 163; CANR 126
Keaton, Buster 1895-1966 .... **CLC 20**
See also CA 194
Keats, John 1795-1821 ...... **NCLC 8, 73, 121; PC 1; WLC**
See also BRW 4; BRWR 1; CDBLB 1789-1832; DA; DA3; DAB; DAC; DAM MST, POET; DLB 96, 110; EXPP; LMFS 1; PAB; PFS 1, 2, 3, 9, 17; RGEL 2; TEA; WLIT 3; WP
Keble, John 1792-1866 .... **NCLC 87**
See also DLB 32, 55; RGEL 2
Keene, Donald 1922- .... **CLC 34**
See also CA 1-4R; CANR 5, 119
Keillor, Garrison .... **CLC 40, 115**
See Keillor, Gary (Edward)
See also AAYA 2; BEST 89:3; BPFB 2; DLBY 1987; EWL 3; SATA 58; TUS
Keillor, Gary (Edward) 1942-
See Keillor, Garrison
See also CA 111; 117; CANR 36, 59, 124; CPW; DA3; DAM POP; MTCW 1, 2

Keith, Carlos
See Lewton, Val
Keith, Michael
See Hubbard, L(afayette) Ron(ald)
Keller, Gottfried 1819-1890 .... **NCLC 2; SSC 26**
See also CDWLB 2; DLB 129; EW; RGSF 2; RGWL 2, 3
Keller, Nora Okja 1965- .... **CLC 109**
See also CA 187
Kellerman, Jonathan 1949- .... **CLC 44**
See also AAYA 35; BEST 90:1; CA 106; CANR 29, 51; CMW 4; CPW; DA3; DAM POP; INT CANR-29
Kelley, William Melvin 1937- .... **CLC 22**
See also BW 1; CA 77-80; CANR 27, 83; CN 7; DLB 33; EWL 3
Kellogg, Marjorie 1922- .... **CLC 2**
See also CA 81-84
Kellow, Kathleen
See Hibbert, Eleanor Alice Burford
Kelly, M(ilton) T(errence) 1947- ...... **CLC 55**
See also CA 97-100; CAAS 22; CANR 19, 43, 84; CN 7
Kelly, Robert 1935- .... **SSC 50**
See also CA 17-20R; CAAS 19; CANR 47; CP 7; DLB 5, 130, 165
Kelman, James 1946- .... **CLC 58, 86**
See also BRWS 5; CA 148; CANR 85; CN 7; DLB 194; RGSF 2; WLIT 4
Kemal, Yashar 1923- .... **CLC 14, 29**
See also CA 89-92; CANR 44; CWW 2
Kemble, Fanny 1809-1893 .... **NCLC 18**
See also DLB 32
Kemelman, Harry 1908-1996 .... **CLC 2**
See also AITN 1; BPFB 2; CA 9-12R; 155; CANR 6, 71; CMW 4; DLB 28
Kempe, Margery 1373(?)-1440(?) ... **LC 6, 56**
See also DLB 146; RGEL 2
Kempis, Thomas a 1380-1471 .... **LC 11**
Kendall, Henry 1839-1882 .... **NCLC 12**
See also DLB 230
Keneally, Thomas (Michael) 1935- ... **CLC 5, 8, 10, 14, 19, 27, 43, 117**
See also BRWS 4; CA 85-88; CANR 10, 50, 74; CN 7; CPW; DA3; DAM NOV; DLB 289; EWL 3; MTCW 1, 2; NFS 17; RGEL 2; RHW
Kennedy, A(lison) L(ouise) 1965- ... **CLC 188**
See also CA 168, 213; CAAE 213; CANR 108; CD 5; CN 7; DLB 271; RGSF 2
Kennedy, Adrienne (Lita) 1931- .... **BLC 2; CLC 66; DC 5**
See also AFAW 2; BW 2, 3; CA 103; CAAS 20; CABS 3; CANR 26, 53, 82; CD 5; DAM MULT; DFS 9; DLB 38; FW
Kennedy, John Pendleton 1795-1870 .... **NCLC 2**
See also DLB 3, 248, 254; RGAL 4
Kennedy, Joseph Charles 1929-
See Kennedy, X. J.
See also CA 1-4R, 201; CAAE 201; CANR 4, 30, 40; CP 7; CWRI 5; MAICYA 2; MAICYAS 1; SATA 14, 86, 130; SATA-Essay 130
Kennedy, William 1928- ... **CLC 6, 28, 34, 53**
See also AAYA 1; AMWS 7; BPFB 2; CA 85-88; CANR 14, 31, 76; CN 7; DA3; DAM NOV; DLB 143; DLBY 1985; EWL 3; INT CANR-31; MTCW 1, 2; SATA 57
Kennedy, X. J. .... **CLC 8, 42**
See Kennedy, Joseph Charles
See also CAAS 9; CLR 27; DLB 5; SAAS 22
Kenny, Maurice (Francis) 1929- ..... **CLC 87; NNAL**
See also CA 144; CAAS 22; DAM MULT; DLB 175

Kent, Kelvin
See Kuttner, Henry
Kenton, Maxwell
See Southern, Terry
Kenyon, Jane 1947-1995 .... **PC 57**
See also AMWS 7; CA 118; 148; CANR 44, 69; CP 7; CWP; DLB 120; PFS 9, 17; RGAL 4
Kenyon, Robert O.
See Kuttner, Henry
Kepler, Johannes 1571-1630 .... **LC 45**
Ker, Jill
See Conway, Jill K(er)
Kerkow, H. C.
See Lewton, Val
Kerouac, Jack 1922-1969 ...... **CLC 1, 2, 3, 5, 14, 29, 61; TCLC 117; WLC**
See Kerouac, Jean-Louis Lebris de
See also AAYA 25; AMWC 1; AMWS 3; BG 3; BPFB 2; CDALB 1941-1968; CPW; DLB 2, 16, 237; DLBD 3; DLBY 1995; EWL 3; GLL 1; LATS 1; LMFS 2; MTCW 2; NFS 8; RGAL 4; TUS; WP
Kerouac, Jean-Louis Lebris de 1922-1969
See Kerouac, Jack
See also AITN 1; CA 5-8R; 25-28R; CANR 26, 54, 95; DA; DA3; DAB; DAC; DAM MST, NOV, POET, POP; MTCW 1, 2
Kerr, (Bridget) Jean (Collins) 1923(?)-2003 .... **CLC 22**
See also CA 5-8R; 212; CANR 7; INT CANR-7
Kerr, M. E. .... **CLC 12, 35**
See Meaker, Marijane (Agnes)
See also AAYA 2, 23; BYA 1, 7, 8; CLR 29; SAAS 1; WYA
Kerr, Robert .... **CLC 55**
Kerrigan, (Thomas) Anthony 1918- .. **CLC 4, 6**
See also CA 49-52; CAAS 11; CANR 4
Kerry, Lois
See Duncan, Lois
Kesey, Ken (Elton) 1935-2001 ... **CLC 1, 3, 6, 11, 46, 64, 184; WLC**
See also AAYA 25; BG 3; BPFB 2; CA 1-4R; 204; CANR 22, 38, 66, 124; CDALB 1968-1988; CN 7; CPW; DA; DA3; DAB; DAC; DAM MST, NOV, POP; DLB 2, 16, 206; EWL 3; EXPN; LAIT 4; MTCW 1, 2; NFS 2; RGAL 4; SATA 66; SATA-Obit 131; TUS; YAW
Kesselring, Joseph (Otto) 1902-1967 .... **CLC 45**
See also CA 150; DAM DRAM, MST
Kessler, Jascha (Frederick) 1929 .... **CLC 4**
See also CA 17-20R; CANR 8, 48, 111
Kettelkamp, Larry (Dale) 1933- .... **CLC 12**
See also CA 29-32R; CANR 16; SAAS 3; SATA 2
Key, Ellen (Karolina Sofia) 1849-1926 .... **TCLC 65**
See also DLB 259
Keyber, Conny
See Fielding, Henry
Keyes, Daniel 1927- .... **CLC 80**
See also AAYA 23; BYA 11; CA 17-20R, 181; CAAE 181; CANR 10, 26, 54, 74; DA; DA3; DAC; DAM MST, NOV; EXPN; LAIT 4; MTCW 2; NFS 2; SATA 37; SFW 4
Keynes, John Maynard 1883-1946 .... **TCLC 64**
See also CA 114; 162, 163; DLBD 10; MTCW 2
Khanshendel, Chiron
See Rose, Wendy

Khayyam, Omar 1048-1131 ... **CMLC 11; PC 8**
See Omar Khayyam
See also DA3; DAM POET
Kherdian, David 1931- .... **CLC 6, 9**
See also AAYA 42; CA 21-24R, 192; CAAE 192; CAAS 2; CANR 39, 78; CLR 24; JRDA; LAIT 3; MAICYA 1, 2; SATA 16, 74; SATA-Essay 125
Khlebnikov, Velimir .... **TCLC 20**
See Khlebnikov, Viktor Vladimirovich
See also DLB 295; EW 10; EWL 3; RGWL 2, 3
Khlebnikov, Viktor Vladimirovich 1885-1922
See Khlebnikov, Velimir
See also CA 117; 217
Khodasevich, Vladislav (Felitsianovich) 1886-1939 .... **TCLC 15**
See also CA 115; EWL 3
Kielland, Alexander Lange 1849-1906 .... **TCLC 5**
See also CA 104
Kiely, Benedict 1919- ... **CLC 23, 43; SSC 58**
See also CA 1-4R; CANR 2, 84; CN 7; DLB 15
Kienzle, William X(avier) 1928-2001 .... **CLC 25**
See also CA 93-96; 203; CAAS 1; CANR 9, 31, 59, 111; CMW 4; DAM POP; INT CANR-31; MSW; MTCW 1, 2
Kierkegaard, Soren 1813-1855 ..... **NCLC 34, 78, 125**
See also EW 6; LMFS 2; RGWL 3; TWA
Kieslowski, Krzysztof 1941-1996 .... **CLC 120**
See also CA 147; 151
Killens, John Oliver 1916-1987 .... **CLC 10**
See also BW 2; CA 77-80; 123; CAAS 2; CANR 26; DLB 33; EWL 3
Killigrew, Anne 1660-1685 .... **LC 4, 73**
See also DLB 131
Killigrew, Thomas 1612-1683 .... **LC 57**
See also DLB 58; RGEL 2
Kim
See Simenon, Georges (Jacques Christian)
Kincaid, Jamaica 1949- ...... **BLC 2; CLC 43, 68, 137**
See also AAYA 13; AFAW 2; AMWS 7; BRWS 7; BW 2, 3; CA 125; CANR 47, 59, 95; CDALBS; CDWLB 3; CLR 63; CN 7; DA3; DAM MULT, NOV; DLB 157, 227; DNFS 1; EWL 3; EXPS; FW; LATS 1; LMFS 2; MTCW 2; NCFS 1; NFS 3; SSFS 5, 7; TUS; WWE 1; YAW
King, Francis (Henry) 1923- ...... **CLC 8, 53, 145**
See also CA 1-4R; CANR 1, 33, 86; CN 7; DAM NOV; DLB 15, 139; MTCW 1
King, Kennedy
See Brown, George Douglas
King, Martin Luther, Jr. 1929-1968 . **BLC 2; CLC 83; WLCS**
See also BW 2, 3; CA 25-28; CANR 27, 44; CAP 2; DA; DA3; DAB; DAC; DAM MST, MULT; LAIT 5; LATS 1; MTCW 1, 2; SATA 14
King, Stephen (Edwin) 1947- .... **CLC 12, 26, 37, 61, 113; SSC 17, 55**
See also AAYA 1, 17; AMWS 5; BEST 90:1; BPFB 2; CA 61-64; CANR 1, 30, 52, 76, 119; CPW; DA3; DAM NOV, POP; DLB 143; DLBY 1980; HGG; JRDA; LAIT 5; MTCW 1, 2; RGAL 4; SATA 9, 55; SUFW 1, 2; WYAS 1; YAW
King, Steve
See King, Stephen (Edwin)
King, Thomas 1943- ..... **CLC 89, 171; NNAL**
See also CA 144; CANR 95; CCA 1; CN 7; DAC; DAM MULT; DLB 175; SATA 96

Kingman, Lee .... **CLC 17**
See Natti, (Mary) Lee
See also CWRI 5; SAAS 3; SATA 1, 67

Kingsley, Charles 1819-1875 .... **NCLC 35**
See also CLR 77; DLB 21, 32, 163, 178, 190; FANT; MAICYA 2; MAICYAS 1; RGEL 2; WCH; YABC 2

Kingsley, Henry 1830-1876 .... **NCLC 107**
See also DLB 21, 230; RGEL 2

Kingsley, Sidney 1906-1995 .... **CLC 44**
See also CA 85-88; 147; CAD; DFS 14; DLB 7; RGAL 4

Kingsolver, Barbara 1955- . **CLC 55, 81, 130**
See also AAYA 15; AMWS 7; CA 129; 134; CANR 60, 96; CDALBS; CPW; CSW; DA3; DAM POP; DLB 206; INT CA-134; LAIT 5; MTCW 2; NFS 5, 10, 12; RGAL 4

Kingston, Maxine (Ting Ting) Hong
1940- .... **AAL; CLC 12, 19, 58, 121; WLCS**
See also AAYA 8, 55; AMWS 5; BPFB 2; CA 69-72; CANR 13, 38, 74, 87, 128; CDALBS; CN 7; DA3; DAM MULT, NOV; DLB 173, 212; DLBY 1980; EWL 3; FW; INT CANR-13; LAIT 5; MAWW; MTCW 1, 2; NFS 6; RGAL 4; SATA 53; SSFS 3

Kinnell, Galway 1927- ..... **CLC 1, 2, 3, 5, 13, 29, 129; PC 26**
See also AMWS 3; CA 9-12R; CANR 10, 34, 66, 116; CP 7; DLB 5; DLBY 1987; EWL 3; INT CANR-34; MTCW 1, 2; PAB; PFS 9; RGAL 4; WP

Kinsella, Thomas 1928- .... **CLC 4, 19, 138**
See also BRWS 5; CA 17-20R; CANR 15, 122; CP 7; DLB 27; EWL 3; MTCW 1, 2; RGEL 2; TEA

Kinsella, W(illiam) P(atrick) 1935- . **CLC 27, 43, 166**
See also AAYA 7; BPFB 2; CA 97-100, 222; CAAE 222; CAAS 7; CANR 21, 35, 66, 75, 129; CN 7; CPW; DAC; DAM NOV, POP; FANT; INT CANR-21; LAIT 5; MTCW 1, 2; NFS 15; RGSF 2

Kinsey, Alfred C(harles)
1894-1956 .... **TCLC 91**
See also CA 115; 170; MTCW 2

Kipling, (Joseph) Rudyard 1865-1936 . **PC 3; SSC 5, 54; TCLC 8, 17; WLC**
See also AAYA 32; BRW 6; BRWC 1, 2; BYA 4; CA 105; 120; CANR 33; CDBLB 1890-1914; CLR 39, 65; CWRI 5; DA; DA3; DAB; DAC; DAM MST, POET; DLB 19, 34, 141, 156; EWL 3; EXPS; FANT; LAIT; LMFS 1; MAICYA 1, 2; MTCW 1, 2; RGEL 2; RGSF 2; SATA 100; SFW 4; SSFS 8; SUFW 1; TEA; WCH; WLIT 4; YABC 2

Kirk, Russell (Amos) 1918-1994 .. **TCLC 119**
See also AITN 1; CA 1-4R; 145; CAAS 9; CANR 1, 20, 60; HGG; INT CANR-20; MTCW 1, 2

Kirkland, Caroline M. 1801-1864 . **NCLC 85**
See also DLB 3, 73, 74, 250, 254; DLBD 13

Kirkup, James 1918- .... **CLC 1**
See also CA 1-4R; CAAS 4; CANR 2; CP 7; DLB 27; SATA 12

Kirkwood, James 1930(?)-1989 .... **CLC 9**
See also AITN 2; CA 1-4R; 128; CANR 6, 40; GLL 2

Kirsch, Sarah 1935- .... **CLC 176**
See also CA 178; CWW 2; DLB 75; EWL 3

Kirshner, Sidney
See Kingsley, Sidney

Kis, Danilo 1935-1989 .... **CLC 57**
See also CA 109; 118; 129; CANR 61; CDWLB 4; DLB 181; EWL 3; MTCW 1; RGSF 2; RGWL 2, 3

Kissinger, Henry A(lfred) 1923- ..... **CLC 137**
See also CA 1-4R; CANR 2, 33, 66, 109; MTCW 1

Kivi, Aleksis 1834-1872 .... **NCLC 30**

Kizer, Carolyn (Ashley) 1925- ... **CLC 15, 39, 80**
See also CA 65-68; CAAS 5; CANR 24, 70; CP 7; CWP; DAM POET; DLB 5, 169; EWL 3; MTCW 2; PFS 18

Klabund 1890-1928 .... **TCLC 44**
See also CA 162; DLB 66

Klappert, Peter 1942- .... **CLC 57**
See also CA 33-36R; CSW; DLB 5

Klein, A(braham) M(oses)
1909-1972 .... **CLC 19**
See also CA 101; 37-40R; DAB; DAC; DAM MST; DLB 68; EWL 3; RGEL 2

Klein, Joe
See Klein, Joseph

Klein, Joseph 1946- .... **CLC 154**
See also CA 85-88; CANR 55

Klein, Norma 1938-1989 .... **CLC 30**
See also AAYA 2, 35; BPFB 2; BYA 6, 7, 8; CA 41-44R; 128; CANR 15, 37; CLR 2, 19; INT CANR-15; JRDA; MAICYA 1, 2; SAAS 1; SATA 7, 57; WYA; YAW

Klein, T(heodore) E(ibon) D(onald)
1947- .... **CLC 34**
See also CA 119; CANR 44, 75; HGG

Kleist, Heinrich von 1777-1811 ...... **NCLC 2, 37; SSC 22**
See also CDWLB 2; DAM DRAM; DLB 90; EW 5; RGSF 2; RGWL 2, 3

Klima, Ivan 1931- .... **CLC 56, 172**
See also CA 25-28R; CANR 17, 50, 91; CDWLB 4; CWW 2; DAM NOV; DLB 232; EWL 3; RGWL 3

Klimentev, Andrei Platonovich
See Klimentov, Andrei Platonovich

Klimentov, Andrei Platonovich
1899-1951 .... **SSC 42; TCLC 14**
See Platonov, Andrei Platonovich; Platonov, Andrey Platonovich
See also CA 108

Klinger, Friedrich Maximilian von
1752-1831 .... **NCLC 1**
See also DLB 94

Klingsor the Magician
See Hartmann, Sadakichi

Klopstock, Friedrich Gottlieb
1724-1803 .... **NCLC 11**
See also DLB 97; EW 4; RGWL 2, 3

Kluge, Alexander 1932- .... **SSC 61**
See also CA 81-84; DLB 75

Knapp, Caroline 1959-2002 .... **CLC 99**
See also CA 154; 207

Knebel, Fletcher 1911-1993 .... **CLC 14**
See also AITN 1; CA 1-4R; 140; CAAS 3; CANR 1, 36; SATA 36; SATA-Obit 75

Knickerbocker, Diedrich
See Irving, Washington

Knight, Etheridge 1931-1991 ... **BLC 2; CLC 40; PC 14**
See also BW 1, 3; CA 21-24R; 133; CANR 23, 82; DAM POET; DLB 41; MTCW 2; RGAL 4

Knight, Sarah Kemble 1666-1727 .... **LC 7**
See also DLB 24, 200

Knister, Raymond 1899-1932 .... **TCLC 56**
See also CA 186; DLB 68; RGEL 2

Knowles, John 1926-2001 ... **CLC 1, 4, 10, 26**
See also AAYA 10; AMWS 12; BPFB 2; BYA 3; CA 17-20R; 203; CANR 40, 74, 76; CDALB 1968-1988; CN 7; DA; DAC; DAM MST, NOV; DLB 6; EXPN; MTCW 1, 2; NFS 2; RGAL 4; SATA 8, 89; SATA-Obit 134; YAW

Knox, Calvin M.
See Silverberg, Robert

Knox, John c. 1505-1572 .... **LC 37**
See also DLB 132

Knye, Cassandra
See Disch, Thomas M(ichael)

Koch, C(hristopher) J(ohn) 1932- .... **CLC 42**
See also CA 127; CANR 84; CN 7; DLB 289

Koch, Christopher
See Koch, C(hristopher) J(ohn)

Koch, Kenneth (Jay) 1925-2002 .... **CLC 5, 8, 44**
See also CA 1-4R; 207; CAD; CANR 6, 36, 57, 97; CD 5; CP 7; DAM POET; DLB 5; INT CANR-36; MTCW 2; SATA 65; WP

Kochanowski, Jan 1530-1584 .... **LC 10**
See also RGWL 2, 3

Kock, Charles Paul de 1794-1871 . **NCLC 16**

Koda Rohan
See Koda Shigeyuki

Koda Rohan
See Koda Shigeyuki
See also DLB 180

Koda Shigeyuki 1867-1947 .... **TCLC 22**
See Koda Rohan
See also CA 121; 183

Koestler, Arthur 1905-1983 ... **CLC 1, 3, 6, 8, 15, 33**
See also BRWS 1; CA 1-4R; 109; CANR 1, 33; CDBLB 1945-1960; DLBY 1983; EWL 3; MTCW 1, 2; RGEL 2

Kogawa, Joy Nozomi 1935- ...... **CLC 78, 129**
See also AAYA 47; CA 101; CANR 19, 62, 126; CN 7; CWP; DAC; DAM MST, MULT; FW; MTCW 2; NFS 3; SATA 99

Kohout, Pavel 1928- .... **CLC 13**
See also CA 45-48; CANR 3

Koizumi, Yakumo
See Hearn, (Patricio) Lafcadio (Tessima Carlos)

Kolmar, Gertrud 1894-1943 .... **TCLC 40**
See also CA 167; EWL 3

Komunyakaa, Yusef 1947- .. **BLCS; CLC 86, 94; PC 51**
See also AFAW 2; AMWS 13; CA 147; CANR 83; CP 7; CSW; DLB 120; EWL 3; PFS 5; RGAL 4

Konrad, George
See Konrad, Gyorgy
See also CWW 2

Konrad, Gyorgy 1933- .... **CLC 4, 10, 73**
See Konrad, George
See also CA 85-88; CANR 97; CDWLB 4; CWW 2; DLB 232; EWL 3

Konwicki, Tadeusz 1926- .... **CLC 8, 28, 54, 117**
See also CA 101; CAAS 9; CANR 39, 59; CWW 2; DLB 232; EWL 3; IDFW 3; MTCW 1

Koontz, Dean R(ay) 1945- .... **CLC 78**
See also AAYA 9, 31; BEST 89:3, 90:2; CA 108; CANR 19, 36, 52, 95; CMW 4; CPW; DA3; DAM NOV, POP; DLB 292; HGG; MTCW 1; SATA 92; SFW 4; SUFW 2; YAW

Kopernik, Mikolaj
See Copernicus, Nicolaus

Kopit, Arthur (Lee) 1937- ...... **CLC 1, 18, 33**
See also AITN 1; CA 81-84; CABS 3; CD 5; DAM DRAM; DFS 7, 14; DLB 7; MTCW 1; RGAL 4
Kopitar, Jernej (Bartholomaus)
1780-1844 .... **NCLC 117**
Kops, Bernard 1926- .... **CLC 4**
See also CA 5-8R; CANR 84; CBD; CN 7; CP 7; DLB 13
Kornbluth, C(yril) M. 1923-1958 .... **TCLC 8**
See also CA 105; 160; DLB 8; SFW 4
Korolenko, V. G.
See Korolenko, Vladimir Galaktionovich
Korolenko, Vladimir
See Korolenko, Vladimir Galaktionovich
Korolenko, Vladimir G.
See Korolenko, Vladimir Galaktionovich
Korolenko, Vladimir Galaktionovich
1853-1921 .... **TCLC 22**
See also CA 121; DLB 277
Korzybski, Alfred (Habdank Skarbek)
1879-1950 .... **TCLC 61**
See also CA 123; 160
Kosinski, Jerzy (Nikodem)
1933-1991 .... **CLC 1, 2, 3, 6, 10, 15, 53, 70**
See also AMWS 7; BPFB 2; CA 17-20R; 134; CANR 9, 46; DA3; DAM NOV; DLB 2; DLBY 1982; EWL 3; HGG; MTCW 1, 2; NFS 12; RGAL 4; TUS
Kostelanetz, Richard (Cory) 1940- .. **CLC 28**
See also CA 13-16R; CAAS 8; CANR 38, 77; CN 7; CP 7
Kostrowitzki, Wilhelm Apollinaris de
1880-1918
See Apollinaire, Guillaume
See also CA 104
Kotlowitz, Robert 1924- .... **CLC 4**
See also CA 33-36R; CANR 36
Kotzebue, August (Friedrich Ferdinand) von
1761-1819 .... **NCLC 25**
See also DLB 94
Kotzwinkle, William 1938- ..... **CLC 5, 14, 35**
See also BPFB 2; CA 45-48; CANR 3, 44, 84, 129; CLR 6; DLB 173; FANT; MAICYA 1, 2; SATA 24, 70, 146; SFW 4; SUFW 2; YAW
Kowna, Stancy
See Szymborska, Wislawa
Kozol, Jonathan 1936- .... **CLC 17**
See also AAYA 46; CA 61-64; CANR 16, 45, 96
Kozoll, Michael 1940(?)- .... **CLC 35**
Kramer, Kathryn 19(?)- .... **CLC 34**
Kramer, Larry 1935- .... **CLC 42; DC 8**
See also CA 124; 126; CANR 60; DAM POP; DLB 249; GLL 1
Krasicki, Ignacy 1735-1801 .... **NCLC 8**
Krasinski, Zygmunt 1812-1859 .... **NCLC 4**
See also RGWL 2, 3
Kraus, Karl 1874-1936 .... **TCLC 5**
See also CA 104; 216; DLB 118; EWL 3
Kreve (Mickevicius), Vincas
1882-1954 .... **TCLC 27**
See also CA 170; DLB 220; EWL 3
Kristeva, Julia 1941- .... **CLC 77, 140**
See also CA 154; CANR 99; DLB 242; EWL 3; FW; LMFS 2
Kristofferson, Kris 1936- .... **CLC 26**
See also CA 104
Krizanc, John 1956- .... **CLC 57**
See also CA 187
Krleza, Miroslav 1893-1981 .... **CLC 8, 114**
See also CA 97-100; 105; CANR 50; CDWLB 4; DLB 147; EW 11; RGWL 2, 3
Kroetsch, Robert 1927- .. **CLC 5, 23, 57, 132**
See also CA 17-20R; CANR 8, 38; CCA 1; CN 7; CP 7; DAC; DAM POET; DLB 53; MTCW 1

Kroetz, Franz
See Kroetz, Franz Xaver
Kroetz, Franz Xaver 1946- .... **CLC 41**
See also CA 130; EWL 3
Kroker, Arthur (W.) 1945- .... **CLC 77**
See also CA 161
Kropotkin, Peter (Alcksieevich)
1842-1921 .... **TCLC 36**
See Kropotkin, Petr Alekseevich
See also CA 119; 219
Kropotkin, Petr Alekseevich
See Kropotkin, Peter (Alcksieevich)
See also DLB 277
Krotkov, Yuri 1917-1981 .... **CLC 19**
See also CA 102
Krumb
See Crumb, R(obert)
Krumgold, Joseph (Quincy)
1908-1980 .... **CLC 12**
See also BYA 1, 2; CA 9-12R; 101; CANR 7; MAICYA 1, 2; SATA 1, 48; SATA-Obit 23; YAW
Krumwitz
See Crumb, R(obert)
Krutch, Joseph Wood 1893-1970 ..... **CLC 24**
See also ANW; CA 1-4R; 25-28R; CANR 4; DLB 63, 206, 275
Krutzch, Gus
See Eliot, T(homas) S(tearns)
Krylov, Ivan Andreevich
1768(?)-1844 .... **NCLC 1**
See also DLB 150
Kubin, Alfred (Leopold Isidor)
1877-1959 .... **TCLC 23**
See also CA 112; 149; CANR 104; DLB 81
Kubrick, Stanley 1928-1999 .... **CLC 16; TCLC 112**
See also AAYA 30; CA 81-84; 177; CANR 33; DLB 26
Kumin, Maxine (Winokur) 1925- ..... **CLC 5, 13, 28, 164; PC 15**
See also AITN 2; AMWS 4; ANW; CA 1-4R; CAAS 8; CANR 1, 21, 69, 115; CP 7; CWP; DA3; DAM POET; DLB 5; EWL 3; EXPP; MTCW 1, 2; PAB; PFS 18; SATA 12
Kundera, Milan 1929- . **CLC 4, 9, 19, 32, 68, 115, 135; SSC 24**
See also AAYA 2; BPFB 2; CA 85-88; CANR 19, 52, 74; CDWLB 4; CWW 2; DA3; DAM NOV; DLB 232; EW 13; EWL 3; MTCW 1, 2; NFS 18; RGSF 2; RGWL 3; SSFS 10
Kunene, Mazisi (Raymond) 1930- ... **CLC 85**
See also BW 1, 3; CA 125; CANR 81; CP 7; DLB 117
Kung, Hans .... **CLC 130**
See Kung, Hans
Kung, Hans 1928-
See Kung, Hans
See also CA 53-56; CANR 66; MTCW 1, 2
Kunikida Doppo 1869(?)-1908
See Doppo, Kunikida
See also DLB 180; EWL 3
Kunitz, Stanley (Jasspon) 1905- .. **CLC 6, 11, 14, 148; PC 19**
See also AMWS 3; CA 41-44R; CANR 26, 57, 98; CP 7; DA3; DLB 48; INT CANR-26; MTCW 1, 2; PFS 11; RGAL 4
Kunze, Reiner 1933- .... **CLC 10**
See also CA 93-96; CWW 2; DLB 75; EWL 3
Kuprin, Aleksander Ivanovich
1870-1938 .... **TCLC 5**
See Kuprin, Aleksandr Ivanovich; Kuprin, Alexandr Ivanovich
See also CA 104; 182

Kuprin, Aleksandr Ivanovich
See Kuprin, Aleksander Ivanovich
See also DLB 295
Kuprin, Alexandr Ivanovich
See Kuprin, Aleksander Ivanovich
See also EWL 3
Kureishi, Hanif 1954(?)- .... **CLC 64, 135**
See also CA 139; CANR 113; CBD; CD 5; CN 7; DLB 194, 245; GLL 2; IDFW 4; WLIT 4; WWE 1
Kurosawa, Akira 1910-1998 ..... **CLC 16, 119**
See also AAYA 11; CA 101; 170; CANR 46; DAM MULT
Kushner, Tony 1957(?)- .... **CLC 81; DC 10**
See also AMWS 9; CA 144; CAD; CANR 74; CD 5; DA3; DAM DRAM; DFS 5; DLB 228; EWL 3; GLL 1; LAIT 5; MTCW 2; RGAL 4
Kuttner, Henry 1915-1958 .... **TCLC 10**
See also CA 107; 157; DLB 8; FANT; SCFW 2; SFW 4
Kutty, Madhavi
See Das, Kamala
Kuzma, Greg 1944- .... **CLC 7**
See also CA 33-36R; CANR 70
Kuzmin, Mikhail (Alekseevich)
1872(?)-1936 .... **TCLC 40**
See also CA 170; DLB 295; EWL 3
Kyd, Thomas 1558-1594 .... **DC 3; LC 22**
See also BRW 1; DAM DRAM; DLB 62; IDTP; LMFS 1; RGEL 2; TEA; WLIT 3
Kyprianos, Iossif
See Samarakis, Antonis
L. S.
See Stephen, Sir Leslie
Labrunie, Gerard
See Nerval, Gerard de
La Bruyere, Jean de 1645-1696 .... **LC 17**
See also DLB 268; EW 3; GFL Beginnings to 1789
Lacan, Jacques (Marie Emile)
1901-1981 .... **CLC 75**
See also CA 121; 104; DLB 296; EWL 3; TWA
Laclos, Pierre Ambroise Francois
1741-1803 .... **NCLC 4, 87**
See also EW 4; GFL Beginnings to 1789; RGWL 2, 3
Lacolere, Francois
See Aragon, Louis
La Colere, Francois
See Aragon, Louis
La Deshabilleuse
See Simenon, Georges (Jacques Christian)
Lady Gregory
See Gregory, Lady Isabella Augusta (Persse)
Lady of Quality, A
See Bagnold, Enid
La Fayette, Marie-(Madelaine Pioche de la Vergne) 1634-1693 .... **LC 2**
See Lafayette, Marie-Madeleine
See also GFL Beginnings to 1789; RGWL 2, 3
Lafayette, Marie-Madeleine
See La Fayette, Marie-(Madelaine Pioche de la Vergne)
See also DLB 268
Lafayette, Rene
See Hubbard, L(afayette) Ron(ald)
La Flesche, Francis 1857(?)-1932 .... **NNAL**
See also CA 144; CANR 83; DLB 175
La Fontaine, Jean de 1621-1695 .... **LC 50**
See also DLB 268; EW 3; GFL Beginnings to 1789; MAICYA 1, 2; RGWL 2, 3; SATA 18
Laforgue, Jules 1860-1887 . **NCLC 5, 53; PC 14; SSC 20**
See also DLB 217; EW 7; GFL 1789 to the Present; RGWL 2, 3

Layamon
See Layamon
See also DLB 146

Lagerkvist, Par (Fabian)
1891-1974 ..... **CLC 7, 10, 13, 54; TCLC 144**
See Lagerkvist, Par
See also CA 85-88; 49-52; DA3; DAM DRAM, NOV; MTCW 1, 2; TWA

Lagerkvist, Par .... **SSC 12**
See Lagerkvist, Paer (Fabian)
See also DLB 259; EW 10; EWL 3; MTCW 2; RGSF 2; RGWL 2, 3

Lagerloef, Selma (Ottiliana Lovisa)
1858-1940 .... **TCLC 4, 36**
See Lagerlof, Selma (Ottiliana Lovisa)
See also CA 108; MTCW 2; SATA 15

Lagerlof, Selma (Ottiliana Lovisa)
See Lagerloef, Selma (Ottiliana Lovisa)
See also CLR 7; SATA 15

La Guma, (Justin) Alex(ander)
1925-1985 . **BLCS; CLC 19; TCLC 140**
See also AFW; BW 1, 3; CA 49-52; 118; CANR 25, 81; CDWLB 3; DAM NOV; DLB 117, 225; EWL 3; MTCW 1, 2; WLIT 2; WWE 1

Laidlaw, A. K.
See Grieve, C(hristopher) M(urray)

Lainez, Manuel Mujica
See Mujica Lainez, Manuel
See also HW 1

Laing, R(onald) D(avid) 1927-1989 . **CLC 95**
See also CA 107; 129; CANR 34; MTCW 1

Lamartine, Alphonse (Marie Louis Prat) de
1790-1869 .... **NCLC 11; PC 16**
See also DAM POET; DLB 217; GFL 1789 to the Present; RGWL 2, 3

Lamb, Charles 1775-1834 ..... **NCLC 10, 113; WLC**
See also BRW 4; CDBLB 1789-1832; DA; DAB; DAC; DAM MST; DLB 93, 107, 163; RGEL 2; SATA 17; TEA

Lamb, Lady Caroline 1785-1828 ... **NCLC 38**
See also DLB 116

Lamb, Mary Ann 1764-1847 .... **NCLC 125**
See also DLB 163; SATA 17

Lame Deer 1903(?)-1976 .... **NNAL**
See also CA 69-72

Lamming, George (William) 1927- ... **BLC 2; CLC 2, 4, 66, 144**
See also BW 2, 3; CA 85-88; CANR 26, 76; CDWLB 3; CN 7; DAM MULT; DLB 125; EWL 3; MTCW 1, 2; NFS 15; RGEL 2

L'Amour, Louis (Dearborn)
1908-1988 .... **CLC 25, 55**
See Burns, Tex; Mayo, Jim
See also AAYA 16; AITN 2; BEST 89:2; BPFB 2; CA 1-4R; 125; CANR 3, 25, 40; CPW; DA3; DAM NOV, POP; DLB 206; DLBY 1980; MTCW 1, 2; RGAL 4

Lampedusa, Giuseppe (Tomasi) di
.... **TCLC 13**
See Tomasi di Lampedusa, Giuseppe
See also CA 164; EW 11; MTCW 2; RGWL 2, 3

Lampman, Archibald 1861-1899 ... **NCLC 25**
See also DLB 92; RGEL 2; TWA

Lancaster, Bruce 1896-1963 .... **CLC 36**
See also CA 9-10; CANR 70; CAP 1; SATA 9

Lanchester, John 1962- .... **CLC 99**
See also CA 194; DLB 267

Landau, Mark Alexandrovich
See Aldanov, Mark (Alexandrovich)

Landau-Aldanov, Mark Alexandrovich
See Aldanov, Mark (Alexandrovich)

Landis, Jerry
See Simon, Paul (Frederick)

Landis, John 1950- .... **CLC 26**
See also CA 112; 122; CANR 128

Landolfi, Tommaso 1908-1979 .... **CLC 11, 49**
See also CA 127; 117; DLB 177; EWL 3

Landon, Letitia Elizabeth
1802-1838 .... **NCLC 15**
See also DLB 96

Landor, Walter Savage
1775-1864 .... **NCLC 14**
See also BRW 4; DLB 93, 107; RGEL 2

Landwirth, Heinz 1927-
See Lind, Jakov
See also CA 9-12R; CANR 7

Lane, Patrick 1939- .... **CLC 25**
See also CA 97-100; CANR 54; CP 7; DAM POET; DLB 53; INT CA-97-100

Lang, Andrew 1844-1912 .... **TCLC 16**
See also CA 114; 137; CANR 85; DLB 98, 141, 184; FANT; MAICYA 1, 2; RGEL 2; SATA 16; WCH

Lang, Fritz 1890-1976 .... **CLC 20, 103**
See also CA 77-80; 69-72; CANR 30

Lange, John
See Crichton, (John) Michael

Langer, Elinor 1939- .... **CLC 34**
See also CA 121

Langland, William 1332(?)-1400(?) ..... **LC 19**
See also BRW 1; DA; DAB; DAC; DAM MST, POET; DLB 146; RGEL 2; TEA; WLIT 3

Langstaff, Launcelot
See Irving, Washington

Lanier, Sidney 1842-1881 . **NCLC 6, 118; PC 50**
See also AMWS 1; DAM POET; DLB 64; DLBD 13; EXPP; MAICYA 1; PFS 14; RGAL 4; SATA 18

Lanyer, Aemilia 1569-1645 ...... **LC 10, 30, 83**
See also DLB 121

Lao-Tzu
See Lao Tzu

Lao Tzu c. 6th cent. B.C.-3rd cent. B.C. .... **CMLC 7**

Lapine, James (Elliot) 1949- .... **CLC 39**
See also CA 123; 130; CANR 54, 128; INT CA-130

Larbaud, Valery (Nicolas)
1881-1957 .... **TCLC 9**
See also CA 106; 152; EWL 3; GFL 1789 to the Present

Lardner, Ring
See Lardner, Ring(gold) W(ilmer)
See also BPFB 2; CDALB 1917-1929; DLB 11, 25, 86, 171; DLBD 16; RGAL 4; RGSF 2

Lardner, Ring W., Jr.
See Lardner, Ring(gold) W(ilmer)

Lardner, Ring(gold) W(ilmer)
1885-1933 .... **SSC 32; TCLC 2, 14**
See Lardner, Ring
See also AMW; CA 104; 131; MTCW 1, 2; TUS

Laredo, Betty
See Codrescu, Andrei

Larkin, Maia
See Wojciechowska, Maia (Teresa)

Larkin, Philip (Arthur) 1922-1985 ... **CLC 3, 5, 8, 9, 13, 18, 33, 39, 64; PC 21**
See also BRWS 1; CA 5-8R; 117; CANR 24, 62; CDBLB 1960 to Present; DA3; DAB; DAM MST, POET; DLB 27; EWL 3; MTCW 1, 2; PFS 3, 4, 12; RGEL 2

La Roche, Sophie von
1730-1807 .... **NCLC 121**
See also DLB 94

Larra (y Sanchez de Castro), Mariano Jose de 1809-1837 .... **NCLC 17, 130**

Larsen, Eric 1941- .... **CLC 55**
See also CA 132

Larsen, Nella 1893(?)-1963 .... **BLC 2; CLC 37; HR 3**
See also AFAW 1, 2; BW 1; CA 125; CANR 83; DAM MULT; DLB 51; FW; LATS 1; LMFS 2

Larson, Charles R(aymond) 1938- ... **CLC 31**
See also CA 53-56; CANR 4, 121

Larson, Jonathan 1961-1996 .... **CLC 99**
See also AAYA 28; CA 156

Las Casas, Bartolome de
1474-1566 .... **HLCS; LC 31**
See Casas, Bartolome de las
See also LAW

Lasch, Christopher 1932-1994 .... **CLC 102**
See also CA 73-76; 144; CANR 25, 118; DLB 246; MTCW 1, 2

Lasker-Schueler, Else 1869-1945 ... **TCLC 57**
See Lasker-Schuler, Else
See also CA 183; DLB 66, 124

Lasker-Schuler, Else
See Lasker-Schueler, Else
See also EWL 3

Laski, Harold J(oseph) 1893-1950 . **TCLC 79**
See also CA 188

Latham, Jean Lee 1902-1995 .... **CLC 12**
See also AITN 1; BYA 1; CA 5-8R; CANR 7, 84; CLR 50; MAICYA 1, 2; SATA 2, 68; YAW

Latham, Mavis
See Clark, Mavis Thorpe

Lathen, Emma .... **CLC 2**
See Hennissart, Martha; Latsis, Mary J(ane)
See also BPFB 2; CMW 4

Lathrop, Francis
See Leiber, Fritz (Reuter, Jr.)

Latsis, Mary J(ane) 1927(?)-1997
See Lathen, Emma
See also CA 85-88; 162; CMW 4

Lattany, Kristin
See Lattany, Kristin (Elaine Eggleston) Hunter

Lattany, Kristin (Elaine Eggleston) Hunter
1931- .... **CLC 35**
See also AITN 1; BW 1; BYA 3; CA 13-16R; CANR 13, 108; CLR 3; CN 7; DLB 33; INT CANR-13; MAICYA 1, 2; SAAS 10; SATA 12, 132; YAW

Lattimore, Richmond (Alexander)
1906-1984 .... **CLC 3**
See also CA 1-4R; 112; CANR 1

Laughlin, James 1914-1997 .... **CLC 49**
See also CA 21-24R; 162; CAAS 22; CANR 9, 47; CP 7; DLB 48; DLBY 1996, 1997

Laurence, (Jean) Margaret (Wemyss)
1926-1987 . **CLC 3, 6, 13, 50, 62; SSC 7**
See also BYA 13; CA 5-8R; 121; CANR 33; DAC; DAM MST; DLB 53; EWL 3; FW; MTCW 1, 2; NFS 11; RGEL 2; RGSF 2; SATA-Obit 50; TCWW 2

Laurent, Antoine 1952- .... **CLC 50**

Lauscher, Hermann
See Hesse, Hermann

Lautreamont 1846-1870 .. **NCLC 12; SSC 14**
See Lautreamont, Isidore Lucien Ducasse
See also GFL 1789 to the Present; RGWL 2, 3

Lautreamont, Isidore Lucien Ducasse
See Lautreamont
See also DLB 217

Laverty, Donald
See Blish, James (Benjamin)

Lavin, Mary 1912-1996 . **CLC 4, 18, 99; SSC 4, 67**
See also CA 9-12R; 151; CANR 33; CN 7; DLB 15; FW; MTCW 1; RGEL 2; RGSF 2

Lavond, Paul Dennis
See Kornbluth, C(yril) M.; Pohl, Frederik

Lawler, Ray
See Lawler, Raymond Evenor
See also DLB 289

Lawler, Raymond Evenor 1922- .... **CLC 58**
See Lawler, Ray
See also CA 103; CD 5; RGEL 2

Lawrence, D(avid) H(erbert Richards)
1885-1930 . **PC 54; SSC 4, 19; TCLC 2, 9, 16, 33, 48, 61, 93; WLC**
See Chambers, Jessie
See also BPFB 2; BRW 7; BRWR 2; CA 104; 121; CDBLB 1914-1945; DA; DA3; DAB; DAC; DAM MST, NOV, POET; DLB 10, 19, 36, 98, 162, 195; EWL 3; EXPP; EXPS; LAIT 2, 3; MTCW 1, 2; NFS 18; PFS 6; RGEL 2; RGSF 2; SSFS 2, 6; TEA; WLIT 4; WP

Lawrence, T(homas) E(dward)
1888-1935 .... **TCLC 18**
See Dale, Colin
See also BRWS 2; CA 115; 167; DLB 195

Lawrence of Arabia
See Lawrence, T(homas) E(dward)

Lawson, Henry (Archibald Hertzberg)
1867-1922 .... **SSC 18; TCLC 27**
See also CA 120; 181; DLB 230; RGEL 2; RGSF 2

Lawton, Dennis
See Faust, Frederick (Schiller)

Layamon fl. c. 1200- .... **CMLC 10**
See Layamon
See also RGEL 2

Laye, Camara 1928-1980 ..... **BLC 2; CLC 4, 38**
See Camara Laye
See also AFW; BW 1; CA 85-88; 97-100; CANR 25; DAM MULT; MTCW 1, 2; WLIT 2

Layton, Irving (Peter) 1912- .... **CLC 2, 15, 164**
See also CA 1-4R; CANR 2, 33, 43, 66, 129; CP 7; DAC; DAM MST, POET; DLB 88; EWL 3; MTCW 1, 2; PFS 12; RGEL 2

Lazarus, Emma 1849-1887 ...... **NCLC 8, 109**

Lazarus, Felix
See Cable, George Washington

Lazarus, Henry
See Slavitt, David R(ytman)

Lea, Joan
See Neufeld, John (Arthur)

Leacock, Stephen (Butler)
1869-1944 .... **SSC 39; TCLC 2**
See also CA 104; 141; CANR 80; DAC; DAM MST; DLB 92; EWL 3; MTCW 2; RGEL 2; RGSF 2

Lead, Jane Ward 1623-1704 .... **LC 72**
See also DLB 131

Leapor, Mary 1722-1746 .... **LC 80**
See also DLB 109

Lear, Edward 1812-1888 .... **NCLC 3**
See also AAYA 48; BRW 5; CLR 1, 75; DLB 32, 163, 166; MAICYA 1, 2; RGEL 2; SATA 18, 100; WCH; WP

Lear, Norman (Milton) 1922- .... **CLC 12**
See also CA 73-76

Leautaud, Paul 1872-1956 .... **TCLC 83**
See also CA 203; DLB 65; GFL 1789 to the Present

Leavis, F(rank) R(aymond)
1895-1978 .... **CLC 24**
See also BRW 7; CA 21-24R; 77-80; CANR 44; DLB 242; EWL 3; MTCW 1, 2; RGEL 2

Leavitt, David 1961- .... **CLC 34**
See also CA 116; 122; CANR 50, 62, 101; CPW; DA3; DAM POP; DLB 130; GLL 1; INT CA-122; MTCW 2

Leblanc, Maurice (Marie Emile)
1864-1941 .... **TCLC 49**
See also CA 110; CMW 4

Lebowitz, Fran(ces Ann) 1951(?)- ... **CLC 11, 36**
See also CA 81-84; CANR 14, 60, 70; INT CANR-14; MTCW 1

Lebrecht, Peter
See Tieck, (Johann) Ludwig

le Carre, John .... **CLC 3, 5, 9, 15, 28**
See Cornwell, David (John Moore)
See also AAYA 42; BEST 89:4; BPFB 2; BRWS 2; CDBLB 1960 to Present; CMW 4; CN 7; CPW; DLB 87; EWL 3; MSW; MTCW 2; RGEL 2; TEA

Le Clezio, J(ean) M(arie) G(ustave)
1940- .... **CLC 31, 155**
See also CA 116; 128; DLB 83; EWL 3; GFL 1789 to the Present; RGSF 2

Leconte de Lisle, Charles-Marie-Rene
1818-1894 .... **NCLC 29**
See also DLB 217; EW 6; GFL 1789 to the Present

Le Coq, Monsieur
See Simenon, Georges (Jacques Christian)

Leduc, Violette 1907-1972 .... **CLC 22**
See also CA 13-14; 33-36R; CANR 69; CAP 1; EWL 3; GFL 1789 to the Present; GLL 1

Ledwidge, Francis 1887(?)-1917 .... **TCLC 23**
See also CA 123; 203; DLB 20

Lee, Andrea 1953- .... **BLC 2; CLC 36**
See also BW 1, 3; CA 125; CANR 82; DAM MULT

Lee, Andrew
See Auchincloss, Louis (Stanton)

Lee, Chang-rae 1965- .... **CLC 91**
See also CA 148; CANR 89; LATS 1

Lee, Don L. .... **CLC 2**
See Madhubuti, Haki R.

Lee, George W(ashington)
1894-1976 .... **BLC 2; CLC 52**
See also BW 1; CA 125; CANR 83; DAM MULT; DLB 51

Lee, (Nelle) Harper 1926- .... **CLC 12, 60; WLC**
See also AAYA 13; AMWS 8; BPFB 2; BYA 3; CA 13-16R; CANR 51, 128; CDALB 1941-1968; CSW; DA; DA3; DAB; DAC; DAM MST, NOV; DLB 6; EXPN; LAIT 3; MTCW 1, 2; NFS 2; SATA 11; WYA; YAW

Lee, Helen Elaine 1959(?)- .... **CLC 86**
See also CA 148

Lee, John .... **CLC 70**

Lee, Julian
See Latham, Jean Lee

Lee, Larry
See Lee, Lawrence

Lee, Laurie 1914-1997 .... **CLC 90**
See also CA 77-80; 158; CANR 33, 73; CP 7; CPW; DAB; DAM POP; DLB 27; MTCW 1; RGEL 2

Lee, Lawrence 1941-1990 .... **CLC 34**
See also CA 131; CANR 43

Lee, Li-Young 1957- .... **CLC 164; PC 24**
See also CA 153; CANR 118; CP 7; DLB 165; LMFS 2; PFS 11, 15, 17

Lee, Manfred B(ennington)
1905-1971 .... **CLC 11**
See Queen, Ellery
See also CA 1-4R; 29-32R; CANR 2; CMW 4; DLB 137

Lee, Shelton Jackson 1957(?)- .. **BLCS; CLC 105**
See Lee, Spike
See also BW 2, 3; CA 125; CANR 42; DAM MULT

Lee, Spike
See Lee, Shelton Jackson
See also AAYA 4, 29

Lee, Stan 1922- .... **CLC 17**
See also AAYA 5, 49; CA 108; 111; CANR 129; INT CA-111

Lee, Tanith 1947- .... **CLC 46**
See also AAYA 15; CA 37-40R; CANR 53, 102; DLB 261; FANT; SATA 8, 88, 134; SFW 4; SUFW 1, 2; YAW

Lee, Vernon .... **SSC 33; TCLC 5**
See Paget, Violet
See also DLB 57, 153, 156, 174, 178; GLL 1; SUFW 1

Lee, William
See Burroughs, William S(eward)
See also GLL 1

Lee, Willy
See Burroughs, William S(eward)
See also GLL 1

Lee-Hamilton, Eugene (Jacob)
1845-1907 .... **TCLC 22**
See also CA 117

Leet, Judith 1935- .... **CLC 11**
See also CA 187

Le Fanu, Joseph Sheridan
1814-1873 .... **NCLC 9, 58; SSC 14**
See also CMW 4; DA3; DAM POP; DLB 21, 70, 159, 178; HGG; RGEL 2; RGSF 2; SUFW 1

Leffland, Ella 1931- .... **CLC 19**
See also CA 29-32R; CANR 35, 78, 82; DLBY 1984; INT CANR-35; SATA 65

Leger, Alexis
See Leger, (Marie-Rene Auguste) Alexis Saint-Leger

Leger, (Marie-Rene Auguste) Alexis Saint-Leger 1887-1975 .. **CLC 4, 11, 46; PC 23**
See Perse, Saint-John; Saint-John Perse
See also CA 13-16R; 61-64; CANR 43; DAM POET; MTCW 1

Leger, Saintleger
See Leger, (Marie-Rene Auguste) Alexis Saint-Leger

Le Guin, Ursula K(roeber) 1929- ..... **CLC 8, 13, 22, 45, 71, 136; SSC 12, 69**
See also AAYA 9, 27; AITN 1; BPFB 2; BYA 5, 8, 11, 14; CA 21-24R; CANR 9, 32, 52, 74; CDALB 1968-1988; CLR 3, 28, 91; CN 7; CPW; DA3; DAB; DAC; DAM MST, POP; DLB 8, 52, 256, 275; EXPS; FANT; FW; INT CANR-32; JRDA; LAIT 5; MAICYA 1, 2; MTCW 1, 2; NFS 6, 9; SATA 4, 52, 99, 149; SCFW; SFW 4; SSFS 2; SUFW 1, 2; WYA; YAW

Lehmann, Rosamond (Nina)
1901-1990 .... **CLC 5**
See also CA 77-80; 131; CANR 8, 73; DLB 15; MTCW 2; RGEL 2; RHW

Leiber, Fritz (Reuter, Jr.)
1910-1992 .... **CLC 25**
See also BPFB 2; CA 45-48; 139; CANR 2, 40, 86; DLB 8; FANT; HGG; MTCW 1, 2; SATA 45; SATA-Obit 73; SCFW 2; SFW 4; SUFW 1, 2

Leibniz, Gottfried Wilhelm von
1646-1716 .... **LC 35**
See also DLB 168

Leimbach, Martha 1963-
See Leimbach, Marti
See also CA 130

Leimbach, Marti .... **CLC 65**
See Leimbach, Martha

Leino, Eino .... **TCLC 24**
See Lonnbohm, Armas Eino Leopold
See also EWL 3

Leiris, Michel (Julien) 1901-1990 ..... **CLC 61**
See also CA 119; 128; 132; EWL 3; GFL 1789 to the Present

Leithauser, Brad 1953- .... **CLC 27**
See also CA 107; CANR 27, 81; CP 7; DLB 120, 282

le Jars de Gournay, Marie
See de Gournay, Marie le Jars

Lelchuk, Alan 1938- .... **CLC 5**
See also CA 45-48; CAAS 20; CANR 1, 70; CN 7

Lem, Stanislaw 1921- ...... **CLC 8, 15, 40, 149**
See also CA 105; CAAS 1; CANR 32; CWW 2; MTCW 1; SCFW 2; SFW 4

Lemann, Nancy (Elise) 1956- .... **CLC 39**
See also CA 118; 136; CANR 121

Lemonnier, (Antoine Louis) Camille
1844-1913 .... **TCLC 22**
See also CA 121

Lenau, Nikolaus 1802-1850 .... **NCLC 16**

L'Engle, Madeleine (Camp Franklin)
1918- .... **CLC 12**
See also AAYA 28; AITN 2; BPFB 2; BYA 2, 4, 5, 7; CA 1-4R; CANR 3, 21, 39, 66, 107; CLR 1, 14, 57; CPW; CWRI 5; DA3; DAM POP; DLB 52; JRDA; MAICYA 1, 2; MTCW 1, 2; SAAS 15; SATA 1, 27, 75, 128; SFW 4; WYA; YAW

Lengyel, Jozsef 1896-1975 .... **CLC 7**
See also CA 85-88; 57-60; CANR 71; RGSF 2

Lenin 1870-1924
See Lenin, V. I.
See also CA 121; 168

Lenin, V. I. .... **TCLC 67**
See Lenin

Lennon, John (Ono) 1940-1980 .. **CLC 12, 35**
See also CA 102; SATA 114

Lennox, Charlotte Ramsay
1729(?)-1804 .... **NCLC 23, 134**
See also DLB 39; RGEL 2

Lentricchia, Frank, (Jr.) 1940- .... **CLC 34**
See also CA 25-28R; CANR 19, 106; DLB 246

Lenz, Gunter .... **CLC 65**

Lenz, Jakob Michael Reinhold
1751-1792 .... **LC 100**
See also DLB 94; RGWL 2, 3

Lenz, Siegfried 1926- .... **CLC 27; SSC 33**
See also CA 89-92; CANR 80; CWW 2; DLB 75; EWL 3; RGSF 2; RGWL 2, 3

Leon, David
See Jacob, (Cyprien-)Max

Leonard, Elmore (John, Jr.) 1925- . **CLC 28, 34, 71, 120**
See also AAYA 22; AITN 1; BEST 89:1, 90:4; BPFB 2; CA 81-84; CANR 12, 28, 53, 76, 96; CMW 4; CN 7; CPW; DA3; DAM POP; DLB 173, 226; INT CANR-28; MSW; MTCW 1, 2; RGAL 4; TCWW 2

Leonard, Hugh .... **CLC 19**
See Byrne, John Keyes
See also CBD; CD 5; DFS 13; DLB 13

Leonov, Leonid (Maximovich)
1899-1994 .... **CLC 92**
See Leonov, Leonid Maksimovich
See also CA 129; CANR 74, 76; DAM NOV; EWL 3; MTCW 1, 2

Leonov, Leonid Maksimovich
See Leonov, Leonid (Maximovich)
See also DLB 272

Leopardi, (Conte) Giacomo
1798-1837 .... **NCLC 22, 129; PC 37**
See also EW 5; RGWL 2, 3; WP

Le Reveler
See Artaud, Antonin (Marie Joseph)

Lerman, Eleanor 1952- .... **CLC 9**
See also CA 85-88; CANR 69, 124

Lerman, Rhoda 1936- .... **CLC 56**
See also CA 49-52; CANR 70

Lermontov, Mikhail Iur'evich
See Lermontov, Mikhail Yuryevich
See also DLB 205

Lermontov, Mikhail Yuryevich
1814-1841 .... **NCLC 5, 47, 126; PC 18**
See Lermontov, Mikhail Iur'evich
See also EW 6; RGWL 2, 3; TWA

Leroux, Gaston 1868-1927 .... **TCLC 25**
See also CA 108; 136; CANR 69; CMW 4; SATA 65

Lesage, Alain-Rene 1668-1747 .... **LC 2, 28**
See also EW 3; GFL Beginnings to 1789; RGWL 2, 3

Leskov, N(ikolai) S(emenovich) 1831-1895
See Leskov, Nikolai (Semyonovich)

Leskov, Nikolai (Semyonovich)
1831-1895 .... **NCLC 25; SSC 34**
See Leskov, Nikolai Semenovich

Leskov, Nikolai Semenovich
See Leskov, Nikolai (Semyonovich)
See also DLB 238

Lesser, Milton
See Marlowe, Stephen

Lessing, Doris (May) 1919- ... **CLC 1, 2, 3, 6, 10, 15, 22, 40, 94, 170; SSC 6, 61; WLCS**
See also AFW; BRWS 1; CA 9-12R; CAAS 14; CANR 33, 54, 76, 122; CD 5; CDBLB 1960 to Present; CN 7; DA; DA3; DAB; DAC; DAM MST, NOV; DLB 15, 139; DLBY 1985; EWL 3; EXPS; FW; LAIT 4; MTCW 1, 2; RGEL 2; RGSF 2; SFW 4; SSFS 1, 12; TEA; WLIT 2, 4

Lessing, Gotthold Ephraim 1729-1781 . **LC 8**
See also CDWLB 2; DLB 97; EW 4; RGWL 2, 3

Lester, Richard 1932- .... **CLC 20**

Levenson, Jay .... **CLC 70**

Lever, Charles (James)
1806-1872 .... **NCLC 23**
See also DLB 21; RGEL 2

Leverson, Ada Esther
1862(?)-1933(?) .... **TCLC 18**
See Elaine
See also CA 117; 202; DLB 153; RGEL 2

Levertov, Denise 1923-1997 .. **CLC 1, 2, 3, 5, 8, 15, 28, 66; PC 11**
See also AMWS 3; CA 1-4R; 178; 163; CAAE 178; CAAS 19; CANR 3, 29, 50, 108; CDALBS; CP 7; CWP; DAM POET; DLB 5, 165; EWL 3; EXPP; FW; INT CANR-29; MTCW 1, 2; PAB; PFS 7, 17; RGAL 4; TUS; WP

Levi, Carlo 1902-1975 .... **TCLC 125**
See also CA 65-68; 53-56; CANR 10; EWL 3; RGWL 2, 3

Levi, Jonathan .... **CLC 76**
See also CA 197

Levi, Peter (Chad Tigar)
1931-2000 .... **CLC 41**
See also CA 5-8R; 187; CANR 34, 80; CP 7; DLB 40

Levi, Primo 1919-1987 ...... **CLC 37, 50; SSC 12; TCLC 109**
See also CA 13-16R; 122; CANR 12, 33, 61, 70; DLB 177; EWL 3; MTCW 1, 2; RGWL 2, 3

Levin, Ira 1929- .... **CLC 3, 6**
See also CA 21-24R; CANR 17, 44, 74; CMW 4; CN 7; CPW; DA3; DAM POP; HGG; MTCW 1, 2; SATA 66; SFW 4

Levin, Meyer 1905-1981 .... **CLC 7**
See also AITN 1; CA 9-12R; 104; CANR 15; DAM POP; DLB 9, 28; DLBY 1981; SATA 21; SATA-Obit 27

Levine, Norman 1924- .... **CLC 54**
See also CA 73-76; CAAS 23; CANR 14, 70; DLB 88

Levine, Philip 1928- .. **CLC 2, 4, 5, 9, 14, 33, 118; PC 22**
See also AMWS 5; CA 9-12R; CANR 9, 37, 52, 116; CP 7; DAM POET; DLB 5; EWL 3; PFS 8

Levinson, Deirdre 1931- .... **CLC 49**
See also CA 73-76; CANR 70

Levi-Strauss, Claude 1908- .... **CLC 38**
See also CA 1-4R; CANR 6, 32, 57; DLB 242; EWL 3; GFL 1789 to the Present; MTCW 1, 2; TWA

Levitin, Sonia (Wolff) 1934- .... **CLC 17**
See also AAYA 13, 48; CA 29-32R; CANR 14, 32, 79; CLR 53; JRDA; MAICYA 1, 2; SAAS 2; SATA 4, 68, 119, 131; SATA-Essay 131; YAW

Levon, O. U.
See Kesey, Ken (Elton)

Levy, Amy 1861-1889 .... **NCLC 59**
See also DLB 156, 240

Lewes, George Henry 1817-1878 ... **NCLC 25**
See also DLB 55, 144

Lewis, Alun 1915-1944 .... **SSC 40; TCLC 3**
See also BRW 7; CA 104; 188; DLB 20, 162; PAB; RGEL 2

Lewis, C. Day
See Day Lewis, C(ecil)

Lewis, C(live) S(taples) 1898-1963 .... **CLC 1, 3, 6, 14, 27, 124; WLC**
See also AAYA 3, 39; BPFB 2; BRWS 3; BYA 15, 16; CA 81-84; CANR 33, 71; CDBLB 1945-1960; CLR 3, 27; CWRI 5; DA; DA3; DAB; DAC; DAM MST, NOV, POP; DLB 15, 100, 160, 255; EWL 3; FANT; JRDA; LMFS 2; MAICYA 1, 2; MTCW 1, 2; RGEL 2; SATA 13, 100; SCFW; SFW 4; SUFW 1; TEA; WCH; WYA; YAW

Lewis, Cecil Day
See Day Lewis, C(ecil)

Lewis, Janet 1899-1998 .... **CLC 41**
See Winters, Janet Lewis
See also CA 9-12R; 172; CANR 29, 63; CAP 1; CN 7; DLBY 1987; RHW; TCWW 2

Lewis, Matthew Gregory
1775-1818 .... **NCLC 11, 62**
See also DLB 39, 158, 178; HGG; LMFS 1; RGEL 2; SUFW

Lewis, (Harry) Sinclair 1885-1951 . **TCLC 4, 13, 23, 39; WLC**
See also AMW; AMWC 1; BPFB 2; CA 104; 133; CDALB 1917-1929; DA; DA3; DAB; DAC; DAM MST, NOV; DLB 9, 102, 284; DLBD 1; EWL 3; LAIT 3; MTCW 1, 2; NFS 15; RGAL 4; TUS

Lewis, (Percy) Wyndham
1884(?)-1957 .. **SSC 34; TCLC 2, 9, 104**
See also BRW 7; CA 104; 157; DLB 15; EWL 3; FANT; MTCW 2; RGEL 2

Lewisohn, Ludwig 1883-1955 .... **TCLC 19**
See also CA 107; 203; DLB 4, 9, 28, 102

Lewton, Val 1904-1951 .... **TCLC 76**
See also CA 199; IDFW 3, 4

Leyner, Mark 1956- .... **CLC 92**
See also CA 110; CANR 28, 53; DA3; DLB 292; MTCW 2

Lezama Lima, Jose 1910-1976 .... **CLC 4, 10, 101; HLCS 2**
See also CA 77-80; CANR 71; DAM MULT; DLB 113, 283; EWL 3; HW 1, 2; LAW; RGWL 2, 3

L'Heureux, John (Clarke) 1934- ...... **CLC 52**
See also CA 13-16R; CANR 23, 45, 88; DLB 244

Liddell, C. H.
See Kuttner, Henry

Lie, Jonas (Lauritz Idemil)
1833-1908(?) .... **TCLC 5**
See also CA 115

Lieber, Joel 1937-1971 .... **CLC 6**
See also CA 73-76; 29-32R

Lieber, Stanley Martin
See Lee, Stan

Lieberman, Laurence (James)
1935- .... **CLC 4, 36**
See also CA 17-20R; CANR 8, 36, 89; CP 7

Lieh Tzu fl. 7th cent. B.C.-5th cent.
B.C. .... **CMLC 27**

Lieksman, Anders
See Haavikko, Paavo Juhani

Li Fei-kan 1904-
See Pa Chin
See also CA 105; TWA

Lifton, Robert Jay 1926- .... **CLC 67**
See also CA 17-20R; CANR 27, 78; INT CANR-27; SATA 66

Lightfoot, Gordon 1938- .... **CLC 26**
See also CA 109

Lightman, Alan P(aige) 1948- .... **CLC 81**
See also CA 141; CANR 63, 105

Ligotti, Thomas (Robert) 1953- ...... **CLC 44; SSC 16**
See also CA 123; CANR 49; HGG; SUFW 2

Li Ho 791-817 .... **PC 13**

Li Ju-chen c. 1763-c. 1830 .... **NCLC 137**

Liliencron, (Friedrich Adolf Axel) Detlev von 1844-1909 .... **TCLC 18**
See also CA 117

Lille, Alain de
See Alain de Lille

Lilly, William 1602-1681 .... **LC 27**

Lima, Jose Lezama
See Lezama Lima, Jose

Lima Barreto, Afonso Henrique de
1881-1922 .... **TCLC 23**
See also CA 117; 181; LAW

Lima Barreto, Afonso Henriques de
See Lima Barreto, Afonso Henrique de

Limonov, Edward 1944- .... **CLC 67**
See also CA 137

Lin, Frank
See Atherton, Gertrude (Franklin Horn)

Lin, Yutang 1895-1976 .... **TCLC 149**
See also CA 45-48; 65-68; CANR 2; RGAL 4

Lincoln, Abraham 1809-1865 .... **NCLC 18**
See also LAIT 2

Lind, Jakov .... **CLC 1, 2, 4, 27, 82**
See Landwirth, Heinz
See also CAAS 4; EWL 3

Lindbergh, Anne (Spencer) Morrow
1906-2001 .... **CLC 82**
See also BPFB 2; CA 17-20R; 193; CANR 16, 73; DAM NOV; MTCW 1, 2; SATA 33; SATA-Obit 125; TUS

Lindsay, David 1878(?)-1945 .... **TCLC 15**
See also CA 113; 187; DLB 255; FANT; SFW 4; SUFW 1

Lindsay, (Nicholas) Vachel
1879-1931 .... **PC 23; TCLC 17; WLC**
See also AMWS 1; CA 114; 135; CANR 79; CDALB 1865-1917; DA; DA3; DAC; DAM MST, POET; DLB 54; EWL 3; EXPP; RGAL 4; SATA 40; WP

Linke-Poot
See Doeblin, Alfred

Linney, Romulus 1930- .... **CLC 51**
See also CA 1-4R; CAD; CANR 40, 44, 79; CD 5; CSW; RGAL 4

Linton, Eliza Lynn 1822-1898 .... **NCLC 41**
See also DLB 18

Li Po 701-763 .... **CMLC 2; PC 29**
See also WP

Lipsius, Justus 1547-1606 .... **LC 16**

Lipsyte, Robert (Michael) 1938- ...... **CLC 21**
See also AAYA 7, 45; CA 17-20R; CANR 8, 57; CLR 23, 76; DA; DAC; DAM MST, NOV; JRDA; LAIT 5; MAICYA 1, 2; SATA 5, 68, 113; WYA; YAW

Lish, Gordon (Jay) 1934- ... **CLC 45; SSC 18**
See also CA 113; 117; CANR 79; DLB 130; INT CA-117

Lispector, Clarice 1925(?)-1977 .... **CLC 43; HLCS 2; SSC 34**
See also CA 139; 116; CANR 71; CDWLB 3; DLB 113; DNFS 1; EWL 3; FW; HW 2; LAW; RGSF 2; RGWL 2, 3; WLIT 1

Littell, Robert 1935(?)- .... **CLC 42**
See also CA 109; 112; CANR 64, 115; CMW 4

Little, Malcolm 1925-1965
See Malcolm X
See also BW 1, 3; CA 125; 111; CANR 82; DA; DA3; DAB; DAC; DAM MST, MULT; MTCW 1, 2

Littlewit, Humphrey Gent.
See Lovecraft, H(oward) P(hillips)

Litwos
See Sienkiewicz, Henryk (Adam Alexander Pius)

Liu, E. 1857-1909 .... **TCLC 15**
See also CA 115; 190

Lively, Penelope (Margaret) 1933- .. **CLC 32, 50**
See also BPFB 2; CA 41-44R; CANR 29, 67, 79; CLR 7; CN 7; CWRI 5; DAM NOV; DLB 14, 161, 207; FANT; JRDA; MAICYA 1, 2; MTCW 1, 2; SATA 7, 60, 101; TEA

Livesay, Dorothy (Kathleen)
1909-1996 .... **CLC 4, 15, 79**
See also AITN 2; CA 25-28R; CAAS 8; CANR 36, 67; DAC; DAM MST, POET; DLB 68; FW; MTCW 1; RGEL 2; TWA

Livy c. 59B.C.-c. 12 .... **CMLC 11**
See also AW 2; CDWLB 1; DLB 211; RGWL 2, 3

Lizardi, Jose Joaquin Fernandez de
1776-1827 .... **NCLC 30**
See also LAW

Llewellyn, Richard
See Llewellyn Lloyd, Richard Dafydd Vivian
See also DLB 15

Llewellyn Lloyd, Richard Dafydd Vivian
1906-1983 .... **CLC 7, 80**
See Llewellyn, Richard
See also CA 53-56; 111; CANR 7, 71; SATA 11; SATA-Obit 37

Llosa, (Jorge) Mario (Pedro) Vargas
See Vargas Llosa, (Jorge) Mario (Pedro)

Llosa, Mario Vargas
See Vargas Llosa, (Jorge) Mario (Pedro)

Lloyd, Manda
See Mander, (Mary) Jane

Lloyd Webber, Andrew 1948-
See Webber, Andrew Lloyd
See also AAYA 1, 38; CA 116; 149; DAM DRAM; SATA 56

Llull, Ramon c. 1235-c. 1316 .... **CMLC 12**

Lobb, Ebenezer
See Upward, Allen

Locke, Alain (Le Roy)
1886-1954 .... **BLCS; HR 3; TCLC 43**
See also BW 1, 3; CA 106; 124; CANR 79; DLB 51; LMFS 2; RGAL 4

Locke, John 1632-1704 .... **LC 7, 35**
See also DLB 31, 101, 213, 252; RGEL 2; WLIT 3

Locke-Elliott, Sumner
See Elliott, Sumner Locke

Lockhart, John Gibson 1794-1854 .. **NCLC 6**
See also DLB 110, 116, 144

Lockridge, Ross (Franklin), Jr.
1914-1948 .... **TCLC 111**
See also CA 108; 145; CANR 79; DLB 143; DLBY 1980; RGAL 4; RHW

Lockwood, Robert
See Johnson, Robert

Lodge, David (John) 1935- .... **CLC 36, 141**
See also BEST 90:1; BRWS 4; CA 17-20R; CANR 19, 53, 92; CN 7; CPW; DAM POP; DLB 14, 194; EWL 3; INT CANR-19; MTCW 1, 2

Lodge, Thomas 1558-1625 .... **LC 41**
See also DLB 172; RGEL 2

Loewinsohn, Ron(ald William)
1937- .... **CLC 52**
See also CA 25-28R; CANR 71

Logan, Jake
See Smith, Martin Cruz

Logan, John (Burton) 1923-1987 .... **CLC 5**
See also CA 77-80; 124; CANR 45; DLB 5

Lo Kuan-chung 1330(?)-1400(?) .... **LC 12**

Lombard, Nap
See Johnson, Pamela Hansford

London, Jack 1876-1916 .. **SSC 4, 49; TCLC 9, 15, 39; WLC**
See London, John Griffith
See also AAYA 13; AITN 2; AMW; BPFB 2; BYA 4, 13; CDALB 1865-1917; DLB 8, 12, 78, 212; EWL 3; EXPS; LAIT 3; NFS 8; RGAL 4; RGSF 2; SATA 18; SFW 4; SSFS 7; TCWW 2; TUS; WYA; YAW

London, John Griffith 1876-1916
See London, Jack
See also CA 110; 119; CANR 73; DA; DA3; DAB; DAC; DAM MST, NOV; JRDA; MAICYA 1, 2; MTCW 1, 2

Long, Emmett
See Leonard, Elmore (John, Jr.)

Longbaugh, Harry
See Goldman, William (W.)

Longfellow, Henry Wadsworth
1807-1882 .... **NCLC 2, 45, 101, 103; PC 30; WLCS**
See also AMW; AMWR 2; CDALB 1640-1865; DA; DA3; DAB; DAC; DAM MST, POET; DLB 1, 59, 235; EXPP; PAB; PFS 2, 7, 17; RGAL 4; SATA 19; TUS; WP

Longinus c. 1st cent. - .... **CMLC 27**
See also AW 2; DLB 176

Longley, Michael 1939- .... **CLC 29**
See also BRWS 8; CA 102; CP 7; DLB 40

Longus fl. c. 2nd cent. - .... **CMLC 7**

Longway, A. Hugh
See Lang, Andrew

Lonnbohm, Armas Eino Leopold 1878-1926
See Leino, Eino
See also CA 123

Lonnrot, Elias 1802-1884 .... **NCLC 53**
See also EFS 1

Lonsdale, Roger ed. .... **CLC 65**

Lopate, Phillip 1943- .... **CLC 29**
See also CA 97-100; CANR 88; DLBY 1980; INT CA-97-100

Lopez, Barry (Holstun) 1945- .... **CLC 70**
See also AAYA 9; ANW; CA 65-68; CANR 7, 23, 47, 68, 92; DLB 256, 275; INT CANR-7, -23; MTCW 1; RGAL 4; SATA 67

Lopez Portillo (y Pacheco), Jose
1920-2004 .... **CLC 46**
See also CA 129; HW 1

Lopez y Fuentes, Gregorio
1897(?)-1966 .... **CLC 32**
See also CA 131; EWL 3; HW 1

Lorca, Federico Garcia
See Garcia Lorca, Federico
See also DFS 4; EW 11; RGWL 2, 3; WP

Lord, Audre
See Lorde, Audre (Geraldine)
See also EWL 3

Lord, Bette Bao 1938- .... **AAL; CLC 23**
See also BEST 90:3; BPFB 2; CA 107; CANR 41, 79; INT CA-107; SATA 58

Lord Auch
See Bataille, Georges

Lord Brooke
See Greville, Fulke

Lord Byron
See Byron, George Gordon (Noel)

Lorde, Audre (Geraldine)
1934-1992 .. **BLC 2; CLC 18, 71; PC 12**
See also Domini, Rey; Lord, Audre
See also AFAW 1, 2; BW 1, 3; CA 25-28R; 142; CANR 16, 26, 46, 82; DA3; DAM MULT, POET; DLB 41; FW; MTCW 1, 2; PFS 16; RGAL 4

Lord Houghton
See Milnes, Richard Monckton

Lord Jeffrey
See Jeffrey, Francis

Loreaux, Nichol .... **CLC 65**

Lorenzini, Carlo 1826-1890
See Collodi, Carlo
See also MAICYA 1, 2; SATA 29, 100

Lorenzo, Heberto Padilla
See Padilla (Lorenzo), Heberto

Loris
See Hofmannsthal, Hugo von

Loti, Pierre .... **TCLC 11**
See Viaud, (Louis Marie) Julien
See also DLB 123; GFL 1789 to the Present

Lou, Henri
See Andreas-Salome, Lou

Louie, David Wong 1954- .... **CLC 70**
See also CA 139; CANR 120

Louis, Adrian C. .... **NNAL**

Louis, Father M.
See Merton, Thomas (James)

Louise, Heidi
See Erdrich, Louise

Lovecraft, H(oward) P(hillips)
1890-1937 .... **SSC 3, 52; TCLC 4, 22**
See also AAYA 14; BPFB 2; CA 104; 133; CANR 106; DA3; DAM POP; HGG; MTCW 1, 2; RGAL 4; SCFW; SFW 4; SUFW

Lovelace, Earl 1935- .... **CLC 51**
See also BW 2; CA 77-80; CANR 41, 72, 114; CD 5; CDWLB 3; CN 7; DLB 125; EWL 3; MTCW 1

Lovelace, Richard 1618-1657 .... **LC 24**
See also BRW 2; DLB 131; EXPP; PAB; RGEL 2

Lowe, Pardee 1904- .... **AAL**

Lowell, Amy 1874-1925 ... **PC 13; TCLC 1, 8**
See also AMW; CA 104; 151; DAM POET; DLB 54, 140; EWL 3; EXPP; LMFS 2; MAWW; MTCW 2; RGAL 4; TUS

Lowell, James Russell 1819-1891 ... **NCLC 2, 90**
See also AMWS 1; CDALB 1640-1865; DLB 1, 11, 64, 79, 189, 235; RGAL 4

Lowell, Robert (Traill Spence, Jr.)
1917-1977 .... **CLC 1, 2, 3, 4, 5, 8, 9, 11, 15, 37, 124; PC 3; WLC**
See also AMW; AMWC 2; AMWR 2; CA 9-12R; 73-76; CABS 2; CANR 26, 60; CDALBS; DA; DA3; DAB; DAC; DAM MST, NOV; DLB 5, 169; EWL 3; MTCW 1, 2; PAB; PFS 6, 7; RGAL 4; WP

Lowenthal, Michael (Francis)
1969- .... **CLC 119**
See also CA 150; CANR 115

Lowndes, Marie Adelaide (Belloc)
1868-1947 .... **TCLC 12**
See also CA 107; CMW 4; DLB 70; RHW

Lowry, (Clarence) Malcolm
1909-1957 .... **SSC 31; TCLC 6, 40**
See also BPFB 2; BRWS 3; CA 105; 131; CANR 62, 105; CDBLB 1945-1960; DLB 15; EWL 3; MTCW 1, 2; RGEL 2

Lowry, Mina Gertrude 1882-1966
See Loy, Mina
See also CA 113

Loxsmith, John
See Brunner, John (Kilian Houston)

Loy, Mina .... **CLC 28; PC 16**
See Lowry, Mina Gertrude
See also DAM POET; DLB 4, 54

Loyson-Bridet
See Schwob, Marcel (Mayer Andre)

Lucan 39-65 .... **CMLC 33**
See also AW 2; DLB 211; EFS 2; RGWL 2, 3

Lucas, Craig 1951- .... **CLC 64**
See also CA 137; CAD; CANR 71, 109; CD 5; GLL 2

Lucas, E(dward) V(errall)
1868-1938 .... **TCLC 73**
See also CA 176; DLB 98, 149, 153; SATA 20

Lucas, George 1944- .... **CLC 16**
See also AAYA 1, 23; CA 77-80; CANR 30; SATA 56

Lucas, Hans
See Godard, Jean-Luc

Lucas, Victoria
See Plath, Sylvia

Lucian c. 125-c. 180 .... **CMLC 32**
See also AW 2; DLB 176; RGWL 2, 3

Lucretius c. 94B.C.-c. 49B.C. .... **CMLC 48**
See also AW 2; CDWLB 1; DLB 211; EFS 2; RGWL 2, 3

Ludlam, Charles 1943-1987 .... **CLC 46, 50**
See also CA 85-88; 122; CAD; CANR 72, 86; DLB 266

Ludlum, Robert 1927-2001 .... **CLC 22, 43**
See also AAYA 10; BEST 89:1, 90:3; BPFB 2; CA 33-36R; 195; CANR 25, 41, 68, 105; CMW 4; CPW; DA3; DAM NOV, POP; DLBY 1982; MSW; MTCW 1, 2

Ludwig, Ken .... **CLC 60**
See also CA 195; CAD

Ludwig, Otto 1813-1865 .... **NCLC 4**
See also DLB 129

Lugones, Leopoldo 1874-1938 .... **HLCS 2; TCLC 15**
See also CA 116; 131; CANR 104; DLB 283; EWL 3; HW 1; LAW

Lu Hsun .... **SSC 20; TCLC 3**
See Shu-Jen, Chou
See also EWL 3

Lukacs, George .... **CLC 24**
See Lukacs, Gyorgy (Szegeny von)

Lukacs, Gyorgy (Szegeny von) 1885-1971
See Lukacs, George
See also CA 101; 29-32R; CANR 62; CDWLB 4; DLB 215, 242; EW 10; EWL 3; MTCW 2

Luke, Peter (Ambrose Cyprian)
1919-1995 .... **CLC 38**
See also CA 81-84; 147; CANR 72; CBD; CD 5; DLB 13

Lunar, Dennis
See Mungo, Raymond

Lurie, Alison 1926- ..... **CLC 4, 5, 18, 39, 175**
See also BPFB 2; CA 1-4R; CANR 2, 17, 50, 88; CN 7; DLB 2; MTCW 1; SATA 46, 112

Lustig, Arnost 1926- .... **CLC 56**
See also AAYA 3; CA 69-72; CANR 47, 102; CWW 2; DLB 232; EWL 3; SATA 56

Luther, Martin 1483-1546 .... **LC 9, 37**
See also CDWLB 2; DLB 179; EW 2; RGWL 2, 3

Luxemburg, Rosa 1870(?)-1919 ..... **TCLC 63**
See also CA 118

Luzi, Mario 1914- .... **CLC 13**
See also CA 61-64; CANR 9, 70; CWW 2; DLB 128; EWL 3

L'vov, Arkady .... **CLC 59**

Lydgate, John c. 1370-1450(?) .... **LC 81**
See also BRW 1; DLB 146; RGEL 2

Lyly, John 1554(?)-1606 .... **DC 7; LC 41**
See also BRW 1; DAM DRAM; DLB 62, 167; RGEL 2

L'Ymagier
See Gourmont, Remy(-Marie-Charles) de

Lynch, B. Suarez
See Borges, Jorge Luis

Lynch, David (Keith) 1946- ...... **CLC 66, 162**
See also AAYA 55; CA 124; 129; CANR 111

Lynch, James
See Andreyev, Leonid (Nikolaevich)

Lyndsay, Sir David 1485-1555 .... **LC 20**
See also RGEL 2

Lynn, Kenneth S(chuyler)
1923-2001 .... **CLC 50**
See also CA 1-4R; 196; CANR 3, 27, 65

Lynx
See West, Rebecca

Lyons, Marcus
See Blish, James (Benjamin)

Lyotard, Jean-Francois
1924-1998 .... **TCLC 103**
See also DLB 242; EWL 3

Lyre, Pinchbeck
See Sassoon, Siegfried (Lorraine)

Lytle, Andrew (Nelson) 1902-1995 ... **CLC 22**
See also CA 9-12R; 150; CANR 70; CN 7; CSW; DLB 6; DLBY 1995; RGAL 4; RHW

Lyttelton, George 1709-1773 .... **LC 10**
See also RGEL 2

Lytton of Knebworth, Baron
See Bulwer-Lytton, Edward (George Earle Lytton)

Maas, Peter 1929-2001 .... **CLC 29**
See also CA 93-96; 201; INT CA-93-96; MTCW 2

Macaulay, Catherine 1731-1791 .... **LC 64**
See also DLB 104

Macaulay, (Emilie) Rose
1881(?)-1958 .... **TCLC 7, 44**
See also CA 104; DLB 36; EWL 3; RGEL 2; RHW

Macaulay, Thomas Babington
1800-1859 .... **NCLC 42**
See also BRW 4; CDBLB 1832-1890; DLB 32, 55; RGEL 2

MacBeth, George (Mann)
1932-1992 .... **CLC 2, 5, 9**
See also CA 25-28R; 136; CANR 61, 66; DLB 40; MTCW 1; PFS 8; SATA 4; SATA-Obit 70

MacCaig, Norman (Alexander)
1910-1996 .... **CLC 36**
See also BRWS 6; CA 9-12R; CANR 3, 34; CP 7; DAB; DAM POET; DLB 27; EWL 3; RGEL 2

MacCarthy, Sir (Charles Otto) Desmond
1877-1952 .... **TCLC 36**
See also CA 167

MacDiarmid, Hugh .... **CLC 2, 4, 11, 19, 63; PC 9**
See Grieve, C(hristopher) M(urray)
See also CDBLB 1945-1960; DLB 20; EWL 3; RGEL 2

MacDonald, Anson
See Heinlein, Robert A(nson)

Macdonald, Cynthia 1928- .... **CLC 13, 19**
See also CA 49-52; CANR 4, 44; DLB 105

MacDonald, George 1824-1905 .... **TCLC 9, 113**
See also BYA 5; CA 106; 137; CANR 80; CLR 67; DLB 18, 163, 178; FANT; MAICYA 1, 2; RGEL 2; SATA 33, 100; SFW 4; SUFW; WCH

Macdonald, John
See Millar, Kenneth

MacDonald, John D(ann) 1916-1986 .... **CLC 3, 27, 44**
See also BPFB 2; CA 1-4R; 121; CANR 1, 19, 60; CMW 4; CPW; DAM NOV, POP; DLB 8; DLBY 1986; MSW; MTCW 1, 2; SFW 4

Macdonald, John Ross
See Millar, Kenneth

Macdonald, Ross ...... **CLC 1, 2, 3, 14, 34, 41**
See Millar, Kenneth
See also AMWS 4; BPFB 2; DLBD 6; MSW; RGAL 4

MacDougal, John
See Blish, James (Benjamin)

MacDougal, John
See Blish, James (Benjamin)

MacDowell, John
See Parks, Tim(othy Harold)

MacEwen, Gwendolyn (Margaret) 1941-1987 .... **CLC 13, 55**
See also CA 9-12R; 124; CANR 7, 22; DLB 53, 251; SATA 50; SATA-Obit 55

Macha, Karel Hynek 1810-1846 .... **NCLC 46**

Machado (y Ruiz), Antonio 1875-1939 .... **TCLC 3**
See also CA 104; 174; DLB 108; EW 9; EWL 3; HW 2; RGWL 2, 3

Machado de Assis, Joaquim Maria 1839-1908 .... **BLC 2; HLCS 2; SSC 24; TCLC 10**
See also CA 107; 153; CANR 91; LAW; RGSF 2; RGWL 2, 3; TWA; WLIT 1

Machaut, Guillaume de c. 1300-1377 .... **CMLC 64**
See also DLB 208

Machen, Arthur .... **SSC 20; TCLC 4**
See Jones, Arthur Llewellyn
See also CA 179; DLB 156, 178; RGEL 2; SUFW 1

Machiavelli, Niccolo 1469-1527 ... **DC 16; LC 8, 36; WLCS**
See also DA; DAB; DAC; DAM MST; EW 2; LAIT 1; LMFS 1; NFS 9; RGWL 2, 3; TWA

MacInnes, Colin 1914-1976 .... **CLC 4, 23**
See also CA 69-72; 65-68; CANR 21; DLB 14; MTCW 1, 2; RGEL 2; RHW

MacInnes, Helen (Clark) 1907-1985 .... **CLC 27, 39**
See also BPFB 2; CA 1-4R; 117; CANR 1, 28, 58; CMW 4; CPW; DAM POP; DLB 87; MSW; MTCW 1, 2; SATA 22; SATA-Obit 44

Mackay, Mary 1855-1924
See Corelli, Marie
See also CA 118; 177; FANT; RHW

Mackenzie, Compton (Edward Montague) 1883-1972 .... **CLC 18; TCLC 116**
See also CA 21-22; 37-40R; CAP 2; DLB 34, 100; RGEL 2

Mackenzie, Henry 1745-1831 .... **NCLC 41**
See also DLB 39; RGEL 2

Mackey, Nathaniel (Ernest) 1947- .... **PC 49**
See also CA 153; CANR 114; CP 7; DLB 169

MacKinnon, Catharine A. 1946- .... **CLC 181**
See also CA 128; 132; CANR 73; FW; MTCW 2

Mackintosh, Elizabeth 1896(?)-1952
See Tey, Josephine
See also CA 110; CMW 4

MacLaren, James
See Grieve, C(hristopher) M(urray)

Mac Laverty, Bernard 1942- .... **CLC 31**
See also CA 116; 118; CANR 43, 88; CN 7; DLB 267; INT CA-118; RGSF 2

MacLean, Alistair (Stuart) 1922(?)-1987 .... **CLC 3, 13, 50, 63**
See also CA 57-60; 121; CANR 28, 61; CMW 4; CPW; DAM POP; DLB 276; MTCW 1; SATA 23; SATA-Obit 50; TCWW 2

Maclean, Norman (Fitzroy) 1902-1990 .... **CLC 78; SSC 13**
See also CA 102; 132; CANR 49; CPW; DAM POP; DLB 206; TCWW 2

MacLeish, Archibald 1892-1982 ... **CLC 3, 8, 14, 68; PC 47**
See also AMW; CA 9-12R; 106; CAD; CANR 33, 63; CDALBS; DAM POET; DFS 15; DLB 4, 7, 45; DLBY 1982; EWL 3; EXPP; MTCW 1, 2; PAB; PFS 5; RGAL 4; TUS

MacLennan, (John) Hugh 1907-1990 .... **CLC 2, 14, 92**
See also CA 5-8R; 142; CANR 33; DAC; DAM MST; DLB 68; EWL 3; MTCW 1, 2; RGEL 2; TWA

MacLeod, Alistair 1936- .... **CLC 56, 165**
See also CA 123; CCA 1; DAC; DAM MST; DLB 60; MTCW 2; RGSF 2

Macleod, Fiona
See Sharp, William
See also RGEL 2; SUFW

MacNeice, (Frederick) Louis 1907-1963 .... **CLC 1, 4, 10, 53**
See also BRW 7; CA 85-88; CANR 61; DAB; DAM POET; DLB 10, 20; EWL 3; MTCW 1, 2; RGEL 2

MacNeill, Dand
See Fraser, George MacDonald

Macpherson, James 1736-1796 .... **LC 29**
See Ossian
See also BRWS 8; DLB 109; RGEL 2

Macpherson, (Jean) Jay 1931- .... **CLC 14**
See also CA 5-8R; CANR 90; CP 7; CWP; DLB 53

Macrobius fl. 430- .... **CMLC 48**

MacShane, Frank 1927-1999 .... **CLC 39**
See also CA 9-12R; 186; CANR 3, 33; DLB 111

Macumber, Mari
See Sandoz, Mari(e Susette)

Madach, Imre 1823-1864 .... **NCLC 19**

Madden, (Jerry) David 1933- .... **CLC 5, 15**
See also CA 1-4R; CAAS 3; CANR 4, 45; CN 7; CSW; DLB 6; MTCW 1

Maddern, Al(an)
See Ellison, Harlan (Jay)

Madhubuti, Haki R. 1942- ... **BLC 2; CLC 6, 73; PC 5**
See Lee, Don L.
See also BW 2, 3; CA 73-76; CANR 24, 51, 73; CP 7; CSW; DAM MULT, POET; DLB 5, 41; DLBD 8; EWL 3; MTCW 2; RGAL 4

Madison, James 1751-1836 .... **NCLC 126**
See also DLB 37

Maepenn, Hugh
See Kuttner, Henry

Maepenn, K. H.
See Kuttner, Henry

Maeterlinck, Maurice 1862-1949 ..... **TCLC 3**
See also CA 104; 136; CANR 80; DAM DRAM; DLB 192; EW 8; EWL 3; GFL 1789 to the Present; LMFS 2; RGWL 2, 3; SATA 66; TWA

Maginn, William 1794-1842 .... **NCLC 8**
See also DLB 110, 159

Mahapatra, Jayanta 1928- .... **CLC 33**
See also CA 73-76; CAAS 9; CANR 15, 33, 66, 87; CP 7; DAM MULT

Mahfouz, Naguib (Abdel Aziz Al-Sabilgi) 1911(?)- .... **CLC 153; SSC 66**
See Mahfuz, Najib (Abdel Aziz al-Sabilgi)
See also AAYA 49; BEST 89:2; CA 128; CANR 55, 101; CWW 2; DA3; DAM NOV; MTCW 1, 2; RGWL 2, 3; SSFS 9

Mahfuz, Najib (Abdel Aziz al-Sabilgi) .... **CLC 52, 55**
See Mahfouz, Naguib (Abdel Aziz Al-Sabilgi)
See also AFW; DLBY 1988; EWL 3; RGSF 2; WLIT 2

Mahon, Derek 1941- .... **CLC 27**
See also BRWS 6; CA 113; 128; CANR 88; CP 7; DLB 40; EWL 3

Maiakovskii, Vladimir
See Mayakovski, Vladimir (Vladimirovich)
See also IDTP; RGWL 2, 3

Mailer, Norman 1923- ... **CLC 1, 2, 3, 4, 5, 8, 11, 14, 28, 39, 74, 111**
See also AAYA 31; AITN 2; AMW; AMWC 2; AMWR 2; BPFB 2; CA 9-12R; CABS 1; CANR 28, 74, 77; CDALB 1968-1988; CN 7; CPW; DA; DA3; DAB; DAC; DAM MST, NOV, POP; DLB 2, 16, 28, 185, 278; DLBD 3; DLBY 1980, 1983; EWL 3; MTCW 1, 2; NFS 10; RGAL 4; TUS

Maillet, Antonine 1929- .... **CLC 54, 118**
See also CA 115; 120; CANR 46, 74, 77; CCA 1; CWW 2; DAC; DLB 60; INT CA-120; MTCW 2

Mais, Roger 1905-1955 .... **TCLC 8**
See also BW 1, 3; CA 105; 124; CANR 82; CDWLB 3; DLB 125; EWL 3; MTCW 1; RGEL 2

Maistre, Joseph 1753-1821 .... **NCLC 37**
See also GFL 1789 to the Present

Maitland, Frederic William 1850-1906 .... **TCLC 65**

Maitland, Sara (Louise) 1950- .... **CLC 49**
See also CA 69-72; CANR 13, 59; DLB 271; FW

Major, Clarence 1936- ... **BLC 2; CLC 3, 19, 48**
See also AFAW 2; BW 2, 3; CA 21-24R; CAAS 6; CANR 13, 25, 53, 82; CN 7; CP 7; CSW; DAM MULT; DLB 33; EWL 3; MSW

Major, Kevin (Gerald) 1949- .... **CLC 26**
See also AAYA 16; CA 97-100; CANR 21, 38, 112; CLR 11; DAC; DLB 60; INT CANR-21; JRDA; MAICYA 1, 2; MAICYAS 1; SATA 32, 82, 134; WYA; YAW

Maki, James
See Ozu, Yasujiro

Malabaila, Damiano
See Levi, Primo

Malamud, Bernard 1914-1986 .. **CLC 1, 2, 3, 5, 8, 9, 11, 18, 27, 44, 78, 85; SSC 15; TCLC 129; WLC**
See also AAYA 16; AMWS 1; BPFB 2; BYA 15; CA 5-8R; 118; CABS 1; CANR 28, 62, 114; CDALB 1941-1968; CPW; DA; DA3; DAB; DAC; DAM MST, NOV,

POP; DLB 2, 28, 152; DLBY 1980, 1986; EWL 3; EXPS; LAIT 4; LATS 1; MTCW 1, 2; NFS 4, 9; RGAL 4; RGSF 2; SSFS 8, 13, 16; TUS

Malan, Herman
See Bosman, Herman Charles; Bosman, Herman Charles

Malaparte, Curzio 1898-1957 .... **TCLC 52**
See also DLB 264

Malcolm, Dan
See Silverberg, Robert

Malcolm X .... **BLC 2; CLC 82, 117; WLCS**
See Little, Malcolm
See also LAIT 5; NCFS 3

Malherbe, Francois de 1555-1628 .... **LC 5**
See also GFL Beginnings to 1789

Mallarme, Stephane 1842-1898 ...... **NCLC 4, 41; PC 4**
See also DAM POET; DLB 217; EW 7; GFL 1789 to the Present; LMFS 2; RGWL 2, 3; TWA

Mallet-Joris, Francoise 1930- .... **CLC 11**
See also CA 65-68; CANR 17; DLB 83; EWL 3; GFL 1789 to the Present

Malley, Ern
See McAuley, James Phillip

Mallon, Thomas 1951- .... **CLC 172**
See also CA 110; CANR 29, 57, 92

Mallowan, Agatha Christie
See Christie, Agatha (Mary Clarissa)

Maloff, Saul 1922- .... **CLC 5**
See also CA 33-36R

Malone, Louis
See MacNeice, (Frederick) Louis

Malone, Michael (Christopher) 1942- .... **CLC 43**
See also CA 77-80; CANR 14, 32, 57, 114

Malory, Sir Thomas 1410(?)-1471(?) . **LC 11, 88; WLCS**
See also BRW 1; BRWR 2; CDBLB Before 1660; DA; DAB; DAC; DAM MST; DLB 146; EFS 2; RGEL 2; SATA 59; SATA-Brief 33; TEA; WLIT 3

Malouf, (George Joseph) David 1934- .... **CLC 28, 86**
See also CA 124; CANR 50, 76; CN 7; CP 7; DLB 289; EWL 3; MTCW 2

Malraux, (Georges-)Andre 1901-1976 .... **CLC 1, 4, 9, 13, 15, 57**
See also BPFB 2; CA 21-22; 69-72; CANR 34, 58; CAP 2; DA3; DAM NOV; DLB 72; EW 12; EWL 3; GFL 1789 to the Present; MTCW 1, 2; RGWL 2, 3; TWA

Malzberg, Barry N(athaniel) 1939- ... **CLC 7**
See also CA 61-64; CAAS 4; CANR 16; CMW 4; DLB 8; SFW 4

Mamet, David (Alan) 1947- .. **CLC 9, 15, 34, 46, 91, 166; DC 4**
See also AAYA 3; CA 81-84; CABS 3; CANR 15, 41, 67, 72, 129; CD 5; DA3; DAM DRAM; DFS 2, 3, 6, 12, 15; DLB 7; EWL 3; IDFW 4; MTCW 1, 2; RGAL 4

Mamoulian, Rouben (Zachary) 1897-1987 .... **CLC 16**
See also CA 25-28R; 124; CANR 85

Mandelshtam, Osip
See Mandelstam, Osip (Emilievich)
See also EW 10; EWL 3; RGWL 2, 3

Mandelstam, Osip (Emilievich) 1891(?)-1943(?) .... **PC 14; TCLC 2, 6**
See Mandelshtam, Osip
See also CA 104; 150; MTCW 2; TWA

Mander, (Mary) Jane 1877-1949 ... **TCLC 31**
See also CA 162; RGEL 2

Mandeville, Bernard 1670-1733 .... **LC 82**
See also DLB 101

Mandeville, Sir John fl. 1350- ...... **CMLC 19**
See also DLB 146

Mandiargues, Andre Pieyre de .... **CLC 41**
See Pieyre de Mandiargues, Andre
See also DLB 83

Mandrake, Ethel Belle
See Thurman, Wallace (Henry)

Mangan, James Clarence 1803-1849 .... **NCLC 27**
See also RGEL 2

Maniere, J.-E.
See Giraudoux, Jean(-Hippolyte)

Mankiewicz, Herman (Jacob) 1897-1953 .... **TCLC 85**
See also CA 120; 169; DLB 26; IDFW 3, 4

Manley, (Mary) Delariviere 1672(?)-1724 .... **LC 1, 42**
See also DLB 39, 80; RGEL 2

Mann, Abel
See Creasey, John

Mann, Emily 1952- .... **DC 7**
See also CA 130; CAD; CANR 55; CD 5; CWD; DLB 266

Mann, (Luiz) Heinrich 1871-1950 ... **TCLC 9**
See also CA 106; 164, 181; DLB 66, 118; EW 8; EWL 3; RGWL 2, 3

Mann, (Paul) Thomas 1875-1955 .... **SSC 5, 70; TCLC 2, 8, 14, 21, 35, 44, 60; WLC**
See also BPFB 2; CA 104; 128; CDWLB 2; DA; DA3; DAB; DAC; DAM MST, NOV; DLB 66; EW 9; EWL 3; GLL 1; LATS 1; LMFS 1; MTCW 1, 2; NFS 17; RGSF 2; RGWL 2, 3; SSFS 4, 9; TWA

Mannheim, Karl 1893-1947 .... **TCLC 65**
See also CA 204

Manning, David
See Faust, Frederick (Schiller)
See also TCWW 2

Manning, Frederic 1882-1935 .... **TCLC 25**
See also CA 124; 216; DLB 260

Manning, Olivia 1915-1980 .... **CLC 5, 19**
See also CA 5-8R; 101; CANR 29; EWL 3; FW; MTCW 1; RGEL 2

Mano, D. Keith 1942- .... **CLC 2, 10**
See also CA 25-28R; CAAS 6; CANR 26, 57; DLB 6

Mansfield, Katherine . **SSC 9, 23, 38; TCLC 2, 8, 39; WLC**
See Beauchamp, Kathleen Mansfield
See also BPFB 2; BRW 7; DAB; DLB 162; EWL 3; EXPS; FW; GLL 1; RGEL 2; RGSF 2; SSFS 2, 8, 10, 11; WWE 1

Manso, Peter 1940- .... **CLC 39**
See also CA 29-32R; CANR 44

Mantecon, Juan Jimenez
See Jimenez (Mantecon), Juan Ramon

Mantel, Hilary (Mary) 1952- .... **CLC 144**
See also CA 125; CANR 54, 101; CN 7; DLB 271; RHW

Manton, Peter
See Creasey, John

Man Without a Spleen, A
See Chekhov, Anton (Pavlovich)

Manzoni, Alessandro 1785-1873 ... **NCLC 29, 98**
See also EW 5; RGWL 2, 3; TWA

Map, Walter 1140-1209 .... **CMLC 32**

Mapu, Abraham (ben Jekutiel) 1808-1867 .... **NCLC 18**

Mara, Sally
See Queneau, Raymond

Maracle, Lee 1950- .... **NNAL**
See also CA 149

Marat, Jean Paul 1743-1793 .... **LC 10**

Marcel, Gabriel Honore 1889-1973 . **CLC 15**
See also CA 102; 45-48; EWL 3; MTCW 1, 2

March, William 1893-1954 .... **TCLC 96**
See also CA 216

Marchbanks, Samuel
See Davies, (William) Robertson
See also CCA 1

Marchi, Giacomo
See Bassani, Giorgio

Marcus Aurelius
See Aurelius, Marcus
See also AW 2

Marguerite
See de Navarre, Marguerite

Marguerite d'Angouleme
See de Navarre, Marguerite
See also GFL Beginnings to 1789

Marguerite de Navarre
See de Navarre, Marguerite
See also RGWL 2, 3

Margulies, Donald 1954- .... **CLC 76**
See also CA 200; DFS 13; DLB 228

Marie de France c. 12th cent. - ..... **CMLC 8; PC 22**
See also DLB 208; FW; RGWL 2, 3

Marie de l'Incarnation 1599-1672 ...... **LC 10**

Marier, Captain Victor
See Griffith, D(avid Lewelyn) W(ark)

Mariner, Scott
See Pohl, Frederik

Marinetti, Filippo Tommaso 1876-1944 .... **TCLC 10**
See also CA 107; DLB 114, 264; EW 9; EWL 3

Marivaux, Pierre Carlet de Chamblain de 1688-1763 .... **DC 7; LC 4**
See also GFL Beginnings to 1789; RGWL 2, 3; TWA

Markandaya, Kamala .... **CLC 8, 38**
See Taylor, Kamala (Purnaiya)
See also BYA 13; CN 7; EWL 3

Markfield, Wallace 1926-2002 .... **CLC 8**
See also CA 69-72; 208; CAAS 3; CN 7; DLB 2, 28; DLBY 2002

Markham, Edwin 1852-1940 .... **TCLC 47**
See also CA 160; DLB 54, 186; RGAL 4

Markham, Robert
See Amis, Kingsley (William)

Markoosie .... **NNAL**
See Patsauq, Markoosie
See also CLR 23; DAM MULT

Marks, J
See Highwater, Jamake (Mamake)

Marks, J.
See Highwater, Jamake (Mamake)

Marks-Highwater, J
See Highwater, Jamake (Mamake)

Marks-Highwater, J.
See Highwater, Jamake (Mamake)

Markson, David M(errill) 1927- .... **CLC 67**
See also CA 49-52; CANR 1, 91; CN 7

Marlatt, Daphne (Buckle) 1942- .... **CLC 168**
See also CA 25-28R; CANR 17, 39; CN 7; CP 7; CWP; DLB 60; FW

Marley, Bob .... **CLC 17**
See Marley, Robert Nesta

Marley, Robert Nesta 1945-1981
See Marley, Bob
See also CA 107; 103

Marlowe, Christopher 1564-1593 . **DC 1; LC 22, 47; PC 57; WLC**
See also BRW 1; BRWR 1; CDBLB Before 1660; DA; DA3; DAB; DAC; DAM DRAM, MST; DFS 1, 5, 13; DLB 62; EXPP; LMFS 1; RGEL 2; TEA; WLIT 3

Marlowe, Stephen 1928- .... **CLC 70**
See Queen, Ellery
See also CA 13-16R; CANR 6, 55; CMW 4; SFW 4

Marmion, Shakerley 1603-1639 .... **LC 89**
See also DLB 58; RGEL 2

Marmontel, Jean-Francois 1723-1799 .. **LC 2**
Maron, Monika 1941- .... **CLC 165**
See also CA 201
Marquand, John P(hillips)
1893-1960 .... **CLC 2, 10**
See also AMW; BPFB 2; CA 85-88; CANR 73; CMW 4; DLB 9, 102; EWL 3; MTCW 2; RGAL 4
Marques, Rene 1919-1979 .. **CLC 96; HLC 2**
See also CA 97-100; 85-88; CANR 78; DAM MULT; DLB 113; EWL 3; HW 1, 2; LAW; RGSF 2
Marquez, Gabriel (Jose) Garcia
See Garcia Marquez, Gabriel (Jose)
Marquis, Don(ald Robert Perry)
1878-1937 .... **TCLC 7**
See also CA 104; 166; DLB 11, 25; RGAL 4
Marquis de Sade
See Sade, Donatien Alphonse Francois
Marric, J. J.
See Creasey, John
See also MSW
Marryat, Frederick 1792-1848 .... **NCLC 3**
See also DLB 21, 163; RGEL 2; WCH
Marsden, James
See Creasey, John
Marsh, Edward 1872-1953 .... **TCLC 99**
Marsh, (Edith) Ngaio 1895-1982 .. **CLC 7, 53**
See also CA 9-12R; CANR 6, 58; CMW 4; CPW; DAM POP; DLB 77; MSW; MTCW 1, 2; RGEL 2; TEA
Marshall, Garry 1934- .... **CLC 17**
See also AAYA 3; CA 111; SATA 60
Marshall, Paule 1929- .. **BLC 3; CLC 27, 72; SSC 3**
See also AFAW 1, 2; AMWS 11; BPFB 2; BW 2, 3; CA 77-80; CANR 25, 73, 129; CN 7; CANR 25, 73, 129; DAM MULT; DLB 33, 157, 227; EWL 3; LATS 1; MTCW 1, 2; RGAL 4; SSFS 15
Marshallik
See Zangwill, Israel
Marsten, Richard
See Hunter, Evan
Marston, John 1576-1634 .... **LC 33**
See also BRW 2; DAM DRAM; DLB 58, 172; RGEL 2
Martha, Henry
See Harris, Mark
Marti, Jose
See Marti (y Perez), Jose (Julian)
See also DLB 290
Marti (y Perez), Jose (Julian)
1853-1895 .... **HLC 2; NCLC 63**
See Marti, Jose
See also DAM MULT; HW 2; LAW; RGWL 2, 3; WLIT 1
Martial c. 40-c. 104 .... **CMLC 35; PC 10**
See also AW 2; CDWLB 1; DLB 211; RGWL 2, 3
Martin, Ken
See Hubbard, L(afayette) Ron(ald)
Martin, Richard
See Creasey, John
Martin, Steve 1945- .... **CLC 30**
See also AAYA 53; CA 97-100; CANR 30, 100; MTCW 1
Martin, Valerie 1948- .... **CLC 89**
See also BEST 90:2; CA 85-88; CANR 49, 89
Martin, Violet Florence 1862-1915 .. **SSC 56; TCLC 51**
Martin, Webber
See Silverberg, Robert
Martindale, Patrick Victor
See White, Patrick (Victor Martindale)

Martin du Gard, Roger
1881-1958 .... **TCLC 24**
See also CA 118; CANR 94; DLB 65; EWL 3; GFL 1789 to the Present; RGWL 2, 3
Martineau, Harriet 1802-1876 ...... **NCLC 26, 137**
See also DLB 21, 55, 159, 163, 166, 190; FW; RGEL 2; YABC 2
Martines, Julia
See O'Faolain, Julia
Martinez, Enrique Gonzalez
See Gonzalez Martinez, Enrique
Martinez, Jacinto Benavente y
See Benavente (y Martinez), Jacinto
Martinez de la Rosa, Francisco de Paula
1787-1862 .... **NCLC 102**
See also TWA
Martinez Ruiz, Jose 1873-1967
See Azorin; Ruiz, Jose Martinez
See also CA 93-96; HW 1
Martinez Sierra, Gregorio
1881-1947 .... **TCLC 6**
See also CA 115; EWL 3
Martinez Sierra, Maria (de la O'LeJarraga)
1874-1974 .... **TCLC 6**
See also CA 115; EWL 3
Martinsen, Martin
See Follett, Ken(neth Martin)
Martinson, Harry (Edmund)
1904-1978 .... **CLC 14**
See also CA 77-80; CANR 34; DLB 259; EWL 3
Martyn, Edward 1859-1923 .... **TCLC 131**
See also CA 179; DLB 10; RGEL 2
Marut, Ret
See Traven, B.
Marut, Robert
See Traven, B.
Marvell, Andrew 1621-1678 .... **LC 4, 43; PC 10; WLC**
See also BRW 2; BRWR 2; CDBLB 1660-1789; DA; DAB; DAC; DAM MST, POET; DLB 131; EXPP; PFS 5; RGEL 2; TEA; WP
Marx, Karl (Heinrich)
1818-1883 .... **NCLC 17, 114**
See also DLB 129; LATS 1; TWA
Masaoka, Shiki -1902 .... **TCLC 18**
See Masaoka, Tsunenori
See also RGWL 3
Masaoka, Tsunenori 1867-1902
See Masaoka, Shiki
See also CA 117; 191; TWA
Masefield, John (Edward)
1878-1967 .... **CLC 11, 47**
See also CA 19-20; 25-28R; CANR 33; CAP 2; CDBLB 1890-1914; DAM POET; DLB 10, 19, 153, 160; EWL 3; EXPP; FANT; MTCW 1, 2; PFS 5; RGEL 2; SATA 19
Maso, Carole 19(?)- .... **CLC 44**
See also CA 170; GLL 2; RGAL 4
Mason, Bobbie Ann 1940- ... **CLC 28, 43, 82, 154; SSC 4**
See also AAYA 5, 42; AMWS 8; BPFB 2; CA 53-56; CANR 11, 31, 58, 83, 125; CDALBS; CN 7; CSW; DA3; DLB 173; DLBY 1987; EWL 3; EXPS; INT CANR-31; MTCW 1, 2; NFS 4; RGAL 4; RGSF 2; SSFS 3,8; YAW
Mason, Ernst
See Pohl, Frederik
Mason, Hunni B.
See Sternheim, (William Adolf) Carl
Mason, Lee W.
See Malzberg, Barry N(athaniel)
Mason, Nick 1945- .... **CLC 35**
Mason, Tally
See Derleth, August (William)

Mass, Anna .... **CLC 59**
Mass, William
See Gibson, William
Massinger, Philip 1583-1640 .... **LC 70**
See also DLB 58; RGEL 2
Master Lao
See Lao Tzu
Masters, Edgar Lee 1868-1950 ...... **PC 1, 36; TCLC 2, 25; WLCS**
See also AMWS 1; CA 104; 133; CDALB 1865-1917; DA; DAC; DAM MST, POET; DLB 54; EWL 3; EXPP; MTCW 1, 2; RGAL 4; TUS; WP
Masters, Hilary 1928- .... **CLC 48**
See also CA 25-28R, 217; CAAE 217; CANR 13, 47, 97; CN 7; DLB 244
Mastrosimone, William 19(?)- .... **CLC 36**
See also CA 186; CAD; CD 5
Mathe, Albert
See Camus, Albert
Mather, Cotton 1663-1728 .... **LC 38**
See also AMWS 2; CDALB 1640-1865; DLB 24, 30, 140; RGAL 4; TUS
Mather, Increase 1639-1723 .... **LC 38**
See also DLB 24
Matheson, Richard (Burton) 1926- ... **CLC 37**
See also AAYA 31; CA 97-100; CANR 88, 99; DLB 8, 44; HGG; INT CA-97-100; SCFW 2; SFW 4; SUFW 2
Mathews, Harry 1930- .... **CLC 6, 52**
See also CA 21-24R; CAAS 6; CANR 18, 40, 98; CN 7
Mathews, John Joseph 1894-1979 .. **CLC 84; NNAL**
See also CA 19-20; 142; CANR 45; CAP 2; DAM MULT; DLB 175
Mathias, Roland (Glyn) 1915- .... **CLC 45**
See also CA 97-100; CANR 19, 41; CP 7; DLB 27
Matsuo Basho 1644-1694 .... **LC 62; PC 3**
See Basho, Matsuo
See also DAM POET; PFS 2, 7
Mattheson, Rodney
See Creasey, John
Matthews, (James) Brander
1852-1929 .... **TCLC 95**
See also DLB 71, 78; DLBD 13
Matthews, Greg 1949- .... **CLC 45**
See also CA 135
Matthews, William (Procter III)
1942-1997 .... **CLC 40**
See also AMWS 9; CA 29-32R; 162; CAAS 18; CANR 12, 57; CP 7; DLB 5
Matthias, John (Edward) 1941- .... **CLC 9**
See also CA 33-36R; CANR 56; CP 7
Matthiessen, F(rancis) O(tto)
1902-1950 .... **TCLC 100**
See also CA 185; DLB 63
Matthiessen, Peter 1927- ... **CLC 5, 7, 11, 32, 64**
See also AAYA 6, 40; AMWS 5; ANW; BEST 90:4; BPFB 2; CA 9-12R; CANR 21, 50, 73, 100; CN 7; DA3; DAM NOV; DLB 6, 173, 275; MTCW 1, 2; SATA 27
Maturin, Charles Robert
1780(?)-1824 .... **NCLC 6**
See also BRWS 8; DLB 178; HGG; LMFS 1; RGEL 2; SUFW
Matute (Ausejo), Ana Maria 1925- .. **CLC 11**
See also CA 89-92; CANR 129; EWL 3; MTCW 1; RGSF 2
Maugham, W. S.
See Maugham, W(illiam) Somerset
Maugham, W(illiam) Somerset
1874-1965 .. **CLC 1, 11, 15, 67, 93; SSC 8; WLC**
See also AAYA 55; BPFB 2; BRW 6; CA 5-8R; 25-28R; CANR 40, 127; CDBLB 1914-1945; CMW 4; DA; DA3; DAB;

DAC; DAM DRAM, MST, NOV; DLB 10, 36, 77, 100, 162, 195; EWL 3; LAIT 3; MTCW 1, 2; RGEL 2; RGSF 2; SATA 54; SSFS 17

Maugham, William Somerset
See Maugham, W(illiam) Somerset

Maupassant, (Henri Rene Albert) Guy de 1850-1893 . **NCLC 1, 42, 83; SSC 1, 64; WLC**
See also BYA 14; DA; DA3; DAB; DAC; DAM MST; DLB 123; EW 7; EXPS; GFL 1789 to the Present; LAIT 2; LMFS 1; RGSF 2; RGWL 2, 3; SSFS 4; SUFW; TWA

Maupin, Armistead (Jones, Jr.) 1944- .... **CLC 95**
See also CA 125; 130; CANR 58, 101; CPW; DA3; DAM POP; DLB 278; GLL 1; INT CA-130; MTCW 2

Maurhut, Richard
See Traven, B.

Mauriac, Claude 1914-1996 .... **CLC 9**
See also CA 89-92; 152; CWW 2; DLB 83; EWL 3; GFL 1789 to the Present

Mauriac, Francois (Charles) 1885-1970 .... **CLC 4, 9, 56; SSC 24**
See also CA 25-28; CAP 2; DLB 65; EW 10; EWL 3; GFL 1789 to the Present; MTCW 1, 2; RGWL 2, 3; TWA

Mavor, Osborne Henry 1888-1951
See Bridie, James
See also CA 104

Maxwell, William (Keepers, Jr.) 1908-2000 .... **CLC 19**
See also AMWS 8; CA 93-96; 189; CANR 54, 95; CN 7; DLB 218, 278; DLBY 1980; INT CA-93-96; SATA-Obit 128

May, Elaine 1932- .... **CLC 16**
See also CA 124; 142; CAD; CWD; DLB 44

Mayakovski, Vladimir (Vladimirovich) 1893-1930 .... **TCLC 4, 18**
See Maiakovskii, Vladimir; Mayakovsky, Vladimir
See also CA 104; 158; EWL 3; MTCW 2; SFW 4; TWA

Mayakovsky, Vladimir
See Mayakovski, Vladimir (Vladimirovich)
See also EW 11; WP

Mayhew, Henry 1812-1887 .... **NCLC 31**
See also DLB 18, 55, 190

Mayle, Peter 1939(?)- .... **CLC 89**
See also CA 139; CANR 64, 109

Maynard, Joyce 1953- .... **CLC 23**
See also CA 111; 129; CANR 64

Mayne, William (James Carter) 1928- .... **CLC 12**
See also AAYA 20; CA 9-12R; CANR 37, 80; 100; CLR 25; FANT; JRDA; MAICYA 1, 2; MAICYAS 1; SAAS 11; SATA 6, 68, 122; SUFW 2; YAW

Mayo, Jim
See L'Amour, Louis (Dearborn)
See also TCWW 2

Maysles, Albert 1926- .... **CLC 16**
See also CA 29-32R

Maysles, David 1932-1987 .... **CLC 16**
See also CA 191

Mazer, Norma Fox 1931- .... **CLC 26**
See also AAYA 5, 36; BYA 1, 8; CA 69-72; CANR 12, 32, 66, 129; CLR 23; JRDA; MAICYA 1, 2; SAAS 1; SATA 24, 67, 105; WYA; YAW

Mazzini, Guiseppe 1805-1872 .... **NCLC 34**

McAlmon, Robert (Menzies) 1895-1956 .... **TCLC 97**
See also CA 107; 168; DLB 4, 45; DLBD 15; GLL 1

McAuley, James Phillip 1917-1976 .. **CLC 45**
See also CA 97-100; DLB 260; RGEL 2

McBain, Ed
See Hunter, Evan
See also MSW

McBrien, William (Augustine) 1930- .... **CLC 44**
See also CA 107; CANR 90

McCabe, Patrick 1955- .... **CLC 133**
See also BRWS 9; CA 130; CANR 50, 90; CN 7; DLB 194

McCaffrey, Anne (Inez) 1926- .... **CLC 17**
See also AAYA 6, 34; AITN 2; BEST 89:2; BPFB 2; BYA 5; CA 25-28R; CANR 15, 35, 55, 96; CLR 49; CPW; DA3; DAM NOV, POP; DLB 8; JRDA; MAICYA 1, 2; MTCW 1, 2; SAAS 11; SATA 8, 70, 116; SFW 4; SUFW 2; WYA; YAW

McCall, Nathan 1955(?)- .... **CLC 86**
See also BW 3; CA 146; CANR 88

McCann, Arthur
See Campbell, John W(ood, Jr.)

McCann, Edson
See Pohl, Frederik

McCarthy, Charles, Jr. 1933-
See McCarthy, Cormac
See also CANR 42, 69, 101; CN 7; CPW; CSW; DA3; DAM POP; MTCW 2

McCarthy, Cormac .... **CLC 4, 57, 101**
See McCarthy, Charles, Jr.
See also AAYA 41; AMWS 8; BPFB 2; CA 13-16R; CANR 10; DLB 6, 143, 256; EWL 3; LATS 1; TCWW 2

McCarthy, Mary (Therese) 1912-1989 .. **CLC 1, 3, 5, 14, 24, 39, 59; SSC 24**
See also AMW; BPFB 2; CA 5-8R; 129; CANR 16, 50, 64; DA3; DLB 2; DLBY 1981; EWL 3; FW; INT CANR-16; MAWW; MTCW 1, 2; RGAL 4; TUS

McCartney, (James) Paul 1942- . **CLC 12, 35**
See also CA 146; CANR 111

McCauley, Stephen (D.) 1955- .... **CLC 50**
See also CA 141

McClaren, Peter .... **CLC 70**

McClure, Michael (Thomas) 1932- ... **CLC 6, 10**
See also BG 3; CA 21-24R; CAD; CANR 17, 46, 77; CD 5; CP 7; DLB 16; WP

McCorkle, Jill (Collins) 1958- .... **CLC 51**
See also CA 121; CANR 113; CSW; DLB 234; DLBY 1987

McCourt, Frank 1930- .... **CLC 109**
See also AMWS 12; CA 157; CANR 97; NCFS 1

McCourt, James 1941- .... **CLC 5**
See also CA 57-60; CANR 98

McCourt, Malachy 1931- .... **CLC 119**
See also SATA 126

McCoy, Horace (Stanley) 1897-1955 .... **TCLC 28**
See also AMWS 13; CA 108; 155; CMW 4; DLB 9

McCrae, John 1872-1918 .... **TCLC 12**
See also CA 109; DLB 92; PFS 5

McCreigh, James
See Pohl, Frederik

McCullers, (Lula) Carson (Smith) 1917-1967 .... **CLC 1, 4, 10, 12, 48, 100; SSC 9, 24; WLC**
See also AAYA 21; AMW; AMWC 2; BPFB 2; CA 5-8R; 25-28R; CABS 1, 3; CANR 18; CDALB 1941-1968; DA; DA3; DAB; DAC; DAM MST, NOV; DFS 5, 18; DLB 2, 7, 173, 228; EWL 3; EXPS; FW; GLL 1; LAIT 3, 4; MAWW; MTCW 1, 2; NFS 6, 13; RGAL 4; RGSF 2; SATA 27; SSFS 5; TUS; YAW

McCulloch, John Tyler
See Burroughs, Edgar Rice

McCullough, Colleen 1938(?)- .. **CLC 27, 107**
See also AAYA 36; BPFB 2; CA 81-84; CANR 17, 46, 67, 98; CPW; DA3; DAM NOV, POP; MTCW 1, 2; RHW

McCunn, Ruthanne Lum 1946- .... **AAL**
See also CA 119; CANR 43, 96; LAIT 2; SATA 63

McDermott, Alice 1953- .... **CLC 90**
See also CA 109; CANR 40, 90, 126; DLB 292

McElroy, Joseph 1930- .... **CLC 5, 47**
See also CA 17-20R; CN 7

McEwan, Ian (Russell) 1948- .... **CLC 13, 66, 169**
See also BEST 90:4; BRWS 4; CA 61-64; CANR 14, 41, 69, 87; CN 7; DAM NOV; DLB 14, 194; HGG; MTCW 1, 2; RGSF 2; SUFW 2; TEA

McFadden, David 1940- .... **CLC 48**
See also CA 104; CP 7; DLB 60; INT CA-104

McFarland, Dennis 1950- .... **CLC 65**
See also CA 165; CANR 110

McGahern, John 1934- ... **CLC 5, 9, 48, 156; SSC 17**
See also CA 17-20R; CANR 29, 68, 113; CN 7; DLB 14, 231; MTCW 1

McGinley, Patrick (Anthony) 1937- . **CLC 41**
See also CA 120; 127; CANR 56; INT CA-127

McGinley, Phyllis 1905-1978 .... **CLC 14**
See also CA 9-12R; 77-80; CANR 19; CWRI 5; DLB 11, 48; PFS 9, 13; SATA 2, 44; SATA-Obit 24

McGinniss, Joe 1942- .... **CLC 32**
See also AITN 2; BEST 89:2; CA 25-28R; CANR 26, 70; CPW; DLB 185; INT CANR-26

McGivern, Maureen Daly
See Daly, Maureen

McGrath, Patrick 1950- .... **CLC 55**
See also CA 136; CANR 65; CN 7; DLB 231; HGG; SUFW 2

McGrath, Thomas (Matthew) 1916-1990 .... **CLC 28, 59**
See also AMWS 10; CA 9-12R; 132; CANR 6, 33, 95; DAM POET; MTCW 1; SATA 41; SATA-Obit 66

McGuane, Thomas (Francis III) 1939- .... **CLC 3, 7, 18, 45, 127**
See also AITN 2; BPFB 2; CA 49-52; CANR 5, 24, 49, 94; CN 7; DLB 2, 212; DLBY 1980; EWL 3; INT CANR-24; MTCW 1; TCWW 2

McGuckian, Medbh 1950- .... **CLC 48, 174; PC 27**
See also BRWS 5; CA 143; CP 7; CWP; DAM POET; DLB 40

McHale, Tom 1942(?)-1982 .... **CLC 3, 5**
See also AITN 1; CA 77-80; 106

McIlvanney, William 1936- .... **CLC 42**
See also CA 25-28R; CANR 61; CMW 4; DLB 14, 207

McIlwraith, Maureen Mollie Hunter
See Hunter, Mollie
See also SATA 2

McInerney, Jay 1955- .... **CLC 34, 112**
See also AAYA 18; BPFB 2; CA 116; 123; CANR 45, 68, 116; CN 7; CPW; DA3; DAM POP; DLB 292; INT CA-123; MTCW 2

McIntyre, Vonda N(eel) 1948- .... **CLC 18**
See also CA 81-84; CANR 17, 34, 69; MTCW 1; SFW 4; YAW

McKay, Claude .... **BLC 3; HR 3; PC 2; TCLC 7, 41; WLC**
See McKay, Festus Claudius
See also AFAW 1, 2; AMWS 10; DAB; DLB 4, 45, 51, 117; EWL 3; EXPP; GLL 2; LAIT 3; LMFS 2; PAB; PFS 4; RGAL 4; WP

McKay, Festus Claudius 1889-1948
See McKay, Claude
See also BW 1, 3; CA 104; 124; CANR 73; DA; DAC; DAM MST, MULT, NOV, POET; MTCW 1, 2; TUS

McKuen, Rod 1933- .... **CLC 1, 3**
See also AITN 1; CA 41-44R; CANR 40

McLoughlin, R. B.
See Mencken, H(enry) L(ouis)

McLuhan, (Herbert) Marshall 1911-1980 .... **CLC 37, 83**
See also CA 9-12R; 102; CANR 12, 34, 61; DLB 88; INT CANR-12; MTCW 1, 2

McManus, Declan Patrick Aloysius
See Costello, Elvis

McMillan, Terry (L.) 1951- . **BLCS; CLC 50, 61, 112**
See also AAYA 21; AMWS 13; BPFB 2; BW 2, 3; CA 140; CANR 60, 104; CPW; DA3; DAM MULT, NOV, POP; MTCW 2; RGAL 4; YAW

McMurtry, Larry (Jeff) 1936- .. **CLC 2, 3, 7, 11, 27, 44, 127**
See also AAYA 15; AITN 2; AMWS 5; BEST 89:2; BPFB 2; CA 5-8R; CANR 19, 43, 64, 103; CDALB 1968-1988; CN 7; CPW; CSW; DA3; DAM NOV, POP; DLB 2, 143, 256; DLBY 1980, 1987; EWL 3; MTCW 1, 2; RGAL 4; TCWW 2

McNally, T. M. 1961- .... **CLC 82**

McNally, Terrence 1939- .... **CLC 4, 7, 41, 91**
See also AMWS 13; CA 45-48; CAD; CANR 2, 56, 116; CD 5; DA3; DAM DRAM; DFS 16; DLB 7, 249; EWL 3; GLL 1; MTCW 2

McNamer, Deirdre 1950- .... **CLC 70**

McNeal, Tom .... **CLC 119**

McNeile, Herman Cyril 1888-1937
See Sapper
See also CA 184; CMW 4; DLB 77

McNickle, (William) D'Arcy 1904-1977 .... **CLC 89; NNAL**
See also CA 9-12R; 85-88; CANR 5, 45; DAM MULT; DLB 175, 212; RGAL 4; SATA-Obit 22

McPhee, John (Angus) 1931- .... **CLC 36**
See also AMWS 3; ANW; BEST 90:1; CA 65-68; CANR 20, 46, 64, 69, 121; CPW; DLB 185, 275; MTCW 1, 2; TUS

McPherson, James Alan 1943- . **BLCS; CLC 19, 77**
See also BW 1, 3; CA 25-28R; CAAS 17; CANR 24, 74; CN 7; CSW; DLB 38, 244; EWL 3; MTCW 1, 2; RGAL 4; RGSF 2

McPherson, William (Alexander) 1933- .... **CLC 34**
See also CA 69-72; CANR 28; INT CANR-28

McTaggart, J. McT. Ellis
See McTaggart, John McTaggart Ellis

McTaggart, John McTaggart Ellis 1866-1925 .... **TCLC 105**
See also CA 120; DLB 262

Mead, George Herbert 1863-1931 . **TCLC 89**
See also CA 212; DLB 270

Mead, Margaret 1901-1978 .... **CLC 37**
See also AITN 1; CA 1-4R; 81-84; CANR 4; DA3; FW; MTCW 1, 2; SATA-Obit 20

Meaker, Marijane (Agnes) 1927-
See Kerr, M. E.
See also CA 107; CANR 37, 63; INT CA-107; JRDA; MAICYA 1; MAICYAS 1; MTCW 1; SATA 20, 61, 99; SATA-Essay 111; YAW

Medoff, Mark (Howard) 1940- .... **CLC 6, 23**
See also AITN 1; CA 53-56; CAD; CANR 5; CD 5; DAM DRAM; DFS 4; DLB 7; INT CANR-5

Medvedev, P. N.
See Bakhtin, Mikhail Mikhailovich

Meged, Aharon
See Megged, Aharon

Meged, Aron
See Megged, Aharon

Megged, Aharon 1920- .... **CLC 9**
See also CA 49-52; CAAS 13; CANR 1; EWL 3

Mehta, Gita 1943- .... **CLC 179**
See also DNFS 2

Mehta, Ved (Parkash) 1934- .... **CLC 37**
See also CA 1-4R, 212; CAAE 212; CANR 2, 23, 69; MTCW 1

Melanchthon, Philipp 1497-1560 .... **LC 90**
See also DLB 179

Melanter
See Blackmore, R(ichard) D(oddridge)

Meleager c. 140B.C.-c. 70B.C. ...... **CMLC 53**

Melies, Georges 1861-1938 .... **TCLC 81**

Melikow, Loris
See Hofmannsthal, Hugo von

Melmoth, Sebastian
See Wilde, Oscar (Fingal O'Flahertie Wills)

Melo Neto, Joao Cabral de
See Cabral de Melo Neto, Joao
See also CWW 2; EWL 3

Meltzer, Milton 1915- .... **CLC 26**
See also AAYA 8, 45; BYA 2, 6; CA 13-16R; CANR 38, 92, 107; CLR 13; DLB 61; JRDA; MAICYA 1, 2; SAAS 1; SATA 1, 50, 80, 128; SATA-Essay 124; WYA; YAW

Melville, Herman 1819-1891 ..... **NCLC 3, 12, 29, 45, 49, 91, 93, 123; SSC 1, 17, 46; WLC**
See also AAYA 25; AMW; AMWR 1; CDALB 1640-1865; DA; DA3; DAB; DAC; DAM MST, NOV; DLB 3, 74, 250, 254; EXPN; EXPS; LAIT 1, 2; NFS 7, 9; RGAL 4; RGSF 2; SATA 59; SSFS 3; TUS

Members, Mark
See Powell, Anthony (Dymoke)

Membreno, Alejandro .... **CLC 59**

Menander c. 342B.C.-c. 293B.C. ..... **CMLC 9, 51; DC 3**
See also AW 1; CDWLB 1; DAM DRAM; DLB 176; LMFS 1; RGWL 2, 3

Menchu, Rigoberta 1959- .. **CLC 160; HLCS 2**
See also CA 175; DNFS 1; WLIT 1

Mencken, H(enry) L(ouis) 1880-1956 .... **TCLC 13**
See also AMW; CA 105; 125; CDALB 1917-1929; DLB 11, 29, 63, 137, 222; EWL 3; MTCW 1, 2; NCFS 4; RGAL 4; TUS

Mendelsohn, Jane 1965- .... **CLC 99**
See also CA 154; CANR 94

Menton, Francisco de
See Chin, Frank (Chew, Jr.)

Mercer, David 1928-1980 .... **CLC 5**
See also CA 9-12R; 102; CANR 23; CBD; DAM DRAM; DLB 13; MTCW 1; RGEL 2

Merchant, Paul
See Ellison, Harlan (Jay)

Meredith, George 1828-1909 ... **TCLC 17, 43**
See also CA 117; 153; CANR 80; CDBLB 1832-1890; DAM POET; DLB 18, 35, 57, 159; RGEL 2; TEA

Meredith, William (Morris) 1919- .... **CLC 4, 13, 22, 55; PC 28**
See also CA 9-12R; CAAS 14; CANR 6, 40, 129; CP 7; DAM POET; DLB 5

Merezhkovsky, Dmitrii Sergeevich
See Merezhkovsky, Dmitry Sergeyevich
See also DLB 295

Merezhkovsky, Dmitry Sergeevich
See Merezhkovsky, Dmitry Sergeyevich
See also EWL 3

Merezhkovsky, Dmitry Sergeyevich 1865-1941 .... **TCLC 29**
See Merezhkovsky, Dmitrii Sergeevich; Merezhkovsky, Dmitry Sergeevich
See also CA 169

Merimee, Prosper 1803-1870 ... **NCLC 6, 65; SSC 7**
See also DLB 119, 192; EW 6; EXPS; GFL 1789 to the Present; RGSF 2; RGWL 2, 3; SSFS 8; SUFW

Merkin, Daphne 1954- .... **CLC 44**
See also CA 123

Merlin, Arthur
See Blish, James (Benjamin)

Mernissi, Fatima 1940- .... **CLC 171**
See also CA 152; FW

Merrill, James (Ingram) 1926-1995 .. **CLC 2, 3, 6, 8, 13, 18, 34, 91; PC 28**
See also AMWS 3; CA 13-16R; 147; CANR 10, 49, 63, 108; DA3; DAM POET; DLB 5, 165; DLBY 1985; EWL 3; INT CANR-10; MTCW 1, 2; PAB; RGAL 4

Merriman, Alex
See Silverberg, Robert

Merriman, Brian 1747-1805 .... **NCLC 70**

Merritt, E. B.
See Waddington, Miriam

Merton, Thomas (James) 1915-1968 . **CLC 1, 3, 11, 34, 83; PC 10**
See also AMWS 8; CA 5-8R; 25-28R; CANR 22, 53, 111; DA3; DLB 48; DLBY 1981; MTCW 1, 2

Merwin, W(illiam) S(tanley) 1927- ... **CLC 1, 2, 3, 5, 8, 13, 18, 45, 88; PC 45**
See also AMWS 3; CA 13-16R; CANR 15, 51, 112; CP 7; DA3; DAM POET; DLB 5, 169; EWL 3; INT CANR-15; MTCW 1, 2; PAB; PFS 5, 15; RGAL 4

Metcalf, John 1938- .... **CLC 37; SSC 43**
See also CA 113; CN 7; DLB 60; RGSF 2; TWA

Metcalf, Suzanne
See Baum, L(yman) Frank

Mew, Charlotte (Mary) 1870-1928 .. **TCLC 8**
See also CA 105; 189; DLB 19, 135; RGEL 2

Mewshaw, Michael 1943- .... **CLC 9**
See also CA 53-56; CANR 7, 47; DLBY 1980

Meyer, Conrad Ferdinand 1825-1898 .... **NCLC 81**
See also DLB 129; EW; RGWL 2, 3

Meyer, Gustav 1868-1932
See Meyrink, Gustav
See also CA 117; 190

Meyer, June
See Jordan, June (Meyer)

Meyer, Lynn
See Slavitt, David R(ytman)

Meyers, Jeffrey 1939- .... **CLC 39**
See also CA 73-76, 186; CAAE 186; CANR 54, 102; DLB 111

Meynell, Alice (Christina Gertrude Thompson) 1847-1922 .... **TCLC 6**
See also CA 104; 177; DLB 19, 98; RGEL 2

Meyrink, Gustav .... **TCLC 21**
See Meyer, Gustav
See also DLB 81; EWL 3

Michaels, Leonard 1933-2003 ..... **CLC 6, 25; SSC 16**
See also CA 61-64; 216; CANR 21, 62, 119; CN 7; DLB 130; MTCW 1

Michaux, Henri 1899-1984 .... **CLC 8, 19**
See also CA 85-88; 114; DLB 258; EWL 3; GFL 1789 to the Present; RGWL 2, 3

Micheaux, Oscar (Devereaux) 1884-1951 .... **TCLC 76**
See also BW 3; CA 174; DLB 50; TCWW 2

Michelangelo 1475-1564 .... **LC 12**
See also AAYA 43

Michelet, Jules 1798-1874 .... **NCLC 31**
See also EW 5; GFL 1789 to the Present

Michels, Robert 1876-1936 .... **TCLC 88**
See also CA 212

Michener, James A(lbert) 1907(?)-1997 .. **CLC 1, 5, 11, 29, 60, 109**
See also AAYA 27; AITN 1; BEST 90:1; BPFB 2; CA 5-8R; 161; CANR 21, 45, 68; CN 7; CPW; DA3; DAM NOV, POP; DLB 6; MTCW 1, 2; RHW

Mickiewicz, Adam 1798-1855 . **NCLC 3, 101; PC 38**
See also EW 5; RGWL 2, 3

Middleton, (John) Christopher 1926- .... **CLC 13**
See also CA 13-16R; CANR 29, 54, 117; CP 7; DLB 40

Middleton, Richard (Barham) 1882-1911 .... **TCLC 56**
See also CA 187; DLB 156; HGG

Middleton, Stanley 1919- .... **CLC 7, 38**
See also CA 25-28R; CAAS 23; CANR 21, 46, 81; CN 7; DLB 14

Middleton, Thomas 1580-1627 ...... **DC 5; LC 33**
See also BRW 2; DAM DRAM, MST; DFS 18; DLB 58; RGEL 2

Migueis, Jose Rodrigues 1901-1980 . **CLC 10**
See also DLB 287

Mikszath, Kalman 1847-1910 .... **TCLC 31**
See also CA 170

Miles, Jack .... **CLC 100**
See also CA 200

Miles, John Russiano
See Miles, Jack

Miles, Josephine (Louise) 1911-1985 .... **CLC 1, 2, 14, 34, 39**
See also CA 1-4R; 116; CANR 2, 55; DAM POET; DLB 48

Militant
See Sandburg, Carl (August)

Mill, Harriet (Hardy) Taylor 1807-1858 .... **NCLC 102**
See also FW

Mill, John Stuart 1806-1873 ... **NCLC 11, 58**
See also CDBLB 1832-1890; DLB 55, 190, 262; FW 1; RGEL 2; TEA

Millar, Kenneth 1915-1983 .... **CLC 14**
See Macdonald, Ross
See also CA 9-12R; 110; CANR 16, 63, 107; CMW 4; CPW; DA3; DAM POP; DLB 2, 226; DLBD 6; DLBY 1983; MTCW 1, 2

Millay, E. Vincent
See Millay, Edna St. Vincent

Millay, Edna St. Vincent 1892-1950 .... **PC 6; TCLC 4, 49; WLCS**
See Boyd, Nancy
See also AMW; CA 104; 130; CDALB 1917-1929; DA; DA3; DAB; DAC; DAM MST, POET; DLB 45, 249; EWL 3; EXPP; MAWW; MTCW 1, 2; PAB; PFS 3, 17; RGAL 4; TUS; WP

Miller, Arthur 1915- ...... **CLC 1, 2, 6, 10, 15, 26, 47, 78, 179; DC 1; WLC**
See also AAYA 15; AITN 1; AMW; AMWC 1; CA 1-4R; CABS 3; CAD; CANR 2, 30, 54, 76; CD 5; CDALB 1941-1968; DA; DA3; DAB; DAC; DAM DRAM, MST; DFS 1, 3, 8; DLB 7, 266; EWL 3; LAIT 1, 4; LATS 1; MTCW 1, 2; RGAL 4; TUS; WYAS 1

Miller, Henry (Valentine) 1891-1980 .... **CLC 1, 2, 4, 9, 14, 43, 84; WLC**
See also AMW; BPFB 2; CA 9-12R; 97-100; CANR 33, 64; CDALB 1929-1941; DA; DA3; DAB; DAC; DAM MST, NOV; DLB 4, 9; DLBY 1980; EWL 3; MTCW 1, 2; RGAL 4; TUS

Miller, Jason 1939(?)-2001 .... **CLC 2**
See also AITN 1; CA 73-76; 197; CAD; DFS 12; DLB 7

Miller, Sue 1943- .... **CLC 44**
See also AMWS 12; BEST 90:3; CA 139; CANR 59, 91, 128; DA3; DAM POP; DLB 143

Miller, Walter M(ichael, Jr.) 1923-1996 .... **CLC 4, 30**
See also BPFB 2; CA 85-88; CANR 108; DLB 8; SCFW; SFW 4

Millett, Kate 1934- .... **CLC 67**
See also AITN 1; CA 73-76; CANR 32, 53, 76, 110; DA3; DLB 246; FW; GLL 1; MTCW 1, 2

Millhauser, Steven (Lewis) 1943- .... **CLC 21, 54, 109; SSC 57**
See also CA 110; 111; CANR 63, 114; CN 7; DA3; DLB 2; FANT; INT CA-111; MTCW 2

Millin, Sarah Gertrude 1889-1968 ... **CLC 49**
See also CA 102; 93-96; DLB 225; EWL 3

Milne, A(lan) A(lexander) 1882-1956 .... **TCLC 6, 88**
See also BRWS 5; CA 104; 133; CLR 1, 26; CMW 4; CWRI 5; DA3; DAB; DAC; DAM MST; DLB 10, 77, 100, 160; FANT; MAICYA 1, 2; MTCW 1, 2; RGEL 2; SATA 100; WCH; YABC 1

Milner, Ron(ald) 1938- .... **BLC 3; CLC 56**
See also AITN 1; BW 1; CA 73-76; CAD; CANR 24, 81; CD 5; DAM MULT; DLB 38; MTCW 1

Milnes, Richard Monckton 1809-1885 .... **NCLC 61**
See also DLB 32, 184

Milosz, Czeslaw 1911- ...... **CLC 5, 11, 22, 31, 56, 82; PC 8; WLCS**
See also CA 81-84; CANR 23, 51, 91, 126; CDWLB 4; CWW 2; DA3; DAM MST, POET; DLB 215; EW 13; EWL 3; MTCW 1, 2; PFS 16; RGWL 2, 3

Milton, John 1608-1674 ..... **LC 9, 43, 92; PC 19, 29; WLC**
See also BRW 2; BRWR 2; CDBLB 1660-1789; DA; DA3; DAB; DAC; DAM MST, POET; DLB 131, 151, 281; EFS 1; EXPP; LAIT 1; PAB; PFS 3, 17; RGEL 2; TEA; WLIT 3; WP

Min, Anchee 1957- .... **CLC 86**
See also CA 146; CANR 94

Minehaha, Cornelius
See Wedekind, (Benjamin) Frank(lin)

Miner, Valerie 1947- .... **CLC 40**
See also CA 97-100; CANR 59; FW; GLL 2

Minimo, Duca
See D'Annunzio, Gabriele

Minot, Susan 1956- .... **CLC 44, 159**
See also AMWS 6; CA 134; CANR 118; CN 7

Minus, Ed 1938- .... **CLC 39**
See also CA 185

Mirabai 1498(?)-1550(?) .... **PC 48**

Miranda, Javier
See Bioy Casares, Adolfo
See also CWW 2

Mirbeau, Octave 1848-1917 .... **TCLC 55**
See also CA 216; DLB 123, 192; GFL 1789 to the Present

Mirikitani, Janice 1942- .... **AAL**
See also CA 211; RGAL 4

Miro (Ferrer), Gabriel (Francisco Victor) 1879-1930 .... **TCLC 5**
See also CA 104; 185; EWL 3

Misharin, Alexandr .... **CLC 59**

Mishima, Yukio ... **CLC 2, 4, 6, 9, 27; DC 1; SSC 4**
See Hiraoka, Kimitake
See also AAYA 50; BPFB 2; GLL 1; MJW; MTCW 2; RGSF 2; RGWL 2, 3; SSFS 5, 12

Mistral, Frederic 1830-1914 .... **TCLC 51**
See also CA 122; 213; GFL 1789 to the Present

Mistral, Gabriela
See Godoy Alcayaga, Lucila
See also DLB 283; DNFS 1; EWL 3; LAW; RGWL 2, 3; WP

Mistry, Rohinton 1952- .... **CLC 71**
See also CA 141; CANR 86, 114; CCA 1; CN 7; DAC; SSFS 6

Mitchell, Clyde
See Ellison, Harlan (Jay)

Mitchell, Emerson Blackhorse Barney 1945- .... **NNAL**
See also CA 45-48

Mitchell, James Leslie 1901-1935
See Gibbon, Lewis Grassic
See also CA 104; 188; DLB 15

Mitchell, Joni 1943- .... **CLC 12**
See also CA 112; CCA 1

Mitchell, Joseph (Quincy) 1908-1996 .... **CLC 98**
See also CA 77-80; 152; CANR 69; CN 7; CSW; DLB 185; DLBY 1996

Mitchell, Margaret (Munnerlyn) 1900-1949 .... **TCLC 11**
See also AAYA 23; BPFB 2; BYA 1; CA 109; 125; CANR 55, 94; CDALBS; DA3; DAM NOV, POP; DLB 9; LAIT 2; MTCW 1, 2; NFS 9; RGAL 4; RHW; TUS; WYAS 1; YAW

Mitchell, Peggy
See Mitchell, Margaret (Munnerlyn)

Mitchell, S(ilas) Weir 1829-1914 .... **TCLC 36**
See also CA 165; DLB 202; RGAL 4

Mitchell, W(illiam) O(rmond) 1914-1998 .... **CLC 25**
See also CA 77-80; 165; CANR 15, 43; CN 7; DAC; DAM MST; DLB 88

Mitchell, William (Lendrum) 1879-1936 .... **TCLC 81**
See also CA 213

Mitford, Mary Russell 1787-1855 ... **NCLC 4**
See also DLB 110, 116; RGEL 2

Mitford, Nancy 1904-1973 .... **CLC 44**
See also CA 9-12R; DLB 191; RGEL 2

Miyamoto, (Chujo) Yuriko 1899-1951 .... **TCLC 37**
See Miyamoto Yuriko
See also CA 170, 174

Miyamoto Yuriko
See Miyamoto, (Chujo) Yuriko
See also DLB 180

Miyazawa, Kenji 1896-1933 .... **TCLC 76**
See Miyazawa Kenji
See also CA 157; RGWL 3

Miyazawa Kenji
See Miyazawa, Kenji
See also EWL 3

Mizoguchi, Kenji 1898-1956 .... **TCLC 72**
See also CA 167

Mo, Timothy (Peter) 1950(?)- ... **CLC 46, 134**
See also CA 117; CANR 128; CN 7; DLB 194; MTCW 1; WLIT 4; WWE 1

Modarressi, Taghi (M.) 1931-1997 ... **CLC 44**
See also CA 121; 134; INT CA-134

Modiano, Patrick (Jean) 1945- .... **CLC 18**
See also CA 85-88; CANR 17, 40, 115; CWW 2; DLB 83; EWL 3

Mofolo, Thomas (Mokopu)
1875(?)-1948 .... **BLC 3; TCLC 22**
See also AFW; CA 121; 153; CANR 83; DAM MULT; DLB 225; EWL 3; MTCW 2; WLIT 2

Mohr, Nicholasa 1938- .... **CLC 12; HLC 2**
See also AAYA 8, 46; CA 49-52; CANR 1, 32, 64; CLR 22; DAM MULT; DLB 145; HW 1, 2; JRDA; LAIT 5; LLW 1; MAICYA 2; MAICYAS 1; RGAL 4; SAAS 8; SATA 8, 97; SATA-Essay 113; WYA; YAW

Moi, Toril 1953- .... **CLC 172**
See also CA 154; CANR 102; FW

Mojtabai, A(nn) G(race) 1938- ..... **CLC 5, 9, 15, 29**
See also CA 85-88; CANR 88

Moliere 1622-1673 ..... **DC 13; LC 10, 28, 64; WLC**
See also DA; DA3; DAB; DAC; DAM DRAM, MST; DFS 13, 18; DLB 268; EW 3; GFL Beginnings to 1789; LATS 1; RGWL 2, 3; TWA

Molin, Charles
See Mayne, William (James Carter)

Molnar, Ferenc 1878-1952 .... **TCLC 20**
See also CA 109; 153; CANR 83; CDWLB 4; DAM DRAM; DLB 215; EWL 3; RGWL 2, 3

Momaday, N(avarre) Scott 1934- ...... **CLC 2, 19, 85, 95, 160; NNAL; PC 25; WLCS**
See also AAYA 11; AMWS 4; ANW; BPFB 2; BYA 12; CA 25-28R; CANR 14, 34, 68; CDALBS; CN 7; CPW; DA; DA3; DAB; DAC; DAM MST, MULT, NOV, POP; DLB 143, 175, 256; EWL 3; EXPP; INT CANR-14; LAIT 4; LATS 1; MTCW 1, 2; NFS 10; PFS 2, 11; RGAL 4; SATA 48; SATA-Brief 30; WP; YAW

Monette, Paul 1945-1995 .... **CLC 82**
See also AMWS 10; CA 139; 147; CN 7; GLL 1

Monroe, Harriet 1860-1936 .... **TCLC 12**
See also CA 109; 204; DLB 54, 91

Monroe, Lyle
See Heinlein, Robert A(nson)

Montagu, Elizabeth 1720-1800 .... **NCLC 7, 117**
See also FW

Montagu, Mary (Pierrepont) Wortley
1689-1762 .... **LC 9, 57; PC 16**
See also DLB 95, 101; RGEL 2

Montagu, W. H.
See Coleridge, Samuel Taylor

Montague, John (Patrick) 1929- ..... **CLC 13, 46**
See also CA 9-12R; CANR 9, 69, 121; CP 7; DLB 40; EWL 3; MTCW 1; PFS 12; RGEL 2

Montaigne, Michel (Eyquem) de
1533-1592 .... **LC 8; WLC**
See also DA; DAB; DAC; DAM MST; EW 2; GFL Beginnings to 1789; LMFS 1; RGWL 2, 3; TWA

Montale, Eugenio 1896-1981 ... **CLC 7, 9, 18; PC 13**
See also CA 17-20R; 104; CANR 30; DLB 114; EW 11; EWL 3; MTCW 1; RGWL 2, 3; TWA

Montesquieu, Charles-Louis de Secondat
1689-1755 .... **LC 7, 69**
See also EW 3; GFL Beginnings to 1789; TWA

Montessori, Maria 1870-1952 ...... **TCLC 103**
See also CA 115; 147

Montgomery, (Robert) Bruce 1921(?)-1978
See Crispin, Edmund
See also CA 179; 104; CMW 4

Montgomery, L(ucy) M(aud)
1874-1942 .... **TCLC 51, 140**
See also AAYA 12; BYA 1; CA 108; 137; CLR 8, 91; DA3; DAB; DAC; DAM MST; DLB 92; DLBD 14; JRDA; MAICYA 1, 2; MTCW 2; RGEL 2; SATA 100; TWA; WCH; WYA; YABC 1

Montgomery, Marion H., Jr. 1925- .... **CLC 7**
See also AITN 1; CA 1-4R; CANR 3, 48; CSW; DLB 6

Montgomery, Max
See Davenport, Guy (Mattison, Jr.)

Montherlant, Henry (Milon) de
1896-1972 .... **CLC 8, 19**
See also CA 85-88; 37-40R; DAM DRAM; DLB 72; EW 11; EWL 3; GFL 1789 to the Present; MTCW 1

Monty Python
See Chapman, Graham; Cleese, John (Marwood); Gilliam, Terry (Vance); Idle, Eric; Jones, Terence Graham Parry; Palin, Michael (Edward)
See also AAYA 7

Moodie, Susanna (Strickland)
1803-1885 .... **NCLC 14, 113**
See also DLB 99

Moody, Hiram (F. III) 1961-
See Moody, Rick
See also CA 138; CANR 64, 112

Moody, Minerva
See Alcott, Louisa May

Moody, Rick .... **CLC 147**
See Moody, Hiram (F. III)

Moody, William Vaughan
1869-1910 .... **TCLC 105**
See also CA 110; 178; DLB 7, 54; RGAL 4

Mooney, Edward 1951-
See Mooney, Ted
See also CA 130

Mooney, Ted .... **CLC 25**
See Mooney, Edward

Moorcock, Michael (John) 1939- ...... **CLC 5, 27, 58**
See Bradbury, Edward P.
See also AAYA 26; CA 45-48; CAAS 5; CANR 2, 17, 38, 64, 122; CN 7; DLB 14, 231, 261; FANT; MTCW 1, 2; SATA 93; SCFW 2; SFW 4; SUFW 1, 2

Moore, Brian 1921-1999 ... **CLC 1, 3, 5, 7, 8, 19, 32, 90**
See Bryan, Michael
See also BRWS 9; CA 1-4R; 174; CANR 1, 25, 42, 63; CCA 1; CN 7; DAB; DAC; DAM MST; DLB 251; EWL 3; FANT; MTCW 1, 2; RGEL 2

Moore, Edward
See Muir, Edwin
See also RGEL 2

Moore, G. E. 1873-1958 .... **TCLC 89**
See also DLB 262

Moore, George Augustus
1852-1933 .... **SSC 19; TCLC 7**
See also BRW 6; CA 104; 177; DLB 10, 18, 57, 135; EWL 3; RGEL 2; RGSF 2

Moore, Lorrie .... **CLC 39, 45, 68**
See Moore, Marie Lorena
See also AMWS 10; DLB 234; SSFS 19

Moore, Marianne (Craig)
1887-1972 ...... **CLC 1, 2, 4, 8, 10, 13, 19, 47; PC 4, 49; WLCS**
See also AMW; CA 1-4R; 33-36R; CANR 3, 61; CDALB 1929-1941; DA; DA3; DAB; DAC; DAM MST, POET; DLB 45; DLBD 7; EWL 3; EXPP; MAWW; MTCW 1, 2; PAB; PFS 14, 17; RGAL 4; SATA 20; TUS; WP

Moore, Marie Lorena 1957- .... **CLC 165**
See Moore, Lorrie
See also CA 116; CANR 39, 83; CN 7; DLB 234

Moore, Thomas 1779-1852 .... **NCLC 6, 110**
See also DLB 96, 144; RGEL 2

Moorhouse, Frank 1938- .... **SSC 40**
See also CA 118; CANR 92; CN 7; DLB 289; RGSF 2

Mora, Pat(ricia) 1942- .... **HLC 2**
See also AMWS 13; CA 129; CANR 57, 81, 112; CLR 58; DAM MULT; DLB 209; HW 1, 2; LLW 1; MAICYA 2; SATA 92, 134

Moraga, Cherrie 1952- ...... **CLC 126; DC 22**
See also CA 131; CANR 66; DAM MULT; DLB 82, 249; FW; GLL 1; HW 1, 2; LLW 1

Morand, Paul 1888-1976 .... **CLC 41; SSC 22**
See also CA 184; 69-72; DLB 65; EWL 3

Morante, Elsa 1918-1985 .... **CLC 8, 47**
See also CA 85-88; 117; CANR 35; DLB 177; EWL 3; MTCW 1, 2; RGWL 2, 3

Moravia, Alberto .... **CLC 2, 7, 11, 27, 46; SSC 26**
See Pincherle, Alberto
See also DLB 177; EW 12; EWL 3; MTCW 2; RGSF 2; RGWL 2, 3

More, Hannah 1745-1833 .... **NCLC 27**
See also DLB 107, 109, 116, 158; RGEL 2

More, Henry 1614-1687 .... **LC 9**
See also DLB 126, 252

More, Sir Thomas 1478(?)-1535 .... **LC 10, 32**
See also BRWC 1; BRWS 7; DLB 136, 281; LMFS 1; RGEL 2; TEA

Moreas, Jean .... **TCLC 18**
See Papadiamantopoulos, Johannes
See also GFL 1789 to the Present

Moreton, Andrew Esq.
See Defoe, Daniel

Morgan, Berry 1919-2002 .... **CLC 6**
See also CA 49-52; 208; DLB 6

Morgan, Claire
See Highsmith, (Mary) Patricia
See also GLL 1

Morgan, Edwin (George) 1920- .... **CLC 31**
See also BRWS 9; CA 5-8R; CANR 3, 43, 90; CP 7; DLB 27

Morgan, (George) Frederick
1922-2004 .... **CLC 23**
See also CA 17-20R; CANR 21; CP 7

Morgan, Harriet
See Mencken, H(enry) L(ouis)

Morgan, Jane
See Cooper, James Fenimore

Morgan, Janet 1945- .... **CLC 39**
See also CA 65-68

Morgan, Lady 1776(?)-1859 .... **NCLC 29**
See also DLB 116, 158; RGEL 2

Morgan, Robin (Evonne) 1941- .... **CLC 2**
See also CA 69-72; CANR 29, 68; FW; GLL 2; MTCW 1; SATA 80**

Morgan, Scott
See Kuttner, Henry

Morgan, Seth 1949(?)-1990 .... **CLC 65**
See also CA 185; 132

Morgenstern, Christian (Otto Josef Wolfgang) 1871-1914 .... **TCLC 8**
See also CA 105; 191; EWL 3

Morgenstern, S.
See Goldman, William (W.)

Mori, Rintaro
See Mori Ogai
See also CA 110

Moricz, Zsigmond 1879-1942 .... **TCLC 33**
See also CA 165; DLB 215; EWL 3

Morike, Eduard (Friedrich)
1804-1875 .... **NCLC 10**
See also DLB 133; RGWL 2, 3

Mori Ogai 1862-1922 .... **TCLC 14**
See Ogai
See also CA 164; DLB 180; EWL 3; RGWL 3; TWA

Moritz, Karl Philipp 1756-1793 .... **LC 2**
See also DLB 94

Morland, Peter Henry
See Faust, Frederick (Schiller)

Morley, Christopher (Darlington)
1890-1957 .... **TCLC 87**
See also CA 112; DLB 9; RGAL 4

Morren, Theophil
See Hofmannsthal, Hugo von

Morris, Bill 1952- .... **CLC 76**

Morris, Julian
See West, Morris L(anglo)

Morris, Steveland Judkins 1950(?)-
See Wonder, Stevie
See also CA 111

Morris, William 1834-1896 . **NCLC 4; PC 55**
See also BRW 5; CDBLB 1832-1890; DLB 18, 35, 57, 156, 178, 184; FANT; RGEL 2; SFW 4; SUFW

Morris, Wright 1910-1998 .. **CLC 1, 3, 7, 18, 37; TCLC 107**
See also AMW; CA 9-12R; 167; CANR 21, 81; CN 7; DLB 2, 206, 218; DLBY 1981; EWL 3; MTCW 1, 2; RGAL 4; TCWW 2

Morrison, Arthur 1863-1945 .... **SSC 40; TCLC 72**
See also CA 120; 157; CMW 4; DLB 70, 135, 197; RGEL 2

Morrison, Chloe Anthony Wofford
See Morrison, Toni

Morrison, James Douglas 1943-1971
See Morrison, Jim
See also CA 73-76; CANR 40

Morrison, Jim .... **CLC 17**
See Morrison, James Douglas

Morrison, Toni 1931- ..... **BLC 3; CLC 4, 10, 22, 55, 81, 87, 173**
See also AAYA 1, 22; AFAW 1, 2; AMWC 1; AMWS 3; BPFB 2; BW 2, 3; CA 29-32R; CANR 27, 42, 67, 113, 124; CDALB 1968-1988; CN 7; CPW; DA; DA3; DAB; DAC; DAM MST, MULT, NOV, POP; DLB 6, 33, 143; DLBY 1981; EWL 3; EXPN; FW; LAIT 2, 4; LATS 1; LMFS 2; MAWW; MTCW 1, 2; NFS 1, 6, 8, 14; RGAL 4; RHW; SATA 57, 144; SSFS 5; TUS; YAW

Morrison, Van 1945- .... **CLC 21**
See also CA 116; 168

Morrissy, Mary 1957- .... **CLC 99**
See also CA 205; DLB 267

Mortimer, John (Clifford) 1923- ..... **CLC 28, 43**
See also CA 13-16R; CANR 21, 69, 109; CD 5; CDBLB 1960 to Present; CMW 4; CN 7; CPW; DA3; DAM DRAM, POP; DLB 13, 245, 271; INT CANR-21; MSW; MTCW 1, 2; RGEL 2

Mortimer, Penelope (Ruth)
1918-1999 .... **CLC 5**
See also CA 57-60; 187; CANR 45, 88; CN 7

Mortimer, Sir John
See Mortimer, John (Clifford)

Morton, Anthony
See Creasey, John

Morton, Thomas 1579(?)-1647(?) .... **LC 72**
See also DLB 24; RGEL 2

Mosca, Gaetano 1858-1941 .... **TCLC 75**

Moses, Daniel David 1952- .... **NNAL**
See also CA 186

Mosher, Howard Frank 1943- .... **CLC 62**
See also CA 139; CANR 65, 115

Mosley, Nicholas 1923- .... **CLC 43, 70**
See also CA 69-72; CANR 41, 60, 108; CN 7; DLB 14, 207

Mosley, Walter 1952- .... **BLCS; CLC 97, 184**
See also AAYA 17; AMWS 13; BPFB 2; BW 2; CA 142; CANR 57, 92; CMW 4; CPW; DA3; DAM MULT, POP; MSW; MTCW 2

Moss, Howard 1922-1987 . **CLC 7, 14, 45, 50**
See also CA 1-4R; 123; CANR 1, 44; DAM POET; DLB 5

Mossgiel, Rab
See Burns, Robert

Motion, Andrew (Peter) 1952- .... **CLC 47**
See also BRWS 7; CA 146; CANR 90; CP 7; DLB 40

Motley, Willard (Francis)
1909-1965 .... **CLC 18**
See also BW 1; CA 117; 106; CANR 88; DLB 76, 143

Motoori, Norinaga 1730-1801 .... **NCLC 45**

Mott, Michael (Charles Alston)
1930- .... **CLC 15, 34**
See also CA 5-8R; CAAS 7; CANR 7, 29

Mountain Wolf Woman 1884-1960 . **CLC 92; NNAL**
See also CA 144; CANR 90

Moure, Erin 1955- .... **CLC 88**
See also CA 113; CP 7; CWP; DLB 60

Mourning Dove 1885(?)-1936 .... **NNAL**
See also CA 144; CANR 90; DAM MULT; DLB 175, 221

Mowat, Farley (McGill) 1921- .... **CLC 26**
See also AAYA 1, 50; BYA 2; CA 1-4R; CANR 4, 24, 42, 68, 108; CLR 20; CPW; DAC; DAM MST; DLB 68; INT CANR-24; JRDA; MAICYA 1, 2; MTCW 1, 2; SATA 3, 55; YAW

Mowatt, Anna Cora 1819-1870 ..... **NCLC 74**
See also RGAL 4

Moyers, Bill 1934- .... **CLC 74**
See also AITN 2; CA 61-64; CANR 31, 52

Mphahlele, Es'kia
See Mphahlele, Ezekiel
See also AFW; CDWLB 3; DLB 125, 225; RGSF 2; SSFS 11

Mphahlele, Ezekiel 1919- ... **BLC 3; CLC 25, 133**
See Mphahlele, Es'kia
See also BW 2, 3; CA 81-84; CANR 26, 76; CN 7; DA3; DAM MULT; EWL 3; MTCW 2; SATA 119

Mqhayi, S(amuel) E(dward) K(rune Loliwe)
1875-1945 .... **BLC 3; TCLC 25**
See also CA 153; CANR 87; DAM MULT

Mrozek, Slawomir 1930- .... **CLC 3, 13**
See also CA 13-16R; CAAS 10; CANR 29; CDWLB 4; CWW 2; DLB 232; EWL 3; MTCW 1

Mrs. Belloc-Lowndes
See Lowndes, Marie Adelaide (Belloc)

Mrs. Fairstar
See Horne, Richard Henry Hengist

M'Taggart, John M'Taggart Ellis
See McTaggart, John McTaggart Ellis

Mtwa, Percy (?)- .... **CLC 47**

Mueller, Lisel 1924- .... **CLC 13, 51; PC 33**
See also CA 93-96; CP 7; DLB 105; PFS 9, 13

Muggeridge, Malcolm (Thomas)
1903-1990 .... **TCLC 120**
See also AITN 1; CA 101; CANR 33, 63; MTCW 1, 2

Muhammad 570-632 .... **WLCS**
See also DA; DAB; DAC; DAM MST

Muir, Edwin 1887-1959 . **PC 49; TCLC 2, 87**
See Moore, Edward
See also BRWS 6; CA 104; 193; DLB 20, 100, 191; EWL 3; RGEL 2

Muir, John 1838-1914 .... **TCLC 28**
See also AMWS 9; ANW; CA 165; DLB 186, 275

Mujica Lainez, Manuel 1910-1984 ... **CLC 31**
See Lainez, Manuel Mujica
See also CA 81-84; 112; CANR 32; EWL 3; HW 1

Mukherjee, Bharati 1940- ..... **AAL; CLC 53, 115; SSC 38**
See also AAYA 46; BEST 89:2; CA 107; CANR 45, 72, 128; CN 7; DAM NOV; DLB 60, 218; DNFS 1, 2; EWL 3; FW; MTCW 1, 2; RGAL 4; RGSF 2; SSFS 7; TUS; WWE 1

Muldoon, Paul 1951- .... **CLC 32, 72, 166**
See also BRWS 4; CA 113; 129; CANR 52, 91; CP 7; DAM POET; DLB 40; INT CA-129; PFS 7

Mulisch, Harry 1927- .... **CLC 42**
See also CA 9-12R; CANR 6, 26, 56, 110; EWL 3

Mull, Martin 1943- .... **CLC 17**
See also CA 105

Muller, Wilhelm .... **NCLC 73**

Mulock, Dinah Maria
See Craik, Dinah Maria (Mulock)
See also RGEL 2

Munday, Anthony 1560-1633 .... **LC 87**
See also DLB 62, 172; RGEL 2

Munford, Robert 1737(?)-1783 .... **LC 5**
See also DLB 31

Mungo, Raymond 1946- .... **CLC 72**
See also CA 49-52; CANR 2

Munro, Alice 1931- .... **CLC 6, 10, 19, 50, 95; SSC 3; WLCS**
See also AITN 2; BPFB 2; CA 33-36R; CANR 33, 53, 75, 114; CCA 1; CN 7; DA3; DAC; DAM MST, NOV; DLB 53; EWL 3; MTCW 1, 2; RGEL 2; RGSF 2; SATA 29; SSFS 5, 13, 19; WWE 1

Munro, H(ector) H(ugh) 1870-1916 .... **WLC**
See Saki
See also CA 104; 130; CANR 104; CDBLB 1890-1914; DA; DA3; DAB; DAC; DAM MST, NOV; DLB 34, 162; EXPS; MTCW 1, 2; RGEL 2; SSFS 15

Murakami, Haruki 1949- .... **CLC 150**
See Murakami Haruki
See also CA 165; CANR 102; MJW; RGWL 3; SFW 4

Murakami Haruki
See Murakami, Haruki
See also DLB 182; EWL 3

Murasaki, Lady
See Murasaki Shikibu

Murasaki Shikibu 978(?)-1026(?) ... **CMLC 1**
See also EFS 2; LATS 1; RGWL 2, 3

Murdoch, (Jean) Iris 1919-1999 ... **CLC 1, 2, 3, 4, 6, 8, 11, 15, 22, 31, 51**
See also BRWS 1; CA 13-16R; 179; CANR 8, 43, 68, 103; CDBLB 1960 to Present; CN 7; CWD; DA3; DAB; DAC; DAM

MST, NOV; DLB 14, 194, 233; EWL 3; INT CANR-8; MTCW 1, 2; NFS 18; RGEL 2; TEA; WLIT 4

Murfree, Mary Noailles 1850-1922 .. **SSC 22; TCLC 135**
See also CA 122; 176; DLB 12, 74; RGAL 4

Murnau, Friedrich Wilhelm
See Plumpe, Friedrich Wilhelm

Murphy, Richard 1927- .... **CLC 41**
See also BRWS 5; CA 29-32R; CP 7; DLB 40; EWL 3

Murphy, Sylvia 1937- .... **CLC 34**
See also CA 121

Murphy, Thomas (Bernard) 1935- ... **CLC 51**
See also CA 101

Murray, Albert L. 1916- .... **CLC 73**
See also BW 2; CA 49-52; CANR 26, 52, 78; CSW; DLB 38

Murray, James Augustus Henry
1837-1915 .... **TCLC 117**

Murray, Judith Sargent
1751-1820 .... **NCLC 63**
See also DLB 37, 200

Murray, Les(lie Allan) 1938- .... **CLC 40**
See also BRWS 7; CA 21-24R; CANR 11, 27, 56, 103; CP 7; DAM POET; DLB 289; DLBY 2001; EWL 3; RGEL 2

Murry, J. Middleton
See Murry, John Middleton

Murry, John Middleton
1889-1957 .... **TCLC 16**
See also CA 118; 217; DLB 149

Musgrave, Susan 1951- .... **CLC 13, 54**
See also CA 69-72; CANR 45, 84; CCA 1; CP 7; CWP

Musil, Robert (Edler von)
1880-1942 .... **SSC 18; TCLC 12, 68**
See also CA 109; CANR 55, 84; CDWLB 2; DLB 81, 124; EW 9; EWL 3; MTCW 2; RGSF 2; RGWL 2, 3

Muske, Carol .... **CLC 90**
See Muske-Dukes, Carol (Anne)

Muske-Dukes, Carol (Anne) 1945-
See Muske, Carol
See also CA 65-68, 203; CAAE 203; CANR 32, 70; CWP

Musset, (Louis Charles) Alfred de
1810-1857 .... **NCLC 7**
See also DLB 192, 217; EW 6; GFL 1789 to the Present; RGWL 2, 3; TWA

Mussolini, Benito (Amilcare Andrea)
1883-1945 .... **TCLC 96**
See also CA 116

Mutanabbi, Al-
See al-Mutanabbi, Ahmad ibn al-Husayn Abu al-Tayyib al-Jufi al-Kindi

My Brother's Brother
See Chekhov, Anton (Pavlovich)

Myers, L(eopold) H(amilton)
1881-1944 .... **TCLC 59**
See also CA 157; DLB 15; EWL 3; RGEL 2

Myers, Walter Dean 1937- .. **BLC 3; CLC 35**
See also AAYA 4, 23; BW 2; BYA 6, 8, 11; CA 33-36R; CANR 20, 42, 67, 108; CLR 4, 16, 35; DAM MULT, NOV; DLB 33; INT CANR-20; JRDA; LAIT 5; MAICYA 1, 2; MAICYAS 1; MTCW 2; SAAS 2; SATA 41, 71, 109; SATA-Brief 27; WYA; YAW

Myers, Walter M.
See Myers, Walter Dean

Myles, Symon
See Follett, Ken(neth Martin)

Nabokov, Vladimir (Vladimirovich)
1899-1977 ...... **CLC 1, 2, 3, 6, 8, 11, 15, 23, 44, 46, 64; SSC 11; TCLC 108; WLC**
See also AAYA 45; AMW; AMWC 1; AMWR 1; BPFB 2; CA 5-8R; 69-72; CANR 20, 102; CDALB 1941-1968; DA; DA3; DAB; DAC; DAM MST, NOV; DLB 2, 244, 278; DLBD 3; DLBY 1980, 1991; EWL 3; EXPS; LATS 1; MTCW 1, 2; NCFS 4; NFS 9; RGAL 4; RGSF 2; SSFS 6, 15; TUS

Naevius c. 265B.C.-201B.C. .... **CMLC 37**
See also DLB 211

Nagai, Kafu .... **TCLC 51**
See Nagai, Sokichi
See also DLB 180

Nagai, Sokichi 1879-1959
See Nagai, Kafu
See also CA 117

Nagy, Laszlo 1925-1978 .... **CLC 7**
See also CA 129; 112

Naidu, Sarojini 1879-1949 .... **TCLC 80**
See also EWL 3; RGEL 2

Naipaul, Shiva(dhar Srinivasa)
1945-1985 .... **CLC 32, 39**
See also CA 110; 112; 116; CANR 33; DA3; DAM NOV; DLB 157; DLBY 1985; EWL 3; MTCW 1, 2

Naipaul, V(idiadhar) S(urajprasad)
1932- .... **CLC 4, 7, 9, 13, 18, 37, 105; SSC 38**
See also BPFB 2; BRWS 1; CA 1-4R; CANR 1, 33, 51, 91, 126; CDBLB 1960 to Present; CDWLB 3; CN 7; DA3; DAB; DAC; DAM MST, NOV; DLB 125, 204, 207; DLBY 1985, 2001; EWL 3; LATS 1; MTCW 1, 2; RGEL 2; RGSF 2; TWA; WLIT 4; WWE 1

Nakos, Lilika 1903(?)-1989 .... **CLC 29**

Napoleon
See Yamamoto, Hisaye

Narayan, R(asipuram) K(rishnaswami)
1906-2001 . **CLC 7, 28, 47, 121; SSC 25**
See also BPFB 2; CA 81-84; 196; CANR 33, 61, 112; CN 7; DA3; DAM NOV; DNFS 1; EWL 3; MTCW 1, 2; RGEL 2; RGSF 2; SATA 62; SSFS 5; WWE 1

Nash, (Frediric) Ogden 1902-1971 . **CLC 23; PC 21; TCLC 109**
See also CA 13-14; 29-32R; CANR 34, 61; CAP 1; DAM POET; DLB 11; MAICYA 1, 2; MTCW 1, 2; RGAL 4; SATA 2, 46; WP

Nashe, Thomas 1567-1601(?) .... **LC 41, 89**
See also DLB 167; RGEL 2

Nathan, Daniel
See Dannay, Frederic

Nathan, George Jean 1882-1958 .... **TCLC 18**
See Hatteras, Owen
See also CA 114; 169; DLB 137

Natsume, Kinnosuke
See Natsume, Soseki

Natsume, Soseki 1867-1916 .... **TCLC 2, 10**
See Natsume Soseki; Soseki
See also CA 104; 195; RGWL 2, 3; TWA

Natsume Soseki
See Natsume, Soseki
See also DLB 180; EWL 3

Natti, (Mary) Lee 1919-
See Kingman, Lee
See also CA 5-8R; CANR 2

Navarre, Marguerite de
See de Navarre, Marguerite

Naylor, Gloria 1950- ..... **BLC 3; CLC 28, 52, 156; WLCS**
See also AAYA 6, 39; AFAW 1, 2; AMWS 8; BW 2, 3; CA 107; CANR 27, 51, 74; CN 7; CPW; DA; DA3; DAC; DAM MST, MULT, NOV, POP; DLB 173; EWL 3; FW; MTCW 1, 2; NFS 4, 7; RGAL 4; TUS

Neff, Debra .... **CLC 59**

Neihardt, John Gneisenau
1881-1973 .... **CLC 32**
See also CA 13-14; CANR 65; CAP 1; DLB 9, 54, 256; LAIT 2

Nekrasov, Nikolai Alekseevich
1821-1878 .... **NCLC 11**
See also DLB 277

Nelligan, Emile 1879-1941 .... **TCLC 14**
See also CA 114; 204; DLB 92; EWL 3

Nelson, Willie 1933- .... **CLC 17**
See also CA 107; CANR 114

Nemerov, Howard (Stanley)
1920-1991 .... **CLC 2, 6, 9, 36; PC 24; TCLC 124**
See also AMW; CA 1-4R; 134; CABS 2; CANR 1, 27, 53; DAM POET; DLB 5, 6; DLBY 1983; EWL 3; INT CANR-27; MTCW 1, 2; PFS 10, 14; RGAL 4

Neruda, Pablo 1904-1973 .. **CLC 1, 2, 5, 7, 9, 28, 62; HLC 2; PC 4; WLC**
See also CA 19-20; 45-48; CAP 2; DA; DA3; DAB; DAC; DAM MST, MULT, POET; DLB 283; DNFS 2; EWL 3; HW 1; LAW; MTCW 1, 2; PFS 11; RGWL 2, 3; TWA; WLIT 1; WP

Nerval, Gerard de 1808-1855 ... **NCLC 1, 67; PC 13; SSC 18**
See also DLB 217; EW 6; GFL 1789 to the Present; RGSF 2; RGWL 2, 3

Nervo, (Jose) Amado (Ruiz de)
1870-1919 .... **HLCS 2; TCLC 11**
See also CA 109; 131; DLB 290; EWL 3; HW 1; LAW

Nesbit, Malcolm
See Chester, Alfred

Nessi, Pio Baroja y
See Baroja (y Nessi), Pio

Nestroy, Johann 1801-1862 .... **NCLC 42**
See also DLB 133; RGWL 2, 3

Netterville, Luke
See O'Grady, Standish (James)

Neufeld, John (Arthur) 1938- .... **CLC 17**
See also AAYA 11; CA 25-28R; CANR 11, 37, 56; CLR 52; MAICYA 1, 2; SAAS 3; SATA 6, 81, 131; SATA-Essay 131; YAW

Neumann, Alfred 1895-1952 .... **TCLC 100**
See also CA 183; DLB 56

Neumann, Ferenc
See Molnar, Ferenc

Neville, Emily Cheney 1919- .... **CLC 12**
See also BYA 2; CA 5-8R; CANR 3, 37, 85; JRDA; MAICYA 1, 2; SAAS 2; SATA 1; YAW

Newbound, Bernard Slade 1930-
See Slade, Bernard
See also CA 81-84; CANR 49; CD 5; DAM DRAM

Newby, P(ercy) H(oward)
1918-1997 .... **CLC 2, 13**
See also CA 5-8R; 161; CANR 32, 67; CN 7; DAM NOV; DLB 15; MTCW 1; RGEL 2

Newcastle
See Cavendish, Margaret Lucas

Newlove, Donald 1928- .... **CLC 6**
See also CA 29-32R; CANR 25

Newlove, John (Herbert) 1938- .... **CLC 14**
See also CA 21-24R; CANR 9, 25; CP 7

Newman, Charles 1938- .... **CLC 2, 8**
See also CA 21-24R; CANR 84; CN 7

Newman, Edwin (Harold) 1919- ...... **CLC 14**
See also AITN 1; CA 69-72; CANR 5

Newman, John Henry 1801-1890 . **NCLC 38, 99**
See also BRWS 7; DLB 18, 32, 55; RGEL 2

Newton, (Sir) Isaac 1642-1727 ...... **LC 35, 53**
See also DLB 252

Newton, Suzanne 1936- .... **CLC 35**
See also BYA 7; CA 41-44R; CANR 14; JRDA; SATA 5, 77

New York Dept. of Ed. .... **CLC 70**

Nexo, Martin Andersen 1869-1954 .... **TCLC 43**
See also CA 202; DLB 214; EWL 3

Nezval, Vitezslav 1900-1958 .... **TCLC 44**
See also CA 123; CDWLB 4; DLB 215; EWL 3

Ng, Fae Myenne 1957(?)- .... **CLC 81**
See also BYA 11; CA 146

Ngema, Mbongeni 1955- .... **CLC 57**
See also BW 2; CA 143; CANR 84; CD 5

Ngugi, James T(hiong'o) . **CLC 3, 7, 13, 182**
See Ngugi wa Thiong'o

Ngugi wa Thiong'o
See Ngugi wa Thiong'o
See also DLB 125; EWL 3

Ngugi wa Thiong'o 1938- ... **BLC 3; CLC 36, 182**
See Ngugi, James T(hiong'o); Ngugi wa Thiong'o
See also AFW; BRWS 8; BW 2; CA 81-84; CANR 27, 58; CDWLB 3; DAM MULT, NOV; DNFS 2; MTCW 1, 2; RGEL 2; WWE 1

Niatum, Duane 1938- .... **NNAL**
See also CA 41-44R; CANR 21, 45, 83; DLB 175

Nichol, B(arrie) P(hillip) 1944-1988 . **CLC 18**
See also CA 53-56; DLB 53; SATA 66

Nicholas of Cusa 1401-1464 .... **LC 80**
See also DLB 115

Nichols, John (Treadwell) 1940- .... **CLC 38**
See also AMWS 13; CA 9-12R, 190; CAAE 190; CAAS 2; CANR 6, 70, 121; DLBY 1982; LATS 1; TCWW 2

Nichols, Leigh
See Koontz, Dean R(ay)

Nichols, Peter (Richard) 1927- .... **CLC 5, 36, 65**
See also CA 104; CANR 33, 86; CBD; CD 5; DLB 13, 245; MTCW 1

Nicholson, Linda ed. .... **CLC 65**

Ni Chuilleanain, Eilean 1942- .... **PC 34**
See also CA 126; CANR 53, 83; CP 7; CWP; DLB 40

Nicolas, F. R. E.
See Freeling, Nicolas

Niedecker, Lorine 1903-1970 ..... **CLC 10, 42; PC 42**
See also CA 25-28; CAP 2; DAM POET; DLB 48

Nietzsche, Friedrich (Wilhelm) 1844-1900 .... **TCLC 10, 18, 55**
See also CA 107; 121; CDWLB 2; DLB 129; EW 7; RGWL 2, 3; TWA

Nievo, Ippolito 1831-1861 .... **NCLC 22**

Nightingale, Anne Redmon 1943-
See Redmon, Anne
See also CA 103

Nightingale, Florence 1820-1910 ... **TCLC 85**
See also CA 188; DLB 166

Nijo Yoshimoto 1320-1388 .... **CMLC 49**
See also DLB 203

Nik. T. O.
See Annensky, Innokenty (Fyodorovich)

Nin, Anais 1903-1977 ..... **CLC 1, 4, 8, 11, 14, 60, 127; SSC 10**
See also AITN 2; AMWS 10; BPFB 2; CA 13-16R; 69-72; CANR 22, 53; DAM NOV, POP; DLB 2, 4, 152; EWL 3; GLL 2; MAWW; MTCW 1, 2; RGAL 4; RGSF 2

Nisbet, Robert A(lexander) 1913-1996 .... **TCLC 117**
See also CA 25-28R; 153; CANR 17; INT CANR-17

Nishida, Kitaro 1870-1945 .... **TCLC 83**

Nishiwaki, Junzaburo
See Nishiwaki, Junzaburo
See also CA 194

Nishiwaki, Junzaburo 1894-1982 .... **PC 15**
See Nishiwaki, Junzaburo; Nishiwaki Junzaburo
See also CA 194; 107; MJW; RGWL 3

Nishiwaki Junzaburo
See Nishiwaki, Junzaburo
See also EWL 3

Nissenson, Hugh 1933- .... **CLC 4, 9**
See also CA 17-20R; CANR 27, 108; CN 7; DLB 28

Nister, Der
See Der Nister
See also EWL 3

Niven, Larry .... **CLC 8**
See Niven, Laurence Van Cott
See also AAYA 27; BPFB 2; BYA 10; DLB 8; SCFW 2

Niven, Laurence Van Cott 1938-
See Niven, Larry
See also CA 21-24R, 207; CAAE 207; CAAS 12; CANR 14, 44, 66, 113; CPW; DAM POP; MTCW 1, 2; SATA 95; SFW 4

Nixon, Agnes Eckhardt 1927- .... **CLC 21**
See also CA 110

Nizan, Paul 1905-1940 .... **TCLC 40**
See also CA 161; DLB 72; EWL 3; GFL 1789 to the Present

Nkosi, Lewis 1936- .... **BLC 3; CLC 45**
See also BW 1, 3; CA 65-68; CANR 27, 81; CBD; CD 5; DAM MULT; DLB 157, 225; WWE 1

Nodier, (Jean) Charles (Emmanuel) 1780-1844 .... **NCLC 19**
See also DLB 119; GFL 1789 to the Present

Noguchi, Yone 1875-1947 .... **TCLC 80**

Nolan, Christopher 1965- .... **CLC 58**
See also CA 111; CANR 88

Noon, Jeff 1957- .... **CLC 91**
See also CA 148; CANR 83; DLB 267; SFW 4

Norden, Charles
See Durrell, Lawrence (George)

Nordhoff, Charles Bernard 1887-1947 .... **TCLC 23**
See also CA 108; 211; DLB 9; LAIT 1; RHW 1; SATA 23

Norfolk, Lawrence 1963- .... **CLC 76**
See also CA 144; CANR 85; CN 7; DLB 267

Norman, Marsha 1947- . **CLC 28, 186; DC 8**
See also CA 105; CABS 3; CAD; CANR 41; CD 5; CSW; CWD; DAM DRAM; DFS 2; DLB 266; DLBY 1984; FW

Normyx
See Douglas, (George) Norman

Norris, (Benjamin) Frank(lin, Jr.) 1870-1902 .... **SSC 28; TCLC 24**
See also AMW; AMWC 2; BPFB 2; CA 110; 160; CDALB 1865-1917; DLB 12, 71, 186; LMFS 2; NFS 12; RGAL 4; TCWW 2; TUS

Norris, Leslie 1921- .... **CLC 14**
See also CA 11-12; CANR 14, 117; CAP 1; CP 7; DLB 27, 256

North, Andrew
See Norton, Andre

North, Anthony
See Koontz, Dean R(ay)

North, Captain George
See Stevenson, Robert Louis (Balfour)

North, Captain George
See Stevenson, Robert Louis (Balfour)

North, Milou
See Erdrich, Louise

Northrup, B. A.
See Hubbard, L(afayette) Ron(ald)

North Staffs
See Hulme, T(homas) E(rnest)

Northup, Solomon 1808-1863 ...... **NCLC 105**

Norton, Alice Mary
See Norton, Andre
See also MAICYA 1; SATA 1, 43

Norton, Andre 1912- .... **CLC 12**
See Norton, Alice Mary
See also AAYA 14; BPFB 2; BYA 4, 10, 12; CA 1-4R; CANR 68; CLR 50; DLB 8, 52; JRDA; MAICYA 2; MTCW 1; SATA 91; SUFW 1, 2; YAW

Norton, Caroline 1808-1877 .... **NCLC 47**
See also DLB 21, 159, 199

Norway, Nevil Shute 1899-1960
See Shute, Nevil
See also CA 102; 93-96; CANR 85; MTCW 2

Norwid, Cyprian Kamil 1821-1883 .... **NCLC 17**
See also RGWL 3

Nosille, Nabrah
See Ellison, Harlan (Jay)

Nossack, Hans Erich 1901-1978 .... **CLC 6**
See also CA 93-96; 85-88; DLB 69; EWL 3

Nostradamus 1503-1566 .... **LC 27**

Nosu, Chuji
See Ozu, Yasujiro

Notenburg, Eleanora (Genrikhovna) von
See Guro, Elena (Genrikhovna)

Nova, Craig 1945- .... **CLC 7, 31**
See also CA 45-48; CANR 2, 53, 127

Novak, Joseph
See Kosinski, Jerzy (Nikodem)

Novalis 1772-1801 .... **NCLC 13**
See also CDWLB 2; DLB 90; EW 5; RGWL 2, 3

Novick, Peter 1934- .... **CLC 164**
See also CA 188

Novis, Emile
See Weil, Simone (Adolphine)

Nowlan, Alden (Albert) 1933-1983 ... **CLC 15**
See also CA 9-12R; CANR 5; DAC; DAM MST; DLB 53; PFS 12

Noyes, Alfred 1880-1958 .... **PC 27; TCLC 7**
See also CA 104; 188; DLB 20; EXPP; FANT; PFS 4; RGEL 2

Nugent, Richard Bruce 1906(?)-1987 ... **HR 3**
See also BW 1; CA 125; DLB 51; GLL 2

Nunn, Kem .... **CLC 34**
See also CA 159

Nwapa, Flora (Nwanzuruaha) 1931-1993 .... **BLCS; CLC 133**
See also BW 2; CA 143; CANR 83; CDWLB 3; CWRI 5; DLB 125; EWL 3; WLIT 2

Nye, Robert 1939- .... **CLC 13, 42**
See also CA 33-36R; CANR 29, 67, 107; CN 7; CP 7; CWRI 5; DAM NOV; DLB 14, 271; FANT; HGG; MTCW 1; RHW; SATA 6

Nyro, Laura 1947-1997 .... **CLC 17**
See also CA 194

Oates, Joyce Carol 1938- .. **CLC 1, 2, 3, 6, 9, 11, 15, 19, 33, 52, 108, 134; SSC 6, 70; WLC**
See also AAYA 15, 52; AITN 1; AMWS 2; BEST 89:2; BPFB 2; BYA 11; CA 5-8R; CANR 25, 45, 74, 113, 129; CDALB 1968-1988; CN 7; CP 7; CPW; CWP; DA; DA3; DAB; DAC; DAM MST, NOV, POP; DLB 2, 5, 130; DLBY 1981; EWL 3; EXPS; FW; HGG; INT CANR-25; LAIT 4; MAWW; MTCW 1, 2; NFS 8; RGAL 4; RGSF 2; SSFS 17; SUFW 2; TUS

O'Brian, E. G.
See Clarke, Arthur C(harles)

O'Brian, Patrick 1914-2000 .... **CLC 152**
See also AAYA 55; CA 144; 187; CANR 74; CPW; MTCW 2; RHW

O'Brien, Darcy 1939-1998 .... **CLC 11**
See also CA 21-24R; 167; CANR 8, 59

O'Brien, Edna 1936- ..... **CLC 3, 5, 8, 13, 36, 65, 116; SSC 10**
See also BRWS 5; CA 1-4R; CANR 6, 41, 65, 102; CDBLB 1960 to Present; CN 7; DA3; DAM NOV; DLB 14, 231; EWL 3; FW; MTCW 1, 2; RGSF 2; WLIT 4

O'Brien, Fitz-James 1828-1862 ..... **NCLC 21**
See also DLB 74; RGAL 4; SUFW

O'Brien, Flann .... **CLC 1, 4, 5, 7, 10, 47**
See O Nuallain, Brian
See also BRWS 2; DLB 231; EWL 3; RGEL 2

O'Brien, Richard 1942- .... **CLC 17**
See also CA 124

O'Brien, (William) Tim(othy) 1946- . **CLC 7, 19, 40, 103**
See also AAYA 16; AMWS 5; CA 85-88; CANR 40, 58; CDALBS; CN 7; CPW; DA3; DAM POP; DLB 152; DLBD 9; DLBY 1980; MTCW 2; RGAL 4; SSFS 5, 15

Obstfelder, Sigbjoern 1866-1900 .... **TCLC 23**
See also CA 123

O'Casey, Sean 1880-1964 .... **CLC 1, 5, 9, 11, 15, 88; DC 12; WLCS**
See also BRW 7; CA 89-92; CANR 62; CBD; CDBLB 1914-1945; DA3; DAB; DAC; DAM DRAM, MST; DLB 10; EWL 3; MTCW 1, 2; RGEL 2; TEA; WLIT 4

O'Cathasaigh, Sean
See O'Casey, Sean

Occom, Samson 1723-1792 .... **LC 60; NNAL**
See also DLB 175

Ochs, Phil(ip David) 1940-1976 .... **CLC 17**
See also CA 185; 65-68

O'Connor, Edwin (Greene) 1918-1968 .... **CLC 14**
See also CA 93-96; 25-28R

O'Connor, (Mary) Flannery 1925-1964 .... **CLC 1, 2, 3, 6, 10, 13, 15, 21, 66, 104; SSC 1, 23, 61; TCLC 132; WLC**
See also AAYA 7; AMW; AMWR 2; BPFB 3; BYA 16; CA 1-4R; CANR 3, 41; CDALB 1941-1968; DA; DA3; DAB; DAC; DAM MST, NOV; DLB 2, 152; DLBD 12; DLBY 1980; EWL 3; EXPS; LAIT 5; MAWW; MTCW 1, 2; NFS 3; RGAL 4; RGSF 2; SSFS 2, 7, 10, 19; TUS

O'Connor, Frank .... **CLC 23; SSC 5**
See O'Donovan, Michael Francis
See also DLB 162; EWL 3; RGSF 2; SSFS 5

O'Dell, Scott 1898-1989 .... **CLC 30**
See also AAYA 3, 44; BPFB 3; BYA 1, 2, 3, 5; CA 61-64; 129; CANR 12, 30, 112; CLR 1, 16; DLB 52; JRDA; MAICYA 1, 2; SATA 12, 60, 134; WYA; YAW

Odets, Clifford 1906-1963 ..... **CLC 2, 28, 98; DC 6**
See also AMWS 2; CA 85-88; CAD; CANR 62; DAM DRAM; DFS 3, 17; DLB 7, 26; EWL 3; MTCW 1, 2; RGAL 4; TUS

O'Doherty, Brian 1928- .... **CLC 76**
See also CA 105; CANR 108

O'Donnell, K. M.
See Malzberg, Barry N(athaniel)

O'Donnell, Lawrence
See Kuttner, Henry

O'Donovan, Michael Francis 1903-1966 .... **CLC 14**
See O'Connor, Frank
See also CA 93-96; CANR 84

Oe, Kenzaburo 1935- .. **CLC 10, 36, 86, 187; SSC 20**
See Oe Kenzaburo
See also CA 97-100; CANR 36, 50, 74, 126; CWW 2; DA3; DAM NOV; DLB 182; DLBY 1994; EWL 3; LATS 1; MJW; MTCW 1, 2; RGSF 2; RGWL 2, 3

Oe Kenzaburo
See Oe, Kenzaburo
See also EWL 3

O'Faolain, Julia 1932- .... **CLC 6, 19, 47, 108**
See also CA 81-84; CAAS 2; CANR 12, 61; CN 7; DLB 14, 231; FW; MTCW 1; RHW

O'Faolain, Sean 1900-1991 ...... **CLC 1, 7, 14, 32, 70; SSC 13; TCLC 143**
See also CA 61-64; 134; CANR 12, 66; DLB 15, 162; MTCW 1, 2; RGEL 2; RGSF 2

O'Flaherty, Liam 1896-1984 .... **CLC 5, 34; SSC 6**
See also CA 101; 113; CANR 35; DLB 36, 162; DLBY 1984; MTCW 1, 2; RGEL 2; RGSF 2; SSFS 5

Ogai
See Mori Ogai
See also MJW

Ogilvy, Gavin
See Barrie, J(ames) M(atthew)

O'Grady, Standish (James) 1846-1928 .... **TCLC 5**
See also CA 104; 157

O'Grady, Timothy 1951- .... **CLC 59**
See also CA 138

O'Hara, Frank 1926-1966 .... **CLC 2, 5, 13, 78; PC 45**
See also CA 9-12R; 25-28R; CANR 33; DA3; DAM POET; DLB 5, 16, 193; EWL 3; MTCW 1, 2; PFS 8, 12; RGAL 4; WP

O'Hara, John (Henry) 1905-1970 . **CLC 1, 2, 3, 6, 11, 42; SSC 15**
See also AMW; BPFB 3; CA 5-8R; 25-28R; CANR 31, 60; CDALB 1929-1941; DAM NOV; DLB 9, 86; DLBD 2; EWL 3; MTCW 1, 2; NFS 11; RGAL 4; RGSF 2

O Hehir, Diana 1922- .... **CLC 41**
See also CA 93-96

Ohiyesa
See Eastman, Charles A(lexander)

Okada, John 1923-1971 .... **AAL**
See also BYA 14; CA 212

Okigbo, Christopher (Ifenayichukwu) 1932-1967 .... **BLC 3; CLC 25, 84; PC 7**
See also AFW; BW 1, 3; CA 77-80; CANR 74; CDWLB 3; DAM MULT, POET; DLB 125; EWL 3; MTCW 1, 2; RGEL 2

Okri, Ben 1959- .... **CLC 87**
See also AFW; BRWS 5; BW 2, 3; CA 130; 138; CANR 65, 128; CN 7; DLB 157, 231; EWL 3; INT CA-138; MTCW 2; RGSF 2; WLIT 2; WWE 1

Olds, Sharon 1942- ..... **CLC 32, 39, 85; PC 22**
See also AMWS 10; CA 101; CANR 18, 41, 66, 98; CP 7; CPW; CWP; DAM POET; DLB 120; MTCW 2; PFS 17

Oldstyle, Jonathan
See Irving, Washington

Olesha, Iurii
See Olesha, Yuri (Karlovich)
See also RGWL 2

Olesha, Iurii Karlovich
See Olesha, Yuri (Karlovich)
See also DLB 272

Olesha, Yuri (Karlovich) 1899-1960 . **CLC 8; SSC 69; TCLC 136**
See Olesha, Iurii; Olesha, Iurii Karlovich; Olesha, Yury Karlovich
See also CA 85-88; EW 11; RGWL 3

Olesha, Yury Karlovich
See Olesha, Yuri (Karlovich)
See also EWL 3

Oliphant, Mrs.
See Oliphant, Margaret (Oliphant Wilson)
See also SUFW

Oliphant, Laurence 1829(?)-1888 .. **NCLC 47**
See also DLB 18, 166

Oliphant, Margaret (Oliphant Wilson) 1828-1897 .... **NCLC 11, 61; SSC 25**
See Oliphant, Mrs.
See also DLB 18, 159, 190; HGG; RGEL 2; RGSF 2

Oliver, Mary 1935- .... **CLC 19, 34, 98**
See also AMWS 7; CA 21-24R; CANR 9, 43, 84, 92; CP 7; CWP; DLB 5, 193; EWL 3; PFS 15

Olivier, Laurence (Kerr) 1907-1989 . **CLC 20**
See also CA 111; 150; 129

Olsen, Tillie 1912- ... **CLC 4, 13, 114; SSC 11**
See also AAYA 51; AMWS 13; BYA 11; CA 1-4R; CANR 1, 43, 74; CDALBS; CN 7; DA; DA3; DAB; DAC; DAM MST; DLB 28, 206; DLBY 1980; EWL 3; EXPS; FW; MTCW 1, 2; RGAL 4; RGSF 2; SSFS 1; TUS

Olson, Charles (John) 1910-1970 .. **CLC 1, 2, 5, 6, 9, 11, 29; PC 19**
See also AMWS 2; CA 13-16; 25-28R; CABS; CANR 35, 61; CAP 1; DAM POET; DLB 5, 16, 193; EWL 3; MTCW 1, 2; RGAL 4; WP

Olson, Toby 1937- .... **CLC 28**
See also CA 65-68; CANR 9, 31, 84; CP 7

Olyesha, Yuri
See Olesha, Yuri (Karlovich)

Olympiodorus of Thebes c. 375-c. 430 .... **CMLC 59**

Omar Khayyam
See Khayyam, Omar
See also RGWL 2, 3

Ondaatje, (Philip) Michael 1943- .... **CLC 14, 29, 51, 76, 180; PC 28**
See also CA 77-80; CANR 42, 74, 109; CN 7; CP 7; DA3; DAB; DAC; DAM MST; DLB 60; EWL 3; LATS 1; LMFS 2; MTCW 2; PFS 8, 19; TWA; WWE 1

Oneal, Elizabeth 1934-
See Oneal, Zibby
See also CA 106; CANR 28, 84; MAICYA 1, 2; SATA 30, 82; YAW

Oneal, Zibby .... **CLC 30**
See Oneal, Elizabeth
See also AAYA 5, 41; BYA 13; CLR 13; JRDA; WYA

O'Neill, Eugene (Gladstone) 1888-1953 ... **DC 20; TCLC 1, 6, 27, 49; WLC**
See also AAYA 54; AITN 1; AMW; AMWC 1; CA 110; 132; CAD; CDALB 1929-1941; DA; DA3; DAB; DAC; DAM

Onetti, Juan Carlos 1909-1994 ... **CLC 7, 10; HLCS 2; SSC 23; TCLC 131**
See also CA 85-88; 145; CANR 32, 63; CDWLB 3; DAM MULT, NOV; DLB 113; EWL 3; HW 1, 2; LAW; MTCW 1, 2; RGSF 2

DRAM, MST; DFS 2, 4, 5, 6, 9, 11, 12, 16; DLB 7; EWL 3; LAIT 3; LMFS 2; MTCW 1, 2; RGAL 4; TUS

O Nuallain, Brian 1911-1966
See O'Brien, Flann
See also CA 21-22; 25-28R; CAP 2; DLB 231; FANT; TEA

Ophuls, Max 1902-1957 .... **TCLC 79**
See also CA 113

Opie, Amelia 1769-1853 .... **NCLC 65**
See also DLB 116, 159; RGEL 2

Oppen, George 1908-1984 ..... **CLC 7, 13, 34; PC 35; TCLC 107**
See also CA 13-16R; 113; CANR 8, 82; DLB 5, 165

Oppenheim, E(dward) Phillips 1866-1946 .... **TCLC 45**
See also CA 111; 202; CMW 4; DLB 70

Opuls, Max
See Ophuls, Max

Origen c. 185-c. 254 .... **CMLC 19**

Orlovitz, Gil 1918-1973 .... **CLC 22**
See also CA 77-80; 45-48; DLB 2, 5

Orris
See Ingelow, Jean

Ortega y Gasset, Jose 1883-1955 ...... **HLC 2; TCLC 9**
See also CA 106; 130; DAM MULT; EW 9; EWL 3; HW 1, 2; MTCW 1, 2

Ortese, Anna Maria 1914-1998 .... **CLC 89**
See also DLB 177; EWL 3

Ortiz, Simon J(oseph) 1941- .... **CLC 45; NNAL; PC 17**
See also AMWS 4; CA 134; CANR 69, 118; CP 7; DAM MULT, POET; DLB 120, 175, 256; EXPP; PFS 4, 16; RGAL 4

Orton, Joe .... **CLC 4, 13, 43; DC 3**
See Orton, John Kingsley
See also BRWS 5; CBD; CDBLB 1960 to Present; DFS 3, 6; DLB 13; GLL 1; MTCW 2; RGEL 2; TEA; WLIT 4

Orton, John Kingsley 1933-1967
See Orton, Joe
See also CA 85-88; CANR 35, 66; DAM DRAM; MTCW 1, 2

Orwell, George ...... **SSC 68; TCLC 2, 6, 15, 31, 51, 128, 129; WLC**
See Blair, Eric (Arthur)
See also BPFB 3; BRW 7; BYA 5; CDBLB 1945-1960; CLR 68; DAB; DLB 15, 98, 195, 255; EWL 3; EXPN; LAIT 4, 5; LATS 1; NFS 3, 7; RGEL 2; SCFW 4; SFW 4; SSFS 4; TEA; WLIT 4; YAW

Osborne, David
See Silverberg, Robert

Osborne, George
See Silverberg, Robert

Osborne, John (James) 1929-1994 .... **CLC 1, 2, 5, 11, 45; WLC**
See also BRWS 1; CA 13-16R; 147; CANR 21, 56; CDBLB 1945-1960; DA; DAB; DAC; DAM DRAM, MST; DFS 4; DLB 13; EWL 3; MTCW 1, 2; RGEL 2

Osborne, Lawrence 1958- .... **CLC 50**
See also CA 189

Osbourne, Lloyd 1868-1947 .... **TCLC 93**

Oshima, Nagisa 1932- .... **CLC 20**
See also CA 116; 121; CANR 78

Oskison, John Milton 1874-1947 .... **NNAL; TCLC 35**
See also CA 144; CANR 84; DAM MULT; DLB 175

Ossian c. 3rd cent. - .... **CMLC 28**
See Macpherson, James

Ossoli, Sarah Margaret (Fuller) 1810-1850 .... **NCLC 5, 50**
See Fuller, Margaret; Fuller, Sarah Margaret
See also CDALB 1640-1865; FW; LMFS 1; SATA 25

Ostriker, Alicia (Suskin) 1937- .... **CLC 132**
See also CA 25-28R; CAAS 24; CANR 10, 30, 62, 99; CWP; DLB 120; EXPP; PFS 19

Ostrovsky, Aleksandr Nikolaevich
See Ostrovsky, Alexander
See also DLB 277

Ostrovsky, Alexander 1823-1886 .. **NCLC 30, 57**
See Ostrovsky, Aleksandr Nikolaevich

Otero, Blas de 1916-1979 .... **CLC 11**
See also CA 89-92; DLB 134; EWL 3

O'Trigger, Sir Lucius
See Horne, Richard Henry Hengist

Otto, Rudolf 1869-1937 .... **TCLC 85**

Otto, Whitney 1955- .... **CLC 70**
See also CA 140; CANR 120

Ouida .... **TCLC 43**
See De la Ramee, Marie Louise (Ouida)
See also DLB 18, 156; RGEL 2

Ouologuem, Yambo 1940- .... **CLC 146**
See also CA 111; 176

Ousmane, Sembene 1923- ... **BLC 3; CLC 66**
See Sembene, Ousmane
See also BW 1, 3; CA 117; 125; CANR 81; CWW 2; MTCW 1

Ovid 43B.C.-17 .... **CMLC 7; PC 2**
See also AW 2; CDWLB 1; DA3; DAM POET; DLB 211; RGWL 2, 3; WP

Owen, Hugh
See Faust, Frederick (Schiller)

Owen, Wilfred (Edward Salter) 1893-1918 ... **PC 19; TCLC 5, 27; WLC**
See also BRW 6; CA 104; 141; CDBLB 1914-1945; DA; DAB; DAC; DAM MST, POET; DLB 20; EWL 3; EXPP; MTCW 2; PFS 10; RGEL 2; WLIT 4

Owens, Louis (Dean) 1948-2002 .... **NNAL**
See also CA 137, 179; 207; CAAE 179; CAAS 24; CANR 71

Owens, Rochelle 1936- .... **CLC 8**
See also CA 17-20R; CAAS 2; CAD; CANR 39; CD 5; CP 7; CWD; CWP

Oz, Amos 1939- ...... **CLC 5, 8, 11, 27, 33, 54; SSC 66**
See also CA 53-56; CANR 27, 47, 65, 113; CWW 2; DAM NOV; EWL 3; MTCW 1, 2; RGSF 2; RGWL 3

Ozick, Cynthia 1928- .... **CLC 3, 7, 28, 62, 155; SSC 15, 60**
See also AMWS 5; BEST 90:1; CA 17-20R; CANR 23, 58, 116; CN 7; CPW; DA3; DAM NOV, POP; DLB 28, 152; DLBY 1982; EWL 3; EXPS; INT CANR-23; MTCW 1, 2; RGAL 4; RGSF 2; SSFS 3, 12

Ozu, Yasujiro 1903-1963 .... **CLC 16**
See also CA 112

Pabst, G. W. 1885-1967 .... **TCLC 127**

Pacheco, C.
See Pessoa, Fernando (Antonio Nogueira)

Pacheco, Jose Emilio 1939- .... **HLC 2**
See also CA 111; 131; CANR 65; DAM MULT; DLB 290; EWL 3; HW 1, 2; RGSF 2

Pa Chin .... **CLC 18**
See Li Fei-kan
See also EWL 3

Pack, Robert 1929- .... **CLC 13**
See also CA 1-4R; CANR 3, 44, 82; CP 7; DLB 5; SATA 118

Padgett, Lewis
See Kuttner, Henry

Padilla (Lorenzo), Heberto 1932-2000 .... **CLC 38**
See also AITN 1; CA 123; 131; 189; EWL 3; HW 1

Page, James Patrick 1944-
See Page, Jimmy
See also CA 204

Page, Jimmy 1944- .... **CLC 12**
See Page, James Patrick

Page, Louise 1955- .... **CLC 40**
See also CA 140; CANR 76; CBD; CD 5; CWD; DLB 233

Page, P(atricia) K(athleen) 1916- ...... **CLC 7, 18; PC 12**
See Cape, Judith
See also CA 53-56; CANR 4, 22, 65; CP 7; DAC; DAM MST; DLB 68; MTCW 1; RGEL 2

Page, Stanton
See Fuller, Henry Blake

Page, Stanton
See Fuller, Henry Blake

Page, Thomas Nelson 1853-1922 .... **SSC 23**
See also CA 118; 177; DLB 12, 78; DLBD 13; RGAL 4

Pagels, Elaine Hiesey 1943- .... **CLC 104**
See also CA 45-48; CANR 2, 51; FW; NCFS 4

Paget, Violet 1856-1935
See Lee, Vernon
See also CA 104; 166; GLL 1; HGG

Paget-Lowe, Henry
See Lovecraft, H(oward) P(hillips)

Paglia, Camille (Anna) 1947- .... **CLC 68**
See also CA 140; CANR 72; CPW; FW; GLL 2; MTCW 2

Paige, Richard
See Koontz, Dean R(ay)

Paine, Thomas 1737-1809 .... **NCLC 62**
See also AMWS 1; CDALB 1640-1865; DLB 31, 43, 73, 158; LAIT 1; RGAL 4; RGEL 2; TUS

Pakenham, Antonia
See Fraser, Antonia (Pakenham)

Palamas, Costis
See Palamas, Kostes

Palamas, Kostes 1859-1943 .... **TCLC 5**
See Palamas, Kostis
See also CA 105; 190; RGWL 2, 3

Palamas, Kostis
See Palamas, Kostes
See also EWL 3

Palazzeschi, Aldo 1885-1974 .... **CLC 11**
See also CA 89-92; 53-56; DLB 114, 264; EWL 3

Pales Matos, Luis 1898-1959 .... **HLCS 2**
See Pales Matos, Luis
See also DLB 290; HW 1; LAW

Paley, Grace 1922- .. **CLC 4, 6, 37, 140; SSC 8**
See also AMWS 6; CA 25-28R; CANR 13, 46, 74, 118; CN 7; CPW; DA3; DAM POP; DLB 28, 218; EWL 3; EXPS; FW; INT CANR-13; MAWW; MTCW 1, 2; RGAL 4; RGSF 2; SSFS 3

Palin, Michael (Edward) 1943- .... **CLC 21**
See Monty Python
See also CA 107; CANR 35, 109; SATA 67

Palliser, Charles 1947- .... **CLC 65**
See also CA 136; CANR 76; CN 7

Palma, Ricardo 1833-1919 .... **TCLC 29**
See also CA 168; LAW

Pamuk, Orhan 1952- .... **CLC 185**
See also CA 142; CANR 75, 127; CWW 2

Pancake, Breece Dexter 1952-1979
See Pancake, Breece D'J
See also CA 123; 109

Pancake, Breece D'J .... **CLC 29; SSC 61**
See Pancake, Breece Dexter
See also DLB 130

Panchenko, Nikolai .... **CLC 59**

Pankhurst, Emmeline (Goulden)
1858-1928 .... **TCLC 100**
See also CA 116; FW

Panko, Rudy
See Gogol, Nikolai (Vasilyevich)

Papadiamantis, Alexandros
1851-1911 .... **TCLC 29**
See also CA 168; EWL 3

Papadiamantopoulos, Johannes 1856-1910
See Moreas, Jean
See also CA 117

Papini, Giovanni 1881-1956 .... **TCLC 22**
See also CA 121; 180; DLB 264

Paracelsus 1493-1541 .... **LC 14**
See also DLB 179

Parasol, Peter
See Stevens, Wallace

Pardo Bazan, Emilia 1851-1921 .... **SSC 30**
See also EWL 3; FW; RGSF 2; RGWL 2, 3

Pareto, Vilfredo 1848-1923 .... **TCLC 69**
See also CA 175

Paretsky, Sara 1947- .... **CLC 135**
See also AAYA 30; BEST 90:3; CA 125; 129; CANR 59, 95; CMW 4; CPW; DA3; DAM POP; INT CA-129; MSW; RGAL 4

Parfenie, Maria
See Codrescu, Andrei

Parini, Jay (Lee) 1948- .... **CLC 54, 133**
See also CA 97-100; CAAS 16; CANR 32, 87

Park, Jordan
See Kornbluth, C(yril) M.; Pohl, Frederik

Park, Robert E(zra) 1864-1944 ..... **TCLC 73**
See also CA 122; 165

Parker, Bert
See Ellison, Harlan (Jay)

Parker, Dorothy (Rothschild)
1893-1967 . **CLC 15, 68; PC 28; SSC 2; TCLC 143**
See also AMWS 9; CA 19-20; 25-28R; CAP 2; DA3; DAM POET; DLB 11, 45, 86; EXPP; FW; MAWW; MTCW 1, 2; PFS 18; RGAL 4; RGSF 2; TUS

Parker, Robert B(rown) 1932- .... **CLC 27**
See also AAYA 28; BEST 89:4; BPFB 3; CA 49-52; CANR 1, 26, 52, 89, 128; CMW 4; CPW; DAM NOV, POP; INT CANR-26; MSW; MTCW 1

Parkin, Frank 1940- .... **CLC 43**
See also CA 147

Parkman, Francis, Jr. 1823-1893 .. **NCLC 12**
See also AMWS 2; DLB 1, 30, 183, 186, 235; RGAL 4

Parks, Gordon (Alexander Buchanan)
1912- .... **BLC 3; CLC 1, 16**
See also AAYA 36; AITN 2; BW 2, 3; CA 41-44R; CANR 26, 66; DA3; DAM MULT; DLB 33; MTCW 2; SATA 8, 108

Parks, Suzan-Lori 1964- .... **DC 23**
See also AAYA 55; CA 201; CD 5; CAD; CWD; RGAL 4;

Parks, Tim(othy Harold) 1954- ...... **CLC 147**
See also CA 126; 131; CANR 77; DLB 231; INT CA-131

Parmenides c. 515B.C.-c.
450B.C. .... **CMLC 22**
See also DLB 176

Parnell, Thomas 1679-1718 .... **LC 3**
See also DLB 95; RGEL 2

Parr, Catherine c. 1513(?)-1548 .... **LC 86**
See also DLB 136

Parra, Nicanor 1914- ... **CLC 2, 102; HLC 2; PC 39**
See also CA 85-88; CANR 32; CWW 2; DAM MULT; DLB 283; EWL 3; HW 1; LAW; MTCW 1

Parra Sanojo, Ana Teresa de la
1890-1936 .... **HLCS 2**
See de la Parra, (Ana) Teresa (Sonojo)
See also LAW

Parrish, Mary Frances
See Fisher, M(ary) F(rances) K(ennedy)

Parshchikov, Aleksei 1954- .... **CLC 59**
See Parshchikov, Aleksei Maksimovich

Parshchikov, Aleksei Maksimovich
See Parshchikov, Aleksei
See also DLB 285

Parson, Professor
See Coleridge, Samuel Taylor

Parson Lot
See Kingsley, Charles

Parton, Sara Payson Willis
1811-1872 .... **NCLC 86**
See also DLB 43, 74, 239

Partridge, Anthony
See Oppenheim, E(dward) Phillips

Pascal, Blaise 1623-1662 .... **LC 35**
See also DLB 268; EW 3; GFL Beginnings to 1789; RGWL 2, 3; TWA

Pascoli, Giovanni 1855-1912 .... **TCLC 45**
See also CA 170; EW 7; EWL 3

Pasolini, Pier Paolo 1922-1975 .. **CLC 20, 37, 106; PC 17**
See also CA 93-96; 61-64; CANR 63; DLB 128, 177; EWL 3; MTCW 1; RGWL 2, 3

Pasquini
See Silone, Ignazio

Pastan, Linda (Olenik) 1932- .... **CLC 27**
See also CA 61-64; CANR 18, 40, 61, 113; CP 7; CSW; CWP; DAM POET; DLB 5; PFS 8

Pasternak, Boris (Leonidovich)
1890-1960 ...... **CLC 7, 10, 18, 63; PC 6; SSC 31; WLC**
See also BPFB 3; CA 127; 116; DA; DA3; DAB; DAC; DAM MST, NOV, POET; EW 10; MTCW 1, 2; RGSF 2; RGWL 2, 3; TWA; WP

Patchen, Kenneth 1911-1972 .... **CLC 1, 2, 18**
See also BG 3; CA 1-4R; 33-36R; CANR 3, 35; DAM POET; DLB 16, 48; EWL 3; MTCW 1; RGAL 4

Pater, Walter (Horatio) 1839-1894 . **NCLC 7, 90**
See also BRW 5; CDBLB 1832-1890; DLB 57, 156; RGEL 2, TEA

Paterson, A(ndrew) B(arton)
1864-1941 .... **TCLC 32**
See also CA 155; DLB 230; RGEL 2; SATA 97

Paterson, Banjo
See Paterson, A(ndrew) B(arton)

Paterson, Katherine (Womeldorf)
1932- .... **CLC 12, 30**
See also AAYA 1, 31; BYA 1, 2, 7; CA 21-24R; CANR 28, 59, 111; CLR 7, 50; CWRI 5; DLB 52; JRDA; LAIT 4; MAICYA 1, 2; MAICYAS 1; MTCW 1; SATA 13, 53, 92, 133; WYA; YAW

Patmore, Coventry Kersey Dighton
1823-1896 .... **NCLC 9**
See also DLB 35, 98; RGEL 2; TEA

Paton, Alan (Stewart) 1903-1988 ...... **CLC 4, 10, 25, 55, 106; WLC**
See also AAYA 26; AFW; BPFB 3; BRWS 2; BYA 1; CA 13-16; 125; CANR 22; CAP 1; DA; DA3; DAB; DAC; DAM MST, NOV; DLB 225; DLBD 17; EWL 3; EXPN; LAIT 4; MTCW 1, 2; NFS 3, 12; RGEL 2; SATA 11; SATA-Obit 56; TWA; WLIT 2; WWE 1

Paton Walsh, Gillian 1937- .... **CLC 35**
See Paton Walsh, Jill; Walsh, Jill Paton
See also AAYA 11; CANR 38, 83; CLR 2, 65; DLB 161; JRDA; MAICYA 1, 2; SAAS 3; SATA 4, 72, 109; YAW

Paton Walsh, Jill
See Paton Walsh, Gillian
See also AAYA 47; BYA 1, 8

Patterson, (Horace) Orlando (Lloyd)
1940- .... **BLCS**
See also BW 1; CA 65-68; CANR 27, 84; CN 7

Patton, George S(mith), Jr.
1885-1945 .... **TCLC 79**
See also CA 189

Paulding, James Kirke 1778-1860 ... **NCLC 2**
See also DLB 3, 59, 74, 250; RGAL 4

Paulin, Thomas Neilson 1949-
See Paulin, Tom
See also CA 123; 128; CANR 98; CP 7

Paulin, Tom .... **CLC 37, 177**
See Paulin, Thomas Neilson
See also DLB 40

Pausanias c. 1st cent. - .... **CMLC 36**

Paustovsky, Konstantin (Georgievich)
1892-1968 .... **CLC 40**
See also CA 93-96; 25-28R; DLB 272; EWL 3

Pavese, Cesare 1908-1950 .... **PC 13; SSC 19; TCLC 3**
See also CA 104; 169; DLB 128, 177; EW 12; EWL 3; RGSF 2; RGWL 2, 3; TWA

Pavic, Milorad 1929- .... **CLC 60**
See also CA 136; CDWLB 4; CWW 2; DLB 181; EWL 3; RGWL 3

Pavlov, Ivan Petrovich 1849-1936 . **TCLC 91**
See also CA 118; 180

Pavlova, Karolina Karlovna
1807-1893 .... **NCLC 138**
See also DLB 205

Payne, Alan
See Jakes, John (William)

Paz, Gil
See Lugones, Leopoldo

Paz, Octavio 1914-1998 . **CLC 3, 4, 6, 10, 19, 51, 65, 119; HLC 2; PC 1, 48; WLC**
See also AAYA 50; CA 73-76; 165; CANR 32, 65, 104; CWW 2; DA; DA3; DAB; DAC; DAM MST, MULT, POET; DLB 290; DLBY 1990, 1998; DNFS 1; EWL 3; HW 1, 2; LAW; LAWS 1; MTCW 1, 2; PFS 18; RGWL 2, 3; SSFS 13; TWA; WLIT 1

p'Bitek, Okot 1931-1982 .... **BLC 3; CLC 96; TCLC 149**
See also AFW; BW 2, 3; CA 124; 107; CANR 82; DAM MULT; DLB 125; EWL 3; MTCW 1, 2; RGEL 2; WLIT 2

Peacock, Molly 1947- .... **CLC 60**
See also CA 103; CAAS 21; CANR 52, 84; CP 7; CWP; DLB 120, 282

Peacock, Thomas Love
1785-1866 .... **NCLC 22**
See also BRW 4; DLB 96, 116; RGEL 2; RGSF 2

Peake, Mervyn 1911-1968 .... **CLC 7, 54**
See also CA 5-8R; 25-28R; CANR 3; DLB 15, 160, 255; FANT; MTCW 1; RGEL 2; SATA 23; SFW 4

Pearce, Philippa
See Christie, Philippa
See also CA 5-8R; CANR 4, 109; CWRI 5; FANT; MAICYA 2

Pearl, Eric
See Elman, Richard (Martin)

Pearson, T(homas) R(eid) 1956- .... **CLC 39**
See also CA 120; 130; CANR 97; CSW; INT CA-130
Peck, Dale 1967- .... **CLC 81**
See also CA 146; CANR 72, 127; GLL 2
Peck, John (Frederick) 1941- .... **CLC 3**
See also CA 49-52; CANR 3, 100; CP 7
Peck, Richard (Wayne) 1934- .... **CLC 21**
See also AAYA 1, 24; BYA 1, 6, 8, 11; CA 85-88; CANR 19, 38, 129; CLR 15; INT CANR-19; JRDA; MAICYA 1, 2; SAAS 2; SATA 18, 55, 97; SATA-Essay 110; WYA; YAW
Peck, Robert Newton 1928- .... **CLC 17**
See also AAYA 3, 43; BYA 1, 6; CA 81-84, 182; CAAE 182; CANR 31, 63, 127; CLR 45; DA; DAC; DAM MST; JRDA; LAIT 3; MAICYA 1, 2; SAAS 1; SATA 21, 62, 111; SATA-Essay 108; WYA; YAW
Peckinpah, (David) Sam(uel)
1925-1984 .... **CLC 20**
See also CA 109; 114; CANR 82
Pedersen, Knut 1859-1952
See Hamsun, Knut
See also CA 104; 119; CANR 63; MTCW 1, 2
Peeslake, Gaffer
See Durrell, Lawrence (George)
Peguy, Charles (Pierre)
1873-1914 .... **TCLC 10**
See also CA 107; 193; DLB 258; EWL 3; GFL 1789 to the Present
Peirce, Charles Sanders
1839-1914 .... **TCLC 81**
See also CA 194; DLB 270
Pellicer, Carlos 1900(?)-1977 .... **HLCS 2**
See also CA 153; 69-72; DLB 290; EWL 3; HW 1
Pena, Ramon del Valle y
See Valle-Inclan, Ramon (Maria) del
Pendennis, Arthur Esquir
See Thackeray, William Makepeace
Penn, William 1644-1718 .... **LC 25**
See also DLB 24
PEPECE
See Prado (Calvo), Pedro
Pepys, Samuel 1633-1703 ... **LC 11, 58; WLC**
See also BRW 2; CDBLB 1660-1789; DA; DA3; DAB; DAC; DAM MST; DLB 101, 213; NCFS 4; RGEL 2; TEA; WLIT 3
Percy, Thomas 1729-1811 .... **NCLC 95**
See also DLB 104
Percy, Walker 1916-1990 .... **CLC 2, 3, 6, 8, 14, 18, 47, 65**
See also AMWS 3; BPFB 3; CA 1-4R; 131; CANR 1, 23, 64; CPW; CSW; DA3; DAM NOV, POP; DLB 2; DLBY 1980, 1990; EWL 3; MTCW 1, 2; RGAL 4; TUS
Percy, William Alexander
1885-1942 .... **TCLC 84**
See also CA 163; MTCW 2
Perec, Georges 1936-1982 .... **CLC 56, 116**
See also CA 141; DLB 83; EWL 3; GFL 1789 to the Present; RGWL 3
Pereda (y Sanchez de Porrua), Jose Maria de 1833-1906 .... **TCLC 16**
See also CA 117
Pereda y Porrua, Jose Maria de
See Pereda (y Sanchez de Porrua), Jose Maria de
Peregoy, George Weems
See Mencken, H(enry) L(ouis)
Perelman, S(idney) J(oseph)
1904-1979 .. **CLC 3, 5, 9, 15, 23, 44, 49; SSC 32**
See also AITN 1, 2; BPFB 3; CA 73-76; 89-92; CANR 18; DAM DRAM; DLB 11, 44; MTCW 1, 2; RGAL 4

Peret, Benjamin 1899-1959 .... **PC 33; TCLC 20**
See also CA 117; 186; GFL 1789 to the Present
Peretz, Isaac Leib 1851(?)-1915
See Peretz, Isaac Loeb
See also CA 201
Peretz, Isaac Loeb 1851(?)-1915 ...... **SSC 26; TCLC 16**
See Peretz, Isaac Leib
See also CA 109
Peretz, Yitzkhok Leibush
See Peretz, Isaac Loeb
Perez Galdos, Benito 1843-1920 ..... **HLCS 2; TCLC 27**
See Galdos, Benito Perez
See also CA 125; 153; EWL 3; HW 1; RGWL 2, 3
Peri Rossi, Cristina 1941- .. **CLC 156; HLCS 2**
See also CA 131; CANR 59, 81; DLB 145, 290; EWL 3; HW 1, 2
Perlata
See Peret, Benjamin
Perloff, Marjorie G(abrielle)
1931- .... **CLC 137**
See also CA 57-60; CANR 7, 22, 49, 104
Perrault, Charles 1628-1703 ... **DC 12; LC 2, 56**
See also BYA 4; CLR 79; DLB 268; GFL Beginnings to 1789; MAICYA 1, 2; RGWL 2, 3; SATA 25; WCH
Perry, Anne 1938- .... **CLC 126**
See also CA 101; CANR 22, 50, 84; CMW 4; CN 7; CPW; DLB 276
Perry, Brighton
See Sherwood, Robert E(mmet)
Perse, St.-John
See Leger, (Marie-Rene Auguste) Alexis Saint-Leger
Perse, Saint-John
See Leger, (Marie-Rene Auguste) Alexis Saint-Leger
See also DLB 258; RGWL 3
Perutz, Leo(pold) 1882-1957 .... **TCLC 60**
See also CA 147; DLB 81
Peseenz, Tulio F.
See Lopez y Fuentes, Gregorio
Pesetsky, Bette 1932- .... **CLC 28**
See also CA 133; DLB 130
Peshkov, Alexei Maximovich 1868-1936
See Gorky, Maxim
See also CA 105; 141; CANR 83; DA; DAC; DAM DRAM, MST, NOV; MTCW 2
Pessoa, Fernando (Antonio Nogueira)
1888-1935 ..... **HLC 2; PC 20; TCLC 27**
See also CA 125; 183; DAM MULT; DLB 287; EW 10; EWL 3; RGWL 2, 3; WP
Peterkin, Julia Mood 1880-1961 ...... **CLC 31**
See also CA 102; DLB 9
Peters, Joan K(aren) 1945- .... **CLC 39**
See also CA 158; CANR 109
Peters, Robert L(ouis) 1924- .... **CLC 7**
See also CA 13-16R; CAAS 8; CP 7; DLB 105
Petofi, Sandor 1823-1849 .... **NCLC 21**
See also RGWL 2, 3
Petrakis, Harry Mark 1923- .... **CLC 3**
See also CA 9-12R; CANR 4, 30, 85; CN 7
Petrarch 1304-1374 .... **CMLC 20; PC 8**
See also DA3; DAM POET; EW 2; LMFS 1; RGWL 2, 3
Petronius c. 20-66 .... **CMLC 34**
See also AW 2; CDWLB 1; DLB 211; RGWL 2, 3
Petrov, Evgeny .... **TCLC 21**
See Kataev, Evgeny Petrovich

Petry, Ann (Lane) 1908-1997 .. **CLC 1, 7, 18; TCLC 112**
See also AFAW 1, 2; BPFB; BW 1, 3; BYA 2; CA 5-8R; 157; CAAS 6; CANR 4, 46; CLR 12; CN 7; DLB 76; EWL 3; JRDA; LAIT 1; MAICYA 1, 2; MAIC-YAS 1; MTCW 1; RGAL 4; SATA 5; SATA-Obit 94; TUS
Petursson, Halligrimur 1614-1674 .... **LC 8**
Peychinovich
See Vazov, Ivan (Minchov)
Phaedrus c. 15B.C.-c. 50 .... **CMLC 25**
See also DLB 211
Phelps (Ward), Elizabeth Stuart
See Phelps, Elizabeth Stuart
See also FW
Phelps, Elizabeth Stuart
1844-1911 .... **TCLC 113**
See Phelps (Ward), Elizabeth Stuart
See also DLB 74
Philips, Katherine 1632-1664 . **LC 30; PC 40**
See also DLB 131; RGEL 2
Philipson, Morris H. 1926- .... **CLC 53**
See also CA 1-4R; CANR 4
Phillips, Caryl 1958- .... **BLCS; CLC 96**
See also BRWS 5; BW 2; CA 141; CANR 63, 104; CBD; CD 5; CN 7; DA3; DAM MULT; DLB 157; EWL 3; MTCW 2; WLIT 4; WWE 1
Phillips, David Graham
1867-1911 .... **TCLC 44**
See also CA 108; 176; DLB 9, 12; RGAL 4
Phillips, Jack
See Sandburg, Carl (August)
Phillips, Jayne Anne 1952- .... **CLC 15, 33, 139; SSC 16**
See also BPFB 3; CA 101; CANR 24, 50, 96; CN 7; CSW; DLBY 1980; INT CANR-24; MTCW 1, 2; RGAL 4; RGSF 2; SSFS 4
Phillips, Richard
See Dick, Philip K(indred)
Phillips, Robert (Schaeffer) 1938- .... **CLC 28**
See also CA 17-20R; CAAS 13; CANR 8; DLB 105
Phillips, Ward
See Lovecraft, H(oward) P(hillips)
Philostratus, Flavius c. 179-c. 244 .... **CMLC 62**
Piccolo, Lucio 1901-1969 .... **CLC 13**
See also CA 97-100; DLB 114; EWL 3
Pickthall, Marjorie L(owry) C(hristie)
1883-1922 .... **TCLC 21**
See also CA 107; DLB 92
Pico della Mirandola, Giovanni
1463-1494 .... **LC 15**
See also LMFS 1
Piercy, Marge 1936- .... **CLC 3, 6, 14, 18, 27, 62, 128; PC 29**
See also BPFB 3; CA 21-24R; 187; CAAE 187; CAAS 1; CANR 13, 43, 66, 111; CN 7; CP 7; CWP; DLB 120, 227; EXPP; FW; MTCW 1, 2; PFS 9; SFW 4
Piers, Robert
See Anthony, Piers
Pieyre de Mandiargues, Andre 1909-1991
See Mandiargues, Andre Pieyre de
See also CA 103; 136; CANR 22, 82; EWL 3; GFL 1789 to the Present
Pilnyak, Boris 1894-1938 . **SSC 48; TCLC 23**
See Vogau, Boris Andreyevich
See also EWL 3
Pinchback, Eugene
See Toomer, Jean
Pincherle, Alberto 1907-1990 ...... **CLC 11, 18**
See Moravia, Alberto
See also CA 25-28R; 132; CANR 33, 63; DAM NOV; MTCW 1

Pinckney, Darryl 1953- .... **CLC 76**
See also BW 2, 3; CA 143; CANR 79

Pindar 518(?)B.C.-438(?)B.C. .... **CMLC 12; PC 19**
See also AW 1; CDWLB 1; DLB 176; RGWL 2

Pineda, Cecile 1942- .... **CLC 39**
See also CA 118; DLB 209

Pinero, Arthur Wing 1855-1934 .... **TCLC 32**
See also CA 110; 153; DAM DRAM; DLB 10; RGEL 2

Pinero, Miguel (Antonio Gomez) 1946-1988 .... **CLC 4, 55**
See also CA 61-64; 125; CAD; CANR 29, 90; DLB 266; HW 1; LLW 1

Pinget, Robert 1919-1997 .... **CLC 7, 13, 37**
See also CA 85-88; 160; CWW 2; DLB 83; EWL 3; GFL 1789 to the Present

Pink Floyd
See Barrett, (Roger) Syd; Gilmour, David; Mason, Nick; Waters, Roger; Wright, Rick

Pinkney, Edward 1802-1828 .... **NCLC 31**
See also DLB 248

Pinkwater, Daniel
See Pinkwater, Daniel Manus

Pinkwater, Daniel Manus 1941- ...... **CLC 35**
See also AAYA 1, 46; BYA 9; CA 29-32R; CANR 12, 38, 89; CLR 4; CSW; FANT; JRDA; MAICYA 1, 2; SAAS 3; SATA 8, 46, 76, 114; SFW 4; YAW

Pinkwater, Manus
See Pinkwater, Daniel Manus

Pinsky, Robert 1940- .... **CLC 9, 19, 38, 94, 121; PC 27**
See also AMWS 6; CA 29-32R; CAAS 4; CANR 58, 97; CP 7; DA3; DAM POET; DLBY 1982; MTCW 2; PFS 18; RGAL 4

Pinta, Harold
See Pinter, Harold

Pinter, Harold 1930- .. **CLC 1, 3, 6, 9, 11, 15, 27, 58, 73; DC 15; WLC**
See also BRWR 1; BRWS 1; CA 5-8R; CANR 33, 65, 112; CBD; CD 5; CDBLB 1960 to Present; DA; DA3; DAB; DAC; DAM DRAM, MST; DFS 3, 4, 5, 7, 14; DLB 13; EWL 3; IDFW 3, 4; LMFS 2; MTCW 1, 2; RGEL 2; TEA

Piozzi, Hester Lynch (Thrale) 1741-1821 .... **NCLC 57**
See also DLB 104, 142

Pirandello, Luigi 1867-1936 .. **DC 5; SSC 22; TCLC 4, 29; WLC**
See also CA 104; 153; CANR 103; DA; DA3; DAB; DAC; DAM DRAM, MST; DFS 4, 9; DLB 264; EW 8; EWL 3; MTCW 2; RGSF 2; RGWL 2, 3

Pirsig, Robert M(aynard) 1928- ... **CLC 4, 6, 73**
See also CA 53-56; CANR 42, 74; CPW 1; DA3; DAM POP; MTCW 1, 2; SATA 39

Pisarev, Dmitrii Ivanovich
See Pisarev, Dmitry Ivanovich
See also DLB 277

Pisarev, Dmitry Ivanovich 1840-1868 .... **NCLC 25**
See Pisarev, Dmitrii Ivanovich

Pix, Mary (Griffith) 1666-1709 .... **LC 8**
See also DLB 80

Pixerecourt, (Rene Charles) Guilbert de 1773-1844 .... **NCLC 39**
See also DLB 192; GFL 1789 to the Present

Plaatje, Sol(omon) T(shekisho) 1878-1932 .... **BLCS; TCLC 73**
See also BW 2, 3; CA 141; CANR 79; DLB 125, 225

Plaidy, Jean
See Hibbert, Eleanor Alice Burford

Planche, James Robinson 1796-1880 .... **NCLC 42**
See also RGEL 2

Plant, Robert 1948- .... **CLC 12**

Plante, David (Robert) 1940- . **CLC 7, 23, 38**
See also CA 37-40R; CANR 12, 36, 58, 82; CN 7; DAM NOV; DLBY 1983; INT CANR-12; MTCW 1

Plath, Sylvia 1932-1963 ..... **CLC 1, 2, 3, 5, 9, 11, 14, 17, 50, 51, 62, 111; PC 1, 37; WLC**
See also AAYA 13; AMWR 2; AMWS 1; BPFB 3; CA 19-20; CANR 34, 101; CAP 2; CDALB 1941-1968; DA; DA3; DAB; DAC; DAM MST, POET; DLB 5, 6, 152; EWL 3; EXPN; EXPP; FW; LAIT 4; MAWW; MTCW 1, 2; NFS 1; PAB; PFS 1, 15; RGAL 4; SATA 96; TUS; WP; YAW

Plato c. 428B.C.-347B.C. ... **CMLC 8; WLCS**
See also AW 1; CDWLB 1; DA; DA3; DAB; DAC; DAM MST; DLB 176; LAIT 1; LATS 1; RGWL 2, 3

Platonov, Andrei
See Klimentov, Andrei Platonovich

Platonov, Andrei Platonovich
See Klimentov, Andrei Platonovich
See also DLB 272

Platonov, Andrey Platonovich
See Klimentov, Andrei Platonovich
See also EWL 3

Platt, Kin 1911- .... **CLC 26**
See also AAYA 11; CA 17-20R; CANR 11; JRDA; SAAS 17; SATA 21, 86; WYA

Plautus c. 254B.C.-c. 184B.C. .... **CMLC 24; DC 6**
See also AW 1; CDWLB 1; DLB 211; RGWL 2, 3

Plick et Plock
See Simenon, Georges (Jacques Christian)

Plieksans, Janis
See Rainis, Janis

Plimpton, George (Ames) 1927-2003 .... **CLC 36**
See also AITN 1; CA 21-24R; CANR 32, 70, 103; DLB 185, 241; MTCW 1, 2; SATA 10

Pliny the Elder c. 23-79 .... **CMLC 23**
See also DLB 211

Pliny the Younger c. 61-c. 112 .... **CMLC 62**
See also AW 2; DLB 211

Plomer, William Charles Franklin 1903-1973 .... **CLC 4, 8**
See also AFW; CA 21-22; CANR 34; CAP 2; DLB 20, 162, 191, 225; EWL 3; MTCW 1; RGEL 2; RGSF 2; SATA 24

Plotinus 204-270 .... **CMLC 46**
See also CDWLB 1; DLB 176

Plowman, Piers
See Kavanagh, Patrick (Joseph)

Plum, J.
See Wodehouse, P(elham) G(renville)

Plumly, Stanley (Ross) 1939- .... **CLC 33**
See also CA 108; 110; CANR 97; CP 7; DLB 5, 193; INT CA-110

Plumpe, Friedrich Wilhelm 1888-1931 .... **TCLC 53**
See also CA 112

Plutarch c. 46-c. 120 .... **CMLC 60**
See also AW 2; CDWLB 1; DLB 176; RGWL 2, 3; TWA

Po Chu-i 772-846 .... **CMLC 24**

Podhoretz, Norman 1930- .... **CLC 189**
See also AMWS 8; CA 9-12R; CANR 7, 78

Poe, Edgar Allan 1809-1849 ..... **NCLC 1, 16, 55, 78, 94, 97, 117; PC 1, 54; SSC 1, 22, 34, 35, 54; WLC**
See also AAYA 14; AMW; AMWC 1; AMWR 2; BPFB 3; BYA 5, 11; CDALB 1640-1865; CMW 4; DA; DA3; DAB; DAC; DAM MST, POET; DLB 3, 59, 73, 74, 248, 254; EXPP; EXPS; HGG; LAIT 2; LATS 1; LMFS 1; MSW; PAB; PFS 1, 3, 9; RGAL 4; RGSF 2; SATA 23; SCFW 2; SFW 4; SSFS 2, 4, 7, 8, 16; SUFW; TUS; WP; WYA

Poet of Titchfield Street, The
See Pound, Ezra (Weston Loomis)

Pohl, Frederik 1919- .... **CLC 18; SSC 25**
See also AAYA 24; CA 61-64, 188; CAAE 188; CAAS 1; CANR 11, 37, 81; CN 7; DLB 8; INT CANR-11; MTCW 1, 2; SATA 24; SCFW 2; SFW 4

Poirier, Louis 1910-
See Gracq, Julien
See also CA 122; 126; CWW 2

Poitier, Sidney 1927- .... **CLC 26**
See also BW 1; CA 117; CANR 94

Pokagon, Simon 1830-1899 .... **NNAL**
See also DAM MULT

Polanski, Roman 1933- .... **CLC 16, 178**
See also CA 77-80

Poliakoff, Stephen 1952- .... **CLC 38**
See also CA 106; CANR 116; CBD; CD 5; DLB 13

Police, The
See Copeland, Stewart (Armstrong); Summers, Andrew James

Polidori, John William 1795-1821 . **NCLC 51**
See also DLB 116; HGG

Pollitt, Katha 1949- .... **CLC 28, 122**
See also CA 120; 122; CANR 66, 108; MTCW 1, 2

Pollock, (Mary) Sharon 1936- .... **CLC 50**
See also CA 141; CD 5; CWD; DAC; DAM DRAM, MST; DFS 3; DLB 60; FW

Pollock, Sharon 1936- .... **DC 20**

Polo, Marco 1254-1324 .... **CMLC 15**

Polonsky, Abraham (Lincoln) 1910-1999 .... **CLC 92**
See also CA 104; 187; DLB 26; INT CA-104

Polybius c. 200B.C.-c. 118B.C. .... **CMLC 17**
See also AW 1; DLB 176; RGWL 2, 3

Pomerance, Bernard 1940- .... **CLC 13**
See also CA 101; CAD; CANR 49; CD 5; DAM DRAM; DFS 9; LAIT 2

Ponge, Francis 1899-1988 .... **CLC 6, 18**
See also CA 85-88; 126; CANR 40, 86; DAM POET; DLBY 2002; EWL 3; GFL 1789 to the Present; RGWL 2, 3

Poniatowska, Elena 1933- . **CLC 140; HLC 2**
See also CA 101; CANR 32, 66, 107; CD-WLB 3; DAM MULT; DLB 113; EWL 3; HW 1, 2; LAWS 1; WLIT 1

Pontoppidan, Henrik 1857-1943 .... **TCLC 29**
See also CA 170

Poole, Josephine .... **CLC 17**
See Helyar, Jane Penelope Josephine
See also SAAS 2; SATA 5

Popa, Vasko 1922-1991 .... **CLC 19**
See also CA 112; 148; CDWLB 4; DLB 181; EWL 3; RGWL 2, 3

Pope, Alexander 1688-1744 ...... **LC 3, 58, 60, 64; PC 26; WLC**
See also BRW 3; BRWC 1; BRWR 1; CD-BLB 1660-1789; DA; DA3; DAB; DAC; DAM MST, POET; DLB 95, 101, 213; EXPP; PAB; PFS 12; RGEL 2; WLIT 3; WP

Popov, Evgenii Anatol'evich
See Popov, Yevgeny
See also DLB 285

Popov, Yevgeny .... **CLC 59**
See Popov, Evgenii Anatol'evich

Poquelin, Jean-Baptiste
See Moliere

Porter, Connie (Rose) 1959(?)- .... **CLC 70**
See also BW 2, 3; CA 142; CANR 90, 109; SATA 81, 129

Porter, Gene(va Grace) Stratton .. **TCLC 21**
See Stratton-Porter, Gene(va Grace)
See also BPFB 3; CA 112; CWRI 5; RHW

Porter, Katherine Anne 1890-1980 ... **CLC 1, 3, 7, 10, 13, 15, 27, 101; SSC 4, 31, 43**
See also AAYA 42; AITN 2; AMW; BPFB 3; CA 1-4R; 101; CANR 1, 65; CDALBS; DA; DA3; DAB; DAC; DAM MST, NOV; DLB 4, 9, 102; DLBD 12; DLBY 1980; EWL 3; EXPS; LAIT 3; MAWW; MTCW 1, 2; NFS 14; RGAL 4; RGSF 2; SATA 39; SATA-Obit 23; SSFS 1, 8, 11, 16; TUS

Porter, Peter (Neville Frederick)
1929- .... **CLC 5, 13, 33**
See also CA 85-88; CP 7; DLB 40, 289; WWE 1

Porter, William Sydney 1862-1910
See Henry, O.
See also CA 104; 131; CDALB 1865-1917; DA; DA3; DAB; DAC; DAM MST; DLB 12, 78, 79; MTCW 1, 2; TUS; YABC 2

Portillo (y Pacheco), Jose Lopez
See Lopez Portillo (y Pacheco), Jose

Portillo Trambley, Estela 1927-1998 .. **HLC 2**
See Trambley, Estela Portillo
See also CANR 32; DAM MULT; DLB 209; HW 1

Posey, Alexander (Lawrence)
1873-1908 .... **NNAL**
See also CA 144; CANR 80; DAM MULT; DLB 175

Posse, Abel .... **CLC 70**

Post, Melville Davisson
1869-1930 .... **TCLC 39**
See also CA 110; 202; CMW 4

Potok, Chaim 1929-2002 ... **CLC 2, 7, 14, 26, 112**
See also AAYA 15, 50; AITN 1, 2; BPFB 3; BYA 1; CA 17-20R; 208; CANR 19, 35, 64, 98; CLR 92; CN 7; DA3; DAM NOV; DLB 28, 152; EXPN; INT CANR-19; LAIT 4; MTCW 1, 2; NFS 4; SATA 33, 106; SATA-Obit 134; TUS; YAW

Potok, Herbert Harold -2002
See Potok, Chaim

Potok, Herman Harold
See Potok, Chaim

Potter, Dennis (Christopher George)
1935-1994 .... **CLC 58, 86, 123**
See also CA 107; 145; CANR 33, 61; CBD; DLB 233; MTCW 1

Pound, Ezra (Weston Loomis)
1885-1972 .. **CLC 1, 2, 3, 4, 5, 7, 10, 13, 18, 34, 48, 50, 112; PC 4; WLC**
See also AAYA 47; AMW; AMWR 1; CA 5-8R; 37-40R; CANR 40; CDALB 1917-1929; DA; DA3; DAB; DAC; DAM MST, POET; DLB 4, 45, 63; DLBD 15; EFS 2; EWL 3; EXPP; LMFS 2; MTCW 1, 2; PAB; PFS 2, 8, 16; RGAL 4; TUS; WP

Povod, Reinaldo 1959-1994 .... **CLC 44**
See also CA 136; 146; CANR 83

Powell, Adam Clayton, Jr.
1908-1972 .... **BLC 3; CLC 89**
See also BW 1, 3; CA 102; 33-36R; CANR 86; DAM MULT

Powell, Anthony (Dymoke)
1905-2000 .... **CLC 1, 3, 7, 9, 10, 31**
See also BRW 7; CA 1-4R; 189; CANR 1, 32, 62, 107; CDBLB 1945-1960; CN 7; DLB 15; EWL 3; MTCW 1, 2; RGEL 2; TEA

Powell, Dawn 1896(?)-1965 .... **CLC 66**
See also CA 5-8R; CANR 121; DLBY 1997

Powell, Padgett 1952- .... **CLC 34**
See also CA 126; CANR 63, 101; CSW; DLB 234; DLBY 01

Powell, (Oval) Talmage 1920-2000
See Queen, Ellery
See also CA 5-8R; CANR 2, 80

Power, Susan 1961- .... **CLC 91**
See also BYA 14; CA 160; NFS 11

Powers, J(ames) F(arl) 1917-1999 ..... **CLC 1, 4, 8, 57; SSC 4**
See also CA 1-4R; 181; CANR 2, 61; CN 7; DLB 130; MTCW 1; RGAL 4; RGSF 2

Powers, John J(ames) 1945-
See Powers, John R.
See also CA 69-72

Powers, John R. .... **CLC 66**
See Powers, John J(ames)

Powers, Richard (S.) 1957- .... **CLC 93**
See also AMWS 9; BPFB 3; CA 148; CANR 80; CN 7

Pownall, David 1938- .... **CLC 10**
See also CA 89-92, 180; CAAS 18; CANR 49, 101; CBD; CD 5; CN 7; DLB 14

Powys, John Cowper 1872-1963 ... **CLC 7, 9, 15, 46, 125**
See also CA 85-88; CANR 106; DLB 15, 255; EWL 3; FANT; MTCW 1, 2; RGEL 2; SUFW

Powys, T(heodore) F(rancis)
1875-1953 .... **TCLC 9**
See also BRWS 8; CA 106; 189; DLB 36, 162; EWL 3; FANT; RGEL 2; SUFW

Prado (Calvo), Pedro 1886-1952 ... **TCLC 75**
See also CA 131; DLB 283; HW 1; LAW

Prager, Emily 1952- .... **CLC 56**
See also CA 204

Pratolini, Vasco 1913-1991 .... **TCLC 124**
See also CA 211; DLB 177; EWL 3; RGWL 2, 3

Pratt, E(dwin) J(ohn) 1883(?)-1964 . **CLC 19**
See also CA 141; 93-96; CANR 77; DAC; DAM POET; DLB 92; EWL 3; RGEL 2; TWA

Premchand .... **TCLC 21**
See Srivastava, Dhanpat Rai
See also EWL 3

Preseren, France 1800-1849 .... **NCLC 127**
See also CDWLB 4; DLB 147

Preussler, Otfried 1923- .... **CLC 17**
See also CA 77-80; SATA 24

Prevert, Jacques (Henri Marie)
1900-1977 .... **CLC 15**
See also CA 77-80; 69-72; CANR 29, 61; DLB 258; EWL 3; GFL 1789 to the Present; IDFW 3, 4; MTCW 1; RGWL 2, 3; SATA-Obit 30

Prevost, (Antoine Francois)
1697-1763 .... **LC 1**
See also EW 4; GFL Beginnings to 1789; RGWL 2, 3

Price, (Edward) Reynolds 1933- ... **CLC 3, 6, 13, 43, 50, 63; SSC 22**
See also AMWS 6; CA 1-4R; CANR 1, 37, 57, 87, 128; CN 7; CSW; DAM NOV; DLB 2, 218, 278; EWL 3; INT CANR-37; NFS 18

Price, Richard 1949- .... **CLC 6, 12**
See also CA 49-52; CANR 3; DLBY 1981

Prichard, Katharine Susannah
1883-1969 .... **CLC 46**
See also CA 11-12; CANR 33; CAP 1; DLB 260; MTCW 1; RGEL 2; RGSF 2; SATA 66

Priestley, J(ohn) B(oynton)
1894-1984 .... **CLC 2, 5, 9, 34**
See also BRW 7; CA 9-12R; 113; CANR 33; CDBLB 1914-1945; DA3; DAM DRAM, NOV; DLB 10, 34, 77, 100, 139; DLBY 1984; EWL 3; MTCW 1, 2; RGEL 2; SFW 4

Prince 1958- .... **CLC 35**
See also CA 213

Prince, F(rank) T(empleton)
1912-2003 .... **CLC 22**
See also CA 101; 219; CANR 43, 79; CP 7; DLB 20

Prince Kropotkin
See Kropotkin, Peter (Aleksieevich)

Prior, Matthew 1664-1721 .... **LC 4**
See also DLB 95; RGEL 2

Prishvin, Mikhail 1873-1954 .... **TCLC 75**
See Prishvin, Mikhail Mikhailovich

Prishvin, Mikhail Mikhailovich
See Prishvin, Mikhail
See also DLB 272; EWL 3

Pritchard, William H(arrison)
1932- .... **CLC 34**
See also CA 65-68; CANR 23, 95; DLB 111

Pritchett, V(ictor) S(awdon)
1900-1997 ... **CLC 5, 13, 15, 41; SSC 14**
See also BPFB 3; BRWS 3; CA 61-64; 157; CANR 31, 63; CN 7; DA3; DAM NOV; DLB 15, 139; EWL 3; MTCW 1, 2; RGEL 2; RGSF 2; TEA

Private 19022
See Manning, Frederic

Probst, Mark 1925- .... **CLC 59**
See also CA 130

Prokosch, Frederic 1908-1989 ...... **CLC 4, 48**
See also CA 73-76; 128; CANR 82; DLB 48; MTCW 2

Propertius, Sextus c. 50B.C.-c.
16B.C. .... **CMLC 32**
See also AW 2; CDWLB 1; DLB 211; RGWL 2, 3

Prophet, The
See Dreiser, Theodore (Herman Albert)

Prose, Francine 1947- .... **CLC 45**
See also CA 109; 112; CANR 46, 95; DLB 234; SATA 101, 149

Proudhon
See Cunha, Euclides (Rodrigues Pimenta) da

Proulx, Annie
See Proulx, E(dna) Annie

Proulx, E(dna) Annie 1935- ...... **CLC 81, 158**
See also AMWS 7; BPFB 3; CA 145; CANR 65, 110; CN 7; CPW 1; DA3; DAM POP; MTCW 2; SSFS 18

Proust, (Valentin-Louis-George-Eugene)
Marcel 1871-1922 .... **TCLC 7, 13, 33; WLC**
See also BPFB 3; CA 104; 120; CANR 110; DA; DA3; DAB; DAC; DAM MST, NOV; DLB 65; EW 8; EWL 3; GFL 1789 to the Present; MTCW 1, 2; RGWL 2, 3; TWA

Prowler, Harley
See Masters, Edgar Lee

Prus, Boleslaw 1845-1912 .... **TCLC 48**
See also RGWL 2, 3

Pryor, Richard (Franklin Lenox Thomas)
1940- .... **CLC 26**
See also CA 122; 152

Przybyszewski, Stanislaw
1868-1927 .... **TCLC 36**
See also CA 160; DLB 66; EWL 3

Pteleon
See Grieve, C(hristopher) M(urray)
See also DAM POET

Puckett, Lute
See Masters, Edgar Lee

Puig, Manuel 1932-1990 .... **CLC 3, 5, 10, 28, 65, 133; HLC 2**
See also BPFB 3; CA 45-48; CANR 2, 32, 63; CDWLB 3; DA3; DAM MULT; DLB 113; DNFS 1; EWL 3; GLL 1; HW 1, 2; LAW; MTCW 1, 2; RGWL 2, 3; TWA; WLIT 1

Pulitzer, Joseph 1847-1911 .... **TCLC 76**
See also CA 114; DLB 23

Purchas, Samuel 1577(?)-1626 .... **LC 70**
See also DLB 151

Purdy, A(lfred) W(ellington)
1918-2000 .... **CLC 3, 6, 14, 50**
See also CA 81-84; 189; CAAS 17; CANR 42, 66; CP 7; DAC; DAM MST, POET; DLB 88; PFS 5; RGEL 2

Purdy, James (Amos) 1923- .... **CLC 2, 4, 10, 28, 52**
See also AMWS 7; CA 33-36R; CAAS 1; CANR 19, 51; CN 7; DLB 2, 218; EWL 3; INT CANR-19; MTCW 1; RGAL 4

Pure, Simon
See Swinnerton, Frank Arthur

Pushkin, Aleksandr Sergeevich
See Pushkin, Alexander (Sergeyevich)
See also DLB 205

Pushkin, Alexander (Sergeyevich)
1799-1837 .... **NCLC 3, 27, 83; PC 10; SSC 27, 55; WLC**
See Pushkin, Aleksandr Sergeevich
See also DA; DA3; DAB; DAC; DAM DRAM, MST, POET; EW 5; EXPS; RGSF 2; RGWL 2, 3; SATA 61; SSFS 9; TWA

P'u Sung-ling 1640-1715 .... **LC 49; SSC 31**

Putnam, Arthur Lee
See Alger, Horatio, Jr.

Puzo, Mario 1920-1999 .... **CLC 1, 2, 6, 36, 107**
See also BPFB 3; CA 65-68; 185; CANR 4, 42, 65, 99; CN 7; CPW; DA3; DAM NOV, POP; DLB 6; MTCW 1, 2; NFS 16; RGAL 4

Pygge, Edward
See Barnes, Julian (Patrick)

Pyle, Ernest Taylor 1900-1945
See Pyle, Ernie
See also CA 115; 160

Pyle, Ernie .... **TCLC 75**
See Pyle, Ernest Taylor
See also DLB 29; MTCW 2

Pyle, Howard 1853-1911 .... **TCLC 81**
See also BYA 2, 4; CA 109; 137; CLR 22; DLB 42, 188; DLBD 13; LAIT 1; MAICYA 1, 2; SATA 16, 100; WCH; YAW

Pym, Barbara (Mary Crampton)
1913-1980 .... **CLC 13, 19, 37, 111**
See also BPFB 3; BRWS 2; CA 13-14; 97-100; CANR 13, 34; CAP 1; DLB 14, 207; DLBY 1987; EWL 3; MTCW 1, 2; RGEL 2; TEA

Pynchon, Thomas (Ruggles, Jr.)
1937- ...... **CLC 2, 3, 6, 9, 11, 18, 33, 62, 72, 123; SSC 14; WLC**
See also AMWS 2; BEST 90:2; BPFB 3; CA 17-20R; CANR 22, 46, 73; CN 7; CPW 1; DA; DA3; DAB; DAC; DAM MST, NOV, POP; DLB 173; EWL 3; MTCW 1, 2; RGAL 4; SFW 4; TUS

Pythagoras c. 582B.C.-c. 507B.C. . **CMLC 22**
See also DLB 176

Q
See Quiller-Couch, Sir Arthur (Thomas)

Qian, Chongzhu
See Ch'ien, Chung-shu

Qian Zhongshu
See Ch'ien, Chung-shu
See also CWW 2

Qroll
See Dagerman, Stig (Halvard)

Quarrington, Paul (Lewis) 1953- ..... **CLC 65**
See also CA 129; CANR 62, 95

Quasimodo, Salvatore 1901-1968 .... **CLC 10; PC 47**
See also CA 13-16; 25-28R; CAP 1; DLB 114; EW 12; EWL 3; MTCW 1; RGWL 2, 3

Quatermass, Martin
See Carpenter, John (Howard)

Quay, Stephen 1947- .... **CLC 95**
See also CA 189

Quay, Timothy 1947- .... **CLC 95**
See also CA 189

Queen, Ellery .... **CLC 3, 11**
See Dannay, Frederic; Davidson, Avram (James); Deming, Richard; Fairman, Paul W.; Flora, Fletcher; Hoch, Edward D(entinger); Kane, Henry; Lee, Manfred B(ennington); Marlowe, Stephen; Powell, (Oval) Talmage; Sheldon, Walter J(ames); Sturgeon, Theodore (Hamilton); Tracy, Don(ald Fiske); Vance, John Holbrook
See also BPFB 3; CMW 4; MSW; RGAL 4

Queen, Ellery, Jr.
See Dannay, Frederic; Lee, Manfred B(ennington)

Queneau, Raymond 1903-1976 ..... **CLC 2, 5, 10, 42**
See also CA 77-80; 69-72; CANR 32; DLB 72, 258; EW 12; EWL 3; GFL 1789 to the Present; MTCW 1, 2; RGWL 2, 3

Quevedo, Francisco de 1580-1645 .... **LC 23**

Quiller-Couch, Sir Arthur (Thomas)
1863-1944 .... **TCLC 53**
See also CA 118; 166; DLB 135, 153, 190; HGG; RGEL 2; SUFW 1

Quin, Ann (Marie) 1936-1973 .... **CLC 6**
See also CA 9-12R; 45-48; DLB 14, 231

Quincey, Thomas de
See De Quincey, Thomas

Quinn, Martin
See Smith, Martin Cruz

Quinn, Peter 1947- .... **CLC 91**
See also CA 197

Quinn, Simon
See Smith, Martin Cruz

Quintana, Leroy V. 1944- ...... **HLC 2; PC 36**
See also CA 131; CANR 65; DAM MULT; DLB 82; HW 1, 2

Quiroga, Horacio (Sylvestre)
1878-1937 .... **HLC 2; TCLC 20**
See also CA 117; 131; DAM MULT; EWL 3; HW 1; LAW; MTCW 1; RGSF 2; WLIT 1

Quoirez, Francoise 1935- .... **CLC 9**
See Sagan, Francoise
See also CA 49-52; CANR 6, 39, 73; CWW 2; MTCW 1, 2; TWA

Raabe, Wilhelm (Karl) 1831-1910 . **TCLC 45**
See also CA 167; DLB 129

Rabe, David (William) 1940- .. **CLC 4, 8, 33; DC 16**
See also CA 85-88; CABS 3; CAD; CANR 59, 129; CD 5; DAM DRAM; DFS 3, 8, 13; DLB 7, 228; EWL 3

Rabelais, Francois 1494-1553 .... **LC 5, 60; WLC**
See also DA; DAB; DAC; DAM MST; EW 2; GFL Beginnings to 1789; LMFS 1; RGWL 2, 3; TWA

Rabinovitch, Sholem 1859-1916
See Aleichem, Sholom
See also CA 104

Rabinyan, Dorit 1972- .... **CLC 119**
See also CA 170

Rachilde
See Vallette, Marguerite Eymery; Vallette, Marguerite Eymery
See also EWL 3

Racine, Jean 1639-1699 .... **LC 28**
See also DA3; DAB; DAM MST; DLB 268; EW 3; GFL Beginnings to 1789; LMFS 1; RGWL 2, 3; TWA

Radcliffe, Ann (Ward) 1764-1823 ... **NCLC 6, 55, 106**
See also DLB 39, 178; HGG; LMFS 1; RGEL 2; SUFW; WLIT 3

Radclyffe-Hall, Marguerite
See Hall, (Marguerite) Radclyffe

Radiguet, Raymond 1903-1923 ...... **TCLC 29**
See also CA 162; DLB 65; EWL 3; GFL 1789 to the Present; RGWL 2, 3

Radnoti, Miklos 1909-1944 .... **TCLC 16**
See also CA 118; 212; CDWLB 4; DLB 215; EWL 3; RGWL 2, 3

Rado, James 1939- .... **CLC 17**
See also CA 105

Radvanyi, Netty 1900-1983
See Seghers, Anna
See also CA 85-88; 110; CANR 82

Rae, Ben
See Griffiths, Trevor

Raeburn, John (Hay) 1941- .... **CLC 34**
See also CA 57-60

Ragni, Gerome 1942-1991 .... **CLC 17**
See also CA 105; 134

Rahv, Philip .... **CLC 24**
See Greenberg, Ivan
See also DLB 137

Raimund, Ferdinand Jakob
1790-1836 .... **NCLC 69**
See also DLB 90

Raine, Craig (Anthony) 1944- .. **CLC 32, 103**
See also CA 108; CANR 29, 51, 103; CP 7; DLB 40; PFS 7

Raine, Kathleen (Jessie) 1908-2003 .. **CLC 7, 45**
See also CA 85-88; 218; CANR 46, 109; CP 7; DLB 20; EWL 3; MTCW 1; RGEL 2

Rainis, Janis 1865-1929 .... **TCLC 29**
See also CA 170; CDWLB 4; DLB 220; EWL 3

Rakosi, Carl .... **CLC 47**
See Rawley, Callman
See also CAAS 5; CP 7; DLB 193

Ralegh, Sir Walter
See Raleigh, Sir Walter
See also BRW 1; RGEL 2; WP

Raleigh, Richard
See Lovecraft, H(oward) P(hillips)

Raleigh, Sir Walter 1554(?)-1618 .... **LC 31, 39; PC 31**
See Ralegh, Sir Walter
See also CDBLB Before 1660; DLB 172; EXPP, PFS 14, TEA

Rallentando, H. P.
See Sayers, Dorothy L(eigh)

Ramal, Walter
See de la Mare, Walter (John)

Ramana Maharshi 1879-1950 .... **TCLC 84**

Ramoacn y Cajal, Santiago
1852-1934 .... **TCLC 93**

Ramon, Juan
See Jimenez (Mantecon), Juan Ramon

Ramos, Graciliano 1892-1953 .... **TCLC 32**
See also CA 167; EWL 3; HW 2; LAW; WLIT 1

Rampersad, Arnold 1941- .... **CLC 44**
See also BW 2, 3; CA 127; 133; CANR 81; DLB 111; INT CA-133

Rampling, Anne
See Rice, Anne
See also GLL 2

Ramsay, Allan 1686(?)-1758 .... **LC 29**
See also DLB 95; RGEL 2

Ramsay, Jay
See Campbell, (John) Ramsey

Ramuz, Charles-Ferdinand
1878-1947 .... **TCLC 33**
See also CA 165; EWL 3

Rand, Ayn 1905-1982 ...... **CLC 3, 30, 44, 79; WLC**
See also AAYA 10; AMWS 4; BPFB 3; BYA 12; CA 13-16R; 105; CANR 27, 73; CDALBS; CPW; DA; DA3; DAC; DAM MST, NOV, POP; DLB 227, 279; MTCW 1, 2; NFS 10, 16; RGAL 4; SFW 4; TUS; YAW

Randall, Dudley (Felker) 1914-2000 . **BLC 3; CLC 1, 135**
See also BW 1, 3; CA 25-28R; 189; CANR 23, 82; DAM MULT; DLB 41; PFS 5

Randall, Robert
See Silverberg, Robert

Ranger, Ken
See Creasey, John

Rank, Otto 1884-1939 .... **TCLC 115**

Ransom, John Crowe 1888-1974 .. **CLC 2, 4, 5, 11, 24**
See also AMW; CA 5-8R; 49-52; CANR 6, 34; CDALBS; DA3; DAM POET; DLB 45, 63; EWL 3; EXPP; MTCW 1, 2; RGAL 4; TUS

Rao, Raja 1909- .... **CLC 25, 56**
See also CA 73-76; CANR 51; CN 7; DAM NOV; EWL 3; MTCW 1, 2; RGEL 2; RGSF 2

Raphael, Frederic (Michael) 1931- ... **CLC 2, 14**
See also CA 1-4R; CANR 1, 86; CN 7; DLB 14

Ratcliffe, James P.
See Mencken, H(enry) L(ouis)

Rathbone, Julian 1935- .... **CLC 41**
See also CA 101; CANR 34, 73

Rattigan, Terence (Mervyn)
1911-1977 .... **CLC 7; DC 18**
See also BRWS 7; CA 85-88; 73-76; CBD; CDBLB 1945-1960; DAM DRAM; DFS 8; DLB 13; IDFW 3, 4; MTCW 1, 2; RGEL 2

Ratushinskaya, Irina 1954- .... **CLC 54**
See also CA 129; CANR 68; CWW 2

Raven, Simon (Arthur Noel)
1927-2001 .... **CLC 14**
See also CA 81-84; 197; CANR 86; CN 7; DLB 271

Ravenna, Michael
See Welty, Eudora (Alice)

Rawley, Callman 1903-
See Rakosi, Carl
See also CA 21-24R; CANR 12, 32, 91

Rawlings, Marjorie Kinnan
1896-1953 .... **TCLC 4**
See also AAYA 20; AMWS 10; ANW; BPFB 3; BYA 3; CA 104; 137; CANR 74; CLR 63; DLB 9, 22, 102; DLBD 17; JRDA; MAICYA 1, 2; MTCW 2; RGAL 4; SATA 100; WCH; YABC 1; YAW

Ray, Satyajit 1921-1992 .... **CLC 16, 76**
See also CA 114; 137; DAM MULT

Read, Herbert Edward 1893-1968 ..... **CLC 4**
See also BRW 6; CA 85-88; 25-28R; DLB 20, 149; EWL 3; PAB; RGEL 2

Read, Piers Paul 1941- .... **CLC 4, 10, 25**
See also CA 21-24R; CANR 38, 86; CN 7; DLB 14; SATA 21

Reade, Charles 1814-1884 .... **NCLC 2, 74**
See also DLB 21; RGEL 2

Reade, Hamish
See Gray, Simon (James Holliday)

Reading, Peter 1946- .... **CLC 47**
See also BRWS 8; CA 103; CANR 46, 96; CP 7; DLB 40

Reaney, James 1926- .... **CLC 13**
See also CA 41-44R; CAAS 15; CANR 42; CD 5; CP 7; DAC; DAM MST; DLB 68; RGEL 2; SATA 43

Rebreanu, Liviu 1885-1944 .... **TCLC 28**
See also CA 165; DLB 220; EWL 3

Rechy, John (Francisco) 1934- ...... **CLC 1, 7, 14, 18, 107; HLC 2**
See also CA 5-8R, 195; CAAE 195; CAAS 4; CANR 6, 32, 64; CN 7; DAM MULT; DLB 122, 278; DLBY 1982; HW 1, 2; INT CANR-6; LLW 1; RGAL 4

Redcam, Tom 1870-1933 .... **TCLC 25**

Reddin, Keith .... **CLC 67**
See also CAD

Redgrove, Peter (William)
1932-2003 .... **CLC 6, 41**
See also BRWS 6; CA 1-4R; 217; CANR 3, 39, 77; CP 7; DLB 40

Redmon, Anne .... **CLC 22**
See Nightingale, Anne Redmon
See also DLBY 1986

Reed, Eliot
See Ambler, Eric

Reed, Ishmael 1938- ...... **BLC 3; CLC 2, 3, 5, 6, 13, 32, 60, 174**
See also AFAW 1, 2; AMWS 10; BPFB 3; BW 2, 3; CA 21-24R; CANR 25, 48, 74, 128; CN 7; CP 7; CSW; DA3; DAM MULT; DLB 2, 5, 33, 169, 227; DLBD 8; EWL 3; LMFS 2; MSW; MTCW 1, 2; PFS 6; RGAL 4; TCWW 2

Reed, John (Silas) 1887-1920 .... **TCLC 9**
See also CA 106; 195; TUS

Reed, Lou .... **CLC 21**
See Firbank, Louis

Reese, Lizette Woodworth 1856-1935 . **PC 29**
See also CA 180; DLB 54

Reeve, Clara 1729-1807 .... **NCLC 19**
See also DLB 39; RGEL 2

Reich, Wilhelm 1897-1957 .... **TCLC 57**
See also CA 199

Reid, Christopher (John) 1949- .... **CLC 33**
See also CA 140; CANR 89; CP 7; DLB 40; EWL 3

Reid, Desmond
See Moorcock, Michael (John)

Reid Banks, Lynne 1929-
See Banks, Lynne Reid
See also AAYA 49; CA 1-4R; CANR 6, 22, 38, 87; CLR 24; CN 7; JRDA; MAICYA 1, 2; SATA 22, 75, 111; YAW

Reilly, William K.
See Creasey, John

Reiner, Max
See Caldwell, (Janet Miriam) Taylor (Holland)

Reis, Ricardo
See Pessoa, Fernando (Antonio Nogueira)

Reizenstein, Elmer Leopold
See Rice, Elmer (Leopold)
See also EWL 3

Remarque, Erich Maria 1898-1970 . **CLC 21**
See also AAYA 27; BPFB 3; CA 77-80; 29-32R; CDWLB 2; DA; DA3; DAB; DAC; DAM MST, NOV; DLB 56; EWL 3; EXPN; LAIT 3; MTCW 1, 2; NFS 4; RGWL 2, 3

Remington, Frederic 1861-1909 ..... **TCLC 89**
See also CA 108; 169; DLB 12, 186, 188; SATA 41

Remizov, A.
See Remizov, Aleksei (Mikhailovich)

Remizov, A. M.
See Remizov, Aleksei (Mikhailovich)

Remizov, Aleksei (Mikhailovich)
1877-1957 .... **TCLC 27**
See Remizov, Alexey Mikhaylovich
See also CA 125; 133; DLB 295

Remizov, Alexey Mikhaylovich
See Remizov, Aleksei (Mikhailovich)
See also EWL 3

Renan, Joseph Ernest 1823-1892 .. **NCLC 26**
See also GFL 1789 to the Present

Renard, Jules(-Pierre) 1864-1910 .. **TCLC 17**
See also CA 117; 202; GFL 1789 to the Present

Renault, Mary .... **CLC 3, 11, 17**
See Challans, Mary
See also BPFB 3; BYA 2; DLBY 1983; EWL 3; GLL 1; LAIT 1; MTCW 2; RGEL 2; RHW

Rendell, Ruth (Barbara) 1930- .. **CLC 28, 48**
See Vine, Barbara
See also BPFB 3; BRWS 9; CA 109; CANR 32, 52, 74, 127; CN 7; CPW; DAM POP; DLB 87, 276; INT CANR-32; MSW; MTCW 1, 2

Renoir, Jean 1894-1979 .... **CLC 20**
See also CA 129; 85-88

Resnais, Alain 1922- .... **CLC 16**

Revard, Carter (Curtis) 1931- .... **NNAL**
See also CA 144; CANR 81; PFS 5

Reverdy, Pierre 1889-1960 .... **CLC 53**
See also CA 97-100; 89-92; DLB 258; EWL 3; GFL 1789 to the Present

Rexroth, Kenneth 1905-1982 .... **CLC 1, 2, 6, 11, 22, 49, 112; PC 20**
See also BG 3; CA 5-8R; 107; CANR 14, 34, 63; CDALB 1941-1968; DAM POET; DLB 16, 48, 165, 212; DLBY 1982; EWL 3; INT CANR-14; MTCW 1, 2; RGAL 4

Reyes, Alfonso 1889-1959 .... **HLCS 2; TCLC 33**
See also CA 131; EWL 3; HW 1; LAW

Reyes y Basoalto, Ricardo Eliecer Neftali
See Neruda, Pablo

Reymont, Wladyslaw (Stanislaw)
1868(?)-1925 .... **TCLC 5**
See also CA 104; EWL 3

Reynolds, Jonathan 1942- .... **CLC 6, 38**
See also CA 65-68; CANR 28

Reynolds, Joshua 1723-1792 .... **LC 15**
See also DLB 104

Reynolds, Michael S(hane)
1937-2000 .... **CLC 44**
See also CA 65-68; 189; CANR 9, 89, 97

Reznikoff, Charles 1894-1976 .... **CLC 9**
See also CA 33-36; 61-64; CAP 2; DLB 28, 45; WP

Rezzori (d'Arezzo), Gregor von
1914-1998 .... **CLC 25**
See also CA 122; 136; 167

Rhine, Richard
See Silverstein, Alvin; Silverstein, Virginia B(arbara Opshelor)

Rhodes, Eugene Manlove
1869-1934 .... **TCLC 53**
See also CA 198; DLB 256

R'hoone, Lord
See Balzac, Honore de

Rhys, Jean 1894(?)-1979 ...... **CLC 2, 4, 6, 14, 19, 51, 124; SSC 21**
See also BRWS 2; CA 25-28R; 85-88; CANR 35, 62; CDBLB 1945-1960; CDWLB 3; DA3; DAM NOV; DLB 36, 117, 162; DNFS 2; EWL 3; LATS 1; MTCW 1, 2; RGEL 2; RGSF 2; RHW; TEA; WWE 1

Ribeiro, Darcy 1922-1997 .... **CLC 34**
See also CA 33-36R; 156; EWL 3

Ribeiro, Joao Ubaldo (Osorio Pimentel)
1941- .... **CLC 10, 67**
See also CA 81-84; EWL 3

Ribman, Ronald (Burt) 1932- .... **CLC 7**
See also CA 21-24R; CAD; CANR 46, 80; CD 5

Ricci, Nino (Pio) 1959- .... **CLC 70**
See also CA 137; CCA 1

Rice, Anne 1941- .... **CLC 41, 128**
See Rampling, Anne
See also AAYA 9, 53; AMWS 7; BEST 89:2; BPFB 3; CA 65-68; CANR 12, 36, 53, 74, 100; CN 7; CPW; CSW; DA3; DAM POP; DLB 292; GLL 2; HGG; MTCW 2; SUFW 2; YAW

Rice, Elmer (Leopold) 1892-1967 ...... **CLC 7, 49**
See Reizenstein, Elmer Leopold
See also CA 21-22; 25-28R; CAP 2; DAM DRAM; DFS 12; DLB 4, 7; MTCW 1, 2; RGAL 4

Rice, Tim(othy Miles Bindon) 1944- .... **CLC 21**
See also CA 103; CANR 46; DFS 7

Rich, Adrienne (Cecile) 1929- ... **CLC 3, 6, 7, 11, 18, 36, 73, 76, 125; PC 5**
See also AMWR 2; AMWS 1; CA 9-12R; CANR 20, 53, 74, 128; CDALBS; CP 7; CSW; CWP; DA3; DAM POET; DLB 5, 67; EWL 3; EXPP; FW; MAWW; MTCW 1, 2; PAB; PFS 15; RGAL 4; WP

Rich, Barbara
See Graves, Robert (von Ranke)

Rich, Robert
See Trumbo, Dalton

Richard, Keith .... **CLC 17**
See Richards, Keith

Richards, David Adams 1950- .... **CLC 59**
See also CA 93-96; CANR 60, 110; DAC; DLB 53

Richards, I(vor) A(rmstrong) 1893-1979 .... **CLC 14, 24**
See also BRWS 2; CA 41-44R; 89-92; CANR 34, 74; DLB 27; EWL 3; MTCW 2; RGEL 2

Richards, Keith 1943-
See Richard, Keith
See also CA 107; CANR 77

Richardson, Anne
See Roiphe, Anne (Richardson)

Richardson, Dorothy Miller 1873-1957 .... **TCLC 3**
See also CA 104; 192; DLB 36; EWL 3; FW; RGEL 2

Richardson (Robertson), Ethel Florence Lindesay 1870-1946
See Richardson, Henry Handel
See also CA 105; 190; DLB 230; RHW

Richardson, Henry Handel .... **TCLC 4**
See Richardson (Robertson), Ethel Florence Lindesay
See also DLB 197; EWL 3; RGEL 2; RGSF 2

Richardson, John 1796-1852 .... **NCLC 55**
See also CCA 1; DAC; DLB 99

Richardson, Samuel 1689-1761 ...... **LC 1, 44; WLC**
See also BRW 3; CDBLB 1660-1789; DA; DAB; DAC; DAM MST, NOV; DLB 39; RGEL 2; TEA; WLIT 3

Richardson, Willis 1889-1977 .... **HR 3**
See also BW 1; CA 124; DLB 51; SATA 60

Richler, Mordecai 1931-2001 .... **CLC 3, 5, 9, 13, 18, 46, 70, 185**
See also AITN 1; CA 65-68; 201; CANR 31, 62, 111; CCA 1; CLR 17; CWRI 5; DAC; DAM MST, NOV; DLB 53; EWL 3; MAICYA 1, 2; MTCW 1, 2; RGEL 2; SATA 44, 98; SATA-Brief 27; TWA

Richter, Conrad (Michael) 1890-1968 .... **CLC 30**
See also AAYA 21; BYA 2; CA 5-8R; 25-28R; CANR 23; DLB 9, 212; LAIT 1; MTCW 1, 2; RGAL 4; SATA 3; TCWW 2; TUS; YAW

Ricostranza, Tom
See Ellis, Trey

Riddell, Charlotte 1832-1906 .... **TCLC 40**
See Riddell, Mrs. J. H.
See also CA 165; DLB 156

Riddell, Mrs. J. H.
See Riddell, Charlotte
See also HGG; SUFW

Ridge, John Rollin 1827-1867 ...... **NCLC 82; NNAL**
See also CA 144; DAM MULT; DLB 175

Ridgeway, Jason
See Marlowe, Stephen

Ridgway, Keith 1965- .... **CLC 119**
See also CA 172

Riding, Laura .... **CLC 3, 7**
See Jackson, Laura (Riding)
See also RGAL 4

Riefenstahl, Berta Helene Amalia 1902-2003
See Riefenstahl, Leni
See also CA 108; 220

Riefenstahl, Leni .... **CLC 16, 190**
See Riefenstahl, Berta Helene Amalia

Riffe, Ernest
See Bergman, (Ernst) Ingmar

Riggs, (Rolla) Lynn 1899-1954 .... **NNAL; TCLC 56**
See also CA 144; DAM MULT; DLB 175

Riis, Jacob A(ugust) 1849-1914 ...... **TCLC 80**
See also CA 113; 168; DLB 23

Riley, James Whitcomb 1849-1916 .... **PC 48; TCLC 51**
See also CA 118; 137; DAM POET; MAICYA 1, 2; RGAL 4; SATA 17

Riley, Tex
See Creasey, John

Rilke, Rainer Maria 1875-1926 .... **PC 2; TCLC 1, 6, 19**
See also CA 104; 132; CANR 62, 99; CDWLB 2; DA3; DAM POET; DLB 81; EW 9; EWL 3; MTCW 1, 2; PFS 19; RGWL 2, 3; TWA; WP

Rimbaud, (Jean Nicolas) Arthur 1854-1891 ... **NCLC 4, 35, 82; PC 3, 57; WLC**
See also DA; DA3; DAB; DAC; DAM MST, POET; DLB 217; EW 7; GFL 1789 to the Present; LMFS 2; RGWL 2, 3; TWA; WP

Rinehart, Mary Roberts 1876-1958 .... **TCLC 52**
See also BPFB 3; CA 108; 166; RGAL 4; RHW

Ringmaster, The
See Mencken, H(enry) L(ouis)

Ringwood, Gwen(dolyn Margaret) Pharis 1910-1984 .... **CLC 48**
See also CA 148; 112; DLB 88

Rio, Michel 1945(?)- .... **CLC 43**
See also CA 201

Rios, Alberto (Alvaro) 1952- .... **PC 57**
See also AMWS 4; CA 113; CANR 34, 79; CP 7; DLB 122; HW 2; PFS 11

Ritsos, Giannes
See Ritsos, Yannis

Ritsos, Yannis 1909-1990 .... **CLC 6, 13, 31**
See also CA 77-80; 133; CANR 39, 61; EW 12; EWL 3; MTCW 1; RGWL 2, 3

Ritter, Erika 1948(?)- .... **CLC 52**
See also CD 5; CWD

Rivera, Jose Eustasio 1889-1928 ... **TCLC 35**
See also CA 162; EWL 3; HW 1, 2; LAW

Rivera, Tomas 1935-1984 .... **HLCS 2**
See also CA 49-52; CANR 32; DLB 82; HW 1; LLW 1; RGAL 4; SSFS 15; TCWW 2; WLIT 1

Rivers, Conrad Kent 1933-1968 .... **CLC 1**
See also BW 1; CA 85-88; DLB 41

Rivers, Elfrida
See Bradley, Marion Zimmer
See also GLL 1

Riverside, John
See Heinlein, Robert A(nson)

Rizal, Jose 1861-1896 .... **NCLC 27**

Roa Bastos, Augusto (Antonio) 1917- .... **CLC 45; HLC 2**
See also CA 131; CWW 2; DAM MULT; DLB 113; EWL 3; HW 1; LAW; RGSF 2; WLIT 1

Robbe-Grillet, Alain 1922- .... **CLC 1, 2, 4, 6, 8, 10, 14, 43, 128**
See also BPFB 3; CA 9-12R; CANR 33, 65, 115; DLB 83; EW 13; EWL 3; GFL 1789 to the Present; IDFW 3, 4; MTCW 1, 2; RGWL 2, 3; SSFS 15

Robbins, Harold 1916-1997 .... **CLC 5**
See also BPFB 3; CA 73-76; 162; CANR 26, 54, 112; DA3; DAM NOV; MTCW 1, 2

Robbins, Thomas Eugene 1936-
See Robbins, Tom
See also CA 81-84; CANR 29, 59, 95; CN 7; CPW; CSW; DA3; DAM NOV, POP; MTCW 1, 2

Robbins, Tom .... **CLC 9, 32, 64**
See Robbins, Thomas Eugene
See also AAYA 32; AMWS 10; BEST 90:3; BPFB 3; DLBY 1980; MTCW 2

Robbins, Trina 1938- .... **CLC 21**
See also CA 128

Roberts, Charles G(eorge) D(ouglas) 1860-1943 .... **TCLC 8**
See also CA 105; 188; CLR 33; CWRI 5; DLB 92; RGEL 2; RGSF 2; SATA 88; SATA-Brief 29

Roberts, Elizabeth Madox 1886-1941 .... **TCLC 68**
See also CA 111; 166; CWRI 5; DLB 9, 54, 102; RGAL 4; RHW; SATA 33; SATA-Brief 27; WCH

Roberts, Kate 1891-1985 .... **CLC 15**
See also CA 107; 116

Roberts, Keith (John Kingston) 1935-2000 .... **CLC 14**
See also CA 25-28R; CANR 46; DLB 261; SFW 4

Roberts, Kenneth (Lewis) 1885-1957 .... **TCLC 23**
See also CA 109; 199; DLB 9; RGAL 4; RHW

Roberts, Michele (Brigitte) 1949- .... **CLC 48, 178**
See also CA 115; CANR 58, 120; CN 7; DLB 231; FW

Robertson, Ellis
See Ellison, Harlan (Jay); Silverberg, Robert

Robertson, Thomas William 1829-1871 .... **NCLC 35**
See Robertson, Tom
See also DAM DRAM

Robertson, Tom
See Robertson, Thomas William
See also RGEL 2

Robeson, Kenneth
See Dent, Lester

Robinson, Edwin Arlington 1869-1935 .... **PC 1, 35; TCLC 5, 101**
See also AMW; CA 104; 133; CDALB 1865-1917; DA; DAC; DAM MST, POET; DLB 54; EWL 3; EXPP; MTCW 1, 2; PAB; PFS 4; RGAL 4; WP

Robinson, Henry Crabb 1775-1867 .... **NCLC 15**
See also DLB 107

Robinson, Jill 1936- .... **CLC 10**
See also CA 102; CANR 120; INT CA-102

Robinson, Kim Stanley 1952- .... **CLC 34**
See also AAYA 26; CA 126; CANR 113; CN 7; SATA 109; SCFW 2; SFW 4
Robinson, Lloyd
See Silverberg, Robert
Robinson, Marilynne 1944- ...... **CLC 25, 180**
See also CA 116; CANR 80; CN 7; DLB 206
Robinson, Smokey .... **CLC 21**
See Robinson, William, Jr.
Robinson, William, Jr. 1940-
See Robinson, Smokey
See also CA 116
Robison, Mary 1949- .... **CLC 42, 98**
See also CA 113; 116; CANR 87; CN 7; DLB 130; INT CA-116; RGSF 2
Rochester
See Wilmot, John
See also RGEL 2
Rod, Edouard 1857-1910 .... **TCLC 52**
Roddenberry, Eugene Wesley 1921-1991
See Roddenberry, Gene
See also CA 110; 135; CANR 37; SATA 45; SATA-Obit 69
Roddenberry, Gene .... **CLC 17**
See Roddenberry, Eugene Wesley
See also AAYA 5; SATA-Obit 69
Rodgers, Mary 1931- .... **CLC 12**
See also BYA 5; CA 49-52; CANR 8, 55, 90; CLR 20; CWRI 5; INT CANR-8; JRDA; MAICYA 1, 2; SATA 8, 130
Rodgers, W(illiam) R(obert) 1909-1969 .... **CLC 7**
See also CA 85-88; DLB 20; RGEL 2
Rodman, Eric
See Silverberg, Robert
Rodman, Howard 1920(?)-1985 .... **CLC 65**
See also CA 118
Rodman, Maia
See Wojciechowska, Maia (Teresa)
Rodo, Jose Enrique 1871(?)-1917 .... **HLCS 2**
See also CA 178; EWL 3; HW 2; LAW
Rodolph, Utto
See Ouologuem, Yambo
Rodriguez, Claudio 1934-1999 .... **CLC 10**
See also CA 188; DLB 134
Rodriguez, Richard 1944- .... **CLC 155; HLC 2**
See also CA 110; CANR 66, 116; DAM MULT; DLB 82, 256; HW 1, 2; LAIT 5; LLW 1; NCFS 3; WLIT 1
Roelvaag, O(le) E(dvart) 1876-1931
See Rolvaag, O(le) E(dvart)
See also CA 117; 171
Roethke, Theodore (Huebner) 1908-1963 .... **CLC 1, 3, 8, 11, 19, 46, 101; PC 15**
See also AMW; CA 81-84; CABS 2; CDALB 1941-1968; DA3; DAM POET; DLB 5, 206; EWL 3; EXPP; MTCW 1, 2; PAB; PFS 3; RGAL 4; WP
Rogers, Carl R(ansom) 1902-1987 .... **TCLC 125**
See also CA 1-4R; 121; CANR 1, 18; MTCW 1
Rogers, Samuel 1763-1855 .... **NCLC 69**
See also DLB 93; RGEL 2
Rogers, Thomas Hunton 1927- .... **CLC 57**
See also CA 89-92; INT CA-89-92
Rogers, Will(iam Penn Adair) 1879-1935 .... **NNAL; TCLC 8, 71**
See also CA 105; 144; DA3; DAM MULT; DLB 11; MTCW 2
Rogin, Gilbert 1929- .... **CLC 18**
See also CA 65-68; CANR 15
Rohan, Koda
See Koda Shigeyuki
Rohlfs, Anna Katharine Green
See Green, Anna Katharine

Rohmer, Eric .... **CLC 16**
See Scherer, Jean-Marie Maurice
Rohmer, Sax .... **TCLC 28**
See Ward, Arthur Henry Sarsfield
See also DLB 70; MSW; SUFW
Roiphe, Anne (Richardson) 1935- .. **CLC 3, 9**
See also CA 89-92; CANR 45, 73; DLBY 1980; INT CA-89-92
Rojas, Fernando de 1475-1541 ... **HLCS 1, 2; LC 23**
See also DLB 286; RGWL 2, 3
Rojas, Gonzalo 1917- .... **HLCS 2**
See also CA 178; HW 2; LAWS 1
Roland, Marie-Jeanne 1754-1793 .... **LC 98**
Rolfe, Frederick (William Serafino Austin Lewis Mary) 1860-1913 .... **TCLC 12**
See Al Siddik
See also CA 107; 210; DLB 34, 156; RGEL 2
Rolland, Romain 1866-1944 .... **TCLC 23**
See also CA 118; 197; DLB 65, 284; EWL 3; GFL 1789 to the Present; RGWL 2, 3
Rolle, Richard c. 1300-c. 1349 .... **CMLC 21**
See also DLB 146; LMFS 1; RGEL 2
Rolvaag, O(le) E(dvart) .... **TCLC 17**
See Roelvaag, O(le) E(dvart)
See also DLB 9, 212; NFS 5; RGAL 4
Romain Arnaud, Saint
See Aragon, Louis
Romains, Jules 1885-1972 .... **CLC 7**
See also CA 85-88; CANR 34; DLB 65; EWL 3; GFL 1789 to the Present; MTCW 1
Romero, Jose Ruben 1890-1952 .... **TCLC 14**
See also CA 114; 131; EWL 3; HW 1; LAW
Ronsard, Pierre de 1524-1585 . **LC 6, 54; PC 11**
See also EW 2; GFL Beginnings to 1789; RGWL 2, 3; TWA
Rooke, Leon 1934- .... **CLC 25, 34**
See also CA 25-28R; CANR 23, 53; CCA 1; CPW; DAM POP
Roosevelt, Franklin Delano 1882-1945 .... **TCLC 93**
See also CA 116; 173; LAIT 3
Roosevelt, Theodore 1858-1919 ..... **TCLC 69**
See also CA 115; 170; DLB 47, 186, 275
Roper, William 1498-1578 .... **LC 10**
Roquelaure, A. N.
See Rice, Anne
Rosa, Joao Guimaraes 1908-1967 ... **CLC 23; HLCS 1**
See Guimaraes Rosa, Joao
See also CA 89-92; DLB 113; EWL 3; WLIT 1
Rose, Wendy 1948- . **CLC 85; NNAL; PC 13**
See also CA 53-56; CANR 5, 51; CWP; DAM MULT; DLB 175; PFS 13; RGAL 4; SATA 12
Rosen, R. D.
See Rosen, Richard (Dean)
Rosen, Richard (Dean) 1949- .... **CLC 39**
See also CA 77-80; CANR 62, 120; CMW 4; INT CANR-30
Rosenberg, Isaac 1890-1918 .... **TCLC 12**
See also BRW 6; CA 107; 188; DLB 20, 216; EWL 3; PAB; RGEL 2
Rosenblatt, Joe .... **CLC 15**
See Rosenblatt, Joseph
Rosenblatt, Joseph 1933-
See Rosenblatt, Joe
See also CA 89-92; CP 7; INT CA 89-92
Rosenfeld, Samuel
See Tzara, Tristan
Rosenstock, Sami
See Tzara, Tristan
Rosenstock, Samuel
See Tzara, Tristan

Rosenthal, M(acha) L(ouis) 1917-1996 .... **CLC 28**
See also CA 1-4R; 152; CAAS 6; CANR 4, 51; CP 7; DLB 5; SATA 59
Ross, Barnaby
See Dannay, Frederic
Ross, Bernard L.
See Follett, Ken(neth Martin)
Ross, J. H.
See Lawrence, T(homas) E(dward)
Ross, John Hume
See Lawrence, T(homas) E(dward)
Ross, Martin 1862-1915
See Martin, Violet Florence
See also DLB 135; GLL 2; RGEL 2; RGSF 2
Ross, (James) Sinclair 1908-1996 ... **CLC 13; SSC 24**
See also CA 73-76; CANR 81; CN 7; DAC; DAM MST; DLB 88; RGEL 2; RGSF 2; TCWW 2
Rossetti, Christina (Georgina) 1830-1894 .... **NCLC 2, 50, 66; PC 7; WLC**
See also AAYA 51; BRW 5; BYA 4; DA; DA3; DAB; DAC; DAM MST, POET; DLB 35, 163, 240; EXPP; LATS 1; MAICYA 1, 2; PFS 10, 14; RGEL 2; SATA 20; TEA; WCH
Rossetti, Dante Gabriel 1828-1882 . **NCLC 4, 77; PC 44; WLC**
See also AAYA 51; BRW 5; CDBLB 1832-1890; DA; DAB; DAC; DAM MST, POET; DLB 35; EXPP; RGEL 2; TEA
Rossi, Cristina Peri
See Peri Rossi, Cristina
Rossi, Jean-Baptiste 1931-2003
See Japrisot, Sebastien
See also CA 201; 215
Rossner, Judith (Perelman) 1935- . **CLC 6, 9, 29**
See also AITN 2; BEST 90:3; BPFB 3; CA 17-20R; CANR 18, 51, 73; CN 7; DLB 6; INT CANR-18; MTCW 1, 2
Rostand, Edmond (Eugene Alexis) 1868-1918 .... **DC 10; TCLC 6, 37**
See also CA 104; 126; DA; DA3; DAB; DAC; DAM DRAM, MST; DFS 1; DLB 192; LAIT 1; MTCW 1; RGWL 2, 3; TWA
Roth, Henry 1906-1995 ..... **CLC 2, 6, 11, 104**
See also AMWS 9; CA 11-12; 149; CANR 38, 63; CAP 1; CN 7; DLB 28; EWL 3; MTCW 1, 2; RGAL 4
Roth, (Moses) Joseph 1894-1939 ... **TCLC 33**
See also CA 160; DLB 85; EWL 3; RGWL 2, 3
Roth, Philip (Milton) 1933- ... **CLC 1, 2, 3, 4, 6, 9, 15, 22, 31, 47, 66, 86, 119; SSC 26; WLC**
See also AMWR 2; AMWS 3; BEST 90:3; BPFB 3; CA 1-4R; CANR 1, 22, 36, 55, 89; CDALB 1968-1988; CN 7; CPW 1; DA; DA3; DAB; DAC; DAM MST, NOV, POP; DLB 2, 28, 173; DLBY 1982; EWL 3; MTCW 1, 2; RGAL 4; RGSF 2; SSFS 12, 18; TUS
Rothenberg, Jerome 1931- .... **CLC 6, 57**
See also CA 45-48; CANR 1, 106; CP 7; DLB 5, 193
Rotter, Pat ed. .... **CLC 65**
Roumain, Jacques (Jean Baptiste) 1907-1944 .... **BLC 3; TCLC 19**
See also BW 1; CA 117; 125; DAM MULT; EWL 3
Rourke, Constance Mayfield 1885-1941 .... **TCLC 12**
See also CA 107; 200; YABC 1

Rousseau, Jean-Baptiste 1671-1741 ...... **LC 9**
Rousseau, Jean-Jacques 1712-1778 .... **LC 14, 36; WLC**
See also DA; DA3; DAB; DAC; DAM MST; EW 4; GFL Beginnings to 1789; LMFS 1; RGWL 2, 3; TWA
Roussel, Raymond 1877-1933 .... **TCLC 20**
See also CA 117; 201; EWL 3; GFL 1789 to the Present
Rovit, Earl (Herbert) 1927- .... **CLC 7**
See also CA 5-8R; CANR 12
Rowe, Elizabeth Singer 1674-1737 ..... **LC 44**
See also DLB 39, 95
Rowe, Nicholas 1674-1718 .... **LC 8**
See also DLB 84; RGEL 2
Rowlandson, Mary 1637(?)-1678 .... **LC 66**
See also DLB 24, 200; RGAL 4
Rowley, Ames Dorrance
See Lovecraft, H(oward) P(hillips)
Rowley, William 1585(?)-1626 .... **LC 100**
See also DLB 58; RGEL 2
Rowling, J(oanne) K(athleen) 1966- .... **CLC 137**
See also AAYA 34; BYA 11, 13, 14; CA 173; CANR 128; CLR 66, 80; MAICYA 2; SATA 109; SUFW 2
Rowson, Susanna Haswell 1762(?)-1824 .... **NCLC 5, 69**
See also DLB 37, 200; RGAL 4
Roy, Arundhati 1960(?)- .... **CLC 109**
See also CA 163; CANR 90, 126; DLBY 1997; EWL 3; LATS 1; WWE 1
Roy, Gabrielle 1909-1983 .... **CLC 10, 14**
See also CA 53-56; 110; CANR 5, 61; CCA 1; DAB; DAC; DAM MST; DLB 68; EWL 3; MTCW 1; RGWL 2, 3; SATA 104
Royko, Mike 1932-1997 .... **CLC 109**
See also CA 89-92; 157; CANR 26, 111; CPW
Rozanov, Vasilii Vasil'evich
See Rozanov, Vassili
See also DLB 295
Rozanov, Vasily Vasilyevich
See Rozanov, Vassili
See also EWL 3
Rozanov, Vassili 1856-1919 .... **TCLC 104**
See Rozanov, Vasilii Vasil'evich; Rozanov, Vasily Vasilyevich
Rozewicz, Tadeusz 1921- ...... **CLC 9, 23, 139**
See also CA 108; CANR 36, 66; CWW 2; DA3; DAM POET; DLB 232; EWL 3; MTCW 1, 2; RGWL 3
Ruark, Gibbons 1941- .... **CLC 3**
See also CA 33-36R; CAAS 23; CANR 14, 31, 57; DLB 120
Rubens, Bernice (Ruth) 1923- .... **CLC 19, 31**
See also CA 25-28R; CANR 33, 65, 128; CN 7; DLB 14, 207; MTCW 1
Rubin, Harold
See Robbins, Harold
Rudkin, (James) David 1936- .... **CLC 14**
See also CA 89-92; CBD; CD 5; DLB 13
Rudnik, Raphael 1933- .... **CLC 7**
See also CA 29-32R
Ruffian, M.
See Hasek, Jaroslav (Matej Frantisek)
Ruiz, Jose Martinez .... **CLC 11**
See Martinez Ruiz, Jose
Ruiz, Juan c. 1283-c. 1350 .... **CMLC 66**
Rukeyser, Muriel 1913-1980 . **CLC 6, 10, 15, 27; PC 12**
See also AMWS 6; CA 5-8R; 93-96; CANR 26, 60; DA3; DAM POET; DLB 48; EWL 3; FW; GLL 2; MTCW 1, 2; PFS 10; RGAL 4; SATA-Obit 22
Rule, Jane (Vance) 1931- .... **CLC 27**
See also CA 25-28R; CAAS 18; CANR 12, 87; CN 7; DLB 60; FW

Rulfo, Juan 1918-1986 .. **CLC 8, 80; HLC 2; SSC 25**
See also CA 85-88; 118; CANR 26; CDWLB 3; DAM MULT; DLB 113; EWL 3; HW 1, 2; LAW; MTCW 1, 2; RGSF 2; RGWL 2, 3; WLIT 1
Rumi, Jalal al-Din 1207-1273 ...... **CMLC 20; PC 45**
See also RGWL 2, 3; WP
Runeberg, Johan 1804-1877 .... **NCLC 41**
Runyon, (Alfred) Damon 1884(?)-1946 .... **TCLC 10**
See also CA 107; 165; DLB 11, 86, 171; MTCW 2; RGAL 4
Rush, Norman 1933- .... **CLC 44**
See also CA 121; 126; INT CA-126
Rushdie, (Ahmed) Salman 1947- .... **CLC 23, 31, 55, 100; WLCS**
See also BEST 89:3; BPFB 3; BRWS 4; CA 108; 111; CANR 33, 56, 108; CN 7; CPW 1; DA3; DAB; DAC; DAM MST, NOV, POP; DLB 194; EWL 3; FANT; INT CA-111; LATS 1; LMFS 2; MTCW 1, 2; RGEL 2; RGSF 2; TEA; WLIT 4; WWE 1
Rushforth, Peter (Scott) 1945- .... **CLC 19**
See also CA 101
Ruskin, John 1819-1900 .... **TCLC 63**
See also BRW 5; BYA 5; CA 114; 129; CDBLB 1832-1890; DLB 55, 163, 190; RGEL 2; SATA 24; TEA; WCH
Russ, Joanna 1937- .... **CLC 15**
See also BPFB 3; CA 5-28R; CANR 11, 31, 65; CN 7; DLB 8; FW; GLL 1; MTCW 1; SCFW 2; SFW 4
Russ, Richard Patrick
See O'Brian, Patrick
Russell, George William 1867-1935
See A.E.; Baker, Jean H.
See also BRWS 8; CA 104; 153; CDBLB 1890-1914; DAM POET; EWL 3; RGEL 2
Russell, Jeffrey Burton 1934- .... **CLC 70**
See also CA 25-28R; CANR 11, 28, 52
Russell, (Henry) Ken(neth Alfred) 1927- .... **CLC 16**
See also CA 105
Russell, William Martin 1947-
See Russell, Willy
See also CA 164; CANR 107
Russell, Willy .... **CLC 60**
See Russell, William Martin
See also CBD; CD 5; DLB 233
Russo, Richard 1949- .... **CLC 181**
See also AMWS 12; CA 127; 133; CANR 87, 114
Rutherford, Mark .... **TCLC 25**
See White, William Hale
See also DLB 18; RGEL 2
Ruyslinck, Ward .... **CLC 14**
See Belser, Reimond Karel Maria de
Ryan, Cornelius (John) 1920-1974 ..... **CLC 7**
See also CA 69-72; 53-56; CANR 38
Ryan, Michael 1946- .... **CLC 65**
See also CA 49-52; CANR 109; DLBY 1982
Ryan, Tim
See Dent, Lester
Rybakov, Anatoli (Naumovich) 1911-1998 .... **CLC 23, 53**
See also CA 126; 135; 172; SATA 79; SATA-Obit 108
Ryder, Jonathan
See Ludlum, Robert
Ryga, George 1932-1987 .... **CLC 14**
See also CA 101; 124; CANR 43, 90; CCA 1; DAC; DAM MST; DLB 60
S. H.
See Hartmann, Sadakichi

S. S.
See Sassoon, Siegfried (Lorraine)
Saba, Umberto 1883-1957 .... **TCLC 33**
See also CA 144; CANR 79; DLB 114; EWL 3; RGWL 2, 3
Sabatini, Rafael 1875-1950 .... **TCLC 47**
See also BPFB 3; CA 162; RHW
Sabato, Ernesto (R.) 1911- .... **CLC 10, 23; HLC 2**
See also CA 97-100; CANR 32, 65; CDWLB 3; DAM MULT; DLB 145; EWL 3; HW 1, 2; LAW; MTCW 1, 2
Sa-Carneiro, Mario de 1890-1916 . **TCLC 83**
See also DLB 287; EWL 3
Sacastru, Martin
See Bioy Casares, Adolfo
See also CWW 2
Sacher-Masoch, Leopold von 1836(?)-1895 .... **NCLC 31**
Sachs, Hans 1494-1576 .... **LC 95**
See also CDWLB 2; DLB 179; RGWL 2, 3
Sachs, Marilyn (Stickle) 1927- .... **CLC 35**
See also AAYA 2; BYA 6; CA 17-20R; CANR 13, 47; CLR 2; JRDA; MAICYA 1, 2; SAAS 2; SATA 3, 68; SATA-Essay 110; WYA; YAW
Sachs, Nelly 1891-1970 .... **CLC 14, 98**
See also CA 17-18; 25-28R; CANR 87; CAP 2; EWL 3; MTCW 2; RGWL 2, 3
Sackler, Howard (Oliver) 1929-1982 .... **CLC 14**
See also CA 61-64; 108; CAD; CANR 30; DFS 15; DLB 7
Sacks, Oliver (Wolf) 1933- .... **CLC 67**
See also CA 53-56; CANR 28, 50, 76; CPW; DA3; INT CANR-28; MTCW 1, 2
Sackville, Thomas 1536-1608 .... **LC 98**
See also DAM DRAM; DLB 62, 132; RGEL 2
Sadakichi
See Hartmann, Sadakichi
Sade, Donatien Alphonse Francois 1740-1814 .... **NCLC 3, 47**
See also EW 4; GFL Beginnings to 1789; RGWL 2, 3
Sade, Marquis de
See Sade, Donatien Alphonse Francois
Sadoff, Ira 1945- .... **CLC 9**
See also CA 53-56; CANR 5, 21, 109; DLB 120
Saetone
See Camus, Albert
Safire, William 1929- .... **CLC 10**
See also CA 17-20R; CANR 31, 54, 91
Sagan, Carl (Edward) 1934-1996 .... **CLC 30, 112**
See also AAYA 2; CA 25-28R; 155; CANR 11, 36, 74; CPW; DA3; MTCW 1, 2; SATA 58; SATA-Obit 94
Sagan, Francoise .... **CLC 3, 6, 9, 17, 36**
See Quoirez, Francoise
See also CWW 2; DLB 83; EWL 3; GFL 1789 to the Present; MTCW 2
Sahgal, Nayantara (Pandit) 1927- .... **CLC 41**
See also CA 9-12R; CANR 11, 88; CN 7
Said, Edward W. 1935-2003 .... **CLC 123**
See also CA 21-24R; 220; CANR 45, 74, 107; DLB 67; MTCW 2
Saint, H(arry) F. 1941- .... **CLC 50**
See also CA 127
St. Aubin de Teran, Lisa 1953-
See Teran, Lisa St. Aubin de
See also CA 118; 126; CN 7; INT CA-126
Saint Birgitta of Sweden c. 1303-1373 .... **CMLC 24**
Sainte-Beuve, Charles Augustin 1804-1869 .... **NCLC 5**
See also DLB 217; EW 6; GFL 1789 to the Present

Saint-Exupery, Antoine (Jean Baptiste Marie Roger) de 1900-1944 .... **TCLC 2, 56; WLC**
See also BPFB 3; BYA 3; CA 108; 132; CLR 10; DA3; DAM NOV; DLB 72; EW 12; EWL 3; GFL 1789 to the Present; LAIT 3; MAICYA 1, 2; MTCW 1, 2; RGWL 2, 3; SATA 20; TWA

St. John, David
See Hunt, E(verette) Howard, (Jr.)

St. John, J. Hector
See Crevecoeur, Michel Guillaume Jean de

Saint-John Perse
See Leger, (Marie-Rene Auguste) Alexis Saint-Leger
See also EW 10; EWL 3; GFL 1789 to the Present; RGWL 2

Saintsbury, George (Edward Bateman) 1845-1933 .... **TCLC 31**
See also CA 160; DLB 57, 149

Sait Faik .... **TCLC 23**
See Abasiyanik, Sait Faik

Saki ...... **SSC 12; TCLC 3**
See Munro, H(ector) H(ugh)
See also BRWS 6; BYA 11; LAIT 2; MTCW 2; RGEL 2; SSFS 1; SUFW

Sala, George Augustus 1828-1895 . **NCLC 46**

Saladin 1138-1193 .... **CMLC 38**

Salama, Hannu 1936- .... **CLC 18**
See also EWL 3

Salamanca, J(ack) R(ichard) 1922- .. **CLC 4, 15**
See also CA 25-28R, 193; CAAE 193

Salas, Floyd Francis 1931- .... **HLC 2**
See also CA 119; CAAS 27; CANR 44, 75, 93; DAM MULT; DLB 82; HW 1, 2; MTCW 2

Sale, J. Kirkpatrick
See Sale, Kirkpatrick

Sale, Kirkpatrick 1937- .... **CLC 68**
See also CA 13-16R; CANR 10

Salinas, Luis Omar 1937- ... **CLC 90; HLC 2**
See also AMWS 13; CA 131; CANR 81; DAM MULT; DLB 82; HW 1, 2

Salinas (y Serrano), Pedro 1891(?)-1951 .... **TCLC 17**
See also CA 117; DLB 134; EWL 3

Salinger, J(erome) D(avid) 1919- .. **CLC 1, 3, 8, 12, 55, 56, 138; SSC 2, 28, 65; WLC**
See also AAYA 2, 36; AMW; AMWC 1; BPFB 3; BYA 11; CA 5-8R; CANR 39, 129; CDALB 1941-1968; CLR 18; CN 7; CPW 1; DA; DA3; DAB; DAC; DAM MST, NOV, POP; DLB 2, 102, 173; EWL 3; EXPN; LAIT 4; MAICYA 1, 2; MTCW 1, 2; NFS 1; RGAL 4; RGSF 2; SATA 67; SSFS 17; TUS; WYA; YAW

Salisbury, John
See Caute, (John) David

Sallust c. 86B.C.-35B.C. .... **CMLC 68**
See also AW 2; CDWLB 1; DLB 211; RGWL 2, 3

Salter, James 1925- .. **CLC 7, 52, 59; SSC 58**
See also AMWS 9; CA 73-76; CANR 107; DLB 130

Saltus, Edgar (Everton) 1855-1921 . **TCLC 8**
See also CA 105; DLB 202; RGAL 4

Saltykov, Mikhail Evgrafovich 1826-1889 .... **NCLC 16**
See also DLB 238:

Saltykov-Shchedrin, N.
See Saltykov, Mikhail Evgrafovich

Samarakis, Andonis
See Samarakis, Antonis
See also EWL 3

Samarakis, Antonis 1919- .... **CLC 5**
See Samarakis, Andonis
See also CA 25-28R; CAAS 16; CANR 36

Sanchez, Florencio 1875-1910 .... **TCLC 37**
See also CA 153; EWL 3; HW 1; LAW

Sanchez, Luis Rafael 1936- .... **CLC 23**
See also CA 128; DLB 145; EWL 3; HW 1; WLIT 1

Sanchez, Sonia 1934- .... **BLC 3; CLC 5, 116; PC 9**
See also BW 2, 3; CA 33-36R; CANR 24, 49, 74, 115; CLR 18; CP 7; CSW; CWP; DA3; DAM MULT; DLB 41; DLBD 8; EWL 3; MAICYA 1, 2; MTCW 1, 2; SATA 22, 136; WP

Sancho, Ignatius 1729-1780 .... **LC 84**

Sand, George 1804-1876 ..... **NCLC 2, 42, 57; WLC**
See also DA; DA3; DAB; DAC; DAM MST, NOV; DLB 119, 192; EW 6; FW; GFL 1789 to the Present; RGWL 2, 3; TWA

Sandburg, Carl (August) 1878-1967 . **CLC 1, 4, 10, 15, 35; PC 2, 41; WLC**
See also AAYA 24; AMW; BYA 1, 3; CA 5-8R; 25-28R; CANR 35; CDALB 1865-1917; CLR 67; DA; DA3; DAB; DAC; DAM MST, POET; DLB 17, 54, 284; EWL 3; EXPP; LAIT 2; MAICYA 1, 2; MTCW 1, 2; PAB; PFS 3, 6, 12; RGAL 4; SATA 8; TUS; WCH; WP; WYA

Sandburg, Charles
See Sandburg, Carl (August)

Sandburg, Charles A.
See Sandburg, Carl (August)

Sanders, (James) Ed(ward) 1939- .... **CLC 53**
See Sanders, Edward
See also BG 3; CA 13-16R; CAAS 21; CANR 13, 44, 78; CP 7; DAM POET; DLB 16, 244

Sanders, Edward
See Sanders, (James) Ed(ward)
See also DLB 244

Sanders, Lawrence 1920-1998 .... **CLC 41**
See also BEST 89:4; BPFB 3; CA 81-84; 165; CANR 33, 62; CMW 4; CPW; DA3; DAM POP; MTCW 1

Sanders, Noah
See Blount, Roy (Alton), Jr.

Sanders, Winston P.
See Anderson, Poul (William)

Sandoz, Mari(e Susette) 1900-1966 .. **CLC 28**
See also CA 1-4R; 25-28R; CANR 17, 64; DLB 9, 212; LAIT 2; MTCW 1, 2; SATA 5; TCWW 2

Sandys, George 1578-1644 .... **LC 80**
See also DLB 24, 121

Saner, Reg(inald Anthony) 1931- .... **CLC 9**
See also CA 65-68; CP 7

Sankara 788-820 .... **CMLC 32**

Sannazaro, Jacopo 1456(?)-1530 .... **LC 8**
See also RGWL 2, 3

Sansom, William 1912-1976 . **CLC 2, 6; SSC 21**
See also CA 5-8R; 65-68; CANR 42; DAM NOV; DLB 139; EWL 3; MTCW 1; RGEL 2; RGSF 2

Santayana, George 1863-1952 .... **TCLC 40**
See also AMW; CA 115; 194; DLB 54, 71, 246, 270; DLBD 13; EWL 3; RGAL 4; TUS

Santiago, Danny .... **CLC 33**
See James, Daniel (Lewis)
See also DLB 122

Santmyer, Helen Hooven 1895-1986 .... **CLC 33; TCLC 133**
See also CA 1-4R; 118; CANR 15, 33; DLBY 1984; MTCW 1; RHW

Santoka, Taneda 1882-1940 .... **TCLC 72**

Santos, Bienvenido N(uqui) 1911-1996 .... **AAL; CLC 22**
See also CA 101; 151; CANR 19, 46; DAM MULT; EWL; RGAL 4; SSFS 19

Sapir, Edward 1884-1939 .... **TCLC 108**
See also CA 211; DLB 92

Sapper .... **TCLC 44**
See McNeile, Herman Cyril

Sapphire
See Sapphire, Brenda

Sapphire, Brenda 1950- .... **CLC 99**

Sappho fl. 6th cent. B.C.- ... **CMLC 3, 67; PC 5**
See also CDWLB 1; DA3; DAM POET; DLB 176; RGWL 2, 3; WP

Saramago, Jose 1922- ..... **CLC 119; HLCS 1**
See also CA 153; CANR 96; DLB 287; EWL 3; LATS 1

Sarduy, Severo 1937-1993 .... **CLC 6, 97; HLCS 2**
See also CA 89-92; 142; CANR 58, 81; CWW 2; DLB 113; EWL 3; HW 1, 2; LAW

Sargeson, Frank 1903-1982 .... **CLC 31**
See also CA 25-28R; 106; CANR 38, 79; EWL 3; GLL 2; RGEL 2; RGSF 2

Sarmiento, Domingo Faustino 1811-1888 .... **HLCS 2**
See also LAW; WLIT 1

Sarmiento, Felix Ruben Garcia
See Dario, Ruben

Saro-Wiwa, Ken(ule Beeson) 1941-1995 .... **CLC 114**
See also BW 2; CA 142; 150; CANR 60; DLB 157

Saroyan, William 1908-1981 ... **CLC 1, 8, 10, 29, 34, 56; SSC 21; TCLC 137; WLC**
See also CA 5-8R; 103; CAD; CANR 30; CDALBS; DA; DA3; DAB; DAC; DAM DRAM, MST, NOV; DFS 17; DLB 7, 9, 86; DLBY 1981; EWL 3; LAIT 4; MTCW 1, 2; RGAL 4; RGSF 2; SATA 23; SATA-Obit 24; SSFS 14; TUS

Sarraute, Nathalie 1900-1999 .... **CLC 1, 2, 4, 8, 10, 31, 80; TCLC 145**
See also BPFB 3; CA 9-12R; 187; CANR 23, 66; CWW 2; DLB 83; EW 12; EWL 3; GFL 1789 to the Present; MTCW 1, 2; RGWL 2, 3

Sarton, (Eleanor) May 1912-1995 ..... **CLC 4, 14, 49, 91; PC 39; TCLC 120**
See also AMWS 8; CA 1-4R; 149; CANR 1, 34, 55, 116; CN 7; CP 7; DAM POET; DLB 48; DLBY 1981; EWL 3; FW; INT CANR-34; MTCW 1, 2; RGAL 4; SATA 36; SATA-Obit 86; TUS

Sartre, Jean-Paul 1905-1980 . **CLC 1, 4, 7, 9, 13, 18, 24, 44, 50, 52; DC 3; SSC 32; WLC**
See also CA 9-12R; 97-100; CANR 21; DA; DA3; DAB; DAC; DAM DRAM, MST, NOV; DFS 5; DLB 72, 296; EW 12; EWL 3; GFL 1789 to the Present; LMFS 2; MTCW 1, 2; RGSF 2; RGWL 2, 3; SSFS 9; TWA

Sassoon, Siegfried (Lorraine) 1886-1967 .... **CLC 36, 130; PC 12**
See also BRW 6; CA 104; 25-28R; CANR 36; DAB; DAM MST, NOV, POET; DLB 20, 191; DLBD 18; EWL 3; MTCW 1, 2; PAB; RGEL 2; TEA

Satterfield, Charles
See Pohl, Frederik

Satyremont
See Peret, Benjamin

Saul, John (W. III) 1942- .... **CLC 46**
See also AAYA 10; BEST 90:4; CA 81-84; CANR 16, 40, 81; CPW; DAM NOV, POP; HGG; SATA 98

Saunders, Caleb
See Heinlein, Robert A(nson)
Saura (Atares), Carlos 1932-1998 .... **CLC 20**
See also CA 114; 131; CANR 79; HW 1
Sauser, Frederic Louis
See Sauser-Hall, Frederic
Sauser-Hall, Frederic 1887-1961 ...... **CLC 18**
See Cendrars, Blaise
See also CA 102; 93-96; CANR 36, 62; MTCW 1
Saussure, Ferdinand de
1857-1913 .... **TCLC 49**
See also DLB 242
Savage, Catharine
See Brosman, Catharine Savage
Savage, Richard 1697(?)-1743 .... **LC 96**
See also DLB 95; RGEL 2
Savage, Thomas 1915-2003 .... **CLC 40**
See also CA 126; 132; 218; CAAS 15; CN 7; INT CA-132; SATA-Obit 147; TCWW 2
Savan, Glenn (?)- .... **CLC 50**
Sax, Robert
See Johnson, Robert
Saxo Grammaticus c. 1150-c.
1222 .... **CMLC 58**
Saxton, Robert
See Johnson, Robert
Sayers, Dorothy L(eigh) 1893-1957 . **SSC 71; TCLC 2, 15**
See also BPFB 3; BRWS 3; CA 104; 119; CANR 60; CDBLB 1914-1945; CMW 4; DAM POP; DLB 10, 36, 77, 100; MSW; MTCW 1, 2; RGEL 2; SSFS 12; TEA
Sayers, Valerie 1952- .... **CLC 50, 122**
See also CA 134; CANR 61; CSW
Sayles, John (Thomas) 1950- . **CLC 7, 10, 14**
See also CA 57-60; CANR 41, 84; DLB 44
Scammell, Michael 1935- .... **CLC 34**
See also CA 156
Scannell, Vernon 1922- .... **CLC 49**
See also CA 5-8R; CANR 8, 24, 57; CP 7; CWRI 5; DLB 27; SATA 59
Scarlett, Susan
See Streatfeild, (Mary) Noel
Scarron 1847-1910
See Mikszath, Kalman
Schaeffer, Susan Fromberg 1941- ...... **CLC 6, 11, 22**
See also CA 49-52; CANR 18, 65; CN 7; DLB 28; MTCW 1, 2; SATA 22
Schama, Simon (Michael) 1945- ...... **CLC 150**
See also BEST 89:4; CA 105; CANR 39, 91
Schary, Jill
See Robinson, Jill
Schell, Jonathan 1943- .... **CLC 35**
See also CA 73-76; CANR 12, 117
Schelling, Friedrich Wilhelm Joseph von
1775-1854 .... **NCLC 30**
See also DLB 90
Scherer, Jean-Marie Maurice 1920-
See Rohmer, Eric
See also CA 110
Schevill, James (Erwin) 1920- .... **CLC 7**
See also CA 5-8R; CAAS 12; CAD; CD 5
Schiller, Friedrich von 1759-1805 ...... **DC 12; NCLC 39, 69**
See also CDWLB 2; DAM DRAM; DLB 94; EW 5; RGWL 2, 3; TWA
Schisgal, Murray (Joseph) 1926- .... **CLC 6**
See also CA 21-24R; CAD; CANR 48, 86; CD 5
Schlee, Ann 1934- .... **CLC 35**
See also CA 101; CANR 29, 88; SATA 44; SATA-Brief 36

Schlegel, August Wilhelm von
1767-1845 .... **NCLC 15**
See also DLB 94; RGWL 2, 3
Schlegel, Friedrich 1772-1829 .... **NCLC 45**
See also DLB 90; EW 5; RGWL 2, 3; TWA
Schlegel, Johann Elias (von)
1719(?)-1749 .... **LC 5**
Schleiermacher, Friedrich
1768-1834 .... **NCLC 107**
See also DLB 90
Schlesinger, Arthur M(eier), Jr.
1917- .... **CLC 84**
See also AITN 1; CA 1-4R; CANR 1, 28, 58, 105; DLB 17; INT CANR-28; MTCW 1, 2; SATA 61
Schlink, Bernhard 1944- .... **CLC 174**
See also CA 163; CANR 116
Schmidt, Arno (Otto) 1914-1979 ...... **CLC 56**
See also CA 128; 109; DLB 69; EWL 3
Schmitz, Aron Hector 1861-1928
See Svevo, Italo
See also CA 104; 122; MTCW 1
Schnackenberg, Gjertrud (Cecelia)
1953- .... **CLC 40; PC 45**
See also CA 116; CANR 100; CP 7; CWP; DLB 120, 282; PFS 13
Schneider, Leonard Alfred 1925-1966
See Bruce, Lenny
See also CA 89-92
Schnitzler, Arthur 1862-1931 ..... **DC 17; SSC 15, 61; TCLC 4**
See also CA 104; CDWLB 2; DLB 81, 118; EW 8; EWL 3; RGSF 2; RGWL 2, 3
Schoenberg, Arnold Franz Walter
1874-1951 .... **TCLC 75**
See also CA 109; 188
Schonberg, Arnold
See Schoenberg, Arnold Franz Walter
Schopenhauer, Arthur 1788-1860 .. **NCLC 51**
See also DLB 90; EW 5
Schor, Sandra (M.) 1932(?)-1990 ..... **CLC 65**
See also CA 132
Schorer, Mark 1908-1977 .... **CLC 9**
See also CA 5-8R; 73-76; CANR 7; DLB 103
Schrader, Paul (Joseph) 1946- .... **CLC 26**
See also CA 37-40R; CANR 41; DLB 44
Schreber, Daniel 1842-1911 .... **TCLC 123**
Schreiner, Olive (Emilie Albertina)
1855-1920 .... **TCLC 9**
See also AFW; BRWS 2; CA 105; 154; DLB 18, 156, 190, 225; EWL 3; FW; RGEL 2; TWA; WLIT 2; WWE 1
Schulberg, Budd (Wilson) 1914- .. **CLC 7, 48**
See also BPFB 3; CA 25-28R; CANR 19, 87; CN 7; DLB 6, 26, 28; DLBY 1981, 2001
Schulman, Arnold
See Trumbo, Dalton
Schulz, Bruno 1892-1942 .. **SSC 13; TCLC 5, 51**
See also CA 115; 123; CANR 86; CDWLB 4; DLB 215; EWL 3; MTCW 2; RGSF 2; RGWL 2, 3
Schulz, Charles M(onroe)
1922-2000 .... **CLC 12**
See also AAYA 39; CA 9-12R; 187; CANR 6; INT CANR-6; SATA 10; SATA-Obit 118
Schumacher, E(rnst) F(riedrich)
1911-1977 .... **CLC 80**
See also CA 81-84; 73-76; CANR 34, 85
Schuyler, George Samuel 1895-1977 .... **HR 3**
See also BW 2; CA 81-84; 73-76; CANR 42; DLB 29, 51
Schuyler, James Marcus 1923-1991 .. **CLC 5, 23**
See also CA 101; 134; DAM POET; DLB 5, 169; EWL 3; INT CA-101; WP

Schwartz, Delmore (David)
1913-1966 ... **CLC 2, 4, 10, 45, 87; PC 8**
See also AMWS 2; CA 17-18; 25-28R; CANR 35; CAP 2; DLB 28, 48; EWL 3; MTCW 1, 2; PAB; RGAL 4; TUS
Schwartz, Ernst
See Ozu, Yasujiro
Schwartz, John Burnham 1965- .... **CLC 59**
See also CA 132; CANR 116
Schwartz, Lynne Sharon 1939- .... **CLC 31**
See also CA 103; CANR 44, 89; DLB 218; MTCW 2
Schwartz, Muriel A.
See Eliot, T(homas) S(tearns)
Schwarz-Bart, Andre 1928- .... **CLC 2, 4**
See also CA 89-92; CANR 109
Schwarz-Bart, Simone 1938- . **BLCS; CLC 7**
See also BW 2; CA 97-100; CANR 117; EWL 3
Schwerner, Armand 1927-1999 .... **PC 42**
See also CA 9-12R; 179; CANR 50, 85; CP 7; DLB 165
Schwitters, Kurt (Hermann Edward Karl Julius) 1887-1948 .... **TCLC 95**
See also CA 158
Schwob, Marcel (Mayer Andre)
1867-1905 .... **TCLC 20**
See also CA 117; 168; DLB 123; GFL 1789 to the Present
Sciascia, Leonardo 1921-1989 .. **CLC 8, 9, 41**
See also CA 85-88; 130; CANR 35; DLB 177; EWL 3; MTCW 1; RGWL 2, 3
Scoppettone, Sandra 1936- .... **CLC 26**
See Early, Jack
See also AAYA 11; BYA 8; CA 5-8R; CANR 41, 73; GLL 1; MAICYA 2; MAICYAS 1; SATA 9, 92; WYA; YAW
Scorsese, Martin 1942- .... **CLC 20, 89**
See also AAYA 38; CA 110; 114; CANR 46, 85
Scotland, Jay
See Jakes, John (William)
Scott, Duncan Campbell
1862-1947 .... **TCLC 6**
See also CA 104; 153; DAC; DLB 92; RGEL 2
Scott, Evelyn 1893-1963 .... **CLC 43**
See also CA 104; 112; CANR 64; DLB 9, 48; RHW
Scott, F(rancis) R(eginald)
1899-1985 .... **CLC 22**
See also CA 101; 114; CANR 87; DLB 88; INT CA-101; RGEL 2
Scott, Frank
See Scott, F(rancis) R(eginald)
Scott, Joan .... **CLC 65**
Scott, Joanna 1960- .... **CLC 50**
See also CA 126; CANR 53, 92
Scott, Paul (Mark) 1920-1978 .... **CLC 9, 60**
See also BRWS 1; CA 81-84; 77-80; CANR 33; DLB 14, 207; EWL 3; MTCW 1; RGEL 2; RHW; WWE 1
Scott, Ridley 1937- .... **CLC 183**
See also AAYA 13, 43
Scott, Sarah 1723-1795 .... **LC 44**
See also DLB 39
Scott, Sir Walter 1771-1832 .... **NCLC 15, 69, 110; PC 13; SSC 32; WLC**
See also AAYA 22; BRW 4; BYA 2; CDBLB 1789-1832; DA; DAB; DAC; DAM MST, NOV, POET; DLB 93, 107, 116, 144, 159; HGG; LAIT 1; RGEL 2; RGSF 2; SSFS 10; SUFW 1; TEA; WLIT 3; YABC 2
Scribe, (Augustin) Eugene 1791-1861 . **DC 5; NCLC 16**
See also DAM DRAM; DLB 192; GFL 1789 to the Present; RGWL 2, 3

Scrum, R.
See Crumb, R(obert)

Scudery, Georges de 1601-1667 .... **LC 75**
See also GFL Beginnings to 1789

Scudery, Madeleine de 1607-1701 .. **LC 2, 58**
See also DLB 268; GFL Beginnings to 1789

Scum
See Crumb, R(obert)

Scumbag, Little Bobby
See Crumb, R(obert)

Seabrook, John
See Hubbard, L(afayette) Ron(ald)

Sealy, I(rwin) Allan 1951- .... **CLC 55**
See also CA 136; CN 7

Search, Alexander
See Pessoa, Fernando (Antonio Nogueira)

Sebastian, Lee
See Silverberg, Robert

Sebastian Owl
See Thompson, Hunter S(tockton)

Sebestyen, Igen
See Sebestyen, Ouida

Sebestyen, Ouida 1924- .... **CLC 30**
See also AAYA 8; BYA 7; CA 107; CANR 40, 114; CLR 17; JRDA; MAICYA 1, 2; SAAS 10; SATA 39, 140; WYA; YAW

Secundus, H. Scriblerus
See Fielding, Henry

Sedges, John
See Buck, Pearl S(ydenstricker)

Sedgwick, Catharine Maria
1789-1867 .... **NCLC 19, 98**
See also DLB 1, 74, 183, 239, 243, 254; RGAL 4

Seelye, John (Douglas) 1931- .... **CLC 7**
See also CA 97-100; CANR 70; INT CA-97-100; TCWW 2

Seferiades, Giorgos Stylianou 1900-1971
See Seferis, George
See also CA 5-8R; 33-36R; CANR 5, 36; MTCW 1

Seferis, George .... **CLC 5, 11**
See Seferiades, Giorgos Stylianou
See also EW 12; EWL 3; RGWL 2, 3

Segal, Erich (Wolf) 1937- .... **CLC 3, 10**
See also BEST 89:1; BPFB 3; CA 25-28R; CANR 20, 36, 65, 113; CPW; DAM POP; DLBY 1986; INT CANR-20; MTCW 1

Seger, Bob 1945- .... **CLC 35**

Seghers, Anna .... **CLC 7**
See Radvanyi, Netty
See also CDWLB 2; DLB 69; EWL 3

Seidel, Frederick (Lewis) 1936- .... **CLC 18**
See also CA 13-16R; CANR 8, 99; CP 7; DLBY 1984

Seifert, Jaroslav 1901-1986 . **CLC 34, 44, 93; PC 47**
See also CA 127; CDWLB 4; DLB 215; EWL 3; MTCW 1, 2

Sei Shonagon c. 966-1017(?) .... **CMLC 6**

Sejour, Victor 1817-1874 .... **DC 10**
See also DLB 50

Sejour Marcou et Ferrand, Juan Victor
See Sejour, Victor

Selby, Hubert, Jr. 1928-2004 ..... **CLC 1, 2, 4, 8; SSC 20**
See also CA 13-16R; CANR 33, 85; CN 7; DLB 2, 227

Selzer, Richard 1928- .... **CLC 74**
See also CA 65-68; CANR 14, 106

Sembene, Ousmane
See Ousmane, Sembene
See also AFW; CWW 2; EWL 3; WLIT 2

Senancour, Etienne Pivert de
1770-1846 .... **NCLC 16**
See also DLB 119; GFL 1789 to the Present

Sender, Ramon (Jose) 1902-1982 ...... **CLC 8; HLC 2; TCLC 136**
See also CA 5-8R; 105; CANR 8; DAM MULT; EWL 3; HW 1; MTCW 1; RGWL 2, 3

Seneca, Lucius Annaeus c. 4B.C.-c. 65 .... **CMLC 6; DC 5**
See also AW 2; CDWLB 1; DAM DRAM; DLB 211; RGWL 2, 3; TWA

Senghor, Leopold Sedar 1906-2001 ... **BLC 3; CLC 54, 130; PC 25**
See also AFW; BW 2; CA 116; 125; 203; CANR 47, 74; DAM MULT, POET; DNFS 2; EWL 3; GFL 1789 to the Present; MTCW 1, 2; TWA

Senna, Danzy 1970- .... **CLC 119**
See also CA 169

Serling, (Edward) Rod(man)
1924-1975 .... **CLC 30**
See also AAYA 14; AITN 1; CA 162; 57-60; DLB 26; SFW 4

Serna, Ramon Gomez de la
See Gomez de la Serna, Ramon

Serpieres
See Guillevic, (Eugene)

Service, Robert
See Service, Robert W(illiam)
See also BYA 4; DAB; DLB 92

Service, Robert W(illiam)
1874(?)-1958 .... **TCLC 15; WLC**
See Service, Robert
See also CA 115; 140; CANR 84; DA; DAC; DAM MST, POET; PFS 10; RGEL 2; SATA 20

Seth, Vikram 1952- .... **CLC 43, 90**
See also CA 121; 127; CANR 50, 74; CN 7; CP 7; DA3; DAM MULT; DLB 120, 271, 282; EWL 3; INT CA-127; MTCW 2; WWE 1

Seton, Cynthia Propper 1926-1982 .. **CLC 27**
See also CA 5-8R; 108; CANR 7

Seton, Ernest (Evan) Thompson
1860-1946 .... **TCLC 31**
See also ANW; BYA 3; CA 109; 204; CLR 59; DLB 92; DLBD 13; JRDA; SATA 18

Seton-Thompson, Ernest
See Seton, Ernest (Evan) Thompson

Settle, Mary Lee 1918- .... **CLC 19, 61**
See also BPFB 3; CA 89-92; CAAS 1; CANR 44, 87, 126; CN 7; CSW; DLB 6; INT CA-89-92

Seuphor, Michel
See Arp, Jean

Sevigne, Marie (de Rabutin-Chantal)
1626-1696 .... **LC 11**
See Sevigne, Marie de Rabutin Chantal
See also GFL Beginnings to 1789; TWA

Sevigne, Marie de Rabutin Chantal
See Sevigne, Marie (de Rabutin-Chantal)
See also DLB 268

Sewall, Samuel 1652-1730 .... **LC 38**
See also DLB 24; RGAL 4

Sexton, Anne (Harvey) 1928-1974 ..... **CLC 2, 4, 6, 8, 10, 15, 53, 123; PC 2; WLC**
See also AMWS 2; CA 1-4R; 53-56; CABS 2; CANR 3, 36; CDALB 1941-1968; DA; DA3; DAB; DAC; DAM MST, POET; DLB 5, 169; EWL 3; EXPP; FW; MAWW; MTCW 1, 2; PAB; PFS 4, 14; RGAL 4; SATA 10; TUS

Shaara, Jeff 1952- .... **CLC 119**
See also CA 163; CANR 109

Shaara, Michael (Joseph, Jr.)
1929-1988 .... **CLC 15**
See also AITN 1; BPFB 3; CA 102; 125; CANR 52, 85; DAM POP; DLBY 1983

Shackleton, C. C.
See Aldiss, Brian W(ilson)

Shacochis, Bob .... **CLC 39**
See Shacochis, Robert G.

Shacochis, Robert G. 1951-
See Shacochis, Bob
See also CA 119; 124; CANR 100; INT CA-124

Shaffer, Anthony (Joshua)
1926-2001 .... **CLC 19**
See also CA 110; 116; 200; CBD; CD 5; DAM DRAM; DFS 13; DLB 13

Shaffer, Peter (Levin) 1926- .. **CLC 5, 14, 18, 37, 60; DC 7**
See also BRWS 1; CA 25-28R; CANR 25, 47, 74, 118; CBD; CD 5; CDBLB 1960 to Present; DA3; DAB; DAM DRAM, MST; DFS 5, 13; DLB 13, 233; EWL 3; MTCW 1, 2; RGEL 2; TEA

Shakespeare, William 1564-1616 .... **WLC**
See also AAYA 35; BRW 1; CDBLB Before 1660; DA; DA3; DAB; DAC; DAM DRAM, MST, POET; DLB 62, 172, 263; EXPP; LAIT 1; LATS 1; LMFS 1; PAB; PFS 1, 2, 3, 4, 5, 8, 9; RGEL 2; TEA; WLIT 3; WP; WS; WYA

Shakey, Bernard
See Young, Neil

Shalamov, Varlam (Tikhonovich)
1907(?)-1982 .... **CLC 18**
See also CA 129; 105; RGSF 2

Shamloo, Ahmad
See Shamlu, Ahmad

Shamlou, Ahmad
See Shamlu, Ahmad

Shamlu, Ahmad 1925-2000 .... **CLC 10**
See also CA 216; CWW 2

Shammas, Anton 1951- .... **CLC 55**
See also CA 199

Shandling, Arline
See Berriault, Gina

Shange, Ntozake 1948- ... **BLC 3; CLC 8, 25, 38, 74, 126; DC 3**
See also AAYA 9; AFAW 1; BW 2; CA 85-88; CABS 3; CAD; CANR 27, 48, 74; CD 5; CP 7; CWD; CWP; DA3; DAM DRAM, MULT; DFS 2, 11; DLB 38, 249; FW; LAIT 5; MTCW 1, 2; NFS 11; RGAL 4; YAW

Shanley, John Patrick 1950- .... **CLC 75**
See also CA 128; 133; CAD; CANR 83; CD 5

Shapcott, Thomas W(illiam) 1935- .. **CLC 38**
See also CA 69-72; CANR 49, 83, 103; CP 7; DLB 289

Shapiro, Jane 1942- .... **CLC 76**
See also CA 196

Shapiro, Karl (Jay) 1913-2000 ...... **CLC 4, 8, 15, 53; PC 25**
See also AMWS 2; CA 1-4R; 188; CAAS 6; CANR 1, 36, 66; CP 7; DLB 48; EWL 3; EXPP; MTCW 1, 2; PFS 3; RGAL 4

Sharp, William 1855-1905 .... **TCLC 39**
See Macleod, Fiona
See also CA 160; DLB 156; RGEL 2

Sharpe, Thomas Ridley 1928-
See Sharpe, Tom
See also CA 114; 122; CANR 85; INT CA-122

Sharpe, Tom .... **CLC 36**
See Sharpe, Thomas Ridley
See also CN 7; DLB 14, 231

Shatrov, Mikhail .... **CLC 59**

Shaw, Bernard
See Shaw, George Bernard
See also DLB 190

Shaw, G. Bernard
See Shaw, George Bernard

Shaw, George Bernard 1856-1950 ..... **DC 23; TCLC 3, 9, 21, 45; WLC**
See Shaw, Bernard
See also BRW 6; BRWC 1; BRWR 2; CA 104; 128; CDBLB 1914-1945; DA; DA3; DAB; DAC; DAM DRAM, MST; DFS 1, 3, 6, 11; DLB 10, 57; EWL 3; LAIT 3; LATS 1; MTCW 1, 2; RGEL 2; TEA; WLIT 4

Shaw, Henry Wheeler 1818-1885 .. **NCLC 15**
See also DLB 11; RGAL 4

Shaw, Irwin 1913-1984 .... **CLC 7, 23, 34**
See also AITN 1; BPFB 3; CA 13-16R; 112; CANR 21; CDALB 1941-1968; CPW; DAM DRAM; POP; DLB 6, 102; DLBY 1984; MTCW 1, 21

Shaw, Robert 1927-1978 .... **CLC 5**
See also AITN 1; CA 1-4R; 81-84; CANR 4; DLB 13, 14

Shaw, T. E.
See Lawrence, T(homas) E(dward)

Shawn, Wallace 1943- .... **CLC 41**
See also CA 112; CAD; CD 5; DLB 266

Shchedrin, N.
See Saltykov, Mikhail Evgrafovich

Shea, Lisa 1953- .... **CLC 86**
See also CA 147

Sheed, Wilfrid (John Joseph) 1930- . **CLC 2, 4, 10, 53**
See also CA 65-68; CANR 30, 66; CN 7; DLB 6; MTCW 1, 2

Sheehy, Gail 1937- .... **CLC 171**
See also CA 49-52; CANR 1, 33, 55, 92; CPW; MTCW 1

Sheldon, Alice Hastings Bradley 1915(?)-1987
See Tiptree, James, Jr.
See also CA 108; 122; CANR 34; INT CA-108; MTCW 1

Sheldon, John
See Bloch, Robert (Albert)

Sheldon, Walter J(ames) 1917-1996
See Queen, Ellery
See also AITN 1; CA 25-28R; CANR 10

Shelley, Mary Wollstonecraft (Godwin) 1797-1851 ...... **NCLC 14, 59, 103; WLC**
See also AAYA 20; BPFB 3; BRW 3; BRWC 2; BRWS 3; BYA 5; CDBLB 1789-1832; DA; DA3; DAB; DAC; DAM MST, NOV; DLB 110, 116, 159, 178; EXPN; HGG; LAIT 1; LMFS 1, 2; NFS 1; RGEL 2; SATA 29; SCFW; SFW 4; TEA; WLIT 3

Shelley, Percy Bysshe 1792-1822 .. **NCLC 18, 93; PC 14; WLC**
See also BRW 4; BRWR 1; CDBLB 1789-1832; DA; DA3; DAB; DAC; DAM MST, POET; DLB 96, 110, 158; EXPP; LMFS 1; PAB; PFS 2; RGEL 2; TEA; WLIT 3; WP

Shepard, Jim 1956- .... **CLC 36**
See also CA 137; CANR 59, 104; SATA 90

Shepard, Lucius 1947- .... **CLC 34**
See also CA 128; 141; CANR 81, 124; HGG; SCFW 2; SFW 4; SUFW 2

Shepard, Sam 1943- .... **CLC 4, 6, 17, 34, 41, 44, 169; DC 5**
See also AAYA 1; AMWS 3; CA 69-72; CABS 3; CAD; CANR 22, 120; CD 5; DA3; DAM DRAM; DFS 3, 6, 7, 14; DLB 7, 212; EWL 3; IDFW 3, 4; MTCW 1, 2; RGAL 4

Shepherd, Michael
See Ludlum, Robert

Sherburne, Zoa (Lillian Morin) 1912-1995 .... **CLC 30**
See also AAYA 13; CA 1-4R; 176; CANR 3, 37; MAICYA 1, 2; SAAS 18; SATA 3; YAW

Sheridan, Frances 1724-1766 .... **LC 7**
See also DLB 39, 84

Sheridan, Richard Brinsley 1751-1816 ..... **DC 1; NCLC 5, 91; WLC**
See also BRW 3; CDBLB 1660-1789; DA; DAB; DAC; DAM DRAM, MST; DFS 15; DLB 89; WLIT 3

Sherman, Jonathan Marc .... **CLC 55**

Sherman, Martin 1941(?)- .... **CLC 19**
See also CA 116; 123; CAD; CANR 86; CD 5; DLB 228; GLL 1; IDTP

Sherwin, Judith Johnson
See Johnson, Judith (Emlyn)
See also CANR 85; CP 7; CWP

Sherwood, Frances 1940- .... **CLC 81**
See also CA 146, 220; CAAE 220

Sherwood, Robert E(mmet) 1896-1955 .... **TCLC 3**
See also CA 104; 153; CANR 86; DAM DRAM; DFS 11, 15, 17; DLB 7, 26, 249; IDFW 3, 4; RGAL 4

Shestov, Lev 1866-1938 .... **TCLC 56**

Shevchenko, Taras 1814-1861 .... **NCLC 54**

Shiel, M(atthew) P(hipps) 1865-1947 .... **TCLC 8**
See Holmes, Gordon
See also CA 106; 160; DLB 153; HGG; MTCW 2; SFW 4; SUFW

Shields, Carol (Ann) 1935-2003 ..... **CLC 91, 113**
See also AMWS 7; CA 81-84; 218; CANR 51, 74, 98; CCA 1; CN 7; CPW; DA3; DAC; MTCW 2

Shields, David (Jonathan) 1956- ...... **CLC 97**
See also CA 124; CANR 48, 99, 112

Shiga, Naoya 1883-1971 ..... **CLC 33; SSC 23**
See Shiga Naoya
See also CA 101; 33-36R; MJW; RGWL 3

Shiga Naoya
See Shiga, Naoya
See also DLB 180; EWL 3; RGWL 3

Shilts, Randy 1951-1994 .... **CLC 85**
See also AAYA 19; CA 115; 127; 144; CANR 45; DA3; GLL 1; INT CA-127; MTCW 2

Shimazaki, Haruki 1872-1943
See Shimazaki Toson
See also CA 105; 134; CANR 84; RGWL 3

Shimazaki Toson .... **TCLC 5**
See Shimazaki, Haruki
See also DLB 180; EWL 3

Shirley, James 1596-1666 .... **LC 96**
See also DLB 58; RGEL 2

Sholokhov, Mikhail (Aleksandrovich) 1905-1984 .... **CLC 7, 15**
See also CA 101; 112; DLB 272; EWL 3; MTCW 1, 2; RGWL 2, 3; SATA-Obit 36

Shone, Patric
See Hanley, James

Showalter, Elaine 1941- .... **CLC 169**
See also CA 57-60; CANR 58, 106; DLB 67; FW; GLL 2

Shreve, Susan Richards 1939- .... **CLC 23**
See also CA 49-52; CAAS 5; CANR 5, 38, 69, 100; MAICYA 1, 2; SATA 46, 95; SATA-Brief 41

Shue, Larry 1946-1985 .... **CLC 52**
See also CA 145; 117; DAM DRAM; DFS 7

Shu-Jen, Chou 1881-1936
See Lu Hsun
See also CA 104

Shulman, Alix Kates 1932- .... **CLC 2, 10**
See also CA 29-32R; CANR 43; FW; SATA 7

Shusaku, Endo
See Endo, Shusaku

Shuster, Joe 1914-1992 .... **CLC 21**
See also AAYA 50

Shute, Nevil .... **CLC 30**
See Norway, Nevil Shute
See also BPFB 3; DLB 255; NFS 9; RHW; SFW 4

Shuttle, Penelope (Diane) 1947- .... **CLC 7**
See also CA 93-96; CANR 39, 84, 92, 108; CP 7; CWP; DLB 14, 40

Shvarts, Elena 1948- .... **PC 50**
See also CA 147

Sidhwa, Bapsy (N.) 1938- .... **CLC 168**
See also CA 108; CANR 25, 57; CN 7; FW

Sidney, Mary 1561-1621 .... **LC 19, 39**
See Sidney Herbert, Mary

Sidney, Sir Philip 1554-1586 . **LC 19, 39; PC 32**
See also BRW 1; BRWR 2; CDBLB Before 1660; DA; DA3; DAB; DAC; DAM MST, POET; DLB 167; EXPP; PAB; RGEL 2; TEA; WP

Sidney Herbert, Mary
See Sidney, Mary
See also DLB 167

Siegel, Jerome 1914-1996 .... **CLC 21**
See Siegel, Jerry
See also CA 116; 169; 151

Siegel, Jerry
See Siegel, Jerome
See also AAYA 50

Sienkiewicz, Henryk (Adam Alexander Pius) 1846-1916 .... **TCLC 3**
See also CA 104; 134; CANR 84; EWL 3; RGSF 2; RGWL 2, 3

Sierra, Gregorio Martinez
See Martinez Sierra, Gregorio

Sierra, Maria (de la O'LeJarraga) Martinez
See Martinez Sierra, Maria (de la O'LeJarraga)

Sigal, Clancy 1926- .... **CLC 7**
See also CA 1-4R; CANR 85; CN 7

Sigourney, Lydia H.
See Sigourney, Lydia Howard (Huntley)
See also DLB 73, 183

Sigourney, Lydia Howard (Huntley) 1791-1865 .... **NCLC 21, 87**
See Sigourney, Lydia H.; Sigourney, Lydia Huntley
See also DLB 1

Sigourney, Lydia Huntley
See Sigourney, Lydia Howard (Huntley)
See also DLB 42, 239, 243

Siguenza y Gongora, Carlos de 1645-1700 .... **HLCS 2; LC 8**
See also LAW

Sigurjonsson, Johann
See Johann Sigurjonsson

Sikelianos, Angelos 1884-1951 .... **PC 29; TCLC 39**
See also EWL 3; RGWL 2, 3

Silkin, Jon 1930-1997 .... **CLC 2, 6, 43**
See also CA 5-8R; CAAS 5; CANR 89; CP 7; DLB 27

Silko, Leslie (Marmon) 1948- .... **CLC 23, 74, 114; NNAL; SSC 37, 66; WLCS**
See also AAYA 14; AMWS 4; ANW; BYA 12; CA 115; 122; CANR 45, 65, 118; CN 7; CP 7; CPW 1; CWP; DA; DA3; DAC; DAM MST, MULT, POP; DLB 143, 175, 256, 275; EWL 3; EXPP; EXPS; LAIT 4; MTCW 2; NFS 4; PFS 9, 16; RGAL 4; RGSF 2; SSFS 4, 8, 10, 11

Sillanpaa, Frans Eemil 1888-1964 ... **CLC 19**
See also CA 129; 93-96; EWL 3; MTCW 1

Sillitoe, Alan 1928- .. **CLC 1, 3, 6, 10, 19, 57, 148**
See also AITN 1; BRWS 5; CA 9-12R, 191; CAAE 191; CAAS 2; CANR 8, 26, 55; CDBLB 1960 to Present; CN 7; DLB 14, 139; EWL 3; MTCW 1, 2; RGEL 2; RGSF 2; SATA 61

Silone, Ignazio 1900-1978 .... **CLC 4**
See also CA 25-28; 81-84; CANR 34; CAP 2; DLB 264; EW 12; EWL 3; MTCW 1; RGSF 2; RGWL 2, 3
Silone, Ignazione
See Silone, Ignazio
Silver, Joan Micklin 1935- .... **CLC 20**
See also CA 114; 121; INT CA-121
Silver, Nicholas
See Faust, Frederick (Schiller)
See also TCWW 2
Silverberg, Robert 1935- .... **CLC 7, 140**
See also AAYA 24; BPFB 3; BYA 7, 9; CA 1-4R; 186; CAAE 186; CAAS 3; CANR 1, 20, 36, 85; CLR 59; CN 7; CPW; DAM POP; DLB 8; INT CANR-20; MAICYA 1, 2; MTCW 1, 2; SATA 13, 91; SATA-Essay 104; SCFW 2; SFW 4; SUFW 2
Silverstein, Alvin 1933- .... **CLC 17**
See also CA 49-52; CANR 2; CLR 25; JRDA; MAICYA 1, 2; SATA 8, 69, 124
Silverstein, Shel(don Allan) 1932-1999 .... **PC 49**
See also AAYA 40; BW 3; CA 107; 179; CANR 47, 74, 81; CLR 5, 96; CWRI 5; JRDA; MAICYA 1, 2; MTCW 2; SATA 33, 92; SATA-Brief 27; SATA-Obit 116
Silverstein, Virginia B(arbara Opshelor) 1937- .... **CLC 17**
See also CA 49-52; CANR 2; CLR 25; JRDA; MAICYA 1, 2; SATA 8, 69, 124
Sim, Georges
See Simenon, Georges (Jacques Christian)
Simak, Clifford D(onald) 1904-1988 . **CLC 1, 55**
See also CA 1-4R; 125; CANR 1, 35; DLB 8; MTCW 1; SATA-Obit 56; SFW 4
Simenon, Georges (Jacques Christian) 1903-1989 .... **CLC 1, 2, 3, 8, 18, 47**
See also BPFB 3; CA 85-88; 129; CANR 35; CMW 4; DA3; DAM POP; DLB 72; DLBY 1989; EW 12; EWL 3; GFL 1789 to the Present; MSW; MTCW 1, 2; RGWL 2, 3
Simic, Charles 1938- .... **CLC 6, 9, 22, 49, 68, 130**
See also AMWS 8; CA 29-32R; CAAS 4; CANR 12, 33, 52, 61, 96; CP 7; DA3; DAM POET; DLB 105; MTCW 2; PFS 7; RGAL 4; WP
Simmel, Georg 1858-1918 .... **TCLC 64**
See also CA 157; DLB 296
Simmons, Charles (Paul) 1924- .... **CLC 57**
See also CA 89-92; INT CA-89-92
Simmons, Dan 1948- .... **CLC 44**
See also AAYA 16, 54; CA 138; CANR 53, 81, 126; CPW; DAM POP; HGG; SUFW 2
Simmons, James (Stewart Alexander) 1933- .... **CLC 43**
See also CA 105; CAAS 21; CP 7; DLB 40
Simms, William Gilmore 1806-1870 .... **NCLC 3**
See also DLB 3, 30, 59, 73, 248, 254; RGAL 4
Simon, Carly 1945- .... **CLC 26**
See also CA 105
Simon, Claude (Henri Eugene) 1913-1984 .... **CLC 4, 9, 15, 39**
See also CA 89-92; CANR 33, 117; DAM NOV; DLB 83; EW 13; EWL 3; GFL 1789 to the Present; MTCW 1
Simon, Myles
See Follett, Ken(neth Martin)
Simon, (Marvin) Neil 1927- ... **CLC 6, 11, 31, 39, 70; DC 14**
See also AAYA 32; AITN 1; AMWS 4; CA 21-24R; CANR 26, 54, 87, 126; CD 5; DA3; DAM DRAM; DFS 2, 6, 12, 18; DLB 7, 266; LAIT 4; MTCW 1, 2; RGAL 4; TUS

Simon, Paul (Frederick) 1941(?)- ..... **CLC 17**
See also CA 116; 153
Simonon, Paul 1956(?)- .... **CLC 30**
Simonson, Rick ed. .... **CLC 70**
Simpson, Harriette
See Arnow, Harriette (Louisa) Simpson
Simpson, Louis (Aston Marantz) 1923- .... **CLC 4, 7, 9, 32, 149**
See also AMWS 9; CA 1-4R; CAAS 4; CANR 1, 61; CP 7; DAM POET; DLB 5; MTCW 1, 2; PFS 7, 11, 14; RGAL 4
Simpson, Mona (Elizabeth) 1957- ... **CLC 44, 146**
See also CA 122; 135; CANR 68, 103; CN 7; EWL 3
Simpson, N(orman) F(rederick) 1919- .... **CLC 29**
See also CA 13-16R; CBD; DLB 13; RGEL 2
Sinclair, Andrew (Annandale) 1935- . **CLC 2, 14**
See also CA 9-12R; CAAS 5; CANR 14, 38, 91; CN 7; DLB 14; FANT; MTCW 1
Sinclair, Emil
See Hesse, Hermann
Sinclair, Iain 1943- .... **CLC 76**
See also CA 132; CANR 81; CP 7; HGG
Sinclair, Iain MacGregor
See Sinclair, Iain
Sinclair, Irene
See Griffith, D(avid Lewelyn) W(ark)
Sinclair, Mary Amelia St. Clair 1865(?)-1946
See Sinclair, May
See also CA 104; HGG; RHW
Sinclair, May .... **TCLC 3, 11**
See Sinclair, Mary Amelia St. Clair
See also CA 166; DLB 36, 135; EWL 3; RGEL 2; SUFW
Sinclair, Roy
See Griffith, D(avid Lewelyn) W(ark)
Sinclair, Upton (Beall) 1878-1968 ..... **CLC 1, 11, 15, 63; WLC**
See also AMWS 5; BPFB 3; BYA 2; CA 5-8R; 25-28R; CANR 7; CDALB 1929-1941; DA; DA3; DAB; DAC; DAM MST, NOV; DLB 9; EWL 3; INT CANR-7; LAIT 3; MTCW 1, 2; NFS 6; RGAL 4; SATA 9; TUS; YAW
Singe, (Edmund) J(ohn) M(illington) 1871-1909 .... **WLC**
Singer, Isaac
See Singer, Isaac Bashevis
Singer, Isaac Bashevis 1904-1991 .. **CLC 1, 3, 6, 9, 11, 15, 23, 38, 69, 111; SSC 3, 53; WLC**
See also AAYA 32; AITN 1, 2; AMW; AMWR 2; BPFB 3; BYA 1, 4; CA 1-4R; 134; CANR 1, 39, 106; CDALB 1941-1968; CLR 1; CWRI 5; DA; DA3; DAB; DAC; DAM MST, NOV; DLB 6, 28, 52, 278; DLBY 1991; EWL 3; EXPS; HGG; JRDA; LAIT 3; MAICYA 1, 2; MTCW 1, 2; RGAL 4; RGSF 2; SATA 3, 27; SATA-Obit 68; SSFS 2, 12, 16; TUS; TWA
Singer, Israel Joshua 1893-1944 .... **TCLC 33**
See also CA 169; EWL 3
Singh, Khushwant 1915- .... **CLC 11**
See also CA 9-12R; CAAS 9; CANR 6, 84; CN 7; EWL 3; RGEL 2
Singleton, Ann
See Benedict, Ruth (Fulton)
Singleton, John 1968(?)- .... **CLC 156**
See also AAYA 50; BW 2, 3; CA 138; CANR 67, 82; DAM MULT
Sinjohn, John
See Galsworthy, John

Sinyavsky, Andrei (Donatevich) 1925-1997 .... **CLC 8**
See Sinyavsky, Andrey Donatovich; Tertz, Abram
See also CA 85-88; 159
Sinyavsky, Andrey Donatovich
See Sinyavsky, Andrei (Donatevich)
See also EWL 3
Sirin, V.
See Nabokov, Vladimir (Vladimirovich)
Sissman, L(ouis) E(dward) 1928-1976 .... **CLC 9, 18**
See also CA 21-24R; 65-68; CANR 13; DLB 5
Sisson, C(harles) H(ubert) 1914-2003 .... **CLC 8**
See also CA 1-4R; 220; CAAS 3; CANR 3, 48, 84; CP 7; DLB 27
Sitting Bull 1831(?)-1890 .... **NNAL**
See also DA3; DAM MULT
Sitwell, Dame Edith 1887-1964 ..... **CLC 2, 9, 67; PC 3**
See also BRW 7; CA 9-12R; CANR 35; CDBLB 1945-1960; DAM POET; DLB 20; EWL 3; MTCW 1, 2; RGEL 2; TEA
Siwaarmill, H. P.
See Sharp, William
Sjoewall, Maj 1935- .... **CLC 7**
See Sjowall, Maj
See also CA 65-68; CANR 73
Sjowall, Maj
See Sjoewall, Maj
See also BPFB 3; CMW 4; MSW
Skelton, John 1460(?)-1529 ..... **LC 71; PC 25**
See also BRW 1; DLB 136; RGEL 2
Skelton, Robin 1925-1997 .... **CLC 13**
See Zuk, Georges
See also AITN 2; CA 5-8R; 160; CAAS 5; CANR 28, 89; CCA 1; CP 7; DLB 27, 53
Skolimowski, Jerzy 1938- .... **CLC 20**
See also CA 128
Skram, Amalie (Bertha) 1847-1905 .... **TCLC 25**
See also CA 165
Skvorecky, Josef (Vaclav) 1924- .... **CLC 15, 39, 69, 152**
See also CA 61-64; CAAS 1; CANR 10, 34, 63, 108; CDWLB 4; DA3; DAC; DAM NOV; DLB 232; EWL 3; MTCW 1, 2
Slade, Bernard .... **CLC 11, 46**
See Newbound, Bernard Slade
See also CAAS 9; CCA 1; DLB 53
Slaughter, Carolyn 1946- .... **CLC 56**
See also CA 85-88; CANR 85; CN 7
Slaughter, Frank G(ill) 1908-2001 ... **CLC 29**
See also AITN 2; CA 5-8R; 197; CANR 5, 85; INT CANR-5; RHW
Slavitt, David R(ytman) 1935- ...... **CLC 5, 14**
See also CA 21-24R; CAAS 3; CANR 41, 83; CP 7; DLB 5, 6
Slesinger, Tess 1905-1945 .... **TCLC 10**
See also CA 107; 199; DLB 102
Slessor, Kenneth 1901-1971 .... **CLC 14**
See also CA 102; 89-92; DLB 260; RGEL 2
Slowacki, Juliusz 1809-1849 .... **NCLC 15**
See also RGWL 3
Smart, Christopher 1722-1771 . **LC 3; PC 13**
See also DAM POET; DLB 109; RGEL 2
Smart, Elizabeth 1913-1986 .... **CLC 54**
See also CA 81-84; 118; DLB 88
Smiley, Jane (Graves) 1949- ...... **CLC 53, 76, 144**
See also AMWS 6; BPFB 3; CA 104; CANR 30, 50, 74, 96; CN 7; CPW 1; DA3; DAM POP; DLB 227, 234; EWL 3; INT CANR-30; SSFS 19

Smith, A(rthur) J(ames) M(arshall)
1902-1980 .... **CLC 15**
See also CA 1-4R; 102; CANR 4; DAC; DLB 88; RGEL 2

Smith, Adam 1723(?)-1790 .... **LC 36**
See also DLB 104, 252; RGEL 2

Smith, Alexander 1829-1867 .... **NCLC 59**
See also DLB 32, 55

Smith, Anna Deavere 1950- .... **CLC 86**
See also CA 133; CANR 103; CD 5; DFS 2

Smith, Betty (Wehner) 1904-1972 .... **CLC 19**
See also BPFB 3; BYA 3; CA 5-8R; 33-36R; DLBY 1982; LAIT 3; RGAL 4; SATA 6

Smith, Charlotte (Turner)
1749-1806 .... **NCLC 23, 115**
See also DLB 39, 109; RGEL 2; TEA

Smith, Clark Ashton 1893-1961 .... **CLC 43**
See also CA 143; CANR 81; FANT; HGG; MTCW 2; SCFW 2; SFW 4; SUFW

Smith, Dave .... **CLC 22, 42**
See Smith, David (Jeddie)
See also CAAS 7; DLB 5

Smith, David (Jeddie) 1942-
See Smith, Dave
See also CA 49-52; CANR 1, 59, 120; CP 7; CSW; DAM POET

Smith, Florence Margaret 1902-1971
See Smith, Stevie
See also CA 17-18; 29-32R; CANR 35; CAP 2; DAM POET; MTCW 1, 2; TEA

Smith, Iain Crichton 1928-1998 .... **CLC 64**
See also BRWS 9; CA 21-24R; 171; CN 7; CP 7; DLB 40, 139; RGSF 2

Smith, John 1580(?)-1631 .... **LC 9**
See also DLB 24, 30; TUS

Smith, Johnston
See Crane, Stephen (Townley)

Smith, Joseph, Jr. 1805-1844 .... **NCLC 53**

Smith, Lee 1944- .... **CLC 25, 73**
See also CA 114; 119; CANR 46, 118; CSW; DLB 143; DLBY 1983; EWL 3; INT CA-119; RGAL 4

Smith, Martin
See Smith, Martin Cruz

Smith, Martin Cruz 1942- .. **CLC 25; NNAL**
See also BEST 89:4; BPFB 3; CA 85-88; CANR 6, 23, 43, 65, 119; CMW 4; CPW; DAM MULT, POP; HGG; INT CANR-23; MTCW 2; RGAL 4

Smith, Patti 1946- .... **CLC 12**
See also CA 93-96; CANR 63

Smith, Pauline (Urmson)
1882-1959 .... **TCLC 25**
See also DLB 225; EWL 3

Smith, Rosamond
See Oates, Joyce Carol

Smith, Sheila Kaye
See Kaye-Smith, Sheila

Smith, Stevie .... **CLC 3, 8, 25, 44; PC 12**
See Smith, Florence Margaret
See also BRWS 2; DLB 20; EWL 3; MTCW 2; PAB; PFS 3; RGEL 2

Smith, Wilbur (Addison) 1933- .... **CLC 33**
See also CA 13-16R; CANR 7, 46, 66; CPW; MTCW 1, 2

Smith, William Jay 1918- .... **CLC 6**
See also AMWS 13; CA 5-8R; CANR 44, 106; CP 7; CSW; CWRI 5; DLB 5; MAICYA 1, 2; SAAS 22; SATA 2, 68

Smith, Woodrow Wilson
See Kuttner, Henry

Smith, Zadie 1976- .... **CLC 158**
See also AAYA 50; CA 193

Smolenskin, Peretz 1842-1885 .... **NCLC 30**

Smollett, Tobias (George) 1721-1771 ... **LC 2, 46**
See also BRW 3; CDBLB 1660-1789; DLB 39, 104; RGEL 2; TEA

Snodgrass, W(illiam) D(e Witt)
1926- .... **CLC 2, 6, 10, 18, 68**
See also AMWS 6; CA 1-4R; CANR 6, 36, 65, 85; CP 7; DAM POET; DLB 5; MTCW 1, 2; RGAL 4

Snorri Sturluson 1179-1241 .... **CMLC 56**
See also RGWL 2, 3

Snow, C(harles) P(ercy) 1905-1980 ... **CLC 1, 4, 6, 9, 13, 19**
See also BRW 7; CA 5-8R; 101; CANR 28; CDBLB 1945-1960; DAM NOV; DLB 15, 77; DLBD 17; EWL 3; MTCW 1, 2; RGEL 2; TEA

Snow, Frances Compton
See Adams, Henry (Brooks)

Snyder, Gary (Sherman) 1930- . **CLC 1, 2, 5, 9, 32, 120; PC 21**
See also AMWS 8; ANW; BG 3; CA 17-20R; CANR 30, 60, 125; CP 7; DA3; DAM POET; DLB 5, 16, 165, 212, 237, 275; EWL 3; MTCW 2; PFS 9, 19; RGAL 4; WP

Snyder, Zilpha Keatley 1927- .... **CLC 17**
See also AAYA 15; BYA 1; CA 9-12R; CANR 38; CLR 31; JRDA; MAICYA 1, 2; SAAS 2; SATA 1, 28, 75, 110; SATA-Essay 112; YAW

Soares, Bernardo
See Pessoa, Fernando (Antonio Nogueira)

Sobh, A.
See Shamlu, Ahmad

Sobh, Alef
See Shamlu, Ahmad

Sobol, Joshua 1939- .... **CLC 60**
See Sobol, Yehoshua
See also CA 200; CWW 2

Sobol, Yehoshua 1939-
See Sobol, Joshua
See also CWW 2

Socrates 470B.C.-399B.C. .... **CMLC 27**

Soderberg, Hjalmar 1869-1941 .... **TCLC 39**
See also DLB 259; EWL 3; RGSF 2

Soderbergh, Steven 1963- .... **CLC 154**
See also AAYA 43

Sodergran, Edith (Irene) 1892-1923
See Soedergran, Edith (Irene)
See also CA 202; DLB 259; EW 11; EWL 3; RGWL 2, 3

Soedergran, Edith (Irene)
1892-1923 .... **TCLC 31**
See Sodergran, Edith (Irene)

Softly, Edgar
See Lovecraft, H(oward) P(hillips)

Softly, Edward
See Lovecraft, H(oward) P(hillips)

Sokolov, Alexander V(sevolodovich) 1943-
See Sokolov, Sasha
See also CA 73-76

Sokolov, Raymond 1941- .... **CLC 7**
See also CA 85-88

Sokolov, Sasha .... **CLC 59**
See Sokolov, Alexander V(sevolodovich)
See also CWW 2; DLB 285; EWL 3; RGWL 2, 3

Sokolov, Sasha .... **CLC 59**

Solo, Jay
See Ellison, Harlan (Jay)

Sologub, Fyodor .... **TCLC 9**
See Teternikov, Fyodor Kuzmich
See also EWL 3

Solomons, Ikey Esquir
See Thackeray, William Makepeace

Solomos, Dionysios 1798-1857 .... **NCLC 15**

Solwoska, Mara
See French, Marilyn

Solzhenitsyn, Aleksandr I(sayevich)
1918- .. **CLC 1, 2, 4, 7, 9, 10, 18, 26, 34, 78, 134; SSC 32; WLC**
See Solzhenitsyn, Aleksandr Isaevich
See also AAYA 49; AITN 1; BPFB 3; CA 69-72; CANR 40, 65, 116; DA; DA3; DAB; DAC; DAM MST, NOV; EW 13; EXPS; LAIT 4; MTCW 1, 2; NFS 6; RGSF 2; RGWL 2, 3; SSFS 9; TWA

Solzhenitsyn, Aleksandr Isaevich
See Solzhenitsyn, Aleksandr I(sayevich)
See also EWL 3

Somers, Jane
See Lessing, Doris (May)

Somerville, Edith Oenone
1858-1949 .... **SSC 56; TCLC 51**
See also CA 196; DLB 135; RGEL 2; RGSF 2

Somerville & Ross
See Martin, Violet Florence; Somerville, Edith Oenone

Sommer, Scott 1951- .... **CLC 25**
See also CA 106

Sondheim, Stephen (Joshua) 1930- . **CLC 30, 39, 147; DC 22**
See also AAYA 11; CA 103; CANR 47, 67, 125; DAM DRAM; LAIT 4

Sone, Monica 1919- .... **AAL**

Song, Cathy 1955- .... **AAL; PC 21**
See also CA 154; CANR 118; CWP; DLB 169; EXPP; FW; PFS 5

Sontag, Susan 1933- .... **CLC 1, 2, 10, 13, 31, 105**
See also AMWS 3; CA 17-20R; CANR 25, 51, 74, 97; CN 7; CPW; DA3; DAM POP; DLB 2, 67; EWL 3; MAWW; MTCW 1, 2; RGAL 4; RHW; SSFS 10

Sophocles 496(?)B.C.-406(?)B.C. .... **CMLC 2, 47, 51; DC 1; WLCS**
See also AW 1; CDWLB 1; DA; DA3; DAB; DAC; DAM DRAM, MST; DFS 1, 4, 8; DLB 176; LAIT 1; LATS 1; LMFS 1; RGWL 2, 3; TWA

Sordello 1189-1269 .... **CMLC 15**

Sorel, Georges 1847-1922 .... **TCLC 91**
See also CA 118; 188

Sorel, Julia
See Drexler, Rosalyn

Sorokin, Vladimir .... **CLC 59**
See Sorokin, Vladimir Georgievich

Sorokin, Vladimir Georgievich
See Sorokin, Vladimir
See also DLB 285

Sorrentino, Gilbert 1929- .. **CLC 3, 7, 14, 22, 40**
See also CA 77-80; CANR 14, 33, 115; CN 7; CP 7; DLB 5, 173; DLBY 1980; INT CANR-14

Soseki
See Natsume, Soseki
See also MJW

Soto, Gary 1952- ... **CLC 32, 80; HLC 2; PC 28**
See also AAYA 10, 37; BYA 11; CA 119; 125; CANR 50, 74, 107; CLR 38; CP 7; DAM MULT; DLB 82; EWL 3; EXPP; HW 1, 2; INT CA-125; JRDA; LLW 1; MAICYA; MAICYAS 1; MTCW 2; PFS 7; RGAL 4; SATA 80, 120; WYA; YAW

Soupault, Philippe 1897-1990 .... **CLC 68**
See also CA 116; 147; 131; EWL 3; GFL 1789 to the Present; LMFS 2

Souster, (Holmes) Raymond 1921- .... **CLC 5, 14**
See also CA 13-16R; CAAS 14; CANR 13, 29, 53; CP 7; DA3; DAC; DAM POET; DLB 88; RGEL 2; SATA 63

Southern, Terry 1924(?)-1995 .... **CLC 7**
See also AMWS 11; BPFB 3; CA 1-4R; 150; CANR 1, 55, 107; CN 7; DLB 2; IDFW 3, 4

Southerne, Thomas 1660-1746 .... **LC 99**
See also DLB 80; RGEL 2

Southey, Robert 1774-1843 .... **NCLC 8, 97**
See also BRW 4; DLB 93, 107, 142; RGEL 2; SATA 54

Southworth, Emma Dorothy Eliza Nevitte 1819-1899 .... **NCLC 26**
See also DLB 239

Souza, Ernest
See Scott, Evelyn

Soyinka, Wole 1934- .. **BLC 3; CLC 3, 5, 14, 36, 44, 179; DC 2; WLC**
See also AFW; BW 2, 3; CA 13-16R; CANR 27, 39, 82; CD 5; CDWLB 3; CN 7; CP 7; DA; DA3; DAB; DAC; DAM DRAM, MST, MULT; DFS 10; DLB 125; EWL 3; MTCW 1, 2; RGEL 2; TWA; WLIT 2; WWE 1

Spackman, W(illiam) M(ode) 1905-1990 .... **CLC 46**
See also CA 81-84; 132

Spacks, Barry (Bernard) 1931- .... **CLC 14**
See also CA 154; CANR 33, 109; CP 7; DLB 105

Spanidou, Irini 1946- .... **CLC 44**
See also CA 185

Spark, Muriel (Sarah) 1918- ..... **CLC 2, 3, 5, 8, 13, 18, 40, 94; SSC 10**
See also BRWS 1; CA 5-8R; CANR 12, 36, 76, 89; CDBLB 1945-1960; CN 7; CP 7; DA3; DAB; DAC; DAM MST, NOV; DLB 15, 139; EWL 3; FW; INT CANR-12; LAIT 4; MTCW 1, 2; RGEL 2; TEA; WLIT 4; YAW

Spaulding, Douglas
See Bradbury, Ray (Douglas)

Spaulding, Leonard
See Bradbury, Ray (Douglas)

Speght, Rachel 1597-c. 1630 .... **LC 97**
See also DLB 126

Spelman, Elizabeth .... **CLC 65**

Spence, J. A. D.
See Eliot, T(homas) S(tearns)

Spencer, Anne 1882-1975 .... **HR 3**
See also BW 2; CA 161; DLB 51, 54

Spencer, Elizabeth 1921- .... **CLC 22; SSC 57**
See also CA 13-16R; CANR 32, 65, 87; CN 7; CSW; DLB 6, 218; EWL 3; MTCW 1; RGAL 4; SATA 14

Spencer, Leonard G.
See Silverberg, Robert

Spencer, Scott 1945- .... **CLC 30**
See also CA 113; CANR 51; DLBY 1986

Spender, Stephen (Harold) 1909-1995 .... **CLC 1, 2, 5, 10, 41, 91**
See also BRWS 2; CA 9-12R; 149; CANR 31, 54; CDBLB 1945-1960; CP 7; DA3; DAM POET; DLB 20; EWL 3; MTCW 1, 2; PAB; RGEL 2; TEA

Spengler, Oswald (Arnold Gottfried) 1880-1936 .... **TCLC 25**
See also CA 118; 189

Spenser, Edmund 1552(?)-1599 ..... **LC 5, 39; PC 8, 42; WLC**
See also BRW 1; CDBLB Before 1660; DA; DA3; DAB; DAC; DAM MST, POET; DLB 167; EFS 2; EXPP; PAB; RGEL 2; TEA; WLIT 3; WP

Spicer, Jack 1925-1965 .... **CLC 8, 18, 72**
See also BG 3; CA 85-88; DAM POET; DLB 5, 16, 193; GLL 1; WP

Spiegelman, Art 1948- .... **CLC 76, 178**
See also AAYA 10, 46; CA 125; CANR 41, 55, 74, 124; MTCW 2; SATA 109; YAW

Spielberg, Peter 1929- .... **CLC 6**
See also CA 5-8R; CANR 4, 48; DLBY 1981

Spielberg, Steven 1947- .... **CLC 20, 188**
See also AAYA 8, 24; CA 77-80; CANR 32; SATA 32

Spillane, Frank Morrison 1918-
See Spillane, Mickey
See also CA 25-28R; CANR 28, 63, 125; DA3; MTCW 1, 2; SATA 66

Spillane, Mickey .... **CLC 3, 13**
See Spillane, Frank Morrison
See also BPFB 3; CMW 4; DLB 226; MSW; MTCW 2

Spinoza, Benedictus de 1632-1677 .. **LC 9, 58**

Spinrad, Norman (Richard) 1940- ... **CLC 46**
See also BPFB 3; CA 37-40R; CAAS 19; CANR 20, 91; DLB 8; INT CANR-20; SFW 4

Spitteler, Carl (Friedrich Georg) 1845-1924 .... **TCLC 12**
See also CA 109; DLB 129; EWL 3

Spivack, Kathleen (Romola Drucker) 1938- .... **CLC 6**
See also CA 49-52

Spoto, Donald 1941- .... **CLC 39**
See also CA 65-68; CANR 11, 57, 93

Springsteen, Bruce (F.) 1949- .... **CLC 17**
See also CA 111

Spurling, (Susan) Hilary 1940- .... **CLC 34**
See also CA 104; CANR 25, 52, 94

Spyker, John Howland
See Elman, Richard (Martin)

Squared, A.
See Abbott, Edwin A.

Squires, (James) Radcliffe 1917-1993 .... **CLC 51**
See also CA 1-4R; 140; CANR 6, 21

Srivastava, Dhanpat Rai 1880(?)-1936
See Premchand
See also CA 118; 197

Stacy, Donald
See Pohl, Frederik

Stael
See Stael-Holstein, Anne Louise Germaine Necker
See also EW 5; RGWL 2, 3

Stael, Germaine de
See Stael-Holstein, Anne Louise Germaine Necker
See also DLB 119, 192; FW; GFL 1789 to the Present; TWA

Stael-Holstein, Anne Louise Germaine Necker 1766-1817 .... **NCLC 3, 91**
See Stael; Stael, Germaine de

Stafford, Jean 1915-1979 .. **CLC 4, 7, 19, 68; SSC 26**
See also CA 1-4R; 85-88; CANR 3, 65; DLB 2, 173; MTCW 1, 2; RGAL 4; RGSF 2; SATA-Obit 22; TCWW 2; TUS

Stafford, William (Edgar) 1914-1993 .... **CLC 4, 7, 29**
See also AMWS 11; CA 5-8R; 142; CAAS 3; CANR 5, 22; DAM POET; DLB 5, 206; EXPP; INT CANR-22; PFS 2, 8, 16; RGAL 4; WP

Stagnelius, Eric Johan 1793-1823 . **NCLC 61**

Staines, Trevor
See Brunner, John (Kilian Houston)

Stairs, Gordon
See Austin, Mary (Hunter)
See also TCWW 2

Stalin, Joseph 1879-1953 .... **TCLC 92**

Stampa, Gaspara c. 1524-1554 .... **PC 43**
See also RGWL 2, 3

Stampflinger, K. A.
See Benjamin, Walter

Stancykowna
See Szymborska, Wislawa

Standing Bear, Luther 1868(?)-1939(?) .... **NNAL**
See also CA 113; 144; DAM MULT

Stannard, Martin 1947- .... **CLC 44**
See also CA 142; DLB 155

Stanton, Elizabeth Cady 1815-1902 .... **TCLC 73**
See also CA 171; DLB 79; FW

Stanton, Maura 1946- .... **CLC 9**
See also CA 89-92; CANR 15, 123; DLB 120

Stanton, Schuyler
See Baum, L(yman) Frank

Stapledon, (William) Olaf 1886-1950 .... **TCLC 22**
See also CA 111; 162; DLB 15, 255; SFW 4

Starbuck, George (Edwin) 1931-1996 .... **CLC 53**
See also CA 21-24R; 153; CANR 23; DAM POET

Stark, Richard
See Westlake, Donald E(dwin)

Staunton, Schuyler
See Baum, L(yman) Frank

Stead, Christina (Ellen) 1902-1983 ... **CLC 2, 5, 8, 32, 80**
See also BRWS 4; CA 13-16R; 109; CANR 33, 40; DLB 260; EWL 3; FW; MTCW 1, 2; RGEL 2; RGSF 2; WWE 1

Stead, William Thomas 1849-1912 .... **TCLC 48**
See also CA 167

Stebnitsky, M.
See Leskov, Nikolai (Semyonovich)

Steele, Sir Richard 1672-1729 .... **LC 18**
See also BRW 3; CDBLB 1660-1789; DLB 84, 101; RGEL 2; WLIT 3

Steele, Timothy (Reid) 1948- .... **CLC 45**
See also CA 93-96; CANR 16, 50, 92; CP 7; DLB 120, 282

Steffens, (Joseph) Lincoln 1866-1936 .... **TCLC 20**
See also CA 117; 198

Stegner, Wallace (Earle) 1909-1993 .. **CLC 9, 49, 81; SSC 27**
See also AITN 1; AMWS 4; ANW; BEST 90:3; BPFB 3; CA 1-4R; 141; CAAS 9; CANR 1, 21, 46; DAM NOV; DLB 9, 206, 275; DLBY 1993; EWL 3; MTCW 1, 2; RGAL 4; TCWW 2; TUS

Stein, Gertrude 1874-1946 ... **DC 19; PC 18; SSC 42; TCLC 1, 6, 28, 48; WLC**
See also AMW; AMWC 2; CA 104; 132; CANR 108; CDALB 1917-1929; DA; DA3; DAB; DAC; DAM MST, NOV, POET; DLB 4, 54, 86, 228; DLBD 15; EWL 3; EXPS; GLL 1; MAWW; MTCW 1, 2; NCFS 4; RGAL 4; RGSF 2; SSFS 5; TUS; WP

Steinbeck, John (Ernst) 1902-1968 ... **CLC 1, 5, 9, 13, 21, 34, 45, 75, 124; SSC 11, 37; TCLC 135; WLC**
See also AAYA 12; AMW; BPFB 3; BYA 2, 3, 13; CA 1-4R; 25-28R; CANR 1, 35; CDALB 1929-1941; DA; DA3; DAB; DAC; DAM DRAM, MST, NOV; DLB 7, 9, 212, 275; DLBD 2; EWL 3; EXPS; LAIT 3; MTCW 1, 2; NFS 1, 5, 7, 17; RGAL 4; RGSF 2; RHW; SATA 9; SSFS 3, 6; TCWW 2; TUS; WYA; YAW

Steinem, Gloria 1934- .... **CLC 63**
See also CA 53-56; CANR 28, 51; DLB 246; FW; MTCW 1, 2

Steiner, George 1929- .... **CLC 24**
See also CA 73-76; CANR 31, 67, 108; DAM NOV; DLB 67; EWL 3; MTCW 1, 2; SATA 62

Steiner, K. Leslie
See Delany, Samuel R(ay), Jr.

Steiner, Rudolf 1861-1925 .... **TCLC 13**
See also CA 107
Stendhal 1783-1842 .. **NCLC 23, 46; SSC 27; WLC**
See also DA; DA3; DAB; DAC; DAM MST, NOV; DLB 119; EW 5; GFL 1789 to the Present; RGWL 2, 3; TWA
Stephen, Adeline Virginia
See Woolf, (Adeline) Virginia
Stephen, Sir Leslie 1832-1904 .... **TCLC 23**
See also BRW 5; CA 123; DLB 57, 144, 190
Stephen, Sir Leslie
See Stephen, Sir Leslie
Stephen, Virginia
See Woolf, (Adeline) Virginia
Stephens, James 1882(?)-1950 .... **SSC 50; TCLC 4**
See also CA 104; 192; DLB 19, 153, 162; EWL 3; FANT; RGEL 2; SUFW
Stephens, Reed
See Donaldson, Stephen R(eeder)
Steptoe, Lydia
See Barnes, Djuna
See also GLL 1
Sterchi, Beat 1949- .... **CLC 65**
See also CA 203
Sterling, Brett
See Bradbury, Ray (Douglas); Hamilton, Edmond
Sterling, Bruce 1954- .... **CLC 72**
See also CA 119; CANR 44; SCFW 2; SFW 4
Sterling, George 1869-1926 .... **TCLC 20**
See also CA 117; 165; DLB 54
Stern, Gerald 1925- .... **CLC 40, 100**
See also AMWS 9; CA 81-84; CANR 28, 94; CP 7; DLB 105; RGAL 4
Stern, Richard (Gustave) 1928- ... **CLC 4, 39**
See also CA 1-4R; CANR 1, 25, 52, 120; CN 7; DLB 218; DLBY 1987; INT CANR-25
Sternberg, Josef von 1894-1969 .... **CLC 20**
See also CA 81-84
Sterne, Laurence 1713-1768 .... **LC 2, 48; WLC**
See also BRW 3; BRWC 1; CDBLB 1660-1789; DA; DAB; DAC; DAM MST, NOV; DLB 39; RGEL 2; TEA
Sternheim, (William Adolf) Carl 1878-1942 .... **TCLC 8**
See also CA 105; 193; DLB 56, 118; EWL 3; RGWL 2, 3
Stevens, Mark 1951- .... **CLC 34**
See also CA 122
Stevens, Wallace 1879-1955 . **PC 6; TCLC 3, 12, 45; WLC**
See also AMW; AMWR 1; CA 104; 124; CDALB 1929-1941; DA; DA3; DAB; DAC; DAM MST, POET; DLB 54; EWL 3; EXPP; MTCW 1, 2; PAB; PFS 13, 16; RGAL 4; TUS; WP
Stevenson, Anne (Katharine) 1933- .. **CLC 7, 33**
See also BRWS 6; CA 17-20R; CAAS 9; CANR 9, 33, 123; CP 7; CWP; DLB 40; MTCW 1; RHW
Stevenson, Robert Louis (Balfour) 1850-1894 ...... **NCLC 5, 14, 63; SSC 11, 51; WLC**
See also AAYA 24; BPFB 3; BRW 5; BRWC 1; BRWR 1; BYA 1, 2, 4, 13; CDBLB 1890-1914; CLR 10, 11; DA; DA3; DAB; DAC; DAM MST, NOV; DLB 18, 57, 141, 156, 174; DLBD 13; HGG; JRDA; LAIT 1, 3; MAICYA 1, 2; NFS 11; RGEL 2; RGSF 2; SATA 100; SUFW; TEA; WCH; WLIT 4; WYA; YABC 2; YAW

Stewart, J(ohn) I(nnes) M(ackintosh) 1906-1994 .... **CLC 7, 14, 32**
See Innes, Michael
See also CA 85-88; 147; CAAS 3; CANR 47; CMW 4; MTCW 1, 2
Stewart, Mary (Florence Elinor) 1916- .... **CLC 7, 35, 117**
See also ΛΛΥΛ 29; BPFB 3; CA 1-4R; CANR 1, 59; CMW 4; CPW; DAB; FANT; RHW; SATA 12; YAW
Stewart, Mary Rainbow
See Stewart, Mary (Florence Elinor)
Stifle, June
See Campbell, Maria
Stifter, Adalbert 1805-1868 .. **NCLC 41; SSC 28**
See also CDWLB 2; DLB 133; RGSF 2; RGWL 2, 3
Still, James 1906-2001 .... **CLC 49**
See also CA 65-68; 195; CAAS 17; CANR 10, 26; CSW; DLB 9; DLBY 01; SATA 29; SATA-Obit 127
Sting 1951-
See Sumner, Gordon Matthew
See also CA 167
Stirling, Arthur
See Sinclair, Upton (Beall)
Stitt, Milan 1941- .... **CLC 29**
See also CA 69-72
Stockton, Francis Richard 1834-1902
See Stockton, Frank R.
See also CA 108; 137; MAICYA 1, 2; SATA 44; SFW 4
Stockton, Frank R. .... **TCLC 47**
See Stockton, Francis Richard
See also BYA 4, 13; DLB 42, 74; DLBD 13; EXPS; SATA-Brief 32; SSFS 3; SUFW; WCH
Stoddard, Charles
See Kuttner, Henry
Stoker, Abraham 1847-1912
See Stoker, Bram
See also CA 105; 150; DA; DA3; DAC; DAM MST, NOV; HGG; SATA 29
Stoker, Bram . **SSC 62; TCLC 8, 144; WLC**
See Stoker, Abraham
See also AAYA 23; BPFB 3; BRWS 3; BYA 5; CDBLB 1890-1914; DAB; DLB 36, 70, 178; LATS 1; NFS 18; RGEL 2; SUFW; TEA; WLIT 4
Stolz, Mary (Slattery) 1920- .... **CLC 12**
See also AAYA 8; AITN 1; CA 5-8R; CANR 13, 41, 112; JRDA; MAICYA 1, 2; SAAS 3; SATA 10, 71, 133; YAW
Stone, Irving 1903-1989 .... **CLC 7**
See also AITN 1; BPFB 3; CA 1-4R; 129; CAAS 3; CANR 1, 23; CPW; DA3; DAM POP; INT CANR-23; MTCW 1, 2; RHW; SATA 3; SATA-Obit 64
Stone, Oliver (William) 1946- .... **CLC 73**
See also AAYA 15; CA 110; CANR 55, 125
Stone, Robert (Anthony) 1937- ... **CLC 5, 23, 42, 175**
See also AMWS 5; BPFB 3; CA 85-88; CANR 23, 66, 95; CN 7; DLB 152; EWL 3; INT CANR-23; MTCW 1
Stone, Ruth 1915- .... **PC 53**
See also CA 45-48; CANR 2, 91; CP 7; CSW; DLB 105; PFS 19
Stone, Zachary
See Follett, Ken(neth Martin)
Stoppard, Tom 1937- ... **CLC 1, 3, 4, 5, 8, 15, 29, 34, 63, 91; DC 6; WLC**
See also BRWS 1; BRWR 2; BRWS 1; CA 81-84; CANR 39, 67, 125; CBD; CD 5; CDBLB 1960 to Present; DA; DA3; DAB; DAC; DAM DRAM, MST; DFS 2, 5, 8, 11, 13, 16; DLB 13, 233; DLBY 1985; EWL 3; LATS 1; MTCW 1, 2; RGEL 2; TEA; WLIT 4

Storey, David (Malcolm) 1933- . **CLC 2, 4, 5, 8**
See also BRWS 1; CA 81-84; CANR 36; CBD; CD 5; CN 7; DAM DRAM; DLB 13, 14, 207, 245; EWL 3; MTCW 1; RGEL 2
Storm, Hyemeyohsts 1935- ... **CLC 3; NNAL**
See also CA 81-84; CANR 45; DAM MULT
Storm, (Hans) Theodor (Woldsen) 1817-1888 .... **NCLC 1; SSC 27**
See also CDWLB 2; DLB 129; EW; RGSF 2; RGWL 2, 3
Storni, Alfonsina 1892-1938 . **HLC 2; PC 33; TCLC 5**
See also CA 104; 131; DAM MULT; DLB 283; HW 1; LAW
Stoughton, William 1631-1701 .... **LC 38**
See also DLB 24
Stout, Rex (Todhunter) 1886-1975 ..... **CLC 3**
See also AITN 2; BPFB 3; CA 61-64; CANR 71; CMW 4; MSW; RGAL 4
Stow, (Julian) Randolph 1935- ... **CLC 23, 48**
See also CA 13-16R; CANR 33; CN 7; DLB 260; MTCW 1; RGEL 2
Stowe, Harriet (Elizabeth) Beecher 1811-1896 .... **NCLC 3, 50, 133; WLC**
See also AAYA 53; AMWS 1; CDALB 1865-1917; DA; DA3; DAB; DAC; DAM MST, NOV; DLB 1, 12, 42, 74, 189, 239, 243; EXPN; JRDA; LAIT 2; MAICYA 1, 2; NFS 6; RGAL 4; TUS; YABC 1
Strabo c. 64B.C.-c. 25 .... **CMLC 37**
See also DLB 176
Strachey, (Giles) Lytton 1880-1932 .... **TCLC 12**
See also BRWS 2; CA 110; 178; DLB 149; DLBD 10; EWL 3; MTCW 2; NCFS 4
Stramm, August 1874-1915 .... **PC 50**
See also CA 195; EWL 3
Strand, Mark 1934- .... **CLC 6, 18, 41, 71**
See also AMWS 4; CA 21-24R; CANR 40, 65, 100; CP 7; DAM POET; DLB 5; EWL 3; PAB; PFS 9, 18; RGAL 4; SATA 41
Stratton-Porter, Gene(va Grace) 1863-1924
See Porter, Gene(va Grace) Stratton
See also ANW; CA 137; CLR 87; DLB 221; DLBD 14; MAICYA 1, 2; SATA 15
Straub, Peter (Francis) 1943- ... **CLC 28, 107**
See also BEST 89:1; BPFB 3; CA 85-88; CANR 28, 65, 109; CPW; DAM POP; DLBY 1984; HGG; MTCW 1, 2; SUFW 2
Strauss, Botho 1944- .... **CLC 22**
See also CA 157; CWW 2; DLB 124
Strauss, Leo 1899-1973 .... **TCLC 141**
See also CA 101; 45-48; CANR 122
Streatfeild, (Mary) Noel 1897(?)-1986 .... **CLC 21**
See also CA 81-84; 120; CANR 31; CLR 17, 83; CWRI 5; DLB 160; MAICYA 1, 2; SATA 20; SATA-Obit 48
Stribling, T(homas) S(igismund) 1881-1965 .... **CLC 23**
See also CA 189; 107; CMW 4; DLB 9; RGAL 4
Strindberg, (Johan) August 1849-1912 ... **DC 18; TCLC 1, 8, 21, 47; WLC**
See also CA 104; 135; DA; DA3; DAB; DAC; DAM DRAM, MST; DFS 4, 9; DLB 259; EW 7; EWL 3; IDTP; LMFS 2; MTCW 2; RGWL 2, 3; TWA
Stringer, Arthur 1874-1950 .... **TCLC 37**
See also CA 161; DLB 92
Stringer, David
See Roberts, Keith (John Kingston)

Stroheim, Erich von 1885-1957 ..... **TCLC 71**
Strugatskii, Arkadii (Natanovich)
    1925-1991 .... **CLC 27**
    See also CA 106; 135; SFW 4
Strugatskii, Boris (Natanovich)
    1933- .... **CLC 27**
    See also CA 106; SFW 4
Strummer, Joe 1953(?)- .... **CLC 30**
Strunk, William, Jr. 1869-1946 .... **TCLC 92**
    See also CA 118; 164; NCFS 5
Stryk, Lucien 1924- .... **PC 27**
    See also CA 13-16R; CANR 10, 28, 55, 110; CP 7
Stuart, Don A.
    See Campbell, John W(ood, Jr.)
Stuart, Ian
    See MacLean, Alistair (Stuart)
Stuart, Jesse (Hilton) 1906-1984 ... **CLC 1, 8, 11, 14, 34; SSC 31**
    See also CA 5-8R; 112; CANR 31; DLB 9, 48, 102; DLBY 1984; SATA 2; SATA-Obit 36
Stubblefield, Sally
    See Trumbo, Dalton
Sturgeon, Theodore (Hamilton)
    1918-1985 .... **CLC 22, 39**
    See Queen, Ellery
    See also AAYA 51; BPFB 3; BYA 9, 10; CA 81-84; 116; CANR 32, 103; DLB 8; DLBY 1985; HGG; MTCW 1, 2; SCFW; SFW 4; SUFW
Sturges, Preston 1898-1959 .... **TCLC 48**
    See also CA 114; 149; DLB 26
Styron, William 1925- .... **CLC 1, 3, 5, 11, 15, 60; SSC 25**
    See also AMW; AMWC 2; BEST 90:4; BPFB 3; CA 5-8R; CANR 6, 33, 74, 126; CDALB 1968-1988; CN 7; CPW; CSW; DA3; DAM NOV, POP; DLB 2, 143; DLBY 1980; EWL 3; INT CANR-6; LAIT 2; MTCW 1, 2; NCFS 1; RGAL 4; RHW; TUS
Su, Chien 1884-1918
    See Su Man-shu
    See also CA 123
Suarez Lynch, B.
    See Bioy Casares, Adolfo; Borges, Jorge Luis
Suassuna, Ariano Vilar 1927- .... **HLCS 1**
    See also CA 178; HW 2; LAW
Suckert, Kurt Erich
    See Malaparte, Curzio
Suckling, Sir John 1609-1642 . **LC 75; PC 30**
    See also BRW 2; DAM POET; DLB 58, 126; EXPP; PAB; RGEL 2
Suckow, Ruth 1892-1960 .... **SSC 18**
    See also CA 193; 113; DLB 9, 102; RGAL 4; TCWW 2
Sudermann, Hermann 1857-1928 .. **TCLC 15**
    See also CA 107; 201; DLB 118
Sue, Eugene 1804-1857 .... **NCLC 1**
    See also DLB 119
Sueskind, Patrick 1949- .... **CLC 44, 182**
    See Suskind, Patrick
Suetonius c. 70-c. 130 .... **CMLC 60**
    See also AW 2; DLB 211; RGWL 2, 3
Sukenick, Ronald 1932- .... **CLC 3, 4, 6, 48**
    See also CA 25-28R; 209; CAAE 209; CAAS 8; CANR 32, 89; CN 7; DLB 173; DLBY 1981
Suknaski, Andrew 1942- .... **CLC 19**
    See also CA 101; CP 7; DLB 53
Sullivan, Vernon
    See Vian, Boris
Sully Prudhomme, Rene-Francois-Armand
    1839-1907 .... **TCLC 31**
    See also GFL 1789 to the Present

Su Man-shu .... **TCLC 24**
    See Su, Chien
    See also EWL 3
Summerforest, Ivy B.
    See Kirkup, James
Summers, Andrew James 1942- .... **CLC 26**
Summers, Andy
    See Summers, Andrew James
Summers, Hollis (Spurgeon, Jr.)
    1916- .... **CLC 10**
    See also CA 5-8R; CANR 3; DLB 6
Summers, (Alphonsus Joseph-Mary Augustus) Montague
    1880-1948 .... **TCLC 16**
    See also CA 118; 163
Sumner, Gordon Matthew .... **CLC 26**
    See Police, The; Sting
Sun Tzu c. 400B.C.-c. 320B.C. .... **CMLC 56**
Surtees, Robert Smith 1805-1864 .. **NCLC 14**
    See also DLB 21; RGEL 2
Susann, Jacqueline 1921-1974 .... **CLC 3**
    See also AITN 1; BPFB 3; CA 65-68; 53-56; MTCW 1, 2
Su Shi
    See Su Shih
    See also RGWL 2, 3
Su Shih 1036-1101 .... **CMLC 15**
    See Su Shi
Suskind, Patrick .... **CLC 182**
    See Sueskind, Patrick
    See also BPFB 3; CA 145; CWW 2
Sutcliff, Rosemary 1920-1992 .... **CLC 26**
    See also AAYA 10; BYA 1, 4; CA 5-8R; 139; CANR 37; CLR 1, 37; CPW; DAB; DAC; DAM MST, POP; JRDA; LATS 1; MAICYA 1, 2; MAICYAS 1; RHW; SATA 6, 44, 78; SATA-Obit 73; WYA; YAW
Sutro, Alfred 1863-1933 .... **TCLC 6**
    See also CA 105; 185; DLB 10; RGEL 2
Sutton, Henry
    See Slavitt, David R(ytman)
Suzuki, D. T.
    See Suzuki, Daisetz Teitaro
Suzuki, Daisetz T.
    See Suzuki, Daisetz Teitaro
Suzuki, Daisetz Teitaro
    1870-1966 .... **TCLC 109**
    See also CA 121; 111; MTCW 1, 2
Suzuki, Teitaro
    See Suzuki, Daisetz Teitaro
Svevo, Italo .... **SSC 25; TCLC 2, 35**
    See Schmitz, Aron Hector
    See also DLB 264; EW 8; EWL 3; RGWL 2, 3
Swados, Elizabeth (A.) 1951- .... **CLC 12**
    See also CA 97-100; CANR 49; INT CA-97-100
Swados, Harvey 1920-1972 .... **CLC 5**
    See also CA 5-8R; 37-40R; CANR 6; DLB 2
Swan, Gladys 1934- .... **CLC 69**
    See also CA 101; CANR 17, 39
Swanson, Logan
    See Matheson, Richard (Burton)
Swarthout, Glendon (Fred)
    1918-1992 .... **CLC 35**
    See also AAYA 55; CA 1-4R; 139; CANR 1, 47; LAIT 5; SATA 26; TCWW 2; YAW
Sweet, Sarah C.
    See Jewett, (Theodora) Sarah Orne
Swenson, May 1919-1989 ...... **CLC 4, 14, 61, 106; PC 14**
    See also AMWS 4; CA 5-8R; 130; CANR 36, 61; DA; DAB; DAC; DAM MST, POET; DLB 5; EXPP; GLL 2; MTCW 1, 2; PFS 16; SATA 15; WP
Swift, Augustus
    See Lovecraft, H(oward) P(hillips)

Swift, Graham (Colin) 1949- ...... **CLC 41, 88**
    See also BRWC 2; BRWS 5; CA 117; 122; CANR 46, 71, 128; CN 7; DLB 194; MTCW 2; NFS 18; RGSF 2
Swift, Jonathan 1667-1745 ..... **LC 1, 42, 101; PC 9; WLC**
    See also AAYA 41; BRW 3; BRWC 1; BRWR 1; BYA 5, 14; CDBLB 1660-1789; CLR 53; DA; DA3; DAB; DAC; DAM MST, NOV, POET; DLB 39, 95, 101; EXPN; LAIT 1; NFS 6; RGEL 2; SATA 19; TEA; WCH; WLIT 3
Swinburne, Algernon Charles
    1837-1909 ... **PC 24; TCLC 8, 36; WLC**
    See also BRW 5; CA 105; 140; CDBLB 1832-1890; DA; DA3; DAB; DAC; DAM MST, POET; DLB 35, 57; PAB; RGEL 2; TEA
Swinfen, Ann .... **CLC 34**
    See also CA 202
Swinnerton, Frank Arthur
    1884-1982 .... **CLC 31**
    See also CA 108; DLB 34
Swithen, John
    See King, Stephen (Edwin)
Sylvia
    See Ashton-Warner, Sylvia (Constance)
Symmes, Robert Edward
    See Duncan, Robert (Edward)
Symonds, John Addington
    1840-1893 .... **NCLC 34**
    See also DLB 57, 144
Symons, Arthur 1865-1945 .... **TCLC 11**
    See also CA 107; 189; DLB 19, 57, 149; RGEL 2
Symons, Julian (Gustave)
    1912-1994 .... **CLC 2, 14, 32**
    See also CA 49-52; 147; CAAS 3; CANR 3, 33, 59; CMW 4; DLB 87, 155; DLBY 1992; MSW; MTCW 1
Synge, (Edmund) J(ohn) M(illington)
    1871-1909 .... **DC 2; TCLC 6, 37**
    See also BRW 6; BRWR 1; CA 104; 141; CDBLB 1890-1914; DAM DRAM; DFS 18; DLB 10, 19; EWL 3; RGEL 2; TEA; WLIT 4
Syruc, J.
    See Milosz, Czeslaw
Szirtes, George 1948- .... **CLC 46; PC 51**
    See also CA 109; CANR 27, 61, 117; CP 7
Szymborska, Wislawa 1923- ... **CLC 99, 190; PC 44**
    See also CA 154; CANR 91; CDWLB 4; CWP; CWW 2; DA3; DAM POET; DLBY 1996; EWL 3; MTCW 2; PFS 15; RGWL 3
T. O., Nik
    See Annensky, Innokenty (Fyodorovich)
Tabori, George 1914- .... **CLC 19**
    See also CA 49-52; CANR 4, 69; CBD; CD 5; DLB 245
Tacitus c. 55-c. 117 .... **CMLC 56**
    See also AW 2; CDWLB 1; DLB 211; RGWL 2, 3
Tagore, Rabindranath 1861-1941 .... **PC 8; SSC 48; TCLC 3, 53**
    See also CA 104; 120; DA3; DAM DRAM, POET; EWL 3; MTCW 1, 2; PFS 18; RGEL 2; RGSF 2; RGWL 2, 3; TWA
Taine, Hippolyte Adolphe
    1828-1893 .... **NCLC 15**
    See also EW 7; GFL 1789 to the Present
Talayesva, Don C. 1890-(?) .... **NNAL**
Talese, Gay 1932- .... **CLC 37**
    See also AITN 1; CA 1-4R; CANR 9, 58; DLB 185; INT CANR-9; MTCW 1, 2
Tallent, Elizabeth (Ann) 1954- .... **CLC 45**
    See also CA 117; CANR 72; DLB 130

Tallmountain, Mary 1918-1997 .... **NNAL**
See also CA 146; 161; DLB 193

Tally, Ted 1952- .... **CLC 42**
See also CA 120; 124; CAD; CANR 125; CD 5; INT CA-124

Talvik, Heiti 1904-1947 .... **TCLC 87**
See also EWL 3

Tamayo y Baus, Manuel 1829-1898 .... **NCLC 1**

Tammsaare, A(nton) H(ansen) 1878-1940 .... **TCLC 27**
See also CA 164; CDWLB 4; DLB 220; EWL 3

Tam'si, Tchicaya
See Tchicaya, Gerald Felix

Tan, Amy (Ruth) 1952- . **AAL; CLC 59, 120, 151**
See also AAYA 9, 48; AMWS 10; BEST 89:3; BPFB 3; CA 136; CANR 54, 105; CDALBS; CN 7; CPW 1; DA3; DAM MULT, NOV, POP; DLB 173; EXPN; FW; LAIT 3, 5; MTCW 2; NFS 1, 13, 16; RGAL 4; SATA 75; SSFS 9; YAW

Tandem, Felix
See Spitteler, Carl (Friedrich Georg)

Tanizaki, Jun'ichiro 1886-1965 ... **CLC 8, 14, 28; SSC 21**
See Tanizaki Jun'ichiro
See also CA 93-96; 25-28R; MJW; MTCW 2; RGSF 2; RGWL 2

Tanizaki Jun'ichiro
See Tanizaki, Jun'ichiro
See also DLB 180; EWL 3

Tanner, William
See Amis, Kingsley (William)

Tao Lao
See Storni, Alfonsina

Tapahonso, Luci 1953- .... **NNAL**
See also CA 145; CANR 72, 127; DLB 175

Tarantino, Quentin (Jerome) 1963- .... **CLC 125**
See also CA 171; CANR 125

Tarassoff, Lev
See Troyat, Henri

Tarbell, Ida M(inerva) 1857-1944 . **TCLC 40**
See also CA 122; 181; DLB 47

Tarkington, (Newton) Booth 1869-1946 .... **TCLC 9**
See also BPFB 3; BYA 3; CA 110; 143; CWRI 5; DLB 9, 102; MTCW 2; RGAL 4; SATA 17

Tarkovskii, Andrei Arsen'evich
See Tarkovsky, Andrei (Arsenyevich)

Tarkovsky, Andrei (Arsenyevich) 1932-1986 .... **CLC 75**
See also CA 127

Tartt, Donna 1963- .... **CLC 76**
See also CA 142

Tasso, Torquato 1544-1595 .... **LC 5, 94**
See also EFS 2; EW 2; RGWL 2, 3

Tate, (John Orley) Allen 1899-1979 .. **CLC 2, 4, 6, 9, 11, 14, 24; PC 50**
See also AMW; CA 5-8R; 85-88; CANR 32, 108; DLB 4, 45, 63; DLBD 17; EWL 3; MTCW 1, 2; RGAL 4; RHW

Tate, Ellalice
See Hibbert, Eleanor Alice Burford

Tate, James (Vincent) 1943- ..... **CLC 2, 6, 25**
See also CA 21-24R; CANR 29, 57, 114; CP 7; DLB 5, 169; EWL 3; PFS 10, 15; RGAL 4; WP

Tauler, Johannes c. 1300-1361 .... **CMLC 37**
See also DLB 179; LMFS 1

Tavel, Ronald 1940- .... **CLC 6**
See also CA 21-24R; CAD; CANR 33; CD 5

Taviani, Paolo 1931- .... **CLC 70**
See also CA 153

Taylor, Bayard 1825-1878 .... **NCLC 89**
See also DLB 3, 189, 250, 254; RGAL 4

Taylor, C(ecil) P(hilip) 1929-1981 .... **CLC 27**
See also CA 25-28R; 105; CANR 47; CBD

Taylor, Edward 1642(?)-1729 .... **LC 11**
See also AMW; DA; DAB; DAC; DAM MST, POET; DLB 24; EXPP; RGAL 4; TUS

Taylor, Eleanor Ross 1920- .... **CLC 5**
See also CA 81-84; CANR 70

Taylor, Elizabeth 1932-1975 ..... **CLC 2, 4, 29**
See also CA 13-16R; CANR 9, 70; DLB 139; MTCW 1; RGEL 2; SATA 13

Taylor, Frederick Winslow 1856-1915 .... **TCLC 76**
See also CA 188

Taylor, Henry (Splawn) 1942- .... **CLC 44**
See also CA 33-36R; CAAS 7; CANR 31; CP 7; DLB 5; PFS 10

Taylor, Kamala (Purnaiya) 1924-2004
See Markandaya, Kamala
See also CA 77-80; NFS 13

Taylor, Mildred D(elois) 1943- .... **CLC 21**
See also AAYA 10, 47; BW 1; BYA 3, 8; CA 85-88; CANR 25, 115; CLR 9, 59, 90; CSW; DLB 52; JRDA; LAIT 3; MAICYA 1, 2; SAAS 5; SATA 135; WYA; YAW

Taylor, Peter (Hillsman) 1917-1994 .. **CLC 1, 4, 18, 37, 44, 50, 71; SSC 10**
See also AMWS 5; BPFB 3; CA 13-16R; 147; CANR 9, 50; CSW; DLB 218, 278; DLBY 1981, 1994; EWL 3; EXPS; INT CANR-9; MTCW 1, 2; RGSF 2; SSFS 9; TUS

Taylor, Robert Lewis 1912-1998 .... **CLC 14**
See also CA 1-4R; 170; CANR 3, 64; SATA 10

Tchekhov, Anton
See Chekhov, Anton (Pavlovich)

Tchicaya, Gerald Felix 1931-1988 .. **CLC 101**
See Tchicaya U Tam'si
See also CA 129; 125; CANR 81

Tchicaya U Tam'si
See Tchicaya, Gerald Felix
See also EWL 3

Teasdale, Sara 1884-1933 .... **PC 31; TCLC 4**
See also CA 104; 163; DLB 45; GLL 1; PFS 14; RGAL 4; SATA 32; TUS

Tecumseh 1768-1813 .... **NNAL**
See also DAM MULT

Tegner, Esaias 1782-1846 .... **NCLC 2**

Teilhard de Chardin, (Marie Joseph) Pierre 1881-1955 .... **TCLC 9**
See also CA 105; 210; GFL 1789 to the Present

Temple, Ann
See Mortimer, Penelope (Ruth)

Tennant, Emma (Christina) 1937- .. **CLC 13, 52**
See also BRWS 9; CA 65-68; CAAS 9; CANR 10, 38, 59, 88; CN 7; DLB 14; EWL 3; SFW 4

Tenneshaw, S. M.
See Silverberg, Robert

Tenney, Tabitha Gilman 1762-1837 .... **NCLC 122**
See also DLB 37, 200

Tennyson, Alfred 1809-1892 ... **NCLC 30, 65, 115; PC 6; WLC**
See also AAYA 50; BRW 4; CDBLB 1832-1890; DA; DA3; DAB; DAC; DAM MST, POET; DLB 32; EXPP; PAB; PFS 1, 2, 4, 11, 15, 19; RGEL 2; TEA; WLIT 4; WP

Teran, Lisa St. Aubin de .... **CLC 36**
See St. Aubin de Teran, Lisa

Terence c. 184B.C.-c. 159B.C. ...... **CMLC 14; DC 7**
See also AW 1; CDWLB 1; DLB 211; RGWL 2, 3; TWA

Teresa de Jesus, St. 1515-1582 .... **LC 18**

Terkel, Louis 1912-
See Terkel, Studs
See also CA 57-60; CANR 18, 45, 67; DA3; MTCW 1, 2

Terkel, Studs .... **CLC 38**
See Terkel, Louis
See also AAYA 32; AITN 1; MTCW 2; TUS

Terry, C. V.
See Slaughter, Frank G(ill)

Terry, Megan 1932- .... **CLC 19; DC 13**
See also CA 77-80; CABS 3; CAD; CANR 43; CD 5; CWD; DFS 18; DLB 7, 249; GLL 2

Tertullian c. 155-c. 245 .... **CMLC 29**

Tertz, Abram
See Sinyavsky, Andrei (Donatevich)
See also CWW 2; RGSF 2

Tesich, Steve 1943(?)-1996 .... **CLC 40, 69**
See also CA 105; 152; CAD; DLBY 1983

Tesla, Nikola 1856-1943 .... **TCLC 88**

Teternikov, Fyodor Kuzmich 1863-1927
See Sologub, Fyodor
See also CA 104

Tevis, Walter 1928-1984 .... **CLC 42**
See also CA 113; SFW 4

Tey, Josephine .... **TCLC 14**
See Mackintosh, Elizabeth
See also DLB 77; MSW

Thackeray, William Makepeace 1811-1863 .... **NCLC 5, 14, 22, 43; WLC**
See also BRW 5; BRWC 2; CDBLB 1832-1890; DA; DA3; DAB; DAC; DAM MST, NOV; DLB 21, 55, 159, 163; NFS 13; RGEL 2; SATA 23; TEA; WLIT 3

Thakura, Ravindranatha
See Tagore, Rabindranath

Thames, C. H.
See Marlowe, Stephen

Tharoor, Shashi 1956- .... **CLC 70**
See also CA 141; CANR 91; CN 7

Thelwell, Michael Miles 1939- .... **CLC 22**
See also BW 2; CA 101

Theobald, Lewis, Jr.
See Lovecraft, H(oward) P(hillips)

Theocritus c. 310B.C.- .... **CMLC 45**
See also AW 1; DLB 176; RGWL 2, 3

Theodorescu, Ion N. 1880-1967
See Arghezi, Tudor
See also CA 116

Theriault, Yves 1915-1983 .... **CLC 79**
See also CA 102; CCA 1; DAC; DAM MST; DLB 88; EWL 3

Theroux, Alexander (Louis) 1939- .... **CLC 2, 25**
See also CA 85-88; CANR 20, 63; CN 7

Theroux, Paul (Edward) 1941- ...... **CLC 5, 8, 11, 15, 28, 46**
See also AAYA 28; AMWS 8; BEST 89:4; BPFB 3; CA 33-36R; CANR 20, 45, 74; CDALBS; CN 7; CPW 1; DA3; DAM POP; DLB 2, 218; EWL 3; HGG; MTCW 1, 2; RGAL 4; SATA 44, 109; TUS

Thesen, Sharon 1946- .... **CLC 56**
See also CA 163; CANR 125; CP 7; CWP

Thespis fl. 6th cent. B.C.- .... **CMLC 51**
See also LMFS 1

Thevenin, Denis
See Duhamel, Georges

Thibault, Jacques Anatole Francois 1844-1924
See France, Anatole
See also CA 106; 127; DA3; DAM NOV; MTCW 1, 2; TWA

Thiele, Colin (Milton) 1920- .... **CLC 17**
See also CA 29-32R; CANR 12, 28, 53, 105; CLR 27; DLB 289; MAICYA 1, 2; SAAS 2; SATA 14, 72, 125; YAW

Thistlethwaite, Bel
See Wetherald, Agnes Ethelwyn

Thomas, Audrey (Callahan) 1935- .... **CLC 7, 13, 37, 107; SSC 20**
See also AITN 2; CA 21-24R; CAAS 19; CANR 36, 58; CN 7; DLB 60; MTCW 1; RGSF 2

Thomas, Augustus 1857-1934 .... **TCLC 97**

Thomas, D(onald) M(ichael) 1935- . **CLC 13, 22, 31, 132**
See also BPFB 3; BRWS 4; CA 61-64; CAAS 11; CANR 17, 45, 75; CDBLB 1960 to Present; CN 7; CP 7; DA3; DLB 40, 207; HGG; INT CANR-17; MTCW 1, 2; SFW 4

Thomas, Dylan (Marlais) 1914-1953 .... **PC 2, 52; SSC 3, 44; TCLC 1, 8, 45, 105; WLC**
See also AAYA 45; BRWS 1; CA 104; 120; CANR 65; CDBLB 1945-1960; DA; DA3; DAB; DAC; DAM DRAM, MST, POET; DLB 13, 20, 139; EWL 3; EXPP; LAIT 3; MTCW 1, 2; PAB; PFS 1, 3, 8; RGEL 2; RGSF 2; SATA 60; TEA; WLIT 4; WP

Thomas, (Philip) Edward 1878-1917 . **PC 53; TCLC 10**
See also BRW 6; BRWS 3; CA 106; 153; DAM POET; DLB 19, 98, 156, 216; EWL 3; PAB; RGEL 2

Thomas, Joyce Carol 1938- .... **CLC 35**
See also AAYA 12, 54; BW 2, 3; CA 113; 116; CANR 48, 114; CLR 19; DLB 33; INT CA-116; JRDA; MAICYA 1, 2; MTCW 1, 2; SAAS 7; SATA 40, 78, 123, 137; SATA-Essay 137; WYA; YAW

Thomas, Lewis 1913-1993 .... **CLC 35**
See also ANW; CA 85-88; 143; CANR 38, 60; DLB 275; MTCW 1, 2

Thomas, M. Carey 1857-1935 .... **TCLC 89**
See also FW

Thomas, Paul
See Mann, (Paul) Thomas

Thomas, Piri 1928- .... **CLC 17; HLCS 2**
See also CA 73-76; HW 1; LLW 1

Thomas, R(onald) S(tuart) 1913-2000 .... **CLC 6, 13, 48**
See also CA 89-92; 189; CAAS 4; CANR 30; CDBLB 1960 to Present; CP 7; DAB; DAM POET; DLB 27; EWL 3; MTCW 1; RGEL 2

Thomas, Ross (Elmore) 1926-1995 .. **CLC 39**
See also CA 33-36R; 150; CANR 22, 63; CMW 4

Thompson, Francis (Joseph) 1859-1907 .... **TCLC 4**
See also BRW 5; CA 104; 189; CDBLB 1890-1914; DLB 19; RGEL 2; TEA

Thompson, Francis Clegg
See Mencken, H(enry) L(ouis)

Thompson, Hunter S(tockton) 1937(?)- .... **CLC 9, 17, 40, 104**
See also AAYA 45; BEST 89:1; BPFB 3; CA 17-20R; CANR 23, 46, 74, 77, 111; CPW; CSW; DA3; DAM POP; DLB 185; MTCW 1, 2; TUS

Thompson, James Myers
See Thompson, Jim (Myers)

Thompson, Jim (Myers) 1906-1977(?) .... **CLC 69**
See also BPFB 3; CA 140; CMW 4; CPW; DLB 226; MSW

Thompson, Judith .... **CLC 39**
See also CWD

Thomson, James 1700-1748 .... **LC 16, 29, 40**
See also BRWS 3; DAM POET; DLB 95; RGEL 2

Thomson, James 1834-1882 .... **NCLC 18**
See also DAM POET; DLB 35; RGEL 2

Thoreau, Henry David 1817-1862 .. **NCLC 7, 21, 61, 138; PC 30; WLC**
See also AAYA 42; AMW; ANW; BYA 3; CDALB 1640-1865; DA; DA3; DAB; DAC; DAM MST; DLB 1, 183, 223, 270, 298; LAIT 2; LMFS 1; NCFS 3; RGAL 4; TUS

Thorndike, E. L.
See Thorndike, Edward L(ee)

Thorndike, Edward L(ee) 1874-1949 .... **TCLC 107**
See also CA 121

Thornton, Hall
See Silverberg, Robert

Thorpe, Adam 1956- .... **CLC 176**
See also CA 129; CANR 92; DLB 231

Thubron, Colin (Gerald Dryden) 1939- .... **CLC 163**
See also CA 25-28R; CANR 12, 29, 59, 95; CN 7; DLB 204, 231

Thucydides c. 455B.C.-c. 395B.C. . **CMLC 17**
See also AW 1; DLB 176; RGWL 2, 3

Thumboo, Edwin Nadason 1933- .... **PC 30**
See also CA 194

Thurber, James (Grover) 1894-1961 .. **CLC 5, 11, 25, 125; SSC 1, 47**
See also AMWS 1; BPFB 3; BYA 5; CA 73-76; CANR 17, 39; CDALB 1929-1941; CWRI 5; DA; DA3; DAB; DAC; DAM DRAM, MST, NOV; DLB 4, 11, 22, 102; EWL 3; EXPS; FANT; LAIT 3; MAICYA 1, 2; MTCW 1, 2; RGAL 4; RGSF 2; SATA 13; SSFS 1, 10, 19; SUFW; TUS

Thurman, Wallace (Henry) 1902-1934 .... **BLC 3; HR 3; TCLC 6**
See also BW 1, 3; CA 104; 124; CANR 81; DAM MULT; DLB 51

Tibullus c. 54B.C.-c. 18B.C. .... **CMLC 36**
See also AW 2; DLB 211; RGWL 2, 3

Ticheburn, Cheviot
See Ainsworth, William Harrison

Tieck, (Johann) Ludwig 1773-1853 .... **NCLC 5, 46; SSC 31**
See also CDWLB 2; DLB 90; EW 5; IDTP; RGSF 2; RGWL 2, 3; SUFW

Tiger, Derry
See Ellison, Harlan (Jay)

Tilghman, Christopher 1946- .... **CLC 65**
See also CA 159; CSW; DLB 244

Tillich, Paul (Johannes) 1886-1965 .... **CLC 131**
See also CA 5-8R; 25-28R; CANR 33; MTCW 1, 2

Tillinghast, Richard (Williford) 1940- .... **CLC 29**
See also CA 29-32R; CAAS 23; CANR 26, 51, 96; CP 7; CSW

Timrod, Henry 1828-1867 .... **NCLC 25**
See also DLB 3, 248; RGAL 4

Tindall, Gillian (Elizabeth) 1938- .... **CLC 7**
See also CA 21-24R; CANR 11, 65, 107; CN 7

Tiptree, James, Jr. .... **CLC 48, 50**
See Sheldon, Alice Hastings Bradley
See also DLB 8; SCFW 2; SFW 4

Tirone Smith, Mary-Ann 1944- .... **CLC 39**
See also CA 118; 136; CANR 113; SATA 143

Tirso de Molina 1580(?)-1648 .... **DC 13; HLCS 2; LC 73**
See also RGWL 2, 3

Titmarsh, Michael Angelo
See Thackeray, William Makepeace

Tocqueville, Alexis (Charles Henri Maurice Clerel Comte) de 1805-1859 .. **NCLC 7, 63**
See also EW 6; GFL 1789 to the Present; TWA

Toer, Pramoedya Ananta 1925- ...... **CLC 186**
See also CA 197; RGWL 3

Toffler, Alvin 1928- .... **CLC 168**
See also CA 13-16R; CANR 15, 46, 67; CPW; DAM POP; MTCW 1, 2

Toibin, Colm
See Toibin, Colm
See also DLB 271

Toibin, Colm 1955- .... **CLC 162**
See Toibin, Colm
See also CA 142; CANR 81

Tolkien, J(ohn) R(onald) R(euel) 1892-1973 .... **CLC 1, 2, 3, 8, 12, 38; TCLC 137; WLC**
See also AAYA 10; AITN 1; BPFB 3; BRWC 2; BRWS 2; CA 17-18; 45-48; CANR 36; CAP 2; CDBLB 1914-1945; CLR 56; CPW 1; CWRI 5; DA; DA3; DAB; DAC; DAM MST, NOV, POP; DLB 15, 160, 255; EFS 2; EWL 3; FANT; JRDA; LAIT 1; LATS 1; LMFS 2; MAICYA 1, 2; MTCW 1, 2; NFS 8; RGEL 2; SATA 2, 32, 100; SATA-Obit 24; SFW 4; SUFW; TEA; WCH; WYA; YAW

Toller, Ernst 1893-1939 .... **TCLC 10**
See also CA 107; 186; DLB 124; EWL 3; RGWL 2, 3

Tolson, M. B.
See Tolson, Melvin B(eaunorus)

Tolson, Melvin B(eaunorus) 1898(?)-1966 .... **BLC 3; CLC 36, 105**
See also AFAW 1, 2; BW 1, 3; CA 124; 89-92; CANR 80; DAM MULT, POET; DLB 48, 76; RGAL 4

Tolstoi, Aleksei Nikolaevich
See Tolstoy, Alexey Nikolaevich

Tolstoi, Lev
See Tolstoy, Leo (Nikolaevich)
See also RGSF 2; RGWL 2, 3

Tolstoy, Aleksei Nikolaevich
See Tolstoy, Alexey Nikolaevich
See also DLB 272

Tolstoy, Alexey Nikolaevich 1882-1945 .... **TCLC 18**
See Tolstoy, Aleksei Nikolaevich
See also CA 107; 158; EWL 3; SFW 4

Tolstoy, Leo (Nikolaevich) 1828-1910 . **SSC 9, 30, 45, 54; TCLC 4, 11, 17, 28, 44, 79; WLC**
See Tolstoi, Lev
See also CA 104; 123; DA; DA3; DAB; DAC; DAM MST, NOV; DLB 238; EFS 2; EW 7; EXPS; IDTP; LAIT 2; LATS 1; LMFS 1; NFS 10; SATA 26; SSFS 5; TWA

Tolstoy, Count Leo
See Tolstoy, Leo (Nikolaevich)

Tomalin, Claire 1933- .... **CLC 166**
See also CA 89-92; CANR 52, 88; DLB 155

Tomasi di Lampedusa, Giuseppe 1896-1957
See Lampedusa, Giuseppe (Tomasi) di
See also CA 111; DLB 177; EWL 3

Tomlin, Lily .... **CLC 17**
See Tomlin, Mary Jean

Tomlin, Mary Jean 1939(?)-
See Tomlin, Lily
See also CA 117

Tomline, F. Latour
See Gilbert, W(illiam) S(chwenck)

Tomlinson, (Alfred) Charles 1927- .... **CLC 2, 4, 6, 13, 45; PC 17**
See also CA 5-8R; CANR 33; CP 7; DAM POET; DLB 40

Tomlinson, H(enry) M(ajor)
1873-1958 .... **TCLC 71**
See also CA 118; 161; DLB 36, 100, 195

Tonna, Charlotte Elizabeth
1790-1846 .... **NCLC 135**
See also DLB 163

Tonson, Jacob fl. 1655(?)-1736 .... **LC 86**
See also DLB 170

Toole, John Kennedy 1937-1969 ..... **CLC 19, 64**
See also BPFB 3; CA 104; DLBY 1981; MTCW 2

Toomer, Eugene
See Toomer, Jean

Toomer, Eugene Pinchback
See Toomer, Jean

Toomer, Jean 1894-1967 .. **BLC 3; CLC 1, 4, 13, 22; HR 3; PC 7; SSC 1, 45; WLCS**
See also AFAW 1, 2; AMWS 3, 9; BW 1; CA 85-88; CDALB 1917-1929; DA3; DAM MULT; DLB 45, 51; EWL 3; EXPP; EXPS; LMFS 2; MTCW 1, 2; NFS 11; RGAL 4; RGSF 2; SSFS 5

Toomer, Nathan Jean
See Toomer, Jean

Toomer, Nathan Pinchback
See Toomer, Jean

Torley, Luke
See Blish, James (Benjamin)

Tornimparte, Alessandra
See Ginzburg, Natalia

Torre, Raoul della
See Mencken, H(enry) L(ouis)

Torrence, Ridgely 1874-1950 .... **TCLC 97**
See also DLB 54, 249

Torrey, E(dwin) Fuller 1937- .... **CLC 34**
See also CA 119; CANR 71

Torsvan, Ben Traven
See Traven, B.

Torsvan, Benno Traven
See Traven, B.

Torsvan, Berick Traven
See Traven, B.

Torsvan, Berwick Traven
See Traven, B.

Torsvan, Bruno Traven
See Traven, B.

Torsvan, Traven
See Traven, B.

Tourneur, Cyril 1575(?)-1626 .... **LC 66**
See also BRW 2; DAM DRAM; DLB 58; RGEL 2

Tournier, Michel (Edouard) 1924- .... **CLC 6, 23, 36, 95**
See also CA 49-52; CANR 3, 36, 74; DLB 83; EWL 3; GFL 1789 to the Present; MTCW 1, 2; SATA 23

Tournimparte, Alessandra
See Ginzburg, Natalia

Towers, Ivar
See Kornbluth, C(yril) M.

Towne, Robert (Burton) 1936(?)- ..... **CLC 87**
See also CA 108; DLB 44; IDFW 3, 4

Townsend, Sue .... **CLC 61**
See Townsend, Susan Lilian
See also AAYA 28; CA 119; 127; CANR 65, 107; CBD; CD 5; CPW; CWD; DAB; DAC; DAM MST; DLB 271; INT CA-127; SATA 55, 93; SATA-Brief 48; YAW

Townsend, Susan Lilian 1946-
See Townsend, Sue

Townshend, Pete
See Townshend, Peter (Dennis Blandford)

Townshend, Peter (Dennis Blandford)
1945- .... **CLC 17, 42**
See also CA 107

Tozzi, Federigo 1883-1920 .... **TCLC 31**
See also CA 160; CANR 110; DLB 264; EWL 3

Tracy, Don(ald Fiske) 1905-1970(?)
See Queen, Ellery
See also CA 1-4R; 176; CANR 2

Trafford, F. G.
See Riddell, Charlotte

Traherne, Thomas 1637(?)-1674 .... **LC 99**
See also BRW 2; DLB 131; PAB; RGEL 2

Traill, Catharine Parr 1802-1899 .. **NCLC 31**
See also DLB 99

Trakl, Georg 1887-1914 .... **PC 20; TCLC 5**
See also CA 104; 165; EW 10; EWL 3; LMFS 2; MTCW 2; RGWL 2, 3

Tranquilli, Secondino
See Silone, Ignazio

Transtroemer, Tomas Gosta
See Transtromer, Tomas (Goesta)

Transtromer, Tomas
See Transtromer, Tomas (Goesta)

Transtromer, Tomas (Goesta)
1931- .... **CLC 52, 65**
See also CA 117; 129; CAAS 17; CANR 115; DAM POET; DLB 257; EWL 3

Transtromer, Tomas Gosta
See Transtromer, Tomas (Goesta)

Traven, B. 1882(?)-1969 .... **CLC 8, 11**
See also CA 19-20; 25-28R; CAP 2; DLB 9, 56; EWL 3; MTCW 1; RGAL 4

Trediakovsky, Vasilii Kirillovich
1703-1769 .... **LC 68**
See also DLB 150

Treitel, Jonathan 1959- .... **CLC 70**
See also CA 210; DLB 267

Trelawny, Edward John
1792-1881 .... **NCLC 85**
See also DLB 110, 116, 144

Tremain, Rose 1943- .... **CLC 42**
See also CA 97-100; CANR 44, 95; CN 7; DLB 14, 271; RGSF 2; RHW

Tremblay, Michel 1942- .... **CLC 29, 102**
See also CA 116; 128; CCA 1; CWW 2; DAC; DAM MST; DLB 60; EWL 3; GLL 1; MTCW 1, 2

Trevanian .... **CLC 29**
See Whitaker, Rod(ney)

Trevor, Glen
See Hilton, James

Trevor, William .. **CLC 7, 9, 14, 25, 71, 116; SSC 21, 58**
See Cox, William Trevor
See also BRWS 4; CBD; CD 5; CN 7; DLB 14, 139; EWL 3; LATS 1; MTCW 2; RGEL 2; RGSF 2; SSFS 10

Trifonov, Iurii (Valentinovich)
See Trifonov, Yuri (Valentinovich)
See also RGWL 2, 3

Trifonov, Yuri (Valentinovich)
1925-1981 .... **CLC 45**
See Trifonov, Iurii (Valentinovich); Trifonov, Yury Valentinovich
See also CA 126; 103; MTCW 1

Trifonov, Yury Valentinovich
See Trifonov, Yuri (Valentinovich)
See also EWL 3

Trilling, Diana (Rubin) 1905-1996 . **CLC 129**
See also CA 5-8R; 154; CANR 10, 46; INT CANR-10; MTCW 1, 2

Trilling, Lionel 1905-1975 .... **CLC 9, 11, 24**
See also AMWS 3; CA 9-12R; 61-64; CANR 10, 105; DLB 28, 63; EWL 3; INT CANR-10; MTCW 1, 2; RGAL 4; TUS

Trimball, W. H.
See Mencken, H(enry) L(ouis)

Tristan
See Gomez de la Serna, Ramon

Tristram
See Housman, A(lfred) E(dward)

Trogdon, William (Lewis) 1939-
See Heat-Moon, William Least
See also CA 115; 119; CANR 47, 89; CPW; INT CA-119

Trollope, Anthony 1815-1882 .... **NCLC 6, 33, 101; SSC 28; WLC**
See also BRW 5; CDBLB 1832-1890; DA; DA3; DAB; DAC; DAM MST, NOV; DLB 21, 57, 159; RGEL 2; RGSF 2; SATA 22

Trollope, Frances 1779-1863 .... **NCLC 30**
See also DLB 21, 166

Trollope, Joanna 1943- .... **CLC 186**
See also CA 101; CANR 58, 95; CPW; DLB 207; RHW

Trotsky, Leon 1879-1940 .... **TCLC 22**
See also CA 118; 167

Trotter (Cockburn), Catharine
1679-1749 .... **LC 8**
See also DLB 84, 252

Trotter, Wilfred 1872-1939 .... **TCLC 97**

Trout, Kilgore
See Farmer, Philip Jose

Trow, George W. S. 1943- .... **CLC 52**
See also CA 126; CANR 91

Troyat, Henri 1911- .... **CLC 23**
See also CA 45-48; CANR 2, 33, 67, 117; GFL 1789 to the Present; MTCW 1

Trudeau, G(arretson) B(eekman) 1948-
See Trudeau, Garry B.
See also CA 81-84; CANR 31; SATA 35

Trudeau, Garry B. .... **CLC 12**
See Trudeau, G(arretson) B(eekman)
See also AAYA 10; AITN 2

Truffaut, Francois 1932-1984 ... **CLC 20, 101**
See also CA 81-84; 113; CANR 34

Trumbo, Dalton 1905-1976 .... **CLC 19**
See also CA 21-24R; 69-72; CANR 10; DLB 26; IDFW 3, 4; YAW

Trumbull, John 1750-1831 .... **NCLC 30**
See also DLB 31; RGAL 4

Trundlett, Helen B.
See Eliot, T(homas) S(tearns)

Truth, Sojourner 1797(?)-1883 ...... **NCLC 94**
See also DLB 239; FW; LAIT 2

Tryon, Thomas 1926-1991 .... **CLC 3, 11**
See also AITN 1; BPFB 3; CA 29-32R; 135; CANR 32, 77; CPW; DA3; DAM POP; HGG; MTCW 1

Tryon, Tom
See Tryon, Thomas

Ts'ao Hsueh-ch'in 1715(?)-1763 .... **LC 1**

Tsushima, Shuji 1909-1948
See Dazai Osamu
See also CA 107

Tsvetaeva (Efron), Marina (Ivanovna)
1892-1941 .... **PC 14; TCLC 7, 35**
See also CA 104; 128; CANR 73; DLB 295; EW 11; MTCW 1, 2; RGWL 2, 3

Tuck, Lily 1938- .... **CLC 70**
See also CA 139; CANR 90

Tu Fu 712-770 .... **PC 9**
See Du Fu
See also DAM MULT; TWA; WP

Tunis, John R(oberts) 1889-1975 ..... **CLC 12**
See also BYA 1; CA 61-64; CANR 62; DLB 22, 171; JRDA; MAICYA 1, 2; SATA 37; SATA-Brief 30; YAW

Tuohy, Frank .... **CLC 37**
See Tuohy, John Francis
See also DLB 14, 139

Tuohy, John Francis 1925-
See Tuohy, Frank
See also CA 5-8R; 178; CANR 3, 47; CN 7

Turco, Lewis (Putnam) 1934- ..... **CLC 11, 63**
See also CA 13-16R; CAAS 22; CANR 24, 51; CP 7; DLBY 1984

Turgenev, Ivan (Sergeevich)
1818-1883 ..... **DC 7; NCLC 21, 37, 122; SSC 7, 57; WLC**
See also DA; DAB; DAC; DAM MST, NOV; DFS 6; DLB 238, 284; EW 6; LATS 1; NFS 16; RGSF 2; RGWL 2, 3; TWA

Turgot, Anne-Robert-Jacques
1727-1781 .... **LC 26**

Turner, Frederick 1943- .... **CLC 48**
See also CA 73-76; CAAS 10; CANR 12, 30, 56; DLB 40, 282

Turton, James
See Crace, Jim

Tutu, Desmond M(pilo) 1931- .. **BLC 3; CLC 80**
See also BW 1, 3; CA 125; CANR 67, 81; DAM MULT

Tutuola, Amos 1920-1997 ..... **BLC 3; CLC 5, 14, 29**
See also AFW; BW 2, 3; CA 9-12R; 159; CANR 27, 66; CDWLB 3; CN 7; DA3; DAM MULT; DLB 125; DNFS 2; EWL 3; MTCW 1, 2; RGEL 2; WLIT 2

Twain, Mark .. **SSC 34; TCLC 6, 12, 19, 36, 48, 59; WLC**
See Clemens, Samuel Langhorne
See also AAYA 20; AMW; AMWC 1; BPFB 3; BYA 2, 3, 11, 14; CLR 58, 60, 66; DLB 11; EXPN; EXPS; FANT; LAIT 2; NCFS 4; NFS 1, 6; RGAL 4; RGSF 2; SFW 4; SSFS 1, 7; SUFW; TUS; WCH; WYA; YAW

Tyler, Anne 1941- . **CLC 7, 11, 18, 28, 44, 59, 103**
See also AAYA 18; AMWS 4; BEST 89:1; BPFB 3; BYA 12; CA 9-12R; CANR 11, 33, 53, 109; CDALBS; CN 7; CPW; CSW; DAM NOV, POP; DLB 6, 143; DLBY 1982; EWL 3; EXPN; LATS 1; MAWW; MTCW 1, 2; NFS 2, 7, 10; RGAL 4; SATA 7, 90; SSFS 17; TUS; YAW

Tyler, Royall 1757-1826 .... **NCLC 3**
See also DLB 37; RGAL 4

Tynan, Katharine 1861-1931 .... **TCLC 3**
See also CA 104; 167; DLB 153, 240; FW

Tyutchev, Fyodor 1803-1873 .... **NCLC 34**

Tzara, Tristan 1896-1963 ..... **CLC 47; PC 27**
See also CA 153; 89-92; DAM POET; EWL 3; MTCW 2

Uchida, Yoshiko 1921-1992 .... **AAL**
See also AAYA 16; BYA 2, 3; CA 13-16R; 139; CANR 6, 22, 47, 61; CDALBS; CLR 6, 56; CWRI 5; JRDA; MAICYA 1, 2; MTCW 1, 2; SAAS 1; SATA 1, 53; SATA-Obit 72

Udall, Nicholas 1504-1556 .... **LC 84**
See also DLB 62; RGEL 2

Ueda Akinari 1734-1809 .... **NCLC 131**

Uhry, Alfred 1936- .... **CLC 55**
See also CA 127; 133; CAD; CANR 112; CD 5; CSW; DA3; DAM DRAM, POP; DFS 11, 15; INT CA-133

Ulf, Haerved
See Strindberg, (Johan) August

Ulf, Harved
See Strindberg, (Johan) August

Ulibarri, Sabine R(eyes)
1919-2003 .... **CLC 83; HLCS 2**
See also CA 131; 214; CANR 81; DAM MULT; DLB 82; HW 1, 2; RGSF 2

Unamuno (y Jugo), Miguel de
1864-1936 .. **HLC 2; SSC 11, 69; TCLC 2, 9, 148**
See also CA 104; 131; CANR 81; DAM MULT, NOV; DLB 108; EW 8; EWL 3; HW 1, 2; MTCW 1, 2; RGSF 2; RGWL 2, 3; TWA

Uncle Shelby
See Silverstein, Shel(don Allan)

Undercliffe, Errol
See Campbell, (John) Ramsey

Underwood, Miles
See Glassco, John

Undset, Sigrid 1882-1949 ..... **TCLC 3; WLC**
See also CA 104; 129; DA; DA3; DAB; DAC; DAM MST, NOV; DLB 293; EW 9; EWL 3; FW; MTCW 1, 2; RGWL 2, 3

Ungaretti, Giuseppe 1888-1970 ... **CLC 7, 11, 15; PC 57**
See also CA 19-20; 25-28R; CAP 2; DLB 114; EW 10; EWL 3; RGWL 2, 3

Unger, Douglas 1952- .... **CLC 34**
See also CA 130; CANR 94

Unsworth, Barry (Forster) 1930- .... **CLC 76, 127**
See also BRWS 7; CA 25-28R; CANR 30, 54, 125; CN 7; DLB 194

Updike, John (Hoyer) 1932- . **CLC 1, 2, 3, 5, 7, 9, 13, 15, 23, 34, 43, 70, 139; SSC 13, 27; WLC**
See also AAYA 36; AMW; AMWC 1; AMWR 1; BPFB 3; BYA 12; CA 1-4R; CABS 1; CANR 4, 33, 51, 94; CDALB 1968-1988; CN 7; CP 7; CPW 1; DA; DA3; DAB; DAC; DAM MST, NOV, POET, POP; DLB 2, 5, 143, 218, 227; DLBD 3; DLBY 1980, 1982, 1997; EWL 3; EXPP; HGG; MTCW 1, 2; NFS 12; RGAL 4; RGSF 2; SSFS 3, 19; TUS

Upshaw, Margaret Mitchell
See Mitchell, Margaret (Munnerlyn)

Upton, Mark
See Sanders, Lawrence

Upward, Allen 1863-1926 .... **TCLC 85**
See also CA 117; 187; DLB 36

Urdang, Constance (Henriette)
1922-1996 .... **CLC 47**
See also CA 21-24R; CANR 9, 24; CP 7; CWP

Uriel, Henry
See Faust, Frederick (Schiller)

Uris, Leon (Marcus) 1924-2003 ... **CLC 7, 32**
See also AITN 1, 2; BEST 89:2; BPFB 3; CA 1-4R; 217; CANR 1, 40, 65, 123; CN 7; CPW 1; DA3; DAM NOV, POP; MTCW 1, 2; SATA 49; SATA-Obit 146

Urista (Heredia), Alberto (Baltazar)
1947- .... **HLCS 1; PC 34**
See Alurista
See also CA 45-48, 182; CANR 2, 32; HW 1

Urmuz
See Codrescu, Andrei

Urquhart, Guy
See McAlmon, Robert (Menzies)

Urquhart, Jane 1949- .... **CLC 90**
See also CA 113; CANR 32, 68, 116; CCA 1; DAC

Usigli, Rodolfo 1905-1979 .... **HLCS 1**
See also CA 131; EWL 3; HW 1; LAW

Ustinov, Peter (Alexander)
1921-2004 .... **CLC 1**
See also AITN 1; CA 13-16R; CANR 25, 51; CBD; CD 5; DLB 13; MTCW 2

U Tam'si, Gerald Felix Tchicaya
See Tchicaya, Gerald Felix

U Tam'si, Tchicaya
See Tchicaya, Gerald Felix

Vachss, Andrew (Henry) 1942- .... **CLC 106**
See also CA 118, 214; CAAE 214; CANR 44, 95; CMW 4

Vachss, Andrew H.
See Vachss, Andrew (Henry)

Vaculik, Ludvik 1926- .... **CLC 7**
See also CA 53-56; CANR 72; CWW 2; DLB 232; EWL 3

Vaihinger, Hans 1852-1933 .... **TCLC 71**
See also CA 116; 166

Valdez, Luis (Miguel) 1940- ..... **CLC 84; DC 10; HLC 2**
See also CA 101; CAD; CANR 32, 81; CD 5; DAM MULT; DFS 5; DLB 122; EWL 3; HW 1; LAIT 4; LLW 1

Valenzuela, Luisa 1938- .... **CLC 31, 104; HLCS 2; SSC 14**
See also CA 101; CANR 32, 65, 123; CDWLB 3; CWW 2; DAM MULT; DLB 113; EWL 3; FW; HW 1, 2; LAW; RGSF 2; RGWL 3

Valera y Alcala-Galiano, Juan
1824-1905 .... **TCLC 10**
See also CA 106

Valerius Maximus fl. 20- .... **CMLC 64**
See also DLB 211

Valery, (Ambroise) Paul (Toussaint Jules)
1871-1945 .... **PC 9; TCLC 4, 15**
See also CA 104; 122; DA3; DAM POET; DLB 258; EW 8; EWL 3; GFL 1789 to the Present; MTCW 1, 2; RGWL 2, 3; TWA

Valle-Inclan, Ramon (Maria) del
1866-1936 .... **HLC 2; TCLC 5**
See also CA 106; 153; CANR 80; DAM MULT; DLB 134; EW 8; EWL 3; HW 2; RGSF 2; RGWL 2, 3

Vallejo, Antonio Buero
See Buero Vallejo, Antonio

Vallejo, Cesar (Abraham)
1892-1938 .... **HLC 2; TCLC 3, 56**
See also CA 105; 153; CANR 81; DAM MULT; DLB 290; EWL 3; HW 1; LAW; RGWL 2, 3

Valles, Jules 1832-1885 .... **NCLC 71**
See also DLB 123; GFL 1789 to the Present

Vallette, Marguerite Eymery
1860-1953 .... **TCLC 67**
See Rachilde
See also CA 182; DLB 123, 192

Valle Y Pena, Ramon del
See Valle-Inclan, Ramon (Maria) del

Van Ash, Cay 1918-1994 .... **CLC 34**
See also CA 220

Vanbrugh, Sir John 1664-1726 .... **LC 21**
See also BRW 2; DAM DRAM; DLB 80; IDTP; RGEL 2

Van Campen, Karl
See Campbell, John W(ood, Jr.)

Vance, Gerald
See Silverberg, Robert

Vance, Jack .... **CLC 35**
See Vance, John Holbrook
See also DLB 8; FANT; SCFW 2; SFW 4; SUFW 1, 2

Vance, John Holbrook 1916-
See Queen, Ellery; Vance, Jack
See also CA 29-32R; CANR 17, 65; CMW 4; MTCW 1

Van Den Bogarde, Derek Jules Gaspard Ulric Niven 1921-1999 .... **CLC 14**
See Bogarde, Dirk
See also CA 77-80; 179

Vandenburgh, Jane .... **CLC 59**
See also CA 168

Vanderhaeghe, Guy 1951- .... **CLC 41**
See also BPFB 3; CA 113; CANR 72

van der Post, Laurens (Jan)
1906-1996 .... **CLC 5**
See also AFW; CA 5-8R; 155; CANR 35; CN 7; DLB 204; RGEL 2

van de Wetering, Janwillem 1931- ... **CLC 47**
See also CA 49-52; CANR 4, 62, 90; CMW 4

Van Dine, S. S. .... **TCLC 23**
See Wright, Willard Huntington
See also MSW

Van Doren, Carl (Clinton)
1885-1950 .... **TCLC 18**
See also CA 111; 168

Van Doren, Mark 1894-1972 .... **CLC 6, 10**
See also CA 1-4R; 37-40R; CANR 3; DLB 45, 284; MTCW 1, 2; RGAL 4

Van Druten, John (William)
1901-1957 .... **TCLC 2**
See also CA 104; 161; DLB 10; RGAL 4

Van Duyn, Mona (Jane) 1921- ...... **CLC 3, 7, 63, 116**
See also CA 9-12R; CANR 7, 38, 60, 116; CP 7; CWP; DAM POET; DLB 5

Van Dyne, Edith
See Baum, L(yman) Frank

van Itallie, Jean-Claude 1936- .... **CLC 3**
See also CA 45-48; CAAS 2; CAD; CANR 1, 48; CD 5; DLB 7

Van Loot, Cornelius Obenchain
See Roberts, Kenneth (Lewis)

van Ostaijen, Paul 1896-1928 .... **TCLC 33**
See also CA 163

Van Peebles, Melvin 1932- .... **CLC 2, 20**
See also BW 2, 3; CA 85-88; CANR 27, 67, 82; DAM MULT

van Schendel, Arthur(-Francois-Emile)
1874-1946 .... **TCLC 56**
See also EWL 3

Vansittart, Peter 1920- .... **CLC 42**
See also CA 1-4R; CANR 3, 49, 90; CN 7; RHW

Van Vechten, Carl 1880-1964 ... **CLC 33; HR 3**
See also AMWS 2; CA 183; 89-92; DLB 4, 9, 51; RGAL 4

van Vogt, A(lfred) E(lton) 1912-2000 . **CLC 1**
See also BPFB 3; BYA 13, 14; CA 21-24R; 190; CANR 28; DLB 8, 251; SATA 14; SATA-Obit 124; SCFW; SFW 4

Vara, Madeleine
See Jackson, Laura (Riding)

Varda, Agnes 1928- .... **CLC 16**
See also CA 116; 122

Vargas Llosa, (Jorge) Mario (Pedro)
1939- .... **CLC 3, 6, 9, 10, 15, 31, 42, 85, 181; HLC 2**
See Llosa, (Jorge) Mario (Pedro) Vargas
See also BPFB 3; CA 73-76; CANR 18, 32, 42, 67, 116; CDWLB 3; DA; DA3; DAB; DAC; DAM MST, MULT, NOV; DLB 145; DNFS 2; EWL 3; HW 1, 2; LAIT 5; LATS 1; LAW; LAWS 1; MTCW 1, 2; RGWL 2; SSFS 14; TWA; WLIT 1

Varnhagen von Ense, Rahel
1771-1833 .... **NCLC 130**
See also DLB 90

Vasiliu, George
See Bacovia, George

Vasiliu, Gheorghe
See Bacovia, George
See also CA 123; 189

Vassa, Gustavus
See Equiano, Olaudah

Vassilikos, Vassilis 1933- .... **CLC 4, 8**
See also CA 81-84; CANR 75; EWL 3

Vaughan, Henry 1621-1695 .... **LC 27**
See also BRW 2; DLB 131; PAB; RGEL 2

Vaughn, Stephanie .... **CLC 62**

Vazov, Ivan (Minchov) 1850-1921 . **TCLC 25**
See also CA 121; 167; CDWLB 4; DLB 147

Veblen, Thorstein B(unde)
1857-1929 .... **TCLC 31**
See also AMWS 1; CA 115; 165; DLB 246

Vega, Lope de 1562-1635 .... **HLCS 2; LC 23**
See also EW 2; RGWL 2, 3

Vendler, Helen (Hennessy) 1933- ... **CLC 138**
See also CA 41-44R; CANR 25, 72; MTCW 1, 2

Venison, Alfred
See Pound, Ezra (Weston Loomis)

Ventsel, Elena Sergeevna 1907-
See Grekova, I.
See also CA 154

Verdi, Marie de
See Mencken, H(enry) L(ouis)

Verdu, Matilde
See Cela, Camilo Jose

Verga, Giovanni (Carmelo)
1840-1922 .... **SSC 21; TCLC 3**
See also CA 104; 123; CANR 101; EW 7; EWL 3; RGSF 2; RGWL 2, 3

Vergil 70B.C.-19B.C. ... **CMLC 9, 40; PC 12; WLCS**
See Virgil
See also AW 2; DA; DA3; DAB; DAC; DAM MST, POET; EFS 1; LMFS 1

Verhaeren, Emile (Adolphe Gustave)
1855-1916 .... **TCLC 12**
See also CA 109; EWL 3; GFL 1789 to the Present

Verlaine, Paul (Marie) 1844-1896 .. **NCLC 2, 51; PC 2, 32**
See also DAM POET; DLB 217; EW 7; GFL 1789 to the Present; LMFS 2; RGWL 2, 3; TWA

Verne, Jules (Gabriel) 1828-1905 ... **TCLC 6, 52**
See also AAYA 16; BYA 4; CA 110; 131; CLR 88; DA3; DLB 123; GFL 1789 to the Present; JRDA; LAIT 2; LMFS 2; MAICYA 1, 2; RGWL 2, 3; SATA 21; SCFW; SFW 4; TWA; WCH

Verus, Marcus Annius
See Aurelius, Marcus

Very, Jones 1813-1880 .... **NCLC 9**
See also DLB 1, 243; RGAL 4

Vesaas, Tarjei 1897-1970 .... **CLC 48**
See also CA 190; 29-32R; DLB 297; EW 11; EWL 3; RGWL 3

Vialis, Gaston
See Simenon, Georges (Jacques Christian)

Vian, Boris 1920-1959(?) .... **TCLC 9**
See also CA 106; 164; CANR 111; DLB 72; EWL 3; GFL 1789 to the Present; MTCW 2; RGWL 2, 3

Viaud, (Louis Marie) Julien 1850-1923
See Loti, Pierre
See also CA 107

Vicar, Henry
See Felsen, Henry Gregor

Vicente, Gil 1465-c. 1536 .... **LC 99**
See also DLB 287; RGWL 2, 3

Vicker, Angus
See Felsen, Henry Gregor

Vidal, Gore 1925- ...... **CLC 2, 4, 6, 8, 10, 22, 33, 72, 142**
See Box, Edgar
See also AITN 1; AMWS 4; BEST 90:2; BPFB 3; CA 5-8R; CAD; CANR 13, 45, 65, 100; CD 5; CDALBS; CN 7; CPW; DA3; DAM NOV, POP; DFS 2; DLB 6, 152; EWL 3; INT CANR-13; MTCW 1, 2; RGAL 4; RHW; TUS

Viereck, Peter (Robert Edwin)
1916- .... **CLC 4; PC 27**
See also CA 1-4R; CANR 1, 47; CP 7; DLB 5; PFS 9, 14

Vigny, Alfred (Victor) de
1797-1863 .... **NCLC 7, 102; PC 26**
See also DAM POET; DLB 119, 192, 217; EW 5; GFL 1789 to the Present; RGWL 2, 3

Vilakazi, Benedict Wallet
1906-1947 .... **TCLC 37**
See also CA 168

Villa, Jose Garcia 1914-1997 .... **AAL; PC 22**
See also CA 25-28R; CANR 12, 118; EWL 3; EXPP

Villa, Jose Garcia 1914-1997
See Villa, Jose Garcia

Villarreal, Jose Antonio 1924- .... **HLC 2**
See also CA 133; CANR 93; DAM MULT; DLB 82; HW 1; LAIT 4; RGAL 4

Villaurrutia, Xavier 1903-1950 ...... **TCLC 80**
See also CA 192; EWL 3; HW 1; LAW

Villaverde, Cirilo 1812-1894 .... **NCLC 121**
See also LAW

Villehardouin, Geoffroi de
1150(?)-1218(?) .... **CMLC 38**

Villiers de l'Isle Adam, Jean Marie Mathias Philippe Auguste 1838-1889 ... **NCLC 3; SSC 14**
See also DLB 123, 192; GFL 1789 to the Present; RGSF 2

Villon, Francois 1431-1463(?) . **LC 62; PC 13**
See also DLB 208; EW 2; RGWL 2, 3; TWA

Vine, Barbara .... **CLC 50**
See Rendell, Ruth (Barbara)
See also BEST 90:4

Vinge, Joan (Carol) D(ennison)
1948- .... **CLC 30; SSC 24**
See also AAYA 32; BPFB 3; CA 93-96; CANR 72; SATA 36, 113; SFW 4; YAW

Viola, Herman J(oseph) 1938- .... **CLC 70**
See also CA 61-64; CANR 8, 23, 48, 91; SATA 126

Violis, G.
See Simenon, Georges (Jacques Christian)

Viramontes, Helena Maria 1954- .... **HLCS 2**
See also CA 159; DLB 122; HW 1; LLW 1

Virgil
See Vergil
See also CDWLB 1; DLB 211; LAIT 1; RGWL 2, 3; WP

Visconti, Luchino 1906-1976 .... **CLC 16**
See also CA 81-84; 65-68; CANR 39

Vitry, Jacques de
See Jacques de Vitry

Vittorini, Elio 1908-1966 .... **CLC 6, 9, 14**
See also CA 133; 25-28R; DLB 264; EW 12; EWL 3; RGWL 2, 3

Vivekananda, Swami 1863-1902 .... **TCLC 88**

Vizenor, Gerald Robert 1934- .... **CLC 103; NNAL**
See also CA 13-16R, 205; CAAE 205; CAAS 22; CANR 5, 21, 44, 67; DAM MULT; DLB 175, 227; MTCW 2; TCWW 2

Vizinczey, Stephen 1933- .... **CLC 40**
See also CA 128; CCA 1; INT CA-128

Vliet, R(ussell) G(ordon)
1929-1984 .... **CLC 22**
See also CA 37-40R; 112; CANR 18

Vogau, Boris Andreyevich 1894-1938
See Pilnyak, Boris
See also CA 123; 218

Vogel, Paula A(nne) 1951- ... **CLC 76; DC 19**
See also CA 108; CAD; CANR 119; CD 5; CWD; DFS 14; RGAL 4

Voigt, Cynthia 1942- .... **CLC 30**
See also AAYA 3, 30; BYA 1, 3, 6, 7, 8; CA 106; CANR 18, 37, 40, 94; CLR 13, 48; INT CANR-18; JRDA; LAIT 5; MAICYA 1, 2; MAICYAS 1; SATA 48, 79, 116; SATA-Brief 33; WYA; YAW

Voigt, Ellen Bryant 1943- .... **CLC 54**
See also CA 69-72; CANR 11, 29, 55, 115; CP 7; CSW; CWP; DLB 120

Voinovich, Vladimir (Nikolaevich)
1932- .... **CLC 10, 49, 147**
See also CA 81-84; CAAS 12; CANR 33, 67; MTCW 1

Vollmann, William T. 1959- .... **CLC 89**
See also CA 134; CANR 67, 116; CPW; DA3; DAM NOV, POP; MTCW 2

Voloshinov, V. N.
See Bakhtin, Mikhail Mikhailovich

Voltaire 1694-1778 .... **LC 14, 79; SSC 12; WLC**
See also BYA 13; DA; DA3; DAB; DAC; DAM DRAM, MST; EW 4; GFL Beginnings to 1789; LATS 1; LMFS 1; NFS 7; RGWL 2, 3; TWA

von Aschendrof, Baron Ignatz
See Ford, Ford Madox

von Chamisso, Adelbert
See Chamisso, Adelbert von

von Daeniken, Erich 1935- .... **CLC 30**
See also AITN 1; CA 37-40R; CANR 17, 44

von Daniken, Erich
See von Daeniken, Erich

von Hartmann, Eduard
1842-1906 .... **TCLC 96**

von Hayek, Friedrich August
See Hayek, F(riedrich) A(ugust von)

von Heidenstam, (Carl Gustaf) Verner
See Heidenstam, (Carl Gustaf) Verner von

von Heyse, Paul (Johann Ludwig)
See Heyse, Paul (Johann Ludwig von)

von Hofmannsthal, Hugo
See Hofmannsthal, Hugo von

von Horvath, Odon
See von Horvath, Odon

von Horvath, Odon
See von Horvath, Odon

von Horvath, Odon 1901-1938 .... **TCLC 45**
See von Horvath, Oedoen
See also CA 118; 194; DLB 85, 124; RGWL 2, 3

von Horvath, Oedoen
See von Horvath, Odon
See also CA 184

von Kleist, Heinrich
See Kleist, Heinrich von

von Liliencron, (Friedrich Adolf Axel) Detlev
See Liliencron, (Friedrich Adolf Axel) Detlev von

Vonnegut, Kurt, Jr. 1922- . **CLC 1, 2, 3, 4, 5, 8, 12, 22, 40, 60, 111; SSC 8; WLC**
See also AAYA 6, 44; AITN 1; AMWS 2; BEST 90:4; BPFB 3; BYA 3, 14; CA 1-4R; CANR 1, 25, 49, 75, 92; CDALB 1968-1988; CN 7; CPW 1; DA; DA3; DAB; DAC; DAM MST, NOV, POP; DLB 2, 8, 152; DLBD 3, DLBY 1980; EWL 3; EXPN; EXPS; LAIT 4; LMFS 2; MTCW 1, 2; NFS 3; RGAL 4; SCFW; SFW 4; SSFS 5; TUS; YAW

Von Rachen, Kurt
See Hubbard, L(afayette) Ron(ald)

von Rezzori (d'Arezzo), Gregor
See Rezzori (d'Arezzo), Gregor von

von Sternberg, Josef
See Sternberg, Josef von

Vorster, Gordon 1924- .... **CLC 34**
See also CA 133

Vosce, Trudie
See Ozick, Cynthia

Voznesensky, Andrei (Andreievich)
1933- .... **CLC 1, 15, 57**
See Voznesensky, Andrey
See also CA 89-92; CANR 37; CWW 2; DAM POET; MTCW 1

Voznesensky, Andrey
See Voznesensky, Andrei (Andreievich)
See also EWL 3

Wace, Robert c. 1100-c. 1175 .... **CMLC 55**
See also DLB 146

Waddington, Miriam 1917- .... **CLC 28**
See also CA 21-24R; CANR 12, 30; CCA 1; CP 7; DLB 68

Wagman, Fredrica 1937- .... **CLC 7**
See also CA 97-100; INT CA-97-100

Wagner, Linda W.
See Wagner-Martin, Linda (C.)

Wagner, Linda Welshimer
See Wagner-Martin, Linda (C.)

Wagner, Richard 1813-1883 ..... **NCLC 9, 119**
See also DLB 129; EW 6

Wagner-Martin, Linda (C.) 1936- .... **CLC 50**
See also CA 159

Wagoner, David (Russell) 1926- .... **CLC 3, 5, 15; PC 33**
See also AMWS 9; CA 1-4R; CAAS 3; CANR 2, 71; CN 7; CP 7; DLB 5, 256; SATA 14; TCWW 2

Wah, Fred(erick James) 1939- .... **CLC 44**
See also CA 107; 141; CP 7; DLB 60

Wahloo, Per 1926-1975 .... **CLC 7**
See also BPFB 3; CA 61-64; CANR 73; CMW 4; MSW

Wahloo, Peter
See Wahloo, Per

Wain, John (Barrington) 1925-1994 . **CLC 2, 11, 15, 46**
See also CA 5-8R; 145; CAAS 4; CANR 23, 54; CDBLB 1960 to Present; DLB 15, 27, 139, 155; EWL 3; MTCW 1, 2

Wajda, Andrzej 1926- .... **CLC 16**
See also CA 102

Wakefield, Dan 1932- .... **CLC 7**
See also CA 21-24R, 211; CAAE 211; CAAS 7; CN 7

Wakefield, Herbert Russell
1888-1965 .... **TCLC 120**
See also CA 5-8R; CANR 77; HGG; SUFW

Wakoski, Diane 1937- ...... **CLC 2, 4, 7, 9, 11, 40; PC 15**
See also CA 13-16R, 216; CAAE 216; CAAS 1; CANR 9, 60, 106; CP 7; CWP; DAM POET; DLB 5; INT CANR-9; MTCW 2

Wakoski-Sherbell, Diane
See Wakoski, Diane

Walcott, Derek (Alton) 1930- ... **BLC 3; CLC 2, 4, 9, 14, 25, 42, 67, 76, 160; DC 7; PC 46**
See also BW 2; CA 89-92; CANR 26, 47, 75, 80; CBD; CD 5; CDWLB 3; CP 7; DA3; DAB; DAC; DAM MST, MULT, POET; DLB 117; DLBY 1981; DNFS 1; EFS 1; EWL 3; LMFS 2; MTCW 1, 2; PFS 6; RGEL 2; TWA; WWE 1

Waldman, Anne (Lesley) 1945- .... **CLC 7**
See also BG 3; CA 37-40R; CAAS 17; CANR 34, 69, 116; CP 7; CWP; DLB 16

Waldo, E. Hunter
See Sturgeon, Theodore (Hamilton)

Waldo, Edward Hamilton
See Sturgeon, Theodore (Hamilton)

Walker, Alice (Malsenior) 1944- .... **BLC 3; CLC 5, 6, 9, 19, 27, 46, 58, 103, 167; PC 30; SSC 5; WLCS**
See also AAYA 3, 33; AFAW 1, 2; AMWS 3; BEST 89:4; BPFB 3; BW 2, 3; CA 37-40R; CANR 9, 27, 49, 66, 82; CDALB 1968-1988; CN 7; CPW; CSW; DA; DA3; DAB; DAC; DAM MST, MULT, NOV, POET, POP; DLB 6, 33, 143; EWL 3; EXPN; EXPS; FW; INT CANR-27; LAIT 3; MAWW; MTCW 1, 2; NFS 5; RGAL 4; RGSF 2; SATA 31; SSFS 2, 11; TUS; YAW

Walker, David Harry 1911-1992 .... **CLC 14**
See also CA 1-4R; 137; CANR 1; CWRI 5; SATA 8; SATA-Obit 71

Walker, Edward Joseph 1934-2004
See Walker, Ted
See also CA 21-24R; CANR 12, 28, 53; CP 7

Walker, George F. 1947- .... **CLC 44, 61**
See also CA 103; CANR 21, 43, 59; CD 5; DAB; DAC; DAM MST; DLB 60

Walker, Joseph A. 1935- .... **CLC 19**
See also BW 1, 3; CA 89-92; CAD; CANR 26; CD 5; DAM DRAM, MST; DFS 12; DLB 38

Walker, Margaret (Abigail)
1915-1998 .... **BLC; CLC 1, 6; PC 20; TCLC 129**
See also AFAW 1, 2; BW 2, 3; CA 73-76; 172; CANR 26, 54, 76; CN 7; CP 7; CSW; DAM MULT; DLB 76, 152; EXPP; FW; MTCW 1, 2; RGAL 4; RHW

Walker, Ted .... **CLC 13**
See Walker, Edward Joseph
See also DLB 40

Wallace, David Foster 1962- ... **CLC 50, 114; SSC 68**
See also AAYA 50; AMWS 10; CA 132; CANR 59; DA3; MTCW 2

Wallace, Dexter
See Masters, Edgar Lee

Wallace, (Richard Horatio) Edgar
1875-1932 .... **TCLC 57**
See also CA 115; 218; CMW 4; DLB 70; MSW; RGEL 2

Wallace, Irving 1916-1990 .... **CLC 7, 13**
See also AITN 1; BPFB 3; CA 1-4R; 132; CAAS 1; CANR 1, 27; CPW; DAM NOV, POP; INT CANR-27; MTCW 1, 2

Wallant, Edward Lewis 1926-1962 ... **CLC 5, 10**
See also CA 1-4R; CANR 22; DLB 2, 28, 143; EWL 3; MTCW 1, 2; RGAL 4

Wallas, Graham 1858-1932 .... **TCLC 91**

Waller, Edmund 1606-1687 .... **LC 86**
See also BRW 2; DAM POET; DLB 126; PAB; RGEL 2

Walley, Byron
See Card, Orson Scott

Walpole, Horace 1717-1797 .... **LC 2, 49**
See also BRW 3; DLB 39, 104, 213; HGG; LMFS 1; RGEL 2; SUFW 1; TEA

Walpole, Hugh (Seymour)
1884-1941 .... **TCLC 5**
See also CA 104; 165; DLB 34; HGG; MTCW 2; RGEL 2; RHW

Walrond, Eric (Derwent) 1898-1966 ... **HR 3**
See also BW 1; CA 125; DLB 51

Walser, Martin 1927- .... **CLC 27, 183**
See also CA 57-60; CANR 8, 46; CWW 2; DLB 75, 124; EWL 3

Walser, Robert 1878-1956 ..... **SSC 20; TCLC 18**
See also CA 118; 165; CANR 100; DLB 66; EWL 3

Walsh, Gillian Paton
See Paton Walsh, Gillian

Walsh, Jill Paton .... **CLC 35**
See Paton Walsh, Gillian
See also CLR 2, 65; WYA

Walter, Villiam Christian
See Andersen, Hans Christian

Walters, Anna L(ee) 1946- .... **NNAL**
See also CA 73-76

Walther von der Vogelweide c.
1170-1228 .... **CMLC 56**

Walton, Izaak 1593-1683 .... **LC 72**
See also BRW 2; CDBLB Before 1660; DLB 151, 213; RGEL 2

Wambaugh, Joseph (Aloysius), Jr.
1937- .... **CLC 3, 18**
See also AITN 1; BEST 89:3; BPFB 3; CA 33-36R; CANR 42, 65, 115; CMW 4; CPW 1; DA3; DAM NOV, POP; DLB 6; DLBY 1983; MSW; MTCW 1, 2

Wang Wei 699(?)-761(?) .... **PC 18**
See also TWA

Warburton, William 1698-1779 .... **LC 97**
See also DLB 104

Ward, Arthur Henry Sarsfield 1883-1959
See Rohmer, Sax
See also CA 108; 173; CMW 4; HGG

Ward, Douglas Turner 1930- .... **CLC 19**
See also BW 1; CA 81-84; CAD; CANR 27; CD 5; DLB 7, 38

Ward, E. D.
See Lucas, E(dward) V(errall)

Ward, Mrs. Humphry 1851-1920
See Ward, Mary Augusta
See also RGEL 2

Ward, Mary Augusta 1851-1920 ... **TCLC 55**
See Ward, Mrs. Humphry
See also DLB 18

Ward, Peter
See Faust, Frederick (Schiller)

Warhol, Andy 1928(?)-1987 .... **CLC 20**
See also AAYA 12; BEST 89:4; CA 89-92; 121; CANR 34

Warner, Francis (Robert le Plastrier)
1937- .... **CLC 14**
See also CA 53-56; CANR 11

Warner, Marina 1946- .... **CLC 59**
See also CA 65-68; CANR 21, 55, 118; CN 7; DLB 194

Warner, Rex (Ernest) 1905-1986 ...... **CLC 45**
See also CA 89-92; 119; DLB 15; RGEL 2; RHW

Warner, Susan (Bogert)
1819-1885 .... **NCLC 31**
See also DLB 3, 42, 239, 250, 254

Warner, Sylvia (Constance) Ashton
See Ashton-Warner, Sylvia (Constance)

Warner, Sylvia Townsend
1893-1978 .. **CLC 7, 19; SSC 23; TCLC 131**
See also BRWS 7; CA 61-64; 77-80; CANR 16, 60, 104; DLB 34, 139; EWL 3; FANT; FW; MTCW 1, 2; RGEL 2; RGSF 2; RHW

Warren, Mercy Otis 1728-1814 ..... **NCLC 13**
See also DLB 31, 200; RGAL 4; TUS

Warren, Robert Penn 1905-1989 .. **CLC 1, 4, 6, 8, 10, 13, 18, 39, 53, 59; PC 37; SSC 4, 58; WLC**
See also AITN 1; AMW; AMWC 2; BPFB 3; BYA 1; CA 13-16R; 129; CANR 10, 47; CDALB 1968-1988; DA; DA3; DAB; DAC; DAM MST, NOV, POET; DLB 2, 48, 152; DLBY 1980, 1989; EWL 3; INT CANR-10; MTCW 1, 2; NFS 13; RGAL 4; RGSF 2; RHW; SATA 46; SATA-Obit 63; SSFS 8; TUS

Warrigal, Jack
See Furphy, Joseph

Warshofsky, Isaac
See Singer, Isaac Bashevis

Warton, Joseph 1722-1800 .... **NCLC 118**
See also DLB 104, 109; RGEL 2

Warton, Thomas 1728-1790 .... **LC 15, 82**
See also DAM POET; DLB 104, 109; RGEL 2

Waruk, Kona
See Harris, (Theodore) Wilson

Warung, Price .... **TCLC 45**
See Astley, William
See also DLB 230; RGEL 2

Warwick, Jarvis
See Garner, Hugh
See also CCA 1

Washington, Alex
See Harris, Mark

Washington, Booker T(aliaferro)
1856-1915 .... **BLC 3; TCLC 10**
See also BW 1; CA 114, 125; DA3; DAM MULT; LAIT 2; RGAL 4; SATA 28

Washington, George 1732-1799 .... **LC 25**
See also DLB 31

Wassermann, (Karl) Jakob
1873-1934 .... **TCLC 6**
See also CA 104; 163; DLB 66; EWL 3

Wasserstein, Wendy 1950- ... **CLC 32, 59, 90, 183; DC 4**
See also CA 121; 129; CABS 3; CAD; CANR 53, 75, 128; CD 5; CWD; DA3; DAM DRAM; DFS 5, 17; DLB 228; EWL 3; FW; INT CA-129; MTCW 2; SATA 94

Waterhouse, Keith (Spencer) 1929- . **CLC 47**
See also CA 5-8R; CANR 38, 67, 109; CBD; CN 7; DLB 13, 15; MTCW 1, 2

Waters, Frank (Joseph) 1902-1995 .. **CLC 88**
See also CA 5-8R; 149; CAAS 13; CANR 3, 18, 63, 121; DLB 212; DLBY 1986; RGAL 4; TCWW 2

Waters, Mary C. .... **CLC 70**
Waters, Roger 1944- .... **CLC 35**

Watkins, Frances Ellen
See Harper, Frances Ellen Watkins

Watkins, Gerrold
See Malzberg, Barry N(athaniel)

Watkins, Gloria Jean 1952(?)- .... **CLC 94**
See also BW 2; CA 143; CANR 87, 126; DLB 246; MTCW 2; SATA 115

Watkins, Paul 1964- .... **CLC 55**
See also CA 132; CANR 62, 98

Watkins, Vernon Phillips
1906-1967 .... **CLC 43**
See also CA 9-10; 25-28R; CAP 1; DLB 20; EWL 3; RGEL 2

Watson, Irving S.
See Mencken, H(enry) L(ouis)

Watson, John H.
See Farmer, Philip Jose

Watson, Richard F.
See Silverberg, Robert

Watts, Ephraim
See Horne, Richard Henry Hengist

Watts, Isaac 1674-1748 .... **LC 98**
See also DLB 95; RGEL 2; SATA 52

Waugh, Auberon (Alexander)
1939-2001 .... **CLC 7**
See also CA 45-48; 192; CANR 6, 22, 92; DLB 14, 194

Waugh, Evelyn (Arthur St. John)
1903-1966 .. **CLC 1, 3, 8, 13, 19, 27, 44, 107; SSC 41; WLC**
See also BPFB 3; BRW 7; CA 85-88; 25-28R; CANR 22; CDBLB 1914-1945; DA; DA3; DAB; DAC; DAM MST, NOV, POP; DLB 15, 162, 195; EWL 3; MTCW 1, 2; NFS 13, 17; RGEL 2; RGSF 2; TEA; WLIT 4

Waugh, Harriet 1944- .... **CLC 6**
See also CA 85-88; CANR 22

Ways, C. R.
See Blount, Roy (Alton), Jr.

Waystaff, Simon
See Swift, Jonathan

Webb, Beatrice (Martha Potter)
1858-1943 .... **TCLC 22**
See also CA 117; 162; DLB 190; FW

Webb, Charles (Richard) 1939- .... **CLC 7**
See also CA 25-28R; CANR 114

Webb, James H(enry), Jr. 1946- ...... **CLC 22**
See also CA 81-84

Webb, Mary Gladys (Meredith)
1881-1927 .... **TCLC 24**
See also CA 182; 123; DLB 34; FW

Webb, Mrs. Sidney
See Webb, Beatrice (Martha Potter)

Webb, Phyllis 1927- .... **CLC 18**
See also CA 104; CANR 23; CCA 1; CP 7; CWP; DLB 53

Webb, Sidney (James) 1859-1947 .. **TCLC 22**
See also CA 117; 163; DLB 190

Webber, Andrew Lloyd .... **CLC 21**
See Lloyd Webber, Andrew
See also DFS 7

Weber, Lenora Mattingly
1895-1971 .... **CLC 12**
See also CA 19-20; 29-32R; CAP 1; SATA 2; SATA-Obit 26

Weber, Max 1864-1920 .... **TCLC 69**
See also CA 109; 189; DLB 296

Webster, John 1580(?)-1634(?) .... **DC 2; LC 33, 84**
See also BRW 2; CDBLB Before 1660; DA; DAB; DAC; DAM DRAM, MST; DFS 17; DLB 58; IDTP; RGEL 2; WLIT 3

Webster, Noah 1758-1843 .... **NCLC 30**
See also DLB 1, 37, 42, 43, 73, 243

Wedekind, (Benjamin) Frank(lin)
1864-1918 .... **TCLC 7**
See also CA 104; 153; CANR 121, 122; CDWLB; DAM DRAM; DLB 118; EW 8; EWL 3; LMFS 2; RGWL 2, 3

Wehr, Demaris .... **CLC 65**

Weidman, Jerome 1913-1998 .... **CLC 7**
See also AITN 2; CA 1-4R; 171; CAD; CANR 1; DLB 28

Weil, Simone (Adolphine)
1909-1943 .... **TCLC 23**
See also CA 117; 159; EW 12; EWL 3; FW; GFL 1789 to the Present; MTCW 2

Weininger, Otto 1880-1903 .... **TCLC 84**

Weinstein, Nathan
See West, Nathanael

Weinstein, Nathan von Wallenstein
See West, Nathanael

Weir, Peter (Lindsay) 1944- .... **CLC 20**
See also CA 113; 123

Weiss, Peter (Ulrich) 1916-1982 .. **CLC 3, 15, 51**
See also CA 45-48; 106; CANR 3; DAM DRAM; DFS 3; DLB 69, 124; EWL 3; RGWL 2, 3

Weiss, Theodore (Russell)
1916-2003 .... **CLC 3, 8, 14**
See also CA 9-12R; 189; 216; CAAE 189; CAAS 2; CANR 46, 94; CP 7; DLB 5

Welch, (Maurice) Denton
1915-1948 .... **TCLC 22**
See also BRWS 8, 9; CA 121; 148; RGEL 2

Welch, James (Phillip) 1940-2003 ..... **CLC 6, 14, 52; NNAL**
See also CA 85-88; 219; CANR 42, 66, 107; CN 7; CP 7; CPW; DAM MULT, POP; DLB 175, 256; LATS 1; RGAL 4; TCWW 2

Weldon, Fay 1931- . **CLC 6, 9, 11, 19, 36, 59, 122**
See also BRWS 4; CA 21-24R; CANR 16, 46, 63, 97; CDBLB 1960 to Present; CN 7; CPW; DAM POP; DLB 14, 194; EWL 3; FW; HGG; INT CANR-16; MTCW 1, 2; RGEL 2; RGSF 2

Wellek, Rene 1903-1995 .... **CLC 28**
See also CA 5-8R; 150; CAAS 7; CANR 8; DLB 63; EWL 3; INT CANR-8

Weller, Michael 1942- .... **CLC 10, 53**
See also CA 85-88; CAD; CD 5

Weller, Paul 1958- .... **CLC 26**
Wellershoff, Dieter 1925- .... **CLC 46**
See also CA 89-92; CANR 16, 37
Welles, (George) Orson 1915-1985 .. **CLC 20, 80**
See also AAYA 40; CA 93-96; 117
Wellman, John McDowell 1945-
See Wellman, Mac
See also CA 166; CD 5
Wellman, Mac .... **CLC 65**
See Wellman, John McDowell; Wellman, John McDowell
See also CAD; RGAL 4
Wellman, Manly Wade 1903-1986 ... **CLC 49**
See also CA 1-4R; 118; CANR 6, 16, 44; FANT; SATA 6; SATA-Obit 47; SFW 4; SUFW
Wells, Carolyn 1869(?)-1942 .... **TCLC 35**
See also CA 113; 185; CMW 4; DLB 11
Wells, H(erbert) G(eorge) 1866-1946 . **SSC 6, 70; TCLC 6, 12, 19, 133; WLC**
See also AAYA 18; BPFB 3; BRW 6; CA 110; 121; CDBLB 1914-1945; CLR 64; DA; DA3; DAB; DAC; DAM MST, NOV; DLB 34, 70, 156, 178; EWL 3; EXPS; HGG; LAIT 3; LMFS 2; MTCW 1, 2; NFS 17; RGEL 2; RGSF 2; SATA 20; SCFW; SFW 4; SSFS 3; SUFW; TEA; WCH; WLIT 4; YAW
Wells, Rosemary 1943- .... **CLC 12**
See also AAYA 13; BYA 7, 8; CA 85-88; CANR 48, 120; CLR 16, 69; CWRI 5; MAICYA 1, 2; SAAS 1; SATA 18, 69, 114; YAW
Wells-Barnett, Ida B(ell) 1862-1931 .... **TCLC 125**
See also CA 182; DLB 23, 221
Welsh, Irvine 1958- .... **CLC 144**
See also CA 173; DLB 271
Welty, Eudora (Alice) 1909-2001 .. **CLC 1, 2, 5, 14, 22, 33, 105; SSC 1, 27, 51; WLC**
See also AAYA 48; AMW; AMWR 1; BPFB 3; CA 9-12R; 199; CABS 1; CANR 32, 65, 128; CDALB 1941-1968; CN 7; CSW; DA; DA3; DAB; DAC; DAM MST, NOV; DLB 2, 102, 143; DLBD 12; DLBY 1987, 2001; EWL 3; EXPS; HGG; LAIT 3; MAWW; MTCW 1, 2; NFS 13, 15; RGAL 4; RGSF 2; RHW; SSFS 2, 10; TUS
Wen I-to 1899-1946 .... **TCLC 28**
See also EWL 3
Wentworth, Robert
See Hamilton, Edmond
Werfel, Franz (Viktor) 1890-1945 ... **TCLC 8**
See also CA 104; 161; DLB 81, 124; EWL 3; RGWL 2, 3
Wergeland, Henrik Arnold 1808-1845 .... **NCLC 5**
Wersba, Barbara 1932- .... **CLC 30**
See also AAYA 2, 30; BYA 6, 12, 13; CA 29-32R, 182; CAAE 182; CANR 16, 38; CLR 3, 78; DLB 52; JRDA; MAICYA 1, 2; SAAS 2; SATA 1, 58; SATA-Essay 103; WYA; YAW
Wertmueller, Lina 1928- .... **CLC 16**
See also CA 97-100; CANR 39, 78
Wescott, Glenway 1901-1987 .. **CLC 13; SSC 35**
See also CA 13-16R; 121; CANR 23, 70; DLB 4, 9, 102; RGAL 4
Wesker, Arnold 1932- .... **CLC 3, 5, 42**
See also CA 1-4R; CAAS 7; CANR 1, 33; CBD; CD 5; CDBLB 1960 to Present; DAB; DAM DRAM; DLB 13; EWL 3; MTCW 1; RGEL 2; TEA
Wesley, John 1703-1791 .... **LC 88**
See also DLB 104

Wesley, Richard (Errol) 1945- .... **CLC 7**
See also BW 1; CA 57-60; CAD; CANR 27; CD 5; DLB 38
Wessel, Johan Herman 1742-1785 .... **LC 7**
West, Anthony (Panther) 1914-1987 .... **CLC 50**
See also CA 45-48; 124; CANR 3, 19; DLB 15
West, C. P.
See Wodehouse, P(elham) G(renville)
West, Cornel (Ronald) 1953- .... **BLCS; CLC 134**
See also CA 144; CANR 91; DLB 246
West, Delno C(loyde), Jr. 1936- .... **CLC 70**
See also CA 57-60
West, Dorothy 1907-1998 .. **HR 3; TCLC 108**
See also BW 2; CA 143; 169; DLB 76
West, (Mary) Jessamyn 1902-1984 ... **CLC 7, 17**
See also CA 9-12R; 112; CANR 27; DLB 6; DLBY 1984; MTCW 1, 2; RGAL 4; RHW; SATA-Obit 37; TCWW 2; TUS; YAW
West, Morris
See West, Morris L(anglo)
See also DLB 289
West, Morris L(anglo) 1916-1999 ..... **CLC 6, 33**
See West, Morris
See also BPFB 3; CA 5-8R; 187; CANR 24, 49, 64; CN 7; CPW; MTCW 1, 2
West, Nathanael 1903-1940 .. **SSC 16; TCLC 1, 14, 44**
See also AMW; AMWR 2; BPFB 3; CA 104; 125; CDALB 1929-1941; DA3; DLB 4, 9, 28; EWL 3; MTCW 1, 2; NFS 16; RGAL 4; TUS
West, Owen
See Koontz, Dean R(ay)
West, Paul 1930- .... **CLC 7, 14, 96**
See also CA 13-16R; CAAS 7; CANR 22, 53, 76, 89; CN 7; DLB 14; INT CANR-22; MTCW 2
West, Rebecca 1892-1983 ... **CLC 7, 9, 31, 50**
See also BPFB 3; BRWS 3; CA 5-8R; 109; CANR 19; DLB 36; DLBY 1983; EWL 3; FW; MTCW 1, 2; NCFS 4; RGEL 2; TEA
Westall, Robert (Atkinson) 1929-1993 .... **CLC 17**
See also AAYA 12; BYA 2, 6, 7, 8, 9, 15; CA 69-72; 141; CANR 18, 68; CLR 13; FANT; JRDA; MAICYA 1, 2; MAICYAS 1; SAAS 2; SATA 23, 69; SATA-Obit 75; WYA; YAW
Westermarck, Edward 1862-1939 . **TCLC 87**
Westlake, Donald E(dwin) 1933- . **CLC 7, 33**
See also BPFB 3; CA 17-20R; CAAS 13; CANR 16, 44, 65, 94; CMW 4; CPW; DAM POP; INT CANR-16; MSW; MTCW 2
Westmacott, Mary
See Christie, Agatha (Mary Clarissa)
Weston, Allen
See Norton, Andre
Wetcheek, J. L.
See Feuchtwanger, Lion
Wetering, Janwillem van de
See van de Wetering, Janwillem
Wetherald, Agnes Ethelwyn 1857-1940 .... **TCLC 81**
See also CA 202; DLB 99
Wetherell, Elizabeth
See Warner, Susan (Bogert)
Whale, James 1889-1957 .... **TCLC 63**
Whalen, Philip (Glenn) 1923-2002 .... **CLC 6, 29**
See also BG 3; CA 9-12R; 209; CANR 5, 39; CP 7; DLB 16; WP

Wharton, Edith (Newbold Jones) 1862-1937 ... **SSC 6; TCLC 3, 9, 27, 53, 129, 149; WLC**
See also AAYA 25; AMW; AMWC 2; AMWR 1; BPFB 3; CA 104; 132; CDALB 1865-1917; DA; DA3; DAB; DAC; DAM MST, NOV; DLB 4, 9, 12, 78, 189; DLBD 13; EWL 3; EXPS; HGG; LAIT 2, 3; LATS 1; MAWW; MTCW 1, 2; NFS 5, 11, 15; RGAL 4; RGSF 2; RHW; SSFS 6, 7; SUFW; TUS
Wharton, James
See Mencken, H(enry) L(ouis)
Wharton, William (a pseudonym) . **CLC 18, 37**
See also CA 93-96; DLBY 1980; INT CA-93-96
Wheatley (Peters), Phillis 1753(?)-1784 ... **BLC 3; LC 3, 50; PC 3; WLC**
See also AFAW 1, 2; CDALB 1640-1865; DA; DA3; DAC; DAM MST, MULT, POET; DLB 31, 50; EXPP; PFS 13; RGAL 4
Wheelock, John Hall 1886-1978 .... **CLC 14**
See also CA 13-16R; 77-80; CANR 14; DLB 45
Whim-Wham
See Curnow, (Thomas) Allen (Monro)
White, Babington
See Braddon, Mary Elizabeth
White, E(lwyn) B(rooks) 1899-1985 .... **CLC 10, 34, 39**
See also AITN 2; AMWS 1; CA 13-16R; 116; CANR 16, 37; CDALBS; CLR 1, 21; CPW; DA3; DAM POP; DLB 11, 22; EWL 3; FANT; MAICYA 1, 2; MTCW 1, 2; NCFS 5; RGAL 4; SATA 2, 29, 100; SATA-Obit 44; TUS
White, Edmund (Valentine III) 1940- .... **CLC 27, 110**
See also AAYA 7; CA 45-48; CANR 3, 19, 36, 62, 107; CN 7; DA3; DAM POP; DLB 227; MTCW 1, 2
White, Hayden V. 1928- .... **CLC 148**
See also CA 128; DLB 246
White, Patrick (Victor Martindale) 1912-1990 ...... **CLC 3, 4, 5, 7, 9, 18, 65, 69; SSC 39**
See also BRWS 1; CA 81-84; 132; CANR 43; DLB 260; EWL 3; MTCW 1; RGEL 2; RGSF 2; RHW; TWA; WWE 1
White, Phyllis Dorothy James 1920-
See James, P. D.
See also CA 21-24R; CANR 17, 43, 65, 112; CMW 4; CN 7; CPW; DA3; DAM POP; MTCW 1, 2; TEA
White, T(erence) H(anbury) 1906-1964 .... **CLC 30**
See also AAYA 22; BPFB 3; BYA 4, 5; CA 73-76; CANR 37; DLB 160; FANT; JRDA; LAIT 1; MAICYA 1, 2; RGEL 2; SATA 12; SUFW 1; YAW
White, Terence de Vere 1912-1994 ... **CLC 49**
See also CA 49-52; 145; CANR 3
White, Walter
See White, Walter F(rancis)
White, Walter F(rancis) 1893-1955 ... **BLC 3; HR 3; TCLC 15**
See also BW 1; CA 115; 124; DAM MULT; DLB 51
White, William Hale 1831-1913
See Rutherford, Mark
See also CA 121; 189
Whitehead, Alfred North 1861-1947 .... **TCLC 97**
See also CA 117; 165; DLB 100, 262

Whitehead, E(dward) A(nthony)
1933- .... **CLC 5**
See also CA 65-68; CANR 58, 118; CBD; CD 5

Whitehead, Ted
See Whitehead, E(dward) A(nthony)

Whiteman, Roberta J. Hill 1947- ...... **NNAL**
See also CA 146

Whitemore, Hugh (John) 1936- .... **CLC 37**
See also CA 132; CANR 77; CBD; CD 5; INT CA-132

Whitman, Sarah Helen (Power)
1803-1878 .... **NCLC 19**
See also DLB 1, 243

Whitman, Walt(er) 1819-1892 .. **NCLC 4, 31, 81; PC 3; WLC**
See also AAYA 42; AMW; AMWR 1; CDALB 1640-1865; DA; DA3; DAB; DAC; DAM MST, POET; DLB 3, 64, 224, 250; EXPP; LAIT 2; LMFS 1; PAB; PFS 2, 3, 13; RGAL 4; SATA 20; TUS; WP; WYAS 1

Whitney, Phyllis A(yame) 1903- .... **CLC 42**
See also AAYA 36; AITN 2; BEST 90:3; CA 1-4R; CANR 3, 25, 38, 60; CLR 59; CMW 4; CPW; DA3; DAM POP; JRDA; MAICYA 1, 2; MTCW 2; RHW; SATA 1, 30; YAW

Whittemore, (Edward) Reed, Jr.
1919- .... **CLC 4**
See also CA 9-12R, 219; CAAE 219; CAAS 8; CANR 4, 119; CP 7; DLB 5

Whittier, John Greenleaf
1807-1892 .... **NCLC 8, 59**
See also AMWS 1; DLB 1, 243; RGAL 4

Whittlebot, Hernia
See Coward, Noel (Peirce)

Wicker, Thomas Grey 1926-
See Wicker, Tom
See also CA 65-68; CANR 21, 46

Wicker, Tom .... **CLC 7**
See Wicker, Thomas Grey

Wideman, John Edgar 1941- ... **BLC 3; CLC 5, 34, 36, 67, 122; SSC 62**
See also AFAW 1, 2; AMWS 10; BPFB 4; BW 2, 3; CA 85-88; CANR 14, 42, 67, 109; CN 7; DAM MULT; DLB 33, 143; MTCW 2; RGAL 4; RGSF 2; SSFS 6, 12

Wiebe, Rudy (Henry) 1934- .. **CLC 6, 11, 14, 138**
See also CA 37-40R; CANR 42, 67, 123; CN 7; DAC; DAM MST; DLB 60; RHW

Wieland, Christoph Martin
1733-1813 .... **NCLC 17**
See also DLB 97; EW 4; LMFS 1; RGWL 2, 3

Wiene, Robert 1881-1938 .... **TCLC 56**

Wieners, John 1934- .... **CLC 7**
See also BG 3; CA 13-16R; CP 7; DLB 16; WP

Wiesel, Elie(zer) 1928- .... **CLC 3, 5, 11, 37, 165; WLCS**
See also AAYA 7, 54; AITN 1; CA 5-8R; CAAS 4; CANR 8, 40, 65; CDALBS; DA; DA3; DAB; DAC; DAM MST, NOV; DLB 83; DLBY 1987; EWL 3; INT CANR-8; LAIT 4; MTCW 1, 2; NCFS 4; NFS 4; RGWL 3; SATA 56; YAW

Wiggins, Marianne 1947- .... **CLC 57**
See also BEST 89:3; CA 130; CANR 60

Wiggs, Susan .... **CLC 70**
See also CA 201

Wight, James Alfred 1916-1995
See Herriot, James
See also CA 77-80; SATA 55; SATA-Brief 44

Wilbur, Richard (Purdy) 1921- ..... **CLC 3, 6, 9, 14, 53, 110; PC 51**
See also AMWS 3; CA 1-4R; CABS 2; CANR 2, 29, 76, 93; CDALBS; CP 7; DA; DAB; DAC; DAM MST, POET; DLB 5, 169; EWL 3; EXPP; INT CANR-29; MTCW 1, 2; PAB; PFS 11, 12, 16; RGAL 4; SATA 9, 108; WP

Wild, Peter 1940- .... **CLC 14**
See also CA 37-40R; CP 7; DLB 5

Wilde, Oscar (Fingal O'Flahertie Wills)
1854(?)-1900 ..... **DC 17; SSC 11; TCLC 1, 8, 23, 41; WLC**
See also AAYA 49; BRW 5; BRWC 1, 2; BRWR 2; BYA 15; CA 104; 119; CANR 112; CDBLB 1890-1914; DA; DA3; DAB; DAC; DAM DRAM, MST, NOV; DFS 4, 8, 9; DLB 10, 19, 34, 57, 141, 156, 190; EXPS; FANT; LAITS 1; RGEL 2; RGSF 2; SATA 24; SSFS 7; SUFW; TEA; WCH; WLIT 4

Wilder, Billy .... **CLC 20**
See Wilder, Samuel
See also DLB 26

Wilder, Samuel 1906-2002
See Wilder, Billy
See also CA 89-92; 205

Wilder, Stephen
See Marlowe, Stephen

Wilder, Thornton (Niven)
1897-1975 .. **CLC 1, 5, 6, 10, 15, 35, 82; DC 1; WLC**
See also AAYA 29; AITN 2; AMW; CA 13-16R; 61-64; CAD; CANR 40; CDALBS; DA; DA3; DAB; DAC; DAM DRAM, MST, NOV; DFS 1, 4, 16; DLB 4, 7, 9, 228; DLBY 1997; EWL 3; LAIT 3; MTCW 1, 2; RGAL 4; RHW; WYAS 1

Wilding, Michael 1942- .... **CLC 73; SSC 50**
See also CA 104; CANR 24, 49, 106; CN 7; RGSF 2

Wiley, Richard 1944- .... **CLC 44**
See also CA 121; 129; CANR 71

Wilhelm, Kate .... **CLC 7**
See Wilhelm, Katie (Gertrude)
See also AAYA 20; BYA 16; CAAS 5; DLB 8; INT CANR-17; SCFW 2

Wilhelm, Katie (Gertrude) 1928-
See Wilhelm, Kate
See also CA 37-40R; CANR 17, 36, 60, 94; MTCW 1; SFW 4

Wilkins, Mary
See Freeman, Mary E(leanor) Wilkins

Willard, Nancy 1936- .... **CLC 7, 37**
See also BYA 5; CA 89-92; CANR 10, 39, 68, 107; CLR 5; CWP; CWRI 5; DLB 5, 52; FANT; MAICYA 1, 2; MTCW 1; SATA 37, 71, 127; SATA-Brief 30; SUFW 2

William of Malmesbury c. 1090B.C.-c. 1140B.C. .... **CMLC 57**

William of Ockham 1290-1349 ..... **CMLC 32**

Williams, Ben Ames 1889-1953 ..... **TCLC 89**
See also CA 183; DLB 102

Williams, C(harles) K(enneth)
1936- .... **CLC 33, 56, 148**
See also CA 37-40R; CAAS 26; CANR 57, 106; CP 7; DAM POET; DLB 5

Williams, Charles
See Collier, James Lincoln

Williams, Charles (Walter Stansby)
1886-1945 .... **TCLC 1, 11**
See also BRWS 9; CA 104; 163; DLB 100, 153, 255; FANT; RGEL 2; SUFW 1

Williams, Ella Gwendolen Rees
See Rhys, Jean

Williams, (George) Emlyn
1905-1987 .... **CLC 15**
See also CA 104; 123; CANR 36; DAM DRAM; DLB 10, 77; IDTP; MTCW 1

Williams, Hank 1923-1953 .... **TCLC 81**
See Williams, Hiram King

Williams, Helen Maria
1761-1827 .... **NCLC 135**
See also DLB 158

Williams, Hiram Hank
See Williams, Hank

Williams, Hiram King
See Williams, Hank
See also CA 188

Williams, Hugo (Mordaunt) 1942- ... **CLC 42**
See also CA 17-20R; CANR 45, 119; CP 7; DLB 40

Williams, J. Walker
See Wodehouse, P(elham) G(renville)

Williams, John A(lfred) 1925- . **BLC 3; CLC 5, 13**
See also AFAW 2; BW 2, 3; CA 53-56, 195; CAAE 195; CAAS 3; CANR 6, 26, 51, 118; CN 7; CSW; DAM MULT; DLB 2, 33; EWL 3; INT CANR-6; RGAL 4; SFW 4

Williams, Jonathan (Chamberlain)
1929- .... **CLC 13**
See also CA 9-12R; CAAS 12; CANR 8, 108; CP 7; DLB 5

Williams, Joy 1944- .... **CLC 31**
See also CA 41-44R; CANR 22, 48, 97

Williams, Norman 1952- .... **CLC 39**
See also CA 118

Williams, Sherley Anne 1944-1999 ... **BLC 3; CLC 89**
See also AFAW 2; BW 2, 3; CA 73-76; 185; CANR 25, 82; DAM MULT, POET; DLB 41; INT CANR-25; SATA 78; SATA-Obit 116

Williams, Shirley
See Williams, Sherley Anne

Williams, Tennessee 1911-1983 . **CLC 1, 2, 5, 7, 8, 11, 15, 19, 30, 39, 45, 71, 111; DC 4; WLC**
See also AAYA 31; AITN 1, 2; AMW; AMWC 1; CA 5-8R; 108; CABS 3; CAD; CANR 31; CDALB 1941-1968; DA; DA3; DAB; DAC; DAM DRAM, MST, DFS 17; DLB 7; DLBD 4; DLBY 1983; EWL 3; GLL 1; LAIT 4; LATS 1; MTCW 1, 2; RGAL 4; TUS

Williams, Thomas (Alonzo)
1926-1990 .... **CLC 14**
See also CA 1-4R; 132; CANR 2

Williams, William C.
See Williams, William Carlos

Williams, William Carlos
1883-1963 .... **CLC 1, 2, 5, 9, 13, 22, 42, 67; PC 7; SSC 31**
See also AAYA 46; AMW; AMWR 1; CA 89-92; CANR 34; CDALB 1917-1929; DA; DA3; DAB; DAC; DAM MST, POET; DLB 4, 16, 54, 86; EWL 3; EXPP; MTCW 1, 2; NCFS 3; PAB; PFS 1, 6, 11; RGAL 4; RGSF 2; TUS; WP

Williamson, David (Keith) 1942- ..... **CLC 56**
See also CA 103; CANR 41; CD 5; DLB 289

Williamson, Ellen Douglas 1905-1984
See Douglas, Ellen
See also CA 17-20R; 114; CANR 39

Williamson, Jack .... **CLC 29**
See Williamson, John Stewart
See also CAAS 8; DLB 8; SCFW 2

Williamson, John Stewart 1908-
See Williamson, Jack
See also CA 17-20R; CANR 23, 70; SFW 4

Willie, Frederick
See Lovecraft, H(oward) P(hillips)

Willingham, Calder (Baynard, Jr.)
1922-1995 .... CLC **5, 51**
See also CA 5-8R; 147; CANR 3; CSW; DLB 2, 44; IDFW 3, 4; MTCW 1

Willis, Charles
See Clarke, Arthur C(harles)

Willy
See Colette, (Sidonie-Gabrielle)

Willy, Colette
See Colette, (Sidonie-Gabrielle)
See also GLL 1

Wilmot, John 1647-1680 .... LC **75**
See Rochester
See also BRW 2; DLB 131; PAB

Wilson, A(ndrew) N(orman) 1950- .. CLC **33**
See also BRWS 6; CA 112; 122; CN 7; DLB 14, 155, 194; MTCW 2

Wilson, Angus (Frank Johnstone)
1913-1991 . CLC **2, 3, 5, 25, 34; SSC 21**
See also BRWS 1; CA 5-8R; 134; CANR 21; DLB 15, 139, 155; EWL 3; MTCW 1, 2; RGEL 2; RGSF 2

Wilson, August 1945- ... BLC **3**; CLC **39, 50, 63, 118; DC 2; WLCS**
See also AAYA 16; AFAW 2; AMWS 8; BW 2, 3; CA 115; 122; CAD; CANR 42, 54, 76, 128; CD 5; DA; DA3; DAB; DAC; DAM DRAM, MST, MULT; DFS 3, 7, 15, 17; DLB 228; EWL 3; LAIT 4; LATS 1; MTCW 1, 2; RGAL 4

Wilson, Brian 1942- .... CLC **12**

Wilson, Colin 1931- .... CLC **3, 14**
See also CA 1-4R; CAAS 5; CANR 1, 22, 33, 77; CMW 4; CN 7; DLB 14, 194; HGG; MTCW 1; SFW 4

Wilson, Dirk
See Pohl, Frederik

Wilson, Edmund 1895-1972 .. CLC **1, 2, 3, 8, 24**
See also AMW; CA 1-4R; 37-40R; CANR 1, 46, 110; DLB 63; EWL 3; MTCW 1, 2; RGAL 4; TUS

Wilson, Ethel Davis (Bryant)
1888(?)-1980 .... CLC **13**
See also CA 102; DAC; DAM POET; DLB 68; MTCW 1; RGEL 2

Wilson, Harriet
See Wilson, Harriet E. Adams
See also DLB 239

Wilson, Harriet E.
See Wilson, Harriet E. Adams
See also DLB 243

Wilson, Harriet E. Adams
1827(?)-1863(?) .... BLC **3**; NCLC **78**
See Wilson, Harriet; Wilson, Harriet E.
See also DAM MULT; DLB 50

Wilson, John 1785-1854 .... NCLC **5**

Wilson, John (Anthony) Burgess 1917-1993
See Burgess, Anthony
See also CA 1-4R; 143; CANR 2, 46; DA3; DAC; DAM NOV; MTCW 1, 2; NFS 15; TEA

Wilson, Lanford 1937- ... CLC **7, 14, 36; DC 19**
See also CA 17-20R; CABS 3; CAD; CANR 45, 96; CD 5; DAM DRAM; DFS 4, 9, 12, 16; DLB 7; EWL 3; TUS

Wilson, Robert M. 1941- .... CLC **7, 9**
See also CA 49-52; CAD; CANR 2, 41; CD 5; MTCW 1

Wilson, Robert McLiam 1964- .... CLC **59**
See also CA 132; DLB 267

Wilson, Sloan 1920-2003 .... CLC **32**
See also CA 1-4R; 216; CANR 1, 44; CN 7

Wilson, Snoo 1948- .... CLC **33**
See also CA 69-72; CBD; CD 5

Wilson, William S(mith) 1932- .... CLC **49**
See also CA 81-84

Wilson, (Thomas) Woodrow
1856-1924 .... TCLC **79**
See also CA 166; DLB 47

Wilson and Warnke eds. .... CLC **65**

Winchilsea, Anne (Kingsmill) Finch
1661-1720
See Finch, Anne
See also RGEL 2

Windham, Basil
See Wodehouse, P(elham) G(renville)

Wingrove, David (John) 1954- .... CLC **68**
See also CA 133; SFW 4

Winnemucca, Sarah 1844-1891 .... NCLC **79**; NNAL
See also DAM MULT; DLB 175; RGAL 4

Winstanley, Gerrard 1609-1676 .... LC **52**

Wintergreen, Jane
See Duncan, Sara Jeannette

Winters, Janet Lewis .... CLC **41**
See Lewis, Janet
See also DLBY 1987

Winters, (Arthur) Yvor 1900-1968 .... CLC **4, 8, 32**
See also AMWS 2; CA 11-12; 25-28R; CAP 1; DLB 48; EWL 3; MTCW 1; RGAL 4

Winterson, Jeanette 1959- .... CLC **64, 158**
See also BRWS 4; CA 136; CANR 58, 116; CN 7; CPW; DLB 207, 261; FANT; FW; GLL 1; MTCW 2; RHW

Winthrop, John 1588-1649 .... LC **31**
See also DLB 24, 30

Wirth, Louis 1897-1952 .... TCLC **92**
See also CA 210

Wiseman, Frederick 1930- .... CLC **20**
See also CA 159

Wister, Owen 1860-1938 .... TCLC **21**
See also BPFB 3; CA 108; 162; DLB 9, 78, 186; RGAL 4; SATA 62; TCWW 2

Wither, George 1588-1667 .... LC **96**
See also DLB 121; RGEL 2

Witkacy
See Witkiewicz, Stanislaw Ignacy

Witkiewicz, Stanislaw Ignacy
1885-1939 .... TCLC **8**
See also CA 105; 162; CDWLB 4; DLB 215; EW 10; EWL 3; RGWL 2, 3; SFW 4

Wittgenstein, Ludwig (Josef Johann)
1889-1951 .... TCLC **59**
See also CA 113; 164; DLB 262; MTCW 2

Wittig, Monique 1935(?)-2003 .... CLC **22**
See also CA 116; 135; 212; CWW 2; DLB 83; EWL 3; FW; GLL 1

Wittlin, Jozef 1896-1976 .... CLC **25**
See also CA 49-52; 65-68; CANR 3; EWL 3

Wodehouse, P(elham) G(renville)
1881-1975 . CLC **1, 2, 5, 10, 22; SSC 2; TCLC 108**
See also AITN 2; BRWS 3; CA 45-48; 57-60; CANR 3, 33; CDBLB 1914-1945; CPW 1; DA3; DAB; DAC; DAM NOV; DLB 34, 162; EWL 3; MTCW 1, 2; RGEL 2; RGSF 2; SATA 22; SSFS 10

Woiwode, L.
See Woiwode, Larry (Alfred)

Woiwode, Larry (Alfred) 1941- ... CLC **6, 10**
See also CA 73-76; CANR 16, 94; CN 7; DLB 6; INT CANR-16

Wojciechowska, Maia (Teresa)
1927-2002 .... CLC **26**
See also AAYA 8, 46; BYA 3; CA 9-12R, 183; 209; CAAE 183; CANR 4, 41; CLR 1; JRDA; MAICYA 1, 2; SAAS 1; SATA 1, 28, 83; SATA-Essay 104; SATA-Obit 134; YAW

Wojtyla, Karol
See John Paul II, Pope

Wolf, Christa 1929- .... CLC **14, 29, 58, 150**
See also CA 85-88; CANR 45, 123; CDWLB 2; CWW 2; DLB 75; EWL 3; FW; MTCW 1; RGWL 2, 3; SSFS 14

Wolf, Naomi 1962- .... CLC **157**
See also CA 141; CANR 110; FW

Wolfe, Gene (Rodman) 1931- .... CLC **25**
See also AAYA 35; CA 57-60; CAAS 9; CANR 6, 32, 60; CPW; DAM POP; DLB 8; FANT; MTCW 2; SATA 118; SCFW 2; SFW 4; SUFW 2

Wolfe, George C. 1954- .... BLCS; CLC **49**
See also CA 149; CAD; CD 5

Wolfe, Thomas (Clayton)
1900-1938 ...... SSC **33**; TCLC **4, 13, 29, 61; WLC**
See also AMW; BPFB 3; CA 104; 132; CANR 102; CDALB 1929-1941; DA; DA3; DAB; DAC; DAM MST, NOV; DLB 9, 102, 229; DLBD 2, 16; DLBY 1985, 1997; EWL 3; MTCW 1, 2; NFS 18; RGAL 4; TUS

Wolfe, Thomas Kennerly, Jr.
1931- .... CLC **147**
See Wolfe, Tom
See also CA 13-16R; CANR 9, 33, 70, 104; DA3; DAM POP; DLB 185; EWL 3; INT CANR-9; MTCW 1, 2; SSFS 18; TUS

Wolfe, Tom .... CLC **1, 2, 9, 15, 35, 51**
See Wolfe, Thomas Kennerly, Jr.
See also AAYA 8; AITN 2; AMWS 3; BEST 89:1; BPFB 3; CN 7; CPW; CSW; DLB 152; LAIT 5; RGAL 4

Wolff, Geoffrey (Ansell) 1937- .... CLC **41**
See also CA 29-32R; CANR 29, 43, 78

Wolff, Sonia
See Levitin, Sonia (Wolff)

Wolff, Tobias (Jonathan Ansell)
1945- .... CLC **39, 64, 172; SSC 63**
See also AAYA 16; AMWS 7; BEST 90:2; BYA 12; CA 114; 117; CAAS 22; CANR 54, 76, 96; CN 7; CSW; DA3; DLB 130; EWL 3; INT CA-117; MTCW 2; RGAL 4; RGSF 2; SSFS 4, 11

Wolfram von Eschenbach c. 1170-c. 1220 .... CMLC **5**
See Eschenbach, Wolfram von
See also CDWLB 2; DLB 138; EW 1; RGWL 2

Wolitzer, Hilma 1930- .... CLC **17**
See also CA 65-68; CANR 18, 40; INT CANR-18; SATA 31; YAW

Wollstonecraft, Mary 1759-1797 .... LC **5, 50, 90**
See also BRWS 3; CDBLB 1789-1832; DLB 39, 104, 158, 252; FW; LAIT 1; RGEL 2; TEA; WLIT 3

Wonder, Stevie .... CLC **12**
See Morris, Steveland Judkins

Wong, Jade Snow 1922- .... CLC **17**
See also CA 109; CANR 91; SATA 112

Woodberry, George Edward
1855-1930 .... TCLC **73**
See also CA 165; DLB 71, 103

Woodcott, Keith
See Brunner, John (Kilian Houston)

Woodruff, Robert W.
See Mencken, H(enry) L(ouis)

Woolf, (Adeline) Virginia 1882-1941 . SSC **7**; TCLC **1, 5, 20, 43, 56, 101, 123, 128; WLC**
See also AAYA 44; BPFB 3; BRW 7; BRWC 2; BRWR 1; CA 104; 130; CANR 64; CDBLB 1914-1945; DA; DA3; DAB; DAC; DAM MST, NOV; DLB 36, 100, 162; DLBD 10; EWL 3; EXPS; FW; LAIT 3; LATS 1; LMFS 2; MTCW 1, 2; NCFS 2; NFS 8, 12; RGEL 2; RGSF 2; SSFS 4, 12; TEA; WLIT 4

Woollcott, Alexander (Humphreys) 1887-1943 .... **TCLC 5**
See also CA 105; 161; DLB 29

Woolrich, Cornell .... **CLC 77**
See Hopley-Woolrich, Cornell George
See also MSW

Woolson, Constance Fenimore 1840-1894 .... **NCLC 82**
See also DLB 12, 74, 189, 221; RGAL 4

Wordsworth, Dorothy 1771-1855 . **NCLC 25, 138**
See also DLB 107

Wordsworth, William 1770-1850 .. **NCLC 12, 38, 111; PC 4; WLC**
See also BRW 4; BRWC 1; CDBLB 1789-1832; DA; DA3; DAB; DAC; DAM MST, POET; DLB 93, 107; EXPP; LATS 1; LMFS 1; PAB; PFS 2; RGEL 2; TEA; WLIT 3; WP

Wotton, Sir Henry 1568-1639 .... **LC 68**
See also DLB 121; RGEL 2

Wouk, Herman 1915- .... **CLC 1, 9, 38**
See also BPFB 2, 3; CA 5-8R; CANR 6, 33, 67; CDALBS; CN 7; CPW; DA3; DAM NOV, POP; DLBY 1982; INT CANR-6; LAIT 4; MTCW 1, 2; NFS 7; TUS

Wright, Charles (Penzel, Jr.) 1935- .. **CLC 6, 13, 28, 119, 146**
See also AMWS 5; CA 29-32R; CAAS 7; CANR 23, 36, 62, 88; CP 7; DLB 165; DLBY 1982; EWL 3; MTCW 1, 2; PFS 10

Wright, Charles Stevenson 1932- ..... **BLC 3; CLC 49**
See also BW 1; CA 9-12R; CANR 26; CN 7; DAM MULT, POET; DLB 33

Wright, Frances 1795-1852 .... **NCLC 74**
See also DLB 73

Wright, Frank Lloyd 1867-1959 .... **TCLC 95**
See also AAYA 33; CA 174

Wright, Jack R.
See Harris, Mark

Wright, James (Arlington) 1927-1980 .... **CLC 3, 5, 10, 28; PC 36**
See also AITN 2; AMWS 3; CA 49-52; 97-100; CANR 4, 34, 64; CDALBS; DAM POET; DLB 5, 169; EWL 3; EXPP; MTCW 1, 2; PFS 7, 8; RGAL 4; TUS; WP

Wright, Judith (Arundell) 1915-2000 .... **CLC 11, 53; PC 14**
See also CA 13-16R; 188; CANR 31, 76, 93; CP 7; CWP; DLB 260; EWL 3; MTCW 1, 2; PFS 8; RGEL 2; SATA 14; SATA-Obit 121

Wright, L(aurali) R. 1939- .... **CLC 44**
See also CA 138; CMW 4

Wright, Richard (Nathaniel) 1908-1960 ... **BLC 3; CLC 1, 3, 4, 9, 14, 21, 48, 74; SSC 2; TCLC 136; WLC**
See also AAYA 5, 42; AFAW 2; AMW; BPFB 3; BW 1; BYA 2; CA 108; CANR 64; CDALB 1929-1941; DA; DA3; DAB; DAC; DAM MST, MULT, NOV; DLB 76, 102; DLBD 2; EWL 3; EXPN; LAIT 3, 4; MTCW 1, 2; NCFS 1; NFS 1, 7; RGAL 4; RGSF 2; SSFS 3, 9, 15; TUS; YAW

Wright, Richard B(ruce) 1937- .... **CLC 6**
See also CA 85-88; CANR 120; DLB 53

Wright, Rick 1945- .... **CLC 35**

Wright, Rowland
See Wells, Carolyn

Wright, Stephen 1946- .... **CLC 33**

Wright, Willard Huntington 1888-1939
See Van Dine, S. S.
See also CA 115; 189; CMW 4; DLBD 16

Wright, William 1930- .... **CLC 44**
See also CA 53-56; CANR 7, 23

Wroth, Lady Mary 1587-1653(?) .... **LC 30; PC 38**
See also DLB 121

Wu Ch'eng-en 1500(?)-1582(?) .... **LC 7**

Wu Ching-tzu 1701-1754 .... **LC 2**

Wulfstan c. 10th cent. -1023 .... **CMLC 59**

Wurlitzer, Rudolph 1938(?)- .... **CLC 2, 4, 15**
See also CA 85-88; CN 7; DLB 173

Wyatt, Sir Thomas c. 1503-1542 . **LC 70; PC 27**
See also BRW 1; DLB 132; EXPP; RGEL 2; TEA

Wycherley, William 1640-1716 .... **LC 8, 21, 102**
See also BRW 2; CDBLB 1660-1789; DAM DRAM; DLB 80; RGEL 2

Wylie, Elinor (Morton Hoyt) 1885-1928 .... **PC 23; TCLC 8**
See also AMWS 1; CA 105; 162; DLB 9, 45; EXPP; RGAL 4

Wylie, Philip (Gordon) 1902-1971 ... **CLC 43**
See also CA 21-22; 33-36R; CAP 2; DLB 9; SFW 4

Wyndham, John .... **CLC 19**
See Harris, John (Wyndham Parkes Lucas) Beynon
See also DLB 255; SCFW 2

Wyss, Johann David Von 1743-1818 .... **NCLC 10**
See also CLR 92; JRDA; MAICYA 1, 2; SATA 29; SATA-Brief 27

Xenophon c. 430B.C.-c. 354B.C. ... **CMLC 17**
See also AW 1; DLB 176; RGWL 2, 3

Xingjian, Gao 1940-
See Gao Xingjian
See also CA 193; RGWL 3

Yakamochi 718-785 .... **CMLC 45; PC 48**

Yakumo Koizumi
See Hearn, (Patricio) Lafcadio (Tessima Carlos)

Yamada, Mitsuye (May) 1923- .... **PC 44**
See also CA 77-80

Yamamoto, Hisaye 1921- .... **AAL; SSC 34**
See also CA 214; DAM MULT; LAIT 4; SSFS 14

Yamauchi, Wakako 1924- .... **AAL**
See also CA 214

Yanez, Jose Donoso
See Donoso (Yanez), Jose

Yanovsky, Basile S.
See Yanovsky, V(assily) S(emenovich)

Yanovsky, V(assily) S(emenovich) 1906-1989 .... **CLC 2, 18**
See also CA 97-100; 129

Yates, Richard 1926-1992 .... **CLC 7, 8, 23**
See also AMWS 11; CA 5-8R; 139; CANR 10, 43; DLB 2, 234; DLBY 1981, 1992; INT CANR-10

Yeats, W. B.
See Yeats, William Butler

Yeats, William Butler 1865-1939 . **PC 20, 51; TCLC 1, 11, 18, 31, 93, 116; WLC**
See also AAYA 48; BRW 6; BRWR 1; CA 104; 127; CANR 45; CDBLB 1890-1914; DA; DA3; DAB; DAC; DAM DRAM, MST, POET; DLB 10, 19, 98, 156; EWL 3; EXPP; MTCW 1, 2; NCFS 3; PAB; PFS 1, 2, 5, 7, 13, 15; RGEL 2; TEA; WLIT 4; WP

Yehoshua, A(braham) B. 1936- .. **CLC 13, 31**
See also CA 33-36R; CANR 43, 90; EWL 3; RGSF 2; RGWL 3

Yellow Bird
See Ridge, John Rollin

Yep, Laurence Michael 1948- .... **CLC 35**
See also AAYA 5, 31; BYA 7; CA 49-52; CANR 1, 46, 92; CLR 3, 17, 54; DLB 52; FANT; JRDA; MAICYA 1, 2; MAICYAS 1; SATA 7, 69, 123; WYA; YAW

Yerby, Frank G(arvin) 1916-1991 ...... **BLC 3; CLC 1, 7, 22**
See also BPFB 3; BW 1, 3; CA 9-12R; 136; CANR 16, 52; CN 7; DAM MULT; DLB 76; INT CANR-16; MTCW 1; RGAL 4; RHW

Yesenin, Sergei Alexandrovich
See Esenin, Sergei (Alexandrovich)

Yesenin, Sergey
See Esenin, Sergei (Alexandrovich)
See also EWL 3

Yevtushenko, Yevgeny (Alexandrovich) 1933- .... **CLC 1, 3, 13, 26, 51, 126; PC 40**
See Evtushenko, Evgenii Aleksandrovich
See also CA 81-84; CANR 33, 54; CWW 2; DAM POET; EWL 3; MTCW 1

Yezierska, Anzia 1885(?)-1970 .... **CLC 46**
See also CA 126; 89-92; DLB 28, 221; FW; MTCW 1; RGAL 4; SSFS 15

Yglesias, Helen 1915- .... **CLC 7, 22**
See also CA 37-40R; CAAS 20; CANR 15, 65, 95; CN 7; INT CANR-15; MTCW 1

Yokomitsu, Riichi 1898-1947 .... **TCLC 47**
See also CA 170; EWL 3

Yonge, Charlotte (Mary) 1823-1901 .... **TCLC 48**
See also CA 109; 163; DLB 18, 163; RGEL 2; SATA 17; WCH

York, Jeremy
See Creasey, John

York, Simon
See Heinlein, Robert A(nson)

Yorke, Henry Vincent 1905-1974 ..... **CLC 13**
See Green, Henry
See also CA 85-88; 49-52

Yosano Akiko 1878-1942 .... **PC 11; TCLC 59**
See also CA 161; EWL 3; RGWL 3

Yoshimoto, Banana .... **CLC 84**
See Yoshimoto, Mahoko
See also AAYA 50; NFS 7

Yoshimoto, Mahoko 1964-
See Yoshimoto, Banana
See also CA 144; CANR 98; SSFS 16

Young, Al(bert James) 1939- ... **BLC 3; CLC 19**
See also BW 2, 3; CA 29-32R; CANR 26, 65, 109; CN 7; CP 7; DAM MULT; DLB 33

Young, Andrew (John) 1885-1971 ...... **CLC 5**
See also CA 5-8R; CANR 7, 29; RGEL 2

Young, Collier
See Bloch, Robert (Albert)

Young, Edward 1683-1765 .... **LC 3, 40**
See also DLB 95; RGEL 2

Young, Marguerite (Vivian) 1909-1995 .... **CLC 82**
See also CA 13-16; 150; CAP 1; CN 7

Young, Neil 1945- .... **CLC 17**
See also CA 110; CCA 1

Young Bear, Ray A. 1950- ... **CLC 94; NNAL**
See also CA 146; DAM MULT; DLB 175

Yourcenar, Marguerite 1903-1987 ... **CLC 19, 38, 50, 87**
See also BPFB 3; CA 69-72; CANR 23, 60, 93; DAM NOV; DLB 72; DLBY 1988; EW 12; EWL 3; GFL 1789 to the Present; GLL 1; MTCW 1, 2; RGWL 2, 3

Yuan, Chu 340(?)B.C.-278(?)B.C. . **CMLC 36**

Yurick, Sol 1925- .... **CLC 6**
See also CA 13-16R; CANR 25; CN 7

Zabolotsky, Nikolai Alekseevich 1903-1958 .... **TCLC 52**
See Zabolotsky, Nikolay Alekseevich
See also CA 116; 164

Zabolotsky, Nikolay Alekseevich
See Zabolotsky, Nikolai Alekseevich
See also EWL 3

Zagajewski, Adam 1945- .... **PC 27**
See also CA 186; DLB 232; EWL 3

Zalygin, Sergei -2000 .... **CLC 59**
Zamiatin, Evgenii
See Zamyatin, Evgeny Ivanovich
See also RGSF 2; RGWL 2, 3
Zamiatin, Evgenii Ivanovich
See Zamyatin, Evgeny Ivanovich
See also DLB 272
Zamiatin, Yevgenii
See Zamyatin, Evgeny Ivanovich
Zamora, Bernice (B. Ortiz) 1938- .. **CLC 89; HLC 2**
See also CA 151; CANR 80; DAM MULT; DLB 82; HW 1, 2
Zamyatin, Evgeny Ivanovich
1884-1937 .... **TCLC 8, 37**
See Zamiatin, Evgenii; Zamiatin, Evgenii Ivanovich; Zamyatin, Yevgeny Ivanovich
See also CA 105; 166; EW 10; SFW 4
Zamyatin, Yevgeny Ivanovich
See Zamyatin, Evgeny Ivanovich
See also EWL 3
Zangwill, Israel 1864-1926 ... **SSC 44; TCLC 16**
See also CA 109; 167; CMW 4; DLB 10, 135, 197; RGEL 2
Zappa, Francis Vincent, Jr. 1940-1993
See Zappa, Frank
See also CA 108; 143; CANR 57
Zappa, Frank .... **CLC 17**
See Zappa, Francis Vincent, Jr.
Zaturenska, Marya 1902-1982 ..... **CLC 6, 11**
See also CA 13-16R; 105; CANR 22
Zayas y Sotomayor, Maria de 1590-c. 1661 .... **LC 102**
See also RGSF 2
Zeami 1363-1443 .... **DC 7; LC 86**
See also DLB 203; RGWL 2, 3

Zelazny, Roger (Joseph) 1937-1995 . **CLC 21**
See also AAYA 7; BPFB 3; CA 21-24R; 148; CANR 26, 60; CN 7; DLB 8; FANT; MTCW 1, 2; SATA 57; SATA-Brief 39; SCFW; SFW 4; SUFW 1, 2
Zhang Ailing 1920(?)-1995
See Chang, Eileen
See also CWW 2; RGSF 2
Zhdanov, Andrei Alexandrovich
1896-1948 .... **TCLC 18**
See also CA 117; 167
Zhukovsky, Vasilii Andreevich
See Zhukovsky, Vasily (Andreevich)
See also DLB 205
Zhukovsky, Vasily (Andreevich)
1783-1852 .... **NCLC 35**
See Zhukovsky, Vasilii Andreevich
Ziegenhagen, Eric .... **CLC 55**
Zimmer, Jill Schary
See Robinson, Jill
Zimmerman, Robert
See Dylan, Bob
Zindel, Paul 1936-2003 ...... **CLC 6, 26; DC 5**
See also AAYA 2, 37; BYA 2, 3, 8, 11, 14; CA 73-76; 213; CAD; CANR 31, 65, 108; CD 5; CDALBS; CLR 3, 45, 85; DA; DA3; DAB; DAC; DAM DRAM, MST, NOV; DFS 12; DLB 7, 52; JRDA; LAIT 5; MAICYA 1, 2; MTCW 1, 2; NFS 14; SATA 16, 58, 102; SATA-Obit 142; WYA; YAW
Zinov'Ev, A. A.
See Zinoviev, Alexander (Aleksandrovich)
Zinoviev, Alexander (Aleksandrovich)
1922- .... **CLC 19**
See also CA 116; 133; CAAS 10

Zizek, Slavoj 1949- .... **CLC 188**
See also CA 201
Zoilus
See Lovecraft, H(oward) P(hillips)
Zola, Emile (Edouard Charles Antoine)
1840-1902 ...... **TCLC 1, 6, 21, 41; WLC**
See also CA 104; 138; DA; DA3; DAB; DAC; DAM MST, NOV; DLB 123; EW 7; GFL 1789 to the Present; IDTP; LMFS 1, 2; RGWL 2; TWA
Zoline, Pamela 1941- .... **CLC 62**
See also CA 161; SFW 4
Zoroaster 628(?)B.C.-551(?)B.C. ... **CMLC 40**
Zorrilla y Moral, Jose 1817-1893 .... **NCLC 6**
Zoshchenko, Mikhail (Mikhailovich)
1895-1958 .... **SSC 15; TCLC 15**
See also CA 115; 160; EWL 3; RGSF 2; RGWL 3
Zuckmayer, Carl 1896-1977 .... **CLC 18**
See also CA 69-72; DLB 56, 124; EWL 3; RGWL 2, 3
Zuk, Georges
See Skelton, Robin
See also CCA 1
Zukofsky, Louis 1904-1978 ... **CLC 1, 2, 4, 7, 11, 18; PC 11**
See also AMWS 3; CA 9-12R; 77-80; CANR 39; DAM POET; DLB 5, 165; EWL 3; MTCW 1; RGAL 4
Zweig, Paul 1935-1984 .... **CLC 34, 42**
See also CA 85-88; 113
Zweig, Stefan 1881-1942 .... **TCLC 17**
See also CA 112; 170; DLB 81, 118; EWL 3
Zwingli, Huldreich 1484-1531 .... **LC 37**
See also DLB 179

Literary Criticism Series
Cumulative Topic Index

This index lists all topic entries in Gale's *Classical and Medieval Literature Criticism* (CMLC), *Contemporary Literary Criticism* (CLC), *Drama Criticism* (DC), *Literature Criticism from 1400 to 1800* (LC), *Nineteenth-Century Literature Criticism* (NCLC), *Short Story Criticism* (SSC), and *Twentieth-Century Literary Criticism* (TCLC). The index also lists topic entries in the Gale Critical Companion Collection, which includes the following publications: *The Beat Generation* (BG), and *Harlem Renaissance* (HR).

Abolitionist Literature of Cuba and Brazil, Nineteenth-Century NCLC 132: 1-94
    overviews, 2-11
    origins and development, 11-23
    sociopolitical concerns, 23-39
    poetry, 39-47
    prose, 47-93

Aborigine in Nineteenth-Century Australian Literature, The NCLC 120: 1-88
    overviews, 2-27
    representations of the Aborigine in Australian literature, 27-58
    Aboriginal myth, literature, and oral tradition, 58-88

Aesopic Fable, The LC 51: 1-100
    the British Aesopic Fable, 1-54
    the Aesopic tradition in non-English-speaking cultures, 55-66
    political uses of the Aesopic fable, 67-88
    the evolution of the Aesopic fable, 89-99

African-American Folklore and Literature TCLC 126: 1-67
    African-American folk tradition, 1-16
    representative writers, 16-34
    hallmark works, 35-48
    the study of African-American literature and folklore, 48-64

Age of Johnson LC 15: 1-87
    Johnson's London, 3-15
    aesthetics of neoclassicism, 15-36
    "age of prose and reason," 36-45
    clubmen and bluestockings, 45-56
    printing technology, 56-62
    periodicals: "a map of busy life," 62-74
    transition, 74-86

Age of Spenser LC 39: 1-70
    overviews and general studies, 2-21
    literary style, 22-34
    poets and the crown, 34-70

AIDS in Literature CLC 81: 365-416

Alcohol and Literature TCLC 70: 1-58
    overview, 2-8
    fiction, 8-48
    poetry and drama, 48-58

American Abolitionism NCLC 44: 1-73
    overviews and general studies, 2-26
    abolitionist ideals, 26-46
    the literature of abolitionism, 46-72

American Autobiography TCLC 86: 1-115
    overviews and general studies, 3-36
    American authors and autobiography, 36-82
    African-American autobiography, 82-114

American Black Humor Fiction TCLC 54: 1-85
    characteristics of black humor, 2-13
    origins and development, 13-38
    black humor distinguished from related literary trends, 38-60
    black humor and society, 60-75
    black humor reconsidered, 75-83

American Civil War in Literature NCLC 32: 1-109
    overviews and general studies, 2-20
    regional perspectives, 20-54
    fiction popular during the war, 54-79
    the historical novel, 79-108

American Frontier in Literature NCLC 28: 1-103
    definitions, 2-12
    development, 12-17
    nonfiction writing about the frontier, 17-30
    frontier fiction, 30-45
    frontier protagonists, 45-66
    portrayals of Native Americans, 66-86
    feminist readings, 86-98
    twentieth-century reaction against frontier literature, 98-100

American Humor Writing NCLC 52: 1-59
    overviews and general studies, 2-12
    the Old Southwest, 12-42
    broader impacts, 42-5
    women humorists, 45-58

American Novel of Manners TCLC 130: 1-42
    history of the Novel of Manners in America, 4-10
    representative writers, 10-18
    relevancy of the Novel of Manners, 18-24
    hallmark works in the Novel of Manners, 24-36
    Novel of Manners and other media, 36-40

American Mercury, The TCLC 74: 1-80

American Popular Song, Golden Age of TCLC 42: 1-49
    background and major figures, 2-34
    the lyrics of popular songs, 34-47

American Proletarian Literature TCLC 54: 86-175
    overviews and general studies, 87-95
    American proletarian literature and the American Communist Party, 95-111
    ideology and literary merit, 111-17
    novels, 117-36
    Gastonia, 136-48
    drama, 148-54
    journalism, 154-9
    proletarian literature in the United States, 159-74

American Realism NCLC 120: 89-246
    overviews, 91-112
    background and sources, 112-72
    social issues, 172-223
    women and realism, 223-45

American Renaissance SSC 64: 46-193
    overviews and general studies, 47-103
    major authors of short fiction, 103-92

American Romanticism NCLC 44: 74-138
    overviews and general studies, 74-84
    sociopolitical influences, 84-104
    Romanticism and the American frontier, 104-15
    thematic concerns, 115-37

American Western Literature TCLC 46: 1-100
    definition and development of American Western literature, 2-7
    characteristics of the Western novel, 8-23
    Westerns as history and fiction, 23-34
    critical reception of American Western literature, 34-41
    the Western hero, 41-73
    women in Western fiction, 73-91
    later Western fiction, 91-9

American Writers in Paris TCLC 98: 1-156
    overviews and general studies, 2-155

Anarchism NCLC 84: 1-97
    overviews and general studies, 2-23
    the French anarchist tradition, 23-56
    Anglo-American anarchism, 56-68
    anarchism: incidents and issues, 68-97

Animals in Literature TCLC 106: 1-120
   overviews and general studies, 2-8
   animals in American literature, 8-45
   animals in Canadian literature, 45-57
   animals in European literature, 57-100
   animals in Latin American literature, 100-06
   animals in women's literature, 106-20

Antebellum South, Literature of the NCLC 112:1-188
   overviews, 4-55
   culture of the Old South, 55-68
   antebellum fiction: pastoral and heroic romance, 68-120
   role of women: a subdued rebellion, 120-59
   slavery and the slave narrative, 159-85

The Apocalyptic Movement TCLC 106: 121-69

Aristotle CMLC 31:1-397
   philosophy, 3-100
   poetics, 101-219
   rhetoric, 220-301
   science, 302-397

Art and Literature TCLC 54: 176-248
   overviews and general studies, 176-93
   definitions, 193-219
   influence of visual arts on literature, 219-31
   spatial form in literature, 231-47

Arthurian Literature CMLC 10: 1-127
   historical context and literary beginnings, 2-27
   development of the legend through Malory, 27-64
   development of the legend from Malory to the Victorian Age, 65-81
   themes and motifs, 81-95
   principal characters, 95-125

Arthurian Revival NCLC 36: 1-77
   overviews and general studies, 2-12
   Tennyson and his influence, 12-43
   other leading figures, 43-73
   the Arthurian legend in the visual arts, 73-6

Australian Cultural Identity in Nineteenth-Century Literature NCLC 124: 1-164
   overviews and general studies, 4-22
   poetry, 22-67
   fiction, 67-135
   role of women writers, 135-64

Australian Literature TCLC 50: 1-94
   origins and development, 2-21
   characteristics of Australian literature, 21-33
   historical and critical perspectives, 33-41
   poetry, 41-58
   fiction, 58-76
   drama, 76-82
   Aboriginal literature, 82-91

Beat Generation, The BG 1:1-562
   the Beat Generation: an overview, 1-137
      primary sources, 3-32
      overviews and general studies, 32-47
      Beat Generation as a social phenomenon, 47-65
      drugs, inspiration, and the Beat Generation, 65-92
      religion and the Beat Generation, 92-124
      women of the Beat Generation, 124-36
   Beat "scene": East and West, 139-259
      primary sources, 141-77
      Beat scene in the East, 177-218
      Beat scene in the West, 218-59
   Beat Generation publishing: periodicals, small presses, and censorship, 261-349
      primary sources, 263-74
      overview, 274-88
      Beat periodicals: "little magazines," 288-311
      Beat publishing: small presses, 311-24
      Beat battles with censorship, 324-49
   performing arts and the Beat Generation, 351-417
      primary sources, 353-58
      Beats and film, 358-81
      Beats and music, 381-415
   visual arts and the Beat Generation, 419-91
      primary sources, 421-24
      critical commentary, 424-90

Beat Generation, Literature of the TCLC 42: 50-102
   overviews and general studies, 51-9
   the Beat generation as a social phenomenon, 59-62
   development, 62-5
   Beat literature, 66-96
   influence, 97-100

The Bell Curve Controversy CLC 91: 281-330

Bildungsroman **in Nineteenth-Century Literature** NCLC 20: 92-168
   surveys, 93-113
   in Germany, 113-40
   in England, 140-56
   female *Bildungsroman*, 156-67

Bloomsbury Group TCLC 34: 1-73
   history and major figures, 2-13
   definitions, 13-7
   influences, 17-27
   thought, 27-40
   prose, 40-52
   and literary criticism, 52-4
   political ideals, 54-61
   response to, 61-71

The Bloomsbury Group TCLC 138: 1-59
   representative members of the Bloomsbury Group, 9-24
   literary relevance of the Bloomsbury Group, 24-36
   Bloomsbury's hallmark works, 36-48
   other modernists studied with the Bloomsbury Group, 48-54

The Blues in Literature TCLC 82: 1-71

Bly, Robert, *Iron John: A Book about Men and Men's Work* CLC 70: 414-62

The Book of J CLC 65: 289-311

Brazilian Literature TCLC 134: 1-126
   overviews and general studies, 3-33
   Brazilian poetry, 33-48
   contemporary Brazilian writing, 48-76
   culture, politics, and race in Brazilian writing, 76-100
   modernism and postmodernism in Brazil, 100-25

British Ephemeral Literature LC 59: 1-70
   overviews and general studies, 1-9
   broadside ballads, 10-40
   chapbooks, jestbooks, pamphlets, and newspapers, 40-69

Buddhism and Literature TCLC 70: 59-164
   eastern literature, 60-113
   western literature, 113-63

The *Bulletin* **and the Rise of Australian Literary Nationalism** NCLC 116: 1-121
   overviews, 3-32
   legend of the nineties, 32-55
   Bulletin style, 55-71
   Australian literary nationalism, 71-98
   myth of the bush, 98-120

Businessman in American Literature TCLC 26: 1-48
   portrayal of the businessman, 1-32
   themes and techniques in business fiction, 32-47

The Calendar LC 55: 1-92
   overviews and general studies, 2-19
   measuring time, 19-28
   calendars and culture, 28-60
   calendar reform, 60-92

Captivity Narratives LC 82: 71-172
   overviews, 72-107
   captivity narratives and Puritanism, 108-34
   captivity narratives and Native Americans, 134-49
   influence on American literature, 149-72

Caribbean Literature TCLC 138: 60-135
   overviews and general studies, 61-9
   ethnic and national identity, 69-107
   expatriate Caribbean literature, 107-23
   literary histoiography, 123-35

Catholicism in Nineteenth-Century American Literature NCLC 64: 1-58
   overviews, 3-14
   polemical literature, 14-46
   Catholicism in literature, 47-57

Celtic Mythology CMLC 26: 1-111
   overviews and general studies, 2-22
   Celtic myth as literature and history, 22-48
   Celtic religion: Druids and divinities, 48-80
   Fionn MacCuhaill and the Fenian cycle, 80-111

Celtic Twilight See Irish Literary Renaissance

Chartist Movement and Literature, The NCLC 60: 1-84
   overview: nineteenth-century working-class fiction, 2-19
   Chartist fiction and poetry, 19-73
   the Chartist press, 73-84

Child Labor in Nineteenth-Century Literature NCLC 108: 1-133
   overviews, 3-10
   climbing boys and chimney sweeps, 10-16
   the international traffic in children, 16-45
   critics and reformers, 45-82
   fictional representations of child laborers, 83-132

Children's Literature, Nineteenth-Century NCLC 52: 60-135
   overviews and general studies, 61-72
   moral tales, 72-89
   fairy tales and fantasy, 90-119
   making men/making women, 119-34

Christianity in Twentieth-Century Literature TCLC 110: 1-79
   overviews and general studies, 2-31
   Christianity in twentieth-century fiction, 31-78

Chronicle Plays LC 89: 1-106
   development of the genre, 2-33
   historiography and literature, 33-56
   genre and performance, 56-88
   politics and ideology, 88-106

The City and Literature TCLC 90: 1-124
   overviews and general studies, 2-9
   the city in American literature, 9-86
   the city in European literature, 86-124

Civic Critics, Russian NCLC 20: 402-46
   principal figures and background, 402-9
   and Russian Nihilism, 410-6
   aesthetic and critical views, 416-45

The Cockney School NCLC 68: 1-64
   overview, 2-7
   Blackwood's Magazine and the contemporary critical response, 7-24
   the political and social import of the Cockneys and their critics, 24-63

Colonial America: The Intellectual Background LC 25: 1-98
    overviews and general studies, 2-17
    philosophy and politics, 17-31
    early religious influences in Colonial America, 31-60
    consequences of the Revolution, 60-78
    religious influences in post-revolutionary America, 78-87
    colonial literary genres, 87-97

Colonialism in Victorian English Literature NCLC 56: 1-77
    overviews and general studies, 2-34
    colonialism and gender, 34-51
    monsters and the occult, 51-76

Columbus, Christopher, Books on the Quincentennial of His Arrival in the New World CLC 70: 329-60

Comic Books TCLC 66: 1-139
    historical and critical perspectives, 2-48
    superheroes, 48-67
    underground comix, 67-88
    comic books and society, 88-122
    adult comics and graphic novels, 122-36

Comedy of Manners LC 92: 1-75
    overviews, 2-21
    comedy of manners and society, 21-47
    comedy of manners and women, 47-74

Commedia dell'Arte LC 83: 1-147
    overviews, 2-7
    origins and development, 7-23
    characters and actors, 23-45
    performance, 45-62
    texts and authors, 62-100
    influence in Europe, 100-46

Connecticut Wits NCLC 48: 1-95
    overviews and general studies, 2-40
    major works, 40-76
    intellectual context, 76-95

Contemporary Feminist Criticism CLC 180: 1-103
    overviews and general studies, 2–59
    modern French feminist theory, 59-102

Contemporary Gay and Lesbian Literature CLC 171: 1-130
    overviews and general studies, 2-43
    contemporary gay literature, 44-95
    lesbianism in contemporary literature, 95-129

Contemporary Southern Literature CLC 167: 1-132
    criticism, 2-131

Crime in Literature TCLC 54: 249-307
    evolution of the criminal figure in literature, 250-61
    crime and society, 261-77
    literary perspectives on crime and punishment, 277-88
    writings by criminals, 288-306

Crime-Mystery-Detective Stories SSC 59:89-226
    overviews and general studies, 90-140
    origins and early masters of the crime-mystery-detective story, 140-73
    hard-boiled crime-mystery-detective fiction, 173-209
    diversity in the crime-mystery-detective story, 210-25

The Crusades CMLC 38: 1-144
    history of the Crusades, 3-60
    literature of the Crusades, 60-116
    the Crusades and the people: attitudes and influences, 116-44

Cyberpunk TCLC 106: 170-366
    overviews and general studies, 171-88
    feminism and cyberpunk, 188-230
    history and cyberpunk, 230-70
    sexuality and cyberpunk, 270-98
    social issues and cyberpunk, 299-366

Cyberpunk Short Fiction SSC 60: 44-108
    overviews and general studies, 46-78
    major writers of cyberpunk fiction, 78-81
    sexuality and cyberpunk fiction, 81-97
    additional pieces, 97-108

Czechoslovakian Literature of the Twentieth Century TCLC 42:103-96
    through World War II, 104-35
    de-Stalinization, the Prague Spring, and contemporary literature, 135-72
    Slovak literature, 172-85
    Czech science fiction, 185-93

Dadaism TCLC 46: 101-71
    background and major figures, 102-16
    definitions, 116-26
    manifestos and commentary by Dadaists, 126-40
    theater and film, 140-58
    nature and characteristics of Dadaist writing, 158-70

Danish Literature See **Twentieth-Century Danish Literature**

Darwinism and Literature NCLC 32: 110-206
    background, 110-31
    direct responses to Darwin, 131-71
    collateral effects of Darwinism, 171-205

Death in American Literature NCLC 92: 1-170
    overviews and general studies, 2-32
    death in the works of Emily Dickinson, 32-72
    death in the works of Herman Melville, 72-101
    death in the works of Edgar Allan Poe, 101-43
    death in the works of Walt Whitman, 143-70

Death in Nineteenth-Century British Literature NCLC 68: 65-142
    overviews and general studies, 66-92
    responses to death, 92-102
    feminist perspectives, 103-17
    striving for immortality, 117-41

Death in Literature TCLC 78:1-183
    fiction, 2-115
    poetry, 115-46
    drama, 146-81

Deconstruction TCLC 138: 136-256
    overviews and general studies, 137-83
    deconstruction and literature, 183-221
    deconstruction in philosophy and history, 221-56

de Man, Paul, Wartime Journalism of CLC 55: 382-424

Detective Fiction, Nineteenth-Century NCLC 36: 78-148
    origins of the genre, 79-100
    history of nineteenth-century detective fiction, 101-33
    significance of nineteenth-century detective fiction, 133-46

Detective Fiction, Twentieth-Century TCLC 38: 1-96
    genesis and history of the detective story, 3-22
    defining detective fiction, 22-32
    evolution and varieties, 32-77
    the appeal of detective fiction, 77-90

Detective Story See **Crime-Mystery-Detective Stories**

Dime Novels NCLC 84: 98-168
    overviews and general studies, 99-123
    popular characters, 123-39
    major figures and influences, 139-52
    socio-political concerns, 152-167

Disease and Literature TCLC 66: 140-283
    overviews and general studies, 141-65
    disease in nineteenth-century literature, 165-81
    tuberculosis and literature, 181-94
    women and disease in literature, 194-221
    plague literature, 221-53
    AIDS in literature, 253-82

El Dorado, The Legend of See **Legend of El Dorado, The**

The Double in Nineteenth-Century Literature NCLC 40: 1-95
    genesis and development of the theme, 2-15
    the double and Romanticism, 16-27
    sociological views, 27-52
    psychological interpretations, 52-87
    philosophical considerations, 87-95

Dramatic Realism NCLC 44: 139-202
    overviews and general studies, 140-50
    origins and definitions, 150-66
    impact and influence, 166-93
    realist drama and tragedy, 193-201

Drugs and Literature TCLC 78: 184-282
    overviews and general studies, 185-201
    pre-twentieth-century literature, 201-42
    twentieth-century literature, 242-82

Dystopias in Contemporary Literature CLC 168: 1-91
    overviews and general studies, 2-52
    dystopian views in Margaret Atwood's *The Handmaid's Tale* (1985), 52-71
    feminist readings of dystopias, 71-90

Eastern Mythology CMLC 26: 112-92
    heroes and kings, 113-51
    cross-cultural perspective, 151-69
    relations to history and society, 169-92

Ecocriticism and Nineteenth-Century Literature NCLC 140: 1-168
    overviews, 3-20
    American literature: Romantics and Realists, 20-76
    American explorers and naturalists, 76-123
    English literature: Romantics and Victorians, 123-67

Ecofeminism and Nineteenth-Century Literature NCLC 136: 1-110
    overviews, 2-24
    the local landscape, 24-72
    travel writing, 72-109

Eighteenth-Century British Periodicals LC 63: 1-123
    rise of periodicals, 2-31
    impact and influence of periodicals, 31-64
    periodicals and society, 64-122

Eighteenth-Century Travel Narratives LC 77: 252-355
    overviews and general studies, 254-79
    eighteenth-century European travel narratives, 279-334
    non-European eighteenth-century travel narratives, 334-55

Electronic "Books": Hypertext and Hyperfiction CLC 86: 367-404
    books vs. CD-ROMs, 367-76
    hypertext and hyperfiction, 376-95
    implications for publishing, libraries, and the public, 395-403

Eliot, T. S., Centenary of Birth CLC 55: 345-75

Elizabethan Drama LC 22: 140-240
    origins and influences, 142-67
    characteristics and conventions, 167-83
    theatrical production, 184-200
    histories, 200-12

comedy, 213-20
tragedy, 220-30

Elizabethan Prose Fiction LC 41: 1-70
overviews and general studies, 1-15
origins and influences, 15-43
style and structure, 43-69

The Emergence of the Short Story in the Nineteenth Century NCLC 140: 169-279
overviews, 171-74
the American short story, 174-214
the short story in Great Britain and Ireland, 214-235
stories by women in English, 235-45
the short story in France and Russia, 245-66
the Latin American short story, 266-77

Enclosure of the English Common NCLC 88: 1-57
overviews and general studies, 1-12
early reaction to enclosure, 12-23
nineteenth-century reaction to enclosure, 23-56

The Encyclopedists LC 26: 172-253
overviews and general studies, 173-210
intellectual background, 210-32
views on esthetics, 232-41
views on women, 241-52

English Abolitionist Literature of the Nineteenth Century NCLC 136: 111-235
overview, 112-35
origins and development, 135-42
poetry, 142-58
prose, 158-80
sociopolitical concerns, 180-95
English abolitionist literature and feminism, 195-233

English Caroline Literature LC 13: 221-307
background, 222-41
evolution and varieties, 241-62
the Cavalier mode, 262-75
court and society, 275-91
politics and religion, 291-306

English Decadent Literature of the 1890s NCLC 28: 104-200
fin de siècle: the Decadent period, 105-19
definitions, 120-37
major figures: "the tragic generation," 137-50
French literature and English literary Decadence, 150-7
themes, 157-61
poetry, 161-82
periodicals, 182-96

English Essay, Rise of the LC 18: 238-308
definitions and origins, 236-54
influence on the essay, 254-69
historical background, 269-78
the essay in the seventeenth century, 279-93
the essay in the eighteenth century, 293-307

English Mystery Cycle Dramas LC 34: 1-88
overviews and general studies, 1-27
the nature of dramatic performances, 27-42
the medieval worldview and the mystery cycles, 43-67
the doctrine of repentance and the mystery cycles, 67-76
the fall from grace in the mystery cycles, 76-88

The English Realist Novel, 1740-1771 LC 51: 102-98
overviews and general studies, 103-22
from Romanticism to Realism, 123-58
women and the novel, 159-175
the novel and other literary forms, 176-197

English Revolution, Literature of the LC 43: 1-58
overviews and general studies, 2-24
pamphlets of the English Revolution, 24-38
political sermons of the English Revolution, 38-48
poetry of the English Revolution, 48-57

English Romantic Hellenism NCLC 68: 143-250
overviews and general studies, 144-69
historical development of English Romantic Hellenism, 169-91
influence of Greek mythology on the Romantics, 191-229
influence of Greek literature, art, and culture on the Romantics, 229-50

English Romantic Poetry NCLC 28: 201-327
overviews and reputation, 202-37
major subjects and themes, 237-67
forms of Romantic poetry, 267-78
politics, society, and Romantic poetry, 278-99
philosophy, religion, and Romantic poetry, 299-324

The Epistolary Novel LC 59: 71-170
overviews and general studies, 72-96
women and the Epistolary novel, 96-138
principal figures: Britain, 138-53
principal figures: France, 153-69

Espionage Literature TCLC 50: 95-159
overviews and general studies, 96-113
espionage fiction/formula fiction, 113-26
spies in fact and fiction, 126-38
the female spy, 138-44
social and psychological perspectives, 144-58

European Debates on the Conquest of the Americas LC 67: 1-129
overviews and general studies, 3-56
major Spanish figures, 56-98
English perceptions of Native Americans, 98-129

European Romanticism NCLC 36: 149-284
definitions, 149-77
origins of the movement, 177-82
Romantic theory, 182-200
themes and techniques, 200-23
Romanticism in Germany, 223-39
Romanticism in France, 240-61
Romanticism in Italy, 261-4
Romanticism in Spain, 264-8
impact and legacy, 268-82

Exile in Literature TCLC 122: 1-129
overviews and general studies, 2-33
exile in fiction, 33-92
German literature in exile, 92-129

Existentialism and Literature TCLC 42: 197-268
overviews and definitions, 198-209
history and influences, 209-19
Existentialism critiqued and defended, 220-35
philosophical and religious perspectives, 235-41
Existentialist fiction and drama, 241-67

Ezra Pound Controversy TCLC 150: 1-132
politics of Ezra Pound, 3-42
anti-semitism of Ezra Pound, 42-57
the Bollingen Award controversy, 57-76
Pound's later writing, 76-104
criticism of *The Pisan Cantos,* 104-32

Familiar Essay NCLC 48: 96-211
definitions and origins, 97-130
overview of the genre, 130-43
elements of form and style, 143-59
elements of content, 159-73
the Cockneys: Hazlitt, Lamb, and Hunt, 173-91
status of the genre, 191-210

Fashion in Nineteenth-Century Literature NCLC 128: 104-93
overviews and general studies, 105-38
fashion and American literature, 138-46
fashion and English literature, 146-74
fashion and French literature, 174-92

The Faust Legend LC 47: 1-117

Fear in Literature TCLC 74: 81-258
overviews and general studies, 81
pre-twentieth-century literature, 123
twentieth-century literature, 182

Feminism in the 1990s: Commentary on Works by Naomi Wolf, Susan Faludi, and Camille Paglia CLC 76: 377-415

Feminist Criticism See Contemporary Feminist Criticism

Feminist Criticism in 1990 CLC 65: 312-60

Fifteenth-Century English Literature LC 17: 248-334
background, 249-72
poetry, 272-315
drama, 315-23
prose, 323-33

Fifteenth-Century Spanish Poetry LC 100:82-173
overviews and general studies, 83-101
the Cancioneros, 101-57
major figures, 157-72

Film and Literature TCLC 38: 97-226
overviews and general studies, 97-119
film and theater, 119-34
film and the novel, 134-45
the art of the screenplay, 145-66
genre literature/genre film, 167-79
the writer and the film industry, 179-90
authors on film adaptations of their works, 190-200
fiction into film: comparative essays, 200-23

Finance and Money as Represented in Nineteenth-Century Literature NCLC 76: 1-69
historical perspectives, 2-20
the image of money, 20-37
the dangers of money, 37-50
women and money, 50-69

Folklore and Literature TCLC 86: 116-293
overviews and general studies, 118-144
Native American literature, 144-67
African-American literature, 167-238
folklore and the American West, 238-57
modern and postmodern literature, 257-91

Food in Literature TCLC 114: 1-133
food and children's literature, 2-14
food as a literary device, 14-32
rituals invloving food, 33-45
food and social and ethnic identity, 45-90
women's relationship with food, 91-132

Food in Nineteenth-Century Literature NCLC 108: 134-288
overviews, 136-74
food and social class, 174-85
food and gender, 185-219
food and love, 219-31
food and sex, 231-48
eating disorders, 248-70
vegetarians, carnivores, and cannibals, 270-87

French Drama in the Age of Louis XIV LC 28: 94-185
overview, 95-127
tragedy, 127-46
comedy, 146-66
tragicomedy, 166-84

French Enlightenment LC 14: 81-145
the question of definition, 82-9

le siècle des lumières, 89-94
women and the salons, 94-105
censorship, 105-15
the philosophy of reason, 115-31
influence and legacy, 131-44

French New Novel TCLC 98: 158-234
overviews and general studies, 158-92
influences, 192-213
themes, 213-33

French Realism NCLC 52: 136-216
origins and definitions, 137-70
issues and influence, 170-98
realism and representation, 198-215

French Revolution and English Literature NCLC 40: 96-195
history and theory, 96-123
romantic poetry, 123-50
the novel, 150-81
drama, 181-92
children's literature, 192-5

Futurism, Italian TCLC 42: 269-354
principles and formative influences, 271-9
manifestos, 279-88
literature, 288-303
theater, 303-19
art, 320-30
music, 330-6
architecture, 336-9
and politics, 339-46
reputation and significance, 346-51

Gaelic Revival See Irish Literary Renaissance

Gates, Henry Louis, Jr., and African-American Literary Criticism CLC 65: 361-405

Gay and Lesbian Literature CLC 76: 416-39

Gay and Lesbian Literature See also Contemporary Gay and Lesbian Literature

German Exile Literature TCLC 30: 1-58
the writer and the Nazi state, 1-10
definition of, 10-4
life in exile, 14-32
surveys, 32-50
Austrian literature in exile, 50-2
German publishing in the United States, 52-7

German Expressionism TCLC 34: 74-160
history and major figures, 76-85
aesthetic theories, 85-109
drama, 109-26
poetry, 126-38
film, 138-42
painting, 142-7
music, 147-53
and politics, 153-8

The Ghost Story SSC 58: 1-142
overviews and general studies, 1-21
the ghost story in American literature, 21-49
the ghost story in Asian literature, 49-53
the ghost story in European and English literature, 54-89
major figures, 89-141

The Gilded Age NCLC 84: 169-271
popular themes, 170-90
Realism, 190-208
Aestheticism, 208-26
socio-political concerns, 226-70

***Glasnost* and Contemporary Soviet Literature** CLC 59: 355-97

Gothic Drama NCLC 132: 95-198
overviews, 97-125
sociopolitical contexts, 125-58
gothic playwrights, 158-97

Gothic Novel NCLC 28: 328-402
development and major works, 328-34

definitions, 334-50
themes and techniques, 350-78
in America, 378-85
in Scotland, 385-91
influence and legacy, 391-400

The Governess in Nineteenth-Century Literature NCLC 104: 1-131
overviews and general studies, 3-28
social roles and economic conditions, 28-86
fictional governesses, 86-131

The Grail Theme in Twentieth-Century Literature TCLC 142: 1-89
overviews and general studies, 2-20
major works, 20-89

Graphic Narratives CLC 86: 405-32
history and overviews, 406-21
the "Classics Illustrated" series, 421-2
reviews of recent works, 422-32

Graphic Novels CLC 177: 163-299
overviews and general studies, 165-198
critical readings of major works, 198-286
reviews of recent graphic novels, 286-299

Graveyard Poets LC 67: 131-212
origins and development, 131-52
major figures, 152-75
major works, 175-212

Greek Historiography CMLC 17: 1-49

Greek Mythology CMLC 26: 193-320
overviews and general studies, 194-209
origins and development of Greek mythology, 209-29
cosmogonies and divinities in Greek mythology, 229-54
heroes and heroines in Greek mythology, 254-80
women in Greek mythology, 280-320

Greek Theater CMLC 51: 1-58
criticism, 2-58

Hard-Boiled Fiction TCLC 118: 1-109
overviews and general studies, 2-39
major authors, 39-76
women and hard-boiled fiction, 76-109

The Harlem Renaissance HR 1: 1-563
overviews and general studies of the Harlem Renaissance, 1-137
primary sources, 3-12
overviews, 12-38
background and sources of the Harlem Renaissance, 38-56
the New Negro aesthetic, 56-91
patrons, promoters, and the New York Public Library, 91-121
women of the Harlem Renaissance, 121-37
social, economic, and political factors that influenced the Harlem Renaissance, 139-240
primary sources, 141-53
overviews, 153-87
social and economic factors, 187-213
Black intellectual and political thought, 213-40
publishing and periodicals during the Harlem Renaissance, 243-339
primary sources, 246-52
overviews, 252-68
African American writers and mainstream publishers, 268-91
anthologies: *The New Negro* and others, 291-309
African American periodicals and the Harlem Renaissance, 309-39
performing arts during the Harlem Renaissance, 341-465
primary sources, 343-48
overviews, 348-64
drama of the Harlem Renaissance, 364-92
influence of music on Harlem Renaissance writing, 437-65
visual arts during the Harlem Renaissance, 467-563
primary sources, 470-71
overviews, 471-517
painters, 517-36
sculptors, 536-58
photographers, 558-63

Harlem Renaissance TCLC 26: 49-125
principal issues and figures, 50-67
the literature and its audience, 67-74
theme and technique in poetry, fiction, and drama, 74-115
and American society, 115-21
achievement and influence, 121-2

Havel, Václav, Playwright and President CLC 65: 406-63

Heroic Drama LC 91: 249-373
definitions and overviews, 251-78
politics and heroic drama, 278-303
early plays: Dryden and Orrery, 303-51
later plays: Lee and Otway, 351-73

Historical Fiction, Nineteenth-Century NCLC 48: 212-307
definitions and characteristics, 213-36
Victorian historical fiction, 236-65
American historical fiction, 265-88
realism in historical fiction, 288-306

Hollywood and Literature TCLC 118: 110-251
overviews and general studies, 111-20
adaptations, 120-65
socio-historical and cultural impact, 165-206
theater and hollywood, 206-51

Holocaust and the Atomic Bomb: Fifty Years Later CLC 91: 331-82
the Holocaust remembered, 333-52
Anne Frank revisited, 352-62
the atomic bomb and American memory, 362-81

Holocaust Denial Literature TCLC 58: 1-110
overviews and general studies, 1-30
Robert Faurisson and Noam Chomsky, 30-52
Holocaust denial literature in America, 52-71
library access to Holocaust denial literature, 72-5
the authenticity of Anne Frank's diary, 76-90
David Irving and the "normalization" of Hitler, 90-109

Holocaust, Literature of the TCLC 42: 355-450
historical overview, 357-61
critical overview, 361-70
diaries and memoirs, 370-95
novels and short stories, 395-425
poetry, 425-41
drama, 441-8

Homosexuality in Nineteenth-Century Literature NCLC 56: 78-182
defining homosexuality, 80-111
Greek love, 111-44
trial and danger, 144-81

Humors Comedy LC 85: 194-324
overviews, 195-251
major figures: Ben Jonson, 251-93
major figures: William Shakespeare, 293-324

Hungarian Literature of the Twentieth Century TCLC 26: 126-88
surveys of, 126-47

Nyugat and early twentieth-century literature, 147-56
mid-century literature, 156-68
and politics, 168-78
since the 1956 revolt, 178-87

Hysteria in Nineteenth-Century Literature NCLC 64: 59-184
the history of hysteria, 60-75
the gender of hysteria, 75-103
hysteria and women's narratives, 103-57
hysteria in nineteenth-century poetry, 157-83

Image of the Noble Savage in Literature LC 79: 136-252
overviews and development, 136-76
the Noble Savage in the New World, 176-221
Rousseau and the French Enlightenment's view of the noble savage, 221-51

Imagism TCLC 74: 259-454
history and development, 260
major figures, 288
sources and influences, 352
Imagism and other movements, 397
influence and legacy, 431

Immigrants in Nineteenth-Century Literature, Representation of NCLC 112: 188-298
overview, 189-99
immigrants in America, 199-223
immigrants and labor, 223-60
immigrants in England, 260-97

Incest in Nineteenth-Century American Literature NCLC 76: 70-141
overview, 71-88
the concern for social order, 88-117
authority and authorship, 117-40

Incest in Victorian Literature NCLC 92: 172-318
overviews and general studies, 173-85
novels, 185-276
plays, 276-84
poetry, 284-318

Indian Literature in English TCLC 54: 308-406
overview, 309-13
origins and major figures, 313-25
the Indo-English novel, 325-55
Indo-English poetry, 355-67
Indo-English drama, 367-72
critical perspectives on Indo-English literature, 372-80
modern Indo-English literature, 380-9
Indo-English authors on their work, 389-404

The Industrial Revolution in Literature NCLC 56: 183-273
historical and cultural perspectives, 184-201
contemporary reactions to the machine, 201-21
themes and symbols in literature, 221-73

The Irish Famine as Represented in Nineteenth-Century Literature NCLC 64: 185-261
overviews and general studies, 187-98
historical background, 198-212
famine novels, 212-34
famine poetry, 234-44
famine letters and eye-witness accounts, 245-61

Irish Literary Renaissance TCLC 46: 172-287
overview, 173-83
development and major figures, 184-202
influence of Irish folklore and mythology, 202-22
Irish poetry, 222-34

Irish drama and the Abbey Theatre, 234-56
Irish fiction, 256-86

Irish Nationalism and Literature NCLC 44: 203-73
the Celtic element in literature, 203-19
anti-Irish sentiment and the Celtic response, 219-34
literary ideals in Ireland, 234-45
literary expressions, 245-73

Irish Novel, The NCLC 80: 1-130
overviews and general studies, 3-9
principal figures, 9-22
peasant and middle class Irish novelists, 22-76
aristocratic Irish and Anglo-Irish novelists, 76-129

Israeli Literature TCLC 94: 1-137
overviews and general studies, 2-18
Israeli fiction, 18-33
Israeli poetry, 33-62
Israeli drama, 62-91
women and Israeli literature, 91-112
Arab characters in Israeli literature, 112-36

Italian Futurism See **Futurism, Italian**

Italian Humanism LC 12: 205-77
origins and early development, 206-18
revival of classical letters, 218-23
humanism and other philosophies, 224-39
humanism and humanists, 239-46
the plastic arts, 246-57
achievement and significance, 258-76

Italian Romanticism NCLC 60: 85-145
origins and overviews, 86-101
Italian Romantic theory, 101-25
the language of Romanticism, 125-45

Jacobean Drama LC 33: 1-37
the Jacobean worldview: an era of transition, 2-14
the moral vision of Jacobean drama, 14-22
Jacobean tragedy, 22-3
the Jacobean masque, 23-36

Jazz and Literature TCLC 102: 3-124

Jewish-American Fiction TCLC 62: 1-181
overviews and general studies, 2-24
major figures, 24-48
Jewish writers and American life, 48-78
Jewish characters in American fiction, 78-108
themes in Jewish-American fiction, 108-43
Jewish-American women writers, 143-59
the Holocaust and Jewish-American fiction, 159-81

Jews in Literature TCLC 118: 252-417
overviews and general studies, 253-97
representing the Jew in literature, 297-351
the Holocaust in literature, 351-416

Journals of Lewis and Clark, The NCLC 100: 1-88
overviews and general studies, 4-30
journal-keeping methods, 30-46
Fort Mandan, 46-51
the Clark journal, 51-65
the journals as literary texts, 65-87

Kabuki LC 73: 118-232
overviews and general studies, 120-40
the development of Kabuki, 140-65
major works, 165-95
Kabuki and society, 195-231

Kit-Kat Club, The LC 71: 66-112
overviews and general studies, 67-88
major figures, 88-107
attacks on the Kit-Kat Club, 107-12

Knickerbocker Group, The NCLC 56: 274-341
overviews and general studies, 276-314
Knickerbocker periodicals, 314-26

writers and artists, 326-40

Künstlerroman TCLC 150: 133-260
overviews and general studies, 135-51
major works, 151-212
feminism in the *Künstlerroman*, 212-49
minority *Künstlerroman*, 249-59

Lake Poets, The NCLC 52: 217-304
characteristics of the Lake Poets and their works, 218-27
literary influences and collaborations, 227-66
defining and developing Romantic ideals, 266-84
embracing Conservatism, 284-303

Language Poets TCLC 126: 66-172
overviews and general studies, 67-122
selected major figures in language poetry, 122-72

Larkin, Philip, Controversy CLC 81: 417-64

Latin American Literature, Twentieth-Century TCLC 58: 111-98
historical and critical perspectives, 112-36
the novel, 136-45
the short story, 145-9
drama, 149-60
poetry, 160-7
the writer and society, 167-86
Native Americans in Latin American literature, 186-97

Law and Literature TCLC 126: 173-347
overviews and general studies, 174-253
fiction critiquing the law, 253-88
literary responses to the law, 289-346

Legend of El Dorado, The LC 74: 248-350
overviews, 249-308
major explorations for El Dorado, 308-50

The Levellers LC 51: 200-312
overviews and general studies, 201-29
principal figures, 230-86
religion, political philosophy, and pamphleteering, 287-311

Literary Criticism in the Nineteenth Century, American NCLC 128: 1-103
overviews and general studies, 2-44
the trancendentalists, 44-65
"young America," 65-71
James Russell Lowell, 71-9
Edgar Allan Poe, 79-97
Walt Whitman, 97-102

Literary Expressionism TCLC 142: 90-185
overviews and general studies, 91-138
themes in literary expressionism, 138-61
expressionism in Germany, 161-84

Literary Marketplace, The Nineteenth-Century NCLC 128: 194-368
overviews and general studies, 197-228
British literary marketplace, 228-66
French literary marketplace, 266-82
American literary marketplace, 282-323
Women in the literary marketplace, 323-67

Literary Prizes TCLC 122: 130-203
overviews and general studies, 131-34
the Nobel Prize in Literature, 135-83
the Pulitzer Prize, 183-203

Literature and Millenial Lists CLC 119: 431-67
The Modern Library list, 433
The Waterstone list, 438-439

Literature in Response to the September 11 Attacks CLC 174: 1-46
Major works about September 11, 2001, 2-22
Critical, artistic, and journalistic responses, 22-45

Literature of the American Cowboy NCLC 96: 1-60

overview, 3-20
cowboy fiction, 20-36
cowboy poetry and songs, 36-59

Literature of the California Gold Rush NCLC 92: 320-85
overviews and general studies, 322-24
early California Gold Rush fiction, 324-44
Gold Rush folklore and legend, 344-51
the rise of Western local color, 351-60
social relations and social change, 360-385

Living Theatre, The DC 16: 154-214

Luddism in Nineteenth-Century Literature NCLC 140: 280-365
overviews, 281-322
the literary response, 322-65

Madness in Nineteenth-Century Literature NCLC 76: 142-284
overview, 143-54
autobiography, 154-68
poetry, 168-215
fiction, 215-83

Madness in Twentieth-Century Literature TCLC 50: 160-225
overviews and general studies, 161-71
madness and the creative process, 171-86
suicide, 186-91
madness in American literature, 191-207
madness in German literature, 207-13
madness and feminist artists, 213-24

Magic Realism TCLC 110: 80-327
overviews and general studies, 81-94
magic realism in African literature, 95-110
magic realism in American literature, 110-32
magic realism in Canadian literature, 132-46
magic realism in European literature, 146-66
magic realism in Asian literature, 166-79
magic realism in Latin-American literature, 179-223
magic realism in Israeli literature and the novels of Salman Rushdie, 223-38
magic realism in literature written by women, 239-326

The Martin Marprelate Tracts LC 101: 165-240
criticism, 166-240

Marxist Criticism TCLC 134: 127-57
overviews and general studies, 128-67
Marxist interpretations, 167-209
cultural and literary Marxist theory, 209-49
Marxism and feminist critical theory, 250-56

The Masque LC 63: 124-265
development of the masque, 125-62
sources and structure, 162-220
race and gender in the masque, 221-64

Medical Writing LC 55: 93-195
colonial America, 94-110
enlightenment, 110-24
medieval writing, 124-40
sexuality, 140-83
vernacular, 185-95

Memoirs of Trauma CLC 109: 419-466
overview, 420
criticism, 429

Metafiction TCLC 130: 43-228
overviews and general studies, 44-85
Spanish metafiction, 85-117
studies of metafictional authors and works, 118-228

Metaphysical Poets LC 24: 356-439
early definitions, 358-67
surveys and overviews, 367-92
cultural and social influences, 392-406
stylistic and thematic variations, 407-38

Missionaries in the Nineteenth-Century, Literature of NCLC 112: 299-392
history and development, 300-16
uses of ethnography, 316-31
sociopolitical concerns, 331-82
David Livingstone, 382-91

Modern Essay, The TCLC 58: 199-273
overview, 200-7
the essay in the early twentieth century, 207-19
characteristics of the modern essay, 219-32
modern essayists, 232-45
the essay as a literary genre, 245-73

Modern French Literature TCLC 122: 205-359
overviews and general studies, 207-43
French theater, 243-77
gender issues and French women writers, 277-315
ideology and politics, 315-24
modern French poetry, 324-41
resistance literature, 341-58

Modern Irish Literature TCLC 102: 125-321
overview, 129-44
dramas, 144-70
fiction, 170-247
poetry, 247-321

Modern Japanese Literature TCLC 66: 284-389
poetry, 285-305
drama, 305-29
fiction, 329-61
western influences, 361-87

Modernism TCLC 70: 165-275
definitions, 166-184
Modernism and earlier influences, 184-200
stylistic and thematic traits, 200-229
poetry and drama, 229-242
redefining Modernism, 242-275

Muckraking Movement in American Journalism TCLC 34: 161-242
development, principles, and major figures, 162-70
publications, 170-9
social and political ideas, 179-86
targets, 186-208
fiction, 208-19
decline, 219-29
impact and accomplishments, 229-40

Multiculturalism CLC 189: 167-254
overviews and general studies, 168-93
the effects of multiculturalism on global literature, 193-213
multicultural themes in specific contemporary works, 213-53

Multiculturalism in Literature and Education CLC 70: 361-413

Music and Modern Literature TCLC 62: 182-329
overviews and general studies, 182-211
musical form/literary form, 211-32
music in literature, 232-50
the influence of music on literature, 250-73
literature and popular music, 273-303
jazz and poetry, 303-28

Mystery Story See Crime-Mystery-Detective Stories

Native American Literature CLC 76: 440-76

Natural School, Russian NCLC 24: 205-40
history and characteristics, 205-25
contemporary criticism, 225-40

Naturalism NCLC 36: 285-382
definitions and theories, 286-305
critical debates on Naturalism, 305-16
Naturalism in theater, 316-32
European Naturalism, 332-61
American Naturalism, 361-72
the legacy of Naturalism, 372-81

Negritude TCLC 50: 226-361
origins and evolution, 227-56
definitions, 256-91
Negritude in literature, 291-343
Negritude reconsidered, 343-58

New Criticism TCLC 34: 243-318
development and ideas, 244-70
debate and defense, 270-99
influence and legacy, 299-315

TCLC 146: 1–108
overviews and general studies, 3–19
defining New Criticism, 19–28
place in history, 28–51
poetry and New Criticism, 51–78
major authors, 78–108

New South, Literature of the NCLC 116: 122-240
overviews, 124-66
the novel in the New South, 166-209
myth of the Old South in the New, 209-39

The New World in Renaissance Literature LC 31: 1-51
overview, 1-18
utopia vs. terror, 18-31
explorers and Native Americans, 31-51

New York Intellectuals and *Partisan Review* TCLC 30: 117-98
development and major figures, 118-28
influence of Judaism, 128-39
Partisan Review, 139-57
literary philosophy and practice, 157-75
political philosophy, 175-87
achievement and significance, 187-97

The New Yorker TCLC 58: 274-357
overviews and general studies, 274-95
major figures, 295-304
New Yorker style, 304-33
fiction, journalism, and humor at *The New Yorker,* 333-48
the new *New Yorker,* 348-56

Newgate Novel NCLC 24: 166-204
development of Newgate literature, 166-73
Newgate Calendar, 173-7
Newgate fiction, 177-95
Newgate drama, 195-204

New Zealand Literature TCLC 134: 258-368
overviews and general studies, 260-300
Maori literature, 300-22
New Zealand drama, 322-32
New Zealand fiction, 332-51
New Zealand poetry, 351 67

Nigerian Literature of the Twentieth Century TCLC 30: 199-265
surveys of, 199-227
English language and African life, 227-45
politics and the Nigerian writer, 245-54
Nigerian writers and society, 255-62

Nihilism and Literature TCLC 110: 328-93
overviews and general studies, 328-44
European and Russian nihilism, 344-73
nihilism in the works of Albert Camus, Franz Kafka, and John Barth, 373-92

Nineteenth-Century Captivity Narratives NCLC 80:131-218
overview, 132-37
the political significance of captivity narratives, 137-67
images of gender, 167-96
moral instruction, 197-217

Nineteenth-Century Euro-American Literary Representations of Native Americans NCLC 104: 132-264

overviews and general studies, 134-53
Native American history, 153-72
the Indians of the Northeast, 172-93
the Indians of the Southeast, 193-212
the Indians of the West, 212-27
Indian-hater fiction, 227-43
the Indian as exhibit, 243-63

Nineteenth-Century Native American Autobiography NCLC 64: 262-389
overview, 263-8
problems of authorship, 268-81
the evolution of Native American autobiography, 281-304
political issues, 304-15
gender and autobiography, 316-62
autobiographical works during the turn of the century, 362-88

Norse Mythology CMLC 26: 321-85
history and mythological tradition, 322-44
Eddic poetry, 344-74
Norse mythology and other traditions, 374-85

Northern Humanism LC 16: 281-356
background, 282-305
precursor of the Reformation, 305-14
the Brethren of the Common Life, the Devotio Moderna, and education, 314-40
the impact of printing, 340-56

Novel of Manners, The NCLC 56: 342-96
social and political order, 343-53
domestic order, 353-73
depictions of gender, 373-83
the American novel of manners, 383-95

Novels of the Ming and Early Ch'ing Dynasties LC 76: 213-356
overviews and historical development, 214-45
major works—overview, 245-85
genre studies, 285-325
cultural and social themes, 325-55

Nuclear Literature: Writings and Criticism in the Nuclear Age TCLC 46: 288-390
overviews and general studies, 290-301
fiction, 301-35
poetry, 335-8
nuclear war in Russo-Japanese literature, 338-55
nuclear war and women writers, 355-67
the nuclear referent and literary criticism, 367-88

Occultism in Modern Literature TCLC 50: 362-406
influence of occultism on literature, 363-72
occultism, literature, and society, 372-87
fiction, 387-96
drama, 396-405

Opium and the Nineteenth-Century Literary Imagination NCLC 20:250-301
original sources, 250-62
historical background, 262-71
and literary society, 271-9
and literary creativity, 279-300

Orientalism NCLC 96: 149-364
overviews and general studies, 150-98
Orientalism and imperialism, 198-229
Orientalism and gender, 229-59
Orientalism and the nineteenth-century novel, 259-321
Orientalism in nineteenth-century poetry, 321-63

The Oxford Movement NCLC 72: 1-197
overviews and general studies, 2-24
background, 24-59
and education, 59-69
religious responses, 69-128
literary aspects, 128-178
political implications, 178-196

The Parnassian Movement NCLC 72: 198-241
overviews and general studies, 199-231
and epic form, 231-38
and positivism, 238-41

Pastoral Literature of the English Renaissance LC 59: 171-282
overviews and general studies, 172-214
principal figures of the Elizabethan period, 214-33
principal figures of the later Renaissance, 233-50
pastoral drama, 250-81

Periodicals, Nineteenth-Century American NCLC 132: 199-374
overviews, chronology, and development, 200-41
literary periodicals, 241-83
regional periodicals, 283-317
women's magazines and gender issues, 317-47
minority periodicals, 347-72

Periodicals, Nineteenth-Century British NCLC 24: 100-65
overviews and general studies, 100-30
in the Romantic Age, 130-41
in the Victorian era, 142-54
and the reviewer, 154-64

Picaresque Literature of the Sixteenth and Seventeenth Centuries LC 78: 223-355
context and development, 224-71
genre, 271-98
the picaro, 299-326
the picara, 326-53

Plath, Sylvia, and the Nature of Biography CLC 86: 433-62
the nature of biography, 433-52
reviews of *The Silent Woman*, 452-61

Political Theory from the 15th to the 18th Century LC 36: 1-55
overview, 1-26
natural law, 26-42
empiricism, 42-55

Polish Romanticism NCLC 52: 305-71
overviews and general studies, 306-26
major figures, 326-40
Polish Romantic drama, 340-62
influences, 362-71

Politics and Literature TCLC 94: 138-61
overviews and general studies, 139-96
Europe, 196-226
Latin America, 226-48
Africa and the Caribbean, 248-60

Popular Literature TCLC 70: 279-382
overviews and general studies, 280-324
"formula" fiction, 324-336
readers of popular literature, 336-351
evolution of popular literature, 351-382

The Portrayal of Jews in Nineteenth-Century English Literature NCLC 72: 242-368
overviews and general studies, 244-77
Anglo-Jewish novels, 277-303
depictions by non-Jewish writers, 303-44
Hebraism versus Hellenism, 344-67

The Portrayal of Mormonism NCLC 96: 61-148
overview, 63-72
early Mormon literature, 72-100
Mormon periodicals and journals, 100-10
women writers, 110-22
Mormonism and nineteenth-century literature, 122-42
Mormon poetry, 142-47

Post-apartheid Literature CLC 187: 284-382
overviews and general studies, 286-318
the post-apartheid novel, 318-65
post-apartheid drama, 365-81

Postcolonial African Literature TCLC 146: 110–239
overviews and general studies, 111–45
ideology and theory, 145–62
postcolonial testimonial literature, 162–99
major authors, 199–239

Postcolonialism TCLC 114: 134-239
overviews and general studies, 135-153
African postcolonial writing, 153-72
Asian/Pacific literature, 172-78
postcolonial literary theory, 178-213
postcolonial women's writing, 213-38

Postmodernism TCLC 90:125-307
overview, 126-166
criticism, 166-224
fiction, 224-282
poetry, 282-300
drama, 300-307

Pre-Raphaelite Movement NCLC 20: 302-401
overview, 302-4
genesis, 304-12
Germ and *Oxford and Cambridge Magazine*, 312-20
Robert Buchanan and the "Fleshly School of Poetry," 320-31
satires and parodies, 331-4
surveys, 334-51
aesthetics, 351-75
sister arts of poetry and painting, 375-94
influence, 394-9

Pre-romanticism LC 40: 1-56
overviews and general studies, 2-14
defining the period, 14-23
new directions in poetry and prose, 23-45
the focus on the self, 45-56

Pre-Socratic Philosophy CMLC 22: 1-56
overviews and general studies, 3-24
the Ionians and the Pythagoreans, 25-35
Heraclitus, the Eleatics, and the Atomists, 36-47
the Sophists, 47-55

Prison in Nineteenth-Century Literature, The NCLC 116: 241-357
overview, 242-60
romantic prison, 260-78
domestic prison, 278-316
America as prison, 316-24
physical prisons and prison authors, 324-56

Protestant Hagiography and Martyrology LC 84: 106-217
overview, 106-37
John Foxe's *Book of Martyrs*, 137-97
martyrology and the feminine perspective, 198-216

Protestant Reformation, Literature of the LC 37: 1-83
overviews and general studies, 1-49
humanism and scholasticism, 49-69
the reformation and literature, 69-82

Psychoanalysis and Literature TCLC 38: 227-338
overviews and general studies, 227-46
Freud on literature, 246-51
psychoanalytic views of the literary process, 251-61
psychoanalytic theories of response to literature, 261-88
psychoanalysis and literary criticism, 288-312
psychoanalysis as literature/literature as psychoanalysis, 313-34

The Quarrel between the Ancients and the Moderns LC 63: 266-381
overviews and general studies, 267-301

Renaissance origins, 301-32
  Quarrel between the Ancients and the Moderns in France, 332-58
  Battle of the Books in England, 358-80
Racism in Literature TCLC 138: 257-373
  overviews and general studies, 257-326
  racism and literature by and about African Americans, 292-326
  theme of racism in literature, 326-773
Rap Music CLC 76: 477-50
Reader-Response Criticism TCLC 146: 240–357
  overviews and general studies, 241–88
  critical approaches to reader response, 288–342
  reader-response interpretation, 342-57
Realism in Short Fiction SSC 63: 128-57
  overviews and general studies, 129-37
  realist short fiction in France, 137-62
  realist short fiction in Russia, 162-215
  realist short fiction in England, 215-31
  realist short fiction in the United States, 231-56
Regionalism and Local Color in Short Fiction SSC 65: 160-289
  overviews and general studies, 163-205
  regionalism/local color fiction of the west, 205-42
  regionalism/local color fiction of the midwest, 242-57
  regionalism/local color fiction of the south, 257-88
Renaissance Natural Philosophy LC 27: 201-87
  cosmology, 201-28
  astrology, 228-54
  magic, 254-86
Representations of the Devil in Nineteenth-Century Literature NCLC 100: 89-223
  overviews and general studies, 90-115
  the Devil in American fiction, 116-43
  English Romanticism: the satanic school, 143-89
  Luciferian discourse in European literature, 189-222
Restoration Drama LC 21: 184-275
  general overviews and general studies, 185-230
  Jeremy Collier stage controversy, 230-9
  other critical interpretations, 240-75
Revenge Tragedy LC 71: 113-242
  overviews and general studies, 113-51
  Elizabethan attitudes toward revenge, 151-88
  the morality of revenge, 188-216
  reminders and remembrance, 217-41
Revising the Literary Canon CLC 81: 465-509
Revising the Literary Canon TCLC 114: 240-84
  overviews and general studies, 241-85
  canon change in American literature, 285-339
  gender and the literary canon, 339-59
  minority and third-world literature and the canon, 359-84
Revolutionary Astronomers LC 51: 314-65
  overviews and general studies, 316-25
  principal figures, 325-51
  Revolutionary astronomical models, 352-64
Robin Hood, Legend of LC 19: 205-58
  origins and development of the Robin Hood legend, 206-20
  representations of Robin Hood, 220-44
  Robin Hood as hero, 244-56

Rushdie, Salman, *Satanic Verses* **Controversy** CLC 55: 214-63; 59:404-56
Russian Nihilism NCLC 28: 403-47
  definitions and overviews, 404-17
  women and Nihilism, 417-27
  literature as reform: the Civic Critics, 427-33
  Nihilism and the Russian novel: Turgenev and Dostoevsky, 433-47
Russian Thaw TCLC 26: 189-247
  literary history of the period, 190-206
  theoretical debate of socialist realism, 206-11
  Novy Mir, 211-7
  Literary Moscow, 217-24
  Pasternak, *Zhivago,* and the Nobel prize, 224-7
  poetry of liberation, 228-31
  Brodsky trial and the end of the Thaw, 231-6
  achievement and influence, 236-46
Salem Witch Trials LC 38: 1-145
  overviews and general studies, 2-30
  historical background, 30-65
  judicial background, 65-78
  the search for causes, 78-115
  the role of women in the trials, 115-44
Salinger, J. D., Controversy Surrounding *In Search of J. D. Salinger* CLC 55: 325-44
Samizdat Literature TCLC 150: 261-342
  overviews and general studies, 262-64
  history and development, 264-309
  politics and Samizdat, 309-22
  voices of Samizdat, 322-42
Sanitation Reform, Nineteenth-Century NCLC 124: 165-257
  overviews and general studies, 166
  primary texts, 186-89
  social context, 189-221
  public health in literature, 221-56
Science and Modern Literature TCLC 90: 308-419
  overviews and general studies, 295-333
  fiction, 333-95
  poetry, 395-405
  drama, 405-19
Science in Nineteenth-Century Literature NCLC 100: 224-366
  overviews and general studies, 225-65
  major figures, 265-336
  sociopolitical concerns, 336-65
Science Fiction, Nineteenth-Century NCLC 24: 241-306
  background, 242-50
  definitions of the genre, 251-56
  representative works and writers, 256-75
  themes and conventions, 276-305
Scottish Chaucerians LC 20: 363-412
Scottish Poetry, Eighteenth-Century LC 29: 95-167
  overviews and general studies, 96-114
  the Scottish Augustans, 114-28
  the Scots Vernacular Revival, 132-63
  Scottish poetry after Burns, 163-66
Sea in Literature, The TCLC 82: 72-191
  drama, 73-9
  poetry, 79-119
  fiction, 119-91
Sea in Nineteenth-Century English and American Literature, The NCLC 104: 265-362
  overviews and general studies, 267-306
  major figures in American sea fiction—Cooper and Melville, 306-29

American sea poetry and short stories, 329-45
  English sea literature, 345-61
Sensation Novel, The NCLC 80: 219-330
  overviews and general studies, 221-46
  principal figures, 246-62
  nineteenth-century reaction, 262-91
  feminist criticism, 291-329
Sentimental Novel, The NCLC 60: 146-245
  overviews and general studies, 147-58
  the politics of domestic fiction, 158-79
  a literature of resistance and repression, 179-212
  the reception of sentimental fiction, 213-44
September 11 Attacks See Literature in Response to the September 11 Attacks
Sex and Literature TCLC 82: 192-434
  overviews and general studies, 193-216
  drama, 216-63
  poetry, 263-87
  fiction, 287-431
Sherlock Holmes Centenary TCLC 26: 248-310
  Doyle's life and the composition of the Holmes stories, 248-59
  life and character of Holmes, 259-78
  method, 278-79
  Holmes and the Victorian world, 279-92
  Sherlockian scholarship, 292-301
  Doyle and the development of the detective story, 301-07
  Holmes's continuing popularity, 307-09
Short-Short Fiction SSC 61: 311-36
  overviews and general studies, 312-19
  major short-short fiction writers, 319-35
The Silver Fork Novel NCLC 88: 58-140
  criticism, 59-139
Slave Narratives, American NCLC 20: 1-91
  background, 2-9
  overviews and general studies, 9-24
  contemporary responses, 24-7
  language, theme, and technique, 27-70
  historical authenticity, 70-5
  antecedents, 75-83
  role in development of Black American literature, 83-8
The Slave Trade in British and American Literature LC 59: 283-369
  overviews and general studies, 284-91
  depictions by white writers, 291-331
  depictions by former slaves, 331-67
Social Conduct Literature LC 55: 196-298
  overviews and general studies, 196-223
  prescriptive ideology in other literary forms, 223-38
  role of the press, 238-63
  impact of conduct literature, 263-87
  conduct literature and the perception of women, 287-96
  women writing for women, 296-98
Social Protest Literature Outside England, Nineteenth-Century NCLC 124: 258-350
  overviews and general studies, 259-72
  oppression revealed, 272-306
  literature to incite or prevent reform, 306-50
Socialism NCLC 88: 141-237
  origins, 142-54
  French socialism, 154-83
  Anglo-American socialism, 183-205
  Socialist-Feminism, 205-36
Southern Gothic Literature TCLC 142: 186-270
  overviews and general studies, 187-97

major authors in southern gothic literature, 197-230
structure and technique in southern gothic literature, 230-50
themes in southern gothic literature, 250-70

Southern Literature *See* **Contemporary Southern Literature**

Southern Literature of the Reconstruction NCLC 108: 289-369
overview, 290-91
reconstruction literature: the consequences of war, 291-321
old south to new: continuities in southern culture, 321-68

Spanish Civil War Literature TCLC 26: 311-85
topics in, 312-33
British and American literature, 333-59
French literature, 359-62
Spanish literature, 362-73
German literature, 373-75
political idealism and war literature, 375-83

Spanish Golden Age Literature LC 23: 262-332
overviews and general studies, 263-81
verse drama, 281-304
prose fiction, 304-19
lyric poetry, 319-31

Spasmodic School of Poetry NCLC 24: 307-52
history and major figures, 307-21
the Spasmodics on poetry, 321-7
Firmilian and critical disfavor, 327-39
theme and technique, 339-47
influence, 347-51

Sports in Literature TCLC 86: 294-445
overviews and general studies, 295-324
major writers and works, 324-402
sports, literature, and social issues, 402-45

Steinbeck, John, Fiftieth Anniversary of *The Grapes of Wrath* CLC 59: 311-54

Sturm und Drang NCLC 40: 196-276
definitions, 197-238
poetry and poetics, 238-58
drama, 258-75

Supernatural Fiction in the Nineteenth Century NCLC 32: 207-87
major figures and influences, 208-35
the Victorian ghost story, 236-54
the influence of science and occultism, 254-66
supernatural fiction and society, 266-86

Supernatural Fiction, Modern TCLC 30: 59-116
evolution and varieties, 60-74
"decline" of the ghost story, 74-86
as a literary genre, 86-92
technique, 92-101
nature and appeal, 101-15

Surrealism TCLC 30: 334-406
history and formative influences, 335-43
manifestos, 343-54
philosophic, aesthetic, and political principles, 354-75
poetry, 375-81
novel, 381-6
drama, 386-92
film, 392-8
painting and sculpture, 398-403
achievement, 403-5

Symbolism, Russian TCLC 30: 266-333
doctrines and major figures, 267-92
theories, 293-8
and French Symbolism, 298-310
themes in poetry, 310-4
theater, 314-20
and the fine arts, 320-32

Symbolist Movement, French NCLC 20: 169-249
background and characteristics, 170-86
principles, 186-91
attacked and defended, 191-7
influences and predecessors, 197-211
and Decadence, 211-6
theater, 216-26
prose, 226-33
decline and influence, 233-47

Television and Literature TCLC 78: 283-426
television and literacy, 283-98
reading vs. watching, 298-341
adaptations, 341-62
literary genres and television, 362-90
television genres and literature, 390-410
children's literature/children's television, 410-25

Theater of the Absurd TCLC 38: 339-415
"The Theater of the Absurd," 340-7
major plays and playwrights, 347-58
and the concept of the absurd, 358-86
theatrical techniques, 386-94
predecessors of, 394-402
influence of, 402-13

Tin Pan Alley *See* **American Popular Song, Golden Age of**

Tobacco Culture LC 55: 299-366
social and economic attitudes toward tobacco, 299-344
tobacco trade between the old world and the new world, 344-55
tobacco smuggling in Great Britain, 355-66

Transcendentalism, American NCLC 24: 1-99
overviews and general studies, 3-23
contemporary documents, 23-41
theological aspects of, 42-52
and social issues, 52-74
literature of, 74-96

Travel Writing in the Nineteenth Century NCLC 44: 274-392
the European grand tour, 275-303
the Orient, 303-47
North America, 347-91

Travel Writing in the Twentieth Century TCLC 30: 407-56
conventions and traditions, 407-27
and fiction writing, 427-43
comparative essays on travel writers, 443-54

Tristan and Isolde Legend CMLC 42: 311-404

Troubadours CMLC 66: 244-383
overviews, 245-91
politics, economics, history, and the troubadours, 291-344
troubadours and women, 344-82

True-Crime Literature CLC 99: 333-433
history and analysis, 334-407
reviews of true-crime publications, 407-23
writing instruction, 424-29
author profiles, 429-33

Twentieth-Century Danish Literature TCLC 142: 271-344
major works, 272-84
major authors, 284-344

Ulysses **and the Process of Textual Reconstruction** TCLC 26:386-416
evaluations of the new *Ulysses,* 386-94
editorial principles and procedures, 394-401
theoretical issues, 401-16

Utilitarianism NCLC 84: 272-340
J. S. Mill's Utilitarianism: liberty, equality, justice, 273-313
Jeremy Bentham's Utilitarianism: the science of happiness, 313-39

Utopianism NCLC 88: 238-346
overviews: Utopian literature, 239-59
Utopianism in American literature, 259-99
Utopianism in British literature, 299-311
Utopianism and Feminism, 311-45

Utopian Literature, Nineteenth-Century NCLC 24: 353-473
definitions, 354-74
overviews and general studies, 374-88
theory, 388-408
communities, 409-26
fiction, 426-53
women and fiction, 454-71

Utopian Literature, Renaissance LC 32: 1-63
overviews and general studies, 2-25
classical background, 25-33
utopia and the social contract, 33-9
origins in mythology, 39-48
utopia and the Renaissance country house, 48-52
influence of millenarianism, 52-62

Vampire in Literature TCLC 46: 391-454
origins and evolution, 392-412
social and psychological perspectives, 413-44
vampire fiction and science fiction, 445-53

Vernacular Bibles LC 67: 214-388
overviews and general studies, 215-59
the English Bible, 259-355
the German Bible, 355-88

Victorian Autobiography NCLC 40: 277-363
development and major characteristics, 278-88
themes and techniques, 289-313
the autobiographical tendency in Victorian prose and poetry, 313-47
Victorian women's autobiographies, 347-62

Victorian Critical Theory NCLC 136: 236-379
overviews and general studies, 237-86
Matthew Arnold, 286-324
Walter Pater and aestheticism, 324-36
other Victorian critics, 336-78

Victorian Fantasy Literature NCLC 60: 246-384
overviews and general studies, 247-91
major figures, 292-366
women in Victorian fantasy literature, 366-83

Victorian Hellenism NCLC 68: 251-376
overviews and general studies, 252-78
the meanings of Hellenism, 278-335
the literary influence, 335-75

Victorian Illustrated Fiction NCLC 120: 247-356
overviews and development, 128-76
technical and material aspects of book illustration, 276-84
Charles Dickens and his illustrators, 284-320
William Makepeace Thackeray, 320-31
George Eliot and Frederic Leighton, 331-51
Lewis Carroll and John Tenniel, 351-56

Victorian Novel NCLC 32: 288-454
development and major characteristics, 290-310
themes and techniques, 310-58
social criticism in the Victorian novel, 359-97
urban and rural life in the Victorian novel, 397-406
women in the Victorian novel, 406-25
Mudie's Circulating Library, 425-34
the late-Victorian novel, 434-51

Vietnamese Literature TCLC 102: 322-386

Vietnam War in Literature and Film CLC 91: 383-437
   overview, 384-8
   prose, 388-412
   film and drama, 412-24
   poetry, 424-35

Violence in Literature TCLC 98: 235-358
   overviews and general studies, 236-74
   violence in the works of modern authors, 274-358

Vorticism TCLC 62: 330-426
   Wyndham Lewis and Vorticism, 330-8
   characteristics and principles of Vorticism, 338-65
   Lewis and Pound, 365-82
   Vorticist writing, 382-416
   Vorticist painting, 416-26

Well-Made Play, The NCLC 80: 331-370
   overviews and general studies, 332-45
   Scribe's style, 345-56
   the influence of the well-made play, 356-69

Women's Autobiography, Nineteenth Century NCLC 76: 285-368
   overviews and general studies, 287-300
   autobiographies concerned with religious and political issues, 300-15
   autobiographies by women of color, 315-38
   autobiographies by women pioneers, 338-51
   autobiographies by women of letters, 351-68

Women's Diaries, Nineteenth-Century NCLC 48: 308-54
   overview, 308-13
   diary as history, 314-25
   sociology of diaries, 325-34
   diaries as psychological scholarship, 334-43
   diary as autobiography, 343-8
   diary as literature, 348-53

Women in Modern Literature TCLC 94: 262-425
   overviews and general studies, 263-86
   American literature, 286-304
   other national literatures, 304-33
   fiction, 333-94
   poetry, 394-407
   drama, 407-24

Women Writers, Seventeenth-Century LC 30: 2-58
   overview, 2-15
   women and education, 15-9
   women and autobiography, 19-31
   women's diaries, 31-9
   early feminists, 39-58

World War I Literature TCLC 34: 392-486
   overview, 393-403
   English, 403-27
   German, 427-50
   American, 450-66
   French, 466-74
   and modern history, 474-82

World War I Short Fiction SSC 71: 187-347
   overviews and general studies, 187-206
   female short fiction writers of World War I, 206-36
   Central Powers
      Czechoslovakian writers of short fiction, 236-44
      German writers of short fiction, 244-61
   Entente/Allied Alliance
      Australian writers of short fiction, 261-73
      English writers of short fiction, 273-305
      French writers of short fiction, 305-11
   Associated Power: American writers of short fiction, 311-46

Yellow Journalism NCLC 36: 383-456
   overviews and general studies, 384-96
   major figures, 396-413

Yiddish Literature TCLC 130: 229-364
   overviews and general studies, 230-54
   major authors, 254-305
   Yiddish literature in America, 305-34
   Yiddish and Judaism, 334-64

Young Playwrights Festival
   1988 CLC 55: 376-81
   1989 CLC 59: 398-403
   1990 CLC 65: 444-8

TCLC Cumulative Nationality Index

AMERICAN

Adams, Andy **56**
Adams, Brooks **80**
Adams, Henry (Brooks) **4, 52**
Addams, Jane **76**
Agee, James (Rufus) **1, 19**
Aldrich, Bess (Genevra) Streeter **125**
Allen, Fred **87**
Anderson, Maxwell **2, 144**
Anderson, Sherwood **1, 10, 24, 123**
Anthony, Susan B(rownell) **84**
Atherton, Gertrude (Franklin Horn) **2**
Austin, Mary (Hunter) **25**
Baker, Ray Stannard **47**
Baker, Carlos (Heard) **119**
Bambara, Toni Cade **116**
Barry, Philip **11**
Baum, L(yman) Frank **7, 132**
Beard, Charles A(ustin) **15**
Becker, Carl (Lotus) **63**
Belasco, David **3**
Bell, James Madison **43**
Benchley, Robert (Charles) **1, 55**
Benedict, Ruth (Fulton) **60**
Benét, Stephen Vincent **7**
Benét, William Rose **28**
Bettelheim, Bruno **143**
Bierce, Ambrose (Gwinett) **1, 7, 44**
Biggers, Earl Derr **65**
Bishop, Elizabeth **121**
Bishop, John Peale **103**
Black Elk **33**
Boas, Franz **56**
Bodenheim, Maxwell **44**
Bok, Edward W. **101**
Bourne, Randolph S(illiman) **16**
Boyd, James **115**
Boyd, Thomas (Alexander) **111**
Bradford, Gamaliel **36**
Brautigan, Richard **133**
Brennan, Christopher John **17**
Brennan, Maeve **124**
Brodkey, Harold (Roy) **123**
Bromfield, Louis (Brucker) **11**
Broun, Heywood **104**
Bryan, William Jennings **99**
Burroughs, Edgar Rice **2, 32**
Burroughs, William S(eward) **121**
Cabell, James Branch **6**
Cable, George Washington **4**
Cahan, Abraham **71**
Caldwell, Erskine (Preston) **117**
Campbell, Joseph **140**
Cardozo, Benjamin N(athan) **65**
Carnegie, Dale **53**
Cather, Willa (Sibert) **1, 11, 31, 99, 132**
Chambers, Robert W(illiam) **41**
Chambers, (David) Whittaker **129**
Chandler, Raymond (Thornton) **1, 7**
Chapman, John Jay **7**
Chase, Mary Ellen **124**
Chesnutt, Charles W(addell) **5, 39**
Childress, Alice **116**
Chopin, Katherine **5, 14, 127**
Cobb, Irvin S(hrewsbury) **77**
Coffin, Robert P(eter) Tristram **95**
Cohan, George M(ichael) **60**
Comstock, Anthony **13**
Cotter, Joseph Seamon Sr. **28**
Cram, Ralph Adams **45**
Crane, (Harold) Hart **2, 5, 80**
Crane, Stephen (Townley) **11, 17, 32**
Crawford, F(rancis) Marion **10**
Crothers, Rachel **19**
Cullen, Countée **4, 37**
Cummings, E. E. **137**
Darrow, Clarence (Seward) **81**
Davis, Rebecca (Blaine) Harding **6**
Davis, Richard Harding **24**
Day, Clarence (Shepard Jr.) **25**
Dent, Lester **72**
De Voto, Bernard (Augustine) **29**
Dewey, John **95**
Dickey, James **151**
Dreiser, Theodore (Herman Albert) **10, 18, 35, 83**
Dulles, John Foster **72**
Dunbar, Paul Laurence **2, 12**
Duncan, Isadora **68**
Dunne, Finley Peter **28**
Eastman, Charles A(lexander) **55**
Eddy, Mary (Ann Morse) Baker **71**
Einstein, Albert **65**
Erskine, John **84**
Faulkner, William **141**
Faust, Frederick (Schiller) **49**
Fenollosa, Ernest (Francisco) **91**
Fields, W. C. **80**
Fisher, Dorothy (Frances) Canfield **87**
Fisher, Rudolph **11**
Fisher, Vardis **140**
Fitzgerald, F(rancis) Scott (Key) **1, 6, 14, 28, 55**
Fitzgerald, Zelda (Sayre) **52**
Fletcher, John Gould **35**
Foote, Mary Hallock **108**
Ford, Henry **73**
Forten, Charlotte L. **16**
Freeman, Douglas Southall **11**
Freeman, Mary E(leanor) Wilkins **9**
Fuller, Henry Blake **103**
Futrelle, Jacques **19**
Gale, Zona **7**
Garland, (Hannibal) Hamlin **3**
Gilman, Charlotte (Anna) Perkins (Stetson) **9, 37, 117**
Ginsberg, Allen **120**
Glasgow, Ellen (Anderson Gholson) **2, 7**
Glaspell, Susan **55**
Goldman, Emma **13**
Green, Anna Katharine **63**
Grey, Zane **6**
Griffith, D(avid) Lewelyn W(ark) **68**
Griggs, Sutton (Elbert) **77**
Guest, Edgar A(lbert) **95**
Guiney, Louise Imogen **41**
Haley, Alex **147**
Hall, James Norman **23**
Handy, W(illiam) C(hristopher) **97**
Harper, Frances Ellen Watkins **14**
Harris, Joel Chandler **2**
Harte, (Francis) Bret(t) **1, 25**
Hartmann, Sadakichi **73**
Hatteras, Owen **18**
Hawthorne, Julian **25**
Hearn, (Patricio) Lafcadio (Tessima Carlos) **9**
Hecht, Ben **101**
Heller, Joseph **131, 151**
Hellman, Lillian (Florence) **119**
Hemingway, Ernest (Miller) **115**
Henry, O. **1, 19**
Hergesheimer, Joseph **11**
Heyward, (Edwin) DuBose **59**
Higginson, Thomas Wentworth **36**
Himes, Chester **139**
Holley, Marietta **99**
Holly, Buddy **65**
Holmes, Oliver Wendell Jr. **77**
Hopkins, Pauline Elizabeth **28**
Horney, Karen (Clementine Theodore Danielsen) **71**
Howard, Robert E(rvin) **8**
Howe, Julia Ward **21**
Howells, William Dean **7, 17, 41**
Huneker, James Gibbons **65**
Hurston, Zora Neale **121, 131**
Ince, Thomas H. **89**
James, Henry **2, 11, 24, 40, 47, 64**
James, William **15, 32**
Jewett, (Theodora) Sarah Orne **1, 22**
Johnson, James Weldon **3, 19**
Johnson, Robert **69**
Kerouac, Jack **117**
Kinsey, Alfred C(harles) **91**
Kirk, Russell (Amos) **119**
Kornbluth, C(yril) M. **8**
Korzybski, Alfred (Habdank Skarbek) **61**
Kubrick, Stanley **112**
Kuttner, Henry **10**
Lardner, Ring(gold) W(ilmer) **2, 14**
Lewis, (Harry) Sinclair **4, 13, 23, 39**
Lewisohn, Ludwig **19**
Lewton, Val **76**
Lindsay, (Nicholas) Vachel **17**
Locke, Alain (Le Roy) **43**
Lockridge, Ross (Franklin) Jr. **111**
London, Jack **9, 15, 39**
Lovecraft, H(oward) P(hillips) **4, 22**
Lowell, Amy **1, 8**
Malamud, Bernard **129**
Mankiewicz, Herman (Jacob) **85**
March, William **96**
Markham, Edwin **47**
Marquis, Don(ald Robert Perry) **7**
Masters, Edgar Lee **2, 25**
Matthews, (James) Brander **95**
Matthiessen, F(rancis) O(tto) **100**
McAlmon, Robert (Menzies) **97**

McCoy, Horace (Stanley) **28**
Mead, George Herbert **89**
Mencken, H(enry) L(ouis) **13**
Micheaux, Oscar (Devereaux) **76**
Millay, Edna St. Vincent **4, 49**
Mitchell, Margaret (Munnerlyn) **11**
Mitchell, S(ilas) Weir **36**
Mitchell, William **81**
Monroe, Harriet **12**
Moody, William Vaughan **105**
Morley, Christopher (Darlington) **87**
Morris, Wright **107**
Muir, John **28**
Murfree, Mary Noailles **135**
Nash, (Frediric) Ogden **109**
Nathan, George Jean **18**
Nemerov, Howard (Stanley) **124F**
Neumann, Alfred **100**
Nisbet, Robert A(lexander) **117**
Nordhoff, Charles (Bernard) **23**
Norris, (Benjamin) Frank(lin Jr.) **24**
O'Connor, Flannery **132**
O'Neill, Eugene (Gladstone) **1, 6, 27, 49**
Oppen, George **107**
Osbourne, Lloyd **93**
Oskison, John Milton **35**
Park, Robert E(zra) **73**
Parker, Dorothy **143**
Patton, George S(mith) Jr. **79**
Peirce, Charles Sanders **81**
Percy, William Alexander **84**
Petry, Ann (Lane) **112**
Phelps, Elizabeth Stuart **113**
Phillips, David Graham **44**
Post, Melville Davisson **39**
Pulitzer, Joseph **76**
Pyle, Ernie **75**
Pyle, Howard **81**
Rawlings, Marjorie Kinnan **4**
Reed, John (Silas) **9**
Reich, Wilhelm **57**
Remington, Frederic **89**
Rhodes, Eugene Manlove **53**
Riggs, (Rolla) Lynn **56**
Riis, Jacob A(ugust) **80**
Riley, James Whitcomb **51**
Rinehart, Mary Roberts **52**
Roberts, Elizabeth Madox **68**
Roberts, Kenneth (Lewis) **23**
Robinson, Edwin Arlington **5, 101**
Rogers, Carl **125**
Rogers, Will(iam Penn Adair) **8, 71**
Roosevelt, Franklin Delano **93**
Roosevelt, Theodore **69**
Rourke, Constance (Mayfield) **12**
Runyon, (Alfred) Damon **10**
Saltus, Edgar (Everton) **8**
Santayana, George **40**
Santmyer, Helen Hooven **133**
Sapir, Edward **108**
Saroyan, William **137**
Schoenberg, Arnold Franz Walter **75**
Sherwood, Robert E(mmet) **3**
Slesinger, Tess **10**
Stanton, Elizabeth Cady **73**
Steffens, (Joseph) Lincoln **20**
Stein, Gertrude **1, 6, 28, 48**
Steinbeck, John **135**
Sterling, George **20**
Stevens, Wallace **3, 12, 45**
Stockton, Frank R. **47**
Stroheim, Erich von **71**
Strunk, William Jr. **92**
Sturges, Preston **48**
Tarbell, Ida M(inerva) **40**
Tarkington, (Newton) Booth **9**
Taylor, Frederick Winslow **76**
Teasdale, Sara **4**
Tesla, Nikola **88**
Thomas, Augustus **97**
Thomas, M. Carey **89**
Thorndike, Edward L(ee) **107**

Thurman, Wallace (Henry) **6**
Torrence, Ridgely **97**
Twain, Mark **6, 12, 19, 36, 48, 59**
Van Doren, Carl (Clinton) **18**
Veblen, Thorstein B(unde) **31**
Walker, Margaret **129**
Washington, Booker T(aliaferro) **10**
Wells, Carolyn **35**
Wells-Barnett, Ida B(ell) **125**
West, Dorothy **108**
West, Nathanael **1, 14, 44**
Whale, James **63**
Wharton, Edith (Newbold Jones) **3, 9, 27, 53, 129, 149**
White, Walter F(rancis) **15**
Williams, Ben Ames **89**
Williams, Hank **81**
Wilson, (Thomas) Woodrow **79**
Wirth, Louis **92**
Wister, Owen **21**
Wolfe, Thomas (Clayton) **4, 13, 29, 61**
Woodberry, George Edward **73**
Woollcott, Alexander (Humphreys) **5**
Wright, Frank Lloyd **95**
Wright, Richard **136**
Wylie, Elinor (Morton Hoyt) **8**

ARGENTINIAN

Arlt, Roberto (Godofredo Christophersen) **29**
Borges, Jorge Luis **109**
Güiraldes, Ricardo (Guillermo) **39**
Hudson, W(illiam) H(enry) **29**
Lugones, Leopoldo **15**
Storni, Alfonsina **5**

AUSTRALIAN

Baynton, Barbara **57**
Franklin, (Stella Maria Sarah) Miles (Lampe) **7**
Furphy, Joseph **25**
Ingamells, Rex **35**
Lawson, Henry (Archibald Hertzberg) **27**
Paterson, A(ndrew) B(arton) **32**
Warung, Price **45**

AUSTRIAN

Beer-Hofmann, Richard **60**
Broch, Hermann **20**
Brod, Max **115**
Freud, Sigmund **52**
Hayek, F(riedrich) A(ugust von) **109**
Hofmannsthal, Hugo von **11**
Kafka, Franz **2, 6, 13, 29, 47, 53, 112**
Kraus, Karl **5**
Kubin, Alfred (Leopold Isidor) **23**
Meyrink, Gustav **21**
Musil, Robert (Edler von) **12, 68**
Pabst, G. W. **127**
Perutz, Leo(pold) **60**
Rank, Otto **115**
Roth, (Moses) Joseph **33**
Schnitzler, Arthur **4**
Steiner, Rudolf **13**
Stroheim, Erich von **71**
Trakl, Georg **5**
Weininger, Otto **84**
Werfel, Franz (Viktor) **8**
Zweig, Stefan **17**

BELGIAN

Bosschere, Jean de **19**
Lemonnier, (Antoine Louis) Camille **22**
Maeterlinck, Maurice **3**
Sarton, May (Eleanor) **120**
van Ostaijen, Paul **33**
Verhaeren, Émile (Adolphe Gustave) **12**

BRAZILIAN

Cunha, Euclides (Rodrigues Pimenta) da **24**
Drummond de Andrade, Carlos **139**
Lima Barreto, Afonso Henrique de **23**
Machado de Assis, Joaquim Maria **10**
Ramos, Graciliano **32**

BULGARIAN

Vazov, Ivan (Minchov) **25**

CANADIAN

Campbell, Wilfred **9**
Carman, (William) Bliss **7**
Carr, Emily **32**
Connor, Ralph **31**
Drummond, William Henry **25**
Duncan, Sara Jeannette **60**
Engel, Marian **137**
Garneau, (Hector de) Saint-Denys **13**
Innis, Harold Adams **77**
Knister, Raymond **56**
Leacock, Stephen (Butler) **2**
Lewis, (Percy) Wyndham **2, 9, 104**
McCrae, John **12**
Montgomery, L(ucy) M(aud) **51, 140**
Nelligan, Emile **14**
Pickthall, Marjorie L(owry) C(hristie) **21**
Roberts, Charles G(eorge) D(ouglas) **8**
Scott, Duncan Campbell **6**
Service, Robert W(illiam) **15**
Seton, Ernest (Evan) Thompson **31**
Stringer, Arthur **37**
Wetherald, Agnes Ethelwyn **81**

CHILEAN

Donoso, José **133**
Godoy Alcayaga, Lucila **2**
Huidobro Fernandez, Vicente Garcia **31**
Prado (Calvo), Pedro **75**

CHINESE

Lin, Yutang **149**
Liu, E. **15**
Lu Hsun **3**
Su Man-shu **24**
Wen I-to **28**

COLOMBIAN

Rivera, José Eustasio **35**

CZECH

Brod, Max **115**
Chapek, Karel **6, 37**
Freud, Sigmund **52**
Hasek, Jaroslav (Matej Frantisek) **4**
Kafka, Franz **2, 6, 13, 29, 47, 53, 112**
Nezval, Vitezslav **44**

DANISH

Brandes, Georg (Morris Cohen) **10**
Hansen, Martin A(lfred) **32**
Jensen, Johannes V. **41**
Nexo, Martin Andersen **43**
Pontoppidan, Henrik **29**

DUTCH

Bok, Edward W. **101**
Couperus, Louis (Marie Anne) **15**
Heijermans, Herman **24**
Hillesum, Etty **49**
van Schendel, Arthur(-Francois-Émile) **56**

ENGLISH

Abbott, Edwin **139**
Abercrombie, Lascelles **141**
Alexander, Samuel **77**
Barbellion, W. N. P. **24**
Baring, Maurice **8**

Baring-Gould, Sabine **88**
Beerbohm, (Henry) Max(imilian) **1, 24**
Bell, Gertrude (Margaret Lowthian) **67**
Belloc, (Joseph) Hilaire (Pierre Sebastien Rene Swanton) **7, 18**
Bennett, (Enoch) Arnold **5, 20**
Benson, A.C. **123**
Benson, E(dward) F(rederic) **27**
Benson, Stella **17**
Bentley, E(dmund) C(lerihew) **12**
Beresford, J(ohn) D(avys) **81**
Besant, Annie (Wood) **9**
Blackmore, R(ichard) D(oddridge) **27**
Blackwood, Algernon (Henry) **5**
Bottomley, Gordon **107**
Bowen, Elizabeth **148**
Braddon, Mary Elizabeth **111**
Bramah, Ernest **72**
Bridges, Robert (Seymour) **1**
Brooke, Rupert (Chawner) **2, 7**
Buchanan, Robert **107**
Burke, Thomas **63**
Butler, Samuel **1, 33**
Butts, Mary **77**
Byron, Robert **67**
Caine, Hall **97**
Carpenter, Edward **88**
Carter, Angela **139**
Chesterton, G(ilbert) K(eith) **1, 6, 64**
Childers, (Robert) Erskine **65**
Churchill, Winston (Leonard Spencer) **113**
Clark, Kenneth Mackenzie **147**
Coleridge, Mary E(lizabeth) **73**
Collier, John **127**
Collingwood, R(obin) G(eorge) **67**
Conrad, Joseph **1, 6, 13, 25, 43, 57**
Coppard, A(lfred) E(dgar) **5**
Corelli, Marie **51**
Crofts, Freeman Wills **55**
Crowley, Aleister **7**
Dale, Colin **18**
Davies, William Henry **5**
Delafield, E. M. **61**
de la Mare, Walter (John) **4, 53**
Dobson, Austin **79**
Doughty, Charles M(ontagu) **27**
Douglas, Keith (Castellain) **40**
Dowson, Ernest (Christopher) **4**
Doyle, Arthur Conan **7**
Drinkwater, John **57**
Dunsany **2, 59**
Eddison, E(ric) R(ucker) **15**
Elaine **18**
Elizabeth **41**
Ellis, (Henry) Havelock **14**
Firbank, (Arthur Annesley) Ronald **1**
Flecker, (Herman) James Elroy **43**
Ford, Ford Madox **1, 15, 39, 57**
Forster, E(dward) M(organ) **125**
Freeman, R(ichard) Austin **21**
Galsworthy, John **1, 45**
Gilbert, W(illiam) S(chwenck) **3**
Gill, Eric **85**
Gissing, George (Robert) **3, 24, 47**
Glyn, Elinor **72**
Gosse, Edmund (William) **28**
Grahame, Kenneth **64, 136**
Granville-Barker, Harley **2**
Gray, John (Henry) **19**
Gurney, Ivor (Bertie) **33**
Haggard, H(enry) Rider **11**
Hall, (Marguerite) Radclyffe **12**
Hardy, Thomas **4, 10, 18, 32, 48, 53, 72, 143**
Henley, William Ernest **8**
Hilton, James **21**
Hodgson, William Hope **13**
Hope, Anthony **83**
Housman, A(lfred) E(dward) **1, 10**
Housman, Laurence **7**
Hudson, W(illiam) H(enry) **29**
Hulme, T(homas) E(rnest) **21**
Hunt, Violet **53**
Jacobs, W(illiam) W(ymark) **22**
James, Montague (Rhodes) **6**
Jerome, Jerome K(lapka) **23**
Johnson, Lionel (Pigot) **19**
Kaye-Smith, Sheila **20**
Keynes, John Maynard **64**
Kipling, (Joseph) Rudyard **8, 17**
Laski, Harold J(oseph) **79**
Lawrence, D(avid) H(erbert Richards) **2, 9, 16, 33, 48, 61, 93**
Lawrence, T(homas) E(dward) **18**
Lee, Vernon **5**
Lee-Hamilton, Eugene (Jacob) **22**
Leverson, Ada **18**
Lindsay, David **15**
Lowndes, Marie Adelaide (Belloc) **12**
Lowry, (Clarence) Malcolm **6, 40**
Lucas, E(dward) V(errall) **73**
Macaulay, (Emilie) Rose **7, 44**
MacCarthy, (Charles Otto) Desmond **36**
Mackenzie, Compton (Edward Montague) **116**
Maitland, Frederic William **65**
Manning, Frederic **25**
Marsh, Edward **99**
McTaggart, John McTaggart Ellis **105**
Meredith, George **17, 43**
Mew, Charlotte (Mary) **8**
Meynell, Alice (Christina Gertrude Thompson) **6**
Middleton, Richard (Barham) **56**
Milne, A(lan) A(lexander) **6, 88**
Moore, G. E. **89**
Morrison, Arthur **72**
Muggeridge, Thomas (Malcom) **120**
Murry, John Middleton **16**
Myers, L(eopold) H(amilton) **59**
Nightingale, Florence **85**
Noyes, Alfred **7**
Oppenheim, E(dward) Phillips **45**
Orwell, George **2, 6, 15, 31, 51, 128, 129**
Owen, Wilfred (Edward Salter) **5, 27**
Pankhurst, Emmeline (Goulden) **100**
Pinero, Arthur Wing **32**
Powys, T(heodore) F(rancis) **9**
Quiller-Couch, Arthur (Thomas) **53**
Richardson, Dorothy Miller **3**
Rolfe, Frederick (William Serafino Austin Lewis Mary) **12**
Rosenberg, Isaac **12**
Ruskin, John **20**
Sabatini, Rafael **47**
Saintsbury, George (Edward Bateman) **31**
Sapper **44**
Sayers, Dorothy L(eigh) **2, 15**
Shiel, M(atthew) P(hipps) **8**
Sinclair, May **3, 11**
Stapledon, (William) Olaf **22**
Stead, William Thomas **48**
Stephen, Leslie **23**
Strachey, (Giles) Lytton **12**
Summers, (Alphonsus Joseph-Mary Augustus) Montague **16**
Sutro, Alfred **6**
Swinburne, Algernon Charles **8, 36**
Symons, Arthur **11**
Thomas, (Philip) Edward **10**
Thompson, Francis (Joseph) **4**
Tolkien, J. R. R. **137**
Tomlinson, H(enry) M(ajor) **71**
Trotter, Wilfred **97**
Upward, Allen **85**
Van Druten, John (William) **2**
Wakefield, Herbert (Russell) **120**
Wallace, (Richard Horatio) Edgar **57**
Wallas, Graham **91**
Walpole, Hugh (Seymour) **5**
Ward, Mary Augusta **55**
Warner, Sylvia Townsend **131**
Warung, Price **45**
Webb, Mary Gladys (Meredith) **24**
Webb, Sidney (James) **22**
Welch, (Maurice) Denton **22**
Wells, H(erbert) G(eorge) **6, 12, 19, 133**
Whitehead, Alfred North **97**
Williams, Charles (Walter Stansby) **1, 11**
Wodehouse, P(elham) G(renville) **108**
Woolf, (Adeline) Virginia **1, 5, 20, 43, 56, 101, 128**
Yonge, Charlotte (Mary) **48**
Zangwill, Israel **16**

ESTONIAN

Talvik, Heiti **87**
Tammsaare, A(nton) H(ansen) **27**

FINNISH

Leino, Eino **24**
Soedergran, Edith (Irene) **31**
Westermarck, Edward **87**

FRENCH

Alain **41**
Apollinaire, Guillaume **3, 8, 51**
Arp, Jean **115**
Artaud, Antonin (Marie Joseph) **3, 36**
Bachelard, Gaston **128**
Barbusse, Henri **5**
Barrès, (Auguste-)Maurice **47**
Barthes, Roland **135**
Benda, Julien **60**
Bergson, Henri(-Louis) **32**
Bernanos, (Paul Louis) Georges **3**
Bernhardt, Sarah (Henriette Rosine) **75**
Bloy, Léon **22**
Bourget, Paul (Charles Joseph) **12**
Claudel, Paul (Louis Charles Marie) **2, 10**
Cocteau, Jean (Maurice Eugene Clement) **119**
Colette, (Sidonie-Gabrielle) **1, 5, 16**
Coppee, Francois **25**
Crevel, Rene **112**
Daumal, Rene **14**
Deleuze, Gilles **116**
Desnos, Robert **22**
Drieu la Rochelle, Pierre(-Eugène) **21**
Dujardin, Edouard (Emile Louis) **13**
Durkheim, Emile **55**
Epstein, Jean **92**
Fargue, Leon-Paul **11**
Feydeau, Georges (Léon Jules Marie) **22**
Genet, Jean **128**
Gide, André (Paul Guillaume) **5, 12, 36**
Giono, Jean **124**
Giraudoux, Jean(-Hippolyte) **2, 7**
Gourmont, Remy(-Marie-Charles) de **17**
Halévy, Elie **104**
Huysmans, Joris-Karl **7, 69**
Jacob, (Cyprien-)Max **6**
Jammes, Francis **75**
Jarry, Alfred **2, 14, 147**
Larbaud, Valery (Nicolas) **9**
Léautaud, Paul **83**
Leblanc, Maurice (Marie Emile) **49**
Leroux, Gaston **25**
Lyotard, Jean-François **103**
Martin du Gard, Roger **24**
Melies, Georges **81**
Mirbeau, Octave **55**
Mistral, Frédéric **51**
Nizan, Paul **40**
Péguy, Charles (Pierre) **10**
Péret, Benjamin **20**
Proust, (Valentin-Louis-George-Eugène-)Marcel **7, 13, 33**
Radiguet, Raymond **29**
Renard, Jules **17**
Rolland, Romain **23**
Rostand, Edmond (Eugene Alexis) **6, 37**
Roussel, Raymond **20**
Saint-Exupéry, Antoine (Jean Baptiste Marie Roger) de **2, 56**

Schwob, Marcel (Mayer André) **20**
Sorel, Georges **91**
Sully Prudhomme, René-François-Armand **31**
Teilhard de Chardin, (Marie Joseph) Pierre **9**
Valéry, (Ambroise) Paul (Toussaint Jules) **4, 15**
Vallette, Marguerite Eymery **67**
Verne, Jules (Gabriel) **6, 52**
Vian, Boris **9**
Weil, Simone (Adolphine) **23**
Zola, Émile (Édouard Charles Antoine) **1, 6, 21, 41**

GERMAN

Adorno, Theodor W(iesengrund) **111**
Andreas-Salome, Lou **56**
Arp, Jean **115**
Auerbach, Erich **43**
Ball, Hugo **104**
Barlach, Ernst (Heinrich) **84**
Benjamin, Walter **39**
Benn, Gottfried **3**
Borchert, Wolfgang **5**
Brecht, (Eugen) Bertolt (Friedrich) **1, 6, 13, 35**
Carossa, Hans **48**
Cassirer, Ernst **61**
Doeblin, Alfred **13**
Einstein, Albert **65**
Ewers, Hanns Heinz **12**
Feuchtwanger, Lion **3**
Frank, Bruno **81**
George, Stefan (Anton) **2, 14**
Goebbels, (Paul) Joseph **68**
Haeckel, Ernst Heinrich (Philipp August) **83**
Hauptmann, Gerhart (Johann Robert) **4**
Heym, Georg (Theodor Franz Arthur) **9**
Heyse, Paul (Johann Ludwig von) **8**
Hitler, Adolf **53**
Horkheimer, Max **132**
Horney, Karen (Clementine Theodore Danielsen) **71**
Huch, Ricarda (Octavia) **13**
Husserl, Edmund (Gustav Albrecht) **100**
Kaiser, Georg **9**
Klabund **44**
Kolmar, Gertrud **40**
Lasker-Schueler, Else **57**
Liliencron, (Friedrich Adolf Axel) Detlev von **18**
Luxemburg, Rosa **63**
Mann, (Luiz) Heinrich **9**
Mann, (Paul) Thomas **2, 8, 14, 21, 35, 44, 60**
Mannheim, Karl **65**
Michels, Robert **88**
Morgenstern, Christian (Otto Josef Wolfgang) **8**
Neumann, Alfred **100**
Nietzsche, Friedrich (Wilhelm) **10, 18, 55**
Ophuls, Max **79**
Otto, Rudolf **85**
Plumpe, Friedrich Wilhelm **53**
Raabe, Wilhelm (Karl) **45**
Rilke, Rainer Maria **1, 6, 19**
Schreber, Daniel Paul **123**
Schwitters, Kurt (Hermann Edward Karl Julius) **95**
Simmel, Georg **64**
Spengler, Oswald (Arnold Gottfried) **25**
Sternheim, (William Adolf) Carl **8**
Strauss, Leo **141**
Sudermann, Hermann **15**
Toller, Ernst **10**
Vaihinger, Hans **71**
von Hartmann, Eduard **96**
Wassermann, (Karl) Jakob **6**
Weber, Max **69**
Wedekind, (Benjamin) Frank(lin) **7**
Wiene, Robert **56**

GHANIAN

Casely-Hayford, J(oseph) E(phraim) **24**

GREEK

Cavafy, C(onstantine) P(eter) **2, 7**
Kazantzakis, Nikos **2, 5, 33**
Palamas, Kostes **5**
Papadiamantis, Alexandros **29**
Sikelianos, Angelos **39**

HAITIAN

Roumain, Jacques (Jean Baptiste) **19**

HUNGARIAN

Ady, Endre **11**
Babits, Mihaly **14**
Csath, Geza **13**
Herzl, Theodor **36**
Horváth, Ödön von **45**
Jozsef, Attila **22**
Karinthy, Frigyes **47**
Mikszath, Kalman **31**
Molnár, Ferenc **20**
Moricz, Zsigmond **33**
Radnóti, Miklós **16**

ICELANDIC

Sigurjonsson, Johann **27**

INDIAN

Chatterji, Saratchandra **13**
Dasgupta, Surendranath **81**
Gandhi, Mohandas Karamchand **59**
Ghose, Aurabinda **63**
Iqbal, Muhammad **28**
Naidu, Sarojini **80**
Premchand **21**
Ramana Maharshi **84**
Tagore, Rabindranath **3, 53**
Vivekananda, Swami **88**

INDONESIAN

Anwar, Chairil **22**

IRANIAN

Hedabayat, Sādeq **21**

IRISH

A.E. **3, 10**
Baker, Jean H. **3, 10**
Cary, (Arthur) Joyce (Lunel) **1, 29**
Gogarty, Oliver St. John **15**
Gregory, Isabella Augusta (Persse) **1**
Harris, Frank **24**
Joyce, James (Augustine Aloysius) **3, 8, 16, 35, 52**
Ledwidge, Francis **23**
Martin, Violet Florence **51**
Martyn, Edward **131**
Moore, George Augustus **7**
O'Faolain, Sean **143**
O'Grady, Standish (James) **5**
Shaw, George Bernard **3, 9, 21, 45**
Somerville, Edith Oenone **51**
Stephens, James **4**
Stoker, Bram **8, 144**
Synge, (Edmund) J(ohn) M(illington) **6, 37**
Tynan, Katharine **3**
Wilde, Oscar (Fingal O'Flahertie Wills) **1, 8, 23, 41**
Yeats, William Butler **1, 11, 18, 31, 93, 116**

ISRAELI

Agnon, S(hmuel) Y(osef) Halevi **151**

ITALIAN

Alvaro, Corrado **60**
Betti, Ugo **5**
Brancati, Vitaliano **12**
Campana, Dino **20**
Carducci, Giosuè (Alessandro Giuseppe) **32**
Croce, Benedetto **37**
D'Annunzio, Gabriele **6, 40**
de Filippo, Eduardo **127**
Deledda, Grazia (Cosima) **23**
Gadda, Carlo Emilio **144**
Gentile, Giovanni **96**
Giacosa, Giuseppe **7**
Jovine, Francesco **79**
Levi, Carlo **125**
Levi, Primo **109**
Malaparte, Curzio **52**
Marinetti, Filippo Tommaso **10**
Montessori, Maria **103**
Mosca, Gaetano **75**
Mussolini, Benito (Amilcare Andrea) **96**
Papini, Giovanni **22**
Pareto, Vilfredo **69**
Pascoli, Giovanni **45**
Pavese, Cesare **3**
Pirandello, Luigi **4, 29**
Protolini, Vasco **124**
Saba, Umberto **33**
Tozzi, Federigo **31**
Verga, Giovanni (Carmelo) **3**

JAMAICAN

De Lisser, H(erbert) G(eorge) **12**
Garvey, Marcus (Moziah Jr.) **41**
Mais, Roger **8**
Redcam, Tom **25**

JAPANESE

Abé, Kōbō **131**
Akutagawa Ryunosuke **16**
Dazai Osamu **11**
Futabatei, Shimei **44**
Hagiwara, Sakutaro **60**
Hayashi, Fumiko **27**
Ishikawa, Takuboku **15**
Kunikida, Doppo **99**
Masaoka, Shiki **18**
Miyamoto, (Chujo) Yuriko **37**
Miyazawa, Kenji **76**
Mizoguchi, Kenji **72**
Mori Ogai **14**
Nagai, Kafu **51**
Nishida, Kitaro **83**
Noguchi, Yone **80**
Santoka, Taneda **72**
Shimazaki Toson **5**
Suzuki, Daisetz Teitaro **109**
Yokomitsu, Riichi **47**
Yosano Akiko **59**

LATVIAN

Berlin, Isaiah **105**
Rainis, Jānis **29**

LEBANESE

Gibran, Kahlil **1, 9**

LESOTHAN

Mofolo, Thomas (Mokopu) **22**

LITHUANIAN

Kreve (Mickevicius), Vincas **27**

MEXICAN

Azuela, Mariano **3**
Gamboa, Federico **36**
Gonzalez Martinez, Enrique **72**
Ibargüengoitia, Jorge **148**
Nervo, (Jose) Amado (Ruiz de) **11**

Reyes, Alfonso **33**
Romero, José Rubén **14**
Villaurrutia, Xavier **80**

NEPALI

Devkota, Laxmiprasad **23**

NEW ZEALANDER

Mander, (Mary) Jane **31**

NICARAGUAN

Darío, Rubén **4**

NORWEGIAN

Bjoernson, Bjoernstjerne (Martinius) **7, 37**
Bojer, Johan **64**
Grieg, (Johan) Nordahl (Brun) **10**
Hamsun, Knut **151**
Ibsen, Henrik (Johan) **2, 8, 16, 37, 52**
Kielland, Alexander Lange **5**
Lie, Jonas (Lauritz Idemil) **5**
Obstfelder, Sigbjoern **23**
Skram, Amalie (Bertha) **25**
Undset, Sigrid **3**

PAKISTANI

Iqbal, Muhammad **28**

PERUVIAN

Arguedas, José María **147**
Palma, Ricardo **29**
Vallejo, César (Abraham) **3, 56**

POLISH

Asch, Sholem **3**
Borowski, Tadeusz **9**
Conrad, Joseph **1, 6, 13, 25, 43, 57**
Peretz, Isaac Loeb **16**
Prus, Boleslaw **48**
Przybyszewski, Stanislaw **36**
Reymont, Wladyslaw (Stanislaw) **5**
Schulz, Bruno **5, 51**
Sienkiewicz, Henryk (Adam Alexander Pius) **3**
Singer, Israel Joshua **33**
Witkiewicz, Stanislaw Ignacy **8**

PORTUGUESE

Pessoa, Fernando (António Nogueira) **27**
Sa-Carniero, Mario de **83**

PUERTO RICAN

Hostos (y Bonilla), Eugenio Maria de **24**

ROMANIAN

Bacovia, George **24**
Caragiale, Ion Luca **76**
Rebreanu, Liviu **28**

RUSSIAN

Aldanov, Mark (Alexandrovich) **23**
Andreyev, Leonid (Nikolaevich) **3**
Annensky, Innokenty (Fyodorovich) **14**
Artsybashev, Mikhail (Petrovich) **31**
Babel, Isaak (Emmanuilovich) **2, 13**
Bagritsky, Eduard **60**
Balmont, Konstantin (Dmitriyevich) **11**
Bely, Andrey **7**
Berdyaev, Nikolai (Aleksandrovich) **67**
Bergelson, David **81**
Blok, Alexander (Alexandrovich) **5**
Bryusov, Valery Yakovlevich **10**
Bulgakov, Mikhail (Afanas'evich) **2, 16**
Bulgya, Alexander Alexandrovich **53**
Bunin, Ivan Alexeyevich **6**
Chekhov, Anton (Pavlovich) **3, 10, 31, 55, 96**
Der Nister **56**
Eisenstein, Sergei (Mikhailovich) **57**
Esenin, Sergei (Alexandrovich) **4**
Fadeyev, Alexander **53**
Gladkov, Fyodor (Vasilyevich) **27**
Gumilev, Nikolai (Stepanovich) **60**
Gurdjieff, G(eorgei) I(vanovich) **71**
Guro, Elena **56**
Hippius, Zinaida **9**
Ilf, Ilya **21**
Ivanov, Vyacheslav Ivanovich **33**
Kandinsky, Wassily **92**
Khlebnikov, Velimir **20**
Khodasevich, Vladislav (Felitsianovich) **15**
Klimentov, Andrei Platonovich **14**
Korolenko, Vladimir Galaktionovich **22**
Kropotkin, Peter (Aleksieevich) **36**
Kuprin, Aleksander Ivanovich **5**
Kuzmin, Mikhail **40**
Lenin, V. I. **67**
Mandelstam, Osip (Emilievich) **2, 6**
Mayakovski, Vladimir (Vladimirovich) **4, 18**
Merezhkovsky, Dmitry Sergeyevich **29**
Nabokov, Vladimir (Vladimirovich) **108**
Olesha, Yuri **136**
Pavlov, Ivan Petrovich **91**
Petrov, Evgeny **21**
Pilnyak, Boris **23**
Prishvin, Mikhail **75**
Remizov, Aleksei (Mikhailovich) **27**
Rozanov, Vassili **104**
Shestov, Lev **56**
Sologub, Fyodor **9**
Stalin, Joseph **92**
Tolstoy, Alexey Nikolaevich **18**
Tolstoy, Leo (Nikolaevich) **4, 11, 17, 28, 44, 79**
Trotsky, Leon **22**
Tsvetaeva (Efron), Marina (Ivanovna) **7, 35**
Zabolotsky, Nikolai Alekseevich **52**
Zamyatin, Evgeny Ivanovich **8, 37**
Zhdanov, Andrei Alexandrovich **18**
Zoshchenko, Mikhail (Mikhailovich) **15**

SCOTTISH

Barrie, J(ames) M(atthew) **2**
Brown, George Douglas **28**
Buchan, John **41**
Cunninghame Graham, Robert (Gallnigad) Bontine **19**
Davidson, John **24**
Doyle, Arthur Conan **7**
Frazer, J(ames) G(eorge) **32**
Lang, Andrew **16**
MacDonald, George **9, 113**
Muir, Edwin **2, 87**
Murray, James Augustus Henry **117**
Sharp, William **39**
Tey, Josephine **14**

SLOVENIAN

Cankar, Ivan **105**

SOUTH AFRICAN

Bosman, Herman Charles **49**
Campbell, (Ignatius) Roy (Dunnachie) **5**
La Guma, Alex **140**
Mqhayi, S(amuel) E(dward) K(rune Loliwe) **25**
Plaatje, Sol(omon) T(shekisho) **73**
Schreiner, Olive (Emilie Albertina) **9**
Smith, Pauline (Urmson) **25**
Vilakazi, Benedict Wallet **37**

SPANISH

Alas (y Urena), Leopoldo (Enrique Garcia) **29**
Aleixandre, Vicente **113**
Barea, Arturo **14**
Baroja (y Nessi), Pio **8**
Benavente (y Martinez), Jacinto **3**
Blasco Ibáñez, Vicente **12**
Echegaray (y Eizaguirre), Jose (Maria Waldo) **4**
García Lorca, Federico **1, 7, 49**
Jiménez (Mantecón), Juan Ramón **4**
Machado (y Ruiz), Antonio **3**
Martinez Sierra, Gregorio **6**
Martinez Sierra, Maria (de la O'LeJarraga) **6**
Miro (Ferrer), Gabriel (Francisco Victor) **5**
Onetti, Juan Carlos **131**
Ortega y Gasset, José **9**
Pereda (y Sanchez de Porrua), Jose Maria de **16**
Pérez Galdós, Benito **27**
Ramoacn y Cajal, Santiago **93**
Salinas (y Serrano), Pedro **17**
Sender, Ramón **136**
Unamuno (y Jugo), Miguel de **2, 9, 148**
Valera y Alcala-Galiano, Juan **10**
Valle-Inclán, Ramón (Maria) del **5**

SWEDISH

Bengtsson, Frans (Gunnar) **48**
Dagerman, Stig (Halvard) **17**
Ekelund, Vilhelm **75**
Heidenstam, (Carl Gustaf) Verner von **5**
Key, Ellen (Karolina Sofia) **65**
Lagerkvist, Pär **144**
Lagerloef, Selma (Ottiliana Lovisa) **4, 36**
Söderberg, Hjalmar **39**
Strindberg, (Johan) August **1, 8, 21, 47**

SWISS

Frisch, Max (Rudolf) **121**
Hesse, Herman **148**
Ramuz, Charles-Ferdinand **33**
Rod, Edouard **52**
Saussure, Ferdinand de **49**
Spitteler, Carl (Friedrich Georg) **12**
Walser, Robert **18**

SYRIAN

Gibran, Kahlil **1, 9**

TURKISH

Sait Faik **23**

UKRAINIAN

Aleichem, Sholom **1, 35**
Bialik, Chaim Nachman **25**

UGANDAN

p'Bitek, Okot **149**

URUGUAYAN

Quiroga, Horacio (Sylvestre) **20**
Sánchez, Florencio **37**

WELSH

Davies, William Henry **5**
Evans, Caradoc **85**
Lewis, Alun **3**
Thomas, Dylan (Marlais) **1, 8, 45, 105**

YUGOSLAVIAN

Andrić, Ivo **135**

TCLC-151 Title Index

"Ad Olam" (Agnon) **151**:11-12, 18-19, 36
"Adultery" (Dickey) **151**:111, 121, 199, 212
"Agadat HaSofer" (Agnon) **151**:35-36
"Agunot" (Agnon) **151**:27-30, 72, 81
Alnilam (Dickey) **151**:153-58, 165, 173, 176, 203, 207, 210, 225
And the Crooked Shall Be Made Straight (Agnon)
  See *Ve-Haya he-Akov le-Mishor*
"Angina" (Dickey) **151**:97, 109
"Apollo" (Dickey) **151**:104, 113, 144, 170
"Approaching Prayer" (Dickey) **151**:180
"At Darien Bridge" (Dickey) **151**:169
Babel to Byzantium (Dickey) **151**:93, 95-96, 98-99, 120, 131-33, 145, 164, 200, 203
"Barnstorming for Poetry" (Dickey) **151**:94
"The Beholders" (Dickey) **151**:163
"Ben sete arim" (Agnon) **151**:21-23
"Betrothed" (Agnon) **151**:45
"Between Two Cities" (Agnon)
  See "Ben sete arim"
"Between Two Prisoners" (Dickey) **151**:199, 216, 224
Bidmi yameha (Agnon) **151**:62-63, 65-68
Billy Goat (Dickey) **151**:136
The Book of Deeds (Agnon)
  See *Sefer HaMa'asim*
"A Book That Was Lost" (Agnon) **151**:72
A Book That Was Lost and Other Stories (Agnon) **151**:72
Born av Tiden (Hamsun) **151**:250
"Bread" (Dickey) **151**:97, 184
The Bridal Canopy (Agnon) **151**:52
Buckdancer's Choice (Dickey) **151**:89-90, 92-93, 95, 98, 100, 102, 108-10, 114, 172, 202-3, 217
"Buckdancer's Choice" (Dickey) **151**:92-93
"Bums, on Waking" (Dickey) **151**:89
Call of the Wild (Dickey) **151**:180
"The Cancer Match" (Dickey) **151**:101, 105, 113-14
Catch-22 (Heller) **151**:298-315, 319-25, 327-32, 334-35, 339-41
"The Celebration" (Dickey) **151**:90-93, 121
The Central Motion: Poems, 1968-1979 (Dickey) **151**:143, 147-48
Chad Gadja: Das Pesachbuch (Agnon) **151**:36
"Chance" (Hamsun) **151**:248
"Chenille" (Dickey) **151**:97, 109, 167
"Cherrylog Road" (Dickey) **151**:89-90, 97, 104, 106, 169
Children of the Age (Hamsun)
  See *Born av Tiden*
"Circuit" (Dickey) **151**:175
Closing Time (Heller) **151**:319, 321-26, 340-41
Collected Works (Hamsun) **151**:242
"The Common Grave" (Dickey) **151**:90, 109
"Crippled Phoenix" (Heller) **151**:308-10, 313, 315
Crux: The Letters of James Dickey (Dickey) **151**:202, 220
"Dancer to Audience" (Dickey) **151**:152
"Dark Ones" (Dickey) **151**:149

Das Buch von den Polnischen Juden (Agnon) **151**:36
"Daughter" (Dickey) **151**:175
"Daybreak" (Dickey) **151**:175
"Deborah and Deirdre as Drunk Bridesmaids Foot-Racing at Daybreak" (Dickey) **151**:152
"Deborah as Scion" (Dickey) **151**:152
"Deborah in Ancient Lingerie, in Thin Oak over Creek" (Dickey) **151**:152
"Dedication, To Ernest Dowson" (Dickey) **151**:213
Deliverance (Dickey) **151**:98, 105, 107, 110, 112, 118, 121, 126, 133, 137, 140, 149, 152, 154-56, 158-62, 173, 179-80, 184-89, 191-94, 196-97, 199, 202-4, 212, 222
"Departure" (Dickey) **151**:167
"Deserted Wives" (Agnon)
  See "Agunot"
"Diabetes, I" (Dickey) **151**:100
"Diabetes" (Dickey) **151**:105, 113, 143
"Different Faces" (Agnon)
  See "Panim aherot"
"Dirge" (Dickey) **151**:213
"The Doctor and His Divorced Wife" (Agnon) **151**:22
"A Dog Sleeping on my Feet" (Dickey) **151**:90
"Drinking from a Helmet" (Dickey) **151**:89, 105
"The Driver" (Dickey) **151**:199
Drowning With Others (Dickey) **151**:90, 99-100, 102, 104-5, 171, 202-3
"The Dusk of Horses" (Dickey) **151**:89, 105
"Eagles" (Dickey) **151**:175
The Eagle's Mile (Dickey) **151**:174-76, 178, 199
"The Eagle's Mile" (Dickey) **151**:175
Editor Lynge (Hamsun) **151**:232
Edo and Enam (Agnon) **151**:41-44
"The Enclosure" (Dickey) **151**:104
"Encounter in the Cage Country" (Dickey) **151**:212
The Enemy from Eden (Dickey) **151**:162
"Entering Scott's Night" (Dickey) **151**:209
"The Escape" (Dickey) **151**:97, 109
"Exchanges" (Dickey) **151**:126, 147, 152
"Expanses" (Dickey) **151**:176
The Eye-Beaters, Blood, Victory, Madness, Buckhead and Mercy (Dickey) **151**:98-103, 108, 113-14, 116, 118, 121, 143-44, 162, 170
"The Eye-Beaters" (Dickey) **151**:98, 100-102, 105, 110, 113-14, 116-17, 144-45, 172
"The Eye of the Fire" (Dickey) **151**:215, 221
"The Face and the Image" (Agnon) **151**:3
"Faces Seen Once" (Dickey) **151**:90
Falling (Dickey) **151**:108
"Falling" (Dickey) **151**:100-101, 109-10, 115, 166, 192, 199, 204, 212
"False Youth: Autumn: Clothes of the Age" (Dickey) **151**:125, 147
"False Youth: Two Seasons" (Dickey) **151**:124, 201

"Farmers" (Dickey) **151**:174
"Fathers and Sons" (Dickey) **151**:90
"Fence Wire" (Dickey) **151**:106
"The Field" (Dickey) **151**:104
"The Fiend" (Dickey) **151**:110, 172, 180, 200, 204
"The Firebombing" (Dickey) **151**:90, 95, 100, 106-8, 139-40, 149, 172, 200, 212, 221
"Fog Envelopes the Animals" (Dickey) **151**:104, 171
"For a Time and Place" (Dickey) **151**:170
"For Robert Bhain Campbell" (Dickey) **151**:171
"For the Death of Lombardi" (Dickey) **151**:126-27, 147
"For the Last Wolverine" (Dickey) **151**:111
"For the Running of the New York City Marathon" (Dickey) **151**:170
Fra det Moderne Amerikas Aandsliv (Hamsun) **151**:231, 241-44, 248, 273
"Fra det ubevidste Sjaeleliv" (Hamsun) **151**:247-48, 254
"Fragment of a Life" (Hamsun) **151**:239
Frida (Hamsun) **151**:231
"The Friend" (Dickey) **151**:90
From the Unconscious Life of the Mind (Hamsun) **151**:254
"From the Unconscious Life of the Mind" (Hamsun)
  See "Fra det ubevidste Sjaeleliv"
"From Time" (Dickey) **151**:174
"Gamecock" (Dickey) **151**:90, 97
"Gib'at hahol" (Agnon) **151**:22
"Gila Bend" (Dickey) **151**:175
"Giving a Son to the Sea" (Dickey) **151**:101
God Knows (Heller) **151**:310, 320
God's Images (Dickey) **151**:152, 162-63, 165-67
"Going Home" (Dickey) **151**:114
Good as Gold (Heller) **151**:294, 296, 320
Growth of the Soil (Hamsun)
  See *Markens grode*
A Guest for the Night (Agnon) **151**:52, 70-71
Ha-panim la-panim (Agnon) **151**:3
"Hadom ve'Khiseh" (Agnon) **151**:36
"Head-Deep in Strange Sounds: Free-Flight Improvisations from the un-English" (Dickey) **151**:147
Head-Deep in Strange Sounds: Free-Flight Improvisations from the unEnglish (Dickey) **151**:162, 171, 174
"The Heaven of Animals" (Dickey) **151**:95, 99, 104, 172
"Hedge Life" (Dickey) **151**:97
Helmets (Dickey) **151**:90, 100, 102, 105-6, 202-3
"Heraldic: Deborah and Horse in Morning Forest" (Dickey) **151**:152
"The Hill of Sand" (Agnon)
  See "Gib'at hahol"
"The Hospital Visit" (Dickey) **151**:204
"The Hospital Window" (Dickey) **151**:121, 203
Hunger (Hamsun) **151**:228-91
"Hunting Civil War Relics at Nimblewill Creek" (Dickey) **151**:98, 170

"Hush hareah" (Agnon) **151**:26, 56, 81, 84
"The Ice Skin" (Dickey) **151**:89
"Ido ve'Enam" (Agnon) **151**:36
"In Lace and Whalebone" (Dickey) **151**:152
In Pursuit of the Grey Soul (Dickey) **151**:162
"In the Marble Quarry" (Dickey) **151**:172, 202
"In the Pocket" (Dickey) **151**:98
In the Prime of Her Life (Agnon)
    See *Bidmi yameha*
"Inside the River" (Dickey) **151**:203
Into the Stone and Other Poems (Dickey) **151**:100, 102-4, 108, 202
The James Dickey Reader (Dickey) **151**:203
Jericho: The South Beheld (Dickey) **151**:152, 162-67
Just Yesterday (Agnon) **151**:45, 52
"Kelev Meshuga" (Agnon) **151**:36
"The Kilikov Trial or a Life for a Life" (Agnon) **151**:73, 77-79
"Kudzu" (Dickey) **151**:199
"Lakes of Värmland" (Dickey) **151**:174
Landstrykere (Hamsun) **151**:255, 261
"The Last Bus" (Agnon) **151**:22
"The Leap" (Dickey) **151**:199
"The Lifeguard" (Dickey) **151**:97-99
"Listening to Foxhounds" (Dickey) **151**:90, 167
"The Little More" (Dickey) **151**:176
"Living There" (Dickey) **151**:101
"Looking for the Buckhead Boys" (Dickey) **151**:100-101, 114, 144
"The Lord in the Air" (Dickey) **151**:113
"The Lyric Beasts" (Dickey) **151**:152
"Mad Dog" (Agnon)
    See "Kelev Meshuga"
"Madness" (Dickey) **151**:98, 113", 166
"Mangham" (Dickey) **151**:97, 114
Markens grode (Hamsun) **151**:232, 234, 261
"May Day Sermon" (Dickey) **151**:105, 109, 115, 152, 166, 169, 172, 212
"Mercy" (Dickey) **151**:143
"Messages" (Dickey) **151**:114, 143
"Metaphor as Pure Adventure" (Dickey) **151**:135
"The Miracle of Danrossane" (Heller) **151**:308-10, 313, 315
"The Mountain Tent" (Dickey) **151**:199
"The Movement of Fish" (Dickey) **151**:104
Mysterier (Hamsun) **151**:231, 234, 238, 250-61
New Ground (Hamsun) **151**:232
"Night Bird" (Dickey) **151**:175
Night (Dickey) **151**:159-60
Night Hurdling (Dickey) **151**:203
No Laughing Matter (Heller) **151**:320, 322
"Notes on the Decline of Courage" (Dickey) **151**:164
"Notes on the Decline of Outrage" (Dickey) **151**:94, 141
Now and Then (Heller) **151**:339-41
Ny Jord (Hamsun) **151**:234, 240
"The Olympian" (Dickey) **151**:170, 176
On Overgrown Paths (Hamsun) **151**:233
"On the Coosawattee" (Dickey) **151**:199
On the Cultural Life of Modern America (Hamsun)
    See *Fra det Moderne Amerikas Aandsliv*
"On Tour" (Hamsun) **151**:239, 245
Only Yesterday (Agnon) **151**:70
The Owl King (Dickey) **151**:162
"The Owl King" (Dickey) **151**:98, 104-5, 114

Pan (Hamsun) **151**:232, 234, 250, 253, 255, 257
"Panim aherot" (Agnon) **151**:22
"The Performance" (Dickey) **151**:97, 104, 106, 124, 168, 199, 212, 215-16
Picture This (Heller) **151**:321-22, 326
"Pine" (Dickey) **151**:98
"Pisces" (Agnon) **151**:72
Poems 1957-1967 (Dickey) **151**:93, 96-100, 108, 110, 118, 121, 133, 199-200
Poems (Dickey) **151**:184
"The Poet Turns on Himself" (Dickey) **151**:132, 142, 145
Poetical Remains (Dickey) **151**:213
"The Poisoned Man" (Dickey) **151**:172
Portrait of the Artist, as an Old Man (Heller) **151**:340-41
"Power and Light" (Dickey) **151**:100, 121, 199, 201
Puella (Dickey) **151**:151-52, 167, 171, 173, 199
"Pursuit from Under" (Dickey) **151**:90, 97, 109
"The Rain Guitar" (Dickey) **151**:127, 147
"The Rain Gutter" (Dickey) **151**:126
"Reincarnation" (Dickey) **151**:90, 172
"Reincarnation (I)" (Dickey) **151**:96, 110
"Reincarnation (II)" (Dickey) **151**:110, 116, 180, 199
"Root-light, or the Lawyer's Daughter" (Dickey) **151**:125, 147, 173
"The Salt Marsh" (Dickey) **151**:169
"The Scarred Girl" (Dickey) **151**:89
"The Seafarer" (Dickey) **151**:174
"Sears" (Dickey) **151**:172
"The Secret of Writing Fables. The Sense of Smell" (Agnon)
    See "Hush hareah"
Sefer HaMa'asim (Agnon) **151**:3, 34, 56
"Sefer HaMa'asim" (Agnon) **151**:36
Segelfoss Town (Hamsun) **151**:234
The Selected Poems (Dickey) **151**:199, 203
"The Self as Agent" (Dickey) **151**:135
Self-Interviews (Dickey) **151**:98-99, 101, 104-5, 110, 131-34, 158-59, 162, 164, 184, 215, 217
"The Sense of Smell" (Agnon)
    See "Hush hareah"
"The Shark's Parlor" (Dickey) **151**:145, 172
"The Sheep Child" (Dickey) **151**:97, 145, 166, 200, 212
"Shevu'at Emunim" (Agnon) **151**:36
Shira (Agnon) **151**:52-54
"Simple Story" (Agnon)
    See "Sippur pasut"
Sippur pasut (Agnon) **151**:45, 51-52
"Sippur pasut" (Agnon) **151**:22
Sirah (Agnon) **151**:22
"Slave Quarters" (Dickey) **151**:95, 110, 121, 170, 200
"Sled Burial, Dream Ceremony" (Dickey) **151**:90, 170
"The Sleep Child" (Dickey) **151**:95
"Sleeping Out on Easter" (Dickey) **151**:103, 199
A Small Book of Tales (Agnon) **151**:73
"Snakebite" (Dickey) **151**:103
"Sne talmide hakamim sehayu be irenu" (Agnon) **151**:21, 23
"Snow on a Southern State" (Dickey) **151**:170
"Snow Thickets" (Dickey) **151**:176

Something Happened (Heller) **151**:310, 319-21, 326, 339
"The Son, the Cave, and the Burning Bush" (Dickey) **151**:135
Sorties (Dickey) **151**:102-3, 132-35, 162, 165, 203
Southern Light (Dickey) **151**:167-68
"Spinning the Crystal Ball" (Dickey) **151**:135
"Spring-Shock" (Dickey) **151**:176
"Springer Mountain" (Dickey) **151**:89
The Strength of Fields (Dickey) **151**:125, 127, 143, 147
"The Strength of Fields" (Dickey) **151**:147, 170
"Sun" (Dickey) **151**:97
The Suspect in Poetry (Dickey) **151**:103, 105, 108, 131-32, 134, 200
"Tacloban" (Dickey) **151**:215
Temol silsom (Agnon) **151**:22, 36
"Them, Crying" (Dickey) **151**:90, 109, 169
"To the Butterflies" (Dickey) **151**:175
To the White Sea (Dickey) **151**:173, 180, 203, 212, 215, 217-18, 220, 223
"Totem-tants" (Agnon) **151**:35
"Translating" (Heller) **151**:308
"Trees and Cattle" (Dickey) **151**:104
Treue: Ein Judisches Sammelsschrift (Agnon) **151**:36
"Turning Away: Variations on Estrangement" (Dickey) **151**:98, 102-3, 113, 116-17
Twenty-One Stories (Agnon) **151**:3
"Two Poems of Going Home" (Dickey) **151**:101, 143, 170
"Two Scholars Who Lived in Our Town" (Agnon)
    See "Sne talmide hakamim sehayu be irenu"
"Two Women" (Dickey) **151**:175
Und das Krumme wird gerade (Agnon)
    See *Vehaya He'akov Lemishor*
"Under Buzzards" (Dickey) **151**:100-101, 113
"Undersea Fragment in Collons" (Dickey) **151**:127
"Variations on Estrangement" (Dickey)
    See "Turning Away: Variations on Estrangement"
Ve-Haya he-Akov le-Mishor (Agnon) **151**:4, 27
"Veer-Voices: Two Sisters under Crows" (Dickey) **151**:152
"The Vegetable King" (Dickey) **151**:104, 199
Vehaya He'akov Lemishor (Agnon) **151**:36-37, 39
Victoria (Hamsun) **151**:232, 234
"A View of Fujiyama after the War" (Dickey) **151**:225
"Walking on Water" (Dickey) **151**:169
Wanderers (Hamsun) **151**:234
"The War Wound" (Dickey) **151**:90, 172, 217
Wayfarer: A Voice from the Southern Mountains (Dickey) **151**:167-68
We Bombed in New Haven (Heller) **151**:320
"The Wedding" (Dickey) **151**:97
The Whole Motion: Collected Poems 1945-1992 (Dickey) **151**:169, 171, 199, 203
Women at the Pump (Hamsun) **151**:234
Yesterday Hertofore (Agnon)
    See *Temol silsom*
The Zodiac (Dickey) **151**:118-24, 128, 141, 143, 145-46, 149-53, 162-63, 167, 172-73, 203

ISBN 0-7876-7050-2